P9-CDL-153

BETHANY

330.9005 D7521 1985

The Dow Jones-Irwin
  business almanac, 1985

The 1985 Dow Jones-Irwin Business and Investment Almanac

The 1985 DOW JONES-IRWIN
Business and Investment Almanac

Edited by

Sumner N. Levine
State University of New York
at Stony Brook
and Editor
Financial Analyst's Handbook
and
The Investment Manager's Handbook

Executive Editor
Caroline Levine

Ref.
330.904
D752
1985

DOW JONES-IRWIN
Homewood, Illinois 60430

© SUMNER N. LEVINE, 1985

All rights reserved. No part of this publication may be
reproduced, stored in a retrieval system, or transmitted,
in any form or by any means, electronic, mechanical,
photocopying, recording, or otherwise, without the prior
written permission of the copyright holder.

This publication is designed to provide accurate and
authoritative information in regard to the subject matter
covered. It is sold with the understanding that the
publisher and editor are not engaged in rendering legal, accounting, or
other professional service. If legal advice or other expert
assistance is required, the service of a competent
professional person should be sought.

*From a Declaration of Principles jointly adopted by a Committee
of the American Bar Association and a Committee of Publishers.*

(casebound)
0–87094–572–6

Printed in the United States of America

1 2 3 4 5 6 7 8 9 0 K 8 7 6 5 4 3 2 1

Contents

Preface

This ninth edition of the annual *Dow Jones-Irwin Business and Investment Almanac* contains a number of new features in response to the rapidly changing business and investment scene as well as updates on our standard features:

- How to Find Computer Software
- 1984 Tax Act
- Comparative Living Costs in U.S. Metropolitan Areas
- Calculating Salary Equivalency Figures
- Selected No Load/Low Load Mutual Fund Families with Switching Privileges
- Real Change in Industry Shipments

The editor and publisher are, of course, pleased with the acceptance of the *Dow Jones-Irwin Business and Investment Almanac* as a standard and unique reference for the business and investment community. As always, we continue to invite suggestions from our readers. All suggestions should be sent to: *Dow Jones-Irwin Business and Investment Almanac,* P.O. Box D, Setauket, New York 11733.

Sumner N. Levine
Editor

References to companies, securities, and other investment information do not constitute a recommendation or endorsement.

Business in Review

1 Leading indicators rose 0.3% in July, signaling that the re'covery's pace will be slower than in the second quarter. Although the index rose for the 11th month in a row, the increase was the weakest since last August. The July rise followed a revised 1.9% gain in June and 1.2% in May.

U.S. and Japanese trade officials have started informal talks aimed at producing an agreement on limiting Japanese car imports for a fourth year. But with the growing recovery in auto sales, further restraints are likely to boost costs and prices and lessen competition in the U.S.

Volatile silver prices have regularly pushed trading volume for the precious metal higher than gold for the first time in four years at the Comex. In the past few weeks, the price of silver has swung as much as 4% during a single trading day.

2 Retailers posted strong sales for August despite sweltering temperatures across most of the country and a hurricane in the Southwest. Shoppers' willingness to spend fueled retailers' optimism about sales and profits through year-end. Sears Roebuck's sales were up 20%, K mart's 16%, Wal-Mart's 41% and Macy's 18%.

An appeals court ruling that Apple Computer's programs for the Apple II personal computer are subject to copyright protection is a blow to makers of machines similar to Apple's.

Construction spending rose 1.7% in July to a seasonally adjusted $267.7 billion annual rate. July's was the fourth consecutive monthly rise, but economists expect smaller increases in months ahead, as high interest rates curb growth.

6 The unemployment rate was unchanged in August from July's adjusted 9.5%, but it is likely to resume its descent soon. Economists warned that the pace of the decline will slow in the next few months, as the recovery slows. They predict a jobless rate of about 9% by year-end.

Lower interest rates look increasingly

likely because of a recent sharp slowdown in money-supply growth and indications that the pace of the economic recovery is easing, many economists and bankers say.

The U.S. Economy didn't improve as rapidly in August as in July, but gains in production were stronger than in any other month this year, according to a monthly survey of corporate purchasing managers.

7 Chrysler emerged from its latest round of negotiations with the UAW with a tentative contract that narrows but doesn't eliminate the company's slight labor cost advantage over its domestic rivals. The accord grants the UAW increases totaling $2.42 an hour over the next two years.

U.S. car sales rose 17.1% in August to 735, 960 units from extremely depressed year-earlier levels. Nearly all of the increase reflected higher sales of domestically produced autos. The pace of last month's sales was the slowest since April.

Home-loan rates are edging lower after rising sharply this summer. Lenders last week quoted an average 13.77% basic interest rate, down from the previous week's 13.78%.

French officials are completing a 1984 austerity budget that calls for public spending limits and heavier taxation for the rich. Bankers and business executives say the tax increases will further sap French morale without solving industry's immediate cash problems.

Two General Dynamics former executives were indicated by a federal grand jury for receiving $2.7 million in kickbacks in connection with shipbuilding projects, including Navy nuclear-submarine contracts. Two former officials of Frigitemp, which acted as a subcontractor, were indicted for arranging and making the kickbacks.

8 Bank of America is applying for a charter to operate in South Dakota, a move that would allow it to enter the insurance underwriting business.

A Texas bank was authorized by the comptroller of the currency to operate an investment-advisory unit. The authorization could elicit protests from the securities industry, which has opposed past incursions by banks into the securities business.

---

*The cut-off date for Business in Review is usually September because of our production schedule. Since the last entry in the previous almanac was August 31, 1983, the current entry commences September 1, 1983.

9 Capital spending by U.S. businesses is expected to increase in coming months, but total 1983 outlays for plant and equipment will be 2.3% less than last year's, according to the Commerce Department's latest survey. Such outlays declined 5.5% in 1982. Fourth-quarter spending is expected to be up 9.2%.

U.S. Steel plans to eliminate as many as 5,000 management employees by early next year, sources said. The cut, representing an estimated one-third of the steel division's white-collar staff, would be part of an effort to return steel operations to health.

Interest rates are too high considering "the current environment of low inflation," Treasury Secretary Regan said. He also said the president expects to decide next week how to respond to a Supreme Court decision that upholds the right of states to tax a share of the world-wide earnings of U.S.-based corporations.

An Agriculture Department report to be released Monday is expected by analysts to say the summer's drought slashed the corn crop by over 1.6 billion bushels and the soybean harvest by over 400 million bushels.

12 GM is pressing the U.S. to raise the limit on Japanese auto imports so it can import cars from its Japanese affiliates for sale here. Other auto makers have been seeking a continuation or reduction of the quotas.

Producer prices increased an adjusted 0.4% in August, indicating that inflation has returned, although at a relatively modest level. Food prices and capital-equipment costs contributed to the increase, which equals 4.8% at an annual rate.

The IMF says the stage has been set for a rise in output and trade world-wide. But in its annual report, the organization warned that the recovery could fizzle if countries, especially the U.S., don't continue their fiscal belt-tightening.

The Eurodollar bond market appears poised for a big rally amid signs that long-term interest rates may decline in the fourth quarter.

13 Chrysler outbid three groups of securities firms, and agreed to pay the U.S. Treasury $311 million to retire 14.4 million warrants were issued three years ago under a $1.2 billion federal bailout package. The auto maker earlier offered as much as $250 million for the warrants.

Drought and a federal program that idled a record amount of farmland nearly halved the projected U.S. corn crop from 1982's record 8.4 billion bushels, the Agriculture Department said. The agency

also said the soybean crop will drop nearly 33% to 1.53 billion bushels because of the worst drought since the Dust Bowl days of the 1930s.

Citibank agreed to pay $323,000 in civil penalties to settle charges that it violated a U.S. law barring U.S. companies from cooperating with the Arab boycott of Israel. FMC Corp. agreed to pay an $8,500 penalty to settle charges that it violated the law. Neither firm admitted or denied having violated the anti-boycott law.

14 Retail sales fell 1.4% in August to $97.6 billion, reflecting a drop in auto sales. Consumer installment credit expanded a record $4.84 billion in July, or at a 16½% annual rate. Half the increase was in auto credit. The sales decline indicates anew that the recovery has slowed, but the economy is expected to grow at a healthy pace through 1983.

Ford said it will increase prices an average of $254, or 2.3%, on 1984 models. As GM had last month, Ford either held the line or raised prices only moderately on small cars while assigning sharp increases on larger cars, which are in strong demand.

Motorists would save about $660 in insurance premiums over 10 years if their autos were equipped with air bags or automatically fastening belts, New York state's insurance superintendent said. In testimony before a Senate panel, he supported a bill requiring auto makers to install air bags, starting with 1986 models.

A $200 million loan to Yugoslavia was released by the Bank for International Settlements. The action frees the last major portion of a $4.5 billion rescue package for the nation.

15 Baldwin-United will sell MGIC Investment, its major asset, signaling a switch in its survival plan. Proceeds apparently will be used to repay part of Baldwin's $1 billion in short-term debt and to pay annuity holders. Baldwin had planned to repay most of that debt with MGIC profits and proceeds from the sale of other assets.

U.S. auto makers' domestic car sales in the first 10 days of September rose 21% to 132,333 units from a year earlier. The figures provide further evidence that sales have slowed since early summer. GM's chairman estimated that U.S. car sales in the 1983 model year will total 8.8 million units, 15% more than in 1982.

Business inventories rose 0.2% in July to an adjusted $506.7 billion, the Commerce Department said.

16 Industrial production rose an adjusted 0.9% in August. Although the increase was healthy, it was the smallest in seven months and is the latest evidence that the recovery has moderated. Output has risen 11.6% since last November but remains 2.2% below the level of July 1981, when the recession began.

Purchases of British slab steel by U.S. Steel Corp. may be thwarted by the Reagan administration. A Commerce Department official said such purchases would threaten a steel import-quota accord the U.S. negotiated with the Common Market last year.

The SEC agreed to an accounting rule change that may boost independent oil companies' earnings next year. The agency agreed to let many oil and gas exploration companies defer leasing, drilling and other "preproduction" expenses for a longer time than they now are allowed.

19 Toyota raised prices of its 1984 cars an average of $271, or 3%. The increase in bigger than recent boosts by GM and Ford and makes the Japanese company's cars more expensive than the U.S. models they compete against. But Toyota's higher prices aren't expected to depress sales.

U.S.-produced cars captured half of the top 10 slots in the EPA's annual fuel-efficiency ratings for new autos, but overall fleet efficiency of Detroit-made vehicles declined from a year ago. The EPA rated Japan's subcompact Honda Civic most fuel-efficient, at an estimated 51 miles a gallon.

Continued gains in manufacturing and an increase in electricity use contributed to August's rise, to an adjusted 76.7%, in the operating rate at U.S. factories, utilities and mines.

The Bank of England begins accepting bids today for the 130 million shares of British Petroleum Britain is selling to raise over $750 million.

The Fed may begin to relax credit policy soon despite the $5.5 billion surge in the money supply reported Friday, many economists said.

20 Housing starts rose 8.4% in August to an adjusted annual rate of 1,935,000 units, despite this summer's rise in mortgage rates. Last month's level was the strongest since December 1978. But a drop in building permits may portend the slowdown in construction that many economists have predicted.

Insurance regulators who control six ailing Baldwin-United units said their plan for "rehabilitating" the units will include paying annuity holders interest rates as low as 3.6% and forbidding complete withdrawals for at least 3½ years.

21 The big board will begin trading stock-index options Friday. Amid charges from rival exchanges that it is engaged in predatory pricing policies, it received SEC approval to let nonmember traders buy and sell its options on the New York Stock Exchange composite index of 1500 stocks without a membership fee.

The Dow Jones Industrial Average rose to a record 1249.19, up 15.25 on volume of 103,050,000 shares. Bond prices surged. The federal funds rate declined, a change some analysts believe indicates that the Fed may be relaxing credit policy.

Ford may be prompted by GM's proposed U.S. small-car venture with Toyota to set up a competing U.S. joint venture with its Japanese affiliate, Toyo Kogyo.

Personal income rose 0.2% in August, and consumer spending fell 0.3%, to an adjusted $2.170 trillion annual pace. The spending decline, the first in over a year, helped boost savings. Economists foresee larger income gains in coming months, and they expect consumer spending to resume its growth soon.

Prepaid union dental plans are losing large sums of money to organized-crime figures aided by corrupt union officials, a Senate panel said. A hearing focused on plans associated with a Las Vegas, Nev., local and an Atlantic City, N.J., local. The plans offer services at a set fee, regardless of whether the services are used.

22 The economy is growing at a strong, 7% annual rate this quarter, the Commerce Department estimated. It said prices are rising at a 3.2% annual rate, the smallest quarterly increase since 1972. The agency said second-quarter corporate profits rose 17.6%, or a record $19 billion, to $127.2 billion at an annual rate.

Big Board short interest rose 5.9%, or 9.3 million shares, in the month ended last Thursday, to a record 168,682,123 shares. Amex short interest fell 2.6%, or 410,078 shares, to 15,122,543 shares.

Eastern Airlines asked its 37,500 employees to accept sharp wage reductions as part of a program to save it over $300 million in 1984. Employee approval for the plan isn't certain.

23 Mexico is allowing the free-rate of exchange of its peso to slip, to avoid sharp future devaluations and to keep its dual-exchange-rate system.

New factory orders for durables rose a modest 0.3% in August, to an adjusted $88.5 billion. Increased orders for autos, metals and nondefense capital goods helped offset a 37.5% plunge in defense orders.

Publicly held companies' holders are likely soon to be getting considerably less information about their executives' pay and benefits, under new rules issued by the SEC.

Supplemental jobless payments would be extended 18 months, under legislation approved by the Senate Finance Committee. The bill is less generous than an extension passed earlier this week by a House panel.

26 Continental Air filed for bankruptcy protection, citing labor costs. The carrier suspended flights to 78 U.S. cities, stranding about 10,000 passengers, flight attendants and pilots, but plans tomorrow to resume service in 25 of those cities. The filing, which doesn't pertain to international flights, will idle 7,800 of Continental's 12,000 employees.

RCA's agreement to sell C.I.T. to Manufacturers Hanover for $1.51 billion would give RCA cash for acquisitions and expansion but could make it vulnerable to a takeover. For Manufacturers, the step furthers a strategy of expanding beyond New York state through activities that aren't subject to the interstate-banking ban.

Consumer prices rose an adjusted 0.4% in August and July and are expected to continue increasing at a measured pace in coming months before accelerating around year-end. The August and July increases reflected higher transportation costs.

Machine-tool orders in August were up 59% from a year earlier, to $137.3 million, but a recovery for the industry is till many months off, machine-tool makers say. Shipments were down 56% from August 1982.

The U.S. car market's strength remains uncertain despite the 6% rise in mid-September's sales, to 164,792 cars, from the year-earlier level. Industry observers called sales relatively low in relation to gains in consumer confidence and the economy. GM posted a sales decline.

27 Santa Fe Industries and Southern Pacific Co. today are expected to announce that they plan to merge. Such a merger would create the nation's third-largest railroad in trackage, with 25,600 miles of road. The system would have combined annual revenue of $4.3 billion.

Baldwin-United was forced into bankruptcy proceedings after two creditor groups failed to agree on sharing Baldwin assets promised as loan collateral to one group. Baldwin's bankruptcy petition said the financial-services company has assets of $9.38 billion. Baldwin's liabilities far exceed those assets, however.

Continental Air will try to resume about half of its flights today and expects its slashed fares to attract hordes of passengers. Many industry executives predict the pared-down carrier may be short-lived, however.

28 Continental Airlines resumed flights as a discount carrier, despite chaotic ticket-purchasing procedures. As rival carriers announced competing $49 fares, industry observers contended Continental, which filed for bankruptcy-law protection last weekend, had little chance for survival.

Eastern Airlines machinists vowed to fight any move by the troubled carrier to file for bankruptcy-law protection and again rejected a call for a 15% pay cut.

Reagan told finance ministers of the IMF that he is impatient with congressional delays in approving a bill to bolster the U.S. contribution to IMF lending resources. He termed a U.S. promise to increase its deposit by $8.4 billion "an unbreakable commitment" and called on "both parties" to approve the measure quickly.

29 Republic Steel agreed to be acquired by LTV for stock valued at $770 million, signaling radical changes in the troubled industry. The merger of the nation's third- and fourth-largest steel makers would challenge U.S. Steel's dominance.

The health of Eastern Airlines rests on the credibility of Frank Borman, chairman. Many employees doubt his warning that if the carrier doesn't win 15% wage cuts it may, like Continental Air, seek bankruptcy-law protection.

Telephone access fees established by the FCC would take effect next year solely for businesses, under legislation approved by a House subcommittee. The bill would prevent a new charge to residential phone users for access to the long-distance network.

The shelf-registration process for underwriting stock sales cut by 29% the fund-raising expenses of big companies using it last year, according to a study by SEC aides.

The merchandise trade deficit for the U.S. widened to a record adjusted $7.19 billion in August as the nation's strong economic expansion continued to spur demand for imports.

30 Boeing received a $560 million order for nine 767 twinjets from Japan Air Lines. It had vied for the work against Europe's Airbus Industrie.

Thatcher backed U.S. arms-control plans but criticized huge deficits.

The British leader's White House meeting was designed to show U.S.-British agreement on the need to deploy U.S.

missiles in Europe this winter unless the U.S. and Soviets reach an arms-control pact. Thatcher added that budget deficits are keeping interest rates high and interfering with the recovery.

But Thatcher apparently felt she failed to change the minds of Reagan and other U.S. officials about deficits.

October 1983

3   U.S. auto makers plan to build 1,983,290 cars in the fourth quarter, 62% more than in the year-earlier period, despite economists' warnings that their goal is too ambitious. The industry plans to eliminate a shortage that it says limited summer sales gains. It predicts fourth-quarter sales of 1,751,000 cars.

Cincinnati Gas said the troubled Zimmer nuclear plant could cost up to $3.5 billion, double its previous estimate. The estimate suggests that much construction must be redone.

The economy remained strong in September, bolstered by a surge in new orders, according to a monthly survey of purchasing managers.

The 0.1% August decline in the index of leading economic indicators was the first decrease in a year and suggests that economic expansion, estimated at a 7% annual rate in the third quarter, will moderate further in coming months. Sales of single-family homes fell 5.1% in August, the second consecutive monthly decline.

Continental Air has begun to implement a long-term survival plan. The carrier, operating under bankruptcy-law protection, kept most of its planes aloft last weekend despite a strike by pilots and flight attendants.

4   Christmas home-computer sales, which account for 40% to 50% of the year's total, will be hurt by a shortage of the machines, retailers predict. The stores expect to fare better than manufacturers, by selling more software and such extra equipment as printers and disk drives.

Factory orders rose 1.1% in August, and construction spending increased 2.4%. Both Commerce Department reports indicate that economic growth has moderated.

5   New-car sales rose 4.9% in the U.S. in September, to 703,507 units, although both domestic and foreign producers were hurt by short supplies. All of the rise was accounted for by U.S.-made models; restrictions on Japanese imports resulted in a sales decline for imports.

Renewable-energy projects and increased conservation must assume an increasingly important role in any long-term energy policy for the U.S., the Reagan administration's updated National Energy Policy asserts. The plan signals a switch from almost complete reliance on such conventional energy sources as oil, natural gas, coal and nuclear power.

Chemical Bank officials said holders of $2.25 billion of defaulted Washington Public Power bonds probably will have to wait at least three years before receiving reimbursement.

A tape-recorded suicide message left last week by Bullion Reserve of North America's chairman may shed light on the fate of up to $60 million in precious metals missing from a Utah depository. The company has filed for bankruptcy-law protection.

6   The budget deficit could narrow sharply to "the area of" $100 billion in fiscal 1985, Treasury Secretary Regan said. Department spokesmen provided only sketchy details to support Regan's projection, which is far lower than the $170.2 billion deficit predicted in July by the Office of Management and Budget.

Continental Air will cut its already reduced flying operations 8% because of effects of a strike by pilots and flight attendants. The carrier planned to increase flights 20% today.

Bank of Montreal agreed to acquire Harris Bankcorp., Chicago's third-largest banking company, for $82 a share, or $546.6 million.

Three precious-metals firms were issued cease-and-desist orders for alleged violations of Florida securities laws. The companies were operated by former employees of the International Gold Bullion Exchange, which was closed by the courts last spring after widespread customer complaints of non-delivery on orders.

The SEC approved a plan to increase the amount of financial data U.S. investors receive from foreign companies whose stock is traded over the counter.

7   Retailers registered strong sales growth for September, the fifth consecutive month of robust gains. The increases furthered their hopes for a strong Christmas season. Sears sales rose 27.5%; Wal-Mart's soared 42%.

Cincinnati Gas said it may scrap its troubled Zimmer nuclear power plant or convert it to alternate fuel because revised cost estimates for completing it create "serious financial problems" for the utility.

Airlines posted strong September traffic gains, reflecting a surge in foreign travel. But the double-digit gains by most major carriers also reflected extremely weak year-earlier results.

Bank of Montreal's move to buy Chicago-based Harris Bankcorp. underscores the discrepancy between the treatment of foreign banks in Canada and Canadian banks abroad. Foreign banks are protesting a Canadian law that limits their growth to 8% of the Canadian banking market.

10 Japan agreed to extend its restraints on auto exports to the U.S. for another year, beginning April 1. But U.S. trade officials said that, to maintain its 22% share of the U.S. market, Japan may want to raise its voluntary limit to 2.2 million cars for the year from 1,680,000.

The civilian unemployment rate, which fell to an adjusted 9.3% of the work force in September, is expected to continue to decline as the pace of the economic recover moderates.

Eastern Air posted a $34.4 million third-quarter loss. Management agreed to drop its threat to take the carrier into bankruptcy proceedings, and union leaders endorsed a management proposal for an audit of company finances. Union acceptance of the audit rests on the success of contract talks between Eastern and the union representing flight attendants.

Carrian Group has been pushed to the verge of failure by Hong Kong's collapsing real-estate market. Bankers Trust and Hong Kong's registrar filed petitions to liquidate two units of Carrian, which had been one of Hong Kong's biggest conglomerates.

Business leaders and government officials at the semiannual session of the Business Council expressed nervousness about the duration of a noninflationary expansion. Fed Chairman Volcker worried that the nation is entering "a testing period" in the fight against inflation.

11 The Dow Jones Industrial Average rose 12.50 points to 1284.65, its third consecutive record, on volume of 67,050,000 shares.

Iran again warned the big Arab oil exporters it will halt oil shipments from the Persian Gulf if Iraq unleashes its new French warplanes. Spot oil prices edged up in anticipation of a possible oil shock.

12 The Supreme Court cleared the way for a new trial to determine damages AT&T must pay MCI for antitrust violations. A federal jury in 1980 awarded $1.8 billion to MCI, but an appeals court ordered a new trial on damages after disagreeing

with a jury finding that AT&T illegally priced long-distance service.

Interest rates climbed, amid speculation that the Fed may be keeping a tight grip on credit because of inflation concerns. The surge in rates jarred financial markets, pushing the Dow Jones Industrial Average down 19.51 points, to 1265.14. Gold fell $5 an ounce, and the U.S. dollar rose.

The IMF effectively cut off further lending to Argentina, which has failed to meet anti-inflation targets.

13 Eastern Air reached a contract settlement with its flight attendants, averting a strike. The settlement clears the way for implementation of another accord, under which Eastern agreed to drop its threat to enter bankruptcy proceedings and its three unions agreed to endorse and act on an analysis of Eastern finances.

The Agriculture Department predicted the nation's 1983 corn crop will total 4.26 billion bushels, 49% less than last year and 3% less than was estimated a month ago. The expected drop reflects the Midwest's drought and a federal land-idling program.

The World Bank is considering creating a semi-independent subsidiary to help raise and channel additional money for use in developing countries.

14 Retail sales rose 1.6% to a seasonally adjusted $99.48 billion in September, as consumers stepped up spending in most categories. Economists predict the gains will continue as employment and income improve further.

The Philippine central bank called a meeting of the nation's major lenders in New York, amid growing signs that the country will ask to reschedule its $18 billion foreign debt.

Home-loan rates declined in the past month and further reductions are likely by year-end. But economists don't expect the declines to prevent an anticipated drop in new-home sales this fall. Lenders last week quoted an average 13.59% basic interest rate, down from 13.65% a week earlier.

U.S. new-car sales rose 45% in the first 10 days of October, to an estimated 191,965 units, from a weak year-earlier period. Sales, at an annual rate, were weaker than the month earlier's but indicate the domestic auto recovery is continuing.

17 Manville and its asbestos-liability creditors met over the weekend to try to resolve their differences before this afternoon, when the construction and forest-products concern is to file its reorganization plan.

First National Bank of Midland's collapse, the second-biggest commercial bank failure in the U.S., resulted largely from a run by large depositors. The FDIC sold deposits and certain assets of the Texas bank, which was declared insolvent Friday, to RepublicBank Corp. of Dallas.

The Philippines' plan to defer principal payments to banks for 90 days on some of its $18 billion foreign debt sparked concern that the debt crisis may be spreading to Asia. The moratorium also adds to pressure on President Marcos to solve the political problems from which the nation's financial crisis springs.

Business inventories' August rise of $6.25 billion, or 1.2%, to an adjusted $512.07 billion was the largest increase in over three years and probably will be followed by additional restocking, many economists say. Separately, consumer installment credit expanded an adjusted $3.39 billion in August, or at a 11.25% annual rate.

Further solid economic growth without a resurgence of inflation was predicted by many economists following government reports that, in September, industrial production climbed a strong 1.5% while producer prices edged up only 0.2%.

18 A Gulf Oil stake of 8.75% has been amassed by a Mesa Petroleum-led group that includes concerns controlled by Canada's Belzberg family. The 14.5 million-share stake was bought for $630 million as an investment, Mesa said. But an SEC filing and Mesa's track record suggest the group wants to reorganize Gulf.

The Transportation Department is considering a public offering of a sizable portion of Conrail as an alternative to selling it to another railroad or selling control to Conrail employees.

Factories, utilities and mines in the U.S. stepped up operations to a seasonally adjusted 78.1% of capacity in September from 77.1% in August, the Fed said.

Short-term interest rates edged lower amid hopes that the recent slowdown in money-supply growth will allow the Fed to further loosen its credit reins.

19 Fed Chairman Volcker said he believes that monetary expansion to help finance large federal budget deficits is "basically unwarranted." Fed officials fear that a sudden expansion of the money supply could generate future inflation.

Digital Equipment said its first-quarter profit fell 65% to 75%. It cited unexpectedly low shipments of personal computers and disk drives. The news sparked a huge stock sell-off; Digital shares fell $21 to $79.25.

IBM introduced two personal computers that make the power and programs of its 370 mainframe machines available to the user at a desk. Analysts viewed the units as threats to office-computer competitors.

The Dow Jones Industrials fell 17.89 points to 1250.81 in reaction to Digital Equipment's disclosure of plunging earnings. Stock options and index futures and options reacted sharply to the slide.

U.S. thrifts appear headed for their first profitable year since 1980 as they posted total after-tax income of $1.1 billion in the first half. But the Federal Home Loan Bank Board said their health remains fragile.

GM agreed to spend at least $42.5 million to hire, train and promote more women and minorities. The accord is the largest settlement of job-bias charges brought by the Equal Employment Opportunity agency.

20 Personal income rose a strong 0.9% in September, to an adjusted $2.781 trillion annual rate, indicating anew that the recovery regained momentum last month. Americans responded to the gain by increasing spending and reducing savings.

Housing starts in September declined 13.4% to 1,652,000 units, the slowest pace since april. A further slowdown in home building is expected in the next few months, reflecting an expected continuation of high home-loan rates.

Gulf Oil hopes that an early December shareholders meeting will force a confrontation with Mesa Petroleum Chairman T. Boone Pickens Jr., who leads a group that has amassed an 8.75% Gulf stake. Gulf's advisers believe Pickens planned to wage a proxy challenge in May.

BankAmerica's net income fell 29% in the third quarter and Continental Illinois Corp.'s plunged 39%, mainly because of problem loans and weak loan demand. First Interstate Bankcorp's net rose 12%.

21 Real GNP grew at a 7.9% annual rate in the third quarter, the Commerce Department said. The rate, stronger than the 7% rise estimated a month ago, reflects higher-than-expected consumer spending. The department said inflation accelerated to an adjusted 3.4% annual rate from 3.3% in the second quarter.

Fed Chairman Paul Volcker said he believes the recent moderation in labor costs and the Fed's monetary policy will result in a 1984 inflation rate lower than the 5% currently forecasted by the Reagan administration.

Seven big securities firms may each have

to return thousands of dollars to buyers of some troubled Baldwin-United annuities. New York Gov. Cuomo said the firms may have violated state law by soliciting buyers for annuities issued by Baldwin units that weren't licensed in New York.

Iraq is diverting its oil traffic from the blocked sea lanes of the Persian Gulf and transporting it by pipelines and trucks, industry sources say. Other Arab producers also want to lessen their dependence on shipping crude through the Persian Gulf, under the gaze of Iran's navy.

24 Lifemark Corp and American Medical International signed a definitive agreement to merge in a transaction valued at $1 billion. The merger, through a stock-swap, would create the second-largest U.S. hospital management concern, behind Hospital Corp. of America.

Many Baldwin-United creditors are writing off their loans to the firm, now that it is operating under bankruptcy-law protection. Some 25 U.S. banks may have to writeoff $172.5 million in short-term Baldwin debt.

25 General Motors profit more than quintupled to a record $736.9 million for the third quarter as sales rose 24%. The auto maker could have earned more if parts shortages hadn't reduced its output. American Motors' operating loss widening to $99.4 million despite a 21% rise in sales.

Trans World Corp is expected to approve spinning off its Trans World Airlines unit tomorrow. Analysts said the move would enhance prospects of the parent, which reported a slight rise in third-quarter earnings.

Hunger in U.S. cities is growing worse despite efforts to feed the needy and despite the economic recovery, the U.S. Conference of Mayors reported. The mayors said the hunger crisis has been worsened by high joblessness, reduced federal benefits and inflation in the cost of necessities.

26 Consumer Prices rose 0.5%, or 6% annually, in September, and further moderate increases are seen. Housing and food costs caused the acceleration in prices. New factory orders for durable goods fell 0.5%, reflecting a sharp drop in orders for motor vehicles and parts.

Domestic car sales rose 41.1% in mid-October, slightly greater than some analysts had expected. The sales were equivalent to an annual rate of 7.6 million units.

Japan won't agree to limit auto exports to the U.S. to 1.8 million cars for 1984 models but has indicated it may accept a 1.9 million-car limit.

27 The Clinch River breeder reactor project, the flagship of the Reagan administration's nuclear research program, was killed by Congress after years of contention. The Senate vote denying further funds for the Tennessee project was 56–40, a wider margin than expected.

Chrysler posted net income for the third quarter of $100.2 million, more than 10 times the year-earlier profit. Revenue rose 14%. The auto maker said it may write down the book value of its 1.8 million Peugeot shares, which could result in a large charge against fourth-quarter profit. Chrysler also said its liabilities exceed assets by over $1 billion.

OPEC is trying to come to grips with alleged production cheating by Saudi Arabia, Iran and Nigeria that is depressing oil prices. The issue will be considered by OPEC's Market Monitoring panel and is expected to be addressed at a Dec. 7 meeting of the cartel in Geneva.

28 Non-farm productivity increased at a 5% annual rate in the third quarter. The moderation of the pace from 6.6% in the second quarter may indicate that the U.S. is moving into the middle stages of economic recovery.

The SEC proposed more stringent rules for most banks that offer full-line brokerage services. The proposal would require such banks to submit to SEC inspections and brokerage-house regulations for the first time.

Ford posted record profit of $333.1 million for the third quarter, reversing a year-earlier loss of $325.4 million. Sales rose 28% to a record $10.29 billion.

Du Pont third-quarter profit surged 60% from weak year-earlier results, with fiber and plastics operations leading the turnaround. Du Pont cited cost-cutting moves and said full-year profit will be "substantially" ahead of 1982's $894 million.

OPEC may have to lower its production ceiling below the 17.5 million barrels a day adopted last March because oil consumption world-wide is dropping, said a member of the cartel's market-monitoring panel.

31 Interest rates may decline in coming months, economists predict. Fears that vigorous economic expansion will stimulate corporate borrowing and push up interest rates aren't likely to be borne out, they say. Their view was bolstered by an unexpectedly large, $2.4 billion drop in the basic money supply measure for the week ended Oct. 19.

Machine-tool orders in September totaled $156 million, up 14% from August and

80% from the depressed year-earlier level. But orders won't return to normal until makers of construction, farm, industrial, aircraft and energy-related equipment resume buying, machine-tool executives say.

Zimmer nuclear plant's partners are to meet today to discuss the future of the stalled project, including a suggestion by Dayton Power that the 97%-complete plant be switched to natural gas and later to coal. Separately, a Nuclear Regulatory Commission report expressed dissatisfaction with agency probes of the plant.

The index of leading economic indicators' 0.9% rise in September suggests the current expansion will enter its second year poised for further solid growth. Growth this quarter will be below the third quarter's 7.9% rate, White House economic adviser Martin Feldstein predicts.

The trade deficit narrowed to an adjusted $5.81 billion in September from a record $7.19 billion in August, indicating that an uneven recovery in U.S. exports may be under way.

November 1983

1 The Supreme Court refused to hear an appeal by a Transamerica unit whose antitrust action seeking $261 million in damages from IBM failed in lower courts. The case was the last of a series in which smaller computer firms accused IBM of curbing competition in the market for disks compatible with its computers.

The Big Three auto makers are expected to post record fourth-quarter profit of $2.3 billion, against a 1982 $187 million loss, despite output problems. The three, trying to run plants at capacity, plan to build 1,964,890 cars this quarter, 20,000 fewer than they planned a month ago but 60% more than were built a year ago.

The value of building contracts awarded in September fell an adjusted 2% from the month earlier, to $17.4 billion, F. W. Dodge said.

2 International Business Machines introduced its first home computer, the long awaited PCjr, whose entry model is priced at a lower-than-expected $669. Units will be on view in December, but won't be sold until 1984.

Shortages of Japanese cars are apt to continue until April 1985 as a result of Japan's agreement with the U.S. to extend export restraints. The agreement is expected to raise prices and boost U.S. carmakers profits.

Reagan told cabinet chiefs to resubmit fiscal 1985 spending plans, cutting them to below the 1985 projections used to prepare this year's budget, White House officials said. "He wants to reassert his image as a budget-cutter as he enters a year in which he may seek reelection," they said.

Construction spending fell 0.8%, in September from August to a $272.7 billion annual rate, suggesting that the residential building boom that began a year ago is slackening.

3 New-home sales rose 13.7% in September to an annual rate of 632,000 houses, after three consecutive months of declines. The strong rise was attributed to aggressive marketing and to the growing attractiveness of adjustable-rate mortgages.

Factory orders rose a strong 1.5% in September to an adjusted $181 billion, foreshadowing continued growth in production and employment. Orders for nondefense capital goods were particularly strong.

U.S. corporate profit rose 29% in the third quarter, their sharpest year-to-year gain in 4½ years, according to a Wall Street Journal survey. Further strong increases are expected this quarter and in 1984. Auto industry profits were especially strong.

Canadian corporate profits soared 137% last quarter, to $1.03 billion (Canadian), according to the survey.

Many of the 22 phone companies to be divested from AT&T Jan. 1 are asking employees to retire early. The Bell System will cut at least 8,000 employees, including managers, from its work force before the divestiture.

4 A deficit-cutting bill was outlined by the Senate Finance panel amid reports that Fed Chairman Volcker had told members forceful deficit-reduction actions must precede any significant interest-rate drop. The three-year, $150 billion measure includes hefty new taxes and big cuts in federal programs, including $28 billion from Social Security.

Greyhound vowed it would resume bus service in about two weeks, with nonunion drivers if necessary. On the first day of a nationwide strike against the No. 1 bus company, traffic on other carriers strengthened and thousands of job applicants lined up outside Greyhound terminals.

Sales of new cars in the U.S. rose more than 31%, to about 855,995 autos, in October from a year earlier, as the domestic industry's recovery continued as predicted. Sales of domestic makes were up more than 36%, and are expected to continue at about the same pace in coming months.

7   IBH holding AG's filing for protection from creditors has sent shock waves around the world, and the web of financial problems linking the huge construction-equipment maker with one of West Germany's largest private banks has triggered Germany's worst bank crisis since 1974. Collapse of IBH could alter radically an industry plagued by overcapacity.

The civilian unemployment rate's 0.5-percentage-point decline in October to a seasonally adjusted 8.8% from September indicates economic growth is continuing to outpace many economists' expectations.

Demand for oil is rising in the U.S. for the first time in five years, but oil executives don't expect prices to rise soon. The U.S. consumed 15.1 million barrels of oil a day from June through September, up 1.6% from 1982. Demand abroad is still falling.

The balance-of-payments deficit on the current account could reach a record $35 billion for 1983, Commerce Secretary Baldrige said. The administration previously estimated the deficit at $30 billion.

Argentina's president-elect, Raul Alfonsin, wants to start anew talks with creditor banks to restructure the nation's $40 billion foreign debt.

8   A GPU unit was charged with criminal misconduct in the operations of the Three Mile Island nuclear plant before the 1979 accident there. A grand jury charged that Metropolitan Edison manipulated and falsified tests pertaining to cooling-system leaks and concealed problems from the NRC. The utility could face fines of $85,000 plus the cost of prosecution.

Interest rates were little changed despite concern about federal borrowing needs. But the dollar strengthened on predictions that U.S. interest rates will rise soon. The Treasury began its delayed quarterly financing operation with the sale of $6.5 billion in notes.

Citicorp plans to buy 29.9% of Vickers da Costa (Holdings) PLC, a British brokerage firm, for $29.7 million. The proposed purchase conforms with its plan to build a global investment-banking business.

9   Hitachi was required to pay IBM about $300 million under a secret agreement that formed the hub of the recent settlement of IBM's suit against Hitachi for alleged theft of technology. Sources close to the companies' talks said that in exchange for the payment IBM agreed to drop its suit, which would have involved disclosures embarrassing to the Japanese conglomerate.

The federal budget deficit won't be reduced to an "acceptable" level through economic growth alone, Martin Feldstein, chairman of Reagan's Council of Economic Advisers, said at a congressional hearing. Feldstein's position is at odds with Treasury Secretary Regan's.

The French steelmaker Creusot-Loire and Manurhin, a big French machine-tool maker, threatened to file for bankruptcy soon unless their financial pressures are eased.

10   Japan agreed with the U.S. on a modest package of steps to strengthen the yen against the dollar. But traders say the accord, reached the first day of Reagan's visit to Japan, will do little to bolster the yen as long as U.S. interest rates remain high. Details of the agreement weren't disclosed.

11   Producer prices for finished goods rose a modest, seasonally adjusted 0.3% in October. Prices didn't show the inflationary upswing some economists had feared. The government also said that retail sales rose 1.1% last month and that consumer credit grew at a 7.9% annual rate in September.

Bond prices soared, on predictions that inflation and money-supply growth will remain under control and interest rates may decline as the economy continues its strong expansion. The optimistic forecasts were spurred by government data on producer prices and retail sales.

U.S. Steel filed countervailing-duty actions against state steelmakers in Mexico, Argentina and Brazil. As part of the domestic industry's campaign to restrict subsidized foreign steel, House Steel Caucus members introduced a measure to limit foreign steel imports to an average 15% of the U.S. market for five years.

14   McDonnell Douglas will halt development of two commercial jets because it can't find customers for them. The move, which could boost earnings, raises the question of whether McDonnell will phase out commercial operations to emphasize more lucrative military production.

The Commerce Department is abandoning its plan to sell the government's weather satellites to a commercial owner because of congressional opposition. But lawmakers are starting to write some rules on selling the Landsat satellite system.

15   Commercial banks in the U.S. have raised

a record $7.6 billion in the first nine months of 1983 through public sales of stock and long-term debt. Spurring the rush for capital are concern over loan losses and desire to be ready for the new opportunities provided by deregulation of banking.

Bond prices declined and some short-term interest rates edged up despite a $2.5 billion plunge in the money supply that sent the measure well below the Fed's target range. The drop isn't expected to encourage the Fed to relax its credit policy.

Business inventories rose an adjusted 0.7% in September to $513.82 billion, reflecting an increase in auto inventories. September's gain was slower than August's, indicating that inventory growth may have peaked in the third quarter.

16 Industrial production rose 0.8% in October, after increasing 1.3% in both September and August. Last month's rise was less than expected, but economists said they were encouraged by continuing strength in business-equipment production.

The White House said it hopes the recent $2.5 billion drop in the money supply doesn't mean the Fed altered its goal of increasing the figure between 5% and 9% in the second half. It called on the central bank to return the figure to that target range.

Sales of U.S.-built autos rose 5.6% in early November from a year earlier, to 198,126 cars. Sales, at an annual rate of 6.9 million units, were about the same as in September and October. GM sales declined 3.4%.

Eight retailing concerns posted fiscal third-quarter earnings gains, reflecting brisk consumer demand. Many expressed optimism about holiday-season sales.

A drop in U.S. exports to Latin America to $30.09 billion from $38.95 billion in 1981 cost nearly 250,000 domestic jobs last year, the New York Fed said. That drop in exports accounted for over 40% of the total decline in U.S. exports last year. The bank said such exports are likely to fall further this year.

Home mortgage rates fell slightly in the past month, but economists predict they will be stable in the near future. An average rate of 13.47% was quoted last week on standard home loans.

17 American telephone estimates that first-quarter dividends for the eight companies that will result from its Jan. 1 breakup will total $1.365 for each predivestiture AT&T share. In a 267-page document filed with the SEC, it also estimated

that in 1984 the "new" AT&T will earn $2.1 billion while the seven regional companies will post combined profits of $6.59 billion.

The futures of phone companies soon to be spun off from AT&T will be determined largely by regulators, who are expected to take a more sympathetic view of the companies after the breakup. Each state commission must grapple with restructuring rates to keep service affordable while letting the companies turn a reasonable profit.

The operating rate at the nation's factories, utilities and mines rose 0.5 percentage point in October, to 78.6% of capacity. The increase was smaller than in the previous seven months, reflecting a moderation in the growth of industrial production.

18 The Big Board is readying itself for Monday's record listing of over 1.6 billion shares of phone company stocks through extra computers and workers and revised work schedules.

Voluminous AT&T disclosures pertaining to the Bell System's Jan. 1 breakup were met cautiously by investors. AT&T stock, bonds and options traded in narrow ranges on unspectacular volume. Meanwhile, rating agencies are reassessing bonds issued by AT&T and its units.

Housing starts declined 3.8% in October from September, to an annual rate of 1,608,000 units. The decline was the second in a row and reflects a summer increase in mortgge rates. Nonetheless, October's rate stood 40.8% above the year earlier's. Building permits rose 3.9% last month.

Morgan Stanley beat 12 other contenders to manage a $4.7 billion Teamsters pension plan, the largest fiduciary-investment account on Wall Street. The plan had been managed by Equitable Life Assurance. The Teamsters' switch follows months of tension over Equitable's handling of certain real estate.

21 The 1.6 billion shares of new phone-company stocks that begin trading today on the New York Stock Exchange will provide many investors with their first experience in buying or selling when-issued stocks.

Japanese investment in Europe may be bolstered by an agreement allowing Japan to export to the Common Market more semi-finished video-tape recorders. Separately, Japan has moved more slowly than expected in gaining even its 2% toehold in the U.S. small-computer market.

22 AT&T led a stock-market rally that pushed

the Dow Jones Industrial Average up 17.78 points, to 1268.80, on volume of 97,740,000 shares. Trading in when-issued shares of the "new" AT&T reached 8,186,900 shares, believed to be a record daily total for an individual Big Board issue.

Personal income last month rose 1.2%, the largest increase in over two years, to $2.819 trillion. The strong growth suggests Americans will continue the buying spree that has fueled the economy's recent rapid growth and also will increase savings, which will help finance huge government budget deficits.

Fed Chairman Volcker dismissed recent White House and congressional complaints that monetary policy is too restrictive. His remarks highlighted a policy debate between those who blame tight monetary policy for high interest rates and those who blame huge federal budget deficits.

23 After-tax profits of U.S. corporations rose 11.6% in the third quarter to annual rate of $141.9 billion. Real GNP grew at a 7.7% rate in the quarter as prices, measured by a GNP-based gauge, increased at a 3.3% rate. Durable-goods orders rose 3% last month, the Commerce Department also said.

25 U.S. new-car sales fell 6.4% in mid-November from last year. The unexpected drop reflected continued shortages of certain popular mid-sized and large autos and, some analysts say, a slight softening in demand.

Consumer price figures in October suggest that inflation is leveling off at an annual rate of 5%. Prices rose last month an adjusted 0.4%, or 4.8% annually. The inflation outlook is benefiting from high productivity increases, moderate pay raises and the dollar's high value abroad.

Debt held by households, nonfinancial businesses and federal, state and local governments grew an adjusted 9.9% annually in the third quarter. The Fed also reported that personal savings totaled $141.7 billion in the second quarter, a $67.6 billion reduction from its August estimates.

Brazil's $3.8 billion debt was rescheduled by Western nations, completing a complex plan to alleviate the country's debt problems.

28 The Philippines plans to seek $3.9 billion in fresh funds by the end of next year. Philippine officials will begin talks Wednesday in New York with commercial banks, which will be asked to provide $1.65 billion.

Machine tool orders rose 70% in October from a year earlier as durable-goods makers continue to increase spending for new production machinery. But the $203.1 million of orders were less than half the monthly average in 1979 and 1980.

The federal budget deficit narrowed to $25.07 billion in October from $26.17 billion a year earlier.

Banks are jumping into venture-capital lending in increasing numbers, shedding their conservative ways for a high-risk business. But industry veterans warn that some of the newcomers are likely to get burned.

29 Gold rose $18.10 an ounce on massive buying triggered mainly by the theft of $40 million of the metal in London over the weekend.

Contracting for new construction fell 3% in October, F.W. Dodge reported. The decline was due to softened demand for housing and a drop in public construction projects.

The basic money-supply measure, M1, fell $300 million in the latest reporting week, putting it at the bottom end of the Fed's target range. But bond prices fell as the credit markets shrugged off the figures.

Coal lands owned by the U.S. have been traded to three railroads in little-noticed land swaps that have angered almost everybody involved except the government and the railroads.

30 Auto makers are questioning the strength of the industry's sales recovery, because November's sales have fallen below the level expected. However, the Big Three still plan an ambitious 58% boost in December production and a 47% increase in 1984 first-quarter output.

The merchandise trade deficit grew to a record $8.97 billion in October. As a result, 1983's trade deficit probably will exceed $70 billion, a Commerce Department official said.

OPEC may be unable to keep oil prices at current levels for the next several years because of internal conflicts and depressed demand, according to a Salomon Brothers report that urges investors to limit exposure in international and domestic oil concerns for as long as 18 months.

The Dow Jones Industrial Average closed at a record 1287.20 points, up 17.38, on a late rally by blue chips. Bond prices also rose.

Evidence of securities fraud by Washington Public Power Supply System, underwriters, accountants and brokers is being sought by the SEC in relation to the system's huge bond default last July.

The SEC authorized the Pacific Stock Exchange to trade an option based on an index of 100 high-technology firms' stock prices. But the SEC ordered tighter margin and position limits than the exchange had sought.

December 1983

1 The index of leading economic indicators rose a healthy 0.8% in October, suggesting that the recovery will continue. The gain, the 14th in a row, represented advances in all major sectors of the economy.

The Transportation Department said it doesn't plan to investigate any possible brake-lockup difficulty on General Motors' A and J cars. The department said it hasn't received any consumer complaints about such a problem.

The growth of non-farm business productivity slowed to a revised, adjusted 3.1% annual rate in the third quarter from the second quarter's 6.6% rate. The growth rate previously was estimated at 5%.

2 Retailers say strong sales during the three-day post-Thanksgiving week-end and November's double-digit sales rises indicate that the December holiday sales season will be the best in five years. Profits are expected to jump 20% to 25% above 1982 levels.

5 Civilian unemployment fell in November to an 8.4% rate, the lowest in two years. The decline from October's 8.8% rate swelled the ranks of economists who say unemployment will be below 8% by Election Day 1984. The White House attributed the drop to Reagan's policies.

The unexpected drop in joblessness led many economists to predict that the Fed will maintain its tight hold on credit for at least a month.

An 8.2% gain in new-home sales in October, to a 660,000-unit annual rate, signals that high mortgage rates don't impede buying as much as expected.

6 Bond prices strengthened after Fed Chairman Volcker said the central bank hasn't made "major" policy changes recently. But economists said Volcker may have been referring to overall economic and monetary goals, rather than daily strategy.

U.S. new-car sales rose 5.8% in November from a year earlier to 590,527 units, after sales strengthened in the last 10 days of the month. November sales reached an annual rate of 6.9 million units, close to the seven million unit rate of recent months.

The Mukluk Field well drilled by Sohio may be dry, according to data disclosed by Diamond Shamrock, a partner in the offshore Alaska drilling program. Another partner, Shell Oil, said results from the well could doom the project, which has cost the industry $1.6 billion in lease acquisitions.

OPEC appears likely to cut prices on crude oil unless escalation of the Iran-Iraq war seriously disrupts world oil-shipping lanes.

7 Capital spending will climb to an annual rate of $324.2 billion in the first half of 1984, according to a Commerce Department survey. That growth projection of 3.9% is well below the 5.6% rise expected for the current quarter but should be large enough to keep the economy expanding steadily.

Airline passenger traffic continued its gains in November, rising an indicated 8%, despite substantially higher fares. With traffic firming and fare wars subsiding, the stocks of several major airlines are poised to soar, industry observers contend.

Trading in aluminum futures is expected to begin tomorrow on the Comex, but most big aluminum makers regard the new market cautiously. Exchange officials hope the new futures contract will become a price-setting mechanism for the industry.

8 Saudi Arabia vowed to block other OPEC members from cutting output to push oil prices higher. The tough stance is likely to lead to a reaffirmation of the status quo at the OPEC meeting that continues today. The Saudi oil minister said his country's resistance to higher prices will continue through 1985.

The U.S. dropped its six-year-old investigation of possible conspiracy among major oil companies to limit production and increase prices of Persian Gulf crude oil. The probe focused most closely on Exxon, Texaco, Standard Oil of California and Mobile.

Home-mortgage rates have remained stable the past month as lenders last week quoted an average 13.4% rate, practically unchanged from a month earlier.

Purchasing managers think the U.S. economy will continue to improve in the next 12 months, according to a semiannual survey.

Citicorp sued to overturn a Massachusetts law that limits bank mergers to within New England. The suit reflects growing animosity by New York banks toward the spread of regional banking laws, which seek to prevent big banks from buying smaller banks around the country.

9 U.S. Steel asked 4,700 workers at five troubled plants for further contract concessions. The steelmaker warned in a letter to employees that noncompetitive labor costs may result in closing all or parts of the plants.

OPEC ministers said they will leave intact their March accord on oil output and pricing. But industry observers said that such action probably won't prevent prices from falling.

12 A defense budget plan calling for a 22% increase in spending for fiscal 1985 will be trimmed by the defense secretary. At a White House meeting with the president, Weinberger agreed to submit a defense spending plan "closer to $300 billion" than the $321.6 billion the Pentagon has sought for months.

The fiscal 1985 budget must include additional taxes, perhaps an unspecified revenue "plug," or a contingency tax, because radical new proposals for cutting domestic spending have been all but ruled out, administration officials said.

Ford plans to install $200 million of steel-processing equipment at its Rouge unit, indicating a long-term commitment to steel operations. The equipment is part of a modernization program Ford promised this fall in return for labor-cost concessions.

Upward pressure on interest rates is apt to continue through year-end, many bankers say. They cite the seasonal surge in private borrowing and the huge supply of Treasury debt securities facing credit markets.

Shell Oil was sued by the Justice Department. The U.S. seeks up to $1.85 billion to cover costs of cleaning up chemical pollution it claims Shell caused on Army land near Denver.

13 Congressional Budget Office Director Rudolph Penner urged that Congress act quickly to cut federal deficits, in order to avoid the damage of higher interest rates.

The British government plans to sell control of British Airways by early 1985, and there are signs that shares might be sold in the U.S. Sale of 100% of the company could raise an estimated $1.14 billion.

The Supreme Court approved the plan under which AT&T will divest itself of its local operating companies Jan. 1. The ruling, which removes the last major hurdle to the Bell System's breakup, rejects challenges to the divestiture plan by California and New York utility regulators.

Consumer installment credit grew a record

$4.89 billion in October, more than twice the September increase, to $371.56 billion. Most of the rise was due to a surge in car sales.

14 Retail sales rose 1.9% in November to $102.46 billion. The gain was more than double the rate expected by many economists. Auto sales, up 5.3% from October, represented much of the gain. Sales were up 1.9% at department stores and 2.8% at general merchandise stores.

Bond prices fell after the government reported retail sales surged 1.9% last month. The sales rise intensified fear that the Fed will rein in credit, pushing up interest rates.

Du Pont said its chemical, plastic and fiber businesses are rebounding sharply from the recession, but soft prices for crude oil and refined petroleum products have hurt its Conoco unit. Edward Jefferson, chairman, also said Du Pont is ahead of schedule on paying its debt and doesn't plan further sales of Conoco assets.

The USW's executive board warned U.S. Steel and other major steelmakers that it will reject demands for further wage-and-benefit concessions. The union's stand could prompt U.S. Steel to close permanently at least five plants.

A fiscal 1985 defense-budget plan calling for about $305 billion in spending has nearly been wrapped up by Reagan, Defense Secretary Weinberger and Budget Director Stockman, administration aides said.

15 A tax increase for 1984 was ruled out by Reagan, but he held open the possibility of a tax boost thereafter, provided Congress first cuts spending. The president said he and advisers "aren't close to any decision" on how to address the issue of taxes in the fiscal 1985 budget.

The Fed moved to control more tightly the financial hybrids that offer banking services without taking on many bank regulations. Companies that own such "non-banks" will have to register as bank holding companies or sell their banking operations.

U.S. auto makers sold 173,062 cars in the first 10 days of December. Deliveries, at an annual rate of 7.3 million cars, conformed to the lackluster pace of recent months and were in line with industry predictions. Sales are expected to continue at that pace through early February.

Britain's state oil company recommended to customers that North Sea oil prices be kept unchanged, with the benchmark grade priced at $30 a barrel. Russia cut the price of its Urals crude by 50 cents a barrel for the second time in two months, to $28.50.

16 First Federal of Chicago will be bought by Citicorp. The Bank Board approved the merger, which would be the largest Bank Board-assisted purchase of a troubled thrift.

A contingency tax is likely to be proposed by the White House in its fiscal 1985 budget. Presidential counselor Meese said such a tax wouldn't take effect before fiscal 1986, which begins Oct. 1, 1985.

Home heating-oil prices have fallen to their lowest level in at least two years because of weakened demand. Standard Oil of California slashed its wholesale price in some locations as much as 1.5 cents a gallon. The lower prices could lead to cuts in world crude-oil prices.

The U.S. economy is continuing to grow at a strong, steady pace as industrial production rose 0.8% in November. But the current-account deficit reached a record $11.98 billion in the third quarter, indicating that the U.S. is borrowing heavily from abroad to sustain that growth.

Argentina may have to suspend interest payments to its foreign creditors unless they restore some trade financing to the country, sources said. The government also is asking banks to delay the deadline for refinancing part of the country's debt.

19 The 0.2% drop in producer prices in November indicates that the 1983 price increase is likely to be the mildest in 19 years. The operating rate at the nation's factories, utilities and mines rose 0.5 percentage point to 79.2% of capacity last month, reflecting moderate but healthy industrial production growth.

Citicorp was allowed by the Federal Home Loan Bank Board to buy New Biscayne Federal Savings, Miami. That was Citicorp's second authorization in two days to buy an out-of-state thrift. It exemplified the spread of interstate banking, despite federal restrictions on it.

Charter Co., two of its units and two chemical firms were charged in a $1.8 billion suit related to health problems of 183 people exposed in Missouri to the toxic chemical dioxin. The suit is the largest filed against makers and haulers of dioxin-laden material.

The federal synfuels program may be phased out by the end of 1984. The government-backed U.S. Synthetic Fuels Corp. is likely by then to have used only two-thirds of the $15 billion Congress has allocated for synfuels projects. Uncommitted funds will be returned to the Treasury.

20 Mexico's bid for new terms on $20 billion of debt was rejected by banks, despite support by the U.S. The Mexican government was able to get banks to consider lending the country about $4 billion in new loans.

21 Housing starts rose 6.4% in November, after two months of declines. This year's performance is expected to be the best since 1979. U.S. personal income increased 0.7% last month and personal spending rose 1.1%, in further signs of continued economic expansion.

22 The economy is growing at a 4.5% annual rate in the fourth quarter, well below the 6% to 7% pace predicted. Prices rose 0.3% in November from October, indicating inflation for 1983 will be the lowest since 1967's 2.9%. The combination of low inflation and slower growth should ease concerns that the economy is overheating, administration officials said.

U.S. Steel is expected to close more plants soon, taking a charge that is apt to exceed $1 billion. The steelmaker wants to emphasize three areas in which competitors with lower production costs are least likely to challenge it: sheet for autos, seamless pipe for energy exploration and plates and beams for construction.

AT&T agreed to buy a 25% stake in Olivetti for $260 million. The purchase will give AT&T a European distribution system and a potential source of office computers. However, AT&T said it hasn't agreed to distribute Olivetti products in the U.S.

Local phone rates for residential users are likely to rise 40% by 1989 but may be offset by long-distance rate cuts, according to an FCC study.

Japan's steelmakers are forcing down prices and curbing deliveries of metallurgical coal for the second time this year, under long-term import contracts with their main suppliers, the U.S., Australia and Canada. Steel producers around the world probably will seek similar price cuts.

Chase Manhattan agreed to buy Rochester, N.Y.-based Lincoln First Banks for $308 million in cash and securities. The step reflects Chase's desire to strengthen operations upstate. Chase said it also is interested in an out-of-state acquisition.

23 Farmers planted 64.9 million acres of winter wheat for next year's harvest, 4% above the year-earlier planting but down 2% from the record 66.5 million acres seeded for 1982.

The Farm Belt was lashed by bitter temperatures and heavy snowfall. Grain prices rose and meat production fell as snowbound farmers failed to ship animals to market. Soybean futures surged on the Chicago Board of Trade as foreign importers stepped up buying in Europe. Durable-goods orders rose 4% in November from October, to $97.08 billion. The big gain reflected a surge in defense orders. Orders for nondefense capital goods fell 4.4%, however. The Commerce Department's chief economist said a continued drop in orders for nondefense capital goods "will be cause for concern."

The FTC tentatively approved by a 3–2 vote a consent decree that clears the way for GM and Toyota to produce cars jointly in the U.S.

27   Toyota seeks a stronger presence in the U.S. than its planned joint production venture with GM, according to documents related to the venture. Provisions of the auto makers' plan apparently allow it to take over the factory to make its own cars for sale in the U.S.

Santa Fe Industries completed its $6.4 billion merger with Southern Pacific into a natural resources holding concern after the ICC lifted an order blocking the merger. The companies' rail operations will stay separate while the ICC decides whether to let them combine, too, forming the nation's third largest rail system.

New-car sales in mid-December rose to 179,749 units, up more than 25% from a year earlier. For all of 1983, U.S. car makers expect sales to total 6.7 million to 6.9 million autos, compared with 5.7 million in 1982.

The value of building contracts rose 4% in November, to $15.4 billion, bringing 1983's 11-month total to a record $178.5 billion, F. W. Dodge said.

Fairchild Semiconductor and other semiconductor makers are under investigation by the Pentagon, which is looking into charges that they may have falsified quality-control data for products sold to the U.S.

The U.S. budget deficit for November narrowed to $21.59 billion from $24.16 billion a year earlier. The administration predicts a fiscal 1984 deficit of $179.67 billion, compared with fiscal 1983's $195.35 billion gap.

Interest rates are apt to decline in coming months despite huge federal borrowing needs, many economists predict. They say the Fed isn't likely to tighten credit as economic growth slows. The Fed disclosed that it maintained its basic credit policies in the September-through-December period.

28   U.S. Steel will close nearly a fifth of its steel-making capacity, taking a $1.2 billion pre-tax charge. It also ended talks for a venture with British Steel, but talks to buy raw steel from the British will continue. About 15,400 of U.S. Steel's 81,000 employees are expected to lose jobs as a result of the closings.

Saudi Arabia appears optimistic that OPEC can prevent crude oil prices from declining in 1984. But Saudi officials say this view is based on the assumption that the nation won't have to bear output cuts alone and that North Sea prices won't fall.

29   Western industrial nations were urged to set tighter controls on social spending. Organization for Economic Cooperation and Development said spending on pensions, health, education and jobless benefits grew nearly twice as fast as the economics of the 24 member nations between 1960 and 1980.

30   The index of leading economic indicators fell 0.4% in November, the first drop since August 1982. Economists agreed the drop didn't mean the recovery is ending. The nation's trade deficit narrowed from October's record, to $7.4 billion. Most of the decline represented a cut in oil imports that is likely to be reversed in the coming cold months.

Charges that the Pentagon's second-ranking official, Deputy Secretary of Defense Paul Thayer, illegally passed on corporate secrets used in stock-market trading while he was chairman of LTV have become the subject of a Justice Department criminal investigation.

Ecuador and Abu Dhabi lowered oil prices as world crude markets remained weak. Major oil companies raised wholesale heating-oil prices in the U.S., but spot and futures-market prices fell, partly because of an industry report showing higher-than-expected inventories.

Lower interest rates are predicted for early 1984 amid further signs that economic growth has moderated. Those signs include the government report that the index of leading economic indicators fell in November.

The dollar declined after the announcement of a $7.4 billion U.S. trade deficit and a 0.4% drop in the leading economic indicators for November. Gold rose $4 an ounce, to $382.50, on the Comex.

Taxes remain the only major issue to be resolved in fiscal 1985's budget. Congress and financial markets are watching the debate between economic adviser Martin Feldstein and Treasury Secretary Regan over the timing of tax boosts and spending cuts. The debate's outcome may indicate the administration's willingness to compromise on the deficit before the 1984 election.

January 1984

1 Effective today is the AT&T breakup, as a result of antitrust action, into a new and much diminished AT&T and seven independent regional telephone companies; Ameritec, Bell Atlantic, Bell South, NYNEX (New York–New England), Pacific Telesis, Southwestern Bell, and U.S. West. The new AT&T retains its long distance lines, Bell Laboratories, and the manufacturing facility, Western Electric.

3 The industrial outlook for 1984 includes an increase in shipments by 87% of U.S. manufacturing industries, according to the Commerce Department. Only 31% will rise to pre-recession levels, however, the agency predicted. Auto shipments are expected to increase 11.1%, after a 33.2% rise in 1983.

Interest rates will decline in the next few months but rebound this year, economists say. Rates are apt to remain in a narrow range, ending 1984 within one percentage point of current levels, according to economists polled by The Wall Street Journal.

Gulf Oil said a preliminary count from a Dec. 2 holders meeting showed that 52.7% of Gulf's shares voted in favor of a management plan to reincorporate in Delaware. The count is a setback for Mesa Petroleum Chairman T. Boone Pickens Jr., who leads a group of dissident Gulf holders.

AT&T agreed to pay former units an estimated $5 billion over three years for billing and collecting payments from long-distance customers.

New-home sales rose 0.5% in November to an annual rate of 638,000 units. The increase follows a 6.4% rise in October and bodes well for further gains in 1984.

4 Factory orders rose 2.2% in November, to $185.85 billion, bolstered by a surge in defense contracts. Orders for nondefense capital goods fell 4.9%. The Commerce Department also said November construction spending on new buildings was unchanged from October's $271.9 billion annual rate.

Merrill Lynch won approval from state regulators to form a bank in New Jersey, a move that further erodes barriers between the banking and securities industries. The bank won't accept checking accounts but will make commercial loans, offer trust-related services and accept time deposits.

The U.S. dollar posted its largest gain in years, currency futures plunged and bond prices declined, reflecting a rise in the interest rate on federal funds. Gold fell $5.90 an ounce and other commodity futures prices tumbled in response to the dollar's strength and uncertainty over the new Nigerian government's oil policy.

Enriched-uranium prices are being cut 2% to 8% by the Energy Department. To boost government sales, the agency also is allowing customers to buy as little as 70% of their originally estimated uranium needs without incurring penalties.

U.S. auto makers built nearly 6.8 million cars last year, up 33% from 1982 production. December output rose about 50% from a year earlier.

5 Getty Oil will be taken private through a $5.3 billion leveraged buyout devised by Pennzoil and Gordon Getty. The buyout, valued at $112.50 a share, will merge Getty Oil into a company owned 57% by a Getty family trust and 43% by Pennzoil. Mr. Getty will be the company's chairman; Pennzoil Chairman J. Hugh Liedtke will be its president.

Retailers expect to report double-digit sales gains today for the five-week December period, the most important month of the industry's year.

TWA said it might sell its big Kansas City, Mo., maintenance base and have outside contractors maintain its jets there. That cost-cutting move would be unprecedented: all major U.S. airlines operate their own maintenance bases.

The Dow Jones Industrial Average rose 16.31 points, its biggest gain in over a month, to 1269.05. Bond prices also strengthened on renewed hope that interest rates will decline in coming months. The U.S. dollar climbed again, setting records against the British pound and the French franc. Gold slipped $1.90 an ounce.

Mutual funds invested in common stocks in 1983 failed to outperform the overall stock market, as measured by the Standard & Poor's 500 index, for the first time in at least a decade. But 1983's leading fund, Oppenheimer Regency, posted a 58.1% gain, compared with average fund gains of 20.2% and S&P's 500 growth of 22.6%.

6 Stock volume soared to a record 159,-990,000 shares, as the Dow-Jones Indus-

trial Average closed up 13.19 points, at 1282.24. Gains were attributed to the return of institutional investors to the market and to a growing belief that interest rates will decline in coming months.

Major retailers' sales surged in December, and heavy spending by shoppers continued after Christmas, suggesting that the sales strength may continue into the second quarter. Sears December sales, including those of the Canadian unit, rose 35%. Dayton Hudson sales were up 25%.

9 Texaco began a $125-a-share cash tender offer for at least 28 million Getty Oil shares as part of its plan to buy the oil company for $9.89 billion of cash and new Texaco debt securities. The acquisition would be the largest in history.

Ford is expected to announce tomorrow that it will invest $400 million to $500 million in Mexico to produce a small car, designed by Japan's Toyo Kogyo, mainly for sale in the U.S.

The SEC found that Bert Lance and Jake Butcher bought shares in Campbell Taggart soon before announcement of merger plans in 1982 boosted its stock price. The purchases followed talks about the stock with a broker who, the SEC says, heard of the merger through a friend of Deputy Defense Secretary Paul Thayer.

The civilian unemployment rate fell to 8.2% of the work force in December from 8.4% in November. The decline of 2½ percentage points from November 1982 was the sharpest annual drop in 30 years.

AT&T told the FCC it could cut basic long-distance rates more than the 10.5% it proposed earlier, while boosting profit on such service.

10 The antitrust division of the Justice Department plans to set up a task force to target industries that are prone to price fixing and to hone techniques for uncovering the practice. Details weren't disclosed, but an official said the division's new head, Paul McGrath, is considering using concealed recording devices on witnesses and soliciting informers.

The Vatican may be near agreement to pay about $300 million of the $1.3 billion debt left by collapsed Banco Ambrosiano S.p.A. Sources said the money would be used to help satisfy claims against the Italian bank by foreign creditor banks.

The Getty family faces a potential legal fight among its members over how the Sarah C. Getty trust will invest the $3.98 billion it is expected to receive from Texaco's pending purchase of Getty Oil.

Oil-industry acquisition fever is strong again, after a lull in 1983. The interest has become more acute as the search for new oil and gas has grown more expensive. Texaco's planned, nearly $10 billion purchase of Getty Oil will give it oil and gas for about one-fourth the drilling cost.

The U.S. dollar gained strength again against European currencies despite reported U.S. and West German intervention to bolster the mark. Bond prices rose, helped by the Fed's large injection of funds into the banking network. Prices of several commodities, including metals, soybeans and cocoa were pushed lower by the dollar's strength.

11 GM detailed a reorganization plan that will change the way it designs and makes cars in North America and announced a plan to realign management. The new Buick-Cadillac-Oldsmobile group will design and make only large cars, while the Chevrolet-Pontiac-GM of Canada group produces small ones.

The Oil, Chemical and Atomic Workers Union accepted from Gulf Oil a two-year contract proposal that offers minimal wage and benefit gains. The union said it expects the settlement to become the pattern for new contracts covering 50,000 of its oil worker members nationwide.

Pennzoil filed suit to block Texaco's proposed $9.89 billion purchase of Getty Oil. Pennzoil is cooperating with federal antitrust regulators who are considering requesting a Senate inquiry into the proposed merger.

Property and casualty insurers' loss reserves were inadequate by more than 10% at the end of 1982 and showed no signs of strengthening in the first nine months of 1983, according to an industry study.

12 Nuclear-accident victims may be awarded extra damages to penalize the companies responsible, the Supreme Court said. The ruling sides with the family of the late Karen Silkwood and reverses an appeals court decision that threw out most of a $10.5 million damage award against Kerr-McGee Corp.

Kuwait agreed to buy Gulf Oil's Italian refining and oil marketing operations for an undisclosed amount. The Middle East country will become the first OPEC member to move into the retail end of the oil business in European markets on a large scale.

Texaco's purchase of Getty is receiving mixed reaction on Wall Street. Texaco will acquire a huge field of low-quality California crude oil and other substantial reserves. Texaco also is acquiring a mangagement team with one of the poorest exploration records of any major oil company.

13 Capital spending in 1984 will rise a strong, inflation-adjusted 9.4% from 1983, to $333.32 billion, the government said. Manufacturers plan to spend $125.98 billion on plants and equipment, up 13% from 1983.

GM is considering importing a new-design small car in the next two years from its 50%-owned South Korean affiliate. Sources said initial annual volume probably wouldn't exceed a modest 50,000 units. The import would join the ambitious lineup of small cars GM plans to sell as part of its so-called Japanese strategy.

Six major brokerage houses were accused in a suit by the state of Massachusetts of "deceptive practices" in the sale of Baldwin-United annuities. The suit names Prudential Bache, E. F. Hutton, Kidder Peabody, Moseley Hallgarten, Paine Webber and Shearson/American Express.

The SEC authorized aides to issue subpoenas compelling witnesses to answer questions and supply documents pertinent to the agency's investigation into Washington Public Power's huge bond default. The step may indicate that the SEC is focusing on specific allegations of wrongdoing.

16 Economic growth showed signs of slowing in December as retail sales increased an unexpectedly slim 0.1% from November, to an adjusted $102.06 billion. Industrial production, up 0.5%, also grew less than expected. And the producer price index for finished goods rose only 0.2%, making 1983 the year with the least wholesale inflation since 1964.

The Common Market's decision to restrict imports of some chemicals and sports products in retaliation for U.S. curbs on specialty-steel imports elicited an expression of disappointment from the U.S. Separately, steelmakers in Belgium and Luxembourg agreed to share capacity cuts as part of a plan to return to profitability.

Domestic sales of U.S.-built cars rose a strong 32% in early January, to 149,136 units, equal to an annual rate of 8.2 million cars. The Big Three auto makers don't expect the annual selling rate to remain above eight million units through the first quarter.

Pressure on the Fed to ease credit conditions may be heightened by fresh evidence that economic growth is moderating. But any such move isn't apt to be made by the central bank for at least a month, many bankers say.

17 Economic growth showed further signs of slowing in 1983's final quarter. The Fed said the nation's factories, mines and utilities operated at 79.4% of capacity in December, up only 0.3 percentage point from November. Business inventories rose only 0.4% in November.

Standard & Poor's cut ratings on debt of nine big bank holding companies, including Bank of Boston, Chase, Chemical New York and Citicorp. S&P said deregulation and "persistent" foreign-lending problems pose increased risk for the industry.

Four big bank holding companies posted fourth-quarter profit gains. First Chicago's net rose 15%; Chase and Irving Bank Corp. both posted gains of 10%. Manufacturers posted a 3% increase and trebled, to $91 million, its provision for loan losses.

18 The Supreme Court decided home use of video recorders to tape TV programs doesn't violate movie and TV producers' copyrights. The ruling is a major victory for Sony. The issue will move to Congress, but persuading legislators to overrule the high court is apt to be difficult for the movie industry.

Chairman Martin Feldstein of the Council of Economic Advisers said the Reagan administration's optimistic long-range economic-growth forecast of 4% a year after 1984 won't be "appropriate" if budget deficits decline only modestly in future years.

Pennzoil again sued to block Texaco's proposed $9.89 billion acquisition of Getty Oil. Pennzoil charged the purchase would violate antitrust law.

19 Housing starts declined 5% in December, to an annual rate of 1,667,000 units, as cold weather impeded builders. But starts for the full year surged 60.3% from 1982's 36-year low, to 1,703,100 units. Housing activity in 1984, barring a jump in home-loan rates, should at least match last year's, economists predict.

IBM profit rose 24% in the fourth quarter, to $1.86 billion, as revenue grew 17%. Th quarter's strength was attributed to IBM's emphasis on sales rather than on leased products. Earnings for the year were up 25% on a 17% revenue gain.

Trading in a "subindex" futures, a stock-index futures contract whose value fluctuates with an index of stock prices within a selected industry, is permitted under a settlement between the SEC and the Commodity Futures Trading Commission.

The Supreme Court gave a boost to mutual-fund investors concerned about the size of fees being paid to fund advisers. Holders who consider fees excessive can take claims to court without first having to ask the fund's board to sue to recover them, the justices ruled. The issue of when fees are excessive wasn't addressed.

20 Access charges for home and small-business phone users will be delayed until 1985. The FCC also agreed to reduce the fee boosts AT&T's long-distance rivals will pay for links to local phone networks. Congressional backers of legislation to halt access charges say they don't plan to drop their efforts, however.

Personal income rose 0.9% in December from November. Personal spending increased an even stronger 1.3%, leading many economists to suggest that last month's 0.1% growth in retail sales understated the economy's strength. Fourth-quarter GNP data are due for release today.

Electric utilities burdened with troubled nuclear power porjects are turning to banks for financing as lower credit ratings nudge them out of the credit markets. Public Service of Indiana, Philadelphia Electric and Lilco seek a combined $2 billion in financing, industry executives say.

23 A conversion of the Zimmer nuclear power plant to burn coal, proposed by Cincinnati Gas and its partners, raises new uncertainties about how the $1.7 billion, 97%-complete plant will be finished. The three Ohio utilities say conversion will cost less than the $1.8 billion needed to make Zimmer acceptable to the NRC.

Sohio said its Mukluk well offshore Alaska is a dry hole and took a $310 million pretax write-off on its investment that will cut 1983 fourth-quarter profit by $163 million. BP plans a $140 million net write-off. Shell doesn't plan a write-off, and two other Mukluk partners, Texaco and Mobil, didn't comment. Diamond Shamrock has written off $200 million.

Trade-balance deterioration helped slow the nation's fourth-quarter economic growth to a 4.5% annual rate, the same as last month's Commerce Department "flash" estimate. Many analysts expected "real" GNP to be higher. Personal spending grew at a hefty 6.5% rate; business investment spending grew at a 22.3% rate.

Citicorp acquired two troubled thrifts, Miami-based New Biscayne Federal and Chicago-based First Federal, after the

Fed gave its approval. The central bank set conditions to bar the big bank from wielding an unfair advantage over competitors. Some opponents pledged to continue legal actions against the acquisitions.

Reagan stood fast in his opposition to tax boosts and belittled the risk of big budget deficits as congressional leaders, preparing to resume legislative sessions today, warned that deficits should be dealt with soon.

24 The Dow Jones Industrial Average closed down 14.66 points, at 1244.45, its sharpest drop since October. Volume slowed to 82,010,000 shares. Analysts cited concern about effects of a slowing economy on corporate profits.

25 Consumer prices rose 3.8% in 1983, the lowest rate since 1972, when price controls were in effect. Prices in December were up 0.3%, equal to a 3.6% annual rate. Prices are apt to be up this month and next, because of the cold, but many economists say 1984 rises won't exceed a 4.5%–5.5% rate.

U.S. auto makers' domestic sales in mid-January rose nearly 26% to an estimated 182,273 units from the weak year-earlier level. The figures represent a continuation of the industry's moderate recovery.

26 Durable goods orders fell 1.1% in December, to $95.42 billion, reflecting a 10.3% drop in defense orders. Non-defense capital-goods orders rose 1.8%. Durables orders rose a healthy 16.9% for all of 1983 compared with 1982's 10.3% drop.

Foreign capital is drawn to the U.S. by the health of the American economy, Treasury Secretary Regan asserted, dismissing European reporters' complaints about budget deficits. He also said his fears over Fed monetary policy have diminished.

23 The manned space station proposed by Reagan is apt to gain support from Congress, despite concern over the estimated $8 billion initial cost. The aerospace industry believes much work on the project will be won by several of the eight big copanies involved in its conceptual phase.

The SEC has issued 18 subpoenas in its widening investigation of Washington Public Power's $2.25 billion bond default.

U.S. auto makers are adhering to their ambitious plans to produce nearly 729,000 cars in February and 2.2 million in the first quarter. Their schedules reflect a belief that sales through the first quarter will run at a 7.5 million-unit annual rate.

Apple Computer won a victory in its fight

to halt pirating of its products in Taiwan, where a court sentenced six computer-company executives to eight-month prison terms for copying Apple software.

30 Texaco agreed to sell Getty Oil's Northeastern and Mid-Atlantic States gasoline marketing assets to Power Test for $90 million. The action is designed to help win antitrust clearance for Texaco's proposed $10.13 billion purchase of Getty. Texaco fourth-quarter profit fell 16%, reflecting an $87 million write-off on the Mukluk hole offshore Alaska.

Machine tool orders were up 25% in December from a year earlier, and orders for all 1983 rose 13% from 1982's depressed level. Machinery producers say January's orders are stronger than December's and predict the nation's factories will benefit this year from higher capital spending.

U.S. trade-balance deterioration is expected to grow more severe in 1984, as imports exceed exports by perhaps $100 billion, Commerce Secretary Baldrige said. The 1983 trade-balance deficit was a record $69.39 billion. December's merchandise-trade deficit narrowed to $6.3 billion from November's $7.4 billion.

Wall Street is nearly unanimous in the conviction that the record-breaking market surge that began in August 1982 hasn't ended. But analysts and investors are divided over whether the market will rise, fall or remain flat in coming months.

The Fed may establish as early as this week an official growth target for the basic money-supply measure. The M1 measure is expected to assume renewed importance in credit-policy formation this year.

31 Non-farm productivity grew at an adjusted 1% annual rate in the fourth quarter, down from the third quarter's revised 2.3% pace. For all of 1983, non-farm productivity rose 3.1%, the steepest gain since 1976.

A telecommunications supply pact between the U.S. and Japan was extended for three years. The accord reduces technical problems U.S. firms have in bidding for supply contracts with the state monopoly, Nippon Telephone, but U.S. concerns face fierce competition from other suppliers.

The Vatican's bank seeks loans totaling as much as $200 million to pay claims resulting from Banco Ambrosiano's collapse, Italian bankers say. The Vatican's bank has sold its stake in the big Italian construction company Vianini S.p.A. for $41 million.

Brazil probably will need $4 billion in new commercial loans in 1985 and is apt to begin talks on those credits in the next three to four months, a former industry minister said.

Colt Industries was pressured to retreat from its threat to halt medical benefits for 4,200 Crucible Steel retirees and their dependents, at least temporarily. Colt was sued by the USW after it said it would halt benefits Feb. 4 for retirees of the unit.

The SEC's accounting-oversight role is being investigated by a House subcommittee, which alleges that the SEC hasn't been tough enough on accounting standard-setters.

February 1984

1 President Reagan's fiscal 1985 budget projects a deficit of $180.4 billion and spending of $925.5 billion, congressional sources say. A deficit-reduction plan totaling $73.6 billion over three years is proposed, and the figures reflect a low tax, high defense spending plan.

Democrats are uncertain whether Reagan's call for a bipartisan budget "summit" is in good faith.

U.S. Steel's loss widened to $983 million in the fourth quarter. The firm took a $1.15 billion charge related to the termination of 15,400 workers and the write-down of assets.

New-home sales rose 28.5% in December from November and 52.7% from year-earlier depressed levels. A 66.1% jump in home-buying in the South was cited. Sales for 1983 rose 51.7% to a four-year high.

The leading economic indicators rose 0.6% in December. The increase in the index is less than the unusually strong average monthly rise of 1.2% in 1983, but enough to suggest that the economy will keep growing.

2 Reagan's budget for fiscal 1985 hints that during a second term, the president would try harder to cut such middle-class entitlements as Social Security and Medicare. Domestic spending cuts of $5 billion are proposed for next year.

Two fiscal accomplishments cherished by Reagan, the military buildup and 1981 tax cuts, are protected. A 14.5% jump in defense spending, to $264.4 billion, is sought. Tax rises are avoided. The budget purports to raise $7.9 billion in fiscal 1985 by curbing tax-shelter and accounting abuses.

U.S Steel proposed to purchase National Steel for $575 million. The acquisiton would strengthen operations in consumer steel, one of the only markets that now is profitable and promises future growth. The proposal is certain to draw close scrutiny from the Justice Department.

3 Most big retailers' January sales gains were smaller than December's robust increases, but merchants remain optimistic about 1984. Sales for Sears rose a strong 26.6%. Associated Dry Goods' sales were up 23.6% and Carter Hawley Hale's rose 23.2%.

The Big Three auto makers are expected to post 1983 fourth-quarter combined earnings exceeding $1.9 billion. That is in contrast to a year-earlier $187 million loss and is far higher than Wall Street had forecast. GM profit is estimated at over $1.1 billion.

Budget deficits are the main cause of high interest rates and the record U.S. trade imbalance, according to the 1984 report of Reagan's Council of Economic Advisers. That analysis, stated repeatedly in the past by Council Chairman Feldstein, differs from the stance of other administration officials, including Treasury Secretary Regan.

Du Pont profit rose 69% to $341 million in the fourth quarter, while Dow Chemical operating profit surged 362% to $60 million. Both predicted continued gains, but said the rebound in chemical operations was partly offset by weakness in petroleum-related businesses and the dollar's strength.

6 A significant interest-rate decline for at least a month or two seems unlikely in light of the economy's continued growth, many bankers say. But a clearer outlook may emerge after this morning, when the Fed announces 1984 money-supply growth targets.

The Fed's policy-making panel, citing inflation risks, voted in December to reject easing of monetary policy, the meeting's minutes disclose.

January new-car sales rose 31%, to 777,929 units. Sales, at an annual rate of 11.2 million cars, were auto makers' strongest in four years.

Many dealers' inventories are bulging with small cars. Flat or falling gasoline prices have lured buyers back to big cars, but Detroit, geared for building small cars, lacks capacity for making larger models.

The unemployment rate fell to an adjusted 8% in January from 8.2% in December, despite a slowing of economic growth. Bureau of Labor Statistics Commissioner Norwood says slower labor-force growth is the main reason for the drop in joblessness.

7 The Fed announced that it will keep a tight rein on the money supply this year. The central bank seeks growth of 6% to 9% in the broader money-supply gauges M2 and M3 from 1983's fourth quarter to this year's fourth quarter. The Fed said it has made considerable progress in curbing inflation but reiterated warnings about high budget deficits.

Interest rates rose and the Dow Jones Industrial Average plunged 22.72 points, to 1174.31, as the Fed resolved publicly to keep its tight grip on credit. The stock market's dive was its biggest in over a year.

Treasury Secretary Regan denied reports that he has demanded the White House fire Martin Feldstein, Reagan's top economist. Feldstein, meanwhile, made light of the dispute among Reagan advisers by noting that all have called big budget deficits unacceptable and advocate a deficit "down payment."

8 General Motors profit rose nearly ninefold in the fourth quarter, to $1.3 billion, and nearly quadrupled for the year, to a record $3.73 billion. The No. 1 auto maker, in a pointed message to the UAW, said it will pay $32 million in March as its first profit-sharing-plan distribution to its half-million U.S. employees.

Wheeling-Pittsburgh Steel and Japan's Nisshin Steel agreed to produce steel together in the U.S., forming the troubled domestic industry's first international partnership. The venture will build a $40 million production line at a Wheeling-Pittsburgh plant in the Ohio River valley.

Japan has been persuaded to retreat from two legislative proposals that would have crippled the ability of U.S. companies to sell computer software and open computerized data-transmission networks in Japan. But the Reagan administration is dissatisfied with Tokyo's policy of buying only Japanese communications satellites.

A record deficit of nearly $40 billion probably was registered last year by the U.S. in its balance of payments on the current account, Commerce Secretary Baldrige said.

The World Bank is issuing $250 million of floating-rate notes that bear interest tied to the yield on U.S. Treasury bills and set a new standard for inexpensive financing in Europe.

9 The stock market plunged and bond prices declined as Treasury Secretary Regan and Fed Chairman Volcker warned that another recession could result from fiscal

and monetary-policy missteps. The Dow Jones Industrial Average fell 24.19 points, its biggest drop in over 15 months, to 1156.30, its lowest close in 10 months.

Chrysler said it must step up cooperation with foreign car makers if it can't block the proposed GM-Toyota joint venture. Chrysler's chairman said the U.S. will lose 300,000 jobs if all domestic auto makers adopt GM's strategy of importing the small cars they sell or the parts for those cars.

France's government approved an industry-modernization plan that will cost taxpayers an estimated $590 million to $710 million over the next few years. Included are federal aid to industries, low-cost loans, outlays for unemployment programs and lost revenue from special tax exemptions.

10 A New York State commission appears likely to recommend that New York state-chartered banks and thrifts be allowed to sell and underwrite all kinds of life and property and casualty insurance and buy or set up insurance companies. Insurers oppose the proposal.

The Dow Jones Industrial Average closed down 3.56 points, at 1152.74. The index has plunged 10.41% since its high this year of 1286.64, reached Jan. 6. Volume surged to 128,190,000 shares, the 12th highest on record.

Bond prices declined for the fifth consecutive day as the federal government completed its $16.25 billion quarterly refunding operation.

13 The producer-price jump of 0.6% in January indicates inflation will be harder to control this year than last. The rise was as big as the entire producer-price-index increase from December 1982 to December 1983. Food prices, accounting for most of the jump, are expected to continue climbing in coming months.

Gulf Oil began a double-barreled defense against a $55-a-share, or $9.24 billion, acquisition strategy by investors led by Mesa Petroleum Chairman T. Boone Pickens, Jr. Gulf sued the group, charging it with market manipulation and other securities-law breaches. Gulf's board also authorized a $1 billion increase in bank credit lines, to $6 billion.

14 Texaco won FTC approval to acquire Getty Oil with provisional acceptance of a consent order requiring divestiture of two refineries and other properties. The $10.1 billion merger will be the U.S.'s largest.

Kodak fourth-quarter profit fell 63% and was down 51% for the year. Kodak cited such cost-cutting programs as layoffs and early-retirement plans and said it expects sharply higher earnings this year.

The Dow Jones Industrial Average fell a further 10.57 points, to close at 1150.13. Declines in corporate and municipal bond prices were attributed to concerns about stronger-than-expected economic growth.

Ford posted record profit of $781 million for the fourth quarter, in contrast to a year-earlier loss. The quarter completed Ford's first profitable year since 1979.

15 Retail sales jumped 2.2% in January and consumer credit expanded a record $6.61 billion in December. The government reports fuel disagreement among economists over economic growth. Some believe growth is at a faster-than-expected 6%-to-7% pace; others contend it has slowed to a 4.5% or 5% annual rate.

The Treasury's proposal to revise the Tax Code will be designed to raise the same amount of revenue as the existing system, a top Treasury official said. Previous administration statements, including those of President Reagan, implied that the tax-system overhaul would be aimed at narrowing federal budget deficits.

U.S. new-car sales rose 33% in early February, to 181,694 units. Sales were equivalent to an annual rate of 7.8 million units, far stronger than a year earlier, but down from late January's rate of nine million units.

Ford said its Rouge Steel unit awarded a $130 million contract for a continuous slab casting plant to a group headed by Mitsubishi International. The plant is part of a modernization plan for the steelmaking unit.

The dollar plunged, despite two U.S. economic reports that foreign-exchange traders said should have reinforced its strength. Gold rose $6.30 an ounce, to $383.50, on the Comex.

IBM, CBS and Sears arranged a videotex venture that will pit IBM against rival AT&T, which has had a two-year head start. The accord represents a switch in allegiance for CBS, which for two years has tested a videotex service with AT&T.

16 A Republic Steel acquisition planned by LTV was opposed by the Justice Department's on the ground that it would excessively increase concentration in three product areas. Antitrust division chief McGrath discounted the firms' claims that the merger would improve their efficiency and slash expenses.

The steel industry's consolidation startegy appears crippled by the Justice

Department's decision. The ruling is widely presumed to kill chances for U.S. Steel's proposed purchase of National Steel.

Industrial production surged 1.1% in January, and business inventories in December rose a modest 0.4%, pushing the ratio of inventories to sales to a record low. January's gains in industrial output and retail sales suggest the economy is growing faster than the fourth quarter's 4.5% pace.

Federal budget deficits aren't causing the stock-market slump and won't cause higher interest rates or threaten the economic recovery, President Reagan insisted. But he said he is sincere in trying to reach at deficit-reduction compromise with congressional Democrats.

The dollar recovered from a sharp midmorning drop. Traders said the currency's decline in recent days, especially against the West German mark, reflected a flight of funds from the U.S. stock market to West German investment instruments, which suddenly have regained favor.

17 Rapid economic growth in January was indicated by government reports that personal income expanded 1.1%, personal spending grew 1.2% and housing starts surged 15% to an annual rate of 1,915,000 units, the highest level since 1978's construction boom. In addition, the operating rate at U.S. factories, mines and utilities climbed to 79.9%.

A credit-tightening move by the Fed appears increasingly likely in light of the economy's robust growth and the latest weekly surge, of $2.5 billion, in the money supply, economists say. Credit-policy concern pushed bond prices lower and interest rates up. The dollar weakened.

LTV officials plan to meet with the Justice Department Wednesday to seek a compromise satisfying broad antitrust objections to LTV's proposed merger with Republic Steel.

Republic Steel faces crucial financial decisions as a result of government objections to a merger with LTV. The nation's fourth-largest steelmaker will have to persuade bankers that it should get the capital for modernization that the LTV merger was designed to provide.

IBM will sell a portable version of its Personal Computer, pressuring makers of IBM look-alikes, including Columbia Data Products, Compaq and Eagle Computer, as well as makers of other portables, including Kaypro. The new computer, available March 1, will sell for $2,795.

21 Corporate profits in the U.S. soared in the fourth quarter, and economists generally expect further strong gains through 1984. After-tax fourth-quarter profits of 529 major corporations surged 64%, compared with a 29% third-quarter rise, a Wall Street Journal survey found.

Canadian corporate profits also rebounded from depressed year-earlier levels. A survey by The Wall Street Journal of 115 companies showed earnings from operations jumped 118% in the fourth quarter and 57% for the year.

The Reagan administration is urging the Fed to supply enough money to keep economic growth on track and to curb its worries about inflation. Recent money-supply growth exceeding a 10% rate was termed "sufficient" by Treasury Secretary Regan, who previously exhorted the Fed to restrict growth to a 4%-to-8% range.

GM plans to cut its U.S. hourly work force of 380,000 by a further 60,000 to 120,000 workers by August 1986, according to an internal company document. The disclosure threatens to complicate GM's relationship with the UAW in new-contract talks beginning in July.

Upward revision of GNP data, showing the economy grew at a 4.9% annual rate in 1983's fourth quarter, reflects stronger investment and less trade deterioration than was initially reported. An estimate last month showed growth at a 4.5% rate.

22 Bond dealers and state officials say the federally required switch to registered bonds in the municipals market is escalating their costs and slowing bond transfers significantly.

American Motors posted profit of $7.4 million for 1983's fourth quarter, after 14 quarters of deficits, and predicted that for 1984 it would post its first annual profit in five years. AMC attributed the turnaround to strong sales of its Jeeps and its Alliance and Encore cars, which have grabbed 10% of the U.S. subcompact market.

Three investor-owned utilities with stakes in Washington Public Power's Unit 3 still hope the mothballed nuclear plant will be completed. Portland General Electric, Puget Sound Power and Washington Water Power say they don't plan to write off their investments, as Pacific Power has.

23 The Supreme Court said companies filing for reorganization in federal bankruptcy court have broad leeway to cancel or alter labor accords. Firms that may reap immediate gains from the ruling include Continental Air and Braniff. The decision doesn't address whether labor cost can serve as the main reason for a bankruptcy filing.

Investors led by Mesa Petroleum Chairman T. Boone Pickens, Jr. said they will offer $65 a share for up to 13.5 million Gulf Corp. shares. The $877 million bid would lift the dissidents' stake to 35.2 million shares, or 21.3%, of the oil giant. Nearly 75% of the bid's cost will be borne by Mesa.

The Congressional Budget Office's director, Rudolf Penner, said Reagan's budget plan will widen deficits through this decade instead of narrowing them, as the administration predicts. The administration says the economy will grow faster and inflation and interest rates will be lower than the nopartisan agency predicts.

U.S.-based multinational firms' shares could benefit from the dollar's month-long decline. The multinationals, including Schering Plough, Polaroid, Dow Chemical and Pan Am, could realize substantial earnings gains when their foreign profits are translated into dollars.

Federal gift taxes must be paid by parents who make interest-free loans to their children, the Supreme Court ruled. The decision supports the position of the IRS, which says over 30 related cases are pending, involving some $5.5 million in taxes.

24 Bond prices fell sharply, but rebounded slightly after the Fed reported a smaller-than-expected rise of $300 million in the nation's money supply for the week ended Feb. 13.

Venezuela's president is expected today to announce austerity measures that the government hopes will help it renegotiate with foreign creditors some of its $27 billion public debt. A currency devaluation is expected.

The dollar declined despite Salomon Brothers chief economist Henry Kaufman's prediction that higher interest rates in the U.S. are imminent. Gold fell only 60 cents an ounce on the Comex, to $399.10, despite Kaufman's forecast. The metal's price has risen 8% since mid-January.

Durable goods orders rose 1.1% in January, reflecting a surge in orders for metals. Despite declines in orders for defense capital goods, business investment is expected to continue to accelerate this year.

U.S. car makers' sales rose 73% in mid-Feb-

ruary. Sales equaled a 9.2 million-unit annual rate. Officials of some producers have raised first-quarter sales estimates. Chrysler posted fourth-quarter profit of $118.3 million and record net of $700.9 million for 1983.

The Transportation department has begun investigating whether GM front wheel drive subcompact and mid-size cars have potentially hazardous brake flaws.

27 Gulf Corp.'s board directed the company's financial advisers to consider a sale of Gulf, an acquisition by it, a leveraged buyout and all other alternatives to the hostile $65-a-share tender offer designed by Mesa Petroleum's chairman. Gulf also sweetened pension and other financial benefits for employees.

The consumer price index's 0.6% surge in January from December suggests that the consumer-spending boom is starting to lift prices. Last month's increase represents an annual rate of 7.2%. A growing group of analysts predicts inflation this year of 6% to 7%.

Interest-rate relief is in sight, argues a small group of economists. The stock market soared 30.47 points, its biggest gain since July 20, on favorable budget-deficit and money-supply reports. Inflation concerns pushed the dollar to its lowest point since last fall against the West German mark and the British pound.

28 The White House rejected a proposal by Senate Budget panel Chairman Domenici (R., N.M.) under which fiscal 1985 defense spending would rise only 5%. The president supports a 13% increase.

Reagan might consider tax increases if big budget deficits remain after further federal spending cuts, Illinois Gov. James Thompson said. The statement triggered an upsurge in the stock market, which closed up 14.86 points, at 1179.96.

29 Volcker warned that Reagan's $100 billion, three-year deficit-reduction plan, weighted heavily toward third-year cuts, won't alleviate current financial-market nervousness. The Fed chairman said further budget cuts could evolve from a bipartisan plan. But talks on the plan collapsed amid partisan bickering. Bonds fell, and the stock market tumbled 22.82 points, to 1157.14.

Most of a deficit-reduction plan to raise about $13 billion over four years by ending several tax-shelter, accounting and corporate-tax "abuses" was approved tentatively by the Senate Finance panel.

Gulf Corp. is offering potential suitors a

chance to study confidential information about it to help pave the way for a possible takeover of the huge oil company. More than a dozen companies have expressed interest in the confidential examination, according to a source close to Gulf.

West Germany's criticisms of U.S. economic policies are being delivered to Reagan, to cabinet members and to Volcker by Chancellor Kohl and Economics Minister Lambsdorff. West Germany fears its economic recovery may be aborted by what it perceives as growing U.S. protectionism.

Common Market ministers approved a five-year, $1.3 billion research program designed to help Europe challenge Japanese and U.S. domination of information technology. Costs will be shared by EC member governments and private industry.

Non-farm business-productivity growth slowed to a revised, adjusted 0.9% annual rate in the fourth quarter from 2.3% in the third quarter.

March 1984

1   A trade deficit of a record $9.47 billion was posted for January, as fast economic growth and the strong dollar caused imports to surge. Leading indicators rose a hefty 1.1%, suggesting that the economy still has considerable momentum.

Arco and Gulf Corp. executives met to discuss a merger. Socal officials prepared for similar talks with Gulf amid speculation that Kuwait Petroleum might be interested in acquiring Gulf's gas stations, refineries and pipelines. In the past year, Kuwait has bought most of Gulf's European marketing and refining assets.

Construction contracts increased an adjusted 12% in January, to $13.75 billion, reflecting improved weather conditions, F. W. Dodge Co. said.

2   Major retailers posted strong sales gains in February. Sears sales were up 10%. J.C. Penney reversed last year's 1.4% decline with a 19% gain, and Montgomery Ward posted a 20% gain after a weak year-earlier 1.9% increase.

U.S. auto makers plan to build more cars in March and the first quarter than they have in five years, but brisker-than-expected sales are outpacing production. Second-quarter sales and output estimates indicate some effort to rebuild inventory.

Interest rates would be reduced one percentage point by narrowing next fiscal year's federal deficit by $50 billion, Fed Chairman Volcker predicted. He said Congress should cut spending before turning to higher taxes, which probably will be needed to make up much of the deficit cut.

Bond prices rose despite a big $1.7 billion money-supply increase in the week ended Feb. 20. The jump in M1 pushed the gauge above Fed targets and could step up pressure for the central bank to tighten its credit rein, some analysts said.

Public Service of New Hampshire said its Seabrook nuclear plant could cost $9 billion, 72% more than its prior estimate. But the utility said it believes management can be improved and the plant built more efficiently.

British Petroleum announced a major energy find, four North Sea natural-gas deposits with recoverable reserves of at least an estimated 2.5 trillion cubic feet. Development of the fields will cost $1.9 billion, BP said.

New construction spending ran at an annual rate of $281.8 billion in January, up 1.4% from December.

5   Strong economic growth continued in February amid evidence of rising prices, according to a monthly survey of purchasing managers.

Congressional passage of a deficit-reduction measure this year appears unlikely despite the assembling of tax-increase measures in the House and Senate. Neither measure is apt to proceed until Republican and Democratic lawmakers agree to cuts in defense and nonmilitary spending.

Factory orders rose a strong 1.2% in January from December, suggesting that economic growth isn't waning. Durable-goods orders rose a surprisingly hefty 2.7%, revised from the 1.1% increase reported two weeks ago. December's increase in factory orders was revised to 1.6% from 1%.

The yen advanced sharply. Support appears to be building in Japan for liberalization of the financial markets. That could broaden the yen's international role and boost its value, and perhaps dampen U.S. consumers' enthusiasm for Japanese products.

Reagan said the strong dollar is a symbol of national success and a boon to the economy. His stance conflicts with concerns voiced by economic adviser Feldstein, Commerce Secretary Baldrige, Trade Representative Brock and Fed Chairman Volcker.

Gains against inflation are threatened by the economy's strong expansion, according to a growing number of economists. Higher interest rates could result. Some analysts forecast a drop in the dollar, which could intensify inflationary pressures.

New-home sales will be strong in the next six months despite a drop of 8% in January, builders predict.

Kentucky's state Senate passed a bill allowing reciprocal interstate banking and other powers that banks contend they need to compete in a deregulated financial environment.

6   Socal agreed to acquire Gulf Corp. for $80 a share, or $13.26 billion, in a transaction that would be the biggest merger in corporate history. Gulf's board agreed to Standard Oil of California's offer after considering a bid from Arco and a leveraged buyout offer from Kohlberg Kravis.

The 13.2 billion dollar takeover of Gulf by Standard Oil of California now tops an earlier record 10.3 billion dollar takeover of Getty Oil by Texaco.

The U.S. has switched to an early-use policy on its 400-million-barrel Strategic Petroleum Reserve. The change would allow the U.S. to make large quantities of stored crude oil available before an interruption of imports could cause shortages.

U.S. new-car sales in February continued January's strong pace, rising to an annual rate of 8.5 million units, the highest monthly sales level since 1979.

7   Texaco bought a 9.9% block of its stock from the Bass family of Texas for $1.28 billion. Texaco shares fell $5.875, signaling that the repurchase made the oil giant a less attractive takeover target. The action followed by one day Socal's accord to buy Gulf, which had been unable to repurchase Gulf shares controlled by hostile suitor T. Boone Pickens, Jr.

Oil industry consolidation is likely to be the subject of extended debate among lawmakers and industry lobbyists, provoked by the FTC's antitrust review of the proposed Socal-Gulf merger. The FTC isn't expected to oppose the $13.4 billion merger.

OPEC stands to benefit from U.S. oil industry mergers, energy experts say. Merger costs diminish the capital available for exploration, increasing reliance on imports. And OPEC can gain strength by buying the refineries and gasoline stations that the FTC insists be divested by merged firms.

Lilco said it is omitting its common stock dividend for the rest of 1984. It also eliminated nearly 1,000 jobs and cut salaries and directors' fees in an effort to cut costs related to its Shoreham nuclear plant.

The New York Stock Exchange's bid to introduce an industry-index option based on phone-company stocks was approved by the SEC. A similar option was approved for the Chicago Board Options Exchange.

8   Volcker commented that the economy looks "very strong, in a number of directions," raising investor fears about higher interest rates. The stock market fell 8.90 points, to 1143.63, on his remarks.

The Fed chairman's comments also depressed bond prices sending yields on some Treasury issues to the highest levels since 1982. Futures in grains, soybeans, metals, livestock, meats and interest-bearing instruments fell. The dollar rebounded, and gold dropped $5.70 an ounce.

Gulf Corp. shares fell $4.50 and the stock of several possible oil-industry takeover targets tumbled amid fears that Congress might block further consolidation of the industry.

Socal said it is willing to shed any Gulf Corp. assets except oil and gas exploration and production properties to win antitrust clearance for its proposed acquisition of Gulf.

OPEC's future looks promising on the eve of a meeting in Vienna of the cartel's Market Monitoring Committee, after three years of uncertain world oil markets and deteriorating sales by OPEC and oil companies.

9   Farm aid would be sweetened under a proposal agreed on by farm-state senators and the administration. The plan, approved by the Agriculture Committee and sent to the Senate floor, would give farmers cash when they trim crop output but would curb price-support subsidies.

Reagan indicated he disagrees with the Justice Department's initial decision to oppose the proposed merger of LTV and Republic Steel. The president said he doesn't believe that merger or the proposed U.S. Steel-National Steel combination would reduce competition to the extent of constituting monopoly.

Economic growth may exceed an annual rate of 6% this quarter, well above the fourth quarter's 4.9% rate, presidential economic adviser Martin Feldstein said. He said the administration's estimate of 4.5% growth for the year seems realistic.

Home mortgage rates slipped in the past month, but some economists say the slide from last summer's peak has struck bottom. Lenders quoted an average rate of

13.23% on standard home loans last week.

13 Investment plans by non-farm businesses for 1984 were boosted 13.6% from last year to $343.6 billion. The Commerce Department estimates that after adjustment for an expected rise in capital goods prices, plant and equipment outlays will rise about 12% this year from 1983.

The U.S. dollar strengthened further in what traders called a technical correction. Gold fell $4.40 an ounce to $396.30 on the Comex. There was speculation that Canada's central bank intervened in foreign-exchange markets to support the Canadian dollar.

Congressional concern over consolidation in the oil industry intensified. Sen. J. Bennett Johnston (D., La.) said he would offer legislation's temporarily banning mergers of the nation's 50 biggest oil concerns, including the proposed Socal-Gulf combination and the Mobil offer.

14 Retail sales slipped 0.2% in February, surprising retailers and economists who thought heavy spending had continued. The Commerce Department revised January sales upward to 3.3%, the largest gain since 1975. The rise previously was reported as 2.2%. December's increase also was revised upward.

The U.S. began its courtroom effort to force GM to recall 1.1 million 1980-model X-cars, because of allegedly defective brakes, and to pay $4 million in fines.

15 Business inventories rose a moderate 0.4% in January, but sales rose even faster, leaving businesses with the lowest inventories-to-sales ratio since the government began keeping records in 1967. Economists said the level reflects lower inflation and higher interest rates.

Empire Savings & Loan was closed by the Federal Home Loan Bank Board after two years of strong growth fueled by brokered deposits. The Texas S&L, which had $308.9 million in deposits, made "speculative loans" that probably will result in "enormous" losses, the Bank Board said.

New-car sales increased 31.5% in early March, to 211,240 units, indicating that Detroit's vigorous rebound is continuing. On an adjusted basis, sales by domestic auto makers ran at an annual pace of 8.1 million units.

16 Industrial production jumped 1.2% in February, providing further evidence that the economy is still booming. Consumer credit in January rose an adjusted $4.34 billion from December, the Fed said.

Texaco is offering $800 million of convertible bonds, the largest such issue ever launched in Europe. The 10-year offering follows Texaco's $10.1 billion takeover of Getty Oil and the $1.28 billion purchase of its shares from the Bass family of Texas.

19 The economy may be overheating, surges in housing starts and the factory operating rate indicated. Housing starts climbed 11.2% and the factory operating rate rose to 80.7% in February. But a moderate 0.4% rise in producer prices gave little evidence that inflation is being rekindled.

Large depositors in two failed banks may lose some of their money, the FDIC said. The banks, Heritage Bank in Anaheim, Calif., and Seminole State National Bank, Seminole, Texas, were closed Friday by the FDIC, which was planning to transfer insured deposits to other banks.

Chicago expects to set a price today on a $260 million issue of daily tender notes, the largest example to date of a new tax-exempt financing technique that, issuers say, provides some of the advantages of long-term financing at sharply lower rates.

The bleak outlook for wheat farmers isn't expected to brighten, even if Congress sweetens 1984 crop-reduction plans, analysts said. A global glut could keep wheat prices depressed.

20 The prime rate was boosted by the nation's major banks to 11½% from 11%, the first increase since August. Other rates climbed, and many economists expect the Fed to increase its discount rate.

The financial markets reflected the rise. The Dow Jones Industrial Average fell nearly 13 points to 1171.38. Bond prices also tumbled. The dollar strengthened slightly against other major currencies.

Personal income rose a solid 0.7% in February, underscoring evidence of a robust expansion. The consumer-led recovery may be slowing, however. The Commerce Department reported that personal consumption dropped 0.7% last month.

The U.S. had a record $15.29 billion deficit in its balance of payments on the current account during the fourth quarter. That brings the deficit for the full year to a record $40.8 billion.

The Congressional Budget Office said Reagan's enlarged plan to cut federal budget deficits isn't nearly as big as the president suggests. The CBO said that even if the plan is adopted, deficits will continue to grow annually to $198 billion in fiscal 1987.

The Supreme Court refused to review an appeals court ruling that struck down a FERC pricing rule for natural gas. The decision clears the way for refunds and reduced prices for natural-gas consumers that could total more than $1 billion.

21 The economy is expanding at an estimated 7.2% annual rate in the first quarter, well above the 5% GNP rate in the fourth quarter and higher than the 6% pace economists expected. The Commerce Department also said after-tax corporate profits fell 0.8% in 1983's fourth quarter.

The Justice Department tentatively agreed to a scaled-down merger of LTV and Republic Steel. Under the accord, the companies would shed one of Republic's plants in Gadsden, Ala., and its specialty operations in Massillon, Ohio.

Delinquent mortgage payments rose 8% in 1983's fourth quarter, but 80% of those were just 30 days or fewer overdue. New foreclosure proceedings declined in the period.

22 Senate foes of mergers in the oil industry abruptly abandoned their opposition to combinations already in the works, but promised to renew their fight against future big oil-company takeovers. They apparently didn't have enough votes to block the Socal-Gulf or Mobil-Superior mergers.

The Supreme Court ruled that internal papers used by outside auditors to outline a corporate client's tax strategy are subject to review by the IRS. Big accounting firms argued that such papers should be privileged.

The Justice Department dropped its opposition to LTV's acquisition of Republic Steel. The move comes after intense criticism from the Reagan administration and the industry. The companies agreed to sell two of Republic's plants to gain clearance.

23 The money supply surged $4 billion in the week ended March 12. The rise in M1 intensifies pressure on the Federal Reserve to tighten its credit grip. Some economists predict that the Fed soon will boost its discount rate to 9% or 9½% from the current 8½% level. Stock prices tumbled, but bond prices rose.

Durable-goods orders fell 1.2% in February, possibly indicating that the hectic pace of economic growth is easing. Many analysts had expected a 1% to 1.5% increase for the month. Nondefense capital goods orders, a barometer of business investment, rose a strong 1.7%.

The steel industry expects more mergers in the wake of government clearance of LTV's bid for Republic Steel. An offer for National Steel, possibly from abroad, and piecemeal solutions by U.S. Steel to revive its operations were projected.

26 The federal reserve has tightened its credit grip in an effort to slow rapid economic expansion, many bankers and economists believe. The move, probably taken earlier this month, is likely to increase interest rates. Some analysts contend that credit will be further tightened this week at meetings of the Fed's policy-making panel.

Consumer prices rose an adjusted 0.4% in February, indicating that rapid economic growth hasn't yet caused a major surge in inflation. The Labor Department attributed the rise to higher food and energy prices during the month.

Manufacturers are gradually building confidence for major spending programs. Machine-tool orders in February more than doubled from the year-earlier total and were up 7% from January. But producers say it may take several months before firms aggressively order new equipment.

The U.S. budget deficit narrowed to $20.38 billion in February from a year earlier. Rising revenue from the rapid economic growth was credited with the improvement.

Sales of U.S.-model cars jumped 33.7% in mid-March from weak year-earlier levels. On an annual-rate basis, the gain was a slight and anticipated softening of the recent pace.

27 American telephone is expected to announce today a commercial line of computers and related office work stations, marking the company's entrance into the office-automation market. The line of products will place AT&T in direct competition with major computer makers.

Federal banking regulators voted essentially to end federal insurance on deposits channeled to banks and S&Ls by independent brokers. The Federal Home Loan Bank Board and the FDIC each approved a rule to eliminate insurance on all but the first $100,000 in brokered funds.

Nigeria will formally offer terms next week for the refinancing of about $5.6 billion in overdue trade bills. Most creditors are expected to agree to the terms.

28 U.S. commercial banks in 1983 posted their second operating-profit decline in two years, but they may be recovering, according to FDIC data. The data disclose that 1983 loan losses totaled $8.4 billion, or 0.69% of average total loans, believed to be the worst since the Depression.

AT&T entered the computer business with a family of six computers ranging from a $340,000 high-powered minicomputer to a $9,950 desktop microcomputer. It also introduced products to link computers to a network.

The Fed drained funds from the banking

network, a step some analysts believe confirms that the central bank has toughened its credit stance. The average yield on the Treasury's auction of $6.02 billion of four-year notes rose to 12.07%, the highest on such an issue since September 1982.

Duty-free privileges of Taiwan, South Korea, Mexico and other developing nations will be cut March 29 by $11.9 billion. The step reduces to $10.7 billion imports eligible for duty-free entry to the U.S. under a nine-year-old program aiding the Third World.

29 The SEC is investigating allegations that a ring of securities traders made illicit profits using information leaked to them by a Wall Street Journal reporter about articles subsequently published in this newspaper.

30 The leading indicators index of the economy rose a strong 0.7% in February, suggesting rapid growth may continue for several months. New-home sales surged 7.7% from January, to an adjusted annual rate of 721,000 units.

The trade deficit grew to a record $10.1 billion in February, and government officials said it is likely to exceed $100 billion for all of 1984.

Royal Dutch/Shell is withdrawing its $5.2 billion merger proposal for Shell Oil and beginning a $55-a-share tender offer for the company, in which it holds 69.5%. The actions followed an announcement that Shell's independent directors rejected as inadequate the Europe-based oil giant's $5.2 billion proposal.

The French government plans a restructuring of the steel industry that will eliminate 20,000 jobs, nearly a quarter of the industry's employment, in the next four years.

Japan is under pressure from the U.S. to eliminate licensing requirements for foreign suppliers of telecommunications services, Commerce Secretary Baldrige said. U.S. firms' entry into Japan's market could narrow the U.S. trade deficit, he said.

April 1984

2 American Telephone plans to ask the FCC for permission to offer complete end-to-end telecommunications services for all agencies of the U.S. government. If approved, the move would, in effect, allow AT&T to reconstitute itself as the old Ma Bell, offering local and long-distance service and phone equipment in a single package.

The economy continued to expand at the end of the first quarter, the nation's purchasing agents said, but increasing prices remain a concern. Production and new orders were strong during the period.

The economy's vigorous expansion is helping increase borrowing, which many analysts predict will push interest rates higher later this year. They said the Fed will be forced to allow sharper rises in rates to keep money-supply growth under control.

A rescue package for Argentina was arranged by four heavily indebted Latin nations and backed by the U.S. Argentina, which owes $43 billion, is sure to be pressured to sign a tough agreement with the IMF.

Attempts by Congress to overhaul federal bankruptcy laws collapsed as rifts opened within organized labor, business groups and GOP senators over a provision relating to the use of the laws to get out of labor pacts.

Large gains in production are seen after the report of a 0.7% rise in factory orders in February. The Commerce Department revised durable goods orders to a 0.9% increase, an unusually large revision from the 1.2% drop estimated earlier.

3 Construction spending in February was 6.9% above the January rate, the biggest monthly rise in more than 30 years. Both new residential and industrial construction gained despite persistently high interest rates.

Rising interest rates helped send stock prices tumbling across a broad front in moderately active trading. Bond prices continued to slump on investor jitters that the Federal Reserve may further tighten its credit grip because of the economy's vigorous growth.

Money-center bank stocks scored gains in yesterday's declining market as investors showed confidence in the $400 million rescue package for Argentina. The dollar climbed sharply against major foreign currencies as a result of the rescue package. Gold plunged $8.20 an ounce to $379.30.

4 Royal Dutch/Shell boosted its $55-a-share, or $5.2 billion, offer for the shares of Shell Oil that it doesn't already own by $3 a share, or $285 million. Shell's independent board previously has said it would recommend a merger at $75 a share, or $7.1 billion.

A farm bill built around cash payments to wheat farmers who idle additional acreage in 1984 and 1985 was sent to President Reagan by the House. Reagan originally had opposed cash payments, and instead sought to pay farmers in surplus crops.

The performance of general equity mutual funds generally trailed the poor stock market in the first quarter, with the average general stock fund off 6.4%. Funds invested in gold, natural resource and international stocks ran far ahead.

The Interior Department said it illegally offered at least 240,000 acres of potentially valuable federal oil and gas leases last year without seeking competitive bids. The noncompetitive lottery was suspended in October because of abuses.

The prime lending rate appears poised for another increase soon, many bankers and economists say. They cited bank's costs and increased loan demand. The rate currently stands at 11½%. Bankers Trust and U.S. Trust boosted their broker-loan rates to 11½% from 11%.

5 Videodisk operations are being phased out by RCA. The company said it would stop making and marketing its videodisk players following a more than $500 million loss over five years, but would continue to press and distribute the disks. RCA also reported a 73% increase in first-quarter net income.

Sales of domestic-make new cars rose 26% in March from the year earlier, but were down markedly from January and February on an annual-rate basis. U.S. auto makers sold 756,164 domestic cars during March.

Home mortgage rates rose during the past month to the highest level since last fall, fueling fears that the housing market may begin cooling. Lenders last week quoted an average 13.55% rate on standard home loans.

Steps by the Common Market to curb imports of corn gluten feed from the U.S. have raised the ire of American agricultural processors. The U.S. grain-processing industry fears a curtailment in one of its few growing export markets.

6 The prime rate was raised by major U.S. banks to 12% from 11½%, bringing the rate to its highest level since November 1982. Most other rates were little changed despite a $2.2 billion jump in the money supply. Stock prices tumbled. The dollar surged against other currencies and futures prices fell.

The nation's retailers posted mixed sales results for March. Dismal weather and the late arrival of Easter were cited. Merchants remained optimistic, however, over the economy generally. Sears Roebuck reported a 2.4% increase in March sales. K mart's sales fell 0.2%.

Occidental Petroleum secretly signed a contract with China to help finance a coal mine, sources said. The pact would be the largest venture that Peking has formed with a foreign company.

9 Rising interest rates are spreading to new-car loans in some areas, causing fear of a drop in consumer demand. The Fed boosted its discount rate to 9% from 8½%, leading some to believe that most rates will edge up in coming months. Analysts see rising rates hurting the housing boom by summer.

The unemployment rate in March, unchanged from February, suggested that the economy's rapid growth may be slowing. The civilian unemployment rate remained at 7.8%.

After-tax profit margins of the nation's manufacturers rose to an average 4.4% of sales in the 1983 fourth quarter. That compared with 4.3% in the previous quarter.

10 Shearson/American Express is negotiating to buy a stake in Lehman Brothers Kuhn Loeb Inc., sources said. It wasn't clear whether Shearson is looking to buy a majority of minority interest in the investment banking firm.

Interest rates declined amid growing expectations that economic expansion is slowing, helping to reduce fears about a resurgence of inflation. The stock market ended mixed in relatively slow trading. The dollar rose against major currencies.

11 Shearson/American Express agreed to acquire Lehman Brothers Kuhn Loeb Inc. for a combined package of convertible debt and installment notes. The transaction is valued at $360 million. The combined company would be called Shearson Lehman/American Express.

The Reagan administrtion cut its projection for the fiscal 1984 budget deficit to $177.8 billion from $183.7 billion. It also raised its estimates for economic growth and interest rates.

The Big Three auto makers are expected to post combined first-period earnings of $3 billion, about triple their year-earlier profits and a record for any quarter. A 43% output rise to meet strong consumer demand is largely responsible for the gain.

General Electric reported a 14% increase in net income for the first quarter. Sales rose 8%. The company's information-services unit also announced a new nationwide network for computer-data communications, which puts GE in the fight for the next big high-technology market.

Warner Communication's record unit received clearance from a federal court to merge with Polygram Records. The joint venture, with sales estimated at about $1 billion, would surpass CBS Inc.'s records unit as the industry leader.

Marsh & McLennan's bond trading losses are being examined by the New York insurance superintendent. Disclosure of the losses, which will result in a $60 million charge against earnings, jarred the credit markets. Prices on some Treasury bonds fell by more than a quarter of a point.

12 U.S. steel shipments rose 21% in the first quarter compared with depressed year earlier results, and mill operating rates climbed to 81% from 57%. But profits remain elusive because of continued weak prices.

Penn Square Bank's failure in 1982 has become the costliest in U.S. history. Losses directly related to the Oklahoma City bank total $1.22 billion and are continuing to mount.

The Canadian government introduced legislation to relax controls on foreign-owned banks operating in Canada. The proposal would let foreign-owned banks increase their share of Canada's banking business to 16% from the current 8%.

GM and Toyota received final approval from the FTC to produce cars jointly in the U.S. The two auto makers plan to make about 250,000 subcompact cars annually. Under the revised consent decree, they must keep records when exchanging data on engineering or development work.

13 The money supply plunged $5 billion in the latest week. Many economists contend that the drop paves the way for lower interest rates. The larger-than-expected decrease in M1 and a steep decline in retail sales pushed bonds higher. A late rally sent the Dow industrials climbing 26.17 points.

Retail sales fell an adjusted 2.2% in March, the largest monthly decline in more than a decade. Analysts refused to attach much significance to the decline, but it seems to provide further evidence that the consumer-spending boom is coming to an end.

The Treasury asked Congress to move swiftly to raise the federal debt ceiling to $1.589 trillion. The agency said the increased limit was needed to avoid the kind of disruption of government services that occurred last fall.

Citicorp is seeking permission from federal regulators to open 10 banks in nine states. Citicorp joins a number of banks requesting new interstate powers through a legal loophole.

16 Domestic auto sales rose 33% in early April, continuing the strong sales pace of early this year. U.S. auto makers said dealers reported 210,395 deliveries in the period.

GM awarded its chairman, Roger B. Smith, a $1.5 million cash-and-stock bonus for last year's strong financial performance. The award, coupled with a $1.4 million bonus for Ford's head, raises questions about curbs on Japanese imports and the need for wage restraint.

Brokers who tout stocks on the basis of false inside data can be sued for financial losses by their clients, an appeals court ruled.

Congress will soon attempt to reconcile the two tax-raising bills that it completed last week. The Senate's three-year, $45 billion tax bill contains dozens of special-interest tax cuts. The House passed a $47.2 billion tax-raising measure. A joint conference is expected next month.

Economic growth in March slowed significantly from the frantic pace of January and February while inflationary pressures rose somewhat. Factory output rose 0.4% during March. Wholesale prices gained 0.5%. Business inventories in February grew 1.8%, the fastest pace since 1974.

17 Three regional phone firms posted strong first-quarter results. Nynex Corp. said net income was $221.7 million. Bell Atlantic earned $235.4 million, and Pacific Telesis reported net of $208 million. The results were the first since the breakup of AT&T.

The factory operating rate in March rose a slim 0.2% from February to 80.9% of capacity. The small gain reflected a modest increase in industrial output. Some analysts said the rate has risen enough in certain industries to prompt investment in plant and equipment.

18 Housing starts plunged almost 27% in March. Bad weather and fear about rising interest rates were cited. Many economists said home-building was simply settling down to a healthy pace after extraordinary growth.

19 American Telephone posted first-quarter net of $226.9 million, or 20 cents a share, on revenue of $8.04 billion. Per-share net was well below what it needs to meet its 1984 profit goal. AT&T also said it would seek to overturn a ruling requiring separation of its competitive and monopoly businesses.

Personal income rose 0.5% in March, the smallest gain in seven months. The moderate rise was another indication that economic growth has slowed from earlier brisk levels. Consumption also slowed slightly, causing the savings rate to edge up to 6.7% of disposable income.

Fears that the economic expansion will generate renewed inflation and higher interest rates sent bond prices tumbling. The market's jitters were intensified by erroneous reports that Fed Chairman Volcker resigned. Stocks also ended lower, with the Dow industrials losing 8.06 points.

Dome Petroleum reached tentative accords with its four main Canadian banks to refinance $2.42 billion (Canadian) of its $5.99 billion of debt.

Public Service of New Hampshire halted work on its troubled Seabrook nuclear project. The utility, plagued by a severe cash-flow problem, immediately laid off 5,200, or 84%, of the plant's workers.

20 Gross national product grew at an 8.3% pace in the first quarter. The rapid growth was well above the 7.2% rate estimated last month, and resulted from an accumulation of business inventories. Economists said the pace is likely to slow sharply in the current quarter.

Major oil firms are expected to report increases of 20% to 30% in first-quarter profit, reflecting improvements in refining and marketing operations, Wall Street analysts said. Increased natural-gas output also is seen aiding the results.

23 Charter Co.'s filing for bankruptcy-law protection is likely to cause a flood of policy redemptions at its insurance units. The subsidiaries, which weren't part of the filing, maintain they can continue operations. Charter cited a loss of trade credit by its oil-refining operations. The filing covered 43 units.

Interest rates are likely to rise even after the long-awaited economic slowdown appears. Bankers and economists said the Federal Reserve will keep credit conditions tight and businesses are seen borrowing heavily.

Argentina is pushing its financial problems into the international political arena. The country hopes to pressure banks into easing repayment terms on its debt by citing its return to democracy.

Long Island Lighting's evacuation plan dilemma is being worked on by the Reagan administration. The plan is a major obstacle to the start-up of the Shoreham nuclear plant.

Public Service of New Hampshire cut payments to the Seabrook nuclear project's construction fund until the utility solves its financial problems.

24 Consumer borrowing surged a record $6.61 billion in February. That followed a revised $4.47 billion jump in January. One economist said the February rise in debt put pressure on interest rates, even though the increase was considered "pretty modest."

Continental Illinois Corp.'s problem loans could exceed the record $2.3 billion reported last week, the bank firm said. It also said it is among the bank lenders to Charter Co., which filed for bankruptcy-law protection.

Socal's proposed merger with Gulf Corp. is likely to get preliminary FTC approval Thursday, sources close to Socal said. Clearance will likely carry the proviso that Socal spin off 4,000 Gulf service stations and a Gulf refinery in the Southeast.

Occidental Petroleum will sign a preliminary joint-venture accord with China to develop a $600 million open-pit coal mine in China's Shanxi province, Occidental's chairman, Armand Hammer, said.

25 U.S. Steel reported net income of $171 million for the first quarter, compared with a $118 million loss a year earlier. Bethlehem Steel reported a deficit of $54.6 million for the period.

Exxon Corp. reported a 39% increase in first-quarter net. Socal's profit rose 22%, Phillips Petroleum posted a 50% gain and Diamond Shamrock's net rose nearly twelvefold.

Cleveland Electric may cancel its Perry nuclear Unit 2, which is 43% complete. The utility cited "uncertainties," including difficulties in obtaining financing.

Consumer prices rose 0.2% in March, reflecting declines in food and fuel-oil prices. Economists, however, don't expect the slim increase to be repeated. Separately, new orders for durable goods climbed 0.8% last month, suggesting a slowing in economic expansion.

National Intergroup agreed to sell a 50% stake in its National Steel unit to Japan's Nippon Kokan for $292 million. National will jointly own the company which will become an independent operation.

26 The Big Board and the CBOE launched formal investigations of unusual trading activity in a stock-index option. The exchanges said they were examining records following a jump in the price of the April call option based on the S&P 100 stock index.

Shell Oil Co.'s net income rose 33% in the first quarter. Gulf Corp. posted a 21% increase, Sun Co. reported a 59% gain and Amerada Hess had an eighteenfold rise.

Du Pont Co.'s first-quarter net jumped 84% from weak year-earlier results. Monsanto posted a 73% gain. Both concerns cited the effects of the economic recovery.

27 Socal's acquisition of Gulf Corp. was tentatively cleared by the FTC. Under the conditional clearance, Socal must sell about $1 billion of Gulf's assets, including 4,200 gasoline stations and 30 supply terminals in the Southeast. The merger would be the largest in U.S. corporate history.

U.S. Synthetic Fuels Corp.'s president, Victor Thompson, resigned amid further allegations that he violated federal ethical guidelines. The charges stem from an SEC probe on his private business activities.

Ford Motor said first-quarter net more than quadrupled to a record $897 million, higher than many analysts expected. Sales jumped nearly 30%.

Mobil Corp. posted a 52% rise in first-quarter net. Sohio's profit climbed 38% and Texaco's edged 1% higher. The results were in line with improvements in the industry.

Productivity of the nation's non-farm businesses grew at an adjusted 2.6% rate in the first quarter, slightly trailing the revised 2.7% pace in the 1983 fourth quarter.

30 U.S. Synthetic Fuels Corp. is likely to be the target of investigations by three congressional panels as allegations of financial scandal continue to grow. Supporters concede that the firm won't survive without changing personnel and policies.

GM said first-quarter net more than doubled to $1.61 billion, its highest profit for any quarter.

The merchandise trade gap widened in March to $10.26 billion from $10.09 billion in February. The performance reflects the nation's vigorous economic growth, demand for imports and a strong dollar.

The Treasury's quarterly refunding package is expected to total between $16 billion and $16.5 billion. Economists warn that the huge borrowing needs will increase pressures for further interest rate boosts.

Machine-tool orders increased 66% in March, continuing the rise from recession levels.

May 1984

1 Leading indicators fell 1.1% in March. The decline in the economic index, the first since August 1982, is another signal of slower growth ahead. Separately, new-home sales dropped 4.9% in March, reflecting harsh weather.

U.S. Synthetic Fuels Corp.'s board discussed conflict-of-interest allegations stemming from its former president's private business activities three months before Victor Thompson resigned. Based on incomplete data, the board didn't find any impropriety.

New-construction contracts fell an adjusted 4% in March, reflecting declines in home building and public-works construction, F. W. Dodge said. For the first quarter, total contracts rose 17%.

2 General Motors is asking its suppliers to trim prices at least 3.3% a year over the next three model years. A significant number of major suppliers, concerned that other car makers may follow, intend to resist the rollback.

GTE Sprint has stopped taking new customers in about 35 to 40 cities or towns because its long-distance telephone network is crowded to capacity. The GTE unit is the nation's third largest long-distance carrier.

Fear that the Fed will tighten credit conditions further, as well as concern that interest rates will rise despite any Federal Reserve moves, sent bond prices lower. Stock prices gained, however, with the Dow Industrials rising 12.25 points.

New factory orders increased a strong 2.2% in March, reflecting a 57.5% jump in defense orders. The gain was the largest since last September. Separately, it was reported that construction spending rose 1.2% in March.

3 Marsh & McLennan discovered more "unauthorized" government-securities trading that will increase its extraordinary after-tax losses to $90 million. The firm's entire treasury department is currently under review.

The government-securities market has become highly volatile. Volume dwarfs the stock market, and there isn't formal federal regulation.

U.S. auto makers plan to build 722,000 cars in May, 22% more than a year earlier. The output pace continues at a five-year high, but capacity limits may prevent the car makers from stockpiling vehicles as a hedge against possible shortages.

Shell Oil said five executives decided to tender their personal holdings in Shell to Royal Dutch/Shell for $58 a share. The announcement follows an independent appraiser's report that put the value of Shell Oil's shares at $81.50 each.

A Federal Reserve official's disclosure that the Fed tightened monetary policy at its

March meeting is causing concern at the central bank and dismay among Treasury aides.

4   Esmark Inc. is considering a proposal from the investment banking firm of Kohlberg Kravis to take the company private at $55 a share. The transaction was valued at $2.3 billion, making it the largest leveraged buyout in history.

The nation's retailers, plagued by harsh weather, reported mostly disappointing sales results for April. Sears Roebuck had a 9.8% increase in April sales and K mart's sales rose 9.6%. Consumer caution also was cited.

Auto sales rose 22% to 894,191 cars in April from a year earlier, the best April results since 1979. Shortages of Japanese cars, however, drove import sales down.

President Reagan sent Congress $13.9 billion in cuts in his record defense budget plan for fiscal 1985. The reductions fulfill a promise to trim his proposed military spending boosts.

The money supply fell an unexpectedly large $3.6 billion, but concern about higher interest rates continued to permeate the credit markets. Stocks closed mixed, with the Dow industrials closing 5.03 points lower.

The outlook for economic recovery this year in the world's industrialized nations has strengthened. Strong growth in corporate profits and rising investment were cited by the OECD.

U.S. Synthetic Fuels Corp.'s inspector general formally requested a criminal investigation by the Justice Department into the private business activities of Victor Thompson, the concern's former president.

7   Economic growth rebounded in April from March's reduced rate, the latest unemployment statistics indicate. The April civilian jobless rate was unchanged at 7.8%.

Corporate profits surged in the first quarter. After-tax earnings from current lines of 510 major firms climbed 57% in the period, and their net rose 58%, a Wall Street Journal survey found. Operating earnings of 154 Canadian companies rose 118%.

Esmark Inc. plans to sell pieces of its business, make major acquisitions and eventually take parts of the company public again once Kohlberg Kravis's $2.4 billion proposed buyout of the firm is completed. Esmark's board has approved the bid.

Lion Capital Group, a small government-securities trading firm, filed for bankruptcy-law protection, leaving a number of public agencies with possible losses in the millions of dollars. The filing was the latest disruption in the government-securities market.

Treasury Secretary Regan said the government is going to have to "rethink" the Social Security system before the decade ends as a means of trimming federal budget deficits. He said rising medical bills are also a target of spending cuts.

Carter Hawley Hale will try to block a preliminary injunction that would severely set back its efforts to avert an unfriendly takeover by Limited Inc. The injunction is being sought by the SEC.

The FDIC said two banks in Wyoming and one each in Minnesota and Texas were closed because of mounting loan losses. The closings bring to 25 the number of failures this year of federally insured banks.

8   Seven chemical firms that produced Agent Orange agreed to pay $180 million to compensate Vietnam veterans for injuries claimed to be related to exposure to dioxin. Details of the out-of-court settlement are expected to be presented for approval within 90 days.

The White House backed away from Treasury Secretary Regan's suggestion that the Social Security system may have to be changed. Other administration officials, though, said the system may be affected next year in a move to trim budget deficits.

The merchandise trade gap widened to a record $25.78 billion in the first quarter from $19.42 billion in the fourth quarter of 1983. Exports grew 4.5%, but imports gained 12.2%.

The dollar rose to a record against the British pound and advanced broadly against other major currencies. The surge was in response to trader expectations of higher U.S. interest rates.

9   The Senate rejected the Democrats' three-year, $200 billion deficit-cutting plan. The 49–49 vote, though, may indicate GOP dissatisfaction with President Reagan's $144 billion deficit-reduction package.

Royal Dutch/Shell's $58-a-share tender offer for Shell Oil was blocked by a Delaware state court. The court barred the offer until Royal Dutch discloses more data about the bid's fairness and resolves certain other "deficiencies."

The prime rate was raised to 12½% from 12% by most major banks, the highest level since October 1982. Further increases are expected. Canadian banks also boosted their lending fee, to 12% from 11½%.

The White House reacted to the increase with sharp criticism of the Fed's credit policies. Rising interest rates are seen as damaging to Reagan's reelection chances.

10 Teledyne Inc. began a tender offer to buy 25% of its common shares for $1 billion. The offer to buy as many as five million shares, at $200 each, is considered one of the biggest stock repurchases in history.

City Investing Co. said a group led by Merrill Lynch Capital Markets offered to acquire the firm in a leveraged buyout valued at $2.3 billion. However, Victor Posner, who holds an 8.5% stake in the firm, is considering making a higher offer.

Martin Feldstein plans to leave his post as chairman of the Council of Economic Advisers July 10. After his resignation announcement, Mr. Feldstein praised the Fed's credit policies, despite escalating White House criticism of the central bank.

The flow of U.S. technology to China is expected to be speeded up under bilateral consultation teams being set by the Reagan administration. The studies will focus on telecommunications, electronics and metallurgy.

Bond prices tumbled as the Treasury proceeded with its massive borrowing program and investors remained concerned that the Fed will tighten its credit grip. Yesterday, the government sold $5.26 billion of 10-year notes at an average rate of 13.16%. Stocks also slid, with the Dow industrials closing 10.78 points lower.

11 American Telephone was ordered by the FCC to cut long-distance phone rates 6.1% as part of a broad revamping of telephone tariffs. The commission also told the Bell regional firms to lower by 8.5% the fees charged for connections to local telephone networks.

Continental Illinois Corp.'s stock and some of its debt securities tumbled in heavy trading. In Big Board composite trading, its stock fell to $12, down $1.125. The decline was ascribed to rumors that the big banking firm's financial position has worsened.

GE Credit Corp. agreed to acquire Employers Reinsurance Corp. for $1.08 billion. The purchase of the Getty Oil unit will broaden the General Electric subsidiary's financial services.

The money supply rose a steeper-than-anticipated $2.4 billion, increasing fears that the Fed would tighten its credit grip further, and sending bonds lower. Investors also shunned the Treasury's $4.75 billion auction of 30-year bonds.

14 Interest rates are headed higher, many bankers and economists warn. They say rates are likely to swing widely as they rise, and that fear about rapid economic expansion will continue to frighten investors from the bond market.

The economy's rapid growth in April had little effect on wholesale prices. The producer-price index was unchanged for the month, as food prices fell. Retail sales jumped 2.9% following a 2% decline in March.

15 Synfuel spending cuts of at least $8 billion in the $14 billion in aid currently available to help proposed projects will be sought by President Reagan. The decision comes in the wake of growing congressional opposition to synfuels subsidies.

AT&T asked the FCC to permit an accounting method that allows faster depreciation of older equipment. Analysts said the request, if granted, could serve as justification for AT&T to boost its long-distance rates. The change would mean an increase of about $960 million a year in depreciation expenses.

Business inventories increased a strong 0.9% in March, indicating businesses still feel a need to build supplies. Separately, consumer debt rose an adjusted $5.87 billion, reflecting heavy borrowing in March.

Bond prices fell sharply and yields on Treasury bonds climbed to their highest levels since the summer of 1982. Many economists contend that rates will rise further on the government's borrowing needs and continued economic growth.

16 Industrial output rose 1.4% in April, apparently reflecting inventory-building and rising demand for capital equipment. The increase verified indications that economic expansion rebounded sharply last month after easing a bit in March.

Five big retailers posted strong gains in first-quarter earnings. Associated Dry Goods reported a 50% increase, May Department Stores' profit gained 35%, Dayton Hudson's rose 25%, R. H. Macy's jumped 24% and Allied's rose 12%. Federated Department Stores' earnings fell 17%.

New-car sales rose a stronger-than-expected 25.5% in early May, indicating that the U.S. auto industry's recovery is continuing. Dealers delivered 238,240 domestic-model new cars during the May 1–10 period.

The FDIC is increasing pressure on some

ailing savings banks to find merger partners. Currently, 23 savings banks are receiving capital assistance from the FDIC, and the agency is convinced that some won't be able to survive independently.

17 A Swiss court ordered five Swiss banks to divulge data on heavy trading in Santa Fe International stock before it was acquired by Kuwait Petroleum in 1981. The order aids the SEC in its probe of illegal stock trading on inside information.

Housing starts jumped 19.33% in April, reflecting a rebound from March's depressed levels. It was the biggest monthly gain since January 1983, but analysts don't expect the pace to continue for long. Separately, the factory operating rate rose 0.9 point in April to 81.9%.

U.S. Synthetic Fuels Corp. director resigned amid conflict-of-interest allegations involving his private business activities. John Carter's resignation leaves five of the seven seats on the board vacant.

18 Continental Illinois will receive a $2 billion capital infusion under an agreement between the FDIC and a group of major banks. A bank group also agreed to boost its credit line to Continental to $5.5 billion from $4.5 billion. Continental, meanwhile, said it is seeking a merger partner.

Bond prices tumbled on worries over the banking system because of the huge credit package for Continental. Adding to the drop was concern over a $4.9 billion jump in M1.

Personal income rose a solid 0.5% in April, aided by strong economic expansion. The rise was damped by a drop in farm income because of a slowing in government payments to farmers. Consumer spending increased 1.1% during the month.

21 Robust economic expansion is increasing pressure on the Federal Reserve to adopt a tighter credit policy. Many bankers and economists, however, think the Fed will delay any significant move because of the financial problems of Continental Illinois.

The economy grew at an adjusted 8.8% annual rate in the first quarter, higher than the previously estimated 8.3% rate. Separately, after-tax corporate profits rose 3.9% in the period, rebounding from a 0.8% drop in 1983's fourth quarter.

LTV and Republic Steel holders approved a proposed merger of the firms. The combination will form the nation's second-largest steelmaker.

Soviet grain output estimates have been cut by some analysts as much as 10%.

Several months of dry weather have pushed the Soviet Union to the brink of severe crop damage, which could boost prices and alter the world wheat-supply outlook.

22 Beatrice Foods said its board will consider today a management recommendation to acquire Esmark Inc. The $56-a-share proposal is valued at $2.5 billion and would top the $2.4 billion leveraged-buy-out offer by Kohlberg Kravis.

Continental Illinois Bank's prospective merger partners won't be promised financial aid, at least so far, the FDIC's chairman said. Four banks have expressed interest in acquiring Continental and have inquired as to what steps the FDIC might take to sweeten the takeover.

23 Consumer prices rose 0.5% in April, indicating some acceleration in inflation. Separately, a 6.4% decline in durable-goods orders hinted that slower economic expansion may lie ahead. The two reports painted a confusing picture for the Fed's policy-making arm, which met this week.

24 U.S. car sales rose 22.1% in mid-May to 226,797 units. The increase was consistent with the recent sales performance and indicates that the auto sales recovery is continuing.

Beatrice Foods arranged $2.8 billion in bank credit to finance its $56-a-share, or about $2.5 billion, tender offer for Esmark Inc. The credit agreement is a sign that Beatrice could pay as much as about $62 a share for Esmark.

25 Money-center banks' stocks plunged amid a general lack of confidence in the financial system and a siege of rumors concerning the soundness of Manufacturers Hanover. The banks denied the rumors, but worries also sent bond prices and the dollar lower.

Continental's rescue package has reassured many commercial customers, who have decided to stick with the bank. But its guaranteed CDs aren't selling well and many bankers are wondering where the financial resources to solve Continental's problems will be found.

The price of prescription drugs is rising sharply. Since 1980, drug prices have risen 37%, while the price of all commodities rose only 13%. Prescription drug sales exceeded $16 billion at wholesale last year.

Esmark Inc. accepted Beatrice Foods Co.'s $60-a-share, or $2.71 billion, offer. In exchange for the sweetened offer, Esmark gave Beatrice the option to buy Esmark's Swift/Hunt-Wesson business for $1.3 billion if Beatrice is outbid for all of Esmark.

29 The Fed's Open Market panel responded to concern that rapid first-quarter growth would fuel inflation and approved a slight tightening of credit conditions at its March 26–27 meeting. But analysts said the Fed will delay further tightening until concern over the banking system eases.

Machine-tool orders rose 23% in April to $255.9 million, indicating that durable-goods manufacturers are continuing to boost spending for new equipment. Machine-tool producers said, however, that companies are mostly ordering individual machines rather than replacing entire plants.

Financier Saul Steinberg is talking with "potential investors" about joining him in a possible bid to take control of Walt Disney Productions. Mr. Steinberg, who owns 12.2% of Disney, said he may acquire as much as 49.9% through a tender offer, merger or open-market purchases.

30 Saul Steinberg said he will attempt to gain enough votes to unseat the current board of Walt Disney Productions. In an SEC filing, Mr. Steinberg, who holds a 12.2% stake in Disney, said he will begin soliciting "consents" from other holders.

Action on a bill to allow Continental Illinois to merge with an out-of-state banking firm is unlikely soon, Illinois state officials said. The lawmakers appear inclined to see if Continental and rival First Chicago can come to terms for a merger.

Bond prices tumbled and yields on some government bonds rose to their highest levels in nearly two years. Many dealers are concerned that a continued surge in M1 will prompt the Fed to further tighten its credit grip to control inflation.

Non-farm productivity grew at an adjusted 3.5% annual rate in the first quarter, surpassing initial estimates and the 2.7% pace of 1983's fourth quarter. The gain reflected increases in output and hours worked.

Washington Public Power's first nuclear plant has begun generating electricity at full power, 12 years after the start of construction. The plant is undergoing tests and won't begin supplying power to commercial customers until summer.

Teledyne Inc. said it would purchase the 8.7 million of its shares tendered prior to last Friday's deadline. Indicated value of the transaction was placed at $1.74 billion.

The U.S. and Japan disclosed details of their accord on liberalizing Japan's financial markets. Under the agreement, Japan would be required to encourage the creation of a worldwide Euroyen market and allow foreign banks greater access to Japan's financial markets.

A. G. Becker Paribas cut its work force by about 10% in reaction to a decline in the fixed-income and securities markets. Other brokerage firms appear to be planning similar reductions in personnel

Grand Metropolitan's U.S. unit agreed in principle to sell its Liggett & Myers Tobacco operation. The buyout group includes the tobacco unit's management.

31 Iran offered to cut its oil price $1.50 to $2 a barrel to revive its oil exports, which have been reduced by attacks on ships going to Iranian ports. Reports of the price cut resulted in a rally on the Big Board and sent gold prices falling.

Oil analysts said that any price cut by Iran isn't likely to put downward pressure on oil prices because the discount would be used to offset higher insurance rates.

The merchandise trade gap widened 19% in April to an adjusted $12.19 billion. Separately, sales of new homes fell 4.9%, indicating that rising interest rates hae started to depress the housing market.

Continental Illinois Corp. probably will need permanent federal aid to effect a merger or survive independently, Continental's chairman told Illinois lawmakers.

Bond prices tumbled on unconfirmed reports that Bolivia will suspend payments on its international debt, and on renewed worries over continued heavy borrowing by the Treasury.

New construction contracts rose an adjusted 1% in April. Gains in housing and commercial and industrial building were largely offset by a drop in public-works construction.

The chemical industry is establishing a program to clean up toxic-waste dumps. Under the voluntary plan, designed to enhance the industry's image, firms have committed $5 million to $10 million annually, which is considered a fraction of the amount needed for the cleanup.

June 1984

1 Leading indicators rose 0.5% in April, suggesting that the economy still has considerable momentum. Factory orders, however, fell 3.6%. The drop was viewed as a sign that interest rates are curbing economic activity.

Sales rose last month for the nation's biggest retailers, but the figures suggest an easing in consumer spending. Sears posted a 6.1% gain from May 1983. K mart reported a 9.7% rise and J. C. Penney, 20%.

U.S. auto makers plan to keep car output close to capacity levels this month. Continued strong sales, however, will prevent the building of inventories as the usual summer plant closings for the changeover of model years begin.

Bond prices rallied sharply on what some analysts said were signs of a long-awaited economic slowdown. The surge came despite a larger-than-expected $3.3 billion jump in the nation's money supply.

Bank stocks tumbled on worries about the international debt crisis and the plight of Continental Illinois. In another sign of market jitters, $250 million of Citicorp floating-rate notes remain unsold.

The economic summit next week in London likely will focus on rising U.S. interest rates, worries about the U.S. financial system following the bailout of Continental Illinois and the escalation of conflict in the Persian Gulf.

4 Interest rates appear poised to decline, at least temporarily, as economic expansion seems to be losing some momentum, a small group of economists said. Others argue that higher rates lie ahead.

Economic expansion continued in May but eased slightly from April's brisk pace, a monthly survey of purchasing agents shows. The survey showed a gain in employment, but slower deliveries for the month.

Unemployment fell to 7.5% of the civilian work force in May, returning the jobless rate to its November 1980 level. However, the number of hours worked and average earnings declined. Separately, construction spending in April rose 0.2%.

5 Producers of industrial goods are asking modest price increases that should bolster profits without creating higher inflation. The discounting of the last couple of years continues on some goods, but purchasing agents have reported the highest prices since January 1981.

Local Bell phone firms plan to modify their existing phone networks to carry computerized data between computers at bargain rates, making a move into local computer-data transmission. An FCC decision on the plan is expected by midsummer.

The dollar eased against most foreign currencies, hitting a six-week low against the West German mark. Gold rose $5.50 to $395.60 an ounce in response to the weaker dollar, lower U.S. interest rates and renewed concern about the Iran-Iraq war.

Bond prices surged amid brisk buying by pension-fund managers and other institutional investors, reflecting growing evidence that the economy is slowing. Rising bond prices pushed stocks higher in active trading.

6 Bond prices fell as traders took profits, ending a three-day rally. Uncertainty over the economic outlook also was cited. Stock prices also declined, with the Dow industrials closing at 1124.89, down 6.68 points.

U.S. car sales rose 22.6% last month to 803,273 cars, led by a larger-than-expected late-May surge. Import sales increased 12.9% compared with May 1983's results, reflecting the availability of Japanese models.

The dollar strengthened against other major currencies following a Saudi Arabian attack on Iranian warplanes and a rise in long-term U.S. rates. Gold's price declined 90 cents to $394.70 an ounce.

7 A U.S. footwear industry request for relief from imports was rejected by the ITC. The commission said that while imports, mainly from Taiwan, South Korea and Brazil, have captured 69% of the U.S. market, the "serious injury" test wasn't met.

Stocks resumed their rally, aided by remarks by Fed Chairman Volcker, who said he saw "indications of progress" in the economy, and headway being made against international debt problems. Bond prices fell on confusion over the outlook for the Fed's credit policy.

IBM soon will be forced to cut prices on its PC line by 25% to 30% to reach its 1984 sales goal, some Wall Street analysts said. They said that dealer surveys show an easing in PC sales growth.

Measures to boost taxes by about $17 billion over four years were tentatively approved by House-Senate conferees, bringing the amount of increased taxes accepted by the conferees to about $31 billion.

8 The money supply fell $2.4 billion. Many analysts had been expecting a small increase. Bond prices surged following the announcement, but ended with small gains.

Home mortgage rates climbed during May to their highest level since fall 1982. Lenders quoted an average interest rate of 14.29% last week on conventional fixed-rate mortgages, up from 13.78% a month earlier.

Many bankruptcies will result from the increasing number of leveraged buyouts and takeovers of firms if interest rates rise significantly or the economy slips into another recession, SEC Chairman John Shad warned.

11 Continental Group embarked on a series of defensive moves as part of an effort to thwart a proposed $2.42 billion takeover by Sir James Goldsmith. Continental retained Morgan Stanley as an adviser and hasn't accepted invitations to enter talks with the financier.

U.S. copper producers expect 60% of the industry to be wiped out by 1990 if the flow of more cheaply produced imports isn't cut sharply. The ITC will meet Thursday to consider proposed copper-import quotas.

Investor Saul Steinberg's $67.50-a-share, or $970 million, bid for 37.9% of Walt Disney Productions stock calls for the dismantling of Disney. If successful, the offer would bring Mr. Steinberg's stake in Disney to 49%.

12 Capital spending will rise 14.8% in 1984 from last year, businesses expect, despite a steady rise in interest rates. The Commerce Department survey suggests that executives are basing their planned spending on economic strength.

Walt Disney Productions purchased Saul Steinberg's 11.1% stake in the company. Disney paid the investor $297.3 million, or $70.83 a share, plus $28 million in expense reimbursement for the common shares.

First Chicago Corp. said it isn't any longer interested in acquiring Continental Illinois. Sources said, however, that First Chicago may again consider an acquisition if the FDIC vows permanent aid.

13 PS of New Hampshire's request for permission to bill customers for its $16.5 million investment in the canceled Pilgrim Unit 2 nuclear plant was rejected. The state's Supreme Court ruled that such a move is barred by state law.

U.S. banks face the prospect of lower earnings for the second consecutive quarter because of Argentina's debt problems. Most bankers are expecting a bailout for Argentina similar to one made in the first quarter.

14 Volcker said he sees "some signs" that the economy is slowing, but he appeared uncertain over whether it will prove lasting or significant. Separately, business inventories rose 1.5% in April and consumer debt expanded an adjusted $6.41 billion during the month.

15 The collapse of Walt Disney's stock price prior to the company announcement that it would purchase investor Saul Steinberg's stake for $325 million is being probed for insider trading abuses by at least five regulators.

The money supply rose $3.1 billion, placing the weekly measure near the upper end of the Fed's target range. Bond prices edged higher, however, on a report that borrowing from the Fed by banks and

savings institutions fell to an average of $512 million in the week.

The Dow Jones Industrial Index fell to 1086 on June 15 closing under 1100 for the first time in 16 months on warnings from Fed Chairman Paul Volker of a credit squeeze which may put further upward pressure on interest rates. However bond prices rose sharply in anticipation of a better market resulting from the elimination of a 30% withholding tax paid by some foreign investors.

18 Industrial output rose 0.4% in May, after climbing 1.1% in April, apparently confirming slower economic expansion. Producer prices remained flat for the second consecutive month. Analysts differ about how much the economy will slow in the months ahead.

Interest rates are likely to rise further this year despite the recent easing in business activity, many bankers and economists said. They contend that economic growth hasn't slowed enough for the Federal Reserve to loosen its credit reins.

The U.S. Treasury's refusal to extend a $300 million loan commitment to Argentina has put pressure on the country to reach an accord with the IMF on an economic austerity program. Banking sources said plans to lend Argentina $125 million to meet interest payments have been dropped.

Bids for Conrail are due by midnight EDT tonight. Already, offers from Conrail employees and Alleghany Corp. are on the table, four more bids are promised and others could arrive, including one involving Marriott Corp.'s president.

The overseas market in Treasury securities is soaring on growing anticipation that the 30% withholding tax on interest on U.S. bonds will be repealed or phased out.

19 Strict limits on the amount of tax benefits that can be taken on company cars were agreed upon by House-Senate conferees. The provision is meant to blunt the tax incentive for businesses to buy "luxury" autos.

Stocks rallied sharply in active trading, with the Dow industrials ending 22.75 points higher at 1109.65. Bonds were little changed. The dollar firmed against other major currencies on higher U.S. interest rates, and gold rose 50 cents an ounce to $371.

The U.S. deficit in the international trade of goods and services was another record in the first quarter, widening to $19.41 billion. The balance-of-payments deficit followed a $17.21 billion deficit in 1983's fourth quarter.

Latin American finance ministers will meet

Thursday and Friday in Colombia. They will be joined by officials of their foreign ministries, underscoring the growing political dimension of the global debt crisis.

British police battled 6,500 stone throwing miners outside a Yorkshire coal processing plant. It was the worst violence in the 99-day coal strike, police said, reporting that union chief Arthur Scargill was among 79 hurt. The strike over proposed pit closings and layoffs is causing patches of hardship throughout Britain.

The operating rate of the nation's factories, mines and utilities rose to 81.7% of capacity in May, from 81.5% in April, reflecting a moderate 0.4% gain in industrial output.

20 Oil prices indirectly are being depressed by the fighting in the Persian Gulf. The Iran-Iraq clash has sparked an increase in OPEC's oil output, currently estimated at more than 18 million barrels daily. The boost is said to put downward pressure on prices.

Personal income rose 0.6% in May and consumption increased a strong 1.1%. Housing starts, however, fell 10.5%, reflecting rising interest rates. Bond prices fell in reaction to the reports, but stocks gained.

Electricity output grew 8% nationwide during the past year, following several years of low growth. The economic recovery and extreme weather were cited.

21 Economic growth is running at a torrid 5.7% annual pace, according to the government's "flash" estimate of second-quarter GNP. The rate, which compares with a revised 9.7% pace for the first period, left analysts even more puzzled about the course of the recovery.

Financial markets were badly shaken. Bond prices plunged. Stocks fell sharply, then rebounded, with the Dow industrials advancing 15.80 points. Interest-rate futures sank, and the dollar soared against other major currencies.

A probe of Continental Illinois was expanded by the SEC to examine the adequacy of the firm's loan-loss provisions over the past several years. The inquiry, begun in March 1983, had centered on possible violation of disclosure rules and possible insider trading abuses.

Argentina is expected to repay its foreign creditor banks about $100 million in overdue interest this week, sources said, leaving about $350 million in interest payments that will be 90 days in arrears by June 30.

22 The money supply rose $3 billion, increasing speculation that the Fed soon will tighten its credit grip in an attempt to slow economic expansion and keep a lid on inflation. The increase pushed the M1

level about the Fed's target range for the first time since late February.

Latin American debtor nations called on industrialized countries and commercial banks to share more of the burden in resolving the international debt crisis.

25 A tax bill that would raise about $50 billion in revenue and trim spending by $11.2 billion through fiscal 1987 was approved by House-Senate conferees. Provisions include the repeal of the 30% withholding tax on interest paid to foreign investors in U.S. securities and a cut in the capital-gains holding period on securities to six months from a year.

Consumer prices rose 0.2% in May, or at a 2.4% annual rate, well below April's increase of 0.5% or 5.6% annually. In addition, average weekly earnings in May fell 1.3%, adding to the picture of low inflation. Separately, May's durable-goods orders rose a solid 3.3%.

Machine tool orders totaled $320.2 million in May, up 27% from April and more than double the year-earlier results.

26 The prime rate was increased to 13% from 12½% by most major banks, bringing the lending fee to its highest level since October 1982. The move was expected because of the recent sharp boosts in banks' costs of raising funds and high loan demand. Many bankers predict further increases this summer.

The dollar soared to records against the British pound and Canadian dollar, and reached a seven-year high against the Swiss franc and its highest level this year against the Japanese yen. Higher U.S. interest rates were cited.

U.S. new-car sales rose 12.4% in mid-June, bringing the sales pace to near the highs of recent months. Auto industry sales climbed to 259,844 units from 205,444 a year earlier.

The U.S. budget deficit widened to a record $33.93 billion in May. The government's budget gap last month compares with a deficit of $29.29 billion a year earlier and a surplus of $11.49 billion in April.

27 Consumers Power will ask its board to approve the cancellation of its Midland, Mich., nuclear project. The utility, which spent $3.6 billion on the plant, had failed to reach an agreement with state regulators over a cost-recovery plan.

Municipal-bond prices fell as more than $1 billion of state and local government bonds flooded the credit market. Dealers expect continued heavy volume because of the anticipated passage of new tax legislation.

Fraudulent trading activities are being probed by at least four major international securities firms. The alleged trading, said to be conducted by employees of the firms, could involve as much as $16 million in losses, market sources said.

AT&T introduced a new line of products including an office-computer network and an IBM-compatible personal computer. Analysts said the network could establish AT&T as a serious rival to IBM.

28 Merrill Lynch disclosed reorganization plans aimed at slashing costs and making it more competitive. The financial-services firm said that the realignment, the result of a two-year study, will cut its work force by 1,500, to 41,500, and help save it $200 million.

Taxes would be raised by $50 billion through fiscal 1987 under a bill passed 268–155 by the House and sent to the Senate. The bill, coupled with measures that would cut spending by $13 billion, is the basis of the "down payment" against deficits that Congress has been working on all year.

Long Island Lighting asked banks for an immediate $200 million credit line to avoid running out of cash by September 1. It cited a severe cash squeeze related to its stalled $4.1 billion Shoreham nuclear power plant.

New construction contracts surged a seasonally adjusted 14% in May from April, to a record $21.9 billion, F.W. Dodge said. Large gains in nonresidential building and public-works projects were cited.

29 General Motors agreed to acquire Electronic Data Systems for as much as $2.55 billion. Through the acquisition, GM's largest, EDS shareholders would be offered cash for their stock or a combination of cash and a class of stock paying dividends tied to EDS earnings.

General Motors faces the threat of a government fine of millions of dollars for failing to comply with water-pollution rules at 10 plants.

A Fed rule permitting bank holding companies to offer discount brokerage services was upheld by the Supreme Court. The decision permits BankAmerica's 1983 purchase of Charles Schwab. But the justices overruled central bank approval of banks' underwriting of commercial paper.

The merchandise trade deficit narrowed in May to $8.84 billion from $12.19 billion, reflecting a 9.8% drop in imports and a 2.4% rise in exports. Analysts were reluctant to read the reduction as more than a temporary gain in the U.S. trade position.

Bond prices continued to decline, despite a $3.1 billion drop in the nation's basic money supply. The drop in M1 returned the measure to the central bank's target range, but many analysts expect a huge rise to be reported next week, pressuring the Fed to tighten credit policy.

July 1984

2 Continental Illinois has sold nearly $5 billion of its assets during the past 60 days, indicating that its $7.5 billion safety net hasn't been sufficient to cover a continuing run on deposits, sources said. The asset sale shows that the run on Continental's deposits has exceeded $10 billion.

Higher interest rates are expected over the next six months by most of the 24 analysts surveyed by the Journal, despite predictions by the White House that rates will fall. The economists also see further increases in the first half of 1985.

The leading indicators fell 0.1% in May, reflecting a large drop in the average workweek. New-home sales declined 4.4%, the third monthly decline in a row. The results suggest that the pace of economic expansion will ease in the months ahead.

Federal budget deficits won't narrow much this year, White House and congressional experts said. The administration puts the fiscal 1984 deficit near $170 billion, down from $177.8 billion. The CBO predicts a budget gap of $174 billion to $175 billion.

The economy continued expanding in June, while the pace of price increases slowed for the second month in a row, a survey of purchasing managers found.

3 Factory orders rose 1.9% in May as durable-goods orders climbed. Construction spending increased 1.8% during the month, mainly because of gains in commercial and industrial building. The results demonstrate continued economic growth despite rising interest rates.

The FDIC cleared a rule that requires banks to report their total amount of brokered deposits as well as the amount of deposits placed by other financial institutions.

Sun Banks plans to merge with Trust Co. of Georgia. The proposal sets in motion the first combination under new interstate banking laws in Georgia and Florida. The new banking firm, SunTrust Banks, would have assets exceeding $14 billion.

Tax-exempt development bonds may flood the market, increasing the loss to the Treasury and pushing tax-exempt interest rates higher as a result of changes in the rules governing the bonds. The new provisions approved by Congress were meant to stem a revenue loss.

Chrysler arranged a $1.1 billion credit line with 57 U.S. and foreign banks. The pact underscores the auto maker's recovery as a creditworthy concern, bankers said.

5 Investor Saul Steinberg said in court papers that he ended his proposed tender offer for Walt Disney Productions only after Disney threatened to load the entertainment company with $2 billion of debt and leave him in sole control.

The steel industry is expected to post its best quarterly earnings since 1981 for the second period. Analysts see the six largest steelmakers reporting combined net of about $200 million for second period.

U.S. auto makers plan to boost production in the third quarter to the highest level since 1978. However, sales are expected to continue to outpace production and further deplete already low inventories.

6 The dollar scored records against the British pound, the French franc and the Canadian dollar as it surged for a third day in a row. Rising U.S. interest rates were cited. The yen withstood the dollar's advance because of continued intervention by the Bank of Japan.

Major retailers posted healthy sales gains in June as consumers continued to spend at levels that should sustain a strong pace through year-end. Sears Roebuck reported a 7.5% gain. Montgomery Ward's sales were up 9.6%, while K mart had a 6.3% increase.

Mortgage rates rose during the past month, with lenders last week quoting an average interest rate of 14.5% on conventional fixed-rate mortgages, up from 14.08% a month earlier. Some analysts, however, see rates soon reaching a plateau.

9 The Federal Reserve is likely to boost its discount rate this month to at least 9½% from 9% to avert renewed inflation stemming from the economy's vigor, some economists said. They warned that even if the Fed decides against any credit tightening, interest rates will rise in coming months.

The jobless rate plunged to 7.1% of the civilian work force in June from 7.5% a month earlier, suggesting that the economy continues at a brisk pace and that industrial output and personal income racked up healthy gains in the month.

The dollar is expected to continue advancing this week despite foreign central bank intervention and interest rate boosts by various nations. While the U.S. isn't expected to act to hold down the dollar, European central bankers may urge the Fed to do so.

Gold's price, which slipped $28 an ounce last week, has metals traders bracing for another slide, while investors see an opportunity to buy.

10 Bond prices soared, but some short-term rates also climbed amid continued uncertainty about the economic outlook and whether the Fed would further tighten its credit grip.

Renovated stores are a focal point of major retailers' changing strategies. Within the last year, three firms have set store remodeling programs that are expected to cost at least $5.4 billion over the next five years.

11 AT&T will freeze the salary structure for its 114,000 managers companywide. The freeze, spurred by a need to trim costs, should save AT&T nearly $184 million in 1985 expenses.

GM's plan to acquire Electronic Data Systems could lead the Big Board to delist GM. At issue is whether GM's plan to issue a new security in connection with the EDS takeover would violate exchange requirements.

Texaco's $10.1 billion takeover of Getty Oil received final approval from the FTC, contingent on some changes in the pact. Under the final accord, Texaco must divest itself of its interest in the Wyco pipeline or all of a number of other facilities.

Diesel-engine sales have been steadily declining as gasoline prices fall, affecting parts suppliers, mechanics and others. After peaking at 6.1% of the new-car market in 1981, diesels sank to a scant 1.5% in the first five months of this year.

European American reported a $137.7 million loss in the second quarter, reflecting $137.8 million of write-offs of bad loans and other charges. The deficit was one of the largest quarterly losses ever for a U.S. bank holding company.

The dollar resumed its upward course, setting records against the British pound, the French franc and the Canadian dollar. It also reached a six-month high against the West German mark. A rise in U.S. interest rates was cited.

12 Steel import quotas and additional tariffs to aid the depressed domestic industry were recommended by the ITC. It conditioned the five-year schedule of assistance on the U.S. industry's willingness to modernize plants and management practices and to cut costs.

The dollar climbed to a 10½-year high against the West German mark and set records against the French franc and Canadian dollar. The British pound managed to stave off the dollar's surge as British banks increased their base lending rate.

Stock prices tumbled broadly and the Dow

industrials fell 18.33 points, their sharpest loss in more than four months. The collapse of drug stocks and ITT's dividend reduction were cited. Meanwhile, some analysts contended that ITT, which grew through a series of acquisitions, may currently be a takeover target itself.

OPEC will allow Nigeria to increase its oil production. The oil ministers, faced with Nigeria's desperate plea and the possibility that it might defy the cartel, agreed to let the country boost output by 150,000 barrels a day by September from its 1.3 million-barrel quota.

Most commodity futures continued to fall broadly as the strong dollar continued to hurt raw-material prices. Trader anticipation that the dollar will remain strong and continue to depress commodity prices was cited.

13 Bankruptcy legislation passed by Congress two weeks ago to smooth the system is causing widespread confusion and could cause once-routine bankruptcy cases to drag on for years, judges, lawyers and legal experts contended.

Manufacturers Hanover's second quarter earnings fell 8.5% because of problem loans to Argentina. Profit at Chemical New York rose 10%, Irving Bank's gained 10% and Marine Midland had a 12% rise. InterFirst Corp. of Dallas posted a 58% drop.

The money supply fell $1.6 billion in the latest week, causing bond prices to surge and raising investor hopes that the decline will reduce pressures on the Fed to tighten its credit conditions further.

Many of Continental Illinois's best lending officers, traders and data processors are leaving the bank firm. The exodus is a growing barrier for attracting a merger partner, and is a considerable obstacle in Continetal's chances of remaining independent.

16 The economy isn't showing signs of a return to the rapid inflation of the 1970s, new economic data indicate. Producer prices were unchanged in June, while industrial production rose 0.5% and retail sales increased 0.8% during the month.

The Fed probably will try to keep short-term interest rates at or slightly above their current high levels, according to economists and sources close to the Fed. It fears that inflation could surge by early 1985.

U.S. car sales increased 32% to 179,026 cars in early July, but industry analysts doubt that the rapid pace can be sustained.

IBM's second-quarter net rose more than 20% to $1.62 billion from $1.34 billion

a year earlier. Revenue increased 17%. Results for the first half were also up sharply.

Price controls on natural-gas exports were eased by the Canadian government, clearing the way for a reduction of as much as 30% in the price paid by U.S. customers.

A Dow Chemical unit will pay $120 million to settle U.S. claims that Bendectin, a drug for the treatment of morning sickness that was discontinued last year, caused birth defects. The payments, into a special fund, will be made over 20 years.

Argentina approved wage increases for both public and private-sector workers. The move comes despite IMF concern that such boosts will fuel Argentina's 580% annual inflation rate.

17 J. P. Morgan posted a drop in second-quarter net of 10% and Chase Manhattan's earnings fell 14%. Both bank firms cited problem loans to Argentina. First Chicago had a 23% gain for the period, and Security Pacific's net increased 5%.

Continental Illinois confirmed that private investors may play a role in recapitalizing the bank firm. Meanwhile, some Continental directors met with federal regulators in Washington as pressure mounted for a solution to the bank's crisis.

Tennessee Valley Authority is considering a staff proposal to abandon four partially completed nuclear plants because energy demand forecasts have declined while construction costs have risen. A final vote on the plan is expected in August.

Most interest rates climbed, with the rate on federal funds hovering between 11⅜% and 11⁷⁄₁₆%, up from Friday's average of 11%. Many investment managers fear that the economy's rapid pace eventually will trigger higher inflation and prompt the Fed to tighten credit.

Kawasaki Steel of Japan agreed to acquire a 25% interest in a venture that will own and operate parts of Kaiser Steel's idled Fontana, Calif., plant. The venture, Pacific Steel, has agreed to buy Kaiser's steelmaking assets for $25 million and an $85 million five-year note.

Consumer credit rose a record $10.23 billion in May, raising concern that borrowing may be getting out of control. Separately, the factory operating rate rose in June to 81.7% of capacity and the growth rate of business inventories in May slowed to 0.9%.

18 The EPA is establishing an array of more

stringent operating, monitoring and inspection standards for the biggest operating hazardous-waste landfills. The agency said the new rules will force the most dangerous dumps to close.

The dollar resumed its climb against other major currencies, with foreign-exchange traders predicting more highs in the days ahead. Gold fell $2.40 an ounce to $346.10 in response to the stronger dollar.

19 The economy may have grown at a brisk 6.8% pace in the second quarter, said Robert Forrestal, president of the Atlanta Federal Reserve Bank. The estimate exceeds the government's 5.7% projection in June, which shocked financial markets.

Housing starts increased 5.3% in June, helped by a 27.2% surge in apartment construction. Many economists, however, predict higher mortgage rates will slow home construction in the second half.

A bill to raise taxes by about $50 billion through fiscal 1987 was signed by President Reagan. The legislation also reduces spending by about $13 billion, largely through changes in Medicare.

20 Continental Illinois's rescue plan remains in flux, although an agreement appears imminent, federal banking regulators said. Talks continued yesterday. In a plan outlined this week, the FDIC would take on many of the bank's shaky loans.

Meanwhile, Continental's foreign loans pose a major dilemma and the FDIC may force the bank to write down their value. Candidates to take the role of chief executive are also being approached.

Chrysler Corp.'s second-quarter net more than doubled to a record $802.9 million. The auto maker also plans to boost output of its minivans by 60% beginning next year.

Of the seven biggest U.S. banks with foreign-exchange operations, four had sizable second-quarter declines in revenue from those operations because of the dollar's strength. A fifth, J. P. Morgan, had a loss. The remaining two said revenue rose.

23 Personal income rose 0.8% in June, twice the May increase. The gain will provide fuel for continued economic expansion in coming weeks. Consumer spending, however, slowed slightly, rising 0.2%.

Manville Corp.'s $315 million insurance settlement for asbestos victims may also aid its insurance firms. Under a provision in the planned pact, the insurers were granted protection against further asbestos-related liabilities.

The SEC is probing what appears to be the largest insider-trading ring ever, involving more than $40 million of trading profits, sources said. The commission is examining over 20 individuals, securities and law firms, including Wachtell Lipton.

Continental Illinois will give the FDIC nonvoting preferred shares equal to about 80% of the bank firm's equity, as part of a rescue plan. The FDIC will assume almost $4 billion in bad loans and infuse the firm with more money.

Continental released an internal report that blames three lending officers for its purchase of $1 billion of loans from the failed Penn Square Bank.

24 The GNP soared at a 7.5% annual rate in the second quarter, outpacing expectations and indicating that the current economic expansion is the strongest since the years immediately following World War II. The first-quarter rate was revised to 10.1% from 9.7%.

Continental Illinois will sell $4.5 billion of bad loans to the FDIC, which will also inject another $1 billion into the bank firm as part of the largest banking rescue ever. The preliminary agreement also would essentially split Continental into two banks.

The dollar soared against most major currencies on news that U.S. GNP advanced by 7.5% in the second quarter. The dollar set a record against the French franc and new highs against the West German mark, Japanese yen and Swiss franc.

25 Consumer prices rose a modest 0.2% in June, or 2% at an annual rate, reflecting a drop in gasoline and clothing prices. The report provides evidence that rapid economic growth hasn't yet pushed prices higher. Separately, durable-goods orders fell 3.2% last month.

Continental Illinois holders could receive as little as one-thousandth of a cent for each of their shares under a federal plan to bail out the bank firm. The alternative, however, is to declare Continental insolvent, which would totally erase holders' equity.

Declines in crude-oil spot prices are raising doubts about the ability of oil firms and producers to keep prices firm. Traders and oil executives say 35% of oil traded in non-communist nations is being discounted.

Leveraged buyouts are running into trouble as banks restrict amounts they will lend for such transactions. Investment bankers Shearson Lehman and Morgan Stanley are considering ending or revising buyout-fund plans.

Shareholders who sell their stock in a buyout face risks. Some lawyers and investment bankers believe those holders could be legally forced to return stock-sale proceeds if the new firm enters bankruptcy-law proceedings.

Reynolds Metals will cut output by 38% at its Troutdale, Ore., plant, idling about 225 workers. The firm cited weak prices and the buildup of aluminum inventories world-wide.

British coal miners stepped up strike actions. Over 50 were arrested in clashes with police near mines and steel works, authorities said. They temporarily closed the northeast Humber suspension bridge, the world's longest, by abandoning cars on it. The walkout over the U.K.'s mine-closing plans has paralyzed two-thirds of the industy.

26 Volcker said the Fed hasn't tightened money and credit conditions substantially since spring. The Federal Reserve chairman also said that the central bank will leave its targets for monetary growth unchanged for the rest of the year.

Bond prices surged on what was interpreted by many investors as reassurance about the economic and inflation outlook. Stocks also ended higher. Interest-rate futures soared, but commodity prices generally ended lower and the dollar weakened.

The FDIC decided to rescue Continental Illinois to avert the risk of a loss of confidence in the U.S. banking system. The bailout, however, which could cost the U.S. as much as $4.5 billion, hasn't much changed the attitude of Continental's customers. Borrowers remain loyal, but some depositors are transferring funds.

27 Continental Illinois's $4.5 billion rescue, formally announced by federal regulators, might take years and more U.S. money before the banking concern could survive without support. Also, Continental said it will post a $1.1 billion loss for the second-quarter.

Continental's turnaround efforts will likely include writing off bad loans and trimming operations, if its new management follows moves made by other troubled banks.

The FCC said a single company can own as many as 36 radio and TV stations. The move ends a 31-year-old rule limiting an owner's holdings to 21 stations, and will allow the major networks and other large firms in the industry to boost their influence.

Ford Motor said net rose 68% in the second quarter to a record $909.1 million. Strong car and truck sales in the U.S. and Canada were cited.

The Justice Department defended its decision against prosecuting General Dynamics on charges of filing false claims to cover cost overruns on Navy nuclear submarines. The agency said it didn't find evidence of criminal intent to defraud the Navy.

General Public Utilities's top executives were all given passing grades for "management integrity" by the NRC staff. It also said the company should be allowed to restart its Three Mile Island Unit 1 nuclear reactor at just 25% of power until NRC probes are completed.

30 General Motors profit surged 54% in the second quarter, to $1.61 billion, or $5.09 a share. Sales grew 11% to $21.58 billion. Low inventories and the profit jump could weaken GM's position in talks with the UAW to replace a contract that expires Sept. 14.

Machine-tool orders in June totaled $192.2 million, up 32% from a year earlier but down 40% from May's exceptionally strong orders. Machinery makers believe an apparent slowdown in durable-goods producers' purchases of new equipment probably is temporary.

Russia slashed the price of its oil exports $1.50 a barrel for the month of August. The cut, bringing Urals crude to $27.50 a barrel, follows an OPEC plea for stable prices. Indiana Standard lowered crude by 35 cents a barrel, to $29.65.

The merchandise trade deficit widened slightly in June to a seasonally adjusted $8.91 billion. May's deficit was $8.84 billion. Imports fell for the second month in a row, but a decline in agricultural exports held total exports below the May level.

Interest rates are apt to be pushed up soon by huge U.S. borrowing needs, many economists say. The Treasury is expected Wednesday to disclose plans to sell as much as $17 billion of new notes and bonds and to outline financing for the quarter.

Economic growth exceeding 6%, after adjustment for inflation, will be projected for this year in the administration's midyear budget review, a budget official said.

31 Oil prices eroded further, with Southland's Citgo unit lowering the price it will pay for certain U.S. crude by as much as $1 a barrel.

World oil markets are threatened by Saudi internal squabbles. The Saudi royal family, overruling Oil Minister Yamani in a planes-for-oil transaction, ordered the nation to exceed oil-output ceilings and to sell extra output in the glutted market.

The EPA proposed reducing the lead in gasoline by 91% starting in 1986 and said it might ban lead altogether by 1995. Slashing lead content "will increase the cost to produce all types of gasoline" and increase crude oil imports, according to the American Petroleum Institute.

Chase Manhattan dismissed 380 employees, including officers, in its consumer banking division, amid signs that further cost-cutting is planned. Chase, stung by sagging earnings, is weighing offering early retirement to 1,000 employees.

GM raised prices on several 1984 models only weeks before it will begin introducing 1985 cars. The increases may be laying the groundwork for further boosts early in the 1985 model year.

Construction contracts in June fell a seasonally adjusted 10% from May, but building in the second quarter and first half reached records nonetheless, F. W. Dodge said.

August 1984

1 Leading indicators of the economy fell 0.9% in June. Such a decline could indicate slowing economic growth. New-home sales rose 0.6% to an annual rate of 620,000 units after falling 4.5% in May. June sales were down 5.3% from a year earlier.

The U.S. dollar soared, setting records against Britain's pound and France's franc and rising above 2.9 West German marks for the first time in 11 years.

U.S. Steel posted profit of $140 million for the second quarter, reversing a year-earlier $112 million deficit. But the company warned it might be only "narrowly profitable" this quarter.

World oil markets are in crisis, and this month will be crucial in determining whether the industry can prevent a general decline in crude prices, warned James E. Lee, chairman of Chevron's Gulf Corp. unit.

Non-farm productivity grew at a 3.3% rate in the second quarter, exceeding the first quarter's revised 2.9% pace. Overall productivity grew at a 2.8% rate, down from a 4% first-quarter rate. Wages and salaries of private-industry workers rose

0.9%, down from the prior quarter's 1.7% increase.

2 Factory orders fell 1.4% in June to an adjusted $191.03 billion as construction spending declined 0.2% to a $310.6 billion rate.

The stock market posted its biggest gain of the summer in response to the government data, which could indicate some moderation in the economy's rapid growth. The Dow Jones Industrial Average closed up 19.33, at 1134.61, on volume of 127,520,000 shares. Bonds also rallied on the news but later lost much of the gains; and precious metals futures soared.

Dome Petroleum signed an accord to restructure $5.2 billion (Canadian) of its $6.2 billion of debt. The pact, which follows nearly two years of negotiations, will reduce Dome's principal payments by $3.5 billion through 1988 but requires that Dome raise $350 million of equity by Oct. 5.

Sallie Mae offered $2 billion face amount of 30-year zero-coupon bonds, the first issue by a U.S. government-chartered agency since the 1984 tax bill repealed withholding tax for foreign investors in U.S. securities. Most of the Student Loan Marketing Association offering was sold abroad.

Argentina will ask creditor banks for a further $1 billion to help it meet IMF austerity requirements, Argentine officials said. The planned move indicates that serious differences remain with the IMF, despite Argentine officials' assurances that an IMF accord by Aug. 15 is certain.

3 Stocks soared, with the Dow Jones Industrial Average closing up 31.47, at 1166.08. The index's jump was the biggest since November 1982. Trading volume rose to a record 172,830,000 shares, as buying by institutional investors flooded the market.

Bond prices surged amid optimism that inflation will remain in check and encourage lower interest rates. M1 dropped an unexpectedly large $1.7 billion. Little change had been expected in the money-supply measure.

IBM and the Common Market settled a four-year-old antitrust case in a compromise that might not alter significantly the way IBM competes in Europe. The pact requires IBM to detail, within four months after announcing a computer, how rivals' machines can mesh with it. IBM might merely delay such announcements to four months before delivery.

Rivals agreed the accord wouldn't give them an advantage, but would ease customers' doubts about connecting competing products with IBM's.

Many major retailers posted moderate sales gains last month, compared with strong July 1983 results. Sears had the most lackluster results, and cited the summer's comparative coolness. Its combined U.S. and Canadian sales rose 1.1% to $1.9 billion.

Synthetic Fuels Corp.'s funding would be cut $5 billion, to $8.25 billion, under a measure approved by the House, which barred the agency from proceeding with two oil-shale projects. The House defeated an administration effort to rescind all but $3.25 billion of the corporation's funds.

Lobbying over Conrail's proposed sale is escalating amid signs of growing division between the government-controlled railroad system's top management and the Transportation Department. At issue is whether the agency should delay plans to sell Conrail this year.

6 The stock market's rally is triggering hopes for a replay of August 1982, when stocks surged out of doldrums into a powerful bull market. May optimists believe falling interest rates and low inflation will continue the uptrend. But others on Wall Street find that prospect unlikely.

Big Board volume Friday soared to 236,570,000 shares, up 37% from the previous day's record. That drove the week's volume to a record 696,162,760 shares. A 36-point leap in the Dow Jones Industrial Average pushed the indicator to 1202.08, up a record 87.46 points for the week.

Corporate net income surged 31% in the second quarter, a Wall Street Journal survey of 518 major corporations found. Canadian profits rose 64%.

July's jump in unemployment to 7.5% from June's 7.1% may bolster Democrats' claims that economic recovery is an illusion. But other data suggest a statistical fluke, not faltering economic growth.

Continental Illinois posted an expected $1.16 billion second-quarter loss, but suggested that the government rescue of the bank holding company could bring about a turnaround as early as the fourth quarter.

New-car sales rose 12.5% in July from a year earlier, to 888,917 units, a sign that rising interest rates and low supplies of some models haven't damped customer interest.

The bond market's rally is likely to deflate soon, say many bankers and economists. They cite high short-term interest rates and rapid economic growth. This week's Treasury auctions of $16.75 billion of notes and bonds are seen as a bond-rally test.

Mortgage rates crept up in July for the fifth month in a row.

AT&T's debt rating was cut by S&P to double-A from the top-notch triple-A it had held since 1956.

7 The stock market's three-day rally slowed on profit-taking and weakness in the bond market. Volume, however, reached 203 million shares. Bond prices slid on investor worries over the interest-rate outlook and U.S. borrowing needs.

Some brokerage firms are posting increases in stock business of 50% to 100% from a week ago, but are divided over advice to investors.

Debtor nations apparently are benefiting from the strong U.S. dollar, which is spurring Third World growth through increased exports. This growth could ease the debt crisis, some bankers say. Separately, banks with international loans fear increasing federal regulatory scrutiny.

Federal budget deficits will grow each year for the rest of the decade, but won't increase as much as previously forecast, the CBO said. The budget office also predicted higher interest rates in the coming years.

8 Financial markets posted gains. Stock prices resisted profit-takers and rose modestly, with the Dow industrials closing at 1204.62, up 1.66. Bonds rebounded as the Treasury began a three-day debt auction and the dollar surged against most other major currencies.

Six banks were charged by the office of the comptroller of the currency with artificially improving their financial statements through dubious transactions. The office obtained consent agreements from the banks, which it declined to identify.

Interest rates are likely to fall, according to a survey of 16 futures analysts by The Wall Street Journal. However, the futures prices of gold, oil and soybeans will also decline, they said. Buying Treasury-bond futures was the favorite trade over the next six months.

Japanese computer firms are advancing into the business of supercomputers, ultrafast machines designed to handle complex problems. But the seriousness of the threat to U.S. makers shouldn't be exaggerated, industry experts believe.

9 The economy is expected to grow at a robust, inflation-adjusted 6.5% this year, up from the 5% rate predicted earlier, Treasury Secretary Regan said. He predicted that inflation would rise just 4.4%, less than the 4.9% previously forecast.

Efforts by oil-producing nations and multinational firms to bolster sagging oil prices appear to be succeeding. Spot and futures prices have been rising following diplomatic initiatives by oil ministers and the temporary closing of major oil fields.

Sizable increases in crops this year are expected to be predicted by the Agriculture Department. Private analysts see an 85% jump in corn production, a 30% rise in soybean output and a 3% gain in wheat.

10 A rally in the bond market reignited stocks and pushed the Dow industrials 27.94 points higher. Bond prices rose on the favorable response that the government's bond auction received, and Treasury-bond futures led many commodity prices higher. The dollar, meanwhile, tumbled.

The money supply declined an unexpectedly large $2.6 billion, easing pressure further on the Fed to tighten credit conditions.

The Canadian government is being urged by some producers to cut its export price for light crude oil, which was trimmed earlier this month 80 cents a barrel. Producers fear output cutbacks unless more oil can be exported to the U.S.

13 Producer prices rose 0.3% last month, or 3.3% at an annual rate after compounding. The increase, though slightly larger than most analysts expected, doesn't indicate a major acceleration in the inflation rate.

The sale of "bearer" securities backed by U.S. bonds should be halted, the Senate said in a nonbinding resolution. The securities allow purchasers to remain anonymous and critics said this permits evasion of U.S. taxes. The resolution, which caused a drop in bond prices, was in response to repackaging of bonds by a Salomon Brothers group.

The forest-products industry is trying to unload its timberland. An estimated six million to nine million acres are for sale in the U.S. as the glut of land has steadily increased and lumber prices have declined.

The bond market's rally in recent weeks could give the economy extra momentum, many economists said. They said the drop in long-term rates will alleviate some strains in the housing market and might prompt firms to boost plant and equipment outlays. However, a continued brisk economy may abort the bond rally.

14 Stauffer Chemical overstated its 1982 earnings by $31.1 million by improperly accounting for certain sales and changes in inventory valuation, the SEC contended. Stauffer settled the suit without admitting or denying guilt and agreed to restate its 1982 and 1983 financial statements.

Business confidence in the economy is beginning to soften as interest rates, despite some recent declines, remain at historically high levels. Purchasing agents said growth in orders and output slowed in July and some firms are operating as though a slowdown could come in 1985.

15 Sales of U.S.-made cars fell 0.8% in early August to 177,182 units, apparently reflecting lower availability of some models and marking the first year-to-year decline in 1984.

U.S. defense contractors hope to use Japanese optical-fiber and other technology to build radar-seeking missiles and manufacturing methods for tanks. The move toward greater cooperation follows last year's change in Japanese government policy.

Retail sales fell 0.9% in July, adding to the evidence that the economy's brisk pace is slowing. Analysts said, however, that consumer spending may surge again this fall. Separately, the Fed said consumer credit grew $7.83 billion in June, indicating an annual growth rate of 22%.

Four financial firms in London, including Mercury Securities and Akroyd & Smithers, agreed to merge. The combination of such leading firms, which probably will be completed in early 1986, would create a British counterpart to big U.S. investment banks.

Equimark Corp. posted a second-quarter net loss of $29.5 million. Separately, Equimark and Marine Midland have been discussing Marine's possible acquisition of as much as 25% of Equimark's Equibank unit. Marine said the talks have ended.

16 Financial Corp. of America, bowing to regulators' demands, restated its earnings for its second quarter to show a loss of $107.5 million. The bank firm had earlier posted profit of $31.1 million. The company, which conceded a loss for the year if interest rates stay at current levels.

Industrial production rose 0.9% in July, indicating that manufacturers are continuing to boost output rapidly despite signs of slower consumer-spending growth. Separately, business inventories in June increased less than 0.1% after rising 0.9% in May.

Federal budget deficits will decline from $174.3 billion in the current fiscal year to $139.3 billion in 1989, according to a prediction by the Reagan administration. The forecast, based on economic assumptions viewed as optimistic, assumes enactment of Reagan's policy proposals.

Fears about the banking system's soundness have played a major role in pushing short-term interest rates higher since May, many bankers and economists said. Some contend, however, that the Fed is responsible for the rise in the federal funds rate.

Rates on long-term bonds have fallen more than 1½ percentage points since May, but most U.S. firms expect further declines and are staying away from the market. The sharp drop in medium- and long-term rates, however, hasn't been accompanied by an equal decrease in the banking rates that affect many consumers.

Stock prices fell to their lowest level since the recent rally began, with the Dow industrials falling 15.13 points to 1198.98. Bond prices also tumbled and the dollar was generally lower against other currencies.

17 Housing starts fell 6.6% in July, reflecting high mortgage rates. The drop followed a revised 5.1% increase in June. Separately, the nation's factories, utilities and mines operated at an 82.5% rate in July, up from a revised 82% in June.

Sale of new government securities, including a bond designed to attract foreign investors by enabling them to purchase securities with some secrecy, is being planned, Treasury Secretary Regan said. He also said that new rules will allow U.S. firms to directly sell "bearer" bonds overseas. Bond prices surged.

20 Charter Co. took a second-quarter writedown of $545 million to reflect expected losses from the sale of its insurance units and the closing of its oil-refining operations. The firm also posted an operating loss of $65.1 million for the quarter.

Walt Disney Productions reversed plans and agreed to cancel its $315 million acquisition of Gibson Greetings. A group led by investor Irwin Jacobs, which holds 6.9% of Disney, had sued to block the acquisition.

Personal income advanced 0.8% in July, but consumer spending expanded at less than half that pace, rising 0.3%. The figures seem to suggest that the consumer-spending boom is slowing, which could ease some of the upward pressure on interest rates.

Slower economic growth, coupled with low inflation, will keep the Fed from tightening its credit grip, bankers and economists said. They contend, however, that the economy is still growing too rapidly for credit conditions to be eased.

Airlines appear assured of receiving immunity from antitrust laws so they can jointly revise schedules to reduce delays at major airports. The U.S. wants the carriers to work on ways to ease the problem and last week 15 airlines agreed to ask the CAB for the right to hold meetings.

Eurodollar futures soon will become the first futures contract to trade around the clock. Contracts based on Eurodollars, already traded in Chicago and London, are set to begin trading September 7 in Singapore.

21 After-tax profits on the books of U.S. corporations grew only 1.5% during the second quarter, sharply slower than the 6.8% gain in the first period. Separately, the gross national product grew an adjusted 7.6% in the second period, against the 7.5% previously estimated.

Financial Corp. of America sold a seven million-share block of American Express common stock in the second largest trade ever on the Big Board. Separately, the Home Loan Bank Board may consider placing a cap on borrowings by FCA's American Savings unit.

OPEC oil production is dropping below the cartel's mandated ceiling of 17.5 million barrels a day, industry sources and OPEC officials said. Export cuts by Iran, Nigeria, Saudi Arabia and the United Arab Emirates were cited.

Securities firms have been promoting the idea that certain corporate pension funds should switch some investments from stocks to bonds. The firms, such as Salomon Brothers and First Boston, reap big trading profits from such transactions.

22 Prudential Insurance agreed to offer job-skills training to 8,000 to 9,000 minority-group members who were rejected for jobs between 1978 and 1983, as part of a Labor Department accord. It also must offer jobs to a portion of those successfully completing the training.

Chrysler and Samsung Group's talks about building cars in South Korea for export to the U.S. are focusing on a 50-50 joint venture with an initial outlay of $400 million, said a source close to Samsung. Any pact, however, could face opposition from the South Korean government.

Stock prices surged in heavy trading, with the Dow Jones Industrial Average rising 22.75 points to close at 1239.73. Analysts attributed the rise to buying by institutional investors, rather than a strong bond market. Bonds continued to adance, but trading was light.

23 Consumer prices rose a slight 0.3% in July, with the rate for service prices outpacing prices for commodities. Separately, durable-goods orders rose 2.2% last month after falling 3% in June, suggesting the economy still has considerable momentum.

Stock prices tumbled in heavy trading, with the Dow Jones Industrials closing 7.95 points lower at 1231.78. A lack of support from the bond market and renewed fears over inflation were cited.

Big U.S. coal producers broke off contract talks with the mine workers union, 40 days before the September 30 strike deadline. The Bituminous Coal Operators said further talks haven't been scheduled.

Thirty oil firms spent about $877 million to acquire 232 federal leases in the Beaufort Sea off Alaska's North Slope. The amount was the second highest spent in a U.S. sale off Alaska and came despite a recent $1.6 billion failure in the area.

New limits on textile imports may be delayed by the Reagan administration because of mounting pressure from foreign governments and U.S. retailers. The restrictions are slated to go into effect September 7. Hong Kong and China have protested the rules.

24 Sales of U.S.-made cars rose 32% in mid-August to 189,209 units, suggesting that the sales decline earlier in the month may have been an abberation. Based on seasonal factors, sales in the period amounted to 8.1 million units at an annual rate.

The U.S. budget deficit in July totaled $16.42 billion, compared with a $21.41 billion deficit a year earlier.

Sales of public housing notes were suspended by HUD because the new tax law raised questions about their tax-exempt status. The IRS is studying the short-term notes and is expected to decide soon if they comply with the new law.

UPI signed an agreement under which its 1,900 employees will take a temporary 25% wage cut in return for a 6.5% stake in the news wire service. The accord with the Wire Service Guild also calls for the dismissal of 100 nonunion workers.

27 Interest rates will edge higher over the next few months even though economic expansion will slow, many analysts said. The borrowing needs of the U.S. and businesses will weigh heavily on the credit markets through year-end, they said.

The Fed's policy-making panel agreed in July that the Fed shouldn't ease its grip on credit, with most members leaning toward tightening monetary policy. Fed Vice Chairman Preston Martin dissented.

AT&T is cutting 11,000 positions at its AT&T Technologies unit in a bid to stay competitive in the growing telecommunications field. The move appears to be aimed at cutting costs at the unit by at least 20%.

Machine tool orders rose 79% in July from a year earlier, but lagged behind the pace of April and May. A large press order by GM aided the July results. Machinery makers hope that a pause in the rise of interest rates will spark an upturn in fourth-quarter orders.

Ambiguities in recent IRS rules over the sale of Treasury and corporate securities to foreign investors may delay bond offerings in Europe and could damage the Treasury's planned test of $1 billion to $2 billion of its new special registered securities.

Soviet purchases of U.S. grain in the past few weeks have led many analysts to predict record American grain sales to the Russians in the coming season. Some analysts expect Soviet purchases to exceed previous record sales by as much as 42%.

28 Interest rates rose on a belief that the Fed wouldn't ease its credit grip soon. Prices of some U.S. government bonds fell nearly a point. Stock prices also declined, with the Dow Jones Industrial Average closing at 1227.92, down 8.61 points, in the lightest trading in nearly a year.

Three big energy banks based in Houston confirmed they were among six banks charged by the comptroller of the currency with using questionable accounting practices to improve their financial reports.

Non-farm productivity grew at an adjusted 4.7% annual rate in the second quarter, higher than the 3.3% pace initially estimated. It was the eighth quarterly gain in a row and the biggest since 1983's second quarter.

29 GM and Ford Motor proposed holding current wages unchanged for the next three years and cutting inflation-protection payments. The UAW, which is holding contract talks with the auto makers, called the offer unacceptable. Neither company promised to keep jobs in the U.S.

New rules governing the sale of U.S. securities abroad were clarified by the IRS, easing foreign bankers' fears about disclosure of the names of their clients. The amendment makes clear that foreign banks are exempt from certain U.S. data-reporting laws.

30 Leading indicators of economic activity fell 0.8% in July. The decline in the index followed a revised 1.3% drop in June, a clear sign of a slowing economy. Separately, the nation's trade deficit grew to a record $14.06 billion in July, and single-family home sales were flat.

Reynolds Metals Co. will trim North American aluminum output another 5% in an effort to stem mounting inventory. The move, the second cutback in a month, indicates that efforts by U.S. producers to curb oversupply haven't yet taken hold.

New construction contracts in July rose an adjusted 3% despite a weak housing market, F. W. Dodge said. Before adjustment, new contracts totaled $19.52 billion, down from $20 billion in June. All categories increased except residential building.

31 Big retailers reported higher sales for August, and a consumer spending surge late in the month boded well for the fall shopping season. K mart's sales rose 8.7%, Sears reported an 8.1% gain and J. C. Penney's increased 8.8%.

Factory orders rose 1% in July after declining 1.6% in June, indicating that the economy still has considerable momentum. However, analysts say, recent figures suggest that the unusually rapid rise in capital outlays by businesses may be slowing.

Washington Public Power's investor-owned utilities are likely to write off their stakes in the system's moth-balled nuclear Unit 3. Analysts said escalating costs are increasing the likelihood that the companies will take the write-offs and cut their losses.

Thomas C. Reed, a former high-level aide to President Reagan, was indicted on charges of insider trading in Amax Inc. securities. The four-count federal indictment charged that Mr. Reed made $431,000 in 1981 by trading on confidential data concerning Social's bid for Amax.

The Boston Stock Exchange and the Montreal Exchange agreed to link their trading floors electronically, in an effort to increase their ability to compete with major exchanges. Separately, the Boston exchange applied to the SEC to trade 66 of the most active over-the-counter stocks.

The Comptroller of the Currency said 528 national banks must raise more than $5.7 billion to comply with proposed new capital requirements. The rules are part of a program to force the banking industry to build up its capital base in light of greater lending risks and higher volatility.

Industry Surveys*

The following provides information about a number of industries as well as financial data on companies in each industry. The meaning of the SIC (Standard Industrial Classification) numbers referred to in the Industrial Trends Tables is given at the end of this section. Financial Ratios are defined in the section *Financial and Investment Terms* (page 363).

EXPLANATIONS OF FINANCIAL AND STOCK MARKET INFORMATION

Most of the tabular content in the stock tables is self-explanatory, but the following notes will help to clarify some of them, as follows:

Earnings Per Share   Earnings per share are on a fully diluted basis, where applicable, and extraordinary items have been excluded.

5-Year Earnings Growth Rate   The compound annual growth rate over the last five years, computed by the least squares method.

---

* The financial data on companies in each industry come from *The Media General Financial Weekly,* Media General Financial Services, 301 E. Grace Street, Richmond, VA 23261; June 25, 1984.

During interim periods, the latest 12 months E.P.S. are used for the sixth point in the equation on a time-weighted basis.

STANDARD FOOTNOTES

General Field Footnotes

NA—Item not applicable to this type of stock.
NC—Data required for calculation currently incomplete in our files.
NE—Negative earnings invalidate calculations.
NS—Negative stockholders equity invalidates calculations
NM—No meaningful figure

Earnings per Share Data

q—First quarter
s—First six months
n—First nine months
f—Fiscal year

Market and Index

N—New York Stock Exchange
A—American Stock Exchange
O—Over-the-Counter
★—Denotes an S&P 500 Stock

CONSTRUCTION: TRENDS AND PROJECTIONS, 1972–84

Item	1972	1977	1978	1979	1981	1982	1983[1]	Compound annual rate of change 1972–83	1984[2]	Percent change 1983–84
Value of new construction put in place (bil $)	124.4	173.8	205.6	230.4	239.4	232.0	265.5	7.1	—	—
Value of new construction put in place (bil 1977 $)	194.0	173.4	182.0	179.0	157.6	150.6	170.2	-1.2	174.1	2
New housing units started (000)	2,379	2,002	2,036	1,760	1,100	1,072	1,710	-3.0	1,710	0
Single-unit structures, privately owned	1,309	1,451	1,433	1,194	705	663	1,080	-1.7	1,100	—
Multi-unit structures, privately owned	1,048	536	587	551	379	400	620	-4.7	600	—
Publicly owned structures	22	15	16	15	16	10	10	-6.9	10	—
Shipments of mobile homes (000 units)[3]	575.9	277.0	275.9	277.4	240.9	238.9	295.0	-5.9	320.0	8
Total employment (000)[3]	5,279	5,612	6,166	6,437	6,060	5,756	6,100	1.3	6,200	2
Construction workers (000)[4]	3,257	3,021	3,354	3,565	3,261	3,004	3,000	-0.7	3,100	3
Self-employed workers (000)[3]	—	950	1,091	1,152	1,152	1,117	1,150	—	1,150	0
Average hourly earnings of construction workers ($)	6.06	8.10	8.66	9.27	10.82	11.62	11.90	6.3	—	—
Composite construction price index (1977 = 100.0)	64.1	100.3	113.0	128.8	151.9	154.1	156.0	8.4	—	—
Producer price index for all construction materials (1977 = 100.0)	61.8	100.0	111.4	122.7	138.1	140.5	144.7	8.0	—	—

Note: The employment data shown here take into account persons who do maintenance and repair work. The data on new construction put in place do not cover maintenance and repair.
[1] Estimate.
[2] Forecast.
[3] Based on household surveys. The total employment figures cover wage and salary workers, self-employed persons, and unpaid family workers. Included in the totals are wage and salary workers who work in construction but who are employed by government such persons accounted for 8 percent of the total employment in 1982 as reported in the household survey.
[4] Based on establishment surveys by the Bureau of Labor Statistics. Excludes white collar workers and all private and public force account workers.

Sources: Bureau of the Census, Bureau of Labor Statistics, and Bureau of Industrial Economics. Estimates and forecasts by the Bureau of Industrial Economics.

Source: *U.S. Industrial Outlook 1984*, U.S. Department of Commerce.

Company and Market	Price to Equity %	P/E Ratio Current -	P/E Ratio 5-Year Average	Latest 12 Months Amount $	Latest 12 Months Change %	5-Year Growth Rate %	Profit Margin %	Return On Assets %	Return On Common Equity %	Debt Equity Ratio %	Dividend Yield %	Market Value $Mil
Residential Construction												
Amer Continental .... O	140	6.1	NC	1.14q	NC	120	5.5	5.4	28.2	271	.0	95
Anthony Ind .... N	115	7.8	9.5	1.58f	410	- 8	2.8	5.4	16.8	102	3.6b	38
Calprop Cp .... A	138	8.2	7.6	.95f	36	- 6	11.8	5.9	12.1	87	.0a	15
Gen Homes .... O	155	8.2	10.1	.79s	NC	89	4.9	6.9	34.0	0	.0	98
Hovnanian Ent .... A	359	8.5	17.7	1.05n	NC	15	3.8	3.3	23.4	435	.0	40
Kaufman Broad .... ★N	83	8.1	15.2	1.36f	NE	- 21	3.9	1.9	13.8	73	3.6	132
Key Company .... A	123	13.1	9.1	.61s	53	- 1	4.3	6.0	10.5	39	3.1	9
Lennar Corp .... N	90	10.6	16.2	1.05q	250	- 11	6.7	1.5	4.2	128	1.8	104
Levitt Cp .... A	139	9.0	12.6	.81q	NC	49	6.4	7.6	24.9	88	.0	25
Natl Homes .... N	116	NE	NC	- .09f	NE	3	- .9	NE	NE	198	.0	24
Oriole Homes .... A	70	11.3	20.9	.61q	65	- 17	1.6	.6	1.8	125	7.3	14
Presley Co .... N	92	7.1	7.0	1.70f	133	- 6	5.9	1.5	5.5	33	2.5	73
Ryan Homes .... ★N	100	6.5	22.3	2.89q	113	- 2	3.5	6.1	16.5	14	5.3	127
Ryland Grp .... N	142	6.1	12.3	2.35q	122	33	4.0	11.5	26.0	21	4.2	86
Shapell Ind .... N	126	8.5	5.2	7.40n	NE	- 20	- 3.7	NE	NE	233	.0	78
Std-Pacific .... N	96	8.8	18.6	1.37f	706	- 15	4.7	.4	1.4	100	3.3	60
Wash Homes .... A	54	3.4	6.1	1.94s	1286	81	4.1	6.3	11.4	65	.0	8
Contractors - General												
Am Med Bldg .... A	47	NE	NM	- .17s	NE	- 35	- 1.8	NE	NE	157	.0	6
Blount B .... A	167	7.6	8.2	1.83f	33	22	2.7	4.7	17.8	53	2.6	157
Dravo Corp .... N	62	NE	16.3	- .69q	NE	- 33	- 1.0	NE	NE	36	4.3	157
Elcor Cp .... N	125	17.0	14.9	.73n	- 19	- 27	1.8	3.4	11.2	98	2.9	43
Fluor Corp .... ★N	80	17.8	13.9	1.00q	- 49	- 7	1.9	2.5	5.8	41	2.3	1,397
Grt Lakes Intl .... N	113	10.5	11.2	3.15q	14	- 8	6.9	5.9	11.6	33	3.3	104
Morrison Knuds .... N	86	7.0	7.2	3.98q	3	10	1.9	4.8	12.7	25	5.0	278
Parsons Corp .... N	289	12.5	10.9	1.91q	10	24	5.5	8.7	22.4	10	4.2	590
Perini Corp .... A	85	10.3	6.3	2.35f	- 49	60	.9	5.9	16.8	15	3.3	78
Seligman&Assc .... A	93	6.8	8.7	.50s	- 7	70	14.8	4.6	13.4	0	.0	6
Stone & Web .... N	101	8.1	8.2	4.17q	- 25	9	9.3	6.4	12.2	8	4.7	243
Turner Cp .... A	161	7.2	5.6	2.92q	4	38	18.3	2.6	22.8	31	5.2	81
Contractors - Special												
ACMAT Corp .... O	325	6.4	7.8	1.52q	83	104	4.6	7.9	29.4	50	.0	11
Am Ship Bldg .... N	151	NE	13.4	- .85q	-100	- 21	-11.4	NE	NE	48	7.3	66
Banister Contl .... N	73	NA	NM	- .94q	-100	29	4.1	4.4	9.5	3	NA	31
Bk Bldg Equip .... A	114	NE	6.3	- .70q	NE	- 30	- 1.1	NE	NE	11	5.9	11
Burnup & Sims Inc ...... O	104	NE	14.1	- .50n	NE	- 26	- 3.5	NE	NE	89	.0	57
Dynalectron .... A	122	11.5	12.5	1.00q	- 18	54	1.8	6.5	16.3	37	2.2	108
Fischbach Cp .... N	106	9.7	7.1	5.31q	- 11	14	2.0	5.3	14.6	26	5.2	187
Goldfield Cp .... A	341	28.1	NM	.04f	0	107	13.9	7.6	14.3	23	.0	27
Kasler Cp .... O	288	18.7	15.2	.79q	- 40	29	3.6	8.2	17.7	0	3.9b	67
KDI Cp .... N	280	11.4	6.8	.88q	76	12	3.4	4.7	16.1	68	1.0	83
McDermott Intl .... ★N	80	8.7	10.6	3.06f	123	11	3.9	1.3	4.1	43	6.8	985
McDowell Ent .... A	76	NE	17.8	- .58f	NE	- 29	- 1.3	NE	NE	4	.0	15
Myers LE Grp .... N	83	19.4	8.8	.60n	NE	- 23	- .5	NE	NE	31	.0	22
Newbery Enrgy .... A	136	5.3	8.4	1.26f	138	30	3.2	2.2	10.8	207	.0	10
SPW Cp .... A	58	NE	36.3	- .37q	-100	- 31	- .3	NE	NE	2	.0	12
Std Shares .... A	113	6.5	6.9	8.93n	45	17	17.3	9.2	12.2	2	.0	153
Tacoma Btbldg .... N	286	NE	6.8	- 5.45q	NE	- 70	-23.4	NE	NE	180	.0	31
Todd Shipyards .... N	117	6.6	5.3	4.84f	- 23	29	3.5	9.5	26.5	32	4.1	146

Building Materials and Supplies

VALUE OF SHIPMENTS OF SELECTED CONSTRUCTION MATERIALS INDUSTRIES, 1982–84 (in millions of 1972 dollars except as noted)

SIC	Industry	1982	Percent change 1981–82	1983[1]	Percent change 1982–83	1984[2]	Percent change 1983–84
3211	Flat glass	950	-8	1,045	10	1,120	7
3241	Cement, hydraulic	1,336	-10	1,456	28	1,560	7
3251	Brick and structural clay tile	263	-14	363	38	390	7
3261	Vitreous plumbing fixtures	214	-13	255	19	272	7
3271	Concrete block and brick	586	-9	691	18	745	8
3272	Concrete Products, N.E.C.	1,640	-2	1,624	-1	1,753	8
3273	Ready-mixed concrete	3,447	-10	3,740	9	4,002	7
3275	Gypsum products	562	-5	703	25	730	4
3431	Metal sanitary ware	223	-7	260	17	277	7
3432	Plumbing fittings and brass goods	589	-8	683	16	725	6
3441	Fabricated structural metal	3,200	-16	3,000	-6	2,950	-2
3444	Sheet metal work	2,330	-11	2,500	7	2,800	12
3448	Prefabricated metal buildings and components	860	-13	870	1	930	7

[1] Estimated.
[2] Forecast.

Source: Bureau of the Census and Bureau of Industrial Economics. Estimates by Bureau of Industrial Economics.

Source: U.S. Industrial Outlook 1984, U.S. Department of Commerce.

HYDRAULIC CEMENT (SIC 3241): TRENDS AND PROJECTIONS 1972-84 (in millions of dollars except as noted)

Item	1972	1977	1979	1981	1982[1]	1983[2]	Compound annual rate of growth 1972-83	1984[3]	Percent change 1983-84
Industry data									
Value of shipments[4]	1,791.2	3,042.3	4,017.1	3,715.4	3,426.0	3,809.0	7.1	—	—
Value of shipments (1972 $)[4]	1,791.2	1,755.5	1,870.2	1,487.3	1,336.0	1,456.0	-1.9	1,560.0	7.1
Total employment (000)	30.0	27.8	30.4	28.1	25.4	23.4	-2.2	26.0	11.1
Production workers (000)	24.3	22.2	24.5	22.3	20.1	18.3	-2.5	21.0	14.8
Average hourly earnings of production workers ($)	5.54	8.56	10.17	12.12	12.92	13.61	8.5	—	—
Capital expenditures	179.5	296.6	282.2	411.3	—	—	—	—	—
Product data									
Value of shipments[5]	1,770.0	2,971.0	3,981.1	3,696.5	3,406.0	3,786.0	7.2	—	—
Value of shipments (1972 $)[5]	1,770.0	1,714.4	1,853.4	1,479.8	1,332.0	1,451.0	-1.8	1,555.0	7.2
Product price index (1972 = 100)	100.0	173.3	214.8	249.8	256.6	259.1	9.0	—	—
Quantity shipped (mil sh tons/incl imp)	82.8	78.7	84.9	71.9	64.6	69.8	-1.5	—	—
Trade									
Value of exports	3.7	23.7	29.5	71.7	43.5	26.0	19.4	—	—
Value of imports	71.8	97.8	305.3	156.2	110.9	190.0	9.2	—	—
Export/shipments ratio	0.002	0.008	0.007	0.019	0.013	0.007	—	—	—
Import/new supply ratio[6]	0.039	0.032	0.071	0.041	0.032	0.048	—	—	—

[1] Estimated except for product price index, exports, and imports.
[2] Estimated.
[3] Forecast.
[4] Value of all products and services sold by industry SIC 3241.
[5] Value of shipments of hydraulic cement products produced by all industries.
[6] New supply is the sum of product shipments plus imports.

Source: Bureau of the Census and Bureau of Industrial Economics. Estimates and forecasts by the Bureau of Industrial Economics.

Source: *U.S. Industrial Outlook 1984*, U.S. Department of Commerce.

Company and Market	Relative Price			Earnings Per Share			Other					
	Price to Equity	P/E Ratio		Latest 12 Months		5-Year Growth Rate	Profit Margin	Return On Assets	Return On Common Equity	Debt Equity Ratio	Dividend Yield	Market Value
		Current	5-Year Average	Amount	Change							
	%	-	-	$	%	%	%	%	%	%	%	$Mil
Cement												
Alpha Portland .... N	91	16.4	41.0	1.40f	1067	- 36	1.6	.2	.5	32	.0	40
Calif Port Cmt .... A	110	41.9	15.9	.60f	NE	- 20	2.7	NE	NE	47	2.4	212
Conrock Co .... A	220	26.4	10.1	1.73f	59	- 7	5.6	5.9	7.5	3	1.3	221
Fla Rock Ind .... A	138	9.2	6.7	3.00s	72	6	6.4	7.2	12.7	34	1.8	123
Giant Portland .... N	120	NE	18.9	- 1.10q	NE	-110	-13.6	NE	NE	143	.0	18
Gifford Hill .... N	89	32.5	18.1	.62q	NE	- 23	.9	.7	1.8	100	2.6	171
Ideal Basic Ind .... ★N	81	NE	6.2	- 2.95q	NE	- 37	- 8.9	NE	NE	122	.0	262
Kaiser Cement .... ★N	59	NE	13.5	- .92f	-100	- 22	- 2.7	1.4	3.4	70	1.1	137
Lafarge Cp .... N	100	NE	NC	- .41f	NE	- 27	- 1.5	NE	NE	88	1.9	396
Lone Star .... ★N	63	18.1	6.6	1.21q	NE	- 21	1.9	1.2	3.9	91	8.7	280
Louisville Cem .... A	83	11.2	17.1	3.09q	NE	- 19	5.1	NE	NE	0	3.6	54
NWn State Port .... O	41	NE	18.3	- 1.99q	NE	- 37	- 6.8	NE	NE	40	.0	16
Puerto Rican C .... N	61	7.8	6.9	1.11f	NE	- 14	3.8	NE	NE	127	.0	17
Tex Ind .... N	140	33.7	9.0	.92n	- 67	- 9	5.8	4.6	11.0	91	2.6b	238
Lumber and Wood Products												
Bohemia Inc .... O	42	NE	6.4	- .21n	NE	- 27	- 1.4	NE	NE	15	4.0b	41
Boise Cascade .... ★N	69	13.4	31.5	2.51q	528	- 17	1.8	2.1	4.7	47	5.7	899
Champ Intl .... ★N	67	16.3	26.1	1.22f	455	- 17	1.9	2.3	5.0	60	2.0	1,092
Etz Lavud Ltd .... A	515	19.7	36.7	1.67n	- 39	66	8.8	13.6	44.5	26	1.2	56
Georgia-Pacifc .... ★N	96	16.6	21.4	1.15q	113	- 18	1.6	2.1	5.2	72	3.1	1,941
La Pacific .... ★N	85	13.9	22.1	1.31q	1091	- 20	2.1	1.8	3.2	25	4.4b	623
MacMlln Bldel .... N	72	NA	4.4	- .68f	NE	- 31	.1	NE	NE	100	NAa	529
Medford Corp .... O	99	7.9	18.0	3.03q	203	- 10	5.0	5.8	12.0	62	2.5	59
Pac Lumber .... N	254	19.0	17.7	1.16f	29	- 9	11.7	8.1	10.4	8	5.5	533
Ply-Gem .... A	211	13.2	7.9	1.33q	125	4	2.6	3.2	12.2	165	1.1	41
Pope & Talbot .... N	85	8.8	19.6	1.80q	89	- 14	3.8	4.8	9.8	58	5.1	94
Potlatch Cp .... ★N	78	12.2	17.7	2.28q	133	- 15	4.5	3.5	7.4	55	5.3	427
Trus Joist Cp .... O	190	14.5	14.9	1.62f	38	- 3	6.4	8.3	13.4	28	1.5	87
Weyerhaeuser .... ★N	112	18.6	20.3	1.47q	133	- 16	4.2	3.4	6.4	41	4.7	3,606
Willamette Ind .... O	94	16.7	29.3	1.48q	63	- 19	1.7	.5	1.3	90	6.1	377

SAWMILLS AND PLANING MILLS (SIC 2421): TRENDS AND PROJECTIONS 1972–84 (in millions of dollars except as noted)

Item	1972	1977	1979	1981	1982[1]	1983[2]	Compound annual rate of growth 1972–83	1984[3]	Percent change 1983–84
Industry data									
Value of shipments[4]	6,484.5	10,866.7	13,991.6	11,836.3	10,959.1	11,897.1	5.7	—	—
Value of shipments (1972 $)[4]	6,484.5	6,449.1	6,480.6	6,008.3	5,820.0	5,910.0	-0.8	6,190.0	4.7
Total employment (000)	166.6	175.2	185.8	161.1	143.5	153.1	-0.8	—	—
Production workers (000)	149.5	155.8	163.5	139.6	123.4	132.1	-1.1	—	—
Average hourly earnings of production workers ($)	3.54	5.14	6.07	6.80	7.32	7.73	7.4	—	—
Capital expenditures	307.1	535.8	734.6	619.6	—	—	—	—	—
Product data									
Value of shipments[5]	6,006.7	10,375.0	13,360.5	11,729.5	10,686.8	11,221.4	5.8	—	—
Value of shipments (1972 $)[5]	6,006.7	6,175.6	6,188.3	5,969.2	5,690.5	5,703.0	-0.5	5,906.0	3.6
Product price index (1972 = 100)	100.0	168.1	216.6	197.0	187.5	203.2	6.7	—	—
Quantity shipped (million board feet)	37,642.0	37,899.0	36,134.0	29,500.0	27,200.0	31,600.0	-1.6	31,100.0	-1.6
Trade									
Value of exports	308.2	720.9	1,188.5	1,196.6	1,027.0	1,100.0	12.2	—	—
Value of imports	1,157.3	2,111.6	2,911.8	2,062.8	1,770.3	2,500.0	7.3	—	—
Export/shipments ratio	0.051	0.069	0.089	0.102	0.096	0.098	—	—	—
Import/new supply ratio[6]	0.162	0.169	0.179	0.150	0.142	0.182	—	—	—

[1] Estimated except for product price index, exports, and imports.
[2] Estimated.
[3] Forecast.
[4] Value of all products and services sold by industry SIC 2421.
[5] Value of shipments of sawmills and planing mills general products produced by all industries.
[6] New supply is the sum of product shipments plus imports.

Source: Bureau of the Census and Bureau of Industrial Economics. Estimates and forecasts by the Bureau of Industrial Economics.

Source: *U.S. Industrial Outlook 1984*, U.S. Department of Commerce.

Chemicals, Plastics and Rubber

CHEMICALS AND ALLIED PRODUCTS (SIC 28): TRENDS AND PROJECTIONS 1972–84 (in millions of dollars except as noted)

Item	1972	1977	1979	1981	1982[1]	1983[2]	Compound annual rate of growth 1972–83	1984[3]	Percent change 1983–84
Industry data									
Value of shipments[4]	57,350	118,074	147,674	180,459	174,310	179,500	10.9	—	—
Value of shipments (1972 $)[4]	57,350	70,698	76,028	75,033	69,690	71,430	2.0	75,510	5.7
Total employment (000)	837	880	925	892	869	846	0.1	859	1.5
Production workers (000)	525	544	570	533	511	496	-0.5	503	1.4
Average hourly earnings of production workers ($)	4.20	6.67	7.61	9.59	—	—	—	—	—
Capital expenditures	2,728	8,199	7,956	9,471	—	—	—	—	—
Trade									
Value of exports[5]	4,143	11,705	19,012	23,371	21,583	19,425	15.1	20,650	6.3
Value of imports[6]	1,993	6,273	7,762	9,637	9,739	8,895	14.6	9,580	7.7

[1] Estimated except for product price index, exports, and imports.
[2] Estimated.
[3] Forecast.
[4] Value of all products and services sold by industry SIC 28
[5] Census Sch. E, Sect. 5, plus 233.1, 266, 267, 651.4
[6] Census Sch. A, Sect. 5, plus 233.1, 266, 651.02

Source: Bureau of the Census and Bureau of Industrial Economics. Estimates and forecasts by the Bureau of Industrial Economics.

Source: *U.S. Industrial Outlook 1984*, U.S. Department of Commerce.

PLASTICS MATERIALS AND RESINS (SIC 2821): TRENDS AND PROJECTIONS 1972–84 (in millions of dollars except as noted)

Item	1972	1977	1979	1981	1982[1]	1983[2]	Compound annual rate of growth 1972–83	1984[3]	Percent change 1983–84
Industry data									
Value of shipments[4]	4,478.2	10,818.2	14,282.4	16,675.5	15,460.0	17,340.0	13.1	—	—
Value of shipments (1972 $)[4]	4,478.2	5,060.0	5,603.1	5,329.3	5,040.0	5,545.0	2.0	5,930.0	6.9
Total employment (000)	54.8	57.2	60.3	57.7	55.2	53.6	−0.2	54.1	0.9
Production workers (000)	35.0	36.7	38.4	35.8	33.9	33.0	−0.5	33.2	0.6
Average hourly earnings of production workers ($)	4.98	7.52	8.86	10.77	11.71	12.66	8.9	—	—
Capital expenditures	253.2	895.2	1,077.1	904.2	—	—	—	—	—
Product data									
Value of shipments[5]	4,486.4	12,181.1	16,964.2	20,172.3	18,180.0	20,400.0	14.8	—	—
Value of shipments (1972 $)[5]	4,486.4	5,546.9	6,487.3	6,319.6	5,930.0	6,520.0	3.5	6,970.0	6.9
Product price index (1972 = 100)	100.0	219.5	261.5	319.1	313.8	312.8	10.9	—	—
Quantity produced (million pounds)	25,921.0	34,623.0	41,871.0	40,600.0	38,000.0	41,900.0	4.5	45,000.0	7.4
Trade									
Value of exports	438.9	1,057.2	2,183.3	2,552.5	2,471.7	2,315.0	16.3	2,400.0	3.7
Value of imports	56.4	106.3	246.4	315.7	292.0	375.0	18.8	430.0	14.7
Export/shipments ratio	0.093	0.081	0.120	0.118	0.136	0.113	—	—	—
Import/new supply ratio[6]	0.010	0.007	0.012	0.013	0.016	0.018	—	—	—

[1] Estimated except for product price index, exports, and imports.
[2] Estimated.
[3] Forecast.
[4] Value of all products and services sold by industry SIC 2821.

[5] Value of shipments of Plastics materials and resins products produced by all industries.
[6] New supply is the sum of product shipments plus imports.

Source: Bureau of the Census and Bureau of Industrial Economics. Estimates and forecasts by the Bureau of Industrial Economics.

Source: U.S. Industrial Outlook 1984, U.S. Department of Commerce.

Company and Market	Relative Price			Earnings Per Share			Other					
	Price to Equity	P/E Ratio		Latest 12 Months		5-Year Growth	Profit	Return	Return On Common	Debt Equity	Dividend	Market
		Current	5-Year Average	Amount	Change	Rate	Margin	On Assets	Equity	Ratio	Yield	Value
	%	-	-	$	%	%	%	%	%	%	%	$Mil
Chemicals, Synthetics												
Air Pd & Chem .... N	126	10.4	10.0	4.08s	28	4	6.7	4.9	10.4	40	2.4	1,319
Am Cyanamid ....★N	153	12.5	10.0	4.00q	59	1	4.7	5.4	10.4	32	3.8	2,456
Big Three Ind .... N	157	21.4	14.0	1.07f	-48	1	6.8	4.1	7.4	32	3.5	969
Cabot Corp .... N	119	13.0	8.9	1.93q	-25	3	4.1	4.9	9.5	36	3.7	805
Celanese Corp ....★N	100	7.9	6.9	8.75q	NE	-8	3.4	3.9	10.4	71	5.8	1,080
Dow Chemical ....★N	111	15.5	11.9	1.84q	19	-14	2.7	2.4	5.8	56	6.3	5,582
DuPont ....★N	96	8.4	8.6	5.40q	53	-4	3.2	4.6	10.0	42	6.2	10,809
Essex Chemical .... N	186	23.8	10.2	.92f	-55	-1	2.0	4.7	16.0	157	3.7b	75
Ethyl Corp .... N	100	7.9	6.5	2.70f	26	4	6.4	6.1	11.8	45	4.0	867
Grace W R ....★N	93	12.9	8.6	3.26f	-37	0	2.6	5.2	11.7	59	6.6	2,042
Hercules Inc ....★N	123	9.6	9.0	3.11q	54	0	5.7	6.9	11.7	27	4.8	1,588
Imperial Chem .... N	95	32.6	25.2	.95f	171	-19	4.8	2.0	4.8	50	4.4	4,673
Koppers Co .... N	98	24.5	18.4	.78q	NE	-25	1.4	NE	NE	51	4.2	547
Liquid Air Cp .... O	113	12.4	9.9	1.85q	-5	-6	5.2	4.5	9.3	50	7.0	289
Monsanto Co ....★N	96	7.9	7.7	5.41q	47	3	5.9	5.7	10.1	26	5.3	3,513
Pacer Tech .... O	394	NE	79.2	-.07s	NE	-31	-18.2	NE	NE	0	.0	10
Pennwalt Corp .... N	89	9.5	8.7	3.68q	50	-7	4.6	5.1	9.4	37	6.3	414
Publicker Ind .... N	66	NE	36.2	-.16n	NE	-6	-2.2	NE	NE	16	.0	28
Regal Intl .... N	132	NE	12.1	-.15f	-100	-13	-13.1	NE	NE	3	.0	15
Reichhold Chm .... N	107	9.6	9.5	2.71q	108	17	2.7	1.9	4.0	35	2.3	191
Rohm & Haas ....★N	159	9.4	8.3	5.90q	51	19	7.3	9.1	15.2	25	2.9	1,435
Stauffer Chem ....★N	76	NE	7.2	-.10q	NE	-28	-.9	NE	NE	33	8.1	789
Stepan Co .... A	93	8.5	8.4	1.78q	17	7	3.0	4.3	10.8	37	4.2	55
Union Carbide ....★N	74	12.4	9.4	4.19q	28	-12	2.4	2.1	4.5	48	6.6	3,647
Witco Chemical .... N	149	8.4	7.2	3.73q	67	6	3.8	4.5	10.0	50	4.7	455
Specialty Chemicals												
Betz Laboratories .... O	294	13.9	15.7	2.14q	10	19	12.4	16.2	20.5	0	4.0	476
Bio-Rad Labs .... A	238	NE	NM	-.15q	-100	-21	.2	.2	.6	170	.0	15
Chemed Cp .... N	324	14.4	19.2	2.03q	21	42	6.4	8.8	21.5	80	5.1	262
Chomerics .... O	578	28.2	22.7	.62q	NE	-37	3.6	NE	NE	220	.0	41
Church & Dwight .... O	175	10.7	7.6	1.64q	21	12	6.6	7.9	15.3	40	3.0	115
Crompt & Knwl .... N	103	11.6	8.4	1.81f	26	-2	2.7	4.0	8.1	39	5.3	67
Dexter Cp .... N	160	10.3	10.1	1.86q	16	4	4.9	6.7	14.7	36	3.7	297
Diamond Crys Salt .... O	76	11.7	9.1	4.12f	18	-4	5.5	4.8	6.5	2	2.9	62
Ferro Corp .... N	98	8.1	9.6	3.35q	150	-7	3.1	3.5	7.4	45	4.4	180
Fuller H B Co .... O	153	10.0	8.0	1.52q	49	16	3.2	6.1	15.0	56	2.0	140
Grt Lks Chem .... A	379	19.3	16.2	1.63f	70	6	10.5	6.9	11.5	28	1.1	461
Hunt Chem .... N	193	20.7	14.5	.95q	12	-6	4.5	6.0	9.2	15	2.5	112
Intl Flav Frag ....★N	278	13.9	13.4	1.88q	8	4	14.8	14.9	19.9	0	4.1	957
Kinark Cp .... A	98	12.5	47.9	.42q	163	10	5.6	3.9	7.5	56	.0	18
Lawter Int .... N	406	15.8	12.6	.83f	41	5	15.9	18.9	25.6	9	4.3	226
LeaRonal Inc .... N	256	15.5	12.6	1.05n	-6	14	4.6	14.3	17.3	6	2.2	98
Loctite Cp .... N	264	14.7	17.4	2.40n	58	-3	7.9	8.0	12.8	12	1.9	352
Lubrizol Corp .... N	184	14.9	13.1	1.46q	18	-9	7.1	7.4	10.3	4	5.0	852
MacDermid Inc .... O	365	14.9	11.0	3.60f	89	5	8.6	9.1	13.2	8	1.9	101
Midwestern Cos .... O	136	.7	NM	1.71n	NC	56	24.1	15.9	63.6	156	.0	12
Morton Thiokol .... N	236	12.7	10.5	6.10n	26	17	5.2	6.8	14.3	27	2.3	1,298
Nalco Chem .... N	263	12.6	13.5	1.83q	12	4	10.8	14.5	20.3	5	5.2	921
NCH Corp .... N	127	15.1	10.1	1.26n	0	-7	4.4	6.1	8.8	5	3.8	208
Nuclear Metals .... O	97	8.0	17.5	1.56s	-20	25	8.8	8.5	14.7	23	.0	34
Oakite Products .... N	157	12.7	10.4	1.89q	27	-5	3.2	6.7	9.3	7	6.3	42
Park Chemical .... A	212	11.6	6.5	1.87f	83	3	8.1	14.4	18.3	0	4.2	15
Petrolite Corp .... O	210	14.2	15.0	1.87s	-13	8	7.7	10.6	14.7	6	3.8	314
Prod Research .... N	182	15.5	16.7	.63q	19	21	6.6	7.7	10.2	6	2.9	75
Quaker Chemical .... O	155	9.6	10.3	2.18q	69	1	6.7	10.0	15.2	10	3.2	73
Sigma-Aldrich .... O	399	19.2	16.1	2.28f	15	23	13.1	14.7	18.1	3	1.1	378
Sun Chem Cp .... N	117	25.1	8.7	1.00q	-44	-14	1.3	1.9	5.9	85	1.9	189
Univar Cp .... N	146	19.5	10.9	.88f	35	-5	.8	1.3	5.2	120	4.0	142

SYNTHETIC RUBBER (SIC 2822): TRENDS AND PROJECTIONS 1972–84 (in millions of dollars except as noted)

Item	1972	1977	1979	1981	1982[1]	1983[2]	Compound annual rate of growth 1972–83	1984[3]	Percent change 1983–84
Industry data									
Value of shipments[4]	1,089.4	1,863.3	2,634.0	2,995.6	2,720.0	2,725.0	8.7	—	—
Value of shipments (1972 $)[4]	1,089.4	1,132.0	1,270.0	1,029.4	920.0	940.0	-1.3	1,025.0	9.0
Total employment (000)	11.8	10.0	12.1	11.2	10.6	9.9	-1.6	10.2	3.0
Production workers (000)	8.2	7.1	8.2	7.3	6.7	6.3	-2.4	6.6	4.8
Average hourly earnings of production workers ($)	5.46	8.85	9.98	12.30	13.48	14.58	9.33	—	—
Capital expenditures	35.5	53.2	66.4	145.5	—	—	—	—	—
Product data									
Value of shipments[5]	1,288.6	2,354.1	3,227.6	3,461.8	3,145.0	3,150.0	8.5	—	—
Value of shipments (1972 $)[5]	1,288.6	1,430.2	1,556.2	1,189.6	1,065.0	1,090.0	-1.5	1,200.0	10.1
Product price index (1972 = 100)	100.0	164.6	207.4	291.0	299.4	290.0	10.2	—	—
Quantity shipped (million pounds)	5,328.0	5,470.0	6,018.0	5,085.0	4,525.0	4,625.0	-1.3	5,100.0	10.3
Trade									
Value of exports	170.6	343.9	622.5	672.5	590.0	500.0	10.3	575.0	15.0
Value of imports	54.3	134.7	176.9	217.2	212.3	225.0	13.8	235.0	4.4
Export/shipments ratio	0.132	0.146	0.193	0.194	—	—	—	—	—
Import/new supply ratio[6]	0.040	0.054	0.052	0.059	—	—	—	—	—

[1] Estimated except for product price index, exports, and imports.
[2] Estimated.
[3] Forecast.
[4] Value of all products and services sold by industry SIC 2822.

[5] Value of shipments of synthetic rubber products produced by all industries.
[6] New supply is the sum of product shipments plus imports.
Source: Bureau of the Census and Bureau of Industrial economics. Estimates and forecasts by the Bureau of Industrial Economics.

Source: *U.S. Industrial Outlook 1984*, U.S. Department of Commerce.

TIRES AND INNER TUBES (SIC 3011): TRENDS AND PROJECTIONS 1972–84 (in millions of dollars except as noted)

Item	1972	1977	1979	1981	1982[1]	1983[2]	Compound annual rate of growth 1972–83	1984[3]	Percent change 1983–84
Industry data									
Value of shipments[4]	5,747.1	8,971.0	9,542.4	9,870.9	10,000.0	10,700.0	5.8	—	—
Value of shipments (1972 $)[4]	5,747.1	5,784.0	5,065.0	4,273.1	4,250.0	4,600.0	-2.0	4,800.0	4.3
Total employment (000)	107.5	114.0	103.2	79.3	76.7	72.1	-3.6	76.0	5.4
Production workers (000)	83.1	88.3	81.0	62.3	61.4	59.3	-3.0	62.0	4.6
Average hourly earnings of production workers ($)	5.38	7.74	9.51	11.89	12.55	13.05	8.40	—	—
Capital expenditures	267.1	289.0	359.6	301.5	—	—	—	—	—
Product data									
Value of shipments[5]	4,898.4	8,127.6	8,959.3	9,576.4	9,700.0	10,375.0	7.1	—	—
Value of shipments (1972 $)[5]	4,898.4	5,240.2	4,755.5	4,145.6	4,125.0	4,475.0	-0.8	4,675.0	4.5
Product price index (1972 = 100)	100.0	155.3	187.6	229.7	234.2	232.0	8.0	—	—
Quantity shipped (millions of units)	234.0	232.0	224.0	188.0	187.0	203.0	-1.3	212.0	4.4
Trade									
Value of exports	100.5	309.0	352.8	583.9	371.9	300.0	—	400.0	33.3
Value of imports	381.5	845.4	1,120.9	1,307.3	1,216.3	1,350.0	—	1,400.0	3.7
Export/shipments ratio	0.021	0.038	0.039	0.061	—	—	—	—	—
Import/new supply ratio[6]	0.075	0.098	0.116	0.127	—	—	—	—	—

[1] Estimated except for product price index, exports, and imports.
[2] Estimated.
[3] Forecast.
[4] Value of all products and services sold by industry SIC 3011.
[5] Value of shipments of tires and inner tubes produced by all industries.
[6] New supply is the sum of product shipments plus imports.

Source: Bureau of the Census and Bureau of Industrial Economics. Estimates and forecasts by the Bureau of Industrial Economics.

Source: *U.S. Industrial Outlook 1984*, U.S. Department of Commerce.

Company and Market		Relative Price			Earnings Per Share			Other					
		Price to Equity %	P/E Ratio Current -	P/E Ratio 5-Year Average -	Latest 12 Months Amount $	Latest 12 Months Change %	5-Year Growth Rate %	Profit Margin %	Return On Assets %	Return On Common Equity %	Debt Equity Ratio %	Dividend Yield %	Market Value $Mil

Tires and Inner Tubes

Company and Market		Price to Equity	Current	5-Year Average	Amount	Change	Growth Rate	Profit Margin	Return On Assets	Return On Common Equity	Debt Equity Ratio	Dividend Yield	Market Value
Alliance Tire	A	57	NE	NM	-.69n	NE	-46	-4.2	NE	NE	17	.0	19
Armstrong Rub	N	44	7.0	5.6	2.46s	18	59	3.0	4.8	9.6	35	2.8	166
Bandag Inc	N	304	11.6	9.5	3.88f	26	26	12.9	16.4	22.5	6	2.4	449
Cooper Tire	N	100	6.5	5.3	2.15q	-4	38	4.7	8.8	15.3	24	2.6	140
Dunlop Holding	A	20	NE	20.4	-.91f	NE	-60	-3.4	NE	NE	122	.0	81
Firestone Tire	*N	64	10.0	8.9	1.72s	-11	36	2.6	3.7	7.7	30	4.7	830
GenCorp	N	79	11.0	9.9	3.16f	26	-6	3.4	4.0	7.9	29	4.3b	746
Goodyear Tire	*N	88	7.6	7.4	3.32f	11	5	3.4	5.5	11.0	22	5.6	2,643
Uniroyal Inc	*N	69	6.8	9.0	1.82q	658	54	2.6	3.5	8.6	55	1.0	417

Rubber and Plastic Products

Company and Market		Price to Equity	Current	5-Year Average	Amount	Change	Growth Rate	Profit Margin	Return On Assets	Return On Common Equity	Debt Equity Ratio	Dividend Yield	Market Value
Am Biltrite	A	63	10.0	10.7	.50q	NE	-34	1.4	2.3	5.3	17	3.0	13
Carlisle Corp	N	162	11.7	9.4	2.45f	-16	12	5.5	8.8	14.0	29	3.4	263
Chelsea Indus	N	99	9.3	7.2	1.74q	-11	-4	3.5	6.0	11.5	35	4.1	44
Crest-Foam	A	109	7.8	9.1	.99q	68	31	3.2	7.1	12.0	16	1.7	10
Dayco Corp	N	66	7.9	17.1	1.94s	1840	-11	.6	.9	2.9	116	1.6	108
Fluorocarbon Co	O	152	13.3	15.2	.75f	63	-6	3.4	4.2	7.1	39	2.0	43
Grt Amer Ind	A	102	7.6	3.9	3.50f	26	0	4.3	6.7	14.2	35	2.2	39
Kleer-Vu Ind	A	170	18.2	10.0	.22f	-19	66	2.3	1.8	4.3	95	1.0	20
Kroy Inc	O	354	10.5	16.1	1.33f	73	78	10.4	10.8	19.7	29	.4	81
NVF Co	N	86	NE	20.0	-.31q	NE	-63	-6.2	NE	NE	436	.0	122
OSullivan Cp	A	460	15.2	7.2	1.97f	48	36	7.9	14.6	20.7	0	2.0b	131
Pantasote Inc	A	75	20.7	17.0	.29f	NE	-24	.8	1.5	3.6	41	.0	23
Plymth Rub A	A	60	NE	91.5	-1.23q	NE	-79	-4.5	NE	NE	0	.0	6
Porex Tech	O	587	54.1	65.2	.37n	NC	10	11.0	5.1	5.9	5	.0	193
Rubbermaid	N	298	15.7	11.8	2.42q	29	18	8.2	11.9	18.1	12	1.9	587
Schulman, A Inc	O	158	7.8	7.2	2.17s	36	21	3.8	8.9	17.9	23	2.1	90
Sealed Air	N	231	15.3	12.8	1.45q	113	11	7.1	8.4	13.4	12	1.6	152
Velcro Industries	O	257	NA	7.3	2.48q	16	15	13.5	10.3	21.1	36	NA	88
Voplex Corp	A	144	10.1	27.6	1.01q	68	1	3.2	7.0	13.5	37	3.1	23

BIOLOGICAL PRODUCTS (SIC 2831): TRENDS AND PROJECTIONS 1972–84 (in millions of dollars except as noted)

Item	1972	1977	1979	1981	1982[1]	1983[2]	Compound annual rate of growth 1972–83	1984[3]	Percent change 1983–84
Industry data									
Value of shipments[4]	360.0	898.5	1,195.8	1,545.2	1,715.0	1,920.0	16.4	—	—
Value of shipments (1972 $)[4]	360.0	628.8	742.3	846.2	888.0	932.0	9.0	978.0	4.9
Total employment (000)	10.1	15.7	18.5	21.8	21.8	22.0	7.3	22.2	0.9
Production workers (000)	5.3	8.8	9.5	11.1	11.0	10.9	6.8	11.1	1.8
Average hourly earnings of production workers ($)	3.88	5.23	5.49	6.53	7.16	7.67	6.4	—	—
Capital expenditures	27.2	35.4	64.0	96.6	—	—	—	—	—
Product data									
Value of shipments[5]	495.1	1,067.5	1,420.6	1,857.4	2,072.0	2,332.0	15.1	—	—
Value of shipments (1972 $)[5]	495.1	747.0	881.8	1,017.2	1,070.0	1,120.0	7.7	1,175.0	4.9
Product price index (1972 = 100)	100.0	142.6	159.5	180.2	191.4	208.2	6.9	—	—
Trade									
Value of exports	58.5	138.4	295.5	384.4	452.2	470.1	20.9	490.0	4.2
Value of imports	7.3	7.1	9.0	28.8	33.9	40.6	16.9	49.0	20.7
Export/shipments ratio	0.118	0.130	0.208	0.207	—	—	—	—	—
Import/new supply ratio[6]	0.015	0.007	0.006	0.015	—	—	—	—	—

[1] Estimated except for product price index, exports, and imports.
[2] Estimated.
[3] Forecast.
[4] Value of all products and services sold by industry SIC 2831.
[5] Value of shipments of biological products produced by all industries.
[6] New supply is the sum of product shipments plus imports.

Source: Bureau of the Census and Bureau of Industrial Economics. Estimates and forecasts by the Bureau of Industrial Economics.

Source: *U.S. Industrial Outlook 1984*, U.S. Department of Commerce.

PHARMACEUTICAL PREPARATIONS (SIC 2834): TRENDS AND PROJECTIONS 1972–84 (in millions of dollars except as noted)

Item	1972	1977	1979	1981	1982[1]	1983[2]	Compound annual rate of growth 1972–83	1984[3]	Percent change 1983–84
Industry data									
Value of shipments[4]	7,149.5	11,459.4	13,738.0	17,503.2	19,990.0	22,000.0	10.8	—	—
Value of shipments (1972 $)[4]	7,149.5	8,821.7	9,320.2	9,702.4	9,820.0	10,100.0	3.2	10,415.0	3.1
Total employment (000)	112.0	126.4	130.0	130.5	129.9	131.0	1.4	131.0	0.0
Production workers (000)	57.0	63.1	66.7	64.8	64.0	63.5	1.0	64.0	0.8
Average hourly earnings of production workers ($)	4.40	6.33	7.41	8.88	9.74	10.48	8.2	—	—
Capital expenditures	166.7	419.3	595.3	729.3	—	—	—	—	—
Product data									
Value of shipments[5]	6,295.4	9,639.5	11,539.1	14,622.7	16,450.0	18,200.0	10.1	—	—
Value of shipments (1972 $)[5]	6,295.4	7,519.1	7,925.2	8,192.0	8,490.0	8,728.0	3.0	9,000.0	3.1
Product price index (1972 = 100)	100.0	128.3	146.0	179.0	197.3	227.0	7.7	—	—
Trade									
Value of exports	181.5	319.7	339.4	532.0	562.8	709.2	13.2	890.0	25.5
Value of imports	14.5	33.9	56.7	52.6	40.7	78.2	16.6	110.0	40.7
Export/shipments ratio	0.029	0.033	0.029	0.036	—	—	—	—	—
Import/new supply ratio[6]	0.002	0.004	0.005	0.004	—	—	—	—	—

[1] Estimated except for product price index, exports, and imports.
[2] Estimated.
[3] Forecast.
[4] Value of all products and services sold by industry SIC 2834.

[5] Value of shipments of pharmaceutical preparations products produced by all industries.
[6] New supply is the sum of product shipments plus imports.
Source: Bureau of the Census and Bureau of Industrial Economics. Estimates and forecasts by the Bureau of Industrial Economics.

Source: *U.S. Industrial Outlook 1984*, U.S. Department of Commerce.

TOILET PREPARATIONS (SIC 2844): TRENDS AND PROJECTIONS 1972-84 (in millions of dollars except as noted)

Item	1972	1977	1979	1981	1982[1]	1983[2]	Compound annual rate of growth 1972-83	1984[3]	Percent change 1983-84
Industry data									
Value of shipments[4]	4,053.0	6,557.2	7,422.2	8,688.2	9,395.0	10,235.0	8.8	—	—
Value of shipments (1972 $)[4]	4,053.0	5,098.9	5,108.2	4,614.0	4,700.0	4,785.0	1.5	4,890.0	2.2
Total employment (000)	48.2	50.9	54.0	54.1	54.5	55.4	1.3	55.0	-0.7
Production workers (000)	31.8	32.8	34.9	33.5	33.7	34.4	0.7	34.2	-0.6
Average hourly earnings of production workers ($)	3.60	5.07	6.12	7.10	7.84	8.51	8.1	—	—
Capital expenditures	71.4	105.6	150.7	197.3	—	—	—	—	—
Product data									
Value of shipments[5]	4,247.0	6,393.5	7,509.5	9,247.5	10,000.0	10,945.0	9.0	—	—
Value of shipments (1972 $)[5]	4,247.0	4,971.6	5,168.3	4,911.0	5,000.0	5,090.0	1.7	5,200.0	2.2
Product price index (1972 = 100)	100.0	128.8	145.7	189.3	205.0	215.0	7.2	—	—
Trade									
Value of exports	53.9	167.8	255.7	370.8	352.7	320.0	17.6	385.0	20.3
Value of imports	20.0	37.0	75.2	102.7	123.6	188.8	22.6	255.0	35.1
Export/shipments ratio	0.013	0.026	0.034	0.040	.035	.029	—	—	—
Import/new supply ratio[6]	0.005	0.006	0.010	0.011	.001	.017	—	—	—

[1] Estimated except for product price index, exports, and imports.
[2] Estimated.
[3] Forecast.
[4] Value of all products and services sold by industry SIC 2844.
[5] Value of shipments of toilet preparations products produced by all industries.
[6] New supply is the sum of product shipments plus imports.

Source: Bureau of the Census and Bureau of Industrial Economics. Estimates and forecasts by the Bureau of Industrial Economics.

Source: *U.S. Industrial Outlook 1984*, U.S. Department of Commerce.

Company and Market		Relative Price — Price to Equity %	P/E Ratio Current	P/E Ratio 5-Year Average	Earnings Per Share — Latest 12 Months Amount $	Latest 12 Months Change %	5-Year Growth Rate %	Profit Margin %	Return On Assets %	Return On Common Equity %	Debt Equity Ratio %	Dividend Yield %	Market Value $Mil
Drug Manufacturers													
A L Labs	A	1066	15.6	NC	.65f	NC	77	3.4	1.7	15.8	532	.0	41
Abbott Labs	★N	382	15.1	13.9	2.97q	20	27	11.9	12.3	24.5	34	2.7	5,419
Alza Cp A	A	G	75.6	NM	.21q	- 77	90	5.8	24.3	G	486	.0	193
Am Home Prod	★N	416	13.7	10.7	4.00f	11	17	12.9	20.3	30.6	0	4.8	8,516
Block Drugs Co	O	151	8.2	6.6	3.28f	11	16	10.0	11.1	15.8	13	3.7b	196
Bolar Pharm	A	593	24.4	21.7	1.16q	30	53	19.2	20.6	23.9	0	.2	122
Bristol-Myers	★N	343	15.3	11.3	3.13q	17	20	10.4	13.6	21.4	5	3.3	6,544
Carter-Wallace	N	110	9.9	12.0	2.25f	302	20	5.4	7.3	10.5	8	2.2	173
Collaborative Rsh	O	1897	NE	NC	- .53s	NC	- 72	-23.8	NE	NE	0	.0	55
Cooper Biomed	O	348	31.9	28.6	.27q	NC	58	10.4	9.8	12.0	2	.0	153
Cooper Labs	N	NA	NA	NA	.00	NC	NC	NA	NA	NA	NA	.5	401
Diagnostic Prods	O	308	16.3	24.0	.49q	- 16	42	18.9	18.4	20.0	0	.0	43
Erbamont	N	166	10.9	19.6	.96q	NC	11	5.4	3.5	11.0	40	1.0	465
Forest Labs	A	516	28.9	25.2	.54f	13	59	13.4	12.3	16.9	12	.0	83
Genentech	O	577	NM	NM	.09q	29	91	2.6	.6	.7	7	.0	531
GNC Inc	N	241	7.9	24.3	.84s	110	55	7.0	16.9	27.4	7	2.4	219
Hybritech	O	339	NM	NC	.01q	NE	27	- 3.1	NE	NE	2	.0	150
ICN Pharm	N	213	35.3	28.5	.23q	- 28	43	5.1	7.0	10.5	17	.0	76
Iroquois Brands	A	135	12.6	15.1	1.87f	267	- 12	2.0	3.7	11.6	128	.0	37
Key Pharm	A	771	23.4	53.1	.55q	45	83	14.8	14.5	31.6	70	1.2	457
Lilly Eli Co	★N	221	10.1	11.4	6.33q	16	12	15.1	13.4	21.6	4	4.5	4,685
Marion Labs	N	645	34.2	28.4	1.12n	70	17	8.2	10.0	13.6	1	1.0	703
Merck & Co	★N	281	14.8	14.5	6.25q	10	7	13.9	10.7	18.5	16	3.2	6,831
Mylan Labs	N	1102	41.9	12.5	.60f	40	107	12.7	19.6	26.0	14	.3	200
Newport Ph	O	413	NE	NC	- .15n	NE	14	- 3.4	NE	NE	21	.0	41
Novo Industri	N	369	14.5	24.2	2.97s	24	77	17.4	12.6	21.3	20	.6	939
Pfizer Inc	★N	252	12.2	13.2	2.82q	27	19	11.9	11.4	20.5	22	3.8	5,505
Reid Prov Labs	O	438	26.9	30.2	.13n	30	56	6.1	9.5	13.5	4	1.4	23
Richardson Vk	N	132	13.3	10.2	1.96s	- 11	- 2	4.6	5.3	10.9	36	5.7	622
Robins, AH	N	97	5.7	7.9	2.38q	9	20	10.3	11.4	16.4	9	5.0	347
Rorer Group	N	297	14.9	11.9	2.08q	13	11	8.9	10.0	19.2	21	3.5	661
Scherer RP Co	N	84	13.6	15.8	.67n	- 37	2	5.2	5.3	10.4	42	3.5	72
Scher Plough	★N	156	11.5	9.9	3.40f	4	- 3	9.9	7.4	14.1	15	4.3	1,976
Searle, GD	★N	347	19.4	13.3	2.39f	- 7	14	11.6	11.1	21.1	31	1.1	2,281
Smith Labs	O	NS	5.2	21.9	.89s	NC	98	37.1	NE	NE	- 241	.0	62
Smithkline Beck	★N	229	9.6	13.2	5.91q	4	17	17.1	15.3	23.6	4	4.9	4,694
Squibb Corp	★N	191	13.2	18.9	3.36q	11	11	9.8	8.9	14.1	17	3.2	2,358
Sterling Drug	★N	175	11.5	10.7	2.27q	6	7	7.2	9.3	15.0	10	4.4	1,593
Syncor Intl	O	228	NE	72.4	- .04s	NE	- 87	- 2.8	NE	NE	3	.0	50
Syntex Corp	N	253	10.3	11.5	4.44s	10	36	17.2	14.9	24.4	19	3.5	1,546
TechAmerica	A	140	37.5	NM	.10f	400	- 2	1.9	.2	.4	30	.0	32
Thompson Med	N	546	12.4	8.1	1.99q	62	70	11.0	20.6	25.6	0	1.6	248
Unimed Inc	O	639	NE	36.7	- .21s	-100	2	37.8	25.0	30.9	0	.0	35
Upjohn Co	★N	196	11.5	10.2	5.91q	39	2	8.1	7.3	15.2	52	3.8	2,069
VLi Cp	O	170	NE	NC	- .40f	NC	- 67	-83.3	NE	NE	0	.0	59
Warner-Lambrt	★N	185	12.5	10.8	2.61q	24	1	6.5	6.9	14.1	42	4.5	2,620
Cosmetics and Grooming Aids													
Alberto-Culver	★N	98	16.2	10.9	1.08q	- 29	9	1.2	2.3	5.7	30	3.1	67
Avon Products	★N	135	9.8	10.5	2.21q	- 14	- 11	5.5	7.2	13.7	26	9.2	1,621
Chesbgh-Pnds	★N	202	11.2	10.0	3.29q	- 5	10	7.6	10.9	19.7	20	5.2	1,324
Conair Cp	N	452	12.6	7.5	1.47q	75	58	7.9	9.8	33.0	132	.6	178
Del Labs	A	110	9.7	9.2	2.66q	34	16	4.2	6.1	13.1	60	2.0	32
Faberge Inc	★N	133	19.2	18.1	1.57f	17	9	3.4	3.7	5.9	14	2.0	169
Gillette Co	★N	193	10.4	8.0	4.60f	7	8	6.7	8.6	19.3	37	5.1	1,463
Helene Curtis	N	163	7.8	6.6	2.84f	190	58	3.1	6.7	19.5	62	.0	87
Johnson Prod	A	57	NM	40.2	.02s	NE	-110	3.5	5.4	7.4	1	.0	12
Lamaur Inc	N	298	17.3	9.5	.92f	18	73	5.1	11.5	18.0	3	1.5	69
Lee Pharm	A	221	NE	19.8	- .31q	NE	- 57	-14.3	NE	NE	27	.0	7
Mary Kay Cos	N	341	10.2	14.6	1.09q	- 14	74	11.3	23.2	37.1	5	1.1	330
MEM Co	A	109	11.5	7.0	2.45f	35	1	5.8	7.8	9.3	1	4.0	45
Minnetonka	O	159	NE	31.5	- .05q	NE	- 35	- 1.8	NE	NE	6	.0	39
Noxell Cp	O	350	13.9	9.8	2.52q	27	24	7.6	14.6	18.7	0	2.2	351
Redken Labs	O	221	12.3	8.3	2.76n	17	21	7.4	10.0	14.9	12	1.5	93
Revlon Inc	★N	144	13.6	11.1	2.80f	26	- 7	4.7	4.6	11.0	34	4.7	1,383

HEALTH AND MEDICAL SERVICES (SIC 80): TRENDS AND PROJECTIONS 1972–84 (in billions of dollars except as noted)

Item	1972	1977	1979	1981	1982[1]	1983[1]	Compound annual rate of growth 1972–83	1984[1]	Percent change 1983–84[1]
Total expenditures	93.5	169.2	215.0	286.6	322.4	354.6	12.9	390.9	10.2
Health services and supplies	86.9	160.1	204.5	273.5	308.3	339.6	13.2	374.8	10.4
Personal health care	80.2	148.7	188.9	255.0	286.9	316.0	13.3	348.9	10.4
Hospital care	34.9	67.8	86.1	118.0	135.5	150.0	14.2	166.3	10.9
Physicians' services	17.2	31.9	40.2	54.8	61.8	68.1	13.3	75.2	10.4
Dentists services	5.6	10.5	13.3	17.3	19.5	21.5	13.0	23.5	9.3
Other professional services	1.8	3.6	4.7	6.4	7.1	7.9	14.4	8.8	11.4
Drugs and medical sundries[2]	9.3	14.1	17.2	21.4	22.4	24.3	9.1	26.6	9.5
Eyeglasses and appliances	2.3	3.7	4.6	5.7	5.7	6.1	9.3	6.7	9.8
Nursing home care	6.5	13.2	17.6	24.2	27.3	29.8	14.9	32.7	9.7
Other health services	2.6	4.1	5.1	7.2	7.6	8.3	11.1	9.1	9.6
Program Administration and net cost of insurance	4.7	7.1	9.3	11.2	12.7	14.1	10.6	15.5	9.9
Government public health activities	2.0	4.3	6.2	7.3	8.6	9.5	15.2	10.4	9.5
Research and medical facilities construction	6.6	9.2	10.5	13.1	14.1	15.0	7.8	16.1	7.3
Research[3]	2.4	3.9	4.8	5.7	5.9	6.2	9.0	6.5	4.8
Construction	4.2	5.3	5.7	7.5	8.2	8.8	7.0	9.6	9.1

[1] Estimated.

[2] Includes only expenditures for prescription drugs, over-the-counter drugs, and medical sundries dispensed through retail channels. Spending for drugs dispensed in hospitals and by physicians are reported within those cost categories.

[3] Research expenditures of drug companies and other manufacturers and providers of medical equipment and supplies are included in the expenditure class in which the product falls and excluded from research expenditures.

Source: Bureau of Data Management and Strategy, U.S. Department of Health and Human Services.

Source: *U.S. Industrial Outlook 1984*, U.S. Department of Commerce.

X-RAY AND ELECTROMEDICAL EQUIPMENT (SIC 3693): TRENDS AND PROJECTIONS 1972–84 (in millions of dollars except as noted)

Item	1972	1977	1979	1981	1982[1]	1983[2]	Compound annual rate of growth 1972–83	1984[3]	Percent change 1983–84
Industry data									
Value of shipments[4]	443.7	1,884.7	2,348.2	3,203.2	3,590.0	4,060.0	22.3	—	—
Value of shipments (1972 $)[4]	443.7	1,273.4	1,286.7	1,374.2	1,455.0	1,537.0	12.0	1,650.0	7.4
Total employment (000)	12.1	30.9	35.7	41.5	41.5	42.7	12.1	44.4	4.0
Production workers (000)	6.9	17.1	18.8	20.7	20.5	21.2	10.7	22.1	4.2
Average hourly earnings of production workers ($)	3.94	5.87	6.44	6.75	6.99	7.27	5.7	—	—
Capital expenditures	8.1	63.4	86.0	155.5	—	—	—	—	—
Product data									
Value of shipments[5]	383.0	1,837.8	2,283.5	3,046.4	3,410.0	3,850.0	23.3	—	—
Value of shipments (1972 $)[5]	383.0	1,241.8	1,251.2	1,306.9	1,382.0	1,458.0	12.9	1,568.0	7.5
Product price index (1972 = 100)[6]	100.0	148.0	182.5	233.1	246.8	264.1	9.2	—	—
Trade									
Value of exports	81.2	337.9	717.4	1,005.9	1,025.5	1,065.0	26.4	1,170.0	9.9
Value of imports	66.2	234.6	274.6	387.7	487.2	670.0	23.4	870.0	29.9
Export/shipments ratio	0.212	0.184	0.314	0.330	0.301	0.277	—	—	—
Import/new supply ratio[7]	0.147	0.113	0.107	0.113	0.125	0.148	—	—	—

[1] Estimated except for product price index, exports, and imports.
[2] Estimated.
[3] Forecast.
[4] Value of all products and services sold by industry SIC 3693.
[5] Value of shipments of X-ray and electromedical products produced by all industries.
[6] Developed by the Office of Research, Analysis, and Statistics, BIE.
[7] New supply is the sum of product shipments plus imports.
Source: Bureau of the Census and Bureau of Industrial Economics. Estimates and forecasts by the Bureau of Industrial Economics.

Source: *U.S. Industrial Outlook 1984*, U.S. Department of Commerce.

SURGICAL AND MEDICAL INSTRUMENTS (SIC 3841): TRENDS AND PROJECTIONS 1972–84 (in millions of dollars except as noted)

Item	1972	1977	1979	1981	1982[1]	1983[2]	Compound annual rate of growth 1972–83	1984[3]	Percent change 1983–84
Industry data									
Value of shipments[4]	961.8	1,833.1	2,253.5	3,158.2	3,475.0	3,890.0	13.5	—	—
Value of shipments (1972 $)[4]	961.8	1,273.0	1,347.0	1,587.0	1,613.0	1,688.0	5.2	1,800.0	6.6
Total employment (000)	34.5	43.2	49.9	54.6	55.1	55.7	4.5	58.2	4.5
Production workers (000)	24.3	29.2	33.6	35.4	35.4	37.0	3.9	38.7	4.6
Average hourly earnings of production workers ($)	3.36	4.55	5.43	6.34	7.07	7.43	7.5	—	—
Capital expenditures	42.0	87.2	142.3	183.7	—	—	—	—	—
Product data									
Value of shipments[5]	984.2	1,891.3	2431.7	3,257.2	3,580.0	4,010.0	13.6	—	—
Value of shipments (1972 $)[5]	984.2	1,313.4	1,453.5	1,636.8	1,662.0	1,740.0	5.3	1,854.0	6.6
Product price index (1972 = 100)[6]	100.0	144.0	167.3	199.0	215.4	230.5	7.9	—	—
Trade									
Value of exports	140.7	400.6	410.3	565.6	605.3	585.0	13.8	615.0	5.1
Value of imports	31.1	99.1	146.1	195.2	221.7	255.0	21.1	295.0	15.7
Export/shipments ratio	0.143	0.212	0.169	0.174	0.169	0.146	—	—	—
Import/new supply ratio[7]	0.031	0.050	0.057	0.057	0.058	0.060	—	—	—

[1] Estimated except for product price index, exports, and imports.
[2] Estimated.
[3] Forecast.
[4] Value of all products and services sold by industry SIC 3841.
[5] Value of shipments of surgical and medical instruments products produced by all industries.
[6] Developed by the Office of Research, Analysis, and Statistics, BIE.
[7] New supply is the sum of product shipments plus imports.

Source: Bureau of the Census and Bureau of Industrial Economics. forecasts by the Bureau of Industrial Economics.

Source: *U.S. Industrial Outlook 1984*, U.S. Department of Commerce.

DENTAL EQUIPMENT AND SUPPLIES (SIC 3843): TRENDS AND PROJECTIONS 1972–84 (in millions of dollars except as noted)

Item	1972	1977	1979	1981	1982[1]	1983[2]	Compound annual rate of growth 1972–83	1984[3]	Percent change 1983–84
Industry data									
Value of shipments[4]	409.2	786.7	1,079.6	1,313.7	1,380.0	1,475.0	12.4	—	—
Value of shipments (1972 $)[4]	409.2	563.5	666.4	658.5	658.0	670.0	4.6	688.0	2.7
Total employment (000)	12.4	16.3	16.2	17.4	17.6	18.0	3.4	18.5	2.8
Production workers (000)	8.5	10.7	10.7	11.4	11.6	11.9	3.1	12.2	2.5
Average hourly earnings of production workers ($)	3.51	4.94	5.58	6.56	7.15	7.55	7.2	—	—
Capital expenditures	14.9	16.2	29.2	19.5	—	—	—	—	—
Product data									
Value of shipments[5]	352.3	660.7	931.0	1,128.3	1,185.0	1,270.0	12.4	—	—
Value of shipments (1972 $)[5]	352.3	473.3	574.7	565.6	565.0	577.0	4.6	593.0	2.8
Product price index (1972 = 100)[6]	100.0	139.6	162.0	199.5	209.7	220.1	7.4	—	—
Trade									
Value of exports	34.3	92.4	101.2	139.7	143.4	155.0	14.7	170.0	9.7
Value of imports	12.7	30.1	41.5	49.9	49.9	55.0	14.3	60.0	9.1
Export/shipments ratio	0.097	0.140	0.109	0.124	0.121	0.122	—	—	—
Import/new supply ratio[7]	0.035	0.044	0.043	0.042	0.040	0.042	—	—	—

[1] Estimated except for product price index, exports, and imports.
[2] Estimated.
[3] Forecast.
[4] Value of all products and services sold by industry SIC 3843.
[5] Value of shipments of dental equipment and supplies products produced by all industries.
[6] Developed by the Office of Research, Analysis, and Statistics, BIE.
[7] New supply is the sum of product shipments plus imports.

Source: Bureau of the Census and Bureau of Industrial Economics.

Source: *U.S. Industrial Outlook 1984*, U.S. Department of Commerce.

Company and Market		Price to Equity %	P/E Ratio Current -	P/E Ratio 5-Year Average -	Latest 12 Months Amount $	Latest 12 Months Change %	5-Year Growth Rate %	Profit Margin %	Return On Assets %	Return On Common Equity %	Debt Equity Ratio %	Dividend Yield %	Market Value $Mil
Medical Instruments and Supplies													
Acme United	A	215	13.2	14.2	1.01q	20	13	7.5	12.4	16.6	9	2.4	43
ADAC Labs	O	89	NE	74.2	- .85s	-100	- 26	6.6	5.9	8.9	3	.0	48
Aff Hosp Prods	A	117	7.8	6.8	2.47q	11	43	5.8	9.6	14.6	5	2.3	30
Am Hosp Sply	★N	176	11.2	13.9	2.98q	20	18	6.4	9.3	15.2	10	3.4	2,461
Am Monitor	O	179	NE	NM	- 1.87n	-100	- 79	- 7.5	NE	NE	65	.0	28
Am Sterilizer	N	115	9.6	8.9	1.66q	1	24	6.1	8.6	12.1	13	2.8	161
Bard C R	★N	219	11.1	12.5	2.22f	22	42	8.4	10.6	16.2	23	1.6	371
Bausch Lomb	N	183	11.0	12.4	1.78q	28	1	7.5	8.6	16.0	30	4.0	566
Baxter Travenol	★N	188	11.2	15.3	1.37q	8	24	11.8	10.3	18.9	20	2.1	2,233
Becton, Dick	★N	117	10.1	12.7	3.34s	45	2	5.0	5.1	9.4	46	3.4	689
Cobe Labs	O	82	9.7	11.9	1.18q	- 20	3	4.7	6.5	9.2	13	.0	50
Coherent Inc	O	247	32.7	28.0	.84s	223	- 3	4.4	4.4	7.3	6	.0	137
Collagen Cp	O	132	35.0	NM	.25s	- 7	72	10.5	3.3	3.5	2	.0	53
CooperVision	N	344	22.4	20.7	1.06q	41	77	10.1	9.4	14.5	9	1.2b	478
Cordis Cp	O	174	6.6	18.1	1.63n	90	26	6.1	5.8	12.6	66	.0	142
Damon Corp	N	137	84.2	NM	.15q	NE	- 14	.5	.5	1.0	50	1.6	85
Datascope Cp	O	203	26.8	23.1	.56n	- 21	9	5.6	5.0	11.9	91	.0	36
Delmed Inc	A	488	NE	62.9	- .80q	-100	- 41	- 9.2	NE	NE	324	.0	103
Diasonics Inc	O	190	NE	NC	- 1.23q	-100	-117	-35.8	10.4	19.9	1	.0	148
Durr Fillauer	O	164	13.9	12.9	.80q	7	22	1.9	5.7	11.8	30	1.3	70
Dynatech Cp	O	341	13.2	19.5	1.08n	77	31	7.5	12.0	22.6	30	.0	115
Electro Biology	O	235	13.5	52.7	.51q	- 9	45	11.7	15.7	18.1	0	.0	40
Electro Nucleonic	O	122	15.5	22.9	.62s	35	32	4.9	4.9	7.0	19	.0	37
Elscint	O	213	9.0	25.2	1.25n	- 11	80	13.6	7.6	17.6	25	.0	181
Everest & Jen	A	112	NE	63.9	- .03q	-100	- 23	.2	.2	.4	65	1.0	24
Fonar Cp	O	7083	NE	NC	- .31s	NE	- 93	-76.5	NE	NE	0	.0	60
Frigitronics	N	197	13.9	10.6	1.68n	18	6	3.9	7.4	11.5	16	2.0	74
Gelman Sci	A	143	18.0	NM	.61s	11	- 2	4.0	5.1	8.5	38	.0	27
Genex Cp	O	311	NE	NC	- .43q	NE	- 84	-61.4	NE	NE	25	.0	118
Hlth Extension	A	423	61.1	53.0	.26q	53	101	2.0	4.0	5.1	3	.0	41
Health-Chem	A	244	38.1	49.3	.20q	300	- 9	2.2	2.1	6.1	106	.0	56
Healthdyne Inc	O	72	57.3	59.1	.12q	- 50	26	4.0	3.0	3.9	9	.0	97
Hillenbrand Ind	N	175	9.9	8.4	1.92q	22	17	8.3	10.2	16.6	24	2.7	378
Intermedics Inc	N	145	NE	20.0	- 1.04s	NE	- 30	- 4.6	4.2	8.3	41	.0	143
Intl Clin Lab	O	190	18.6	19.9	.90s	25	39	6.7	5.7	8.0	17	.0	114
Intl Hydron	A	NS	28.7	36.8	.34q	NC	83	8.9	NE	NE	- 15	.0	109
IPCO Corp	N	119	11.7	13.6	1.06n	116	77	3.2	5.6	9.8	29	2.4	67
Jensen Inds	A	127	6.5	16.7	2.16f	58	17	8.9	10.5	12.8	1	.0	15
Johnsn & John	★N	201	10.8	14.0	2.95q	11	14	9.2	12.3	18.1	6	3.5	6,075
Laser Indus	A	567	44.1	56.9	.32n	NE	25	7.3	4.3	7.7	9	.0	44
Lumex	A	204	13.4	16.9	.73q	- 5	35	6.8	9.2	15.5	46	.8	37
Medex	O	517	19.2	25.6	.39n	8	55	11.8	16.0	27.7	38	.5	28
Mediq	A	360	17.6	14.3	.81q	25	93	9.1	6.6	19.4	120	1.1	93
Medtronic Inc	N	160	7.9	13.0	3.64f	9	21	14.0	13.0	18.5	5	2.5	466
Mtn Med Equip	A	205	7.9	23.5	.71n	- 9	84	14.7	14.3	30.3	23	.0	30
Natl Patent	A	350	13.5	89.7	1.20f	118	45	12.0	6.0	11.8	66	.6	172
Newport Cp	O	491	34.3	19.4	.63s	26	88	23.1	11.1	11.7	0	.3	202
NMS	O	592	NE	NM	- .18n	NC	- 72	- 9.1	NE	NE	0	.0	20
Omega Optical	O	192	81.3	27.7	.10s	25	- 20	1.1	1.5	2.6	47	3.7	30
Puritan Bennett	O	99	23.0	19.3	.87f	NE	- 16	2.4	NE	NE	10	2.0	58

Company and Market	Relative Price			Earnings Per Share			Other					
	Price to Equity	P/E Ratio		Latest 12 Months		5-Year Growth	Profit	Return	Return On Common	Debt Equity	Dividend	Market
		Current	5-Year Average	Amount	Change	Rate	Margin	On Assets	Equity	Ratio	Yield	Value
	%	·	·	$	%	%	%	%	%	%	%	$Mil
St Jude Med .... O	210	14.3	40.9	1.00q	64	108	16.8	12.4	13.3	0	.0	68
Sci Leasing .... A	299	16.1	17.5	1.71n	44	119	13.4	2.4	11.9	296	.0	82
Stryker Cp .... O	329	17.6	18.7	1.22q	21	35	8.3	13.6	17.9	0	.0	106
Survival Tech .... O	260	83.3	27.0	.09s	-79	-7	3.5	5.8	12.0	36	.0	20
Sybron Corp .... N	83	16.1	17.4	1.07q	215	-14	2.2	2.6	5.9	49	6.3	171
Tambrands Inc .... N	324	10.7	9.8	4.90q	22	10	14.8	20.9	28.6	0	5.7	578
Unit Industl .... N	222	10.0	9.7	1.70q	24	35	5.8	10.0	21.5	3	2.8	172
US Surgical .... O	119	11.3	27.0	1.07n	60	23	5.8	3.8	7.9	77	.0	131
USR Ind .... A	89	4.8	14.6	.94n	4600	59	6.1	3.0	3.4	2	.0	5
West Co .... N	187	10.9	9.1	2.09q	38	23	8.6	10.7	16.9	22	1.9	180
Xonics .... O	18	NE	NC	-1.19n	NE	17	.1	.1	.5	132	.0	5

Institutional Services

Company and Market	Price to Equity	Current	5-Year Average	Amount	Change	Rate	Margin	On Assets	Equity	Ratio	Yield	Value
Am Med Intl .... ★N	230	12.7	14.6	1.88s	13	39	7.6	6.5	21.0	140	2.5	1,899
Am Surgery .... O	6875	NE	NC	-.31q	NC	-57	-07.7	NE	NE	420	.0	41
Auto Med Labs .... O	192	NE	NM	-.33f	NE	-61	-7.1	NE	NE	49	.0	7
Beverly Enterp .... N	179	19.0	14.7	1.45f	9	47	3.2	2.5	9.2	211	1.0	682
Care Cp .... A	277	8.9	11.5	.88n	110	62	3.3	4.5	23.5	288	.0	16
Cetus Corp .... O	202	NE	NM	-.03s	NE	20	-16.3	NE	NE	0	.0	254
Charter Med .... A	481	15.1	13.9	1.54s	33	106	7.5	6.7	28.4	217	.9	458
Chemex Pharma .... O	G	NE	NM	-.24s	NE	-49	-87.5	NE	NE	0	.0	28
Commun Psych .... N	441	23.1	16.9	1.51q	30	65	19.5	13.0	17.1	14	.8	692
Comprhen Care .... O	232	17.4	23.1	1.18n	18	77	12.5	9.0	10.7	6	1.6	233
Diagnostic Data .... O	927	NM	NC	.04n	NE	-6	-10.5	NE	NE	0	.0	27
Enzo Biochem .... O	805	NE	NC	-.09s	NE	-112	-43.5	NE	NE	0	.0	144
Forum Grp .... O	179	13.5	37.2	.38f	46	85	6.4	2.1	8.4	264	1.2	115
Grtwst Hosp .... N	203	22.3	24.1	.60s	43	-12	2.6	2.0	4.2	67	.0	68
Hazleton Labs .... N	74	NE	19.6	-.06n	-100	-10	3.7	3.3	4.9	14	3.4	39
HBO Co .... O	1024	32.1	30.7	.67q	168	63	14.8	14.1	21.9	11	.7	351
HealthAmerica Cp .... O	1267	55.5	41.0	.86q	NC	56	6.3	11.3	19.8	10	.0	410
Hosp Cp Am .... ★N	230	14.1	15.3	2.97q	23	52	6.2	6.0	15.5	109	1.2	3,615
Humana Inc .... ★N	425	15.0	15.5	1.80s	22	86	9.1	7.2	26.4	175	2.2	2,590
Manor Care Inc .... N	369	15.9	14.0	1.23n	27	97	5.0	3.8	18.4	305	1.1	344
Maxicare Hlth .... O	1629	52.1	43.3	.35f	NC	114	2.7	4.8	14.9	76	.0	295
Metrocare Inc .... A	197	16.7	12.8	1.08n	96	54	5.7	4.7	7.2	21	.0	25
Natl Med Care .... N	210	11.2	11.4	1.26f	22	5	7.4	8.4	16.8	36	3.5	259
Natl Med Ent .... ★N	206	12.1	15.6	1.70n	23	53	5.3	4.9	14.4	131	2.1	1,362
Nelson Rsh&Dev .... O	375	NM	NM	.05q	NC	98	18.2	.8	.8	0	.0	98
Omnicare Inc .... N	191	8.9	17.2	1.74q	14	48	8.9	13.7	20.8	22	5.9	163
Pearle Hlth Svc .... O	135	14.1	14.2	1.38q	NC	39	7.8	9.1	17.5	40	.0	255
Quality Care .... O	1523	29.9	38.9	.28f	100	23	2.3	4.2	19.4	169	.0	65
ServiceMaster .... O	1069	23.6	22.6	1.22q	20	36	3.7	27.1	43.7	0	3.6	623
Summit Hlth .... O	844	16.5	17.0	.41s	NC	66	5.7	13.0	44.5	43	.7	211
Unit Medical .... A	264	15.8	15.3	.79q	23	23	12.8	11.8	16.5	8	.0a	29
Univ Health .... O	170	17.5	21.2	.70q	-20	61	3.6	2.2	9.8	283	.0	169

STEEL MILL PRODUCTS (SIC'S 3312, 3315–17): TRENDS AND PROJECTIONS 1972–84 (in millions of dollars except as noted)

Item	1972	1977	1979	1981	1982[1]	1983[2]	Compound annual rate of growth 1972–83	1984[3]	Percent change 1983–84
Industry Data									
Value of shipments[4]	28,102	49,651	165,952	68,963	50,881	60,442	7.2	—	—
Value of shipments (1972$)[4]	28,102	27,798	30,409	26,609	18,521	21,045	-2.6	24,051	14
Total employment (000)	543	521	535	469	365	330	-4.4	—	—
Production workers (000)	438	411	426	362	269	243	-5.2	—	—
Average hourly earnings of production workers ($)	5.76	9.95	12.17	15.06	16.04	16.41	10.0	—	—
Capital expenditures	1,032	2,390	2,568	3,090	—	—	—	—	—
Product data									
Value of shipments[5]	25,035	44,919	60,069	63,315	45,568	54,112	7.3	—	—
Value of shipments (1972$)[5]	25,035	25,179	27,720	24,532	17,075	19,404	-2.3	22,176	14
Product price index (1972 = 100)[5]	100.0	179.1	217.6	258.5	268.2	273.0	—	—	—
Quantity shipped (000 net tons)	91,805	91,147	100,262	88,450	61,567	70,000	-2.4	80,000	14
Trade									
Value of exports	627	1,096	1,793	2,170	1,395	775	1.9	1,048	35
Value of imports	2,725	5,337	6,967	10,127	8,804	7,491	9.6	8,597	15
Export/shipments ratio	0.025	0.024	0.030	0.034	0.031	0.014	—	—	—
Import/new supply ratio[6]	0.098	0.106	0.104	0.138	0.162	0.122	—	—	—

[1] Estimated except for product price index, exports, and imports.
[2] Estimated.
[3] Forecast.
[4] Value of all products and services sold by industry SIC's 3312, 3315–17.
[5] Value of shipments of steel mill products produced by all industries.
[6] New supply is the sum of product shipments plus imports.

Source: Bureau of the Census and Bureau of Industrial Economics. Estimates and forecasts by the Bureau of Industrial Economics.

Source: *U.S. Industrial Outlook 1984*, U.S. Department of Commerce.

Company and Market		Relative Price			Earnings Per Share			Other					
		Price to Equity	P/E Ratio		Latest 12 Months		5-Year Growth Rate	Profit Margin	Return On Assets	Return On Common Equity	Debt Equity Ratio	Dividend Yield	Market Value
			Current	5-Year Average	Amount	Change							
		%	-	-	$	%	%	%	%	%	%	%	$Mil
Iron Mining													
Clevel-Cliffs Ir	N	77	NM	40.6	.16f	NE	-22	.6	NE	NE	24	5.0	249
Grt N Iron Ore	N	252	10.5	8.6	1.85n	-29	1	58.3	28.7	30.2	0	.0	29
Hanna Mining	N	50	NE	7.1	-2.84f	NE	-33	-18.8	NE	NE	21	2.1	190
Inspiration Rsc	N	50	NE	NC	-3.32q	NC	-37	-10.9	NE	NE	68	.0a	261
Iron and Steel Furnaces, Mills, Foundries													
Amcast	O	204	21.1	16.0	1.10s	NE	59	2.0	2.5	4.6	27	1.7	152
Ampco-Pitts	N	95	NE	6.8	-.32f	NE	-22	-.7	NE	NE	123	1.4	112
Armco Inc	★N	82	NE	6.7	-4.21f	NE	-27	-6.6	NE	NE	67	2.6	1,010
Athlone Indus	N	103	NE	5.7	-.59f	NE	-19	-.2	NE	NE	134	7.4	50
Bethlehem Stl	★N	83	NE	5.9	-6.65q	NE	-93	-6.4	NE	NE	104	3.1	908
Bundy Corp	N	79	7.1	40.4	2.05n	88	-3	2.0	2.7	4.9	27	5.5	50
Carpenter Tech	N	131	12.5	11.4	3.49n	88	-7	4.0	3.5	5.5	21	4.8	380
Cascade Stl Rolling	O	130	12.2	13.5	.88q	138	-12	2.8	3.7	8.8	54	2.2b	34
CCX Inc	N	82	NE	6.3	-.89s	NE	-50	-17.3	NE	NE	1	.0a	19
Chromalloy Am	N	63	NE	8.6	-3.05f	NE	-29	-4.9	NE	NE	90	.0	175
Copperweld Cp	N	94	NE	5.5	-2.56f	NE	-24	-6.8	NE	NE	55	3.1	160
Cyclops Corp	N	65	NE	9.0	-.72f	NE	-22	-.2	NE	NE	36	3.3	120
Eastmet Corp	O	84	NE	97.1	-2.67q	NE	-59	-8.5	NE	NE	107	.0	44
Foote Minl	A	71	NE	10.1	-.63q	NE	-37	-2.8	NE	NE	37	.0	60
Foster L B	O	76	NE	7.4	-1.30n	-100	-36	-1.7	NE	NE	90	1.7	58
Friedman Ind	A	94	26.2	10.6	.31n	-50	-8	1.9	2.2	2.5	10	3.4b	27
Grant Indus	A	132	9.8	9.7	.91s	3	1	5.1	6.0	13.2	79	.0a	22
Harsco Corp	N	101	13.5	8.6	1.54q	-5	-9	3.3	4.0	7.0	31	5.8	396
Hofmann Indus	A	94	9.4	22.9	.61n	1120	-23	.5	.7	1.7	59	.0	11
Inland Steel	★N	46	NE	13.2	-3.67q	NE	-46	-3.6	NE	NE	70	2.4	517
Interlake Inc	★N	84	9.4	12.5	5.02q	710	1	2.7	3.4	7.0	35	5.5	253
KeyCn n	N	NA	NA	NA	.00	NC	NC	NA	NA	NA	NA	.0	8
Laclede Steel	O	60	11.7	42.2	1.26f	NE	-33	1.5	NE	NE	53	.0	40
Lindberg Corp	N	156	NE	56.0	-.33q	NE	-31	-5.3	NE	NE	34	24.2	35
Lukens Inc	N	53	NE	18.2	-1.77q	NE	-39	-3.2	NE	NE	69	3.1	66
Natl Intergrp	★N	48	NE	5.8	-9.46f	NE	-37	-5.9	NE	NE	67	1.0	523
Natl-Standard	N	63	10.7	24.4	1.30s	NE	-31	-.4	NE	NE	18	2.9	57
NWn Stl & Wr	N	50	NE	6.8	-2.89s	NE	-34	-11.4	NE	NE	4	.0	113
Ohio Ferro Alloys	O	63	NE	17.7	-4.80q	NE	-74	-20.9	NE	NE	71	.0	6
Proler Intl	N	73	52.3	16.8	.65n	-56	-10	1.6	1.0	1.4	12	4.1	56
Quanex Corp	N	120	52.6	7.4	.19q	NE	-32	-1.2	NE	NE	144	.0	107
Rep Steel	★N	27	NE	4.9	-21.32f	NE	-45	-13.5	NE	NE	61	2.2	409
Sharon Steel	A	177	NE	73.2	-.73q	NE	-70	-8.4	NE	NE	492	.0	195
Tubos Mexico	A	25	2.9	8.2	1.27f	-46	NC	2.4	3.6	8.6	6	.0	61
Union El Steel	O	155	18.5	12.6	2.13f	395	-12	7.5	6.0	8.3	26	3.0	60
US Steel Corp	★N	58	NE	7.6	-9.55q	NE	-62	-6.9	NE	NE	157	4.0	2,642
Valley Inds	N	62	NE	10.0	-.56q	NE	-37	-3.9	NE	NE	57	.0	34
Weld Tube Am	A	74	20.8	11.7	.53f	NE	-16	2.7	2.3	3.8	24	.9	22
Wheel-Pitts St	★N	25	NE	26.5	-14.72f	NE	-49	-7.0	NE	NE	142	.0	86
Worthington Ind	O	276	14.4	13.5	1.47n	27	8	4.4	6.6	15.6	68	2.7	391

PRIMARY COPPER (SIC 3331): TRENDS AND PROJECTIONS 1972–84 (in millions of dollars except as noted)

Item	1972	1977	1979	1981	1982[1]	1983[2]	Compound annual rate of growth 1972–83	1984[3]	Percent change 1983–84
Industry data									
Value of shipments[4]	2,771.1	3,918.1	5,646.3	5,366.2	3,595.4	4,404.4	4.3	—	—
Value of shipments (1972 $)[4]	2,771.1	3,032.6	3,182.6	3,356.0	2,755.9	3,133.5	1.1	3,040.0	-3.0
Total employment (000)	17.2	13.1	11.9	10.7	8.6	7.0	-7.8	8.0	14.3
Production workers (000)	14.4	10.6	9.8	8.5	6.6	5.2	-8.8	6.2	19.2
Average hourly earnings of production workers ($)	4.82	8.13	9.99	12.62	13.63	14.34	10.4	—	—
Capital expenditures	119.7	D	90.8	D	—	—	—	—	—
Product data									
Value of shipments[5]	2,898.7	3,923.8	4,432.8	5,470.8	2,668.5	3,384.5	1.4	—	—
Value of shipments (1972 $)[5]	2,898.7	3,006.7	2,488.9	3,317.6	1,900.0	2,225.0	-2.4	2,340.0	5.2
Product price index (1972 = 100)	100.0	130.2	177.6	164.2	142.2	156.6	4.2	—	—
Trade									
Value of exports	190.5	82.4	156.8	73.0	49.3	50.2	-11.4	54.0	7.6
Value of imports	246.8	502.8	436.6	647.6	394.7	860.4	12.0	636.7	-26.0
Export/shipments ratio	0.066	0.021	0.035	0.013	0.018	0.015	—	—	—
Import/new supply ratio[6]	0.078	0.114	0.090	0.106	0.129	0.203	—	—	—

[1] Estimated except for product price index, exports, and imports.
[2] Estimated.
[3] Forecast.
[4] Value of all products and services sold by industry SIC 3331.
[5] Value of shipments of primary copper products produced by all industries.
[6] New supply is the sum of product shipments plus imports.

Source: Bureau of the Census and Bureau of Industrial Economics. Estimates and forecasts by the Bureau of Industrial Economics.

Source: *U.S. Industrial Outlook 1984*, U.S. Department of Commerce.

Company and Market		Relative Price			Earnings Per Share			Other					
		Price to Equity %	P/E Ratio Current -	P/E Ratio 5-Year Average -	Latest 12 Months Amount $	Latest 12 Months Change %	5-Year Growth Rate %	Profit Margin %	Return On Assets %	Return On Common Equity %	Debt Equity Ratio %	Dividend Yield %	Market Value $Mil
Copper Mining													
Atlas Consol B	A	188	31.3	23.1	.06f	NE	- 26	2.4	1.4	6.3	251	.0	157
Campbell Rsc	N	72	NA	15.6	- .24s	NE	- 25	- 3.2	NE	NE	65	NAa	88
Marindqe Mine	A	10	NE	5.6	- 3.29f	NE	- 83	-57.8	NE	NE	241	.0	23
Newmont Mng	*N	75	24.3	17.1	1.51q	- 22	- 15	7.3	2.5	3.6	13	2.7	1,109
O'Okiep Copp	A	69	NE	8.9	- 2.57q	NE	- 46	-18.5	NE	NE	44	.0	26
Ranchers Expl	A	289	13.7	20.3	1.92n	83	16	13.2	6.7	15.7	61	1.1	150
Copper Refining													
ASARCO Inc	*N	67	NE	13.9	- .30q	NE	- 26	3.9	2.6	5.7	48	1.7	682
Phelps Dodge	*N	45	NE	10.5	- 2.76f	NE	- 31	- 6.5	NE	NE	61	.0	436
Revere Copper	N	149	6.1	6.8	2.02f	NE	- 59	2.8	4.0	30.0	5	.0	70
Aluminum Refining													
Alcan Alum	*N	98	18.5	17.6	1.53q	NE	- 21	1.1	.9	2.1	54	4.2	2,750
Alum Co Am	*N	82	9.4	9.0	3.42q	NE	- 16	3.1	2.6	5.2	52	3.7	2,600
Kaiser Alum	*N	47	NE	5.3	- 1.69f	NE	- 30	- 3.3	NE	NE	76	4.1	628
Reynolds Metal	*N	50	NE	5.4	- 4.73f	NE	- 26	- 2.7	NE	NE	82	3.6	575

ALUMINUM: TRENDS AND PROJECTIONS 1972–84 (in millions of dollars except as noted)

Item	1972	1977	1979	1981	1982	1983[1]	Compound annual rate of growth 1972–83	1984[2]	Percent change 1983–84
Value of product shipments[3]	6,600	13,116	19,880	20,485	14,721	21,100	11.0	24,700	17.1
Value of product shipments (1972 $)[3]	6,600	7,113	7,777	7,382	5,165	7,500	1.0	8,200	9.3
Product price index (1972 = 100)									
SIC 3334	100.0	213.0	311.0	334.6	306.2	—	—	—	—
SIC 3353	100.0	187.1	241.4	269.3	276.7	—	—	—	—
SIC 3354	100.0	166.7	228.4	244.6	243.1	—	—	—	—
SIC 3355	100.0	174.9	219.6	242.8	252.3	—	—	—	—
SIC 3361	100.0	189.8	256.1	258.4	262.8	—	—	—	—
Quantity shipped (million pounds)	12,049	12,986	14,199	13,477	11,777	13,190	1.0	14,100	6.9
Total employment (000)									
SIC 3334	25.6	28.6	32.8	30.3	24.1	19.3	–3.0	21.0	8.8
SIC 3353, 3354, 3355, 3361	109.3	114.8	122.2	118.9	106.3	101.4	–1.0	110	8.5
Production workers (000)									
SIC 3334	20.0	22.8	25.7	23.3	17.7	14.0	–3.0	16.0	14.3
SIC 3353, 3354, 3355, 3361	88.8	94.0	98.1	95.3	83.7	80.5	–1.0	87.0	8.1
Average hourly earnings of production workers ($)									
SIC 3334	5.61	9.37	13.23	14.45	15.55	16.36	10.0	—	—
SIC 3353	5.43	9.49	12.96	14.65	16.03	17.18	11.0	—	—
SIC 3354	3.83	6.00	7.98	8.53	8.99	9.55	9.0	—	—
SIC 3355	4.87	8.19	10.43	11.38	12.0	12.74	9.0	—	—
SIC 3361	4.19	6.15	7.64	8.40	8.95	9.45	8.0	—	—
Capital expenditures									
SIC 3334	136.5	158.7	216.6	458.6	—	—	—	—	—
SIC 3353, 3354, 3355, 3361	170.9	343.1	682.5	621.4	—	—	—	—	—
Value of exports	207	515	2,026	1,254.7	1,004	720	—	960	33.3
Value of imports	374	758	871	1,316.1	1,444.4	800	—	1,420	77.5
Export/shipments ratio	.031	.039	.102	.061	.068	.034	—	—	—
Import/new supply ratio	.057	.058	.048	.060	.089	.037	—	—	—

[1] Estimated.

[2] Forecast.

[3] Value estimated by Bureau of Industrial Economics (BIE). Includes imports and represents shipments to consuming industries and exports; includes shipments of aluminum products made by all industries. Covers SIC Codes 3334, 3353, 3354, 3355, 3361 and parts of 3341, 3357, 3399 and 3463.

Note: Description of SIC Codes used: 3334 primary aluminum production; 3353 aluminum sheet, plate and foil; 3354 aluminum extruded products; 3355 aluminum rolling and drawing, n.e.c.; 3361 aluminum foundries (castings).

Source: Bureau of the Census and Bureau of Industrial Economics. Estimates and forecasts by the Bureau of Industrial Economics.

Source: U.S. Industrial Outlook 1984, U.S. Department of Commerce.

Energy: Coal, Oil, and Gas

CONSUMPTION BY FUEL TYPE AND SECTOR 1973–1982 [Quadrillon (10^{15}) BTU]

	Residential and Commercial*				Transportation***		
Total	Coal	Natural Gas (Dry)	Petroleum	Total	Coal	Natural Gas (Dry)	Petroleum
1973	R0.259	7.626	4.391	1973	0.003	0.743	R17.821
1974	R0.260	7.518	3.996	1974	0.002	0.685	R17.396
1975	R0.212	7.581	3.805	1975	0.001	0.595	R17.610
1976	R0.206	7.866	4.181	1976	(1)	0.559	R18.499
1977	R0.207	7.461	4.206	1977	(1)	0.543	R19.230
1978	R0.215	7.624	4.070	1978	(1)	0.539	R20.019
1979	R0.188	7.891	3.448	1979	(1)	0.612	R19.817
1980	R0.147	7.539	3.035	1980	(1)	R0.648	R19.009
1981	R0.171	R7.249	R2.634	1981	(1)	R0.658	R18.800
1982	R0.189	R7.443	R2.449	1982	(1)	R0.613	R18.417
1983	.193	7.088	2.326	1983	(1)	0.576	18.381

* Geographic coverage: the 50 United States and District of Columbia.
The Residential and Commercial Sector consists of housing units, non-manufacturing business establishments (e.g., wholesale and retail businesses), health and educational institutions, and government office buildings.
R = Revised data.
*** Geographic coverage: the 50 United States and District of Columbia.
Totals may not equal sum of components due to independent rounding.
The Transportation Sector consists of both private and public passenger and freight transportation, as well as government transportation, including military operations.
R = Revised data.
[1] Since 1976 coal use by transportation section has been negligible.

	Industrial**				Electric Utilities****		
Total	Coal	Natural Gas (Dry)	Petroleum	Total	Coal	Natural Gas (Dry)	Petroleum
1973	R3.984	10.388	R9.113	1973	8.658	3.748	3.515
1974	R3.800	10.003	R8.698	1974	8.535	3.519	3.365
1975	R3.602	8.532	R8.151	1975	8.786	3.240	3.166
1976	R3.595	8.761	R9.018	1976	9.720	3.152	3.477
1977	R3.394	8.636	R9.786	1977	10.243	3.284	4.901
1978	R3.258	8.539	R9.890	1978	10.236	3.297	3.987
1979	R3.532	8.549	R10.576	1979	11.264	3.609	3.283
1980	R3.103	8.394	R9.524	1980	12.122	3.807	2.634
1981	R3.109	R8.265	R8.295	1981	12.583	3.764	2.202
1982	R2.520	R7.116	R7.798	1982	R12.526	3.336	1.568
1983	2.422	6.745	7.734	1983	13.234	3.014	1.543

** Geographic coverage: the 50 United States and District of Columbia.
The Industrial Sector is made up of construction, manufacturing, agriculture, and mining establishments.
R = Revised data.
**** Geographic coverage: the 50 United States and District of Columbia.
Totals may not equal sum of components due to independent rounding.
[1] Includes petroleum products reported as "oil consumed at steam units" through 1979 and "heavy oil" from 1980 forward, which are assumed to be residual fuel oil; petroleum products reported as "oil consumed by gas turbine and internal combustion units" through 1979 and "light oil" from 1980 forward, which are assumed to be distillate fuel oil and kerosene; and petroleum coke.
R = Revised data.
Source: *Monthly Energy Review*, U.S. Department of Energy, Energy Information Administration, March 1984.

PETROLEUM—CRUDE OIL[1] SUPPLY AND DISPOSITION

| | | Field Production | | Supply | | |
		Total Domestic	Alaskan	Imports Total	SPR[2]	Other
				Thousand barrels per day		
1973	AVERAGE	9,208	198	3,244		3,244
1974	AVERAGE	8,774	193	3,477		3,477
1975	AVERAGE	8,375	191	4,105		4,105
1976	AVERAGE	8,132	173	5,287		5,287
1977	AVERAGE	8,245	464	6,615	21	6,594
1978	AVERAGE	8,707	1,229	6,356	162	6,195
1979	AVERAGE	8,552	1,401	6,519	67	6,452
1980	AVERAGE	8,597	1,617	5,263	44	5,219
1981	AVERAGE	8,572	1,609	4,396	256	4,141
1982	AVERAGE	8,649	1,696	3,488	165	3,323
1983	AVERAGE	8,656	1,715	3,303	234	3,069

Geographic coverage: the 50 United States and the District of Columbia.
[1] Includes lease condensate.
[2] Strategic Petroleum Reserve.
Source: *Monthly Energy Review*, U.S. Department of Energy, Energy Information Administration, March 1984.

		Relative Price			Earnings Per Share			Other					
		Price to Equity	P/E Ratio Current	5-Year Average	Latest 12 Months Amount	Change	5-Year Growth Rate	Profit Margin	Return On Assets	Return On Common Equity	Debt Equity Ratio	Dividend Yield	Market Value
Company and Market		%	-	-	$	%	%	%	%	%	%	%	$Mil

Oil and Natural Gas Producers

Company and Market		Price to Equity	Current	5-Year Average	Amount	Change	Growth Rate	Profit Margin	Return On Assets	Return On Common Equity	Debt Equity Ratio	Dividend Yield	Market Value
Adobe Oil Gas	A	155	13.5	19.2	1.45q	- 3	18	14.4	6.0	11.7	39	1.2	314
Argo Pet	A	243	NE	65.6	- .27q	NE	- 91	-10.7	NE	NE	263	.0	59
Asamera Inc	A	329	NE	29.4	- .70q	NE	- 49	- 4.8	NE	NE	39	1.4	305
Barnwell Indus	A	NS	7.1	31.6	1.37q	10	69	11.7	6.6	NS	- 560	2.1	14
Baruch-Foster	A	238	15.6	13.5	.77f	- 17	24	15.4	7.5	15.6	79	.0a	29
Buttes Gas Oil	N	84	NE	10.4	- .84f	-100	- 23	- 2.6	1.1	10.7	685	.0	31
Cdn Occid Pet	A	155	NA	9.9	1.91q	46	38	16.8	5.9	11.8	36	NA	713
Cdn Pac Enter	N	89	NA	17.1	.66q	12	- 19	.7	.5	2.1	133	NA	2,636
Coastal Corp	N	134	5.7	7.0	5.71q	88	8	1.5	2.0	12.5	188	1.2	671
Consol O & G	A	576	NE	NM	- .17f	NE	- 5	4.2	.9	10.3	880	.0	93
Crystal Oil	A	510	NE	NM	- .65q	NE	- 60	- 4.7	NE	NE	790	3.6	209
Damson Oil	A	63	15.2	66.4	.42q	- 32	38	10.2	2.9	10.9	156	.0	48
Dome Petrol	A	85	NA	12.8	- 4.92q	NE	- 89	42.6	NE	NE	593	NA	637
Dorchstr Gas	A	228	55.3	12.2	.38s	- 60	- 9	1.3	3.4	11.1	90	.8	365
Dyco Petroleum	N	148	10.0	14.3	1.28q	- 32	21	18.1	4.3	14.4	183	2.2	94
Ensource Inc	N	119	27.5	92.4	.10f	233	- 22	7.2	1.6	4.3	71	.0	100
Enstar Cp	N	120	15.5	8.4	1.05f	- 43	10	8.6	5.7	14.1	91	2.6	251
Equity Oil	O	273	15.8	31.6	.49q	40	- 4	25.9	8.9	12.9	0	2.6	91
Felmont Oil	A	317	21.2	19.3	1.50q	4	16	18.8	8.9	13.4	8	.3	331
Forest Oil Corp	O	185	24.6	41.2	1.03q	- 46	11	5.5	1.4	7.9	348	3.9	162

		Relative Price			Earnings Per Share			Other					
Company and Market		Price to Equity	P/E Ratio Current	5-Year Average	Latest 12 Months Amount	Change	5-Year Growth Rate	Profit Margin	Return On Assets	Return On Common Equity	Debt Equity Ratio	Dividend Yield	Market Value
		%	-	-	$	%	%	%	%	%	%	%	$Mil
Gulf Appld Tech	O	68	NE	12.9	-.66f	-100	-20	-13.2	NE	NE	11	2.5	27
Hamilton Oil	O	122	20.5	15.9	.84f	68	-15	9.0	2.5	4.7	34	.6	234
Inexco Oil	N	109	20.8	19.5	.56q	-3	-2	7.2	1.5	4.8	150	1.2	285
MAPCO	N	119	12.1	11.0	2.20q	-9	-8	2.4	3.1	7.9	80	3.8	767
May Petrol	O	59	NE	44.1	-1.41q	NE	-46	-36.4	.5	1.3	98	.0	57
Maynard Oil	O	96	NE	24.3	-.50q	NE	-44	-12.5	NE	NE	32	.0	33
MCO Holding	A	107	11.8	10.7	1.09q	-6	14	6.9	1.8	10.9	267	.0	83
Mitchell Energy	A	176	12.8	11.7	1.48q	-15	7	7.8	3.7	14.0	166	1.3	911
N Cdn Oils	A	89	NA	11.2	2.81f	36	50	42.3	7.3	16.4	86	NA	90
Numac O & G	A	253	NA	42.7	.58f	263	-6	27.8	1.5	3.5	69	NA	273
Occidental Pet	★N	107	14.6	15.8	2.01q	NE	-14	2.4	1.0	5.9	164	8.5	2,936
Page Pete	A	NS	NM	NC	-7.58f	NE	-121	-57.3	NE	NE	-230	.0	3
Pauley Petroleum	O	141	2.4	16.6	4.07s	NE	117	4.2	9.6	42.1	200	.0	29
Petro-Lewis	A	53	NE	15.2	-.25n	-100	-1	9.2	2.8	19.5	428	.0a	91
Prairie Oil Roy	A	154	NA	10.6	3.24f	11	58	46.0	11.2	18.3	0	NA	48
Presidio Oil	A	128	23.9	NM	.22n	144	68	12.5	2.7	4.0	23	.0	29
Ranger Oil	N	199	11.5	26.9	.61f	33	81	34.4	6.8	15.7	31	.0	484
Scurry Rainbow	A	145	NA	11.0	1.67s	17	34	28.5	10.6	18.9	6	NA	172
Southland Roy	N	586	13.1	27.9	1.09q	68	-2	15.6	4.2	26.9	395	.6	619
Statex Pet	A	150	NE	22.8	-.47s	NE	-30	-13.8	NE	NE	15	.0	31
Summit En	A	77	55.2	NM	.12s	-66	-19	13.9	3.9	4.9	0	.0	17
Sundance Oil	A	NS	NM	77.1	.07q	NE	-3	.9	.5	NS	-561	.0	85
Superior Oil	★N	235	24.9	16.0	1.71q	34	0	9.6	4.5	9.7	55	.5	5,408
Tesoro Petrol	N	56	7.3	5.7	2.40s	-10	-1	1.7	4.8	11.2	25	2.3	242
Tex Am Energy	A	141	8.0	12.7	.97q	59	14	3.2	3.5	17.1	234	.0a	53
Tex Oil & Gas	★N	416	15.4	14.4	1.53s	18	28	16.1	10.1	24.8	57	.8	4,960
Tex Pacific	N	922	18.3	20.6	1.99q	54	13	59.9	40.9	51.8	0	1.1	151
Tipperary Cp	O	72	NE	NM	-.06s	NE	-22	.2	.1	.1	77	.0a	56
Tosco Corp	N	15	NE	15.7	-4.62f	-100	-32	-3.3	.8	3.6	143	.0	43
Total Petro NA	A	129	NE	16.9	-.23q	NE	-56	-1.5	NE	NE	185	2.4	218
Towner Pete	A	36	NE	36.8	-2.75n	NC	-105	1.8	.6	3.2	221	.0	17
Transcont Engy	A	35	NE	12.4	-4.10q	NE	-80	-66.6	NE	NE	364	.0	6
Univ Rsourcs	A	71	NE	17.2	-.77q	-100	-31	-16.1	NE	NE	96	.0	66
Wichita Indus	A	190	NE	40.4	-.22f	NE	-28	-7.3	NE	NE	90	.0a	14
Wilshire Oil	N	415	29.3	34.9	.29q	-6	21	20.8	1.9	12.5	149	1.1	71
Wiser Oil	O	219	16.9	14.1	1.26q	-8	-2	21.8	11.1	13.7	0	4.1	193
Woods Petrol	N	214	19.4	19.4	1.19q	-36	-5	19.0	6.1	10.7	17	3.1	273

Company and Market		Relative Price — Price to Equity %	P/E Ratio Current -	P/E Ratio 5-Year Average -	Earnings Per Share — Latest 12 Months Amount $	Earnings Per Share — Latest 12 Months Change %	5-Year Growth Rate %	Profit Margin %	Return On Assets %	Return On Common Equity %	Debt Equity Ratio %	Dividend Yield %	Market Value $Mil
Oil Refineries and Marketing Companies													
Adam Rsc En	A	NS	12.0	13.0	.25q	0	27	2.3	11.2	NS	- 152	.0	20
Amerada Hess	★N	89	11.4	9.0	2.43f	46	- 8	2.4	2.3	5.4	69	4.0	2,290
Am Petrofina	A	111	10.0	7.8	6.02q	68	- 2	2.7	4.0	9.5	51	5.3	652
Ashland Oil	N	63	8.5	10.9	2.91s	- 35	- 8	1.2	2.4	8.9	62	6.4	689
Atlantic Rchfld	★N	112	7.4	7.5	6.03f	- 9	13	6.0	7.7	17.1	40	6.7	11,029
British Petrol	N	84	9.2	6.3	2.80n	- 20	- 2	2.7	2.7	8.3	44	6.5	11,751
Charter Co	N	10	1.3	9.0	1.80f	112	- 16	.9	1.8	5.7	72	42.1	39
Crown Ctrl Ptrl	A	60	12.5	27.8	1.46q	NE	- 24	.2	.6	2.1	89	4.4	114
Diamond Shmrk	N	88	12.0	10.5	1.59q	- 19	- 11	2.8	1.9	4.2	67	9.2	2,420
Exxon	★N	116	6.4	5.9	6.31q	24	8	5.6	7.9	16.9	16	8.4	34,055
Gulf Canada	A	127	NA	14.0	.98q	- 5	- 4	4.4	4.3	9.3	36	NA	2,986
Holly Corp	A	134	31.6	12.5	.36s	- 64	- 6	1.5	3.7	9.4	3	2.1	93
Husky Oil Ltd	A	129	NA	20.6	.45f	200	- 14	3.0	2.0	8.9	186	NA	691
Imperial Oil	A	105	NA	10.3	2.30q	24	- 8	3.8	4.1	7.8	28	NA	4,407
Kerr-McGee	N	96	11.9	10.3	2.55q	- 28	- 1	3.4	6.0	13.6	49	3.6	1,603
Mobil Corp	★N	79	7.3	6.5	3.70f	27	- 1	2.8	4.3	10.8	39	8.1	10,984
Murphy Oil	N	124	9.4	8.3	3.56q	- 14	13	5.6	4.7	13.4	27	3.0	1,220
Pacific Rscs	N	112	6.4	11.3	1.28n	45	12	.8	1.8	11.3	176	.0a	115
Pennzoil Co	★N	136	9.3	9.7	3.50q	- 3	- 3	7.1	4.6	13.4	92	6.8	1,672
Phibro Salomon	★N	170	8.6	8.1	3.12q	14	17	1.6	1.1	21.0	31	2.0	3,809
Phillips Petrol	★N	88	7.5	7.4	4.71f	11	- 3	4.8	5.5	11.7	36	6.8	5,439
Quaker St Oil	N	130	10.5	11.1	1.60q	- 10	6	4.1	6.6	12.9	32	5.1	335
Royal Dutch	★N	78	5.9	4.3	8.06f	- 13	4	99.8	12.8	13.2	0	5.9	12,799
Shell Oil Co	★N	152	10.1	7.9	5.53q	14	13	8.3	7.4	14.4	23	3.6	17,309
Shell Transport	N	87	7.0	6.0	4.90s	- 33	2	99.5	10.9	11.3	0	5.8	9,529
Std Oil Cal	★N	84	7.4	6.7	4.65f	15	2	5.8	6.6	11.3	13	6.9	11,846
Std Oil Ind	★N	131	8.7	8.4	6.39f	2	11	7.0	7.2	15.0	31	5.4	16,347
Std Oil Ohio	★N	64	5.9	6.8	7.15q	- 1	17	14.9	10.6	21.4	47	6.2	10,463
Sun Co Inc	★N	115	12.0	7.8	4.24q	2	- 3	2.9	4.5	10.5	41	4.5	5,884
Texaco Canada	A	186	NA	10.2	3.09q	37	14	6.0	10.5	18.9	5	NA	3,382
Texaco	★N	60	7.1	5.5	4.81q	1	- 2	3.1	4.5	8.4	19	8.7	8,022
U S Indus	N	119	16.1	8.0	1.39f	40	- 5	2.9	4.5	7.6	22	3.4	456
Unocal Cp	★N	125	9.5	8.1	3.60f	- 22	14	5.9	9.4	16.9	27	2.9	5,949
Other Mining Including Coal													
Eastern Gas Fl	★N	100	10.2	9.2	2.22q	- 20	9	3.6	3.4	8.2	52	5.7	520
N Amer Coal	★N	168	7.6	8.3	6.10f	- 4	25	4.7	2.2	23.5	687	2.2	148
Northgate Exp	N	62	NA	12.3	- .95f	NE	- 48	-16.0	NE	NE	135	NA	41
Penn Va	O	134	12.1	23.2	3.36q	29	17	29.2	9.0	12.2	21	3.5b	153
Pittston Co	★N	73	NE	17.4	- 1.89f	NE	- 28	- 5.8	NE	NE	45	.0	455
Placer Develop	A	114	NA	13.7	.78q	NE	- 17	11.4	3.4	5.0	19	NA	667
Pyro Engy Cp	N	260	9.3	29.4	.79f	172	32	12.5	3.6	10.6	135	.0	111
US Energy Cp	O	72	15.5	NM	.21f	- 54	63	22.2	2.7	4.6	61	.0	9
Westmoreland Coal	★O	90	12.8	NM	1.91f	68	63	2.8	3.8	7.0	25	1.2	197

Machinery: Metal Working

METAL CUTTING MACHINE TOOLS (SIC 3541): TRENDS AND PROJECTIONS 1972–84 (in millions of dollars except as noted)

Item	1972	1977	1979	1981	1982[1]	1983[2]	Compound annual rate of growth 1972–83	1984[3]	Percent change 1983–84
Industry data									
Value of shipments[4]	1,418.1	2,819.1	4,389.0	5,865.3	4,125.0	2,100.0	3.6	—	—
Value of shipments (1972 $)[4]	1,418.1	1,706.5	2,095.0	2,226.8	1,496.0	734.0	-5.8	833.0	13.5
Total employment (000)	52.5	59.5	69.1	74.3	59.5	45.0	-1.4	47.0	4.4
Production workers (000)	33.4	37.3	45.7	47.9	35.7	24.0	-3.0	26.0	8.3
Average hourly earnings of production workers ($)	4.78	7.08	8.21	9.79	10.51	10.76	7.7	—	—
Capital expenditures	35.2	82.2	147.6	233.2	—	—	—	—	—
Product data									
Value of shipments[5]	1,258.5	2,560.5	4,127.5	5,554.0	3,925.0	1,950.0	4.1	—	—
Value of shipments (1972 $)[5]	1,258.5	1,549.9	1,970.2	2,108.6	1,423.0	682.0	-5.4	767.0	12.5
Product price index (1972 = 100)	100.0	168.4	217.3	280.3	299.5	307.0	10.7	—	—
Quantity shipped (units over $2,500 each)[4]	41,829.0	59,500.0	59,453.0	59,260.0	35,535.0	18,000.0	-7.4	20,500.0	13.9
Trade									
Value of exports	189.8	317.7	550.3	978.9	654.1	400.0	7.0	425.0	6.3
Value of imports	104.6	383.3	984.6	1,497.9	1,271.3	900.0	21.6	1,080.0	20.0
Export/shipments ratio	0.151	0.124	0.133	0.176	0.166	0.205	—	—	—
Import/new supply ratio[6]	0.077	0.130	0.193	0.212	0.244	0.315	—	—	—

[1] Estimated except for product price index, exports, and imports.
[2] Estimated.
[3] Forecast.
[4] Value of all products and services sold by industry SIC 3541.
[5] Value of shipments of metal-cutting machine tools products produced by all industries.
[6] New supply is the sum of product shipments plus imports.

Source: Bureau of the Census and Bureau of Industrial Economics. Estimates and forecasts by the Bureau of Industrial Economics.

Source: *U.S. Industrial Outlook 1984*, U.S. Department of Commerce.

METAL FORMING MACHINE TOOLS (SIC 3542): TRENDS AND PROJECTIONS 1972–84 (in millions of dollars except as noted)

Item	1972	1977	1979	1981	1982[1]	1983[2]	Compound annual rate of growth 1972–83	1984[3]	Percent change 1983–84
Industry data									
Value of shipments[4]	696.3	1,130.6	1,663.5	1,615.7	1,200.0	800.0	1.3	—	—
Value of shipments (1972 $)[4]	696.3	625.3	703.1	542.7	375.0	239.0	–9.3	254.0	6.3
Total employment (000)	24.1	23.7	27.0	24.0	20.6	16.5	–3.4	17.5	6.1
Production workers (000)	16.6	16.1	18.7	16.0	12.5	9.5	–4.9	10.5	10.5
Average hourly earnings of production workers ($)	4.72	6.69	8.14	9.57	10.30	10.66	7.7	—	—
Capital expenditures	17.5	24.7	58.1	63.0	—	—	—	—	—
Product data									
Value of shipments[5]	670.1	1,114.7	1,634.8	1,652.1	1,200.0	775.0	1.3	247.0	6.5
Value of shipments (1972 $)[5]	670.1	616.5	691.0	555.0	375.0	232.0	–9.2	—	—
Product price index (1972 = 100)	100.0	184.8	236.5	298.9	318.0	330.5	11.5	—	—
Quantity shipped (units over $2,500 each)[2]	21,803.0	32,770.0	30,133.0	22,114.0	16,561.0	13,500.0	–4.3	14,850.0	10.0
Trade									
Value of exports	123.6	207.1	343.3	471.4	371.9	250.0	6.6	270.0	8.0
Value of imports	35.1	93.0	236.4	224.3	228.5	290.0	21.2	335.0	15.5
Export/shipments ratio	0.184	0.186	0.210	0.285	0.309	0.322	—	—	—
Import/new supply ratio[6]	0.040	0.056	0.093	0.083	0.159	0.272	—	—	—

[1] Estimated except for product price index, exports, and imports.
[2] Estimated.
[3] Forecast.
[4] Value of all products and services sold by industry SIC 3542.
[5] Value of shipments of metal-forming machine tools products produced by all industries.
[6] New supply is the sum of product shipments plus imports.

Source: Bureau of the Census and Bureau of Industrial Economics. Estimates and forecasts by the Bureau of Industrial Economics.

Source: *U.S. Industrial Outlook 1984*, U.S. Department of Commerce.

Company and Market	Relative Price			Earnings Per Share			Other					
	Price to Equity	P/E Ratio		Latest 12 Months		5-Year Growth Rate	Profit Margin	Return On Assets	Return On Common Equity	Debt Equity Ratio	Dividend Yield	Market Value
		Current	5-Year Average	Amount	Change							
	%	-	-	$	%	%	%	%	%	%	%	$Mil

Machine Tools and Accessories

Company and Market	Price to Equity	Current	5-Year Average	Amount	Change	5-Year Growth Rate	Profit Margin	Return On Assets	Return On Common Equity	Debt Equity Ratio	Dividend Yield	Market Value
Acme-Clevelnd ★N	88	NE	6.2	-2.19q	-100	-29	-7.4	NE	NE	30	1.9b	100
Aro Corp N	93	23.8	18.5	.84f	190	-15	2.4	2.7	3.8	18	5.0	48
Barden Corp O	110	11.6	7.5	2.03q	-41	-4	6.4	6.7	8.6	7	4.3	42
Brenco Inc O	163	NE	53.8	-.21f	-100	-22	-13.5	NE	NE	0	3.0	79
Brown & Shrpe ★N	62	NE	8.0	-.31f	NE	-27	-.8	NE	NE	60	1.5	43
Chi Pneu Tool ★N	98	25.8	10.3	.92q	NE	-29	-2.7	NE	NE	44	.0	117
Cinn Milacron ★N	197	NE	14.4	-.16q	-100	-23	-1.8	NE	NE	33	2.8	585
Cross Trecker ★O	121	NE	22.7	-.12s	-100	-13	2.5	1.3	1.8	6	3.9	251
Ex-Cell-O ★N	106	9.7	7.7	3.29q	-11	2	4.9	6.8	10.9	12	5.0	454
Fedl-Mogul N	166	12.9	8.6	2.74n	14	0	3.9	5.1	10.5	53	4.0	466
Gleason Cp N	89	NE	6.8	-.43q	NE	-31	-2.4	NE	NE	30	.0	82
Ill Tool Wk N	188	13.4	9.6	1.72f	8	2	8.6	9.9	13.0	3	2.8	574
Lodge & Ship A	84	NE	9.5	-.68f	NE	-31	-15.6	NE	NE	35	.0	12
LSB Ind Inc A	77	NE	8.0	-1.54f	NE	-60	-10.0	NE	NE	837	.0	7
Monarch Mach ★N	90	NM	46.5	.09q	-92	-16	.9	.6	.7	0	4.6	63
New Hamp Ball A	129	12.7	10.5	2.08s	-23	7	7.4	8.8	12.0	16	3.0	44
Omark Ind N	117	12.6	10.7	1.83n	158	-9	2.7	2.8	4.9	36	4.5	163
Ransburg Corp A	107	NE	52.9	-.41q	-100	-21	.6	.5	.8	7	5.5	104
Regal-Beloit A	233	18.2	11.0	.83f	69	-3	5.7	7.7	12.8	34	3.7	46
Spectra-Phys N	158	40.7	65.7	.59s	1375	-20	.8	.8	1.2	38	.0	141
Timken Co ★N	80	32.9	NM	1.61q	NE	-22	.1	.0	.1	6	3.4	621
Wedco Inc A	152	NE	13.3	-.03s	NC	34	-5.9	NE	NE	43	.0	4

Electronic Components and Equipment

ELECTRONIC COMPONENTS (SIC 367): TRENDS AND PROJECTIONS 1972–84 (in millions of dollars except as noted)

Item	1972	1977	1979	1981	1982[1]	1983[2]	Compound annual rate of growth 1972–83	1984[3]	Percent change 1983–84
Industry data									
Value of shipments[4]	8,826	15,390	22,708	30,422	32,124	36,729	13.8	42,256	15.0
Value of shipments (1972$)[4]	8,826	13,814	20,127	25,377	26,965	31,048	12.1	36,332	17.0
Total employment (000)	336	374	468	504	509	518	4.0	534	3.1
Production workers (000)	234	258	325	326	321	329	3.1	337	2.4
Average hourly earnings of production workers ($)	3.38	4.38	5.48	6.92	7.49	8.02	8.2	—	—
Capital expenditures	344	783	1591	2459	2493	2723	20.7	—	—
Product data									
Value of shipments[5]	8,561	14,275	21,649	29,280	31,006	35,538	13.8	41,148	15.8
Value of shipments (1972$)[5]	8,561	12,690	18,794	23,317	25,061	29,410	11.2	34,314	16.7
Product price index (1972 = 100)[6]	100.0	116.3	132.5	119.9	119.1	118.3	1.5	—	—
Trade									
Value of exports	957	2,682	3,905	5,218	5,487	5,851	17.9	6,749	15.3
Value of imports	520	2,108	3,562	4,933	5,686	6,770	26.3	8,375	23.7
Export/shipments ratio	0.112	0.188	0.180	0.178	0.177	0.165	—	—	—
Import/new supply ratio[7]	0.057	0.124	0.141	0.144	0.155	0.160	—	—	—

[1] Estimated except for product price index, exports, and imports.
[2] Estimated.
[3] Forecast.
[4] Value of all products and services sold by industry SIC 367
[5] Value of shipments of electronic components produced by all industries.
[6] Developed by the Office of Research, Analysis, and Statistics, BIE.
[7] New supply is the sum of product shipments plus imports.

Source: Bureau of the Census and Bureau of Industrial Economics. Estimates & forecasts by the Bureau of Industrial Economics

Source: *U.S. Industrial Outlook 1984*, U.S. Department of Commerce.

RADIO AND TV COMMUNICATION EQUIPMENT (SIC 3662): TRENDS AND PROJECTIONS 1972–84 (in millions of dollars except as noted)

Item	1972	1977	1979	1981	1982[1]	1983[2]	Compound annual rate of growth 1972–83	1984[3]	Percent change 1983–84
Industry data									
Value of shipments[4]	9,140.2	14,886.0	19,623.5	27,054.2	30,800.0	35,100.0	13.0	—	—
Value of shipments (1972 $)[4]	9,140.2	11,285.8	14,493.0	17,728.8	18,500.0	20,100.0	7.4	22,000.0	9.5
Total employment (000)	319.2	334.0	386.3	426.9	453.1	471.4	3.6	490.0	3.9
Production workers (000)	161.9	172.4	198.9	217.7	224.8	229.7	3.2	235.0	2.3
Average hourly earnings of production workers ($)	4.51	6.27	7.08	8.76	9.74	10.76	8.2	—	—
Capital expenditures	212.2	471.4	808.4	1373.7	—	—	—	—	—
Product data									
Value of shipments[5]	8,376.6	14,051.0	18,582.0	26,709.6	30,100.0	34,300.0	13.7	—	—
Value of shipments (1972 $)[5]	8,376.6	10,652.8	13,723.8	17,503.0	18,100.0	19,600.0	8.0	21,000.0	7.1
Product price index (1972 = 100)[6]	100.0	131.9	135.4	152.6	166.5	178.0	5.4	—	—
Trade									
Value of exports	609.0	1,400.0	1,781.0	2,305.0	2,402.0	2,510.0	13.7	2,600.0	3.6
Value of imports	256.0	1,207.0	941.0	1,741.0	2,022.0	2,040.0	20.8	2,100.0	2.9
Export/shipments ratio	0.073	0.100	0.096	0.087	0.087	0.073		—	
Import/new supply ratio[7]	0.030	0.079	0.048	0.062	0.063	0.056			

[1] Estimated except for product price index, exports, and imports.
[2] Estimated.
[3] Forecast.
[4] Value of all products and services sold by industry SIC 3662.
[5] Value of shipments of radio and TV communication equipment products produced by all industries.
[6] Developed by the Office of Research, Analysis, and Statistics, BIE.
[7] New supply is the sum of product shipments plus imports.
Source: Bureau of the Census and Bureau of Industrial Economics. Estimates and forecasts by the Bureau of Industrial Economics.

Source: *U.S. Industrial Outlook 1984*, U.S. Department of Commerce.

		Relative Price		Earnings Per Share			Other					
		Price to Equity	P/E Ratio		Latest 12 Months		5-Year Growth	Profit	Return On Assets	Return On Common Equity	Debt Equity Ratio	Dividend Yield	Market Value
Company and Market		Equity	Current	Average	Amount	Change	Rate	Margin	On Assets	Equity	Ratio	Yield	Value
		%	-	-	$	%	%	%	%	%	%	%	$Mil

Electronic Equipment Manufacturers

Company and Market		Price to Equity	Current	Average	Amount	Change	Rate	Margin	On Assets	Equity	Ratio	Yield	Value
Adams Russell	A	245	15.6	18.6	1.16s	20	35	7.2	6.2	14.8	86	.6	110
Adv Micro Dev	★N	925	39.0	32.6	.82n	141	28	5.9	6.8	11.5	20	.0	1,725
Alpha Indus	A	211	17.4	18.8	.79f	5	25	9.3	9.1	11.4	10	.4	97
Am Precision	A	268	26.9	8.8	.84f	-28	5	5.3	7.7	9.6	1	1.2	42
Analog Devices	N	407	22.7	26.5	1.08s	116	51	8.6	8.3	12.2	18	.0	615
Anaren Micrwve	O	322	21.2	32.4	.43n	30	66	6.8	6.1	12.6	59	.0	39
Andrew Corp	O	294	16.0	18.8	1.91s	20	48	10.2	11.6	17.1	15	.0	305
Anthem Elects	A	497	13.1	16.7	.83f	246	26	5.8	7.5	11.1	20	.4	78
Applied Mater	O	323	34.3	37.7	.91q	NE	-19	2.9	2.7	5.0	26	.0	208
ArgoSysts Inc	O	418	22.4	33.0	.78s	15	85	10.4	10.0	16.7	0	.0	113
Augat	N	303	19.5	19.0	1.60q	31	9	11.6	10.8	13.8	5	1.0	515
Avantek Inc	O	459	34.5	29.2	.67q	8	35	10.0	10.0	12.6	2	.0	432
Avnet Inc	N	223	18.1	14.5	1.88s	29	3	4.3	7.1	9.5	3	1.5	1,193
AVX Corp	N	226	21.7	21.1	.98f	128	-11	5.4	2.1	4.6	98	1.5	188
Aydin Cp	N	211	9.6	14.0	2.93f	34	88	9.2	10.0	22.5	9	.0	131
Barnes Engin	A	NS	NE	24.5	-1.11s	NE	-102	-19.2	NE	NE	-341	.0	5
Birdview Satellite	O	3875	96.9	NM	.02f	NE	49	.9	NE	NE	175	.0	15
BMC Ind Inc	N	137	10.3	10.4	1.66f	25	14	5.0	4.4	8.3	25	2.8	88
Burr-Brown	O	259	22.2	23.9	.99q	NC	18	6.5	5.9	10.3	19	.0	109
Calif Microwv	O	284	17.3	51.5	.71n	13	32	5.3	9.7	15.4	7	.0	100
Cetec Corp	A	119	11.4	11.8	.71q	73	10	1.9	4.7	9.3	31	2.5	18
Chyron Cp	A	500	21.3	17.2	.80n	29	61	25.4	17.7	20.7	0	.4	104
Cognitronics	A	164	13.5	19.3	.38q	15	25	6.5	4.9	8.2	0	.0	11
Cohu Inc	A	120	10.3	10.9	.78q	47	16	6.1	8.1	10.3	0	2.5	14
Comdial Cp	O	128	NE	NM	-1.03q	-100	-2	.7	.8	1.4	5	.0	101
Commun Ind	O	308	17.5	20.4	1.23q	16	36	16.8	13.1	16.7	5	1.6	220
Comtech Inc	O	72	20.8	18.3	.09q	-79	33	3.8	3.3	14.0	197	.0	9
CTS Corp	N	98	16.2	13.8	1.61f	-10	-6	3.0	4.4	5.9	4	3.8	150
Cubic Corp	A	166	8.4	9.1	2.27s	5	30	6.9	10.6	20.7	28	2.1	151
Dale Electronic	A	208	7.5	8.0	2.61q	139	31	8.3	12.2	23.7	49	1.6	70
Designatronics	A	112	9.2	8.3	.49s	-6	49	6.9	10.3	13.4	7	.0a	10
Digital Switch	O	254	20.4	45.3	1.15q	NC	77	19.5	4.5	5.6	8	.0	509
Diodes Inc	A	473	13.1	35.0	.43n	72	66	7.6	12.8	22.7	0	.0	10
Drexler Technlgy	O	182	63.2	43.8	.17f	-55	-6	4.1	5.7	6.6	0	.0	45
E Systems	N	347	16.3	15.9	1.73q	31	52	6.0	13.5	20.9	3	1.8	825
EDO Cp	N	209	12.6	10.4	1.25q	20	82	9.1	6.7	16.1	7	1.5	132
EECO Inc	A	181	24.4	20.4	.59q	NE	-14	.3	.3	.5	18	2.2	36
EG & G Inc	N	386	17.6	17.0	1.56q	16	27	5.2	13.7	21.7	5	1.5	830
Espey Mfg El	A	326	11.2	11.9	2.54s	40	82	18.0	22.3	25.5	0	1.2	35
Fluke, John	A	237	19.1	18.0	1.33q	28	3	5.6	6.4	11.3	32	.0a	200
Gen Instrument	★N	117	13.9	13.8	1.62n	-50	19	10.5	12.6	17.0	6	2.2	709
GenRad	N	216	19.4	26.7	1.22q	69	10	8.6	8.3	11.5	5	.4	368
Granger Assc	A	452	29.5	26.0	.84s	71	50	12.5	11.2	12.9	1	.0	324
GTI Corp	A	139	NM	NM	.04q	-50	-17	NC	.0	.0	21	.0	13
Gulton Ind	N	114	10.4	8.3	1.51f	9	-5	3.0	5.2	10.1	24	3.8	51
Harris Cp	★N	128	15.6	18.0	1.65n	-4	-5	3.5	3.7	7.9	33	3.4	1,027
Hazeltine Corp	N	362	56.1	17.5	.47q	-39	-6	1.8	2.5	5.8	0	1.2	164
Helionetics Inc	A	508	25.5	43.1	.48q	118	71	12.9	8.6	18.8	12	.0	60
Hi-G Inc	A	306	NE	7.2	-6.91f	NE	-64	-36.5	NE	NE	427	.0	16
Integrated Device	O	NS	NE	NC	-.30n	NC	-18	-14.6	NE	NE	-51	.0	109

Company and Market		Relative Price			Earnings Per Share			Other					
		Price to Equity	P/E Ratio		Latest 12 Months		5-Year Growth Rate	Profit Margin	Return On Assets	Return On Common Equity	Debt Equity Ratio	Dividend Yield	Market Value
			Current	5-Year Average	Amount	Change							
		%	-	-	$	%	%	%	%	%	%	%	$Mil
Intel Corp	★O	314	23.2	32.4	1.36q	258	10	10.3	6.9	10.4	11	.0	3,519
Intl Rectifier	N	506	58.8	9.8	.37n	NE	-27	-3.2	NE	NE	140	.0	152
Jetronic Ind	A	117	15.4	12.2	.35f	52	-8	1.6	1.7	5.3	27	.0a	10
King Radio	A	111	NE	22.0	-.85q	NE	-29	-3.1	NE	NE	15	1.0	52
Koss Cp	O	66	NE	9.4	-.25n	-100	-18	NC	.0	.0	42	.0	7
KRATOS Inc	O	NS	NE	11.2	-8.09f	NE	-52	-15.2	NE	NE	-11	.0	6
Kyocera Cp	N	524	29.0	19.8	1.77s	2	31	12.0	10.5	12.9	0	.6	3,546
La Pointe Inds	A	116	18.2	43.9	.22s	NC	25	1.2	1.7	4.2	33	.0	3
Loral Corp	N	293	17.2	15.5	1.45f	25	16	8.1	8.2	15.2	15	1.8	573
LSI Logic	O	NS	25.5	55.1	.54q	NE	70	28.7	NE	NE	-98	.0	354
Lynch Com Sy	A	160	21.0	25.8	.78q	66	-3	3.4	3.8	7.0	50	.6	46
M/A - Com	★N	210	25.2	25.2	.76q	-22	17	4.9	4.8	8.0	33	1.2	824
Marshall Ind	A	485	9.5	20.0	2.49n	NE	63	1.1	2.7	11.5	34	.0	82
Materials Rsh	A	196	NE	37.1	-.78q	-100	-36	-5.3	NE	NE	13	.7	68
Matsushita Elec	N	157	14.0	11.1	4.90f	25	12	4.6	5.3	11.4	3	.6	10,684
Micro Mask	O	161	18.1	14.7	.69s	-21	-3	6.2	7.7	10.7	14	.0a	24
Millicom Inc	O	600	NE	NC	-.61q	NE	-101	-20.0	NE	NE	88	.0	49
Mitel Cp	N	92	NA	47.7	-.51f	-100	-16	-5.7	NE	NE	66	NA	269
Molex Inc	O	658	21.8	16.4	1.79n	77	32	12.5	13.1	18.6	5	.1	779
MSI Data	A	142	9.1	11.7	1.63f	18	4	6.7	9.9	13.1	2	2.7	37
Natl Semicon	★N	273	26.0	14.0	.49n	NE	-15	-1.4	NE	NE	44	.0	1,088
Northn Telecom	★N	121	16.7	13.3	2.05f	63	27	6.9	6.2	15.1	24	1.2	3,856
Oak Ind	N	71	NE	30.0	-9.44q	NE	-86	-39.0	NE	NE	263	.0	61
Paradyne Cp	N	170	NM	52.2	.04q	-97	3	1.8	1.4	1.9	15	.0	340
Park Electro	N	433	19.4	18.0	1.32n	140	74	3.0	6.2	10.7	14	.0	88
Penril Corp	A	130	12.6	11.3	1.04n	55	-3	3.6	3.4	7.0	78	1.5	27
Pico Prods	A	110	35.2	28.1	.22n	-24	28	7.8	3.2	3.7	7	.0	27
Plantronics	N	126	15.0	15.1	1.08n	-23	-3	6.4	6.2	8.7	14	1.0	106
Plessey Co Ltd	N	351	15.6	14.2	1.86n	13	20	7.7	8.4	20.3	8	3.2	2,125
Porta Syst	A	313	NM	36.6	.07q	-85	-8	2.6	2.0	3.5	0	.0	53
Radiation Syst	O	231	12.6	16.2	.91n	-4	40	15.8	10.9	15.6	9	.0	52
Ragen Cp	O	190	NM	53.4	.03q	-50	-25	1.1	1.0	2.5	78	.0	23
Ramtek Corp	O	59	NE	29.3	-.21s	-100	-18	1.9	1.8	2.3	8	.0	20
REDM Ind Inc	A	144	8.0	7.4	1.58q	15	23	6.4	10.4	15.3	17	.0	18
Regency Electro	O	182	9.3	13.5	.82n	67	15	8.0	11.9	15.6	5	2.6	82
RMS	A	104	NE	20.7	-.07f	NE	-20	-.5	NE	NE	32	.0	8
Robinson Nugent	O	304	17.3	20.1	.91n	98	16	8.0	9.8	14.8	20	.4	107
Rogers Corp	A	215	15.1	40.5	1.78q	334	5	4.3	6.0	12.9	51	.4	78
Sanders Assoc	N	285	18.1	17.1	2.38n	25	23	6.4	7.9	13.2	4	1.0	817
Sci-Atlanta	★N	122	16.1	NM	.56n	NE	-2	.1	.1	.2	6	1.3	210
Scope Inc	O	117	34.1	66.9	.11q	NE	-73	.9	1.4	2.6	28	.0	7
Seeq Technology	O	NS	NE	NC	-4.28s	NC	-51	-00.0	NE	NE	-70	.0	136
Semtech Cp	A	82	NE	56.1	-.72q	-100	-50	-6.1	NE	NE	3	.0a	8
Sensormatic Elec	O	167	9.7	26.2	.81n	-5	56	26.6	11.0	20.0	47	.6	219
Servo Cp Am	A	114	11.7	13.0	.75s	436	69	2.5	3.9	8.2	29	.0	6
SFE Tech	O	211	19.2	17.2	.82s	49	31	6.7	5.2	7.5	23	.6b	93
Silicon Gen	O	789	25.0	21.3	.53s	104	40	15.2	17.1	23.5	6	.0	152
Silicon Systs	O	589	NE	52.2	-.02q	NE	-48	-11.0	NE	NE	21	.0	130
Siliconix Inc	O	237	10.6	83.6	1.54q	1000	19	11.9	13.8	19.9	0	.0	99
Siltec Cp	O	128	31.7	NM	.30q	NE	-20	2.5	2.2	4.2	36	.0	33
Solitron Device	A	113	24.5	18.3	.25n	NE	-15	-5.5	NE	NE	65	.0	29

(Continued)

Company and Market		Price to Equity %	P/E Ratio Current -	P/E Ratio 5-Year Average -	Latest 12 Months Amount $	Latest 12 Months Change %	5-Year Growth Rate %	Profit Margin %	Return On Assets %	Return On Common Equity %	Debt Equity Ratio %	Dividend Yield %	Market Value $Mil
			Relative Price		**Earnings Per Share**				**Other**				

Electronic Equipment Manufacturers

Company and Market		Price to Equity	P/E Current	P/E 5-Yr Avg	Amount	Change	5-Yr Growth	Profit Margin	Return On Assets	Return On Common Equity	Debt Equity Ratio	Dividend Yield	Market Value
Spectrum Control	O	288	20.0	22.9	.35q	3	24	10.2	6.9	14.0	47	.7	37
Std Microsystems	O	305	31.3	28.8	.74f	111	24	17.3	9.4	9.4	6	.0	248
Sterling Extr	A	175	7.5	8.8	1.26s	152	79	3.5	3.2	8.3	69	.0	6
Sun Electric	N	90	NE	10.8	-.46s	NE	-33	-2.0	NE	NE	51	.0	73
Sunair Electron	A	194	13.1	11.2	.60s	7	11	19.9	16.2	17.7	0	3.0	38
T-BAR Inc	A	270	29.2	36.8	.33q	1000	-10	2.3	1.4	3.4	58	.0a	37
TDK Cp	N	319	18.9	14.8	2.10f	-3	17	7.8	10.0	17.1	1	.6	2,175
Tech Sym	A	220	13.9	17.1	1.14q	34	103	9.5	10.6	14.2	12	.0	96
Technicom Intl	A	878	15.3	51.6	.27q	35	93	4.9	5.6	8.5	0	.0	77
Technitrol	A	142	6.4	5.8	1.46f	92	53	9.0	16.1	21.8	9	2.6	10
Technodyne Inc	A	74	4.6	9.3	.57q	NC	-5	5.1	6.2	10.3	37	.0	13
Tech for Commun	O	188	11.5	16.4	.89s	-33	61	19.0	11.5	23.4	6	.0	32
Tektronix Inc	★N	163	17.9	15.4	3.15n	-3	-4	4.1	4.5	7.4	23	1.8	1,082
TeleConcepts	A	76	9.5	69.8	.54q	-36	86	5.8	6.0	9.4	8	.0	16
Telescience Inc	A	623	NE	24.7	-1.78f	-100	-37	-11.3	NE	NE	0	.0	52
Tellabs Inc	O	427	21.1	22.1	1.10q	77	55	15.2	13.9	17.3	9	.0	318
Tex Inst	★N	259	NE	16.1	-3.07q	-100	-30	-3.2	NE	NE	19	1.5	3,115
Texscan Cp	A	171	11.7	23.5	.98n	18	59	10.4	11.0	13.9	2	.0	72
TII Ind	A	198	11.2	12.3	.97n	NE	-2	-9.4	NE	NE	2	.0a	31
Torotel Inc	A	233	NE	52.6	-.15n	NE	-38	-5.5	NE	NE	47	.0	18
Trans-Lux Cp	A	81	7.9	8.0	1.37q	1	10	8.9	7.4	10.9	27	.9	19
Unitrode Cp	N	358	19.9	14.1	1.32q	23	25	10.5	12.0	17.5	14	.8	342
Varian Assoc	N	248	17.5	32.2	2.40s	44	26	5.5	7.0	11.6	12	.6	905
Vicon	A	144	11.7	13.4	.62s	82	7	5.0	5.3	11.1	48	.0	17
Vishay Inter	N	179	11.1	12.6	1.47n	17	13	10.4	8.7	12.5	11	.0a	63
VLSI Tech	O	451	NE	NC	-.21q	NE	0	-18.7	NE	NE	29	.0	289
VMX Inc	O	351	NC	NC	.00f	NC	23	1.0	1.0	.6	0	.0	58
Wavetek	O	94	16.1	20.0	.48s	-11	-2	5.6	5.0	6.4	4	.0	70
Webcor Eltrn	A	68	5.7	19.3	.72n	80	82	4.8	5.0	6.3	0	.0	14
Western Digital	A	423	29.8	NM	.26s	NE	38	4.4	NE	NE	21	.0	119
Wyle Labs	N	146	10.9	15.7	1.33q	NE	-8	2.4	5.1	9.6	36	2.2	105
Xicor Inc	O	464	NE	NC	-.42q	NE	-74	-49.0	NE	NE	32	.0	152

Radio, TV, Phonograph, Stereo

Company and Market		Price to Equity	P/E Current	P/E 5-Yr Avg	Amount	Change	5-Yr Growth	Profit Margin	Return On Assets	Return On Common Equity	Debt Equity Ratio	Dividend Yield	Market Value
Andrea Radio	A	153	12.4	13.5	.88f	2	33	9.1	10.3	11.1	0	6.6	6
Armatron Intl	A	126	9.4	7.7	1.16s	-3	60	6.6	8.8	11.1	12	.0	27
Compact Video	O	86	54.2	22.5	.09n	NE	-30	2.4	1.9	3.8	60	.0	19
Craig Corp	N	59	NE	15.6	-2.62n	NE	-68	-11.8	NE	NE	0	.0	11
Emerson Radio	N	565	16.5	84.2	.53n	NE	34	3.3	6.7	14.4	49	.0	125
Esquire Radio	A	81	6.5	5.3	4.68f	8	16	3.4	8.2	11.7	0	2.4	15
Microdyne	O	107	25.8	26.0	.31q	-26	-11	5.9	3.8	4.1	2	.8	37
Motorola Inc	★N	207	13.9	13.7	2.46q	63	10	5.6	7.5	12.5	13	1.9	4,036
Pioneer Elec	N	211	NM	56.0	.16f	NE	-20	.7	.9	1.6	1	.8	1,251
Sony Corp	N	197	19.9	18.9	.74q	28	0	2.7	3.7	9.7	12	1.1	3,406
Superscope	N	59	NE	NC	-.19f	NE	17	-1.2	NE	NE	1	.0	10
Wells Gard El	A	91	NE	53.4	-.11q	-100	15	.4	25.7	33.8	0	.0	15
Zenith Eltrns	★N	144	10.5	13.5	2.34q	NE	12	3.4	6.3	12.3	28	.0	541

Computing Equipment

COMPUTING EQUIPMENT (SIC 3573): TRENDS AND PROJECTIONS 1972–84 (in millions of dollars except as noted)

Item	1972	1977	1979	1981	1982[1]	1983[2]	Compound annual rate of growth 1972–83	1984[3]	Percent change 1983–84
Industry data									
Value of shipments[4]	6,471	12,924	21,466	32,032	35,700	41,055	—	—	—
Value of shipments (1972 $)[4]	6,471	12,924	21,466	32,032	35,700	41,055	18.3	48,440	18.0
Total employment (000)	145	193	274	321	336	348	8.3	362	4.0
Production workers (000)	65	86	122	136	138	140	7.2	143	2.1
Average hourly earnings of production workers ($)	4.19	5.68	6.34	8.05	8.52	9.15	7.4	—	—
Capital expenditures	213	652	1,317	2,125	—	—	—	—	—
Product data									
Value of shipments[5]	6,108	12,673	20,399	30,157	33,550	38,580	18.2	45,500	17.9
Value of shipments (1972 $)[5]	6,108	12,673	20,399	30,157	33,550	38,580	—	—	—
Product price index (1972 = 100)	100.0	100.0	100.0	100.0	100.0	100.0	—	—	—
Trade									
Value of exports	1,341	3,264	5,389	8,493	8,957	10,300	20.4	12,360	20.0
Value of imports	174[7]	253[7]	969	1,646	2,295	4,100	33.2	6,470	58.0
Export/shipments ratio	0.219	0.258	0.264	0.282	0.267	0.267	—	—	—
Import/new supply ratio[6]	0.028	0.020	0.045	0.052	0.064	0.096	—	—	—

[1] Estimated except for product price index, exports, and imports.
[2] Estimated.
[3] Forecast.
[4] Value of all products and services sold by industry SIC 3573.
[5] Value of shipments of products produced by all industries.
[6] New supply is the sum of product shipments plus imports.
[7] Does not include parts for computer equipment.
Source: Bureau of the Census and Bureau of Industrial Economics. Estimates and forecasts by the Bureau of Industrial Economics.

Source: *U.S. Industrial Outlook 1984*, U.S. Department of Commerce.

Company and Market	Relative Price			Earnings Per Share			Other					
	Price to Equity	P/E Ratio Current	5-Year Average	Latest 12 Months Amount	Change	5-Year Growth Rate	Profit Margin	Return On Assets	Return On Common Equity	Debt Equity Ratio	Dividend Yield	Market Value
	%	-	-	$	%	%	%	%	%	%	%	$Mil

Computers, Subsystems and Peripherals

Company and Market												
Amdahl Corp .... A	124	12.8	45.6	.93q	417	0	5.6	6.0	11.6	15	1.7	461
Analogic Corp .... O	208	13.7	23.1	.95s	25	44	11.7	10.4	13.3	11	.0	237
Andersn Jacob .... A	134	5.7	25.3	1.53n	206	18	3.6	3.5	11.1	52	.0a	23
Apollo Cptr .... O	951	55.1	69.2	.44q	120	60	13.9	11.6	14.6	2	.0	734
Apple Compt .... ★O	449	40.9	53.7	.70s	- 49	57	7.8	13.8	20.3	0	.0	1,701
Applied Magnet .... N	84	11.3	15.3	1.04s	- 12	7	6.6	5.6	7.3	3	.0a	77
Audiotronics Cp .... A	104	NE	12.6	- .01n	-100	- 25	- 1.8	NE	NE	0	2.2b	9
Barry Wright .... N	273	16.2	13.0	1.68q	29	16	8.4	11.8	15.4	2	1.8	244
Beehive Intl .... A	58	NE	NM	- .14s	NE	11	.3	.3	.6	19	.0	9
Burroughs Cp .... ★N	107	11.4	16.9	4.63q	105	- 9	4.5	4.7	8.6	25	4.9	2,391
C COR Electronics .... O	116	14.6	22.7	.60s	- 53	59	13.7	11.8	13.5	2	.0	31
C 3 Inc .... N	178	21.5	24.0	.47f	- 55	27	7.0	11.8	18.6	4	.0	97
Centronics Data .... N	137	NE	11.2	- 3.85s	NE	- 51	-16.2	NE	NE	55	.0	118
Cipher Data .... O	309	29.0	32.8	.75n	70	114	6.8	5.0	5.6	0	.0	286
Compaq Cptr .... O	200	54.8	90.4	.13f	NC	NC	4.2	3.9	5.2	0	.0	181
Compucorp .... O	93	NE	NM	- 1.12q	-100	- 65	-12.0	6.8	12.0	37	.0	13
Compuscan Inc .... O	199	20.4	71.8	.19n	0	29	5.6	6.5	8.3	1	.0	24
Comp & Commun .... O	231	NE	18.2	- 2.95q	-100	- 73	-30.5	NE	NE	3	.0	112
Comp Automation .... O	40	NE	13.6	- 2.93n	-100	- 41	- .8	NE	NE	7	.0	12
Comp Consoles .... A	235	15.2	19.2	1.17q	225	63	10.0	11.2	18.0	17	.0	197
Cptr Memories .... O	128	42.9	NM	.14f	17	110	3.0	2.3	2.7	0	.0	67
Comp Prods .... O	349	20.3	20.4	.77q	51	39	9.9	11.9	15.7	10	.0	142
Computervision .... ★N	507	29.4	26.4	1.34q	22	37	8.8	10.1	16.0	15	.0	1,113
Control Data .... ★N	68	7.8	8.3	4.14q	4	8	3.5	1.8	8.9	258	2.0	1,241
Convergent Tech .... O	223	34.4	55.5	.40f	- 5	69	9.1	5.8	6.7	0	.0	499
Corvus Systs .... O	98	NC	55.6	.00n	-100	20	9.2	9.1	10.5	1	.0	41
Cray Research .... N	419	28.0	27.0	1.77f	28	107	15.4	9.4	15.1	22	.0	721
Data General .... ★N	234	33.1	18.4	1.46s	175	- 12	2.8	2.7	4.9	30	.0	1,100
Data Switch Cp .... O	931	24.3	33.1	.72q	53	121	16.9	15.1	21.2	4	.0	151
Datapoint Cp .... ★N	129	16.5	75.9	1.28n	266	- 9	1.5	1.4	2.5	37	.0	427
Dataproducts .... A	203	15.2	21.6	1.26f	80	6	6.5	5.5	8.2	17	.8	395
Dataram Cp .... A	166	15.0	11.5	.55n	NE	- 14	8.0	8.2	11.1	0	.0a	18
Decision Data .... O	181	13.7	30.1	.74q	57	121	5.1	8.2	11.9	2	.0	77
Denelcor Inc .... O	426	NE	NC	- 1.82q	NE	- 75	-83.3	NE	NE	6	.0	61
Digital Equip .... ★N	136	18.7	14.9	4.59s	- 26	7	6.6	6.2	8.0	3	.0	4,847
Dysan Corp .... O	100	NE	48.3	- .82s	-100	- 24	4.3	3.2	4.3	11	.0	182
Electron Assoc .... N	157	NE	14.4	- 4.31f	-100	- 46	-29.9	NE	NE	4	.0	15
Electron Mem .... N	86	14.4	30.1	.45q	246	- 2	4.2	4.5	8.0	49	.0	35
Electron Modules .... O	189	NE	17.0	- .45s	-100	- 26	- 2.8	NE	NE	4	.0	64
Elron Electronic .... O	240	23.7	9.6	.39n	- 86	37	17.3	14.6	37.9	59	.0a	97
Emulex Cp .... O	732	22.2	26.4	.81n	108	107	18.1	16.0	19.3	0	.0	214
Esprit Syst .... A	2344	46.9	65.6	.12n	NC	NC	3.9	3.8	33.3	222	.0	21
Float Pt Sys .... N	167	9.5	22.3	1.70s	36	78	13.1	10.6	15.1	3	.0	146
Fortune Systs .... O	87	NE	NC	- .97q	NE	- 25	-28.3	NE	NE	5	.0	79
Gandalf Tech .... O	264	NA	27.2	.28s	- 53	19	6.3	6.5	9.3	14	NA	106
Gen Automation .... O	371	NE	41.9	- 2.13s	NE	- 56	-17.8	NE	NE	204	.0	25

Company and Market		Relative Price			Earnings Per Share			Other					
		Price to Equity	P/E Ratio		Latest 12 Months		5-Year Growth Rate	Profit Margin	Return On Assets	Return On Common Equity	Debt Equity Ratio	Dividend Yield	Market Value
			Current	5-Year Average	Amount	Change							
		%	-	-	$	%	%	%	%	%	%	%	$Mil
Gen Datacomm	N	522	26.1	30.7	.57s	1040	5	4.1	3.5	9.1	106	.0	203
Genisco Tech	A	115	17.4	17.3	.41s	- 43	7	3.3	4.3	6.1	18	.0	19
Honeywell Inc	★N	107	9.8	8.5	5.38q	16	0	4.0	4.9	10.0	30	3.6	2,472
Information Intl	O	133	13.4	20.3	.84n	- 13	11	8.7	9.4	10.9	0	1.8	29
Infotron Systs	O	295	20.6	55.1	1.41q	74	73	12.1	10.9	12.6	0	.0	145
Intecom Inc	O	250	31.4	NM	.33q	83	69	12.7	6.5	7.9	0	.0	318
Intelligent Sys	O	338	17.0	26.2	.84f	95	67	10.0	14.6	19.4	0	.0	158
Intergraph Cp	O	1569	43.8	53.7	1.01n	146	77	8.4	10.8	19.9	3	.0	1,129
Intermec Cp	O	620	25.2	24.2	.66f	38	36	11.5	13.9	18.6	0	.0	75
Intl Bus Mach	★N	277	11.2	11.3	9.39q	22	18	13.7	14.7	23.6	12	3.6	64,279
Intertec Data	A	73	NE	25.1	- .66n	-100	3	6.2	3.4	4.0	5	.0	22
ISC Systems	O	465	26.8	49.3	.57n	78	57	5.0	6.1	8.3	12	.0	224
Kaypro Cp	O	1151	10.4	23.8	.42s	NC	58	15.8	25.2	96.0	6	.0	158
Key Tronic	O	240	11.0	26.4	1.23n	NC	82	6.5	6.5	10.5	21	.0	119
Lee Data	O	150	7.4	24.3	1.25f	36	100	17.8	17.2	21.5	1	.0	123
Lexidata Cp	O	161	70.8	23.9	.09s	- 53	14	- .8	NE	NE	3	.0	37
LTX	O	356	26.6	33.0	.63n	80	43	5.0	5.0	6.9	9	.0	129
Mgmnt Assist	N	232	NE	NM	- .37s	-100	- 25	NC	.0	.0	94	.0	184
Masstor Sys	O	NS	NE	NC	- .71q	NE	7	-43.6	8.4	NS	- 10	.0	55
Micom Syst	O	991	30.0	24.6	1.34f	46	56	15.6	19.1	22.9	0	.0	614
Miniscribe Cp	O	228	23.9	74.6	.22q	NC	101	3.7	4.7	6.7	0	.0	96
Modular Comp	N	84	NE	33.8	- 4.16q	NC	- 69	-31.8	NE	NE	10	.0	39
Mohawk Data	N	88	15.2	14.0	.66n	- 27	- 4	3.1	3.3	6.9	62	.0	145
Monolithic Mem	O	269	17.9	25.1	1.05s	338	72	9.7	6.4	8.2	5	.0	337
Natl Micronetics	O	173	17.3	30.3	.49n	4	12	6.3	6.2	8.7	17	.0	67
NBI Inc	N	260	20.6	48.3	1.09n	54	66	3.8	2.9	5.3	52	.0	227
Network Sys	O	582	46.0	62.6	.50q	61	81	21.3	10.3	11.6	0	.0	499
Onyx IMI Inc	O	102	NM	32.8	.01q	- 98	68	5.0	8.0	11.6	0	.0	32
Par Tech Cp	O	492	19.3	36.2	.83q	41	88	14.6	16.7	22.7	0	.0	122
Priam Cp	O	152	12.9	76.8	.62n	NC	73	4.4	3.0	3.5	6	.0	124
Prime Computer	N	229	18.9	22.9	.68f	- 31	34	6.3	7.3	12.1	6	.0	610
Printronix	O	171	11.5	16.9	1.70f	12	28	6.7	9.6	12.3	2	.0	89
Quantum Cp	O	330	17.0	NM	1.03n	- 29	62	16.7	12.4	14.4	0	.0	161
Recog Equip	N	133	19.0	20.0	.56q	NE	- 72	2.7	2.8	5.3	37	.0	80
Rolm Corp	★N	229	28.0	27.2	1.42n	- 23	32	7.1	6.8	9.3	6	.0	919
SCI Systs	O	384	20.5	23.4	.70s	59	81	3.6	5.3	15.0	91	.0	183
Seagate Tech	O	411	13.1	69.2	.87n	295	81	11.9	8.3	10.9	6	.0	498
Sperry Corp	★N	75	11.2	8.8	3.49n	10	- 7	2.1	2.0	4.5	36	4.9	2,069
Storage Technl	★N	62	NE	12.1	- .28f	-100	- 8	- 1.1	5.2	11.7	62	.0	338
Stratus Cptr	O	424	NM	NM	.10f	NC	30	8.3	3.7	3.9	1	.0	183
Sykes Data	O	121	NE	NM	- .30f	-100	- 19	-11.5	NE	NE	20	.0	38
System Indus	O	95	19.1	29.6	.38s	NC	- 14	1.5	1.8	2.6	0	.0	31
Tab Products	A	218	11.2	10.6	1.38n	66	22	4.2	8.4	14.0	24	.8	67
Tandem Cpt	★O	297	32.9	36.5	.71s	- 4	56	7.4	7.4	9.9	8	.0	933
Tandon Cp	O	189	14.9	45.3	.53q	29	113	7.8	7.7	11.2	0	.0	400
TEC Inc	A	171	NE	16.9	- .04n	NE	- 35	- 6.8	NE	NE	26	.0	9
Televideo Syst	O	183	10.9	48.3	.56q	27	121	13.3	12.5	16.1	0	.0	255
Telex Corp	N	356	11.0	19.9	2.48f	42	115	11.1	13.6	22.2	37	.0	395
Timeplex Inc	N	257	25.6	28.7	.60n	62	40	7.8	4.6	6.9	25	.0	126
TRW Inc	★N	144	11.2	10.7	5.72q	38	1	3.6	6.0	12.4	16	4.4	2,322

(*Continued*)

Company and Market		Relative Price			Earnings Per Share			Other					
		Price to Equity	P/E Ratio Current	P/E Ratio 5-Year Average	Latest 12 Months Amount	Latest 12 Months Change	5-Year Growth Rate	Profit Margin	Return On Assets	Return On Common Equity	Debt Equity Ratio	Dividend Yield	Market Value
		%	-	-	$	%	%	%	%	%	%	%	$Mil
Computers, Subsystems and Peripherals													
Ultimate Cp	A	1010	23.8	35.6	.86n	91	79	13.1	12.1	23.2	0	.0	200
Ungermann Bass	O	486	98.2	NM	.14f	600	51	5.5	2.7	3.0	3	.0	230
Valid Logic	O	NS	NM	NM	.08f	NC	113	5.6	NE	NE	-20	.0	162
Vector Graphic	O	25	NE	25.5	-1.17n	NE	-59	-8.9	13.0	16.6	0	.0	5
Verbatim Cp	A	379	17.5	31.5	.60n	3	56	11.9	14.1	22.6	6	.0	239
Vermont Resch	A	102	NE	13.6	-.96q	-100	-32	-14.9	NE	NE	3	.0	12
Vernitron Corp	A	128	12.7	10.4	1.02f	-4	8	4.9	6.0	10.0	25	1.2	82
Visual Tech	O	127	11.2	20.0	.87f	12	67	7.8	7.4	10.2	4	.0	46
Wang Labs	*A	390	19.9	26.3	1.39n	29	74	9.9	9.0	16.2	39	.4	3,869
Wespercorp	A	77	NE	16.4	-2.39s	-100	-53	-22.1	NE	NE	28	.0	10
Wicat Systs	O	NS	NE	NC	-.31n	NC	4	-16.2	NE	NE	-446	.0	43
Xebec	O	160	13.0	47.0	.69s	103	89	6.8	4.2	5.3	2	.0	117
Zentec	O	198	NE	29.2	-.98q	-100	-44	-17.0	NE	NE	7	.0	17
Electronic Controls and Instruments													
AccuRay Cp	O	189	13.4	13.0	1.36q	20	86	4.5	6.1	13.3	53	.9	76
Ametek Inc	N	306	16.7	12.5	1.48f	18	11	7.2	10.4	18.3	27	3.2	537
Autom Switch	A	217	17.8	14.5	1.94f	-4	2	10.0	10.9	12.2	0	2.9	287
Bowmar Instr	A	488	NE	49.1	-.39s	NE	-71	-5.3	NE	NE	289	.0	18
Clarostat Mfg	A	159	9.6	11.3	2.85q	88	44	5.6	6.8	8.5	4	2.2	13
CompuDyne	A	69	18.1	6.8	.38q	-62	-5	1.0	1.4	8.0	157	.0	7
Conrac Corp	N	97	11.9	11.9	1.04q	-17	8	5.0	6.4	8.9	10	3.2	76
Daniel Inds	N	104	39.4	14.8	.27q	-83	-7	2.3	2.3	3.5	19	1.7b	103
Dynascan Cp	O	58	10.3	13.0	.58q	-44	48	5.1	8.3	18.6	0	.0a	27
EIP Microwave	O	435	15.2	39.9	.66s	6	34	8.2	15.8	28.8	0	1.0	23
Electron Cp A	A	169	52.5	14.1	.35q	52	-27	-9.5	NE	NE	95	7.6	33
Energy Conv Dev	O	598	NE	52.0	-1.16s	NE	3	-27.7	NE	NE	12	.0	128
Fischer & Port	A	91	37.5	54.2	.43q	NE	-15	.2	.5	1.2	48	.0a	56
Frequency Elec	A	170	16.1	30.0	1.02n	-11	119	17.4	8.2	10.2	14	.0	50
Hewlett-Pack	*N	320	21.1	18.8	1.72q	10	27	9.2	10.4	15.0	2	.5	9,085
Instron Corp	A	191	14.1	76.4	1.35q	165	-10	3.6	4.8	11.7	28	1.5	38
Johnson Contr	N	134	9.4	8.9	4.49s	20	7	4.5	6.4	14.1	25	3.9	595
KLA Instruments	O	945	49.2	60.8	.48n	78	63	12.4	8.4	11.7	0	.0	236
Knogo Corp	A	252	17.5	24.6	.68f	113	-11	12.7	3.6	7.0	68	.0	60
Kollmorgen Cp	N	269	23.7	19.3	1.15q	32	-1	3.4	4.9	9.2	30	1.2	260
Liebert Cp	O	366	22.5	26.1	.89s	25	78	6.5	9.0	14.2	15	.3	295
Mangood Corp	A	382	32.6	10.1	.84f	4	21	2.9	5.4	11.1	20	.0	17
Mark Products	A	131	NM	68.0	.02f	NE	-8	.9	NE	NE	35	.0	29
Measurex Corp	N	158	20.2	20.9	.83q	NE	-17	3.9	NE	NE	12	.6	145
MTS Systems Cp	O	125	13.2	12.3	1.70s	67	-10	3.6	3.3	7.5	42	1.4	40
Nicolet Instr	N	205	24.8	49.5	.56n	30	-5	.6	.7	1.4	46	.6	85
Nuclear Data	A	84	NE	12.3	-1.28f	NE	-31	-4.9	NE	NE	32	.0	14
Pac Scientific	N	138	7.6	10.6	1.65q	-6	23	13.7	12.0	22.3	64	3.2	67
Robertshaw	N	139	8.3	9.5	3.71q	151	15	4.2	7.5	13.1	25	3.2	166
Tenney Engr	A	241	16.1	13.6	.24q	14	8	4.2	5.6	14.3	93	.0	11
Teradyne Inc	N	486	27.4	28.8	1.01f	321	6	8.5	2.1	4.4	81	.0	597
Tesdata Sys	O	66	NE	36.4	-1.99q	NE	-67	-11.0	NE	NE	0	.0	4
Veeco Instrs	N	285	16.2	18.6	1.24s	35	4	8.3	9.4	14.9	14	1.6	194

MEASURING AND CONTROLLING INSTRUMENTS (SICs 3822–4, 3829): TRENDS AND PROJECTIONS 1972–84 (in millions of dollars except as noted)

Item	1972	1977	1979	1981	1982[1]	1983[2]	Compound annual rate of growth 1972–83	1984[3]	Percent change 1983–84
Industry data									
Value of shipments[4]	2,499	5,149	6,319	7,766	7,684	7,352	10.3	7,633	3.8
Value of shipments (1972$)[4]	2,499	3,946	4,299	4,547	4,238	3,878	4.1	3,813	−1.7
Total employment (000)	99.9	133.7	139.1	132.1	123.4	117.1	1.5	116.8	−0.3
Production workers (000)	60.9	81.0	83.4	79.1	71.3	66.1	0.7	65.6	−0.8
Average hourly earning of production workers ($)	3.86	5.49	6.27	7.49	8.18	8.63	7.6	—	—
Capital expenditures	67.1	169.0	222.8	292.7	—	—	—	—	—
Product data									
Value of shipments[5]	2,366	4,875	6,122	7,769	7,591	7,172	10.6	7,372	2.8
Value of shipments (1972$)[5]	2,366	3,699	4,128	4,512	4,150	3,750	4.3	3,650	−2.7
Product price index (1972 = 100)	N.A.	N.A.	N.A.	N.A.	N.A.	N.A.	—	—	—
Trade									
Value of exports	428	906	1,164	1,648	1,549	1,416	11.5	1,405	−0.8
Value of imports	64	149	176	306	284	306	15.3	325	6.2
Export/shipments ratio	.181	.186	.190	.212	.204	.197	0.8	.190	—
Import/new supply ratio[6]	.026	.030	.028	.038	.036	.041	4.2	.042	—

[1] Estimated except for product price index, exports, and imports
[2] Estimated.
[3] Forecast.
[4] Value of all products and services sold by industry SICs 3822-4, 3829.
[5] Value of shipments of products produced by all industries.
[6] New supply is the sum of product shipments plus imports.

Source: Bureau of the Census and Bureau of Industrial Economics. Estimates & forecasts by the Bureau of Industrial Economics.

Source: *U.S. Industrial Outlook 1984*, U.S. Department of Commerce.

TEXTILE MILL PRODUCTS (SIC 22): TRENDS AND PROJECTIONS 1972–83 (in millions of dollars except as noted)

Item	1972	1977	1979	1981	1982[1]	1983[2]	Compound annual rate of growth 1972–83
Industry data							
Value of shipments[3]	28,063.9	40,550.5	45,135.5	50,262.2	47,217.0	51,088.8	—
Value of shipments (1972 $)[3]	28,063.9	30,360.9	30,957.4	28,895.9	26,642.0	28,959.8	0.3
Total employment (000)	952.6	875.6	842.1	785.2	716.1	698.9	—
Production workers (000)	836.0	764.6	732.3	678.5	612.0	600.4	2.8
Average hourly earnings of production workers ($)	2.75	3.99	4.66	5.52	5.83	6.14	—
Capital expenditures	1,127.4	1,223.3	1,329.3	1,724.8	1,471.3	1,449.2	—
Product data							
Product price index (1972 = 100)	N.A.	100.0	106.8	127.3	129.5	128.8	—
Trade							
Value of exports	744.6	1,857.3	3,028.9	3,474.2	2,649.6	2,114.4	—
Value of imports	1,496.7	1,764.8	2,213.8	3,014.7	2,772.2	3,099.3	—
Export/shipments ratio	0.027	0.046	0.067	0.069	0.056	0.041	—
Import/new supply ratio[4]	0.051	0.042	0.047	0.057	0.055	0.057	—

[1] Estimated except for product price index, exports, and imports.
[2] Estimated.
[3] Value of all products and services sold by industry SIC 22.
[4] New supply is the sum of industry shipments plus imports.

Source: Bureau of the Census and Bureau of Industrial Economics. Estimates by International Trade Administration (OTEXA).

Source: *U.S. Industrial Outlook 1984*, U.S. Department of Commerce.

WEAVING MILLS, SYNTHETICS (SIC 2221): TRENDS AND PROJECTIONS 1972–83 (in millions of dollars except as noted)

Item	1972	1977	1979	1981	1982[1]	1983[2]	Compound annual rate of growth 1972–83
Industry data							
Value of shipments[3]	3,856.6	6,325.9	7,291.5	8,725.7	7,704.5	8,213.0	—
Value of shipments (1972 $)[3]	3,856.6	4,675.5	4,632.5	4,678.7	4,120.1	4,329.2	1.1
Total employment (000)	149.7	151.0	145.1	141.5	121.8	107.7	−2.9
Production workers (000)	134.9	134.6	128.9	125.0	106.5	94.4	−3.2
Average hourly earnings of production workers ($)	2.82	4.24	5.05	6.03	6.41	6.86	8.42
Capital expenditures	136.2	260.2	264.6	408.7	—	—	—
Product data							
Value of shipment[4]	4,118.5	7,287.3	8,398.1	10,177.6	8,844.8	9,287.0	—
Value of shipments (1972 $)[4]	4,118.5	5,618.6	5,606.2	5,759.8	4,952.3	5,253.4	—
Product price index (1972 = 100)	100.0	131.6	154.8	183.3	185.3	183.5	—
Trade							
Value of exports	147.1	349.5	601.8	736.2	487.3	399.6	—
Value of imports	219.9	324.4	437.7	702.5	654.9	685.0	—
Export/shipments ratio	0.037	0.053	0.080	0.081	0.064	0.052	—
Import/new supply ratio[4]	0.052	0.047	0.055	0.072	0.076	0.076	—

[1] Estimated except for product price index, exports, and imports.
[2] Estimated.
[3] Value of all products and services sold by industry SIC 2221.
[4] Value of shipments of products produced by all industries.
[5] New supply is the sum of product shipments plus imports.

Source: Bureau of the Census and Bureau of Industrial Economics. Estimates by International Trade Administration (OTEXA).

Source: *U.S. Industrial Outlook 1984*, U.S. Department of Commerce.

WEAVING MILLS, COTTON (SIC 2211): TRENDS AND PROJECTIONS 1972–83 (in millions of dollars except as noted)

Item	1972	1977	1979	1981	1982[2]	1983[1]	Compound annual rate of growth 1972–83
Industry data							
Value of shipments[3]	2,660.6	4,431.2	4,864.8	5,284.8	4,941.3	5,331.7	—
Value of shipments (1972 $)[3]	2,660.6	2,594.4	2,505.0	2,306.8	2,247.1	2,395.8	–1.0
Total employment (000)	121.3	117.2	111.0	100.4	90.5	81.5	–3.6
Production workers (000)	112.1	107.2	100.6	90.3	80.4	72.5	–3.9
Average hourly earnings of production workers ($)	2.78	4.21	5.01	5.86	6.19	6.65	8.26
Capital expenditures	72.7	187.2	185.3	289.2	—	—	—
Product data							
Value of shipment[4]	2,595.5	4,024.0	4,299.9	4,551.4	4,200.9	4,415.2	—
Value of shipments (1972 $)[4]	2,595.5	2,268.3	2,138.2	1,942.6	1,892.3	2,038.9	—
Product price index (1972 = 100)	100.0	179.9	203.6	238.9	229.1	223.2	—
Trade							
Value of exports	204.3	438.3	623.4	339.6	241.3	182.4	—
Value of imports	254.3	339.8	367.3	597.1	474.9	436.9	—
Export/shipments ratio	0.078	0.106	0.141	0.072	0.054	0.038	—
Import/new supply ratio[4]	0.089	0.076	0.077	0.112	0.098	0.086	—

[1] Estimated except for product price index, exports, and imports.
[2] Estimated.
[3] Value of all products and services sold by industry SIC 2211.
[4] Value of shipments of products produced by all industries.
[5] New supply is the sum of product shipments plus imports.
Source: Bureau of the Census and Bureau of Industrial Economics. Estimates by International Trade Administration (OTEXA).

Source: *U.S. Industrial Outlook 1984*, U.S. Department of Commerce.

WEAVING AND FINISHING MILLS, WOOL (SIC 2231): TRENDS AND PROJECTIONS 1972–83 (in millions of dollars except as noted)

Item	1972	1977	1979	1981	1982[1]	1983[2]	Compound annual rate of growth 1972–83
Industry data							
Value of shipments[3]	450.1	583.3	662.6	844.2	769.8	828.3	—
Value of shipments (1972 $)[3]	450.1	424.2	420.4	468.2	425.8	451.8	—
Total employment (000)	19.4	14.6	15.4	14.4	13.0	11.6	−4.6
Production workers (000)	16.5	12.6	13.2	12.3	11.1	10.0	−4.5
Average hourly earnings of production workers ($)	2.85	4.08	4.71	5.71	6.16	6.48	7.74
Capital expenditures	11.6	14.9	21.8	18.2	—	—	—
Product data							
Value of shipment[4]	440.7	581.3	684.5	885.5	811.2	842.8	+3.9
Value of shipments (1972 $)[4]	440.7	422.8	434.3	491.1	452.8	479.1	+5.8
Product price index (1972 = 100)	100.0	138.3	159.0	181.9	183.0	179.5	—
Trade							
Value of exports	1.5	3.1	3.2	6.2	5.8	4.4	—
Value of imports	32.0	67.1	80.0	107.9	114.5	116.8	—
Export/shipments ratio	0.005	0.008	0.006	0.009	0.009	0.008	—
Import/new supply ratio[4]	0.091	0.138	0.134	0.139	0.154	0.164	—

[1] Estimated except for product price index, exports, and imports.
[2] Estimated.
[3] Value of all products and services sold by industry SIC 2231.
[4] Value of shipments of products produced by all industries.
[5] New supply is the sum of product shipments plus imports.

Source: Bureau of the Census and Bureau of Industrial Economics Estimates by International Trade Administration (OTEXA).

Source: *U.S. Industrial Outlook 1984*, U.S. Department of Commerce.

KNIT FABRIC MILLS (SIC 2257-58): TRENDS AND PROJECTIONS 1972-83 (in millions of dollars except as noted)

Item	1972	1977	1979	1981	1982[1]	1983[2]	Compound annual rate of growth 1972-83
Industry data							
Value of shipments[3]	3,796.5	4,597.0	4,817.5	4,633.1	4,137.4	4,385.6	—
Value of shipments (1972 $)[3]	3,796.5	3,756.4	3,691.6	3,068.1	2,810.4	2,962.2	-2.2
Total employment (000)	90.1	75.5	72.3	62.2	55.8	55.3	-5.7
Production workers (000)	75.7	64.0	61.2	52.8	47.2	46.8	—
Average hourly earnings of production workers ($)	2.98	4.21	4.91	5.45	5.70	6.05	6.66
Capital expenditures	270.1	91.6	85.6	106.5	—	—	—
Product data							
Value of shipment[4]	3,209.3	4,254.8	4,360.8	4,313.2	3,868.9	3,965.6	—
Value of shipments (1972 $)[4]	3,209.3	3,485.8	3,341.3	2,855.8	2,615.9	2,765.0	—
Product price index (1972 = 100)	100.0	122.7	128.3	148.6	145.8	141.1	—
Trade							
Value of exports	21.4	42.7	55.3	72.7	55.6	48.6	—
Value of imports	123.0	32.5	22.4	15.9	17.6	12.2	—
Export/shipments ratio	0.007	0.010	0.013	0.017	0.014	0.012	—
Import/new supply ratio[4]	0.037	0.008	0.005	0.004	0.005	0.003	—

[1] Estimated except for product index, exports, and imports.
[2] Estimated.
[3] Value of all products and services sold by industry SIC 2257-58.
[4] Value of shipments of products produced by all industries.
[5] New supply is the sum of product shipments plus imports.

Source: Bureau of the Census and Bureau of Industrial Economics. Estimates by International Trade Administration (OTEXA).

Source: *U.S. Industrial Outlook 1984*, U.S. Department of Commerce.

Company and Market		Relative Price			Earnings Per Share			Other					
		Price to Equity	P/E Ratio Current	P/E Ratio 5-Year Average	Latest 12 Months Amount	Latest 12 Months Change	5-Year Growth Rate	Profit Margin	Return On Assets	Return On Common Equity	Debt Equity Ratio	Dividend Yield	Market Value
		%	-	-	$	%	%	%	%	%	%	%	$Mil
Weaving Mills													
Avondale Mills	A	88	5.3	24.3	3.40n	47	42	3.5	.4	.5	9	4.4	72
Belding Hemin	N	103	7.7	8.9	1.75f	187	10	4.5	3.3	4.7	16	3.0	39
Bibb Co	O	45	8.5	7.7	2.31f	34	19	1.3	2.1	4.0	28	3.0	27
Burlington Inds	★N	63	6.1	8.5	4.27s	162	8	3.0	4.0	7.4	40	6.2	756
Chatham Mfg	O	77	8.7	9.8	2.50f	155	0	4.0	6.9	8.8	12	3.9	39
Collins & Aikm	★N	186	7.9	7.0	4.47f	103	46	5.2	6.0	11.5	36	2.8	378
Concord Fab	A	84	7.0	7.1	1.38s	112	60	1.7	3.9	6.9	23	.0	17
Courtaulds Ltd	A	87	6.3	8.4	.26n	86	- 6	1.7	2.7	9.1	73	3.7	444
Crompton Co	A	30	NE	4.5	- 8.78s	NE	- 58	- 8.5	NE	NE	99	.0	12
Crown Crafts	A	85	7.7	16.9	1.10f	NE	- 2	3.1	NE	NE	39	.0	6
Fab Indus	A	117	7.9	4.4	2.27q	21	5	8.2	8.8	13.8	3	1.7	68
Fieldcrest Mill	N	81	9.3	8.7	3.94q	99	- 11	2.6	4.3	8.1	39	5.4	141
Graniteville	N	70	NE	25.2	- .51f	NE	- 39	- 1.0	NE	NE	56	.0	70
Lowenstn Sons	★N	108	6.9	7.4	7.96q	80	58	3.8	4.6	9.1	44	3.3	185
Riegel Textile	N	66	15.2	8.3	1.73q	- 30	- 12	1.6	2.4	4.4	38	6.9	101
Ruddick Corp	A	132	10.1	6.1	2.81s	9	13	2.0	6.1	14.0	59	2.7	100
Springs Indus	★N	75	8.6	6.0	4.15f	- 1	6	4.1	6.2	8.9	11	4.3	314
Stevens JP	★N	67	13.8	11.8	1.49s	42	- 12	1.0	1.6	3.4	53	5.8	377
Unit Mer Mfrs	N	63	57.7	4.2	.21n	NE	- 36	- 1.3	NE	NE	69	.0	99
Vertipile Inc	A	104	15.6	12.9	.44f	300	- 14	2.5	4.6	6.9	14	1.5	9
West Point-P	★N	98	6.8	6.6	5.89n	31	16	4.3	7.4	12.3	25	1.7	419
Wright Wm Co	O	68	4.7	8.3	1.90n	192	35	5.3	8.2	11.3	2	4.2	19
Knitting Mills													
Adams-Millis	N	100	10.3	7.6	1.56q	47	10	4.1	6.2	9.4	20	1.8	36
Aileen Inc	N	46	NE	25.9	- .27s	NE	23	- .4	NE	NE	11	.0	15
Alba-Waldens	A	99	6.3	9.1	1.56f	42	38	5.6	6.0	11.4	18	2.1	18
Damon Creatn	A	58	25.0	13.0	.28f	- 26	- 6	.8	2.4	3.5	14	.0	8
Guilford Mills	N	151	6.9	5.9	3.22n	96	7	6.0	9.3	14.4	12	2.4	174
Lehigh Valley	N	NS	NE	13.2	- .14f	NE	- 31	- 4.1	NE	NE	- 900	.0	24
Nantucket ind	A	258	9.5	9.7	.87f	78	53	5.3	6.2	18.8	96	.0	16
Russell Corp	A	139	8.9	7.7	1.37q	19	13	8.4	10.1	15.4	17	2.4	241
Stanwood Cp	A	64	11.8	14.9	.88q	42	- 12	.4	.6	1.6	73	.0	16
Texfi Ind	N	110	NE	30.6	- .05s	NE	16	1.2	2.4	13.4	284	.0	15
Unifi Inc	O	97	5.8	7.5	1.54n	34	54	4.7	8.0	13.7	36	.0	64
V.F. Corp	★N	197	6.4	5.8	3.76q	22	88	10.8	21.1	29.9	11	4.2	789

APPAREL AND OTHER TEXTILE PRODUCTS (SIC 23): TRENDS AND PROJECTIONS 1972–84 (in millions of dollars except as noted)

Item	1972	1977	1979	1981	1982[1]	1983[2]	Compound annual rate of growth 1972–83	1984[3]	Percent change 1983–84
Industry data									
Value of shipments[3]	27.810	40.109	43.030	49.823	49.916	51.768	—	—	—
Value of shipments (1972 $)[3]	27.810	30.450	29.763	29.497	28.720	28.824	0.3	—	—
Total employment (000)	1,382.7	1,316.2	1,304.2	1,304.3	1,244.4	1,163.7	–1.7	—	—
Production workers (000)	1,208.0	1,129.4	1,116.7	1,059.5	983.8	971.7	–2.0	—	—
Average hourly earnings of production workers ($)	2.59	3.62	4.23	4.97	5.20	5.34	6.8	—	—
Capital expenditures	363.4	456.6	523.8	646.0	—	—	—	—	—
Trade[4]									
Value of exports	309.6	524.1	772.1	1,032.1	774.9	616.3	—	—	—
Value of imports	1,982.6	3,649.7	5,015.0	6,756.1	7,386.1	8,577.5	—	—	—
Export/shipments ratio	0.011	0.013	0.018	0.021	0.016	0.012	—	—	—
Import/new supply ratio[5]	0.067	0.083	0.104	0.119	0.129	0.142	—	—	—

[1] Estimated except for exports, and imports.
[2] Estimated.
[3] Value of all products and services sold by industry SIC 23.
[4] Includes apparel only.
[5] New supply is the sum of product shipments plus imports.
Source: Bureau of the Census and Bureau of Industrial Economics. Estimates by International Trade Administration (OTEXA).

Source: U.S. Industrial Outlook 1984, U.S. Department of Commerce.

MEN'S AND BOYS' OUTERWEAR (SIC 2311-21-27-28): TRENDS AND PROJECTIONS 1972-84 (in millions of dollars except as noted)

Item	1972	1977	1979	1981	1982[1]	1983[2]	Compound annual rate of growth 1972-83	1984[3]	Percent change 1983-84
Industry data									
Value of shipments[3]	7,984	11,062	11,667	13,474	13,078	13,779	—	—	—
Value of shipments (1972 $)[3]	7,984	7,391	7,097	7,200	6,742	6,820	-1.4	—	—
Total employment (000)	420.3	383.7	361.8	345.1	324.3	309.5	-2.5	—	—
Production workers (000)	368.8	332.2	311.7	296.1	277.7	270.0	-2.8	—	—
Average hourly earnings of production workers ($)	92.9	118.6	146.2	157.5	—	—	—	—	—
Capital expenditures	92.9	118.6	146.2	157.5	—	—	—	—	—
Trade									
Value of exports	84.6	192.0	334.2	411.5	263.1	191.1	—	—	—
Value of imports	669.2	1,746.5	2,336.2	2,929.3	3,307.9	3,776.6	—	—	—
Export/shipments ratio	0.011	0.017	0.029	0.031	0.020	0.014	—	—	—
Import/new supply ratio[4]	0.070	0.118	0.147	0.157	0.177	0.192	—	—	—

[1] Estimated except for exports, and imports.
[2] Estimated.
[3] Value of all products and services sold by industry SIC 2311, 2321, 2327, and 2328.
[4] New supply is the sum of product shipments plus imports.
Source: Bureau of the Census and Bureau of Industrial Economics. Estimates by International Trade Administration (OTEXA).

Source: *U.S. Industrial Outlook 1984*, U.S. Department of Commerce.

WOMEN'S AND MISSES' OUTERWEAR (SIC 233): TRENDS AND PROJECTIONS 1972–84 (in millions of dollars except as noted)

Item	1972	1977	1979	1981	1982[1]	1983[2]	Compound annual rate of growth 1972–83	1984[3]	Percent change 1983–84
Industry data									
Value of shipments[3]	8.278	12.720	13.207	16.093	17.332	17.811	—	—	—
Value of shipments (1972 $)[3]	8.278	10.808	10.381	10.779	11.060	11.042	2.7	—	—
Total employment (000)	422.2	426.7	434.6	411.3	386.9	387.4	−0.8	—	—
Production workers (000)	374.0	369.1	374.8	353.0	329.7	328.1	−1.2	—	—
Average hourly earnings of production workers ($)	2.71	3.65	4.23	4.95	5.13	5.24	6.2	—	—
Capital expenditures	98.3	133.6	145.8	220.3	—	—	—	—	—
Trade[4]									
Value of exports	20.4	66.5	105.0	138.5	119.1	70.9	—	—	—
Value of imports	291.3	757.9	1,248.7	1,419.6	1,977.0	2,378.9	—	—	—
Export/shipments ratio	0.004	0.009	0.015	0.016	0.013	0.007	—	—	—
Import/new supply ratio	0.049	0.065	0.101	0.100	0.126	0.145	—	—	—

[1] Estimated except for product price index, exports, and imports.
[2] Estimated.
[3] Value of all products and services sold by industry SIC 233.
[4] Includes only SIC 2331, 2335 and 2337.
[5] New supply is the sum of product shipments plus imports.

Source: Bureau of the Census and Bureau of Industrial Economics. Estimates by International Trade Administration (OTEXA).

Source: U.S. Industrial Outlook 1984, U.S. Department of Commerce.

Textile Manufacturers

Company and Market		Relative Price — Price to Equity %	P/E Ratio Current	P/E Ratio 5-Year Average	Earnings Per Share — Latest 12 Months Amount $	Earnings Per Share — Latest 12 Months Change %	5-Year Growth Rate %	Profit Margin %	Return On Assets %	Return On Common Equity %	Debt Equity Ratio %	Dividend Yield %	Market Value $Mil
After Six Inc	A	111	9.7	58.2	1.37n	25	5	4.8	4.3	10.7	120	.9	21
Angelica	N	179	11.0	10.3	1.65q	8	31	6.9	10.0	16.2	30	2.6	168
Barco of Cal	A	67	15.5	15.2	.25n	-51	10	3.3	5.1	6.6	1	3.1	8
Bassett Walker	O	164	7.2	9.4	2.77q	5	55	12.2	19.2	22.2	1	2.2	203
Blue Bell Inc	★N	122	10.7	7.1	4.03q	27	- 6	4.1	7.1	11.1	13	4.6	470
BTK	A	NS	NE	5.5	- 3.40s	NE	-120	-16.6	NE	NE	-1168	.0a	4
Champ Prods	A	58	11.8	13.1	1.11q	136	- 15	1.7	3.0	4.9	26	5.5	21
Cluett Peabody	★N	92	8.6	6.4	2.96f	15	14	3.2	6.2	12.1	31	3.6	211
Eagle Clothes	A	384	7.3	24.2	.46q	12	32	2.7	5.8	59.1	157	.0	22
Farah Mfg	N	279	7.6	11.5	2.64s	73	56	7.1	7.0	15.7	68	4.4	126
Garan Inc	A	150	8.0	5.4	3.73s	22	23	6.8	10.9	16.8	16	4.0b	97
Genesco Inc	★N	253	12.5	20.4	.59n	NE	59	- .5	NE	NE	330	.0	111
Hampton Ind	A	84	8.9	4.8	1.09q	40	1	2.1	4.3	8.1	51	.0a	28
Jon Logan	★N	139	9.8	8.8	2.59q	30	67	4.9	6.4	10.5	17	2.1	179
Kellwood Co	N	101	6.5	47.2	4.05f	28	90	2.5	3.8	12.2	62	3.8	94
Kennington Ltd	O	77	16.4	9.3	.55f	25	- 15	6.8	3.5	3.8	0	.0	51
Levi Strauss	★N	108	6.7	8.5	4.03q	16	- 1	7.1	10.6	18.5	21	6.8	1,027
Littlefield Adam	A	37	NE	80.6	- .67q	-100	- 34	- 2.8	.0	.0	32	.0	3
Liz Claiborne	O	980	14.8	10.5	2.61q	75	70	9.8	24.2	34.2	0	.0	405
Manhattan Ind	N	104	6.6	5.7	2.93q	60	114	2.7	5.8	15.8	70	1.5b	85
Movie Star Inc	A	90	9.0	9.0	2.22s	222	- 7	.9	1.6	3.3	20	3.0	17
Munsingwear	N	111	18.8	11.7	.88f	NE	- 71	1.8	3.3	6.0	46	.0	31
Noel Industries	N	50	16.3	40.0	.20q	NE	26	1.1	2.3	5.2	9	.0	4
Oxford Inds	N	139	5.7	6.6	2.26n	26	69	4.4	12.2	21.2	20	3.1	150
Palm Beach	N	111	7.1	6.6	3.89q	62	- 2	2.9	6.2	15.2	81	4.4	101
Phil-Van Heu	N	84	6.2	6.3	2.77f	92	30	3.4	7.3	13.9	22	2.3	104
Russ Togs	N	127	8.1	5.8	2.29f	21	20	4.8	8.9	13.5	7	4.1	95
Salant Corp	N	69	28.6	11.0	.35f	- 74	- 4	.6	1.0	2.3	51	4.0	33
Sanmark Star	A	211	11.5	17.2	.39s	56	105	5.6	9.0	15.1	13	.0a	25
Superior Surg	A	102	9.2	7.0	1.27q	41	12	3.5	6.1	10.4	33	2.8	28
Tultex Corp	A	148	9.0	6.2	1.30q	- 24	26	5.1	8.0	20.5	57	3.7	106
Warnaco Inc	N	141	8.1	6.0	2.87q	16	30	5.7	10.2	17.2	18	3.8	233
Wayne Goss	N	56	10.1	8.8	1.19q	8	32	2.5	4.4	7.4	46	1.7	16
Wilson Bros	A	392	NE	18.4	- .15q	NC	17	1.7	NE	NE	594	.0	9
Winter, Jack	N	91	18.6	NM	.39q	160	75	3.2	3.1	4.5	1	.0	26
Wolf, Howard	A	77	20.8	30.9	.18n	350	- 8	NC	.0	.0	2	.0	4
Work Wear Inc	A	74	6.3	10.0	1.94q	159	7	2.6	4.1	10.6	107	3.9	38

Household Appliances and Furniture

HOUSEHOLD APPLIANCES (SIC 363): TRENDS AND PROJECTIONS 1972–84 (in millions of dollars except as noted)

Item	1972	1977	1979	1981	1982[1]	1983[2]	Compound annual rate of growth 1972–83	1984[3]	Percent change 1983–84
Industry data									
Value of industry shipments (SIC 363)[4]	6,940.2	10,736.6	12,740.9	13,108.1	12,746.0	15,026.0	7.3	—	—
Cooking equipment (3631)	939.8	1,707.2	2,353.4	2,525.9	2,485.5	3,124.0	11.5	—	—
Refrigerators—freezers (3632)	1,719.7	2,576.6	2,683.8	2,702.9	2,615.9	3,106.0	5.5	—	—
Laundry equipment (3633)	1,356.5	1,792.8	2,214.7	2,259.0	2,306.5	2,790.0	6.8	—	—
Electric housewares (3634)	1,615.0	2,531.2	2,868.9	3,078.4	2,915.5	3,236.0	6.5	—	—
Vacuum cleaners (3635)	467.7	639.9	796.1	769.8	763.8	827.0	5.3	—	—
Sewing machines (3636)	159.6	304.9	399.0	309.7	285.1	289.0	5.5	—	—
Household appliances n.e.c. (3639)	681.9	1,184.0	1,424.9	1,462.4	1,373.7	1,654.0	8.4	—	—
Value of industry shipments (1972 $) (SIC 363)[4]	6,940.2	8,013.8	8,556.6	7,568.6	6,959.6	7,880.0	1.2	8,600.0	9.1
Cooking equipment (1972 $) (3631)	939.8	1,209.1	1,519.3	1,421.4	1,331.3	1,580.0	4.8	1,775.0	12.3
Refrigerators—freezers (1972 $) (3632)	1,719.7	1,848.4	1,775.0	1,526.2	1,358.9	1,535.0	-1.0	1,660.0	8.1
Laundry equipment (1972 $) (3633)	1,356.5	1,279.7	1,434.4	1,255.7	1,198.2	1,380.0	.2	1,500.0	8.7
Electric housewares (1972 $) (3634)	1,615.0	2,088.4	2,068.4	1,885.1	1,727.2	1,885.0	1.4	2,035.0	8.0
Vacuum cleaners (1972 $) (3635)	467.7	516.5	585.8	500.2	484.0	523.0	1.0	560.0	7.1
Sewing machines (1972 $) (3636)	159.6	201.1	222.5	142.9	125.0	127.0	-2.0	130.0	2.4
Household appliances, n.e.c. (1972 $) (3639)	681.9	870.6	950.6	837.1	735.0	850.0	-2.0	940.0	10.6
Total employment (000)	163.0	162.2	161.4	148.3	127.8	135.5	-1.7	—	—
Production workers (000)	131.1	128.6	126.9	116.3	96.7	102.0	-2.3	—	—
Average hourly earnings of production workers ($)	3.85	5.57	6.56	7.73	8.18	8.74	7.7	—	—
Capital expenditures	151.9	207.0	236.0	304.6	—	—	—	—	—

Product data

Value of product shipments (SIC 363)[5]	6,592.1	10,167.2	12,025.9	12,410.1	12,050.3	14,216.0	7.2	—	—
Cooking equipment (3631)	1,027.0	1,806.5	2,212.1	2,477.2	2,437.6	3,064.0	10.4	—	—
Refrigerators—freezers (3632)	1,419.4	2,005.6	2,314.4	2,402.9	2,325.6	2,762.0	6.2	—	—
Laundry equipment (3633)	1,289.9	1,697.3	1,883.4	1,881.4	1,921.0	2,325.0	5.5	—	—
Electric housewares (3634)	1,448.0	2,304.0	2,730.4	2,874.1	2,722.1	3,022.0	6.9	—	—
Vacuum cleaners (3635)	439.2	710.4	860.2	831.0	824.8	893.0	6.7	—	—
Sewing machines (3636)	152.1	260.4	323.2	241.1	221.2	223.0	3.5	—	—
Household appliances n.e.c. (3639)	816.5	1,383.0	1,702.2	1,702.4	1,598.0	1,927.0	8.1	—	—
Value of shipments (1972 $) (SIC 363)[5]	6,592.7	7,592.7	8,097.2	7,182.3	6,598.9	7,478.0	1.2	8,165.0	9.2
Cooking equipment (1972 $) (3631)	1,027.0	1,279.4	1,428.1	1,394.0	1,305.6	1,550.0	3.8	1,740.0	12.3
Refrigerators—freezers (1972 $) (3632)	1,419.4	1,438.7	1,530.7	1,356.8	1,208.1	1,365.0	-0.4	1,475.0	8.1
Laundry equipment (1972 $) (3633)	1,289.9	1,211.5	1,219.8	1,045.8	997.9	1,150.0	-1.0	1,250.0	8.7
Electric housewares (1972 $) (3634)	1,448.0	1,901.0	1,968.6	1,760.0	1,612.6	1,760.0	1.8	1,900.0	8.0
Vacuum cleaners (1972 $) (3635)	439.2	573.4	633.0	540.0	522.7	565.0	2.3	605.0	7.1
Sewing machines (1972 $) (3636)	152.1	171.8	180.3	111.2	97.0	98.0	-3.9	100.0	2.0
Household appliances, n.e.c. (1972 $) (3639)	816.5	1,016.9	1,135.6	974.5	855.0	990.0	1.8	1,095.0	10.6
Product price index (1972 = 100)	100.0	134.8	149.5	174.1	185.0	192.5	—	—	—

Trade

Value of exports	275.8	778.7	1,060.5	1,342.5	1,115.5	940.0	11.8	—	—
Value of imports	439.2	829.3	957.5	1,147.3	1,180.1	1,540.0	12.1	—	—
Export/shipments ratio	.042	.076	.089	.108	.092	.066	—	—	—
Import/new supply ratio[6]	.062	.075	.084	.094	.089	.098	—	—	—

n.e.c. = not elsewhere classified.
n.a. = not available or insignificant.
[1] Estimated except for product price change, exports and imports.
[2] Estimated.
[3] Forecast.
[4] Value of all products and services sold by industry SIC 363.
[5] Value of shipments of household appliances produced by all industries.
[6] New supply is the sum of product shipments plus imports.

Source: Bureau of the Census and Bureau of Industrial Economics. Estimates and forecasts by the Bureau of Industrial Economics.

Source: *U.S. Industrial Outlook 1984*, U.S. Department of Commerce.

HOUSEHOLD FURNITURE (SIC 251): TRENDS AND PROJECTIONS 1972–84 (in millions of dollars except as noted)

Item	1972	1977	1979	1981	1982[1]	1983[2]	Compound annual rate of growth 1972–83	1984[3]	Percent change 1983–84
Industry data									
Value of shipments[4]									
Household furniture (SIC 251)	7,409.6	10,392.1	12,466.4	13,658.4	12,515.0	14,213.0	6.1	—	—
Wood furniture (SIC 2511)	2,870.0	4,148.8	4,942.3	5,321.7	4,752.2	5,370.0	5.8	—	—
Upholstered furniture (SIC 2512)	2,104.7	2,931.0	3,641.6	3,860.0	3,551.2	4,165.0	6.4	—	—
Metal furniture (SIC 2514)	890.4	1,307.1	1,506.9	1,545.5	1,329.2	1,479.6	4.7	—	—
Bedding (SIC 2515)	1,041.7	1,398.5	1,760.1	2,171.8	2,150.0	2,410.2	7.9	—	—
Wood TV-radio cabinets (SIC 2517)	330.2	304.8	261.7	291.9	277.2	295.9	-0.1	—	—
Household furniture, n.e.c. (SIC 2519)	172.6	301.9	353.8	467.5	455.2	492.3	10.0	—	—
Value of shipments (1972 $)[4]									
Household furniture (1972 $)	7,409.6	7,538.0	7,904.5	7,397.0	6,480.0	7,238.0	-0.2	7,929.0	9.5
Wood (1972 $)	2,870.0	2,959.2	3,009.9	2,689.1	2,312.6	2,567.0	-1.0	2,826.0	10.1
Upholstered (1972 $)	2,104.7	2,171.1	2,465.5	2,254.7	1,988.7	2,286.9	0.8	2,495.0	9.1
Metal (1972 $)	890.4	904.6	862.6	814.8	692.5	768.7	-1.3	840.0	9.3
Bedding (1972 $)	1,041.7	1,068.4	1,182.1	1,259.0	1,142.0	1,255.0	1.7	1,378.0	9.8
Wood TV-radio cabinets (1972 $)	330.2	216.9	159.4	146.0	131.4	137.8	-7.6	150.0	8.8
Household furniture, n.e.c. (1972 $)	172.6	217.8	225.0	233.4	212.8	222.6	2.3	240.0	7.8
Total employment (000)	317.4	309.7	315.5	292.2	265.0	280.0	-1.1	—	—
Production workers (000)	272.4	265.3	267.9	246.4	220.0	233.5	-1.4	—	—
Average hourly earnings of production workers	2.85	3.95	4.55	5.33	5.65	5.92	6.9	—	—
Capital expenditures	212.1	211.1	290.9	296.3	—	—	—	—	—

Product data

Value of shipments									
Household furniture[5]	7,129.5	9,934.7	11,961.1	13,211.6	12,104.1	13,745.7	6.1	—	—
Wood	2,716.8	3,890.7	4,738.1	5,220.3	4,661.7	5,267.7	6.2	—	—
Upholstered	1,990.5	2,735.7	3,241.5	3,562.5	3,277.5	3,844.0	6.1	—	—
Metal	859.3	1,231.2	1,431.3	1,498.0	1,288.3	1,434.0	4.7	—	—
Bedding	1,079.6	1,481.5	1,905.3	2,220.3	2,198.1	2,464.0	7.8	—	—
Wood TV-radio cabinets	293.0	312.8	320.9	296.9	282.0	301.0	.2	—	—
Household furniture, n.e.c.	190.3	281.8	324.0	413.6	396.5	435.0	7.8	—	—
Value of product shipments (1972 $)[5]									
Household furniture (1972 $)	7,129.5	7,211.7	7,578.6	7,132.5	6,248.5	6,979.5	-1.9	7,646.0	9.5
Wood (1972 $)	2,716.8	2,775.1	2,885.6	2,635.5	2,266.5	2,515.8	-.7	2,770.0	10.1
Upholstered (1972 $)	1,990.5	2,026.4	2,194.7	2,080.9	1,835.4	2,110.6	0.5	2,302.0	9.1
Metal (1972 $)	859.3	852.0	819.3	789.1	670.7	744.5	-1.3	814.0	9.3
Bedding (1972 $)	1,079.6	1,131.8	1,279.6	1,257.2	1,140.3	1,253.2	1.4	1,376.0	9.8
Wood TV-radio cabinets (1972 $)	293.0	222.6	195.4	148.5	133.7	140.2	-6.5	152.0	8.6
Household furniture, n.e.c. (1972 $)	190.3	203.8	204.0	221.3	202.0	215.2	1.1	232.0	7.8
Producer Price index (1972 = 100)									
Household furniture	100.0	137.9	158.5	188.5	198.3	202.2	6.6	—	—
Wood	100.0	140.4	164.2	200.0	210.0	215.6	7.2	—	—
Upholstered	100.0	135.0	148.5	172.2	179.8	183.4	5.7	—	—
Metal	100.0	144.3	174.5	185.7	187.7	188.0	5.9	—	—
Bedding	100.0	131.2	149.4	189.5	206.8	213.0	7.1	—	—
Trade									
Value of exports	32.0	136.0	176.0	280.0	253.0	225.0	19.4	—	—
Value of imports	204.0	464.0	783.0	989.0	1,110.0	1,440.0	19.4	—	—
Export/shipments ratio	0.00	0.01	0.02	0.02	0.02	0.02	13.4	—	—
Imports/new supply ratio[6]	0.03	0.04	0.06	0.07	0.08	0.10	11.7	—	—

n.e.c. = not elsewhere classified
[1] Estimated except for product price changes, exports, and imports.
[2] Estimated.
[3] Forecast.
[4] Value of all products and services by industry SIC 251.
[5] Value of shipments of household furniture produced by all industries.
[6] New supply is the sum of product shipments and imports.

Source: Bureau of the Census and Bureau of Industrial Economics. Estimates by BIE.

Source: *U.S. Industrial Outlook 1984*, U.S. Department of Commerce.

Company and Market		Relative Price			Earnings Per Share			Other					
		Price to Equity	P/E Ratio Current	P/E Ratio 5-Year Average	Latest 12 Months Amount	Latest 12 Months Change	5-Year Growth Rate	Profit Margin	Return On Assets	Return On Common Equity	Debt Equity Ratio	Dividend Yield	Market Value
		%	-	-	$	%	%	%	%	%	%	%	$Mil
Appliances													
Health-Mor	A	95	9.1	7.3	1.18q	39	- 9	9.3	8.9	10.1	0	5.2	19
Hoover Co	O	168	9.9	14.2	2.47q	225	- 7	3.8	7.5	14.2	8	4.1	302
Magic Chef	N	125	4.9	13.7	5.21n	174	36	3.4	6.2	12.9	42	3.1	246
Maytag Co	★N	242	8.8	9.9	4.37f	63	6	10.2	18.8	27.3	11	7.6	536
Mor-Flo Inds	O	107	5.4	11.0	2.31q	82	103	3.0	5.3	19.4	113	.1	36
Natl Presto	N	130	11.4	7.0	2.11f	- 14	26	15.2	11.4	14.1	5	4.2	177
Preway Inc	O	98	11.9	12.2	.65f	- 38	- 13	4.7	4.6	8.3	41	6.5b	22
Rangaire	O	76	12.2	13.0	.49s	17	- 6	2.2	3.5	6.3	34	4.0b	23
Roper Corp	★N	103	6.1	9.9	2.35s	218	22	2.4	5.5	13.0	50	4.5	91
Scott & Fetzer	N	159	11.5	7.7	4.49q	31	0	4.5	6.3	13.1	32	3.5	342
Scovill Inc	N	118	10.4	8.5	2.25f	44	- 9	3.4	5.1	10.3	36	6.5	284
Whirlpool Cp	★N	146	8.1	8.0	4.81q	18	15	6.1	11.1	16.7	6	5.1	1,425
Furniture and Home Furnishings													
Am Furniture	O	83	7.9	19.1	1.15q	26	5	2.6	4.3	7.8	40	3.1	22
Bassett Furniture	★O	133	8.2	7.8	3.91q	27	12	9.4	13.3	15.7	0	4.8	271
Berkline Corp	O	65	8.2	45.0	1.07n	257	- 13	1.0	2.3	3.9	17	5.7	13
Flexsteel Ind	O	136	7.1	7.4	1.62n	64	11	5.4	9.6	13.6	17	4.2	55
Henredon Furn	O	151	10.8	10.1	2.66f	3	5	10.5	11.7	13.9	7	3.3	150
La-Z-Boy Chair	O	140	6.1	7.6	4.87n	152	25	6.5	9.1	13.2	12	4.2	137
Lane Co Inc	O	153	9.7	6.5	3.52f	47	15	8.0	9.5	10.7	0	3.3	175
Leggett Platt	N	152	8.7	7.8	1.95q	39	20	4.4	7.7	16.3	56	2.6	155
Levitz Furn	N	192	9.3	10.8	3.37f	215	4	4.3	2.4	5.8	91	2.3	257
Ohio Mattress	A	420	18.9	8.4	.76q	36	37	7.8	12.6	20.4	21	2.8	232
Rowe Furn	O	84	5.8	13.1	1.12q	149	74	4.0	6.8	12.6	38	2.6	16
Rymer Co	N	896	NE	NC	- .92n	NE	13	- 5.3	NE	NE	417	.0	21
Triangle Home	A	132	14.8	22.1	.38s	NC	63	1.9	5.6	7.8	18	.0	7

SELECTED MERCHANDISE CATEGORIES (SIC'S 52, 59, 5311, 56, 5812, 5813): TRENDS AND PROJECTIONS 1972–84
(in millions of current dollars except as noted)

Item	1972	1977	1979	1981	1982[1]	1983[2]	Compound annual rate of growth 1972–83[2]	1984[2]	Percent change 1983–84
Retail trade total									
Sales	449,064	725,220	900,558	1,047,573	1,075,679	1,167,111	8.9	1,266,315	8.5
Total employment (000)	11,836	13,808	14,989	15,189	15,122	15,228	2.3	15,335	0.7
Average hourly earnings	2.75	3.85	4.53	5.25	5.47	—	—	—	—
Department stores									
Sales	49,105	76,469	89,159	103,673	107,030	115,592	8.1	124,839	8.0
Total employment (000)	1,706	1,786	1,878	1,872	1,855	1,866	.8	1,990	0.6
Average hourly earnings	2.62	3.71	4.38	5.15	5.39	—	—	—	—
Apparel and accessory stores									
Sales	24,127	35,565	43,422	50,270	51,991	54,591	7.7	57,321	5.0
Total employment (000)	784	870	949	968	942	949	2.0	955	.7
Average hourly earnings	2.52	3.45	4.01	4.65	4.85	—	—	—	—
Eating and drinking places									
Sales	36,180	63,276	82,270	98,585	107,357	118,093	11.4	129,902	10.0
Total employment (000)	2,860	3,949	4,513	4,750	4,820	4,892	5.0	4,965	1.5
Average hourly earnings	2.07	2.93	3.45	3.95	4.09	—	—	—	—

[1] Estimated by Bureau of Industrial Economics.
[2] Forecast by Bureau of Industrial Economics.

Sources: Bureau of the Census, Bureau of Labor Statistics, and Bureau of Industrial Economics.

Source: *U.S. Industrial Outlook 1984*, U.S. Department of Commerce.

FOOD RETAILING (SIC 54): TRENDS AND PROJECTIONS 1972–83 (in millions of dollars except as noted)

Item	1972	1977	1979	1980	1981	1982	1983[1]	Compound annual rate of growth 1972–83
Industry Sales								
All food retailing establishment	93,327	157,941	199,210	222,687	241,102	252,802	261,726	9.8
Grocery stores	86,690	147,759	186,488	207,775	224,952	236,489	245,688	9.9
Other retail food stores	6,637	10,182	12,722	14,912	16,150	16,313	16,038	8.4
Employment and earnings								
Total employment (000)	1,807	2,106	2,298	2,384	2,448	2,458	2,470	2.9
Nonsupervisory workers (000)	1,677	1,942	2,121	2,202	2,270	2,277	2,285	2.9
Average hourly earnings, nonsupervisory ($)	3.09	4.77	5.67	6.24	6.85	7.21	7.43	8.3

[1] Estimate.

Source: Bureau of the Census, Bureau of Labor Statistics, and Bureau of Industrial Economics. Estimates by the Bureau of Industrial Economics.

Source: *U.S. Industrial Outlook 1984*, U.S. Department of Commerce.

Company and Market		Relative Price Price to Equity %	P/E Ratio Current -	P/E Ratio 5-Year Average -	Earnings Per Share Latest 12 Months Amount $	Earnings Per Share Latest 12 Months Change %	5-Year Growth Rate %	Profit Margin %	Return On Assets %	Return On Common Equity %	Debt Equity Ratio %	Dividend Yield %	Market Value $Mil
Food Chain Stores													
Albertson's Inc	N	206	10.9	9.0	2.25q	17	20	1.6	7.5	17.9	51	2.8	809
Arden Group Inc	O	85	16.1	16.2	.63n	- 28	47	.6	2.2	8.0	124	.0	28
Big V Supmkt	A	137	12.5	7.0	.80q	- 38	4	1.0	6.6	13.8	45	4.0b	55
Borman's Inc	N	67	NE	15.8	- 3.89f	-100	- 43	- 1.1	NE	NE	116	.0	16
Bruno's Inc	O	387	15.3	13.8	.99n	15	45	2.5	11.3	21.9	22	1.6	269
CasaBlanca Ind	A	163	7.6	26.0	.76s	NC	63	33.3	4.1	5.5	2	.0a	24
Circle K Cp	N	396	15.0	20.3	1.62n	500	5	2.0	8.5	21.8	59	3.0	279
Cullum Companies	O	138	10.1	7.8	1.44n	- 15	9	1.2	6.0	16.2	95	3.9	119
Farm Fresh	O	285	18.8	25.0	.81q	11	49	2.4	6.1	14.1	89	.0a	143
Fst Nat Supermkts	O	82	4.9	5.8	2.70s	35	60	.6	3.7	17.3	140	2.0	38
Fisher Foods	N	57	NM	78.2	.04f	- 95	- 4	.1	2.1	5.2	47	.0	41
Food Lion	O	495	17.5	16.5	.53f	26	35	2.4	10.3	22.4	23	.4	485
Foodarama	A	41	NE	NM	- .23q	-100	- 25	NC	2.1	5.5	65	.0	9
Gen Host	N	131	11.0	6.6	1.39f	30	22	2.7	3.9	12.1	138	2.4	193
Giant Food A	A	178	8.5	5.4	2.77f	9	42	2.1	8.5	20.9	58	3.4	343
Grt A & P Tea	*N	151	18.0	12.4	.84f	47	15	.6	2.6	8.4	69	.0	567
Hannaford Bros	A	154	9.6	5.5	2.85q	- 1	25	1.5	6.4	15.2	66	3.3	97
Jewel Co	*N	176	13.0	6.6	5.59q	- 5	9	1.4	6.0	18.4	74	3.6	849
Kroger	*N	141	13.3	8.0	2.53q	- 36	- 2	.8	3.6	11.8	82	5.9	1,510
Lucky Stores	*N	156	8.0	8.7	2.02f	7	3	1.3	6.1	18.6	77	7.1	824
Marsh Supmkts	O	123	34.0	12.6	.43f	- 67	- 6	.3	3.2	10.4	129	3.3	55
Mott's Super	A	107	27.6	8.8	.43q	- 60	- 9	.5	3.1	4.9	9	1.7	33
Munford Inc	N	167	10.1	15.2	1.85q	8	120	1.9	6.4	18.8	70	2.9b	74
Natl Conv Str	N	307	13.9	10.7	1.08n	21	22	2.2	5.3	19.1	172	2.7	230
Pantry Pride	N	124	8.2	18.0	.41s	NE	29	1.0	3.7	15.4	161	.0	73
Penn Traffic	A	78	6.6	6.0	3.05f	21	0	1.2	5.2	11.9	72	6.0	42
Pneumo Corp	N	222	10.0	8.4	2.70q	44	91	2.9	7.3	20.0	56	2.2	397
Pueblo Intl	N	102	12.8	7.4	.84f	33	- 3	.7	1.8	6.1	105	1.5	40
Safeway Stores	*N	110	7.3	7.1	3.26f	7	3	1.0	3.9	13.5	110	6.3	1,390
Seaway Food Town	O	75	16.9	4.9	.77s	- 58	- 7	.7	2.9	8.9	96	5.2	29
Shop & Go	O	286	11.9	8.4	1.16n	25	31	3.2	12.2	19.8	17	1.7	93
Shopwell Inc	A	58	11.4	9.3	.89q	- 61	28	.4	3.4	12.7	129	1.6	16
Southland Corp	*N	101	8.1	8.4	3.30q	14	16	1.5	4.0	12.3	105	3.4	1,259
Stop & Shop	N	234	10.1	5.8	4.10f	25	51	1.8	5.6	19.2	118	2.4	479
Sunshine-Jr	A	140	13.8	8.0	1.07f	2	- 3	1.1	6.1	10.1	12	3.3	25
Supermkts Gen	N	175	10.9	6.7	2.19q	6	22	1.2	5.4	16.8	78	1.8	423
Thriftmart	A	97	35.2	8.6	1.81f	- 68	- 8	.3	1.8	3.3	21	2.8	42
Victory Markets	O	125	7.5	6.0	1.81q	6	69	.9	5.7	17.2	70	3.0b	21
Waldbaum Inc	O	86	6.3	4.8	2.58f	- 15	27	.9	6.2	16.6	84	.0a	88
Weis Markets	N	230	12.5	9.4	2.54q	18	21	5.6	14.8	17.6	0	.0	652
Winn-Dixie A	*N	199	10.4	9.4	2.67n	0	10	1.6	9.8	19.5	18	5.6	1,126

Company and Market	Relative Price			Earnings Per Share			Other					
	Price to Equity	P/E Ratio Current	P/E Ratio 5-Year Average	Latest 12 Months Amount	Latest 12 Months Change	5-Year Growth Rate	Profit Margin	Return On Assets	Return On Common Equity	Debt Equity Ratio	Dividend Yield	Market Value
	%	-	-	$	%	%	%	%	%	%	%	$Mil
Department Stores												
Alexander's Inc .... N	180	25.0	12.6	1.02s	32	16	.9	2.6	7.2	116	.0	115
Allied Stores .... ★N	103	7.6	6.5	5.61f	35	5	3.5	3.8	10.0	91	4.7	896
Almy Stores Inc .... A	63	NE	37.1	-.13n	-100	-27	-.6	NE	NE	34	.0	14
Ames Dept St .... N	411	16.5	7.4	3.07f	54	37	3.1	7.7	15.6	48	.8	329
Assoc Dry Gds .... ★N	106	9.0	7.3	5.95f	38	23	3.1	5.8	14.9	57	4.1	825
Carson Pir Sc .... N	114	12.6	8.8	3.04f	35	-6	1.7	2.7	8.3	111	3.1	185
Carter Hawley .... ★N	91	10.6	9.6	1.90f	24	-7	1.9	3.3	8.7	67	6.1	711
Crowley Milner .... A	67	6.4	4.7	3.54f	58	-4	2.1	4.3	10.5	78	4.4	12
Dayton Hudson .... ★N	203	12.5	9.5	2.57q	21	27	3.5	6.8	15.8	49	2.0	3,117
Dillard Dept A .... A	176	9.0	5.3	5.75q	42	79	4.0	7.6	18.4	59	.6	323
Elder Beerman Str .... O	75	5.0	5.9	2.54f	303	9	2.5	4.9	16.2	97	1.7b	34
Fedrtd Dep Str .... ★N	110	7.7	7.8	6.22q	23	12	3.6	5.1	11.1	33	5.0	2,331
Grand Centl .... A	110	NE	12.0	-.50s	NE	-41	-1.2	NE	NE	251	.0	25
Hecks Inc .... N	97	11.4	14.0	1.04q	46	-9	2.2	3.8	8.5	68	2.4	110
Higbee Co .... O	98	8.6	15.0	4.51q	42	63	2.9	2.4	5.6	74	2.6	55
Holmes, D.H. .... O	93	6.3	5.9	2.88f	26	15	3.3	6.1	13.1	53	5.6	61
Jacobson Stores .... O	99	8.4	10.4	1.54q	185	27	1.5	2.8	11.9	190	3.1	26
Jamesway Corp .... N	178	9.6	6.6	1.74q	25	19	2.8	5.5	13.4	77	.6	99
Macy, R.H. .... ★N	257	11.2	9.0	4.35n	23	34	5.4	9.9	19.5	22	2.1	2,469
May Dept Strs .... ★N	139	8.4	6.8	6.68q	32	18	4.4	6.5	16.0	49	4.3	1,616
Mercantile Strs .... ★N	162	8.9	6.5	5.65f	20	26	5.1	8.8	15.1	27	2.4	742
Penney, JC .... ★N	124	8.7	7.0	6.25f	6	14	3.9	6.4	13.3	43	4.3	4,044
Sears, Roebuck .... ★N	118	8.3	8.9	3.95q	46	12	3.7	2.9	13.7	76	5.4	11,610
Strawbrid & Cloth .... O	107	8.7	5.4	3.97f	47	25	3.8	5.3	13.1	78	2.4b	170
Wieboldt .... N	59	NE	12.5	-1.17n	NE	-66	-1.7	NE	NE	110	.0	21
Woodwd & Lothrop .... O	173	13.6	6.9	4.23q	38	9	3.8	5.1	12.4	64	2.4	215
Discount and Variety Stores												
Best Products .... N	92	10.3	11.1	1.40f	-14	-4	1.8	3.1	8.8	74	1.7	388
Cook United .... N	295	NE	16.1	-9.94f	NE	-65	-12.0	NE	NE	1174	.0a	21
Dollar General Cp .... O	284	14.3	8.6	.97q	26	48	4.4	9.8	19.7	47	1.4	217
Family Dollar .... N	571	20.0	12.1	1.05s	54	33	5.9	13.9	22.4	0	.8	400
Gaylords Natl .... A	66	17.4	26.6	.43s	330	-14	.1	.2	.7	90	.0	9
Glosser Bros .... A	130	8.1	8.2	1.85n	91	5	1.4	7.7	12.0	12	2.7	34
K mart Cp .... ★N	134	9.0	9.8	3.90q	66	10	2.6	6.0	16.7	86	4.0	3,950
Marcade Grp .... N	80	NE	10.2	-.84q	NE	-63	-4.5	NE	NE	119	.0	21
Murphy, GC .... N	105	8.4	7.7	4.22f	42	85	1.9	3.8	8.8	53	3.9	144
Nichols, SE .... A	68	3.8	18.1	1.52q	63	40	2.5	6.6	17.4	82	.0	27
Pic 'n Save .... O	473	17.2	12.6	1.20q	29	73	16.5	21.8	26.8	1	.0	645
Rose's Stores .... O	56	7.6	4.7	2.30q	65	48	2.6	9.9	17.6	15	2.2	179
SCOA Inds .... N	230	11.8	8.7	2.12f	12	14	3.2	8.3	20.4	78	2.7	472
Service Mdse .... O	153	9.1	9.5	1.40q	19	17	3.1	5.9	17.8	61	.6	384
Three D Depts .... A	176	10.5	6.2	.62s	22	20	3.9	9.5	15.7	24	.9	11
Vornado Inc .... N	163	17.5	30.0	1.64q	89	15	8.3	2.4	5.1	95	.0	117
Wal-Mart Strs .... ★N	783	27.3	16.5	1.51q	56	111	4.2	11.9	26.6	52	.5	5,752
Wilson H J .... O	74	10.2	14.7	1.13f	57	-7	1.7	2.5	7.4	113	1.7	89
Woolworth FW .... ★N	112	9.5	7.1	3.81q	35	-8	2.2	3.3	8.2	52	4.9	1,141
Zayre Corp .... N	169	11.0	7.5	3.37q	49	57	2.3	6.8	15.5	49	1.1b	73

MOTOR VEHICLES AND CAR BODIES (SIC 3711): TRENDS AND PROJECTIONS 1972–84 (in millions of dollars except as noted)

Item	1972	1977	1979	1981	1982[1]	1983[2]	Compound annual rate of growth 1972–83	1984[3]	Percent change 1983–84
Industry data									
Value of shipments[4]	42,905.6	76,517.8	85,147.4	74,273.1	70,625.0	97,920.0	7.8	—	—
Value of shipments (1972 $)[4]	42,905.6	57,188.2	54,863.0	40,520.0	36,670.0	48,830.0	1.2	54,250.0	11.1
Total employment (000)	339.2	343.6	348.5	271.9	243.6	265.0	-2.2	275.0	3.8
Production workers (000)	284.0	289.9	292.0	223.4	198.0	223.0	-2.2	232.0	4.0
Average hourly earnings of production workers ($)	5.79	9.23	10.99	13.94	14.76	15.05	9.1	—	—
Capital expenditures	917.2	1,706.1	1,905.6	4,697.2	—	—	—	—	—
Product data									
Value of shipments[5]	41,045.9	72,979.1	80,133.1	69,457.0	68,880.0	92,745.0	7.7	—	—
Value of shipments (1972 $)[5]	41,045.9	54,543.4	51,632.2	37,892.5	34,725.0	46,250.0	1.1	51,385.0	11.1
Product price index (1972 = 100)	100.0	133.3	153.9	184.3	193.9	191.2	6.1	—	—
Trade[6]									
Value of exports	732.5	2,571.8	3,172.1	2,826.0	2,211.0	1,097.0	3.7	1,124.0	2.5
Value of imports	3,452.0	7,602.2	12,741.1	15,858.0	16,529.0	18,381.0	16.4	20,829.0	13.3
Export/shipments ratio	0.018	0.035	0.040	0.041	0.032	0.012	—	—	—
Import/new supply ratio[7]	0.078	0.094	0.137	0.186	0.194	0.165	—	—	—

[1] Estimated except for product price index, exports, and imports.
[2] Estimated.
[3] Forecast.
[4] Value of all products and services sold by industry SIC 3711.
[5] Value of shipments of motor vehicles and car bodies products produced by all industries.
[6] Excludes Canada.
[7] New supply is the sum of product shipments plus imports.

Source: Bureau of the Census and Bureau of Industrial Economics. Estimates and forecasts by the Bureau of Industrial Economics.

Source: *U.S. Industrial Outlook 1984*, U.S. Department of Commerce.

MOTOR VEHICLE PARTS AND ACCESSORIES (SIC 3714): TRENDS AND PROJECTIONS 1972–84 (in millions of dollars except as noted)

Item	1972	1977	1979	1981	1982[1]	1983[2]	Compound annual rate of growth 1972–83	1984[3]	Percent change 1983–84
Industry data									
Value of shipments[4]	18,333.5	35,750.8	39,807.2	37,080.9	34,600.0	46,300.0	8.8	17,400.0	10.8
Value of shipments (1972 $)[4] ..	18,333.5	22,027.6	20,852.4	13,893.2	12,000.0	15,700.0	−1.4	340.0	2.1
Total employment (000)	400.9	450.7	459.0	359.4	322.9	333.0	−1.7	269.0	2.7
Production workers (000)	332.3	372.5	372.9	285.2	250.8	262.0	−2.1		
Average hourly earnings of production workers ($)	5.20	8.09	9.40	11.55	12.13	12.83	8.6		
Capital expenditures	1,113.1	1,833.2	2,750.7	3,309.4	—	—	—		
Product data									
Value of shipments[5]	19,417.0	37,841.8	42,906.5	40,214.9	37,500.0	50,250.0	9.0	18,900.0	11.2
Value of shipments (1972 $)[5] ..	19,417.0	23,316.0	22,475.9	15,067.4	13,000.0	17,000.0	−1.2		
Product price index (1972 = 100) ..	100.0	162.3	190.7	266.6	288.5	295.6	10.4		
Trade[6]									
Value of exports	563.4	1,548.7	2,071.0	3,302.7	2,767.4	1,890.9	11.6		
Value of imports	520.9	1,331.8	2,460.7	2,713.3	2,885.1	4,177.1	20.8		
Export/shipments ratio[7]	0.029	0.041	0.048	0.082	0.074	0.038	—		
Import/new supply ratio[7] ...	0.026	0.034	0.054	0.063	0.071	0.077	—		

[1] Estimated except for product price index, exports, and imports.
[2] Estimated.
[3] Forecast.
[4] Value of all products and services sold by industry SIC 3714.
[5] Value of shipments of motor vehicle parts and accessories products produced by all industries.
[6] Excludes Canada.
[7] New supply is the sum of product shipments plus imports.

Source: Bureau of the Census and Bureau of Industrial Economics. Estimates and forecasts by the Bureau of Industrial Economics.

Source: *U.S. Industrial Outlook 1984*, U.S. Department of Commerce.

Company and Market	Relative Price			Earnings Per Share			Other					
	Price to Equity	P/E Ratio		Latest 12 Months		5-Year Growth	Profit Margin	Return On Assets	Return On Common Equity	Debt Equity Ratio	Dividend Yield	Market Value
		Current	5-Year Average	Amount	Change	Rate						
	%	-	-	$	%	%	%	%	%	%	%	$Mil
Auto Manufacturers												
Am Motors ....★N	253	NE	3.9	- 2.01q	NE	- 57	- 7.9	NE	NE	469	.0	454
Chrysler Cp ....★N	NS	4.2	10.6	6.02q	201	28	2.3	NE	NE	- 663	3.2	3,047
Ford Motor Co ....★N	108	3.4	3.7	10.62f	NE	- 19	4.3	NE	NE	39	4.4	6,567
Ford of Can ....A	81	NA	23.3	14.46f	NE	1	1.4	5.3	16.3	16	NA	593
Gen Motors ....★N	101	4.4	17.6	14.87q	212	13	5.0	8.2	18.2	17	5.9	20,640
Honda Motor ....N	173	10.8	9.7	4.46f	25	34	4.0	6.7	16.7	35	.8	4,174
Mack Trucks ....O	92	9.3	19.7	1.77q	NC	78	- 2.2	NE	NE	27	.0	500
Automotive Parts and Accessories												
Allen Group ....N	128	19.3	10.9	1.03f	NE	- 22	1.8	3.0	6.5	44	2.5b	129
Arvin Indus ....N	92	9.8	10.3	2.28f	65	- 8	3.0	5.6	10.1	40	5.0	167
Barnes Group ....N	113	13.9	19.5	1.40f	300	- 16	2.3	NE	NE	55	4.1	141
Buell Indus ....A	117	8.3	12.2	3.00q	131	11	4.9	6.5	9.2	8	2.0	33
Champ Parts ....O	58	23.8	24.3	.21f	- 78	- 23	.4	3.0	11.3	229	2.0	10
Champ Spark ....★N	94	9.6	12.2	.92q	156	- 12	3.1	4.5	7.4	6	4.5	341
Dana Corp ....★N	117	9.3	11.4	2.50q	184	- 8	3.8	5.2	9.8	29	5.2	1,306
Donaldson ....N	113	14.6	11.2	1.26n	NE	- 16	- 1.7	NE	NE	26	3.6	96
Dyneer Corp ....A	119	10.8	10.5	1.76s	184	- 8	2.1	2.9	6.0	36	3.7	64
Eaton Corp ....★N	133	8.4	14.8	4.89q	1938	- 7	4.1	4.8	11.1	42	2.9	1,309
Echlin Mfg ....★N	210	12.2	16.6	1.93s	56	10	5.4	7.7	13.2	28	3.2	488
Facet Entprs ....N	62	9.9	NM	1.09q	51	90	2.1	2.9	5.6	51	.0	32
Fruehauf Cp ....★N	83	72.3	30.3	.42f	NE	- 25	.4	.5	1.8	104	1.3	380
Guardian Inds ....N	206	9.5	8.9	1.72q	9	20	8.1	8.1	18.6	65	2.0	372
Hastings Mfg ....A	151	7.6	5.9	5.01q	108	39	3.8	6.1	8.9	7	1.7	16
Hayes Albion ....N	91	NE	NM	- 1.84q	NE	- 95	- 7.6	NE	NE	48	.0	37
Hoover Univ ....N	175	8.8	7.7	2.58q	34	2	4.2	5.8	12.4	48	4.1	310
Howell Ind ....A	157	10.8	50.1	.79s	NE	6	.3	.9	1.3	0	.0	12
Kysor Ind ....N	118	14.5	39.5	1.00f	1900	- 17	2.5	NE	NE	65	2.8	43
Mr Gasket ....O	639	13.1	19.9	.88n	NC	68	10.5	11.6	31.1	90	.0	121
Premier Ind ....N	346	17.5	14.5	1.76n	19	15	9.8	13.9	16.8	0	1.6	638
Raymark Cp ....N	62	NE	11.5	- 5.80f	NE	- 45	- 4.4	5.0	14.1	79	.0	40
Sealed Power ....★N	141	9.0	8.3	2.66q	39	9	6.9	9.7	14.0	9	3.3	293
Seaport Cp ....A	75	25.0	63.5	.08f	700	85	.7	.7	1.8	22	.0	4
Sheller-Globe ....N	87	6.4	9.1	2.85s	108	9	2.7	4.0	8.4	56	3.8	163
Simpson Indust ....O	157	13.5	49.0	1.04n	225	- 12	.3	.5	.8	11	5.7	59
Smith AO ....A	50	5.1	8.3	2.74q	NE	- 18	1.6	3.1	6.6	35	3.4	103
Sparton Corp ....N	210	10.3	10.5	1.45s	31	49	6.5	13.5	19.0	0	3.2	102
Std Motor Prd ....N	242	10.3	9.0	1.76q	41	72	10.2	14.0	21.5	21	1.8	237
Std Products ....A	182	5.2	5.7	3.41n	85	61	4.8	10.7	22.0	31	4.5	114
Superior Ind Int ....A	176	8.0	16.7	1.03f	94	- 13	5.0	6.2	11.2	26	.0a	34
Trico Prods ....O	79	NE	9.4	- 1.22n	NE	- 33	- 9.4	NE	NE	0	.7	70
Wynn's Intl ....N	97	9.8	10.3	1.82q	139	- 7	3.4	5.3	9.4	19	3.4	66

TELEPHONE AND TELEGRAPH SERVICES (4811 & 4821): TRENDS AND PROJECTIONS 1972–84 (in millions of dollars except as noted)

Item	1972	1977	1979	1981	1982[1]	1983[2]	Compound annual rate of growth 1972–83	1984[2]	Percent change 1983–84
Operating Revenues:									
Domestic telephone & telegraph	25,750	44,100	54,754	70,837	78,886	86,870	—	—	—
International telephone & telegraph	663	1,339	1,906	2,250	2,325	2,500	—	—	—
Operating Revenues (1972 $):									
Domestic telephone & telegraph	25,750	38,150	48,957	53,664	56,752	59,500	7.9	62,475	5.0
International telephone & telegraph[3]	663	1,339	1,906	2,250	2,325	2,500	12.8	2,875	15.0
No. of telephone (000) (Dec.)	131,998	162,037	175,162	181,892	183,530	189,000	3.3	203,200	7.5
Total employment[4] (000)	1,002	975	1,070	1,095	1,100	1,110	0.9	1,120	0.9
Production workers (000)	790	738	789	796	790	790	0.0	790	—
Average hourly earnings (Dec. $)	4.10	6.91	8.09	9.90	10.65[5]	11.18	9.5	11.74	5.0
Year-to-year percent change in average hourly earnings (Dec.-Dec.)	13.6	9.0	7.6	12.2	6.2	7.5	—	—	—
Year-to-year percent change in productivity output per employee hour	4.8	7.2	4.7	5.4	5.2	—	—	—	—
Industry price index	100	115.6	118.4	132.0	139.0	146.0	—	—	—
Year-to-year percent change in industry price index (Dec.-Dec.)[6]	—	1.6	2.4	8.4	5.3	5.0	—	—	—
Capital expenditures	10,500	14,700	20,180	23,340	22,525	21,125	6.6	—	—
Gross cumulative plant investment[7]	84,400	131,200	155,200	186,800	202,350	216,925	9.0	—	—

[1] Estimated by Bureau of Industrial Economics (BIE).
[2] Forecast.
[3] Price indices for international services have declined slightly since 1972.
[4] Includes both telephone and telegraph workers.
[5] As of July 1983.
[6] Implicit price deflator for gross revenues originating in telephone and telegraph services.
[7] Does not include domestic or international telegraph carriers.

Source: Bureau of the Census; Bureau of Labor Statistics. Bureau of Industrial Economics estimates, Federal Communications Commission, AT&T, U.S. Independent Telephone Association, Industry Publications and Annual Reports.

Source: *U.S. Industrial Outlook 1984*, U.S. Department of Commerce.

Company and Market		Relative Price — Price to Equity %	P/E Ratio Current -	P/E Ratio 5-Year Average -	Earnings Per Share — Latest 12 Months Amount $	Change %	5-Year Growth Rate %	Other — Profit Margin %	Return On Assets %	Return On Common Equity %	Debt Equity Ratio %	Dividend Yield %	Market Value $Mil
Communications													
Acton Cp	A	265	NE	38.1	-1.29q	-100	-43	-23.3	1.4	7.6	302	.0a	35
Allnet CommunSvc	O	349	20.1	53.5	.18q	NC	71	3.6	6.0	14.4	44	.0	123
ALLTEL Cp	N	107	7.8	7.6	2.71q	2	4	9.1	4.0	14.9	161	8.5b	396
Am Tel & T	★N	NA	NA	NA	.00f	NC	NC	NA	NA	NA	NA	7.0	16,515
Ameritech Cp	★N	NA	NA	NA	.00	NC	NC	NA	NA	NA	NA	9.0	6,484
Bell Atlantic	★N	NA	NA	NA	.00	NC	NC	NA	NA	NA	NA	9.1	6,881
Bell Canada	N	95	NA	6.6	3.37f	13	10	8.4	5.0	14.0	83	NA	5,053
BellSouth	★N	NA	NA	NA	.00	NC	NC	NA	NA	NA	NA	9.0	8,478
Centel Cp	N	132	8.3	8.0	4.19q	7	8	8.7	4.7	15.3	110	6.7	956
Century Tel	N	86	8.3	7.6	1.00f	-17	0	10.6	3.4	14.9	221	9.5	71
Cinn Bell	N	86	6.6	6.5	5.31f	24	-2	11.6	5.7	13.3	57	8.3	216
Cmwth Tel Ent	O	113	6.6	7.9	3.55q	18	19	8.2	4.0	15.2	181	6.4	60
COMSAT	N	81	8.9	11.8	2.70f	0	4	11.4	5.3	8.1	2	5.0	436
Contl Telecom	N	110	7.6	7.9	2.50q	16	5	8.2	4.1	14.3	135	9.1	1,331
Coradian Corp	A	602	NE	19.2	-2.77n	NE	-97	-12.8	NE	NE	2350	.0	3
Electrospace Sys	O	998	24.5	16.5	.95f	27	57	10.1	14.5	32.0	9	.3	196
Equatorial Commun	O	549	NM	NM	.19q	NC	112	7.8	2.9	3.2	4	.0	252
GTE Cp	★N	110	7.5	7.6	4.98q	13	6	7.4	4.0	14.9	136	8.1	7,102
Herit Comm	N	271	30.5	28.9	.52f	-2	117	5.1	3.8	11.3	98	.3	118
Inter Tel	O	184	NE	66.9	-.29q	-100	-35	-4.7	NE	NE	30	.0	40
Lincoln Telecom	O	102	7.3	6.9	3.47q	17	5	11.2	5.0	13.3	81	7.8	104
Magnetics Cont	O	184	13.5	14.3	.87q	1	20	7.2	9.1	15.1	17	.0	67
MCI Communicatn	★O	157	11.4	27.1	.67f	-17	72	9.4	4.4	13.7	152	.0	1,790
NYNEX Cp	★N	NA	NA	NA	.00	NC	NC	NA	NA	NA	NA	9.6	6,144
Pac Telecom	O	131	7.3	7.5	1.92f	19	31	18.5	7.5	17.9	63	5.1	524
Pacific Telesis	★N	NA	NA	NA	.00	NC	NC	NA	NA	NA	NA	9.7	5,481
Philipp LD Tel	A	33	5.4	4.5	.44s	-33	-13	13.4	.0	20.2	460	18.9	39
Rochester Tele	N	122	8.2	7.7	3.40f	8	9	12.4	6.9	14.4	62	8.1	285
So N Eng Tel	N	105	7.5	7.1	3.99q	20	8	10.2	5.7	14.4	69	8.8	878
Swtrn Bell	★N	NA	NA	NA	.00	NC	NC	NA	NA	NA	NA	9.6	5,686
Telecom Plus	O	249	NE	24.6	-.85q	-100	-64	-16.4	4.5	8.9	13	.0	223
Telephone Data	A	116	10.6	11.4	.92f	-6	9	8.9	2.3	10.5	249	3.8	71
TIE Comm	A	184	12.0	20.3	1.17q	113	88	10.8	9.8	14.2	7	.0	461
U S Telephone	O	347	NE	NC	-.19q	NE	-69	-3.5	1.2	5.0	204	.0	69
Unit Telecom	N	95	6.8	7.9	2.72q	5	4	9.4	4.7	14.1	107	9.9	1,570
Univ Commun	A	273	16.0	25.4	.60s	22	54	7.5	5.3	15.4	93	.0	69
US West Inc	★N	NA	NA	NA	.00	NC	NC	NA	NA	NA	NA	9.1	5,819
Wstn Union Cp	N	76	NE	11.8	-3.59q	-100	-38	-5.7	NE	NE	111	6.0	560

COMMERCIAL BANKING: TRENDS AND PROJECTIONS 1972–1984 (in billions of dollars except as noted)

Item	1972	1977	1979	1981	1982	1983[1]	Compound annual rate of growth 1972–83	1984[1]	Percent change 1983–84
Assets	739	1,166	1,351	1,652	1,820	1,966	9.3	2,123	8
Loans	415	680	860	926	1,001	1,061	8.9	1,156	9
Investments	184	259	283	341	370	414	7.7	447	8
Deposits	616	939	1,031	1,240	1,362	1,498	8.4	1,648	10
Employment (000)	1,105	1,238	1,369	1,482	1,506	1,530	3.0	1,553	2

[1] Estimated by Bureau of Industrial Economics.

Source: Board of Governors of the Federal Reserve System. Bureau of Labor Statistics. and Bureau of Industrial Economics.

Source: *U.S. Industrial Outlook 1984*, U.S. Department of Commerce.

SAVINGS AND LOAN INDUSTRY (SIC 612): TRENDS AND PROJECTIONS 1972–84 (in billions of current dollars except as noted)

Item	1972	1978	1979	1981	1982	1983ᵉ	Compound annual rate of growth 1972–83	1984ᵉ	Percent change 1983–84
Assets	236	448	568	651	693	830	12.1	905	9.0
Mortgages	200	385	486	532	531	590	10.3	649	10.0
Total savings	201	377	461	512	550	640	11.1	717	12.0
Mortgage originations	50	105	99	52	53	109	7.3	125	15.0
Net new savings	24	32	15	−25	−6	55	7.8	45	−18.0
Employment (000)	129	208	242	269	274	295	7.8	313	6.0

ᵉ Estimate.

Note: Includes data for FSLIC-insured federal savings banks, most of which converted from savings and loan association status.

Source: Federal Home Loan Bank Board and Bureau of Labor Statistics.

Source: *U.S. Industrial Outlook 1984*, U.S. Department of Commerce.

Company and Market		Relative Price — Price to Equity %	Relative Price — P/E Ratio Current	Relative Price — P/E Ratio 5-Year Average	Earnings Per Share — Latest 12 Months Amount $	Earnings Per Share — Latest 12 Months Change %	Earnings Per Share — 5-Year Growth Rate %	Other — Profit Margin %	Other — Return On Assets %	Other — Return On Common Equity %	Other — Debt Equity Ratio %	Other — Dividend Yield %	Other — Market Value $Mil
Middle Atlantic Banks													
Bank of NY Co	N	75	5.8	5.8	4.88q	12	18	6.8	.7	16.1	17	6.5	422
Bankers Tr NY	★N	76	5.0	4.4	8.30f	19	20	6.6	.6	15.5	26	5.9	1,242
Chase Manhttn	★N	45	3.8	4.9	10.44f	43	11	5.0	.5	14.1	45	9.2	1,365
Chem NY Corp	★N	60	4.4	4.7	6.02f	18	19	6.2	.6	15.5	36	8.9	1,188
Citicorp	★N	74	5.2	6.0	6.06q	9	15	5.0	.6	16.4	233	6.6	3,893
Citizen Fst Bcp	A	110	8.0	5.4	2.48f	11	3	7.8	.7	13.8	2	5.1b	69
Contl Bncp	O	99	7.0	5.8	3.82q	-7	3	9.3	.9	13.5	2	7.6b	221
CoreStates Fnl	O	100	6.1	4.5	5.45q	9	16	9.3	1.0	16.3	39	5.6	512
Equimark Corp	N	29	NE	7.3	-3.58q	-100	-67	-3.3	NE	NE	20	.0	18
Fidelcor Inc	O	80	4.7	4.9	8.09q	38	96	8.9	.8	19.2	41	5.8	197
Fst Natl State	N	77	5.1	4.5	7.08q	6	18	9.0	.7	17.4	33	7.3	388
Fst Penn Cp	★N	60	NE	14.5	-.74q	NE	-4	-2.9	NE	NE	127	.0	85
Horizon Bncp	N	117	7.2	5.0	2.72f	25	14	9.1	.8	13.8	14	5.3	159
HUBCO Inc	A	77	7.7	5.9	1.22f	17	24	6.4	.6	10.0	0	6.0	16
Irving Bk Cp	N	60	5.1	4.5	10.02q	8	7	5.0	.5	12.5	46	7.2	448
IVB Fncl	O	69	7.7	6.9	2.91q	70	-10	4.8	.5	10.5	18	9.8	66
Key Banks	N	80	6.5	4.5	2.85q	14	11	9.7	.9	12.9	24	5.9	206
Lincoln First Bks	O	111	9.8	5.1	7.04f	7	11	6.1	.6	12.0	39	2.9	238
Mfrs Hanover	★N	40	3.1	4.8	8.37f	8	9	5.1	.5	14.8	108	12.2	1,040
Marine Midland	N	41	4.4	4.7	4.61q	0	16	4.7	.4	10.7	57	7.9	387
Mellon Natl	★N	68	5.4	5.5	6.68q	-8	11	7.3	.7	13.3	42	7.1	938
Meridian Bncp	O	77	6.1	3.6	4.72f	0	10	8.1	.9	12.6	22	7.6	197
Midlantic Banks	O	105	6.5	3.3	3.45f	16	6	9.5	.8	14.7	22	4.5	351
Morgan, J.P.	★N	83	5.7	6.3	11.08q	9	12	8.0	.8	15.0	18	6.4	2,554
Natl Cm Bk NJ	O	117	7.3	6.1	5.81q	18	5	10.7	1.0	15.2	0	6.0	108
Norstar Bncp	N	89	6.9	5.8	4.44q	-1	13	12.4	1.1	13.4	24	7.2b	388
PNC Fnl Cp	O	104	6.9	4.9	5.60q	9	17	9.6	1.0	15.3	54	5.5	796
Rep NY	N	89	5.9	5.4	5.47f	4	19	8.6	.8	17.3	69	4.9	436
Sterling Bncp	N	127	10.0	14.2	1.00f	-8	110	8.5	1.0	14.6	63	7.2	50
Union Natl Cp	O	79	8.2	5.5	3.66q	-7	1	7.0	.6	9.0	0	6.1	120
Unit Jer Bank	N	97	7.2	4.9	3.65f	15	13	6.9	.7	14.9	21	5.3	155
US Trust Cp	O	149	10.8	7.9	3.62f	14	19	6.5	.7	13.7	31	4.1	177
Pacific States Banks													
Bancal TriState	N	110	9.5	9.1	5.25f	193	0	6.5	.7	12.3	21	2.4	245
Bancp Hawaii Inc	O	80	5.4	5.6	3.50q	-2	7	9.0	.9	15.0	22	6.5	165
BankAmerica	★N	50	7.3	7.8	2.00q	-21	-11	2.9	.3	8.8	55	10.4	2,200
Calif Fst Bk	O	72	9.3	7.4	1.78f	62	-10	3.9	.4	7.6	4	6.5	170
City Natl Corp	O	151	10.0	9.4	2.37q	26	4	8.0	.8	14.6	6	3.7	180
Crocker Natl	N	29	NE	6.5	-7.34q	-100	-32	-.4	NE	NE	17	7.1	345
Fst Hawaiian	O	104	6.7	5.8	6.25n	17	10	7.9	.8	15.7	41	6.2	140
Fst Interstate	★N	69	5.7	5.8	5.72f	7	3	5.7	.6	12.6	73	7.2	1,347
Orbanco Fnl Svcs	O	43	NE	5.8	-3.29f	-100	-20	-5.2	NE	NE	203	.0	37
Rainier Bcp	O	90	7.1	6.1	5.15q	20	6	6.8	.7	11.9	18	4.8	354
Security Pac	N	88	5.9	5.0	7.23f	11	13	6.1	.7	14.8	20	5.7	1,570
US Bancorp	O	67	6.6	6.8	2.74n	-16	5	8.0	.8	10.9	43	5.5	323
Wells Fargo	N	65	5.4	5.2	6.11q	7	3	5.2	.6	12.9	128	6.6	782

Life Insurance

LIFE INSURANCE (SIC 6311): TRENDS AND PROJECTIONS 1972–84 (in millions of dollars except as noted)

Item	1972	1977	1979	1981	1982	1983[1]	Compound annual growth rate 1972–83	1984[2]	Percent change 1983–84
Premium receipts	44.4	72.3	84.9	103.6	118.1	134.0	10.6	150.0	11.9
New life insurance purchases	208.7	369.8	492.8	831.1	837.9	845.0	13.6	930.0	1.1
Life insurance in force	1,628.8	2,582.8	3,222.3	4,063.6	4,476.7	4,937.0	10.6	5,430.0	10.1
Total benefits payable	18.6	26.5	38.0	43.4	48.0	53.0	10.0	58.0	9.4
Life insurance assets	239.7	351.7	432.3	525.8	588.2	660.0	9.6	740.0	12.1
Total employment (000)[3]	567.7	519.7	540.0	535.3	539.5	540.0	-0.5	540.0	0.0

[1] Estimates by Bureau of Industrial Economics.
[2] Forecast.
[3] Home office personnel only.

Source: *U.S. Industrial Outlook 1984*, U.S. Department of Commerce.

Company and Market		Relative Price			Earnings Per Share			Other					
		Price to Equity	P/E Ratio Current	P/E Ratio 5-Year Average	Latest 12 Months Amount	Change	5-Year Growth Rate	Profit Margin	Return On Assets	Return On Common Equity	Debt Equity Ratio	Dividend Yield	Market Value
		%	-	-	$	%	%	%	%	%	%	%	$Mil
Life, Accident and Health													
Academy Ins Grp	O	154	8.1	12.6	1.11q	31	67	14.4	5.3	17.6	15	2.2	140
Aetna Life Cas	★N	73	14.8	8.1	2.04q	-52	-15	2.3	.7	7.9	10	8.7	3,010
Alleghany Corp	N	170	13.4	8.4	5.43n	-3	16	4.3	1.3	16.2	5	1.5	609
Am Family Cp	N	138	9.8	7.3	1.84q	40	-1	4.4	2.3	13.5	10	3.3	320
Am Heritage Lf	N	120	10.9	8.2	2.39f	6	10	4.5	2.4	11.0	0	4.1	83
Am Income Life	O	144	7.6	7.4	1.59q	15	26	17.8	6.0	18.2	0	2.5	163
Am Natl Ins	O	80	7.5	6.1	3.40q	41	10	12.4	2.7	10.1	0	3.8	739
Benef Std A	A	179	24.0	9.5	1.91f	68	-6	4.8	1.5	7.4	21	.9	129
Busn Mens Assur	O	91	6.7	6.3	5.71f	30	4	9.3	2.6	10.5	5	5.0	205
Capital Holdg	★N	108	7.4	6.9	4.43q	9	13	7.8	2.6	13.3	36	4.5	853
CIGNA Cp	★N	49	6.2	7.7	5.26f	-18	-19	3.2	1.1	8.2	9	7.9	2,400
Colonial Penn	N	128	9.6	6.7	2.84q	34	-12	3.8	4.2	13.6	0	5.1	439
Combined Intl	N	140	8.0	6.5	4.04q	21	6	10.6	5.2	20.7	5	6.4	886
Equitable of Iowa	O	52	5.9	7.1	3.08f	79	-4	5.1	1.3	9.8	2	7.0	114
First Executive	O	103	11.5	10.5	1.00f	27	98	3.3	.9	9.0	0	.0	516
Fremont Genl	O	134	68.5	12.5	.23s	-80	-9	1.2	.7	4.4	42	3.0	170
Home Beneficial	O	82	6.7	5.5	2.84f	11	16	21.3	4.0	12.2	0	4.2	234
ICH Corp	A	150	8.7	5.2	3.47f	10	49	9.4	1.8	17.3	128	.8	234
Indep Ins Grp	O	75	5.5	5.8	3.85q	22	5	7.1	2.8	13.2	3	6.3	154
Jackson Natl Lf	O	262	13.4	8.4	2.23f	3	52	4.7	2.0	19.7	7	.0	183
Jefferson-Pilot	★N	90	9.1	6.8	4.74q	18	3	10.6	3.0	9.7	0	4.6	915
Kansas City Life	O	64	9.4	6.9	6.19q	-25	-3	7.6	1.3	7.2	3	4.5	149
Liberty Corp	N	102	11.4	8.2	2.08q	54	-6	6.9	2.3	8.7	39	3.0	237
Life Inv Inc	O	128	11.9	11.0	3.06q	22	10	4.3	1.6	9.5	20	.7	350
Lincoln Nat	★N	92	8.1	6.6	4.13q	51	3	4.3	1.5	11.0	17	5.0	1,411
Manhattan Natl	N	76	14.8	10.4	1.02q	10	9	1.9	.5	5.1	0	2.1	74
Monarch Capital	O	100	9.1	7.3	3.60q	25	2	7.1	2.0	10.0	1	4.3	287
Monumental Cp	O	73	10.8	9.5	2.09f	3	-6	5.5	1.2	6.9	2	5.3	147
NWn Natl Life	O	56	10.8	9.3	3.85n	85	-6	.6	.2	1.9	27	3.6	146
Old Rep Intl	O	112	7.1	5.0	4.65f	19	-3	12.5	4.2	16.9	22	2.7	339
Orion Cap Cp	N	80	12.9	13.2	1.77q	-12	10	3.5	1.9	7.4	20	3.3	128
Provident Lf Acc	O	93	6.8	6.1	10.11q	43	9	7.8	2.8	13.0	0	4.2	640
Southland Fincl	O	153	NE	10.0	-.72f	NE	-24	-9.4	NE	NE	266	2.5	341
Torchmark Cp	N	53	8.4	6.6	2.73q	3	17	8.6	3.0	12.0	11	4.3	873
Travelers Corp	★N	78	7.0	5.5	4.08f	11	-2	2.9	1.0	11.2	2	6.7	2,396
Unit Cos Fincl	A	156	8.3	6.3	4.31f	26	29	5.7	1.0	15.9	26	2.8b	51
U S Hlth Care	O	656	65.8	54.6	.46q	NC	68	3.5	5.4	7.5	0	.0	280
USLIFE Corp	★N	73	6.8	6.2	3.64q	5	0	8.2	2.6	13.2	44	3.9	456
Wash Natl Cp	N	59	9.7	9.8	1.86f	-9	-7	2.7	.7	6.6	4	6.0	198
Westbridge Cap	A	164	8.1	4.6	1.02f	-4	57	7.0	4.8	17.1	0	.0a	34
Williams A L	O	743	26.2	38.9	.42q	NC	71	16.2	4.1	5.0	0	.0	237

STANDARD INDUSTRIAL CLASSIFICATION (SIC) CODES*

1972 Code	SIC Title
2011	MEAT PACKING PLANTS
2013	SAUSAGE & OTHER PREPARED MEATS
2016	POULTRY DRESSING PLANTS
2017	POULTRY & EGG PROCESSING
2021	CREAMERY BUTTER
2022	CHEESE, NATURAL & PROCESSED
2023	CONDENSED & EVAPORATED MILK
2024	ICE CREAM & FROZEN DESSERTS
2026	FLUID MILK
2032	CANNED SPECIALTIES
2033	CANNED FRUITS & VEGETABLES
2034	DEHYDRATED FRUITS, VEGETABLES, SOUPS
2035	PICKLES, SAUCES, SALAD DRESSINGS
2037	FROZEN FRUITS & VEGETABLES
2038	FROZEN SPECIALTIES
2041	FLOUR & OTHER GRAIN MILL PRODUCTS
2043	CEREAL BREAKFAST FOODS
2044	RICE MILLING
2045	BLENDED & PREPARED FLOUR
2046	WET CORN MILLING
2047	DOG, CAT, & OTHER PET FOOD
2048	PREPARED FEEDS NEC
2051	BREAD, CAKE & RELATED PRODUCTS
2052	COOKIES & CRACKERS
2061	RAW CANE SUGAR
2062	CANE SUGAR REFINING
2063	BEET SUGAR
2065	CONFECTIONERY PRODUCTS
2066	CHOCOLATE & COCOA PRODUCTS
2067	CHEWING GUM
2074	COTTONSEED OIL MILLS
2075	SOYBEAN OIL MILLS
2076	VEGETABLE OIL MILLS NEC
2077	ANIMAL & MARINE FATS & OILS
2079	SHORTENING & COOKING OILS
2082	MALT BEVERAGES
2083	MALT
2084	WINES, BRANDY, & BRANDY SPIRITS
2085	DISTILLED LIQUOR EXC BRANDY
2086	BOTTLED & CANNED SOFT DRINKS
2087	FLAVORING EXTRACTS & SIRUPS NEC
2091	CANNED & CURED SEAFOODS
2092	FRESH OR FROZEN PKGD FISH
2095	ROASTED COFFEE
2097	MANUFACTURED ICE
2098	MACARONI & SPHAGHETTI
2099	FOOD PREPARATIONS NEC
2211	WEAVING MILLS, COTTON
2221	WEAVING MILLS, SYNTHETICS
2231	WEAVING & FINISHING MILLS, WOOL
2257	CIRCULAR KNIT FABRIC MILLS
2258	WARP KNIT FABRIC MILLS
2281	YARN MILLS, EXC WOOL
2283	WOOL YARN MILLS
2284	THREAD MILLS
2311	MEN'S & BOY'S SUITS & COATS
2321	MEN'S & BOYS' SHIRTS & NIGHTWEAR
2327	MEN'S & BOYS' SEPARATE TROUSERS
2328	MEN'S & BOYS' WORK CLOTHING
2331	WOMEN'S & MISSES' BLOUSES & WAISTS
2335	WOMEN'S & MISSES' DRESSES
2337	WOMEN'S & MISSES' SUITS & COATS
2361	CHILDREN'S DRESSES & BLOUSES
2421	SAWMILLS & PLANING MILLS, GENERAL
2426	HARDWOOD DIMENSION & FLOORING
2435	HARDWOOD VENEER & PLYWOOD
2436	SOFTWOOD VENEER & PLYWOOD
2451	MOBILE HOMES
2511	WOOD HOUSEHOLD FURNITURE
2512	UPHOLSTERED HOUSEHOLD FURNITURE
2514	METAL HOUSEHOLD FURNITURE
2515	MATTRESSES & BEDSPRINGS
2517	WOOD TV & RADIO CABINETS
2519	HOUSEHOLD FURNITURE NEC
2541	WOOD PARTITIONS & FIXTURES
2611	PULPMILLS
2621	PAPERMILLS, EXC BUILDING PAPER
2631	PAPERBOARD MILLS
2641	PAPER COATING & GLAZING
2642	ENVELOPES
2643	BAGS, EXC TEXTILE BAGS
2645	DIE CUT PAPER & BOARD
2646	PRESSED & MOLDED PULP GOODS
2647	SANITARY PAPER PRODUCTS
2648	STATIONERY PRODUCTS
2649	CONVERTED PAPER PRODUCTS NEC
2651	FOLDING PAPERBOARD BOXES
2652	SET-UP PAPERBOARD BOXES
2653	CORRUGATED & SOLID FIBER BOXES
2654	SANITARY FOOD CONTAINERS
2655	FIBER CANS, DRUMS, & SIMILAR PRODUCTS
2661	BUILDING PAPER & BUILDING BOARD MILLS
2711	NEWSPAPERS
2721	PERIODICALS
2731	BOOK PUBLISHING
2732	BOOK PRINTING
2741	MISCELLANEOUS PUBLISHING
2751	COMMERCIAL PRINTING, LETTERPRESS
2752	COMMERCIAL PRINTING, LITHOGRAPHIC
2753	ENGRAVING & PLATE PRINTING
2754	COMMERCIAL PRINTING, GRAVURE
2761	MANIFOLD BUSINESS FORMS
2771	GREETING CARD PUBLISHING
2782	BLANKBOOKS & LOOSELEAF BINDERS
2789	BOOKBINDING & RELATED WORK
2791	TYPESETTING
2793	PHOTOENGRAVING
2794	ELECTROTYPING & STEREOTYPING
2795	LITHOGRAPHIC PLATEMAKING SERVICES
2812	ALKALIES & CHLORINE
2816	INORGANIC PIGMENTS
2819	INDUSTRIAL INORGANIC CHEMICALS NEC
2821	PLASTICS MATERIALS & RESINS
2822	SYNTHETIC RUBBER
2823	CELLULOSIC MAN-MADE FIBERS
2824	ORGANIC FIBERS, NONCELLULOSIC
2831	BIOLOGICAL PRODUCTS
2841	SOAP & OTHER DETERGENTS
2843	SURFACE ACTIVE AGENTS
2844	TOILET PREPARATIONS

* For the name and telephone number of the specialist in the Bureau of Industrial Economics (U.S. Department of Commerce) covering a particular industry call 202-377-4356.

1972 Code	SIC Title	1972 Code	SIC Title
2851	PAINTS & ALLIED PRODUCTS	3483	AMMUNITION, EXC FOR SMALL ARMS NEC
2865	CYCLIC CRUDES & INTERMEDIATES	3484	SMALL ARMS
2869	INDUSTRIAL ORGANIC CHEMICALS NEC	3511	TURBINES & TURBINE GENERATOR SETS
2873	NITROGENOUS FERTILIZERS	3523	FARM MACHINERY & EQUIPMENT
2879	AGRICULTURAL CHEMICALS NEC	3524	LAWN & GARDEN EQUIPMENT
2895	CARBON BLACK	3531	CONSTRUCTION MACHINERY
2911	PETROLEUM REFINING		
3011	TIRES & INNER TUBES	3532	MINING MACHINERY
3041	RUBBER & PLASTICS HOSE & BELTING	3533	OILFIELD MACHINERY
3069	FABRICATED RUBBER PRODUCTS NEC	3534	ELEVATORS & MOVING STAIRWAYS
		3541	MACHINE TOOLS, METAL-CUTTING TYPES
3079	MISCELLANEOUS PLASTICS PRODUCTS	3542	MACHINE TOOLS, METAL-FORMING TYPES
3131	BOOT & SHOE CUT STOCK & FINDINGS	3544	SPECIAL DIES, TOOLS, JIGS, & FIXTURES
3142	HOUSE SLIPPERS	3545	MACHINE TOOL ACCESSORIES
3144	WOMEN'S FOOTWEAR EXC ATHLETIC	3551	FOOD PRODUCTS MACHINERY
3149	FOOTWEAR, EXC RUBBER, NEC	3552	TEXTILE MACHINERY
3151	LEATHER GLOVES & MITTENS	3555	PRINTING TRADES MACHINERY
3161	LUGGAGE	3561	PUMPS & PUMPING EQUIPMENT
3171	WOMEN'S HANDBAGS & PURSES		
3172	PERSONAL LEATHER GOODS NEC	3563	AIR & GAS COMPRESSORS
3199	LEATHER GOODS NEC	3564	BLOWERS & FANS
		3567	INDUSTRIAL FURNACES & OVENS
3211	FLAT GLASS	3573	ELECTRONIC COMPUTING EQUIPMENT
3221	GLASS CONTAINERS	3574	CALCULATING & ACCOUNTING MACHINES
3241	CEMENT, HYDRAULIC	3585	REFRIGERATION & HEATING EQUIPMENT
3261	VITREOUS PLUMBING FIXTURES	3612	TRANSFORMERS
3262	VITREOUS CHINA FOOD UTENSILS	3613	SWITCHGEAR & SWITCHBOARD APPARATUS
3263	FINE EARTHENWARE FOOD UTENSILS	3623	WELDING APPARATUS, ELECTRIC
3271	CONCRETE BLOCK & BRICK	3631	HOUSEHOLD COOKING EQUIPMENT
3272	CONCRETE PRODUCTS NEC		
3273	READY-MIXED CONCRETE	3632	HOUSEHOLD REFRIGERATORS & FREEZERS
3312	BLAST FURNACES & STEEL MILLS	3633	HOUSEHOLD LAUNDRY EQUIPMENT
		3634	ELECTRICAL HOUSEWARES & FANS
3313	ELECTROMETALLURGICAL PRODUCTS	3635	HOUSEHOLD VACUUM CLEANERS
3315	STEEL WIRE & RELATED PRODUCTS	3636	SEWING MACHINES
3316	COLD FINISHING OF STEEL SHAPES	3639	HOUSEHOLD APPLIANCES NEC
3317	STEEL PIPE & TUBES	3643	CURRENT CARRYING WIRING DEVICES
3321	GRAY IRON FOUNDRIES	3644	NONCURRENT CARRYING WIRING DEVICES
3322	MALLEABLE IRON FOUNDRIES	3645	RESIDENTIAL LIGHTING FIXTURES
3324	STEEL INVESTMENT FOUNDRIES	3646	COMMERCIAL LIGHTING FIXTURES
3325	STEEL FOUNDRIES NEC		
3331	PRIMARY COPPER	3648	LIGHTING EQUIPMENT NEC
3332	PRIMARY LEAD	3651	RADIO & TV RECEIVING SETS
		3652	PHONOGRAPH RECORDS
3333	PRIMARY ZINC	3661	TELEPHONE & TELEGRAPH APPARATUS
3334	PRIMARY ALUMINUM	3662	RADIO & TV COMMUNICATION EQUIPMENT
3339	PRIMARY NONFERROUS METALS NEC	3671	ELECTRON TUBES, RECEIVING TYPE
3341	SECONDARY NONFERROUS METALS	3672	CATHODE RAY TELEVISION TUBES
3351	COPPER ROLLING & DRAWING	3673	ELECTRON TUBES, TRANSMITTING
3353	ALUMINUM SHEET, PLATE, & FOIL	3674	SEMICONDUCTORS & RELATED DEVICES
3354	ALUMINUM EXTRUDED PRODUCTS	3675	ELECTRONIC CAPACITORS
3355	ALUMINUM ROLLING & DRAWING NEC		
3357	NONFERROUS WIREDRAWING & INSULAT-ING	3676	ELECTRONIC RESISTORS
		3677	ELECTRONIC COILS & TRANSFORMERS
		3678	ELECTRONIC CONNECTORS
3361	ALUMINUM FOUNDRIES (CASTINGS)	3679	ELECTRONIC COMPONENTS NEC
3362	BRASS, BRONZE, & COPPER FOUNDRIES	3693	X-RAY APPARATUS & TUBES
3369	NONFERROUS FOUNDRIES NEC	3711	MOTOR VEHICLES & CAR BODIES
3398	METAL HEAT TREATING	3713	TRUCK & BUS BODIES (INCL MOTOR HOMES)
3399	PRIMARY METAL PRODUCTS NEC	3715	TRUCK TRAILERS
3411	METAL CANS	3721	AIRCRAFT
3431	METAL SANITARY WARE	3724	AIRCRAFT ENGINES & ENGINE PARTS
3432	PLUMBING FITTINGS & BRASS GOODS	3728	AIRCRAFT EQUIPMENT NEC
3433	HEATING EQUIPMENT EXC ELECTRIC	3731	SHIP BUILDING AND REPAIR
3441	FABRICATED STRUCTURAL METAL	3743	RAILROAD EQUIPMENT
3443	FABRICATED PLATEWORK (BOILER SHOPS)	3751	MOTORCYCLES, BICYCLES & PARTS
3462	IRON & STEEL FORGINGS	3761	GUIDED MISSILES & SPACE VEHICLES
3463	NONFERROUS FORGINGS	3764	SPACE PROPULSION UNITS & PARTS
3465	AUTOMOTIVE STAMPINGS	3769	SPACE VEHICLE EQUIPMENT NEC
3482	SMALL ARMS AMMUNITION	3811	ENGINEERING & SCIENTIFIC INSTRUMENTS

1972 Code	SIC Title	1972 Code	SIC Title
3822	ENVIRONMENTAL CONTROLS	3843	DENTAL EQUIPMENT & SUPPLIES
3823	PROCESS CONTROL INSTRUMENTS	3911	JEWELRY, PRECIOUS METAL
3824	FLUID METERS & COUNTING DEVICES	3914	SILVERWARE & PLATED WARE
3825	INSTRUMENTS TO MEASURE ELECTRICITY	3942	DOLLS
3829	MEASURING & CONTROLLING DEVICES NEC	3944	GAMES, TOYS, & CHILDREN'S VEHICLES
3832	OPTICAL INSTRUMENTS & LENSES	3949	SPORTING & ATHLETIC GOODS NEC
3841	SURGICAL & MEDICAL INSTRUMENTS	3961	COSTUME JEWELRY

Source: *U.S. Industrial Outlook.*

Real Change in Industry Shipments

The standard measure of real shipments in this section is the 1972 dollar. This constant dollar yardstick is an attempt to provide a means of getting at "real" growth by eliminating the distorting effects of price change. While the 1972 constant dollar measures may have little meaning to the manufacturer who does business in current dollars, their relative magnitudes over time can provide a reasonably firm basis of judgment for business decisions. By converting real shipments measures to index numbers, the relative movements are highlighted.

The choice of a base year in such a data series is arbitrary, affecting only the perspective. In the table that follows, the year 1983 is used as the base (1983 = 100) to facilitate comparisons from a present day perspective.

The indices in the table are constructed using the 1972 dollar measures. For example, the Trends and Projections table for the Cereal and Breakfast Foods industry (SIC 2043) shows that the real industry shipments (in 1972 dollars) for 1981, 1982, and 1983 were $1.493, $1.537, and $1.543 billion, respectively. The corresponding entries in the table below are constructed by dividing each of these shipment values by the 1983 value and then multiplying by 100 to yield indices of 97, 100, and 100. The shipment data in the Trends and Projections tables were supplemented with strictly comparable data for additional years and industries.

The 1983-based retrospective is given in terms of index numbers rather than aggregates (constant-dollar values) for two reasons:

First, index numbers show at a glance the direction of changes. An index value

Source: *U.S. Industrial Outlook 1984*, U.S. Department of Commerce.

greater than 100 indicates a volume of shipments larger than that in 1983, the reference year, while an index value less than 100 indicates a smaller volume of shipments than in 1983.

Second, the index number approach enables comparison of the relative changes between industries. For example, the 1982 index of the Creamery Butter industry (SIC 2021) is 103, while the 1982 index for the Natural and Processed Cheese industry (SIC 2022) is 93, indicating that real shipments in the butter industry declined about 3 percent from 1982 to 1983, while real shipments in the cheese industry increased about 7 percent from 1982 to 1983.

The estimated 1983 industry shipments in the table are in millions of current (1983) dollars. This permits a quick comparison of industries based on their current shipments, and also, their relative performance over the years. For example, as noted above, the cheese industry grew relatively more slowly than the butter industry shrank in 1983. The 1983 values show that the cheese industry is roughly 10 times the size of the butter industry ($12.8 billion versus $1.3 billion); the recent growth of the cheese industry has more than offset the shrinkage of the butter industry. A comparison of the real shipment levels of butter and cheese in 1972 shows that butter shipments in 1972 were approximately $1.8 billion in 1983 dollars (1.44 × $1.3) while cheese shipments were approximately $7.5 billion in 1983 dollars, (.58 × $12.8), or approximately four times the volume of butter shipments.

INDICES OF REAL INDUSTRY SHIPMENTS (1983 = 100)

SIC	Title	Y58	Y63	Y67	Y72	Y73	Y74	Y75	Y76	Y77	Y78	Y79	Y80	Y81	Y82	Y83	Y84	Value 83$
2011	Meatpacking plants	62	74	83	93	87	93	87	99	94	94	94	94	98	97	100	100	46,258.0
2013	Sausages and other prepared meats	44	57	67	81	70	80	76	87	107	99	97	103	100	96	100	100	12,018.5
2016	Poultry dressing plants	30	42	55	59	70	61	58	67	69	73	82	88	97	95	100	103	8,326.6
2017	Poultry and egg processing	17	18	29	62	51	54	55	65	57	59	76	78	85	95	100	103	1,487.4
2021	Creamery butter	239	231	195	144	134	137	141	138	106	109	99	97	100	103	100	99	1,267.6
2022	Natural and processed cheese	28	34	41	58	59	65	66	71	70	69	70	76	83	93	100	106	12,846.4
2023	Condensed and evaporated milk	74	83	92	88	75	79	81	77	95	94	89	92	96	100	100	100	4,842.2
2024	Ice cream and frozen desserts	79	89	81	87	92	92	95	95	97	94	96	95	96	97	100	102	3,177.5
2026	Fluid milk	97	94	97	101	104	107	109	111	113	111	105	106	103	103	100	99	17,779.8
2032	Canned specialties	54	77	83	101	112	101	101	105	98	104	99	98	99	99	100	101	4,078.4
2033	Canned fruits and vegetables	74	83	97	97	104	101	99	102	103	104	107	104	100	98	100	101	9,555.3
2034	Dehydrated fruits, vegetables, and soup	53	68	81	89	88	98	100	111	100	107	82	103	97	99	100	101	1,644.0
2035	Pickles, sauces, and salad dressing	37	52	53	62	61	59	59	60	100	104	106	107	99	100	100	101	4,107.8
2037	Frozen fruits and vegetables	33	39	59	83	87	89	89	95	96	105	99	102	99	98	100	103	5,136.2
2038	Frozen specialties	19	30	53	90	102	102	94	104	108	116	108	103	96	98	100	100	5,138.9
2043	Cereal breakfast foods	42	54	58	73	80	79	82	87	94	93	98	96	97	100	100	100	4,186.4
2051	Bread, cake, and related products	102	103	107	109	108	107	108	112	107	105	103	101	100	98	100	100	13,414.5
2052	Cookies and crackers	72	83	90	96	97	92	90	91	92	95	100	98	99	99	100	101	4,866.0
2065	Confectionery products	47	51	63	68	70	73	65	66	76	80	81	87	93	96	100	103	7,224.0
2082	Malt beverages	36	42	52	64	69	73	73	77	83	90	91	94	97	98	100	101	11,545.0
2084	Wines, brandy, and brandy spirits	28	37	41	68	73	92	76	77	88	92	103	103	101	101	100	101	2,667.0
2085	Distilled liquor, except brandy	43	50	64	81	81	81	77	76	82	91	95	100	97	99	100	100	3,889.0
2086	Bottled and canned soft drinks	38	43	57	78	87	81	83	84	91	97	99	96	90	95	100	103	18,209.0
2111	Cigarettes	84	100	106	111	119	119	124	126	120	116	108	124	122	112	100	97	11,674.0
2121	Cigars	32	235	238	203	196	172	157	139	121	126	111	105	106	104	100	92	283.0
2131	Chewing and smoking tobacco	123	83	65	76	79	71	82	85	94	101	106	103	105	98	100	99	766.0
2141	Tobacco stemming and redrying	136	155	139	135	128	141	132	135	119	118	104	106	105	104	100	99	2,981.5
2211	Weaving mills—cotton	141	155	165	111	100	96	88	96	108	97	103	102	96	94	100	—	5,331.7
2221	Weaving mills—manmade fibers	29	42	59	89	85	80	85	99	108	101	81	87	108	95	100	—	8,213.0
2231	Weaving and finishing mills—wool	237	249	249	100	98	104	94	103	94	95	93	91	104	94	100	—	828.3
2281	Yarn mills, except wool	40	50	64	97	95	90	90	96	108	111	106	99	97	92	100	—	4,691.9
2283	Wool yarn mills	147	207	192	111	69	74	82	86	68	65	101	99	97	93	100	—	378.2
2311	Men's and boys' suits and coats	142	157	177	163	161	143	128	131	142	124	116	119	117	106	100	—	2,956.3
2321	Men's and boys' shirts and nightwear	62	78	82	106	108	100	94	105	97	103	99	101	106	98	100	—	3,783.3
2327	Men's and boys' separate trousers	43	78	103	147	153	147	140	122	106	115	110	102	104	102	100	—	2,251.4
2328	Men's and boys work clothing	42	47	62	80	77	68	80	88	98	99	97	95	99	93	100	—	4,788.1
2331	Women's and misses' blouses	28	35	41	63	66	72	77	83	96	101	97	92	97	104	100	—	3,405.0
2335	Women's and misses' dresses	78	92	117	117	127	113	112	115	115	118	103	103	101	107	100	—	5,030.0
2337	Women's and misses suits and coats	58	68	72	60	65	63	65	71	89	87	86	87	98	100	100	—	4,283.1
2341	Women's and children's underwear	58	69	76	84	88	88	78	80	90	96	99	104	101	101	100	—	2,809.3
2361	Children's dresses and blouses	64	76	81	88	89	89	69	73	90	95	90	92	97	102	100	—	1,210.4
2386	Leather and sheep lined clothing	117	93	149	221	205	264	301	267	182	165	117	142	133	106	100	97	181.0
2411	Logging camps and log contractors	40	50	57	61	63	70	76	74	87	83	83	100	97	87	100	109	8,143.0

SIC	Industry																	Value
2421	Sawmills and planing mills—general	88	94	97	110	103	97	93	105	109	107	110	108	102	98	100	105	1,1897.1
2426	Hardwood dimension and flooring	84	109	101	113	110	91	92	100	104	112	100	90	89	87	100	109	1,143.3
2431	Millwork	58	62	68	106	96	79	77	85	95	92	91	83	83	77	100	108	6,566.0
2435	Hardwood veneer and plywood	40	67	87	89	97	90	83	86	101	101	101	97	99	97	100	105	1,559.7
2436	Softwood veneer and plywood	32	51	70	89	82	76	76	88	92	95	90	83	84	83	100	105	4,444.5
2439	Structural wood members, nec	41	22	38	88	88	78	84	103	112	132	126	105	94	91	100	101	970.2
2448	Wood pallets and skids	10	21	35	47	55	60	64	71	88	94	90	96	96	94	100	102	994.3
2491	Wood preserving	56	65	84	78	74	100	86	78	91	96	93	108	105	96	100	105	1,350.0
2492	Particleboard	7	11	10	107	114	112	88	98	115	119	119	97	94	83	100	105	590.9
2611	Pulpmills	49	77	87	76	82	86	71	89	93	101	101	100	99	83	100	106	3,150.0
2621	Papermills, except building paper	48	55	64	73	82	88	73	85	88	97	97	97	100	95	100	105	21,400.0
2631	Paperboard mills	35	51	62	84	92	98	80	86	90	94	94	94	94	93	100	106	11,300.0
2641	Paper coating and glazing	44	64	81	93	101	97	85	95	99	103	106	102	104	96	100	104	5,039.8
2642	Envelopes	39	50	62	80	83	85	74	77	87	97	97	98	99	95	100	104	1,692.0
2643	Bags, except textile bags	48	62	68	87	91	103	96	100	95	99	99	101	99	98	100	103	5,800.0
2645	Die-cut paper and board	36	53	79	88	90	84	76	83	83	102	102	92	97	95	100	104	1,828.5
2646	Pressed and molded pulp goods	89	126	159	155	149	155	147	145	154	137	119	107	104	101	100	99	233.9
2647	Sanitary paper products	33	43	52	68	74	83	79	82	83	88	94	93	96	97	100	104	9,112.0
2648	Stationery products	64	73	103	110	116	113	106	113	108	116	105	103	100	98	100	102	929.6
2649	Converted paper products, nec	35	41	38	60	72	68	62	72	95	101	93	98	99	97	100	104	2,668.8
2651	Folding paperboard boxes	60	77	84	98	98	93	92	105	120	129	114	112	100	99	100	102	3,983.0
2652	Setup paperboard boxes	161	152	179	168	154	154	130	141	120	122	113	105	104	99	100	102	503.0
2653	Corrugated and solid fiber boxes	39	52	68	84	91	91	81	89	98	103	101	96	109	95	100	105	1,1065.0
2654	Sanitary food containers	69	91	108	132	130	129	121	128	124	121	122	111	100	103	100	99	2,753.0
2655	Fiber cans, drums and similar products	34	55	79	98	111	107	92	96	96	99	105	99	100	97	100	103	1,560.0
2661	Building paper and board mills	113	103	130	147	156	154	131	126	103	98	105	92	82	94	100	102	680.0
2711	Newspapers	59	65	75	86	88	88	82	84	88	90	92	93	96	97	100	103	24,250.0
2721	Periodicals	41	50	66	61	65	65	62	68	77	86	93	93	98	98	100	104	1,1479.4
2731	Book publishing	58	71	83	90	81	87	81	84	96	100	96	95	98	98	100	102	8,050.0
2732	Book printing	49	66	87	74	85	73	77	78	94	99	93	93	96	98	100	104	3,050.0
2741	Miscellaneous publishing	41	47	66	87	85	73	70	74	95	92	95	100	98	98	100	102	3,205.0
2761	Manifold business forms	24	37	51	65	74	85	71	71	84	89	96	94	95	97	100	105	5,480.0
2771	Greeting card publishing	38	41	56	67	68	70	61	63	71	74	78	82	90	95	100	106	2,414.6
2795	Lithograph platemaking services	11	19	22	33	35	41	39	46	66	74	77	86	89	92	100	107	1,435.0
2812	Alkalies and chlorine	114	151	161	182	186	208	176	183	170	163	122	116	107	95	100	105	1,483.0
2813	Industrial gases	30	46	64	68	78	70	66	78	90	92	101	95	108	98	100	103	1,791.0
2816	Inorganic pigments	83	96	102	141	148	165	119	123	110	115	113	107	107	93	100	105	1,835.0
2819	Industrial inorganic chemicals, nec	66	77	85	95	101	108	94	108	121	129	126	121	108	107	100	110	10,859.0
2821	Plastics materials and resins	19	30	44	81	89	89	65	80	91	99	101	90	96	91	100	107	17,340.0
2822	Synthetic rubber	56	79	100	116	123	122	107	118	120	119	135	112	110	98	100	109	2,725.0
2823	Cellulosic manmade fibers	125	133	158	97	103	130	108	116	122	127	133	126	120	95	100		1,252.3
2824	Organic fibers - noncellulosic	8	20	33	60	77	73	79	84	96	103	112	103	99	89	100	105	9,575.6
2831	Biological products	6	10	17	39	41	52	53	55	67	72	80	72	91	89	100	105	1,920.0
2833	Medicinals and botanicals	12	15	22	25	32	49	46	57	66	66	75	86	92	95	100	104	3,720.0
2834	Pharmaceutical preparations	25	34	48	71	75	78	80	86	87	92	92	95	96	97	100	103	22,000.0
2841	Soap and other detergents	41	55	64	77	84	84	78	81	84	89	89	95	94	97	100	103	10,773.0

INDICES OF REAL INDUSTRY SHIPMENTS (1983 = 100)—(continued)

SIC	Title	Y58	Y63	Y67	Y72	Y73	Y74	Y75	Y76	Y77	Y78	Y79	Y80	Y81	Y82	Y83	Y84	Value 83$
2842	Polishes and sanitation goods	33	43	62	85	88	84	84	87	89	95	93	88	92	97	100	103	5,645.0
2843	Surface active agents	14	19	30	41	42	68	51	58	62	72	75	84	93	96	100	104	2,515.0
2844	Toilet preparations	27	43	57	85	91	94	93	102	107	112	107	97	96	98	100	102	10,235.0
2851	Paints and allied products	52	70	78	90	96	95	85	94	100	103	107	98	101	94	100	105	9,600.0
2861	Gum and wood chemicals	58	65	60	62	64	57	42	61	58	64	53	65	108	98	100	102	610.0
2865	Cyclic crudes and intermediates	44	64	84	112	129	107	97	114	137	140	116	113	111	99	100	105	6,750.0
2869	Industrial organic chemicals, nec	23	40	54	87	98	94	75	88	102	105	112	98	101	96	100	109	34,000.0
2873	Nitrogenous fertilizers	25	40	59	80	92	101	100	110	117	123	120	131	124	114	100	110	2,964.0
2874	Phosphatic fertilizers	57	80	99	105	115	139	120	136	140	142	147	155	138	116	100	115	2,937.0
2875	Fertilizers, mixing only	66	91	103	110	123	123	125	131	151	135	148	147	131	115	100	110	1,762.0
2879	Agricultural chemicals, nec	29	44	72	82	93	125	102	92	90	95	104	99	126	111	100	112	4,905.0
2891	Adhesives and sealants	26	42	57	81	96	97	82	88	101	107	120	100	99	90	100	107	2,910.0
2892	Explosives	90	99	226	121	124	130	123	112	114	109	116	117	108	103	100	105	919.0
2893	Printing ink	66	78	106	105	108	85	79	80	98	111	111	101	97	97	100	103	1,560.0
2895	Carbon black	59	82	92	130	136	122	80	95	120	126	114	83	110	93	100	109	615.0
2899	Chemical preparations, nec	47	52	67	83	77	66	68	86	90	106	127	107	108	95	100	104	6,180.0
2911	Petroleum refining	56	65	76	91	86	95	97	109	114	115	123	110	106	103	100	106	171,839.0
3011	Tires and inner tubes	57	74	88	125	140	132	114	114	126	118	110	88	93	92	100	104	10,700.0
3021	Rubber and plastics footwear	87	124	148	143	129	129	112	105	92	88	83	88	102	100	100	100	705.0
3041	Rubber and plastic hose and belting	70	116	140	129	129	138	122	132	152	160	162	130	132	105	100	106	1,820.0
3069	Fabricated rubber products, nec	59	80	95	105	118	110	97	105	115	117	119	108	114	96	100	104	6,400.0
3079	Miscellaneous plastics products	13	21	37	64	75	70	60	70	88	96	94	90	95	92	100	108	37,000.0
3111	Leather tanning and finishing	144	137	144	124	112	117	118	135	123	118	84	97	100	95	100	98	1,900.0
3142	House slippers	174	183	222	153	148	146	121	122	147	150	153	172	138	124	100	101	197.0
3143	Men's footwear, except athletic	114	117	148	139	136	129	123	125	122	117	104	109	118	93	100	101	2,178.0
3144	Women's footwear, except athletic	174	168	186	155	148	131	109	113	125	121	112	113	119	108	100	97	1,723.0
3149	Footwear, except rubber, nec	135	134	107	108	112	117	171	175	101	104	97	116	109	97	100	96	810.0
3151	Leather gloves and mittens	133	189	170	164	178	230	96	108	172	145	130	114	117	105	100	97	161.7
3161	Luggage	61	67	99	96	104	100	123	136	116	121	140	145	125	109	100	99	815.0
3171	Women's handbags and purses	74	84	93	102	97	97	132	134	132	148	120	112	107	97	100	101	605.0
3172	Personal leather goods, nec	69	73	86	105	118	123	90	112	144	153	143	121	115	106	100	98	385.0
3211	Flat glass	45	67	71	90	102	88	121	120	124	130	113	100	99	91	100	107	1,840.0
3221	Glass containers	61	75	96	112	117	113	109	111	122	118	115	109	107	103	100	101	5,535.0
3241	Hydraulic cement	100	109	113	123	131	128	110	121	129	130	128	116	102	92	100	107	3,809.0
3251	Brick and structural clay tile	112	118	123	141	135	129	117	98	107	111	113	101	84	73	100	107	987.0
3261	Vitreous plumbing fixtures	65	77	77	106	113	117	91	83	94	92	113	102	96	84	100	103	613.0
3262	Vitreous china food utensils	73	75	86	76	83	79	70	138	93	94	92	104	101	96	100	103	295.7
3263	Fine earthenware food utensils	216	234	173	196	217	229	197	112	144	141	127	113	118	103	100	97	97.3
3271	Concrete block and brick	79	96	99	124	125	119	110	104	111	124	115	106	93	85	100	108	1,576.0
3272	Concrete products, nec	56	72	91	121	128	116	106	104	111	111	116	105	103	101	100	108	3,830.0

SIC	Industry																	Value
3273	Ready-mixed concrete	61	81	92	108	112	109	99	99	112	121	123	107	102	92	100	107	9,073.0
3275	Gypsum products	60	67	63	91	96	84	68	79	89	99	100	85	84	80	100	104	1,750.0
3331	Primary copper	52	64	49	88	98	87	79	84	97	106	102	92	107	88	100	97	4,404.4
3332	Primary lead	122	110	100	137	170	172	151	138	102	115	112	163	113	101	100	105	687.4
3333	Primary zinc	343	399	409	371	362	319	199	250	225	231	272	195	184	123	100	138	246.0
3411	Metal cans	61	67	87	105	110	105	104	106	111	111	110	102	101	99	100	106	11,475.0
3431	Metal sanitary ware	92	103	115	142	132	124	89	105	112	120	113	93	93	86	100	107	638.0
3432	Plumbing fittings and brass goods	61	71	73	104	105	89	89	106	108	110	110	94	94	86	100	106	1,655.0
3441	Fabricated structural metal	88	91	124	131	135	122	110	110	108	110	122	130	126	107	100	98	7,300.0
3444	Sheet metalwork	52	62	84	107	127	110	87	101	104	110	110	108	105	93	100	112	6,750.0
3448	Prefabricated metal buildings	26	30	72	70	102	95	64	74	115	126	122	112	113	99	100	107	2,030.0
3451	Screw machine products	67	79	122	96	127	109	78	88	105	119	129	122	115	96	100	109	2,378.0
3452	Bolts, nuts, rivets, and washers	92	107	129	121	137	135	101	116	129	141	148	137	134	100	100	107	3,441.9
3465	Automotive stampings	50	79	87	112	122	104	110	110	125	128	115	88	87	77	100	111	11,425.0
3494	Valves and pipe fittings	56	67	85	91	101	101	89	93	104	110	116	115	118	109	100	106	8,370.0
3519	Internal combustion engines, nec	37	51	67	88	104	113	90	114	133	152	144	130	130	112	100	114	9,723.5
3523	Farm machinery and equipment	85	89	123	116	141	154	102	161	168	152	179	158	154	108	100	104	9,938.6
3524	Lawn and garden equipment	27	36	44	101	109	131	100	98	104	118	148	118	97	96	100	108	2,388.2
3531	Construction machinery	93	108	149	171	198	213	192	184	208	237	223	195	187	108	100	105	9,649.9
3532	Mining machinery	81	84	115	125	137	157	175	170	160	146	143	146	141	120	100	104	1,945.6
3533	Oilfield machinery	30	33	38	45	52	65	72	70	76	89	95	106	136	139	100	106	8,918.3
3541	Metal-cutting machine tools	152	214	349	193	243	272	261	222	232	268	285	296	303	204	100	113	2,100.0
3542	Metal-forming machine tools	201	266	368	291	350	369	305	270	262	276	294	268	227	157	100	106	800.0
3544	Special dies, tools, and jigs	68	80	116	113	132	127	95	105	115	124	132	128	128	96	100	105	5,250.0
3546	Power driven handtools	29	43	55	68	86	95	80	81	119	132	140	132	112	95	100	106	2,080.0
3551	Food products machinery	74	95	117	109	129	140	127	121	132	149	142	133	119	100	100	112	2,176.0
3552	Textile machinery	116	161	198	182	194	207	162	160	140	138	136	135	128	105	100	104	1,083.0
3554	Paper industries machinery	123	145	170	114	128	81	124	125	109	110	126	123	113	104	100	98	1,344.0
3555	Printing trades machinery	44	56	86	75	82	81	75	76	88	97	106	112	112	97	100	105	2,370.0
3561	Pumps and pumping equipment	41	49	63	72	79	80	80	84	87	91	97	98	98	99	100	103	6,934.2
3562	Ball and roller bearings	60	102	146	144	168	167	144	147	152	162	171	149	148	109	100	109	2,961.0
3563	Air and gas compressors	34	42	61	56	65	77	70	77	85	91	100	98	101	99	100	102	3,310.8
3564	Blowers and fans	46	57	89	106	126	110	110	115	107	108	113	112	110	104	100	98	1,947.0
3567	Industrial furnaces and ovens	118	144	218	152	166	187	157	150	150	147	167	163	145	117	100	100	827.0
3573	Electronic computing equipment	1	3	7	16	18	22	21	25	31	40	52	65	78	87	100	118	41,055.0
3579	Office machines and typewriters, etc.	27	34	51	53	64	70	62	67	88	93	97	101	103	98	100	103	3,857.0
3612	Transformers	47	63	96	122	134	134	104	118	118	126	132	132	127	114	100	102	2,745.0
3623	Electric welding apparatus	40	55	82	92	100	108	91	90	100	109	111	104	113	97	100	104	1,600.0
3643	Current-carrying wiring devices	66	77	88	110	126	137	85	109	109	108	125	119	113	94	100	103	2,817.1
3644	Noncurrent-carrying wiring divices	75	87	104	110	123	105	88	97	104	112	127	120	116	107	100	103	2,192.1
3645	Residential lighting fixtures	67	86	103	121	126	97	80	94	103	107	101	94	88	85	100	106	1,503.0
3646	Commercial lighting fixtures	45	65	88	108	116	103	87	101	100	109	121	121	119	106	100	103	1,476.0
3648	Lighting equipment, nec	35	49	66	102	112	100	77	68	89	106	114	118	117	96	100	103	1,077.0
3651	Radio and television receiving sets	17	28	51	63	74	69	62	72	86	95	95	96	101	90	100	105	6,996.0
3661	Telephone and telegraph apparatus	21	31	46	67	73	79	59	55	73	81	96	104	106	98	100	105	12,991.8
3662	Radio and TV communication equipment	16	42	51	45	47	47	49	51	56	63	72	84	88	92	100	109	35,100.0

INDICES OF REAL INDUSTRY SHIPMENTS (1983 = 100)—(concluded)

SIC	Title	Y58	Y63	Y67	Y72	Y73	Y74	Y75	Y76	Y77	Y78	Y79	Y80	Y81	Y82	Y83	Y84	Value 83$
3671	Electron tubes	72	74	117	108	119	103	91	100	107	108	113	114	101	97	100	102	2,360.7
3674	Semiconductors and related devices	1	3	5	14	18	20	15	22	28	40	53	65	75	84	100	121	14,141.0
3675	Electronic capacitors	28	48	78	77	103	103	75	91	103	110	117	105	98	95	100	106	1,272.3
3676	Electronic resistors	26	58	85	82	106	99	76	84	99	95	102	113	105	98	100	101	812.0
3677	Electronic coils and transformers	48	78	147	105	116	112	84	89	96	97	110	106	105	96	100	104	856.3
3678	Electronic connectors	7	15	41	38	51	54	49	53	64	76	91	98	97	91	100	111	2,649.1
3679	Electronic components, nec	7	14	39	42	47	40	42	50	64	62	76	81	87	90	100	112	14,637.8
3693	X-ray apparatus and tubes	10	14	20	29	32	39	43	45	83	82	84	79	89	95	100	107	4,060.0
3711	Motor vehicles and car bodies	21	54	65	88	102	83	79	102	117	121	112	81	83	75	100	111	97,920.0
3713	Truck and bus bodies	22	34	49	89	90	75	79	99	139	155	110	89	90	81	100	121	4,300.0
3714	Motor vehicle parts and accessories	99	103	93	117	134	119	99	123	140	147	133	98	88	76	100	111	46,300.0
3715	Truck trailers	51	80	107	138	166	179	90	118	161	193	219	157	125	98	100	125	2,045.0
3721	Aircraft	64	62	102	67	78	77	73	73	75	79	95	101	100	87	100	104	35,426.0
3724	Aircraft engines and engine parts	70	79	94	85	99	97	87	85	88	96	111	122	121	98	100	98	12,900.0
3728	Aircraft equipment, nec	77	77	132	84	93	91	88	80	83	87	106	121	104	97	100	93	9,400.0
3731	Ship building and repairing	56	57	81	83	94	101	105	104	107	105	107	114	124	117	100	86	9,882.6
3751	Motorcycles, bicycles, and parts	24	41	62	113	120	139	101	97	119	135	136	118	112	89	100	111	1,321.0
3761	Guided missiles and space vehicles	75	100	132	95	104	109	104	95	82	86	92	94	91	241	100	105	11,500.0
3764	Space propulsion units and parts	215	241	288	86	110	91	77	68	70	75	78	89	94	99	100	107	2,410.0
3769	Space vehicle equipment, nec	331	302	161	145	135	94	89	94	39	40	44	46	119	113	100	92	1,500.0
3825	Instruments to measure electricity	24	25	36	41	48	53	51	52	58	67	75	90	93	98	100	105	6,878.0
3841	Surgical and medical instruments	11	22	34	57	65	69	69	78	75	78	80	88	94	96	100	107	3,890.0
3842	Surgical appliances and supplies	21	27	35	55	56	52	60	57	62	68	75	75	88	94	100	108	5,990.0
3843	Dental equipment and supplies	19	24	35	61	69	86	79	82	84	91	99	102	98	98	100	103	1,475.0
3861	Photographic equipment and supplies	14	21	37	57	64	70	64	71	78	87	95	92	94	100	100	103	18,100.0
3911	Jewelry and precious metal	80	111	160	180	169	137	137	171	181	154	132	83	96	94	100	103	3,225.0
3914	Silverware and plated ware	187	196	241	199	201	134	120	133	143	149	127	76	102	93	100	104	600.0
3931	Musical instruments	61	77	95	132	132	133	117	138	129	135	127	120	114	101	100	103	1,086.0
3942	Dolls	46	71	50	54	52	62	49	58	78	72	70	63	72	96	100	104	598.4
3944	Games, toys, and childrens' vehicles	28	41	52	66	72	64	57	63	75	75	84	82	95	100	100	102	5,262.0
3949	Sporting and athletic goods, nec	36	42	48	91	83	80	88	88	93	97	97	95	97	95	100	106	3,537.0
3961	Costume jewelry	46	48	62	70	71	78	101	90	103	107	105	113	105	97	100	104	1,017.0

Source: *U.S. Industrial Outlook 1984*, U.S. Department of Commerce.

PRESENT VALUE OF $1

Periods until Payment	1%	2%	4%	6%	8%	10%	12%	14%	15%	16%	18%	20%	22%	24%	25%	26%	28%	30%	35%	40%	45%	50%
1	0.990	0.980	0.962	0.943	0.926	0.909	0.893	0.877	0.870	0.862	0.847	0.833	0.820	0.806	0.800	0.794	0.781	0.769	0.741	0.714	0.690	0.667
2	0.980	0.961	0.925	0.890	0.857	0.826	0.797	0.769	0.756	0.743	0.718	0.694	0.672	0.650	0.640	0.630	0.610	0.592	0.549	0.510	0.476	0.444
3	0.971	0.942	0.889	0.840	0.794	0.751	0.712	0.675	0.658	0.641	0.609	0.579	0.551	0.524	0.512	0.500	0.477	0.455	0.406	0.364	0.328	0.296
4	0.961	0.924	0.855	0.792	0.735	0.683	0.636	0.592	0.572	0.552	0.516	0.482	0.451	0.423	0.410	0.397	0.373	0.350	0.301	0.260	0.226	0.198
5	0.951	0.906	0.822	0.747	0.681	0.621	0.567	0.519	0.497	0.476	0.437	0.402	0.370	0.341	0.328	0.315	0.291	0.269	0.223	0.186	0.156	0.132
6	0.942	0.888	0.790	0.705	0.630	0.564	0.507	0.456	0.432	0.410	0.370	0.335	0.301	0.275	0.262	0.250	0.227	0.207	0.165	0.133	0.108	0.088
7	0.933	0.871	0.760	0.665	0.583	0.513	0.452	0.400	0.376	0.354	0.314	0.279	0.249	0.222	0.210	0.198	0.178	0.159	0.122	0.095	0.074	0.059
8	0.923	0.853	0.731	0.627	0.540	0.467	0.404	0.351	0.327	0.305	0.266	0.233	0.204	0.179	0.168	0.157	0.139	0.123	0.091	0.068	0.051	0.039
9	0.914	0.837	0.703	0.592	0.500	0.424	0.361	0.308	0.284	0.263	0.225	0.194	0.167	0.144	0.134	0.125	0.108	0.094	0.067	0.048	0.035	0.026
10	0.905	0.820	0.676	0.558	0.463	0.386	0.322	0.270	0.247	0.227	0.191	0.162	0.137	0.116	0.107	0.099	0.085	0.073	0.050	0.035	0.024	0.017
11	0.896	0.804	0.650	0.527	0.429	0.350	0.287	0.237	0.215	0.195	0.162	0.135	0.112	0.094	0.086	0.079	0.066	0.056	0.037	0.025	0.017	0.012
12	0.887	0.788	0.625	0.497	0.397	0.319	0.257	0.208	0.187	0.168	0.137	0.112	0.092	0.076	0.069	0.062	0.052	0.043	0.027	0.018	0.012	0.008
13	0.879	0.773	0.601	0.469	0.368	0.290	0.229	0.182	0.163	0.145	0.116	0.093	0.075	0.061	0.055	0.050	0.040	0.033	0.020	0.013	0.008	0.005
14	0.870	0.758	0.577	0.442	0.340	0.263	0.205	0.160	0.141	0.125	0.099	0.078	0.062	0.049	0.044	0.039	0.032	0.025	0.015	0.009	0.006	0.003
15	0.861	0.743	0.555	0.417	0.315	0.239	0.183	0.140	0.123	0.108	0.084	0.065	0.051	0.040	0.035	0.031	0.025	0.020	0.011	0.006	0.004	0.002
16	0.853	0.728	0.534	0.394	0.292	0.218	0.163	0.123	0.107	0.093	0.071	0.054	0.042	0.032	0.028	0.025	0.019	0.015	0.008	0.005	0.003	0.002
17	0.844	0.714	0.513	0.371	0.270	0.198	0.146	0.108	0.093	0.080	0.060	0.045	0.034	0.026	0.021	0.020	0.015	0.012	0.006	0.003	0.002	0.001
18	0.836	0.700	0.494	0.350	0.250	0.180	0.130	0.095	0.081	0.069	0.051	0.038	0.028	0.021	0.018	0.016	0.012	0.009	0.005	0.002	0.001	0.001
19	0.828	0.686	0.475	0.331	0.232	0.164	0.116	0.083	0.070	0.060	0.043	0.031	0.023	0.017	0.014	0.012	0.009	0.007	0.003	0.002	0.001	0.001
20	0.820	0.673	0.456	0.312	0.215	0.149	0.104	0.073	0.061	0.051	0.037	0.026	0.019	0.014	0.012	0.010	0.007	0.005	0.002	0.001	0.001	
21	0.811	0.660	0.439	0.294	0.199	0.135	0.093	0.064	0.053	0.044	0.031	0.022	0.015	0.011	0.009	0.008	0.006	0.004	0.002	0.001		
22	0.803	0.647	0.422	0.278	0.184	0.123	0.083	0.056	0.046	0.038	0.026	0.018	0.013	0.009	0.007	0.006	0.004	0.003	0.001	0.001		
23	0.795	0.634	0.406	0.262	0.170	0.112	0.074	0.049	0.040	0.033	0.022	0.015	0.010	0.007	0.006	0.005	0.003	0.002	0.001			
24	0.788	0.622	0.390	0.247	0.158	0.102	0.066	0.043	0.035	0.028	0.019	0.013	0.008	0.006	0.005	0.004	0.003	0.002	0.001			
25	0.780	0.610	0.375	0.233	0.146	0.092	0.059	0.038	0.030	0.024	0.016	0.010	0.007	0.005	0.004	0.003	0.002	0.001	0.001			
26	0.772	0.598	0.361	0.220	0.135	0.084	0.053	0.033	0.026	0.021	0.014	0.009	0.006	0.004	0.003	0.002	0.002	0.001				
27	0.764	0.586	0.347	0.207	0.125	0.076	0.047	0.029	0.023	0.018	0.011	0.007	0.005	0.003	0.002	0.002	0.001	0.001				
28	0.757	0.574	0.333	0.196	0.116	0.069	0.042	0.026	0.020	0.016	0.010	0.006	0.004	0.003	0.002	0.002	0.001	0.001				
29	0.749	0.561	0.321	0.185	0.107	0.063	0.037	0.022	0.017	0.014	0.008	0.005	0.004	0.002	0.002	0.001	0.001					
30	0.742	0.552	0.308	0.174	0.099	0.057	0.033	0.020	0.015	0.012	0.007	0.004	0.003	0.002	0.001	0.001	0.001					
40	0.672	0.453	0.208	0.097	0.046	0.022	0.011	0.005	0.004	0.003	0.001	0.001										
50	0.608	0.372	0.141	0.054	0.021	0.009	0.003	0.001	0.001	0.001												

Source: By permission, from Robert N. Anthony, Management Accounting: Text and Cases, rev. ed. (Homewood, Ill.: Richard D. Irwin, Inc., 1960), p. 656.

Financial Statement Ratios by Industry

Many quantitative indicators are used to assess the financial strength of an enterprise and the success of its operations. The simplest is to assemble related financial items, such as sales and profits, and express the relationship in the form of a ratio. Using these ratios, various aspects of corporate operations may be compared with the performance of other corporations or groups of corporations of similar size or in a similar industry.

The Quarterly Financial Report's (QFR) ratio formatted income statement and selected balance sheet ratios are expressed as a percent of net sales and total assets, respectively. The operating and financial characteristics of the respective industries and asset size groups are thus reduced to a common denominator to facilitate analysis.

The ratio tables include the following additional basic operating ratios:

1. *Annual rate of profit on stockholders' equity at end of the period.* This ratio is obtained by multiplying income for the quarter before or after domestic taxes [including branch income (loss) and equity in the earnings of nonconsolidated subsidiaries net of foreign taxes] by four, to put it on an annual basis, and then dividing by stockholders' equity at the end of the quarter. It measures the rate of return which accrues to stockholders on their investment.

2. *Annual rate of profit on total assets.* This ratio is obtained by multiplying income, as defined in deriving the rate of profit on stockholders' equity, both before and after taxes, by four and then dividing by total assets at the end of the quarter. This ratio measures the productivity of assets in terms of producing income.

3. *Total current assets to total current liabilities.* This ratio is obtained by dividing total current assets by total current liabilities. It measures the ability to discharge current maturing obligations from existing current assets.

4. *Total cash, U.S. government and other securities to current liabilities.* This ratio is obtained by dividing total cash, U.S. government and other securities by total current liabilities. It measures the ability to discharge current liabilities from liquid assets.

5. *Total stockholders' equity to total debt.* This ratio is obtained by dividing total stockholders' equity by the total of short-term loans,

current installments on long-term debt, and long-term debt due in more than one year. It indicates the extent of leverage financing used.

DESCRIPTION OF THE SAMPLE

The sample on which the QFR estimates for mining, wholesale and retail trade are based is a composite sample selected from two mutually exclusive sampling frames. Prior to the third quarter 1977, the sample drawn for manufacturing estimates was similarly based. The frame from which the major portion of the sample continues to be selected consists of the Internal Revenue Service file of those corporate entities which are required to file Form 1120 or 1120-S and which also have as their principal industrial activity manufacturing, mining, or wholesale or retail trade. The IRS file is sampled once each year. At the time the sample is selected, the file does not contain those corporate entities whose first income tax return has not been processed. In addition, several months elapse between the selection of this sample and its introduction into the QFR program. To keep the mining and wholesale and retail trade QFR sample as up to date as possible, a separate sample is drawn each calendar quarter from a frame comprising applications for a Federal Social Security Employer's Identification Number filed with the Social Security Administration (SSA) during the previous quarter by new corporations. In processing the composite list of sample companies, a screening technique is used to insure that corporations drawn from the SSA frame could not have been drawn from the IRS frame.

Stratification is used in the sample selection process. In sampling from the IRS frame, stratification by industry and size is employed. In sampling from the SSA frame, stratification is by division and size alone. The measures of size used in the IRS frame are total assets and gross receipts while the measure of size used in the SSA frame is number of employees. Beginning with the third quarter 1977, the strata comprised of manufacturing firms with assets of less than $250,000 and the strata which contained corporations in the SSA frame are estimated by multivariate techniques. The sampling fractions applied to the other various industry-size strata vary according to both industry and size. They range from approximately one out of 850 to one out of one. Nearly all corporations whose operations are within the scope of the QFR and which have total assets greater than $50 million

Source: Quarterly Financial Report, Bureau of the Census. The exhibits in this section are from the same FTC publication.

are included in the sample. Corporations whose total assets are between $10 million and $50 million and whose receipts exceed the estimated average value for a corporation with $25 million in assets in its industry are also in the sample. Thus, for the most part, corporations with assets over $25 million are permanent sample members with a one out of one sampling fraction.

In those industry-size strata for which the sampling fraction is less than one out of one, a replacement scheme is utilized which provides that one eighth of the sample is replaced each quarter. Corporations removed are those that have been in the reporting group longest (usually eight quarters). Therefore, samples of small corporations for adjacent quarters are seven-eighths identical; for quarters ending nine months apart they are five-eighths identical; etc.

Industry Contents

TABLE 1—INCOME STATEMENT
FOR CORPORATIONS INCLUDED IN ESIC MAJOR GROUPS 20 AND 21

	Food and Kindred Products [1]				
	1Q 1983	2Q 1983	3Q 1983	4Q 1983	1Q 1984
	(percent of net sales)				
INCOME STATEMENT IN RATIO FORMAT					
Net sales, receipts, and operating revenues	100.0	100.0	100.0	100.0	100.0
Less: Depreciation, depletion, and amortization of property, plant and equipment	2.2	2.2	2.1	2.1	2.2
Less: All other operating costs and expenses	93.5	92.9	92.8	92.5	92.7
Income (or loss) from operations	4.3	5.0	5.1	5.4	5.1
Non-operating income (expense)	-0.4	0.4	0.4	0.4	0.2
Income (or loss) before income taxes	3.9	5.4	5.5	5.8	5.4
Less: Provision for current and deferred domestic income taxes	1.7	2.0	2.0	1.8	2.1
Income (or loss) after income taxes	2.2	3.4	3.5	4.0	3.3
	(percent)				
OPERATING RATIOS (see explanatory notes)					
Annual rate of profit on stockholders' equity at end of period:					
Before income taxes	14.08	19.95	20.84	22.00	19.78
After taxes	8.03	12.51	13.18	15.15	12.07
Annual rate of profit on total assets:					
Before income taxes	6.84	9.83	10.28	10.80	9.59
After taxes	3.90	6.16	6.50	7.44	5.85
BALANCE SHEET RATIOS (based on succeeding table)					
Total current assets to total current liabilities	1.55	1.63	1.59	1.59	1.56
Total cash, U.S. Government and other securities to total current liabilities	0.19	0.22	0.22	0.23	0.21
Total stockholders' equity to total debt	1.77	1.87	1.88	1.87	1.80

[1] During the first quarter of 1984, a considerable number of companies were reclassified by industry. To provide comparability, the four quarters of 1983 have been restated to reflect these reclassifications.

TABLE 2—BALANCE SHEET
FOR CORPORATIONS INCLUDED IN ESIC MAJOR GROUPS 20 AND 21

	Food and Kindred Products [1]				
	1Q 1983	2Q 1983	3Q 1983	4Q 1983	1Q 1984
	(percent of total assets)				
SELECTED BALANCE SHEET RATIOS					
Total cash, U.S. Government and other securities	5.0	5.5	5.4	5.7	5.2
Trade accounts and trade notes receivable	13.1	13.5	14.0	13.6	13.4
Inventories	18.3	17.2	17.2	18.1	17.9
Total current assets	39.8	39.7	39.6	40.2	39.0
Net property, plant and equipment	36.2	36.4	35.7	35.4	36.0
Short-term debt including installments on long-term debt	7.4	6.6	6.5	6.5	6.9
Total current liabilities	25.6	24.4	24.9	25.3	25.0
Long-term debt	19.9	19.8	19.8	19.7	20.0
Total liabilities	51.4	50.7	50.7	50.9	51.5
Stockholders' equity	48.6	49.3	49.3	49.1	48.5

[1] During the first quarter of 1984, a considerable number of companies were reclassified by industry. To provide comparability, the four quarters of 1983 have been restated to reflect these reclassifications.

	Food and Kindred Products¹ Assets Under $25 Million					Tobacco Manufactures					Tobacco Manufactures Assets Under $25 Million				
	1Q 1983	2Q 1983	3Q 1983	4Q 1983	1Q 1984	1Q 1983	2Q 1983	3Q 1983	4Q 1983	1Q 1984	1Q 1983	2Q 1983	3Q 1983	4Q 1983	1Q 1984
	(percent of net sales)					(percent of net sales)					(percent of net sales)				
	100.0	100.0	100.0	100.0	100.0	100.0	100.0	100.0	100.0	100.0	100.0	100.0	100.0	100.0	100.0
	1.7	1.9	1.8	1.8	1.9	3.5	3.0	3.4	3.9	3.7	1.8	1.2	2.3	1.7	2.2
	95.4	95.1	95.3	94.3	95.0	80.3	77.9	76.9	75.8	79.1	87.2	93.6	87.6	91.1	84.5
	2.8	3.1	2.9	3.9	3.0	16.2	19.1	19.7	20.3	17.2	11.0	5.3	10.2	7.3	13.3
	-0.3	-0.2	-0.2	-0.3	-0.3	1.0	0.0	2.5	-0.8	0.4	-2.6	-1.8	-1.3	-0.6	0.0
	2.5	2.9	2.6	3.6	2.7	17.2	19.1	22.2	19.5	17.6	8.4	3.4	8.9	6.7	13.3
	1.0	1.3	1.1	1.4	1.3	6.4	7.6	8.5	7.0	6.8	4.2	1.4	3.1	3.3	5.5
	1.5	1.5	1.5	2.2	1.4	10.8	11.4	13.7	12.5	10.7	4.2	2.0	5.8	3.4	7.8
	(percent)					(percent)					(percent)				
	18.00	19.19	19.50	25.14	18.60	25.93	31.23	33.17	28.53	26.00	22.39	12.65	29.10	34.62	34.34
	10.65	10.35	11.01	15.23	9.45	16.34	18.69	20.47	18.35	15.88	11.15	7.55	18.83	17.46	20.20
	8.62	9.42	9.06	12.15	8.71	12.55	15.44	16.73	15.78	14.33	9.44	6.08	15.32	18.94	19.61
	5.13	5.08	5.12	7.36	4.42	7.91	9.24	10.32	10.16	8.75	4.70	3.63	9.91	9.55	11.53
	1.69	1.73	1.69	1.70	1.64	1.56	1.52	1.46	1.75	1.60	1.81	2.08	2.28	2.46	2.53
	0.29	0.30	0.28	0.28	0.27	0.06	0.06	0.05	0.10	0.08	0.19	0.24	0.29	0.45	0.31
	1.65	1.83	1.60	1.76	1.56	1.97	2.16	2.41	2.31	2.14	1.08	1.42	1.86	1.82	2.13

	Food and Kindred Products¹ Assets Under $25 Million					Tobacco Manufactures					Tobacco Manufactures Assets Under $25 Million				
	1Q 1983	2Q 1983	3Q 1983	4Q 1983	1Q 1984	1Q 1983	2Q 1983	3Q 1983	4Q 1983	1Q 1984	1Q 1983	2Q 1983	3Q 1983	4Q 1983	1Q 1984
	(percent of total assets)					(percent of total assets)					(percent of total assets)				
	9.8	10.0	9.5	9.6	9.3	1.6	1.7	1.5	1.9	1.7	7.9	8.3	8.2	10.8	8.1
	22.3	22.8	22.6	22.5	21.7	5.0	6.2	5.1	6.5	6.4	9.3	12.3	14.6	13.4	18.5
	22.4	21.7	22.1	22.1	22.1	24.1	21.7	21.7	22.3	22.1	57.2	51.1	41.3	33.5	37.9
	57.9	58.2	58.0	57.7	56.5	41.8	40.1	39.5	32.9	32.3	75.3	72.7	65.4	59.3	65.7
	36.8	36.7	36.5	36.6	38.0	26.6	27.2	27.5	30.2	30.3	21.8	23.4	31.8	37.5	29.8
	12.9	11.2	11.4	11.5	12.7	3.6	2.9	3.2	3.6	6.8	24.1	18.0	10.1	10.0	10.7
	34.4	33.6	34.4	34.0	34.5	26.7	26.3	27.0	18.9	20.2	41.6	35.0	28.7	24.1	26.0
	16.2	15.6	17.6	16.0	17.3	21.0	19.9	17.8	20.4	18.9	15.2	15.8	18.2	20.0	16.2
	52.1	50.9	53.5	51.7	53.2	51.6	50.6	49.6	44.7	44.9	57.9	51.9	47.4	45.3	42.9
	47.9	49.1	46.5	48.3	46.8	48.4	49.4	50.4	55.3	55.1	42.2	48.1	52.6	54.7	57.1

TABLE 3—INCOME STATEMENT
FOR CORPORATIONS INCLUDED IN ESIC MAJOR GROUPS 22 AND 26

	Textile Mill Products [1]				
	1Q 1983	2Q 1983	3Q 1983	4Q 1983	1Q 1984
	(percent of net sales)				
INCOME STATEMENT IN RATIO FORMAT					
Net sales, receipts, and operating revenues	100.0	100.0	100.0	100.0	100.0
Less: Depreciation, depletion, and amortization of property, plant and equipment	3.0	2.6	2.6	2.4	2.5
Less: All other operating costs and expenses	92.4	90.9	90.5	91.2	90.8
Income (or loss) from operations	4.6	6.5	6.9	6.4	6.6
Non-operating income (expense)	-0.6	-0.2	-0.4	-0.8	-0.7
Income (or loss) before income taxes	4.1	6.3	6.5	5.6	5.9
Less: Provision for current and deferred domestic income taxes	1.7	2.4	2.6	2.5	2.6
Income (or loss) after income taxes	2.3	3.9	3.9	3.1	3.3
	(percent)				
OPERATING RATIOS (see explanatory notes)					
Annual rate of profit on stockholders' equity at end of period:					
Before income taxes	13.76	23.15	24.05	20.58	21.14
After taxes	7.97	14.27	14.44	11.25	11.86
Annual rate of profit on total assets:					
Before income taxes	7.11	11.81	12.11	10.69	10.73
After taxes	4.12	7.28	7.27	5.84	6.02
BALANCE SHEET RATIOS (based on succeeding table)					
Total current assets to total current liabilities	2.50	2.35	2.33	2.35	2.36
Total cash, U.S. Government and other securities to total current liabilities	0.32	0.28	0.28	0.30	0.24
Total stockholders' equity to total debt	1.95	1.91	1.87	2.07	1.96

[1] During the first quarter of 1984, a considerable number of companies were reclassified by industry. To provide comparability, the four quarters of 1983 have been restated to reflect these reclassifications.

TABLE 4—BALANCE SHEET
FOR CORPORATIONS INCLUDED IN ESIC MAJOR GROUPS 22 AND 26

	Textile Mill Products [1]				
	1Q 1983	2Q 1983	3Q 1983	4Q 1983	1Q 1984
	(percent of total assets)				
SELECTED BALANCE SHEET RATIOS					
Total cash, U.S. Government and other securities	7.6	7.3	7.4	7.8	6.4
Trade accounts and trade notes receivable	22.9	24.7	26.3	24.6	24.6
Inventories	27.0	27.1	26.1	25.9	28.0
Total current assets	60.2	61.4	61.6	60.9	61.5
Net property, plant and equipment	33.6	32.3	31.2	31.5	30.5
Short-term debt including installments on long-term debt	6.2	7.7	7.8	7.1	6.9
Total current liabilities	24.1	26.1	26.4	25.9	26.0
Long-term debt	20.4	18.9	19.1	18.2	19.0
Total liabilities	48.3	49.0	49.6	48.1	49.2
Stockholders' equity	51.7	51.0	50.4	51.9	50.8

[1] During the first quarter of 1984, a considerable number of companies were reclassified by industry. To provide comparability, the four quarters of 1983 have been restated to reflect these reclassifications.

	Textile Mill Products Assets Under $25 Million					Paper and Allied Products [1]					Paper and Allied Products Assets Under $25 Million				
	1Q 1983	2Q 1983	3Q 1983	4Q 1983	1Q 1984	1Q 1983	2Q 1983	3Q 1983	4Q 1983	1Q 1984	1Q 1983	2Q 1983	3Q 1983	4Q 1983	1Q 1984
(percent of net sales)						(percent of net sales)					(percent of net sales)				
	100.0	100.0	100.0	100.0	100.0	100.0	100.0	100.0	100.0	100.0	100.0	100.0	100.0	100.0	100.0
	2.2	2.0	1.8	1.7	1.6	4.1	4.0	4.1	3.8	4.0	2.4	2.3	2.4	2.3	2.6
	93.9	91.9	91.7	93.6	92.1	90.9	90.2	90.0	89.5	88.9	92.7	92.5	93.5	93.7	92.6
	3.9	6.2	6.5	4.7	6.3	4.9	5.8	5.9	6.7	7.1	4.9	5.1	4.1	4.0	4.8
	-0.7	-0.1	-0.3	-0.2	0.1	-0.7	-0.7	0.1	-1.0	-1.0	-0.6	-0.3	-0.8	-0.7	-0.5
	3.2	6.0	6.2	4.5	6.5	4.2	5.2	5.9	5.7	6.1	4.3	4.9	3.3	3.3	4.3
	1.5	2.3	2.5	2.5	2.8	1.3	1.8	1.8	1.8	2.5	1.6	2.0	1.4	1.6	1.8
	1.7	3.7	3.7	2.0	3.6	2.9	3.3	4.1	3.9	3.6	2.7	2.9	1.8	1.7	2.5
(percent)						(percent)					(percent)				
	15.25	31.46	32.84	22.40	30.74	9.65	12.59	14.50	14.06	15.55	20.75	23.93	16.79	20.39	25.09
	8.03	19.27	19.72	9.82	17.39	6.67	8.34	10.09	9.63	9.11	12.94	14.16	9.42	10.50	14.52
	7.37	14.06	14.94	11.10	15.63	4.86	6.19	7.22	6.98	7.65	9.48	10.07	7.09	7.68	9.94
	3.87	8.61	8.97	4.87	8.74	3.36	4.00	5.02	4.78	4.48	5.91	5.96	3.98	3.95	5.75
	2.11	1.87	1.86	2.01	1.99	1.88	1.84	1.84	1.79	1.81	2.12	1.91	1.96	1.70	1.77
	0.35	0.26	0.26	0.32	0.24	0.31	0.28	0.22	0.19	0.19	0.40	0.34	0.26	0.16	0.17
	1.75	1.50	1.56	2.00	2.32	1.78	1.72	1.77	1.78	1.76	1.41	1.23	1.21	1.03	1.15

	Textile Mill Products Assets Under $25 Million					Paper and Allied Products [1]					Paper and Allied Products Assets Under $25 Million				
	1Q 1983	2Q 1983	3Q 1983	4Q 1983	1Q 1984	1Q 1983	2Q 1983	3Q 1983	4Q 1983	1Q 1984	1Q 1983	2Q 1983	3Q 1983	4Q 1983	1Q 1984
(percent of total assets)						(percent of total assets)					(percent of total assets)				
	11.4	9.7	9.5	11.4	9.0	5.2	5.0	3.9	3.4	3.4	11.8	11.4	8.1	5.8	6.1
	24.1	27.3	29.4	27.3	28.1	12.2	13.1	13.4	13.1	13.7	25.4	26.0	26.2	27.2	28.5
	29.?	30.0	27.6	28.0	32.2	12.6	12.7	12.5	12.9	13.0	21.0	22.2	23.7	25.7	25.0
	68.9	70.0	69.1	70.9	73.6	31.9	32.7	31.9	31.3	32.3	62.8	63.7	61.5	61.1	64.1
	26.9	25.4	24.7	23.3	20.9	56.6	56.5	57.0	58.1	57.2	32.8	32.3	34.9	35.5	31.8
	9.9	13.5	13.1	10.9	11.0	3.3	3.7	3.3	3.3	3.3	9.9	12.2	10.5	12.2	12.2
	32.6	37.4	37.0	35.2	37.1	17.0	17.8	17.4	17.5	17.8	29.6	33.4	31.4	35.9	36.2
	17.6	16.4	16.1	13.9	10.9	24.9	24.9	24.9	24.8	24.7	22.5	22.1	24.3	24.5	22.3
	51.7	55.3	54.5	50.4	49.2	49.6	50.8	50.2	50.3	50.8	54.3	57.9	57.7	62.3	60.4
	48.3	44.7	45.5	49.6	50.8	50.4	49.2	49.8	49.7	49.2	45.7	42.1	42.3	37.7	39.6

TABLE 5—INCOME STATEMENT
FOR CORPORATIONS INCLUDED IN ESIC MAJOR GROUPS 27 AND 28

	Printing and Publishing [1]				
	1Q 1983	2Q 1983	3Q 1983	4Q 1983	1Q 1984
	(percent of net sales)				
INCOME STATEMENT IN RATIO FORMAT					
Net sales, receipts, and operating revenues	100.0	100.0	100.0	100.0	100.0
Less: Depreciation, depletion, and amortization of property, plant and equipment	3.3	3.2	3.2	3.2	3.3
Less: All other operating costs and expenses	88.2	86.3	86.1	85.8	87.1
Income (or loss) from operations	8.5	10.5	10.7	11.1	9.7
Non-operating income (expense)	-0.3	0.0	0.0	-0.1	-0.1
Income (or loss) before income taxes	8.2	10.5	10.7	11.0	9.5
Less: Provision for current and deferred domestic income taxes	3.5	4.5	4.7	4.5	4.0
Income (or loss) after income taxes	4.7	6.0	6.0	6.4	5.6
	(percent)				
OPERATING RATIOS (see explanatory notes)					
Annual rate of profit on stockholders' equity at end of period:					
Before income taxes	24.25	31.57	31.71	34.05	27.95
After taxes	13.85	18.13	17.79	19.95	16.34
Annual rate of profit on total assets:					
Before income taxes	11.58	15.40	15.36	16.27	13.53
After taxes	6.61	8.85	8.62	9.53	7.91
BALANCE SHEET RATIOS (based on succeeding table)					
Total current assets to total current liabilities	1.83	1.87	1.87	1.78	1.88
Total cash, U.S. Government and other securities to total current liabilities	0.41	0.44	0.43	0.41	0.44
Total stockholders' equity to total debt	2.02	2.10	2.07	2.03	2.07

[1] During the first quarter of 1984, a considerable number of companies were reclassified by industry. To provide comparability, the four quarters of 1983 have been restated to reflect these reclassifications.

TABLE 6—BALANCE SHEET
FOR CORPORATIONS INCLUDED IN ESIC MAJOR GROUPS 27 AND 28

	Printing and Publishing [1]				
	1Q 1983	2Q 1983	3Q 1983	4Q 1983	1Q 1984
	(percent of total assets)				
SELECTED BALANCE SHEET RATIOS					
Total cash, U.S. Government and other securities	9.6	10.1	9.9	10.2	10.2
Trade accounts and trade notes receivable	19.4	19.0	19.8	20.2	19.5
Inventories	9.7	9.4	9.3	9.2	9.5
Total current assets	43.2	42.9	43.4	44.0	43.7
Net property, plant and equipment	34.2	34.1	33.9	33.9	33.3
Short-term debt including installments on long-term debt	4.0	4.0	4.1	4.5	4.0
Total current liabilities	23.7	22.9	23.2	24.7	23.3
Long-term debt	19.6	19.3	19.5	19.1	19.4
Total liabilities	52.2	51.2	51.5	52.2	51.6
Stockholders' equity	47.8	48.8	48.5	47.8	48.4

[1] During the first quarter of 1984, a considerable number of companies were reclassified by industry. To provide comparability, the four quarters of 1983 have been restated to reflect these reclassifications.

	Printing and Publishing Assets Under $25 Million					Chemicals and Allied Products [1]					Chemicals and Allied Products Assets Under $25 Million				
	1Q 1983	2Q 1983	3Q 1983	4Q 1983	1Q 1984	1Q 1983	2Q 1983	3Q 1983	4Q 1983	1Q 1984	1Q 1983	2Q 1983	3Q 1983	4Q 1983	1Q 1984
	(percent of net sales)					(percent of net sales)					(percent of net sales)				
	100.0	100.0	100.0	100.0	100.0	100.0	100.0	100.0	100.0	100.0	100.0	100.0	100.0	100.0	100.0
	3.0	2.8	2.9	2.8	2.9	4.4	4.2	4.1	4.4	4.1	2.1	1.9	2.0	1.9	2.0
	91.6	89.5	90.6	90.5	90.6	88.6	88.4	87.9	89.3	86.8	92.0	89.0	90.8	92.8	91.5
	5.4	7.7	6.4	6.6	6.6	7.0	7.4	8.0	6.4	9.1	5.9	9.1	7.3	5.2	6.5
	-0.1	-0.1	-0.3	-0.3	-0.6	1.2	1.2	1.3	0.9	1.4	0.7	-0.4	-0.4	-0.8	-0.4
	5.4	7.6	6.1	6.4	6.0	8.2	8.5	9.2	7.2	10.4	6.6	8.7	6.8	4.4	6.1
	2.0	2.6	2.5	2.3	2.0	2.5	2.6	3.0	2.0	3.5	3.2	3.7	2.8	1.9	2.6
	3.3	5.0	3.6	4.1	4.0	5.7	6.0	6.2	5.2	6.9	3.4	5.0	4.0	2.5	3.4
	(percent)					(percent)					(percent)				
	24.71	34.79	27.54	30.74	26.76	16.56	18.02	19.62	15.42	22.61	27.95	41.43	31.70	21.52	27.94
	15.34	22.99	16.21	19.87	17.78	11.57	12.60	13.29	11.07	14.96	14.55	23.80	18.48	12.28	15.86
	10.66	15.70	12.36	13.16	12.21	8.58	9.32	10.11	7.99	11.67	13.74	19.33	15.43	9.82	12.78
	6.62	10.37	7.27	8.50	8.12	6.00	6.52	6.84	5.74	7.72	7.15	11.10	8.99	5.60	7.25
	1.83	1.97	1.85	1.76	1.90	1.73	1.73	1.68	1.67	1.65	1.89	1.87	1.90	1.75	1.81
	0.44	0.54	0.48	0.41	0.45	0.20	0.20	0.20	0.20	0.20	0.32	0.28	0.28	0.28	0.27
	1.47	1.55	1.52	1.40	1.54	2.10	2.13	2.15	2.26	2.23	2.17	1.99	2.33	2.32	2.12

	Printing and Publishing Assets Under $25 Million					Chemicals and Allied Products [1]					Chemicals and Allied Products Assets Under $25 Million				
	1Q 1983	2Q 1983	3Q 1983	4Q 1983	1Q 1984	1Q 1983	2Q 1983	3Q 1983	4Q 1983	1Q 1984	1Q 1983	2Q 1983	3Q 1983	4Q 1983	1Q 1984
	(percent of total assets)					(percent of total assets)					(percent of total assets)				
	14.0	16.1	14.8	13.6	13.7	4.1	4.2	4.5	4.4	4.4	11.6	10.2	10.5	11.3	10.4
	25.5	25.3	25.4	26.1	25.7	14.0	14.3	15.0	14.6	15.2	26.6	29.4	29.2	27.4	27.7
	13.5	11.8	11.9	12.5	13.3	15.1	14.8	14.3	14.4	14.4	25.0	24.0	24.9	26.2	25.2
	58.1	58.4	57.6	57.8	57.7	36.2	36.5	36.6	36.4	37.0	68.3	68.7	65.9	69.8	68.6
	32.6	31.9	32.7	33.1	33.6	42.4	42.2	41.8	41.7	40.8	25.7	25.4	25.7	24.5	25.5
	8.7	7.9	8.8	10.1	9.2	3.9	3.6	4.2	3.5	4.3	9.1	8.2	7.6	6.9	7.0
	31.8	29.7	31.1	32.9	30.3	20.9	21.0	21.8	21.8	22.4	36.1	36.7	36.8	39.8	37.9
	20.6	21.1	20.7	20.5	20.6	20.8	20.7	19.9	19.3	18.9	13.6	15.3	13.3	12.8	14.7
	56.9	54.9	55.1	57.2	54.4	48.2	48.3	48.5	48.2	48.4	50.9	53.3	51.3	54.4	54.3
	43.1	45.1	44.9	42.8	45.6	51.8	51.7	51.5	51.8	51.6	49.1	46.7	48.7	45.6	45.7

TABLE 7—INCOME STATEMENT
FOR CORPORATIONS INCLUDED IN ESIC MAJOR GROUPS 28.1 AND 28.3

	Industrial Chemicals and Synthetics [1] [2]				
	1Q 1983	2Q 1983	3Q 1983	4Q 1983	1Q 1984
	(percent of net sales)				
INCOME STATEMENT IN RATIO FORMAT					
Net sales, receipts, and operating revenues	100.0	100.0	100.0	100.0	100.0
Less: Depreciation, depletion, and amortization of property, plant and equipment	5.8	5.4	5.4	5.9	5.5
Less: All other operating costs and expenses	89.7	88.9	88.8	89.0	86.2
Income (or loss) from operations	4.6	5.8	5.7	5.1	8.4
Non-operating income (expense)	-0.4	0.0	0.0	-1.6	0.3
Income (or loss) before income taxes	4.1	5.8	5.7	3.4	8.7
Less: Provision for current and deferred domestic income taxes	0.8	1.3	1.4	0.8	3.0
Income (or loss) after income taxes	3.4	4.6	4.3	2.6	5.7
	(percent)				
OPERATING RATIOS (see explanatory notes)					
Annual rate of profit on stockholders' equity at end of period:					
Before income taxes	8.31	12.41	12.12	7.48	18.99
After taxes	6.78	9.74	9.07	5.75	12.37
Annual rate of profit on total assets:					
Before income taxes	4.02	6.03	5.89	3.67	9.28
After taxes	3.28	4.73	4.41	2.82	6.05
BALANCE SHEET RATIOS (based on succeeding table)					
Total current assets to total current liabilities	1.58	1.57	1.54	1.55	1.52
Total cash, U.S. Government and other securities to total current liabilities	0.12	0.12	0.13	0.14	0.12
Total stockholders' equity to total debt	1.79	1.85	1.89	2.03	2.01

[1] Included in Chemicals and Allied Products.
[2] During the first quarter of 1984, a considerable number of companies were reclassified by industry. To provide comparability, the four quarters of 1983 have been restated to reflect these reclassifications.

TABLE 8—BALANCE SHEET
FOR CORPORATIONS INCLUDED IN ESIC MAJOR GROUPS 28.1 AND 28.3

	Industrial Chemicals and Synthetics [1] [2]				
	1Q 1983	2Q 1983	3Q 1983	4Q 1983	1Q 1984
	(percent of total assets)				
SELECTED BALANCE SHEET RATIOS					
Total cash, U.S. Government and other securities	2.5	2.6	2.7	3.1	2.7
Trade accounts and trade notes receivable	13.7	14.3	15.1	15.2	15.7
Inventories	13.6	13.3	12.7	12.6	12.7
Total current assets	32.5	32.7	33.0	33.3	33.6
Net property, plant and equipment	48.7	48.5	48.0	48.0	47.2
Short-term debt including installments on long-term debt	3.5	3.2	3.7	3.1	3.8
Total current liabilities	20.6	20.8	21.4	21.5	22.1
Long-term debt	23.5	23.1	22.0	21.1	20.5
Total liabilities	51.6	51.5	51.4	50.9	51.1
Stockholders' equity	48.4	48.5	48.6	49.1	48.9

[1] Included in Chemicals and Allied Products.
[2] During the first quarter of 1984, a considerable number of companies were reclassified by industry. To provide comparability, the four quarters of 1983 have been restated to reflect these reclassifications.

Industrial Chemicals and Synthetics [1] Assets Under $25 Million					Drugs [1][2]					Drugs [1] Assets Under $25 Million				
1Q 1983	2Q 1983	3Q 1983	4Q 1983	1Q 1984	1Q 1983	2Q 1983	3Q 1983	4Q 1983	1Q 1984	1Q 1983	2Q 1983	3Q 1983	4Q 1983	1Q 1984
(percent of net sales)					(percent of net sales)					(percent of net sales)				
100.0	100.0	100.0	100.0	100.0	100.0	100.0	100.0	100.0	100.0	100.0	100.0	100.0	100.0	100.0
3.3	3.3	3.0	2.9	3.3	2.9	2.8	2.8	2.8	2.9	2.7	2.2	2.0	2.0	2.0
89.3	90.4	88.9	93.0	90.7	84.1	86.0	83.9	86.9	83.5	85.2	87.9	90.3	85.9	87.7
7.4	6.3	8.1	4.0	6.0	13.1	11.2	13.3	10.3	13.6	12.1	9.9	7.6	12.1	10.4
0.2	-0.6	-0.8	-1.2	-0.9	6.7	6.6	6.4	8.7	6.0	0.6	0.7	0.3	-3.7	-0.9
7.7	5.7	7.2	2.9	5.1	19.8	17.7	19.6	19.0	19.7	12.7	10.6	7.9	8.4	9.4
2.8	1.9	2.4	1.4	2.1	6.0	5.6	6.7	4.8	6.1	6.0	4.5	3.7	3.5	3.9
4.9	3.8	4.8	1.5	3.0	13.7	12.1	13.0	14.1	13.5	6.8	6.1	4.2	4.9	5.5
(percent)					(percent)					(percent)				
25.04	21.77	26.96	13.35	23.86	30.03	26.32	30.69	29.81	30.02	34.18	38.83	26.20	31.47	31.15
15.90	14.48	17.89	6.81	13.90	20.85	17.96	20.29	22.24	20.65	18.14	22.34	14.05	18.31	18.26
13.47	10.23	13.70	5.85	9.35	18.07	15.62	17.97	17.52	17.71	19.97	20.59	15.03	17.13	17.35
8.55	6.80	9.09	2.98	5.45	12.55	10.66	11.88	13.07	12.18	10.60	11.85	8.06	9.97	10.17
2.04	1.95	2.15	1.69	1.66	1.76	1.69	1.59	1.62	1.63	2.48	2.21	2.54	2.29	2.18
0.52	0.44	0.40	0.20	0.13	0.23	0.19	0.18	0.18	0.20	0.61	0.30	0.43	0.37	0.45
2.17	1.56	1.94	1.63	1.19	3.07	2.88	2.85	2.99	3.06	3.33	2.78	3.46	3.95	3.57

Industrial Chemicals and Synthetics [1] Assets Under $25 Million					Drugs [1][2]					Drugs [1] Assets Under $25 Million				
1Q 1983	2Q 1983	3Q 1983	4Q 1983	1Q 1984	1Q 1983	2Q 1983	3Q 1983	4Q 1983	1Q 1984	1Q 1983	2Q 1983	3Q 1983	4Q 1983	1Q 1984
(percent of total assets)					(percent of total assets)					(percent of total assets)				
14.8	13.0	11.6	7.1	4.3	4.9	4.2	4.2	4.1	4.5	14.4	9.0	12.4	11.3	13.2
23.3	22.4	24.3	25.0	24.9	13.6	13.4	13.6	13.3	13.6	19.4	24.9	24.4	24.3	22.4
17.4	18.4	19.4	21.2	20.4	14.5	14.8	14.4	14.4	13.5	22.6	30.4	33.0	31.1	26.1
58.5	57.4	61.9	59.8	56.5	37.1	36.7	36.3	36.6	36.3	58.4	66.9	72.5	69.0	64.1
36.0	38.0	34.5	36.7	38.7	28.5	28.8	28.7	29.3	29.0	26.8	22.7	24.7	22.0	26.7
8.7	8.1	7.5	8.1	8.5	5.5	6.0	6.6	6.0	6.2	3.4	3.1	3.7	2.0	3.1
28.6	29.5	28.8	35.4	34.1	21.1	21.7	22.9	22.5	22.3	23.5	30.2	28.5	30.1	29.4
16.1	22.1	18.6	18.8	24.6	14.1	14.5	14.0	13.5	13.0	14.1	16.0	12.9	11.6	12.6
46.2	53.0	49.2	56.2	60.8	39.8	40.6	41.4	41.2	41.0	41.6	47.0	42.6	45.6	44.3
53.8	47.0	50.8	43.8	39.2	60.2	59.4	58.6	58.8	59.0	58.4	53.0	57.4	54.4	55.7

TABLE 9—INCOME STATEMENT
FOR CORPORATIONS INCLUDED IN ESIC MAJOR GROUPS 29 AND 30

	Petroleum and Coal Products [1]				
	1Q 1983	2Q 1983	3Q 1983	4Q 1983	1Q 1984
	(percent of net sales)				
INCOME STATEMENT IN RATIO FORMAT					
Net sales, receipts, and operating revenues	100.0	100.0	100.0	100.0	100.0
Less: Depreciation, depletion, and amortization of property, plant and equipment	5.6	5.4	5.4	6.0	5.9
Less: All other operating costs and expenses	90.3	87.5	86.4	87.5	87.2
Income (or loss) from operations	4.2	7.1	8.2	6.5	6.9
Non-operating income (expense)	2.4	1.3	1.9	3.0	1.7
Income (or loss) before income taxes	6.5	8.4	10.1	9.5	8.5
Less: Provision for current and deferred domestic income taxes	1.7	2.7	3.1	2.4	2.9
Income (or loss) after income taxes	4.8	5.7	7.0	7.1	5.6
	(percent)				
OPERATING RATIOS (see explanatory notes)					
Annual rate of profit on stockholders' equity at end of period:	13.39	17.56	20.59	19.30	16.98
Before income taxes					
After taxes	9.94	11.92	14.22	14.37	11.15
Annual rate of profit on total assets:	6.68	8.71	10.32	9.75	8.30
Before income taxes					
After taxes	4.96	5.91	7.13	7.26	5.45
BALANCE SHEET RATIOS (based on succeeding table)					
Total current assets to total current liabilities	0.94	0.95	1.01	0.98	1.02
Total cash, U.S. Government and other securities to total current liabilities	0.13	0.14	0.15	0.15	0.20
Total stockholders' equity to total debt	2.62	2.61	2.77	2.92	2.39

[1] During the first quarter of 1984, a considerable number of companies were reclassified by industry. To provide comparability, the four quarters of 1983 have been restated to reflect these reclassifications.

TABLE 10—BALANCE SHEET
FOR CORPORATIONS INCLUDED IN ESIC MAJOR GROUPS 29 AND 30

	Petroleum and Coal Products [1]				
	1Q 1983	2Q 1983	3Q 1983	4Q 1983	1Q 1984
	(percent of total assets)				
SELECTED BALANCE SHEET RATIOS					
Total cash, U.S. Government and other securities	2.6	2.9	2.9	3.0	3.7
Trade accounts and trade notes receivable	8.1	8.3	8.1	8.5	7.7
Inventories	6.2	6.2	6.3	5.8	5.6
Total current assets	19.2	19.4	19.3	18.9	18.6
Net property, plant and equipment	58.8	58.8	58.4	58.2	56.1
Short-term debt including installments on long-term debt	4.8	4.6	3.7	3.6	3.6
Total current liabilities	20.3	20.4	19.2	19.3	18.3
Long-term debt	14.2	14.3	14.4	13.7	16.8
Total liabilities	50.1	50.4	49.9	49.5	51.1
Stockholders' equity	49.9	49.6	50.1	50.5	48.9

[1] During the first quarter of 1984, a considerable number of companies were reclassified by industry. To provide comparability, the four quarters of 1983 have been restated to reflect these reclassifications.

	Petroleum and Coal Products [1] Assets Under $25 Million					Rubber and Misc. Plastics Products [1]					Rubber and Misc. Plastics Products [1] Assets Under $25 Million				
	1Q 1983	2Q 1983	3Q 1983	4Q 1983	1Q 1984	1Q 1983	2Q 1983	3Q 1983	4Q 1983	1Q 1984	1Q 1983	2Q 1983	3Q 1983	4Q 1983	1Q 1984
(percent of net sales)						(percent of net sales)					(percent of net sales)				
	100.0	100.0	100.0	100.0	100.0	100.0	100.0	100.0	100.0	100.0	100.0	100.0	100.0	100.0	100.0
	2.5	2.6	2.1	2.0	2.5	3.3	3.0	2.9	2.8	2.8	2.9	2.6	2.6	2.6	2.3
	97.6	95.6	93.2	92.4	97.3	91.1	90.9	90.6	91.2	90.9	89.7	90.8	91.3	92.3	90.5
	-0.1	1.8	4.6	5.6	0.3	5.6	6.2	6.5	6.0	6.3	7.4	6.6	6.1	5.2	7.2
	-0.6	0.2	-0.2	-0.9	-0.9	-0.4	-0.3	0.0	-0.1	0.5	-0.3	-0.9	-0.6	-0.4	0.5
	-0.8	2.1	4.4	4.7	-0.6	5.2	5.8	6.6	5.9	6.8	7.1	5.8	5.5	4.8	7.7
	1.1	1.1	1.8	2.7	0.9	1.9	2.3	2.6	2.2	2.5	2.5	2.4	2.3	1.8	2.8
	-1.9	1.0	2.6	2.0	-1.5	3.3	3.5	4.0	3.7	4.3	4.6	3.4	3.2	3.0	4.9
(percent)						(percent)					(percent)				
	-3.43	8.22	24.26	25.97	-2.07	16.48	20.08	22.93	20.25	22.89	33.13	29.75	27.26	24.27	37.97
	-8.54	3.96	14.42	11.16	-5.29	10.38	12.14	13.83	12.73	14.58	21.68	17.51	15.63	14.97	24.35
	-1.51	4.07	11.10	11.35	-0.99	8.04	9.79	11.17	10.12	11.32	15.21	13.35	12.21	11.17	17.55
	-3.75	1.97	6.59	4.88	-2.54	5.06	5.92	6.74	6.36	7.21	9.96	7.86	7.00	6.89	11.26
	1.51	1.63	1.61	1.52	1.37	1.92	1.95	1.95	1.89	1.91	1.86	1.83	1.86	1.83	1.92
	0.31	0.23	0.22	0.23	0.26	0.24	0.28	0.28	0.30	0.23	0.28	0.29	0.29	0.32	0.28
	1.53	2.25	1.93	1.42	1.68	1.98	2.05	2.10	2.36	2.24	1.53	1.56	1.57	1.75	1.70

	Petroleum and Coal Products [1] Assets Under $25 Million					Rubber and Misc. Plastics Products [1]					Rubber and Misc. Plastics Products [1] Assets Under $25 Million				
	1Q 1983	2Q 1983	3Q 1983	4Q 1983	1Q 1984	1Q 1983	2Q 1983	3Q 1983	4Q 1983	1Q 1984	1Q 1983	2Q 1983	3Q 1983	4Q 1983	1Q 1984
(percent of total assets)						(percent of total assets)					(percent of total assets)				
	12.8	8.2	8.6	9.5	9.4	6.4	7.3	7.6	8.3	6.4	9.4	9.9	9.7	11.1	9.8
	27.0	25.1	30.0	32.2	22.5	23.3	23.2	24.5	23.2	24.6	28.2	28.8	30.3	29.7	31.4
	18.0	18.0	16.8	16.5	15.3	18.8	18.3	17.9	18.1	19.2	20.4	19.8	20.3	20.4	21.4
	61.4	58.9	62.7	61.5	50.1	51.1	51.3	52.4	51.8	52.8	61.6	62.2	63.4	64.1	66.2
	34.3	29.9	28.3	29.3	31.8	36.4	35.7	35.3	35.1	34.1	33.7	32.1	31.3	30.4	28.8
	16.0	10.8	11.5	17.8	15.3	6.2	5.0	4.8	4.5	5.1	11.0	9.7	9.7	9.5	10.0
	40.8	36.2	38.9	40.6	36.5	26.6	26.3	26.9	27.3	27.6	33.1	33.9	34.1	35.0	34.4
	12.8	11.2	12.2	12.9	13.3	18.6	18.7	18.3	16.6	16.9	19.1	19.2	18.9	16.7	17.3
	56.1	50.4	54.3	56.3	52.0	51.2	51.2	51.3	50.0	50.5	54.1	55.1	55.2	54.0	53.8
	43.9	49.6	45.7	43.7	48.0	48.8	48.8	48.7	50.0	49.5	45.9	44.9	44.8	46.0	46.2

TABLE 11—INCOME STATEMENT
FOR CORPORATIONS INCLUDED IN ESIC MAJOR GROUPS 32 AND 33

	Stone, Clay and Glass Products [1]				
	1Q 1983	2Q 1983	3Q 1983	4Q 1983	1Q 1984
	(percent of net sales)				
INCOME STATEMENT IN RATIO FORMAT					
Net sales, receipts, and operating revenues	100.0	100.0	100.0	100.0	100.0
Less: Depreciation, depletion, and amortization of property, plant and equipment	5.4	4.6	4.1	4.4	4.5
Less: All other operating costs and expenses	94.4	89.3	88.6	89.6	91.8
Income (or loss) from operations	0.2	6.1	7.3	6.0	3.7
Non-operating income (expense)	-2.6	-1.1	-0.6	-1.1	-0.6
Income (or loss) before income taxes	-2.4	5.0	6.7	4.9	3.1
Less: Provision for current and deferred domestic income taxes	0.4	2.1	2.3	1.7	1.7
Income (or loss) after income taxes	-2.8	3.0	4.4	3.3	1.4
	(percent)				
OPERATING RATIOS (see explanatory notes)					
Annual rate of profit on stockholders' equity at end of period:					
Before income taxes	-4.98	12.37	17.80	12.07	7.43
After taxes	-5.76	7.31	11.57	8.04	3.45
Annual rate of profit on total assets:					
Before income taxes	-2.43	5.98	8.67	6.00	3.64
After taxes	-2.81	3.53	5.64	4.00	1.69
BALANCE SHEET RATIOS (based on succeeding table)					
Total current assets to total current liabilities	2.01	2.03	2.10	2.08	1.95
Total cash, U.S. Government and other securities to total current liabilities	0.28	0.27	0.32	0.36	0.27
Total stockholders' equity to total debt	1.61	1.63	1.70	1.83	1.77

[1] During the first quarter of 1984, a considerable number of companies were reclassified by industry. To provide comparability, the four quarters of 1983 have been restated to reflect these reclassifications.

TABLE 12—BALANCE SHEET
FOR CORPORATIONS INCLUDED IN ESIC MAJOR GROUPS 32 AND 33

	Stone, Clay and Glass Products [1]				
	1Q 1983	2Q 1983	3Q 1983	4Q 1983	1Q 1984
	(percent of total assets)				
SELECTED BALANCE SHEET RATIOS					
Total cash, U.S. Government and other securities	5.2	5.2	6.0	6.7	5.4
Trade accounts and trade notes receivable	15.1	16.7	17.6	16.0	16.2
Inventories	15.1	14.5	13.9	14.2	15.3
Total current assets	37.8	39.0	39.8	39.3	39.4
Net property, plant and equipment	48.5	46.7	45.9	46.0	45.6
Short-term debt including installments on long-term debt	5.2	4.5	4.0	4.0	4.8
Total current liabilities	18.8	19.2	18.9	18.9	20.2
Long-term debt	25.0	25.1	24.7	23.2	22.9
Total liabilities	51.2	51.7	51.3	50.3	51.0
Stockholders' equity	48.8	48.3	48.7	49.7	49.0

[1] During the first quarter of 1984, a considerable number of companies were reclassified by industry. To provide comparability, the four quarters of 1983 have been restated to reflect these reclassifications.

Stone, Clay and Glass Products — Assets Under $25 Million / Primary Metal Industries¹ / Primary Metal Industries¹ — Assets Under $25 Million

(percent of net sales)

	Stone, Clay and Glass Products, Assets Under $25 Million					Primary Metal Industries¹					Primary Metal Industries¹, Assets Under $25 Million				
	1Q 1983	2Q 1983	3Q 1983	4Q 1983	1Q 1984	1Q 1983	2Q 1983	3Q 1983	4Q 1983	1Q 1984	1Q 1983	2Q 1983	3Q 1983	4Q 1983	1Q 1984
	100.0	100.0	100.0	100.0	100.0	100.0	100.0	100.0	100.0	100.0	100.0	100.0	100.0	100.0	100.0
	5.0	3.7	3.1	3.3	3.4	4.8	4.4	4.4	4.0	3.9	2.9	2.8	2.8	2.6	2.7
	96.7	89.3	88.0	91.5	95.3	99.3	95.4	95.0	94.7	92.4	93.1	92.6	92.7	92.3	91.0
	-1.7	7.0	8.9	5.2	1.3	-4.1	0.1	0.6	1.3	3.7	4.0	4.7	4.5	5.1	6.3
	-1.0	-0.8	-0.5	-0.9	0.0	-1.4	-3.1	-3.1	-9.8	-1.3	-0.8	0.1	-0.2	-0.3	-0.2
	-2.7	6.2	8.4	4.2	1.3	-5.5	-2.9	-2.5	-8.5	2.4	3.3	4.7	4.3	4.9	6.1
	0.7	2.7	2.8	1.8	2.0	-1.5	-0.6	-0.2	-1.2	0.8	2.1	1.9	2.3	1.9	2.3
	-3.5	3.4	5.7	2.4	-0.7	-3.9	-2.3	-2.3	-7.3	1.5	1.2	2.8	2.0	2.9	3.8

(percent)

	1Q 1983	2Q 1983	3Q 1983	4Q 1983	1Q 1984	1Q 1983	2Q 1983	3Q 1983	4Q 1983	1Q 1984	1Q 1983	2Q 1983	3Q 1983	4Q 1983	1Q 1984
	-7.74	24.64	35.97	16.52	5.04	-12.48	-7.47	-6.44	-24.38	7.13	12.86	18.85	17.19	21.51	25.80
	-9.83	13.71	24.15	9.51	-2.48	-9.00	-5.91	-5.84	-21.06	4.56	4.56	11.20	8.06	13.06	16.10
	-3.82	11.29	17.27	7.84	2.46	-4.95	-2.97	-2.54	-9.25	2.88	5.75	8.95	8.13	9.84	12.12
	-4.85	6.29	11.60	4.51	-1.21	-3.57	-2.35	-2.31	-7.99	1.71	2.04	5.32	3.81	5.97	7.56
	1.96	1.85	2.05	2.12	2.13	1.64	1.62	1.62	1.62	1.61	1.91	2.01	1.87	1.81	1.85
	0.38	0.33	0.40	0.46	0.44	0.19	0.18	0.15	0.16	0.15	0.34	0.39	0.32	0.36	0.39
	1.54	1.46	1.65	1.69	1.73	1.15	1.19	1.17	1.15	1.15	1.42	1.69	1.76	1.69	1.86

Stone, Clay and Glass Products — Assets Under $25 Million / Primary Metal Industries¹ / Primary Metal Industries¹ — Assets Under $25 Million

(percent of total assets)

	Stone, Clay and Glass Products, Assets Under $25 Million					Primary Metal Industries¹					Primary Metal Industries¹, Assets Under $25 Million				
	1Q 1983	2Q 1983	3Q 1983	4Q 1983	1Q 1984	1Q 1983	2Q 1983	3Q 1983	4Q 1983	1Q 1984	1Q 1983	2Q 1983	3Q 1983	4Q 1983	1Q 1984
	10.6	10.1	11.4	12.9	12.1	4.0	3.8	3.1	3.4	3.5	10.5	11.8	10.4	12.6	13.8
	21.7	25.7	27.6	25.4	23.2	12.6	13.4	14.2	14.8	15.6	24.0	26.2	27.0	26.7	27.3
	18.4	17.5	16.4	16.9	19.0	16.1	15.6	15.4	15.6	16.1	20.7	20.3	20.5	20.5	20.4
	54.5	57.3	59.0	58.7	58.2	34.5	34.3	34.4	35.4	37.1	59.4	61.7	60.8	62.6	64.7
	40.3	37.4	36.6	36.0	36.4	50.7	51.0	50.8	49.8	48.3	35.0	32.1	33.8	31.7	29.5
	11.3	10.5	8.5	7.8	7.8	4.4	4.1	4.1	3.8	4.0	9.4	8.4	9.3	9.9	10.0
	27.7	30.9	28.7	27.7	27.3	21.1	21.2	21.2	21.9	23.0	31.1	30.6	32.6	34.5	35.1
	20.7	23.0	20.7	20.2	20.5	30.0	29.2	29.5	29.2	28.6	21.9	19.7	17.5	17.2	15.2
	50.7	54.2	52.0	52.5	51.1	60.3	60.2	60.5	62.1	62.4	55.3	52.5	52.7	54.3	53.0
	49.3	45.8	48.0	47.5	48.9	39.7	39.8	39.5	37.9	37.6	44.7	47.5	47.3	45.7	47.0

TABLE 13—INCOME STATEMENT
FOR CORPORATIONS INCLUDED IN ESIC MAJOR GROUPS 33.1–2 AND 33.5–6

	Iron and Steel [1]				
	1Q 1983	2Q 1983	3Q 1983	4Q 1983	1Q 1984
	(percent of net sales)				
INCOME STATEMENT IN RATIO FORMAT					
Net sales, receipts, and operating revenues	100.0	100.0	100.0	100.0	100.0
Less: Depreciation, depletion, and amortization of property, plant and equipment	5.2	4.8	4.7	4.1	4.0
Less: All other operating costs and expenses	100.4	96.3	95.1	96.1	92.9
Income (or loss) from operations	−5.7	−1.1	0.2	−0.2	3.1
Non-operating income (expense)	−1.8	−3.4	−3.9	−12.5	−1.4
Income (or loss) before income taxes	−7.4	−4.5	−3.7	−12.6	1.7
Less: Provision for current and deferred domestic income taxes	−2.1	−0.6	−0.2	−2.2	0.5
Income (or loss) after income taxes	−5.4	−3.9	−3.5	−10.4	1.2
	(percent)				
OPERATING RATIOS (see explanatory notes)					
Annual rate of profit on stockholders' equity at end of period:					
Before income taxes	−18.87	−12.82	−10.97	−43.58	6.12
After taxes	−13.66	−11.16	−10.43	−35.87	4.20
Annual rate of profit on total assets:					
Before income taxes	−6.75	−4.60	−3.90	−14.44	2.01
After taxes	−4.89	−4.01	−3.70	−11.89	1.38
BALANCE SHEET RATIOS (based on succeeding table)					
Total current assets to total current liabilities	1.57	1.55	1.57	1.55	1.55
Total cash, U.S. Government and other securities to total current liabilities	0.21	0.20	0.15	0.16	0.16
Total stockholders' equity to total debt	0.99	1.03	1.01	0.96	0.99

[1] Included in Primary Metal Industries.
[2] During the first quarter of 1984, a considerable number of companies were reclassified by industry. To provide comparability, the four quarters of 1983 have been restated to reflect these reclassifications.

TABLE 14—BALANCE SHEET
FOR CORPORATIONS INCLUDED IN ESIC MAJOR GROUPS 33.1–2 AND 33.5–6

	Iron and Steel [1]				
	1Q[3] 1983	2Q 1983	3Q 1983	4Q 1983	1Q 1984
	(percent of total assets)				
SELECTED BALANCE SHEET RATIOS					
Total cash, U.S. Government and other securities	4.8	4.5	3.4	3.6	4.0
Trade accounts and trade notes receivable	12.4	13.0	14.2	14.9	15.6
Inventories	16.0	15.6	15.9	15.9	16.5
Total current assets	34.8	34.5	34.8	36.0	37.9
Net property, plant and equipment	54.3	54.5	54.0	52.9	51.3
Short-term debt including installments on long-term debt	3.7	3.3	3.4	3.0	2.9
Total current liabilities	22.1	22.2	22.2	23.2	24.4
Long-term debt	32.3	31.5	31.9	31.4	30.5
Total liabilities	64.2	64.1	64.5	66.9	67.1
Stockholders' equity	35.8	35.9	35.5	33.1	32.9

[1] Included in Primary Metal Industries.
[2] During the first quarter of 1984, a considerable number of companies were reclassified by industry. To provide comparability, the four quarters of 1983 have been restated to reflect these reclassifications.
[3] Revised

	Iron and Steel Assets Under $25 Million [1]					Nonferrous Metals [1][2]					Nonferrous Metals [1][2] Assets Under $25 Million			
1Q 1983	2Q 1983	3Q 1983	4Q 1983	1Q 1984	1Q 1983	2Q 1983	3Q 1983	4Q 1983	1Q 1984	1Q 1983	2Q 1983	3Q 1983	4Q 1983	1Q 1984
(percent of net sales)					(percent of net sales)					(percent of net sales)				
100.0	100.0	100.0	100.0	100.0	100.0	100.0	100.0	100.0	100.0	100.0	100.0	100.0	100.0	100.0
4.0	3.5	3.4	3.1	3.1	4.1	3.8	3.9	3.9	3.7	2.0	2.1	2.3	2.2	2.4
93.4	94.5	94.1	93.7	92.2	97.6	93.9	94.8	92.2	91.6	92.9	90.9	91.4	91.1	89.9
2.6	1.9	2.5	3.2	4.7	-1.6	2.3	1.3	3.9	4.8	5.1	7.0	6.3	6.7	7.7
-1.4	-0.3	-0.2	-1.3	-0.8	-0.7	-2.6	-1.7	-4.9	-1.2	-0.3	0.4	-0.1	0.7	0.3
1.2	1.6	2.3	1.9	3.8	-2.3	-0.4	-0.4	-1.0	3.5	4.8	7.4	6.2	7.4	8.0
1.1	0.8	1.6	1.4	1.5	-0.7	-0.7	-0.3	0.8	1.4	2.8	2.9	2.9	2.3	3.0
0.1	0.8	0.7	0.5	2.3	-1.6	0.3	0.0	-1.8	2.1	1.9	4.5	3.3	5.1	5.0
(percent)					(percent)					(percent)				
4.09	5.43	8.99	8.28	15.68	-4.50	-0.78	-0.78	-2.19	8.28	21.35	33.78	25.46	33.68	34.61
0.27	2.62	2.69	2.18	9.56	-3.18	0.67	-0.10	-3.94	4.97	8.70	20.75	13.46	23.06	21.79
1.78	2.65	3.98	3.68	7.14	-2.07	-0.36	-0.36	-1.00	3.73	9.77	15.56	12.89	15.80	16.73
0.12	1.28	1.19	0.97	4.35	-1.46	0.31	-0.05	-1.79	2.24	3.98	9.56	6.81	10.82	10.53
1.82	2.03	1.79	1.77	1.73	1.75	1.74	1.71	1.73	1.73	1.99	2.00	1.95	1.85	1.95
0.35	0.43	0.31	0.32	0.34	0.15	0.14	0.14	0.16	0.14	0.33	0.35	0.33	0.40	0.44
1.36	1.81	1.53	1.59	1.86	1.45	1.49	1.48	1.49	1.44	1.50	1.58	2.07	1.80	1.87

	Iron and Steel [1] Assets Under $25 Million					Nonferrous Metals [1][2]					Nonferrous Metals [1][2] Assets Under $25 Million			
1Q 1983	2Q 1983	3Q 1983	4Q 1983	1Q 1984	1Q 1983	2Q 1983	3Q 1983	4Q 1983	1Q 1984	1Q 1983	2Q 1983	3Q 1983	4Q 1983	1Q 1984
(percent of total assets)					(percent of total assets)					(percent of total assets)				
10.0	11.8	9.9	10.1	11.7	2.8	2.8	2.7	3.1	2.8	10.9	11.8	11.1	15.0	15.7
21.6	24.2	25.6	26.1	26.6	12.8	14.0	14.3	14.6	15.5	26.3	28.4	28.5	27.3	28.0
16.5	16.2	18.0	18.4	18.4	16.4	15.5	14.7	15.1	15.6	24.8	24.6	23.5	22.5	22.3
52.7	55.6	56.3	56.8	59.9	33.9	33.9	33.6	34.5	35.8	66.2	68.1	65.9	68.2	69.2
42.5	36.9	37.7	36.1	33.3	44.9	45.4	45.6	44.8	43.6	27.3	27.1	29.3	27.4	25.9
7.8	6.5	8.6	8.6	8.3	5.4	5.2	5.3	5.0	5.8	11.1	10.4	10.2	11.2	11.6
29.0	27.3	31.5	32.0	34.6	19.3	19.5	19.6	20.0	20.8	33.2	34.1	33.8	37.0	35.5
24.3	20.5	20.4	19.5	16.2	26.2	25.7	25.9	25.7	25.6	19.5	18.9	14.3	14.8	14.3
56.3	51.1	55.7	55.5	54.5	54.1	54.0	54.0	54.4	54.9	54.3	53.9	49.4	53.1	51.7
43.7	48.9	44.3	44.5	45.5	45.9	46.0	46.0	45.6	45.1	45.7	46.1	50.6	46.9	48.3

TABLE 15—INCOME STATEMENT
FOR CORPORATIONS INCLUDED IN ESIC MAJOR GROUPS 34 AND 35

	Fabricated Metal Products [1]				
	1Q 1983	2Q 1983	3Q 1983	4Q 1983	1Q 1984
	(percent of net sales)				
INCOME STATEMENT IN RATIO FORMAT					
Net sales, receipts, and operating revenues	100.0	100.0	100.0	100.0	100.0
Less: Depreciation, depletion, and amortization of property, plant and equipment	3.3	3.1	3.0	2.9	2.9
Less: All other operating costs and expenses	92.8	91.4	90.8	91.8	90.6
Income (or loss) from operations	3.9	5.6	6.2	5.3	6.5
Non-operating income (expense)	-0.8	-0.3	-1.0	-0.2	-0.7
Income (or loss) before income taxes	3.1	5.3	5.2	5.1	5.9
Less: Provision for current and deferred domestic income taxes	1.8	2.3	2.4	1.9	2.4
Income (or loss) after income taxes	1.4	3.0	2.8	3.2	3.5
	(percent)				
OPERATING RATIOS (see explanatory notes)					
Annual rate of profit on stockholders' equity at end of period:					
Before income taxes	8.91	16.39	16.29	16.35	19.18
After taxes	3.93	9.36	8.80	10.21	11.34
Annual rate of profit on total assets:					
Before income taxes	4.26	7.86	7.75	7.79	9.06
After taxes	1.88	4.49	4.18	4.86	5.36
BALANCE SHEET RATIOS (based on succeeding table)					
Total current assets to total current liabilities	1.87	1.91	1.91	1.96	1.86
Total cash, U.S. Government and other securities to total current liabilities	0.29	0.31	0.32	0.35	0.30
Total stockholders' equity to total debt	1.88	1.90	1.85	1.87	1.86

[1] During the first quarter of 1984, a considerable number of companies were reclassified by industry. To provide comparability, the four quarters of 1983 have been restated to reflect these reclassifications.

TABLE 16—BALANCE SHEET
FOR CORPORATIONS INCLUDED IN ESIC MAJOR GROUPS 34 AND 35

	Fabricated Metal Products [1]				
	1Q 1983	2Q 1983	3Q 1983	4Q 1983	1Q 1984
	(percent of total assets)				
SELECTED BALANCE SHEET RATIOS					
Total cash, U.S. Government and other securities	8.4	8.8	9.1	9.7	8.8
Trade accounts and trade notes receivable	21.4	22.0	22.7	21.8	22.9
Inventories	21.5	20.9	20.4	20.8	21.0
Total current assets	53.4	54.1	54.6	54.6	55.1
Net property, plant and equipment	32.3	31.5	30.7	30.6	29.8
Short-term debt including installments on long-term debt	6.2	6.4	6.6	6.3	6.8
Total current liabilities	28.6	28.4	28.5	27.9	29.6
Long-term debt	19.2	18.9	19.0	19.2	18.5
Total liabilities	52.1	52.1	52.5	52.4	52.8
Stockholders' equity	47.9	47.9	47.5	47.6	47.2

[1] During the first quarter of 1984, a considerable number of companies were reclassified by industry. To provide comparability, the four quarters of 1983 have been restated to reflect these reclassifications.

	Fabricated Metal Products [1] Assets Under $25 Million					Machinery, Except Electrical [1]					Machinery, Except Electrical [1] Assets Under $25 Million				
	1Q 1983	2Q 1983	3Q 1983	4Q 1983	1Q 1984	1Q 1983	2Q 1983	3Q 1983	4Q 1983	1Q 1984	1Q 1983	2Q 1983	3Q 1983	4Q 1983	1Q 1984
	(percent of net sales)					(percent of net sales)					(percent of net sales)				
	100.0	100.0	100.0	100.0	100.0	100.0	100.0	100.0	100.0	100.0	100.0	100.0	100.0	100.0	100.0
	3.1	2.9	2.8	2.7	2.7	5.2	4.8	4.7	4.5	4.4	3.5	3.4	3.5	3.2	3.3
	93.3	91.9	90.8	90.9	90.7	90.6	86.9	88.9	87.6	89.0	92.7	92.4	92.1	94.5	93.2
	3.6	5.2	6.5	6.4	6.6	4.2	6.3	6.3	7.9	6.6	3.8	4.1	4.4	2.3	3.5
	-1.0	-0.6	-0.5	-0.5	-0.6	0.7	0.0	0.6	0.8	0.9	-0.6	-0.6	-0.8	-0.5	-0.7
	2.7	4.6	6.0	5.9	6.1	4.9	6.3	6.9	8.7	7.5	3.2	3.5	3.6	1.7	2.8
	1.7	2.4	2.8	2.6	2.6	1.8	2.2	2.7	3.1	3.1	2.1	2.4	2.2	2.1	2.3
	1.0	2.2	3.1	3.4	2.5	3.1	4.1	4.2	5.6	4.4	1.1	1.1	1.4	-0.4	0.5
	(percent)					(percent)					(percent)				
	9.39	17.90	22.83	23.95	24.51	8.46	11.63	12.56	16.82	14.43	9.47	11.06	11.26	5.41	9.82
	3.43	8.58	11.99	13.56	13.99	5.39	7.54	7.71	10.89	8.42	3.33	3.43	4.39	-1.24	1.87
	4.65	8.78	11.32	11.76	11.95	4.58	6.36	6.97	9.45	7.92	4.80	5.38	5.54	2.78	4.61
	1.70	4.21	5.95	6.66	6.82	2.92	4.13	4.28	6.12	4.62	1.68	1.67	2.16	-0.64	0.88
	2.05	2.07	2.13	2.13	2.04	1.97	2.00	2.04	2.12	2.01	2.20	2.13	2.14	2.26	2.08
	0.33	0.36	0.39	0.40	0.36	0.31	0.32	0.34	0.37	0.31	0.52	0.47	0.47	0.50	0.39
	1.77	1.76	1.83	1.78	1.79	2.52	2.61	2.71	2.95	2.86	1.73	1.60	1.72	1.91	1.64

	Fabricated Metal Products [1] Assets Under $25 Million					Machinery, Except Electrical [1]					Machinery, Except Electrical [1] Assets Under $25 Million				
	1Q 1983	2Q 1983	3Q 1983	4Q 1983	1Q 1984	1Q 1983	2Q 1983	3Q 1983	4Q 1983	1Q 1984	1Q 1983	2Q 1983	3Q 1983	4Q 1983	1Q 1984
	(percent of total assets)					(percent of total assets)					(percent of total assets)				
	10.2	11.0	11.9	12.3	11.5	7.8	7.9	8.1	8.6	7.8	15.5	14.6	15.0	15.1	12.7
	25.4	26.2	27.0	26.0	27.4	17.2	17.6	17.8	18.4	18.9	21.9	22.0	22.7	23.4	24.2
	24.3	23.7	23.2	23.3	22.7	21.2	20.9	20.5	20.3	20.8	25.3	25.7	26.5	26.3	27.5
	62.8	64.0	65.1	64.7	64.7	49.2	49.2	49.4	50.0	50.5	66.1	66.0	67.7	69.1	68.5
	31.3	30.3	28.9	29.5	29.0	29.9	29.4	28.9	27.8	27.2	28.5	27.5	26.8	25.6	26.2
	9.9	9.5	9.3	9.1	9.3	5.3	4.9	4.7	3.6	4.0	11.3	12.0	10.7	10.3	10.8
	30.6	30.9	30.6	30.4	31.7	25.0	24.6	24.2	23.6	25.2	30.0	31.0	31.7	30.6	32.9
	18.2	18.4	17.8	18.6	17.9	16.1	16.0	15.8	15.6	15.2	17.9	18.4	17.7	16.4	17.8
	50.5	51.0	50.4	50.9	51.3	45.8	45.3	44.5	43.8	45.1	49.4	51.3	50.8	48.6	53.0
	49.5	49.0	49.6	49.1	48.7	54.2	54.7	55.5	56.2	54.9	50.6	48.7	49.2	51.4	47.0

TABLE 17—INCOME STATEMENT
FOR CORPORATIONS INCLUDED IN ESIC MAJOR GROUPS 36 AND 37

	Electrical and Electronic Equipment [1]				
	1Q 1983	2Q 1983	3Q 1983	4Q 1983	1Q 1984
	(percent of net sales)				
INCOME STATEMENT IN RATIO FORMAT					
Net sales, receipts, and operating revenues	100.0	100.0	100.0	100.0	100.0
Less: Depreciation, depletion, and amortization of property, plant and equipment	3.7	3.4	3.6	3.2	3.3
Less: All other operating costs and expenses	91.5	91.7	92.0	90.8	90.3
Income (or loss) from operations	4.8	4.9	4.5	6.0	6.4
Non-operating income (expense)	0.8	0.4	1.0	1.0	1.0
Income (or loss) before income taxes	5.6	5.3	5.4	7.0	7.5
Less: Provision for current and deferred domestic income taxes	2.1	2.1	1.6	2.2	2.5
Income (or loss) after income taxes	3.5	3.2	3.9	4.8	5.0
	(percent)				
OPERATING RATIOS (see explanatory notes)					
Annual rate of profit on stockholders' equity at end of period					
Before income taxes	13.88	13.69	13.66	18.75	19.58
After taxes	8.66	8.18	9.75	12.93	13.00
Annual rate of profit on total assets:					
Before income taxes	6.68	6.58	6.63	9.07	9.36
After taxes	4.17	3.93	4.73	6.25	6.22
BALANCE SHEET RATIOS (based on succeeding table)					
Total current assets to total current liabilities	1.65	1.65	1.66	1.64	1.59
Total cash, U.S. Government and other securities to total current liabilities	0.22	0.22	0.23	0.23	0.19
Total stockholders' equity to total debt	2.72	2.80	2.83	3.02	2.90

[1] During the first quarter of 1984, a considerable number of companies were reclassified by industry. To provide comparability, the four quarters of 1983 have been restated to reflect these reclassifications.

TABLE 18—BALANCE SHEET
FOR CORPORATIONS INCLUDED IN ESIC MAJOR GROUPS 36 AND 37

	Electrical and Electronic Equipment [1]				
	1Q 1983	2Q 1983	3Q 1983	4Q 1983	1Q 1984
	(percent of total assets)				
SELECTED BALANCE SHEET RATIOS					
Total cash, U.S. Government and other securities	7.4	7.7	7.8	7.8	6.7
Trade accounts and trade notes receivable	19.4	20.1	20.5	21.0	20.6
Inventories	24.2	23.9	23.6	23.3	24.4
Total current assets	55.5	56.4	56.4	56.7	56.8
Net property, plant and equipment	26.4	25.8	25.7	25.8	25.6
Short-term debt including installments on long-term debt	4.9	4.9	5.1	4.7	5.4
Total current liabilities	33.6	34.1	33.9	34.6	35.7
Long-term debt	12.7	12.3	12.1	11.3	11.1
Total liabilities	51.9	51.9	51.5	51.6	52.2
Stockholders' equity	48.1	48.1	48.5	48.4	47.8

[1] During the first quarter of 1984, a considerable number of companies were reclassified by industry. To provide comparability, the four quarters of 1983 have been restated to reflect these reclassifications.

Electrical and Electronic Equipment¹ — Assets Under $25 Million

(percent of net sales)

1Q 1983	2Q 1983	3Q 1983	4Q 1983	1Q 1984
100.0	100.0	100.0	100.0	100.0
2.7	2.6	2.4	2.5	2.4
93.5	92.6	92.8	91.4	92.2
3.9	4.7	4.7	6.2	5.4
-1.3	-1.0	-1.1	-0.8	-0.6
2.6	3.7	3.7	5.4	4.9
2.2	2.4	2.2	2.7	2.7
0.4	1.3	1.5	2.6	2.1

(percent)

1Q 1983	2Q 1983	3Q 1983	4Q 1983	1Q 1984
9.83	15.04	14.69	20.93	20.76
1.53	5.37	5.95	10.28	9.10
4.40	6.73	6.62	9.62	9.03
0.69	2.40	2.68	4.73	3.96
2.05	2.02	2.00	2.08	1.95
0.35	0.34	0.32	0.36	0.30
1.49	1.53	1.54	1.62	1.47

Transportation Equipment¹

(percent of net sales)

1Q 1983	2Q 1983	3Q 1983	4Q 1983	1Q 1984
100.0	100.0	100.0	100.0	100.0
4.2	3.9	3.8	3.6	3.7
92.5	90.0	91.6	89.7	88.8
3.3	6.1	4.6	6.7	7.5
1.1	1.2	1.1	1.5	2.0
4.4	7.3	5.7	8.2	9.5
1.4	2.5	1.8	3.3	3.5
3.0	4.8	3.9	4.9	6.0

(percent)

1Q 1983	2Q 1983	3Q 1983	4Q 1983	1Q 1984
16.11	28.76	20.17	31.94	37.68
11.01	18.88	13.76	19.19	23.99
5.92	10.98	7.90	12.54	14.49
4.05	7.21	5.39	7.53	9.22
1.23	1.23	1.24	1.27	1.26
0.15	0.16	0.14	0.21	0.22
2.27	2.67	2.90	3.06	3.14

Transportation Equipment¹ — Assets Under $25 Million

(percent of net sales)

1Q 1983	2Q 1983	3Q 1983	4Q 1983	1Q 1984
100.0	100.0	100.0	100.0	100.0
2.5	2.3	2.2	2.4	2.1
92.4	89.8	91.6	93.4	91.5
5.1	7.9	6.3	4.3	6.4
-0.9	-0.4	0.3	-0.7	-0.1
4.3	7.4	6.5	3.6	6.3
2.5	3.0	2.6	1.9	2.4
1.8	4.4	3.9	1.7	3.9

(percent)

1Q 1983	2Q 1983	3Q 1983	4Q 1983	1Q 1984
17.03	33.26	25.55	15.12	31.92
7.02	19.80	15.33	7.09	19.86
7.33	14.46	12.00	7.01	13.55
3.02	8.61	7.20	3.29	8.43
2.11	2.07	2.22	2.05	1.96
0.30	0.32	0.42	0.34	0.24
1.41	1.47	1.67	1.72	1.47

Electrical and Electronic Equipment¹ — Assets Under $25 Million

(percent of total assets)

1Q 1983	2Q 1983	3Q 1983	4Q 1983	1Q 1984
11.8	12.1	11.5	12.6	11.2
25.5	26.2	26.4	26.5	27.5
27.3	28.0	28.5	27.5	28.4
59.3	71.3	71.6	72.2	72.3
25.7	24.3	23.1	23.2	23.5
11.0	11.5	11.8	11.0	12.8
33.5	35.3	35.8	34.8	37.1
19.0	17.8	17.6	17.2	16.8
65.3	55.3	54.9	54.0	56.5
14.7	44.7	45.1	46.0	43.5

Transportation Equipment¹

(percent of total assets)

1Q 1983	2Q 1983	3Q 1983	4Q 1983	1Q 1984
6.0	6.9	5.6	8.5	9.8
11.9	12.7	13.5	13.0	14.7
29.6	28.8	28.8	28.3	27.9
50.8	51.6	51.3	52.8	55.1
29.7	29.2	29.1	28.4	26.1
3.6	3.6	3.0	2.9	3.2
41.1	41.9	41.2	41.6	43.8
12.6	10.7	10.5	9.9	9.1
63.2	61.8	60.8	60.7	61.6
36.8	38.2	39.2	39.3	38.4

Transportation Equipment¹ — Assets Under $25 Million

(percent of total assets)

1Q 1983	2Q 1983	3Q 1983	4Q 1983	1Q 1984
9.8	10.4	12.7	11.4	8.6
20.5	20.1	18.8	20.1	23.3
31.7	30.4	30.5	29.4	32.6
68.9	68.2	68.3	68.3	70.8
24.6	24.3	23.6	24.2	22.8
9.5	9.4	8.5	9.2	9.7
32.6	33.0	30.7	33.3	36.1
21.0	20.0	19.7	17.8	19.2
57.0	56.5	53.0	53.6	57.5
43.0	43.5	47.0	46.4	42.5

TABLE 19—INCOME STATEMENT
FOR CORPORATIONS INCLUDED IN ESIC MAJOR GROUPS 37.1 AND 37.7

	Motor Vehicles and Equipment [1][2]				
	1Q 1983	2Q 1983	3Q 1983	4Q 1983	1Q 1984
	(percent of net sales)				
INCOME STATEMENT IN RATIO FORMAT					
Net sales, receipts, and operating revenues	100.0	100.0	100.0	100.0	100.0
Less: Depreciation, depletion, and amortization of property, plant and equipment	5.3	4.8	4.5	4.1	4.1
Less: All other operating costs and expenses	92.1	88.6	91.6	87.7	87.5
Income (or loss) from operations	2.7	6.6	3.9	8.1	8.3
Non-operating income (expense)	2.2	1.8	1.8	2.3	2.9
Income (or loss) before income taxes	4.8	8.5	5.7	10.5	11.3
Less: Provision for current and deferred domestic income taxes	1.2	2.8	1.4	4.3	4.0
Income (or loss) after income taxes	3.7	5.7	4.2	6.2	7.3
	(percent)				
OPERATING RATIOS (see explanatory notes)					
Annual rate of profit on stockholders' equity at end of period:					
Before income taxes	18.00	35.14	20.97	43.79	48.94
After taxes	13.58	23.61	15.64	25.94	31.72
Annual rate of profit on total assets:					
Before income taxes	7.69	15.71	9.59	20.11	22.18
After taxes	5.80	10.56	7.15	11.91	14.38
BALANCE SHEET RATIOS (based on succeeding table)					
Total current assets to total current liabilities	1.13	1.14	1.16	1.25	1.30
Total cash, U.S. Government and other securities to total current liabilities	0.24	0.26	0.17	0.31	0.41
Total stockholders' equity to total debt	2.78	3.42	3.76	3.94	4.21

[1] Included in Transportation Equipment.
[2] During the first quarter of 1984, a considerable number of companies were reclassified by industry. To provide comparability, the four quarters of 1983 have been restated to reflect these reclassifications.

TABLE 20—BALANCE SHEET
FOR CORPORATIONS INCLUDED IN ESIC MAJOR GROUPS 37.1 AND 37.7

	Motor Vehicles and Equipment [1][2]				
	1Q 1983	2Q 1983	3Q 1983	4Q 1983	1Q 1984
	(percent of total assets)				
SELECTED BALANCE SHEET RATIOS					
Total cash, U.S. Government and other securities	8.1	8.8	5.7	10.3	14.7
Trade accounts and trade notes receivable	11.8	13.5	14.5	12.9	15.3
Inventories	12.9	12.2	13.4	14.2	13.4
Total current assets	37.6	39.2	39.1	42.0	47.1
Net property, plant and equipment	35.6	34.8	34.5	33.3	29.6
Short-term debt including installments on long-term debt	4.1	4.3	3.1	3.2	3.0
Total current liabilities	33.3	34.4	33.6	33.5	36.1
Long-term debt	11.3	8.7	9.0	8.6	7.9
Total liabilities	57.3	55.3	54.3	54.1	54.7
Stockholders' equity	42.7	44.7	45.7	45.9	45.3

[1] Included in Transportation Equipment.
[2] During the first quarter of 1984, a considerable number of companies were reclassified by industry. To provide comparability, the four quarters of 1983 have been restated to reflect these reclassifications.

Motor Vehicles and Equipment [1] [2] Assets Under $25 Million					Aircraft, Guided Missiles and Parts [1] [2]					Aircraft, Guided Missiles and Parts [1] [2] Assets Under $25 Million				
1Q 1983	2Q 1983	3Q 1983	4Q 1983	1Q 1984	1Q 1983	2Q 1983	3Q 1983	4Q 1983	1Q 1984	1Q 1983	2Q 1983	3Q 1983	4Q 1983	1Q 1984
(percent of net sales)					(percent of net sales)					(percent of net sales)				
100.0	100.0	100.0	100.0	100.0	100.0	100.0	100.0	100.0	100.0	100.0	100.0	100.0	100.0	100.0
2.2	2.0	1.8	1.8	1.7	2.7	2.6	2.8	2.8	2.9	4.2	4.7	3.9	4.9	4.6
91.3	89.2	91.3	91.6	89.4	93.2	92.1	91.8	91.5	90.9	90.9	84.4	90.7	87.3	88.0
6.5	8.8	6.9	6.6	8.8	4.1	5.3	5.4	5.7	6.1	4.9	10.9	5.4	7.8	7.3
-0.5	0.1	0.3	-0.5	-0.5	0.1	0.7	0.7	0.5	0.7	-3.6	-3.5	1.0	-2.1	0.5
6.1	8.9	7.2	6.2	8.3	4.2	6.1	6.1	6.2	6.9	1.3	7.4	6.3	5.7	7.8
2.8	3.5	2.5	1.6	2.6	1.7	2.2	2.5	2.3	2.7	3.2	2.6	4.5	3.2	3.6
3.3	5.4	4.7	4.6	5.7	2.4	3.8	3.6	4.0	4.2	-1.9	4.7	1.8	2.4	4.3
(percent)					(percent)					(percent)				
26.99	40.66	33.25	30.92	47.80	15.09	22.00	20.40	21.64	22.31	4.68	26.07	22.27	15.35	25.78
14.73	24.62	21.58	23.11	32.80	8.81	13.89	11.95	13.78	13.56	-6.70	18.05	6.40	6.60	14.01
12.30	19.45	16.33	13.99	20.53	4.94	7.46	7.11	7.54	7.47	1.46	9.54	7.98	6.97	10.44
6.71	11.78	10.60	10.46	14.09	2.88	4.71	4.16	4.80	4.54	-2.08	6.13	2.29	3.00	5.67
1.88	1.79	1.91	1.85	1.74	1.29	1.28	1.28	1.27	1.21	1.93	2.02	1.99	1.72	1.92
0.20	0.23	0.31	0.24	0.12	0.07	0.09	0.10	0.13	0.09	0.27	0.34	0.34	0.30	0.27
1.94	2.26	2.62	2.02	1.93	2.57	3.06	3.38	3.74	3.58	0.71	0.80	0.85	1.54	1.14

Motor Vehicles and Equipment [1] [2] Assets Under $25 Million					Aircraft, Guided Missiles and Parts [1] [2]					Aircraft, Guided Missiles and Parts [1] [2] Assets Under $25 Million				
1Q 1983	2Q 1983	3Q 1983	4Q 1983	1Q 1984	1Q 1983	2Q 1983	3Q 1983	4Q 1983	1Q 1984	1Q 1983	2Q 1983	3Q 1983	4Q 1983	1Q 1984
(percent of total assets)					(percent of total assets)					(percent of total assets)				
7.3	8.4	10.8	8.9	5.1	3.5	4.7	5.2	6.8	5.0	8.8	10.6	10.5	10.4	8.8
25.4	24.7	23.3	24.0	27.3	11.5	11.5	12.1	12.4	13.1	14.1	13.2	13.6	15.4	17.8
32.6	28.2	29.6	30.5	33.9	49.6	48.2	47.1	45.3	46.1	36.5	35.8	35.2	29.4	32.8
68.8	65.1	67.0	67.4	70.4	66.3	66.1	65.6	65.7	65.5	63.1	63.4	62.2	59.5	62.1
22.7	23.4	20.9	22.2	22.4	20.9	20.9	21.1	20.9	20.2	30.7	29.8	30.4	31.8	30.0
9.0	9.5	6.7	7.9	8.7	2.5	2.3	2.2	1.8	2.8	11.8	12.1	11.9	12.1	11.0
36.6	36.3	35.0	36.5	40.6	51.4	51.6	51.3	51.8	54.1	32.7	31.3	31.3	34.7	32.4
14.4	11.7	12.0	14.5	13.4	10.2	8.8	8.1	7.4	6.6	31.7	30.4	30.5	17.4	24.5
54.4	52.2	50.9	54.7	57.0	67.3	66.1	65.2	65.2	66.5	68.9	66.0	64.2	54.6	59.5
45.6	47.8	49.1	45.3	43.0	32.7	33.9	34.8	34.8	33.5	31.1	34.0	35.8	45.4	40.5

TABLE 21—INCOME STATEMENT
FOR CORPORATIONS INCLUDED IN ESIC MAJOR GROUP 38
AND OTHER DURABLE MANUFACTURING INDUSTRIES

	Instruments and Related Products [1]				
	1Q 1983	2Q 1983	3Q 1983	4Q 1983	1Q 1984
	(percent of net sales)				
INCOME STATEMENT IN RATIO FORMAT					
Net sales, receipts, and operating revenues	100.0	100.0	100.0	100.0	100.0
Less: Depreciation, depletion, and amortization of property, plant and equipment	4.7	4.2	4.3	4.2	4.5
Less: All other operating costs and expenses	89.2	88.1	86.6	88.5	86.5
Income (or loss) from operations	6.1	7.7	9.0	7.4	9.0
Non-operating income (expense)	2.9	2.1	2.7	2.0	2.2
Income (or loss) before income taxes	9.0	9.8	11.7	9.4	11.2
Less: Provision for current and deferred domestic income taxes	2.6	3.1	3.7	2.8	4.1
Income (or loss) after income taxes	6.4	6.7	8.0	6.6	7.1
	(percent)				
OPERATING RATIOS (see explanatory notes)					
Annual rate of profit on stockholders' equity at end of period:					
Before income taxes	15.07	16.49	19.79	17.04	18.79
After taxes	10.65	11.28	13.57	11.92	11.90
Annual rate of profit on total assets:					
Before income taxes	9.55	10.72	12.87	10.87	11.98
After taxes	6.75	7.33	8.83	7.61	7.59
BALANCE SHEET RATIOS (based on succeeding table)					
Total current assets to total current liabilities	2.41	2.48	2.50	2.44	2.49
Total cash, U.S. Government and other securities to total current liabilities	0.33	0.32	0.36	0.43	0.40
Total stockholders' equity to total debt	4.36	4.96	5.08	4.90	4.79

[1] During the first quarter of 1984, a considerable number of companies were reclassified by industry. To provide comparability, the four quarters of 1983 have been restated to reflect these reclassifications.

TABLE 22—BALANCE SHEET
FOR CORPORATIONS INCLUDED IN ESIC MAJOR GROUP 38
AND OTHER DURABLE MANUFACTURING INDUSTRIES

	Instruments and Related Products [1]				
	1Q 1983	2Q 1983	3Q 1983	4Q 1983	1Q 1984
	(percent of total assets)				
SELECTED BALANCE SHEET RATIOS					
Total cash, U.S. Government and other securities	6.7	6.3	7.1	8.8	8.1
Trade accounts and trade notes receivable	16.7	17.7	18.5	18.0	18.2
Inventories	21.1	21.1	19.8	19.2	19.9
Total current assets	48.8	49.2	49.7	50.2	50.3
Net property, plant and equipment	30.8	30.6	30.2	29.6	29.2
Short-term debt including installments on long-term debt	2.9	2.7	2.7	2.8	2.8
Total current liabilities	20.3	19.8	19.9	20.6	20.2
Long-term debt	11.5	10.4	10.2	10.3	10.5
Total liabilities	36.6	35.0	35.0	36.2	36.3
Stockholders' equity	63.4	65.0	65.0	63.8	63.7

[1] During the first quarter of 1984, a considerable number of companies were reclassified by industry. To provide comparability, the four quarters of 1983 have been restated to reflect these reclassifications.

	Instruments and Related Products[1] Assets Under $25 Million					Other Durable Mfg. Industries[1]					Other Durable Mfg. Industries[1] Assets Under $25 Million				
	1Q 1983	2Q 1983	3Q 1983	4Q 1983	1Q 1984	1Q 1983	2Q 1983	3Q 1983	4Q 1983	1Q 1984	1Q 1983	2Q 1983	3Q 1983	4Q 1983	1Q 1984
(percent of net sales)															
	100.0	100.0	100.0	100.0	100.0	100.0	100.0	100.0	100.0	100.0	100.0	100.0	100.0	100.0	100.0
	2.6	2.4	2.8	2.6	2.6	3.3	3.0	2.9	2.8	2.9	2.4	2.2	2.1	2.1	2.2
	90.2	92.4	90.5	92.9	89.0	92.3	90.2	91.7	91.0	91.6	93.7	92.1	92.9	92.3	93.6
	7.2	5.2	6.7	4.5	8.4	4.4	6.8	5.3	6.1	5.5	3.9	5.7	4.9	5.6	4.2
	-1.0	-1.2	-0.5	-1.2	-0.3	-0.9	-0.8	-0.9	-1.0	-1.2	-0.4	-0.3	-0.3	-0.2	-0.3
	6.2	4.1	6.3	3.3	8.0	3.6	6.0	4.4	5.2	4.3	3.5	5.4	4.7	5.4	4.0
	2.7	2.2	2.8	2.0	3.7	1.6	2.4	2.1	2.1	2.0	1.7	2.1	1.9	2.0	1.7
	3.5	1.9	3.5	1.3	4.4	2.0	3.6	2.3	3.1	2.3	1.8	3.3	2.8	3.4	2.3
(percent)															
	24.35	13.14	19.52	10.90	24.06	11.41	21.03	15.99	19.31	15.17	15.83	24.89	22.80	28.72	19.05
	13.83	5.37	10.86	4.28	13.10	6.32	12.75	8.41	11.51	8.13	8.22	15.12	13.53	18.15	10.95
	10.71	6.93	10.12	5.63	12.70	5.28	9.82	7.39	8.88	6.99	7.16	11.64	10.42	12.99	.8.72
	6.08	3.15	5.63	2.21	6.91	2.93	5.96	3.89	5.30	3.75	3.72	7.07	6.18	8.21	5.01
	1.94	2.33	2.24	2.24	2.51	2.04	2.06	1.95	2.01	1.94	1.95	1.96	1.89	1.93	1.94
	0.33	0.39	0.37	0.40	0.49	0.28	0.28	0.27	0.29	0.25	0.32	0.30	0.30	0.30	0.28
	1.36	2.14	2.04	2.06	2.10	1.46	1.51	1.51	1.49	1.49	1.41	1.53	1.52	1.46	1.46

	Instruments and Related Products[1] Assets Under $25 Million					Other Durable Mfg. Industries[1]					Other Durable Mfg. Industries Assets Under $25 Million				
	1Q 1983	2Q 1983	3Q 1983	4Q 1983	1Q 1984	1Q 1983	2Q 1983	3Q 1983	4Q 1983	1Q 1984	1Q 1983	2Q 1983	3Q 1983	4Q 1983	1Q 1984
(percent of total assets)															
	11.3	11.5	11.6	12.9	14.2	7.1	7.0	7.2	7.7	6.9	10.9	10.4	10.6	10.4	9.6
	23.9	23.7	25.6	26.5	26.1	19.0	20.2	20.7	20.0	20.5	25.1	26.8	26.4	25.2	25.9
	30.2	31.3	30.2	28.8	29.2	20.8	20.5	20.5	20.9	21.7	27.0	26.6	26.6	27.3	28.4
	67.6	69.2	70.1	71.4	72.6	51.1	52.1	52.5	52.8	53.1	66.8	66.8	67.3	67.4	67.3
	24.9	23.7	22.7	22.9	20.6	39.6	38.7	38.4	38.2	38.0	27.6	27.5	27.4	27.6	27.5
	12.9	9.1	10.3	10.4	8.6	8.2	8.2	9.1	8.7	9.8	13.1	12.9	13.5	13.4	13.9
	34.8	29.7	31.3	32.0	29.0	25.1	25.3	27.0	26.3	27.3	34.4	34.1	35.6	35.0	34.7
	19.5	15.6	15.1	14.7	16.6	23.4	22.7	21.5	22.2	21.2	18.9	17.5	16.5	17.7	17.4
	56.0	47.2	48.2	48.3	47.2	53.7	53.3	53.8	54.0	53.9	54.8	53.2	54.3	54.8	54.2
	44.0	52.8	51.8	51.7	52.8	46.3	46.7	46.2	46.0	46.1	45.2	46.8	45.7	45.2	45.8

TABLE 23—INCOME STATEMENT
FOR CORPORATIONS INCLUDED IN ESIC MAJOR GROUP 20, ASSETS $25 MILLION AND OVER

	Food and Kindred Products [1]				
	1Q 1983	2Q 1983	3Q 1983	4Q 1983	1Q 1984
INCOME STATEMENT IN RATIO FORMAT	(percent of net sales)				
Net sales, receipts, and operating revenues	100.0	100.0	100.0	100.0	100.0
Less: Depreciation, depletion, and amortization of property, plant and equipment	2.4	2.2	2.2	2.2	2.3
Less: All other operating costs and expenses	92.9	92.3	92.1	92.1	92.1
Income (or loss) from operations	4.7	5.5	5.7	5.8	5.7
Non-operating income (expense)	-1.1	-0.1	-0.1	-0.4	-0.3
Income (or loss) before income taxes	3.7	5.4	5.6	5.4	5.4
Net income (or loss) of foreign branches and equity in earnings (losses) of non-consolidated subsidiaries (net of foreign taxes)	0.6	0.7	0.7	1.0	0.7
Less: Provision for current and deferred domestic income taxes	1.8	2.2	2.2	1.9	2.3
Income (or loss) after income taxes	2.4	3.9	4.0	4.5	3.8
OPERATING RATIOS (see explanatory notes)	(percent)				
Annual rate of profit on stockholders' equity at end of period:					
Before income taxes	13.56	20.05	21.01	21.59	19.93
After taxes	7.68	12.79	13.45	15.14	12.41
Annual rate of profit on total assets:					
Before income taxes	6.60	9.88	10.44	10.62	9.70
After taxes	3.73	6.30	6.69	7.45	6.04

[1] During the first quarter of 1984, a considerable number of companies were reclassified by industry. To provide comparability, the four quarters of 1983 have been restated to reflect these reclassifications.

TABLE 24—INCOME STATEMENT
FOR CORPORATIONS INCLUDED IN ESIC MAJOR GROUP 21, ASSETS $25 MILLION AND OVER

	Tobacco Manufactures				
	1Q 1983	2Q 1983	3Q 1983	4Q 1983	1Q 1984
INCOME STATEMENT IN RATIO FORMAT	(percent of net sales)				
Net sales, receipts, and operating revenues	100.0	100.0	100.0	100.0	100.0
Less: Depreciation, depletion, and amortization of property, plant and equipment	3.5	3.0	3.4	3.9	3.7
Less: All other operating costs and expenses	80.2	77.7	76.8	75.5	79.1
Income (or loss) from operations	16.3	19.2	19.8	20.5	17.2
Non-operating income (expense)	-2.3	-3.7	-1.2	-3.6	-3.2
Income (or loss) before income taxes	13.9	15.5	18.6	16.9	14.0
Net income (or loss) of foreign branches and equity in earnings (losses) of non-consolidated subsidiaries (net of foreign taxes)	3.4	3.7	3.7	2.8	3.6
Less: Provision for current and deferred domestic income taxes	6.4	7.7	8.6	7.0	6.9
Income (or loss) after income taxes	10.9	11.5	13.8	12.7	10.8
OPERATING RATIOS (see explanatory notes)	(percent)				
Annual rate of profit on stockholders' equity at end of period:					
Before income taxes	25.95	31.33	33.18	28.50	25.96
After taxes	15.36	18.75	20.48	18.36	15.85
Annual rate of profit on total assets:					
Before income taxes	12.57	15.49	16.73	15.77	14.30
After taxes	7.93	9.27	10.33	10.16	8.73

TABLE 25—INCOME STATEMENT
FOR CORPORATIONS INCLUDED IN ESIC MAJOR GROUP 22, ASSETS $25 MILLION AND OVER

	Textile Mill Products [1]				
	1Q 1983	2Q 1983	3Q 1983	4Q 1983	1Q 1984
	(percent of net sales)				
INCOME STATEMENT IN RATIO FORMAT					
Net sales, receipts and operating revenues	100.0	100.0	100.0	100.0	100.0
Less: Depreciation, depletion, and amortization of property, plant and equipment	3.4	3.0	3.1	2.8	3.1
Less: All other operating costs and expenses	91.4	90.3	89.7	89.7	90.1
Income (or loss) from operations	5.1	6.7	7.2	7.5	6.8
Non-operating income (expense)	+0.6	-0.2	-0.7	-1.3	-1.4
Income (or loss) before income taxes	4.5	6.4	6.6	6.2	5.5
Net income (or loss) of foreign branches and equity in earnings (losses) of non-consolidated subsidiaries (net of foreign taxes)	0.1	0.0	0.2	0.1	0.1
Less: Provision for current and deferred domestic income taxes	1.8	2.4	2.7	2.5	2.5
Income (or loss) after income taxes	2.8	4.0	4.1	3.7	3.1
	(percent)				
OPERATING RATIOS (see explanatory notes)					
Annual rate of profit on stockholders' equity at end of period:					
Before income taxes	13.18	20.04	20.28	19.85	17.18
After taxes	7.95	12.39	12.47	11.83	9.66
Annual rate of profit on total assets:					
Before income taxes	7.00	10.79	10.90	10.51	8.72
After taxes	4.23	6.68	6.54	6.26	4.90

[1] During the first quarter of 1984, a considerable number of companies were reclassified by industry. To provide comparability, the four quarters of 1983 have been restated to reflect these reclassifications.

TABLE 26—INCOME STATEMENT
FOR CORPORATIONS INCLUDED IN ESIC MAJOR GROUP 26, ASSETS $25 MILLION AND OVER

	Paper and Allied Products [1]				
	1Q 1983	2Q 1983	3Q 1983	4Q 1983	1Q 1984
	(percent of net sales)				
INCOME STATEMENT IN RATIO FORMAT					
Net sales, receipts, and operating revenues	100.0	100.0	100.0	100.0	100.0
Less: Depreciation, depletion, and amortization of property, plant and equipment	4.5	4.4	4.5	4.2	4.3
Less: All other operating costs and expenses	90.5	89.6	89.2	88.5	88.1
Income (or loss) from operations	4.9	6.0	6.3	7.3	7.6
Non-operating income (expense)	-1.0	-1.1	0.0	-1.3	-1.4
Income (or loss) before income taxes	4.0	4.9	6.3	6.1	6.2
Net income (or loss) of foreign branches and equity in earnings (losses) of non-consolidated subsidiaries (net of foreign taxes)	0.2	0.3	0.3	0.1	0.3
Less: Provision for current and deferred domestic income taxes	1.3	1.8	1.9	1.9	2.7
Income (or loss) after income taxes	3.0	3.4	4.7	4.4	3.8
	(percent)				
OPERATING RATIOS (see explanatory notes)					
Annual rate of profit on stockholders' equity at end of period:					
Before income taxes	8.58	11.41	14.27	13.55	14.76
After taxes	6.06	7.51	10.15	9.56	8.67
Annual rate of profit on total assets:					
Before income taxes	4.36	5.71	7.23	6.90	7.41
After taxes	3.08	3.76	5.15	4.87	4.35

[1] During the first quarter of 1984, a considerable number of companies were reclassified by industry. To provide comparability, the four quarters of 1983 have been restated to reflect these reclassifications.

TABLE 27—INCOME STATEMENT
FOR CORPORATIONS INCLUDED IN ESIC MAJOR GROUP 27,
ASSETS $25 MILLION AND OVER

	Printing and Publishing [1]				
	1Q 1983	2Q 1983	3Q 1983	4Q 1983	1Q 1984
INCOME STATEMENT IN RATIO FORMAT	(percent of net sales)				
Net sales. receipts, and operating revenues	100.0	100.0	100.0	100.0	100.0
Less: Depreciation. depletion. and amortization of property, plant and equipment	3.5	3.5	3.4	3.4	3.5
Less: All other operating costs and expenses	86.1	84.4	83.5	83.1	85.1
Income (or loss) from operations	10.4	12.1	13.1	13.5	11.4
Non-operating income (expense)	-0.5	-0.3	-0.3	-0.6	-0.1
Income (or loss) before income taxes	9.9	11.8	12.8	12.9	11.3
Net income (or loss) of foreign branches and equity in earnings (losses) of non-consolidated subsidiaries (net of foreign taxes)	0.1	0.4	0.5	0.6	0.2
Less: Provision for current and deferred domestic income taxes	4.4	5.6	5.9	5.8	5.0
Income (or loss) after income taxes	5.5	6.6	7.3	7.7	6.5
OPERATING RATIOS (see explanatory notes)	(percent)				
Annual rate of profit on stockholders' equity at end of period:					
Before income taxes	24.10	30.55	33.02	35.04	28.31
After taxes	13.36	16.60	18.29	19.98	15.91
Annual rate of profit on total assets:					
Before income taxes	11.92	15.30	16.41	17.34	13.96
After taxes	6.61	8.31	9.09	9.89	7.84

[1] During the first quarter of 1984, a considerable number of companies were reclassified by industry. To provide comparability, the four quarters of 1983 have been restated to reflect these reclassifications.

TABLE 28—INCOME STATEMENT
FOR CORPORATIONS INCLUDED IN ESIC MAJOR GROUP 28,
ASSETS $25 MILLION AND OVER

	Chemicals and Allied Products [1]				
	1Q 1983	2Q 1983	3Q 1983	4Q 1983	1Q 1984
INCOME STATEMENT IN RATIO FORMAT	(percent of net sales)				
Net sales. receipts, and operating revenues	100.0	100.0	100.0	100.0	100.0
Less: Depreciation. depletion. and amortization of property, plant and equipment	4.6	4.5	4.4	4.7	4.3
Less: All other operating costs and expenses	88.2	88.3	87.5	88.8	86.3
Income (or loss) from operations	7.1	7.2	8.1	6.5	9.3
Non-operating income (expense)	-0.5	-0.7	-0.5	-1.0	-0.5
Income (or loss) before income taxes	6.6	6.4	7.6	5.5	8.8
Net income (or loss) of foreign branches and equity in earnings (losses) of non-consolidated subsidiaries (net of foreign taxes)	1.8	2.1	1.9	2.0	2.0
Less: Provision for current and deferred domestic income taxes	2.4	2.4	3.0	2.1	3.6
Income (or loss) after income taxes	6.0	6.1	6.5	5.5	7.3
OPERATING RATIOS (see explanatory notes)	(percent)				
Annual rate of profit on stockholders' equity at end of period:					
Before income taxes	16.01	16.84	18.97	15.12	22.37
After taxes	11.42	12.04	13.01	11.02	14.92
Annual rate of profit on total assets:					
Before income taxes	8.32	8.76	9.80	7.89	11.61
After taxes	5.94	6.26	6.72	5.75	7.75

[1] During the first quarter of 1984, a considerable number of companies were reclassified by industry. To provide comparability, the four quarters of 1983 have been restated to reflect these reclassifications.

TABLE 29—INCOME STATEMENT
FOR CORPORATIONS INCLUDED IN ESIC MAJOR GROUP 28.1,
ASSETS $25 MILLION AND OVER

	Industrial Chemicals and Synthetics [1]				
	1Q 1983	2Q 1983	3Q 1983	4Q 1983	1Q 1984
INCOME STATEMENT IN RATIO FORMAT	(percent of net sales)				
Net sales, receipts, and operating revenues	100.0	100.0	100.0	100.0	100.0
Less: Depreciation, depletion, and amortization of property, plant and equipment	5.8	5.4	5.5	6.0	5.5
Less: All other operating costs and expenses	89.7	88.8	88.8	88.9	86.0
Income (or loss) from operations	4.5	5.7	5.6	5.1	8.4
Non-operating income (expense)	-1.4	-1.1	-0.8	-2.4	-0.9
Income (or loss) before income taxes	3.1	4.6	4.8	2.7	7.5
Net income (or loss) of foreign branches and equity in earnings (losses) of non-consolidated subsidiaries (net of foreign taxes)	0.9	1.2	0.9	0.8	1.3
Less: Provision for current and deferred domestic income taxes	0.7	1.2	1.4	0.8	3.1
Income (or loss) after income taxes	3.3	4.6	4.3	2.7	5.7
OPERATING RATIOS (see explanatory notes)	(percent)				
Annual rate of profit on stockholders' equity at end of period:					
Before income taxes	7.95	12.22	11.74	7.37	18.91
After taxes	6.58	9.64	8.84	5.73	12.35
Annual rate of profit on total assets:					
Before income taxes	3.84	5.94	5.70	3.63	9.28
After taxes	3.18	4.68	4.29	2.82	6.06

[1] During the first quarter of 1984, a considerable number of companies were reclassified by industry. To provide comparability, the four quarters of 1983 have been restated to reflect these reclassifications.

TABLE 30—INCOME STATEMENT
FOR CORPORATIONS INCLUDED IN ESIC MAJOR GROUP 28.3,
ASSETS $25 MILLION AND OVER

	Drugs [1]				
	1Q 1983	2Q 1983	3Q 1983	4Q 1983	1Q 1984
INCOME STATEMENT IN RATIO FORMAT	(percent of net sales)				
Net sales, receipts, and operating revenues	100.0	100.0	100.0	100.0	100.0
Less: Depreciation, depletion, and amortization of property, plant and equipment	2.9	2.9	2.9	2.8	3.0
Less: All other operating costs and expenses	84.0	85.9	83.5	87.0	83.3
Income (or loss) from operations	13.1	11.2	13.6	10.2	13.8
Non-operating income (expense)	1.2	-0.3	0.0	2.9	0.7
Income (or loss) before income taxes	14.3	10.9	13.5	13.2	14.5
Net income (or loss) of foreign branches and equity in earnings (losses) of non-consolidated subsidiaries (net of foreign taxes)	5.8	7.3	6.8	6.4	5.7
Less: Provision for current and deferred domestic income taxes	6.0	5.7	6.8	4.8	6.2
Income (or loss) after income taxes	14.0	12.4	13.5	14.6	13.9
OPERATING RATIOS (see explanatory notes)	(percent)				
Annual rate of profit on stockholders' equity at end of period:					
Before income taxes	29.94	26.03	30.81	29.78	29.99
After taxes	20.91	17.86	20.46	22.33	20.70
Annual rate of profit on total assets:					
Before income taxes	18.03	15.49	18.05	17.53	17.72
After taxes	12.59	10.63	11.99	13.14	12.23

[1] During the first quarter of 1984, a considerable number of companies were reclassified by industry. To provide comparability, the four quarters of 1983 have been restated to reflect these reclassifications.

TABLE 31—INCOME STATEMENT
FOR CORPORATIONS INCLUDED IN ESIC MAJOR GROUP 29,
ASSETS $25 MILLION AND OVER

	Petroleum and Coal Products [1]				
	1Q 1983	2Q 1983	3Q 1983	4Q 1983	1Q 1984
INCOME STATEMENT IN RATIO FORMAT	(percent of net sales)				
Net sales, receipts, and operating revenues	100.0	100.0	100.0	100.0	100.0
Less: Depreciation, depletion, and amortization of property, plant and equipment	5.6	5.4	5.4	6.1	5.9
Less: All other operating costs and expenses	90.2	87.4	86.3	87.4	87.2
Income (or loss) from operations	4.2	7.2	8.2	6.5	6.9
Non-operating income (expense)	0.6	-0.5	0.1	0.8	-0.3
Income (or loss) before income taxes	4.8	6.7	8.4	7.4	6.7
Net income (or loss) of foreign branches and equity in earnings (losses) of non-consolidated subsidiaries (net of foreign taxes)	1.8	1.8	1.7	2.2	1.9
Less: Provision for current and deferred domestic income taxes	1.7	2.7	3.1	2.4	2.9
Income (or loss) after income taxes	4.9	5.8	7.0	7.2	5.7
OPERATING RATIOS (see explanatory notes)	(percent)				
Annual rate of profit on stockholders' equity at end of period:					
Before income taxes	13.46	17.61	20.57	19.26	17.08
After taxes	10.03	11.96	14.22	14.38	11.24
Annual rate of profit on total assets:					
Before income taxes	6.72	8.73	10.31	9.74	8.35
After taxes	5.00	5.93	7.13	7.28	5.49

[1] During the first quarter of 1984, a considerable number of companies were reclassified by industry. To provide comparability, the four quarters of 1983 have been restated to reflect these reclassifications.

TABLE 32—INCOME STATEMENT
FOR CORPORATIONS INCLUDED IN ESIC MAJOR GROUP 30,
ASSETS $25 MILLION AND OVER

	Rubber and Misc. Plastics Products [1]				
	1Q 1983	2Q 1983	3Q 1983	4Q 1983	1Q 1984
INCOME STATEMENT IN RATIO FORMAT	(percent of net sales)				
Net sales, receipts, and operating revenues	100.0	100.0	100.0	100.0	100.0
Less: Depreciation, depletion, and amortization of property, plant and equipment	3.6	3.3	3.1	3.0	3.2
Less: All other operating costs and expenses	92.3	90.9	90.0	90.4	91.3
Income (or loss) from operations	4.1	5.8	6.9	6.6	5.6
Non-operating income (expense)	-1.2	-0.6	-0.2	-0.7	-0.2
Income (or loss) before income taxes	2.9	5.2	6.7	5.9	5.3
Net income (or loss) of foreign branches and equity in earnings (losses) of non-consolidated subsidiaries (net of foreign taxes)	0.6	0.7	0.7	0.9	0.8
Less: Provision for current and deferred domestic income taxes	1.4	2.3	2.8	2.4	2.2
Income (or loss) after income taxes	2.1	3.6	4.6	4.3	3.8
OPERATING RATIOS (see explanatory notes)	(percent)				
Annual rate of profit on stockholders' equity at end of period:					
Before income taxes	8.88	16.00	20.99	18.58	16.57
After taxes	5.21	9.87	13.03	11.80	10.48
Annual rate of profit on total assets:					
Before income taxes	4.46	8.10	10.64	9.63	8.44
After taxes	2.62	5.00	6.60	6.11	5.34

[1] During the first quarter of 1984, a considerable number of companies were reclassified by industry. To provide comparability, the four quarters of 1983 have been restated to reflect these reclassifications.

TABLE 33—INCOME STATEMENT
FOR CORPORATIONS INCLUDED IN ESIC MAJOR GROUP 32, ASSETS $25 MILLION AND OVER

	Stone, Clay and Glass Products [1]				
	1Q 1983	2Q 1983	3Q 1983	4Q 1983	1Q 1984
INCOME STATEMENT IN RATIO FORMAT	(percent of net sales)				
Net sales, receipts, and operating revenues	100.0	100.0	100.0	100.0	100.0
Less: Depreciation, depletion, and amortization of property, plant and equipment	5.6	5.0	4.6	4.9	5.0
Less: All other operating costs and expenses	93.4	89.3	88.8	88.7	90.3
Income (or loss) from operations	1.0	5.7	6.6	6.4	4.7
Non-operating income (expense)	-3.7	-1.8	-1.1	-1.7	-1.4
Income (or loss) before income taxes	-2.8	3.9	5.4	4.7	3.3
Net income (or loss) of foreign branches and equity in earnings (losses) of non-consolidated subsidiaries (net of foreign taxes)	0.5	0.5	0.4	0.6	0.5
Less: Provision for current and deferred domestic income taxes	0.2	1.7	2.1	1.6	1.5
Income (or loss) after income taxes	-2.5	2.8	3.7	3.7	2.3
	(percent)				
OPERATING RATIOS (see explanatory notes)					
Annual rate of profit on stockholders' equity at end of period:					
Before income taxes	-4.24	9.32	13.12	10.98	8.00
After taxes	-4.66	5.71	8.33	7.68	4.86
Annual rate of profit on total assets:					
Before income taxes	-2.06	4.57	6.42	5.52	3.92
After taxes	-2.27	2.80	4.07	3.86	2.38

[1] During the first quarter of 1984, a considerable number of companies were reclassified by industry. To provide comparability, the four quarters of 1983 have been restated to reflect these reclassifications.

TABLE 34—INCOME STATEMENT
FOR CORPORATIONS INCLUDED IN ESIC MAJOR GROUP 33, ASSETS $25 MILLION AND OVER

	Primary Metal Industries [1]				
	1Q 1983	2Q 1983	3Q 1983	4Q 1983	1Q 1984
INCOME STATEMENT IN RATIO FORMAT	(percent of net sales)				
Net sales, receipts, and operating revenues	100.0	100.0	100.0	100.0	100.0
Less: Depreciation, depletion, and amortization of property, plant and equipment	5.1	4.6	4.6	4.2	4.0
Less: All other operating costs and expenses	100.2	95.8	95.3	95.0	92.6
Income (or loss) from operations	-5.2	-0.4	0.2	0.8	3.4
Non-operating income (expense)	-1.8	-3.1	-3.4	-10.2	-1.2
Income (or loss) before income taxes	-7.0	-3.6	-3.2	-9.4	2.2
Net income (or loss) of foreign branches and equity in earnings (losses) of non-consolidated subsidiaries (net of foreign taxes)	0.4	-0.3	-0.1	-0.7	-0.3
Less: Provision for current and deferred domestic income taxes	-2.0	-1.0	-0.6	-1.5	0.7
Income (or loss) after income taxes	-4.6	-3.0	-2.8	-8.6	1.2
	(percent)				
OPERATING RATIOS (see explanatory notes)					
Annual rate of profit on stockholders' equity at end of period:					
Before income taxes	-14.34	-9.51	-8.19	-27.98	5.49
After taxes	-9.99	-7.24	-6.87	-23.74	3.55
Annual rate of profit on total assets:					
Before income taxes	-5.64	-3.74	-3.20	-10.48	2.03
After taxes	-3.93	-2.84	-2.68	-8.89	1.31

[1] During the first quarter of 1984, a considerable number of companies were reclassified by industry. To provide comparability, the four quarters of 1983 have been restated to reflect these reclassifications.

TABLE 35—INCOME STATEMENT
FOR CORPORATIONS INCLUDED IN ESIC MAJOR GROUPS 33.1–2,
ASSETS $25 MILLION AND OVER

	Iron and Steel				
	1Q 1983	2Q 1983	3Q 1983	4Q 1983	1Q 1984
INCOME STATEMENT IN RATIO FORMAT	(percent of net sales)				
Net sales, receipts, and operating revenues	100.0	100.0	100.0	100.0	100.0
Less: Depreciation, depletion, and amortization of property, plant and equipment	5.3	4.9	4.8	4.2	4.1
Less: All other operating costs and expenses	101.0	96.5	95.2	96.3	92.9
Income (or loss) from operations	-6.4	-1.4	0.0	-0.4	3.0
Non-operating income (expense)	-1.5	-2.8	-3.5	-12.2	-0.8
Income (or loss) before income taxes	-7.9	-4.2	-3.4	-12.6	2.2
Net income (or loss) of foreign branches and equity in earnings (losses) of non-consolidated subsidiaries (net of foreign taxes)	-0.3	-0.8	-0.7	-1.3	-0.7
Less: Provision for current and deferred domestic income taxes	-2.4	-0.7	-0.3	-2.5	0.4
Income (or loss) after income taxes	-5.9	-4.3	-3.8	-11.3	1.1
OPERATING RATIOS (see explanatory notes)	(percent)				
Annual rate of profit on stockholders' equity at end of period:					
Before income taxes	-20.35	-14.15	-12.29	-47.18	5.40
After taxes	-14.55	-12.17	-11.30	-38.52	3.80
Annual rate of profit on total assets:					
Before income taxes	-7.20	-4.98	-4.31	-15.36	1.74
After taxes	-5.15	-4.29	-3.96	-12.54	1.22

TABLE 36—INCOME STATEMENT
FOR CORPORATIONS INCLUDED IN ESIC MAJOR GROUPS 33,5–6,
ASSETS $25 MILLION AND OVER

	Nonferrous Metals [1]				
	1Q 1983	2Q 1983	3Q 1983	4Q 1983	1Q 1984
INCOME STATEMENT IN RATIO FORMAT	(percent of net sales)				
Net sales, receipts, and operating revenues	100.0	100.0	100.0	100.0	100.0
Less: Depreciation, depletion, and amortization of property, plant and equipment	4.5	4.1	4.2	4.2	3.9
Less: All other operating costs and expenses	98.6	94.5	95.4	92.4	91.9
Income (or loss) from operations	-3.1	1.4	0.4	3.3	4.1
Non-operating income (expense)	-2.4	-3.9	-3.2	-6.4	-2.1
Income (or loss) before income taxes	-5.5	-2.5	-2.8	-3.1	2.0
Net income (or loss) of foreign branches and equity in earnings (losses) of non-consolidated subsidiaries (net of foreign taxes)	1.6	0.6	1.2	0.4	0.6
Less: Provision for current and deferred domestic income taxes	-1.4	-1.3	-0.9	0.5	1.1
Income (or loss) after income taxes	-2.4	-0.5	-0.7	-3.1	1.5
OPERATING RATIOS (see explanatory notes)	(percent)				
Annual rate of profit on stockholders' equity at end of period:					
Before income taxes	-6.66	-3.65	-2.98	-5.38	5.59
After taxes	-4.19	-1.09	-4.24	-6.34	3.25
Annual rate of profit on total assets:					
Before income taxes	-3.07	-1.68	-1.36	-2.45	2.50
After taxes	-1.92	-0.46	-0.56	-2.88	1.46

[1] During the first quarter of 1984, a considerable number of companies were reclassified by industry. To provide comparability, the four quarters of 1983 have been restated to reflect these reclassifications.

TABLE 37—INCOME STATEMENT
FOR CORPORATIONS INCLUDED IN ESIC MAJOR GROUP 34, ASSETS $25 MILLION AND OVER

	Fabricated Metal Products [1]				
	1Q 1983	2Q 1983	3Q 1983	4Q 1983	1Q 1984
INCOME STATEMENT IN RATIO FORMAT	(percent of net sales)				
Net sales, receipts, and operating revenues	100.0	100.0	100.0	100.0	100.0
Less: Depreciation, depletion, and amortization of property, plant and equipment	3.5	3.3	3.4	3.1	3.2
Less: All other operating costs and expenses	92.3	90.8	90.8	92.9	90.4
Income (or loss) from operations	4.2	5.9	5.9	4.0	6.5
Non-operating income (expense)	-0.8	-0.9	-2.4	-0.2	-1.4
Income (or loss) before income taxes	3.4	5.0	3.4	3.8	5.0
Net income (or loss) of foreign branches and equity in earnings (losses) of non-consolidated subsidiaries (net of foreign taxes)	0.3	1.0	0.9	0.3	0.6
Less: Provision for current and deferred domestic income taxes	1.8	2.1	1.9	1.1	2.2
Income (or loss) after income taxes	1.8	3.9	2.4	2.9	3.5
OPERATING RATIOS (see explanatory notes)	(percent)				
Annual rate of profit on stockholders' equity at end of period:					
Before income taxes	8.54	15.23	11.26	10.69	15.11
After taxes	4.30	9.92	6.35	7.72	9.33
Annual rate of profit on total assets:					
Before income taxes	3.99	7.21	5.19	4.98	6.97
After taxes	2.01	4.68	2.92	3.60	4.30

[1] During the first quarter of 1984, a considerable number of companies were reclassified by industry. To provide comparability, the four quarters of 1983 have been restated to reflect these reclassifications.

TABLE 38—INCOME STATEMENT
FOR CORPORATIONS INCLUDED IN ESIC MAJOR GROUP 35, ASSETS $25 MILLION AND OVER

	Machinery, Except Electrical [1]				
	1Q 1983	2Q 1983	3Q 1983	4Q 1983	1Q 1984
INCOME STATEMENT IN RATIO FORMAT	(percent of net sales)				
Net sales, receipts, and operating revenues	100.0	100.0	100.0	100.0	100.0
Less: Depreciation, depletion, and amortization of property, plant and equipment	5.7	5.1	5.1	4.8	4.7
Less: All other operating costs and expenses	90.0	87.9	88.1	85.9	87.9
Income (or loss) from operations	4.3	7.0	6.9	9.3	7.4
Non-operating income (expense)	-1.6	-2.7	-1.5	-2.0	-0.8
Income (or loss) before income taxes	2.6	4.3	5.3	7.3	6.6
Net income (or loss) of foreign branches and equity in earnings (losses) of non-consolidated subsidiaries (net of foreign taxes)	2.8	2.7	2.5	3.2	2.2
Less: Provision for current and deferred domestic income taxes	1.6	2.2	2.8	3.3	3.3
Income (or loss) after income taxes	3.7	4.9	5.0	7.2	5.4
OPERATING RATIOS (see explanatory notes)	(percent)				
Annual rate of profit on stockholders' equity at end of period:					
Before income taxes	8.30	11.73	12.74	18.46	15.05
After taxes	5.72	8.13	8.18	12.63	9.30
Annual rate of profit on total assets:					
Before income taxes	4.55	6.53	7.20	10.52	8.45
After taxes	3.13	4.53	4.62	7.19	5.23

[1] During the first quarter of 1984, a considerable number of companies were reclassified by industry. To provide comparability, the four quarters of 1983 have been restated to reflect these reclassifications.

TABLE 39—INCOME STATEMENT
FOR CORPORATIONS INCLUDED IN ESIC MAJOR GROUP 36,
ASSETS $25 MILLION AND OVER

	Electrical and Electronic Equipment [1]				
	1Q 1983	2Q 1983	3Q 1983	4Q 1983	1Q 1984
INCOME STATEMENT IN RATIO FORMAT	(percent of net sales)				
Net sales, receipts, and operating revenues	100.0	100.0	100.0	100.0	100.0
Less: Depreciation, depletion, and amortization of property, plant and equipment	3.8	3.5	3.8	3.4	3.5
Less: All other operating costs and expenses	91.2	91.6	91.8	90.7	89.9
Income (or loss) from operations	5.0	5.0	4.4	6.0	6.6
Non-operating income (expense)	0.0	-0.5	0.1	0.3	0.1
Income (or loss) before income taxes	5.0	4.4	4.6	6.2	6.6
Net income (or loss) of foreign branches and equity in earnings (losses) of non-consolidated subsidiaries (net of foreign taxes)	1.1	1.1	1.2	1.0	1.3
Less: Provision for current and deferred domestic income taxes	2.1	2.0	1.4	2.1	2.5
Income (or loss) after income taxes	4.0	3.5	4.3	5.2	5.5
OPERATING RATIOS (see explanatory notes)	(percent)				
Annual rate of profit on stockholders' equity at end of period:					
Before income taxes	14.30	13.55	13.55	18.50	19.45
After taxes	9.40	8.47	10.16	13.23	13.42
Annual rate of profit on total assets:					
Before income taxes	6.94	6.55	6.63	9.00	9.40
After taxes	4.56	4.10	4.97	6.44	6.48

[1] During the first quarter of 1984, a considerable number of companies were reclassified by industry. To provide comparability, the four quarters of 1983 have been restated to reflect these reclassifications.

TABLE 40—INCOME STATEMENT
FOR CORPORATIONS INCLUDED IN ESIC MAJOR GROUP 37,
ASSETS $25 MILLION AND OVER

	Transportation Equipment [1]				
	1Q 1983	2Q 1983	3Q 1983	4Q 1983	1Q 1984
INCOME STATEMENT IN RATIO FORMAT	(percent of net sales)				
Net sales, receipts, and operating revenues	100.0	100.0	100.0	100.0	100.0
Less: Depreciation, depletion, and amortization of property, plant and equipment	4.3	4.0	3.9	3.7	3.8
Less: All other operating costs and expenses	92.5	90.0	91.6	89.5	88.7
Income (or loss) from operations	3.2	6.0	4.5	6.8	7.6
Non-operating income (expense)	-0.6	-0.3	-0.1	-0.7	0.1
Income (or loss) before income taxes	2.5	5.8	4.4	6.2	7.6
Net income (or loss) of foreign branches and equity in earnings (losses) of non-consolidated subsidiaries (net of foreign taxes)	1.9	1.5	1.2	2.3	2.1
Less: Provision for current and deferred domestic income taxes	1.3	2.5	1.8	3.3	3.5
Income (or loss) after income taxes	3.1	4.8	3.9	5.1	6.2
OPERATING RATIOS (see explanatory notes)	(percent)				
Annual rate of profit on stockholders' equity at end of period:					
Before income taxes	16.07	28.56	19.91	32.73	37.94
After taxes	11.20	18.84	13.69	19.75	24.17
Annual rate of profit on total assets:					
Before income taxes	5.87	10.85	7.74	12.76	14.52
After taxes	4.09	7.15	5.32	7.70	9.25

[1] During the first quarter of 1984, a considerable number of companies were reclassified by industry. To provide comparability, the four quarters of 1983 have been restated to reflect these reclassifications.

TABLE 41—INCOME STATEMENT
FOR CORPORATIONS INCLUDED IN ESIC MAJOR GROUP 37.1,
ASSETS $25 MILLION AND OVER

	Motor Vehicles and Equipment [1]				
	1Q 1983	2Q 1983	3Q 1983	4Q 1983	1Q 1984
INCOME STATEMENT IN RATIO FORMAT	(percent of net sales)				
Net sales, receipts, and operating revenues	100.0	100.0	100.0	100.0	100.0
Less: Depreciation, depletion, and amortization of property, plant and equipment	5.4	4.9	4.6	4.2	4.2
Less: All other operating costs and expenses	92.1	88.6	91.6	87.6	87.5
Income (or loss) from operations	2.5	6.6	3.8	8.2	8.3
Non-operating income (expense)	-0.5	-0.2	0.2	-0.8	0.2
Income (or loss) before income taxes	2.0	6.4	4.0	7.4	8.6
Net income (or loss) of foreign branches and equity in earnings (losses) of non-consolidated subsidiaries (net of foreign taxes)	2.8	2.1	1.7	3.2	2.8
Less: Provision for current and deferred domestic income taxes	1.1	2.8	1.4	4.4	4.0
Income (or loss) after income taxes	3.7	5.7	4.2	6.3	7.4
OPERATING RATIOS (see explanatory notes)	(percent)				
Annual rate of profit on stockholders' equity at end of period:					
Before income taxes	17.64	34.94	20.51	44.19	48.97
After taxes	13.53	23.57	15.42	26.03	31.69
Annual rate of profit on total assets:					
Before income taxes	7.51	15.59	9.36	20.30	22.23
After taxes	5.76	10.54	7.03	11.96	14.39

[1] During the first quarter of 1984, a considerable number of companies were reclassified by industry. To provide comparability, the four quarters of 1983 have been restated to reflect these reclassifications.

TABLE 42—INCOME STATEMENT
FOR CORPORATIONS INCLUDED IN ESIC MAJOR GROUP 37.7,
ASSETS $25 MILLION AND OVER

	Aircraft, Guided Missiles and Parts [1]				
	1Q 1983	2Q 1983	3Q 1983	4Q 1983	1Q 1984
INCOME STATEMENT IN RATIO FORMAT	(percent of net sales)				
Net sales, receipts, and operating revenues	100.0	100.0	100.0	100.0	100.0
Less: Depreciation, depletion, and amortization of property, plant and equipment	2.6	2.5	2.8	2.7	2.9
Less: All other operating costs and expenses	93.3	92.3	91.8	91.6	91.0
Income (or loss) from operations	4.1	5.2	5.4	5.6	6.1
Non-operating income (expense)	-0.5	0.2	0.2	-0.1	0.2
Income (or loss) before income taxes	3.6	5.4	5.6	5.5	6.3
Net income (or loss) of foreign branches and equity in earnings (losses) of non-consolidated subsidiaries (net of foreign taxes)	0.6	0.6	0.6	0.7	0.6
Less: Provision for current and deferred domestic income taxes	1.7	2.2	2.5	2.2	2.7
Income (or loss) after income taxes	2.5	3.8	3.7	4.0	4.2
OPERATING RATIOS (see explanatory notes)	(percent)				
Annual rate of profit on stockholders' equity at end of period:					
Before income taxes	15.30	21.85	20.35	21.82	22.22
After taxes	9.12	13.78	12.09	13.98	13.55
Annual rate of profit on total assets:					
Before income taxes	5.01	7.40	7.08	7.55	7.40
After taxes	2.99	4.67	4.21	4.84	4.51

[1] During the first quarter of 1984, a considerable number of companies were reclassified by industry. To provide comparability, the four quarters of 1983 have been restated to reflect these reclassifications.

TABLE 43—INCOME STATEMENT
FOR CORPORATIONS INCLUDED IN MINING,
ALL WHOLESALE TRADE AND ESIC MAJOR GROUPS 50, 51
ASSETS $25 MILLION AND OVER

	All Mining [1]				
	1Q 1983	2Q 1983	3Q 1983	4Q 1983	1Q 1984
	(percent of net sales)				
INCOME STATEMENT IN RATIO FORMAT					
Net sales, receipts, and operating revenues	100.0	100.0	100.0	100.0	100.0
Less: Depreciation, depletion, and amortization of property, plant and equipment	16.6	15.5	15.4	15.4	15.5
Less: All other operating costs and expenses	73.8	73.9	73.9	76.1	74.9
Income (or loss) from operations	9.7	10.6	10.8	8.5	9.5
Non-operating income (expense)	−3.1	−4.4	−3.9	−6.0	−0.5
Income (or loss) before income taxes	6.6	6.2	6.9	2.5	9.0
Less: Provision for current and deferred domestic income taxes	2.8	3.1	2.9	2.6	3.5
Income (or loss) after income taxes	3.8	3.1	4.0	−0.1	5.5
	(percent)				
OPERATING RATIOS (see explanatory notes)					
Annual rate of profit on stockholders' equity at end of period:					
Before income taxes	8.22	7.35	8.15	3.05	11.07
After taxes	4.68	3.71	4.70	−0.11	6.76
Annual rate of profit on total assets:					
Before income taxes	3.09	2.80	3.16	1.17	4.24
After taxes	1.76	1.41	1.82	−0.04	2.59
BALANCE SHEET RATIOS (based on succeeding table)					
Total current assets to total current liabilities	1.19	1.22	1.24	1.23	1.11
Total cash, U.S. Government and other securities to total current liabilities	0.24	0.29	0.29	0.31	0.27
Total stockholders' equity to total debt	0.96	0.99	1.02	1.01	1.01

[1] During the first quarter of 1984, a considerable number of companies were reclassified by industry. To provide comparability, the four quarters of 1983 have been restated to reflect these reclassifications.

TABLE 44—BALANCE SHEET
FOR CORPORATIONS INCLUDED IN MINING,
ALL WHOLESALE TRADE AND ESIC MAJOR GROUPS 50, 51,
ASSETS $25 MILLION AND OVER

	All Mining [1]				
	1Q 1983	2Q 1983	3Q 1983	4Q 1983	1Q 1984
	(percent of total assets)				
SELECTED BALANCE SHEET RATIOS					
Total cash, U.S. Government and other securities	4.0	4.7	4.7	5.0	4.7
Trade accounts and trade notes receivable	9.1	8.7	8.7	8.5	8.6
Inventories	4.9	4.6	4.3	4.1	4.0
Total current assets	19.9	19.7	19.7	19.7	19.4
Net property, plant and equipment	66.5	66.6	66.1	65.9	66.2
Short-term debt including installments on long-term debt	5.5	5.7	5.4	4.9	5.9
Total current liabilities	16.8	16.2	15.9	16.0	17.4
Long-term debt	33.3	33.1	32.6	32.8	31.8
Total liabilities	62.4	61.9	61.3	61.7	61.7
Stockholders' equity	37.6	38.1	38.7	38.3	38.3

[1] During the first quarter of 1984, a considerable number of companies were reclassified by industry. To provide comparability, the four quarters of 1983 have been restated to reflect these reclassifications.

	All Wholesale Trade [1]					Wholesale Trade, Durable Goods [1]					Wholesale Trade, Nondurable Goods [1]			
1Q 1983	2Q 1983	3Q 1983	4Q 1983	1Q 1984	1Q 1983	2Q 1983	3Q 1983	4Q 1983	1Q 1984	1Q 1983	2Q 1983	3Q 1983	4Q 1983	1Q 1984
(percent of net sales)					(percent of net sales)					(percent of net sales)				
100.0	100.0	100.0	100.0	100.0	100.0	100.0	100.0	100.0	100.0	100.0	100.0	100.0	100.0	100.0
0.9	0.9	0.9	0.9	0.9	1.1	1.1	1.1	1.1	1.1	0.8	0.8	0.8	0.8	0.8
97.6	97.4	96.9	97.1	96.8	96.5	96.4	96.0	95.7	95.3	98.3	98.0	97.5	98.0	97.7
1.5	1.7	2.2	2.0	2.4	2.4	2.5	2.9	3.2	3.7	0.9	1.2	1.7	1.3	1.6
-0.4	-0.2	-0.4	-0.3	-0.2	-1.0	-0.5	-0.7	-0.7	-0.3	-0.1	-0.1	-0.2	-0.1	0.0
1.1	1.5	1.8	1.7	2.2	1.5	2.1	2.1	2.5	3.3	0.9	1.1	1.5	1.2	1.5
0.6	0.6	0.8	0.7	1.0	1.0	1.0	1.2	1.4	1.8	0.3	0.3	0.6	0.4	0.5
0.5	0.9	0.9	0.9	1.2	0.4	1.0	1.0	1.1	1.6	0.6	0.8	0.9	0.8	1.0
(percent)					(percent)					(percent)				
9.81	13.42	15.77	15.49	19.41	9.85	14.06	14.56	16.81	21.86	9.78	12.82	16.98	14.14	16.86
4.73	8.11	8.37	8.73	10.73	2.94	6.91	6.49	7.64	10.29	6.44	9.25	10.24	9.83	11.19
3.26	4.49	5.29	5.25	6.96	3.25	4.87	5.02	5.89	8.26	3.27	4.15	5.55	4.63	5.74
1.59	2.71	2.81	2.96	3.85	0.97	2.40	2.24	2.68	3.89	2.16	2.99	3.35	3.22	3.81
1.39	1.38	1.39	1.40	1.44	1.53	1.54	1.54	1.55	1.62	1.26	1.24	1.24	1.25	1.28
0.16	0.17	0.17	0.18	0.16	0.19	0.22	0.23	0.24	0.23	0.13	0.12	0.12	0.11	0.11
0.91	0.95	0.95	0.98	1.10	0.83	0.54	0.94	0.98	1.17	1.00	0.97	0.96	0.99	1.02

	All Wholesale Trade[1]					Wholesale Trade, Durable Goods[1]					Wholesale Trade, Nondurable Goods[1]			
1Q 1983	2Q 1983	3Q 1983	4Q 1983	1Q 1984	1Q 1983	2Q 1983	3Q 1983	4Q 1983	1Q 1984	1Q 1983	2Q 1983	3Q 1983	4Q 1983	1Q 1984
(percent of total assets)					(percent of total assets)					(percent of total assets)				
7.2	7.8	8.1	8.2	7.4	8.7	10.4	10.7	11.3	10.3	5.9	5.6	5.7	5.3	4.8
25.3	25.6	25.3	25.3	25.7	26.3	25.9	27.1	27.0	27.6	24.4	25.5	23.6	23.8	23.9
26.9	26.1	27.3	28.1	28.0	31.4	31.0	31.1	31.1	31.2	22.8	21.8	23.8	25.2	25.0
63.5	63.7	64.8	65.7	65.2	70.5	71.5	72.8	73.3	73.2	57.1	56.8	57.2	58.5	57.7
22.8	23.0	22.2	21.5	21.6	19.3	20.0	19.1	19.0	18.6	26.0	25.7	25.1	23.8	24.3
18.9	18.1	19.2	18.5	17.3	22.0	21.0	21.5	21.1	18.2	15.9	15.5	16.8	16.3	16.3
45.6	46.1	46.7	47.0	45.2	46.1	46.4	47.2	47.1	45.2	45.2	45.9	46.3	46.9	45.2
17.5	17.0	16.2	15.8	15.5	17.7	15.9	15.3	14.8	13.9	17.4	17.9	17.3	16.7	17.0
66.8	66.6	66.4	66.1	64.1	67.0	65.3	65.5	64.9	62.2	66.5	67.7	67.3	67.2	66.0
33.2	33.4	33.6	33.9	35.9	33.0	34.7	34.5	35.1	37.8	33.5	32.3	32.7	32.8	34.0

General Business and Economic Indicators

SELECTED BUSINESS STATISTICS

SEASONALLY ADJUSTED WHERE APPLICABLE — SHADED AREA DENOTES RECESSIONS/DEPRESSIONS

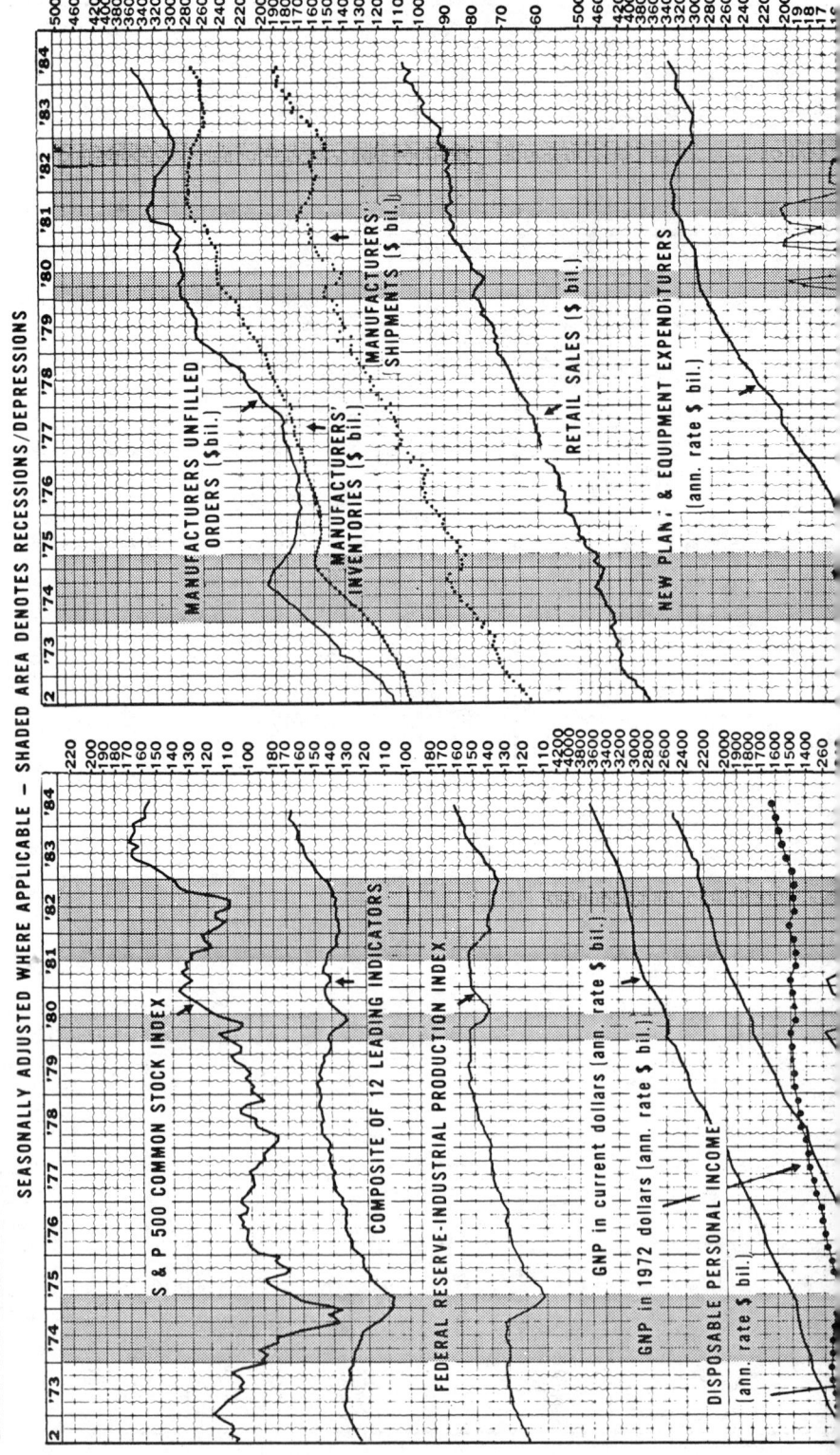

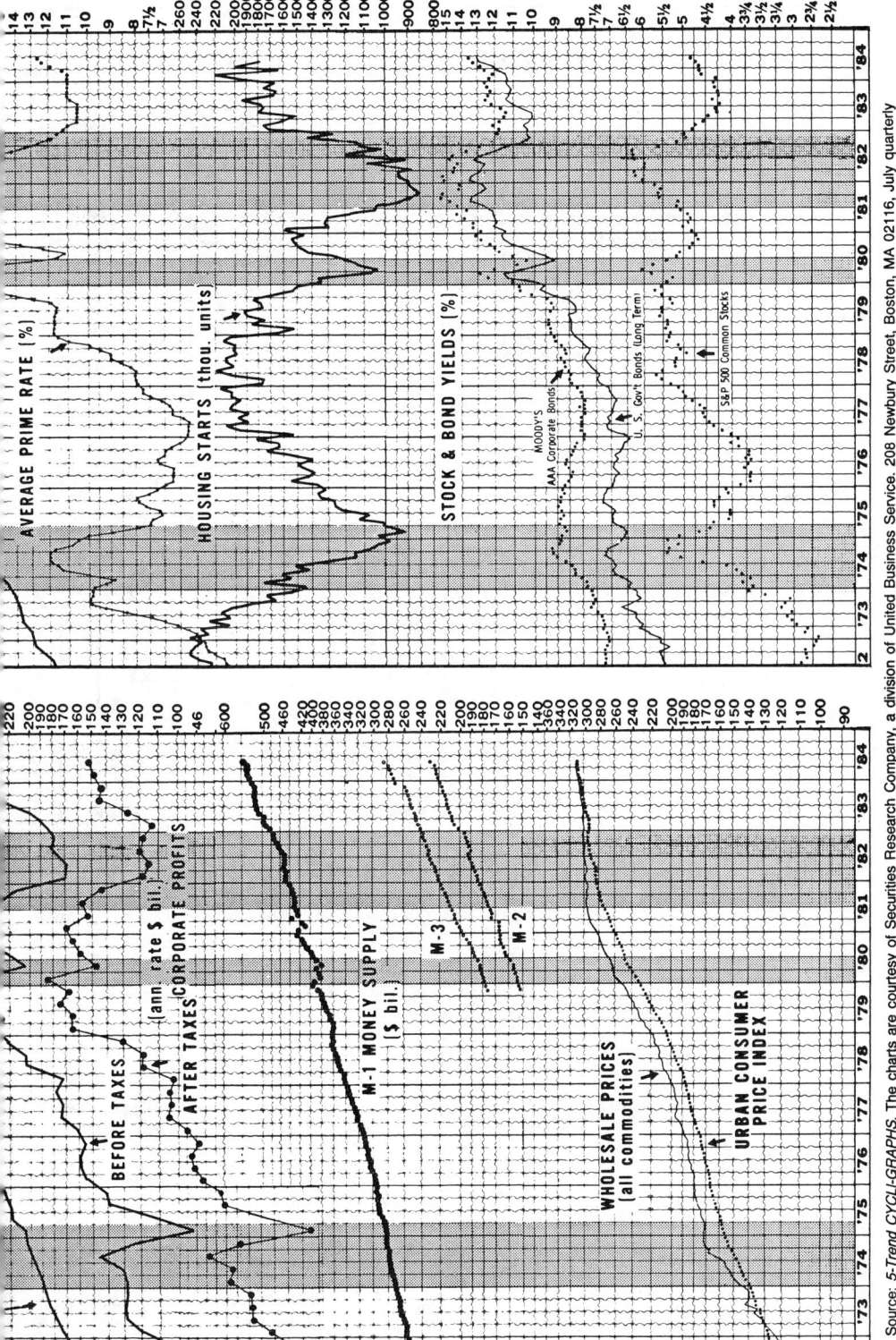

Source: *5-Trend CYCLI-GRAPHS*. The charts are courtesy of Securities Research Company, a division of United Business Service. 208 Newbury Street, Boston, MA 02116, July quarterly edition, 1984.

COMPOSITE INDEXES AND THEIR COMPONENTS

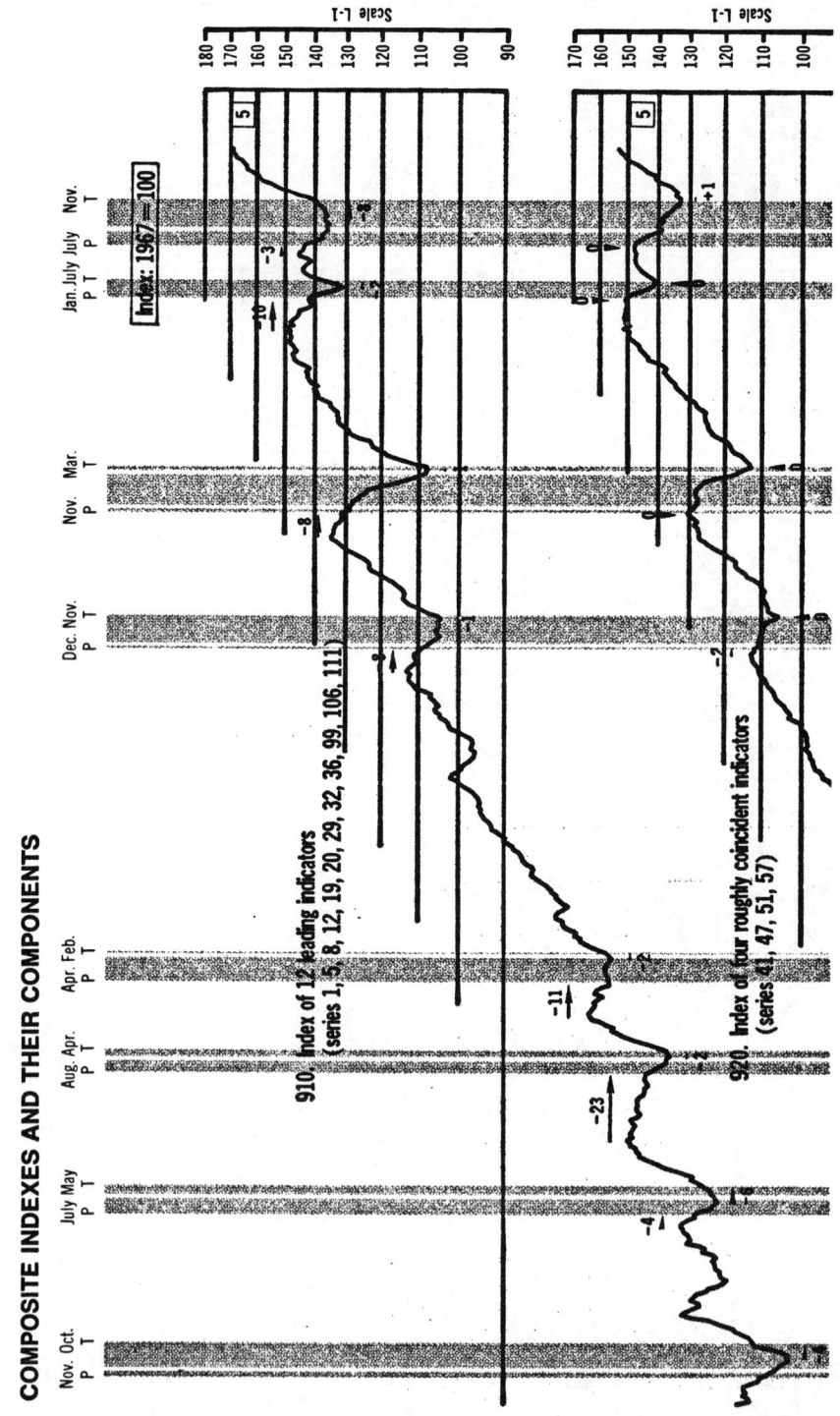

910. Index of 12 leading indicators
(series 1, 5, 8, 12, 19, 20, 29, 32, 36, 99, 106, 111)

920. Index of four roughly coincident indicators
(series 41, 47, 51, 57)

Index: 1967=100

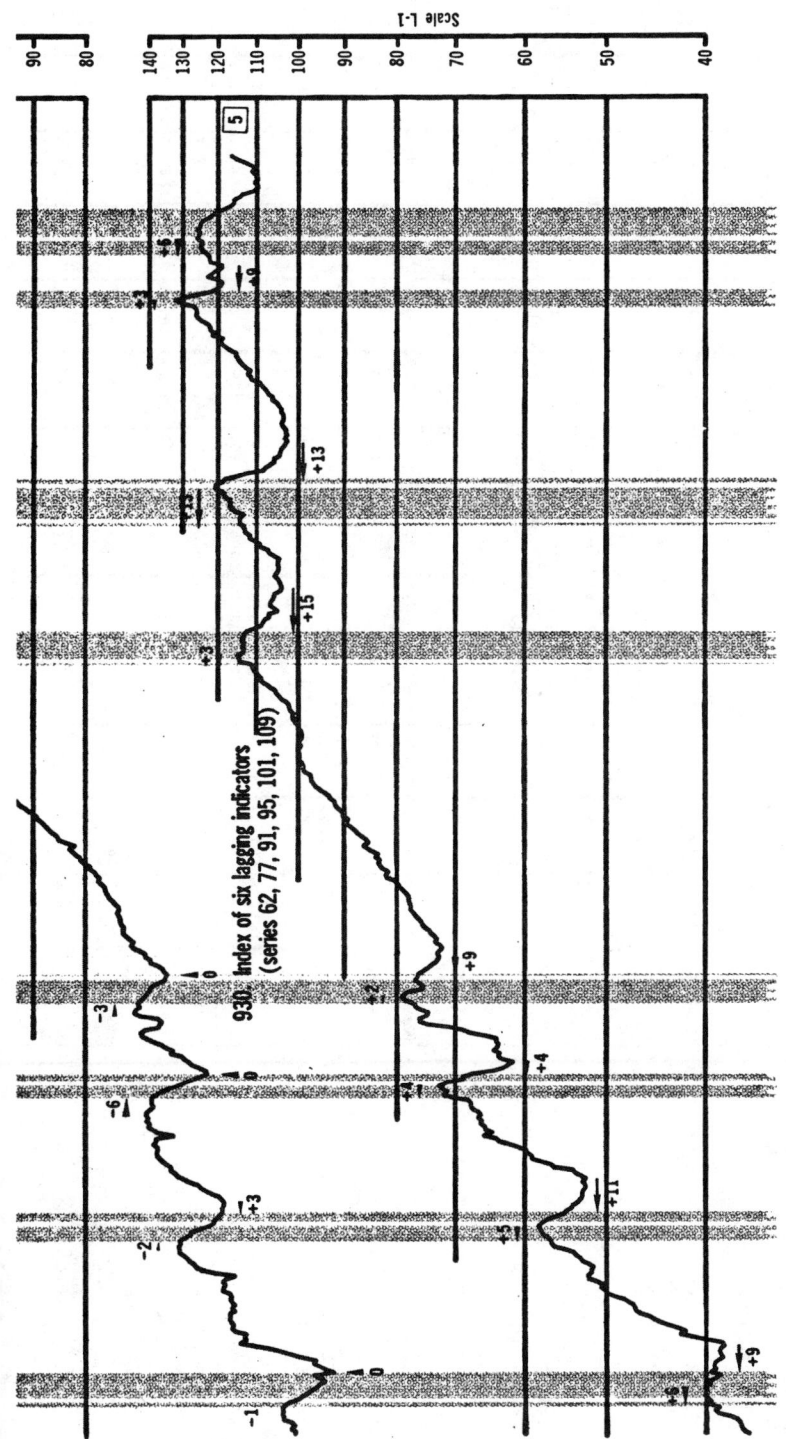

930. Index of six lagging indicators
(series 62, 77, 91, 95, 101, 109)

NOTE: Numbers entered on the chart indicate length of leads (−) and lags (+) in months from reference turning dates.

Source: *Business Conditions Digest*, U.S. Department of Commerce, Bureau of Economic Analysis.

SUMMARY OF RECENT DATA AND CURRENT CHANGES FOR PRINCIPAL INDICATORS

Series title and timing classification		Unit of measure	Basic data								Percent change				Series number
			Annual average		3d Q 1983	4th Q 1983	1st Q 1984	Mar. 1984	Apr. 1984	May 1984	Mar. to Apr. 1984	Apr. to May 1984	3d Q to 4th Q 1983	4th Q to 1st Q 1984	
			1982	1983											
I. CYCLICAL INDICATORS															
A. Composite Indexes															
910 Twelve leading indicators	L,L,L	1967=100	136.8	156.2	159.3	163.3	166.4	167.4	168.3	168.2	0.5	-0.1	2.5	1.9	910
920 Four roughly coincident indicators	C,C,C	do	136.3	139.8	141.4	145.7	150.3	150.9	152.2	153.0	0.9	0.5	3.0	3.2	920
930 Six lagging indicators	Lg,Lg,Lg	do	123.0	111.8	110.0	110.5	113.2	113.2	115.2	116.4	1.8	1.0	0.5	1.1	930
940 Ratio, coincident index to lagging index	L,L,L	do	110.9	125.1	128.6	131.8	134.6	133.3	132.1	131.4	-0.9	-0.5	2.5	2.1	940
Leading Indicator Subgroups:															
913 Marginal employment adjustments	L,L,L	do	NA	NA	NA	NA	NA	NA	NA	NA	NA	NA	NA	NA	913
914 Capital investment commitments	L,L,L	do	104.3	108.8	109.3	110.1	111.3	111.1	111.1	111.2	0.1	0.	0.7	1.1	914
915 Inventory investment and purchasing	L,L,L	do	97.2	103.0	104.3	106.1	106.8	107.5	107.7	107.7	0.2	0.	1.7	0.7	915
916 Profitability	L,L,L	do	93.7	105.0	107.3	109.5	NA	NA	NA	NA	NA	NA	2.1	NA	916
917 Money and financial flows	L,L,L	do	122.8	130.7	131.5	132.3	135.0	136.5	137.3	NA	NA	NA	0.6	2.0	917
B. Cyclical Indicators by Economic Process															
B1. Employment and Unemployment															
Marginal Employment Adjustments:															
*1. Average workweek, prod. workers, mfg.	L,L,L	Hours	38.9	40.1	40.4	40.6	40.8	40.7	41.2	40.7	1.2	-1.2	0.5	0.5	1
21. Avg weekly overtime, prod. workers, mfg.	L,C,L	do	2.3	3.0	3.1	3.3	3.5	3.5	3.7	3.4	0.2	-0.3	0.2	0.2	21
5. Avg weekly initial claims (inverted)	L,C,L	Thousands	578	426	392	382	352	348	360	348	-3.4	3.3	2.6	7.9	5
Job Vacancies:															
60. Ratio, help-wanted advertising to unemployment[1]	L,Lg,U	Ratio	0.243	0.271	0.278	0.362	0.420	0.421	0.418	0.437	-0.003	0.019	0.084	0.058	60
46. Help-wanted advertising	L,Lg,U	1967=100	86	96	98	115	125	124	124	125	0.	0.8	17.3	8.7	46
Comprehensive Employment:															
48. Employee-hours in nonagri. establishments	U,C,C	Ar. bil. hrs.	165.78	167.89	169.05	171.00	174.03	173.66	176.50	176.07	1.6	-0.2	1.2	1.8	48
42. Persons engaged in nonagri. activities	U,C,C	Millions	96.12	97.45	98.11	99.22	100.42	100.86	101.01	101.90	0.9	0.9	1.1	1.2	42
*41. Employees on nonagri. payrolls	C,C,C	do	89.57	90.14	90.40	91.69	92.76	93.06	93.46	93.69	0.4	0.2	1.4	1.2	41
40. Employees in mining, mfg. construction	L,C,U	Thousands	23,813	23,394	23,538	24,050	24,518	24,595	24,763	24,856	0.7	0.4	2.2	1.9	40
90. Ratio, civilian employment to total population of working age	U,Lg,U	Percent	57.05	57.15	57.47	57.86	58.32	58.49	58.59	59.04	0.10	0.45	0.39	0.46	90
Comprehensive Unemployment:															
37 Total unemployed (inverted*)	L,Lg,U	Thousands	10,678	10,717	10,529	9,507	8,866	8,772	8,843	8,514	-0.8	3.7	9.7	6.7	37
43 Unemployment rate, total (inverted*)	L,Lg,U	Percent	9.7	9.6	9.4	8.5	7.9	7.8	7.8	7.5	0.3	0.3	0.9	0.6	43
45 Avg weekly insured unemployment rate (inv*)	L,Lg,U	do	4.6	3.8	3.5	3.3	2.9	2.9	2.8	2.7	0.1	0.1	0.3	0.3	45
91 Avg duration of unemployment (inverted)	Lg,Lg,Lg	Weeks	15.6	20.0	20.5	20.0	19.4	18.8	18.5	18.4	1.6	0.5	0.3	3.0	91
44 Unemployment rate, 15 weeks and over (inv*)	Lg,Lg,Lg	Percent	3.2	3.8	3.7	3.1	2.7	2.5	2.5	2.5	0.	0.	0.6	0.4	44

B2. Production and Income

No.	Series	Code	Unit	1	2	3	4	5	6	7	8	9	10	11	12
	Comprehensive Output and Income:														
50	GNP in 1972 dollars	C.C.C.	Ar., bil. dol.	2.3	1.2			1356.5	1352.1	1346.0	1609.3	1572.5	1553.4	1535.3	1485.4
52	Personal income in 1972 dollars	C.C.C.	do	2.3	2.0	0.3	0.5				1341.6	1311.8	1286.6	1285.2	1256.1
*51	Pers. income less transfer pay., 1972 dollars	C.C.C.	do	2.7	2.2	0.4	0.5	1166.8	1162.6	1157.1	1152.8	1123.0	1099.0	1096.0	1073.8
53	Wages and salaries in mining, mfg. and construction, 1972 dollars	C.C.C.	do	1.9	1.2	0.3	1.0	229.9	229.3	227.1	227.0	222.8	220.1	217.8	216.3
	Industrial Production:														
*47	Industrial production, total	C.C.C.	1967=100	2.8	2.4	0.4	1.1	163.2	162.5	160.8	159.8	155.5	151.8	147.6	138.6
73	Industrial production, durable mfrs.	C.C.C.	do	4.4	3.4	0.5	1.3	154.0	153.2	151.2	150.1	143.8	139.1	134.5	124.7
74	Industrial production-nondurable mfrs	C.L.L.	do	1.1	1.2	0.2	1.2	180.2	179.9	177.8	176.7	174.8	172.7	168.1	156.2
49	Value of goods output, 1972 dollars	C.C.C.	Ar., bil. dol.	3.6	2.5						742.7	716.8	699.0	688.6	661.6
	Capacity Utilization:														
83	Capacity utilization rate, mfg., BEA	L.C.U.	Percent	NA	1	NA		NA			NA	77	76	74	70
82	Capacity utilization rate, mfg., FRB	L.C.U.	do	1.8	1.5	NA					80.7	78.9	77.4	75.2	71.1
84	Capacity utilization rate, materials, FRB	L.C.U.	do	2.0	2.1	NA					81.6	79.6	77.5	75.2	70.0

B3. Consumption, Trade, Orders, and Deliveries

No.	Series	Code	Unit	1	2	3	4	5	6	7	8	9	10	11	12
	Orders and Deliveries:														
6	New orders, durable goods	L.L.L.	Bil dol	5.4	8.6	3.3	-6.5	101.55	98.32	105.18	102.32	97.07	89.40	87.85	75.00
7	New orders, durable goods, 1972 dollars	L.L.L.	do	4.7	8.2	3.2	-6.7	41.84	40.53	43.43	42.48	40.59	37.50	37.01	32.47
*8	New orders, cons. goods and mtls., 1972 dol	L.L.L.	do	3.9	4.8	1.6	-0.6	37.92	37.31	37.52	38.17	36.73	35.04	34.12	29.44
25	Change in unfilled orders, durable goods'	L.L.L.	do	1.67	1.98	0.78	-5.57	3.40	2.62	8.19	6.13	4.46	2.48	2.69	-1.81
96	Mfrs' unfilled orders, durable goods'	L.L.g.U.	Bil dol. EOP	5.8	4.4	1.0	0.8	343.72	340.32	337.70	337.70	319.30	305.94	319.30	287.01
*32	Vendor performance' (1)	L.L.L.	Percent	5	5	-1	-1	70	71	72	68	63	58	54	37
	Consumption and Trade:														
56	Manufacturing and trade sales	C.C.C.	Bil dol	3.2	3.7	NA	0.7	NA	404.62	401.90	400.62	388.23	374.23	367.06	343.34
*57	Manufacturing and trade sales, 1972 dollars	C.C.C.	do	2.8	2.6	NA	0.7	NA	173.40	172.16	172.37	167.73	163.43	161.16	152.07
75	Industrial production, consumer goods	C.L.C.	1967=100	1.7	0.5	0.	1.1	161.7	161.1	160.0	159.6	156.9	156.1	151.7	142.6
54	Sales of retail stores	C.L.U.	Bil dol	3.0	2.9	0.2	1.1	107.29	107.10	103.87	105.32	101.75	98.88	97.83	89.55
59	Sales of retail stores, 1972 dollars	U.L.U.	do	3.0	2.5	0.	3.1	51.48	51.46	49.89	50.66	49.19	47.97	47.67	44.62
55	Personal consumption expenditures, automobiles	L.C.C.	Ar., bil dol	9.3	7.2						108.4	99.2	92.5	90.9	73.9
58	Index of consumer sentiment (1)	L.L.L.	IQ 1966=100	8.7	-0.1	2.1	-4.9	98.1	96.1	101.0	99.5	91.5	91.6	87.5	68.0

B4. Fixed Capital Investment

No.	Series	Code	Unit	1	2	3	4	5	6	7	8	9	10	11	12
	Formation of Business Enterprises:														
*12	Net business formation	L.L.L.	1967=100	0.1	2.0	-2.0	0.9	116.2	118.6	117.6	117.5	117.4	115.1	114.8	113.2
13	New business incorporations	L.L.L.	Number	NA	1.2	NA	NA	NA	NA	NA	NA	51,213	50,625	50,162	47,153
	Business Investment Commitments:														
10	Contracts and orders, plant and equipment	L.L.L.	Bil dol	4.4	6.4	15.6	-4.2	34.15	29.55	30.85	30.12	28.84	27.10	26.69	24.79
*20	Contracts and orders, plant and equipment, 1972 dollars	L.L.L.	do	7.3	3.3	14.9	-7.0	16.97	14.77	15.88	15.38	14.33	13.87	13.56	12.40
24	New orders, capital goods indus., nondefense	L.L.L.	do	5.2	6.8	10.7	-3.6	28.64	25.88	26.86	26.32	25.02	23.42	22.73	20.63
27	New orders, capital goods industries, nondefense, 1972 dollars	L.L.L.	do	8.7	3.2	10.9	-6.8	14.70	13.26	14.23	13.81	12.71	12.31	11.87	10.62

SUMMARY OF RECENT DATA AND CURRENT CHANGES FOR PRINCIPAL INDICATORS (continued)

Series title and timing classification	Unit of measure	Basic data — Annual average 1982	1983	3d Q 1983	4th Q 1983	1st Q 1984	Mar. 1984	Apr. 1984	May 1984	Mar. to Apr. 1984	Apr. to May 1984	3d Q to 4th Q 1983	4th Q 1983 to 1st Q 1984	Series number
I. CYCLICAL INDICATORS—Con.														
B4. Fixed Capital Investment—Con.														
Business Investment Commitments—Con.:														
9. Construction contracts, commercial and industrial buildings, floor space ... L.C.U.	Mil. sq. ft	57.38	63.86	65.41	70.63	71.28	73.63	80.03	84.39	8.7	5.4	8.0	0.9	9
11. Newly approved capital appropriations, mfg. ... U.Lg.U.	Bil. dol	21.28	22.04	22.20	25.17	27.88	...	...	...	...	...	13.4	10.8	11
97. Backlog of capital appropriations, mfg³ ... C.Lg.Lg.	Bil. dol. EOP	70.76	73.67	72.17	73.67	80.00	...	...	...	...	...	2.1	8.6	97
Business Investment Expenditures:														
61. Business expend., new plant and equipment ... C.Lg.Lg.	A.r., bil. dol	282.71	269.22	270.05	283.96	293.15	...	...	...	...	...	5.2	3.2	61
69. Machinery and equipment sales and business construction expenditures ... C.Lg.U.	do	325.66	321.39	323.86	340.40	350.72	362.54	358.41	NA	-1.1	NA	5.1	3.0	69
76. Industrial production, business equipment ... C.Lg.U.	1967 = 100	157.9	153.3	156.2	164.2	171.6	172.3	173.8	175.4	0.9	0.9	5.1	4.5	76
86. Nonresid. fixed investment, total, 1972 dollars ... C.Lg.C.	A.r., bil. dol	166.1	168.4	170.1	180.7	187.6	...	...	...	...	...	6.2	3.8	86
Residential Construction Commitments and Investment:														
28. New private housing units started, total ... L.L.L.	A.r., thousands	1,062	1,703	1,782	1,699	1,968	1,662	1,990	1,782	19.7	-10.5	-4.7	15.8	28
*29. New building permits, private housing ... L.L.L.	1967 = 100	80.7	129.4	133.6	132.0	146.1	139.5	142.0	141.0	1.8	-0.7	-1.2	10.7	29
89. Fixed investment, residential, 1972 dollars ... L.L.L.	A.r., bil. dol	37.8	52.7	56.8	55.8	59.2	...	...	...	...	...	-1.8	6.1	89
B5. Inventories and Inventory Investment														
Inventory Investment:														
30. Change in business inventories, 1972 dollars¹ ... L.L.L.	do	-9.4	-2.1	3.8	8.7	30.7	...	...	...	...	...	4.9	22.0	30
*36. Change in inventories on hand and on order, 1972 dollars¹ (smoothed⁴) ... L.L.L.	do	-14.43	2.85	10.72	20.37	23.80	29.42	32.39	NA	2.97	NA	9.65	3.43	36
31. Change in mfg. and trade inventories¹ ... L.L.L.	do	-18.1	8.8	25.5	29.4	73.7	66.6	97.7	NA	31.1	NA	3.9	44.3	31
38. Change in materials on hand and on order¹ ... L.L.L.	Bil. dol	-2.13	1.46	2.07	2.23	2.78	2.76	1.95	NA	-0.81	NA	0.16	0.55	38
Inventories on Hand and on Order:														
71. Mfg. and trade inventories, book value⁵ ... Lg.Lg.Lg.	Bil. dol. EOP	505.55	514.34	506.98	514.34	532.77	532.77	540.90	NA	1.5	NA	1.5	3.6	71
70. Mfg. and trade inventories, 1972 dollars⁵ ... Lg.Lg.Lg.	do	261.21	261.65	259.29	261.65	266.78	266.78	269.48	NA	1.0	NA	0.9	2.0	70
65. Mfrs.' inventories of finished goods⁵ ... Lg.Lg.Lg.	do	85.02	80.87	81.72	80.87	82.87	82.87	84.06	NA	1.4	NA	-1.0	2.5	65
*77. Ratio, constant-dollar inventories to sales, mfg. and trade⁵ ... Lg.Lg.Lg.	Ratio	1.75	1.61	1.58	1.56	1.54	1.55	1.55	NA	0.	NA	-0.02	-0.02	77
78. Stocks of materials and supplies on hand and on order, mfg.¹ ... L.Lg.Lg.	Bil. dol. EOP	191.12	208.59	201.91	208.59	216.92	216.92	218.87	NA	0.9	NA	3.3	4.0	78

B6. Prices, Costs, and Profits

Series	Code	Unit	V1	V2	V3	V4	V5	V6	V7	V8	V9	V10	V11	V12	No.
Sensitive Commodity Prices:															
98. Change in producer prices, sensitive materials[1]	L,L,L	Percent	-0.38	1.23	0.44	0.96	0.29	0.61	-0.45	-0.51	-0.06	-1.06	0.52	-0.67	98
23. Spot market prices, raw industrials ⑬	U,L,L	1967=100	242.5	258.5	263.0	278.5	285.5	289.2	288.6	289.5	0.3	-0.2	5.9	2.5	23
*99. Change in sensitive materials prices (smoother)[1]	L,L,L	Percent	-0.67	1.03	1.00	0.93	0.52	0.34	0.39	0.27	-0.12	0.05	-0.07	-0.41	99
Stock Prices:															
*19. Stock prices, 500 common stocks ⑬	L,L,L	1941-43=10	119.71	160.41	165.51	165.75	160.36	157.44	157.60	156.55	-0.7		0.1	-3.3	19
Profits and Profit Margins:															
16. Corporate profits after taxes	L,L,L	A.r., bil. dol.	115.1	130.6	144.1	142.9	151.6	...	...	...	...	...	-0.8	6.1	16
18. Corporate profits after taxes, 1972 dollars	L,L,L	do	55.6	62.1	68.5	67.5	71.5	...	...	...	...	...	-1.5	5.9	18
79. Corp. profits after taxes with IVA and CCAdj	L,C,L	do	105.6	152.2	163.4	182.9	188.0	...	...	...	...	...	11.9	3.3	79
80. ....do........ 1972 dollars	L,C,L	do	51.1	72.5	77.2	86.8	89.7	...	...	...	...	...	11.6	3.3	80
15. Profits (after taxes) per dollar of sales, mfg.	L,L,L	Cents	3.4	4.0	4.2	4.5	4.9	...	...	...	...	...	0.3	0.4	15
26. Ratio, price to unit labor cost, nonfarm business	L,L,L	1977=100	96.2	97.6	98.0	98.5	98.4	...	...	...	...	...	0.5	-0.1	26
Cash Flows:															
34. Net cash flow, corporate	L,L,L	A.r., bil. dol	267.3	319.8	341.1	348.5	361.7	...	...	...	...	...	2.2	3.8	34
35. Net cash flow, corporate, 1972 dollars	L,L,L	do	125.2	150.1	160.4	163.8	170.1	...	...	...	...	...	2.1	3.8	35
Unit Labor Costs and Labor Share:															
63. Unit labor cost, private business sector	Lg,Lg,Lg	1977=100	153.3	157.1	156.9	157.9	158.6	...	...	...	...	...	0.6	0.4	63
68. Labor cost per unit of real gross domestic product, nonfin. corporations	Lg,Lg,Lg	do	1.397	1.418	1.412	1.416	1.423	...	...	...	...	...	0.3	0.5	68
62. Labor cost per unit of output, manufacturing	Lg,Lg,Lg	Dollars													62
a) Actual data	Lg,Lg,Lg	1967=100	228.0	226.1	222.8	223.3	225.3	225.4	225.6	225.1	-0.2	0.1	0.2	0.9	62
*b) Actual data as percent of trend	Lg,Lg,Lg	Percent	101.0	93.0	90.5	89.9	89.5	89.0	88.5	87.8	-0.7	-0.5	-0.6	-0.4	62
64. Compensation of employees as percent of national income[?]	Lg,Lg,Lg	do	76.1	75.1	74.9	74.2	73.3	...	...	...	...	...	-0.7	-0.9	64

B7. Money and Credit

Series	Code	Unit	V1	V2	V3	V4	V5	V6	V7	V8	V9	V10	V11	V12	No.
Money:															
85. Change in money supply (M1)[3]	L,L,L	do	0.70	0.75	0.52	0.41	0.62	0.43	0.04	1.06	-0.39	1.02	-0.11	0.21	85
102. Change in money supply (M2)[3]	L,C,U	do	0.75	0.93	0.48	0.75	0.51	0.33	0.55	0.78	0.22	0.23	0.27	-0.24	102
104. Change in total liquid assets (smoother)[3]	L,L,L	do	0.86	0.81	0.83	0.71	0.88	0.91	1.00	NA	0.09	NA	-0.12	0.17	104
105. Money supply (M1), 1972 dollars	L,L,L	Bil. dol	198.7	213.8	216.1	216.3	217.6	218.0	217.1	219.0	-0.4	0.9	0.1	0.6	105
*106. Money supply (M2), 1972 dollars	L,L,L	do	814.3	888.8	893.0	902.1	906.6	908.3	909.2	914.5	-0.1	0.6	1.0	0.5	106
Velocity of Money:															
107. Ratio, GNP to money supply (M1)[3]	C,C,C	Ratio	6.705	6.502	6.502	6.566	6.664	...	...	...	...	...	0.064	0.098	107
108. Ratio, personal income to money supply (M2)[3]	C,Lg,C	do	1.373	1.296	1.293	1.300	1.318	1.320	1.321	1.318	0.001	-0.003	0.007	0.018	108
Credit Flows:															
33. Change in mortgage debt[3]	L,L,L	A.r., bil. dol	-5.13	36.67	48.23	83.70	90.43	109.46	98.96	82.67	NA	NA	35.47	6.73	33
112. Change in business loans[3]	L,L,L	do	17.32	3.66	0.20	25.66	120.73	53.77	76.90	NA	-21.77	-16.29	25.46	28.01	112
113. Change in consumer installment credit[3]	L,L,L	do	13.36	39.77	41.41	62.78	70.44	53.77	70.44	NA	6.46	NA	21.37	5.01	113
*111. Change in credit outstanding[3]	L,L,L	A.r., percent	1.9	4.9	5.9	10.8	14.8	20.2	20.9	NA	-0.7	NA	4.9	-22.7	111
110. Total private borrowing	L,L,L	A.r., bil. dol	262.99	386.61	362.20	512.88	396.58	...	...	...	...	...	41.6	...	110
Credit Difficulties:															
14. Liabilities of business failures (inv.[4]) ⑩	L,L,L	Mil. dol	NA	NA	NA	NA	NA	NA	NA	NA	NA	NA	NA	0.09	14
39. Delinquency rate, installment loans (inv.[4])[5]	L,L,L	Percent, EOP	2.18	1.94	1.88	1.94	1.85	1.85	NA	NA	0.09	NA	-0.06	...	39

SUMMARY OF RECENT DATA AND CURRENT CHANGES FOR PRINCIPAL INDICATORS (continued)

Series title and timing classification	Unit of measure	Timing	Annual average 1982	Annual average 1983	Basic data 3d Q 1983	4th Q 1983	1st Q 1984	Mar. 1984	Apr. 1984	May 1984	% chg Mar. to Apr. 1984	% chg Apr. to May 1984	% chg 3d Q to 4th Q 1983	% chg 4th Q 1983 to 1st Q 1984	Series number
I. CYCLICAL INDICATORS—Con.															
B7. Money and Credit—Con.															
Bank Reserves:															
93. Free reserves (inverted)[1] [2]	Mil. dol.	L,U,U	-692	-545	-982	-300	15	-196	-795	-2,385	599	1,590	-682	-315	93
94. Borrowing from the Federal Reserve[1] [2]	do.	L,Lg,U	1,052	1,034	1,465	831	740	905	1,285	2,964	380	1,679	-634	-91	94
Interest Rates:															
119. Federal funds rate[1] [2]	Percent	L,Lg,Lg	12.26	9.09	9.46	9.43	9.69	9.91	10.29	10.32	0.38	0.03	-0.03	0.26	119
114. Treasury bill rate[1] [2]	do.	C,Lg,Lg	10.72	8.62	9.19	8.79	9.13	9.44	9.69	9.90	0.25	0.21	-0.40	0.34	114
116. Corporate bond yields[1] [2]	do.	Lg,Lg,Lg	14.68	12.25	12.68	12.76	12.94	13.36	13.64	14.41	0.28	0.77	-0.08	0.18	116
115. Treasury bond yields[1] [2]	do.	C,Lg,Lg	12.23	10.84	11.26	11.32	11.54	11.90	12.17	12.89	0.27	0.72	0.06	0.22	115
117. Municipal bond yields[1] [2]	do.	U,Lg,Lg	11.66	9.51	9.61	9.77	9.73	9.93	9.96	10.49	0.03	0.53	0.16	-0.04	117
118. Mortgage yields, residential[1] [2]	do.	Lg,Lg,Lg	15.30	13.11	13.85	13.24	13.32	13.68	13.80	15.01	0.12	1.21	-0.61	-0.08	118
67. Bank rates on short-term business loans[1] [2]	do.	Lg,Lg,Lg	14.69	10.64	11.09	10.95	11.06						-0.14	0.11	67
*109. Average prime rate charged by banks[1] [2]	do.	Lg,Lg,Lg	14.86	10.79	10.80	11.00	11.07	11.21	11.93	12.39	0.72	0.46	-0.20	0.07	109
Outstanding Debt:															
66. Consumer installment credit³	Bil. dol., EOP	Lg,Lg,Lg	348.94	388.72	373.02	388.72	405.66	405.66	412.07	NA	1.6	NA	4.2	4.4	66
72. Commercial and industrial loans outstanding	Bil. dol.	Lg,Lg,Lg	268.24	264.94	262.47	265.41	274.22	282.27	290.51	297.40	2.9	2.4	1.1	3.3	72
*101. Commercial and industrial loans outstanding, 1972 dollars	do.	Lg,Lg,Lg	106.74	104.13	102.70	103.35	105.58	108.06	111.10	113.64	2.8	2.3	0.6	2.2	101
*95. Ratio, consumer install. credit to pers. income³	Percent	Lg,Lg,Lg	13.13	13.35	13.39	13.51	13.65	13.78	13.92	NA	0.14	NA	0.12	0.14	95
II. OTHER IMPORTANT ECONOMIC MEASURES															
B. Prices, Wages, and Productivity															
B1. Price Movements															
310. Implicit price deflator, GNP	1972=100.		206.9	215.6	216.4	218.5	220.6						1.0	1.0	310
320. Consumer price index (CPI), all items [2]	1967=100.		289.1	298.4	300.5	303.1	306.4	307.3	308.8	309.7	0.5	0.3	0.9	1.1	320
320c. Change in CPI, all items, S/A	Percent		0.3	0.3	0.4	0.3	0.4	0.2	0.5	0.2	0.3	-0.3	-0.1	-0.1	320
322. CPI, food	1967=100.		285.7	291.7	291.4	294.3	301.4	301.8	301.7	300.9	0.	-0.3	0.9	2.4	322
330. Producer price index (PPI), all commodities [2]	do.		299.3	303.1	304.4	305.9	309.3	311.1	311.4	311.7	0.1	0.1	0.5	1.1	330
335. PPI, industrial commodities [2]	do.		312.3	315.8	317.0	318.4	320.5	321.9	322.5	323.3	0.2	0.2	0.4	0.7	335
331. PPI, crude materials	do.		319.5	323.6	323.9	331.1	334.4	337.7	337.5	334.3	-0.1	-0.9	2.2	1.0	331
332. PPI, intermediate materials	do.		310.4	312.4	313.6	316.6	317.8	319.1	319.3	320.2	0.1	0.2	1.0	0.4	332
333. PPI, capital equipment	do.		279.6	287.3	288.3	289.1	291.8	292.9	293.8	294.4	0.3	0.2	0.3	0.9	333
334. PPI, finished consumer goods	do.		280.9	284.6	285.4	286.5	289.9	291.3	290.9	290.6	-0.1	-0.1	0.4	1.2	334

B2. Wages and Productivity

No.	Series	Unit	(1)	(2)	(3)	(4)	(5)	(6)	(7)	(8)	(9)	(10)	(11)	(12)
340	Average hourly earnings, production workers, private nonfarm economy	1977=100	0.9	1.0	-0.1	0.5	159.7	159.9	159.1	158.7	157.3	155.7	155.1	148.3
341	Real average hourly earnings, production workers, private nonfarm economy	do	0.2	0.1	-0.5	0.3	94.9	95.4	95.1	94.9	94.7	94.6	94.8	93.4
345	Average hourly compensation, nonfarm business	do	1.3	0.1	...	...	...	...	...	167.8	165.6	163.7	163.0	154.4
346	Real average hourly compensation, nonfarm business	do	0.1	0.1	...	...	...	...	...	99.3	99.2	99.1	99.2	96.9
370	Output per hour, private business sector	do	0.9	1.1	...	...	...	...	...	106.3	105.3	104.2	103.8	101.2
358	Output per hour, nonfarm business sector	do	0.9	0.7	...	...	...	...	...	105.6	104.7	104.0	103.4	100.2

C. Labor Force, Employment, and Unemployment

No.	Series	Unit	(1)	(2)	(3)	(4)	(5)	(6)	(7)	(8)	(9)	(10)	(11)	(12)
441	Total civilian labor force	Millions	0.5	1.0	0.5	0.3	113.80	113.24	112.91	112.61	112.01	112.06	111.55	110.20
442	Total civilian employment	do	1.2	1.0	0.9	0.2	105.29	104.40	104.14	103.74	102.50	101.53	100.83	99.53
37	Number of persons unemployed	Thousands	-6.7	-9.7	-3.7	0.8	8,514	8,843	8,772	8,866	9,507	10,529	10,717	10,678
444	Unemployed males, 20 years and over	do	-9.8	-10.6	-5.7	1.9	3,861	4,095	4,020	4,149	4,599	5,144	5,257	5,089
445	Unemployed females, 20 years and over	do	-3.2	-8.2	-1.9	1.3	3,124	3,186	3,144	3,149	3,254	3,545	3,632	3,613
446	Unemployed persons, 16-19 years of age	do	-5.2	-10.1	-2.1	-2.9	1,529	1,562	1,608	1,568	1,654	1,840	1,829	1,977
447	Number unemployed, full-time workers	do	-7.4	-10.6	-4.6	1.3	7,058	7,398	7,301	7,372	7,959	8,899	9,075	9,006

Labor Force Participation Rates:

No.	Series	Unit	(1)	(2)	(3)	(4)	(5)	(6)	(7)	(8)	(9)	(10)	(11)	(12)
451	Males, 20 years and over	Percent	-0.1	-0.2	0.	0.	78.3	78.3	78.3	78.3	78.4	78.6	78.5	78.7
452	Females, 20 years and over	do	0.	-0.1	0.5	0.3	54.2	53.7	53.4	53.2	53.2	53.3	53.1	52.7
453	Both sexes, 16-19 years of age	do	0.4	-0.7	0.	0.2	54.4	54.4	54.2	53.7	53.3	54.0	53.5	54.1

D. Government Activities
D1. Receipts and Expenditures

No.	Series	Unit	(1)	(2)	(3)	(4)	(5)	(6)	(7)	(8)	(9)	(10)	(11)	(12)
500	Federal Government surplus or deficit	A.r. bil dol	19.1	-2.5	...	...	...	...	...	-170.7	-189.8	-187.3	-181.6	-147.1
501	Federal Government receipts	do	4.6	1.9	...	...	...	...	...	687.9	657.5	645.2	644.7	617.4
502	Federal Government expenditures	do	1.3	1.8	...	...	...	...	...	858.7	847.3	832.5	826.3	764.4
510	State and local government surplus or deficit	do	2.4	2.6	...	...	...	...	...	60.5	58.1	55.5	51.4	31.3
511	State and local government receipts	do	2.7	1.6	...	...	...	...	...	514.2	500.7	492.1	483.5	439.1
512	State and local government expenditures	do	2.5	1.3	...	...	...	...	...	453.7	442.7	437.1	432.0	407.8

D2. Defense Indicators

No.	Series	Unit	(1)	(2)	(3)	(4)	(5)	(6)	(7)	(8)	(9)	(10)	(11)	(12)
517	Defense Department obligations incurred	Mil dol	2.5	8.9	NA	-18.2	NA	19,185	23,445	22,419	21,882	20,095	20,635	18,908
525	Defense Department prime contract awards	do	51.8	-13.0	NA	NA	NA	...	11,779	14,380	9,474	10,888	10,787	10,718
548	New orders, defense products	1967=100	9.8	36.2	-10.9	-45.9	5,564	6,248	11,539	8,479	9,723	5,669	6,772	6,256
557	Output of defense and space equipment	do	4.1	2.8	0.8	2.1	133.8	132.7	130.0	129.3	124.2	120.8	119.9	109.4
570	Employment in defense products industries	Thousands	1.4	1.2	NA	0.5	NA	1,407	1,400	1,391	1,372	1,356	1,355	1,371
564	National defense purchases	A.r. bil dol	3.1	2.5	...	...	...	...	...	212.7	206.3	201.2	200.3	179.4

E. U.S. International Transactions
E1. Merchandise Trade

No.	Series	Unit	(1)	(2)	(3)	(4)	(5)	(6)	(7)	(8)	(9)	(10)	(11)	(12)
602	Exports, excluding military aid shipments, total	Mil dol	3.6	2.1	NA	-1.2	NA	17,522	17,727	17,755	17,131	16,775	16,722	17,694
604	Exports of domestic agricultural products	do	7.8	-1.1	NA	-9.2	NA	3,030	3,336	3,330	3,088	3,122	3,011	3,053
606	Exports of nonelectrical machinery	do	5.1	3.7	NA	1.2	NA	3,811	3,764	3,874	3,686	3,554	3,536	4,007
612	General imports, total	do	12.9	5.1	NA	6.0	NA	28,368	26,771	26,501	23,475	22,331	21,513	20,329
614	Imports of petroleum and products	do	0.2	-10.3	NA	20.1	NA	6,348	5,287	4,667	4,660	5,195	4,383	4,964
616	Imports of automobiles and parts	do	5.1	-24.2	NA	7.6	NA	4,011	3,728	3,609	3,434	2,766	2,935	2,442

SUMMARY OF RECENT DATA AND CURRENT CHANGES FOR PRINCIPAL INDICATORS (concluded)

Series title	Unit of measure	Annual average 1981	Annual average 1982	Annual average 1983	Basic data 4th Q 1982	Basic data 1st Q 1983	Basic data 2d Q 1983	Basic data 3d Q 1983	Basic data 4th Q 1983	Basic data 1st Q 1984	Pct change 2d Q to 3d Q 1983	Pct change 3d Q to 4th Q 1983	Pct change 4th Q to 1st Q 1984	Series number
II. OTHER IMPORTANT ECONOMIC MEASURES—Con.														
E2. Goods and Services Movements Except Transfers Under Military Grants														
667. Balance on goods and services[1]	Bil. dol	3.28	-0.28	-8.23	-3.91	-1.37	-7.71	-9.70	-14.13	-17.26	-1.99	-4.43	-3.13	667
668. Exports of goods and services	do	93.93	87.36	83.05	80.94	81.11	81.36	84.83	84.91	90.62	4.3	0.1	6.7	668
669. Imports of goods and services	do	90.65	87.65	91.28	84.84	82.48	89.07	94.53	99.04	107.88	6.1	4.8	8.9	669
622. Merchandise trade balance[1]	do	-7.00	-9.12	-15.26	-11.44	-9.28	-14.87	-17.50	-19.41	-25.64	-2.63	-1.91	-6.23	622
618. Merchandise exports	do	59.27	52.80	50.06	48.52	49.25	48.74	50.44	51.83	54.16	3.5	2.8	4.5	618
620. Merchandise imports	do	66.27	61.92	65.33	59.76	58.52	63.62	67.94	71.24	79.80	6.8	4.9	12.0	620
651. Income on U.S. investments abroad	do	21.60	20.96	19.25	19.16	17.62	18.97	20.80	19.61	22.79	9.6	-5.7	16.2	651
652. Income on foreign investments in the U.S.	do	13.09	14.01	13.37	13.24	12.38	13.00	13.63	14.49	15.17	4.8	6.3	4.7	652
A. National Income and Product														
A1. GNP and Personal Income														
200. GNP, current dollars	A.r. bil. dol	2954.1	3073.0	3310.5	3109.6	3171.5	3272.0	3362.2	3436.2	3550.1	2.8	2.2	3.3	200
50. GNP, 1972 dollars	do	1513.8	1485.4	1535.3	1480.7	1490.1	1525.1	1553.4	1572.5	1609.3	1.9	1.2	2.3	50
217. Per capita GNP, 1972 dollars	A.r. dollars	6,584	6,399	6,552	6,355	6,382	6,518	6,622	6,688	6,830	1.6	1.0	2.1	217
213. Final sales, 1972 dollars	A.r. bil dol	1505.3	1494.8	1537.4	1503.4	1505.5	1530.0	1554.7	1563.7	1578.6	1.3	0.9	1.0	213
224. Disposable personal income, current dollars	do	2047.6	2176.0	2335.6	2227.8	2255.9	2301.0	2361.7	2423.9	2504.9	2.6	2.6	3.3	224
225. Disposable personal income, 1972 dollars	do	1054.7	1060.2	1094.6	1066.1	1073.8	1083.0	1100.1	1121.5	1148.6	1.6	1.9	2.4	225
227. Per capita disposable personal income, 1972 dollars	A.r. dollars	4,587	4,567	4,672	4,576	4,599	4,629	4,690	4,769	4,875	1.3	1.7	2.2	227
A2. Personal Consumption Expenditures														
230. Total, current dollars	A.r. bil dol	1857.2	1991.9	2158.0	2046.9	2073.0	2147.0	2181.1	2230.8	2286.2	1.6	2.3	2.5	230
231. Total, 1972 dollars	do	956.8	970.2	1011.4	979.6	986.5	1010.6	1016.0	1032.2	1048.3	0.5	1.6	1.6	231
232. Durable goods, current dollars	do	236.1	244.5	279.4	252.1	258.5	277.7	282.8	298.6	315.1	1.8	5.6	5.5	232
233. Durable goods, 1972 dollars	do	141.2	139.8	156.3	143.2	145.8	156.5	157.9	165.2	174.0	0.9	4.6	5.3	233
236. Nondurable goods, current dollars	do	733.9	761.0	804.1	773.0	777.1	799.6	814.8	825.0	843.2	1.9	1.3	2.2	236
238. Nondurable goods, 1972 dollars	do	362.5	364.2	376.1	366.0	368.9	374.7	378.1	382.5	387.3	0.9	1.2	1.3	238
237. Services, current dollars	do	887.1	986.4	1074.5	1021.8	1037.4	1069.7	1083.5	1107.3	1127.9	1.3	2.2	1.9	237
239. Services, 1972 dollars	do	453.1	466.2	479.0	470.4	472.0	479.4	480.1	484.4	486.9	0.1	0.9	0.5	239
A3. Gross Private Domestic Investment														
240. Total, current dollars	do	474.9	414.5	471.9	377.4	404.1	450.1	501.1	532.5	604.6	11.3	6.3	13.5	240
241. Total, 1972 dollars	do	227.6	194.5	219.0	178.4	190.0	210.2	230.2	245.2	277.4	9.8	6.3	13.1	241
242. Total fixed investment, current dollars	do	456.5	439.1	478.4	433.8	443.5	464.6	492.5	512.8	533.5	6.0	4.1	4.0	242
243. Total fixed investment, 1972 dollars	do	219.1	203.9	221.1	201.1	205.4	215.6	227.0	236.5	246.7	5.3	4.2	4.3	243
245. Change in business inventories, current dollars[1]	do	18.5	-24.5	-6.4	-56.4	-39.4	-14.5	8.5	19.6	71.0	23.0	11.1	51.4	245
30. Change in business inventories, 1972 dollars[1]	do	8.5	-9.4	-2.1	-22.7	-15.4	-5.4	3.8	8.7	30.7	9.2	4.9	22.0	30

A4. Government Purchases of Goods and Services

Series	Title	Unit													Series
260.	Total, current dollars	do	595.7	649.2	689.5	679.7	677.4	683.4	698.3	699.0	707.6	2.2	0.1	1.2	260
261.	Total, 1972 dollars	do	286.5	291.8	293.1	299.7	292.9	292.1	295.2	292.3	291.0	1.1	-1.0	-0.4	261
262.	Federal Government, current dollars	do	110.4	258.4	274.8	279.2	273.5	273.7	278.1	274.2	271.8	1.6	-1.4	-0.8	262
263.	Federal Government, 1972 dollars	do	116.6	116.6	117.8	124.4	118.4	117.6	118.9	116.4	113.8	1.1	-2.1	-2.2	263
266.	State and local governments, current dollars	do	366.5	390.5	414.7	400.5	404.0	409.7	420.2	424.9	435.7	2.6	1.1	2.5	266
267.	State and local governments, 1972 dollars	do	176.1	175.2	175.3	175.2	174.5	174.5	176.3	175.9	177.2	1.0	-0.2	0.7	267

A5. Foreign Trade

Series	Title	Unit													Series
250.	Net exports of goods and services, current dollars[2]	do	26.3	17.4	-9.0	5.6	17.0	-8.5	-18.3	-26.1	-48.2	-9.8	-7.8	-22.1	250
255.	Net exports of goods and services, 1972 dollars[2]	do	43.0	28.9	11.8	23.0	20.5	12.3	11.4	2.8	-7.5	-0.9	-8.6	-10.3	255
252.	Exports of goods and services, current dollars	do	368.8	347.6	335.4	321.6	326.9	327.1	341.1	346.5	355.8	4.3	1.6	2.7	252
256.	Exports of goods and services, 1972 dollars	do	159.7	147.3	138.7	136.1	137.3	136.2	140.7	140.6	144.4	3.3	-0.1	2.7	256
253.	Imports of goods and services, current dollars	do	342.5	330.2	344.4	316.1	309.9	335.6	359.4	372.6	407.0	7.1	3.7	9.2	253
257.	Imports of goods and services, 1972 dollars	do	116.7	118.4	126.9	113.5	116.8	123.9	129.2	137.8	151.9	4.3	6.7	10.2	257

A6. National Income and Its Components

Series	Title	Unit													Series
220.	National income	do	2373.0	2450.4	2650.2	2474.0	2528.5	2612.8	2686.9	2772.4	2883.3	2.8	3.2	4.0	220
280.	Compensation of employees	do	1769.2	1865.7	1990.0	1889.0	1923.7	1968.7	2011.8	2056.6	2113.4	2.2	2.2	2.8	280
282.	Proprietors' income with IVA and CCAdj	do	120.2	109.0	128.5	116.2	120.6	127.2	126.7	139.4	169.3	-0.4	10.0	21.4	282
284.	Rental income of persons with CCAdj	do	41.4	49.9	54.8	52.3	54.8	53.9	56.2	57.0		-1.6	4.3	1.4	284
286.	Corporate profits with IVA and CCAdj	do	192.3	164.8	229.1	161.9	181.8	218.0	248.4	268.2	281.6	13.8	8.0	5.0	286
288.	Net interest	do	249.9	261.1	247.5	254.7	248.3	243.8	246.1	251.9	262.0	0.9	2.4	4.0	288

A7. Saving

Series	Title	Unit													Series
290.	Gross saving (private and government)	do	483.8	405.8	439.6	351.3	398.5	420.6	455.4	484.0	537.6	8.3	6.3	11.1	290
295.	Business saving	do	374.4	396.2	456.2	405.8	419.7	443.4	471.4	490.2	499.5	6.3	4.0	1.9	295
292.	Personal saving	do	135.3	125.4	113.6	120.8	121.7	91.5	115.8	125.6	148.4	26.6	8.5	18.2	292
298.	Government surplus or deficit[2]	do	-26.9	15.8	-130.2	-175.3	-142.9	-114.4	-131.8	-131.8	-110.2	-17.4	0.3	21.6	298
293.	Personal saving rate[3]	Percent	6.6	5.8	4.9	5.4	5.4	4.0	4.9	5.2	5.9	0.9	0.3	0.7	293

NOTE: Series are seasonally adjusted except for those, indicated by ⓤ, that appear to contain no seasonal movement. Series indicated by an asterisk (*) are included in the major composite indexes. Dollar values are in current dollars unless otherwise specified. For complete series titles and sources, see "Titles and Sources of Series" at the back of this issue. NA, not available. a, anticipated. EOP, end of period. A.r., annual rate. S/A, seasonally adjusted (used for special emphasis). IVA, inventory valuation adjustment. CCAdj, capital consumption adjustment.

The three-part timing code indicates the timing classification of the series at peaks, at troughs, and at all turns. L, leading. C, roughly coincident. Lg, lagging. U, unclassified.

[1] For a few series, data shown here are rounded to fewer digits than those shown elsewhere in BCD. Annual figures published by the source agencies are used if available.
[2] Differences rather than percent changes are shown for this series.
[3] Inverted series. Since this series tends to move counter to movements in general business activity, signs of the changes are reversed.
[4] End-of-period series. The annual figures (and quarterly figures for monthly series) are the last figures for the period.
[5] This series is a weighted 4-term moving average (with weights 1, 2, 2, 1) placed on the terminal month of the span.

"Series 9. Raw data provided by F.W. Dodge Division, McGraw-Hill Information Systems Company, and seasonally adjusted by Bureau of Economic Analysis."
"Series 23, permission of Commodity Research Bureau, Inc., 75 Montgomery Street, Jersey City, NJ 07302."

Source: *Business Conditions Digest*, U.S. Department of Commerce, Bureau of Economic Analysis.

GROSS NATIONAL PRODUCT

BILLIONS OF DOLLARS (RATIO SCALE)

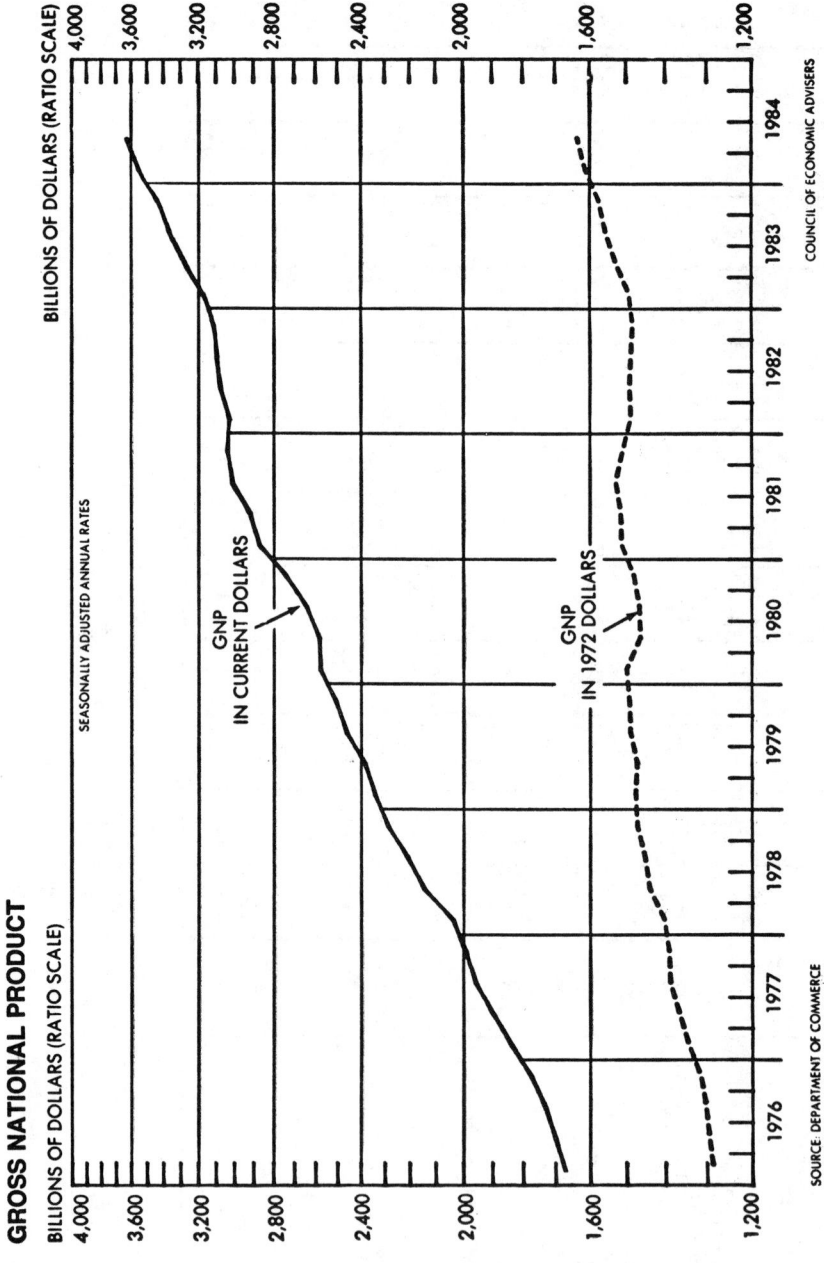

BILLIONS OF DOLLARS (RATIO SCALE)

SEASONALLY ADJUSTED ANNUAL RATES

GNP
IN CURRENT DOLLARS

GNP
IN 1972 DOLLARS

SOURCE: DEPARTMENT OF COMMERCE

COUNCIL OF ECONOMIC ADVISERS

[Billions of current dollars; quarterly data at seasonally adjusted annual rates]

Period	Gross national product	Personal consumption expenditures	Gross private domestic investment	Exports and imports of goods and services				Government purchases of goods and services					Final sales
				Net exports	Exports	Imports	Total	Total	Federal			State and local	
									Total	National defense	Non-defense		
1972	1,185.9	737.1	195.0	0.7	77.5	76.7	253.1	101.7	73.1	28.5	151.4	1,175.7	
1973	1,326.4	812.0	229.8	14.2	109.6	95.4	270.4	102.0	72.8	29.1	168.5	1,307.9	
1974	1,434.2	888.1	228.7	13.4	146.2	132.8	304.1	111.0	77.0	33.9	193.1	1,420.1	
1975	1,549.2	976.4	206.1	26.8	154.9	128.1	339.9	122.7	83.0	39.7	217.2	1,556.1	
1976	1,718.0	1,084.3	257.9	13.8	170.9	157.1	362.1	129.2	86.0	43.2	232.9	1,706.2	
1977	1,918.3	1,204.4	324.1	−4.0	182.7	186.7	393.8	143.4	92.8	50.6	250.4	1,895.3	
1978	2,163.9	1,346.5	386.6	−1.1	218.7	219.8	431.9	153.6	100.3	53.3	278.3	2,137.4	
1979	2,417.8	1,507.2	423.0	13.2	281.4	268.1	474.4	168.3	111.8	56.5	306.0	2,403.5	
1980	2,631.7	1,668.1	401.9	23.9	338.8	314.8	537.8	197.0	131.2	65.9	340.8	2,641.5	
1981	2,954.1	1,857.2	474.9	26.3	368.8	342.5	595.7	229.2	154.0	75.2	366.5	2,935.6	
1982	3,073.0	1,991.9	414.5	17.4	347.6	330.2	649.2	258.7	179.4	79.3	390.5	3,097.5	
1983	3,310.5	2,158.0	471.9	−9.0	335.4	344.4	689.5	274.8	200.3	74.5	414.7	3,316.9	
1982: I	3,021.4	1,938.9	422.9	29.9	358.4	328.5	629.8	249.7	168.1	81.7	380.0	3,047.1	
II	3,070.2	1,972.8	432.5	33.3	364.5	331.2	631.6	244.1	175.2	68.9	387.5	3,081.4	
III	3,090.7	2,008.8	425.3	.9	346.0	345.0	655.7	261.7	183.6	78.1	394.0	3,095.6	
IV	3,109.6	2,046.9	377.4	5.6	321.6	316.1	679.7	279.2	190.8	88.5	400.5	3,165.9	
1983: I	3,171.5	2,073.0	404.1	17.0	326.9	309.9	677.4	273.5	194.4	79.1	404.0	3,210.9	
II	3,272.0	2,147.0	450.1	−8.5	327.1	335.6	683.4	273.7	199.4	74.3	409.7	3,286.6	
III	3,362.2	2,181.1	501.1	−18.3	341.1	359.4	698.3	278.1	201.2	76.9	420.2	3,353.7	
IV	3,436.2	2,230.9	532.5	−26.1	346.5	372.6	699.0	274.1	206.3	67.8	424.9	3,416.6	
1984: Iʳ	3,550.1	2,286.2	604.6	−48.2	358.8	407.0	707.6	271.9	212.7	59.2	435.7	3,479.1	
IIᵖ	3,624.6												

*Very preliminary ("flash") estimate.

Source: Economic Indicators, Council of Economic Advisers.

Source: Department of Commerce, Bureau of Economic Analysis.

GROSS NATIONAL PRODUCT IN 1972 DOLLARS

[Billions of 1972 dollars; quarterly data at seasonally adjusted annual rates]

Period	Gross national product	Personal consumption expenditures	Gross private domestic investment — Nonresidential fixed	Gross private domestic investment — Residential fixed	Gross private domestic investment — Change in business inventories	Net exports	Exports of goods and services — Exports	Exports of goods and services — Imports	Government purchases of goods and services — Total	Government purchases of goods and services — Federal Total	Government purchases of goods and services — Federal National defense	Government purchases of goods and services — Federal Non-defense	Government purchases of goods and services — State and local	Final sales
1972	1,185.9	737.1	121.0	63.8	10.2	0.7	77.5	76.7	253.1	101.7	73.1	28.5	151.4	1,175.7
1973	1,254.3	767.9	138.1	62.3	17.2	15.5	97.3	81.8	253.3	95.9	68.3	27.6	157.4	1,237.1
1974	1,246.3	762.8	135.7	48.2	11.6	27.8	108.5	80.7	260.3	96.6	66.9	29.7	163.6	1,234.7
1975	1,231.6	779.4	119.3	42.2	-6.7	32.2	103.5	71.4	265.2	97.4	66.4	31.0	167.8	1,238.4
1976	1,298.2	823.1	125.6	51.2	7.8	25.4	110.1	84.7	265.2	96.8	64.9	31.8	168.4	1,290.4
1977	1,369.7	864.3	140.3	60.7	13.3	22.0	112.9	90.9	269.2	100.4	65.4	35.0	168.8	1,356.4
1978	1,438.6	903.2	158.3	62.4	16.0	24.0	126.7	102.7	274.6	100.3	65.7	34.7	174.3	1,422.6
1979	1,479.4	927.6	169.9	59.1	7.3	37.2	146.2	109.0	278.3	102.1	67.4	34.8	176.2	1,472.2
1980	1,475.0	931.8	165.8	47.1	-4.4	50.3	159.1	108.8	284.3	106.4	70.0	36.4	177.9	1,479.4
1981	1,513.8	956.8	174.4	44.7	8.5	43.0	159.7	116.7	286.5	110.4	73.6	36.8	176.1	1,505.3
1982	1,485.4	970.2	166.1	37.8	-9.4	28.9	147.3	118.4	291.8	116.6	78.8	37.8	175.2	1,494.8
1983	1,535.3	1,011.4	168.4	52.7	-2.1	11.8	138.7	126.9	293.1	117.8	84.3	33.6	175.3	1,537.4
1982: I	1,485.8	961.4	173.6	36.3	-10.2	35.2	151.8	116.6	289.4	114.5	75.5	39.1	174.9	1,495.9
II	1,489.3	968.8	167.1	37.8	-3.4	33.4	154.5	121.1	285.8	110.3	77.8	32.5	175.4	1,492.7
III	1,485.7	971.0	163.3	36.5	-1.3	24.0	146.4	122.4	292.2	116.9	80.4	36.5	175.3	1,487.0
IV	1,480.7	979.6	160.5	40.6	-22.7	23.0	136.5	113.5	299.7	124.4	81.4	43.0	175.2	1,503.4
1983: I	1,490.1	986.7	159.9	45.5	-15.4	20.5	137.3	116.8	292.9	118.4	82.7	35.7	174.5	1,505.5
II	1,525.1	1,010.6	163.0	52.6	-5.4	12.3	136.2	123.9	292.1	117.6	84.2	33.4	174.5	1,530.5
III	1,553.4	1,016.0	170.1	56.8	3.8	11.4	140.7	129.2	295.2	118.9	84.2	34.7	176.3	1,549.7
IV	1,572.5	1,032.2	180.7	55.8	8.7	2.8	140.6	137.8	292.3	116.4	85.8	30.5	175.9	1,563.7
1984: I'	1,609.3	1,048.3	187.6	59.2	30.7	-7.5	144.4	151.9	291.0	113.8	87.1	26.6	177.2	1,578.6
II*	1,631.6													

'Very preliminary ("flash") estimate.

Source: *Economic Indicators*, Council of Economic Advisers.

Source: Department of Commerce, Bureau of Economic Analysis.

SELECTED COMPONENTS OF GNP

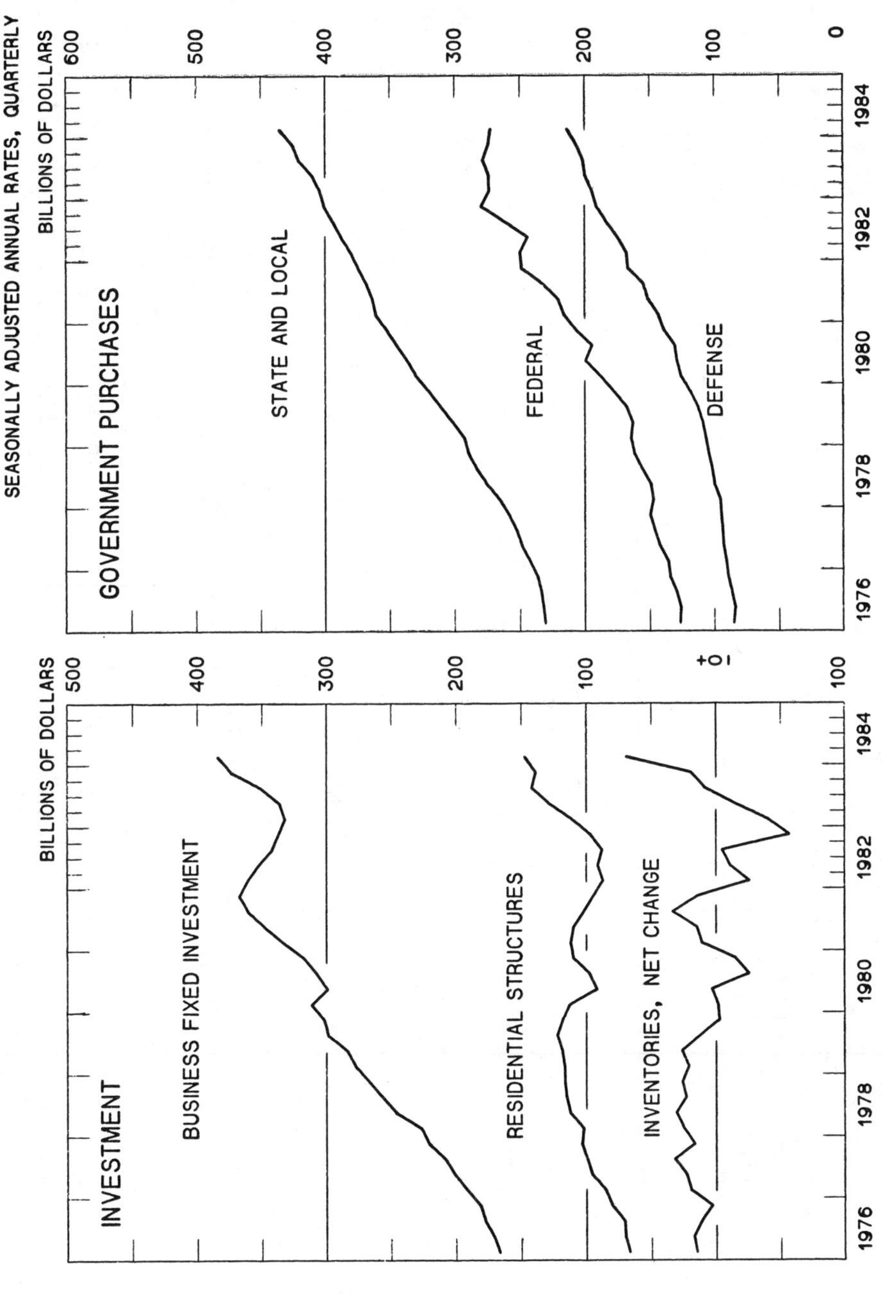

SEASONALLY ADJUSTED ANNUAL RATES, QUARTERLY

BILLIONS OF DOLLARS

GOVERNMENT PURCHASES

STATE AND LOCAL

FEDERAL

DEFENSE

600
500
400
300
200
100
0

1976   1978   1980   1982   1984

BILLIONS OF DOLLARS

500
400
300
200
100
+0
100

INVESTMENT

BUSINESS FIXED INVESTMENT

RESIDENTIAL STRUCTURES

INVENTORIES, NET CHANGE

1976   1978   1980   1982   1984

Source: Federal Reserve Chart Book, Board of Governors of the Federal Reserve System.

CORPORATE PROFITS

BILLIONS OF DOLLARS

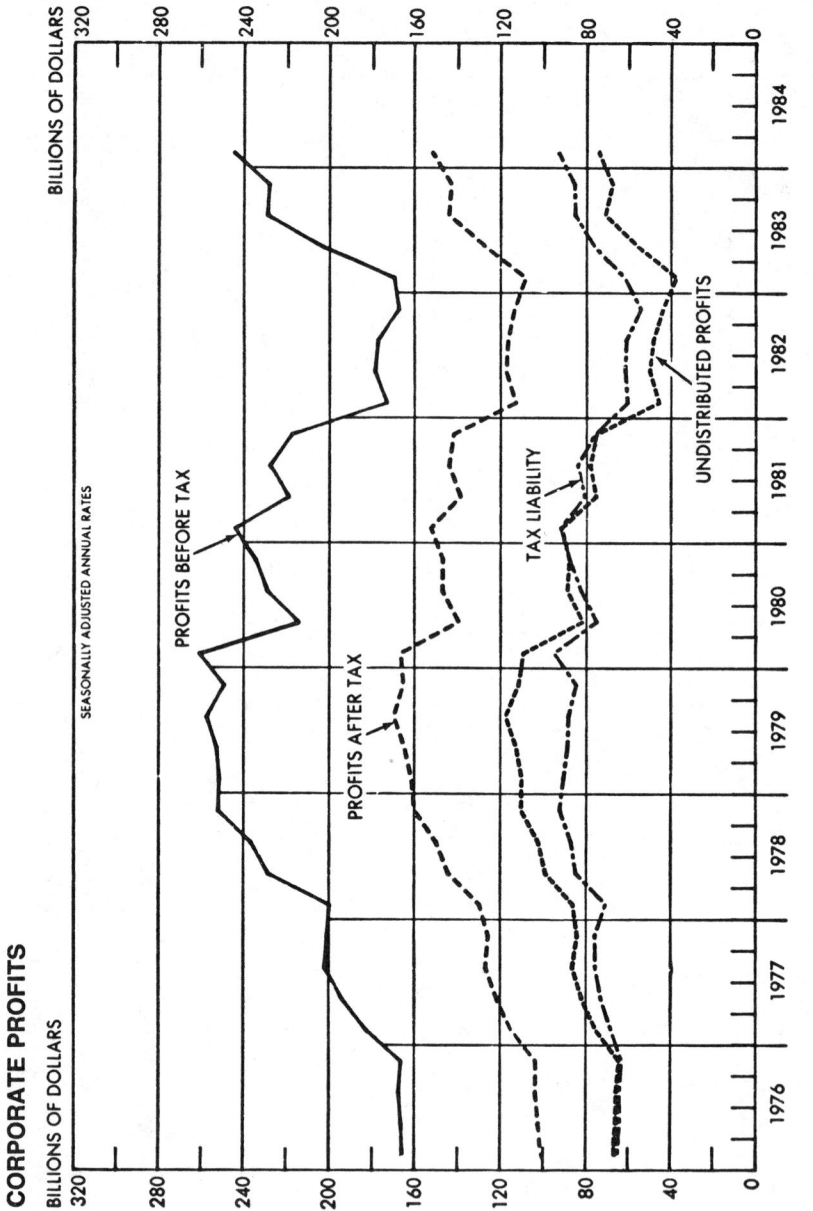

BILLIONS OF DOLLARS

SEASONALLY ADJUSTED ANNUAL RATES

PROFITS BEFORE TAX

PROFITS AFTER TAX

TAX LIABILITY

UNDISTRIBUTED PROFITS

SOURCE: DEPARTMENT OF COMMERCE

COUNCIL OF ECONOMIC ADVISERS

[Billions of dollars; quarterly data at seasonally adjusted annual rates]

Period	Profits (before tax) with inventory valuation adjustment [1]						Profits before tax	Tax liability	Profits after tax			Inventory valuation adjustment
	Total [2]	Domestic industries							Total	Dividends	Undistributed profits	
		Total	Financial	Nonfinancial								
				Total [3]	Manufacturing	Wholesale and retail trade						
1972	94.0	85.3	15.3	70.0	40.7	13.4	100.6	41.6	58.9	24.4	34.5	−6.6
1973	105.6	92.0	15.9	76.0	45.5	13.9	125.6	49.0	76.6	27.0	49.6	−20.0
1974	96.7	80.4	15.0	65.4	39.0	12.5	136.7	51.6	85.1	29.9	55.2	−40.0
1975	120.6	107.6	11.8	95.8	52.6	21.3	132.1	50.6	81.5	30.8	50.7	−11.6
1976	151.6	137.4	17.1	120.3	69.2	22.4	166.3	63.8	102.5	37.4	65.1	−14.7
1977	178.5	163.4	23.1	140.3	78.3	26.6	194.7	72.7	122.0	40.8	81.2	−16.2
1978	205.1	185.4	31.0	154.4	86.9	26.9	229.1	83.2	145.9	47.0	98.9	−24.0
1979	209.6	179.0	30.3	148.6	85.6	27.1	252.7	87.6	165.1	52.7	112.4	−43.1
1980	191.7	161.9	26.9	134.9	72.9	23.6	234.6	84.8	149.8	58.6	91.2	−42.9
1981	203.3	179.7	20.3	159.4	86.7	32.8	227.0	82.8	144.1	64.7	79.5	−23.6
1982	165.9	144.1	20.9	123.2	59.0	27.6	174.2	59.2	115.1	68.7	46.4	−8.4
1983	198.3	176.9	31.5	145.4	72.0	34.7	207.5	76.9	130.6	73.3	57.3	−9.2
1982: I	167.7	147.0	15.5	131.5	60.9	30.2	173.2	60.3	112.9	67.7	45.2	−5.5
II	170.3	148.5	20.4	128.1	61.4	27.4	178.8	61.4	117.4	67.8	49.5	−8.5
III	168.3	147.6	22.2	125.4	65.5	25.2	177.3	60.8	116.5	68.8	47.7	−9.0
IV	157.2	133.1	25.5	107.6	48.3	27.5	167.5	54.0	113.5	70.4	43.1	−10.3
1983: I	168.0	147.8	29.8	118.0	53.7	27.8	169.7	61.5	108.2	71.4	36.7	−1.7
II	192.7	172.2	33.8	138.4	68.1	33.9	203.3	76.0	127.2	72.0	55.2	−10.6
III	210.8	187.4	31.9	155.5	78.2	36.7	229.1	84.9	144.1	73.7	70.4	−18.3
IV	222.0	200.3	30.6	169.6	88.1	40.2	228.2	85.3	142.9	75.9	67.0	−6.3
1984: I r	231.8	209.7	31.1	178.6	92.3	41.2	244.3	92.7	151.6	78.2	73.4	−12.5

[1] See p. 199 for profits with inventory valuation and capital consumption adjustments.

[2] Includes rest of the world, not shown separately.

[3] Includes industries not shown separately.

Source: Department of Commerce, Bureau of Economic Analysis.

Source: Economic Indicators, Council of Economic Advisers.

Price Data

Definitions are applicable to the exhibit on page 191.

Price data are gathered by the Bureau of Labor Statistics from retail and primary markets in the United States. Price indexes are given in relation to a base period (1967 = 100, unless otherwise noted).

DEFINITIONS

The **Consumer Price Index** is a monthly statistical measure of the average change in prices in a fixed market basket of goods and services. Effective with the January 1978 index, the Bureau of Labor Statistics began publishing CPI's for two groups of the population. It introduced a CPI for All Urban Consumers, covering 80 percent of the total noninstitutional population, and revised CPI for Urban Wage Earners and Clerical Workers, covering about half the new index population. The All Urban Consumers index covers in addition to wage earners and clerical workers, professional, managerial, and technical workers, the self-employed, short-term workers, the unemployed, retirees, and others not in the labor force.

The CPI is based on prices of food, clothing, shelter, fuel, drugs, transportation fares, doctor's and dentist's fees, and other goods and services that people buy for day-to-day living. The quantity and quality of these items are kept essentially unchanged between major revisions so that only price changes will be measured. Data are collected from more than 24,000 retail establishments and 24,000 tenants in 85 urban areas across the country. All taxes directly associated with the purchase and use of items are included in the index. Because the CPI's are based on the expenditures of two population

Source: *Monthly Labor Review*, U.S. Department of Labor, Bureau of Labor Statistics.

groups in 1972–73, they may not accurately reflect the experience of individual families and single persons with different buying habits.

Though the CPI is often called the "Cost-of-Living Index," it measures only price change, which is just one of several important factors affecting living costs. Area indexes do not measure differences in the level of prices among cities. They only measure the average change in prices for each area since the base period.

NOTES ON THE DATA

Beginning with the May 1978 issue of the *Review*, regional CPI's cross classified by population size, were introduced. These indexes enable users in local areas for which an index is not published to get a better approximation of the CPI for their area by using the appropriate population size class measure for their region. The cross-classified indexes are published bimonthly.

For details concerning the 1978 revision of the CPI see *The Consumer Price Index: Concepts and Content Over the Years*, Report 517, revised edition (Bureau of Labor Statistics, May 1978).

As of January 1976, the Producer Price Index incorporated a revised weighting structure reflecting 1972 values of shipments. Additional data and analysis on price changes are provided in the *CPI Detailed Report* and *Producer Prices and Price Indexes*, both monthly publications of the Bureau.

For a discussion of the general method of computing producer, and industry price indexes, see *BLS Handbook of Methods*, Bulletin 2134–1 (Bureau of Labor Statistics, 1982), chapters 7. For consumer prices see *BLS Handbook of Methods for Surveys and Studies* (1976), Chapter 13. See also John F. Early, "Improving the Measurement of Producer Price Change," *Monthly Labor Review*, April 1978. For industry prices, see also Bennett R. Moss, "Industry and Sector Price Indexes," *Monthly Labor Review*, August 1965.

URBAN WAGE EARNERS AND CLERICAL WORKERS, U.S. CITY AVERAGE—GENERAL SUMMARY

[1967 = 100 unless otherwise specified]

General summary	AUC 1983 Feb.	AUC 1983 Sept.	AUC 1983 Oct.	AUC 1983 Nov.	AUC 1983 Dec.	AUC 1984 Jan.	AUC 1984 Feb.	UWE 1983 Feb.	UWE 1983 Sept.	UWE 1983 Oct.	UWE 1983 Nov.	UWE 1983 Dec.	UWE 1984 Jan.	UWE 1984 Feb.
All items	293.2	301.8	302.6	303.1	303.5	305.2	306.6	292.3	300.8	301.3	301.4	301.5	302.7	303.3
Food and beverages	281.6	285.3	285.7	285.3	286.5	291.6	294.2	282.1	285.6	285.9	285.6	286.8	291.9	294.4
Housing	318.5	326.4	326.8	327.0	327.4	329.2	331.0	317.6	325.3	325.2	324.5	324.2	324.7	324.2
Apparel and upkeep	192.0	200.4	200.7	200.7	199.3	196.4	196.2	191.0	199.3	199.8	199.7	198.1	195.3	195.4
Transportation	289.9	303.7	305.0	306.3	306.3	306.0	305.8	291.1	305.5	306.9	306.9	308.2	307.9	307.7
Medical care	351.3	361.2	362.9	364.9	366.2	369.5	373.2	348.9	359.2	360.9	362.9	364.3	367.5	371.3
Entertainment	243.1	247.5	249.1	249.5	249.5	249.9	251.5	239.5	244.1	245.4	245.7	245.8	246.2	247.7
Other goods and services	281.6	294.4	296.8	298.1	298.6	300.5	301.5	279.6	292.0	294.1	295.5	295.9	298.1	299.2
Commodities	266.7	274.5	275.0	275.2	275.5	276.8	278.3	267.8	275.9	276.1	276.2	276.3	277.3	278.0
Commodities less food and beverages	255.2	265.1	265.8	266.3	266.0	265.2	266.0	257.1	267.3	267.1	267.5	267.1	266.4	266.2
Nondurables less food and beverages	265.2	275.8	275.2	274.5	273.5	272.3	274.0	266.9	277.9	277.4	276.6	275.4	274.2	276.0
Durables	247.1	256.4	258.7	261.0	261.8	261.4	260.9	247.8	257.0	257.7	258.7	258.9	258.4	256.9
Services	338.9	349.0	350.2	351.0	351.6	353.9	355.3	337.8	346.9	348.1	348.2	348.4	349.8	350.1
Rent, residential	233.1	239.5	240.4	241.3	242.0	242.9	243.6	232.5	238.9	239.8	240.7	241.3	242.3	242.9
Household services less rent of shelter (12/82 = 100)	101.0	105.1	104.8	104.2	104.1	105.1	105.7							
Transportation services	299.9	305.4	307.8	310.1	310.8	314.1	314.4	296.9	301.4	303.9	306.0	306.9	310.3	310.6
Medical care services	381.5	391.0	392.9	395.0	396.3	400.2	404.4	378.2	388.3	390.2	392.3	393.8	397.5	401.8
Other services	272.6	282.5	285.2	286.5	287.2	288.0	289.1	270.2	279.6	282.2	283.6	284.3	285.0	286.1
Special indexes:														
All items less food	292.6	302.3	303.2	303.9	304.0	304.8	305.9	291.9	301.5	302.1	302.3	302.1	302.3	302.4
All items less homeowners' costs	100.2	103.2	103.5	103.6	103.7	104.3	104.8							
All items less mortgage interest costs								279.0	287.5	288.1	288.3	288.5	290.0	290.9
Commodities less food	253.2	262.9	263.6	264.1	263.8	263.0	263.8	255.0	264.9	265.1	264.9	264.9	264.2	264.1
Nondurables less food	260.5	270.6	270.2	269.5	268.5	267.4	269.1	262.2	272.8	272.3	271.5	271.5	269.4	271.1
Nondurables less food and apparel	299.9	311.0	310.2	309.3	308.6	308.6	311.2							
Nondurables	274.6	281.8	281.7	281.1	281.2	283.2	285.3	275.6	282.8	282.7	282.1	282.2	284.1	286.3
Services less rent of shelter (12/82 = 100)	101.0	104.2	104.5	104.7	104.8	105.7	106.3							
Services less medical care	332.2	342.2	343.3	344.1	344.5	346.6	347.8	331.2	341.0	342.0	342.8	343.2	345.3	346.5
Domestically produced farm foods	266.6	269.2	268.5	267.7	269.7	277.2	280.7	266.0	268.9	268.2	267.4	269.4	277.0	280.3
Selected beef cuts	272.0	267.5	265.6	265.3	265.5	274.6	280.8	273.5	267.9	266.1	265.8	266.0	275.2	281.3
Energy[1]	406.7	429.3	425.1	419.9	418.0	416.7	420.2	406.9	430.2	425.8	420.8	418.7	417.0	420.2
Energy commodities[1]	401.6	422.1	418.2	414.4	411.8	409.9	414.5	401.9	423.4	419.6	415.8	412.9	410.7	414.7
All items less energy	284.7	292.1	293.4	294.4	295.0	297.0	298.2	283.0	290.3	291.3	291.8	292.1	293.5	293.8
All items less food and energy	282.0	290.2	291.8	293.2	293.6	294.6	295.5	280.2	288.3	289.5	290.3	290.3	290.7	290.4
Commodities less food and energy	237.9	246.2	247.6	248.9	249.0	248.3	248.5	237.9	246.2	247.1	247.8	247.7	247.2	246.6
Services less energy	332.9	341.6	343.3	344.9	345.5	348.1	349.5	331.4	339.0	340.8	341.6	341.8	343.3	343.6
Purchasing power of the consumer dollar, 1967 = $1	$0.341	$0.331	$0.330	$0.330	$0.329	$0.328	$0.326	$0.342	$0.332	$0.332	$0.332	$0.332	$0.330	$0.330

[1] Excludes motor oil, coolant, and other products as of January 1983.

Source: Monthly Labor Review, U.S. Department of Labor, Bureau of Labor Statistics.

CHANGES IN CURRENT- AND CONSTANT-DOLLAR WAGE AND SALARY COMPONENT OF THE EMPLOYMENT COST INDEX AND IN THE CONSUMER PRICE INDEX FOR ALL URBAN CONSUMERS, 1976–83*

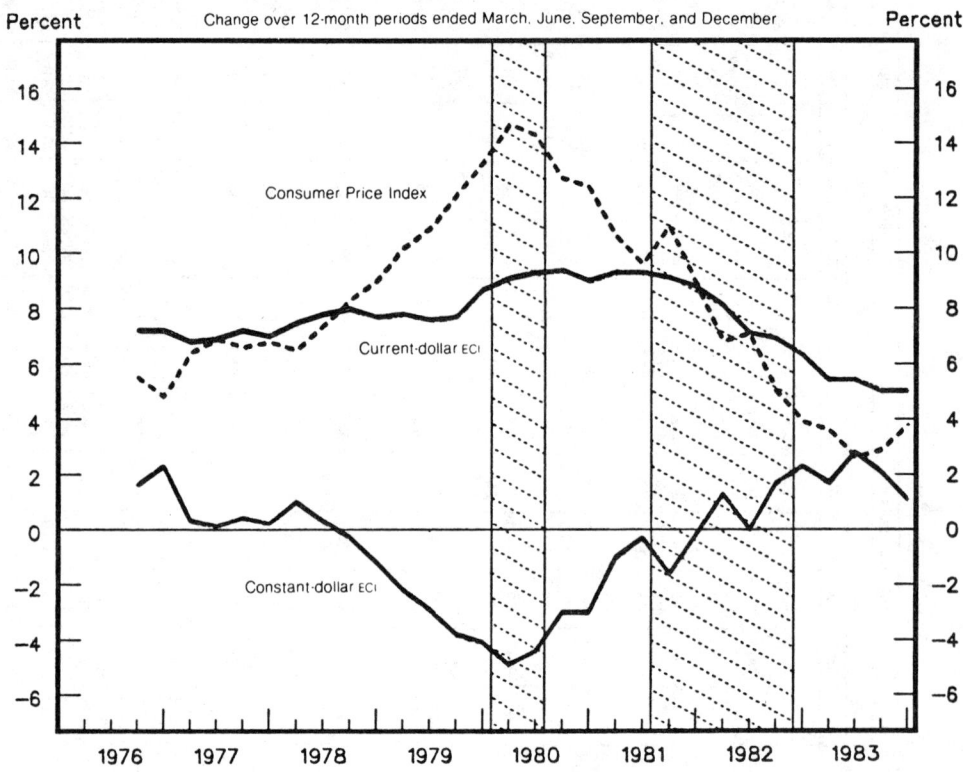

Percent   Change over 12-month periods ended March, June, September, and December   Percent

NOTE: Shaded areas indicate recessionary period.

   * Employment Cost Index [ECI] measures the purchasing power of wages and salary by collecting wage rates for specific occupations and using fixed occupation and industry weights in the calculation of indexes.

   Source: *Monthly Labor Review,* Department of Labor, Bureau of Labor Statistics.

PERCENT CHANGES IN SELECTED CONSUMER PRICE INDEXES (CPI-U), 1982–83

Index	Relative Importance Dec. 1983	Percent change Dec. 1981 to Dec. 1982	Percent change Dec. 1982 to Dec. 1983	Contribution Dec. 1981 to Dec. 1982	Contribution Dec. 1982 to Dec. 1983	Compound annual rate, seasonally adjusted except as noted, for 3 months ended— 1983 March	June	Sept.	Dec.
All Items	100.0	3.9	3.8	100.0	100.0	1.2	5.4	4.5	4.0
Food	18.7	3.1	2.6	13.4	12.9	3.2	1.7	1.1	4.3
Commodities less food and energy	26.5	5.8	5.0	48.8	34.4	5.7	3.2	6.8	4.6
Energy	11.9	1.3	-.5	3.7	-1.5	-23.3	19.1	3.4	1.7
Services less energy	42.9	3.4	4.8	34.1	54.2	4.3	4.8	5.2	5.3
All Items	100.0	3.9	3.8	100.0	100.0	1.2	5.4	4.5	4.0
Services	47.5	4.3	4.8	47.5	59.2	4.4	4.8	5.1	4.9
Commodities	52.4	3.6	2.9	52.5	40.8	-1.6	5.8	4.4	3.3
All Items	100.0	3.9	3.8	100.0	100.0	1.2	5.4	4.5	4.0
Food and beverages	19.8	3.2	2.7	14.4	13.9	3.3	1.9	1.1	4.3
Food at home	12.6	2.2	1.9	6.6	6.3	3.6	.6	-.4	3.7
Food away from home	6.1	5.0	4.1	6.8	6.6	2.6	4.0	4.5	5.4
Alcoholic beverages	1.1	4.0	3.4	1.0	1.0	4.4	3.6	3.7	1.8
Housing	37.6	3.6	3.5	43.5	34.8	1.8	4.6	4.3	3.5
Shelter	21.5	2.4	4.7	19.7	26.6	3.6	5.4	5.6	4.4
Renters' costs[1]	7.0	—	5.1	—	9.3	4.5	4.8	6.8	4.3
Rent, residential[1]	6.0	6.6	4.9	8.7	7.6	4.9	4.0	6.2	4.2
Homeowners' costs[1]	13.9	—	4.5	—	16.6	3.6	5.3	5.2	3.9
Homeownership		1.4	—	9.3	—	—	—	—	—
Fuel and other utilities	8.2	9.7	1.8	17.3	3.9	-2.6	5.0	4.0	1.0
Household furnishings and operation	7.9	3.5	2.0	6.5	4.4	-1.4	1.9	1.5	3.4
Apparel and upkeep	5.1	1.6	2.9	2.0	4.0	2.9	4.4	3.9	.6
Apparel commodities	4.4	.9	2.5	.9	2.9	2.9	4.0	3.7	-.4
Apparel services	.8	6.2	5.0	1.1	1.0	3.4	6.2	5.3	5.1
Transportation	21.8	1.7	3.9	8.6	22.4	-6.6	10.9	7.6	4.4
Private transportation[1]	20.3	1.4	3.8	6.4	20.9	-7.1	11.2	7.7	4.5
Public transportation[1]	1.5	6.5	3.8	2.2	1.5	-1.2	7.8	6.1	2.6
Medical care	6.1	11.0	6.4	13.8	10.1	8.9	5.8	6.0	4.8
Medical care commodities	1.0	9.6	7.6	2.0	1.9	8.3	7.3	6.8	7.8
Medical care services	5.1	11.2	6.1	11.8	8.1	9.1	5.5	5.7	4.4
Entertainment	4.2	5.6	3.9	5.2	4.3	4.7	2.0	4.3	4.6
Other goods and services	5.2	12.1	8.0	12.6	10.5	9.8	6.7	7.4	7.9

[1]Not seasonally adjusted.

Source: *Monthly Labor Review*, U.S. Department of Labor, Bureau of Labor Statistics.

Comparative Living Costs
in U.S. Metropolitan Areas

The chart below, computed by the U.S. Bureau of Labor Statistics, will help you compare living costs city by city.[1] Dollar figures in the righthand columns represent the average middle and upper income budgets in metropolitan areas around the country. Nationwide, total expenditures for a middle income family of four average $25,407. An upper income budget is $38,060. Since these figures are equivalent to an index of 100 (within 1%) at their respective income levels, the lefthand columns enable you to determine at a glance if a city is more or less expensive than average.

	MIDDLE INCOME		UPPER INCOME	
	OVERALL INDEX	AVERAGE BUDGET	OVERALL INDEX	AVERAGE BUDGET
Atlanta..................	92	$23,273	91	$34,623
Baltimore	99	$25,114	100	$38,090
Boston...................	115	$29,213	118	$44,821
Buffalo..................	104	$26,473	102	$38,919
Chicago.................	100	$25,358	98	$37,368
Cincinnati	100	$25,475	96	$36,599
Cleveland	101	$25,598	98	$37,487
Dallas	89	$22,678	89	$33,769
Denver..................	98	$24,820	97	$36,979
Detroit	99	$25,208	99	$37,721
Honolulu	126	$31,893	132	$50,317
Houston	93	$23,601	91	$34,728
Kansas City.............	97	$24,528	97	$36,988
Los Angeles	98	$25,025	101	$38,516
Milwaukee..............	106	$26,875	104	$39,709
Minneapolis-St. Paul	102	$25,799	102	$38,698
New York	116	$29,540	124	$47,230
Philadelphia	105	$26,567	104	$39,560
Pittsburgh	97	$24,717	96	$36,714
St. Louis	96	$24,498	94	$35,965
San Diego	98	$24,776	99	$37,722
San Francisco...........	107	$27,082	107	$40,906
Seattle..................	102	$25,881	98	$37,396
Washington, D.C.	108	$27,352	108	$41,137

[1]Food, rental & homeownership, transportation, clothing, taxation, personal and medical care costs are included. Homeownership costs are based on the assumption that the family bought its home six years ago. This data is based on Autumn 1981 Bureau of Labor Statistics figures, the most recent release of four-person family budget data.

Source: *MBA Employment Guide.* Copyright 1984. Reprinted courtesy of the Association of MBA Executives, New York, NY.

Calculating Salary Equivalency Figures

How do you compare salary offers in different cities? If you are offered $25,000 in Cleveland, how much is an equivalent salary in Detroit considering the different cost of living in both cities? The table on the previous page and the examples below give the answer.

Examples:

1. What is the Denver equivalent of a $30,000 offer in New York using the middle income budget?

$$\frac{\text{Denver} \quad 98}{\text{New York* } 116} \times \$30,000 = \$25,345$$

An offer of $25,345 in Denver is the same as a $30,000 offer in New York.

---

* The denominator of this fraction is always the Bureau of Labor Statistics' index of the city with the given salary.

Source: *MBA Employment Guide.* Copyright 1984. Reprinted courtesy of the Association of MBA Executives, New York, NY.

2. What is the New York equivalent of a $30,000 Denver offer using the middle income budget?

$$\frac{\text{New York } 116}{\text{Denver} \quad 98} \times \$30,000 = \$35,510$$

You need to earn $35,510 in New York to be equivalent to a $30,000 offer in Denver.

3. I've received a job offer of $25,000 in Washington, D.C. What is an equivalent offer in Atlanta using the upper income budget?

$$\frac{\text{Atlanta} \quad 91}{\text{Wash., D.C. } 108} \times \$25,000 = \$21,065$$

An offer of $21,065 in Atlanta is equivalent to an offer of $25,000 in Washington, D.C.

4. What is the Seattle equivalent of a $35,000 offer in Boston using the upper income budget?

$$\frac{\text{Seattle } 98}{\text{Boston } 118} \times \$35,000 = \$29,068$$

An offer of $35,000 in Boston is equivalent to an offer of $29,068 in Seattle.

Purchasing Power of the Dollar: 1940 to 1983

[1967 = $1.00. Producer prices prior to 1961, and consumer prices prior to 1964, exclude Alaska and Hawaii. For 1940 and 1945, producer prices based on all commodities index; subsequent years based on finished goods index. Obtained by dividing the average price index for the 1967 base period (100.0) by the price index for a given period and expressing the result in dollars and cents. Annual figures are based on average of monthly data]

YEAR	ANNUAL AVERAGE AS MEASURED BY—		YEAR	ANNUAL AVERAGE AS MEASURED BY—		YEAR	ANNUAL AVERAGE AS MEASURED BY—	
	Producer prices	Consumer prices		Producer prices	Consumer prices		Producer prices	Consumer prices
1940	$2.469	$2.381	1958	$1.073	$1.155	1970	$.907	$.860
1945	1.832	1.855	1959	1.075	1.145	1971	.880	.824
1948	1.252	1.387	1960	1.067	1.127	1972	.853	.799
1949	1.289	1.401	1961	1.067	1.116	1973	.782	.752
1950	1.266	1.387	1962	1.064	1.104	1974	.678	.678
1951	1.156	1.295	1963	1.067	1.091	1975	.612	.621
1952	1.163	1.258	1964	1.063	1.076	1976	.586	.587
1953	1.175	1.248	1965	1.045	1.058	1977	.550	.551
1954	1.172	1.242	1966	1.012	1.029	1978	.510	.512
1955	1.170	1.247	1967	1.000	1.000	1979	.459	.461
1956	1.138	1.229	1968	.972	.960	1980	.405	.406
1957	1.098	1.186	1969	.938	.911	1981	.371	.367
						1982	.356	.346
						1983, May	.352	.337

Source: U.S. Bureau of Labor Statistics. Monthly data in U.S. Bureau of Economic Analysis, *Survey of Current Business.*

Source: *Statistical Abstracts of the United States, 1984.*

CONSUMER PRICES

INDEX, 1967 = 100 (RATIO SCALE)

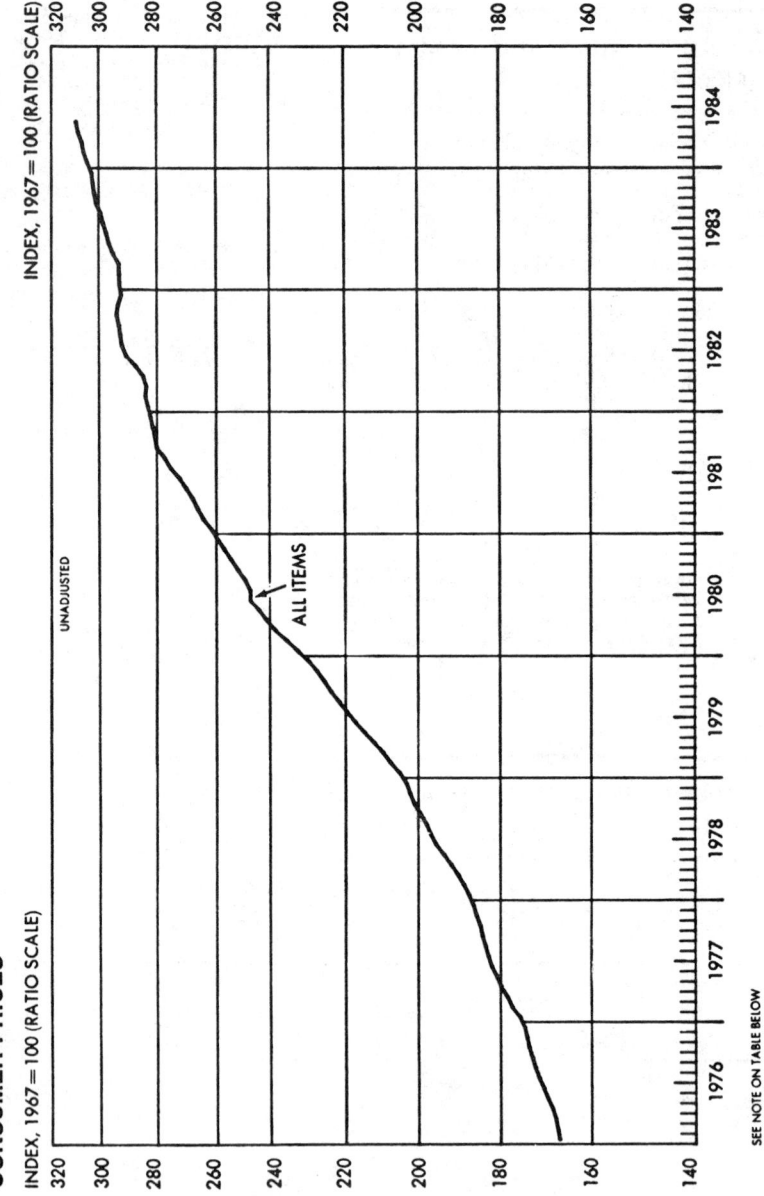

INDEX, 1967 = 100 (RATIO SCALE)

UNADJUSTED

ALL ITEMS

1976   1977   1978   1979   1980   1981   1982   1983   1984

SEE NOTE ON TABLE BELOW
SOURCE: DEPARTMENT OF LABOR

COUNCIL OF ECONOMIC ADVISERS

[1967=100, except as noted; monthly data seasonally adjusted, except as noted]

Period	All items[1]	Food	Housing Total[1]	Shelter Total	Shelter Renters' costs[2]	Shelter Homeowners' costs[2]	Maintenance and repairs	Fuel and other utilities	Apparel and upkeep	Transportation Total[1]	Transportation New cars	Transportation Motor fuel[3]	Medical care	Energy[4]	All items less food, energy, and shelter
	NSA				NSA	NSA	NSA								
Rel. imp.[5]	100.0	18.7	37.6	21.5	7.0	14.0	0.5	8.2	5.2	21.8	3.5	5.9	6.1	11.9	47.9
1976	170.5	180.8	174.6	179.0			199.6	182.7	147.6	165.5	135.7	177.9	184.7	189.3	159.9
1977	181.5	192.2	186.5	191.1			214.7	202.2	154.2	177.2	142.9	188.2	202.4	207.3	169.5
1978	195.4	211.4	202.8	210.4			233.0	216.0	159.6	185.5	153.8	196.3	219.4	220.4	179.1
1979	217.4	234.5	227.6	239.7			256.4	239.3	166.6	212.0	166.0	265.6	239.7	275.9	191.5
1980	246.8	254.6	263.3	281.7			285.7	278.6	178.4	249.7	179.3	369.1	265.9	361.1	208.3
1981	272.4	274.6	293.5	314.7			314.4	319.2	186.9	280.0	190.2	410.0	294.5	410.0	228.1
1982	289.1	285.7	314.7	337.0			334.1	350.8	191.8	291.5	197.6	389.4	328.7	416.1	245.6
1983	298.4	291.7	323.1	344.8	103.0	102.5	346.3	370.3	196.5	298.4	202.6	376.4	357.3	419.3	258.4
1983: May	297.1	292.1	321.1	342.3	102.2	102.0	344.3	368.4	195.7	296.4	201.1	379.8	354.8	420.5	256.3
June	298.1	291.5	321.9	343.3	102.5	102.2	345.1	369.3	196.3	297.3	201.3	381.0	356.5	421.6	257.1
July	299.3	291.2	323.2	345.1	103.1	102.7	345.1	370.7	197.3	298.7	201.7	382.5	358.5	423.2	258.4
Aug	300.3	291.7	324.1	346.3	103.6	103.0	347.9	371.9	197.9	300.8	203.3	383.7	360.3	424.6	259.7
Sept	301.8	292.3	325.3	348.0	104.2	103.5	346.6	372.9	198.2	302.8	204.9	383.7	361.7	425.1	260.9
Oct	302.6	293.5	326.0	349.3	104.6	103.9	351.1	372.2	198.2	304.4	205.5	383.2	362.9	424.2	262.2
Nov	303.1	294.1	327.4	350.7	105.0	104.3	353.4	374.4	198.5	305.5	205.3	381.6	364.7	424.5	263.5
Dec	303.5	295.4	328.1	351.8	105.3	104.5	354.7	373.8	198.5	306.1	205.7	379.8	366.0	423.3	264.2
1984: Jan	305.2	300.2	329.6	353.0	105.7	104.9	356.7	378.2	199.0	306.7	205.6	375.9	368.6	421.7	265.8
Feb	306.6	302.2	331.1	353.8	106.0	105.1	353.5	384.8	198.5	306.6	206.4	370.5	371.5	422.7	266.7
Mar	307.3	301.8	331.2	355.3	106.5	105.6	355.3	380.9	198.6	309.4	207.4	374.0	373.5	421.8	267.8
Apr	308.8	301.7	333.3	357.6	107.4	106.2	356.3	383.9	198.5	311.2	207.6	375.4	375.3	424.7	269.1
May	309.7	300.9	334.1	358.7	107.8	106.5	357.3	384.6	198.6	312.7	207.2	376.1	377.3	425.4	270.0

[1] Includes items not shown separately.
[2] December 1982=100.
[3] Includes direct pricing of diesel and gasohol beginning September 1981.
[4] Fuel oil, coal, and bottled gas; gas (piped) and electricity; and motor fuel. Motor oil, coolant, etc. also included through 1982.
[5] Relative importance, December 1983.

NOTE.—NSA indicates data are not seasonally adjusted.
Data beginning 1978 are for all urban consumers; earlier data are for urban wage earners and clerical workers.
Data beginning 1983 incorporate a rental equivalence measure for homeownership costs and therefore are not strictly comparable with figures for earlier periods.
Source: Department of Labor, Bureau of Labor Statistics.

Source: Economic Indicators, Council of Economic Advisers.

CONSUMER PRICE INDEX—U.S. CITY AVERAGE, AND SELECTED AREAS

[1967 = 100 unless otherwise specified]

Area[1]	All Urban Consumers							Urban Wage Earners and Clerical Workers						
	Feb. 1983	Sept. 1983	Oct. 1983	Nov. 1983	Dec. 1983	Jan. 1984	Feb. 1984	Feb. 1983	Sept. 1983	Oct. 1983	Nov. 1983	Dec. 1983	Jan. 1984	Feb. 1984
U.S. city average[2]	293.2	301.8	302.6	303.1	303.5	305.2	306.6	292.3	300.8	301.3	301.4	301.5	302.7	303.3
Anchorage, Alaska (10/67 = 100)	...	267.9	...	270.4	...	271.5	...	...	260.8	...	264.0	...	264.0	...
Atlanta, Ga.	295.1	...	304.4	304.7	307.3	307.6	309.3	297.0	299.5	306.3	302.4	309.7	303.8	309.6
Baltimore, Md.	...	302.9	304.7	294.0	...	307.6	...	...	288.6	...	292.5	...	294.4	...
Boston, Mass.	280.3	290.6	288.5	294.0	288.2	296.6	290.5	276.5	288.6	286.8	292.5	285.6	294.4	285.9
Buffalo, N.Y.	...	...	...	...	...	...	...	...	...	...	...	...	...	...
Chicago, Ill.-Northwestern Ind.	293.7	303.0	302.3	303.9	303.9	305.2	305.0	291.4	299.1	294.5	295.7	294.2	298.3	296.9
Cincinnati, Ohio-Ky.-Ind.	318.8	314.6	...	316.8	...	318.4	331.1	313.5	311.2	317.6	316.0	314.9	313.4	318.2
Cleveland, Ohio	304.5	332.5	332.5	...	330.7	...	322.7	298.1	...	314.7	...	313.5	...	317.7
Dallas-Ft. Worth, Tex.	318.5	318.5	318.5	317.6	317.6	...	322.7	298.1	...	...	...	...	336.0	...
Denver-Boulder, Colo.	339.4	339.4	339.8	339.8	...	343.0	...	337.3	...	...	338.4	...	...	...
Detroit, Mich.	292.3	299.2	298.2	299.9	300.1	301.3	303.1	287.1	304.6	298.9	301.8	301.3	307.9	304.7
Honolulu, Hawaii	270.4	...	276.4	...	278.4	...	280.7	274.8	...	285.9	...	288.2	...	284.3
Houston, Tex.	317.3	...	324.3	...	320.7	...	323.6	317.4	...	322.4	...	317.9	...	323.5
Kansas City, Mo.-Kansas	292.3	296.4	303.3	293.9	303.0	299.1	306.4	289.0	...	303.9	299.3	300.0	290.2	296.6
Los Angeles-Long Beach, Anaheim, Calif.	286.8	296.4	297.0	296.5	297.7	299.1	300.2	290.1	296.7	299.0	297.8	299.9	293.2	299.0
Miami, Fla. (11/77 = 100)	162.9	162.9	...	164.0	...	165.0	...	164.3	...	164.9	...	...	165.9	...
Milwaukee, Wis.	313.9	313.9	...	312.5	...	314.0	319.6	309.0	329.1	312.7	328.9	312.5	327.5	318.6
Minneapolis-St. Paul, Minn.-Wis.	305.8	292.1	316.8	293.9	317.5	...	299.6	279.6	288.1	288.7	287.3	288.2	290.2	290.5
New York, N.Y.-Northeastern N.J.	283.2	297.2	292.9	288.5	294.3	291.0	299.0	...	290.0	288.7	290.9	...	293.2	...
Northeast, Pa. (Scranton)	...	...	...	...	...	...	...	...	290.0	...	...	...	...	...
Philadelphia, Pa.-N.J.	282.0	291.2	291.2	291.7	291.8	294.4	296.4	283.3	294.2	294.2	294.8	294.3	296.7	298.5
Pittsburgh, Pa.	304.8	293.3	313.7	...	314.3	295.1	315.5	296.6	304.7	304.7	...	302.6	289.5	299.6
Portland, Oreg.-Wash.	293.3	302.0	...	293.9	...	300.9	...	...	299.1	...	289.6	...	296.8	...
St. Louis, Mo.-Ill.	302.0	...	...	299.6	...	346.6	...	...	323.9	...	299.3	...	296.8	...
San Diego, Calif.	340.4	340.4	...	342.3	...	346.6	...	...	323.9	...	323.7	...	329.6	...
San Francisco-Oakland, Calif.	...	308.8	305.7	309.5	307.3	311.1	311.7	297.3	297.7	301.4	299.0	306.1	299.4	308.7
Seattle-Everett, Wash.	308.8	308.8	...	309.5	...	311.1	...	...	300.9	...	302.7	...	308.1	...
Washington, D.C.-Md.-Va.	297.0	297.0	...	298.6	...	303.4	...	293.9	300.9	301.4	299.0	306.1	...	...

[1] The areas listed include not only the central city but the entire portion of the Standard Metropolitan Statistical Area, as defined for the 1970 Census of Population, except that the Standard Consolidated Area is used for New York and Chicago.
[2] Average of 85 cities.

Source: *Monthly Labor Review*, U.S. Department of Labor, Bureau of Labor Statistics.

NATIONAL INCOME

[Billions of dollars; quarterly data at seasonally adjusted annual rates]

Period	National income	Compensation of employees [1]	Proprietors' income with inventory valuation and capital consumption adjustments		Rental income of persons with capital consumption adjustment	Corporate profits with inventory valuation and capital consumption adjustments					Net interest
			Farm	Nonfarm		Total	Profits with inventory valuation adjustment and without capital consumption adjustment			Capital consumption adjustment	
							Total	Profits before tax	Inventory valuation adjustment		
1972	963.6	718.0	18.7	58.1	21.0	96.6	94.0	100.6	−6.6	2.7	51.2
1973	1,086.2	801.3	32.8	61.0	22.6	108.3	105.6	125.6	−20.0	2.7	60.2
1974	1,160.7	877.5	26.5	62.2	23.5	94.9	96.7	136.7	−40.0	−1.8	76.1
1975	1,239.4	931.4	24.6	65.4	23.0	110.5	120.6	132.1	−11.6	−10.1	84.5
1976	1,379.2	1,036.3	19.1	75.0	23.5	138.1	151.6	166.3	−14.7	−13.5	87.2
1977	1,550.5	1,152.1	19.1	84.8	24.8	167.3	178.5	194.7	−16.2	−11.3	102.5
1978	1,760.3	1,301.1	26.3	92.2	26.6	192.4	205.1	229.1	−24.0	−12.7	121.7
1979	1,966.7	1,458.1	31.9	100.2	27.9	194.8	209.6	252.7	−43.1	−14.8	153.8
1980	2,116.6	1,599.6	21.8	95.6	31.5	175.4	191.7	234.6	−42.9	−16.3	192.6
1981	2,373.0	1,769.2	30.5	89.7	41.4	192.3	203.3	227.0	−23.6	−11.0	249.9
1982	2,450.4	1,865.7	21.5	87.4	49.9	164.8	165.9	174.2	−8.4	−1.1	261.1
1983	2,650.2	1,990.2	20.9	107.6	54.8	229.1	198.3	207.5	−9.2	30.8	247.5
1982: I	2,419.7	1,834.2	27.4	83.7	47.4	162.0	167.7	173.2	−5.5	−5.6	265.0
II	2,448.9	1,859.5	16.8	88.1	49.0	166.8	170.3	178.8	−8.5	−3.5	268.3
III	2,458.9	1,879.5	15.8	87.8	50.9	168.5	168.3	177.3	−9.0	.1	256.4
IV	2,474.0	1,889.0	26.0	90.2	52.3	161.9	157.2	167.5	−10.3	4.7	254.7
1983: I	2,528.5	1,923.7	22.2	98.4	54.1	181.8	168.0	169.7	−1.7	13.9	248.3
II	2,612.8	1,968.7	21.0	106.2	54.8	218.2	192.7	203.3	−10.6	25.6	243.8
III	2,686.9	2,011.8	15.5	111.2	53.9	248.4	210.8	229.1	−18.3	37.6	246.1
IV	2,772.4	2,056.6	25.0	114.5	56.2	268.2	222.0	228.2	−6.3	46.2	251.9
1984: I r	2,883.3	2,113.4	47.9	121.4	57.0	281.6	231.6	244.3	−12.5	49.8	262.0

1 Includes employer contributions for social insurance.

Source: Economic Indicators, Council of Economic Advisers.

Source: Department of Commerce, Bureau of Economic Analysis.

SELECTED UNEMPLOYMENT RATES

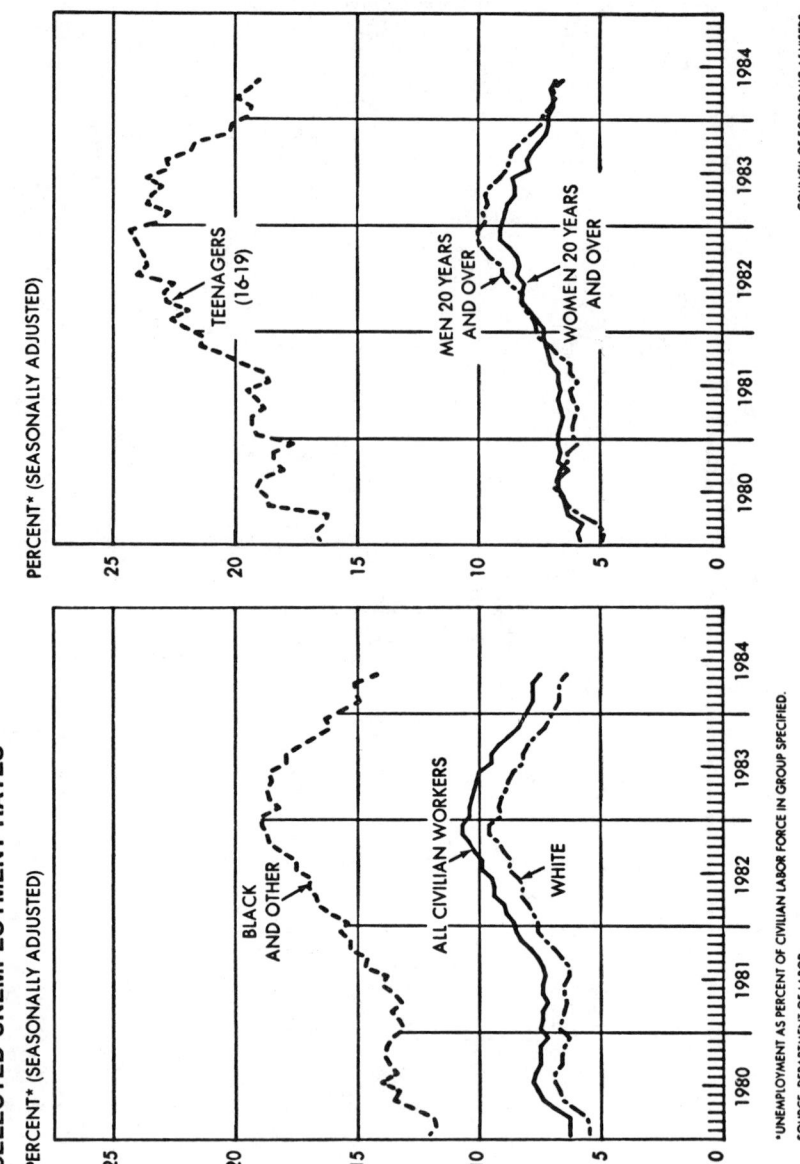

PERCENT* (SEASONALLY ADJUSTED)

PERCENT* (SEASONALLY ADJUSTED)

TEENAGERS (16-19)

MEN 20 YEARS AND OVER

WOMEN 20 YEARS AND OVER

BLACK AND OTHER

ALL CIVILIAN WORKERS

WHITE

*UNEMPLOYMENT AS PERCENT OF CIVILIAN LABOR FORCE IN GROUP SPECIFIED.

SOURCE: DEPARTMENT OF LABOR

COUNCIL OF ECONOMIC ADVISERS

[Monthly data seasonally adjusted]

Unemployment rate (percent of civilian labor force in group)

Period	Unemployment rate, all workers [1]	By sex and age				By race			By selected groups					Labor force time lost (percent) [2]
		All civilian workers	Men 20 years and over	Women 20 years and over	Both sexes 16–19 years	White	Black and other		Experienced wage and salary workers	Married men, spouse present	Women who maintain families	Full-time workers	Part-time workers	
							Total	Black						
1978	6.0	6.1	4.3	6.0	16.4	5.2	11.9	12.8	5.6	2.8	8.5	5.6	9.0	6.5
1979	5.8	5.8	4.2	5.7	16.1	5.1	11.3	12.3	5.5	2.8	8.3	5.3	8.8	6.3
1980	7.0	7.1	5.9	6.4	17.8	6.3	13.1	14.3	6.9	4.2	9.2	6.9	8.8	7.9
1981	7.5	7.6	6.3	6.8	19.6	6.7	14.2	15.6	7.3	4.3	10.4	7.3	9.4	8.5
1982	9.5	9.7	8.8	8.3	23.2	8.6	17.3	18.9	9.3	6.5	11.7	9.6	10.5	11.0
1983	9.5	9.6	8.9	8.1	22.4	8.4	17.8	19.5	9.2	6.5	12.2	9.5	10.4	10.9
1983: May	9.9	10.1	9.5	8.5	23.0	8.8	18.5	20.3	9.8	7.0	12.7	10.0	10.9	11.5
June	9.8	10.0	9.1	8.6	23.6	8.6	18.6	20.3	9.4	6.7	12.5	9.7	11.8	11.1
July	9.3	9.5	9.1	7.9	22.7	8.2	17.9	19.6	9.1	6.2	11.8	9.4	10.2	10.7
Aug	9.3	9.5	8.7	8.0	22.8	8.2	17.9	19.8	9.1	6.3	11.8	9.3	10.2	10.7
Sept	9.1	9.2	8.6	7.8	21.8	8.0	17.3	18.9	8.8	6.1	12.0	9.1	10.1	10.5
Oct	8.7	8.8	8.2	7.5	21.6	7.7	16.7	18.3	8.5	5.7	11.4	8.7	10.0	10.0
Nov	8.3	8.4	7.8	7.2	20.2	7.3	16.1	17.7	8.1	5.5	10.5	8.2	9.8	9.7
Dec	8.1	8.2	7.4	7.1	20.1	7.1	16.3	17.8	7.9	5.2	10.9	8.0	9.8	9.4
1984: Jan	7.9	8.0	7.3	7.1	19.4	6.9	15.6	16.7	7.6	5.0	10.7	7.8	9.2	9.2
Feb	7.7	7.8	7.0	6.9	19.3	6.7	14.9	16.2	7.4	4.9	11.0	7.5	-9.3	8.9
Mar	7.7	7.8	6.8	6.9	19.9	6.7	15.1	16.6	7.2	4.7	11.0	7.5	9.2	8.8
Apr	7.7	7.8	6.9	7.0	19.4	6.7	15.1	16.8	7.3	4.7	10.5	7.6	9.1	8.9
May	7.4	7.5	6.5	6.8	19.0	6.4	14.2	15.8	6.9	4.5	9.8	7.2	9.3	8.5

[1] Unemployed as percent of total labor force including resident Armed Forces.
[2] Aggregate hours lost by the unemployed and persons on part time for economic reasons as percent of potentially available labor force hours.

Source: Department of Labor, Bureau of Labor Statistics.

Source: *Economic Indicators*, Council of Economic Advisers.

MONEY STOCK, LIQUID ASSETS, AND DEBT MEASURES

BILLIONS OF DOLLARS*(RATIO SCALE)

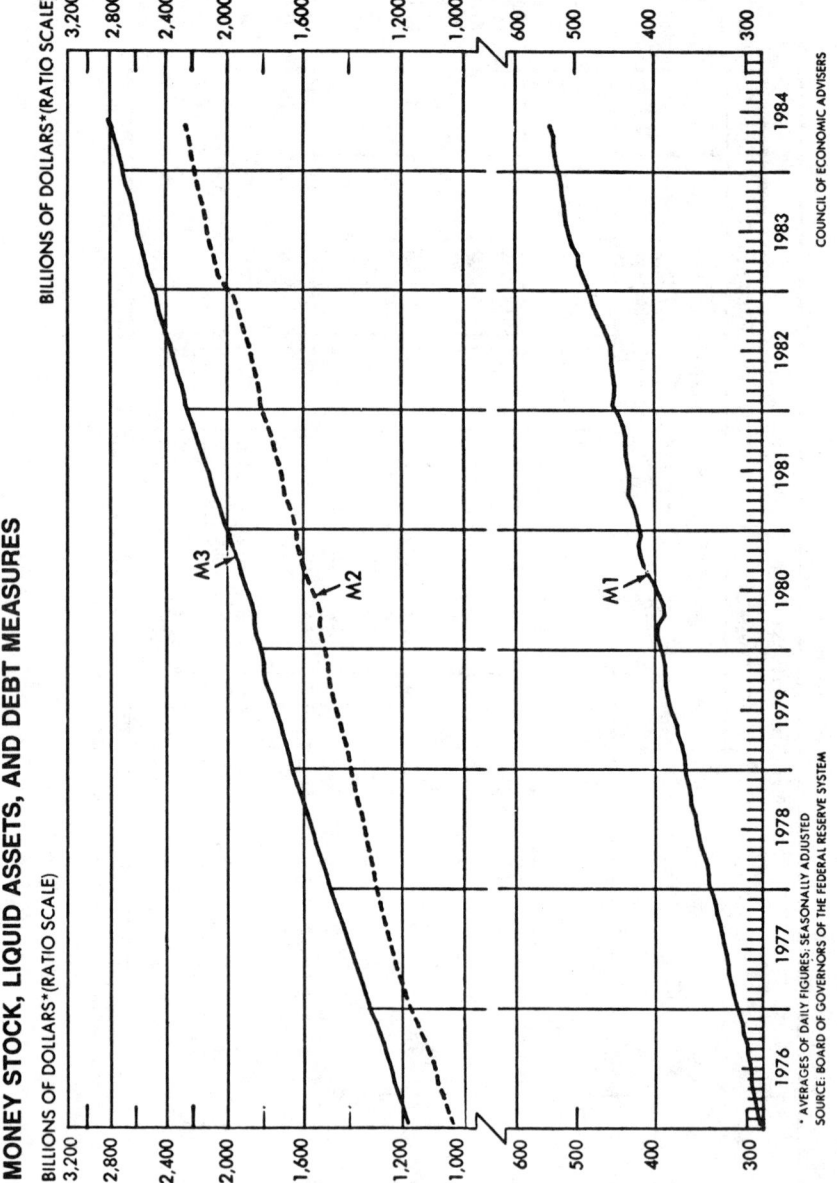

* AVERAGES OF DAILY FIGURES; SEASONALLY ADJUSTED
SOURCE: BOARD OF GOVERNORS OF THE FEDERAL RESERVE SYSTEM

COUNCIL OF ECONOMIC ADVISERS

[Averages of daily figures, except as noted; billions of dollars, seasonally adjusted]

Period	M1 Sum of currency, demand deposits, travelers' checks, and other checkable deposits (OCDs)	M2 M1 plus overnight RPs and Eurodollars, MMMF balances (general purpose and broker/dealer), MMDAs, and savings and small time deposits	M3 M2 plus large time deposits, term RPs, term Eurodollars, and institution-only MMMF balances	L M3 plus other liquid assets	Debt Debt of domestic nonfinancial sectors (monthly average)[1]	Percent change from year or 6 months earlier[2] M1	Percent change from year or 6 months earlier[2] M2	Percent change from year or 6 months earlier[2] M3	Percent change from year or 6 months earlier[2] Debt
1976: Dec	310.4	1,163.6	1,311.9	1,516.6	r2,507.5	6.6	13.7	11.9	10.7
1977: Dec	335.4	1,286.7	1,472.9	1,704.7	r2,823.1	8.1	10.6	12.3	r12.6
1978: Dec	363.1	1,389.1	1,647.1	1,910.6	r3,194.2	8.3	8.0	11.8	r13.1
1979: Dec	389.1	1,498.5	1,804.8	2,117.1	r3,578.1	7.2	7.9	9.6	12.0
1980: Dec	414.9	1,632.6	1,989.8	2,326.0	r3,920.8	6.6	8.9	10.3	r9.6
1981: Dec	441.9	1,796.6	2,236.7	2,598.4	r4,301.3	6.5	10.0	12.4	9.7
1982: Dec	480.5	1,965.3	2,460.3	2,868.7	r4,691.7	8.7	9.4	10.0	r9.1
1983: Dec r	525.3	2,196.2	2,706.8	3,176.9	5,203.9	9.3	11.7	10.0	10.9
1983: May	506.6	2,102.2	2,571.0	3,003.3	r4,877.0	13.1	16.7	10.2	r9.9
June	510.9	2,117.0	2,593.0	3,033.1	r4,931.4	13.1	16.0	11.1	r10.5
July	514.9	2,126.6	2,604.0	3,059.7	r4,984.0	12.7	11.1	9.4	r11.2
Aug	517.4	2,135.3	2,617.2	3,075.1	r5,025.2	11.0	8.1	8.1	r11.7
Sept r	518.9	2,147.9	2,636.4	3,097.6	5,066.4	9.3	7.9	8.4	11.8
Oct r	521.6	2,167.2	2,656.4	3,114.0	5,109.2	9.7	8.4	8.5	11.7
Nov r	523.0	2,182.1	2,688.5	3,146.5	5,152.5	6.6	7.7	9.3	11.6
Dec r	525.3	2,196.2	2,706.8	3,176.9	5,203.9	5.7	7.6	9.0	11.4
1984: Jan r	530.0	2,206.8	2,721.8	3,197.5	5,260.3	6.0	7.7	9.3	11.4
Feb r	532.9	2,222.5	2,744.6	3,227.1	5,317.2	6.1	8.3	10.0	12.0
Mar r	535.2	2,230.0	2,766.0	3,269.5	5,371.2	6.4	7.8	10.1	12.4
Apr r	535.4	2,242.5	2,790.7	3,298.3	5,430.9	5.4	7.1	10.4	13.0
May p	541.0	2,259.6	2,814.5			7.0	7.2	9.6	

[1] Consists of outstanding credit market debt of the U.S. Government, State and local governments, and private nonfinancial sectors; data from flow of funds accounts. Beginning with this issue, data are on a monthly-average basis rather than end-of-month basis.

[2] Annual changes are from December to December and monthly changes are from 6 months earlier at a seasonally adjusted annual rate.

NOTE.—The nontransactions portion of M2 is now seasonally adjusted as a whole to reduce distortions caused by substantial portfolio shifts arising from regulatory and financial changes in recent years, especially shifts to MMDAs in 1983. A similar procedure is being used to seasonally adjust the remaining nontransactions balances in M3.

Source: Board of Governors of the Federal Reserve System.

Source: *Economic Indicators*, Council of Economic Advisers.

Monetary Aggregates Defined

Money supply data has been revised and expanded to reflect the Federal Reserve's redefinition of the monetary aggregates. The redefinition was prompted by the emergence in recent years of new monetary assets—for example, negotiable order of withdrawal (NOW) accounts and money-market mutual fund shares—and alterations in the basic character of established monetary assets—for example, the growing similarity of and substitution between the deposits of thrift institutions and those of commercial banks.

M1-A has been discontinued with M1-B now designated as "M-1." M-1 is currency in circulation plus all checking accounts including those which pay interest, such as NOW accounts. M-1 excludes deposits due to foreign commercial banks and official institutions.

M-2 as redefined adds to M1-B overnight repurchase agreements (RPs) issued by commercial banks and certain overnight Eurodollars (those issued by Carribbean branches of member banks) held by U.S. nonbank residents, money-market mutual fund shares, and savings and small-denomination time deposits (those issued in denominations of less than $100,000) at all depository institutions. Depository institutions are commercial banks (including U.S. agencies and branches of foreign banks, Edge Act Corporations, and foreign investment companies), mutual savings banks, savings and loan associations, and credit unions.

M-3 as redefined is equal to new M-2 plus large-denomination time deposits (those issued as in denominations of $100,000 or more) at all depository institutions (including negotiable CDs) plus term RPs issued by commercial banks and savings and loan associations.

L, the very broad measure of liquid assets, equals new M-3 plus other liquid assets consisting of other Eurodollar holdings of U.S. nonbank residents, bankers acceptances, commercial paper, savings bonds, and marketable liquid Treasury obligations.

Federal Budget: Procedure and Timetable

Congressional Budget Timetable

CONGRESSIONAL BUDGET ACT OF 1974: THE NEW BUDGET PROCESS IN TEN STEPS

1. To give Congress an earlier and better start in reviewing and reshaping the budget, the Executive Branch must submit a "current services budget" by November 10th for the new fiscal year that starts the following October 1st. The current services budget should project the spending required to maintain ongoing programs throughout the following fiscal year at existing commitment levels, or at commitment levels specified by existing legislation based on current economic assumptions. The Joint Economic Committee should review and assess the current services budget and report to Congress by December 31st.

2. The President will continue to submit his new budget to Congress in late January or early February. In addition to the traditional budget totals and breakdowns, the budget document must include a list of existing "tax expenditures"—i.e., estimates of revenues lost to the Treasury through preferential tax treatment—as well as any proposed changes in tax expenditures. The budget must also contain estimates of expenditures for programs for which funds are appropriated one year in advance and five-year budget projections of all federal spending under existing programs.

3. Reports of all standing committees to the House and Senate Budget Committees of the spending plans of those committees on all matters under their jurisdiction, including spending under new legislation, are required by March 15th for the upcoming fiscal year.

4. An annual report of the Congressional Budget Office to the Budget Committees on alternative budget levels and national budget priorities is required on or before April 1st.

5. By April 15th, the Budget Committees must report concurrent resolutions to the House and Senate floors, and Congress will have to clear the initial budget resolution by May 15th. This initial budget resolution sets target totals for appropriations, outlays, taxes, the budget surplus or deficit, and the federal debt. Within these overall targets, the resolution will break down appropriations and outlays by the functional categories used in the President's budget document, as well as by classifications used by the appropriations subcommittees for the 13 appropriations bills. The resolution will include any recommended changes in tax revenues and in the level of the federal debt ceiling.

6. Committees report bills or resolutions authorizing new budget authority by May 15th.

7. The basic appropriations process proceeds within the Appropriations Committees, but is subject to targets of the budget resolution.

8. Scorekeeping reports will be issued periodically by the Congressional Budget Office on the status of budget authority, revenue, outlays and debt legislation, comparing the amounts and changes in such legislation with the First Congressional Budget Resolution.

9. Subject to prior authorization, all appropriations bills have to be cleared by the middle of September—no later than the seventh day after Labor Day. By September 15th, after finishing action on all appropriations and other spending bills, Congress must adopt a second, and final, budget resolution that may either affirm or revise the budget targets set by the initial resolution. This resolution must provide for a final budget reconciliation by changing either one or more of the following: (1) appropriations (both for the upcoming fiscal year or carried over from previous fiscal years) and/or entitlements; (2) revenues; and (3) the public debt. The final resolution will direct the committees that have jurisdiction over these matters to report the necessary legislative changes. The Budget Committees will then combine these changes and report them to the floor in the form of a reconciliation bill.

If Congress has withheld all appropriations and entitlement bills from the President until passage of the final reconciliation bill, then this bill becomes the final budget legislation, subject to Presidential signature (or veto). If, on the other hand, each individual appropriations bill has been signed by the President upon passage by the Congress, the final reconciliation bill—upon signature by the President—supersedes all the previously passed individual bills.

10. The new fiscal year begins on October 1st.

FEDERAL BUDGET: PROCEDURE AND TIMETABLE

Congressional Budget Timetable

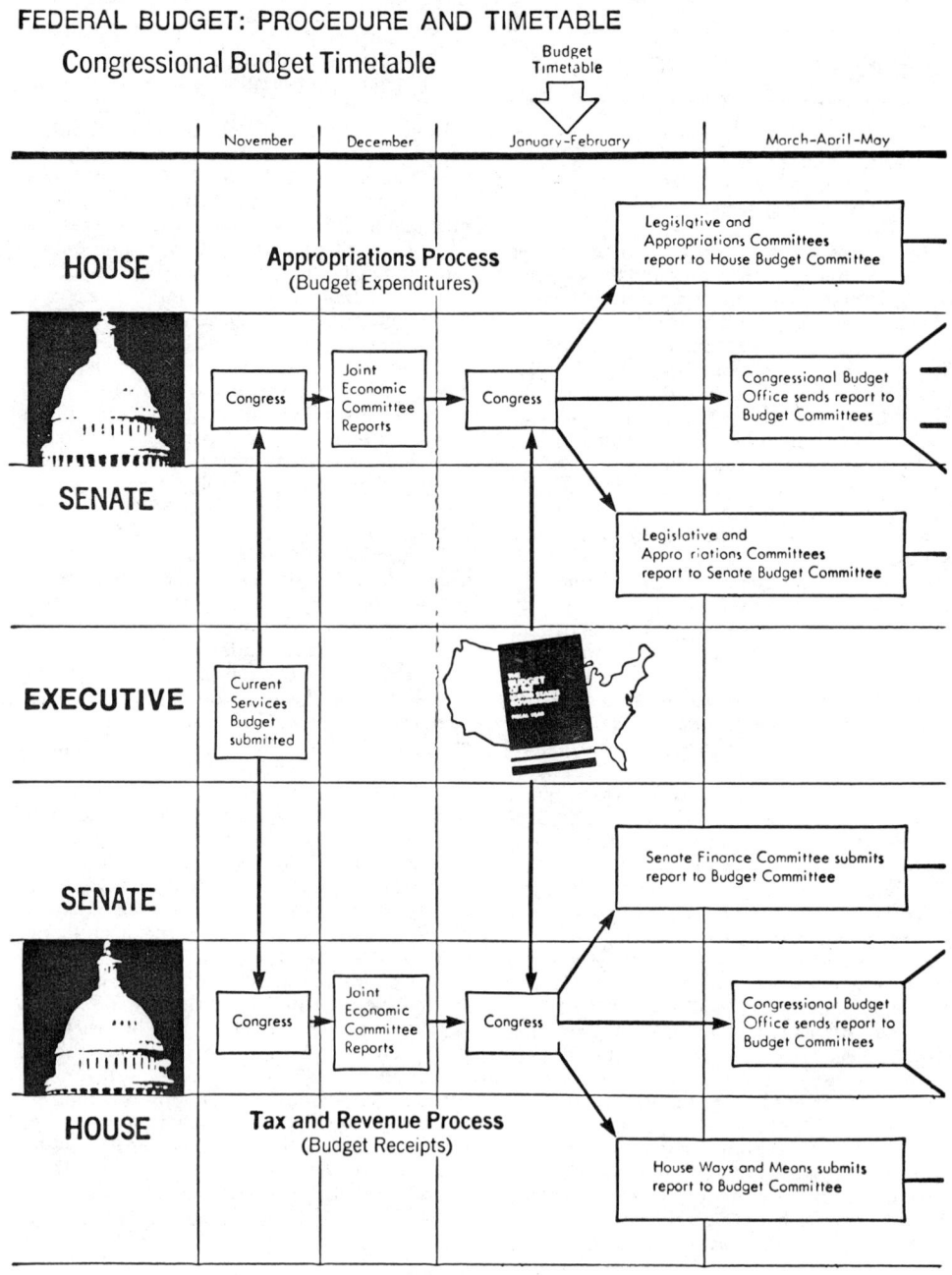

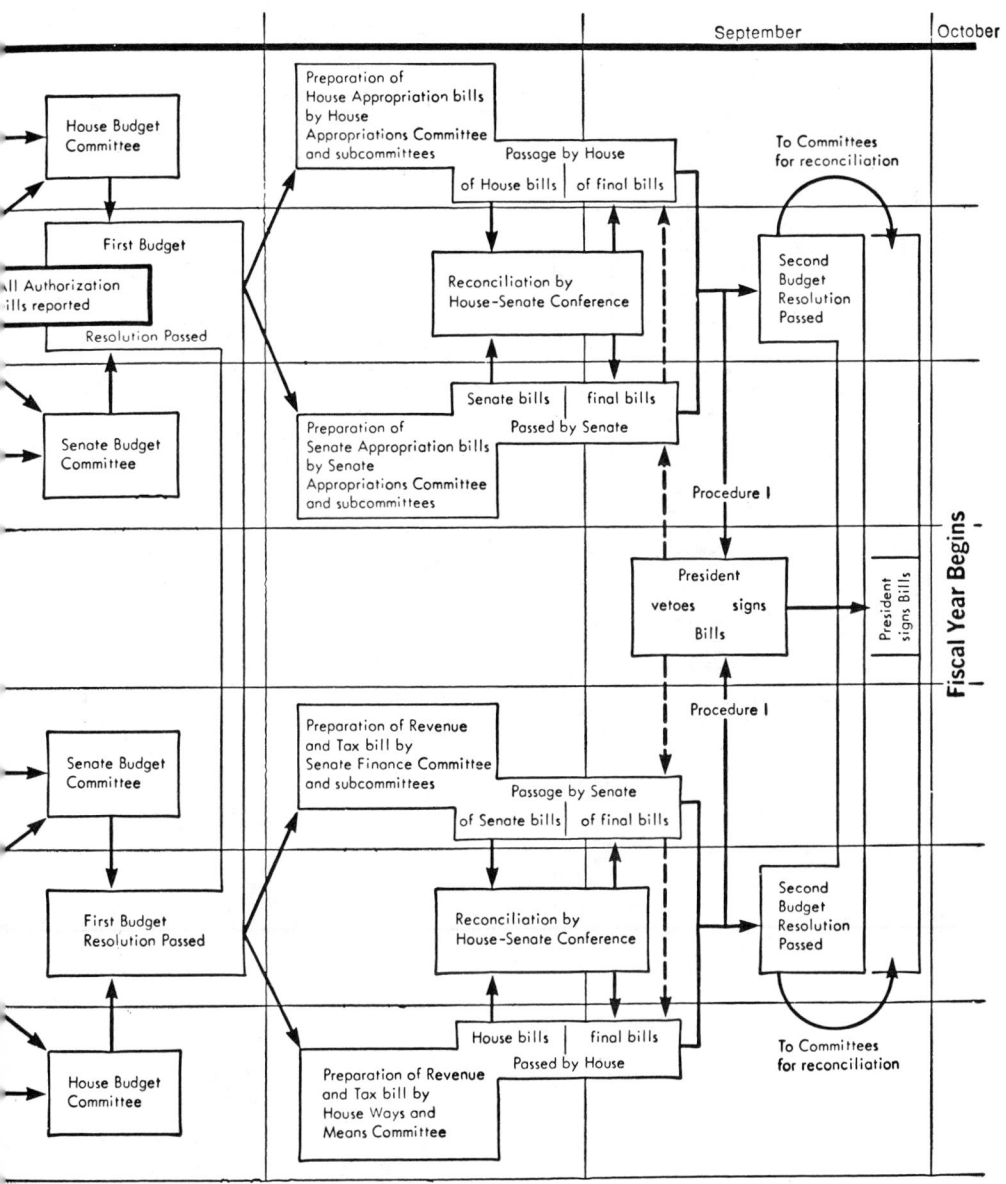

September | October

House Budget Committee

Preparation of House Appropriation bills by House Appropriations Committee and subcommittees

Passage by House of House bills | of final bills

To Committees for reconciliation

First Budget

All Authorization bills reported

Resolution Passed

Reconciliation by House-Senate Conference

Second Budget Resolution Passed

Senate Budget Committee

Senate bills | final bills Passed by Senate

Preparation of Senate Appropriation bills by Senate Appropriations Committee and subcommittees

Procedure I

President vetoes   signs Bills

President signs Bills

Fiscal Year Begins

Procedure I

Senate Budget Committee

Preparation of Revenue and Tax bill by Senate Finance Committee and subcommittees

Passage by Senate of Senate bills | of final bills

First Budget Resolution Passed

Reconciliation by House-Senate Conference

Second Budget Resolution Passed

House Budget Committee

House bills | final bills Passed by House

Preparation of Revenue and Tax bill by House Ways and Means Committee

To Committees for reconciliation

Source: The Conference Board, "The Federal Budget: Its Impact on the Economy," Michael E. Levy, assisted by Delos R. Smith.

U.S. BUDGET RECEIPTS AND OUTLAYS (millions of dollars)

Source or type	Fiscal year 1981	Fiscal year 1982	Fiscal year 1983	Calendar year 1982 H1	Calendar year 1982 H2	Calendar year 1983 H1	1984 Feb.	1984 Mar.	1984 Apr.
RECEIPTS									
1 All sources	**599,272**	**617,766**	**600,563**	**322,478**	**286,338**	**306,331**	**47,886**	**44,464**	**80,180**
2 Individual income taxes, net	285,917	297,744	288,938	150,565	145,676	144,550	22,190	12,895	39,192
3 Withheld	256,332	267,513	266,010	133,575	131,567	135,531	23,523	26,877	22,321
4 Presidential Election Campaign Fund	41	39	36	34	5	30	4	9	5
5 Nonwithheld	76,844	84,691	83,586	66,174	20,040	63,014	1,501	2,776	31,993
6 Refunds	47,299	54,498	60,692	49,217	5,938	54,024	2,838	16,766	15,127
Corporation income taxes									
7 Gross receipts	73,733	65,991	61,780	37,836	25,661	33,522	1,892	9,441	11,786
8 Refunds	12,596	16,784	24,758	8,028	11,467	13,809	1,833	1,476	2,691
9 Social insurance taxes and contributions, net	182,720	201,498	209,001	108,079	94,278	110,521	19,972	17,702	26,036
10 Payroll employment taxes and contributions[1]	156,932	172,744	179,010	88,795	85,063	90,912	16,774	16,704	18,532
11 Self-employment taxes and contributions[2]	6,041	7,941	6,756	7,357	177	6,427	523	433	4,637
12 Unemployment insurance	15,763	16,600	18,799	9,809	6,857	11,146	2,308	191	2,501
13 Other net receipts[3]	3,984	4,212	4,436	2,119	2,181	2,196	369	373	366
14 Excise taxes	40,839	36,311	35,300	17,525	16,556	16,904	2,693	2,870	3,042
15 Customs deposits	8,083	8,854	8,655	4,310	4,299	4,010	839	974	937
16 Estate and gift taxes	6,787	7,991	6,053	4,208	3,445	2,883	570	523	505
17 Miscellaneous receipts[4]	13,790	16,161	15,594	7,984	7,891	7,751	1,613	1,535	1,374

OUTLAYS

18 All types	657,204	728,424	795,917	348,683	390,847	396,477	68,267	73,020	68,687
19 National defense	159,765	187,418	210,461	93,154	100,419	105,072	18,515	19,516	18,711
20 International affairs	11,130	9,982	8,927	5,183	4,406	4,705	780	1,180	973
21 General science, space, and technology	6,359	7,070	7,777	3,370	3,903	3,486	721	611	685
22 Energy	10,277	4,674	4,035	2,946	2,059	2,073	34	265	57
23 Natural resources and environment	13,525	12,934	12,676	5,636	6,940	5,892	790	861	923
24 Agriculture	5,572	14,875	22,173	7,087	13,260	10,154	1,737	1,315	1,364
25 Commerce and housing credit	3,946	3,865	4,721	1,408	2,244	2,164	−648	224	−22
26 Transportation	23,381	20,560	21,231	9,915	10,686	9,918	1,517	1,555	1,716
27 Community and regional development	9,394	7,165	7,302	3,055	4,186	3,124	524	514	481
28 Education, training, employment, social services	31,402	26,300	25,726	12,607	12,187	12,801	2,305	2,172	2,210
29 Health	26,858	27,435	28,655 }	150,001[5]	172,852	184,207	2,540	2,729	2,577
30 Social security and medicare	178,733	202,531	223,311 }				19,164	20,192	19,405
31 Income security	85,514	92,084	106,211 }				8,585	9,791	8,677
32 Veterans benefits and services	22,988	23,955	24,845	112,782	13,241	11,334	2,108	3,293	891
33 Administration of justice ...	4,696	4,671	5,014	2,334	2,373	2,522	505	435	476
34 General government	4,614	4,726	4,991	2,400	2,322	2,434	495	585	265
35 General-purpose fiscal assistance	6,856	6,393	6,287	3,325	3,152	3,124	201	86	1,219
36 Net interest[6]	68,726	84,697	89,774	41,883	44,948	42,358	9,801	8,592	9,211
37 Undistributed offsetting receipts[7]	−16,509	−13,270	−21,424	−6,490	−8,333	−8,885	−1,407	−824	−1,130

1. Old-age, disability, and hospital insurance, and railroad retirement accounts.
2. Old-age, disability, and hospital insurance.
3. Federal employee retirement contributions and civil service retirement and disability fund.
4. Deposits of earnings by Federal Reserve Banks and other miscellaneous receipts.
5. In accordance with the Social Security Amendments Act of 1983, the Treasury now provides social security and medicare outlays as a separate function. Before February 1984, these outlays were included in the income security and health functions.
6. Net interest function includes interest received by trust funds.
7. Consists of rents and royalties on the outer continental shelf and U.S. government contributions for employee retirement.

SOURCE. "Monthly Treasury Statement of Receipts and Outlays of the U.S. Government" and the *Budget of the U.S. Government, Fiscal Year 1985.*

Source: *Federal Reserve Bulletin*, Board of Governors of the Federal Reserve.

Largest Companies

The 100 Largest U.S. Industrial Corporations (ranked by sales)

Rank '83	'82	Company	Sales ($000)	Assets ($000)	Rank	Net Income ($000)	Rank	Stockholders' Equity ($000)	Rank
1	1	Exxon (New York)	88,561,134*	62,962,990	1	4,977,957	2	29,443,095	1
2	2	General Motors (Detroit)	74,581,600	45,694,500	2	3,730,200	3	20,766,600	3
3	3	Mobil (New York)	54,607,000*	35,072,000	4	1,503,000	11	13,952,000	6
4	5	Ford Motor (Dearborn, Mich.)	44,454,600	23,868,900	9	1,866,900	6	7,545,300	14
5	6	International Business Machines (Armonk, N.Y.)	40,180,000	37,243,000	3	5,485,000	1	23,219,000	2
6	4	Texaco (Harrison, N.Y.)	40,068,000	27,199,000	5	1,233,000	12	14,726,000	4
7	8	E. I. du Pont de Nemours (Wilmington, Del.)	35,378,000	24,432,000	7	1,127,000	13	11,472,000	8
8	10	Standard Oil (Indiana) (Chicago)	27,635,000*	25,805,000	6	1,868,000	5	12,440,000	7
9	7	Standard Oil of California (San Francisco)	27,342,000	24,010,000	8	1,590,000	8	14,106,000	5
10	11	General Electric (Fairfield, Conn.)	26,797,000	23,288,000	10	2,024,000	4	11,270,000	10
11	9	Gulf Oil Pittsburgh)	26,581,000*	20,964,000	13	978,000	14	10,128,000	12
12	12	Atlantic Richfield (Los Angeles)	25,147,036	23,282,307	11	1,547,875	9	10,888,138	11
13	13	Shell Oil (Houston)	19,678,000	22,169,000	12	1,633,000	7	11,359,000	9
14	15	Occidental Petroleum (Los Angeles)	19,115,700	11,775,400	21	566,700**	25	2,640,900	50
15	14	U.S. Steel (Pittsburgh)	16,869,000	19,314,000	14	(1,161,000)	489	5,355,000	20
16	17	Phillips Petroleum (Bartlesville, Okla.)	15,249,000	13,094,000	18	721,000	18	6,149,000	16
17	18	Sun (Radnor, Pa.)	14,730,000	12,466,000	19	453,000	34	5,236,000	21
18	20	United Technologies (Hartford)	14,669,265	8,720,059	32	509,173	28	3,783,755	31
19	19	Tenneco (Houston)	14,353,000	17,994,000	15	716,000	19	5,822,000	18
20	16	ITT (New York)[1]	14,155,408	13,966,744	17	674,510	21	6,106,084	17
21	29	Chrysler (Highland Park, Mich.)	13,240,399	6,772,300	38	700,900**	20	1,143,058	126
22	23	Procter & Gamble (Cincinnati)[2]	12,452,000	8,135,000	34	866,000	17	4,601,000	27
23	25	R. J. Reynolds Industries (Winston-Salem, N.C.)[3]	11,957,000¶*	9,874,000	26	881,000	16	5,223,000	22
24	24	Getty Oil (Los Angeles)	11,600,024	10,385,050	23	494,314	29	5,402,707	19
25	21	Standard Oil (Ohio) (Cleveland)	11,599,000	16,362,000	16	1,512,000	10	8,094,000	13
26	22	AT&T Technologies (New York)[4]	11,154,700	9,087,500	30	50,700	229	4,621,300	26
27	34	Boeing (Seattle)	11,129,000	7,471,000	36	355,000	44	3,038,000	40
28	27	Dow Chemical (Midland, Mich.)	10,951,000	11,981,000	20	334,000**	47	5,047,000	24
29	49	Allied (Morris Township, N.J.)[5]	10,351,000	7,647,000	35	98,000	145	2,747,000	46
30	26	Eastman Kodak (Rochester, N.Y.)	10,170,000	10,928,000	22	565,000	26	7,520,000	15
31	28	Unocal (Los Angeles)[6]	10,065,600	9,228,000	29	625,900	24	5,180,100	23
32	37	Goodyear Tire & Rubber (Akron, Ohio)	9,735,800	5,985,500	44	305,500**	49	3,016,200	42
33	30	Dart & Kraft (Northbrook, Ill.)	9,714,000	5,418,100	49	435,100	38	2,922,700	43
34	31	Westinghouse Electric (Pittsburgh)	9,532,600	8,569,000	33	449,000	36	3,410,300	35
35	32	Philip Morris (New York)	9,465,600*	9,667,000	27	903,500	15	4,033,700	30
36	35	Beatrice Foods (Chicago)[8]	9,188,200	4,731,700	58	43,200	252	2,214,800	60
37	33	Union Carbide (Danbury, Conn.)	9,001,100	10,295,300	24	79,200‡	168	4,928,800	25
38	38	Xerox (Stamford, Conn.)	8,463,500	9,296,900	28	466,400	32	4,222,400	28

Employees		Net Income as Percent of				Earnings per Share			Growth Rate 1973–83		Total Return to Investors				Indus-try Code
		Sales		Stockholders' Equity							1983		1973–83 Average		
Number	Rank	%	Rank	%	Rank	'83/$	'82/$	'73/$	%	Rank	%	Rank	%	Rank	
156,000†	9	5.6	135	7.8§	324	5.78	4.82	2.72	7.81	195	36.05	185	12.39	285	29
691,000†	1	5.0	171	18.0	75	11.84	3.09	8.34	3.57	266	23.73	274	12.75	275	40
178,100	7	2.8	330	10.8	241	3.70	3.31	2.08	5.90	231	22.39	288	15.17	221	29
380,077†	2	4.2	219	24.7	16	10.29	(3.64)	4.87	7.77	199	65.43	70	14.22	237	40
369,545	3	13.7	9	23.6	23	9.04	7.39	2.70	12.85	98	30.61	227	11.30	306	44
54,683	62	3.1	302	8.4	307	4.80	4.92	4.75	0.10	325	24.90	267	10.21	322	29
159,231	8	3.2	290	9.8	269	4.70	3.75	4.01	1.59	302	51.92	110	5.39	390	28
56,734	55	6.8	90	15.0	128	6.39	6.25	1.83	13.30	90	34.72	196	11.90	295	29
40,091	92	5.8	123	11.3	229	4.65	4.03	2.48	6.47	220	15.70	329	13.53	253	29
340,000†	4	7.6	70	18.0	76	4.45	4.00	1.60	10.74	127	27.38	245	10.91	314	36
42,700	83	3.7	253	9.7	274	5.83	4.98	4.06	3.68	262	54.54	102	13.97	243	29
49,693	70	6.2	114	14.2	154	6.03	6.61	1.19	17.62	43	8.69	374	8.70	348	29
35,185	113	8.3	52	14.4	151	5.28	5.19	1.23	15.64	61	13.11	346	13.79	247	29
41,369	87	3.0	310	7.8§	325	2.03**	0.69	1.05	6.81	216	38.61	172	19.00	153	10
98,722†	19	—		—		(12.07)	(3.99)	4.01	—		49.40	121	8.32	358	29
28,400	143	4.7	190	11.7	215	4.71	4.23	1.52	11.94	110	12.49	350	4.10	408	29
37,804	104	3.1	303	8.7	298	3.84	4.49	2.25	5.48	238	46.77	130	10.80	316	29
193,700	6	3.5	263	13.5	177	7.94	8.74	2.46	12.43	101	32.54	213	25.26	73	41
97,000	20	5.0	175	11.2§	230	4.75	5.74	2.86	5.20	245	35.10	192	12.97	269	29
278,000	5	4.8	187	11.1	234	4.50	4.75	4.22	0.64	317	52.03	108	13.24	264	36
81,478†	29	5.3	153	51.1§	1	5.79**	1.84	4.80	1.89	294	55.63	97	10.00	328	40
61,700	50	7.0	87	18.8	57	5.22	4.69	1.84	10.99	122	0.25	410	5.75	384	43
96,228	21	7.4	75	15.7§	115	7.25	7.82	2.94	9.43	157	25.10	265	17.45	179	21
19,440	192	4.3	212	9.1§	286	6.24	8.61	1.88	12.72	100	107.68	13	12.02	292	29
44,000	77	13.0	12	18.7	61	6.14	7.63	0.61**	26.03	12	32.91	208	12.22	288	29
142,000†	11	0.5	419	1.1	415	N.A.	N.A.	N.A.	—		—		—		36
84,600†	28	3.2	287	11.7	218	3.67	3.02	0.53	21.27	29	33.28	205	36.92	14	41
54,500	64	3.1	306	6.6	361	1.71**	2.07**	1.49	1.35	308	35.94	186	5.90	383	28
117,750	15	1.0	402	1.2§	414	0.13	6.22	3.45	(27.95)	387	79.61	30	6.53	378	37
125,500	14	5.6	136	7.5	333	3.41	7.12	4.05	(1.71)	342	(7.35)	439	(0.38)	438	38
20,304	187	6.2	109	12.1	208	3.60	4.63	1.38	10.10	140	22.54	286	13.50	254	29
128,760†	13	3.1	295	10.1	260	3.06**	3.59	2.53	1.92	293	(9.21)	443	14.22	236	30
77,139†	37	4.5	200	14.9	136	7.92	6.40	3.70[7]	7.91	190	2.87	399	11.79	297	20
132,927†	12	4.7	191	13.2	185	5.08	5.16	1.82	10.81	125	45.47	136	14.27	234	36
68,000	47	9.6	39	22.4	29	7.17	6.23	1.35	18.13	42	24.21	271	12.72	277	21
78,000†	34	0.5	418	2.0	407	0.27	3.80**	1.36	(14.93)	378	42.34	153	9.29	338	20
99,506	18	0.9	404	1.6	410	1.13‡	4.47	4.78	(13.43)	376	25.11	264	12.61	279	28
104,007	16	5.5	138	9.9§	267	4.42	5.00	3.80	1.52	303	40.47	165	(4.88)	453	38

The 100 Largest Industrials *(continued)*

Rank '83	'82	Company	Sales ($000)	Assets ($000)	Rank	Net Income ($000)	Rank	Stockholders' Equity ($000)	Rank
39	40	Amerada Hess (New York)	8,368,946	6,217,098	42	205,347	72	2,525,663	52
40	53	Union Pacific (New York)	8,352,585	10,218,416	25	296,886	53	4,056,481	29
41	39	General Foods (White Plains, N.Y.)[9]	8,256,433	4,309,598	70	288,525	54	1,872,120	75
42	43	McDonnell Douglas (St. Louis)	8,111,000	4,791,800	57	274,900	59	2,067,900	65
43	42	Rockwell International (Pittsburgh)[10]	8,097,900	5,231,100	52	389,100	43	2,367,300	56
44	41	PepsiCo (Purchase, N.Y.)	7,895,936	4,638,340	61	284,111	57	1,794,158	79
45	36	Ashland Oil (Russell, Ky.)[10]	7,852,299	4,107,839	74	102,833	137	1,084,824	140
46	46	General Dynamics (St. Louis)	7,146,300	2,836,200	112	286,600	56	1,260,600	109
47	44	Minnesota Mining & Manufacturing (St. Paul)	7,039,000	5,760,000	47	667,000	22	3,698,000	32
48	48	Coca-Cola (Atlanta)	6,990,992	5,227,822	53	558,787	27	2,920,756	44
49	51	Consolidated Foods (Chicago)[2]	6,572,298	2,616,340	127	171,255	91	935,016	164
50	56	Lockheed (Burbank, Calif.)	6,490,300	2,829,600	114	262,800	60	826,200	183
51	62	Georgia-Pacific (Atlanta)	6,469,000	4,979,000	56	105,000	135	2,013,000	69
52	47	Monsanto (St. Louis)	6,299,000	6,427,000	39	402,000	41	3,667,000	33
53	50	W. R. Grace (New York)	6,219,500	5,034,600	55	159,715	102	2,182,300	61
54	69	Signal Companies (La Jolla, Calif.)[11]	6,151,000	5,203,000	54	103,000	136	2,633,000	51
55	77	Anheuser-Busch (St. Louis)	6,034,200*	4,330,200	69	348,000	45	1,766,500	81
56	52	Nabisco Brands (Parsippany, N.J.)	5,985,200	3,625,500	84	322,600	48	1,710,800	83
57	55	Johnson & Johnson (New Brunswick, N.J.)	5,972,900	4,461,500	64	489,000	31	3,026,500	41
58	54	Coastal (Houston)	5,963,074	3,338,392	93	93,695	149	572,007	229
59	58	Raytheon (Lexington, Mass.)	5,937,264	3,728,700	81	300,147	52	1,887,441	74
60	59	Honeywell (Minneapolis)	5,753,100	4,675,400	60	231,200	69	2,313,700	57
61	88	Charter (Jacksonville, Fla.)	5,565,643	1,813,199	175	53,895	218	614,127	217
62	63	General Mills (Minneapolis)[12]	5,550,800	2,943,900	103	245,100	63	1,227,400	115
63	66	TRW (Cleveland)	5,492,998	3,321,383	94	205,160	73	1,615,979	86
64	45	Caterpillar Tractor (Peoria, Ill.)	5,424,000	6,968,000	37	(345,000)	482	3,337,000	36
65	74	Aluminum Co. of America (Pittsburgh)	5,263,400	6,266,800	41	174,200	89	3,227,500	38
66	57	Sperry (New York)[9]	5,076,000	5,330,300	50	118,100	119	2,398,900	55
67	60	Gulf & Western Industries (New York)[13]	5,072,459¶	4,418,176	67	(212,053)	480	1,893,924	73
68	67	Continental Group (Stamford, Conn.)	4,942,000	3,653,000	83	199,000	77	1,532,000	88
69	64	Bethlehem Steel (Bethlehem, Pa.)	4,898,200	4,457,400	65	(163,500)**	477	1,313,100	103
70	82	Weyerhaeuser (Tacoma, Wash.)	4,882,629	5,945,634	45	204,843	75	3,223,347	39
71	71	Ralston Purina (St. Louis)[0]	4,872,400	2,101,200	155	256,000	61	1,104,100	138
72	70	Colgate-Palmolive (New York)	4,864,798	2,663,965	123	197,834	78	1,341,668	101
73	76	American Home Products (New York)	4,856,501	3,086,029	100	627,233	23	2,048,889	67
74	68	Litton Industries (Beverly Hills, Calif.)[13]	4,719,206	3,999,403	76	231,560	68	1,829,661	77
75	81	Hewlett-Packard (Palo Alto, Calif.)[14]	4,710,000	4,161,000	73	432,000	39	2,887,000	45
76	80	Control Data (Minneapolis)	4,582,800	8,777,600	31	161,700	100	1,825,500	78
77	79	Texas Instruments (Dallas)	4,579,800	2,713,300	122	(145,400)	473	1,202,700	119
78	65	LTV (Dallas)	4,577,800	4,406,300	68	(180,700)‡	479	1,142,000	127
79	90	American Brands (New York)	4,436,452*	4,303,874	71	390,298	42	2,085,147	64
80	91	International Paper (New York)	4,357,100	5,617,100	48	254,900	62	3,321,200	37
81	98	Motorola (Schaumburg, Ill.)	4,328,000	3,236,000	97	244,000	64	1,948,000	71
82	85	Burroughs (Detroit)	4,296,500	4,098,200	75	196,900	79	2,231,900	59
83	102	Archer-Daniels-Midland (Decatur, Ill.)[2]	4,291,957	2,549,910	131	110,185	130	1,449,963	95

Employees Number	Rank	Net Income as Percent of — Sales %	Rank	Stockholders' Equity %	Rank	Earnings per Share '83/$	'82/$	'73/$	Growth Rate 1973–83 %	Rank	Total Return to Investors 1983 %	Rank	1973–83 Average %	Rank	Industry Code
8,082†	355	2.5	347	8.1	316	2.43	2.00	4.41	(5.80)	359	20.40	304	8.74	347	29
46,897†	72	3.6	257	6.6§	363	2.40	3.38	1.40	5.52	237	11.81	352	11.73	299	29
60,000	53	3.5	261	15.4	121	5.73	4.05	2.21	10.00	142	35.71	188	14.32	232	20
74,466	40	3.4	270	13.3	180	6.91	5.44	3.26	7.80	196	44.35	141	18.00	168	41
102,707	17	4.8	186	16.4	100	2.52	2.16	1.06	9.02	163	59.32	88	24.83	77	41
154,000	10	3.6	256	15.8	112	3.01	2.40	1.12	10.39	137	11.52	353	8.95	343	49
28,976	138	1.3	394	6.3§	368	2.46	5.29	2.25	0.91	312	5.17	390	12.54	281	29
92,600	24	4.0	231	22.7	27	5.30	2.41	0.79	21.00	33	78.95	33	32.01	27	41
85,702	27	9.5	40	18.0	72	5.67	5.37	2.62	8.03	188	14.40	336	4.35	404	38
40,000	94	8.0	62	19.1	53	4.10	3.95	1.80	8.58	174	8.04	375	2.93	418	49
93,300	23	2.6	339	18.3	68	5.75	5.39	2.51	8.64	172	20.38	305	16.75	193	20
71,800	44	4.1	227	31.5§	4	4.18	3.65	0.49**	23.82	18	63.82	75	43.46	5	41
39,000	99	1.6	381	5.2	383	0.97	1.44‡	1.79	(5.93)	360	(3.43)	428	4.64	400	26
50,889	68	6.4	103	11.0	235	9.78	8.79	6.90	3.55	267	43.48	143	12.07	291	28
78,500	33	2.6	340	7.3	339	3.28	6.62	2.86	1.38	307	25.21	262	12.79	273	28
55,000	60	1.7	379	3.9	394	0.90	1.56	0.79	1.29	309	35.60	190	20.88	129	41
39,320	97	5.8	127	18.0§	73	6.50	5.97	1.46	16.11	51	(0.59)	412	9.78	332	49
69,700	45	5.4	147	18.9	56	4.86	4.83	1.32	13.90	82	17.61	314	15.19	220	20
77,400	36	8.2	55	16.2	107	2.57	2.52	0.86	11.53	112	(15.47)	452	2.75	420	42
5,484	420	1.6	385	15.3§	123	4.02	2.65	1.76	8.61	173	72.74	46	17.93	170	29
76,100	39	5.1	167	15.9	111	3.55	3.78	0.77	16.51	47	(0.50)	411	21.78	113	36
93,514	22	4.0	230	10.0	265	5.03	6.08	2.73	6.30	224	56.49	93	10.35	320	44
4,800	438	1.0	401	8.8	297	2.01	1.04	0.92	8.11	184	11.36	355	17.86	175	29
81,186	30	4.4	205	20.0	47	4.89	4.46	1.40	13.32	88	11.16	356	10.33	321	20
88,374	26	3.7	249	12.7	192	5.53	5.49	2.95	6.49	218	21.66	294	21.42	119	40
58,402†	54	—		—		(3.74)	(2.04)	2.88	—		21.50	296	4.18	407	45
39,100†	98	3.3	276	5.4	379	2.15	0.11**	1.54	3.36	269	48.63	124	10.92	313	33
77,493	35	2.3	350	4.9	387	2.65	5.25	2.62	0.11	324	45.86	134	3.89	410	44
79,150	32	—		—		(2.86)	2.17	1.34	—		84.55	26	20.39	140	23
39,700	95	4.0	228	11.5§	223	3.66	3.20	2.17	5.38	242	66.47	66	17.63	177	34
52,800†	66	—		—		(3.92)**	(33.64)	4.72	—		51.17	114	4.80	397	33
40,018	93	4.2	220	6.3§	367	1.36	1.12	2.74	(6.77)	364	(2.64)	426	1.71	426	26
56,200	58	5.3	155	23.2	25	2.58	0.66	0.74	13.30	91	63.37	79	11.27	307	20
43,000†	80	4.1	225	14.8	144	2.42	2.41	1.31	6.33	223	15.97	327	3.66	412	43
54,680	63	12.9	13	30.6	6	4.00)	3.59	1.25	12.33	103	16.26	323	6.58	377	42
69,200	46	4.9	181	12.7	193	5.52	7.54	0.82	21.01	32	47.11	129	30.51	32	36
72,000	43	9.2	43	15.0	133	1.69	1.52	0.24	21.75	24	16.53	321	15.91	214	44
55,858	59	3.5	258	8.9	291	4.20	4.11	1.86	8.46	178	23.47	278	11.13	309	44
80,696	31	—		—		(6.09)	6.10	3.67	—		4.46	392	4.29	405	36
37,300	105	—		—		(3.64)‡	(3.20)	5.16**	—		63.74	77	7.28	371	33
74,000	41	8.8	46	18.1§	71	6.76	6.55	2.45	10.68	131	36.89	181	22.15	109	21
33,600	121	5.9	121	6.9§	354	4.61	2.94	3.60	2.50	281	26.93	250	6.14	380	26
88,800	25	5.6	134	12.5	195	6.26	4.87	2.95	7.81	194	58.45	90	12.86	272	36
63,800	48	4.6	198	8.8	295	4.60	2.80	3.00	4.35	253	26.89	251	(4.14)	451	44
8,670	337	2.6	341	7.6	331	1.34	1.93	0.30	16.11	50	(1.67)	423	15.44	217	20

The 100 Largest Industrials *(concluded)*

Rank			Sales	Assets		Net Income		Stockholders' Equity	
'83	'82	Company	($000)	($000)	Rank	($000)	Rank	($000)	Rank
84	95	Digital Equipment (Maynard, Mass.)[2]	4,271,854	4,541,085	62	283,622	58	3,541,282	34
85	84	Borden (New York)	4,264,771	2,720,471	121	189,069	84	1,391,039	100
86	101	Champion International (Stamford, Conn.)	4,263,999	3,575,743	88	82,160	164	1,782,186	80
87	61	Armco (Middletown, Ohio)	4,164,600	3,609,000	86	(672,500)	488	1,288,900	106
88	117	Esmark (Chicago)[14]	4,037,386	3,661,673	82	117,348	120	1,031,001	146
89	121	Diamond Shamrock (Dallas)[15]	4,026,107	6,024,441	43	(56,163)	456	2,743,327	47
90	87	CPC International (Englewood Cliffs, N.J.)	4,010,900	2,482,800	133	136,200	110	1,306,000	104
91	106	Time Inc. (New York)	3,990,435¶	2,273,316	142	168,934	92	881,445	174
92	75	Deere (Moline, Ill.)[14]	3,967,934	5,880,012	46	23,285	341	2,275,967	58
93	104	Bristol-Myers (New York)	3,971,005	3,007,265	102	407,961	40	1,907,909	72
94	108	Martin Marietta (Bethesda, Md.)	3,899,2580	2,737,651	118	141,331	106	845,356	181
95	96	Firestone Tire & Rubber (Akron, Ohio)[14]	3,866,000	2,729,000	119	111,000	128	1,291,000	105
96	94	IC Industries (Chicago)	3,864,100	3,985,100	77	92,700	152	1,225,100	116
97	122	North American Philips (New York)	3,799,825	2,252,493	144	95,712	146	883,874	173
98	97	Agway (DeWitt, N.Y.)[2]	3,768,212	1,416,547	209	N.A.[16]		290,931	340
99	114	Pfizer (New York)	3,750,000	3,936,100	78	447,100	37	2,180,800	62
100	103	H. J. Heinz (Pittsburgh)[17]	3,738,445	2,178,693	150	214,250	71	1,138,707	128

The Definitions and concepts underlying the figures in this directory are explained on page 215.
¶ Includes sales from discontinued operations of at least 10%; see the explanation of "sales" on page 215.
N.A. Not available.
* Does not include excise taxes; see the explanation of "sales" on page 215.
** Reflects an extraordinary credit of at least 10%; see the explanations of "net income" and "earnings per share" on pages 215, 216.
† Average for the year; see the reference to "employees" on page 215.
‡ Reflects an extraordinary charge of at least 10%; see the explanations of "net income" and "earnings per share" on pages 215, 216.
§ Dividends paid by company on its mandatory redeemable preferred stock were subtracted from net income in calculating this figure.
[1] Name changed from International Telephone & Telegraph December 31, 1983.
[2] Figures are for fiscal year ended June 30, 1983.
[3] Figures include Heublein (1982 rank: 204) acquired October 12, 1982.
[4] Name changed from Western Electric January 3, 1984.
[5] Figures include Bendix (1982 rank: 86), acquired January 31, 1983.

| Employees | | Net Income as Percent of | | | | Earnings per Share | | | Growth Rate 1973–83 | | Total Return to Investors | | | | Indus- try Code |
| | | Sales | | Stockholders' Equity | | | | | | | 1983 | | 1973–83 Average | | |
Num- ber	Rank	%	Rank	%	Rank	'83/$	'82/$	'73/$	%	Rank	%	Rank	%	Rank	
73,000	42	6.6	96	8.0	320	5.00	7.53	0.72	21.38	27	(27.64)	458	7.80	361	44
32,600	122	4.4	203	13.6	172	6.56	5.81	2.37	10.72	129	23.64	275	16.73	195	20
39,681	96	1.9	367	4.6	390	1.22	0.45	2.71	(7.67)	367	23.26	280	11.41	303	26
48,071	71	—	—			(10.27)	(5.41)	2.25	—		29.92	235	10.05	325	33
60,000	51	2.9	316	11.2§	231	3.66	3.39	0.99	13.99	80	50.37	117	26.10	62	20
13,364	247	—	—			(0.71)	2.94	1.42	—		3.64	397	9.97	329	29
38,000	102	3.4	269	10.4	250	2.81	4.80	1.59	5.83	233	(2.28)	425	16.88	190	20
18,000	208	4.2	216	18.6§	62	2.65	2.45	1.14	8.75	169	22.54	285	27.54	48	27
45,728	74	0.6	412	1.0	417	0.34	0.78	2.88	(19.22)	382	33.90	201	8.61	350	45
36,500	109	10.4	28	21.4	34	3.00	2.59	0.79	14.27	76	29.11	238	17.28	184	42
42,800	82	3.6	255	16.7	92	4.23	1.95	1.13	14.08	79	27.01	248	25.64	67	41
60,000	52	2.9	321	8.6	300	2.26	0.11**	2.89	(2.43)	346	23.51	277	11.05	311	30
40,807	89	2.4	348	6.9§	356	4.73	2.03	3.42	3.30	271	43.06	148	16.00	212	20
56,500	56	2.5	344	8.1§	317	6.75	5.33	3.78	5.97	229	67.88	62	20.94	128	36
17,953	209	—	—			N.A.	N.A.	N.A.	—		—		—		29
40,700	90	11.9	16	20.5	40	2.73	2.13	0.87	12.12	107	7.18	380	8.41	357	42
43,452	79	5.7	129	18.8§	58	4.51	4.10	0.47‡	25.29	15	45.70	135	17.97	169	20

6 Name changed from Union Oil of California April 25, 1983.
7 Figure is for Kraftco.
8 Figures are for fiscal year ended February 28, 1983.
9 Figures are for fiscal year ended March 31, 1983.
10 Figures are for fiscal year ended September 30, 1983.
11 Figures include Wheelabrator-Frye (1982 rank: 227), acquired February 1, 1983.
12 Figures are for fiscal year ended May 31, 1983.
13 Figures are for fiscal year ended July 31, 1983.
14 Figures are for fiscal year ended October 31, 1983.
15 Figures include Natomas (1982 rank: 214), acquired August 31, 1983.
16 Cooperatives provide only "net margin" figures, which are not comparable with the net income figures in these listings.
17 Figures are for fiscal year ended April 30, 1983

Source: Reprinted from the FORTUNE Directory by permission; © 1984 Time Inc. All rights reserved.

NOTES TO THE FORTUNE DIRECTORY

Sales All companies on the list must have derived more than 50% of their sales from manufacturing and/or mining. Sales include rental and other revenues but exclude dividends, interest, and other non-operating revenues. Sales of subsidiaries are included when they are consolidated. Sales from discontinued operations are included when these figures are published. When the sales are at least 10% higher for this reason, there is a symbol (¶) next to the sales figure. All figures are for the year ending December 31, 1983, unless otherwise noted. Sales figures do not include excise taxes collected by the manufacturer, and so the figures for some corporations—most of which sell gasoline, liquor, or tobacco—may be lower than those published by the corporations themselves. When they are at least 5% lower for this reason, there is an asterisk (*) next to the sales figures.

Assets are those shown at the company's year-end.

Net Income is shown after taxes and after extraordinary credits or charges when any are shown on the income statement. A double asterisk (**) signifies an extraordinary credit reflecting at least 10 percent of the net income shown, a double dagger (‡) an extraordinary charge of at least 10 percent. Figures in parentheses indicate a loss.

Stockholders' Equity is the sum of capital stock, surplus, and retained earnings at the company's year-end. Redeemable preferred stock is excluded when its redemption is either mandatory or outside the control of the company, except in the case of cooperatives. For purposes of calculating "net income as percent of stockholders' equity," any dividends paid on redeemable preferred stock, if that stock's redemption is either mandatory or outside the control of the company, have been subtracted from the net income figure.

Employees The figure shown is a year-end total except when it is followed by a dagger (†), in which case it is an average for the year.

Earnings per Share For all companies, the figures shown are the "primary" earnings per share that appear on the company's income statement. These figures are based on a weighted average of the number of common shares and common-stock equivalents outstanding during the year. "Common-stock equivalents" generally include (a) convertible securities whose cash yield is less than two-thirds of the prime rate at the time the securities were issued and (b) options and warrants when the effect of their inclusion in the computation would reduce the "primary" earnings per share. Per-share earnings for 1982 and 1983 are adjusted for stock splits and stock dividends. They are not restated for mergers, acquisitions, or accounting changes made after 1973. A double asterisk (**) signifies an extraordinary credit reflecting at least 10 percent of the net income shown, a double dagger (‡) an extraordinary charge of at least 10 percent. Results are listed as not available (N.A.) where the companies are cooperatives, joint ventures, or wholly owned subsidiaries of other companies, or if the figures were not published in 1973. The growth rate is the average annual growth, compounded. No growth rate is given if the company had a loss in either 1973 or 1983.

Total Return to Investors includes both price appreciation and dividend yield, to an investor in the company's stock. The figures shown assume sales at the end of 1983 of stock owned at the end of 1973 or 1982. It has been assumed that any proceeds from cash dividends, the sale of rights and warrant offerings, and stock received in spin-offs were reinvested at the end of the year in which they were received. Returns are adjusted for stock splits, stock dividends, recapitalizations, and corporate reorganizations as they occur; however, no effort has been made to reflect the cost of brokerage commissions or of taxes. Results are listed as not available (N.A.) where shares are not publicly traded or traded on only a limited basis. If companies have more than one class of shares outstanding, only the more widely held and actively traded has been considered.

Total-return percentages shown are the returns received by the hypothetical investor described above. The ten-year figures are annual averages, compounded. If corporations were substantially reorganized—e.g., because of mergers—the predecessor companies used in calculating total return are the same as those cited in the footnotes to the earnings-per-share figures.

Industry Code numbers used in the directory indicate which industry represents the greatest volume of industrial sales for each company. The numbers refer to the industry groups below, which are based on categories established by the U.S. Office of Management and Budget and issued by the Federal Statistical Policy and Standards Office. The median figures in the tables refer only to results of companies among the 500; no attempt has been made to calculate medians in groups with fewer than four companies.

Code No.	Industry
10	Mining, crude-oil production
20	Food
21	Tobacco
22	Textiles, vinyl flooring
23	Apparel
25	Furniture
26	Paper, fiber, and wood products
27	Publishing, printing
28	Chemicals
29	Petroleum refining
30	Rubber, plastic products
31	Leather
32	Glass, concrete, abrasives, gypsum
33	Metal manufacturing
34	Metal products
36	Electronics, appliances
37	Shipbuilding, railroad and transportation equipment
38	Measuring, scientific, photographic equipment
40	Motor vehicles
41	Aerospace
42	Pharmaceuticals
43	Soaps, cosmetics
44	Office equipment (includes computers)
45	Industrial and farm equipment
46	Jewelry, silverware
47	Musical instruments, toys, sporting goods
49	Beverages

INDUSTRIAL PRODUCTION AND CONSUMER PRICES—MAJOR INDUSTRIAL COUNTRIES

[1967=100]

Period	Industrial production (seasonally adjusted)							Consumer prices (unadjusted)						
	United States	Canada	Japan	France	Germany	Italy	United Kingdom	United States [1]	Canada	Japan	France	Germany	Italy	United Kingdom
1977	138.2	152.7	189.7	152	152.0	145.1	124.2	181.5	185.9	243.0	214.5	155.9	255.2	292.4
1978	146.1	157.8	201.1	155	154.1	147.9	127.8	195.4	202.5	252.3	233.9	160.2	286.2	316.6
1979	152.5	167.6	215.3	163	161.5	157.6	132.9	217.4	221.0	261.3	259.1	166.8	328.5	359.0
1980	147.0	165.1	225.2	161	162.0	166.5	124.1	246.8	243.5	282.3	294.2	175.9	398.0	423.6
1981	151.0	166.6	227.5	160	159.1	162.7	119.5	272.4	273.9	296.2	332.7	186.3	472.4	473.9
1982	138.6	148.8	228.4	158	154.5	159.1	121.6	289.1	303.5	304.1	373.1	196.2	549.4	514.7
1983 ᵖ	147.6	157.6	236.5	159	155.5	150.7	125.1	298.4	321.0	309.7	407.9	202.1	631.8	538.3
1983: May	144.4	153.5	231.1	160	153.7	148.5	124.2	297.1	317.9	312.0	404.5	201.1	628.2	536.4
June	146.4	157.1	233.3	157	159.2	145.1	122.3	298.1	321.5	309.7	406.9	201.8	632.2	537.7
July	149.7	157.8	234.0	160	154.5	146.9	125.7	299.3	322.9	308.3	410.4	202.6	638.5	540.6
Aug	151.8	160.8	241.2	160	155.2	134.9	125.2	300.3	324.5	307.4	412.8	203.2	641.1	543.0
Sept	153.8	163.8	244.8	157	157.1	151.1	126.4	301.8	324.5	311.4	416.0	203.6	649.4	545.4
Oct	155.0	164.4	241.4	155	157.5	148.6	126.8	302.6	326.5	314.2	419.2	203.6	660.4	547.3
Nov	155.3	165.9	246.4	161	160.2	152.8	127.2	303.1	326.5	312.2	420.9	204.1	667.0	549.2
Dec	156.2	ʳ167.1	248.2	160	161.0	146.0	129.0	303.5	327.5	311.4	422.4	204.5	670.3	550.7
1984: Jan	158.5	ʳ171.0	250.2	161	161.0	129.7	305.2	329.2	312.3	425.4	205.6	678.3	550.4
Feb	ʳ160.0	165.2	257.0	159	164.4		ʳ127.4	306.6	331.1	314.2	428.0	206.2	685.8	552.6
Mar	ʳ160.8	165.5	ʳ254.1	162	ʳ158.9		125.7	307.3	331.9	ʳ315.1	431.0	206.3	690.6	554.4
Apr ᵖ	ʳ162.5		257.9	157	159.6			308.8	332.7	315.9	433.6	206.8	695.4	561.8
May ᵖ	163.2							309.7	333.3				699.6	563.9

[1] Beginning January 1978 data relate to all urban consumers.

Source: Economic Indicators, Council of Economic Advisers.

Source: National sources as reported by Department of Commerce, International Trade Administration, Office of Trade Information and Analysis, Trade Performance Division, in International Economic Indicators.

The 100 Largest International Industrial Corporations (ranked by sales)

Rank '83	'82	Company	Country	Industry	Sales[1] ($000)	Assets[2] ($000)	Net Income[3] ($000)	Stock-Holders' Equity[4] ($000)	Employees
1	1	Royal Dutch/Shell Group	Neth./Britain	Petroleum	80,550,885	70,809,976	4,174,736	28,400,049	156,000
2	2	British Petroleum	Britain	Petroleum	49,194,886	39,443,061	1,562,873	13,989,557	131,600
3	3	ENI[5]	Italy	Petroleum	25,022,358[6]	19,263,164[6]	(928,925)[6]	2,776,268[6]	133,999[6]
4	4	IRI[5]	Italy	Metal mfg.—steel; shipbldg.; elec.; aerospace	24,518,447	N.A.	N.A.	N.A.	515,900
5	5	Unilever	Britain/Neth.	Food products; soaps, cosmetics	20,291,583	11,217,192	583,614	4,425,623	267,000
6	16	Toyota Motor[7]	Japan	Motor vehicles	19,741,094	13,454,451	918,421	7,897,789	57,800
7	6	Française des Pétroles	France	Petroleum	18,350,186[6]	11,008,398[6]	101,548[6]	2,771,446[6]	46,824[6]
8	8	Elf-Aquitaine[5]	France	Petroleum	18,021,116[6]	18,021,116[6]	488,451[6]	4,089,622[6]	77,600[6]
9	20	Matsushita Electric Industrial[8]	Japan	Electronics, appliances	16,719,440	14,624,255	766,060	6,789,888	124,825
10	7	Petrobrás (Petróleo Brasileiro)[5]	Brazil	Petroleum	16,258,011	14,038,029	485,888	4,265	56,835
11	13	Philips' Gloeilampenfabrieken	Netherlands	Electronics, appliances	16,176,941	15,596,995	226,631	4,999,020	343,000
12	21	Pemex (Petróleos Mexicanos)[5]	Mexico	Petroleum	16,140,013[*,9]	32,598,710[*,9]	(5,238)[*,9]	13,966,462[*,9]	157,000[*,9]
13	12	Hitachi[10]	Japan	Electronics, appliances; office equipment	15,804,301	17,402,603	603,287	542,460	155,582
14	9	Siemens[11]	Germany	Electronics; computers	15,724,273	15,368,048	296,074	3,860,570	313,000
15	10	Nissan Motor[10]	Japan	Motor vehicles	15,697,733	13,440,318	416,337	4,783,485	108,102
16	18	Volkswagenwerk	Germany	Motor vehicles	15,693,352	10,590,384	(51,083)	2,295,548	231,710
17	14	Daimler-Benz	Germany	Motor vehicles and parts	15,660,437	9,110,732	404,580	2,688,446	184,877
18	24	Bayer	Germany	Chemicals	14,615,594[6]	10,966,403[6]	295,899[6]	2,659,316[6]	174,760[6]
19	23	Hoechst	Germany	Chemicals	14,558,235[6]	9,734,862[6]	128,987[6]	2,280,991[6]	179,849[6]
20	15	Renault[5]	France	Motor vehicles and parts	14,467,765[6]	10,816,437[6]	(206,769)[6]	1,339,412[6]	210,000[6]
21	19	Fiat	Italy	Motor vehicles and parts	14,466,548	N.A.	N.A.	N.A.	243,808
22	25	Nestlé	Switzerland	Food products; beverages	13,303,618[6]	9,402,937[6]	600,360[6]	4,935,291[6]	140,400[6]
23	27	BASF	Germany	Chemicals	13,250,424[6]	8,026,053[6]	202,464[6]	2,889,658[6]	114,128[6]
24	32	Volvo	Sweden	Motor vehicles and parts; energy	12,963,008	6,679,900	26,588	696,629	76,206
25	29	Imperial Chemical Industries	Britain	Chemicals	12,750,075	11,061,881	573,003	4,850,913	117,900
26	17	BAT Industries	Britain	Tobacco	12,083,087	10,021,156	475,987	4,961,227	187,173
27	26	Mitsubishi Heavy Industries[10]	Japan	Motor vehicles; industrial equipment	11,916,259	17,390,937	98,396	1,402,573	96,562
28	22	Nippon Steel[10]	Japan	Metal manufacturing—steel	11,605,901	15,873,126	142,467	2,715,410	74,153
29	28	Thyssen[11]	Germany	Metal mfg.—steel; industrial equipment	11,301,248	6,773,527	(221,491)	863,329	137,537
30	33	Peugeot	France	Motor vehicles and parts	11,244,484[6]	7,635,393[6]	(339,804)[6]	685,303[6]	203,000[6]
31	45	General Motors of Canada	Canada	Motor vehicles and parts	11,200,522[12]	2,432,815	548,098	1,188,705	43,410
32	30	Idemitsu Kosan[10]	Japan	Petroleum	10,770,203[9]	6,944,080[9]	137,253[9]	133,291[9]	7,041[9]
33	31	Kuwait Petroleum[5,7]	Kuwait	Petroleum	10,744,273	13,799,974	1,055,827	9,028,429	14,240
34	36	Canadian Pacific	Canada	Metal manufacturing—steel; mining	10,351,766	14,143,792	116,498	3,256,385	121,127
35	34	Toshiba[10]	Japan	Electronics, appliances	9,482,937	9,794,498	154,041	1,767,565	103,000
36	39	Esso UK[13]	Britain	Petroleum	9,448,316	5,793,872	635,856	405,450	6,619
37	41	Hyundai Group	South Korea	Shipbuilding; motor vehicles; industrial equip.	9,300,429	69,800,475	149,494	1,156,319	146,000
38	2	India Oil[10]	India	Petroleum	9,069,891	2,618,119	121,447	695,685	27,927

		Company	Country	Industry					
40	37	Petrofina	Belgium	Petroleum	6,11,574	275,617	5,576,152	1,211,472	2,100
41	38	National Coal Board[5,10]	Britain	Mining—coal	8,242,117	(185,498)	8,158,197	(42,992)	268,000
42	35	CGE (Cie. Générale d'Electricité)[5]	France	Electronics, appliances	8,195,173[6]	52,611[6]	10,125,987[6]	715,585[6]	148,700[6]
43	42	General Electric Co.[10]	Britain	Electronics; industrial equipment	7,730,745	649,409	6,788,071	3,361,865	178,000
44	44	Saint-Gobain[5]	France	Building materials; metal products	7,595,596[6]	53,135[6]	6,047,510[6]	1,597,001[6]	133,583[6]
45	46	Veba Oel	Germany	Petroleum; chemicals	7,570,949[6]	5,208[6]	2,440,560[6]	526,568[6]	23,225[6]
46	60	Rio Tinto-Zinc	Britain	Mining—alum., lead, zinc, copper, iron	7,292,903	170,082	11,089,170	2,975,430	73,844
47	53	Imperial Oil	Canada	Petroleum	7,236,088[12]	235,280	6,467,658	3,399,759	14,732
48	48	Ruhrkohle	Germany	Mining—coal	7,195,761	15,293	7,167,315	242,536	130,001
49	67	Samsung Group	South Korea	Electronics, appliances; food prod.; textiles	7,167,315	81,568	5,452,795	790,851	102,255
50	82	Lucky Group	South Korea	Petroleum; electronics, appliances	7,159,333	70,391	4,124,667	708,052	53,005
51	55	Ciba-Geigy	Switzerland	Chemicals; pharmaceuticals	7,018,167	369,452	9,054,612	5,539,697	79,173
52	57	Montedison	Italy	Chemicals	7,014,483[6]	(211,882)[6]	6,458,333[6]	737,923[6]	72,813[6]
53	68	Ford Motor of Canada	Canada	Motor vehicles and parts	6,961,541[12]	123,806	1,813,258	591,884	33,500
54	54	DSM[5]	Netherlands	Natural gas; chemicals	6,926,030[6]	57,328[6]	3,348,380[6]	708,105[6]	27,885[6]
55	104	YPF (Yacimientos Petrolíferos)[5]	Argentina	Petroleum	6,782,765	(4,643,995)	11,147,265	N.A.	32,773
56	52	Fried. Krupp	Germany	Metal mfg.—steel; industrial equipment	6,761,591	(117,952)	3,713,962	608,259	69,291
57	69	Barlow Rand[11]	South Africa	Food products; mining—coal, chrome, gold	6,747,692	222,370	5,123,868	1,391,198	139,261
58	47	Maruzen Oil[10]	Japan	Petroleum	6,638,171	42,852	3,964,393	(347,795)	3,586
59	90	VÖEST-Alpine[5]	Austria	Metal manufacturing	6,632,500	(2,062)	5,229,414	25,274	72,288
60	50	Thomson[5,15]	France	Electronics, appliances	6,492,743[6]	(140,776)[6]	6,635,753[6]	331,494[6]	110,000[6]
61	51	Esso	Germany	Petroleum	6,397,340[12]	117,459	1,907,043	478,349	4,216
62	•	Daewoo Industrial	South Korea	Shipbldg.; textiles; elec. appl.; indus. equip.	6,313,466	68,648	5,153,847	710,547	15,000
63	49	Nippon Kokan[10]	Japan	Metal manufacturing—steel	6,267,271	103,815	10,658,335	1,232,937	38,577
64	62	Sunkyong	South Korea	Petroleum; textiles; chemicals	6,210,191	41,050	2,362,308	374,259	19,001
65	63	Mitsubishi Electric[10]	Japan	Electronics, appliances	6,127,766	140,347	5,945,184	1,277,460	64,432
66	94	Toyo Kogyo[16]	Japan	Motor vehicles	6,050,038	113,444	3,502,786	879,547	40,000
67	64	Grand Metropolitan[11]	Britain	Beverages; food products	6,044,617	325,078	5,223,229	2,345,997	136,297
68	11	Petróleos de Venezuela[5]	Venezuela	Petroleum	6,012,156	712,041	8,292,709	7,085,769	44,475
69	91	Adam Opel	Germany	Motor vehicles and parts	5,871,961*	N.A.	N.A.	N.A.	59,379
70	80	NEC[10,12]	Japan	Electronics, appliances	5,783,079	132,372	6,909,038	1,198,975	73,080
71	77	Rhône-Poulenc[5]	France	Chemicals	5,656,879[6]	12,857[6]	4,726,095[6]	935,213[6]	81,000[6]
72	72	George Weston Holdings[10]	Britain	Food products	5,642,132	102,271	2,153,792	712,202	68,924
73	74	Robert Bosch	Germany	Motor vehicle parts; electronics, appliances	5,618,211	78,491	4,001,070	1,236,017	109,725
74	76	Nippon Mining[10]	Japan	Petroleum; metal manufacturing—nonferrous	5,612,031	19,481	4,068,402	282,439	8,415
75	65	Schlumberger	Neth. Antilles	Measuring and scientific equipment	5,513,246	1,084,299	8,353,239	5,818,860	69,000
76	56	Mannesmann	Germany	Metal products; industrial equipment	5,509,361	29,903	3,788,126	1,129,056	104,795
77	58	Sumitomo Metal Industries[10]	Japan	Metal manufacturing—steel	5,492,402	129,106	9,059,498	1,358,264	35,693
78	70	Ford Motor	Britain	Motor vehicles	5,434,433[12]	(156,136)	4,654,960	1,762,121	63,900
79	59	British Steel[5,10]	Britain	Metal manufacturing—steel	5,399,489	(1,452,230)	5,185,785	3,205,165	81,100
80	78	Michelin	France	Rubber products	5,390,093[6]	(285,757)[6]	6,677,475[6]	1,326,921[6]	120,000[6]
81	79	Chinese Petroleum[5]	Taiwan	Petroleum	5,313,672[9]	432,414[9]	4,018,348[9]	1,986,934[9]	19,521[9]
82	88	Akzo Group	Netherlands	Chemicals	5,283,786	149,954	3,532,103	968,975	66,300
83	75	Toa Nenryo Kogyo	Japan	Petroleum	5,259,645	166,030	3,435,183	929,443	3,936
84	95	Ford-Werke	Germany	Motor vehicles and parts	5,227,533[12]	58,961	2,030,776	393,688	48,029
85	85	BL[5]	Britain	Motor vehicles	5,185,374	(229,656)	3,635,717	981,649	101,346

The 100 Largest International Industrial Corporations (ranked by sales) (concluded)

Rank '83	'82	Company	Country	Industry	Sales[1] ($000)	Assets[2] ($000)	Net Income[3] ($000)	Stock-Holders' Equity[4] ($000)	Employees
86	97	Brown Boveri	Switzerland	Electrical and industrial equip., electronics	5,074,257[6]	7,480,037[*,6]	140,449[6]	436,439[6]	90,600[6]
87	87	Daikyo Oil[10]	Japan	Petroleum	5,004,090	2,220,042	41,628	49,476	1,956
88	61	Gutehoffnungshütte[7]	Germany	Industrial and transportation equipment	4,988,056	4,870,412	(34,998)	592,478	62,670
89	89	Mitsubishi Oil[10]	Japan	Petroleum	4,916,879	3,425,059	92,758	71,720	3,376
90	86	Kobe Steel[10]	Japan	Metal manufacturing—steel	4,885,412[9]	7,041,975[9]	47,369[9]	749,531[9]	32,760[9]
91	109	Sanyo Electric[18]	Japan	Electronics, appliances	4,774,860	4,426,275	142,342	1,442,396	22,776
92	114	BMW (Bayerische Motoren Werke)	Germany	Motor vehicles and parts	4,675,261	2,128,292	114,163	590,880	43,169
93	121	Texaco Canada	Canada	Petroleum	4,645,570[12]	2,642,025	279,091	1,464,042	3,904
94	99	Dalgety[7]	Britain	Food products	4,587,804	1,303,203	51,657	478,909	21,243
95	71	Kawasaki Steel[10]	Japan	Metal manufacturing—steel	4,581,474[9]	7,479,854[9]	74,896[9]	1,326,711[9]	29,268[9]
96	103	Sony[16,19]	Japan	Electronics, appliances	4,544,500	5,258,009	123,876	2,043,542	42,654
97	101	Thorn EMI[10]	Britain	Electronics, appliances	4,538,679	2,721,573	68,016	896,468	91,544
98	83	AEG-Telefunken	Germany	Electronics, appliances	4,512,314[6]	3,242,906[6]	21,880[6]	299,528[6]	76,600[6]
99	125	Degussa[11]	Germany	Metal products; chemicals	4,420,680	1,434,073	35,814	259,322	21,369
100	98	ENPETROL[5]	Spain	Petroleum; chemicals	4,399,869	2,255,673	2,775	523,930	7,683

* Not on last year's list.

N.A. Not available.

e Fortune estimate.

[1] All companies on the list must have derived more than 50% of their sales from manufacturing and/or mining. Sales do not include excise taxes or customs duties levied according to either volume or value of sales, and so the figures for some companies—most of which sell gasoline, liquor, or tobacco—may be lower than those published by the companies themselves. Unless otherwise noted, figures exclude intracompany transactions and include consolidated subsidiaries more than 50% owned, either fully or on a prorated basis. Figures have been converted to dollars using an exchange rate that consists of the average rate in the official exchange market during each company's fiscal year (ended December 31, 1983, unless otherwise noted).

[2] Total shown at each company's year-end. Figures have been converted to dollars at the market rate prevailing at each company's year-end.

[3] After taxes, minority interest, and extraordinary items. Figures have been converted to dollars at the average market rate during each company's fiscal year. Figures in parentheses are losses.

[4] Total at each company's year-end. Figures have been converted to dollars at the market rate prevailing at each company's year-end. Minority interest is not included.

[5] Government-owned.

[6] Also includes certain subsidiaries owned 50% or less, either fully or on a prorated basis.

[7] Figures are for fiscal year ended June 30, 1983.

[8] Figures are for fiscal year ended November 20, 1983.

[9] Parent only.

[10] Figures are for fiscal year ended March 31, 1983.

[11] Figures are for fiscal year ended September 30, 1983.

[12] Revenues include certain sales to foreign affiliates of the U.S. parent company.

[13] Name changed from Esso Petroleum on January 1, 1983.

[14] Figures are for fiscal year ended February 28, 1983.

[15] Name changed from Thomson-Brandt on December 20, 1983.

[16] Figures are for fiscal year ended October 31, 1983.

[17] Name changed from Nippon Electric on April 1, 1983.

[18] Figures are for fiscal year ended November 30, 1983.

[19] Includes only wholly owned subsidiaries.

Source: Reprinted from the FORTUNE Directory by permission: © 1984 Time Inc. All rights reserved.

The 25 Largest Industrial Companies in the World (ranked by sales)

Rank '83	Rank '82	Company	Headquarters	Sales ($000)	Net Income ($000)
1	1	Exxon	New York	88,561,134	4,977,957
2	2	Royal Dutch/Shell Group	The Hague/London	80,550,885	4,174,736
3	3	General Motors	Detroit	74,581,600	3,730,200
4	4	Mobil	New York	54,607,000	1,503,000
5	5	British Petroleum	London	49,194,886	1,562,873
6	7	Ford Motor	Dearborn, Mich.	44,454,600	1,866,900
7	8	International Business Machines	Armonk, N.Y.	40,180,000	5,485,000
8	6	Texaco	Harrison, N.Y.	40,068,000	1,233,000
9	10	E.I. du Pont de Nemours	Wilmington, Del.	35,378,000	1,127,000
10	12	Standard Oil (Ind.)	Chicago	27,635,000	1,868,000
11	9	Standard Oil of California	San Francisco	27,342,000	1,590,000
12	14	General Electric	Fairfield, Conn.	26,797,000	2,024,000
13	11	Gulf Oil	Pittsburgh	26,581,000	978,000
14	15	Atlantic Richfield	Los Angeles	25,147,036	1,547,875
15	13	ENI	Rome	25,022,358	(928,925)
16	16	IRI	Rome	24,518,447	N.A.
17	17	Unilever	London/Rotterdam	20,291,583	583,614
18	33	Toyota Motor	Toyota City (Japan)	19,741,094	918,421
19	18	Shell Oil	Houston	19,678,000	1,633,000
20	22	Occidental Petroleum	Los Angeles	19,115,700	566,700
21	19	Française des Pétroles	Paris	18,350,186	101,548
22	23	Elf-Aquitaine	Paris	18,188,156	488,451
23	21	U.S. Steel	Pittsburgh	16,869,000	(1,161,000)
24	39	Matsushita Electric Industrial	Osaka (Japan)	16,719,440	766,060
25	20	Petrobrás (Petróleo Brasileiro)	Rio de Janeiro	16,258,011	485,888

Source: Reprinted from the *FORTUNE Directory* by permission; © 1984 Time Inc. All rights reserved.

The 25 Largest Diversified Service Companies (ranked by sales)

Rank			Sales[1]	Assets		Net Income		Stockholders' Equity	
'83	'82	Company	($000)	($000)	Rank	($000)	Rank	($000)	Rank
1	1	Phibro-Salomon (New York)	29,757,000	42,017,000	1	470,000	2	2,240,000	2
2	2	RCA (New York)	8,977,300	7,656,100	3	240,800	4	1,981,400	3
3	5	City Investing (New York)	5,948,000	8,361,000	2	175,000	7	1,556,000	6
4	4	Halliburton (Dallas)	5,522,178	5,833,794	4	275,815	2	3,571,527	1
5	3	Fluor (Irvine, Calif.)[2]	5,300,452	4,084,920	5	27,700	52	1,747,249	4
6	7	Super Valu Stores (Eden Prairie, Minn.)[3]	5,197,081	857,671	48	68,031	24	327,924	46
7	10	Fleming Companies (Oklahoma City)	4,898,175	678,675	54	41,710	43	262,506	50
8	6	Farmland Industries (Kansas City, Mo.)[5]	4,688,893	1,709,080	19	N.A.[4]		502,622	25
9	8	McKesson (San Francisco)[6,7]	4,570,030	1,372,812	23	56,493	29	510,092	24
10	9	CBS (New York)	4,458,359	2,989,842	7	187,198	6	1,440,461	7
11	•	Greyhound (Phoenix)[8]	4,061,153	1,964,963	15	105,499**	16	1,101,409	12
12	11	American Hospital Supply (Evanston, Ill.)	3,310,500	2,280,000	11	211,900	5	1,396,800	9
13	12	Hospital Corp. of America (Nashville)	3,202,988	4,083,373	6	243,218	3	1,570,908	5
14	14	American Broadcasting (New York)	2,940,137	2,090,538	14	159,834	10	1,214,011	10
15	17	Tesoro Petroleum (San Antonio)[9]	2,813,755	1,003,713	38	48,397	36	435,298	33
16	13	Alco Standard (Valley Forge, Pa.)[9]	2,785,938	1,059,544	35	56,853	28	408,952	36
17	15	Associated Milk Producers (San Antonio)	2,699,730	382,649	72	N.A.[4]		111,356	81
18	24	Malone & Hyde (Memphis)[10]	2,601,335	467,951	66	34,014	51	187,148	63
19	21	Harvest States (St. Paul)[11,12]	2,355,443	528,982	58	N.A.[4]		169,764	66
20	25	Ryder System (Miami)	2,341,978	2,256,633	12	101,094	19	646,910	16
21	28	Wetterau (Hazelwood, Mo.)[6]	2,276,622	407,027	68	15,415	65	146,684	69
22	23	Amfac (Honolulu)	2,253,102	1,439,510	21	(68,026)	89	443,678	30
23	19	Morrison-Knudsen (Boise)	2,165,987	859,022	47	41,512	44	325,469	47
24	26	IU International (Wilmington, Del.)	2,083,933	1,155,955	32	44,943	38	383,072	40
25	29	Genuine Parts (Atlanta)	2,068,231	867,721	45	103,634	17	636,218	17

The definitions and concepts underlying the figures in this directory are explained on page 215.

• Not on last year's list.

N.A. Not available.

** Reflects an extraordinary credit of at least 10%; see the explanations of "net income" and "earnings per share" on pages 215, 216.

† Average for the year; see the reference to "employees" on page 215.

§ Dividends paid by company on its mandatory redeemable preferred stock were subtracted from net income in calculating this figure.

‡ Reflects an extraordinary charge of at least 10%; see the explanations of "net income" and "earnings per share" on pages 215, 216.

[1] Net sales include all operating revenues and revenues from discontinued operations when they are published. All figures are for the fiscal year ending December 31, 1983, unless otherwise noted. Sales of subsidiaries are included when they are consolidated. All companies on the list must have derived more than 50% of their revenues from non-manufacturing and/or non-mining businesses. Excluded (but eligible for the lists that follow) are companies deriving more than 50% of their revenues solely from banking, life insurance, finance, retailing, transportation, or utilities.

Employees		Net Income as Percent of				Earnings per Share			Growth Rate 1973–83		Total Return to Investors			
		Sales		Stockholders' Equity							1983		1973–83 Average	
Number	Rank	%	Rank	%	Rank	'83($)	'82($)	'73($)	%	Rank	%	Rank	%	Rank
6,700	56	1.6	59	21.0	14	3.35	2.48	0.44	22.37	13	30.83	29	31.38	12
110,500	1	2.7	44	9.0§	65	2.10	2.03	2.39	(1.29)	70	58.44	13	12.68	59
63,200	5	2.9	41	11.3	53	4.04	3.64	2.57	4.63	62	30.79	30	22.31	36
73,165	2	5.0	28	7.7	70	2.33	4.21	0.84	10.74	43	18.80	48	4.48	79
34,123	13	0.5	77	1.6	80	0.35	1.94	0.23	4.34	63	(7.44)	77	5.31	77
21,391	23	1.3	61	20.8	15	1.85	1.77	0.27	21.05	16	15.29	53	34.31	9
11,910	40	0.9	70	15.9	27	2.36	1.98	0.71	12.76	36	30.02	31	24.65	30
8,432	44	—		—		N.A.	N.A.	N.A.	—		—		—	
12,700	38	1.2	65	11.1§	54	3.36	4.59	2.05	5.07	60	5.03	62	20.11	43
60,781	6	4.2	34	13.0	42	6.31	4.01	3.27	6.79	57	15.56	52	14.99	53
33,624†	14	2.6	45	9.5§	62	2.22**	2.34	1.81	2.06	66	54.06	15	14.48	56
33,600	15	6.4	19	15.2	34	2.86	3.18	0.75	14.27	32	0.83	70	6.28	75
71,000	3	7.6	14	15.5	31	2.80	2.25	0.27	26.35	7	(4.42)	75	20.51	42
13,700	32	5.4	25	13.2	41	5.45	5.54	1.86	11.35	42	(0.69)	71	17.88	47
3,200	79	1.7	58	10.5§	60	3.05	2.90	1.90	4.82	61	(14.67)	82	(2.39)	83
14,492	30	2.0	54	13.7§	38	2.70	2.95	0.82	12.66	39	19.60	46	31.22	13
3,629	74	—		—		N.A.	N.A.	N.A.	—		—		—	
7,900	47	1.3	62	18.2	19	2.12	1.76	0.60	13.45	35	21.33	43	15.88	51
3,400†	76	—		—		N.A.	N.A.	N.A.	—		—		—	
22,904	21	4.3	33	15.6	29	4.43	3.73	1.20	14.00	33	21.58	41	12.80	58
7,574	49	0.7	73	10.5	59	1.91	0.25	0.97	7.06	56	10.07	56	9.40	68
26,300	20	—		—		(4.70)	2.27	2.36	—		19.00	47	14.80	55
19,670	24	1.9	57	12.8	45	3.97	3.86	0.99	14.93	28	21.42	42	17.82	48
35,000	11	2.2	51	11.7	50	1.74	1.44	2.31	(2.79)	73	95.95	4	14.84	54
13,100	34	5.0	27	16.3	25	2.87	2.77	0.87	12.72	37	2.45	66	10.08	66

² Figures are for fiscal year ending October 31, 1983.
³ Figures are for fiscal year ending February 28, 1983.
⁴ Cooperatives provide only net margin figures, which are not comparable with their net income figure in these listings.
⁵ Figures are for fiscal year ending August 31, 1983.
⁶ Figures are for fiscal year ending March 31, 1983.
⁷ Name changed from Foremost-McKesson on July 27, 1973.
⁸ Company was No. 78 on the 1982 FORTUNE 500.
⁹ Figures are for fiscal year ending September 30, 1983.
¹⁰ Figures are for fiscal year ending June 30, 1983.
¹¹ Figures are for fiscal year ending May 31, 1983.
¹² Name changed from Grain Terminal Association on June 1, 1983.

Source: Reprinted from the *FORTUNE Directory* by permission; © 1984 Time Inc. All rights reserved.

The 25 Largest Commercial Banking Companies (ranked by assets)

Rank '83	Rank '82	Company	Assets[1] ($000)	Deposits ($000)	Deposits Rank	Loans[2] ($000)	Loans Rank	Employees Number	Employees Rank
1	1	Citicorp (New York)	134,655,000	79,794,000	2	90,283,000	1	63,700	2
2	2	BankAmerica Corp. (San Francisco)[3]	121,175,689	95,750,672	1	81,326,825	2	91,068	1
3	3	Chase Manhattan Corp. (New York)	81,921,449	56,299,557	3	55,329,418	3	37,230	3
4	4	Manufacturers Hanover Corp. (New York)	64,332,306	42,284,115	4	47,852,437	4	28,250	5
5	5	J. P. Morgan & Co. (New York)	58,023,000	38,070,000	5	32,974,000	6	12,965	12
6	6	Chemical New York Corp.	51,164,860	32,452,401	6	33,327,585	5	19,464	7
7	8	First Interstate Bancorp. (Los Angeles)	44,422,997	32,030,652	7	25,459,185	9	31,719†	4
8	7	Continental Illinois Corp. (Chicago)	42,097,371	29,431,468	8	30,776,484	7	12,189	13
9	10	Security Pacific Corp. (Los Angeles)	40,382,185	27,824,915	9	28,342,676	8	28,157	6
10	9	Bankers Trust New York Corp.	40,003,359	22,829,079	11	23,383,213	10	11,653	15
11	11	First Chicago Corp.	36,323,324	27,680,040	10	22,032,326	11	11,154	16
12	13	Wells Fargo & Co. (San Francisco)	27,017,621	20,360,996	12	20,068,019	12	16,200	9
13	15	Mellon National Corp. (Pittsburgh)[4]	26,432,958	15,692,507	16	15,247,385	14	11,939	14
14	12	Crocker National Corp. (San Francisco)	23,393,460	18,927,793	13	15,995,055	13	14,256	10
15	16	Marine Midland Banks (Buffalo)[5]	22,872,245	16,077,465	15	13,049,884	16	11,132†	17
16	14	InterFirst Corp. (Dallas)	21,736,000	16,909,000	14	14,363,000	15	10,625	19
17	22	First Bank System (Minneapolis)	20,871,147	13,430,315	20	10,985,466	21	9,805†	20
18	20	Norwest Corp. (Minneapolis)[6]	19,854,235	13,552,190	19	12,082,588	17	17,721	8
19	18	Bank of Boston Corp.[7]	19,538,382	12,380,924	23	11,760,081	19	14,000	11
20	19	Texas Commerce Bancshares (Houston)	19,499,000	13,051,000	21	11,535,000	20	7,939	27
21	21	RepublicBank Corp. (Dallas)	19,081,721	13,907,085	17	11,780,652	18	8,417	24
22	17	Irving Bank Corp. (New York)	18,586,055	12,609,924	22	10,363,526	22	9,600	21
23	23	First City Bancorp. of Texas (Houston)	17,262,782	13,713,645	18	10,234,753	23	8,533	23
24	25	NBD Bancorp. (Detroit)	13,244,777	8,946,664	26	5,679,587	29	6,690	33
25	26	NCNB Corp. (Charlotte, N.C.)	12,807,706	8,812,998	27	6,867,374	26	7,635	28

N.A. Not available.
** Reflects an extraordinary credit of at least 10%; see the explanations of "net income" and "earnings per share" on pages 215, 216.
   † Average for the year; see the reference to "employees" on page 215.
   § Dividends paid by company on its mandatory redeemable preferred stock were subtracted from net income in calculating this figure.
   [1] As of December 31, 1983.

Net Income ($000)	Rank	Stockholders' Equity ($000)	Rank	Net Income as Percent of Equity %	Rank	Earnings per Share '83($)	'82($)	'73($)	Growth Rate: 1973–83 %	Rank	Total Return to Investors 1983 %	Rank	1973–83 Average %	Rank
860,000	1	5,771,000	1	14.8§	20	6.48	5.60	2.11	11.87	14	19.89	73	2.34	82
390,468	4	5,136,162	2	7.6	86	2.18	3.03	1.60	3.11	81	11.28	82	3.77	77
429,607	3	3,425,825	3	12.5§	48	10.96	7.73	5.10	7.95	56	0.00	91	4.76	73
336,964	5	2,671,065	5	12.6	46	8.37	7.78	3.44	9.30	37	(1.41)	93	7.12	66
460,000	2	3,319,000	4	13.9	27	10.52	9.53	3.84	10.60	24	5.30	88	4.37	75
305,563	6	2,305,332	6	13.3	38	9.50	8.41	3.23	11.38	18	16.42	77	12.98	44
247,404	9	2,091,663	7	11.8	55	5.76	5.35	2.21	10.07	31	39.73	49	15.83	22
108,319	19	1,821,574	8	5.9	90	2.63	1.95	2.47	0.61	88	17.18	76	4.48	74
264,267	7	1,781,639	10	14.8	19	7.23	6.53	2.07	13.33	7	72.48	11	19.75	3
261,239	8	1,790,111	9	14.6	22	8.55	8.34	2.88	11.51	17	27.61	65	14.92	32
183,534	11	1,742,070	11	10.5	72	3.92	3.33	2.30	5.45	74	46.79	34	2.35	81
154,900	13	1,347,771	13	11.5	59	6.03	5.81	2.21	10.56	25	54.59	21	11.86	49
183,815	10	1,383,073	12	12.9§	43	7.44	6.83	3.30**	8.47	49	41.10	44	15.05	31
(10,423)	98	1,228,446	14	—		(0.63)	3.62	3.12	—		0.09	90	8.97	58
101,085	20	1,046,010	18	9.7	78	4.85	4.54	3.65	2.88	82	39.47	50	8.22	61
(172,000)	100	1,079,000	17	—		(2.82)	3.80	1.06	—		(22.92)	95	0.47	85
129,747	16	1,105,334	16	11.7	56	8.46	7.66	3.51	9.20	38	57.63	17	4.36	76
125,202	17	1,130,062	15	11.1	66	4.05	3.08	1.94	7.64	57	43.86	39	6.07	69
135,736	14	1,007,352	20	13.5	34	7.40	6.67	2.85	10.00	32	26.28	68	10.85	53
177,000	12	1,019,000	19	17.4	4	5.50	5.35	1.14	17.04	2	14.13	80	8.44	60
130,168	15	977,222	21	13.3	36	4.60	5.18	1.27	13.77	4	7.49	85	8.07	62
92,464	23	816,391	23	11.3	64	9.72	9.13	3.70	10.14	28	37.13	55	15.15	30
49,785	42	886,072	22	5.6	91	1.23	3.52	1.23	(0.04)	89	(8.30)	94	3.74	79
81,689	31	797,648	24	10.2	75	6.75	6.69	3.35	7.24	62	56.35	20	16.15	20
92,162	24	608,687	29	15.1	17	3.68	3.18	1.55	9.03	42	51.49	25	1.24	84

² Net of unearned discount and loan loss reserve. Figure includes lease financing.
³ Company acquired Seafirst Corp. (1982 rank: No. 28) on July 1, 1983.
⁴ Company acquired Girard (1982 rank: No. 66) on April 6, 1983.
⁵ Company is 51% owned by the Hongkong & Shanghai Banking Corp.
⁶ Name changed from Northwest Bancorp. on May 2, 1983.
⁷ Name changed from First National Boston Corp. on April 1, 1983.

Source: Reprinted from the *FORTUNE Directory* by permission; © 1984 Time Inc. All rights reserved.

The 25 Largest Life Insurance Companies (ranked by Assets)

Rank			Assets	Premium and Annuity Income[2]		Net Investment Income	
1983	1982	Company	($000)	($000)	Rank	($000)	Rank
1	1	Prudential (Newark)*	72,248,810	9,514,847	1	4,265,237	2
2	2	Metropolitan (New York)*	60,598,562	5,947,671	2	4,749,002	1
3	3	Equitable Life Assurance (New York)*	43,305,559	1,102,684	16	2,580,860	3
4	4	Aetna Life (Hartford)[7]	31,414,088	3,693,699	4	1,588,435	6
5	5	New York Life*	24,288,095	3,554,362	5	1,811,404	4
6	6	John Hancock Mutual (Boston)*	23,458,537	2,397,284	7	1,394,447	8
7	7	Travelers (Hartford)[8]	20,741,507	3,976,185	3	1,713,995	5
8	8	Connecticut General Life (Bloomfield)[9]	17,424,833	3,036,377	6	1,157,902	9
9	9	Teachers Insurance & Annuity (New York)	16,143,856	1,641,832	11	1,551,249	7
10	10	Northwestern Mutual (Milwaukee)*	14,480,689	2,012,505	8	1,005,841	10
11	11	Massachusetts Mutual (Springfield)*	12,172,745	1,306,586	13	871,100	12
12	12	Bankers Life (Des Moines)*	11,358,456	1,961,454	9	903,663	11
13	13	Mutual of New York*	9,284,182	1,004,018	18	651,406	14
14	14	New England Mutual (Boston, Mass.)*	8,487,638	1,645,748	10	669,279	13
15	15	Mutual Benefit (Newark)*	7,898,157	1,135,331	15	630,582	15
16	16	Connecticut Mutual (Hartford)*	6,753,954	944,840	19	478,667	16
17	18	Stare Farm Life (Bloomington, Ill.)	4,979,900	944,221	20	384,565	17
18	17	Lincoln National Life (Fort Wayne, Ind.)[10]	4,681,607	1,051,476	17	321,848	19
19	20	Continental Assurance (Chicago)[11]	4,077,317	1,198,304	14	169,014	41
20	19	Penn Mutual (Philadelphia)*	3,960,275	357,801	42	268,677	21
21	23	Nationwide Life (Columbus, Ohio)	3,938,289	435,140	37	194,533	36
22	21	Phoenix Mutual (Hartford)*	3,808,291	630,858	27	264,032	22
23	25	National Life & Accident (Nashville)[12]	3,526,819	504,885	35	235,016	28
24	22	Western & Southern Life (Cincinnati)*	3,422,095	373,267	41	225,740	29
25	33	Variable Annuity Life (Houston)[12]	3,384,084	485,780	36	299,929	20

See notes on page 215.
Data for all companies are on the statutory accounting basis required by state insurance regulatory authorities.
N.A. Not available.
* Indicates a mutual company.
[1] As of December 31, 1983.
[2] Includes premium income from life, accident, and health policies, annuities, and from contributions to deposit administration funds.
[3] After dividends to policyholders and federal income taxes, excluding capital gains and losses. Figures in parentheses indicate a loss.

Net Gain from Operations[3] ($000)	Rank Mutual	Rank Stock	Life Insurance in Force[4] ($000)	Rank	Increase in Life Insurance in Force[5] ($000)	Rank	Percent	Rank	Employees[6] Number	Rank
187,623	1		509,963,512	1	27,655,523	1	5.7	32	59,347	1
37,926	10		450,908,885	2	24,280,107	2	5.7	33	40,000	3
56,468	3		238,425,689	3	10,078,169	8	4.4	35	22,836	4
259,240		1	198,734,099	4	18,590,573	4	10.3	22	16,611	8
54,154	5		172,050,634	5	20,975,502	3	13.9	15	19,320	6
31,900	12		153,182,732	6	6,180,253	13	4.2	36	19,977	5
154,877		4	130,630,639	8	(7,224,466)	49	—		42,966	2
249,432		2	104,804,346	9	8,140,262	11	8.4	26	10,512	10
37,629		11	12,544,006	42	1,642,290	30	15.1	10	2,133	40
49,414	6		92,622,381	11	13,281,662	5	16.7	7	7,265	16
72,516	2		61,574,596	13	4,075,322	25	7.1	29	9,808	11
13,891	17		52,251,774	15	5,071,771	16	10.8	21	7,230	17
32,431	11		51,548,474	17	5,757,004	14	12.6	19	7,538	14
48,070	7		40,916,608	20	4,603,293	22	12.7	18	7,618	13
40,110	9		51,816,886	16	642,294	37	1.3	40	4,610	22
45,125	8		40,251,365	21	5,035,287	18	14.3	12	5,827	20
121,248		5	73,657,948	12	9,141,184	9	14.2	13	17,329	7
167,030		3	103,513,639	10	11,988,776	7	13.1	17	4,196	25
12,612		15	35,231,590	26	4,808,484	19	15.8	9	N.A.	
10,786	19		21,596,818	29	598,370	39	2.9	38	3,438	30
17,700		14	15,906,047	37	770,872	36	5.1	34	6,355	19
10,762	20		49,001,338	18	6,961,138	12	16.6	8	3,285	32
72,210		8	19,686,431	33	(737,233)	46	—		6,776	18
54,227	4		19,267,903	34	2,465,958	28	14.7	11	7,404	15
(19,958)		23	4,082	49	(1,032)	42	—		999	43

[4] Face value of all life policies as of December 31, 1983.
[5] Change between December 31, 1982, and December 31, 1983.
[6] Includes home office, field force, and full-time agents.
[7] Wholly owned by Aetna Life & Casualty.
[8] Wholly owned by Travelers Corp.
[9] Wholly owned by CIGNA.
[10] Wholly owned by Lincoln National.
[11] Wholly owned by a subsidiary of Loews.
[12] Wholly owned by American General.

Source: Reprinted from the FORTUNE Directory by permission; © 1984 Time Inc. All rights reserved.

The 100 Largest Brokerage Houses

Rank 1983	Rank 1984	Name of Firm	Total Capital	Equity Capital	Subordinated Debt	Excess Net Capital	Number of Employees	Number of Offices	Number of Registered Representatives
1	1	Merrill Lynch & Co.	$2,023,731,000	$1,888,019,000	$135,712,000	$ 16,139,000	43,064	1,007	10,700
2	2	Salomon Brothers Holding Co.	1,279,600,000	1,181,300,000	98,300,000	335,400,000	2,878	9	812
3	3	Shearson/American Express	1,056,555,000	710,345,000	346,210,000	184,855,000	13,465	364	4,758
9	4	Dean Witter Financial Services Group	964,543,000	961,226,000	3,317,000	69,674,000	17,200	483	5,900
4	5	E. F. Hutton Group	746,480,000	587,382,000	159,098,000	48,287,000	15,824	400	6,082
5	6	Goldman, Sachs & Co.	712,000,000[1]	502,000,000	210,000,000	528,941,537	3,251	16	887
8	7	Paine Webber Inc.	499,125,000	329,301,000	169,824,000	56,809,606	11,383	282	4,176
6	8	Prudential-Bache Securities	493,744,000	478,236,000	15,508,000	17,621,000	11,300	300	4,800
7	9	First Boston Inc. (Consolidated)	424,400,000	385,800,000	38,600,000	184,700,000	2,248	18	760
10	10	Bear, Stearns & Co.	420,000,000	291,175,000	128,825,000	248,667,000	3,640	12	900
14	11	Drexel Burnham Lambert Group	407,359,000	320,311,000	87,048,000	73,477,000	5,310	54	1,600
11	12	Donaldson, Lufkin & Jenrette	337,866,000	181,703,000	156,163,000	77,300,000	3,786	25	425
13	13	Morgan Stanley Inc.	290,900,000	206,700,000	84,200,000	71,668,996	2,413	7	780
16	14	Lehman Brothers Kuhn Loeb	290,123,307	215,123,307	75,000,000	55,928,937	2,906	11	495
12	15	Stephens	275,598,477	275,598,477	—	55,373,941	176	1	91
15	16	Becker Paribas	226,734,000	176,334,000	50,400,000	62,467,000	2,300	19	355
18	17	Kidder, Peabody & Co.	223,294,000[2]	178,279,000	45,015,000	33,995,000	5,513	73	2,009
22	18	Thomson McKinnon Inc.	214,079,000	199,079,000	15,000,000	113,500,000	4,119	138	1,831
17	19	Smith Barney Inc.	203,000,000	166,000,000	37,000,000	55,000,000	5,400	105	1,850
23	20	Spear, Leeds & Kellogg	203,000,000	140,000,000	63,000,000	10,111,196	1,208	10	120
19	21	A. G. Edwards & Sons	172,591,000[2]	172,591,000	—	89,004,000	4,093	234	1,985
24	22	L. F. Rothschild, Unterberg, Towbin	154,932,685	129,552,685	25,380,000	53,224,000	1,767	12	705
21	23	Allen & Co.	150,054,976	148,007,760	—	—	NA	1	4
20	24	Shelby Cullom Davis & Co.	148,007,760	148,007,760	—	—	13	2	5
28	25	Oppenheimer & Co.	142,265,611	81,439,611	60,826,000	44,182,671	1,800	9	476
27	26	John Nuveen & Co.	97,398,000	97,398,000	—	58,456,000	470	15	158
26	27	Neuberger & Berman	92,362,352	92,362,352	—	44,288,257	355	2	37
35	28	Cowen & Co.	76,326,427	69,846,427	6,480,000	34,409,691	1,004	16	458
30	29	Alex. Brown & Sons	74,912,000	71,432,000	3,480,000	24,496,000	1,083	20	330
64	30	Janney Montgomery Scott	73,511,057	73,511,057	—	16,369,363	955	29	426
29	31	Aubrey G. Lanston & Co.	73,500,000[3]	73,500,000	—	—	58	3	NA
32	32	Bateman Eichler, Hill Richards	73,432,000	25,694,000	47,738,000	12,215,000	1,240	35	572
31	33	McMahan, Brafman, Morgan & Co.	72,336,000	72,336,000	—	24,247,000	83	3	12
44	34	Dillon, Read & Co.	64,866,117	52,366,117	12,500,000	24,625,998	469	4	176
40	35	Allen & Co. Inc.	63,567,000[2]	58,567,000	5,000,000	12,371,000	191	2	65
42	36	Prescott, Ball & Turben	63,170,964	58,170,964	5,000,000	11,595,154	1,031	39	319
58	37	Advest Group	60,395,000	32,688,000	27,707,000	24,743,000	1,356	50	532

56	38	Charles Schwab Corp.	59,007,443	32,742,443	26,265,000	9,519,394	1,375	78	510
37	39	Wertheim & Co. Inc.	58,400,000	51,600,000	6,800,000	5,600,000	515	6	89
34	40	Brown Brothers Harriman & Co.	57,833,088	57,833,088	—	—	1,128	10	220
33	41	Stern Brothers & Co.	57,152,800	57,152,800	—	28,600,000	84	6	30
67	42	Jefferies Group Inc.	51,582,000	51,582,000	—	33,950,000	315	8	116
45	43	Van Kampen Merritt	50,914,990	50,914,990	—	33,071,444	175	5	85
38	44	Carl Marks & Co.	50,272,706	50,272,706	—	12,976,076	100	1	32
36	45	Glickenhaus & Co.	48,107,000	48,107,000	—	21,392,000	59	2	2
41	46	Ziegler Co.	47,260,230	47,260,023	—	27,268,622	360	31	50
60	47	Moseley, Hallgarten, Estabrook & Weeden Holding Corp.	44,359,000	33,709,000	10,650,000	13,731,000	963	38	604
—	48	Gruss & Co.	43,284,215	43,284,215	—	15,325,111	9	1	6
49	49	M. A. Schapiro & Co.	42,114,000	42,114,000	—	17,706,000	24	1	5
43	50	Nomura Securities International	41,926,570	41,926,570	—	25,449,422	192	5	58
47	51	William Blair & Co.	41,724,953	41,724,953	—	25,847,799	339	3	115
48	52	Piper, Jaffray Inc.	41,575,940	41,075,940	500,000	11,696,000	1,423	44	538
—	53	Fidelity Brokerage Services	41,371,000	41,371,000	—	14,035,000	466	28	145
50	54	Dain Bosworth	39,389,000	34,751,000	4,638,000	9,811,000	1,310	49	533
62	55	Herzfeld & Stern	37,522,235	37,522,235	—	3,800,000	790	10	385
52	56	J. C. Bradford & Co.	37,081,277	35,081,277	2,000,000	7,317,455	939	44	371
54	57	Ohio Co.	36,347,075	36,347,075	—	12,394,393	458	47	160
59	58	Wedbush, Noble, Cooke	36,247,000	35,469,000	778,000	22,612,000	506	20	225
68	59	Blunt Ellis & Loewi	35,327,740	25,327,740	10,000,000	5,500,000	1,188	65	471
53	60	Atlantic Capital Corp.	33,193,153	33,193,153	—	27,428,900	92	1	19
39	61	Easton & Co.	32,168,000	30,343,000	1,825,000	17,793,000	35	3	6
51	62	Gruntal Financial Corp.	30,924,420	30,924,420	—	11,548,462	892	22	324
71	63	Mabon, Nugent & Co.	30,631,968	30,631,968	—	7,779,719	430	2	145
66	64	Arnhold & S. Bleichroeder	30,629,259	30,629,259	—	8,812,636	150	1	44
61	65	Eppler, Guerin & Turner	30,448,895	30,448,895	—	21,083,000	435	26	210
55	66	Lazard Freres & Co.	30,000,000	30,000,000	—	12,181,192	413	1	69
63	67	Interstate Securities Corp.	29,250,632	25,600,632	3,650,000	5,744,191	769	54	378
57	68	Rothschild	28,877,549	14,877,549	14,000,000	2,080,178	143	1	12
—	69	Montgomery Securities	27,391,447	25,266,447	2,125,000	12,048,358	279	1	60
86	70	Boettcher & Co.	26,000,000	6,000,000	20,000,000	13,769,950	1,000	30	315
84	71	McDonald & Co.	25,497,917	25,497,917	—	15,774,582	384	21	105
—	72	Morgan, Keegan & Co.	25,275,753	25,275,753	—	19,254,142	338	12	132
—	73	Crowell Weedon & Co.	24,752,863	23,762,863	990,000	7,426,416	329	9	138
83	74	Edward D. Jones & Co.	24,250,000	23,770,000	480,000	11,814,000	1,481	673	736
65	75	Daiwa Securities America	24,000,000	24,000,000	—	—	66	2	16
69	76	Albert Fried & Co.	23,986,545*	23,566,545	420,000	17,258,000	15	1	NA
74	77	Robert W. Baird & Co.	23,934,000	23,934,000	—	14,518,000	530	27	191
99	78	Stifel Financial Corp.	23,550,951	23,550,951	—	2,345,961	760	42	400
75	79	Tucker, Anthony & R. L. Day	23,479,742	20,399,742	3,080,000	7,538,299	1,130	31	560
97	80	Nikko Securities Co. International	22,684,000	22,684,000	—	17,950,792	65	3	35
78	81	Keefe, Bruyette & Woods	22,659,000	19,353,000	3,306,000	16,075,000	95	3	43

The 100 Largest Brokerage Houses (concluded)

Rank 1982	Rank 1983	Name of Firm	Total Capital	Equity Capital	Subordinated Debt	Excess Net Capital	Number of Employees	Number of Offices	Number of Registered Representatives
73	82	Legg Mason Wood Walker	22,424,515	16,942,015	5,482,500	6,219,757	726	30	309
70	83	Wepco Holding Co.	22,007,000	22,007,000	—	—	154	6	61
72	84	Rauscher Pierce Refsnes	21,288,979	19,903,279	1,385,700	2,654,257	1,019	29	373
—	85	Clayton Brown & Associates	20,592,929	20,592,929	—	10,042,071	105	5	59
91	86	Herzog Heine Geduld	19,563,370	18,404,800	1,158,570	6,545,260	347	4	53
85	87	Ryan, Beck & Co.	19,441,000	19,441,000	—	13,341,000	125	2	40
79	88	Gintel & Co.	19,222,000	18,122,000	1,100,000	10,817,000	186	3	65
77	89	Asiel & Co.	18,763,058	17,763,058	1,000,000	9,618,532	199	1	58
92	90	Furman Selz Mager Dietz & Birney	18,381,000	18,381,000	—	8,697,000	105	1	35
80	91	Sutro & Co.	17,466,313	13,466,313	4,000,000	735,670	828	21	279
76	92	Ernst & Co.	17,415,440	17,215,440	200,000	4,359,986	211	3	45
88	93	J. J. B. Hillard, W. L. Lyons	16,442,021	13,723,086	2,718,935	4,138,090	590	34	230
—	94	Raymond, James & Associates	16,411,198	16,411,198	—	6,025,173	648	29	300
—	95	Cantor Fitzgerald & Co.	15,956,992	15,956,992	—	8,825,429	200	5	72
87	96	First Manhattan Co.	15,400,000	15,400,000	—	9,000,000	198	2	65
81	97	Underwood, Neuhaus & Co.	15,270,498	14,245,752	1,024,844	3,747,844	394	9	192
82	98	Yamaichi International (America)	14,800,000	14,800,000	—	4,148,153	51	2	23
94	99	Josephthal & Co.	14,430,985	9,975,985	4,455,000	1,999,670	416	13	148
93	100	First of Michigan Corp.	14,364,944	14,364,944	—	1,956,025	475	27	267

[1] All figures as of 11/25/83
[2] All figures as of 11/30/83
[3] All figures as of 4/30/83
[4] All figures as of 10/31/83

Source: *Institutional Investor*, Ranking America's Biggest Brokers, April 1984.

Top Growth Companies (500 with sales of more than $25 million)

Rank	Company	Exchange	5-Year EPS Growth %	Latest 12-Month EPS	Year to Date Price Change
1	Jet American Airlines	O	123	3.35	(38.0)
2	Nutri/System	N	123	1.46	(52.6)
3	Ultra Systems	O	123	0.72	(13.2)
4	Synergex	O	122	0.87	(27.3)
5	TeleVideo Systems	O	122	0.56	(53.5)
6	Basix	N	121	0.82	(20.9)
7	Data Switch	O	121	0.72	(35.8)
8	Decision Data Computer	O	121	0.74	(20.5)
9	Mgmt. Science America	O	121	0.63	(42.5)
10	MCI Communications	O	121	0.86	(43.5)
11	CalFed	O	120	4.56	(42.9)
12	Clow Corp.	O	120	1.16	(26.7)
13	MCO Resources	A	120	0.13	(13.8)
14	Adage Inc.	O	119	0.92	(41.7)
15	Caressa	N	118	1.86	(17.9)
16	Diceon Electronics	O	118	0.87	0.0
17	Great Amer. Mgmt. & Invst.	O	118	1.33	(23.9)
18	Paine Webber	N	118	2.90	(23.6)
19	American Century	N	117	1.10	(26.9)
20	Heritage Communications	N	117	0.52	(4.5)
21	Aydin	N	116	3.31	(36.2)
22	Charter Medical	A	116	1.42	37.9
23	Cencor Inc.	O	115	1.86	(6.3)
24	Metro. Fed. S&L	O	115	4.10	(32.7)
25	AFG Industries	O	114	1.54	(17.1)
26	Cipher Data Products	O	114	0.75	(5.1)
27	Maxicare Health Products	O	114	0.35	47.9
28	Rent-A-Center	O	114	0.69	(23.2)
29	Tandon Corp.	O	113	0.53	(56.3)
30	Pauley Petroleum	O	112	3.22	(30.5)
31	Pick 'n' Save	O	111	1.17	(17.0)
32	Wal-Mart Stores	N	111	1.51	(8.7)
33	Ohio Art Co.	A	110	1.28	(1.1)
34	Sterling Bancorp	N	110	1.00	4.9
35	Bally's Park Place	N	108	0.86	(5.0)
36	St. Jude Medical	O	108	1.00	(28.6)
37	Subaru of America	O	108	8.50	(1.5)
38	Bell National	O	107	2.93	(59.3)
39	Cray Research	N	107	1.77	(25.8)
40	Emulex	O	107	0.81	(16.3)
41	Mylan Laboratories	O	107	0.60	50.9
42	Pasquale Food	O	107	0.39	56.3
43	Donaldson, Lufkin & Jen.	N	105	1.71	7.8
44	Brinkman, L.D.	O	105	0.79	(18.6)
45	Sanmark-Stardust	A	105	0.39	(28.8)
46	VSE Corp.	O	105	2.12	(16.7)
47	Acmat Corp.	O	104	1.52	(23.5)
48	Aeronca	A	104	0.76	(11.4)
49	Care Enterprises	O	104	0.50	(28.2)
50	Conair	N	104	1.30	(1.4)
51	First Financial	O	103	3.48	(33.3)
52	FoxMeyer	O	103	1.43	(10.4)
53	Fuqua Industries	N	103	3.12	(20.6)

Top Growth Companies (500 with sales of more than $25 million) *(continued)*

Rank	Company	Exchange	5-Year EPS Growth %	Latest 12-Month EPS	Year to Date Price Change
54	General Dynamics	N	103	5.30	(21.7)
55	Geriatric & Medical Ctrs.	O	103	0.45	(12.2)
56	Mor-Flo Industries	O	103	2.31	(33.3)
57	Tech-Sym	A	103	1.14	(29.9)
58	Wards Co.	A	103	1.23	(4.6)
59	Envirodyne	O	102	0.27	29.4
60	Lake Shore Mines	A	102	2.11	(9.4)
61	Smith Labs	O	102	1.03	(41.5)
62	Commodore Int'l	N	101	4.09	(41.0)
63	Cosmo Communications	O	101	1.33	(48.3)
64	Mickleberry	N	101	0.66	(11.0)
65	Miniscribe	O	101	0.22	(55.2)
66	Systems & Computer Tech.	O	101	0.59	(22.9)
67	CCX Network	O	100	0.51	1.9
68	Computer Data Systems	O	100	0.93	(25.8)
69	Green Tree Accept.	O	100	1.95	(33.8)
70	Technical Communications	O	100	0.43	(62.7)
71	Carrols	N	99	0.57	(16.0)
72	Genovese Drug Stores	A	99	0.96	(33.8)
73	Grumman	N	99	3.81	(5.7)
74	Price Co.	O	99	1.35	(9.7)
75	Crime Control	O	98	1.01	10.2
76	First Executive	O	98	1.00	(25.7)
77	Northern Air Freight	O	98	0.43	(50.0)
78	Esmark	N	97	3.78	37.6
79	Ketchum & Co.	A	97	0.96	(24.8)
80	Manor Care	N	97	1.23	(4.7)
81	Pope, Evans & Robbins	A	97	0.22	(23.8)
82	Crown Books	O	96	0.73	(28.9)
83	Nuclear Pharmacy	O	96	0.13	(13.8)
84	Quick & Reilly	N	96	1.13	5.6
85	Textone	O	96	2.14	(20.9)
86	Eagle Computer	O	95	0.11	(70.0)
87	Winnebago Industries	N	95	0.84	(32.1)
88	Conquest Exploration	A	94	0.17	15.7
89	Nike Inc.	O	94	1.30	(32.8)
90	U.S. Health Care Sys.	O	94	0.37	22.9
91	University Fed. Savings	O	94	1.08	(46.5)
92	Mediq Inc.	A	93	0.81	(4.8)
93	Morgan Keegan	O	93	1.34	(24.4)
94	Oak Hill Sportswear	O	93	0.71	(48.1)
95	Integrated Resources	N	92	3.30	(32.7)
96	Mentor Co.	O	92	0.20	(32.1)
97	Triton Energy	N	92	1.70	(6.7)
98	Berg Enterprises	N	91	1.55	(35.7)
99	Genentech	O	91	0.09	(13.8)
100	Monfort of Colorado	O	91	3.15	0.0
101	Munford Inc.	N	91	1.82	(12.0)
102	Pneumo	N	91	2.70	(20.3)
103	Electrospace Sys.	O	90	0.90	(6.5)
104	Facet Enterprises	N	90	1.09	(39.2)
105	Greenman Bros.	A	90	1.03	(16.2)
106	Lockheed	N	90	4.14	(14.4)
107	Sippican Ocean Sys.	O	90	0.82	(28.1)
108	Sunrise S&L	O	90	4.76	(41.8)
109	General Homes	O	89	0.79	(28.2)
110	Int'l Leasing	O	89	1.03	(15.5)

Rank	Company	Exchange	5-Year EPS Growth %	Latest 12-Month EPS	Year to Date Price Change
111	Jones & Vining	O	89	0.83	(11.9)
112	Thompson Medical	N	89	1.65	25.7
113	Treco Inc.	O	89	0.67	(7.7)
114	Xebec	O	89	0.69	(46.5)
115	Agency Rent-A-Car	O	88	1.40	(33.2)
116	DWG Corp.	A	88	0.87	(3.0)
117	Par Technology	O	88	0.83	7.1
118	Payco American	O	88	1.25	(21.3)
119	TIE/Communications	A	88	1.17	(56.9)
120	VF Corp.	N	88	3.76	(21.2)
121	Gemco	A	87	0.68	(37.8)
122	Rodine PLC.	O	87	0.82	(43.4)
123	Student Loan Mktg.	N	87	1.54	(10.0)
124	Accuray	O	86	1.36	(38.9)
125	Concept Development	O	86	0.57	25.4
126	Continental Info Sys.	O	86	1.37	(26.0)
127	GRI Corp.	A	86	0.57	(28.9)
128	Humana	N	86	1.80	16.0
129	Seagate Technology	O	86	0.70	(27.0)
130	Trak Auto	O	86	0.83	(37.2)
131	Valmac Industries	A	86	0.83	(4.9)
132	ArgoSystems	O	85	0.78	(31.8)
133	CPI Corp.	O	85	1.45	(21.0)
134	Forum Group	O	85	0.38	(6.3)
135	Jefferson Smurfit	O	85	1.26	(16.8)
136	Murphy, G.C.	N	85	4.22	0.0
137	Comdisco	N	84	1.45	(36.8)
138	Mountain Medical Equip.	A	84	0.71	(48.5)
139	Phillips-Van Heusen	N	84	2.51	(6.7)
140	Telerate	N	84	0.57	(34.4)
141	Nature's Bounty	O	83	0.32	(32.4)
142	DEA Inc.	A	83	1.54	(18.6)
143	State Street Boston	O	83	4.18	13.8
144	Technical Tape	A	83	0.82	(26.6)
145	Zenith Labs	O	83	0.73	26.9
146	Boothe Financial	O	82	2.56	17.3
147	Key Tronic	O	82	1.23	(37.6)
148	Micom Systems	O	82	1.20	(14.0)
149	Standard Motor Products	N	82	1.60	(8.2)
150	Webcor Electronics	A	82	0.72	(55.6)
151	Champion Home Builders	A	81	0.21	(34.3)
152	Fidelcor	O	81	8.15	(4.8)
153	First Boston	N	81	6.12	(13.2)
154	Int'l Hydron	A	81	0.39	(28.0)
155	Leucadia National	N	81	2.32	(2.2)
156	Network Systems	O	81	0.50	(1.2)
157	Olga Company	O	81	4.69	(1.1)
158	Pulte Home	N	81	1.56	(51.0)
159	Ranger Oil	N	81	0.61	(34.1)
160	Earl Schelb	A	81	1.53	(16.2)
161	SCI Systems	O	81	0.70	(38.9)
162	Sparkman Energy	A	81	1.66	(9.4)
163	Washington Homes	A	81	1.94	(43.0)
164	Eiscint Ltd.	O	80	1.25	(18.9)
165	Holly Sugar	N	80	5.52	10.3
166	Horizon Ind.	O	80	1.47	(50.0)
167	Masland, C.H.	A	80	1.04	(26.3)

Top Growth Companies (500 with sales of more than $25 million) *(continued)*

Rank	Company	Exchange	5-Year EPS Growth %	Latest 12-Month EPS	Year to Date Price Change
168	Radice	O	80	1.13	(27.1)
169	Seagram Company	N	80	2.95	(11.4)
170	Beck/Arnley	O	79	1.25	(16.7)
171	Carteret S&L	O	79	4.38	(31.3)
172	Dillard Dept. Stores	A	79	5.75	(15.6)
173	Dreyfus Corp.	N	79	3.03	3.7
174	Falstaff Brewing	O	79	0.38	(18.8)
175	Hasbro Industries	A	79	2.41	24.1
176	North Atlantic Ind.	O	79	0.76	(26.6)
177	Oxford Industries	N	79	2.23	(22.5)
178	Sherwin-Williams	N	79	2.20	(5.7)
179	Ultimate Corp.	A	79	0.86	0.0
180	Gibson Greetings	O	78	2.22	(9.5)
181	Liebert Corp.	O	78	0.89	(16.7)
182	Micropolis	O	78	0.43	(44.6)
183	A.L. Labs	A	77	0.65	0.0
184	Comprehensive Care	O	77	1.18	(8.2)
185	CooperVision	N	77	1.06	57.4
186	Florida Federal S&L	O	77	3.41	(7.4)
187	Groman Corp.	O	77	1.06	(17.1)
188	Intergraph	O	77	1.01	(9.1)
189	IPCO Corp.	N	77	1.06	(8.1)
190	Ladd Furniture	O	77	2.14	(20.0)
191	Novo Industri	N	77	2.97	(21.9)
192	Alaska Pacific Bancorp	O	76	2.51	0.2
193	Buffton	O	76	0.10	(9.1)
194	Burlington Coat Factory	O	76	1.26	(29.7)
195	Deb Shops	O	76	1.49	(33.3)
196	Hogan Systems	O	76	0.55	(41.9)
197	Hyde Athletic	O	76	1.03	(34.3)
198	Sargent Industries	A	76	0.77	(20.0)
199	Second Nat'l Bldg. & Loan	O	75	3.87	(22.7)
200	AGS Computers	O	75	1.27	(40.7)
201	Altos Systems	O	75	0.56	(5.1)
202	Cerberonics	O	75	0.78	(48.9)
203	Echo Bay Mine	A	75	0.10	18.3
204	Gott Corp.	O	75	0.92	(19.2)
205	Sensormatic Electronics	O	75	0.95	(66.5)
206	Southern Hospitality	O	75	0.31	(11.1)
207	Winter, Jack Inc.	N	75	0.39	(22.2)
208	Canandalgua Wine	A	74	3.78	(0.4)
209	Carling O'Keefe	N	74	2.52	(25.0)
210	Mary Kay Cosmetics	N	74	1.09	(20.5)
211	Park Electrochemical	N	74	1.32	(27.6)
212	Rowe Furniture	O	74	1.12	1.8
213	Saye Energy	A	74	1.52	(22.5)
214	Sun City Industries	A	74	1.04	(7.5)
215	Toys R Us	N	74	1.70	8.3
216	United First Fed. S&L	O	74	0.22	16.5
217	Wang Laboratories	A	74	1.39	(31.2)
218	Builders Transport	O	73	2.20	(31.3)
219	Infotron Systems	O	73	1.41	(24.8)
220	Lamaur	N	73	0.92	(12.0)
221	Priam Corp.	O	73	0.62	(37.2)
222	Sterling Software	O	73	0.82	(18.2)
223	Caesars New Jersey	A	72	0.65	(11.9)

Rank	Company	Exchange	5-Year EPS Growth %	Latest 12-Month EPS	Year to Date Price Change
224	Connelly Containers	A	72	0.50	(15.7)
225	Eaton Vance	O	72	1.92	(14.6)
226	Great Bay Casino	O	72	1.79	(8.1)
227	Helen of Troy	O	72	0.64	(12.5)
228	IRE Financial	O	72	0.45	(16.7)
229	Legg Mason	N	72	1.30	(13.5)
230	Systematics General	O	72	0.61	(20.5)
231	Warehouse Enter.	A	72	1.07	(16.9)
232	Whitehall	N	72	3.09	(45.1)
233	Aeroflex Labs	N	71	1.01	(39.4)
234	Allnet Communications	O	71	0.18	(27.3)
235	Apple Computer	O	71	0.95	20.5
236	HEI Corp.	O	71	0.94	(20.0)
237	Computer Associates	O	71	0.84	(37.5)
238	Gulfstream Aerospace	N	71	1.62	(2.3)
239	Horn & Hardart	A	71	1.16	(23.6)
240	Micro-D	O	71	0.32	(20.6)
241	Moseley Hallgarten	O	71	0.47	(12.5)
242	Williams, A.L.	O	71	0.42	(26.0)
243	Diversifoods	O	70	0.99	(16.1)
244	Glendale Fed. S&L	O	70	2.54	(26.9)
245	Home Health Care	O	70	0.11	(20.0)
246	Interface Flooring	O	70	0.91	(59.5)
247	Jonathan Logan	N	70	2.52	34.2
248	Knoll Int'l	A	70	0.82	(34.4)
249	Liz Claiborne	O	70	2.61	2.9
250	Regis Corp.	O	70	1.38	9.3
251	Republic Health	O	70	1.17	(10.9)
252	Teleconcepts	A	70	0.66	(50.7)
253	Ally & Gargano	O	69	1.23	(39.5)
254	Ask Computer Sys.	O	69	0.50	(19.4)
255	Bliss, A.T.	O	69	3.15	(47.4)
256	Comcast	O	69	1.07	(22.3)
257	Convergent Technologies	O	69	0.40	(47.9)
258	Hale Systems	O	69	0.56	(15.8)
259	InteCom	O	69	0.33	(35.2)
260	National Health	O	69	1.01	(10.0)
261	Prime Motor Inns	N	69	1.09	(10.2)
262	SEI Corp.	O	69	0.89	(46.1)
263	Victory Markets	O	69	1.81	(12.3)
264	Amfesco Ind.	N	68	2.06	(35.7)
265	Florafax Int'l	O	68	0.49	(18.4)
266	Mr. Gasket	O	68	0.88	(30.4)
267	Onyx IMI	O	68	0.01	(63.2)
268	Oxoco	O	68	1.14	(15.2)
269	Pandick	N	68	1.37	(25.1)
270	Visual Technology	O	68	0.87	(31.9)
271	Academy Insurance	O	67	1.11	(36.8)
272	AirCal	O	67	0.85	(14.9)
273	American Carriers	O	67	1.85	(55.1)
274	Bolar Pharmaceutical	A	67	1.15	13.0
275	Chi-Chi's	O	67	0.53	(43.4)
276	Comdata Network	O	67	0.55	(34.0)
277	Compucare	O	67	0.46	(44.6)
278	Consolidated Products	O	67	0.29	(45.2)
279	Dart Drug	O	67	9.37	33.3
280	Intelligent Systems	O	67	0.84	(14.5)

Top Growth Companies (500 with sales of more than $25 million) *(continued)*

Rank	Company	Exchange	5-Year EPS Growth %	Latest 12-Month EPS	Year to Date Price Change
281	Biosearch Medical	O	66	0.04	(25.8)
282	Diodes	A	66	0.43	(30.2)
283	Etz Lavud Ltd.	A	66	1.67	5.6
284	NBI Inc.	N	66	1.09	(29.4)
285	Optel	O	66	2.70	(8.5)
286	Pacific Gas Transmission	A	66	2.75	(5.3)
287	Presidio Oil	A	66	0.19	16.7
288	Silicon Valley	O	66	0.84	(10.8)
289	Summit Health	O	66	0.41	9.6
290	Swedlow	O	66	1.21	13.2
291	WCS Int'l	O	66	0.12	(11.1)
292	Yankee Oil & Gas	A	66	1.22	(30.6)
293	Alamco	A	65	0.54	(5.3)
294	Ault Inc.	O	65	0.33	(62.3)
295	Booth Inc.	O	65	0.58	0.0
296	Clayton Homes	O	65	0.99	(26.1)
297	Coachmen Ind.	N	65	3.06	(36.5)
298	Community Psych.	N	65	1.51	(10.1)
299	Digital Switch	O	65	0.98	(41.3)
300	Home Depot	N	65	0.41	(25.7)
301	Pancho's Mexican Buffet	O	65	0.49	(10.3)
302	Pansophic Systems	O	65	0.97	(36.7)
303	Singer	N	65	0.64	(10.4)
304	Southmark	N	65	1.81	(26.6)
305	Action Industries	A	64	1.34	14.6
306	Applied Data Research	A	64	1.28	(35.9)
307	C 3	N	64	0.94	(37.1)
308	LSI Logic	O	64	0.44	(30.0)
309	Manhattan Industries	N	64	2.79	(17.1)
310	Saga Corp.	N	64	2.27	(9.2)
311	Sedco	N	64	6.02	0.3
312	Systems Integrators	O	64	0.74	(9.8)
313	Telepictures	O	64	1.01	(6.9)
314	Williams-Sonoma	O	64	0.30	(18.2)
315	Computer Consoles	A	63	1.17	(17.7)
316	Diebold	O	63	6.06	(4.0)
317	HBO & Co.	N	63	0.67	(1.8)
318	Higbee	O	63	4.51	0.0
319	Jeffrey Martin	O	63	0.83	(43.9)
320	Lowenstein, M.	N	63	6.62	1.9
321	Marshall Ind.	A	63	2.49	(29.1)
322	Matrix Corp.	A	63	0.74	(30.2)
323	Motor Club of America	O	63	1.99	14.5
324	Sandgate	A	63	2.76	42.9
325	Consolidated Capital	O	63	1.04	(12.2)
326	Spectro Industries	A	63	1.78	(3.1)
327	Thetford	O	63	1.40	(43.1)
328	Westmoreland Coal	O	63	1.91	1.0
329	Alpha Microsystems	O	62	1.46	(23.3)
330	American Stores	N	62	3.61	(24.9)
331	Bay Financial	N	62	3.78	13.3
332	Care Corp.	A	62	0.88	(35.4)
333	Financial Corp. of Am.	N	62	4.57	(29.6)
334	Golden Nugget	N	62	1.09	(25.0)
335	Quantum	O	62	1.03	(12.0)
336	Sunstates	N	62	0.98	(18.2)
337	Telex	N	62	2.32	(16.9)

Rank	Company	Exchange	5-Year EPS Growth %	Latest 12-Month EPS	Year to Date Price Change
338	Washington Fed. S&L	O	62	4.90	(26.3)
339	American Fed. S&L	O	61	3.56	(27.0)
340	Atwood Oceanics	O	61	2.62	4.3
341	General Defense	A	61	1.45	(31.3)
342	Lee Data	O	61	1.25	(48.6)
343	MDC	N	61	1.17	(30.2)
344	Policy Mgmt. Systems	O	61	0.63	(11.6)
345	Raymond Engineering	O	61	1.69	0.0
346	Rhodes Inc.	O	61	1.17	(31.1)
347	Standard Products	A	61	3.41	(36.9)
348	Standun Inc.	O	61	0.97	(20.3)
349	Technicom Int'l	A	61	0.34	(69.2)
350	Tellabs	O	61	0.99	(24.2)
351	Telxon	O	61	0.75	(11.6)
352	Unity Buying Service	A	61	2.50	9.6
353	Universal Health Services	O	61	0.70	10.9
354	Air Midwest	O	60	1.29	11.1
355	Apollo Computer	O	60	0.44	(13.5)
356	Armatron Int'l	A	60	1.16	2.3
357	Aviation Group	O	60	1.30	(17.9)
358	CompuShop	O	60	0.42	(45.8)
359	Concord Fabrics	A	60	1.38	14.3
360	DBA Systems	O	60	0.76	(22.0)
361	Dreyer's Grand Ice Cream	O	60	0.74	(16.1)
362	First Nat'l Supermarkets	O	60	2.70	(21.4)
363	Int'l King's Table	O	60	1.40	(17.4)
364	Key Pharmaceuticals	A	60	0.51	(25.7)
365	Paco Pharmaceuticals	O	60	0.94	(12.3)
366	Perini	A	60	2.35	12.8
367	Softech	O	60	0.47	(49.2)
368	Amcast Industrial	O	59	1.10	6.0
369	Armstrong Rubber	N	59	2.46	(4.1)
370	City Federal S&L	O	59	2.18	(22.5)
371	DST Systems	O	59	0.96	(44.8)
372	Falcon Oil & Gas	O	59	0.05	33.3
373	First Data	O	59	0.88	(3.6)
374	FMI Financial	O	59	0.14	(21.7)
375	Home Federal S&L	O	59	2.30	(19.4)
376	Medicare Glaser	O	59	0.44	(30.3)
377	Naugles	O	59	0.65	(56.6)
378	Optical Radiation	O	59	0.76	10.8
379	Savings Bank-Puget Sd.	O	59	3.47	(14.2)
380	Texscan Corp.	A	59	0.98	(34.0)
381	Todd Shipyards	N	59	4.64	4.0
382	BankAmerica Realty	N	58	2.70	(3.4)
383	Casey's General Stores	O	58	0.87	4.3
384	Cooper Tire & Rubber	N	58	2.15	(12.6)
385	Farah Mfg.	N	58	2.45	(19.0)
386	Floating Point Systems	N	58	1.47	(55.6)
387	Helene Curtis	N	58	2.84	(39.4)
388	Kaypro	O	58	0.42	(32.1)
389	Mediflex Systems	O	58	0.58	19.3
390	Monolithic Memories	O	58	0.81	(34.4)
391	Scan Optics	O	58	0.63	(15.0)
392	Thousand Trails	O	58	1.81	13.0
393	United Presidential	O	58	0.57	(21.3)

Top Growth Companies (500 with sales of more than $25 million) *(concluded)*

Rank	Company	Exchange	5-Year EPS Growth %	Latest 12-Month EPS	Year to Date Price Change
394	Ashton-Tate	O	57	0.68	(32.7)
395	Grolier	N	57	1.02	(2.9)
396	Helix Technology	O	57	1.30	(20.0)
397	Int'l Dairy Queen	O	57	3.10	9.9
398	ISC Systems	O	57	0.57	2.0
399	Kinder-Care Learning	O	57	0.82	(14.7)
400	People Express Airlines	O	57	0.31	(41.9)
401	Quotron Systems	O	57	0.73	(51.9)
402	Rax Restaurants	O	57	0.63	(26.8)
403	Scope Industries	A	57	3.31	(6.4)
404	Seton Co.	A	57	2.00	23.1
405	Westbridge Capital	A	57	1.02	(14.6)
406	Zayre	N	57	3.37	(18.6)
407	Cullinet Software	N	56	0.94	(23.3)
408	EDO	N	56	1.14	(16.4)
409	Fay's Drugs	O	56	0.60	(29.2)
410	Great American Federal	O	56	2.70	(9.9)
411	HealthAmerica	O	56	0.86	77.3
412	Kroy	O	56	1.33	(50.5)
413	Verbatim	A	56	0.60	(39.0)
414	Vicorp Restaurants	O	56	0.90	(15.7)
415	Tandem Computers	O	56	0.71	(45.2)
416	Bassett Walker	O	55	2.77	(6.6)
417	Federal Express	N	55	2.39	(31.4)
418	GNC Inc.	N	55	0.84	(44.8)
419	Nelson Research	O	55	0.05	(42.3)
420	Pier 1 Imports	N	55	1.32	(14.2)
421	Russell, Burdsall & Ward	A	55	0.08	(13.5)
422	Junstar Foods	O	55	1.12	(20.8)
423	Tandy	N	55	2.80	(39.2)
424	Teleflex	A	55	1.83	(24.0)
425	Affiliated Hospital Products	A	54	2.41	(16.7)
426	Amedco	A	54	0.91	(3.3)
427	Canadian Marconi	A	54	1.17	(15.0)
428	Dollar General	O	54	0.97	(15.2)
429	Dynalectron	A	54	1.00	(14.0)
430	Hechinger	O	54	0.90	(12.7)
431	Intermountain Gas	O	54	4.10	27.0
432	Minstar	O	54	0.74	19.1
433	Systematics	O	54	0.52	(32.1)
434	Trazonic	A	54	1.48	(6.7)
435	Unifi Inc.	O	54	1.54	(43.5)
436	Uniroyal	N	54	1.82	(41.2)
437	Universal Comm. Sys.	A	54	0.60	(19.0)
438	Cycare Sys.	O	53	1.02	(6.8)
439	First City Properties	N	53	0.41	23.1
440	National Medical Ent.	N	53	1.70	(8.2)
441	Golden Enterprises	O	53	1.22	(2.7)
442	Syntrex	O	53	0.40	(31.9)
443	Technitrol	A	53	1.46	(28.7)
444	Valley National	O	53	6.01	9.3
445	Watkins-Johnson	N	53	1.60	(21.3)
446	E-Systems	N	52	1.73	(22.2)
447	Hospital Corp. of America	N	52	2.97	1.6
448	Jackson Nat'l Life	O	52	2.23	5.2
449	Telecredit	A	52	1.07	(24.7)
450	Laidlaw Industries	O	51	0.67	(15.9)

Rank	Company	Exchange	5-Year EPS Growth %	Latest 12-Month EPS	Year to Date Price Change
451	Louisiana Land Offshore	O	51	1.95	0.0
452	Optical Coating Lab	O	51	1.25	(4.5)
453	Stop & Shop	N	51	4.10	(25.5)
454	Ungerman-Bass	O	51	0.14	(5.8)
455	Granger Associates	A	50	0.84	(18.8)
456	Lumex	A	50	0.79	(44.4)
457	Nat'l Patent Dev.	A	50	0.73	(54.5)
458	North Canadian Oils	A	50	2.81	7.8
459	Weyenberg Shoe	O	50	6.91	6.7
460	American Medical Int'l	N	49	2.14	(3.1)
461	Computer Language	O	49	0.59	(68.1)
462	EAC Industries	A	49	1.05	(32.1)
463	Farm Fresh	O	49	0.83	(18.2)
464	ICH Corp.	A	49	3.47	5.3
465	Ocean Drilling & Exp.	N	49	2.31	9.9
466	Sparton	N	49	1.45	(26.3)
467	Andrew Corp.	O	49	1.91	(23.7)
468	Atlantic Research	O	48	1.95	(5.1)
469	Bruno's	O	48	0.95	(11.0)
470	Cordura	N	48	1.44	(13.8)
471	CPT Corp.	O	48	0.99	1.0
472	Dynascan	O	48	0.58	(55.9)
473	Firestong Tire & Rubber	N	48	2.01	(27.0)
474	Foster Medical	O	48	0.35	20.4
475	Grand Auto	A	48	1.71	(19.6)
476	Omnicare	N	48	1.74	(40.4)
477	Value Line	O	48	1.12	(5.1)
478	Xidex	O	48	0.84	(29.7)
479	Arden Group	O	47	0.63	6.0
480	Beverly Enterprises	N	47	1.45	0.5
481	Computer Horizons	O	47	0.91	(28.2)
482	De Rose Industries	A	47	0.75	(47.0)
483	Matrix Science	O	47	1.57	(32.9)
484	Valspar	A	47	1.79	(9.2)
485	Collins & Aikman	N	46	4.47	(18.9)
486	Evans & Sutherland	O	46	1.10	(42.6)
487	Lynden	O	46	3.32	(5.4)
488	Mid-America Petroleum	O	46	0.04	(25.0)
489	National City Lines	O	46	3.77	(3.6)
490	Safety-Kleen	N	46	1.71	(3.7)
491	Brand Insulations	O	45	1.21	(22.7)
492	Brunswick	N	45	2.92	(14.3)
493	Canadian Occid. Petroleum	A	45	1.90	(7.6)
494	Citizens & Southern	O	45	1.96	(9.6)
495	Communications Systems	O	45	1.41	3.9
496	Data I/O Corp.	O	45	0.84	(42.4)
497	Electro-Biology	O	45	0.51	(35.2)
498	Electro-Rent Corp.	O	45	1.23	(25.0)
499	McCormick & Co.	O	45	4.92	(4.1)
500	Analog Devices	N	44	0.91	(31.2)

A: American Stock Exchange.   O: Over the counter.   N: New York Stock Exchange.

Source: Reprinted by permission of *Financial World*.

Major Certified Public Accounting (CPA) Firms*

Alexander Grant & Company
605 Third Avenue
New York, NY 10016
212-599-0100

Altschuler Melvoin and Glasser
69 West Washington Street
Chicago, IL 60602
312-236-9500

Arthur Andersen & Company[1]
69 West Washington Street
Chicago, IL 60602
312-346-6262

Arthur Young & Company[1]
277 Park Avenue
New York, NY 10017
212-922-2000

Baird, Kurtz & Dobson
928 Grand Avenue
Kansas City, MO 64106
816-221-7544

Cherry, Bekaert & Holland
1 NCNB Plaza
Charlotte, NC 28280
704-377-3741

Clifton, Gunderson & Co.
808 Commercial National Bank Building
Peoria, IL 61602
309-671-4511

Coopers & Lybrand[1]
1251 Avenue of the Americas
New York, NY 10020
212-536-2000

Crowe, Chizek and Company
330 East Jefferson Boulevard
South Bend, IN 46624
219-232-3992

Deloitte Haskins & Sells[1]
1114 Avenue of the Americas
New York, NY 10036
219-790-0500

Fox and Company
1660 Lincoln Street
Denver, CO 80264
303-861-5555

Ernst & Whinney[1]
2000 National City Center
Cleveland, OH 44114
216-861-5000

Kenneth Leventhal & Company
2049 Century Park East
Los Angeles, CA 90067
213-277-0880

Laventhol & Horwath
1845 Walnut Street
Philadelphia, PA 19103
215-299-1700

Main Hurdman
55 East 52nd Street
New York, NY 10055
212-909-5000

McGladrey Hendrickson & Pullen
640 Capital Square
4th & Locust
Des Moines, IA 50309
515-284-8660

Moss Adams & Co.
2830 Bank of California Center
Seattle, WA 98164
206-223-1820

Geo. S. Olive & Company
320 North Meridian Street
Indianapolis, IN 46204
317-267-8400

Oppenheim, Appel, Dixon & Co.
One New York Plaza
New York, NY 10004
212-422-1000

Pannell, Kerr, Forster & Co.
420 Lexington Avenue
New York, NY 10017
212-867-8000

Peat, Marwick, Mitchell & Co.[1]
345 Park Avenue
New York, NY 10022
212-758-9700

---

* Firms with the largest number of American Institute of Certified Public Accountants (AICPA) members.
[1] One of the "Big 8" accounting firms.
Source: American Institute of Certified Public Accountants.

Plante & Moran
26211 Central Park Boulevard
Southfield, MI 48037
313-352-2500

Price Waterhouse & Co.[1]
1251 Avenue of the Americas
New York, NY 10020
212-489-8900

Seidman & Seidman
110 Union Bank Building
Grand Rapids, MI 49503
616-744-2111

Touche Ross & Company[1]
1633 Broadway
New York, NY 10019
212-489-1600

Capital Sources for Startup Companies and Small Businesses

Sources of Venture Capital

INTRODUCTION

What Is An SBIC?

Although individual investors have been providing venture capital for new and small business in the United States for many years, no institutional sources of such financing existed until 1958 when Congress passed the Small Business Investment Act.

Small business investment companies (SBICs) and minority enterprise small business investment companies (MESBICs) are financial institutions created to make equity capital and long-term credit (with maturities of at least 5 years) available to small, independent businesses. SBICs are licensed by the Federal Government's Small Business Administration, but they are privately-organized and privately-managed firms which set their own policies and make their own investment decisions. In return for pledging to finance only small businesses, SBICs may qualify for long-term loans from SBA. Although all SBICs will consider applications for funds from socially and economically disadvantaged entrepreneurs. MESBICs normally make all their investments in this area.

What Have SBICs Done?

To date, SBICs have disbursed over $4.5-billion by making over 66,000 loans and investments. The concerns they have financed have far out-performed all national averages as measured by increases in assets, sales, profits, and new employment.

Need Money? Which SBIC Should You See?

This Directory of members of the National Association of Small Business Investment Companies (NASBIC) lists over 350 SBICs and MESBICs. They represent approximately 90% of the industry's resources and are located in all parts of the country.

In using this Directory, you should consider the following factors:

A. *Geography:* Generally speaking, SBICs are more likely to make loans and investments near their offices, even though many of them operate regionally or even nationally. Therefore, it would probably be wise to contact first those SBICs closest to your business.

B. *Investment Policy:* Even though most SBICs have both equity investments and straight loans in their portfolios, each of them has a policy on which type of financing it prefers. This Directory utilizes a code symbol which indicates that policy; you should match your requirements with that information.

C. *Industry Preferences:* Here again, SBICs differ widely. Because of the expertise of its officers and directors, an SBIC often specializes in making loans and investments in certain industries. This Directory indicates such specialization.

D. *Size of Financing:* Because they differ in size and investment policies, SBICs establish different dollar limits on the financings they make. This Directory has a symbol showing the preferred maximum size of loan or investment for each SBIC.

It should be emphasized that the information given in the Directory should be considered only as a general guide. Every SBIC departs from its usual policies in special cases. Furthermore, SBICs often work together in making loans or investments in greater amounts than any of them could make separately. No SBIC should be ruled out as a possible source of financing, since this Directory is designed to give you an idea about which ones are *most likely* to be interested in your application.

Is Your Firm Eligible for SBIC Financing?

Probably so, since the overwhelming majority of all business firms qualify as small. As a general rule, companies are eligible if they have net worth under $6-million and average after-tax earnings of less than $2-million during the past two years. *In addition,* your firm may qualify as small either under an employment standard or amount of annual sales. Both these standards vary from industry to industry.

A phone call or a note to any NASBIC member—or to our Washington office—will clear up the eligibility question quickly.

Source: *Venture Capital, Where to Find It,* National Association of Small Business Investment Companies, 618 Washington Building, Washington, D.C. 20005.

242

How Do You Present Your Case To An SBIC?

There is nothing mysterious about asking an SBIC for money. You should prepare a report on your operations, financial condition, and requirements. Specifically, the report should include detailed information on key personnel, products, proposed new product lines, patent positions, market data and competitive position, distribution and sales methods, and other pertinent materials.

How Long Will It Take?

There are no hard and fast rules about the length of time it will take an SBIC to investigate and close a transaction. Ordinarily, an initial response, either positive or negative, is made quickly. On the other hand, the thorough study an SBIC must make before it can make a final decision could take several weeks.

Naturally, a well-documented presentation on your part will reduce the amount of time the SBIC will require.

How Are SBIC Financings Structured?

Every single SBIC financing is tailored individually to meet your needs and to make the best use of the SBIC's funds. You and the SBIC will negotiate the terms. The SBIC might buy shares of your stock or it might make a straight loan.

Usually, SBICs are interested in generating capital gains, so they will purchase stock in your company or advance funds through a note, or debenture, with conversion privileges or rights to buy stock at a predetermined later date.

How Can SBIC Money Provide Additional Credit Lines?

If the SBIC money is provided to you in a subordinated position, it will often do double or triple duty. Industry averages show that for every SBIC dollar placed with a small business concern, two additional senior dollars become available from commercial banks or other sources.

Are There Unique Advantages To SBIC Financing?

Yes, indeed! Before it receives its license, an SBIC must prove that its management and directors are experienced individuals with a broad range of business and professional talents.

This expertise will be applied to assist your business, supplementing the skills of your own management team. Here again, the actual pattern of management and financial counseling will be cut to fit each specific situation.

SBICs can make only long-term loans or equity investments; therefore, their interests and yours will coincide—both of you will want your firm to grow and prosper.

Will I Be Treated Fairly?

As mentioned above, SBICs are licensed by the Federal Government only after their officers and directors have been carefully screened. Furthermore, all the SBICs listed in this Directory are NASBIC members and all have voluntarily subscribed to the Association's Code of Ethics and Trade Practice Rules.

The Code provides, in part, that "the constant goal of each SBIC shall be to improve the welfare of the small business concerns which it serves. Each SBIC shall promote and maintain ethical standards of conduct and deal fairly and honestly with all small business concerns seeking its assistance."

What Is NASBIC?

It is the national trade association which represents the overwhelming majority of all active SBICs and MESBICs. It was formed in 1958, soon after the passage of the Small Business Investment Act, and has worked on behalf of small business generally and the SBIC industry in particular for 25 years.

In addition to providing educational and informational services for its members, NASBIC presses for a rational legal and regulatory framework for the industry. It also cooperates closely with other independent business associations in advancing the interests of small business on the Federal level.

Need More Information?

Contact any SBIC in this Directory. Write the National Association of Small Business Investment Companies (NASBIC), 618 Washington Building, Washington, D.C. 20005.

EXPLANATION OF CODES

Preferred Limit for Loans or Investments

A—up to $100,000
B—up to $250,000
C—up to $500,000
D—up to $1-million
E—Above $1-million

Investment Policy

·   —Will consider either loans or investments
· · —Prefers to make long-term loans
· · · —Prefers financings with right to acquire stock interest

Industry Preferences

1. Communications
2. Construction & Development
3. Natural Resources
4. Hotels, Motels & Restaurants
5. Manufacturing & Processing

6. Medical & Other Health Services
7. Recreation & Amusements
8. Research & Technology
9. Retailing, Wholesaling & Distribution
10. Service Trades
11. Transportation
12. Diversified

MESBIC—an SBIC which concentrates in placing its loans and investments with

a small businessperson who is socially
or economically disadvantaged

Non-SBIC Members

This Directory also lists a number of Associate and Sustaining Members of NASBIC. Some
of these firms are non-SBIC venture capitalists
who also invest in small businesses. Others are
firms which provide professional services to
SBICs and to small business concerns.

ALABAMA
First SBIC of Alabama
Mr. David C. DeLaney, Pres.
16 Midtown Park E.
Mobile, AL 36606
(205) 476-0700
C ** 12

Tuskegee Capital Corp.
Mr. E. Taylor Harmon, Pres.
PO Drawer GG
Tuskegee Institute, AL 36088
(205) 727-2850
MESBIC A * 2,5,12

ALASKA
Alaska Business Investment Corp.
Mr. James L. Cloud, VP
301 W. Northern Lights Blvd.
PO Box 600
Anchorage, AK 99510
(907) 265-2816
C * 1,5,6,8,12

Alaska Pacific Inv. Corp.
Mr. Robert R. Richards, Pres.
PO Box 420
Anchorage, AK 99510
(907) 276-0002
A *** 12

Calista Business Investment Corp.
Mr. Alex Raider, Pres.
516 Denali St.
Anchorage, AK 99501
(907) 279-5516
MESBIC B * 12

ARIZONA
Rocky Mountain Equity Corp.
Mr. Anthony J. Nicoli, Pres.
4530 N. Central Ave., Ste. 3
Phoenix, AZ 85012
(602) 274-7558
A * 4,7,8,10

Sun Belt Capital Corporation
Mr. Brian Burch, VP
14255 N. 76th Pl., Ste A-1
Scottsdale, AZ 85260
(602) 998-4444
A * 2,9,10

ARKANSAS
Capital Management Services, Inc.
Mr. David L. Hale, Pres.
1910 N. Grant, Ste. 200
Little Rock, AR 72207
(501) 664-8613
MESBIC A *** 12

First SBIC of Arkansas, Inc.
Mr. Fred C. Burns, Pres.
1400 Worthen Bank Bldg.
Little Rock, AR 72201
(501) 378-1876
A *** 12

Independence Financial
Services, Inc.
Mr. Preston Grace, Jr., Pres.
PO Box 3878
Batesville, AR 72503
(501) 793-4533
D * 12

Kar-Mal Venture Capital, Inc.
Mr. Thomas Karam, Pres.
610 Plaza West Bldg.
Little Rock, AR 72205
(501) 661-0010
MESBIC B *** 12

Power Ventures, Inc.
Mr. Dorsey D. Glover, Pres.
829 Highway 270 N.
PO Box 518
Malvern, AR 72104
(501) 332-3695
MESBIC A *** 12

CALIFORNIA
AMF Financial, Inc.
Mr. William A. Temple, Pres.
9910-D Mira Mesa Blvd.
San Diego, CA 92131
(619) 695-0233
A *** 12

Branch Office
Atalanta Investment Co., Inc.
Mr. Alan W. Livingston, Pres.
141 El Camino Dr.
Los Angeles, CA 90212
(213) 273-1730
D *** 1,2,5,6,7,8
(Main office in NY)

Bay Venture Group
Mr. William Chandler, Gen. Ptnr.
One Embarcadero Ctr., Ste. 3303
San Francisco, CA 94111
(415) 989-7680
B *** 1,6,8

Beverly Glen Venture Capital
Mr. Herman Jacobs, Pres.
1964 Westwood Blvd., Ste. 450
Los Angeles, CA 90025
(213) 550-0431
B * 5,12

Brantman Capital Corp.
Mr. W.T. Brantman, Pres.
PO Box 877
Tiburon, CA 94920
(415) 435-4747
A *** 1,4,5,6,8,9,10,11,12

Brentwood Associates
Mr. Timothy Pennington, Gen Ptnr
11661 San Vicente Blvd. Ste. 707
Los Angeles, CA 90049
(213) 826-6581
E *** 1,8

Business Equity and
Development Corp.
Mr. Ricardo J. Olivarez, Pres.
1411 W. Olympic Blvd., Ste. 200
Los Angeles, CA 90015
(213) 385-0351
MESBIC B *** 1,5,6,12

Cal Fed Venture Capital Corp.
Ms. Anna Henry, Pres.
5670 Wilshire Blvd., Ste. 2135
Los Angeles, CA 90036
(213) 932-4077
C *** 1,5,6,7,8,9,10,12

California Capital Investors, Ltd
Mr. Arthur Bernstein, Gen. Ptnr.
11812 San Vicente Blvd.
Los Angeles, CA 90049
(213) 820-7222
B *** 1,5,6,11,12

California Partners
Mr. Alan R. Brudos, Sec.
3000 Sand Hill Rd.
Bldg. 2, Ste. 260
Menlo Park, CA 94025
(415) 854-1555
A *** 1,8

CFB Venture Capital Corporation
Mr. Piet Westerbeek III, CFO
530 B St., 2nd Fl.
San Diego, CA 92101
(619) 230-3304
C * 1,6,8

Charterway Investment Corp.
Mr. Harold Chuang, Pres.
222 S. Hill St., Ste. 800
Los Angeles, CA 90012
(213) 687-8534
B *** 2,4,5,7,9

Churchill International
Oceanic Capital Corp.
Mr. Robert C. Weeks, Pres.
545 Middlefield Rd., Ste. 160
Menlo Park, CA 94025
(415) 328-4401
C * 1,5,8

Churchill International
Pan American Investment Co.
Mr. Robert C. Weeks, Mng. Dir.
545 Middlefield Rd., Ste. 160
Menlo Park, CA 94025
(415) 328-4401
D * 1,5,8

Branch Office
Citicorp Venture Capital, Ltd.
Mr. Peter G. Gerry, Pres.
44 Montgomery St.
San Francisco, CA 94104
(415) 954-1154
E *** 1,3,5,6,8,10,11
(Main office in NY)

City Ventures, Inc.
Mr. Neill B. Lawton, Pres.
404 N. Roxbury Dr., Ste. 800
Beverly Hills, CA 90210
(213) 550-0416
D *** 1,5,6,8,12

Continental Investors, Inc.
Mr. Lac Thantrong, Pres.
8781 Seaspray Dr.
Huntington Beach, CA 92646
(714) 964-5207
MESBIC B * 4,6,9,10,12

anch Office
rnell Capital Corp.
. Alan B. Newman
49 Century Park E., 12th Fl.
ntury City, CA 90067
13) 277-7993
*** 4,9,12
ain office in NY)

ocker Ventures, Inc.
. Jordan Burkart, VP
e Montgomery St.
n Francisco, CA 94104
15) 983-3636
* 12

osspoint Investment Corp.
. Max S. Simpson, Pres.
15 Corporation Way
Box 10101
lo Alto, CA 94303
15) 964-3545
*** 1,5,6

velopers Equity Cap. Corp.
. Larry Sade, Pres.
201 Wilshire Blvd., Ste. 204
everly Hills, CA 90210
13) 278-3611
* 2,4,6

nterprise Venture Cap. Corp.
. Ernest de la Ossa, Pres.
22 The Alameda, Ste. 306
n Jose, CA 95126
408) 249-3507
* 1,4,5,6,8,10,12

quitable Capital Corp.
. John C. Lee, Pres.
55 Sansome St., Ste. 200
n Francisco, CA 94111
15) 434-4114
SBIC B * 1,2,11,12

rst Interstate Capital
. David B. Jones, Pres.
5 S. Figueroa, Ste. 1900
s Angeles, CA 90071
13) 622-1922
*** 12

rst SBIC of California
. Timothy Hay, Pres.
. Gregory Forrest, Sr. VP
. Michael Cronin, VP
. Brian Jones, VP
. James McElwee, VP
00 MacArthur Blvd., Ste. 950
ewport Beach, CA 92660
14) 754-4780
*** 12

anch Office
irst SBIC of California
. John D. Padgett, VP
. Tony Stevens, VP
5th Fl., H25-4
33 S. Hope St.
s Angeles, CA 90071
13) 613-5215
*** 12

lover Capital Corp.
. J. David Ray, Pres.
00 E. Dominquez St.
arson, CA 90746
13) 532-6187
* 1,3,6,7,8,12

amco Capital
. William R. Hambrecht, Pres.
35 Montgomery St.
n Francisco, CA 94104
15) 986-5500
*** 1,6,8

JB Enterprises, Ltd.
. Jack M. Atkin, Gen. Mgr.
878 Doyle St.
meryville, CA 94608
15) 428-2181
SBIC A * 2,5,9,12

Imperial Ventures, Inc.
Mr. Donald B. Prell, Pres.
9920 S. LaCienega Blvd., 14th Fl
Inglewood, CA 90301
(213) 417-5888
A * 12

Ivanhoe Venture Cap., Ltd.
Brigadier Gen. Alan R. Toffler
  Managing Partner
737 Pearl St., Ste. 201
La Jolla, CA 92037
(619) 454-8882
C *** 1,5,6,12

Lasung Investment & Finance Co.
Mr. Jung Su Lee, Pres.
3600 Wilshire Blvd., Ste.1410
Los Angeles, CA 90010
(213) 384-7548
MESBIC B * 9,12

Latigo Capital Partners
Mr. Donald Peterson, Gen. Ptnr.
23410 Civic Ctr. Way, Ste. E-2
Malibu, CA 90265
(213) 456-5054
C * 1,6,8

Marwit Capital Corp.
Mr. Martin Witte, Pres.
180 Newport Ctr. Dr., Ste. 200
Newport Beach, CA 92660
(714) 640-6234
D *** 1,2,4,5,6,8,12

MCA New Ventures, Inc.
Mr. W. Roderick Hamilton, Pres.
100 Universal City Pl.
Universal City, CA 91608
(213) 508-2933
MESBIC C * 1,12

Merrill, Pickard, Anderson
  & Eyre
Mr. Steven L. Merrill, Mng. Ptnr.
Two Palo Alto Sq., Ste. 425
Palo Alto, CA 94306
(415) 856-8880
E *** 1,6,8

Metropolitan Venture Co.
Mr. Rudolph J. Lowy, Chmn.
8383 Wilshire Blvd., Ste. 360
Beverly Hills, CA 90211
(213) 651-2175
B *** 1,2,6,8

Myriad Capital, Inc.
Mr. Kuo-Hung Chen, Sec.
8820 S. Sepulveda Blvd., Ste. 204
Los Angeles, CA 90045
(213) 641-7936
MESBIC E * 12

Branch Office
Nelson Capital Corp.
Mr. Norman Tulchin, Chmn.
1901 Ave. of the Stars, Ste. 584
Los Angeles, CA 90067
(213) 556-1944
E * 12
(Main Office in NY)

New West Ventures
Mr. Tim Haidinger, Pres.
180 Newport Ctr. Dr., Ste. 200
Newport Beach, CA 92660
(714) 759-0884
E *** 1,5,6,9,11,12

Opportunity Capital Corp.
Mr. J. Peter Thompson, Pres.
50 California St., Ste. 2505
San Francisco, CA 94111
(415) 421-5935
MESBIC B *** 1,5,11

PCF Venture Capital Corporation
Mr. Miguel L. Guerrero, Pres.
3420 E. Third Ave., Ste. 200
Foster City, CA 94404
(415) 571-5411
B * 1,6

San Joaquin Capital Corp.
Mr. Chester W. Troudy, Pres.
PO Box 2538
1675 Chester Ave., Ste. 330
Bakersfield, CA 93303
(805) 323-7581
B *** 5,8,9,12

San Jose SBIC, Inc.
Mr. Robert T. Murphy, Pres.
100 Park Ctr. Pl., Ste. 427
San Jose, CA 95113
(408) 293-8052/7708
B * 1,5,6,8,12

Seaport Ventures, Inc.
Mr. Michael Stolper, Pres.
770 B St., Ste. 420
San Diego, CA 92101
(619) 232-4069
B *** 12

Space Ventures, Inc.
Mr. Leslie R. Brewer, Pres.
3931 MacArthur Blvd., Ste. 212
Newport Beach, CA 92660
(714) 851-0855
MESBIC C *** 12

Union Venture Corp.
Mr. Brent T. Rider, Pres.
445 S. Figueroa St.
Los Angeles, CA 90071
(213) 236-6292
E *** 1,5,6,8,12

Unity Capital Corp.
Mr. Frank W. Owen, Pres.
4343 Morena Blvd., Ste. 3A
San Diego, CA 92117
(619) 275-6030
MESBIC B *** 1,2,8,12

Vista Capital Corp.
Mr. Fred J. Howden, Jr., Chmn.
701 "B" St., Ste. 760
San Diego, CA 92101
(619) 236-1900
D *** 1,3,5,6,8,12

Wells Fargo Equity Corp.
Mr. Michael F. Park, Sr. VP
Mr. Louis Gerken, VP
One Embarcadero Ctr., Ste. 1814
San Francisco, CA 94111
(415) 396-3291
D *** 12

Wesco Capital, Ltd.
Mr. Peter J. Madigan, Gen. Ptnr.
3471 Via Lido, Ste. 204
Newport Beach, CA 92663
(714) 673-4733
B *** 12

Westamco Investment Co.
Mr. Leonard G. Muskin, Pres.
8929 Wilshire Blvd., Ste. 400
Beverly Hills, CA 90211
(213) 652-8288
B * 2,4,6,7,9,12

Branch Office
Wood River Capital Corp.
3000 Sand Hill Rd., Ste. 280
Menlo Park, CA 94025
(415) 854-7145
C *** 1,5,6
(Main Office in NY)

Yosemite Capital Investment
Mr. J. Horace Hampton, Pres.
448 Fresno St.
Fresno, CA 93706
(209) 485-2431
MESBIC A *** 12

COLORADO
Colorado Growth Capital, Inc.
Mr. Nicholas Davis, Chmn./Pres.
1600 Broadway, Ste. 2125
Denver, CO 80202
(303) 629-0205
B *** 5,12

Enervest, Inc.
Mr. Mark Kimmel, Pres.
7000 E. Bellevue Ave., Ste. 310
Englewood, CO 80111
(303) 771-9650
D *** 1,5,6,8

Mile Hi SBIC
Mr. Joseph Chavez, Inv. Adv.
1355 S. Colorado Blvd., Ste. 400
Denver, CO 80222
(303) 830-0087
MESBIC B *** 1,5,6,8,12

Branch Office
Norwest Venture Cap. Mgmt., Inc.
Mr. Larry R. Wonnacott, V.P.
Mr. Mark Dubovy, V.P.
1801 California St., Ste. 585
City Center Four
Denver, CO 80202
(303) 297-0537
E *** 1,5,8
(Main Office in MN)

CONNECTICUT
Asset Capital & Management Corp.
Mr. Robert N. Nolting, VP
608 Ferry Blvd.
Stratford, CT 06497
(203) 375-0299
C ** 1,6

Capital Resource Co.
  of Connecticut
Mr. I. Martin Fierberg, Ptnr.
699 Bloomfield Ave.
Bloomfield, CT 06002
(203) 243-1114
B * 12

The First Connecticut SBIC
Mr. James Breiner, Chmn.
Mr. David Engelson, Pres.
177 State St.
Bridgeport, CT 06604
(203) 366-4726
D * 1,2,4,5,6,9,12

Marcon Capital Corp.
Mr. Martin Cohen, Pres.
49 Riverside Ave.
Westport, CT 06880
(203) 226-7751
A ** 1,9,10

Northeastern Capital Corp.
Mr. Louis W. Mingione, VP
310 Main St.
East Haven, CT 06512
(203) 469-7901
A * 12

Regional Financial Enterprises
Mr. Robert M. Williams, Chmn.
51 Pine St.
New Canaan, CT 06840
(203) 966-2800
E *** 1,5,6,8,9,12

SBIC of Connecticut
Mr. Kenneth F. Zarrilli, Pres.
1115 Main St., Rm. 610
Bridgeport, CT 06604
(203) 367-3282
A ** 12

DISTRICT OF COLUMBIA
Allied Capital Corp.
Mr. George C. Williams, Pres.
Mr. David Gladstone, Exec. VP
1625 I St., NW, Ste. 603
Washington, DC 20006
(202) 331-1112
C *** 12

Broadcast Capital, Inc.
Mr. John E. Oxendine, Pres.
1771 N St., NW, Ste. 420
Washington, DC 20036
(202) 293-3575
MESBIC C *** 1

Capital Investment Co. of Wash.
Mr. John Katkish, Pres.
1208 - 30th St., NW
Washington, DC 20007
(202) 333-2281
A * 2,6

Branch Office
Continental Investors, Inc.
Mr. Lac Thantrong, Pres.
2020 K Street, NW, Ste. 350
Washington, DC 20006
(202) 466-3709
MESBIC B * 4,6,9,10,12
(Main Office in CA)

Fulcrum Venture Cap. Corp.
Mr. Divakar Kamath, VP
2021 K St., NW, Ste. 301
Washington, DC 20006
(202) 833-9590
MESBIC B *** 1,5,6,9,11,12

Snycom Capital Corp.
Mr. Herbert P. Wilkins, Pres.
1625 I St., NW, Ste. 412
Washington, DC 20006
(202) 293-9428
MESBIC C *** 1

FLORIDA
Branch Office
Allied Capital Corp.
Mr. G. Cabell Williams, Asst. VP
One Financial Pl., Ste. 1614
Ft. Lauderdale, FL 33394
(305) 763-8484
C *** 12
(Main Office in DC)

Caribank Capital Corp.
Mr. Michael E. Chaney, Pres.
255 E. Dania Beach Blvd.
Dania, FL 33004
(305) 925-2211/ext.400
C *** 1,3,5,6,8

CUBICO, Ltd.
Mr. Anthony G. Marina, Pres.
7425 NW 79th St.
Miami, FL 33166
(305) 885-8881
MESBIC B * 12

First American Investment Corp.
Mr. Joseph N. Hardin, Jr., Pres.
3250 Mary St., Ste. 308
Coconut Grove, FL 33133
(305) 441-0881
C *** 2,8,12

First Tampa Capital Corp.
Mr. Thomas L. du Pont, Pres.
4600 N. Dale Mabry Hwy.
Tampa, FL 33614
(813) 879-4058
B *** 12

Ideal Financial Corp.
Mr. Mario Pineda, Gen. Mgr.
85 Grand Canal Dr., Ste. 105
Miami, FL 33144
(305) 264-1468
MESBIC B * 12

J & D Capital Corp.
Mr. Jack Carmel, Pres.
12747 Biscayne Blvd.
North Miami, FL 33181
(305) 893-0303
B * 5,9,12

Mansfield Capital Corp.
Mr. Stephen H. Farrington, Pres.
2900 14th St., N
Naples, FL 33940
(813) 263-3660
A * 12

Market Capital Corp.
Mr. E.E. Eads, Pres.
PO Box 22667
Tampa, FL 33622
(813) 248-5781
A * 2,9

Massachusetts Capital Corp.
Ms. Mary Helen Blakeslee, Pres.
3250 Mary St., Ste. 308
Coconut Grove, FL 33133
(305) 441-0924
C * 1,5,6,8

Safeco Capital, Inc.
Dr. Rene J. Leonard, Pres.
835 SW 37th Ave.
Miami, FL 33135
(305) 443-7953
MESBIC B *** 12

Servico Capital Corp.
Mr. Gary O. Marino, Pres.
1601 Belvedere Rd., Ste. 201
West Palm Beach, FL 33406
(305) 689-4906
A * 1,4,5,11

Small Business Assistance Corp.
  of Panama City, FL
Mr. Charles S. Smith, Pres.
2612 W. 15th St., PO Box 1627
Panama City, FL 32401
(904) 785-9577
C * 12

Southeast Venture Capital, Inc.
Mr. C.L. Hofmann, Pres.
100 S. Biscayne Blvd.
Miami, FL 33131
(305) 577-4680
D *** 1,5,6,8,11,12

Branch Office
Threshold Ventures, Inc.
Mr. T. Denny Sanford, Chmn.
2566D McMullen Booth Rd.
Clearwater, FL 33519
(813) 797-7697
B *** 1,5,6,9,12
(Main office in MN)

Trans Florid' Capital Corp.
Mr. Alex Echevarria, VP
1450 Avenida Madruga, #402
Coral Gables, FL 33146
(305) 665-5489
MESBIC B * 12

Universal Financial Services, Inc
Mr. Norman Zipkin, Pres.
225 NE 35th St., Ste. B
Miami, FL 33137
(305) 573-6326
MESBIC B * 12

Venture Group, Inc.
Mr. Ellis W. Hitzing, Pres.
5433 Buffalo Ave.
Jacksonville, FL 32208
(904) 355-6265
MESBIC A * 9

enture Opportunities Corp.
r. A. Fred March, Pres.
44 Brickell Ave., Ste. 930
iami, FL 33131
305) 358-0359
ESBIC B *** 1,2,5,12

erde Capital Corp.
r. Jose Dearing, Pres.
701 Sunset Dr., State 104
outh Miami, FL 33143
305) 666-8789
ESBIC B * 2,5,9,12

estern Financial Cap. Corp.
r. Fredric M. Rosemore, Pres.
2550 Biscayne Blvd., Ste. 406
. Miami, FL 33181
305) 891-0823
** 6,12

EORGIA
ffiliated Investment Fund, Ltd.
r. Samuel Weissman, Pres.
225 Shurfine Dr.
ollege Park, GA 30337
404) 766-0221
** 9

entral Georgia Capital
 Funding Corp.
r. H. Edward Downey, Pres.
O Box 218
llenwood, GA 30349
404) 474-2892
ESBIC B * 12

ighty Capital Corp.
r. Gary Korynoski, VP/Gen. Mgr.
0 Technology Park
tlanta - Ste. 100
orcross, GA 30092
404) 448-2232
9,10

unbelt Funding Corp.
r. Charles H. Jones, Pres.
O Box 7006
acon, GA 31298
912) 474-5137
ESBIC A * 12

AWAII
acific Venture Capital, Ltd.
r. Dexter J. Taniguchi, Pres.
405 N. King St., Ste. 302
onolulu, HI 96817
808) 847-6502
ESBIC A *** 12

DAHO
irst Idaho Venture Capital Corp.
r. Ron Twilegar, Pres.
00 W. Washington
oise, ID 83701
208) 345-3460
*** 12

LLINOIS
bbott Capital Corp.
r. Richard E. Lassar, Pres.
933 Lawler Ave., Ste. 125
kokie, IL 60077
312) 982-0404
*** 1,6,10

lpha Capital Corp.
r. Andrew H. Kalnow, Pres.
 First National Pl. Ste. 1400
hicago, IL 60602
312) 372-1556
*** 12

usiness Ventures, Inc.
r. Milton Lefton, Pres.
0 N. Wacker Dr., Ste. 550
hicago, IL 60606
312) 346-1580
* 12

CEDCO Capital Corp.
Mr. J.C. Taylor, VP/Gen.Mgr.
180 N. Michigan Ave., Ste. 333
Chicago, IL 60601
(312) 984-5971
MESBIC A * 12

Chicago Community Ventures Inc.
Ms. Phyllis George, Pres.
108 N. State St., Ste. 902
Chicago, IL 60602
(312) 726-6084
MESBIC B *** 4,5,12

Combined Opportunities, Inc.
Mr. E. Patric Jones, Pres.
1525 E. 53rd St.
Chicago, IL 60615
(312) 752-5355
MESBIC B * 12

Continental Illinois Venture Corp.
Mr. John L. Hines, Pres.
231 S. LaSalle St.
Chicago, IL 60697
(312) 828-8021
E *** 1,5,6,7,8,9,10

First Capital Corp. of Chicago
Mr. John A. Canning, Jr., Pres.
One First National Pl., Ste. 2628
Chicago, IL 60670
(312) 732-5400
E *** 12

Frontenac Capital Corp.
Mr. David A.R. Dullum, Pres.
208 S. LaSalle St., Rm. 1900
Chicago, IL 60604
(312) 368-0044
C *** 1,5,6,8,12

FUND'S Inc.
Mr. William R. Breihan, Gen. Mgr.
1930 George St.
Melrose Park, IL 60068
(312) 921-5100
A * 6,9

Golder, Thoma & Cressey
Mr. Stanley C. Golder, Gen. Ptnr.
120 S. LaSalle St., Ste. 630
Chicago, IL 60603
(312) 853-3322
D *** 1,5,6,11,12

Heizer Corp.
Mr. E.F. Heizer, Jr., Chmn./Pres.
20 N. Wacker Dr., Ste. 4100
Chicago, IL 60606
(312) 641-2200
E *** 1,4,5,6,7,8,9,12

Mesirow Capital Corp.
Mr. James C. Tyree, Exec. VP
135 S. LaSalle St., Ste. 3713
Chicago, IL 60603
(312) 443-5757
E *** 1,4,5,6,7,9,10,11,12

Branch Office
Nelson Capital Corp.
Mr. Irwin B. Nelson, Pres.
8550 W. Bryn Mawr Ave., Ste. 515
Chicago, IL 60631
(312) 693-5990
E * 12
(Main Office in NY)

Tower Ventures, Inc.
Mr. James M. Troka, Pres.
Sears Tower, BSC 43-50
Chicago, IL 60684
(312) 875-0583
MESBIC B * 12

The Urban Fund of Illinois, Inc.
Mr. E. Patric Jones, Pres.
1525 E. 53rd St.
Chicago, IL 60615
(312) 752-5355
MESBIC B * 12

Walnut Capital Corp.
Mr. Burton W. Kanter, Chmn.
Three First Nat'l. Pl., 22nd Fl.
Chicago, IL 60602
(312) 269-1732
C *** 12
(Branch Office in NY)

INDIANA
First Indiana Equity Group
Mr. Samuel Sutphin
20 N. Meridian St., 3rd Fl.
Indianapolis, IN 46240
(317) 635-4551
B * 12

Heritage Venture Group, Inc.
Mr. Arthur A. Angotti, Pres.
One Indiana Sq., Ste. 2400
Indianapolis, IN 46204
(317) 635-5696
D *** 1,5,6

Mt. Vernon Venture Capital Co.
Mr. Thomas Grande, Gen. Mgr.
9102 N Meridian St., PO Box 40177
Indianapolis, IN 46240
(317) 846-5106
B * 12

White River Capital Corp.
Mr. John H. Cragoe, Pres.
Mr. David J. Blair, VP
500 Washington St.
Columbus, IN 47201
(812) 376-1759
B *** 1,5,6,8,9,10,11,12

IOWA
R.W. Allsop Capital Corp.
Mr. Robert W. Allsop, Pres.
Mr. Paul D. Rhines, Exec. VP
2750 First Ave., NE, Ste. 210
Cedar Rapids, IA 52402
(319) 363-8971
C *** 1,5,6,12

MorAmerica Capital Corp.
Mr. Jerry M. Burrows, Pres.
300 American Bldg.
Cedar Rapids, IA 52401
(319) 363-8249
D *** 1,5,6,9,12

KANSAS
Branch Office
R.W. Allsop Capital Corp.
Mr. Larry C. Maddox, VP
35 Corporate Woods, Ste. 244
9101 W. 110th St.
Overland Park, KS 66210
(913) 642-4719
C *** 1,5,6,12
(Main office in Iowa)

Kansas Venture Capital, Inc.
Mr. George L. Doak, Pres.
First Nat'l Bank Tower, Ste. 1030
One Townsite Pl.
Topeka, KS 66603
(913) 233-1368
B *** 5

KENTUCKY
Blackburn-Sanford Venture
 Capital Corp.
Mr. Charles Arensberg, Gen. Mgr.
3120 First National Tower
Louisville, KY 40202
(502) 585-9612
C *** 1,4,5,9,11,12

Equal Opportunity Finance, Inc.
Mr. Frank P. Justice, Pres.
420 Hurstbourne Ln., Ste. 201
Louisville, KY 40222
(502) 423-1943
MESBIC B * 12

Financial Opportunities, Inc.
Mr. Gary F. Duerr, Gen. Mgr.
981 S. Third St.
Louisville, KY 40203
(502) 584-1281
A * 12

Mountain Ventures, Inc.
Mr. Frederick Beste III, Pres.
Box 628, 911 N. Main St.
London, KY 40741
(606) 878-6635
D *** 1,3,5,6,7,8,11,12

LOUISIANA
Business Capital Corp.
Mr. David R. Burrus, Pres.
PO Drawer 57329
New Orleans, LA 70157
(504) 581-4002
MESBIC E * 2,4,12

Caddo Capital Corp.
Mr. Thomas L. Young, Jr., Pres.
3010 Knight St., Ste. 240
Shreveport, LA 71105
(318) 869-1689
A *** 6,8

Capital Equity Corp.
Mr. Arthur Mitchell, Sr. VP
1885 Wooddale Blvd.
Baton Rouge, LA 70806
(504) 924-9205
B *** 6,12

Commercial Capital, Inc.
Mr. A.R. Blossman, Sr., Treas.
200 Belle Terre Blvd.
Covington, LA 70433
(504) 892-4921
A * 12

Dixie Business Investment Co.
Mr. L. Wayne Baker, Pres.
PO Box 588
Lake Providence, LA 71254
(318) 559-1558
A * 12

EDICT Investment Corp.
Mr. Gregory G. Johnson, Exec. VP
2908 S. Carrollton Ave.
New Orleans, LA 70118
(504) 861-2364
MESBIC A ** 12

First Southern Capital Corp.
Mr. John H. Crabtree, Pres.
6161 Perkins Rd., Ste. 2-C
Baton Rouge, LA 70808
(504) 769-3004
D * 1,3,5,6,8,11,12

Louisiana Equity Capital Corp.
Mr. Melvin L. Rambin, Pres.
451 Florida St.
Baton Rouge, LA 70801
(504) 389-4421
C ** 5,9,10

Savings Venture Capital Corp.
Mr. David R. Dixon, Exec. VP
6001 Financial Pl.
Shreveport, LA 71130
(318) 687-8996
B ** 12

Walnut Street Capital Co.
Mr. William D. Humphries
   Managing General Partner
702 Cotton Exchange Bldg.
New Orleans, LA 70130
(504) 525-2112
D *** 12

MAINE
Maine Capital Corp.
Mr. David M. Coit, Exec. VP
70 Center St.
Portland, ME 04101
(207) 772-1001
B *** 12

MARYLAND
Albright Venture Capital, Inc.
Mr. William A. Albright, Pres.
8005 Rappahannock Ave.
Jessup, MD 20794
(301) 799-7935
MESBIC B ** 2,4,5,6,9,10,12

Greater Washington Investors, Inc
Mr. Don A. Christensen, Pres.
5454 Wisconsin Ave., Ste. 1565
Chevy Chase, MD 20815
(301) 656-0626
D *** 1,5,6,8,12

Suburban Capital Corp.
Mr. Henry P. Linsert, Jr., Pres.
6610 Rockledge Dr.
Bethesda, MD 20817
(301) 493-7025
D *** 1,6,8,12

MASSACHUSETTS
Advent III Capital Company
Mr. David D. Croll, Mng. Ptnr.
45 Milk St.
Boston, MA 02109
(617) 338-0800
E * 1,3,5,6,8,12

Advent IV Capital Company
Mr. David D. Croll, Mng. Ptnr.
45 Milk St.
Boston, MA 02109
(617) 338-0800
E * 1,3,5,6,8,12

Alta Capital Corp.
Mr. William P. Egan, Pres.
One Post Office Sq., Ste. 3800
Boston, MA 02109
(617) 482-8020
B *** 1,6,8,12

Atlas Capital Corp.
Mr. Herbert Carver, Treas.
55 Court St., Ste. 200
Boston, MA 02108
(617) 482-1218
B ** 12

Branch Office
Boston Hambro Capital Co.
Mr. Robert Sherman, VP
One Boston Pl., Ste. 723
Boston, MA 02106
(617) 722-7055
D *** 1,5,6,9,12
(Main Office in NY)

Chestnut Capital Corp.
Mr. David D. Croll, Chmn/CEO
45 Milk St.
Boston, MA 02109
(617) 338-0800
E * 1,3,5,6,8,12

Branch Office
Churchill International
  Pan American Investment Co.
Dr. Terry K. Dorsey, Inv. Dir.
Nine Riverside Rd.
Weston, MA 02193
(617) 893-6555
D * 1,5,8
(Main Office in CA)

Devonshire Capital Company
Mr. David D. Croll, Mng. Ptnr.
45 Milk St.
Boston, MA 02109
(617) 338-0800
E * 1,3,5,6,8,12

First Capital Corp. of Boston
Mr. Bruce G. Rossiter, Pres.
100 Federal St.
Boston, MA 02110
(617) 434-2442
D *** 5,6,8,12

Branch Office
First Capital Corp. of Chicago
Mr. Kevin M. McCafferty, VP
200 Claredon St.
Boston, MA 02116
(617) 247-4856
E *** 1,6,8,9
(Main Office in IL)

Massachusetts Venture
  Capital Corp.
Ms. Irene E. Sax
59 Temple Pl.
Boston, MA 02111
(617) 426-0208
MESBIC B * 12

New England Capital Corp.
Mr. Z. David Patterson, Exec. VP
One Washington Mall
Boston, MA 02108
(617) 722-6400
C *** 1,5,6

New England MESBIC, Inc.
Dr. Jeff Yeh, Gen. Mgr.
50 Kearney Rd., Ste. 3
Needham, MA 02194
(617) 449-2066
MESBIC A * 2,4,5,6,8,9,12

Orange Nassau Capital Corp.
Mr. Joost E. Tjaden, Pres.
One Post Office Sq., Ste. 1760
Boston, MA 02109
(617) 451-6220
C *** 1,3,5,6,8,9,12

Transatlantic Capital Corp.
Mr. Bayard Henry, Pres.
Mr. John O. Flender, VP/Treas.
24 Federal St.
Boston, MA 02110
(617) 482-0015
C *** 1,5,6,8,10,11,12

UST Capital Corp.
Mr. Richard Kohn, VP
30 Court St.
Boston, MA 02108
(617) 726-7137
B *** 1,6,8,12

Worcester Capital Corp.
Mr. W. Kenneth Kidd, VP
446 Main St.
Worcester, MA 01608
(617) 793-4508
A *** 1,6,8

MICHIGAN
Comerica Capital Corp.
Mr. John D. Berkaw, Pres.
243 W. Congress, PO Box 59
Detroit, MI 48231
(313) 222-3907
C *** 1,5,6,8,12

Detroit Metropolitan SBIC
Ms. Charlotte Doud
150 Michigan Ave.
Detroit, MI 48226
(313) 964-4000
B * 12

Doan Resources Corp.
Mr. Ian R.N. Bund, Pres.
333 E. Main St., PO Box 1431
Midland, MI 48640
(517) 631-2471
D *** 1,5,6,8

Federated Capital Corp.
Mr. Jack Takala, VP Fin.
20000 W. Twelve Mile Rd.
Southfield, MI   48076
(313) 557-9100
A * 12

Metro-Detroit Investment Co.
Mr. William J. Fowler, Pres.
30777 Northwestern, Ste. 300
Farmington Hills, MI   48018
(313) 851-6300
MESBIC A ** 9

Michigan Cap. & Service, Inc.
Mr. Joseph F. Conway, Pres.
440 City Ctr. Bldg.
Ann Arbor, MI   48104
(313) 663-0702
D * 1,5,6,8,12

Michigan Tech Capital Corp.
Mr. Edward J. Koepel, Pres.
PO Box 20
Hubbell, MI   49934
(906) 487-2643
A * 3,5,8

Motor Enterprises, Inc.
Mr. James Kobus, Mgr.
3044 W. Grand Blvd., Rm 13-152
Detroit, MI   48202
(313) 556-4273
MESBIC B ** 5,12

Mutual Investment Co., Inc.
Mr. Timothy J. Taylor, Treas.
18501 W. Ten Mile Rd.
Southfield, MI   48075
(313) 559-5210
MESBIC B * 9

Tyler Refrigeration Cap. Corp.
Mr. Gary J. Slock, Pres.
1329 Lake St.
Niles, MI   49120
(616) 683-1610
A * 10

MINNESOTA
Control Data Capital Corp.
Mr. W.D. Anderson, Sec./Treas.
3600 W. 78th St., 7th Fl.
Minneapolis, MN   55435
(612) 921-4391
C * 1,5,6,12

Eagle Ventures, Inc.
Mr. Lawrence L. Horsch, Pres.
700 Soo Line Bldg.
Minneapolis, MN   55402
(603) 339-9693
B *** 1,6,8

FBS Venture Capital Co.
Mr. Donald Soukup, Mng. Agent
7515 Wayzata Blvd.
Minneapolis, MN   55426
(612) 544-2754
D *** 1,5,6,8

First Midwest Capital Corp.
Mr. Alan K. Ruvelson, Chmn.
Mr. Thomas M. Neitge, Pres.
1010 Plymouth Bldg., 12 S 6th St.
Minneapolis, MN   55402
(612) 339-9391
C *** 1,5,6,7,8,9,10,12

Northland Capital Corp.
Mr. George G. Barnum, Jr., Pres.
613 Missabe Bldg., 277 W. 1st St.
Duluth, MN   55802
(218) 722-0545
B *** 12

North Star Ventures, Inc.
Mr. Terrence W. Glarner, Pres.
1501 First Bank Place W.
Minneapolis, MN   55402
(612) 333-1133
D *** 1,5,6,7,8,12

Norwest Growth Fund, Inc.
Mr. Robert F. Zicarelli, Chmn.
1730 Midwest Plaza Bldg.
801 Nicollet Mall
Minneapolis, MN   55402
(612) 372-8770
E *** 1,6,8,12

P.R. Peterson Venture
   Capital Corp.
Mr. P.R. Peterson, Pres.
7301 Washington Ave. S.
Edina, MN   55435
(612) 941-8282
A * 5,6,8

Retailers Growth Fund, Inc.
Mr. Cornell L. Moore, Pres.
5100 Gamble Dr., Ste. 380
Minneapolis, MN   55416
(612) 546-8989
A ** 9,11,12

Shared Ventures, Inc.
Mr. Howard Weiner, Pres.
6550 York Ave. S., Ste. 419
Edina, MN   55435
(612) 925-3411
B *** 12

Threshold Ventures, Inc.
Mr. Michael J. Meyer, Pres.
430 Oak Grove St., Ste. 303
Minneapolis, MN   55403
(612) 874-7199
B *** 1,5,6,9,12

MISSISSIPPI
Invesat Capital Corp.
Mr. J. Thomas Noojin, Pres.
162 E. Amite St., Ste. 204
PO Box 3288
Jackson, MS   39207
(601) 969-3242
D *** 12

Vicksburg SBIC
Mr. David L. May, Pres.
PO Box 1240
302 First National Bank Bldg.
Vicksburg, MS   39180
(601) 636-4762
A * 12

MISSOURI
Branch Office
R.W. Allsop Capital Corp.
Mr. Robert L. Kuk, VP
111 W. Port Plaza, Ste. 600
St. Louis, MO   63146
(314) 434-1688
C *** 1,5,6,12
(Main Office in Iowa)

Bankers Capital Corp.
Mr. Raymond E. Glasnapp, Pres.
4049 Pennsylvania Ave., Ste. 304
Kansas City, MO   64111
(816) 531-1600
A * 12

Capital For Business, Inc.
Mr. James Hebenstreit, Pres.
720 Main St.
Executive Plaza Bldg.
Kansas City, MO   64105
(816) 234-2381
D *** 5,12

Branch Office
Capital For Business, Inc.
Mr. James Hebenstreit, Pres.
7931 Forsyth Blvd.
St. Louis, MO   63105
(314) 725-0900
D *** 5,12

Intercapco West, Inc.
Mr. Thomas E. Phelps, Pres.
7800 Bonhomme Ave.
St. Louis, MO   63105
(314) 863-0600
A *** 12

Branch Office:
MorAmerica Capital Corp.
Mr. Kevin F. Mullane, VP
Ste. 2724 - Commerce Tower
911 Main St.
Kansas City, MO   64105
(816) 842-0114
D *** 1,5,6,9,12
(Main Office in Iowa)

MONTANA
Rocky Mountain Ventures, Ltd.
Mr. James H. Koessler, Pres.
315 Securities Bldg.
Billings, MT   59101
(406) 256-1984
D * 12

NEBRASKA
Community Equity Corp. of NE
Mr. Herbert M. Patten, Sec.
6421 Ames Ave.
Omaha, NE   68104
(402) 455-7722
MESBIC A ** 12

NEVADA
United Capital Corp. of Illinois
Mr. Seth L. Atwood, Pres.
PO Box 109, 2001 Foothill Rd.
Genoa, NV   89411
(702) 782-5114
C * 1,4,5,12

NEW HAMPSHIRE
Granite State Capital, Inc.
Mr. Stuart D. Pompian, Mng. Dir.
10 Fort Eddy Rd.
Concord, NH   03301
(603) 228-9090
B *** 12

Hampshire Capital Corp.
Mr. Philip G. Baker, Pres.
One Middle St., PO Box 468
Portsmouth, NH   03801
(603) 431-1415
A *** 12

NEW JERSEY
Engle Investment Co.
Mr. Murray Hendel, Pres.
35 Essex St.
Hackensack, NJ   07601
(201) 489-3583
B * 12

ESLO Capital Corp.
Mr. Ronald Lokos, CEO
485 Morris Ave.
Springfield, NJ   07081
(201) 467-2545
A * 12

First Princeton Capital Corp.
Mr. S. Lawrence Goldstein, Pres.
227 Hamburg Tpke.
Pompton Lakes, NJ 07442
(201) 831-0330
D *** 1,2,5,9,10,11,12

Lloyd Capital Corp.
Mr. Solomon T. Scharf, Pres.
77 State Hghwy. 5, PO Box 180
Edgewater, NJ 07020
(201) 947-6000
C ** 2,4,5,9,10,12

Monmouth Capital Corp.
Mr. Eugene W. Landy, Pres.
Mr. Charles P. Kaempffer, Exec VP
PO Box 335 - 125 Wyckoff Rd.
Eatontown, NJ 07724
(201) 542-4927
C * 12

Raybar SBIC
Mr. Patrick McCort, VP
255 W. Spring Valley Ave.
Maywood, NJ 07607
(201) 368-2280
B *** 12

Rutgers Minority Investment Co.
Mr. Oscar Figueroa, Pres.
180 University Ave., 3rd Fl.
Newark, NJ 07102
(201) 648-5627
MESBIC B *** 1,5,6,9,12

Unicorn Ventures, Ltd.
Mr. Frank P. Diassi, Gen. Ptnr.
Mr. Arthur B. Baer, Gen. Ptnr.
14 Commerce Dr.
Cranford, NJ 07016
(201) 276-7880
C *** 12

Venray Capital Corp.
Mr. Raymond Skiptunis, Pres.
981 Rt. #22, PO Box 6817
Bridgewater, NJ 08807
(201) 725-1020
B *** 12

NEW MEXICO
Albuquerque SBIC
Mr. Albert T. Ussery, Pres.
501 Tijeras Ave., NW, Ste. 202
PO Box 487
Albuquerque, NM 87103
(505) 247-0145
A *** 12

Associated SW Investors, Inc.
Mr. John R. Rice, Pres.
2425 Alamo, SE
Albuquerque, NM 87106
(505) 842-5955
MESBIC C * 1,5,6,12

Equity Capital Corp.
Mr. Jerry A. Henson, Pres.
231 Washington Ave., Ste. 2
Santa Fe, NM 87501
(505) 988-4273
B *** 12

Fluid Capital Corp.
Mr. George T. Slaughter, Pres.
8421 B Montgomery Blvd., NE
Albuquerque, NM 87111
(505) 292-4747
A *** 1,2,4,5,12

Fluid Financial Corp.
Mr. George T. Slaughter, Pres.
8421 B Montgomery Blvd, NE
Albuquerque, NM 87111
(505) 292-4747
MESBIC A *** 1,2,4,5,12

New Mexico Capital Corp.
Mr. Phillip G. Larson, Chmn.
2900 Louisiana Blvd., NE, #201
Albuquerque, NM 87110
(505) 884-3600
C *** 12

Southwest Capital Investments
Mr. Martin J. Roe, Pres./Treas.
3500 Commanche Rd., NE, Bldg. E
Albuquerque, NM 87107
(505) 884-7161
C * 12

Venture Capital Corp. of NM
Mr. Gary L. McPherson, Chmn.
5301 Central Ave., NE, Ste. 1600
Albuquerque, NM 87108
(505) 266-0066
A *** 4,12

NEW YORK
American Commercial Capital Corp.
Mr. Gerald J. Grossman, Pres.
310 Madison Ave., Ste. 1304
New York, NY 10017
(212) 986-3305
B ** 1,2,4,5,7,11,12

AMEV Capital Corp.
Mr. Martin S. Orland, Pres.
Two World Trade Ctr., Ste. 9766
New York, NY 10048
(212) 775-1912
D *** 1,4,5,6,7,8,9,11,12

Amistad DOT Venture Capital Inc.
Mr. Percy E. Sutton, Pres.
801 Second Ave., Ste. 303
New York, NY 10017
(212) 697-9210
MESBIC C * 1,5,8,11

Atalanta Investment Co., Inc.
Mr. L. Mark Newman, Chmn.
450 Park Ave., Ste. 1802
New York, NY 10022
(212) 832-1104
D *** 1,2,5,6,7,8

BanCap Corp.
Mr. William L. Whitely, Pres.
155 E. 42nd St., Ste. 305
New York, NY 10017
(212) 687-6470
MESBIC B *** 1,5,6,12

Beneficial Capital Corp.
Mr. John J. Hoey, Pres.
645 Fifth Ave.
New York, NY 10022
(212) 752-1291
B *** 12

Bohlen Capital Corp.
Mr. Harvey J. Wertheim, Pres.
767 Third Ave.
New York, NY 10017
(212) 838-7776
D *** 1,5,6,8

Boston Hambro Capital Co.
Mr. Edwin A. Goodman, Pres.
17 E. 71st St.
New York, NY 10021
(212) 288-7778
D *** 1,5,6,9,12

BT Capital Corp.
Mr. James G. Hellmuth, Pres.
280 Park Ave.
New York, NY 10017
(212) 850-1916
E *** 5,12

The Central New York SBIC, Inc.
Mr. Albert Wertheimer, Pres.
351 S. Warren St., Ste. 204
Syracuse, NY 13202
(315) 478-5026
A ** 1,4,7

Citicorp Venture Capital
Mr. Peter G. Gerry, Pres.
399 Park Ave., 20th Fl.
New York, NY 10043
(212) 559-1117
E *** 1,3,5,6,8,10,11

Clinton Capital Corp.
Mr. Mark Scharfman, Pres.
35 Middagh St.
Brooklyn, NY 11201
(212) 858-0920
D * 12

CMNY Capital Co., Inc.
Mr. Robert Davidoff, VP
77 Water St.
New York, NY 10005
(212) 437-7078
C *** 1,5,6,7,12

College Venture Equity Corp.
Mr. Francis M. Williams, Pres.
256 3rd St., PO Box 135
Niagara Falls, NY 14305
(716) 285-8455
A *** 2,6,7,11

Cornell Capital Corp.
Mr. Barry M. Bloom, Pres.
Mr. Alan B. Newman
230 Park Ave., Ste. 3440
New York, NY 10169
(212) 490-9198
D *** 4,9,12

County Capital Corp.
Mr. Myron Joffe, Pres.
25 Main St.
Southampton, NY 11968
(516) 283-2943
A * 2,4,6,11,12

EAB Venture Corp.
Mr. Richard C. Burcaw, Pres.
90 Park Ave.
New York, NY 10016
(212) 687-6010
C * 1,3,5,6,9,10,11,12

Edwards Capital Co.
Mr. Edward Teitlebaum, Mng. Ptnr
215 Lexington Ave., Rm. 805
New York, NY 10016
(212) 686-2568
C ** 11

Elk Associates Funding Corp.
Mr. Gary C. Granoff, Pres.
31 East Mall
Plainview, NY 11803
(516) 249-3387
MESBIC A ** 11

Branch Office
Engle Investment Co.
Mr. Murray Hendel, Pres
135 W. 50th St.
New York, NY 10020
(212) 757-9580
B * 12
(Main Office in NJ)

Equico Capital Corp.
Mr. Duane E. Hill, Pres./CEO
1290 Ave. of the Americas
Ste. 3400
New York, NY 10019
(212) 554-8413
MESBIC C *** 12

Equities Capital Co., Inc.
Mr. Leon Scharf, Pres.
890 West End Ave.
New York, NY 10025
(212) 866-6008
A ** 12

uropean Development Cap. Corp.
r. Harvey J. Wertheim, Pres.
67 Third Ave.
ew York, NY 10017
212) 838-7776
 *** 1,5,6,8

airfield Equity Corp.
r. Matthew A. Berdon, Pres.
00 E. 42nd St.
ew York, NY 10017
212) 867-0150
 *** 1,5,6,9,10

erranti High Technology, Inc.
r. Sanford R. Simon, Pres.
05 Park Ave.
ew York, NY 10022
212) 688-9828
 *** 1,8,12

ifty-Third Street Ventures
r. Alan J. Patricof, Chmn.
45 Madison Ave., 15th Fl.
ew York, NY 10022
212) 753-6300
 *** 1,6,9

ranch Office
he First Connecticut SBIC
r. James Breiner, Chmn.
r. David Engelson, Pres.
80 Fifth Ave.
ew York, NY 10153
212) 355-6540
 * 1,2,4,5,6,9,12
Main office in CT)

.H. Foster & Co., Ltd.
r. John H. Foster, Ptnr.
37 Madison Ave.
ew York, NY 10022
212) 753-4810
 *** 1,3,5,6,8,11

he Franklin Corp.
r. Herman E. Goodman, Pres.
185 Ave. of Americas, 27th Fl.
ew York, NY 10036
212) 719-4844
 * 1,2,4,5,6,7,8,11,12

undex Capital Corp.
r. Howard F. Sommer, Pres.
25 Northern Blvd.
reat Neck, NY 11746
516) 466-8550
 * 12

enesee Funding, Inc.
r. A. Keene Bolton, Pres.
te. 1450 - 183 E. Main St.
ochester, NY 14604
716) 262-4716
 * 12

anover Capital Corp.
r. John A. Selzer, VP
50 E. 58th St., Ste. 3520
ew York, NY 10155
212) 486-2411
 *** 5,12

eller Capital Services
r. Jack A. Prizzi, Exec. VP
01 Park Ave.
ew York, NY 10178
212) 880-7047
 *** 1,5,6,8,9,11,12

olding Capital Mgmt. Corp.
r. James W. Donaghy, VP
85 Fifth Ave., 14th Fl.
ew York, NY 10022
212) 486-6670
 *** 1,2,3,5,6,9,10,12

Ibero-American Investors Corp.
Mr. Emilio L. Serrano, Pres./CEO
Chamber of Commerce Bldg.
55 St. Paul St.
Rochester, NY 14604
(716) 262-3440
MESBIC A * 5

Intercoastal Capital Corp.
Mr. Herbert Krasnow, Pres.
380 Madison Ave., 18th Fl.
New York, NY 10017
(212) 986-0482
D * 1,2,4,5,6,7,10,11,12

Intergroup Venture Cap. Corp.
Mr. Ben Hauben, Pres.
230 Park Ave., Ste. 210
New York, NY 10169
(212) 661-5428
A * 12

Int'l. Paper Cap. Formation, Inc.
Mr. Bernard Riley, Chmn.
77 W. 45th St.
New York, NY 10036
(212) 536-6606
MESBIC B * 12

Irving Capital Corp.
Mr. J. Andrew McWethy, Exec. VP
1290 Ave. of Americas, 3rd Fl.
New York, NY 10019
(212) 922-8790
E *** 12

Japanese American Capital Corp.
Mr. Benjamin Lin, Pres.
120 Broadway, Rm. 1755
New York, NY 10271
(212) 964-4077
MESBIC A * 2,4,6,12

Key Venture Capital Corp.
Mr. John M. Lang, Pres.
Mr. Mark R. Hursty
60 State St.
Albany, NY 12207
(518) 447-3180
B *** 8,12

Korean Capital Corp.
Ms. Min ja OH, Pres.
144-43 25th Rd.
Flushing, NY 11354
(212) 762-8866
MESBIC C * 12

Kwiat Capital Corp.
Mr. Jeffrey M. Greene, Pres.
576 Fifth Ave.
New York, NY 10036
(212) 391-2461
C *** 1,5,6,7,8,12

Lincoln Capital Corp.
Mr. Martin Lifton, Pres.
41 E. 42nd St., Ste. 1510
New York, NY 10017
(212) 697-0610
B ** 12

M & T Capital Corp.
Mr. Joseph V. Parlato, Pres.
One M & T Pl.
Buffalo, NY 14240
(716) 842-5881
D *** 1,5,6,8,9,10,11,12

Medallion Funding Corp.
Mr. Alvin Murstein, Pres.
205 E. 42nd St., Ste. 2020
New York, NY 10017
(212) 682-3300
MESBIC A ** 11

Midland Venture Capital, Ltd.
Mr. Edwin B. Hathaway, Asst. VP
950 Third Ave.
New York, NY 10022
(212) 753-7799
E *** 3,5

Minority Equity Capital Co., Inc.
Mr. Patrick Owen Burns, Pres.
275 Madison Ave., Ste. 1901
New York, NY 10016
(212) 686-9710
MESBIC C *** 1,5,6,9,12

Multi-Purpose Capital Corp.
Mr. Eli B. Fine, Pres.
31 S. Broadway
Yonkers, NY 10701
(914) 963-2733
A *** 12

Nelson Capital Corp.
Mr. Irwin B. Nelson, Pres.
591 Stewart Ave.
Garden City, NY 11530
(516) 222-2555
E * 12

New Oasis Capital Corp.
Mr. James Huang, Pres.
114 Liberty St., Ste. 304
New York, NY 10006
(212) 394-2804
MESBIC B * 12

New Publications Fund, Inc.
Mr. Richard Ekstract, Pres.
350 E. 81st St.
New York, NY 10028
(212) 734-4440
B * 1

Noro Capital Ltd.
Mr. Harvey J. Wertheim, Gen Ptnr
767 Third Ave.
New York, NY 10017
(212) 838-7776
D *** 1,5,6,8

North American Funding Corp.
Mr. Franklin Wong, VP
177 Canal St.
New York, NY 10013
(212) 226-0080
MESBIC A * 12

North Street Capital Corp.
Mr. Ralph L. McNeal, Sr., Pres.
250 North St., RA-6S
White Plains, NY 10625
(914) 335-6306
MESBIC B *** 12

NPD Capital, Inc.
Mr. David A. Rapaport, VP
375 Park Ave., Ste. 2201
New York, NY 10152
(212) 826-8500
B *** 6,8,12

NYBDC Capital Corp.
Mr. Marshall R. Lustig, Pres.
41 State St.
Albany, NY 12207
(518) 463-2268
A *** 3,5,6,8,9,10,12

Pan Pac Capital Corp.
Dr. In-Ping J. Lee, Pres.
120 Broadway
New York, NY 10271
(212) 966-2296
MESBIC A * 12

Pioneer Investors Corp.
Mr. James G. Niven, Pres.
113 E. 55th St.
New York, NY 10022
(212) 980-9090
C *** 1,3,5,6,8,9

Questech Capital Corp.
Dr. Earl W. Brian, Pres.
600 Madison Ave.
New York, NY 10022
(212) 758-8522
D *** 1,5,6,8

R & R Financial Corp.
Mr. Herbert Glick
1451 Broadway
New York, NY 10036
(212) 790-1400
A * 12

Rand Capital Corp.
Mr. George F. Rand III, Chmn.
Mr. Donald A. Ross, Pres.
Mr. Keith B. Wiley, VP
1300 Rand Bldg.
Buffalo, NY 14203
(716) 853-0802
C *** 1,5,8,9

Realty Growth Capital Corp.
Mr. Lawrence A. Benenson, Pres.
575 Lexington Ave.
New York, NY 10022
(212) 755-9044
A ** 2,11

Retzloff Capital Corp.
Mr. James K. Hines, Pres.
PO Box 41250
Houston, TX 77240
(713) 466-4633
C *** 12

Peter J. Schmitt Co., Inc.
Mr. Denis G. Riley, Mgr.
355 Harlem Road, PO Box 2
Buffalo, NY 14240
(716) 821-1400
A ** 9

Securities First Corp.
Mr. Norman M. Kanterman, Treas.
c/o Jericho Management Associates
41-11 39th St.
Long Island City, NY 14240
(212) 392-7000
D ** 11,12

Sherwood Business Capital Corp.
Mr. Anthony R. Russo, Pres.
175 Main St.
White Plains, NY 10601
(914) 761-1946
D *** 12

Small Business Electronics
  Investment Corp.
Mr. Stanley Meisels, Pres.
60 Cutter Mill Rd.
Great Neck, NY 11021
(516) 466-6451
A ** 12

Southern Tier Capital Corp.
Mr. Milton Brizel, Pres.
55 S. Main St.
Liberty, NY 12754
(914) 292-3030
A * 12

Sprout Capital Corp.
Mr. Richard E. Kroon, Pres.
140 Broadway, 48th Fl.
New York, NY 10005
(212) 902-2482
D *** 1,5,6,8,9

Tappan Zee Capital Corp.
Mr. Jack Birnberg, Exec. VP
120 N. Main St.
New City, NY 10956
(914) 634-8890
A ** 12

Taroco Capital Corp.
Mr. David R.C. Chang, Pres.
19 Rector St., 35th Fl.
New York, NY 10006
(212) 344-6690
MESBIC A * 12

TLC Funding Corp.
Mr. Philip G. Kass, Pres.
141 S. Central Ave.
Hartsdale, NY 10530
(914) 683-1144
B *** 5,6,9,10,12

Transportation SBIC, Inc.
Mr. Melvin L. Hirsch, Pres.
122 E. 42nd St., 46th Fl.
New York, NY 10168
(212) 986-6050
MESBIC B ** 11

Transworld Ventures, Ltd.
Mr. Jack H. Berger, Pres.
331 W. End Ave., Ste. 1A
New York, NY 10023
(212) 496-1010
A *** 5,10,12

Van Rietschoten Capital Corp.
Mr. Harvey J. Wertheim, Pres.
767 Third Ave.
New York, NY 10017
(212) 838-7776
D *** 1,5,6,8

Vega Capital Corp.
Mr. Victor Harz, Pres.
720 White Plains Rd.
Scarsdale, NY 10583
(914) 472-8550
D * 12

Venture SBIC, Inc.
Mr. Arnold Feldman, Pres.
249-12 Jericho Tpke.
Bellerose, NY 11426
(516) 352-0068
B * 12

Branch Office
Walnut Capital Corp.
Mr. Burton W. Kanter, Chmn.
110 E. 59th St., 37th Fl.
New York, NY 10022
(212) 980-4665
C *** 12
(Main Office in IL)

Watchung Capital Corp.
Mr. Thomas S.T. Jeng, Pres.
431 Fifth Ave., 5th Fl.
New York, NY 10016
(212) 889-3466
MESBIC A * 12

Winfield Capital Corp.
Mr. Stanley Pechman, Pres.
237 Mamaroneck Ave.
White Plains, NY 10605
(914) 949-2600
D *** 12

Wood River Capital Corp.
Ms. Elizabeth W. Smith, Exec. VP
645 Madison Ave.
New York, NY 10022
(212) 750-9420
C *** 1,5,6

Yang Capital Corp.
Mr. Maysing Yang, Pres.
41-40 Kissena Blvd.
Flushing, NY 11355
(516) 482-1578
(212) 445-4585
MESBIC B *** 2,6

NORTH CAROLINA
Delta Capital, Inc.
Mr. Alex B. Wilkins, Jr., Pres.
227 N. Tryon St., Ste 201
Charlotte, NC 28202
(704) 372-1410
C *** 12

Heritage Capital Corp.
Mr. J. Randolph Gregory, Pres
2290 First Union Pl.
Charlotte, NC 28282
(704) 334-2867
C *** 12

Kitty Hawk Capital, Ltd.
Mr. Walter Wilkinson Jr.
  General Partner
2030 One Tryon Ctr.
Charlotte, NC 28284
(704) 333-3777
C *** 1,5,6,9,12

Vanguard Investment Co., Inc.
Mr. Marion Rex Harris, Pres.
4517 Bragg Blvd., Ste. 3
Fayetteville, NC 28303
(919) 864-4447
MESBIC B *** 1,5,8,11,12

NORTH DAKOTA
Dakota First Capital Corp.
Mr. Alexander P. McDonald, Pres.
51 Broadway, Ste. 601
Fargo, ND 58102
(701) 237-0450
A *** 1,5,8,12

OHIO
Center City Minority
  Enterprises Investment Co.
Mr. Claude Patmon, Pres.
40 S. Main St., Ste. 762
Dayton, OH 45402
(513) 229-2416
MESBIC A * 12

Clarion Capital Corp.
Mr. Morton A. Cohen, Pres.
1801 E. 12th St., Ste. 201
Cleveland, OH 44114
(216) 687-1096
C *** 5,6,8,12

First Ohio Capital Corp.
Mr. Michael Aust, Gen. Mgr.
606 Madison Ave.
Toledo, OH 43604
(419) 259-7146
B *** 12

Glenco Enterprises, Inc.
Dr. Lewis F. Wright, Jr., VP
1464 E. 105th St., Ste. 101
Cleveland, OH 44106
(216) 721-1200
MESBIC A *** 12

Gries Investment Co.
Mr. Robert D. Gries, Pres.
720 Statler Office Tower
Cleveland, OH 44115
(216) 861-1146
B *** 12

Intercapco, Inc.
Mr. Robert B. Haas, Pres.
One Erieview Pl.
Cleveland, OH 44114
(216) 241-7170
D *** 1,3,5,6,8,9,12

Miami Valley Capital, Inc.
Mr. Everett F. Telljohann, Pres.
131 N. Ludlow, Ste. 315
Dayton OH 45402
(513) 222-7222
B *** 5

National City Capital Corp.
Mr. Michael Sherwin, Pres.
623 Euclid Ave.
Cleveland, OH 44114
(216) 575-2491
C *** 1,5,12

Branch Office:
RIHT Capital Corp.
Mr. Peter Van Oosterhout, Pres.
796 Huntington Bldg.
Cleveland, OH 44115
(216) 781-3655
D *** 12
(Main Office in RI)

Tamco Investors SBIC, Inc.
Mr. Nathan H. Monus, Pres.
375 Victoria Rd., PO Box 1588
Youngstown, OH 44501
(216) 792-3811
A ** 9

Tomlinson Capital Corp.
Mr. Donald R. Calkins, VP
3055 E. 63rd St.
Cleveland, OH 44127
(216) 271-2103
B *** 12

OKLAHOMA
Alliance Business Investment Co
Mr. Barry M. Davis, Pres.
One Williams Ctr., Ste. 2000
Tulsa, OK 74172
(918) 584-3581
D *** 1,3,5,6,8,11,12

Bartlesville Investment Corp.
Mr. J.L. Diamond, Pres.
PO Box 548
Bartlesville, OK 74003
(918) 333-3022
A * 2,3

First OK Investment Cap. Corp.
Mr. O. Stuart Brown, Pres.
PO Box 25189
Oklahoma City, OK 73125
(405) 272-4660
D *** 1,3,4,5,6,7,9

Investment Capital, Inc.
Mr. James J. Wasson, Pres.
300 N. Harrison
Cushing, OK 74023
(918) 225-5850
B * 12

Southwest Venture Capital, Inc.
Mr. Donald J. Rubottom, Pres.
4120 E. 51st St., Ste. E
Tulsa, OK 74135
(918) 742-3177
A *** 12

Utica Investment Corp.
Mr. David D. Nunneley, Pres.
1924 South Utica
Tulsa, OK 74104
(918) 749-9976
A *** 2,3,5,10,12

OREGON
Branch Office
First Interstate Capital, Inc.
Mr. Wayne B. Kingsley, Exec. VP
1300 S.W. Fifth Ave., Ste. 2323
Portland, OR 97201
(503) 223-4334
E *** 1,5,6,8
(Main office in CA)

Northern Pacific Cap. Corp.
Mr. John Tennant, Jr., Pres.
1201 S.W. 12th Ave.
Portland, OR 97202
(503) 241-1255
B *** 5,9,11

Branch Office:
Norwest Growth Fund, Inc.
Mr. Anthony Miadich, VP
1300 S.W. Fifth Ave., Ste. 3018
Portland, OR 97201
(503) 223-6622
E *** 1,6,8,12
(Main Office in MN)

PENNSYLVANIA
Alliance Enterprise Corp.
Mr. Duane C. McKnight, VP
1801 Market St., 3rd Fl.
Philadelphia, PA 19103
(215) 972-4230
MESBIC C * 2,5,6,9,10,12

American Venture Capital Co.
Mr. Knute Albrecht, Pres./CEO
Ste. 122, Blue Bell W.
Blue Bell, PA 19422
(215) 278-8907
B *** 12

Branch Office
First SBIC of California
Mr. Daniel A. Dye, VP
PO Box 512
Washington, PA 15301
(412) 223-0707
E *** 12
(Main Office in CA)

First Valley Capital Corp.
Mr. Carl B. Bear, Pres.
One Bethlehem Pl.
Bethlehem, PA 18018
(215) 865-8675
C *** 5,6,7,9,10,11

Greater Philadelphia Venture
  Capital Corp., Inc.
Mr. Martin Newman, Pres.
225 S. 15th St., Ste. 920
Philadelphia, PA 19102
(215) 732-1666
(215) 732-3415
MESBIC B *** 1,4,6,7,12

PNC Capital Corp.
Mr. David McL. Hillman, Exec. VP
Fifth Ave. & Wood St. - PNB Bldg.
Pittsburgh, PA 15222
(412) 355-2245
C * 1,5,6,8,9

PUERTO RICO
First Puerto Rico Capital, Inc.
Mr. Eliseo E. Font, Pres.
PO Box 1300
Mayaguez, PR 00709
(809) 832-9171
MESBIC A * 12

North America Investment Corp.
Sr. Santiago Ruiz-Betancourt
  Pres.
Banco Popular Ctr., Ste. 1710
Hato Rey, PR 00928
(809) 754-6177
MESBIC B *** 5,6,9,10,12

Venture Capital P.R., Inc.
Mr. Manuel L. Prats, Inv. Adv.
Banco Cooperativo Plz, Ste. 604-B
Hato Rey, PR 00917
(809) 751-8040
MESBIC A * 2,5,12

RHODE ISLAND
Fleet Venture Resources, Inc.
Mr. Robert M. Van Degna, Pres.
111 Westminster St.
Providence, RI 02903
(401) 278-6770
C *** 1,6,8

Narragansett Capital Corp.
Mr. Arthur D. Little, Chmn.
40 Westminster St.
Providence, RI 02903
(401) 751-1000
E *** 1,5,6,9

Old Stone Capital Corp.
Mr. Bruce D. Moger, Pres.
150 S. Main St.
Providence, RI 02901
(401) 278-2544
E *** 12

RIHT Capital Corp.
Mr. Peter Van Oosterhout, Pres.
Mr. Robert A. Comey, VP
One Hospital Trust Plaza
Providence, RI 02903
(401) 278-8819
D *** 12

SOUTH CAROLINA
Carolina Venture Capital Corp.
Mr. Thomas Harvey III, Pres.
14 Archer Rd., PO Box 3110
Hilton Head Island, SC 29928
(803) 842-3101
B *** 1,2,4,7,11,12

Reedy River Ventures
Mr. Jack Sterling, Pres.
PO Box 17526
Greenville, SC 29606
(803) 297-9198
B *** 12

TENNESSEE
Chickasaw Capital Corp.
Mr. Wayne J. Haskins, Pres.
PO Box 387, 67 Madison
Memphis, TN 38147
(901) 523-6404
MESBIC A *** 5,6,12

DeSoto Capital Corp.
Mr. William B. Rudner, Pres.
5050 Poplar Ave., Ste. 2429
Memphis, TN 38157
(901) 682-9072
A *** 12

Financial Resources, Inc.
Mr. Milton C. Picard, Chmn.
2800 Sterick Bldg.
Memphis, TN 38103
(901) 527-9411
B *** 1,5,6,8,10,12

Inverness Capital Corp.
Mr. Floyd W. Kephart, Jr., Pres.
127 Woodmont Blvd.
Nashville, TN 37205
(615) 297-1970
C *** 5,6,8

Suwannee Capital Corp.
Mr. Peter R. Pettit, Pres.
1991 Corporate Ave.
Memphis, TN 38132
(901) 345-4235
B ** 9

Tennessee Equity Capital Corp.
Mr. Walter S. Cohen, Pres.
1102 Stonewall Jackson Ct.
Nashville, TN 37220
(615) 373-4502
MESBIC C *** 12

Valley Capital Corp.
Ste. 806, Krystal Bldg.
Chattanooga, TN 37402
(615) 265-1557
MESBIC A *** 1,5,8,9,10,11

West Tennessee Venture
  Capital Corp.
Mr. Bennie L. Marshall, Mgr.
Ste. 1701, Sterick Bldg.
8 N. Third St.
Memphis, TN 38103
(901) 527-6091
MESBIC B * 1,6,12

TEXAS
Branch Office
Alliance Business Investment Co
2660 S. Tower, Pennzoil Pl.
Houston, TX 77002
(713) 224-8224
D *** 1,3,5,6,11,12

Allied Bancshares Capital Corp.
Mr. D. Kent Anderson, Chmn.
Mr. Philip A. Tuttle, Pres.
PO Box 3326
Houston, TX 77001
(713) 224-6611
C * 3,5,10,12

American Energy Investment Corp
Mr. Robert J. Moses, Pres.
1010 Lamar, Ste. 1680
Houston, TX 77002
(713) 651-0220
C * 3

Americap Corp.
Mr. James L. Hurn, Pres.
6363 Woodway, Ste. 200
Houston, TX 77057
(713) 780-8084
B *** 3,12

BancTexas Capital Inc.
Mr. Byron G. Berger, Exec. VP
1601 Elm St., PO Box 2249
Dallas, TX 75221
(214) 969-6382
B *** 1,3,5,6,8,12

Bow Lane Capital Corp.
Mr. Stuart Schube, Pres.
2401 Fountainview, Ste. 950
Houston, TX 77057
(713) 977-7421
E *** 1,6,8,12

Branch Office
Bow Lane Capital Corp.
Mr. Hugh Batey
3305 Graybuck Rd.
Austin, TX 78748
(512) 456-8698
E *** 1,6,8,12

Brittany Capital Corp.
Mr. Robert E. Clements, Pres.
2424 LTV Tower, 1525 Elm St.
Dallas, TX 75201
(214) 742-5810
B *** 12

Business Capital Corp.
   of Arlington
Mr. Keith Martin, Pres.
1112 Copeland Rd., Ste.420
Arlington, TX 76011
(817) 261-4936
B *** 1,5,9

Capital Marketing Corp.
Mr. John King Myrick, Pres.
PO Box 1000
Keller, TX 76248
(214) 281-4417
E ** 2,12

Central Texas SBIC
Mr. David G. Horner, Pres.
514 Austin Ave.
Waco, TX 76710
(817) 753-6461
A * 12

Charter Venture Group, Inc.
Mr. Kent E. Smith, Pres.
5150 N. Shepherd, Ste. 218
PO Box 10816
Houston, TX 77018
(713) 699-3588
B *** 12

CSC Capital Corp.
Mr. William R. Thomas, Pres.
Mr. J. Bruce Duty, VP
12900 Preston Rd., Ste. 700
Dallas, TX 75230
(214) 233-8242
D *** 1,3,5,6,8,9,11,12

Energy Assets, Inc.
Mr. L.E. Simmons, VP
1800 S. Tower, Pennzoil Pl.
Houston, TX 77002
(713) 236-9999
A * 3

Energy Capital Corp.
Mr. Herbert Poyner, Jr.,Pres.
953 Esperson Bldg.
Houston, TX 77002
(713) 236-0006
D * 3

Enterprise Capital Corp.
Mr. Fred S. Zeidman, Pres.
3401 Allen Pkwy., Ste. 108
Houston, TX 77019
(713) 524-5170
E *** 1,2,5,6,12

Equity Capital Corp. of Texas
Mr. John M. Fooshee, Pres.
5333 Spring Valley Rd.
Dallas, TX 75240
(214) 991-2961
B *** 4,9,12

Evergreen Capital Co., Inc.
Mr. Richard Shen-Lim Lin, Pres.
8502 Tybor, Ste. 201
Houston, TX 77074
(713) 778-9889
MESBIC B *** 12

First City Capital Corp.
Mr. William E. Ladin, Pres.
One West Loop S., Ste. 809
Houston, TX 77027
(713) 623-6151
D *** 12

FSA Capital, Ltd.
Mr. G. Felder Thornhill, Pres.
PO Box 1987
Austin, TX 78767
(512) 472-6720
C * 1,3,6,8,12

Grocers SBIC
Mr. Milton Levit, Pres.
3131 E. Holcombe Blvd.
Houston, TX 77021
(713) 747-7913
B ** 9

InterFirst Venture Corp.
Mr. J.A. O'Donnell, Pres.
PO Box 83644
Dallas, TX 75283
(214) 744-8050
E *** 1,2,3,6,12

Livingston Capital Ltd.
Mr. J. Livingston Kosberg, Pres.
5701 Woodway, Ste. 332
Houston, TX 77057
(713) 977-4040
D *** 12

Mapleleaf Capital Corp.
Mr. Michael P. Zuk, Pres.
One West Loop S., Ste. 603
Houston, TX 77027
(713) 627-0752
C *** 3,8,10,12

Mercantile Dallas Corp.
Mr. J. Wayne Gaylord, Exec. VP
PO Box 222090
Dallas, TX 75222
(214) 741-1469
D * 5,6,12

MESBIC Financial Corp. of Dallas
Mr. Walter W. Durham, Pres.
7701 N Stemmons Freeway, Ste. 836
Dallas, TX 75247
(214) 637-0445
MESBIC C *** 12

MESBIC Financial Corp. of Houston
Mr. Richard Rothfeld, Pres.
1801 Main St., Ste. 320
Houston, TX 77002
(713) 228-8321
MESBIC B * 5,8,9,10,11,12

MESBIC of San Antonio, Inc.
Mr. Ruben M. Saenz, VP
2300 W. Commerce
San Antonio, TX 78207
(512) 224-0909
MESBIC A *** 2,3,4,5,6,9,12

Omega Capital Corp.
Mr. Ted E. Moor, Jr., Pres.
755 S. 11th St., Ste. 250
Beaumont, TX 77701
(409) 835-5928
A * 12

Red River Ventures, Inc.
Mr. Thomas Schnitzius, Pres.
2050 Houston Natural Gas Bldg.
Houston, TX 77002
(713) 658-9806
C *** 3,8

Republic Venture Group, Inc.
Mr. Robert H. Wellborn, Pres.
PO Box 225961
Dallas, TX 75265
(214) 653-5078
E * 1,2,3,5,6,11,12

Retail Capital Corp.
Mr. William J. Boschma, Pres.
7915 FM 1960 W., Ste. 300
Houston, TX 77070
(713) 890-4242
A * 9

Retzloff Capital Corp.
Mr. James K. Hines, Pres.
PO Box 41250
Houston, TX 77240
(713) 466-4633
C *** 12

Rice Country Capital, Inc.
Mr. W. H. Harrison, Jr., Pres.
PO Box 215
Eagle Lake, TX 77434
(409) 234-2504
A * 12

Rust Capital Ltd.
Mr. Jeffery C. Garvey, Pres.
114 W. 7th St., Ste. 1300
Austin, TX 78701
(512) 479-0055
D *** 1,4,5,6,12

San Antonio Venture Group, Inc.
Mr. Domingo Bueno, Pres.
2300 W. Commerce
San Antonio, TX 78207
(512) 224-0909
B *** 12

SBI Capital Corp.
Mr. William E. Wright, Pres.
6305 Beverly Hill Ln.
Houston, TX 77057
(713) 975-1188
D *** 1,3,4,5,6,8,12

Southern Orient Capital Corp.
Mr. Min-Hsiung Liang, Pres.
2419 Fannin, Ste. 200
Houston, TX 77002
(713) 225-3369
MESBIC A * 4,9,10,12

Southwestern Venture Capital
   of Texas, Inc.
Mr. J.A. Bettersworth, Pres.
PO Box 1169
Seguin, TX 78155
(512) 379-0380
B * 12

ranch Office
outhwestern Venture Capital
of Texas, Inc.
r. James A. Bettersworth, Pres.
orth Frost Center
250 N.E. Loop 410, Ste. 300
an Antonio, TX 78209
* 12

inwestern Capital Corp.
r. Floyd W. Collins, VP
te. 816, South Tower
720 Stemmons Freeway
allas, TX 75207
214) 638-2100
*** 1,3,5,6,8,12

exas Capital Corp.
r. W. Grogan Lord, Chmn.
33 Clay St., Ste. 2100
ouston, TX 77002
713) 658-9961
*** 1,6

exas Commerce Investment Co.
r. Fred Lummis, VP
07 Travis St., 7th Fl.
0 Box 2558
ouston, TX 77002
713) 236-5332
*** 1,2,6,8

rammell Crow Investment Corp.
r. Henry Billingsley, Pres.
001 Bryan, Ste. 3900
allas, TX 75201
214) 747-0643
** 2

SM Corp.
r. L. Joe Justice, Inv. Adv,
44 Executive Ctr. Blvd., Ste. 222
l Paso, TX 79902
915) 533-6375
* 5,9

nited Oriental Cap. Co.
r. Don J. Wang, Pres.
3432 Hempstead Hwy.
ouston, TX 77040
713) 462-6264
SBIC B * 12

ERMONT
ermont Investment Capital, Inc.
r. Harold Jacobs, Pres.
ox 590
outh Royalton, VT 05068
802) 763-7716
* 12

IRGINIA
asic Investment Corp.
r. Frank Luwis, Pres.
723 Whittier Ave.
cLean, VA 22101
703) 356-4300
SBIC A * 12

ast West United Investment Co.
r. Doug Bui, Pres.
723 Whittier Ave., Ste.206
cLean, VA 22101
703) 821-6616
SBIC A * 4,9,12

ames River Capital Associates
r. A. Hugh Ewing, III, Pres.
S. 12th St.
ichmond, VA 23219
804) 643-7358
*** 1,5,6,8,9,12

etropolitan Capital Corp.
s. M.A. Riebe, Pres.
550 Huntington Ave.
lexandria, VA 22303
703) 960-4698
*** 12

Norfolk Investment Co., Inc.
Mr. Kirk W. Saunders, Pres.
100 W. Plume St., Ste. 208
Norfolk, VA 23502
(804) 623-1042
MESBIC A *** 1,5,6,8,11,12

Tidewater SBIC
Mr. Robert H. Schmidt, Pres.
1106 Maritime Tower
Norfolk, VA 23510
(804) 627-2315
A * 12

WASHINGTON
Capital Resource Corp.
Mr. Theodore M. Wight, Pres.
1001 Logan Bldg.
Seattle, WA 98101
(206) 623-6550
B *** 1,5,6,8,9,12

Clifton Capital Corp.
Mr. John S. Wiborg, VP
1408 Washington Bldg.
Tacoma, WA 98406
(206) 272-1875
A *** 1,5,9,12

Peoples Capital Corp.
Mr. Robert E. Karns, Pres.
2411 Fourth Ave., Ste. 990
Seattle, WA 98121
(206) 344-8105
A *** 1,5,12

Seafirst Capital Corp.
Mr. Steven G. Blanchard, Pres.
Fourth & Blanchard Bldg.
Seattle, WA 98121
(206) 583-3278
C * 2,5,6

Seattle Trust Capital Corp.
Mr. Willard E. Skeel, Jr., VP
804 Second Ave.
Seattle, WA 98104
(206) 223-2237
B *** 12

Washington Trust Equity Corp.
Mr. Jack Snead, Pres.
PO Box 2127
Spokane, WA 99210
(509) 455-4106
B *** 1,5,6,9,10,11,12

WISCONSIN
Branch Office
R.W. Allsop Capital Corp.
Mr. Gregory B. Bultman, VP
Ste. 1501, 815 E. Mason St.
PO Box 1368
Milwaukee, WI 53201
(414) 271-6510
C *** 1,5,6,12
(Main Office in Iowa)

Bando-McGlocklin Investment
Company, Inc.
Mr. Sal Bando, Pres.
13555 Bishops Ct., Ste. 205
Brookfield, WI 53005
(414) 784-9010
D ** 5,6,9,10

CERTCO Capital Corp.
Mr. Donald E. Watzke, Pres.
PO Box 7368
Madison, WI 53707
(608) 271-4500
A ** 9

Madison Capital Corp.
Mr. Roger H. Ganser, Exec. VP
102 State St.
Madison, WI 53703
(608) 256-2799
B *** 1,5,6,8,10,11

Branch Office:
MorAmerica Capital Corp.
Mr. Steven H. Massey
  Investment Analyst
600 East Mason St.
Milwaukee, WI 53202
(414) 276-3839
D *** 1,5,6,9,12
(Main Office in Iowa)

SC Opportunities, Inc.
Mr. Robert Ableman, VP/Sec.
1112 7th Ave.
Monroe, WI 53566
(608) 325-3134
MESBIC A *** 9

Super Market Investors, Inc.
Mr. John W. Andorfer, Pres.
c/o ROUNDY's, Inc.
PO Box 473, 11300 W. Burleigh St.
Milwaukee, WI 53201
(414) 783-4956
A ** 9

WYOMING
Capital Corp. of Wyoming, Inc.
Mr. Larry J. McDonald, Exec. VP
PO Box 612
Casper, WY 82602
(307) 234-5438
A * 12

NON-SBIC MEMBERS
Allstate Insurance Co. -
  Venture Capital Division
Mr. Charles L. Rees, Dir.
Allstate Plaza E-2
Northbrook, IL 60062
(312) 291-5681
E *** 1,5,6

Arthur Andersen & Co.
Mr. Richard J. Strotman, Ptnr.
33 W. Monroe St.
Chicago, IL 60603
(312) 580-0033

Atlantic Venture Partners
Mr. Robert H. Pratt, Gen. Ptnr.
PO Box 1493
Richmond, VA 23212
(804) 644-5496
D *** 12

Bacon Stifel Nicolaus
Mr. George Hendrick, 1st VP
208 S. LaSalle St., Ste. 400
Chicago, IL 60604
(312) 368-0050

Beacon Partners
Mr. Leonard Vignola, Mng. Ptnr.
111 Hubbard Ave.
Stamford, CT 06905
(203) 348-8858
D * 1,4,5,6,7,8,9,10,11,12

William Blair Venture Partners
Mr. Samuel B. Guren, Gen. Ptnr.
135 S. LaSalle St.
Chicago, IL 60603
(312) 236-1600
D *** 12

Bridge Capital Advisors, Inc.
Mr. Donald P. Remey, Mng. Dir.
Mr. Hoyt J. Goodrich, Mng. Dir.
50 Broadway
New York, NY 10004
(212) 514-6700
E *** 1,5,6,8,10,12

Broventure Capital Management
Mr. William M. Gust, Ptnr.
16 W. Madison St.
Baltimore, MD 21201
(301) 727-4520
D *** 1,5,6,8

Brownstein, Zeidman & Schomer
Mr. Thomas C. Evans, Ptnr.
1025 Conn. Ave., NW, Ste. 900
Washington, DC 20036
(202) 457-6560

Canadian Enterprise Dev. Corp Ltd
Mr. Gerald D. Sutton, Pres.
199 Bay St., Ste. 1103
Toronto, Ontario M5J 1L4
(416) 366-7607
C *** 1,6,8

Capital Publishing Corp.
Mr. Stanley E. Pratt, Pres.
16 Laurel Avenue, PO Box 348
Wellesley Hills, MA 02181
(617) 431-8100

Capital Services & Resources, Inc
Mr. Charles Y. Bancroft, Treas.
5159 Wheelis Dr., Ste. 104
Memphis, TN 38117
(901) 761-2156
D * 1,5,6,12

Cardinal Development Cap. Fund I
Mr. Richard Bannon, Ptnr.
155 E Broad St.
Columbus, OH 43215
(614) 464-5552
D * 1,4,5,6,8,9

The Charles River Partnerships
Mr. John T. Neises, Gen. Ptnr.
Mr. Richard Burnes Jr, Gen. Ptnr.
Mr. Robert F. Higgins, Gen. Ptnr.
133 Federal St., Ste. 602
Boston, MA 02110
(617) 482-9370
E *** 1,6,8

Commonwealth Development Finance
  Company Limited (CFC)
Mr. Peter Duce, Pres.
One London Bridge Walk
London, England SE1 2SS
(01) 407-9711
E *** 12

Corp. For Innovation Development
Mr. Marion C. Dietrich, Pres.
One North Capitol Ave., Ste. 520
Indianapolis, IN 46204
(317) 635-7325
C *** 1,5,6,8

Criterion Venture Partners
Mr. Gregory A. Rider, Gen. Ptnr.
4300 Capital Bank Plaza
Houston, TX 77002
(713) 751-2400
D *** 1,3,5,6,8,9,11

Deloitte, Haskins & Sells
Mr. Daniel A. Bailey, Ptnr.
One World Trade Ctr.
New York, NY 10048
(212) 669-5140

Development Credit Corp. of MD
Mr. W.G. Brooks Thomas, Pres.
40 W. Chesapeake Ave., Ste. 211
PO Box 10629
Towson, MD 20204
(301) 828-47.11
D ** 12

The Early Stages Partnership
Mr. W.P. Lanphear IV, Ptnr.
244 California St., Ste. 300
San Francisco, CA 94111
(415) 986-5700
C *** 1,9

EastWest Capital Corp.
Mr. Charles H. Bruce, Pres.
390 Union Blvd., Ste. 390
Denver, CO 80228
(303) 986-1113
C * 1,5,6,8,9,12

Enterprise Finance Capital
  Development Corp.
Mr. Robert N. Hampton, Pres.
PO Box 5840
Snowmass Village, CO 81615
(303) 923-4144
B ** 12

Enventure Capital Group, Inc.
Mr. Ronald E. Allen, CEO
1000 Guaranty Bldg.
Church & Pearl Streets
Buffalo, NY 14202
(714) 849-9329
C *** 1,2,3,5,6,8

EntreSource
Mr. S. Albert Hanser, Gen. Ptnr.
1300 First Bank Pl. W.
Minneapolis, MN 55402
(612) 375-9655
C * 1,3,5,6,7,8

Equity Resource Company, Inc.
Mr. Michael J. Hammes, VP
202 S. Michigan St.
South Bend, IN 46624
(219) 237-5344
B *** 12

Ernst & Whinney
Mr. Oscar Jimenez, Ptnr.
515 S. Flower St., Ste. 2700
Los Angeles, CA 90071
(213) 621-1666

Exchange Nat'l. Bank of Chicago
Mr. Joseph Chevalier, VP
120 LaSalle St.
Chicago, IL 60603
(312) 781-7046

Executive Capital Corp.
Mr. John A. Hall, Jr., Pres.
4144 N. Central Expy., Ste. 1222
Dallas, TX 75204
(214) 823-6990
C *** 1,2,5,9,12

Fine & Ambrogne
Mr. Arnold M. Zaff, Ptnr.
133 Federal St.
Boston, MA 02110
(617) 482-0100

Fine Art Funds Inc.
Mr. Stephen Maitland-Lewis, Pres.
25 E. 77th St.
New York, NY 10021
(212) 737-2330
B ** 12

The First Nat'l. Bank of Atlanta
Mr. Richard S. Downey, VP
Two Peachtree St., Ste. 212
Atlanta, GA 30383
(404) 588-6504

The First Worcester SBIC
Mr. Carl Cervini, Pres.
420 Boston Tpke.
Shrewsbury, MA 01545
(617) 842-4000
C *** 4,5,8,9

G.E. Venture Capital Corporation
Mr. Harry T. Rein, Pres.
Mr. Robert L. Burr, Sen. VP
3000 Sand Hill Road
Bldg 1, Ste. 230
Menlo Park, CA 94025
(415) 854-8092

Harrison Capital, Inc.
Mr. W. T. Corl, Pres.
2000 Westchester Ave.
White Plains, NY 10650
(914) 253-7845
D *** 12

Hawley & Associates
Mr. Frank J. Hawley, Jr., Pres.
999 Summer St.
Stamford, CT 06905
(203) 348-6669
D *** 1,2,3,5,6,11,12

Haynes and Boone
Mr. Marc H. Folladori, Corp. Div
4300 InterFirst Two
Dallas, TX 75270
(214) 744-0550

Helms, Mulliss & Johnston
Mr. B. Bernard Burns, Jr., Ptnr.
227 N. Tryon St., PO Box 31247
Charlotte, NC 28231
(704) 372-9510

IEG Venture Partners
Mr. F. I. Blair, Man. Ptnr.
Three First Nat'l. Pl., Ste. 140
Chicago, IL 60602
(312) 899-0185
D *** 1,3,6,8

Investment Management Group of
  the First Nat'l. Bank of Chicag
Mr. Daniel O'Connell, VP
Three First Nat'l. Pl., Ste. 014
Chicago, IL 60607
(312) 732-7974
D *** 12

Investors in Industry
Mr. David R. Shaw, Pres.
99 High St., Ste. 1200
Boston, MA 02110
(617) 542-8560
E *** 12

JVIG U.S. Management, Inc.
Mr. John Ross, CEO
1008 N. Bowen Rd.
Arlington, TX 76012
(817) 860-5222
E ** 12

Knight & Irish Associates, Inc.
Dr. Joan S. Irish, Pres.
420 Lexington Ave., Ste. 2358
New York, NY 10170
(212) 490-0135

Leighton, Lemov, Jacobs & Buckle
Mr. James L. Watts
2033 M St. NW
Washington, D.C. 20036
(202) 785-4800

Lewis, D'Amato, Brisbois &
  Bisgaard
William F. Greenhalgh, Esq.
261 S. Figueroa St., Ste. 300
Los Angeles, CA 90012
(213) 628-7777

Lord, Bissell & Brook
Mr. John K. O'Connor, Ptnr.
115 S. LaSalle St.
Chicago, IL 60603
(312) 443-0265

M&I Capital Corporation
Mr. Daniel P. Howell, Asst. VP
770 N. Water St.
Milwaukee, WI 53201
(414) 765-7800
C *** 6,12

Marine Venture Capital, Inc.
Mr. H. Wayne Foreman, Pres.
111 E. Wisconsin Ave.
Milwaukee, WI 53202
(414) 765-2151
C *** 1,5,6,12

Herbert B. Max, Esq.
77 Water St.
New York, NY 10005
(212) 437-7132

Med-Wick Associates, Inc.
Mr. A.A.T. Wickersham, Chmn/Pres
1902 Fleet National Bank Bldg.
Providence, RI 02903
(401) 751-5270

Menlo Ventures
Mr. Kirk L. Knight, Gen. Ptnr.
3000 Sand Hill Rd.
Menlo Park, CA 94025
(415) 854-8540
E *** 1,5,6,8

New Enterprise Associates
Mr. Charles Newhall III,
  General Partner
300 Cathedral St., Ste 110
Baltimore, MD 21201
(301) 244-0115
E * 1,6

Nippon Inv. & Fin. Co. Ltd.
Mr. Yasutoshi Sasada, Pres.
1-25-1 Nishi-Shinjuku, Shinjuku-ku
Tokyo 160 Japan
(03) 349-0961
B * 12

NMB Participatie B.V.
Mr. Michiel A. de Haan, Drs.
Eekholt 26, DIEMEN-Zuid
PO Box 1800
1000 BV AMSTERDAM
The Netherlands
(020) 903311
D * 12

North American Capital Corp.
Mr. Stanley P. Roth, Chmn.
510 Broad Hollow Rd., Ste. 205
Melville, NY 11747
(516) 752-9696
E * 12

North American Capital Group
Mr. Gregory I. Kravitt, Pres.
449 N. Wells St., Ste 1E
Chicago, IL 60610
(312) 645-0831
E *** 1,2,4,5,6,9,10,12

I. Gordon Odell & Company
Mr. I. Gordon Odell, Pres.
77 N. Oak Knoll Ave., Ste. 108
Pasadena, CA 91101
(213) 793-6858

Opportunity Capital, Inc.
Mr. Chip Glaser, Pres.
8300 Norman Ctr. Dr., #838
Bloomington, MN 55437
(612) 893-9270
B *** 4,6,8,12

Oxford Partners
Mr. Kenneth Rind, Gen. Ptnr.
Mr. Cornelius T. Ryan, Gen. Ptnr.
Mr. William Lonergah, Gen. Ptnr.
72 Cummings Point Rd.
Stamford, CT 06902
(203) 964-0592
E *** 1,6,8

Parker Hyde Corp.
Mr. Anthony W. Parker, Pres.
2000 L St., N.W., Ste. 200
Washington, D.C. 20036
(202) 466-3810
C * 12

Pathfinder Venture Cap. Fund
Mr. A.J.Greenshields, Gen.Ptnr.
7300 Metro Blvd., Ste. 585
Minneapolis, MN 55435
(612) 835-1121
E *** 1,5,6,8,12

Peat, Marwick, Mitchell & Co.
Mr. Donald T. Briggs, Jr., Ptnr.
Three Embarcadero Ctr.
San Francisco, CA 94111
(415) 335-5300

Peat, Marwick, Mitchell & Co.
Mr. Paul H. Phillips, Ptnr.
1700 IDS Center
Minneapolis, MN 55402
(612) 341-2222

Peat, Marwick, Mitchell & Co.
Mr. Edgar R. Wood, Jr., Ptnr.
1800 First Union Pl.
Charlotte, NC 28282
(704) 335-5300

Pennsylvania Dev. Credit Corp.
Mr. C. Drew Moyer, Exec. VP
2595 Interstate Dr., Ste. 103
Harrisburg, PA 17110
(717) 652-9434
B ** 5,9

Pepper, Hamilton & Scheetz
Mr. Michael B. Staebler, Ptnr.
36th Fl., 100 Renaissance Ctr.
Detroit, MI 48226
(313) 259-7110

Peregrine Associates
Mr. Gene I. Miller, Gen. Ptnr.
606 Wilshire Blvd., Ste. 602
Santa Monica, CA 90401
(213) 458-1441
E *** 1,5,6,8,9,10,12

Pernovo, Inc.
Mr. Robert P. Whipple, Exec. VP
15233 Ventura Blvd., Ste. 716
Sherman Oaks, CA 91403
(213) 789-0666

Plante and Moran
Mr. Robert C. Law, Dir.
220 E. Huron St., Ste. 600
Ann Arbor, MI 48104
(313) 665-9494

Price Waterhouse
Mr. L. Michael Larrenaga
5950 Canoga Ave., Ste. 100
Woodland Hills, CA 91367
(213) 704-1117

Quidnet Capital Corp.
Mr. Reid White, Pres.
909 State Rd.
Princeton, NJ 08540
(609) 924-7665
B *** 1,3,5,6,9,12

Richards, O'Neil & Allegaeret
Mr. Craigh Leonard, Ptnr.
660 Madison Ave.
New York, NY 10021
(212) 207-1200

Rodi, Pollock, Pettker,
  Galbraith & Phillips
Michael P. Ridley, Esq.
611 W. 6th St., Ste. 1600
Los Angeles, CA 90017
(213) 680-0823

L.F. Rothschild, Unterberg, Towbin
Mr. T.I. Unterberg, Mng. Dir.
55 Water St.
New York, NY 10041
(212) 425-3300
C *** 1,6,8,9,11

Scientific Advances, Inc.
Mr. Charles G. James, Pres.
601 W. Fifth Ave.
Columbus, OH 43201
(614) 294-5541
D *** 1,5,6,8

Security Pacific Bus. Credit, Inc.
Mr. Robert Spitalnic, VP
228 E. 45th St.
New York, NY 10017
(212) 309-9302

The Small Business Advocacy, Inc.
Mr. Marc E. Brown, Pres.
526 Nilles Rd., Ste. 5
Fairfield, OH 45014
(513) 829-0800
C *** 1,3,5,6,7,8,9

Standard Ventures, Ltd.
Mr. Michael R. Thomas, Mng. Ptnr.
225 Peachtree St., N.E.
Atlanta, GA 30303
(404) 577-8773
D ** 12

Stephenson Merchant Banking
Mr. A. Emmet Stephenson, Sr. Ptnr.
899 Logan St.
Denver, CO 80203
(303) 837-1700
C *** 1,3,5,6,9,10

Steuben Partners
Mr. Amory Houghton, Jr., Chmn.
717 Fifth Ave.
New York, NY 10022
(212) 752-1100
E * 1,3,5,6,8,10,11,12

TDH Capital Corp.
Mr. J. Mahlon Buck, Jr., Pres.
Box 234, Two Radnor Corp. Ctr.
Radnor, PA 19089
(215) 293-9787
D *** 12

Technology Transfer Institute
Mr. Shingo Tanaka, Exec. Mng. Dir.
Kokusai Shin Akasaka West Bldg.
12F 1-20, Akasaka 6-chome
Minato-ku, Tokyo 107
(03) 585-6451

Tulsa Industrial Authority
Mr. Rick L. Weddle, Gen. Mgr.
616 S. Boston
Tulsa, OK 74119
(918) 585-1201
E ** 5,6

The Venture Capital Fund
  of New England
Mr. Richard Farrell, Gen.Ptnr.
100 Franklin St.
Boston, MA 02110
(617) 451-2575
C *** 1,8,12

Venture Capital International
Mr. Robert S. Froug, Pres.
720 S. Colorado Blvd., Ste. 940
Denver, CO 80222
(303) 759-4860
C * 5,6,7,8,10,11,12

Venture Founders Corp.
Mr. Alexander Dingee, Jr., Pres
100 Fifth Ave.
Waltham, MA 02154
(617) 890-1000
D *** 1,5,6,8

Vista Ventures
Mr. Gerald Bay, Mng. Gen. Ptnr.
1600 Summer St.
Stamford, CT 06905
(203) 359-3500
D *** 1,5,6,8

Whitehead Associates
Mr. Joseph A. Orlando, Pres.
15 Valley Dr.
Greenwich, CT 06830
(203) 629-4633
D *** 12

```
Arthur Young & Co.                Arthur Young & Co.                  Arthur Young & Co.
Mr. Jerome S. Engel, Ptnr.        Mr. John Spencer, Jr., Ptnr.        Mr. Dennis Serlen, Ptnr.
One Post St.                      235 Peachtree St., NE               277 Park Ave.
San Francisco, CA  94104          2100 Gas Light Tower                New York, NY  10172
(415) 393-2733                    Atlanta, GA  30043                  (212) 407-1611
                                  (404) 581-1300

Arthur Young & Co.                Arthur Young & Co.                  Arthur Young & Co.
Mr. Robert J. Brennan, Ptnr.      Mr. Al Boos, Ptnr.                  Mr. Robert M. Feerick, Ptnr.
1111 Summer St.                   200 Lomas Blvd., N.W., Ste. 300     777 E. Wisconsin Ave.
Stamford, CT  06905               Albuquerque, NM  87102             Milwaukee, WI  53202
(203) 356-1800                    (505) 842-9273                      (414) 273-3340
```

Small Business Administration (SBA) Field Offices

Alabama
908 South 20th Street
Birmingham, Alabama 35256
205/254-1344

Alaska
Federal Building
701 C Street, Box 67
Anchorage, Alaska 99513
907/271-4022

Box 14
101 12th Avenue
Fairbanks, Alaska 99701
907/456-0211

Arizona
3030 North Central Avenue
Phoenix, Arizona 85012
602/241-2206

301 West Congress St.
Federal Bldg., Box 33
Tucson, Arizona 85701
602/792-6715

Arkansas
320 W. Capitol Ave., Suite 601
Little Rock, Arkansas 72201
501/378-5871

California
2202 Monterey Street
Fresno, California 93721
209/487-5791

660 J Street, Suite 215
Sacramento, California
95814
916/484-4726

880 Front Street
San Diego, California 92188
619/293-5440

*450 Golden Gate Avenue
P.O. Box 36044
San Francisco, California
94102
415/556-7487

211 Main St., 4th Floor
San Francisco, California
94105
415/974-0649

350 S. Figueroa St.
Los Angeles, California 90071
213/688-2956

Fidelity Federal Bldg.
2700 North Main St.
Santa Ana, California 92701
714/836-2494

111 West St. John Street
San Jose, California 95113
408/275-7584

Colorado
*Executive Tower Building
1405 Curtis Street
Denver, Colorado 80202-2395
303/837-5441

721 19th Street
Denver, Colorado 80202
303/837-2607

Connecticut
One Hartford Square W.
Hartford, Connecticut 06106
203/244-4041

Delaware
844 King Street
Lockbox 16
Wilmington, Delaware 19801
302/573-6294

Source: Small Business Administration.   * Regional Office

District of Columbia
1111 18th St., N.W.
Washington, D.C. 20036
202/634-1818

Florida
400 West Bay Street
P.O. Box 35067
Jacksonville, Florida 32202
904/791-3782

2222 Ponce De Leon Blvd.
Coral Gables, Florida 33134
305/350-5521

700 Twiggs Street
Tampa, Florida 33602
813/228-2594

3500 45th Street
West Palm Beach, Florida
33407
305/689-2223

Georgia
*1375 Peachtreet Street, N.E.
Atlanta, Georgia 30367
404/881-4943

1720 Peachtree Road, N.W.
Atlanta, Georgia 30309
404/881-4325

Guam
Pacific News Bldg., Rm. 508
238 O'Hara Street
Agana, Guam 96910
671/472-7277

Hawaii
300 Ala Moana
P.O. Box 2213
Honolulu, Hawaii 96850
808/546-8950

Idaho
1005 Main Street
Boise, Idaho 83702
208/334-1096

Illinois
*219 South Dearborn Street
Chicago, Illinois 60604
312/353-4544

219 South Dearborn Street
Chicago, Illinois 60604
312/353-4528

Washington Building
Four North Old State

Capitol Plaza
Springfield, Illinois 62701
217/492-4416

Indiana
501 E. Monroe Street
South Bend, Indiana 46601
219/236-8361

New Federal Bldg.
575 N. Pennsylvania Street
Indianapolis, Indiana 46209
317/269-7278

Iowa
210 Walnut Street
Des Moines, Iowa 50309
515/284-4567

373 Collins Road, N.E.
Cedar Rapids, Iowa 52402
319/399-2571

Kansas
Main Place Bldg.
110 East Waterman Street
Wichita, Kansas 67202
316/269-6273

Kentucky
Federal Office Bldg.
P.O. Box 3517
Louisville, Kentucky 40201
502/582-5971

Louisiana
Ford-Fisk Bldg.
1661 Canal Street
New Orleans, Louisiana
70112
504/589-6685

500 Fannin Street
Federal Bldg. & Courthouse
Shreveport, Louisiana 71101
318/226-5196

Maine
40 Western Avenue
Augusta, Maine 04330
207/622-8378

Maryland
8600 LaSalle Road
Towson, Maryland 21204
301/962-4392

Massachusetts
*60 Batterymarch Street
Boston, Massachusetts
02110
617/223-2100

---

* Regional Office

150 Causeway Street
Boston, Massachusetts 02114
617/223–2100

302 High Street
Holyoke, Massachusetts
01040
413/536–8770

Michigan
477 Michigan Avenue
McNamara Bldg.
Detroit, Michigan 48226
313/226–6075

220 W. Washington St.
Marquette, Michigan 49885
906/225–1108

Minnesota
610-C Butler Square
100 North 6th Street
Minneapolis, Minnesota
55403
612/349–3550

Mississippi
Gulf National Life
Insurance Bldg.
111 Fred Haise Blvd.
Biloxi, Mississippi 39530
601/435–3676

100 West Capitol St.
New Federal Bldg.
Jackson, Mississippi 39269
601/960–4371

Missouri
*911 Walnut Street
Kansas City, Missouri 64106
816/374–3316

818 Grand Avenue
Kansas City, Missouri 64106
816/374–5557

815 Olive Street
St. Louis, Missouri 63101
314/425–6600

Federal Court House Bldg.
339 Broadway
Cape Girardeau, Missouri
63701
314/335–6039

309 North Jefferson
Springfield, Missouri 65806
417/864–7670

Montana
301 South Park Avenue
Helena, Montana 59601
406/449–5381

Nebraska
Empire State Building
19th & Farnam Streets
Omaha, Nebraska 68102
402/221–4691

Nevada
Box 7527—Downtown
Station
301 East Stewart
Las Vegas, Nevada 89101
702/385–6611

P.O. Box 3216
50 S. Virginia Street
Reno, Nevada 89505
702/784–5268

New Hampshire
55 Pleasant Street
Concord, New Hampshire
03301
603/224–4724

New Jersey
1800 East Davis Street
Camden, New Jersey 08104
609/757–5183

60 Park Place
Newark, New Jersey 07102
201/645–3683

New Mexico
Patio Plaza Building
5000 Marble Ave., N.E.
Albuquerque, N.M. 87110
505/766–3430

New York
*26 Federal Plaza
New York, New York 10278
212/264–7772

445 Broadway
Albany, New York 12210
518/472–6300

111 West Huron Street
Buffalo, New York 14202
716/846–4301

180 Clemens Center Pkwy.
Elmira, New York 14901
607/733–4686

---

* Regional Office

35 Pinelaw Road
Melville, New York 11747
516/454-0764
26 Federal Plaza
New York, New York 10278
212/264-1766

100 State Street
Rochester, New York 14614
716/263-6700

100 South Clinton St.
Federal Bldg.
Syracuse, New York 13260
315/423-5382

North Carolina
230 S. Tryon Street
Charlotte, North Carolina
28202
704/371-6561

215 South Evans Street
Greenville, North Carolina
27834
919/752-3798

North Dakota
P.O. Box 3086
Fargo, North Dakota 58102
701/237-5131

Ohio
1240 East 9th St.
AJC Federal Bldg.
Cleveland, Ohio 44199
216/522-4180

85 Marconi Boulevard
Columbus, Ohio 43215
614/469-6860

550 Main Street
Cincinnati, Ohio 45202
513/684-2814

Oklahoma
200 N.W. 5th Street
Oklahoma City, Oklahoma
73102
405/231-4301

333 W. Fourth Street
Tulsa, Oklahoma 74103
918/581-7495

Oregon
1220 S.W. Third Ave.
Federal Building
Portland, Oregon 97202
503/423-5221

Pennsylvania
*One Bala Cynwyd Plaza
231 St. Asaphs Road
Bala Cynwyd, Pennsylvania
19004
215/596-5889

One Bala Cynwyd Plaza
231 St. Asaphs Rd.
Bala Cynwyd, Pennsylvania
19004
215/597-3311

100 Chestnut Street
Harrisburg, Pennsylvania
17101
717/782-3840

960 Penn Avenue
Convention Tower
Pittsburgh, Pennsylvania
15222
412/644-2780

Penn Place
20 N. Pennsylvania Avenue
Wilkes-Barre, Pennsylvania
18702
717/826-6497

Puerto Rico
Federal Building
Carlos Chardon Avenue
Hato Rey, Puerto Rico 00919
809/753-4572

Rhode Island
40 Fountain Street
Providence, Rhode Island
02903
401/528-4586

South Carolina
1835 Assembly Street
P.O. Box 2786
Columbia, South Carolina
29201
803/765-5376

South Dakota
101 South Main Avenue
Sioux Falls, South Dakota
57102
605/336-2980

Tennessee
404 James Robertson
Parkway
Nashville, Tennessee 37219
615/251-5881

---

* Regional Office

Texas
Federal Building
300 East 8th Street
Austin, Texas 78701
512/482-7811

3105 Leopard Street
P.O. Box 9253
Corpus Christi, Texas 78408
512/888-3331

*8625 King George Drive
Bldg. C
Dallas, Texas 75235-3391
214/767-7643

1100 Commerce Street
Dallas, Texas 75242
214/767-0605

4100 Rio Bravo Street
Pershing W. Bldg.
El Paso, Texas 79902
915/543-7586

222 E. Van Buren St.
Harlingen, Texas 78550
512/423-4533

2525 Murthworth
Houston, Texas 77054
713/660-2409

1611 10th Street
Lubbock, Texas 79401
806/743-7466

100 South Washington Street
Marshall, Texas 75670
214/935-5257

727 E. Durango St.
Federal Bldg.
San Antonio, Texas 78206
512/229-6270

Utah
125 South State Street
Salt Lake City, Utah 84138
801/524-5800

Vermont
87 State Street
Montpelier, Vermont 05602
802/229-0538

Virginia
400 North 8th Street
P.O. Box 10126

Richmond, Virginia 23240
804/771-2617

Virgin Islands
Veterans Drive
St. Thomas, Virgin Islands
00801
809/774-8530

P.O. Box 4010
Christiansted, Virgin Islands
00820
809/773-3480

Washington
*710 2nd Avenue
Seattle, Washington 98104
206/442-5676

915 Second Avenue
Seattle, Washington 98174
206/442-5534

651 U.S. Courthouse
P.O. Box 2167
Spokane, Washington 99210
509/456-3781

West Virginia
109 North 3rd Street
Clarksburg, West Virginia
26301
304/623-5631

Charleston National Plaza
Charleston, West Virginia
25301
304/343-6181

Wisconsin
500 South Barstow Street
Eau Claire, Wisconsin 54701
715/834-9012

212 E. Washington Ave.
Madison, Wisconsin 53703
608/264-5205

310 West Wisconsin Avenue
Milwaukee, Wisconsin 53202
414/291-3941

Wyoming
P.O. Box 2839
Casper, Wyoming 82602
307/261-5761

---

* Regional Office

Executive Search Firms

Members of the Association of Executive Search Consultants, Inc. are indicated by superscript 1 and members of the Association of Management Consulting Firms, Inc. are indicated by superscript 2.

Association of Executive Search Consultants, Inc.
151 Railroad Avenue
Greenwich, CT 06830
(203) 661–6606

Association of Management Consulting Firms
230 Park Avenue
New York, NY 10169
(212) 697–9693

Information regarding a firm's area of specialization as well as a listing of its domestic and foreign branches can be obtained from the individual firm or from the appropriate organization given above.

A useful source for information on executive recruitment is *Executive Recruiting News*, published monthly by Kennedy & Kennedy, Inc., Templeton Road, Fitzwilliam, NH 03447, (603–585–2200).

American Executive Management, Inc.
30 Federal Street
Salem, MA 01970
(617) 744–5923

Antell, Nagel, Moorhead & Associates
280 Park Avenue
New York, NY 10169
(212) 678–1744

D. P. Baiocchi Associates
150 North Wacker Drive
Chicago, IL 60606
(312) 443–0070

Barger & Sargeant, Inc.[1]
5 Warren Street
Concord, NH 03301
(603) 224–7753

Battalia & Associates, Inc.[1]
275 Madison Avenue
New York, NY 10016
(212) 683–9440

J. W. Bauder Associates, Inc.[1]
16475 Dallas Parkway
Dallas, TX 75248
(214) 931–1111

Bentley & Evans, Inc.
One Penn Plaza
New York, NY 10119
(212) 371–1212

Billington, Fox & Ellis, Inc.[1]
20 North Wacker Drive
Chicago, IL 60606
(312) 236–5000

Bowden & Company, Inc.[1]
5000 Rockside Road
Cleveland, OH 44131
(216) 447–1800

Boyden Associates, Inc.
260 Madison Avenue
New York, NY 10016
(212) 949–7600

The Brand Company, Inc.
12740 North River Road
Mequon, WI 53092
(414) 242–6203

Thomas A. Buffum Assoc.[1]
1 Post Office Square
Boston, MA 02109
(617) 423–4100

The Caldwell Partners[1]
64 Prince Arthur Avenue
Toronto, Ontario M5R 1B4
(416) 920–7702

Canny, Bowen Inc.
425 Park Avenue
New York, NY 10022
(212) 986–8653

David Chambers & Associates, Inc.
6 East 43rd Street
New York, NY 10017
(212) 986–8653

Christenson & Montgomery, Inc.[1]
250 Madison Avenue
Morristown, NJ 07960
(201) 540–1444

William H. Clark Associates, Inc.
330 Madison Avenue
New York, NY 10017
(212) 661–8760

---

† CPA firm with an executive search department.

Coopers & Lybrand†
1251 Avenue of the Americas
New York, NY 10022
(212) 536–3021

Allan Cox & Associates
410 North Michigan Avenue
Chicago, IL 60611
(312) 644–2360

Thorndike Deland Associates[1]
1440 Broadway
New York, NY 10018
(212) 840–8100

Devine, Baldwin & Peters, Inc.[1]
250 Park Avenue
New York, NY 10177
(212) 867–5235

Robert W. Dingman Co., Inc.[1]
32131 West Lindero Canyon Road
Westlake Village, CA 91361
(213) 991–5950

Eastman & Beaudine, Inc.[1]
111 West Monroe Street
Chicago, IL 60603
(312) 726–8195

Leon A. Farley Associates[1]
468 Jackson Street
San Francisco, CA 94111
(415) 777-2888

Fleming Associates[1]
1428 Franklin Street
P.O. Box 604
Columbus, IN 47201
(812) 376–9061

Foster & Associates, Inc.[1]
One Market Plaza
Steuart Street Tower
San Francisco, CA 94105
(415) 777–0330

Walter Frederick Friedman and Company,
Inc.[2]
111 Northfield Avenue
West Orange, NJ 07052
(201) 325–3700

Garofolo, Curtiss & Company[1]
366 West Lancaster Avenue
Ardmore, PA 19003
(215) 896–5080

Robert L. Gette
400 Beach Road
Tequesta, FL 33458
(305) 746–6240

N. W. Gibson Int'l, Inc.
5900 Wilshire Boulevard
Los Angeles, CA 90036
(213) 930–1100

Golightly and Company, International, Inc.[2]
Personnel Services Division
One Rockefeller Plaza
New York, NY 10020
(212) 245–0900

Goodrich & Sherwood
521 Fifth Avenue
New York, NY 10017
(212) 697–4131

Gould & McCoy Inc.[1]
551 Madison Avenue
New York, NY 10022
(212) 688–8671

Halbrecht Associates, Inc.
1200 Summer Street
Stamford, CT 06905
(203) 327–5630

Haley Associates, Inc.[1]
375 Park Avenue
New York, NY 10152
(212) 421–7860

Harris & U'Ren, Inc.[1]
101 North First Avenue
Phoenix, AZ 85003
(602) 257–1072

Haskell & Stern Associates, Inc.[1]
529 Fifth Avenue
New York, NY 10017
(212) 687–7292

Heidrick Partners, Inc.[1]
20 North Wacker Drive
Chicago, IL 60606
(312) 845–9700

Helmich, Miller & Pasek, Inc.[1]
5725 East River Road
Chicago, IL 60631
(312) 693–6270

Herbert Davis & Company[2]
111 Charlotte Place
Englewood Cliffs, NJ 07632
(201) 871–1760

Hodge-Cronin & Associates, Inc.[1]
9575 West Higgins Road
Rosemont, IL 60018
(312) 692–2041

Houze, Shourds & Montgomery, Inc.[1]
27520 Hawthorne Boulevard

Rolling Hills Estates, CA 90274
(213) 373–0961

Daniel D. Howard Associates, Inc.[2]
307 North Michigan Avenue
Chicago, IL 60601
(312) 372–7041

Ward Howell International, Inc.[1]
99 Park Avenue
New York, NY 10016
(212) 697–3730

Interface Group, Ltd.
3238 Prospect Street, NW
Washington, DC 20007
(202) 965–1100

International Management Advisors, Inc.[1]
767 Third Avenue
New York, NY 10017
(212) 758–7770

Charles Irish Company, Inc.[1]
420 Lexington Avenue
New York, NY 10170
(212) 490–0040

Johnson, Smith & Knisely, Inc.
275 Madison Avenue
New York, NY 10016
(212) 686–9760

Kearney: Executive Search Group[1,2]
222 South Riverside Plaza
Chicago, IL 60606
(312) 648–0111

Keating, Grimm & Leeper, Inc.
717 Fifth Avenue
New York, NY 10022
(212) 758–2300

Kensington Management Consultants, Inc.[1,2]
25 Third Street
Stamford, CT 06905
(203) 327–9860

Korn/Ferry International
277 Park Avenue
New York, NY 10017
(212) 371–3770

Kors Marlar Savage & Associates
1980 South Post Oak Boulevard
Houston, TX 77056

Krall Management Incorporated[2]
Valley Forge Plaza
1150 First Avenue
King of Prussia, PA 19406
(215) 687–8410

Kremple & Meade[1]
1900 Avenue of the Stars
Los Angeles, CA 90067
(213) 456–6451

Kunzer Associates, Ltd.[1]
208 South LaSalle Street
Chicago, IL 60604
(312) 641–0010

Lamalie Associates, Inc.[1]
101 Park Avenue
New York, NY 10178
(212) 953–7900

Lauer, Sbarbaro Assoc., Inc.[1]
1 North LaSalle Street
Chicago, IL 60602
(312) 372–7050

Laurence L. Lapham Associates, Inc.[1]
230 Park Avenue
New York, NY 10169
(212) 599–0644

Lawrence-Leiter and Company[2]
427 West Twelfth Street
Kansas City, MO 64105
(816) 474–8340

Locke & Associates[1]
3145 NCNB Plaza
Charlotte, NC 28280
(704) 372–6600

John Lucht Consultancy, Inc.[1]
645 Fifth Avenue
New York, NY 10022
(212) 935–4660

Management Advisors of Princeton, Inc.
228 Alexander Street
Princeton, NJ 08540
(609) 921–3622

McFeely Wackerle Associates[1]
20 North Wacker Drive
Chicago, IL 60606
(312) 641–2977

Christopher Mill & Partners[1]
The Garden House
11a Calonne Road
Wimbledon, London
SW19 5HH England

Harold A. Miller Associates[1]
Fearrington Box 53
Pittsboro, NC 27312
(919) 542–5115

Moriarty/Fox, Inc.[1]
20 North Wacker Drive

Chicago, IL 60606
(312) 332–4600

MSL International Consultants[2]
1 Dag Hammarskjold Plaza
New York, NY 10017
(212) 644–5656

Nordeman Grumm, Inc.—MBA Resources
717 Fifth Avenue
New York, NY 10022
(212) 935–1000

Oliver & Rozner Associates, Inc.[1]
598 Madison Avenue
New York, NY 10022
(212) 688–1850

Ott & Associates, Inc.
201 South Lake Avenue
Pasadena, CA 91101
(213) 578–0551

PA Executive Search Inc.
200 Park Avenue
New York, NY 10166
(212) 599–4774

Parker, Eldridge, Sholl & Gordon, Inc.
440 Totten Pond Road
Boston, MA 02154
(617) 890–0340

Peat Marwick Mitchell & Co.†
303 East Wacker Drive
Chicago, IL 60601
(312) 938–1000

Pinsker & Shattuck, Inc.[1]
100 Bush Street
San Francisco, CA 94104
(415) 421–6264

Paul R. Ray & Co., Inc.
1208 Ridglea Bank Building
Fort Worth, TX 76116
(817) 731–4111

Rath & Strong, Inc.[2]
21 Worthen Road
Lexington, MA 02173
(617) 861–1700

Robison, Sockwell & McAulay[1]
3100 NCNB Plaza
Charlotte, NC 28280
(704) 376–0059

Ropes Associates, Inc.[1]
One Financial Plaza
Fort Lauderdale, FL 33394
(305) 525–6600

Russell Reynolds Associates, Inc.[1]
245 Park Avenue
New York, NY 10167
(212) 953–4300

Ryan/Parmenter & Associates, Inc.[1]
P.O. Box 253
Westfield, NJ 07090
(201) 232–5720

Schwarzkopf Consultants, Inc.[1]
15285 Watertown Plank Road
Elm Grove, WI 53122
(414) 784–4200

Skott/Edwards Consultants, Inc.
230 Park Avenue
New York, NY 10169
(212) 697–7640

Spencer Stuart & Associates
55 East 52nd Street
New York, NY 10055
(212) 407–0200

John W. Siller & Associates, Inc.[1]
5261 North Port Washington Road
P.O. Box 17526
Milwaukee, WI 53217
(414) 962–9400

Paul Stafford Associates, Ltd.[1]
45 Rockefeller Plaza
New York, NY 10111
(212) 765–7700

S. K. Stewart & Associates[1]
P.O. Box 40110
Cincinnati, OH 45240
(513) 771–2250

TASA, Inc[1]
875 Third Avenue
New York, NY 10022
(212) 486–1490

Tully and Hobart, Inc.[1]
333 North Michigan Avenue
Chicago, IL 60601
(312) 372–0300

K. W. Tunnell Company, Inc.[2]
Valley Forge Plaza
1150 First Avenue
King of Prussia, PA 19406
(215) 337–0820

Robert M. Wald and Associates, Inc.[2]
45 Mercantile Place
Pasadena, CA 91105
(213) 792–7111

Emanuel Weintraub Associates, Inc.[2]
Polygon Plaza
2050 Center Avenue
Ft. Lee, NJ 07024
(201) 947–2404

Werner Management Consultants, Inc.[2]
111 West 40th Street
New York, NY 10018
(212) 730–1280

Arthur Young Executive Resource Consultants†
299 Park Avenue
New York, NY 10017
(212) 407–1515

E. N. Wilkins and Co., Inc.[1]
7131 Sears Tower
Chicago, IL 60606
(312) 930–1036

William R. Wilkinson & Company[1]
P.O. Box 326
Orinda, CA 94563
(415) 254–2770

William H. Willis, Inc.[1]
445 Park Avenue
New York, NY 10022
(212) 752–3456

Witt Associates, Inc.[1]
1415 West 22nd Street
Oak Brook, IL 60521
(312) 325–5070

Yelverton & Company[1]
350 Sacramento Street
San Francisco, CA 94104
(415) 981–6060

Charles Zabriskie Associates, Inc.
919 Third Avenue
New York, NY 10022
(212) 980–0700

Egon Zehnder International Inc.
645 Fifth Avenue
New York, NY 10022
(212) 838–9199

Returns on Various Types of Investments*

R. S. Salomon, Jr.
Mallory J. Lennox

This report details our eighth annual survey of returns provided by a broad array of tangible assets—collectibles, commodities and real estate—as well as financial assets. Figure 1 provides performance statistics for 14 investment categories for four intervals: 15 years, 10 years, five years and one year. We have listed the assets according to their 15-year performance. Figure 2 compares the one-year return and rankings for the period ended June 1, 1984, with last year's results. Since the protection and enhancement of purchasing power is a primary investment goal, we have included the CPI on both tables as a benchmark for determining whether a particular asset has provided a real return to investors over the period being measured. The inflation scorecard at the bottom of Figure 1 tallies the number of assets in each category where returns beat inflation rates. Real returns proved particularly elusive over the past 12 months. Despite the fact that inflation was a modest 4.6%, only four of the 14 asset categories provided real returns: old masters, Treasury bills, coins, and housing. That compares with 11 out of 14 assets that provided returns in excess of inflation over the 15-year period and ten out of 14 categories over the ten-year period, when inflation was running at much higher levels. While it may seem counterintuitive that lower rates of inflation would be harder to beat than higher rates, we note that roughly 70% (ten out of 14) of the survey categories are tangible assets, which benefit from higher inflation expectations.

Although investors tend to group tangible assets together in opposition to financial assets, there are, in fact, three fairly distinct categories of tangible assets: collectibles, commodities and real estate. While all three types of tangibles tend to rise in value when inflation rates are

high, they can respond in quite disparate ways to other economic trends.

The results of this year's survey demonstrate some of these differences. The moderate price increases of the past 12 months were accompanied by record real rates of interest and concomitant strength in the dollar. High interest rates add substantially to the carrying costs of commodities, diminishing net returns. If interest rates are rising because of rampant inflation, the resultant rise in the price of the commodity is likely to compensate for the higher costs. But the combination of record carrying costs on a real basis and only modest inflation is especially unattractive for commodity investors. Add a strong dollar to the picture and you have a very negative environment for gold in particular. None of the commodity-related assets provided real returns this year.

In the real estate market, rising real costs could potentially swamp investment returns in periods of stable or declining prices. However, the changes in the nature of mortgage instruments from primarily fixed rate to primarily variable rates has muted the effect of rising rates on home prices. By lowering the initial cost, variable-rate instruments have made housing more affordable to more people, and thus they have stimulated demand.

Rising interest rates have much less of an effect on the market for collectibles than on either the real estate or commodity markets. Rising real rates diminish the relative attractiveness of collectibles compared with financial assets, but they do not increase carrying costs, since purchases are rarely, if ever, financed by borrowing. In one area, old masters, high interest rates have actually helped to foster a renaissance in prices. The category took the number one spot in this year's survey with a return of 14.3%. High U.S. interest rates have contributed to the strength in the dollar over the past 12 months. Industry sources tell us that Americans have been arriving in force at European art auctions to take advantage of the significant opportunities offered by currency differentials.

In theory, collectibles are priced according to their scarcity and quality, but the concept of both criteria can change over time. Changes in quality standards present a particular problem when attempting to measure historic returns for an asset. Such calculations compare

* Although the information in this report has been obtained from sources which Salomon Brothers Inc believes to be reliable, we do not guarantee its accuracy and such information may be incomplete or condensed. All opinions and estimates included in this report constitute our judgment as of this date and are subject to change without notice. This report is for information purposes only and is not intended as an offer or solicitation with respect to the purchase or sale of any security.

Editor's Note: Stock returns are for the S&P 500 and include appreciation plus dividends. Bond returns are for Salomon Brothers Index and include appreciation plus interest.

Source: *Financial Assets—A Temporary Setback*, by R. S. Salomon, Jr. and Mallory J. Lennox © Salomon Brothers Inc., June 8, 1984.

Figure 1. Compounded Annual Rates of Return

	15 Years	Rank	10 Years	Rank	5 Years	Rank	1 Year	Rank
Oil	20.4%	1	10.1%	4	14.8%	2	0.0%	8
Coins	17.3	2	21.4	1	11.3	5	7.4	3
Gold	16.3	3	9.5	6	7.4	8	(4.0)	12
U.S. Stamps	16.1	4	17.1	2	9.8	6	(4.0)	13
Chinese Ceramics	13.7	5	5.9	14	15.7	1	3.0	6
Silver	11.7	6	7.2	12	2.4	13	(25.2)	15
Diamonds	10.4	7	9.8	5	6.1	9	0.0	7
Farmland	9.6	8	9.4	7	3.3	12	(0.7)	9
Treasury Bills	9.0	9	10.1	3	12.7	4	9.4	2
Old Masters	8.5	10	9.1	8	1.5	14	14.3	1
Housing	8.5	11	8.6	10	5.8	10	5.5	4
CPI	**7.2**	**12**	**7.9**	**11**	**7.9**	**7**	**4.6**	**5**
Bonds	5.7	13	6.3	13	4.6	11	(7.2)	14
Stocks	5.3	14	9.0	9	13.5	3	(1.2)	10
Foreign Exchange	3.0	15	0.9	15	(4.9)	15	(3.0)	11

Inflation Scorecard (Number of Assets That Outperformed Inflation)

Tangibles	10 out of 10	8 out of 10	4 out of 10	3 out of 10
• Collectibles	4 out of 4	3 out of 4	3 out of 4	2 out of 4
• Commodities	4 out of 4	3 out of 4	1 out of 4	0 out of 4
• Real Estate	2 out of 2	2 out of 2	0 out of 2	1 out of 2
Financials	1 out of 4	2 out of 4	2 out of 4	1 out of 4

a All returns are for the period ended June 1. 1984. based on latest available data.

past bids with current bids for items of the same quality ranking. Accordingly, if the quality ranking of an asset changes during the holding period, the actual return to the investor may be substantially different from that implied by historical performance measurements. For example, quality grading in the numismatic market has become much stricter over the past 15 years. Based on our survey of compound annual returns, which measures price changes in coins of a given quality, coins have ranked in the top five categories for all four periods. However, returns to individual investors who held this same basket of coins could be substantially less

Figure 2. One-Year Rankings, 1984 vs. 1983

	This Year (Period Ended 1 June 1984)		Last Year (Period Ended 1 Jun 1983)	
	Return	Rank	Return	Rank
Old Masters	14.3%	1	1.7%	10
Treasury Bills	9.4	2	10.8	6
Coins	7.4	3	16.8	5
Housing	5.5	4	2.1	9
CPI	4.6	5	3.9	8
Chinese Ceramics	3.0	6	0.0	11
Diamonds	0.0	7	6.1a	7
Oil	0.0	8	(14.7)	15
Farmland	(0.7)	9	(5.7)	13
Stocks	(1.2)	10	51.8	2
Foreign Exchange	(3.0)	11	(4.3)	12
Gold	(4.0)	12	28.6	4
U.S. Stamps	(4.0)	13	(6.2)	14
Bonds	(7.2)	14	39.0	3
Silver	(25.2)	15	109.5	1

a Reflects revision in diamond index, return from June 1, 1982, to June 1, 1983, was previously estimated at 0.0%.

than those indicated, if one or more coins no longer met the stricter criteria for the quality ranking that it was originally assigned.

Factors Favorable for Tangible Assets
Escalating rate of inflation
Rising taxes
Increasing government regulation
Political instability
An economy favoring consumption
Fear of personal harm

Factors Favorable for Financial Assets
Increasing confidence in money (i.e., declining rate of inflation)
Reduced government intervention in the private sector
Sustained economic growth
Improving productivity
Political stability
An economy favoring savings and investment

Of the factors listed above, inflation is probably the most important. yet, based on the results of this year's survey, the market seems to have developed a split personality over this issue. The poor showing of tangible assets (only three out of ten provided a real return) would suggest that investors are not willing to assume that inflation will rise fast enough to compensate for the higher carrying costs imposed by current levels of real interest rates. Yet the performance of stocks (ranked tenth) and bonds (ranked fourteenth) suggests that participants in the financial markets are very worried about a resurgence of inflation and a concomitant rise in interest rate levels. The beneficiary of this confusion has been Treasury bills, which ranked second this year, with a return of 9.4%. In our view, the continued discipline of high real interest rates, export competition and the deregulation that has already taken place across broad industry sectors will continue to hamper pricing flexibility in the U.S. economy and provide continued incentive to corporations to increase efficiencies. We look for inflation to average about 4.5% this year, as measured by the GNP deflator, compared with 4.2% in 1983.

It continues to be our view that the factors favorable for financial assets will dominate the investment environment for some time to come. There are, however, some trends, which we view as temporary, that could color investment opinion near term: expectations of a tax hike after the presidential election; the Government's expanding role in the banking area, both with regard to domestic problems and the LDC crisis; and a persistently low savings rate, despite very real inducements to save. On the political stability/instability front, we note with interest that while a number of things are exploding in the Middle East, oil prices are not one of them. Indeed, Iran has lowered its price to compensate for the increase in insurance rates for tankers and cargo.

As with tangible assets, some distinctions also need to be made among categories of financial assets. Although we anticipate an economic environment that generally favors financial assets over tangibles, we do not expect all categories to provide real returns over the next 12 months. Our evaluation of the relative attractiveness of financial assets is predicated on the following assumptions: real interest rates will remain high, nominal rates will rise, and the improvement in the quality of earnings that has already taken place will persist. Although the dollar is expected to weaken somewhat from current levels, high real U.S. interest rates will provide support, and we do not anticipate a substantial falloff relative to major currencies. Accordingly, the basket of currencies measured in the survey is likely to continue to rank toward the bottom of the list. If the rate on long-term Government bonds rises by 125 basis points or more over the next 12 months from its current level of 13.4%, the depreciation in price would be sufficient to wipe out a real return. Given current credit conditions, both at home and abroad, we believe this is very likely to occur. Thus, in our opinion, the best opportunities for real returns lie with stocks and Treasury bills. Furthermore, we believe that the returns on stocks will beat those on Treasury bills. While rising interest rates certainly have a negative effect on stock prices, improvements in the quality of earnings have, historically, had as much of an impact, if not more, on stock prices. It is our contention that the market is currently undervaluing the improvement in the quality of earnings. Based on historical relationships, given the improvement in earnings quality that has already taken place, multiples should expand even in a climate of rising interest rates. We expect this upward bias in valuation levels to result in a total return for the S&P 500 of 20%25% over the next 12 months.

Stock Market

STOCK EXCHANGES

Common Stocks (shares of ownership in a corporation) are traded on several exchanges. The best known are the New York Stock Exchange and the American Stock Exchange, both located in Manhattan's financial district. Generally, the stocks of the largest companies are traded on the New York Stock Exchange, while somewhat smaller companies are traded on the American Exchange. There are also a number of regional exchanges such as the Midwest Exchange in Chicago and the Pacific Exchange in San Francisco. These exchanges trade stocks of local corporations as well as stocks listed on the New York and American Exchanges.

In addition, there is the Over-The Counter-Market (OTC) which, unlike the exchanges previously mentioned, does not have a specific location but consists of a network of brokers and dealers linked by telephone and private wires. Smaller or relatively new companies are traded on the OTC. Trading information for many (but far from all) stocks on the OTC market is collected and displayed on a computerized system, the National Association of Security Dealers Automatic Quote System (NASDAQ).

Large institutional traders (mutual and pension funds, insurance companies, etc.) often trade blocks of stocks directly with one another. This information is collected and displayed on the Instinet System.

MAJOR STOCK EXCHANGES

UNITED STATES

AMERICAN STOCK EXCHANGE, INC.
86 Trinity Place
New York, New York 10006

BOSTON STOCK EXCHANGE, INC.
53 State Street
Boston, Massachusetts 02109

THE CINCINNATI STOCK EXCHANGE, INC.
205 Dixie Terminal Building
Cincinnati, Ohio 45202

INTERMOUNTAIN STOCK EXCHANGE, INC.
39 Exchange Place
Salt Lake City, Utah 84111

MIDWEST STOCK EXCHANGE, INC.
120 South LaSalle Street
Chicago, Illinois 60603

NEW YORK STOCK EXCHANGE, INC.
11 Wall Street
New York, New York 10005

PACIFIC STOCK EXCHANGE, INC.
301 Pine Street
San Francisco, California 94104
and
618 South Spring Street
Los Angeles, California 90014

PHILADELPHIA STOCK EXCHANGE, INC.
17th Street & Stock Exchange Place
Philadelphia, Pennsylvania 19103

SPOKANE STOCK EXCHANGE, INC.
225 Peyton Building
Spokane, Washington 99201

CANADA

ALBERTA STOCK EXCHANGE
201 Sun Oil Building
500–4th Ave. S.W.
Calgary, Alberta T2P 2V6

MONTREAL STOCK EXCHANGE
The Stock Exchange Tower
800 Victoria Square
Montreal, Quebec H4Z 1A9

TORONTO STOCK EXCHANGE
234 Bay Street
Toronto, Ontario M5J 1R1

VANCOUVER STOCK EXCHANGE
536 Howe Street
Vancouver, B.C. V6C 2E1

WINNIPEG STOCK EXCHANGE
420, 167 Lombard Avenue
Winnipeg, Manitoba R3B OT

Investment Returns on Stocks, Bonds, and Bills

*Roger G. Ibbotson**

Our look at history consists of examining the returns of five capital market sectors. We measure total returns (capital gains plus income) on common stocks, long-term corporate bonds, long-term government bonds, U.S. Treasury bills, and rates of inflation on consumer goods. Comparing the returns from the various sectors gives us insights into the returns available from taking risk and the relationships between capital market returns and inflation.

THE RISKS AND REWARDS

We display graphically the rewards and risks available from the U.S. capital markets over the past 58 years. Exhibit 1 shows the growth of an investment in common stocks, long-term government bonds, and Treasury bills as well

* Professor, Graduate School of Business, University of Chicago, Chicago, Illinois.

EXHIBIT 1: WEALTH INDEXES OF INVESTMENTS IN THE U.S. CAPITAL MARKETS, 1926–1983 (assumed initial investment of $1.00 at year-end 1925, includes reinvestment income)

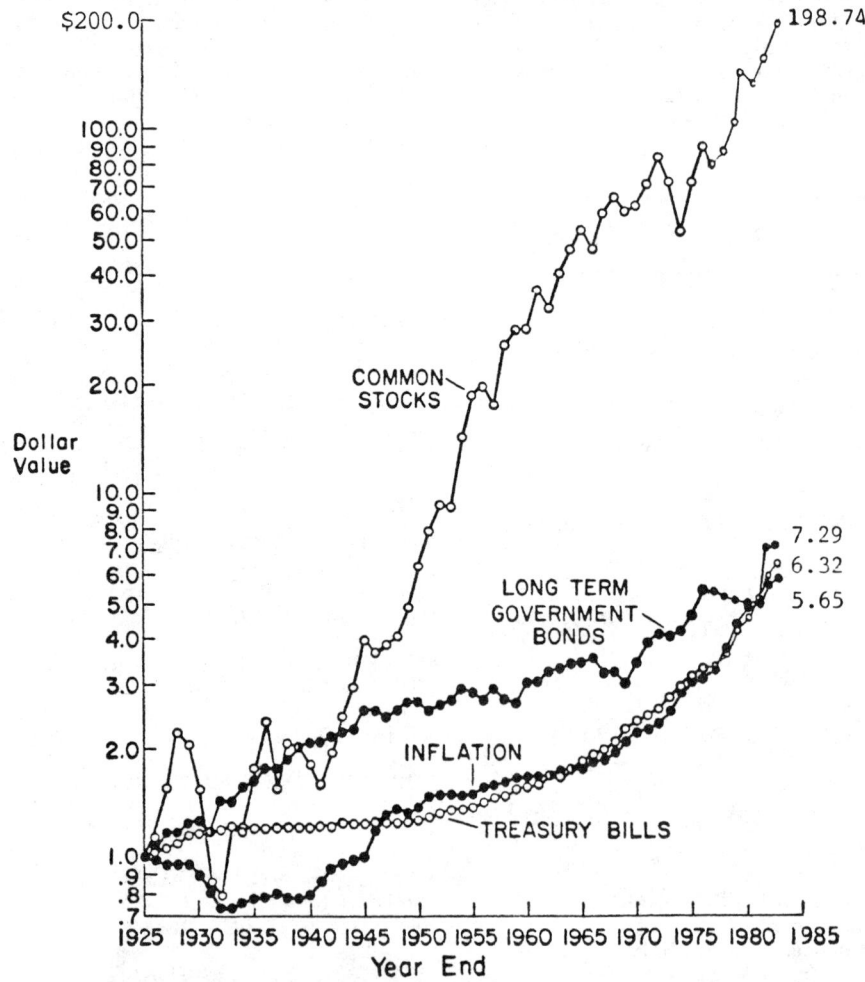

Source: Roger G. Ibbotson and Rex A. Sinquefield, *Stocks, Bonds, Bills, and Inflation: The Past and The Future* (1982 Edition), Financial Analysts Research Foundation (Charlottesville, Va.: 1982); for 1926–1981; *Stocks, Bonds, Bills, and Inflation: 1984 Yearbook*, published by R. G. Ibbotson Associates [8 S. Michigan Avenue, Suite 707, Chicago, IL. 60603], 1984, for updates.

EXHIBIT 2: BASIC SERIES: TOTAL ANNUAL RETURNS, 1926–1983

SERIES	GEOMETRIC MEAN	ARITHMETIC MEAN	STANDARD DEVIATION	DISTRIBUTION
COMMON STOCKS	9.6%	11.8%	21.4%	
LONG TERM CORPORATE BONDS	4.2	4.4	7.6	
LONG TERM GOVERNMENT BONDS	3.5	3.7	7.4	
U.S. TREASURY BILLS	3.1	3.2	3.2	
INFLATION	3.0	3.1	5.0	

-90x   0x   +90x

Source: Ibbotson, Roger G. and Rex A. Sinquefield, *Stocks, Bonds, Bills and Inflation: The Past and The Future*, 1982 edition, Financial Analysts Research Foundation (Charlottesville, Va.: 1982); updates by R. G. Ibbotson Associates, Inc., Chicago.

as the increase in the inflation index over the 58-year period. Each of the series is initiated at $1 at year-end 1925. The vertical scale is logarithmic so that equal distances represent equal percentage changes anywhere along the axis. The graph vividly portrays that common stocks were the big winner over the entire period. If $1 were invested in stocks at year-end 1925 and all dividends reinvested, the dollar investment would have grown to $198.74 by year-end 1983. This phenomenal growth was not without substantial risk, especially during the earlier portion of the period. In contrast, long-term government bonds (with a constant 20-year maturity) exhibited much less risk, but grew to only $7.29.

A virtually riskless strategy (for those with short-term time horizons) has been to buy U.S. Treasury bills. However, Treasury bills have had a marked tendency to track inflation, with the result that their real (inflation adjusted) return is near zero for the entire 1926–1983 period. Note that the tracking is only prevalent over the latter portion of the period. During periods of deflation (such as the late 1920s and early 1930s) the Treasury bill returns were near zero, but not negative, since no one intentionally buys securities with negative yields. Beginning in the early 1940s, the yields (returns) on Treasury bills were pegged by the government at low rates while high inflation was experienced. The government pegging ended with

the U.S. Treasury-Federal Reserve Accord in March 1951.

We summarize the investment returns in Exhibit 2 by presenting the average annual returns over the 1926–1983 period. Common stocks returned a compounded (geometric mean) total return of 9.6 percent per year. The annual compound return from capital appreciation alone was 4.5 percent. After adjusting for inflation, annual compounded total returns were 6.3 percent per year.*

The average total return over any single year (arithmetic mean) for stocks was 11.8 percent, with positive returns recorded in nearly two-thirds of the years (38 out of 58 years). The risk or degree of return fluctuation is measured by standard deviation as 21.4 percent. The frequency distribution (histogram) counts the

* Editor's note: Over the current decade the compounded growth rate for common stock with dividends reinvested after adjusting for inflation has been considerably less than the long-term value of 6.3 percent. Thus from the beginning of 1974 to the end of 1983 the compounded growth rate before adjusting for inflation has been 10.6 percent for common stock as compared to 6.4 percent for long-term corporate bonds and 8.6 percent for U.S. Treasury bills. All figures neglect taxes. The inflation rate during this period was 8.2 percent. After inflationary adjustments and income taxes, it is evident that all of these investments resulted in a net loss in terms of real income. Assuming a 40 percent tax rate and an 8 percent inflation rate, investments must earn 13.3 percent before taxes to break even.

number of years the returns fell in each 5 percent return increment. Note the wide variations in common stock returns relative to the other capital market sectors. Annual stock returns ranged from 54.0 percent in 1933 to −43.3 percent in 1931.

A simple example illustrates the difference between geometric and arithmetic means. Suppose $1 were invested in a common stock portfolio that experiences successive annual returns of +50 percent and −50 percent. At the end of the first year, the portfolio is worth $1.50. At the end of the second year, the portfolio is worth $0.75. The annual arithmetic mean is 0 percent, whereas the annual geometric mean (compounded return) is −13.4 percent. Naturally, it is the geometric mean that more directly measures the change in wealth over more than one period. On the other hand, the arithmetic mean is a better representation of typical performance over any single annual period.

The other capital market sectors also had returns commensurate with their risks. Long-term corporate bonds outperformed the default-free, long-term government bonds, which in turn outperformed the essentially riskless U.S. Treasury bills. Over the entire period the riskless U.S. Treasury bills had a return almost identical with the inflation rate. Thus, we again note that the real rate of interest (the inflation-adjusted riskless rate) has been on average very near 0 percent historically.

MEASUREMENT OF THE FIVE SERIES

The returns were computed by compounding monthly returns, with no adjustments made for transactions costs or taxes. We describe each of the five total return series which are listed annually in Exhibit 3.

Common Stocks

The total return index is based upon Standard & Poor's (S&P) Composite Index with dividends reinvested monthly. To the extent that the 500 stocks currently included in the S&P Composite Index (prior to March 1957, there were 90 stocks) are representative of all stocks

in the United States, the market value weighting scheme allows the returns of the index to correspond to the aggregate stock market returns in the U.S. economy.

Long-Term Corporate Bonds

We measure the total returns of a corporate bond index with approximately 20 years to maturity. We use Salomon Brothers' High-Grade Long-Term Corporate Bond Index from its beginning in 1969 through 1983. For the period 1946–68 we backdate Salomon Brothers' index using Salomon Brothers' monthly yield data and similar methodology. For the period 1926–45 we compute returns using Standard & Poor's monthly high-grade corporate composite bond yield data, assuming a 4 percent coupon and a 20-year maturity.

Long-Term Government Bonds

To measure the total returns of long-term U.S. government bonds, we use the bond data obtained from the U.S. Government Bond File (constructed by Lawrence Fisher) at the Center for Research in Security Prices (CRSP) at the University of Chicago. We attempt to maintain a 20-year bond portfolio whose returns do not reflect the potential tax benefits, impaired negotiability, or the special redemption or call privileges frequently characterizing government bond prices and yields.

U.S. Treasury Bills

For the U.S. Treasury bill index, we again use the data in the CRSP U.S. Government Bond File. We measure one-month holding period returns for the shortest-term bills not less than one month in maturity. Since U.S. Treasury bills were not initiated until 1929, we use short-term coupon bonds whenever bill quotes are unavailable.

Consumer Price Index

We utilize the Consumer Price Index (CPI) to measure inflation. The CPI is constructed by the U.S. Department of Labor, Bureau of Labor Statistics, Washington, D.C.

EXHIBIT 3: BASIC SERIES, INDEXES OF YEAR-END CUMULATIVE WEALTH, 1925–1983 (year-end 1925 = 1.000)

Year	Common Stocks Total Returns	Common Stocks Capital Appreciation Only	Long-Term Government Bonds Total Returns	Long-Term Government Bonds Capital Appreciation Only	Long-Term Corporate Bonds Total Returns	U.S. Treasury Bills Total Returns	Consumer Price Index Rates of Inflation
1925	1.000	1.000	1.000	1.000	1.000	1.000	1.000
1926	1.116	1.057	1.078	1.039	1.074	1.033	0.985
1927	1.535	1.384	1.174	1.095	1.154	1.065	0.965
1928	2.204	1.908	1.175	1.061	1.186	1.099	0.955
1929	2.018	1.681	1.215	1.059	1.225	1.152	0.957
1930	1.516	1.202	1.272	1.072	1.323	1.179	0.899
1931	0.859	0.636	1.204	0.981	1.299	1.192	0.814
1932	0.789	0.540	1.407	1.108	1.439	1.204	0.730
1933	1.214	0.792	1.406	1.073	1.588	1.207	0.734
1934	1.197	0.745	1.547	1.146	1.808	1.209	0.749
1935	1.767	1.053	1.624	1.170	1.982	1.211	0.771
1936	2.367	1.346	1.746	1.225	2.116	1.213	0.780
1937	1.538	0.827	1.750	1.194	2.174	1.217	0.804
1938	2.016	1.035	1.847	1.228	2.307	1.217	0.782
1939	2.008	0.979	1.957	1.271	2.399	1.217	0.778
1940	1.812	0.829	2.076	1.319	2.480	1.217	0.786
1941	1.602	0.681	2.095	1.305	2.548	1.218	0.862
1942	1.927	0.766	2.162	1.315	2.614	1.221	0.942
1943	2.427	0.915	2.207	1.310	2.688	1.225	0.972
1944	2.906	1.041	2.270	1.314	2.815	1.229	0.993
1945	3.965	1.361	2.513	1.423	2.930	1.233	1.015
1946	3.645	1.199	2.511	1.392	2.980	1.238	1.199
1947	3.853	1.199	2.445	1.327	2.911	1.244	1.307
1948	4.065	1.191	2.528	1.340	3.031	1.254	1.343
1949	4.829	1.313	2.691	1.395	3.132	1.268	1.318
1950	6.360	1.600	2.692	1.366	3.198	1.283	1.395
1951	7.888	1.863	2.586	1.281	3.112	1.302	1.477
1952	9.336	2.082	2.616	1.262	3.221	1.324	1.490
1953	9.244	1.944	2.711	1.270	3.331	1.348	1.499
1954	14.108	2.820	2.906	1.325	3.511	1.360	1.492
1955	18.561	3.564	2.868	1.271	3.527	1.381	1.497
1956	19.778	3.658	2.708	1.164	3.287	1.415	1.540
1957	17.648	3.134	2.910	1.208	3.573	1.459	1.587
1958	25.298	4.327	2.733	1.097	3.494	1.482	1.615
1959	28.322	4.694	2.671	1.029	3.460	1.526	1.639
1960	28.455	4.554	3.039	1.124	3.774	1.566	1.663
1961	36.106	5.607	3.068	1.092	3.956	1.600	1.674
1962	32.955	4.945	3.280	1.122	4.270	1.643	1.695
1963	40.469	5.879	3.319	1.092	4.364	1.695	1.723
1964	47.139	6.642	3.436	1.084	4.572	1.754	1.743
1965	53.008	7.244	3.460	1.047	4.552	1.823	1.777
1966	47.674	6.295	3.586	1.036	4.560	1.910	1.836
1967	59.104	7.560	3.257	0.895	4.335	1.991	1.892
1968	65.642	8.139	3.248	0.846	4.446	2.094	1.981
1969	60.059	7.210	3.083	0.754	4.086	2.232	2.102
1970	62.465	7.222	3.457	0.791	4.837	2.378	2.218
1971	71.406	8.001	3.914	0.843	5.370	2.482	2.292
1972	84.956	9.252	4.136	0.840	5,760	2.577	2.371
1973	72.500	7.645	4.090	0.775	5.825	2.756	2.579
1974	53.311	5.373	4.268	0.748	5.647	2.976	2.894
1975	73.144	7.068	4.661	0.754	6.474	3.149	3.097
1976	90.584	8.422	5.441	0.815	7.681	3.309	3.246
1977	84.076	7.453	5.405	0.750	7.813	3.479	3.466
1978	89.592	7.532	5.342	0.682	7.807	3.728	3.778
1979	106.112	8.459	5.277	0.615	7.481	4.115	4.281
1980	140.513	10.639	5.069	0.530	7.285	4.578	4.812
1981....	133.615	9.605	5.162	0.475	7.215	5.251	5.242
1982	162.221	11.023	7.245	0.589	10.374	5.805	5.445
1983....	198.744	12.926	7.294	0.530	10.862	6.317	5.652

Source: Ibbotson and Sinquefield, *Stocks, Bonds, Bills, and Inflation.*

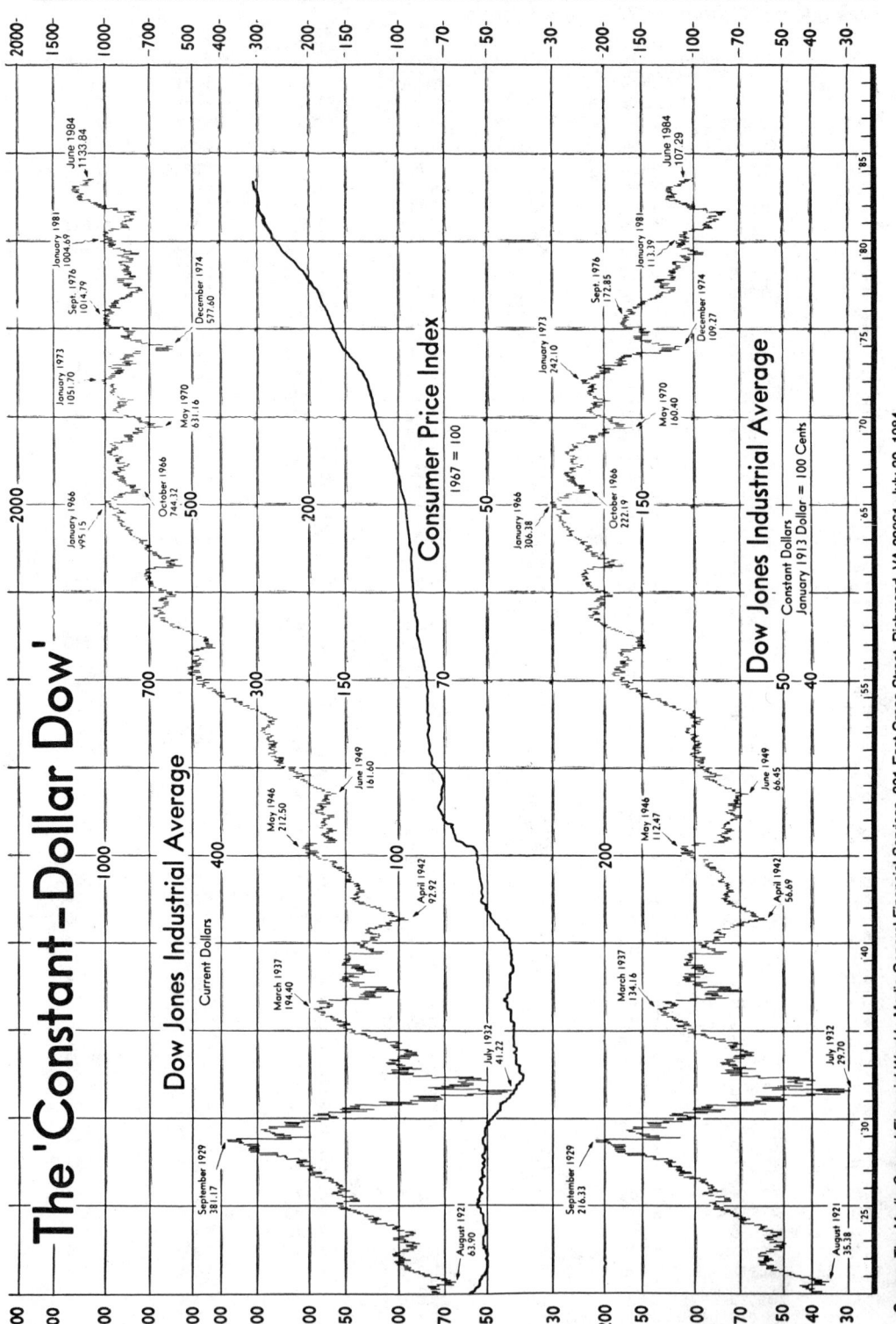

The 'Constant-Dollar Dow'

Dow Jones Industrial Average

Current Dollars

September 1929
381.17

August 1921
63.90

July 1932
41.22

March 1937
194.40

April 1942
92.92

May 1946
212.50

June 1949
161.60

January 1966
995.15

October 1966
744.32

May 1970
631.16

January 1973
1051.70

December 1974
577.60

Sept. 1976
1014.79

January 1981
1004.69

June 1984
1133.84

Consumer Price Index

1967 = 100

Dow Jones Industrial Average

Constant Dollars
January 1913 Dollar = 100 Cents

September 1929
216.33

August 1921
35.38

July 1932
29.70

March 1937
134.16

April 1942
56.69

May 1946
112.47

June 1949
66.45

January 1966
306.38

October 1966
222.19

May 1970
160.40

January 1973
242.10

December 1974
109.27

Sept. 1976
172.85

January 1981
113.39

June 1984
107.29

Source: The Media General Financial Weekly, Media General Financial Services, 301 East Grace Street, Richmond, VA 23261, July 30, 1984.

PORTFOLIOS WITHOUT MANAGEMENT

Cumulative Without Dividends — Annual Compound Growth Rate

	1974-1983			1975-1983			1976-1983			1977-1983			1978-1983			1979-1983			1980-1983			1981-1983			1982-1983			First Quarter 1984		
	1800 Cos.	1000 Cos.	500 Cos.	1800 Cos.	1000 Cos.	500 Cos.	1800 Cos.	1000 Cos.	500 Cos.	1800 Cos.	1000 Cos.	500 Cos.	1800 Cos.	1000 Cos.	500 Cos.	1800 Cos.	1000 Cos.	500 Cos.	1800 Cos.	1000 Cos.	500 Cos.	1800 Cos.	1000 Cos.	500 Cos.	1800 Cos.	1000 Cos.	500 Cos.	1800 Cos.	1000 Cos.	500 Cos.
Top 5 %	19.5	16.8	13.7	26.1	22.7	19.0	22.9	19.4	15.7	20.7	17.3	13.8	23.3	20.5	17.4	26.1	23.2	20.1	25.1	22.1	18.8	24.8	21.6	17.6	35.9	32.1	27.8	0.8	1.8	0.8
Top 10 %	18.7	16.1	13.1	25.1	22.0	18.3	22.0	18.7	15.0	19.7	16.5	13.0	22.3	19.6	16.5	24.9	22.1	19.1	23.7	20.9	17.7	23.3	20.4	16.3	33.9	30.3	26.2	1.8	2.6	1.6
Top 15 %	18.1	15.6	12.6	24.6	21.4	17.9	21.4	18.1	14.6	19.1	15.9	12.5	21.5	18.9	15.9	24.0	21.4	18.4	24.0	20.2	17.0	22.3	19.5	15.5	32.5	29.1	25.1	2.5	3.1	2.1
Top 20 %	17.7	15.2	12.3	24.1	21.0	17.5	20.9	17.7	14.2	18.6	15.5	12.1	21.0	18.4	15.5	23.4	20.9	17.9	22.1	19.5	16.5	21.5	18.8	14.9	31.5	28.1	24.1	3.0	3.6	2.6
Top 25 %	17.3	14.8	12.0	23.7	20.7	17.2	20.5	17.4	13.9	18.0	15.1	11.8	20.6	18.1	15.1	22.8	20.4	17.4	21.0	19.0	16.0	20.8	18.2	14.3	30.5	27.2	23.3	3.5	3.9	2.9
Top 30 %	17.0	14.6	11.8	23.1	20.1	17.0	20.1	17.0	13.6	17.7	14.8	11.5	20.1	17.6	14.8	22.3	19.9	17.0	21.5	18.6	15.6	20.2	17.6	13.9	29.6	26.5	22.7	3.8	4.2	3.2
Top 35 %	16.7	14.3	11.5	22.8	19.9	16.7	19.5	16.7	13.3	17.4	14.5	11.2	19.7	17.3	14.5	21.9	19.5	16.7	21.0	18.1	15.2	19.6	17.1	13.4	28.8	25.9	22.1	4.2	4.5	3.5
Top 40 %	16.4	14.0	11.3	22.2	19.6	16.5	19.5	16.5	13.1	17.1	14.2	11.0	19.3	16.9	14.2	21.5	19.2	16.4	20.0	17.7	14.8	19.1	16.6	13.1	28.2	25.2	21.5	4.5	4.8	3.8
Top 45 %	16.1	13.8	11.1	22.2	19.3	16.0	18.9	16.2	12.9	16.8	13.9	10.8	19.0	16.6	13.9	21.0	18.8	16.0	19.6	17.4	14.5	18.5	16.2	12.6	27.5	24.6	21.0	4.9	5.1	4.0
Top 50 %	15.9	13.6	10.9	21.9	19.1	15.8	18.9	16.0	12.6	16.4	13.6	10.5	18.6	16.3	13.6	20.6	18.4	15.7	19.1	17.0	14.1	18.1	15.9	12.3	26.9	24.0	20.5	5.2	5.3	4.3
Top 55 %	15.6	13.3	10.5	21.3	18.9	15.6	18.6	15.7	12.4	16.1	13.4	10.3	18.3	16.0	13.3	20.2	18.1	15.4	18.7	16.6	13.9	17.6	15.4	11.9	25.9	23.5	19.9	5.5	5.6	4.5
Top 60 %	15.3	13.1	10.5	21.3	18.6	15.3	18.3	15.5	12.2	15.8	13.1	10.0	17.9	15.7	13.1	19.8	17.8	15.1	18.3	16.2	13.5	17.1	15.0	11.5	25.6	22.9	19.4	5.8	5.9	4.8
Top 65 %	15.1	12.8	10.2	21.0	18.3	15.1	18.0	15.2	11.9	15.5	12.8	9.8	17.6	15.4	12.8	19.4	17.4	14.7	17.4	15.8	13.2	16.6	14.5	11.1	24.1	21.7	18.3	6.1	6.2	5.0
Top 70 %	14.8	12.6	10.0	20.7	18.1	14.8	17.4	14.9	11.7	15.2	12.5	9.5	17.2	15.0	12.5	19.0	17.0	14.4	17.4	15.4	12.8	16.0	14.1	10.7	23.3	21.0	17.7	6.4	6.5	5.3
Top 75 %	14.4	12.3	9.8	20.3	17.7	14.5	17.4	14.6	11.4	14.8	12.2	9.2	16.8	14.7	12.1	18.5	16.5	13.9	16.9	14.9	12.4	15.5	13.6	10.3	22.3	20.2	17.0	6.8	7.1	5.6
Top 80 %	14.1	12.0	9.5	19.9	17.3	14.2	16.6	14.3	11.1	14.4	11.9	8.9	16.4	14.3	11.7	18.1	16.1	13.6	16.3	14.5	12.0	14.9	13.1	9.8	21.7	19.3	17.0	7.2	7.1	5.9
Top 85 %	13.7	11.7	9.2	19.3	16.9	13.8	16.6	13.9	10.8	14.0	11.5	8.5	15.8	13.8	11.3	17.5	15.6	13.1	15.7	13.9	11.5	14.1	12.4	9.3	21.5	19.3	16.2	7.6	7.5	6.3
Top 90 %	13.2	11.2	8.8	18.5	16.1	13.1	16.3	13.5	10.3	13.6	11.0	8.1	15.2	13.2	10.8	16.7	14.9	12.5	15.2	13.2	10.9	13.2	11.5	8.5	21.5	18.2	15.3	8.2	8.0	6.8
Top 95 %	12.5	10.6	8.2	18.5	16.1	13.1	15.3	12.8	9.7	12.6	10.2	7.4	14.2	12.4	10.0	15.7	14.0	11.7	13.8	12.1	9.9	11.9	10.4	7.5	18.4	16.6	14.0	9.1	8.8	7.4
S&P 500 Index	5.4	4.0		10.2	8.3		7.8	5.0		6.3	3.3		9.6	7.2		11.4	9.4		11.2	10.7		6.7	9.3		16.0	19.9		-3.5	-7.4	
Dow Ind. Avg.																														

Cumulative With Dividends — Annual Compound Growth Rate

	1974-1983			1975-1983			1976-1983			1977-1983			1978-1983			1979-1983			1980-1983			1981-1983			1982-1983			First Quarter 1984		
	1800 Cos.	1000 Cos.	500 Cos.	1800 Cos.	1000 Cos.	500 Cos.	1800 Cos.	1000 Cos.	500 Cos.	1800 Cos.	1000 Cos.	500 Cos.	1800 Cos.	1000 Cos.	500 Cos.	1800 Cos.	1000 Cos.	500 Cos.	1800 Cos.	1000 Cos.	500 Cos.	1800 Cos.	1000 Cos.	500 Cos.	1800 Cos.	1000 Cos.	500 Cos.	1800 Cos.	1000 Cos.	500 Cos.
Top 5 %	24.2	21.8	18.9	30.8	27.8	24.3	27.5	24.4	20.9	25.3	22.3	19.0	28.1	25.7	22.8	30.8	28.4	25.5	29.7	27.1	24.1	29.3	26.6	22.9	40.2	36.9	33.0	0.0	0.8	0.3
Top 10 %	23.4	21.1	18.3	29.9	27.1	23.6	26.6	23.6	20.2	24.3	21.5	18.2	27.0	24.8	21.8	29.6	27.4	24.4	27.8	26.0	23.1	27.8	25.4	21.6	37.8	35.1	31.2	0.9	1.6	0.5
Top 15 %	22.8	20.6	17.8	29.3	26.5	23.2	26.0	23.1	19.7	23.7	20.9	17.7	26.3	24.1	21.4	28.7	26.6	23.9	27.4	25.2	22.4	26.8	24.5	20.7	36.8	33.9	30.2	1.6	2.2	1.1
Top 20 %	22.4	20.2	17.5	28.9	26.1	22.8	25.5	22.7	19.3	23.0	20.5	17.3	25.7	23.6	20.9	28.1	26.1	23.4	26.7	24.6	21.8	26.3	23.8	20.1	35.6	32.9	29.2	2.1	2.4	1.5
Top 25 %	21.7	19.9	17.2	28.5	25.8	22.5	25.1	22.3	19.0	22.7	20.1	17.0	25.3	23.2	20.5	27.5	25.6	22.9	26.1	24.1	21.3	25.2	23.2	19.6	34.6	32.1	28.5	2.6	2.9	1.8
Top 30 %	21.3	19.6	17.0	28.1	25.5	22.2	24.4	22.0	18.7	22.3	19.8	16.7	24.8	22.8	20.2	27.0	25.1	22.5	25.5	23.6	20.9	24.6	22.6	19.1	33.1	31.3	27.9	3.0	3.3	2.1
Top 35 %	21.4	19.3	16.7	27.8	24.9	22.0	24.1	21.7	18.5	22.0	19.5	16.4	24.4	22.5	19.9	26.6	24.6	22.1	24.6	23.2	20.5	24.0	22.1	18.7	33.1	30.7	26.6	3.4	3.6	2.4
Top 40 %	21.1	19.1	16.5	27.2	24.7	21.5	24.1	21.4	18.1	21.6	19.2	16.1	24.0	22.1	19.6	26.2	24.4	21.5	24.1	22.8	20.2	23.5	21.6	18.3	32.4	30.0	26.1	3.7	3.8	2.7
Top 45 %	20.8	18.8	16.3	27.2	24.4	21.5	23.8	21.2	18.0	21.3	18.9	16.0	23.7	21.8	19.3	25.7	24.0	21.3	24.1	22.4	19.8	23.0	21.2	17.9	31.8	29.4	25.6	4.0	4.1	3.0
Top 50 %	20.6	18.6	16.1	26.9	24.2	21.0	23.5	20.9	17.8	20.8	18.6	15.7	23.3	21.5	19.0	25.3	23.7	20.8	23.7	22.1	19.5	22.5	20.8	17.5	31.1	28.8	25.0	4.3	4.4	3.0
Top 55 %	20.3	18.4	15.8	26.6	23.9	20.8	23.2	20.7	17.5	20.7	18.4	15.5	23.0	21.2	18.7	24.9	23.3	20.5	23.3	21.7	19.2	22.5	20.4	17.1	30.4	28.3	25.0	4.4	4.7	3.5
Top 60 %	20.0	18.1	15.6	26.3	23.7	20.6	22.9	20.4	17.3	20.4	18.1	15.2	22.6	20.9	18.5	24.5	23.0	20.2	22.8	21.3	18.9	21.5	19.9	16.7	29.8	27.7	24.5	4.7	4.9	3.7
Top 65 %	19.5	17.6	15.2	25.7	23.4	20.1	22.3	19.9	17.1	19.8	17.8	15.0	22.2	20.5	18.2	24.1	22.6	19.8	22.4	20.9	18.5	20.5	19.5	16.2	29.1	27.1	24.0	5.0	5.2	4.0
Top 70 %	19.1	17.4	14.7	25.0	23.1	20.1	22.3	19.6	16.8	19.4	17.5	14.7	21.9	20.1	17.9	23.7	22.2	19.4	21.9	20.6	18.1	20.5	19.0	15.5	28.4	26.5	23.4	5.3	5.4	4.3
Top 75 %	18.8	17.0	14.7	25.0	22.8	19.7	21.6	19.2	16.5	19.0	17.2	14.4	21.5	19.8	17.5	23.2	21.7	19.0	21.4	20.0	17.7	19.2	18.5	15.0	27.6	25.9	22.8	5.6	5.8	4.6
Top 80 %	18.4	16.7	14.3	24.6	22.4	19.4	21.2	18.9	16.2	18.6	16.9	14.1	21.1	19.5	17.2	22.7	21.3	18.6	20.9	19.5	17.3	19.2	18.0	14.4	26.7	25.1	22.1	6.0	5.8	4.9
Top 85 %	17.9	16.2	13.9	24.0	21.9	19.0	20.7	18.4	15.9	18.0	16.5	13.7	20.5	19.0	16.7	22.2	20.8	18.0	20.2	19.0	16.7	17.6	17.3	13.6	25.7	24.1	21.3	6.4	6.6	5.3
Top 90 %	17.1	15.6	13.4	23.2	21.2	18.4	19.9	17.7	14.8	18.0	15.9	13.3	19.9	18.4	16.2	21.4	20.1	17.6	19.5	18.2	16.1	16.3	16.4	12.6	24.5	23.0	20.4	7.4	7.1	5.7
Top 95 %	17.1	15.6	13.4	23.2	21.2	18.4	19.9	17.7	17.7	17.1	15.2	15.2	18.9	17.6	15.4	20.4	19.2	17.0	18.4	17.1	15.1	16.3	15.2	12.6	22.7	21.4	19.0	8.3	7.9	6.4
S&P 500 Index	10.6	9.8		15.7	14.3		13.3	11.0		11.8	9.4		15.4	13.6		17.3	15.9		16.9	17.2		12.2	15.6		22.1	26.7		-2.4	-6.4	
Dow Ind. Avg.																														

RETURNS ON PORTFOLIOS WITHOUT MANAGEMENT (continued)

Annual Without Dividends — Percent Change

	1974			1975			1976			1977			1978			1979			1980			1981			1982			1983		
	1800 Cos.	1000 Cos.	500 Cos.	1800 Cos.	1000 Cos.	500 Cos.	1800 Cos.	1000 Cos.	500 Cos.	1800 Cos.	1000 Cos.	500 Cos.	1800 Cos.	1000 Cos.	500 Cos.	1800 Cos.	1000 Cos.	500 Cos.	1800 Cos.	1000 Cos.	500 Cos.	1800 Cos.	1000 Cos.	500 Cos.	1800 Cos.	1000 Cos.	500 Cos.	1800 Cos.	1000 Cos.	500 Cos.
Top 5 %	-18.6	-17.9	-18.7	68.5	63.8	60.4	50.7	44.7	38.4	12.6	5.3	-1.1	18.2	14.4	10.6	41.3	37.7	35.8	35.0	31.5	29.8	11.6	9.1	4.3	38.5	35.5	32.6	41.4	35.5	28.8
Top 10%	-21.3	-21.0	-20.5	64.9	60.6	57.3	47.2	42.1	36.1	10.7	3.9	-2.3	16.0	12.3	7.8	37.5	34.4	31.6	32.1	28.9	26.3	9.4	7.4	2.8	35.1	32.3	29.4	38.6	33.7	27.2
Top 15%	-22.9	-22.6	-21.8	61.8	58.4	55.1	45.2	40.3	34.4	9.4	3.0	-3.1	14.6	11.1	7.0	35.3	32.1	29.3	30.0	27.2	26.1	8.1	6.0	1.8	32.8	30.3	27.5	36.9	32.1	26.0
Top 20%	-24.1	-23.7	-22.7	59.8	56.7	53.6	43.4	39.0	33.3	8.4	1.6	-3.8	13.5	10.1	6.2	33.4	30.5	27.4	28.5	25.9	25.0	7.0	5.1	1.1	31.2	28.6	25.9	35.5	30.7	25.2
Top 25%	-25.0	-24.5	-23.5	58.1	55.3	52.2	41.0	37.8	32.3	7.5	1.0	-4.3	12.6	9.3	6.2	32.1	29.1	26.1	27.2	24.8	23.0	6.1	4.3	0.4	29.7	27.2	24.5	34.0	29.7	24.4
Top 30%	-25.8	-25.3	-24.1	56.6	54.1	51.0	40.1	36.8	30.6	6.7	0.4	-4.8	11.8	8.6	5.6	30.9	28.0	24.9	26.2	23.8	23.0	5.2	3.6	-0.3	28.4	25.9	23.4	33.3	28.8	23.7
Top 35%	-26.6	-25.9	-24.7	55.3	53.3	50.3	39.2	35.9	30.6	6.1	0.4	-5.2	11.1	7.9	5.0	29.7	26.9	23.9	25.2	23.1	21.4	4.5	2.9	-0.8	28.1	25.1	23.4	33.1	28.0	23.0
Top 40%	-27.2	-26.6	-25.3	54.0	51.9	48.9	39.2	35.1	29.9	5.4	-0.2	-5.6	10.2	7.3	4.4	28.5	25.9	23.0	24.2	22.1	21.4	3.8	2.2	-1.4	26.0	23.9	21.3	31.3	27.3	22.4
Top 45%	-27.8	-27.2	-25.9	52.8	50.9	47.0	38.3	34.3	29.2	4.9	-0.7	-6.0	9.4	6.7	3.9	27.4	25.0	22.4	23.3	21.1	20.0	3.1	1.6	-1.9	23.9	23.1	20.4	30.6	26.6	21.9
Top 50%	-28.5	-27.7	-26.4	51.5	49.9	47.0	37.5	33.6	28.0	4.2	-1.3	-6.5	8.7	6.1	3.0	26.4	23.6	21.3	23.3	20.3	20.0	2.4	1.0	-2.4	23.9	22.1	19.5	29.7	25.9	21.3
Top 55%	-29.2	-28.9	-26.9	50.3	49.0	45.2	36.7	32.8	28.0	3.6	-1.7	-6.8	8.1	5.6	3.0	25.4	23.3	20.6	21.6	19.5	19.3	1.7	0.4	-2.9	23.1	21.2	19.5	28.9	25.2	20.7
Top 60%	-29.8	-28.9	-27.5	49.1	48.0	45.2	35.8	32.1	27.2	3.0	-2.2	-7.2	7.5	5.0	2.5	24.4	22.4	19.9	20.6	18.7	18.6	1.0	-0.2	-3.9	21.8	20.3	17.8	28.1	24.5	20.1
Top 65%	-31.0	-30.0	-28.0	47.8	46.9	44.1	34.9	31.3	26.5	2.7	-2.7	-7.6	6.9	4.4	2.0	23.5	21.5	19.1	19.8	17.9	17.1	0.2	-0.8	-4.5	20.8	19.3	16.0	27.3	23.8	19.5
Top 70%	-31.6	-30.6	-28.6	46.5	45.9	43.2	34.0	30.5	25.7	1.8	-3.3	-8.0	6.3	3.8	1.5	22.5	20.7	18.3	18.8	17.1	16.2	-0.5	-1.3	-5.1	19.7	18.4	16.0	26.4	23.1	18.9
Top 75%	-32.3	-31.3	-29.2	45.1	44.7	42.1	33.1	29.7	24.9	1.1	-3.9	-8.5	5.5	3.1	0.9	21.4	19.7	17.5	17.7	16.1	15.0	-1.3	-2.1	-5.9	18.6	17.3	15.0	25.4	22.3	18.3
Top 80%	-32.5	-31.3	-29.9	43.8	43.5	41.0	32.1	28.7	24.1	0.4	-4.5	-9.0	4.7	2.4	0.3	20.2	18.6	16.5	16.7	15.2	14.4	-3.1	-2.9	-6.6	17.3	16.2	13.9	24.5	21.4	17.6
Top 85%	-33.2	-32.1	-30.7	43.8	42.0	41.0	30.8	27.7	23.1	-0.5	-5.1	-9.6	3.8	1.6	-0.5	18.9	17.4	15.4	15.3	14.1	12.7	-3.1	-3.8	-7.6	15.8	14.8	12.7	23.1	20.4	16.7
Top 90%	-33.3	-33.1	-31.6	39.9	40.1	39.1	29.4	26.4	21.8	-1.5	-5.9	-10.3	2.5	1.0	-1.3	17.2	15.9	14.1	13.7	13.1	12.0	-4.4	-5.0	-7.6	14.0	13.1	11.2	23.1	19.1	15.7
Top 95%	-35.9	-34.6	-32.9	37.0	37.5	35.4	27.1	24.6	19.7	-3.1	-7.1	-11.4	1.0	-1.0	-2.5	14.9	13.9	12.2	11.4	10.7	11.2	-6.1	6.7	-9.0	11.4	10.8	8.9	19.3	17.3	14.1
S&P 500 Index	-29.7			31.5			19.1			-11.5			1.1			12.3			25.8			-9.7			14.8			17.3		
Dow Ind. Avg.	-27.6			38.3			17.9			-17.3			-3.1			4.2			14.9			-9.2			19.6			20.3		

Annual With Dividends — Percent Change

	1974			1975			1976			1977			1978			1979			1980			1981			1982			1983		
	1800 Cos.	1000 Cos.	500 Cos.	1800 Cos.	1000 Cos.	500 Cos.	1800 Cos.	1000 Cos.	500 Cos.	1800 Cos.	1000 Cos.	500 Cos.	1800 Cos.	1000 Cos.	500 Cos.	1800 Cos.	1000 Cos.	500 Cos.	1800 Cos.	1000 Cos.	500 Cos.	1800 Cos.	1000 Cos.	500 Cos.	1800 Cos.	1000 Cos.	500 Cos.	1800 Cos.	1000 Cos.	500 Cos.
Top 5 %	-14.0	-13.3	-14.1	74.6	70.1	66.6	55.2	49.2	43.1	16.5	9.4	3.1	22.9	19.3	15.8	46.5	43.5	41.8	39.8	36.8	35.3	16.6	14.4	9.9	43.0	40.6	38.0	45.4	40.0	33.7
Top 10%	-17.0	-16.5	-15.9	70.4	66.9	63.7	51.7	46.7	40.8	14.5	7.8	1.9	20.7	17.4	14.2	42.8	40.2	37.6	37.0	34.2	33.1	14.3	12.7	8.3	39.6	37.4	34.7	42.5	37.7	32.0
Top 15%	-18.6	-18.1	-17.1	67.8	64.8	61.5	49.6	45.6	39.1	13.2	6.9	1.1	19.3	16.1	13.1	40.7	37.8	35.1	34.9	32.6	31.6	13.0	11.4	7.3	37.3	35.4	32.8	40.8	36.2	31.0
Top 20%	-19.8	-19.2	-18.1	65.8	63.0	59.9	48.0	43.6	37.9	12.3	6.3	0.4	18.3	15.2	12.2	38.8	36.3	33.5	33.3	31.2	30.5	11.8	10.4	6.5	35.7	33.7	31.3	39.4	35.2	30.1
Top 25%	-20.8	-20.1	-18.9	64.1	61.6	58.4	46.7	42.4	37.0	11.4	5.6	-0.2	17.4	14.4	11.4	37.4	34.9	32.1	32.1	30.1	29.5	10.9	9.5	5.8	34.2	32.3	29.9	38.4	34.2	29.3
Top 30%	-21.6	-20.9	-19.6	62.7	60.4	56.1	45.6	41.4	35.3	10.5	5.0	-0.7	16.6	13.6	10.8	36.1	33.8	30.9	31.1	29.0	28.6	10.0	8.8	5.2	32.9	31.1	28.8	37.5	33.4	28.6
Top 35%	-22.3	-21.5	-20.2	61.4	59.2	56.2	44.6	40.5	34.6	9.9	4.4	-1.2	15.8	13.0	10.3	35.0	32.7	29.9	30.1	28.2	27.7	9.3	8.1	4.6	31.7	30.0	27.7	36.3	32.5	28.0
Top 40%	-23.0	-22.2	-20.8	60.0	58.2	54.3	43.8	39.7	33.9	8.7	3.8	-1.6	15.0	12.4	9.7	33.9	31.8	28.2	29.2	27.4	26.8	8.5	7.4	4.0	29.5	28.1	25.8	36.3	31.8	27.4
Top 45%	-23.7	-22.8	-21.4	58.7	57.2	54.1	42.8	38.9	33.3	8.1	3.3	-2.0	14.0	11.8	9.2	32.8	30.8	28.2	28.3	26.5	26.3	7.8	6.8	3.5	28.5	28.1	25.8	34.5	31.1	26.8
Top 50%	-24.3	-23.4	-21.9	57.6	56.2	53.3	42.0	38.2	32.6	7.5	2.7	-2.4	13.4	11.2	8.7	31.7	30.0	26.6	27.3	25.7	25.0	7.1	6.2	2.4	28.1	26.3	24.1	34.0	30.4	26.2
Top 55%	-24.5	-23.5	-22.5	56.3	55.2	52.4	41.2	37.4	32.6	6.9	2.3	-2.8	12.9	10.6	8.3	30.7	29.0	25.9	26.5	24.9	25.0	6.4	5.5	1.9	27.4	26.3	24.1	32.8	29.7	25.6
Top 60%	-25.6	-24.0	-23.0	55.1	54.2	51.4	40.4	36.7	31.9	6.3	1.8	-3.2	12.3	10.0	7.8	29.8	28.2	25.1	25.6	24.1	24.1	5.7	4.9	1.3	26.3	25.4	23.1	32.1	29.0	25.0
Top 65%	-26.3	-25.1	-23.6	53.8	53.2	50.4	39.5	35.9	31.0	5.7	1.3	-3.6	11.6	9.5	7.3	28.9	27.4	24.5	24.7	23.4	23.5	4.9	4.3	0.7	25.3	24.4	22.2	30.4	28.3	24.4
Top 70%	-26.9	-25.7	-24.2	52.4	52.1	49.4	38.6	35.1	30.2	5.0	0.8	-4.0	11.1	8.9	6.8	27.8	26.5	24.3	23.7	22.4	21.3	4.1	3.6	0.1	24.2	23.4	21.3	30.4	27.7	23.8
Top 75%	-27.6	-26.4	-24.8	51.2	52.1	47.1	37.6	34.2	29.4	4.2	-0.5	-4.5	9.4	7.5	6.2	26.8	25.5	23.5	22.7	21.5	21.9	2.9	2.1	-0.7	22.4	22.4	20.3	28.3	26.8	23.2
Top 80%	-28.3	-27.1	-25.5	49.7	49.7	47.1	36.6	32.2	27.6	3.4	-1.2	-5.1	8.5	6.7	4.9	24.3	24.5	22.5	21.6	20.6	21.0	1.5	1.1	-1.5	21.8	21.3	19.3	27.0	26.0	22.4
Top 85%	-28.3	-27.9	-26.3	48.0	48.4	46.4	35.4	32.2	26.3	2.6	-1.2	-5.6	7.3	5.6	4.1	22.6	21.7	21.4	20.3	19.4	20.0	0.1	-0.1	-2.5	19.8	18.1	18.0	26.0	25.0	21.6
Top 90%	-30.4	-29.0	-27.3	45.9	46.4	44.2	33.8	30.9	26.3	2.2	-2.0	-6.4	5.6	5.6	4.1	22.6	21.7	20.1	18.7	18.2	18.7	0.1	-0.1	-2.5	18.5	18.1	16.4	25.5	23.6	20.5
Top 95%	-32.0	-30.5	-28.6	43.0	43.6	41.5	31.5	29.0	24.2	0.7	-3.2	-7.4	5.6	4.2	2.8	20.3	19.7	18.2	16.4	16.2	16.9	-1.8	-1.7	-4.0	15.7	15.9	14.2	23.3	21.8	18.9
S&P 500 Index	-26.5			37.3			24.0			-7.2			6.4			18.7			32.4			-5.3			21.5			22.6		
Dow Ind. Avg.	-23.8			45.0			23.0			-12.9			2.8			10.7			22.2			-3.7			27.2			26.1		

The data on this page represent an analytical device that enables the user to measure relative fund performance on a scientific grading system.

The tables were developed with three precepts in mind.

• While it is often done, comparing fund performance with stock market indexes can be highly misleading.

• Comparison with what other funds have done can be equally misleading.

• The only true way to measure the performance of managed funds is to compare the performance of those funds with the results achieved by other funds totally without management.

The problem with using index comparison is vividly illustrated by looking at the 1981 section of the tables, excluding dividends (lower right).

Here we see that the Standard & Poor's 500 stock index declined 9.7 percent, without inclusion of dividends. The Dow Jones industrial average was off 9.2 percent.

The performance of both was substantially worse than the median performance of our random portfolios, off only 2.4 at the 500 company level, but up 1.0 percent at the 1,000 company level and up 2.4 percent at the 1,800 company level.

Stated quite simply, while few investors could duplicate the S&P 500 or the Dow average in a portfolio, an investor could have thrown darts at a stock page and performed better than the two popular measures of stock perfor-

mance, the S&P 500 or the Dow, for 1981.

To obtain the results of unmanaged funds for comparison, it is necessary to duplicate the investment process and then measure the results.

This we have done in Portfolios Without Management by generating 30,000 random portfolios each year from 1974 on, with 35 stocks in each portfolio selected at random at the beginning of each year.

Scientific random sampling methods have been used at all times to eliminate any bias in our results. We chose to generate a very large number of portfolios each year to reduce sampling error to a small fraction of a percentage point.

We have applied this process to 10,000 portfolios in each of three separate company-size groups: the largest 1,800 companies, the largest 1,000 companies, and the largest 500 companies, based on annual revenue.

Performance results have been measured and are reported separately for each group and time period, with and without dividends, and these results are presented in these tables so the user can select the group deemed most appropriate for his analytical purpose.

These tables are remarkably easy to use. For any fund performance in any specific period, you need only look at the table for that period and simply read the relative score for this particular performance result.

With no more effort than that, you have a scientific

rating of the fund's relative performance in the specified period.

You can use the ratings to analyze the performance of a given fund over a period of years, with or without dividends, both on an annual and cumulative basis.

The ratings also enable you to quickly compare the relative performance of one fund against others in any time period.

And you may also find it instructive to rate the equity component of a fund for comparison with the performance of the fund as a whole.

To illustrate how easy it is to use this report, let's take a simple example.

In 1981, let's say that you have a fund with an 8.3 percent gain, including dividends.

You simply look at the appropriate year in the bottom table, and note that the portfolio ranks between the 45 and 40 percent group.

This tells you immediately that your fund out-performed approximately 60 percent of the portfolios without management, and but did not achieve the performance of the top 40 percent.

You also can see at a glance that median performance at the top 50 percent level was 7.1 percent in the 1,800 company group, 6.2 percent in the 1,000 company group and 2.9 percent in the 500 company group, so your fund was well above the median in all three groups.

Source: *The Media General Financial Weekly*, Media General Financial Services, 301 East Grace Street, Richmond, VA 23261, June 4, 1984.

THE MAJOR MARKET AVERAGES

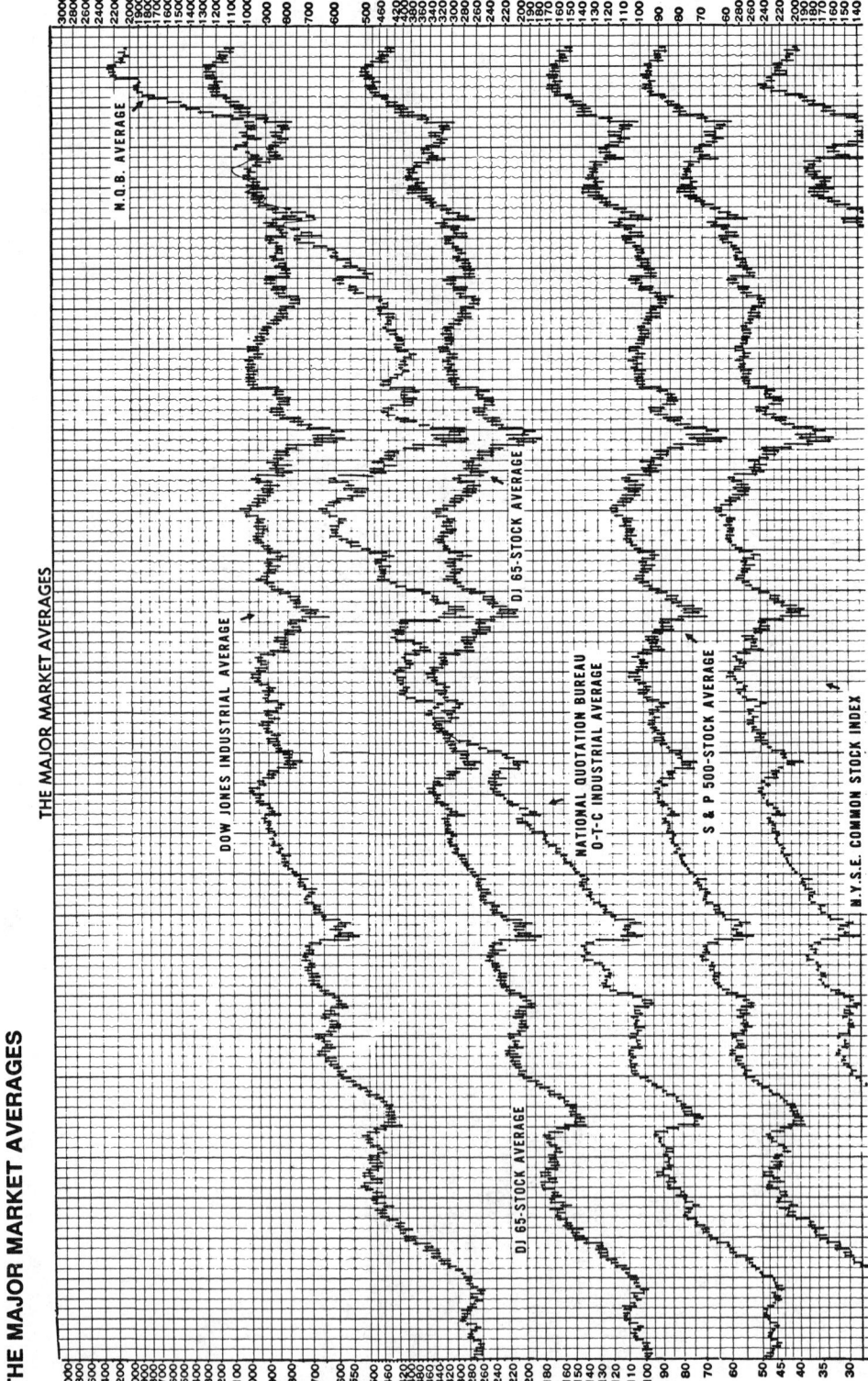

THE MAJOR MARKET AVERAGES

N.Q.B. AVERAGE

DOW JONES INDUSTRIAL AVERAGE

DJ 65-STOCK AVERAGE

DJ 65-STOCK AVERAGE

NATIONAL QUOTATION BUREAU
O-T-C INDUSTRIAL AVERAGE

S & P 500-STOCK AVERAGE

N.Y.S.E. COMMON STOCK INDEX

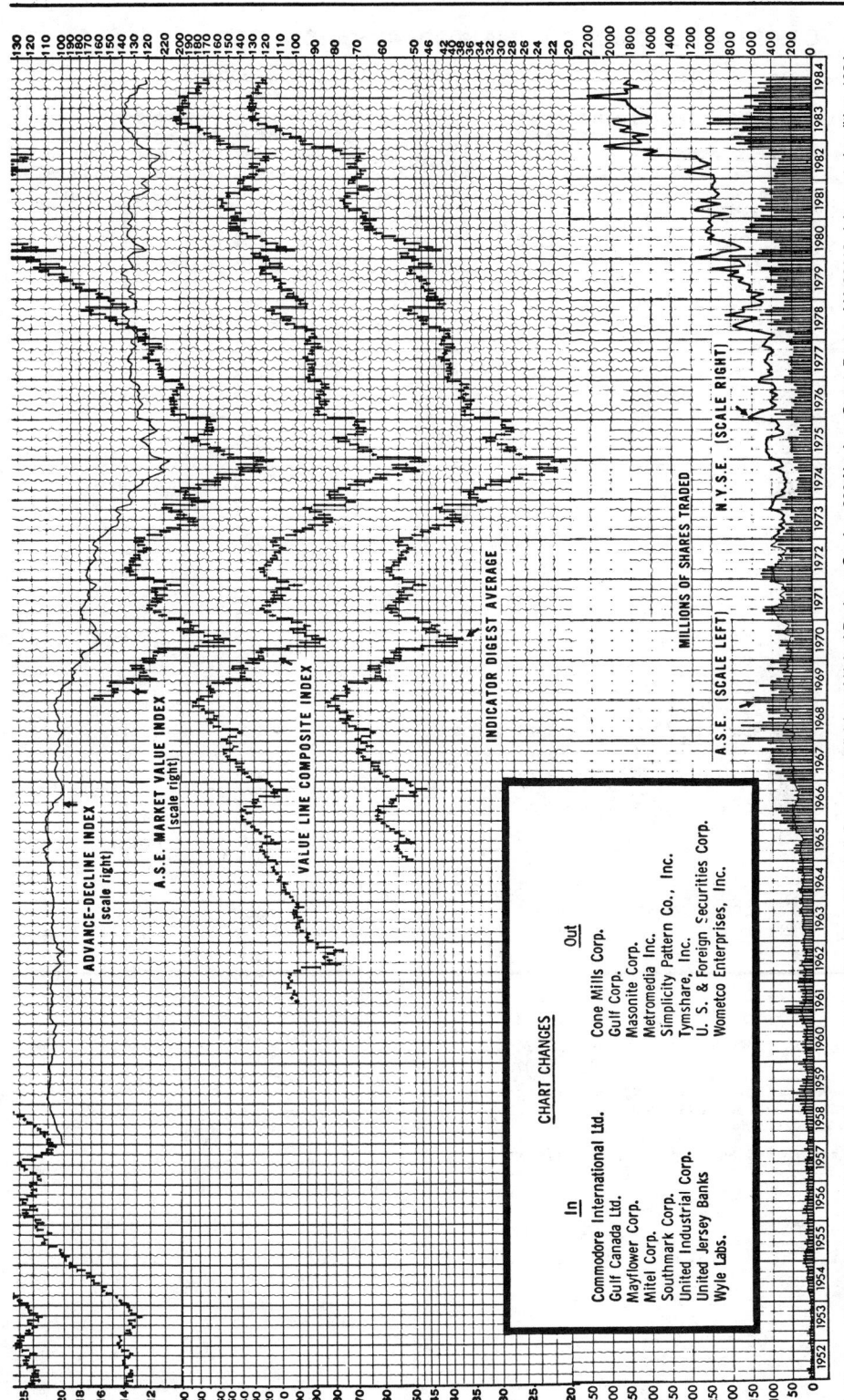

ADVANCE-DECLINE INDEX
(scale right)

A.S.E. MARKET VALUE INDEX
(scale right)

VALUE LINE COMPOSITE INDEX

INDICATOR DIGEST AVERAGE

MILLIONS OF SHARES TRADED

N.Y.S.E. (SCALE RIGHT)

A.S.E. (SCALE LEFT)

CHART CHANGES

In	Out
Commodore International Ltd.	Cone Mills Corp.
Gulf Canada Ltd.	Gulf Corp.
Mayflower Corp.	Masonite Corp.
Mitel Corp.	Metromedia Inc.
Southmark Corp.	Simplicity Pattern Co., Inc.
United Industrial Corp.	Tymshare, Inc.
United Jersey Banks	U. S. & Foreign Securities Corp.
Wyle Labs.	Wometco Enterprises, Inc.

Source: 5-Trend CYCLI-GRAPHS. The charts are courtesy of Securities Research Company, a division of United Business Service, 208 Newbury Street, Boston, MA 02116, July quarterly edition, 1984.

NEW YORK STOCK EXCHANGE CASH DIVIDENDS AND YIELDS

Calendar year	Common stocks				Preferred stocks			
	Number of issues listed at year end	Number paying cash dividends during year	Estimated aggregate cash payments (millions)	Median yield[*]	Number of issues listed at year end	Number paying cash dividends during year	Estimated aggregate cash payments (millions)	Median yield[*]
1929	842	554	$ 2,711	N/A	N/A	N/A	N/A	N/A
1930	848	576	2,667	N/A	N/A	N/A	N/A	N/A
1935	776	387	1,336	N/A	N/A	N/A	N/A	N/A
1940	829	577	2,099	6.1%	N/A	N/A	N/A	N/A
1945	881	746	2,275	3.6	388	341	$ 337	4.2%
1950	1,039	930	5,404	6.7	433	405	379	4.3
1951	1,054	961	5,467	6.5	441	406	380	4.6
1952	1,067	975	5,595	6.0	455	433	378	4.4
1953	1,069	964	5,874	6.3	461	443	383	4.7
1954	1,076	968	6,439	4.7	456	436	368	4.2
1955	1,076	982	7,488	4.6	432	412	336	4.2
1956	1,077	975	8,341	5.2	425	411	333	4.9
1957	1,098	991	8,807	6.1	424	409	335	4.9
1958	1,086	961	8,711	4.1	421	406	331	4.9
1959	1,092	953	9,337	3.8	415	403	337	5.1
1960	1,126	981	9,872	4.2	402	391	331	5.0
1961	1,145	981	10,430	3.3	396	381	341	4.8
1962	1,168	994	11,203	3.8	391	369	336	4.6
1963	1,194	1,032	12,096	3.6	378	359	342	4.6
1964	1,227	1,066	13,555	3.3	379	364	352	4.5
1965	1,254	1,111	15,302	3.2	373	358	388	4.7
1966	1,267	1,127	16,151	4.1	398	385	431	5.4
1967	1,255	1,116	16,866	3.2	445	432	596	5.8
1968	1,253	1,104	18,124	2.6	514	500	894	5.2
1969	1,290	1,121	19,404	3.6	499	487	1,142	6.8
1970	1,330	1,120	19,781	3.7	510	498	1,233	6.9
1971	1,399	1,132	20,256	3.2	528	499	1,360	6.7
1972	1,478	1,195	21,490	3.0	525	496	1,375	6.7
1973	1,536	1,276	23,627	5.0	522	497	1,487	8.0
1974	1,543	1,308	25,662	7.4	537	520	1,616	10.2
1975	1,531	1,273	26,901	5.0	580	552	1,682	9.3
1976	1,550	1,304	30,608	4.0	608	592	1,802	8.0
1977	1,549	1,360	36,270	4.5	628	619	1,954	8.4
1978	1,552	1,373	41,151	4.8	642	626	1,974	9.4
1979	1,536	1,359	46,937	5.0	656	644	2,225	10.9
1980	1,540	1,361	53,072	4.6	688	676	2,338	12.6
1981	1,534	1,337	60,628	5.0	686	676	2,637	14.1
1982	1,499	1,287	62,224	4.1	726	715	3,554	12.0
1983	1,518	1,259	67,102	3.5	789	776	4,562	11.9

[*] Based on cash payments during the year and price at end of year for dividend-paying stocks only.

N/A-Not Available.

Source: New York Stock Exchange *1984 Fact Book.*

Stock Market Averages by Industry Group

These definitions apply to the following charts.

Price scale: The price ranges are always read from the scale at the right-hand side of each chart. This scale is equal to 15 times the earnings and dividend scale at the left, so when the price range bars and the earnings line coincide, it shows the price is at 15 times earnings. When the price is above the earnings line, the ratio of price to earnings is greater than 15 times earnings; when below, it is less.

Monthly price ranges represented by the solid vertical bars show the highest and lowest point of each month's transactions. Cross-bars indicate the month's closing price.

Monthly ratio-cator: The plottings for this line are obtained by dividing the closing price of the stock by the closing price of the Dow Jones Industrial Average on the say day. The resulting percentage is multiplied by a factor of 4.5 to bring the line closer to the price bars and is read from the right-hand scale. The plotting indicates whether the stock has kept pace, outperformed, or lagged behind the general market as represented by the DJIA.

Volume: The number of shares traded each month is shown by vertical bars at the bottom of each chart on an arithmetical scale.

Source: *5-Trend CYCLI-GRAPHS.* The charts are courtesy of Securities Research Company, a division of United Business Service, 208 Newbury Street, Boston, MA 02116, July quarterly edition, 1984.

STOCK MARKET AVERAGES BY INDUSTRY GROUP

PRICES & EARNS. SOURCE: S&P

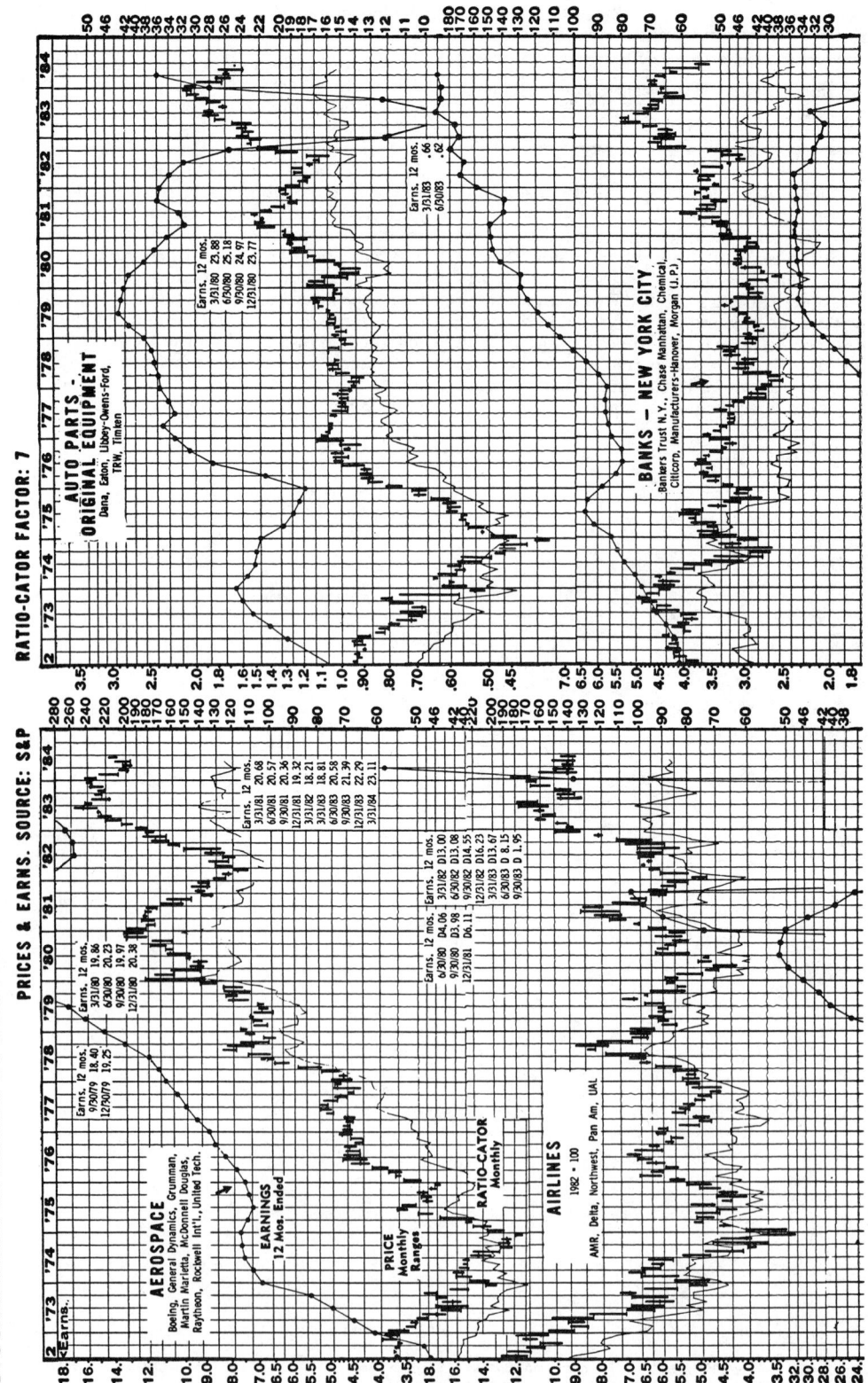

RATIO-CATOR FACTOR: 7

AUTO PARTS - ORIGINAL EQUIPMENT
Dana, Eaton, Libbey-Owens-Ford, TRW, Timken

Earns. 12 mos.
3/31/80 23.88
6/30/80 25.18
9/30/80 24.97
12/31/80 23.77

Earns. 12 mos.
3/31/83 .66
6/30/83 .62

BANKS — NEW YORK CITY
Bankers Trust N.Y., Chase Manhattan, Chemical, Citicorp, Manufacturers-Hanover, Morgan (J.P.)

AEROSPACE
Boeing, General Dynamics, Grumman, Martin Marietta, McDonnell Douglas, Raytheon, Rockwell Int'l, United Tech.

Earns. 12 mos.
9/30/79 18.40
12/30/79 19.25

Earns. 12 mos.
3/31/80 19.86
6/30/80 20.23
9/30/80 19.97
12/31/80 20.38

EARNINGS
12 Mos. Ended

Earns. 12 mos.
3/31/81 20.68
6/30/81 20.57
9/30/81 20.36
12/31/81 19.32
3/31/82 18.21
6/30/82 18.81
9/30/82 20.58
12/31/82 21.39
3/31/83 22.29
9/30/83 23.11
3/31/84

PRICE
Monthly Ranges

RATIO-CATOR
Monthly

Earns. 12 mos.
6/30/80 D4.06
9/30/80 D3.98
12/31/80 D6.11

Earns. 12 mos.
3/31/82 D3.00
6/30/82 D3.08
9/30/82 D4.55
12/31/82 D6.23
3/31/83 D13.67
6/30/83 D 8.15
9/30/83 D 1.95

AIRLINES
1982 = 100
AMR, Delta, Northwest, Pan Am, UAL

284

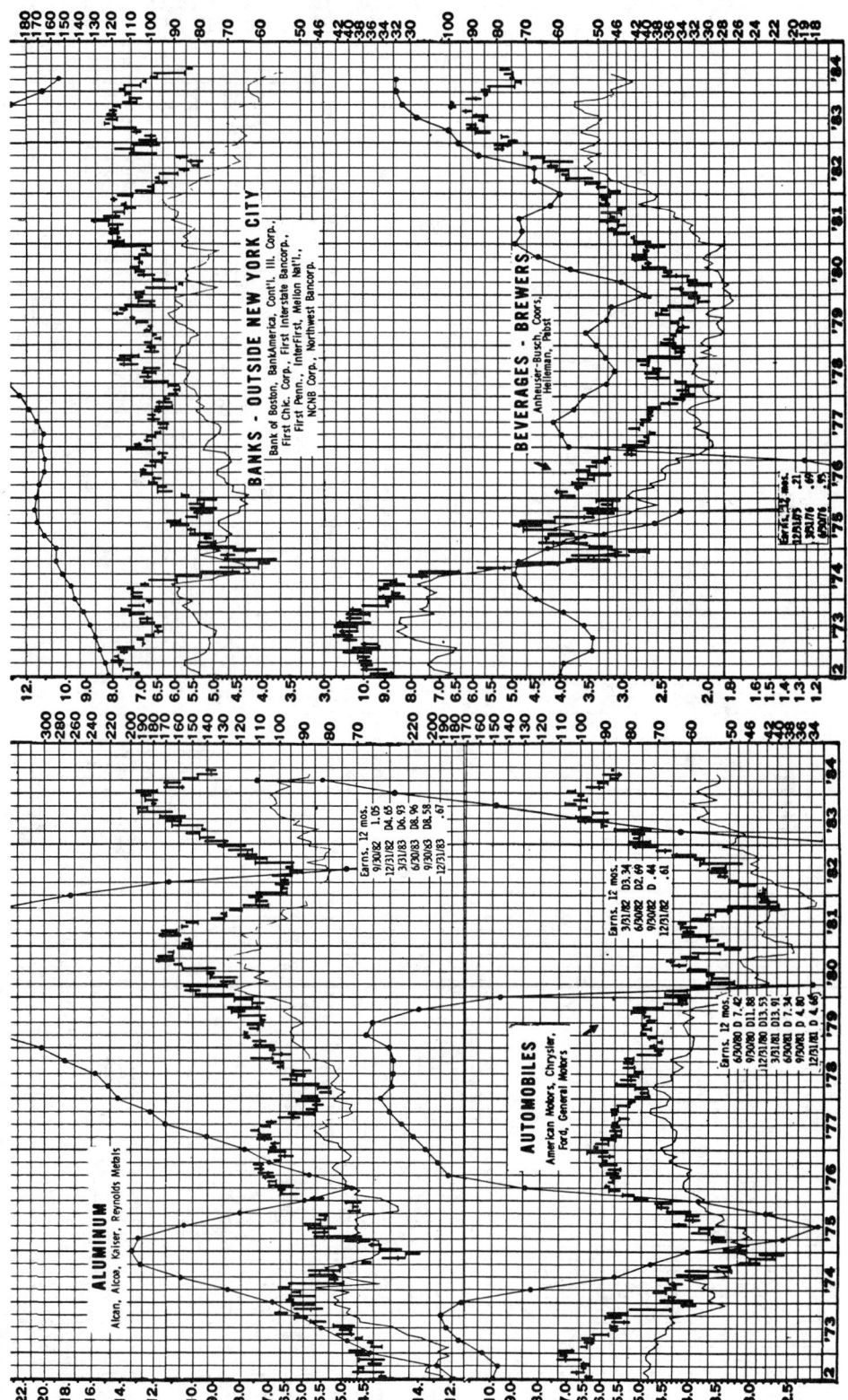

ALUMINUM
Alcan, Alcoa, Kaiser, Reynolds Metals

AUTOMOBILES
American Motors, Chrysler,
Ford, General Motors

Earns. 12 mos.
9/30/82 1.05
12/31/82 D4.65
3/31/83 D6.93
6/30/83 D8.96
9/30/83 D8.58
12/31/83 .67

Earns. 12 mos.
3/31/82 D3.34
6/30/82 D2.69
9/30/82 D. 44
12/31/82 D. 61

Earns. 12 mos.
6/30/80 D 7.42
9/30/80 D11.88
12/31/80 D13.53
3/31/81 D13.91
6/30/81 D 7.34
9/30/81 D 4.80
12/31/81 D 4.46

BANKS - OUTSIDE NEW YORK CITY
Bank of Boston, BankAmerica, Cont'l. Ill. Corp.,
First Chic. Corp., First Interstate Bancorp.,
First Penn., InterFirst, Mellon Nat'l.,
NCNB Corp., Northwest Bancorp.

BEVERAGES - BREWERS
Anheuser-Busch, Coors,
Heileman, Pabst

Earns. 12 mos.
12/31/75 .21
12/31/76 .64
6/30/76 .15

285

STOCK MARKET AVERAGES BY INDUSTRY GROUP *(continued)*

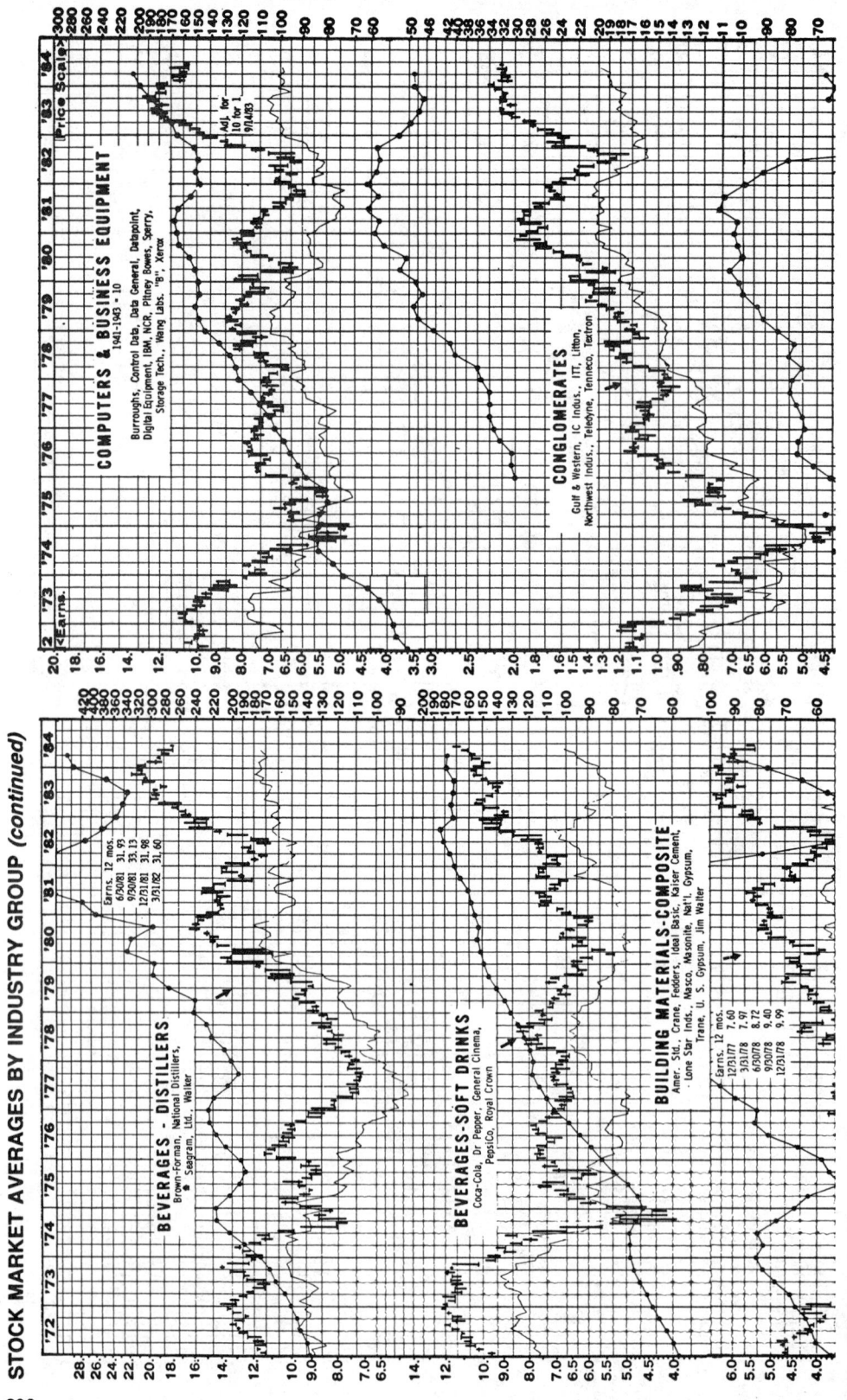

COMPUTERS & BUSINESS EQUIPMENT
1941-1943 = 10

Burroughs, Control Data, Data General, Datapoint, Digital Equipment, IBM, NCR, Pitney Bowes, Sperry, Storage Tech., Wang Labs. "B", Xerox

Adj. for 10 for 1 9/14/83

CONGLOMERATES

Gulf & Western, IC Indus., ITT, Litton, Northwest Indus., Teledyne, Tenneco, Textron

BEVERAGES – DISTILLERS

Brown-Forman, National Distillers, Seagram, Ltd. Walker

Earns. 12 mos.	
6/30/81	31.93
9/30/81	33.13
12/31/81	31.98
3/31/82	31.60

BEVERAGES-SOFT DRINKS

Coca-Cola, Dr Pepper, General Cinema, PepsiCo, Royal Crown

BUILDING MATERIALS-COMPOSITE

Amer. Std., Crane, Fedders, Ideal Basic, Kaiser Cement, Lone Star Inds., Masco, Masonite, Nat'l. Gypsum, Trane, U. S. Gypsum, Jim Walter

Earns. 12 mos.	
12/31/77	7.60
3/31/78	7.97
6/30/78	8.72
9/30/78	9.40
12/31/78	9.99

286

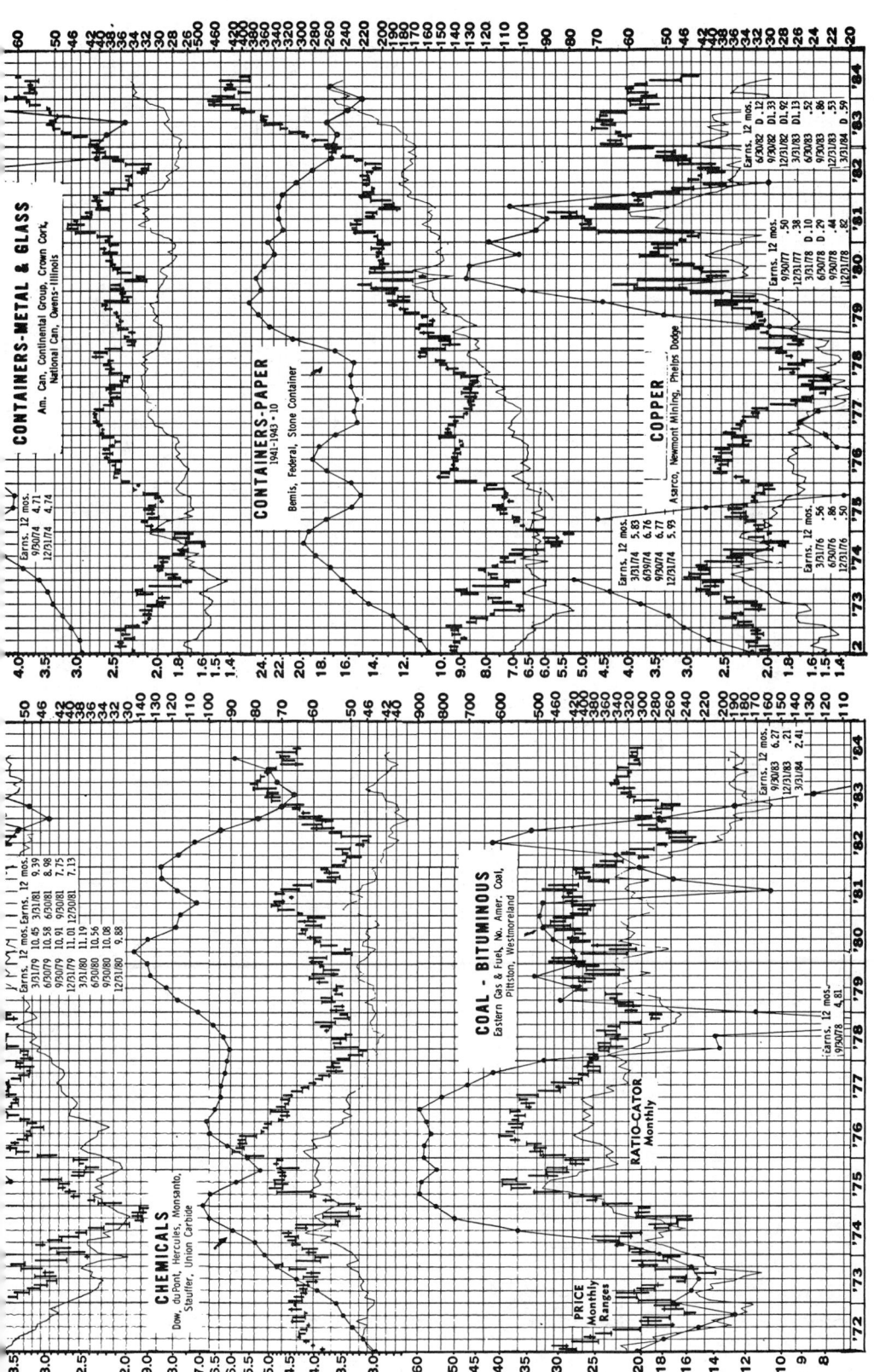

CONTAINERS-METAL & GLASS
Am. Can, Continental Group, Crown Cork, National Can, Owens-Illinois

Earns, 12 mos.
9/30/74   4.71
12/31/74   4.74

CONTAINERS-PAPER
1941-1943 · 10
Bemis, Federal, Stone Container

Earns, 12 mos.
3/31/74   5.83
6/30/74   6.76
9/30/74   6.77
12/31/74   5.93

COPPER
Asarco, Newmont Mining, Phelps Dodge

Earns, 12 mos.
3/31/76   .56
6/30/76   .86
9/30/76   .50
12/31/76   .50

Earns, 12 mos.
6/30/82   D .12
9/30/82   D1.33
12/31/82   D1.92
3/31/83   D1.13
6/30/83   .52
9/30/83   .86
12/31/83   .53
3/31/84   D .59

Earns, 12 mos.
9/30/77   .50
12/31/77   .38
3/31/78   D .10
6/30/78   D .29
9/30/78   .44
12/31/78   .82

CHEMICALS
Dow, duPont, Hercules, Monsanto, Stauffer, Union Carbide

Earns, 12 mos. Earns, 12 mos.
3/31/79   10.45   3/31/81   9.39
6/30/79   10.58   6/30/81   8.98
9/30/79   10.91   9/30/81   7.75
12/31/79 11.01   12/31/81 7.13
3/31/80   11.19
6/30/80   10.56
9/30/80   10.08
12/31/80   9.88

COAL - BITUMINOUS
Eastern Gas & Fuel, No. Amer. Coal, Pittston, Westmoreland

RATIO-CATOR
Monthly

Earns, 12 mos.
9/30/78   4.81

Earns, 12 mos.
9/30/83   6.27
12/31/83 6.21
3/31/84   2.41

PRICE
Monthly
Ranges

287

STOCK MARKET AVERAGES BY INDUSTRY GROUP *(continued)*

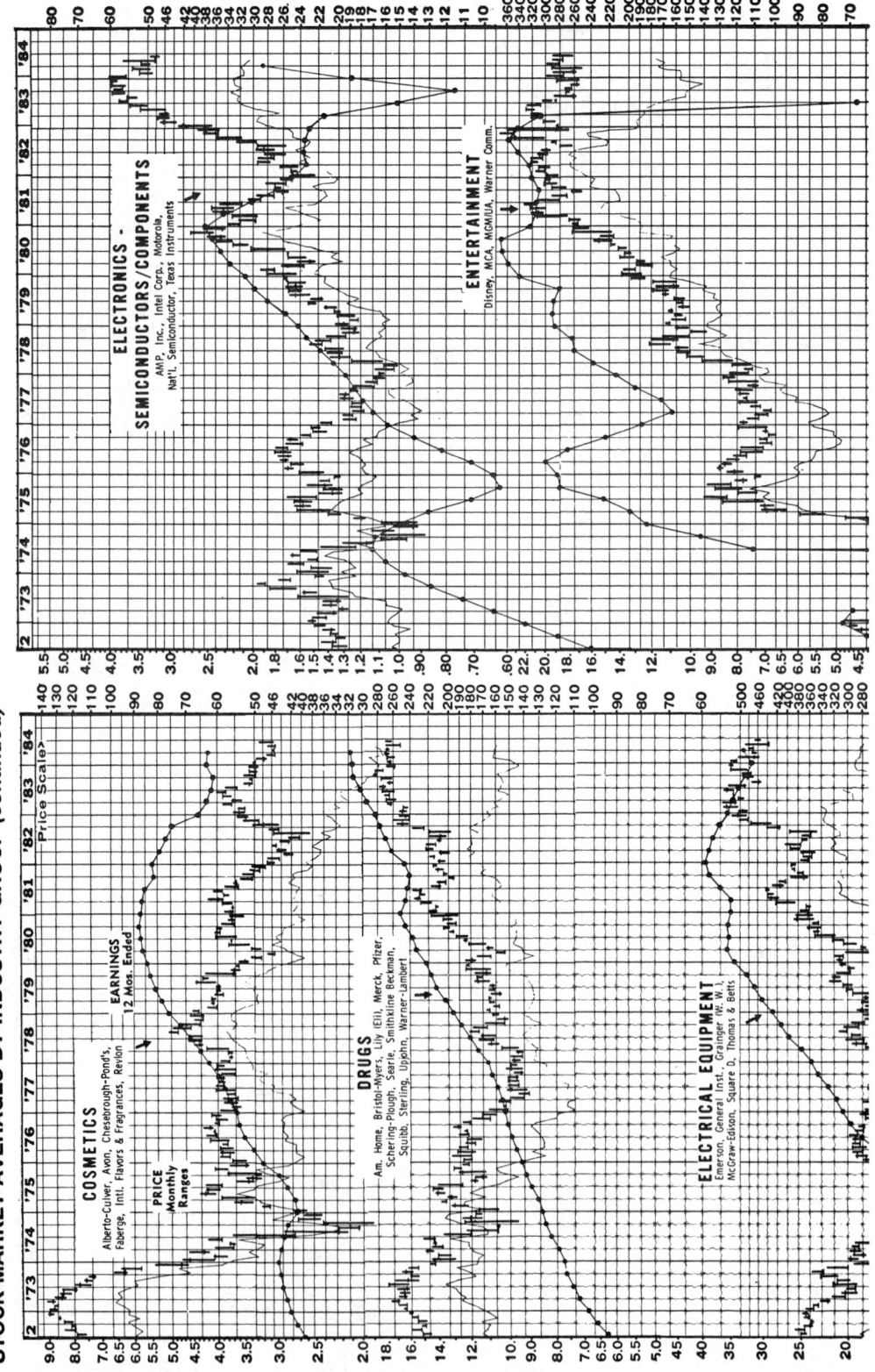

COSMETICS
Alberto-Culver, Avon, Chesebrough-Pond's, Faberge, Intl. Flavors & Fragrances, Revlon

PRICE
Monthly
Ranges

EARNINGS
12 Mos. Ended

Price Scale▷

DRUGS
Am. Home, Bristol-Myers, Lily (Eli), Merck, Pfizer, Schering-Plough, Searle, Smithkline Beckman, Squibb, Sterling, Upjohn, Warner-Lambert

ELECTRICAL EQUIPMENT
Emerson, General Inst., Grainger (W. W.), McGraw-Edison, Square D, Thomas & Betts

ELECTRONICS – SEMICONDUCTORS/COMPONENTS
AMP, Inc., Intel Corp., Motorola, Nat'l. Semiconductor, Texas Instruments

ENTERTAINMENT
Disney, MCA, MGM/UA, Warner Comm.

288

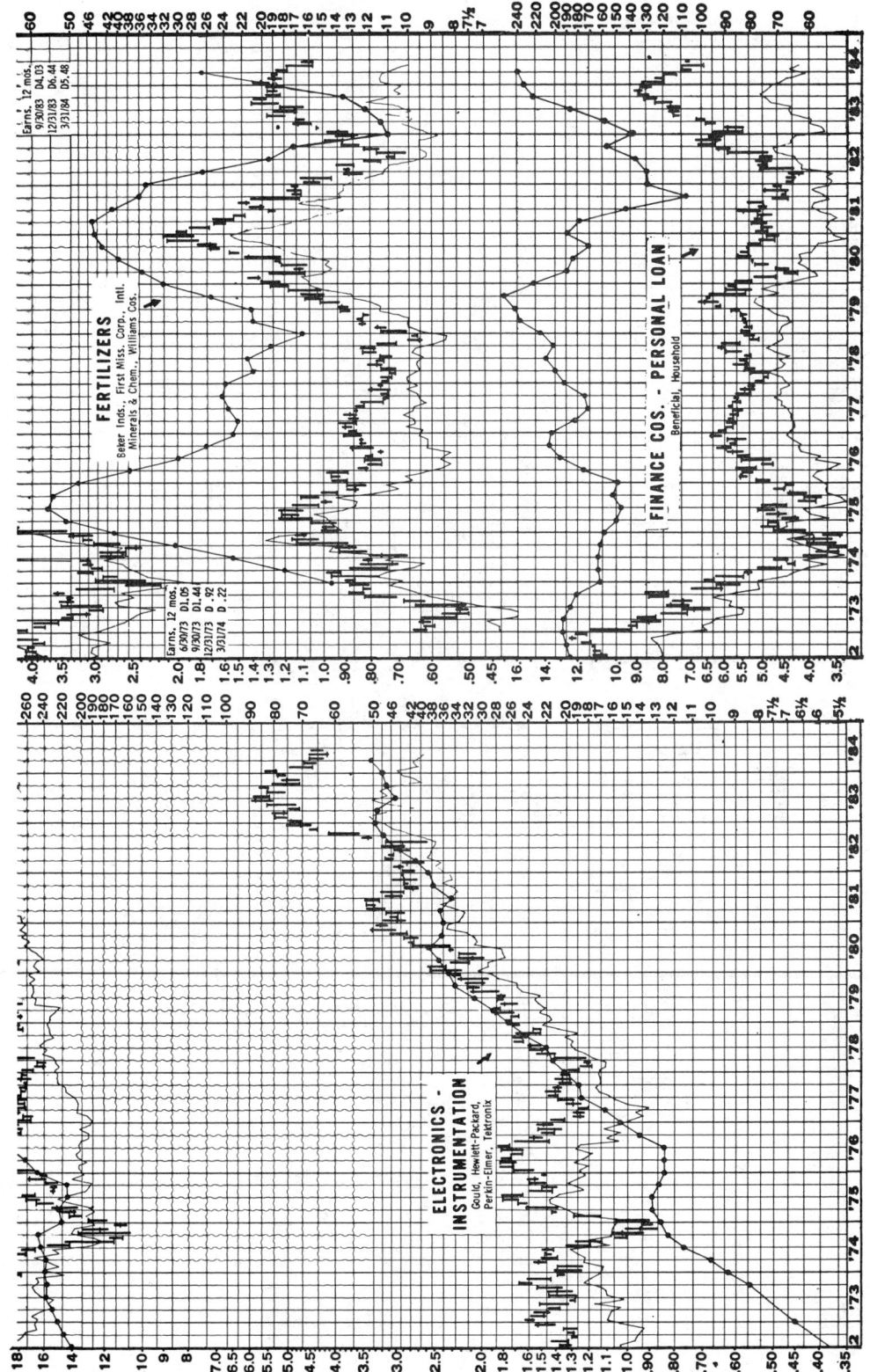

FERTILIZERS
Beker Inds., First Miss. Corp., Intl.
Minerals & Chem., Williams Cos.

Earns. 12 mos.
9/30/83 D4.03
12/31/83 D6.44
3/31/84 D5.48

Earns. 12 mos.
6/30/73 D1.05
9/30/73 D1.44
12/31/73 D .92
3/31/74 D .22

FINANCE COS. - PERSONAL LOAN
Beneficial, Household

ELECTRONICS -
INSTRUMENTATION
Gould, Hewlett-Packard,
Perkin-Elmer, Tektronix

289

STOCK MARKET AVERAGES BY INDUSTRY GROUP *(continued)*

HOSPITAL MANAGEMENT
— Am. Med. Intl., Hospital Corp. of Am.,
Humana Inc., Natl. Med. Enter.

<Earns.

HOSPITAL SUPPLIES
— Abbott Labs., Am. Hosp., Bard (C. R.),
Baxter Travenol, Becton Dickinson, Johnson & Johnson

(Price Scale)>

FOODS-COMPOSITE
1941-1943 = 10

Earns. 12 mos.	
3/31/81	10.64
6/30/81	10.96
9/30/81	11.24
12/31/81	11.43

Amstar, Archer Daniels Midland, Beatrice Foods, Borden, CPC Intl., Campbell
Soup, Carnation, ConAgra, Consolidated Foods, Dart & Kraft, Gen. Foods,
Gen. Mills, Gerber Prod., Heinz (H. J.), Hershey Foods, Kellogg, Nabisco
Brands, Pillsbury, Quaker Oats, Ralston Purina, Wrigley (Wm.)

Earns. 12 mos.	
3/31/82	11.48
6/30/82	11.70
9/30/82	11.32
12/31/82	11.63
3/31/83	10.95
6/30/83	11.25
9/30/83	12.44
12/31/83	13.85

FOREST PRODUCTS
— Boise Cascade, Champion Int'l., Evans
Products, Georgia-Pacific, Louisiana-
Pacific, Potlatch Corp., Weyerhaeuser

Earns. 12 mos.	
12/31/82	.36
3/31/83	.35
6/30/83	.51
9/30/83	.66

GOLD MINING
1982 = 100

— ASA Ltd., Campbell Red Lake,
Dome, Homestake Mining

290

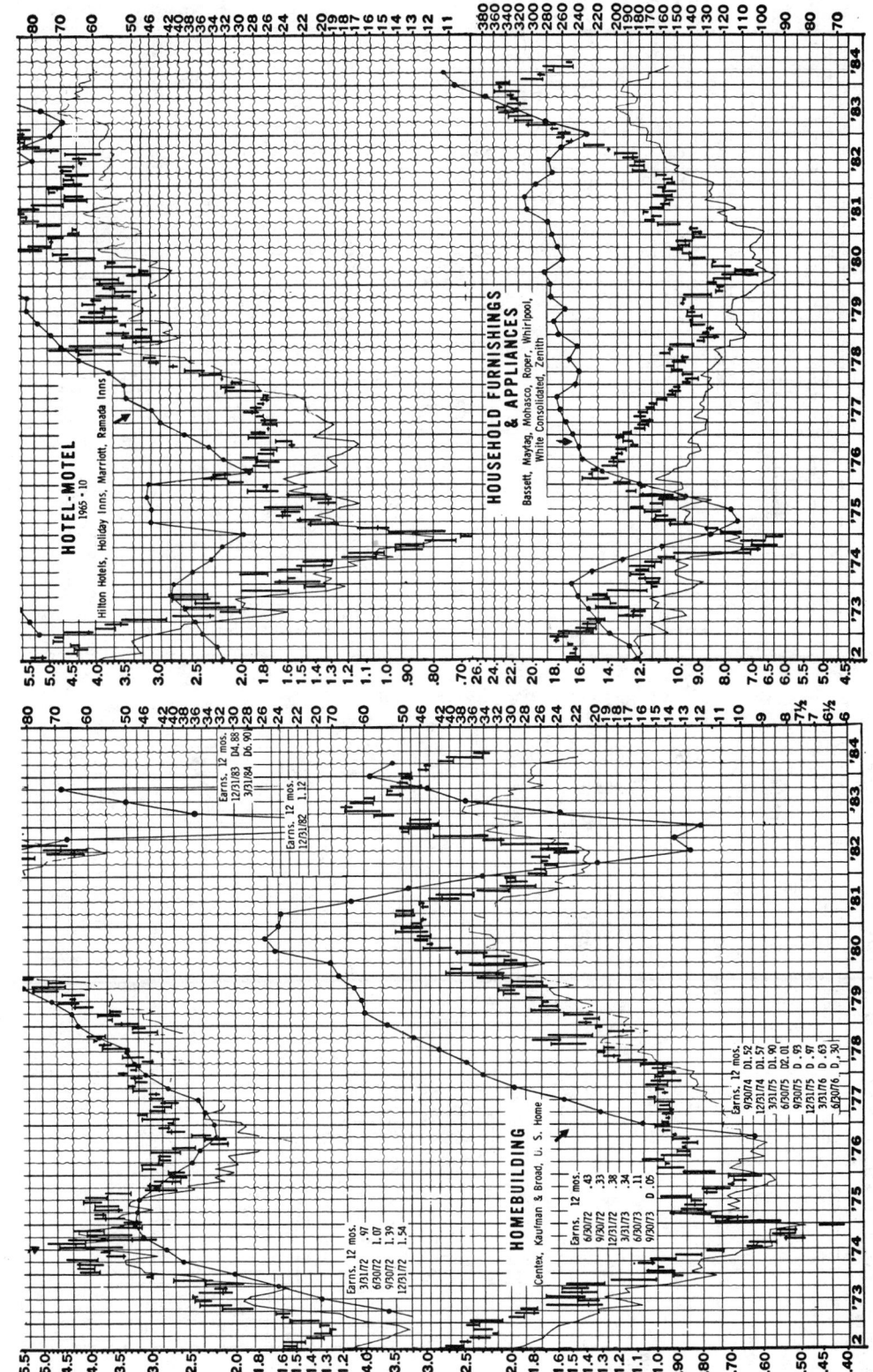

HOTEL-MOTEL
1965 = 10

Hilton Hotels, Holiday Inns, Marriott, Ramada Inns

HOUSEHOLD FURNISHINGS & APPLIANCES

Bassett, Maytag, Mohasco, Roper, Whirlpool, White Consolidated, Zenith

HOMEBUILDING

Centex, Kaufman & Broad, U. S. Home

Earns. 12 mos.
3/31/72   .97
6/30/72   1.07
9/30/72   1.39
12/31/72 1.54

Earns. 12 mos.
6/30/72   .43
9/30/72   .33
12/31/72   .38
3/31/73   .34
6/30/73   .11
9/30/73   D .05

Earns. 12 mos.
9/30/74   D1.52
12/31/74 D1.57
3/31/75   D1.90
6/30/75   D2.01
9/30/75   D .93
12/31/75 D .97
3/31/76   D .63
6/30/76   D .30

Earns. 12 mos.
12/31/83 D4.88
3/31/84   D6.90

Earns. 12 mos.
12/31/82 1.12

STOCK MARKET AVERAGES BY INDUSTRY GROUP *(continued)*

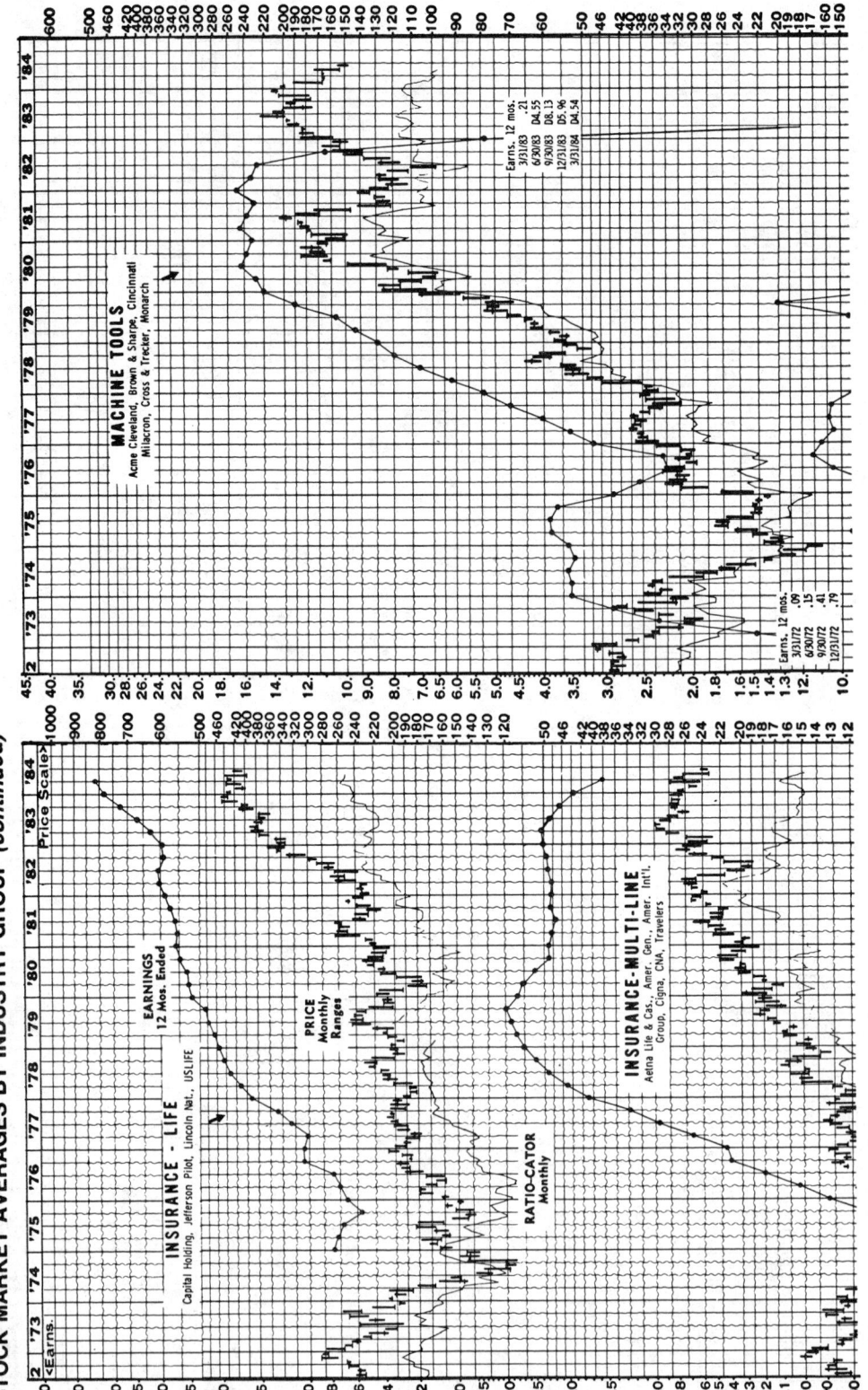

INSURANCE - LIFE
Capital Holding, Jefferson Pilot, Lincoln Nat'l, USLIFE

EARNINGS
12 Mos. Ended

PRICE
Monthly
Ranges

RATIO-CATOR
Monthly

INSURANCE - MULTI-LINE
Aetna Life & Cas., Amer. Gen., Amer. Int'l.
Group, Cigna, CNA, Travelers

MACHINE TOOLS
Acme Cleveland, Brown & Sharpe, Cincinnati
Milacron, Cross & Trecker, Monarch

Earns. 12 mos.
3/31/83   .21
6/30/83   D4.55
9/30/83   D8.13
12/31/83 D5.96
3/31/84   D4.54

Earns. 12 mos.
3/31/72   .09
6/30/72   .15
9/30/72   .41
12/31/72   .79

292

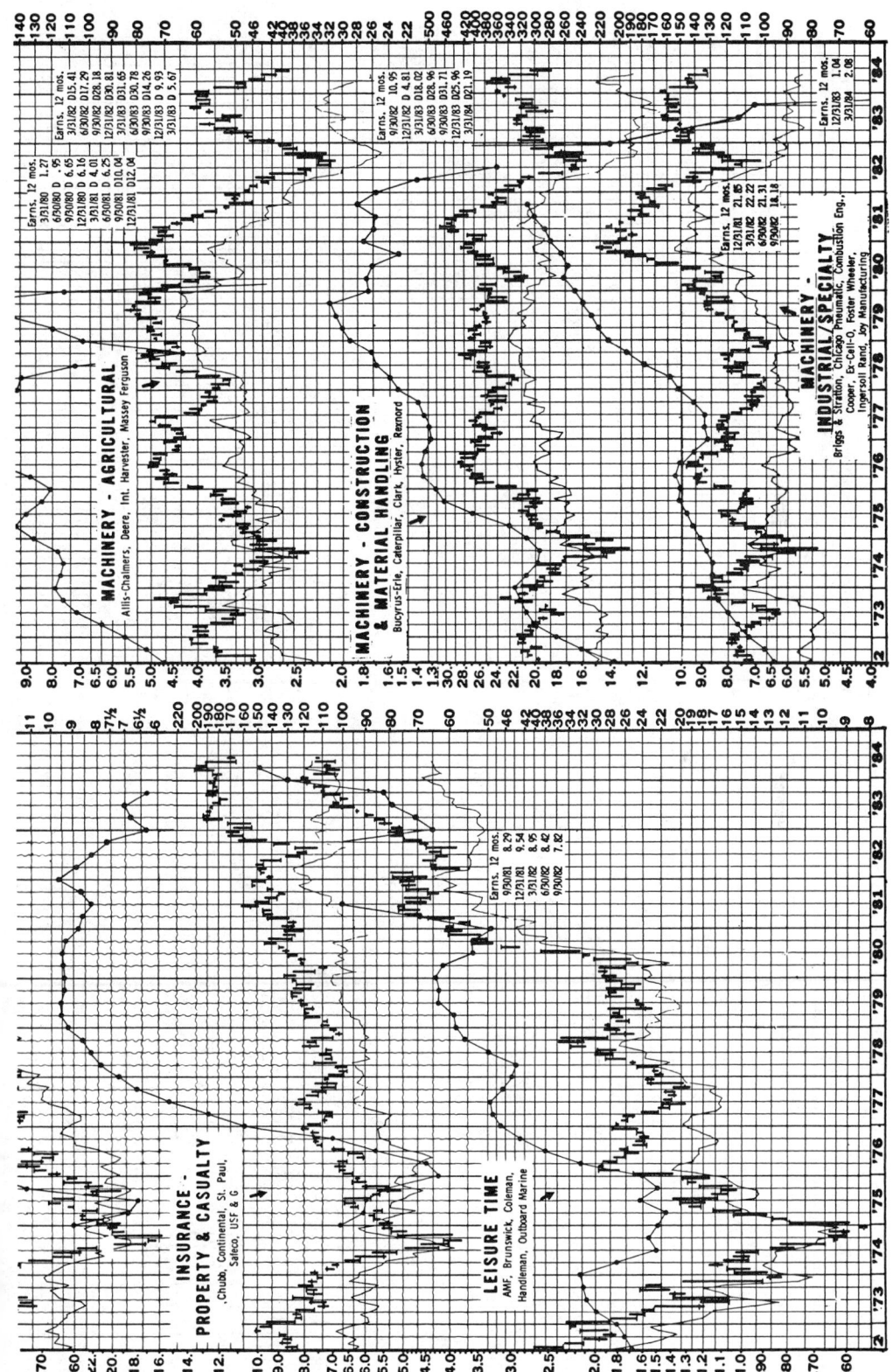

MACHINERY - AGRICULTURAL
Allis-Chalmers, Deere, Int. Harvester, Massey Ferguson

Earns. 12 mos.
3/31/80   1.27
6/30/80 D .95
9/30/80 D 6.65
12/31/80 D 6.16
3/31/81 D 4.01
6/30/81 D 6.25
9/30/81 D10.04
12/31/81 D12.04

MACHINERY - CONSTRUCTION
& MATERIAL HANDLING
Bucyrus-Erie, Caterpillar, Clark, Hyster, Rexnord

Earns. 12 mos.
9/30/82   10.95
12/31/82 D 4.81
3/31/83 D18.02
6/30/83 D28.96
9/30/83 D31.71
12/31/83 D25.96
3/31/84 D21.19

MACHINERY -
INDUSTRIAL/SPECIALTY
Briggs & Stratton, Chicago Pneumatic, Combustion Eng.,
Cooper, Ex-Cell-O, Foster Wheeler,
Ingersoll Rand, Joy Manufacturing

Earns. 12 mos.
12/31/83 1.04
3/31/84   2.08

Earns, 12 mos.
3/31/82   15.41
6/30/82   17.29
9/30/82   28.18
12/31/82 30.81
3/31/83   31.65
6/30/83   30.78
9/30/83   14.26
12/31/83 D 9.93
3/31/83   D 5.67

Earns. 12 mos.
12/31/81 21.85
3/31/82   22.22
6/30/82   21.31
9/30/82   14.18

INSURANCE -
PROPERTY & CASUALTY
.Chubb, Continental, St. Paul,
Safeco, USF & G

LEISURE TIME
AMF, Brunswick, Coleman,
Handleman, Outboard Marine

Earns. 12 mos.
9/30/81   8.29
12/31/81 9.54
3/31/82   8.95
6/30/82   8.42
9/30/82   7.82

293

STOCK MARKET AVERAGES BY INDUSTRY GROUP (continued)

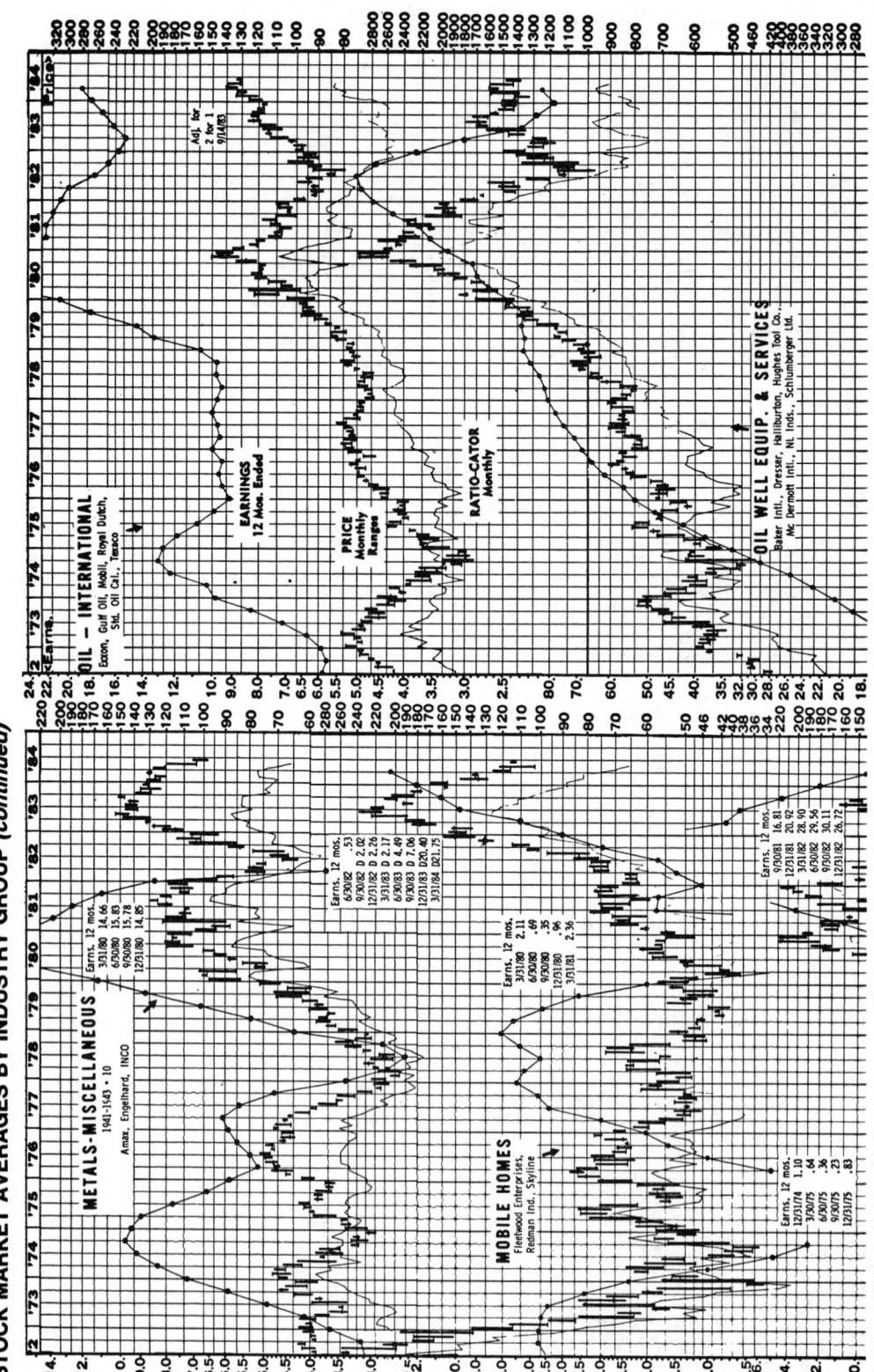

OIL – INTERNATIONAL
Exxon, Gulf Oil, Mobil, Royal Dutch, Std. Oil Cal., Texaco

EARNINGS
12 Mos. Ended

PRICE
Monthly
Ranges

RATIO-CATOR
Monthly

Adj. for 1
2 for 1
9/14/83

OIL WELL EQUIP. & SERVICES
Baker Intnl., Dresser, Halliburton, Hughes Tool Co.
Mc Dermott Intnl., NL Inds., Schlumberger Ltd.

Earns. 12 mos.	
9/30/81	16.81
12/31/81	20.92
3/31/82	28.90
6/30/82	29.56
9/30/82	30.11
12/31/82	26.72

METALS–MISCELLANEOUS
1941-1943 = 10
Amax, Engelhard, INCO

Earns. 12 mos.	
3/31/80	14.66
6/30/80	15.83
9/30/80	15.78
12/31/80	14.85

Earns. 12 mos.	
6/30/82	2.53
9/30/82	2.02
12/31/82	2.26
3/31/83	2.17
6/30/83	4.49
9/30/83	7.06
12/31/83	D20.40
3/31/84	D21.75

MOBILE HOMES
Fleetwood Enterprises,
Redman Ind., Skyline

Earns. 12 mos.	
3/31/80	2.11
6/30/80	.69
9/30/80	.35
12/31/80	.96
3/31/81	2.56

Earns. 12 mos.	
12/31/74	1.10
3/30/75	.64
6/30/75	.36
9/30/75	.23
12/31/75	.83

294

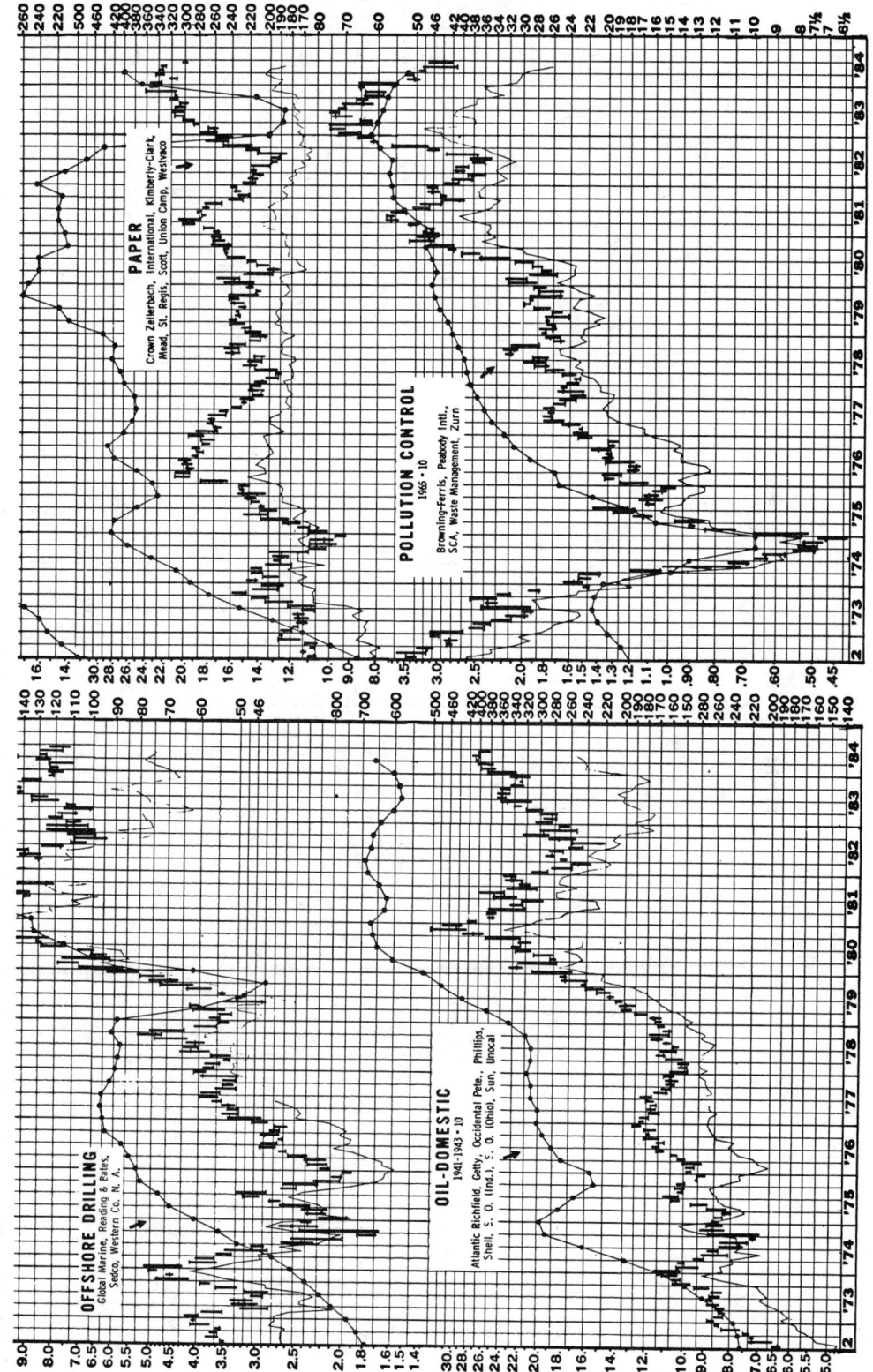

OFFSHORE DRILLING
Global Marine, Reading & Bates, Sedco, Western Co. N. A.

OIL–DOMESTIC
1941–1943 = 10
Atlantic Richfield, Getty, Occidental Pete., Phillips, Shell, S. O. (Ind.), S. O. (Ohio), Sun, Unocal

PAPER
Crown Zellerbach, International, Kimberly-Clark, Mead, St. Regis, Scott, Union Camp, Westvaco

POLLUTION CONTROL
1965 = 10
Browning-Ferris, Peabody Intl., SCA, Waste Management, Zurn

STOCK MARKET AVERAGES BY INDUSTRY GROUP (continued)

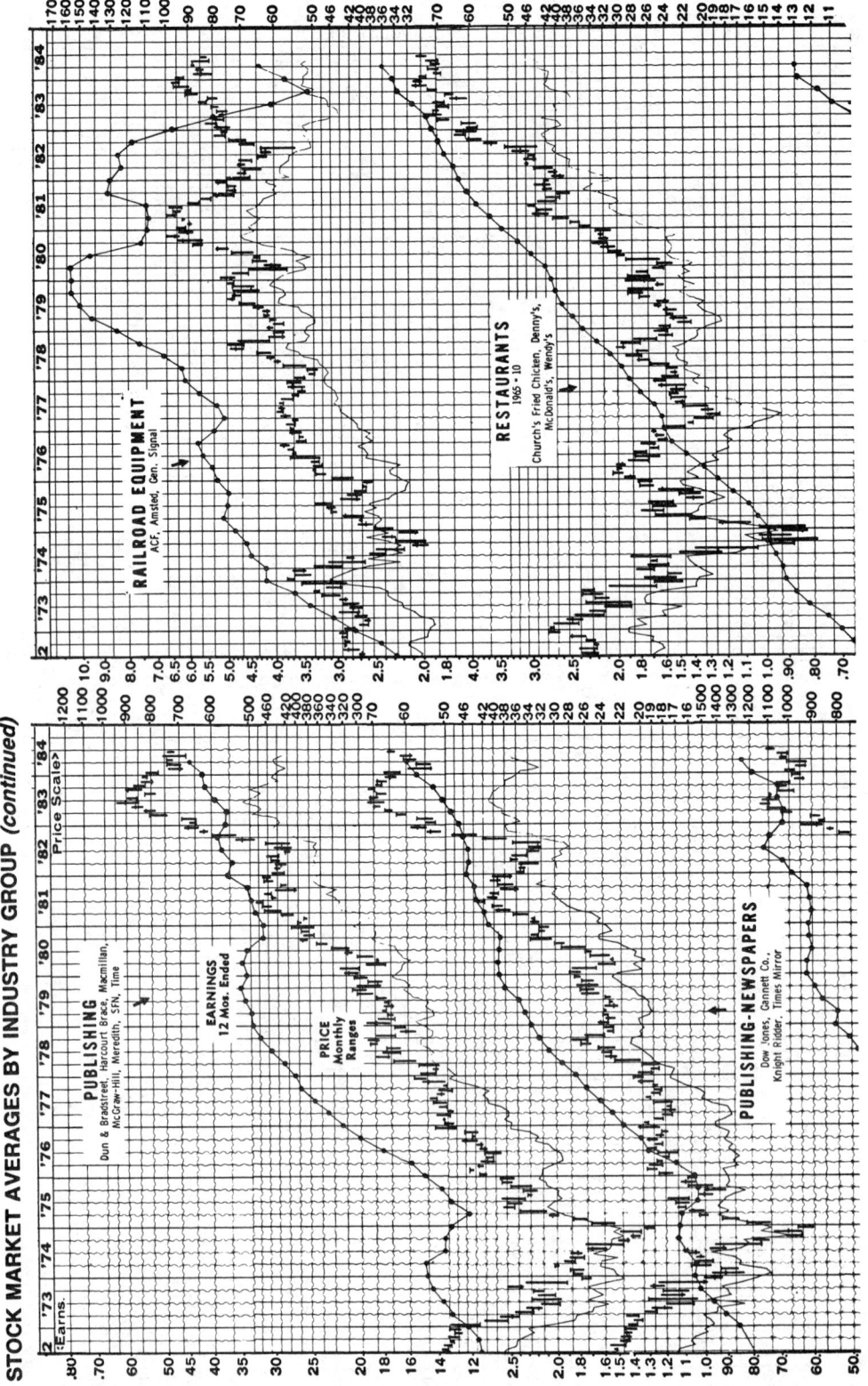

PUBLISHING
Dun & Bradstreet, Harcourt Brace, Macmillan, McGraw-Hill, Meredith, SFN, Time

EARNINGS
12 Mos. Ended

PRICE
Monthly Ranges

PUBLISHING-NEWSPAPERS
Dow Jones, Gannett Co., Knight Ridder, Times Mirror

RAILROAD EQUIPMENT
ACF, Amsted, Gen. Signal

RESTAURANTS
1965 - 10
Church's Fried Chicken, Denny's, McDonald's, Wendy's

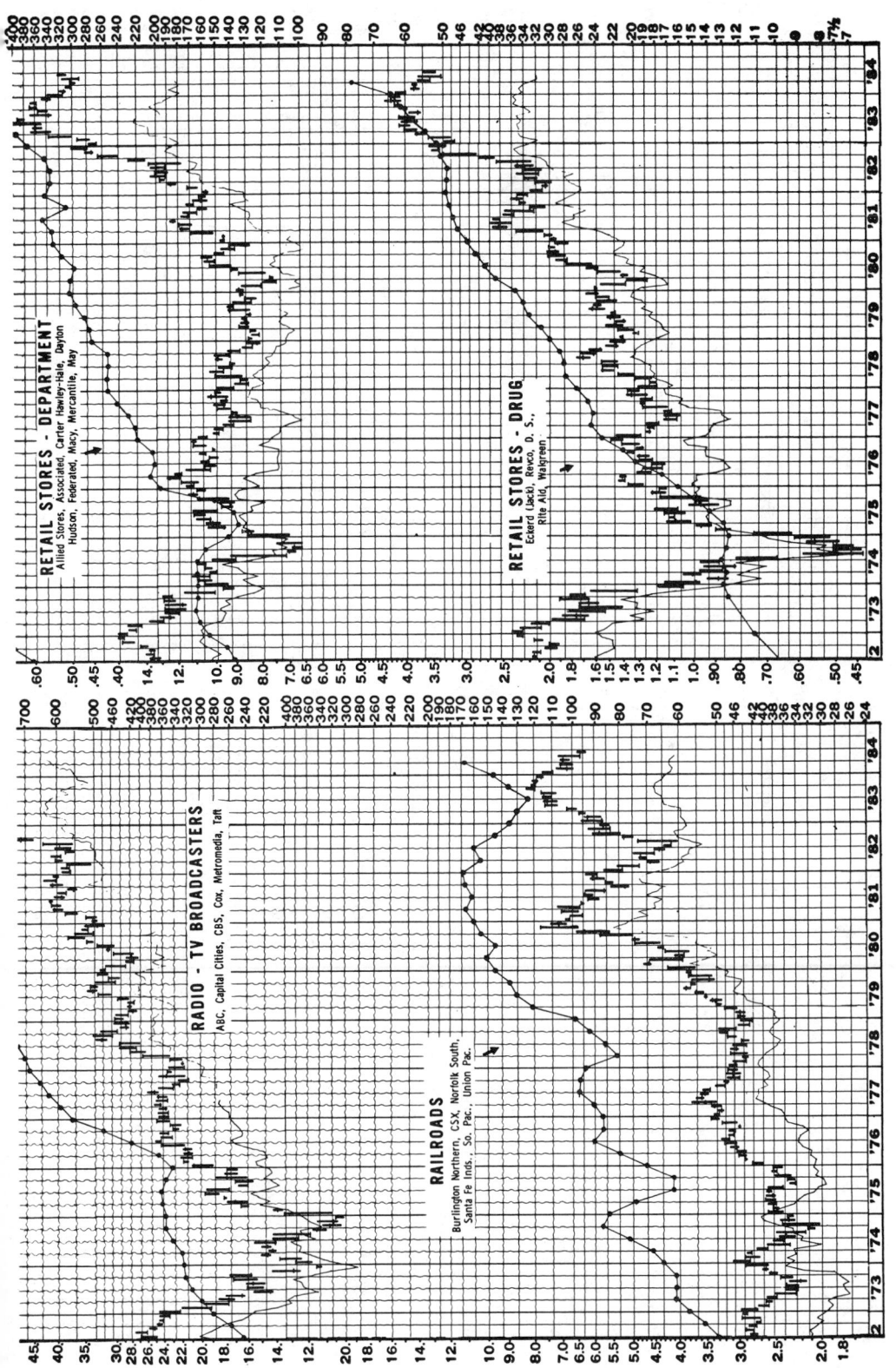

RETAIL STORES - DEPARTMENT
Allied Stores, Associated, Carter Hawley-Hale, Dayton Hudson, Federated, Macy, Mercantile, May

RETAIL STORES - DRUG
Eckerd (Jack), Revco, D. S.,
Rite Aid, Walgreen.

RADIO - TV BROADCASTERS
ABC, Capital Cities, CBS, Cox, Metromedia, Taft

RAILROADS
Burlington Northern, CSX, Norfolk South,
Santa Fe Inds., So. Pac., Union Pac.

297

STOCK MARKET AVERAGES BY INDUSTRY GROUP (continued)

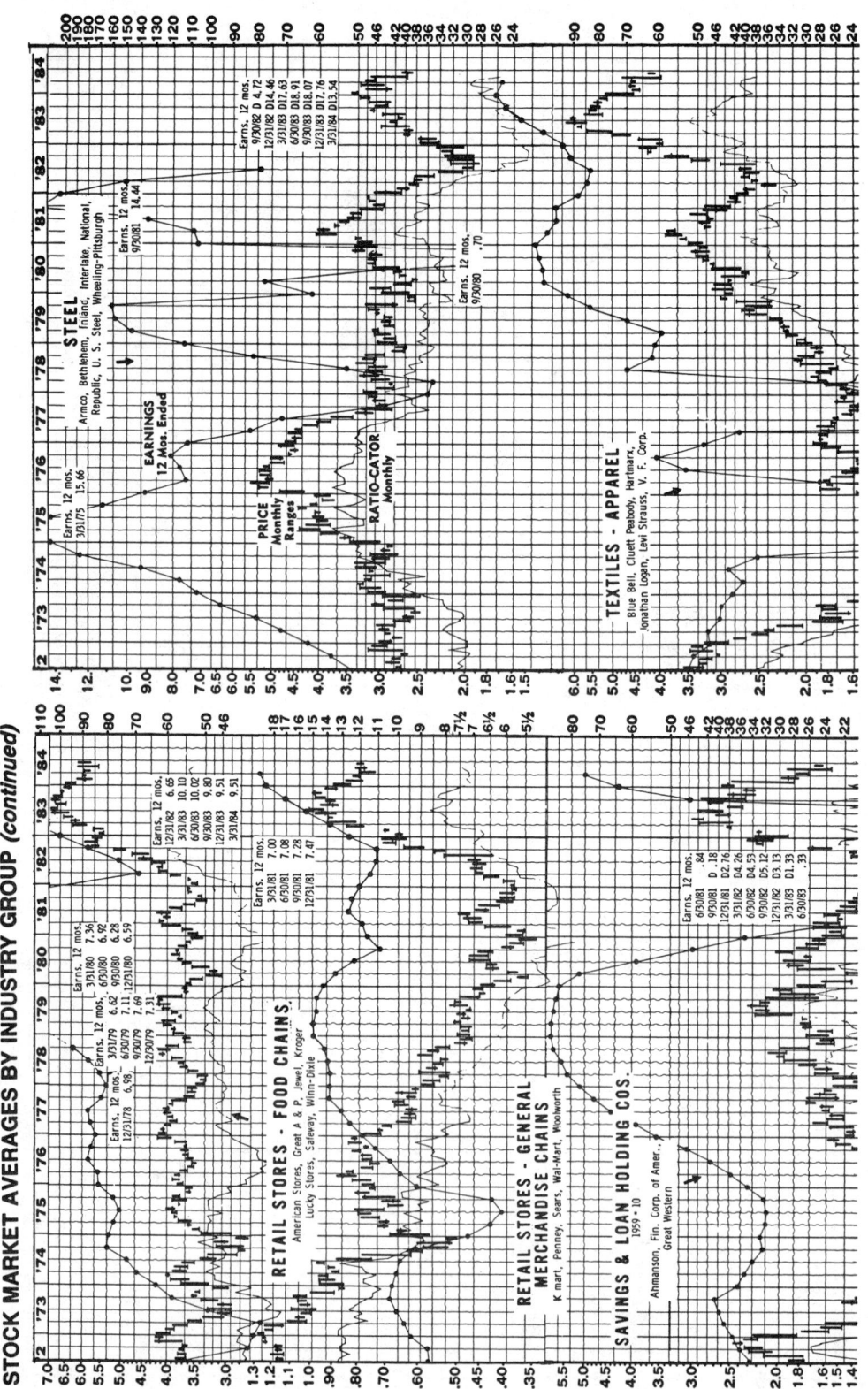

STEEL
Armco, Bethlehem, Inland, Interlake, National, Republic, U. S. Steel, Wheeling-Pittsburgh

Earns. 12 mos.
3/31/75   15.66

Earns. 12 mos.   14.44
9/30/81

Earns. 12 mos.
9/30/82   D 4.72
12/31/82   D14.46
3/31/83   D17.63
6/30/83   D18.91
9/30/83   D18.07
12/31/83   D17.76
3/31/84   D13.54

EARNINGS
12 Mos. Ended

PRICE
Monthly
Ranges

RATIO-CATOR
Monthly

Earns. 12 mos.
9/30/80   .70

TEXTILES - APPAREL
Blue Bell, Cluett Peabody, Hartmarx, Jonathan Logan, Levi Strauss, V. F. Corp.

RETAIL STORES - FOOD CHAINS
American Stores, Great A & P, Jewel, Kroger
Lucky Stores, Safeway, Winn-Dixie

Earns. 12 mos.   3/31/80   7.36
Earns. 12 mos.   6/30/80   6.92
12/31/79   7.31   9/30/80   6.28
9/30/79   7.69   12/31/80   6.59
6/30/79   7.11
3/31/79   6.62
Earns. 12 mos.
12/31/78   6.98

Earns. 12 mos.
3/31/81   7.00
6/30/81   7.08
9/30/81   7.28
12/31/81   7.47

Earns. 12 mos.
12/31/82   6.65
3/31/83   10.10
6/30/83   10.02
9/30/83   9.80
12/31/83   9.51
3/31/84   9.51

RETAIL STORES - GENERAL MERCHANDISE CHAINS
K mart, Penney, Sears, Wal-Mart, Woolworth

SAVINGS & LOAN HOLDING COS.
1959 - 10
Ahmanson, Fin. Corp. of Amer.,
Great Western

Earns. 12 mos.
6/30/81   .84
9/30/81   D. 18
12/31/81   D2.76
3/31/82   D4.26
6/30/82   D4.53
9/30/82   D5.12
12/31/82   D3.13
3/31/83   D1.33
6/30/83   .33

298

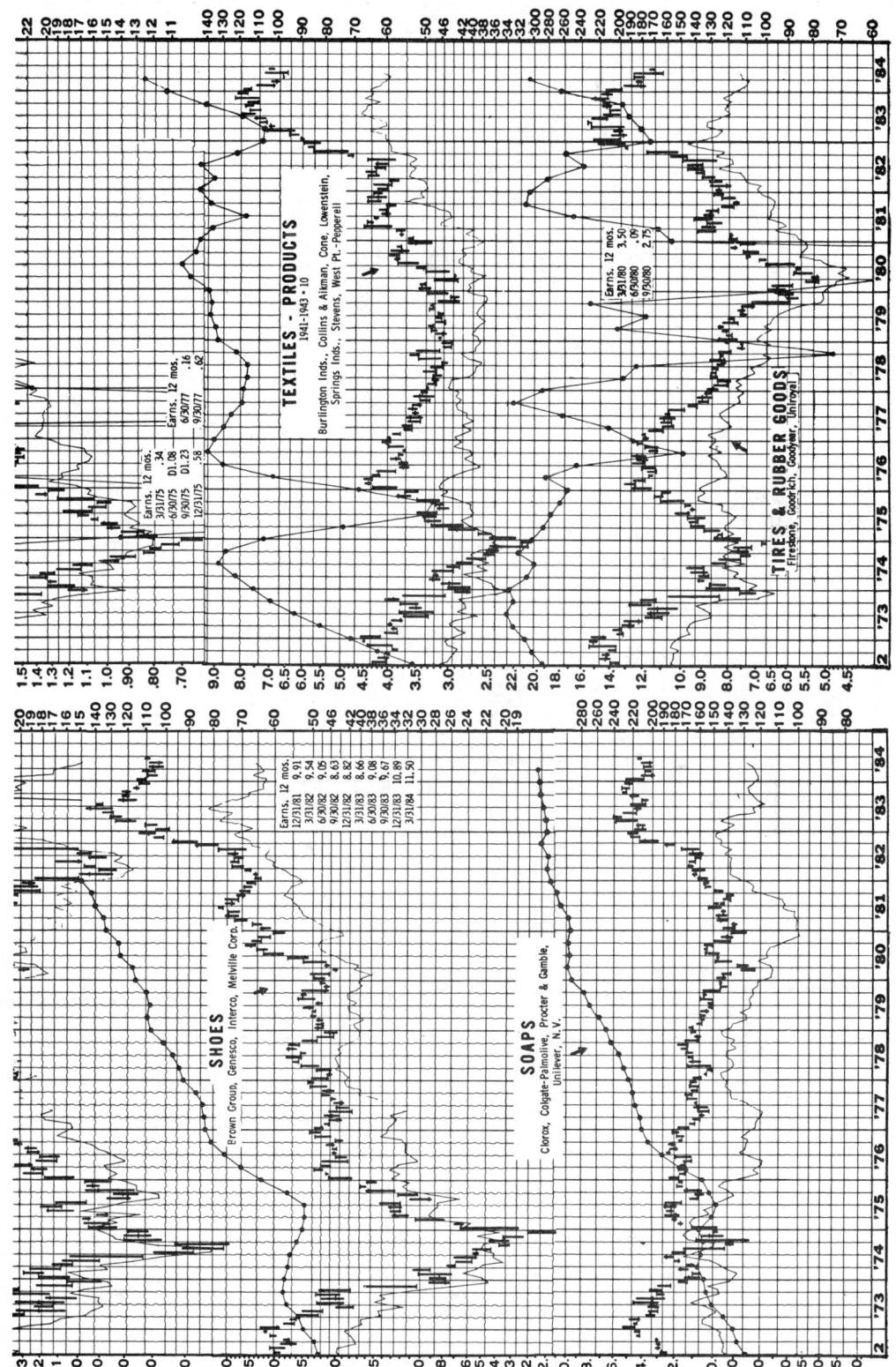

TEXTILES - PRODUCTS
1941-1943 • 10

Burlington Inds., Collins & Aikman, Cone, Lowenstein,
Springs Inds., Stevens, West Pt.-Pepperell

Earns. 12 mos.
3/31/75   D1.08
-6/30/75   .34
9/30/75   D1.23
12/31/75   .58

Earns. 12 mos.
6/30/77   .16
9/30/77   .62

Earns. 12 mos.
3/31/80   3.50
6/30/80   .09
9/30/80   2.75

TIRES & RUBBER GOODS
Firestone, Goodrich, Goodyear, Uniroyal

SHOES
Brown Group, Genesco, Interco, Melville Corp.

Earns. 12 mos.
12/31/81   9.91
3/31/82   9.54
6/30/82   9.05
9/30/82   8.63
12/31/82   8.82
3/31/83   8.66
6/30/83   9.08
9/30/83   9.67
12/31/83 10.89
3/31/84   11.50

SOAPS
Clorox, Colgate-Palmolive, Procter & Gamble,
Unilever, N.V.

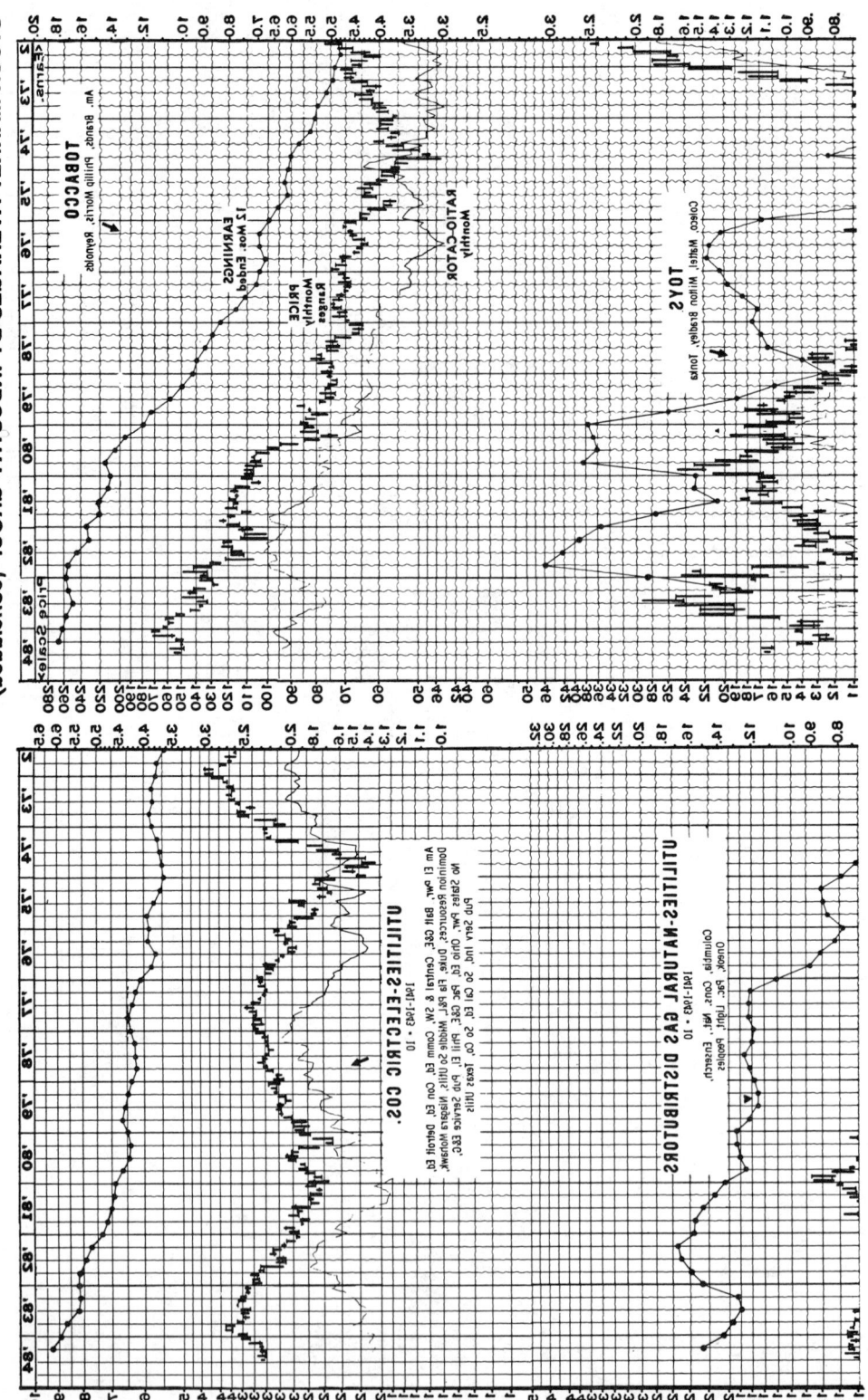

STOCK MARKET AVERAGES BY INDUSTRY GROUP (concluded)

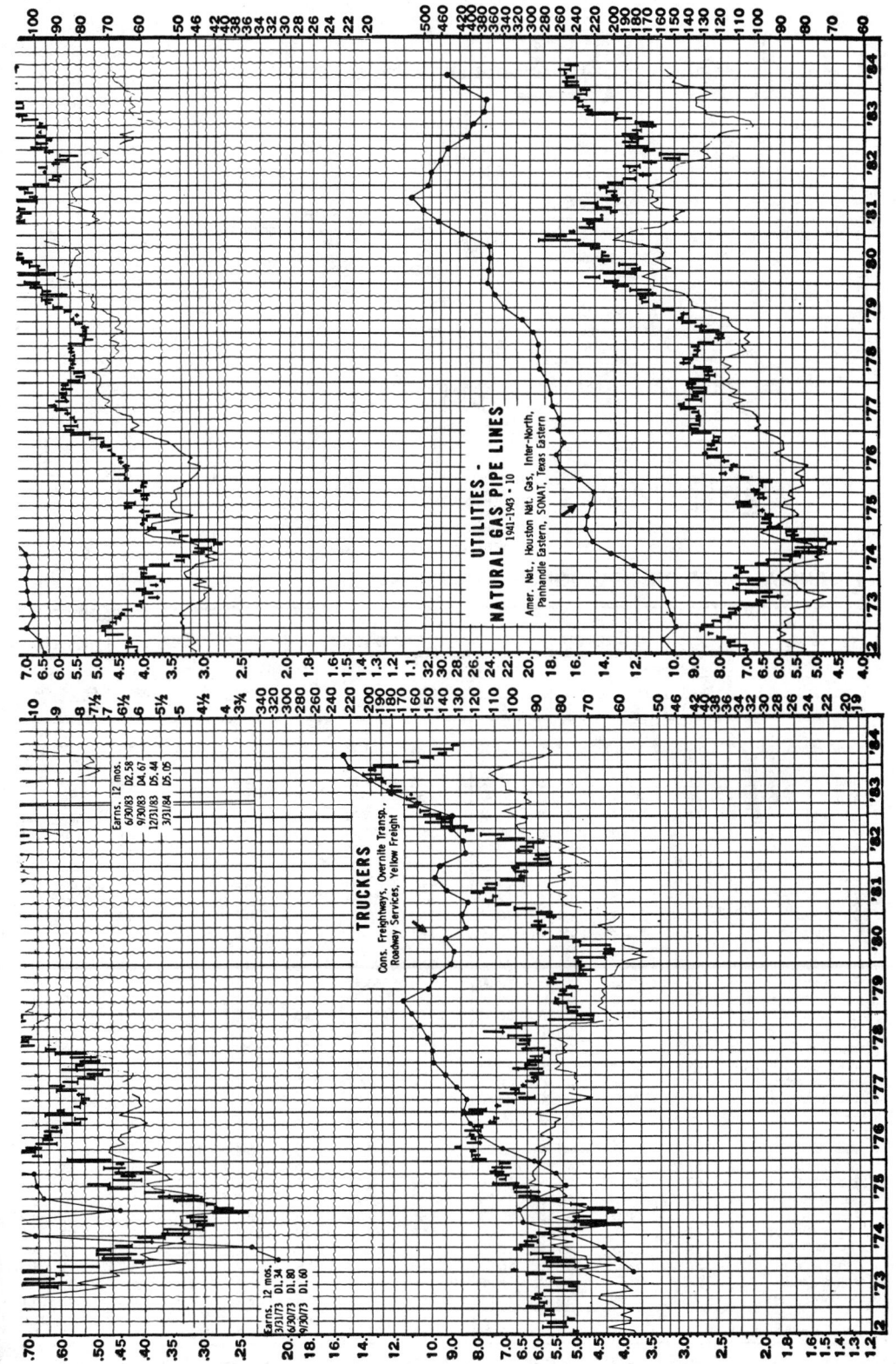

TRUCKERS

Cons. Freightways, Overnite Transp.,
Roadway Services, Yellow Freight

Earns. 12 mos.
3/31/73   D1.34
6/30/73   D1.80
9/30/73   D1.60

UTILITIES -
NATURAL GAS PIPE LINES
1941-1943 - 10

Amer. Nat., Houston Nat. Gas, Inter-North,
Panhandle Eastern, SONAT, Texas Eastern

Earns. 12 mos.
6/30/83   D2.58
9/30/83   D4.67
12/31/83 D5.44
3/31/84   D5.05

Components Dow Jones Stock Averages

Industrials

Allied Corp.	General Electric	Owens-Illinois
Aluminum Co.	General Foods	Procter & Gamb
Amer Brands	General Motors	Sears Roebuck
Amer Can	Goodyear	Std Oil of Calif
Amer Express	Inco	Texaco
Amer Tel & Tel	IBM	Union Carbide
Bethlehem Steel	Inter Harvester	United Technologies
Du Pont	Inter Paper	US Steel
Eastman Kodak	Merck	Westinghouse El
Exxon	Minnesota M&M	Woolworth

Transportation

AMR Corp.	Eastern Air Lines	Southern Pacific
Burlington North	Norfolk Southern	Transway Int'l
CSX Corp	Northwest Air	Trans World
Canadian Pacific	Overnite Trans	UAL Inc
Carolina Freight	Pan Am World Air	Union Pac Corp
Consolid Freight	Rio Grande Indus	USAir Group
Delta Air Lines	Santa Fe Indust	

Utilities

Am Elec Power	Consol Nat Gas	Panhandle E Cp
Cleveland E III	Detroit Edison	Peoples Energy
Colum-Gas Sys	Houston Indust	Phila Elec
Comwlth Edison	Niag Mohawk P	Pub Serv E&G
Consol Edison	Pacific Gas & El	Sou Cal Edison

Source: Reprinted by courtesy of Barron's *National Business and Financial Weekly*.

FINANCIAL DATA ON DOW JONES INDUSTRIALS

	History				Earnings			P/E Ratio			Dvds	
	52-Week		5-Year		Last	%	5-Yr.		5-Year Avg		Indic.	
	High	Low	High	Low	12Mos	Ch	Growth	Today	High	Low	Amt	Yield
	$	$	$	$	$	%	%	-	-	-	$	%
Dow Jones Ind. ...	1287.20	1086.57	1287.20	759.13	90.84	208.97	-12	12.3	42.6	9.4	57.66	5.2
Allied Corp	38.78	28.63	41.19	19.00	4.49	-2.18	2	6.6	7.7	4.6	1.80	6.1
Alum Co Am	48.63	30.75	48.63	21.88	4.37	NE	-13	7.4	10.9	7.0	1.20	3.7
Am Brands	62.50	48.75	62.50	23.81	6.59	3.29	10	8.6	7.5	5.3	3.75	6.6
Am Can	55.00	39.00	55.00	25.75	3.92	250.00	-12	10.9	13.9	9.7	2.90	6.8
Am Express Co ...	45.88	25.00	49.59	12.25	2.27	-29.06	2	12.2	11.3	6.8	1.28	4.6
Am Tel & T	21.25	14.88	21.25	14.88	NA	NA	NA	NA	NA	NA	1.20	6.7
Bethlehem Stl	29.50	16.13	32.00	14.50	-6.65	NE	-93	NE	7.0	4.7	.60	3.7
Chevron Cp	40.25	31.25	58.75	22.19	4.65	15.38	2	6.7	8.2	5.1	2.40	7.7
DuPont	59.00	42.38	59.00	30.00	5.40	52.54	-4	8.4	10.4	6.8	3.00	6.6
Eastman Kodak	77.50	60.25	98.13	42.88	3.41	-52.11	-3	21.8	14.6	9.9	3.55	4.8
Exxon	43.13	34.75	44.38	24.38	6.31	24.21	8	6.4	6.8	4.9	3.40	8.4
Gen Electric	59.00	46.00	59.00	22.00	4.72	11.85	13	10.9	10.8	7.6	2.00	3.9
Gen Foods	56.00	42.88	56.00	23.50	7.12	26.24	8	7.7	7.5	5.3	2.50	4.5
Gen Motors	80.50	61.00	80.50	33.88	14.87	212.39	13	4.6	22.1	13.1	3.85	5.7
Goodyear Tire	34.25	23.00	36.88	10.75	3.32	11.04	5	7.2	9.0	5.7	1.40	5.8
Inco Ltd	18.75	8.63	33.25	7.88	-2.23	NE	-61	NE	13.2	8.0	.20	2.2
Intl Bus Mach	134.25	99.00	134.25	48.38	9.82	21.38	17	11.1	13.5	9.1	3.80	3.5
Intl Harvester	14.75	5.13	45.50	2.75	-7.34	NE	-110	NE	3.8	2.9	.00	.0
Intl Paper	60.00	46.00	60.00	30.50	3.44	18.21	-10	13.9	13.3	9.3	2.40	5.0
Merck & Co	104.63	78.25	104.63	58.25	6.25	10.23	7	13.2	16.5	12.4	3.00	3.6
Minn Mng Mfg	89.50	69.25	90.50	45.88	5.84	8.15	3	13.1	13.1	9.4	3.40	4.5
Owens-Illinois	41.63	31.13	41.63	17.38	3.19	168.07	-8	11.3	11.2	7.8	1.68	4.7
Proct & Gambl	60.25	45.63	63.25	31.38	5.29	4.34	12	10.2	11.8	8.9	2.60	4.8
Sears, Roebuck ...	42.75	29.50	45.13	14.38	3.95	45.76	12	8.2	10.7	7.0	1.76	5.4
Texaco	48.38	32.00	54.38	23.63	4.81	1.26	-6	6.7	6.5	4.4	3.00	9.3
Union Carbide	72.88	47.75	73.88	34.00	4.19	27.74	-12	11.7	11.0	7.7	3.40	6.9
US Steel Corp	33.25	22.00	35.25	16.00	-9.55	NE	-62	NE	9.2	5.9	1.00	4.4
Utd Technol	37.19	28.50	38.38	15.63	3.89	17.88	9	8.7	9.3	5.9	1.40	4.1
Westinghouse	28.38	19.75	28.38	8.25	2.68	-4.63	8	8.1	8.0	5.1	1.00	4.6
Woolworth FW	39.38	29.88	39.38	15.88	3.81	35.11	-8	9.2	8.8	5.3	1.80	5.1
Unweighted Avg. ..	52.57	37.90	56.35	23.73	3.55	36.55	-5	9.7	10.6	7.0	2.18	5.1

Source: *The Media General Financial Weekly*, Media General Financial Services, 301 East Grace Street, Richmond, VA 23261, July 30, 1984.

DOW JONES INDUSTRIAL, TRANSPORTATION AND UTILITY AVERAGES

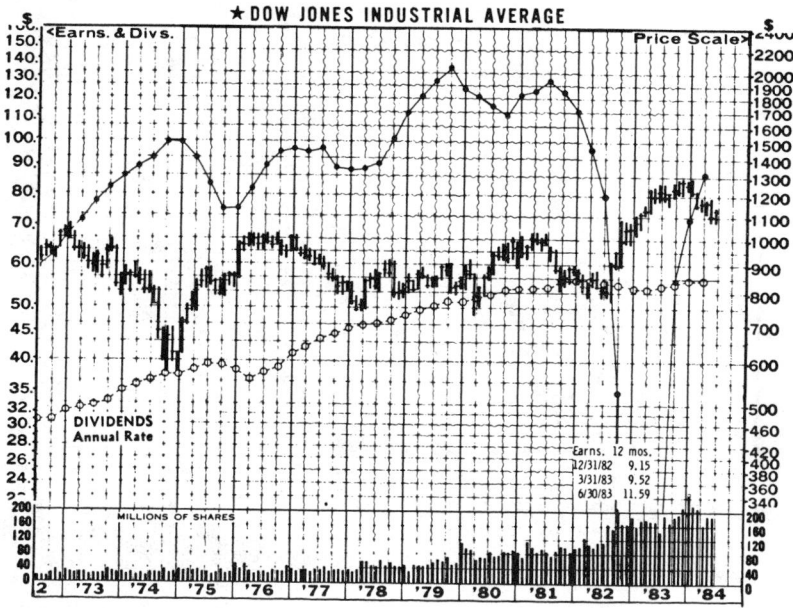

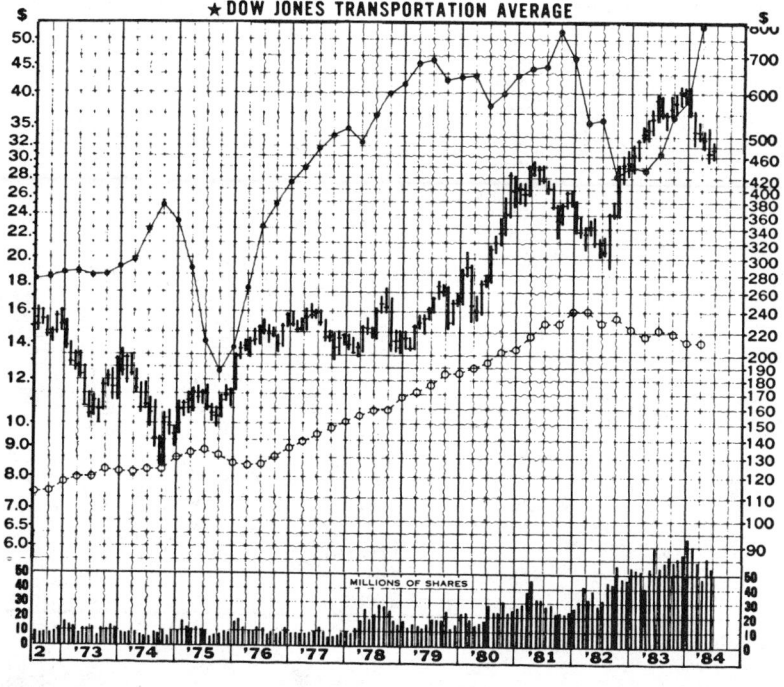

DOW JONES INDUSTRIAL, TRANSPOR-
TATION AND UTILITY AVERAGES *(continued)*

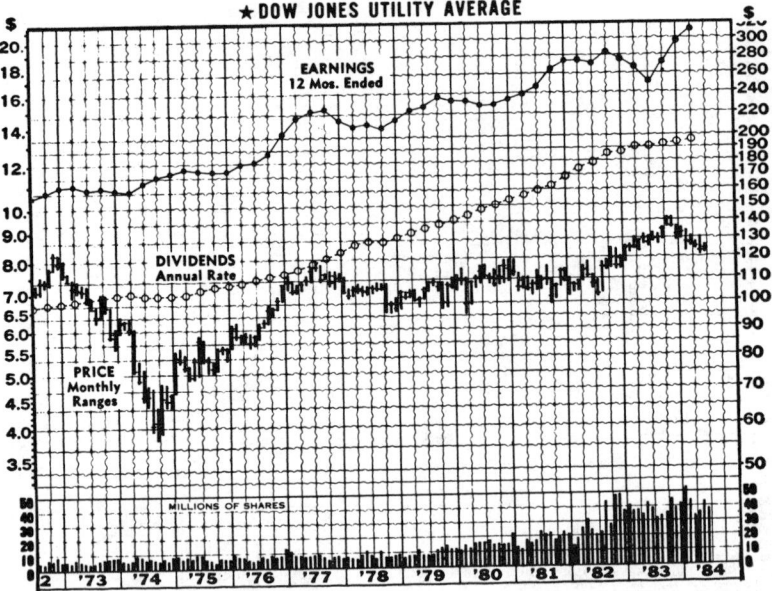

Source: *5-Trend CYCLI-GRAPHS.* The charts are courtesy of Securities Research Company, a division of United Business Service, 208 Newbury Street, Boston, MA 02116, July quarterly edition, 1984.

SHARES SOLD ON REGISTERED EXCHANGES

Year	Number of shares (millions)			Percent of total		
	NYSE	**ASE**	**Other exchanges**	**NYSE**	**ASE**	**Other exchanges**
1935	513.6	84.7	63.6	77.6%	12.8%	9.6%
1940	282.7	47.9	41.4	76.0	12.9	11.1
1945	496.0	152.4	96.1	66.6	20.5	12.9
1950	655.3	114.9	86.9	76.5	13.4	10.1
1955	820.5	243.9	148.0	67.7	20.1	12.2
1960	958.3	300.6	129.6	69.0	21.6	9.3
1965	1,809.4	582.2	195.3	69.9	22.5	7.5
1966	2,204.8	730.9	252.2	69.2	22.9	7.9
1967	2,885.8	1,290.2	327.8	64.1	28.6	7.3
1968	3,298.7	1,570.7	442.6	62.1	29.6	8.3
1969	3,173.6	1,341.0	448.8	63.9	27.0	9.0
1970	3,213.1	878.5	444.1	70.8	19.4	9.8
1971	4,265.3	1,049.3	601.1	72.1	17.7	10.2
1972	4,496.2	1,103.2	699.8	71.4	17.5	11.1
1973	4,336.6	740.4	653.2	75.7	12.9	11.4
1974	3,821.9	475.3	541.9	79.0	9.8	11.2
1975	5,056.5	540.9	637.6	81.1	8.7	10.2
1976	5,649.2	637.0	749.5	80.3	9.1	10.7
1977	5,613.3	651.9	758.2	79.9	9.3	10.8
1978	7,618.0	992.2	872.6	80.3	10.5	9.2
1979	8,675.3	1,161.3	1,026.2	79.9	10.7	9.4
1980	12,389.9	1,658.8	1,437.0	80.0	10.7	9.3
1981	12,843.1	1,472.3	1,594.9	80.7	9.3	10.0
1982	18,210.8	1,582.6	2,662.1	81.1	7.0	11.9
1983	24,253.5	2,209.4	3,683.8	80.5	7.3	12.2

Source: New York Stock Exchange *1984 Fact Book.*

MARKET VALUE OF SHARES SOLD ON REGISTERED EXCHANGES

Year	Market value (millions)			Percent of total		
	NYSE	ASE	Other exchanges	NYSE	ASE	Other exchanges
1935	$ 13,335	$ 1,205	$ 736	87.3%	7.9%	4.8%
1940	7,166	643	595	85.3	7.7	7.0
1945	13,462	1,728	1,036	83.0	10.6	6.4
1950	18,725	1,481	1,571	86.0	6.8	7.2
1955	32,745	2,593	2,530	86.5	6.8	6.7
1960	37,960	4,176	3,083	83.9	9.2	6.8
1965	73,200	8,612	7,402	82.0	9.7	8.3
1966	98,565	14,130	10,339	80.1	11.5	8.4
1967	125,329	23,111	13,318	77.5	14.3	8.2
1968	144,978	34,775	16,605	73.8	17.7	8.5
1969	129,603	30,074	15,621	73.9	17.2	8.9
1970	103,063	14,266	13,579	78.7	10.9	10.4
1971	147,098	17,664	20,169	79.5	9.6	10.9
1972	159,700	20,453	23,873	78.3	10.0	11.7
1973	146,451	10,430	21,156	82.3	5.9	11.9
1974	99,178	5,048	14,023	83.9	4.3	11.9
1975	133,819	5,678	17,595	85.2	3.6	11.2
1976	164,545	7,468	22,956	84.4	3.8	11.8
1977	157,250	8,532	21,421	84.0	4.6	11.4
1978	210,426	15,204	23,625	84.4	6.1	9.5
1979	251,098	20,596	28,279	83.7	6.9	9.4
1980	397,670	34,696	43,485	83.6	7.3	9.1
1981	415,913	26,385	48,390	84.8	5.4	9.9
1982	514,263	20,731	69,054	85.1	3.4	11.4
1983	815,113	31,501	110,505	85.2	3.3	11.5

Source: Securities & Exchange Commission.

Source: New York Stock Exchange *1984 Fact Book.*

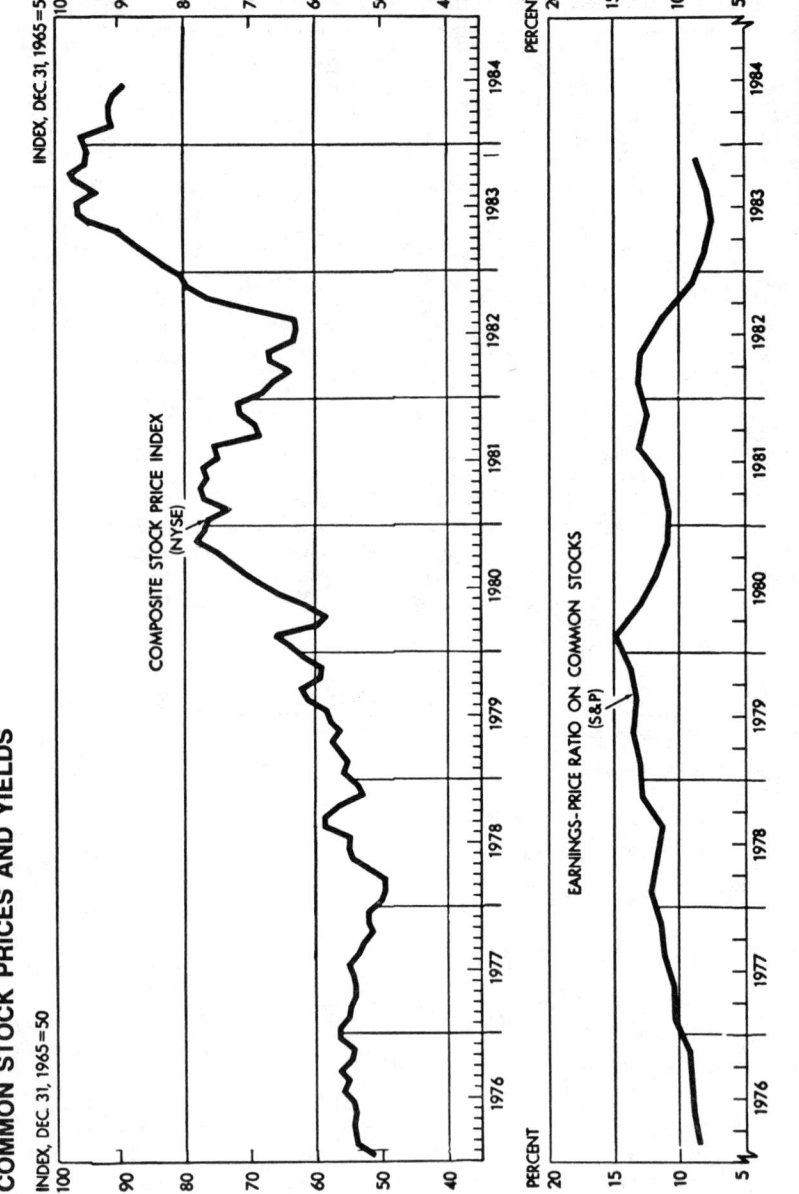

COMMON STOCK PRICES AND YIELDS

INDEX, DEC. 31, 1965=50

COMPOSITE STOCK PRICE INDEX (NYSE)

EARNINGS-PRICE RATIO ON COMMON STOCKS (S&P)

SOURCES: NEW YORK STOCK EXCHANGE AND STANDARD & POOR'S CORPORATION

COUNCIL OF ECONOMIC ADVISERS

| Period | Common stock prices [1] | | | | | | | Common stock yields (percent) [5] | |
| | New York Stock Exchange indexes (Dec. 31, 1965=50) [2] | | | | | Dow-Jones industrial average [3] | Standard & Poor's composite index (1941–43=10) [4] | Dividend-price ratio | Earnings-price ratio |
	Composite	Industrial	Transportation	Utility	Finance				
1978	53.70	58.23	43.50	39.22	56.65	820.23	96.02	5.28	12.03
1979	58.32	64.76	47.34	38.20	61.42	844.40	103.01	5.47	13.46
1980	68.10	78.70	60.61	37.35	64.25	891.41	118.78	5.26	12.66
1981	74.02	85.44	72.61	38.91	73.52	932.92	128.05	5.20	11.96
1982	68.93	78.18	60.41	39.75	71.99	884.36	119.71	5.81	11.60
1983	92.63	107.45	89.36	47.00	95.34	1,190.34	160.41	4.40	8.04
1983: June	96.43	112.52	92.22	46.76	101.22	1,221.47	166.39	4.26	7.49
July	96.74	113.21	92.91	46.61	99.60	1,213.93	166.96	4.21	
Aug	93.96	109.50	88.06	46.94	95.76	1,189.21	162.42	4.35	
Sept	96.70	112.76	94.56	48.16	97.00	1,237.04	167.16	4.24	8.01
Oct	96.78	112.87	95.41	48.73	94.79	1,252.20	167.65	4.25	
Nov	95.36	110.77	97.68	48.50	94.48	1,250.01	165.23	4.31	
Dec	94.92	110.65	98.79	47.00	94.25	1,257.64	164.36	4.32	8.52
1984: Jan	96.16	112.16	97.98	47.43	95.79	1,258.89	166.39	4.27	
Feb	90.60	105.44	86.33	45.67	89.95	1,164.46	157.25	4.59	
Mar	90.66	105.92	86.10	44.83	89.50	1,161.97	157.44	4.63	
Apr	90.67	106.56	83.61	43.86	88.22	1,152.71	157.60	4.64	
May	90.07	105.94	81.62	r44.22	85.06	1,143.42	156.55	4.72	
June p	88.28	104.03	79.30	43.67	80.75	1,120.57	153.12	4.86	
Week ended:									
1984: May 26	87.91	103.39	78.18	43.64	81.95	1,113.25	152.92	4.83	
June 2	86.95	102.36	78.02	43.16	79.84	1,108.26	151.11	4.93	
9	89.00	104.94	80.78	43.74	81.58	1,130.80	154.62	4.79	
16	87.36	102.90	77.93	43.47	79.55	1,104.24	151.36	4.89	
23	88.58	104.33	79.14	43.94	81.22	1,123.08	153.63	4.82	

[1] Average of daily closing prices.
[2] Includes all the stocks (more than 1,500) listed on the NYSE.
[3] Includes 30 stocks.
[4] Includes 500 stocks.
[5] Standard & Poor's series. Dividend-price ratios based on Wednesday closing prices. Earnings-price ratios based on prices at end of quarter.

NOTE.—All data relate to stocks listed on the New York Stock Exchange (NYSE).

Sources: New York Stock Exchange, Dow-Jones & Company, Inc., and Standard & Poor's Corporation.

Source: *Economic Indicators*, Council of Economic Advisers.

NEW SECURITY ISSUES OF CORPORATIONS (Millions of dollars)

Type of issue or issuer, or use	1981	1982	1983	1983					1984		
				Aug.	Sept.	Oct.	Nov.	Dec.	Jan.	Feb.	Mar.
1 All issues[1,2]	70,441	84,198	98,845	5,941	6,568	6,897r	8,103	6,812	7,691	7,629r	5,442
2 Bonds	45,092	53,636	47,266	2,547	2,865	3,055	4,075	3,173	5,648	5,250r	3,346
Type of offering											
3 Public	38,103	43,838	47,266	2,547	2,865	3,055	4,075	3,173	5,648	5,250r	3,346
4 Private placement	6,989	9,798	n.a.	n.a.	n.a.	n.a.	n.a.	n.a.	n.a.	n.a.	n.a.
Industry group											
5 Manufacturing	12,325	13,123	8,133	200	282	367	22	423	179	452	68
6 Commercial and miscellaneous	5,229	5,681	5,374	458	353	114	23	201	976	626	258
7 Transportation	2,052	1,474	1,086	0	0	0	111	105	10	75	180
8 Public utility	8,963	12,155	7,066	355	590	510	910	120	325	385	521
9 Communication	4,280	2,265	3,380	0	100	50	0	0	210	0	200
10 Real estate and financial	12,243	18,938	22,227	1,534	1,540	2,014	3,009	2,324	3,948	3,712r	2,119
11 Stocks[3]	25,349	30,562	51,579	3,394	3,703	3,842	4,028	3,639	2,043	2,379	2,096
Type											
12 Preferred	1,797	5,113	7,213	247	644	300	433	253	305	425	227
13 Common	23,552	25,449	44,366	3,147	3,059	3,542	3,595	3,386	1,738	1,954	1,869
Industry group											
14 Manufacturing	5,074	5,649	14,135	1,309	962	744	498	649	427	299	387
15 Commercial and miscellaneous	7,557	7,770	13,112	743	997	868	1,498	852	465	616	486
16 Transportation	779	709	2,729	145	165	305	192	413	54	15	105
17 Public utility	5,577	7,517	5,001	263	200	588	622	245	225	45	134
18 Communication	1,778	2,227	1,822	236	0	36	13	12	30	20	18
19 Real estate and financial	4,584	6,690	14,780	698	1,379	1,301	1,145	1,468	842	1,384	966

1. Figures, which represent gross proceeds of issues maturing in more than one year, sold for cash in the United States, are principal amount or number of units multiplied by offering price. Excludes offerings of less than $100,000, secondary offerings, undefined or exempted issues as defined in the Securities Act of 1933, employee stock plans, investment companies other than closed-end, intracorporate transactions, and sales to foreigners.

2. Data for 1983 include only public offerings.
3. Beginning in August 1981, gross stock offerings include new equity volume from swaps of debt for equity.

SOURCE. Securities and Exchange Commission and the Board of Governors of the Federal Reserve System.

Source: *Federal Reserve Bulletin*, Board of Governors of the Federal Reserve.

How to Understand and Analyze Financial Statement‚

Fred B. Renwick†

Analyzing financial statements in corporate annual reports can be easy, fun, and rewarding, if you know what to look for. This short essay explains in a nutshell what to look for and how to analyze financial statements.

Only four statements are important to understand and analyze, namely:

- The *balance sheet*, which states the financial condition of the corporation as of one particular date: the date posted at the top of the statement.
- The *income statement*, which shows the amount of earnings for the year currently ending, and conveys information regarding the efficiency and profitability of the business.
- The *statement of retained earnings*, which gives further information regarding one of the lines on the balance sheet, and also shows the division of net income for the year between dividend payout to stockholders and earnings retained and reinvested in the business.
- The *statement of sources and uses of funds*, which gives further information regarding total current assets and total current liabilities as stated on the balance sheet; and shows the net changes during the year in working capital.

Additionally, corporate annual reports usually contain supplementary information which expands upon items in the four basic statements, and includes: (1) a letter or report of independent accountants and auditors addressed to stockholders and directors of the company certifying and validating the figures in the four statements, (2) notes which report material information regarding line items in each statement, (3) segment information which summarizes selected information by industry and geographic segments, (4) restatement pursuant to Financial Accounting Standards Board (FASB) *Statement of Financial Accounting Standards No. 33* to account for effects of inflation and changing prices on items in the four primary statements, and (5) a long-term (5 or 10-year) summary of selected items from the four primary statements.

The following section explains each statement in detail, Section II explains how to ana-

lyze the statements, Section III explains notes and supplementary information.

1. FOUR FINANCIAL STATEMENTS: WHAT TO LOOK FOR

BALANCE SHEETS

Exhibit 1 shows a balance sheet for Universal Manufacturing Corporation (UMC), a hypothetical company which produces and distributes goods and services in the health industry. Universal's single line of business is divided into two industry segments: human and animal health products, and environmental health products and services.

Observe the format of Universal's balance sheet, the *report form*, where total assets, $26 million, are itemized first and total financing (total liabilities and stockholders' equity), $26 million, are itemized below the asset section. Some corporations prefer to use the *account form*, where assets are listed on the left side of the form and liabilities and owners' equity sections are listed to the right of the asset section. UMC is using the *report form*.

The balance sheet shows the ownership of total corporate assets as of the date of the statement. For example, the following calculation implies that if UMC's tangible assets were liquidated as of the date posted at the top of the balance sheet, $17.8 million would be available for distribution among the preferred and common stockholders.

Total assets owned by UMC	$26,000,000
Less: Intangibles	200,000
Total tangible assets owned by UMC	$25,800,000
Amount required to pay total liabilities	8,000,000
Amount remaining for the stockholders	$17,800,000

Further, the above example illustrates a critical point: the difference between *current market value* (the amount UMC's assets would really bring if sold) versus the *accounting book value* (the $17.8 million). Relationships exist between market and book values, but accounting statements (except for FASB *No. 33*) are factual reports of *book*, not *market*, values of corporate assets.

The following paragraphs explain each line entry on balance sheets.

Starting at the top of the balance sheet, after the name of the corporation, title, and date of the statement, total assets are itemized, with current assets (total, $13.6 million) always first.

* See also the definition of financial terms, page 363.

† Fred B. Renwick is Professor of Finance at the Graduate School of Business Administration, New York University, New York, N.Y.

EXHIBIT 1

UNIVERSAL MANUFACTURING CORPORATION
Balance Sheet
December 31, 1983

Assets	1983	1982
Current assets		
Cash	$ 350,000	$ 250,000
Marketable securities at cost		
(market value: 1983, $2,980,000; 1982, $1,900,000)	2,850,000	1,830,000
Accounts receivable		
Less: Allowance for bad debt: 1983, $24,000; 1982, $21,000	4,800,000	4,370,000
Inventories	5,600,000	4,950,000
Total current assets	$13,600,000	$11,400,000
Fixed assets (property, plant, and equipment)		
Land	$ 734,000	$ 661,000
Building	5,762,000	5,258,000
Machinery	11,435,000	10,011,000
Office equipment	614,000	561,000
	18,545,000	16,491,000
Less: Accumulated depreciation	6,435,000	5,671,000
Net fixed assets	12,110,000	10,820,000
Prepayments and deferred charges	90,000	61,600
Intangibles (goodwill, patent, trademarks)	200,000	200,000
Total assets	$26,000,000	$22,481,600

Liabilities	1983	1982
Current liabilities		
Accounts payable	$ 2,910,000	$ 2,300,000
Notes payable	1,420,000	730,000
Accrued expenses payable	430,000	350,000
Federal income taxes payable	1,240,000	1,320,000
Total current liabilities	$ 6,000,000	$ 4,700,000
Long-term liabilities		
First mortgage bonds, 8% interest, due 2003	$ 2,000,000	$ 2,000,000
Total liabilities	$ 8,000,000	$ 6,700,000
Stockholders' Equity		
Capital stock		
Preferred stock, 6% cumulative, $100 par value each;		
authorized, issued, and outstanding 13,600 shares	1,360,000	1,360,000
Common stock, 30 cents par value each; authorized, issued,		
and outstanding 760,000 shares	228,000	228,000
Capital surplus	1,112,000	1,112,000
Accumulated retained earnings	15,300,000	13,081,600
Total stockholders' equity	$18,000,000	$15,781,600
Total liabilities and stockholders' equity	$26,000,000	$22,481,600

Current assets consist of:

1. *Cash,* $350,000, which is what you would expect, namely pocket-book currency and coins in the treasurer's office, plus demand deposits at a commercial bank. Cash is synonymous with liquidity,

2. *Marketable securities,* $2.85 million, which usually are cash equivalents or highly liquid securities such as Treasury Bills of the federal government or negotiable certificates of deposit (CDs), or demand notes issued by large corporations,

3. *Accounts receivable,* $4.8 million, which consist of payments due from customers who purchased UMC's goods and services on credit and have not paid yet but are scheduled to pay within the next few months. Since a small fraction of customers might never pay (because of death, financial disaster, flood, or other catastrophe), an allowance is made, $24,000, pursuant to good accounting practices for bad debts,

4. *Inventories,* $5.6 million, which consist of (a) finished goods in stock and ready for sale or shipment, (b) work and merchandise in process, and (c) supplies and raw materials inventories; and are priced on the balance sheet at the lower of cost or market on either a first-in-first-out (Fifo) or last-in-first-out (Lifo) basis. Pricing policy is usually stated in a note.

Total current assets, $13.6 million, are the sum of the four aforecited figures and usually are earmarked for use within the coming 12 months. In other words, *current* means within the next 12 months.

Fixed assets (property, plant and equipment) are the permanent tangible capital owned by the business, and are listed *at cost* (original purchase price) next on the balance sheet; and consists of:

1. *Land*, $734,000, or ground upon which buildings or other assets such as forests, air or water rights, and the like are built,
2. *Building*, $5.762 million, which are structures such as offices, warehouses, and the like where business is conducted,
3. *Machinery*, $11.435 million, which are mechanical apparatuses for increasing productivity and economic efficiency,
4. *Office equipment*, $614,000, which is what you would expect, namely desks, typewriters, copiers, and the like.

Accumulated depreciation, $6.435 million, is the total depreciation (deterioration of property, plant, and equipment due to physical wear and tear) accumulated to date for accounting purposes against UMC's assets. It is important to know about three concepts of depreciation, namely: (1) depreciation calculated for tax purposes which is figured pursuant to the Tax Code to benefit from allowable accelerated rates of depreciation, (2) accounting depreciation, which can be either straight-line or accelerated and is usually explained in a note, (3) economic depreciation, which comes from technological obsolescence and deterioration in ability to continue generating future income at current rates due to changes in demand and markets for the goods and services produced by UMC. The balance sheet states only number two, accounting depreciation.

Net fixed assets, $12,110,000, are the sum of the four above figures, minus accounting depreciation; and are used by the business to generate future (beyond the coming 12 months) income.

Prepayments and deferred charges, $90,000, state total amounts paid in advance for assets not yet obtained (such as paid-up premiums on a fire insurance policy covering the next five years, or rental paid on computers for the next three years); and for benefits to be received in future years for expenditures already made (such as for research and development, moving the business to a new location, or expenses incurred in bringing a new product to market).

Intangibles, $200,000, are assets such as goodwill, trademarks, franchises, patents, copyrights, and the like which have no physical existence; yet are valuable in producing business income.

Total assets, $26 million, are current, plus fixed, plus prepayments and deferred charges, plus intangibles; and state the size of the business and are the total property owned by the business.

Look next at the lower part of the balance sheet, which concerns the financing of the business. Financing must come from either borrowing (liabilities) or ownership equity.

Underneath the asset section of the balance sheet (or on the right side if the company uses the account form), total current liabilities, $6 million, always are itemized next, then long-term liabilities, $2 million, then finally stockholders' equity of $18 million.

Total current liabilities consist of bills due and payable by UMC within the next 12 months, all of which fall into one of four categories:

1. *Accounts payable*, $2.91 million, which are bills currently owed and due to creditors,
2. *Notes payable*, $1.42 million, which are current obligations owed to a bank or other short-term lender,
3. *Accrued expenses payable*, $430,000, include wages due employees, fees to attorneys, current pension or retirement obligations, and the like.
4. *Federal income taxes payable*, $1.24 million, is the current tax payable to the Internal Revenue Service, and is sufficiently important to merit a line of its own on the corporate balance sheet.

Long-term liabilities, $2 million for UMC, can include straight debt (like UMC's which pays 8 percent interest and matures in 2003), convertible bonds (bonds which pay interest like straight bonds but are convertible upon demand of the bond owner into a stated number of shares of common stock), or "other" long-term debt (like pollution control and industrial revenue bonds or sinking-fund debentures). UMC has only straight debt outstanding.

Total liabilities, $8 million, are the sum of current and long-term liabilities and constitute the total financing obtained from borrowings.

Stockholders' equity, $18 million consists of:

1. *Capital stock*, $1.588 million, which includes both preferred stock and common stock but no convertible preferred stock and no warrants or rights to purchase either bonds or common stock,
2. *Capital surplus*, $1.112 million, which is the amount paid in by shareholders over the par or legal value of 30 cents for each common share,
3. *Accumulated retained earnings*, $15.3 million, which are earnings not paid out in dividends but have been retained and reinvested in the business. Further information regarding accumulated retained earnings since inception of the business is set forth below in the *statement of retained earnings*.

Capital stock represents proprietary interest in the company, is represented by stock certificates authorized and issued by the company, and can belong to either of several classes, including:

1. *Preferred stock,* which has preference or takes priority over other shares regarding dividend payout (6 percent in UMC's case), and which can be cumulative, which means that if the company fails to pay dividends for whatever reason for any year, then the 6 percent of $100 or $6 per preferred share accumulates on the books and must be paid before common stockholders can receive future dividends. Total preferred stock authorized and issued by UMC is $100 per share times 13,600 shares or $1.36 million.

2. *Common stock,* which represents the remaining ownership of the company and is entitled to receive a dividend along with fluctuations in value of the stock. Par value is the legal stated value of each common share; so the par value (30 cents per share times 760,000 shares or $228,000) plus the additional amount or capital surplus ($1.112 million) together state the amount UMC received upon issuing 760,000 shares, namely $1.34 million divided by 760,000 or $1.76 per share.

The bottom line, *total liabilities and stockholders equity,* states the financing of the corporation, and shows where UMC obtained the $26 million to buy the total assets itemized at the top of the balance sheet.

We turn next to income statements.

INCOME STATEMENTS

Exhibit 2 shows UMC's income statement, where the important items to look for, after the name of the company, the title, and date of the statement at the heading, are:

1. *Net sales,* which is where most of the business revenue comes from for most businesses, except rental and leasing companies, $23,850,000.

2. *Net Operating Income* (NOI) or profit before interest and taxes, which states profit from business operations, without regard to financing, $5,878,000.

3. *Total Income* before interest and taxes, which states the return on total capital available to the business during the year, $6,220,000.

4. *Less:* provision for federal income tax, $2,240,000.

5. *Total Income,* after tax but before interest deduction, which states the after-tax profitability of the corporation and is widely used in computing cost of capital for a business enterprise, $3,980,000.

EXHIBIT 2

UNIVERSAL MANUFACTURING CORPORATION
Consolidated Income Statement
December 31, 1983 and 1982

	1983	1982
Net sales	$23,850,000	$19,810,000
Cost of sales and operating expenses		
Cost of goods sold	8,940,000	7,209,000
Depreciation	800,000	750,000
Selling and administrating expenses	8,232,000	6,814,000
Operating profit	$ 5,878,000	$ 5,037,000
Other income		
Dividends and interest	342,000	183,000
Total income	$ 6,220,000	$ 5,220,000
Less: Interest on bonds	160,000	160,000
Income before provision for federal income tax	$ 6,060,000	$ 5,060,000
Provision for federal income tax	2,240,000	1,980,000
Net profit for year	$ 3,820,000	$ 3,080,000
Common shares outstanding	760,000	760,000
Net earnings per share	$ 4.92	$ 3.95

Statement of Accumulated Retained Earnings

	1983	1982
Balance January 1	$13,081,600	$11,413,200
Net profit for year	3,820,000	3,080,000
Total	$16,901,600	$14,493,200
Less: Dividends paid on		
Preferred stock	81,600	81,600
Common stock	1,520,000	1,330,000
Balance December 31	$15,300,000	$13,081,600

6. *Net income* (NI) or profit for the year, which states earnings after taxes and after all fixed charges. The net profit for the year is available for (a) dividend payout to preferred stockholders, (b) dividend payout to common stockholders, and (c) retention and reinvestment in the business, $3,820,000.
7. *Net earnings per share* (EPS), which equals total earnings available for distribution to common stockholders ($3.82 million minus 6% dividend owed on 13,600 shares of $100 par value preferred stock, or $3,738,400), divided by 760,000 common shares outstanding, $4.92.

$3,820,000 − 0.06(13,600)($100) =
$3,738,400
$3,738,400/760,000 =
$4.92 per share

Cost of sales and operating expenses falls into one of three categories:

1. *Cost of goods sold*, which states the amount of labor, material, and other expenses in producing the items sold, $8,940,000.
2. *Depreciation expense*, which states the amount of capital (producer's durables) consumed in producing the goods and services sold and which must be replaced or restored to its original capacity, $800,000.
3. *Selling and administrating expenses*, which includes office expenses, executives salaries, salespersons salaries, advertising and promotion expenses and the like, $8,232,000.

Operating profit, also called net operating income, $5.878 million, is the income from business operations, and is an important indicator of how efficiently the fixed assets were employed during the year.
Other income, $342,000, is from UMC's marketable securities of $1.83 million at cost as of one year ago.
Total income, $6.22 million, is the sum of operating profit from the business and income from other sources.
Interest on bonds, $160,000, (8 percent of 2 million) is itemized next on the income statement, followed by:

Income after interest, before tax	$6,060,000
Provision for federal income tax	2,240,000
Net profit for the year	3,820,000
Net earnings per share	$4.92

We turn next to statements of accumulated retained earnings.

STATEMENTS OF ACCUMULATED RETAINED EARNINGS

The bottom part of Exhibit 2 contains the accumulated retained earnings statement for UMC, and shows at the beginning of the balance, since the starting date of the business to January 1 of the current year, $13,081,600— to which is added the net profit for the year, $3,820,000, to get total accumulated retained earnings of $16,901,600.
Dividends paid to stockholders are itemized next:

Preferred stock dividend: 6 percent of $1,360,000	$ 81,600
Common stock dividend: $2.00 per share declared times 760,000 shares	1,520,000
Total dividends paid	$1,601,600

Balance, December 31 (15.3 million) equals the difference between the total available ($16,901,600) and total dividends paid. Retained earnings are an important source of finance of corporate capital assets.
We turn next to statements of sources and uses of funds.

STATEMENT OF SOURCE AND APPLICATION OF FUNDS

Exhibit 3 is a statement of source and application or use of funds for UMC. Ordinarily, *funds* imply cash; but in a broader sense, *funds* include cash equivalents and substitutes for cash, such as short-term credit, notes, and account payable and accrued liabilities to meet the short-term financing needs of the business. So *funds* in the broader sense imply net working capital, which is the difference between current assets and current liabilities.
Sources of funds in general include transactions which increase the amount of working capital, such as:

1. Net profit from operations.
2. Sale or consumption of noncurrent assets.
3. Long-term borrowing.
4. Issuing additional shares of capital stock.
5. Annual depreciation.

Uses of funds in general include transactions which decrease working capital, such as:

1. Declaring cash dividends.
2. Repaying long-term debt.
3. Buying noncurrent assets.
4. Repurchasing outstanding capital stock.

In the case of UMC and Exhibit 3, funds were provided by net income, $3.82 million, and current depreciation expense, $800,000. Some analysts worry that depreciation is not cash, depreciation is a bookkeeping entry. But the capital was consumed in the process of producing the goods and services sold; so the business pays the cash to itself to ultimately replace the consumed capital. Depreciation expense is a source of funds.
Total funds provided for UMC are $4,620,000.

EXHIBIT 3

UNIVERSAL MANUFACTURING CORPORATION
Statement of Source and Application of Funds
December 31, 1983

	1983	
Funds were provided by		
Net income	$3,820,000	
Depreciation	800,000	
Total		$4,620,000
Funds were used for		
Dividends on preferred stock	$ 81,600	
Dividends on common stock	1,520,000	
Plant and equipment	1,720,300	
Sundry assets	398,100	
Total		$3,720,000
Increase in Working Capital		$ 900,000
Analysis of changes in working capital—1983		
Changes in current assets		
Cash	$ 100,000	
Marketable securities	1,020,000	
Accounts receivable	430,000	
Inventories	650,000	
Total		$2,200,000
Changes in current liabilities		
Accounts payable	$ 610,000	
Notes payable	690,000	
Accrued expenses payable	80,000	
Federal income tax payable	(80,000)	
Total		$1,300,000

Uses of funds are itemized next, where all uses fall into one of four categories:

Dividends on preferred stock	$ 81,600
Dividends on common stock	1,520,000
Plant and equipment	1,720,300
Sundry assets	398,100
Total uses or application of funds	$3,720,000

Increase in working capital, $900,000, is the difference between the total funds provided, $4.62 million, and the total funds used, $3.72 million.

An *analysis of changes in working capital* for the year is included in the statement of source and application of funds, and gives further information regarding the $900,000 increase in working capital, which is explained by analyzing changes in current assets together with changes in current liabilities.

Changes in current assets total $2.2 million, itemized as follows:

1. *Cash* increased from $250,000 to $350,000, giving a net change of $100,000,
2. *Marketable securities* increased from $1.83 million to $2.85 million, giving a net change of $1.02 million,
3. *Accounts receivable* increased from $4.37 million to $4.8 million, giving a net change of $430,000,
4. *Inventories* increased from $4.95 million to

$5.6 million, giving a net change of $650,000.

Changes in current liabilities total $1.3 million, itemized as follows:

1. *Accounts payable* increased from $2.3 million to $2.91 million, giving a net change of $610,000,
2. *Notes payable* increased from $730,000 to $1.42 million, giving a net change of $690,000,
3. *Accrued expenses payable* increased from $350,000 to $430,000, giving a net change of $80,000,
4. *Federal income taxes payable* decreased from $1.32 million to $1.24 million, giving a net change of ($80,000).

The difference between the changes in current assets ($2.2 million) and changes in current liabilities ($1.3 million) equals the $900,000 increase in working capital.

We turn next to understanding more regarding how to analyze financial statements.

II. ANALYZING FINANCIAL STATEMENTS

The analysis of all four statements consists primarily of calculating ratios; but other methods including the time trend of the ratio, information theory, and flow-of-funds analysis are sometimes used. We shall limit our analysis to using ratios.[1]

In general, financial analysts, investors, creditors, and others look for two kinds of information regarding business enterprises:

1. *Risk*, including financial, business, market, and country or political risks,
2. *Return*, including productivity, efficiency, and profitability of corporate capital investments.

A third factor, *growth rate*, is important too, primarily because high steady growth is usually worth more than low or no growth.

BALANCE SHEET RATIOS

Balance sheet ratios belong to one of the three following categories:

1. *Liquidity and turnover ratios*, which indicate the ability of the corporation to pay current liabilities,
2. *Capitalization*, also called *leverage*, or *debt ratios*, which is the amount of borrowing relative to other factors such as total capitalization, total assets, or total equity,
3. *Net asset ratios*, which indicate the amount of assets backing each class of outstanding securities.

Liquidity ratios are calculated to judge whether the corporation owns sufficient cash and cash-equivalents or substitutes to comfortably pay short-term obligations, and include:

1. *Current liquidity*, the ability to pay current liabilities from current assets:

Current ratio:

$$\frac{\text{Current assets}}{\text{Current liabilities}} = \frac{\$13,600,000}{\$\ 6,000,000} = 2.3 \text{ to } 1$$

In total dollar amounts, the numerator in the current ratio, minus the denominator, states *net working capital*, where

Total current assets	$13,600,000
Less: Total current liabilities	6,000,000
Working capital	$ 7,600,000

2. *Quick asset* (sometimes called *acid test*) *ratio:*

$$\frac{\text{Quick assets}}{\text{Current liabilities}} = \frac{\$8,000,000}{\$6,000,000} = 1.33$$

Where quick assets are total current assets minus inventories, because inventories usually are less liquid than either cash, marketable securities, or accounts receivable:

Total current assets	$13,600,000
Less: Inventories	5,600,000
Quick assets	$8,000,000
Less: Total current liabilities	6,000,000
Net quick assets	$2,000,000

3. The *cash plus marketable securities ratio* indicates the firm's ability to pay current liabilities without relying on either inventories or accounts receivable:

$$\frac{\text{Cash plus marketable securities}}{\text{Total current liabilities}} = \frac{\$3,200,000}{\$6,000,000}$$
$$= 0.53$$

Liquidity and turnover of inventories ratios indicate how close inventories approximate true liquidity through total sales, and are the three following figures:

1. *Inventory as a percent of total current assets:*

$$\frac{\text{Inventory}}{\text{Total current assets}} = \frac{\$5,600,000}{\$13,600,000}$$
$$= 41.18 \text{ percent}$$

2. *Cost of goods sold*, including depreciation and capital consumption, *to average inventory ratio:*

$$\frac{\substack{\text{Cost of goods sold} \\ \text{plus depreciation}}}{\text{Inventory}} = \frac{\$9,740,000}{\$5,600,000} = 1.74$$

3. *Inventory turnover ratio:*

$$\frac{\text{Net sales}}{\text{Inventory}} = \frac{\$23,850,000}{\$5,600,000} = 4.26 \text{ times}$$

Liquidity of receivables ratios indicate how close accounts receivable approximate true liquidity through total sales, and are the two following figures:

1. *Average collection period ratio*, which indicates the number of day's sales in accounts receivables:

$$\frac{\text{Receivables} \times \text{Days in year}}{\text{Annual sales}} =$$
$$\frac{\$4,800,000 \times 360}{\$23,850,000} = 72.45$$

2. *Accounts receivable turnover ratio:*

$$\frac{\text{Annual sales}}{\text{Accounts receivable}} = \frac{\$23,850,000}{\$4,800,000} = 4.97$$

Liquidity and turnover of tangible and fixed asset ratios indicate relationships between total sales and total assets, and are given by the following two figures:

1. *Fixed asset turnover ratio:*

$$\frac{\text{Sales}}{\text{Net fixed assets}} = \frac{\$23,850,000}{\$12,110,000} = 1.97$$

2. *Total asset turnover ratio:*

$$\frac{\text{Net sales}}{\text{Average total tangible assets}} = \frac{\$23,850,000}{\$25,800,000}$$
$$= 0.9244$$

Capitalization ratios include:

1. Debt ratio:

$$\frac{\text{Total liabilities}}{\text{Total assets}} = \frac{\$8,000,000}{\$26,000,000} = 30.77 \text{ percent}$$

2. Current liabilities as a percent of total liabilities:

$$\frac{\text{Current liabilities}}{\text{Total liabilities}} = \frac{\$6,000,000}{\$8,000,000} = 75 \text{ percent}$$

3. Debt-to-net-worth ratio:

$$\frac{\text{Total liabilities}}{\text{Net Worth}} = \frac{\$8,000,000}{\$18,000,000} = 0.4444$$

4. Long-term debt capitalization ratio:

$$\frac{\text{Long-term debt}}{\text{Total capitalization}} = \frac{\$2,000,000}{\$19,800,000}$$
$$= 10.10 \text{ percent}$$

5. Preferred stock ratio:

$$\frac{\text{Preferred stock}}{\text{Total capitalization}} = \frac{\$1,360,000}{\$19,800,000}$$
$$= 6.87 \text{ percent}$$

6. Common stock ratio:

$$\frac{\text{Common stock plus accumulated earnings}}{\text{Total capitalization}} = \frac{\$16,440,000}{\$19,800,000}$$
$$= 83.03 \text{ percent}$$

7. Summary:

Total assets	$26,000,000	
Less: Intangibles	$ 200,000	
Less: Total current liabilities	$ 6,000,000	
Total capitalization	$19,800,000	100.00%
Bonds (long-term debt)	2,000,000	10.10
Preferred stock	1,360,000	6.87
Common stock (including capital surplus and retained earnings)	16,440,000	83.03

8. Long-term debt as a percent of total liabilities:

$$\frac{\text{Long-term debt}}{\text{Total liabilities}} = \frac{\$2,000,000}{\$8,000,000} = 25.00 \text{ percent}$$

Net asset value ratios include:

1. Net asset value per $1,000 bond; $9,900 per bond.

$$\frac{\begin{array}{c}\text{Net tangible assets}\\\text{available to meet}\\\text{bondholders' claims}\end{array}}{\begin{array}{c}\text{Number of \$1,000}\\\text{bonds outstanding}\end{array}} = \frac{\$19,800,000}{2,000,000}$$

where the numerator is calculated as follows:

Total assets	$26,000,000
Less: Intangibles	200,000
Total tangible assets	$25,800,000
Less: Current liabilities	6,000,000
Net tangible assets available to meet bondholders' claims	$19,800,000

2. Net asset value per share of preferred stock: $1,308.82

$$\frac{\begin{array}{c}\text{Net assets backing}\\\text{the preferred stock}\\\text{Number of shares}\\\text{of preferred stock}\\\text{outstanding}\end{array}}{} = \frac{\$17,800,000}{13,600}$$

where the numerator is calculated as follows:

Total assets	$26,000,000
Less: Intangibles	200,000
Total tangible assets	$25,800,000
Less: Current liabilities	6,000,000
Less: Long-term liabilities	2,000,000
Net assets backing the preferred stock	$17,800,000

3. Net book value per share of common stock: $21.63

$$\frac{\begin{array}{c}\text{Net assets available}\\\text{for the common stock}\\\text{Total number of}\\\text{shares outstanding}\end{array}}{} = \frac{\$16,440,000}{760,000} = \$21.63$$

where the numerator is calculated as follows:

Total assets	$26,000,000
Less: Intangibles	200,000
Total tangible assets	$25,800,000
Less: Current liabilities	6,000,000
Less: Long-term liabilities	2,000,000
Less preferred stock	1,360,000
Net assets available for the common stock	$16,440,000

Finally, estimate the youngest average plant age by dividing the current (1983) depreciation expense accrual ($800,000 from the Statement of Source and Application of Funds) into accumulated depreciation ($6,435,000 from the Balance Sheet) to get 8.04 years. Because some plants and pieces of equipment may have been fully written off over time, we can say that UMC's Fixed Assets, on average, are over 8 years old.

INCOME STATEMENT RATIOS

Income statement ratios belong to one of the two following categories:

1. *Coverage,* which analyzes financial risk by relating the financial charges of a corporation to its ability to service them.
2. *Productivity* or *capital efficiency ratios,* which relate income to total sales and to investment.

Coverage ratios include:

1. Interest coverage ratio: 38.875

$$\frac{\text{Net operating income before interest and taxes}}{\text{Interest charges on bonds}} = \frac{\$6,220,000}{\$160,000} = 38.875$$

2. Cash flow coverage ratio, which indicates the firm's ability to service debt, which is related to both interest and principal payments and is not met out of earnings per se, but out of cash: 19.5 times.

$$\frac{\text{Annual cash flow before interest and taxes}}{\text{Interest on bonds plus principal repayments}/(1-T)} = \frac{\$7,020,000}{\$\ 360,000} = 19.5$$

where:

Net operating income before interest and taxes	$6,220,000
Plus annual depreciation expense	800,000
Annual cash flow before interest and taxes	$7,020,000
Face value 20-year 8% bonds due 2003	$2,000,000
Annual Repayment rate after taxes $2,000,000 divided by 20 years	100,000
Before tax annual bond repayment rate $100,000 divided by 1 minus the effective tax rate, say 50 %	$200,000
Plus: 8% interest on $2,000,000	160,000
Interest plus principal repayments	$360,000

Since interest payments are made before taxes, the adjustment is necessary to convert principal repayments which are made after taxes to before-tax equivalents.

3. Preferred dividend coverage ratio: 46.81

$$\frac{\text{Income available for paying preferred dividends}}{\text{Total dividends to preferred shareholders}} = \frac{\$3,820,000}{\$81,600} = 46.81$$

4. Earnings per common share: $4.92

$$\frac{\text{Earnings available for distribution to common shareholders}}{\text{Total number of common shares outstanding}} = \frac{\$3,738,400}{760,000} = \$4.92$$

where:

Net profit for the year	$3,820,000
Less: Dividend requirements on preferred stock	81,600
Earnings available for common stock	$3,738,400

5. Primary earnings for the year: $4.94

$$\frac{\text{Earnings for the year}}{\text{Common stock plus stock equivalents}} = \frac{\$3,820,000}{773,500} = \$4.94$$

Assuming the 13,600 preferred shares had been convertible and converted, on a share-for-share basis, into common stock.

$$13,600 + 760,000 = 773,600 \text{ common shares after conversion}$$

6. Fully diluted earnings per share: $4.79

$$\frac{\text{Adjusted earnings}}{\text{Adjusted shares outstanding}} = \frac{\$3,900,000}{813,600}$$
$$= \$4.79$$

where:

Earnings for the year	$3,820,000
Plus: interest on convertible bonds....	$ 160,000
Less: income tax applicable to interest deduction	80,000
Adjusted earnings for the year..........	$3,900,000
Common shares outstanding	760,000
Preferred convertible stock equivalent common shares	13,600
Twenty common shares per $1,000 convertible bond (2,000) outstanding ..	40,000
Adjusted shares outstanding	813,600

7. Summary:

Earnings per share	$4.92
Primary earnings	4.94
Fully diluted earnings......	4.79

8. Price-earnings ratio: Approximately 15 times

$$\frac{\text{Market price of stock}}{\text{Earnings per share}} = \frac{\$72.25}{\$4.92} = 14.69$$

Productivity or capital efficiency ratios include:

1. Operating margin of profit: 24.65%.

$$\frac{\text{Operating profit}}{\text{Sales}} = \frac{\$5,878,000}{\$23,850,000} = 24.65\%$$

Previous year:

$$= \frac{\$5,037,000}{\$19,810,000} = 25.43\%$$

2. Operating cost ratio: 75.35%.

	Amount	Ratio
Net sales	$23,850,000	100.00%
Operating costs	17,972,000	75.35
Operating profit	$ 5,878,000	24.65%

3. Net profit ratio: 16.02%.

$$\frac{\text{Net profit for the year}}{\text{Net sales}} = \frac{\$3,820,000}{\$23,850,000} = 16.02\%$$

Previous year: 15.55%

$$= \frac{\$3,080,000}{\$19,810,000} = 15.55\%$$

RATIOS FROM STATEMENTS OF ACCUMULATED RETAINED EARNINGS

Retained earnings statements ratios belong to one of the two following categories:

1. Dividend payout ratio.
2. Earnings retention ratio.

The dividend payout ratio for UMC is: 40.66%.

$$\frac{\text{Dividends paid to}}{\substack{\text{common stockholders} \\ \text{Income available for} \\ \text{common stockholders}}} = \frac{\$1,520,000}{\$3,738,400} = 40.66\%$$

where:

Net profit for the year	$3,820,000
Dividends on preferred stock	81,600
Earnings available for common	$3,738,400

The earnings retention ratio for UMC is: 59.34%.

$$\frac{\text{Earnings retained}}{\substack{\text{Earnings available} \\ \text{for payout}}} = \frac{\$2,218,400}{\$3,738,400} = 59.34\%$$

where:

Net profit for the year	$3,820,000
Less: Dividends paid on preferred stock	$ 81,600
Less: Dividends paid on common stock	1,520,000
Earnings retained	$2,218,400

Summary:

Dividend payout ratio	40.66%
Earnings retention ratio	59.34
Earnings available	100.00%

Dividends per share: $2.00.

$$\frac{\substack{\text{Total dividends} \\ \text{paid to common} \\ \text{shareholders}}}{\substack{\text{Number of} \\ \text{common shares} \\ \text{outstanding}}} = \frac{\$1,520,000}{760,000} = \$2.00$$

Balance December 31, $15,300,000.

RATIOS FROM STATEMENTS OF SOURCE AND APPLICATION OF FUNDS

Since an analysis was stated directly on the statement of source and use of funds in Exhibit 3, that part of the analysis is completed; however we still need to calculate profitability ratios which belong to one of the two following categories:

1. Return on assets.
2. Return on equity.

Return on assets ratios include:
Return on total assets: 27.67%.

$$\frac{\text{Total income}}{\text{Last year's total assets}} = \frac{\$6,220,000}{\$22,481,600}$$
$$= 27.67\%$$

After tax return on total assets: 17.70%.

$$\frac{\substack{\text{Total income after tax} \\ \text{but before interest}}}{\text{Last year's total assets}} = \frac{\$3,980,000}{\$22,481,600}$$
$$= 17.70\%$$

where:

Total income	$6,220,000
Less: Provision for total taxes	2,240,000
After tax total income	$3,980,000

Return on equity ratio: 25.92%.

$$\frac{\substack{\text{Income available for} \\ \text{distribution to common} \\ \text{stockholders}}}{\substack{\text{Last year's total} \\ \text{equity of common} \\ \text{stockholders}}} = \frac{\$3,738,400}{\$14,421,600}$$
$$= 25.92\%$$

where:

Last year's total stockholder equity	$15,781,600
Less: Preferred stock value	1,360,000
Last year's common stock equity	$14,421,600

We turn next to further discussion of notes and supplemental information.

III. NOTES AND SUPPLEMENTAL INFORMATION

As explained in the introduction, financial statements in corporate annual reports usually are accompanied by:

- A *report of independent accountants and auditors* certifying the statements conform to generally accepted accounting principles and that generally accepted auditing standards and procedures were used.
- *Notes* which further explain details and disclose relevant information regarding line items on all four statements.
- *Segment information*, which summarizes selected items by business, industry, and geographic segment.
- A *restatement* of almost everything in current (in contrast with the traditional historical original purchase) prices, and to account for the effects of inflation on items reported in the standard statements.
- *Long-term record* summarizing selected items over a five- or ten-year time span.

EXHIBIT 4
SEGMENT REPORTING AND FOREIGN OPERATIONS

| | Industry Segments | | | Geographic Segments | | | | |
| | | | | | Foreign | | | |
	Segment No. 1	Segment No. 2	Consolidated	Domestic	OECD	Other	Eliminations	Consolidated
1983								
Sales, unaffiliated customers	$20,044,000	$3,806,000	$23,850,000	$12,647,000	$ 9,029,000	$2,175,000		$23,850,000
Sales, intersegment				2,171,000	346,000	21,000	($2,539,000)	
Total sales	$20,044,000	$3,806,000	$23,850,000	$14,818,000	$ 9,375,000	$2,196,000	($2,539,000)	$23,850,000
Pretax operating income	5,435,000	443,000	5,878,000	3,690,000	1,820,000	211,000	157,000	5,878,000
Identifiable assets at December 31	21,700,000	4,300,000	26,000,000	16,549,000	10,168,000	2,353,000	(3,070,000)	26,000,000
Depreciation expense	666,000	134,000	800,000					
Capital spending	1,884,300	234,100	2,118,400					
1982								
Sales, unaffiliated customers	$16,629,000	$3,181,000	$19,810,000	$10,519,000	$ 7,511,000	$1,780,000		$19,810,000
Sales, intersegment				2,614,000	246,000	14,000	($2,878,000)	
Total sales	$16,629,000	$3,181,000	$19,810,000	$13,133,000	$ 7,757,000	$1,794,000	($2,878,000)	$19,810,000
Pretax operating income	4,627,000	410,000	5,037,000	3,512,000	1,449,000	126,000	(50,000)	5,037,000
Identifiable assets at December 31	19,027,000	3,473,000	22,500,000	14,728,000	8,660,000	2,005,000	(2,893,000)	22,500,000
Depreciation expense	611,000	127,000	738,000					
Capital spending	1,751,000	190,000						
1981								
Sales, unaffiliated customers	$14,461,000	$2,779,000	$17,240,000	$ 9,504,000	$ 6,152,000	$1,584,000		$17,240,000
Sales, intersegment				2,677,000	155,000	3,000	($2,835,000)	
Total sales	$14,461,000	$2,779,000	$17,240,000	$12,181,000	$ 6,307,000	$1,587,000	($2,835,000)	$17,240,000
Pretax operating income	4,163,000	378,000	4,541,000	3,552,000	1,234,000	119,000	(364,000)	4,541,000
Identifiable assets at December 31	16,614,000	3,341,000	19,955,000	13,627,000	7,818,000	1,590,000	(3,179,000)	19,955,000
Depreciation expense	551,000	102,000	653,000					
Capital spending	1,969,000	238,000	2,207,000					

REPORT OF INDEPENDENT ACCOUNTANTS

A typical report of independent accountants is addressed to the stockholders and board of directors of the corporation and will read as follows:

"In our opinion, the accompanying consolidated financial statements, appearing on pages — through —, present fairly the financial position of Universal Manufacturing Corporation and its subsidiary companies at December 31, 1983 and 1982, and the results of their operations and changes in financial position for the years then ended,

in conformity with generally accepted accounting principles consistently applied. Also, in our opinion, the five-year comparative consolidated summary of operations presents fairly the financial information included therein. Our examinations of these statements were made in accordance with generally accepted auditing standards and accordingly included such tests of the accounting records and such other auditing procedures as we considered necessary in the circumstances."

The report will be signed with the name and address of the accounting firm and dated.

EXHIBIT 5

UNIVERSAL MANUFACTURING CORPORATION
SCHEDULE OF INCOME FROM CONTINUING OPERATIONS
AND OTHER CHANGES IN SHAREHOLDERS' EQUITY
ADJUSTED FOR EFFECTS OF CHANGING PRICES
For the Year Ended December 31, 1983

		Adjusted for	
	As Reported (historical cost)	General Inflation (constant 1983 $)	Specific (current) Costs
Income from continuing operations			
Net sales	$23,850,000		
Other income	342,000		
Total revenue from continuing operations	$24,192,000	$24,192,000	$24,192,000
Costs and other deductions			
Depreciation expenses	800,000	1,076,000	1,115,000
Other costs and expenses	17,172,000	17,699,000	17,273,000
Interest expense	160,000	160,000	160,000
Federal and foreign income taxes	2,240,000	2,240,000	2,240,000
Total costs and other deductions	$20,372,000	$21,175,000	$20,788,000
Net income from continuing operations	$ 3,820,000	$ 3,017,000	$ 3,404,000
Purchasing power gain on net monetary liabilities (Net amounts owed)		1,000	1,000
Increase in current cost of inventories and property, plant and equipment during 1983			1,911,000
Less: effect of increase in general price level during 1983			2,788,000
Excess of increase in specific prices over increase in the general price level			($ 877,000)
Net income	$ 3,820,000		
Adjusted net income		$ 3,018,000	
Net change in shareholders' equity from above	$ 3,820,000	$ 3,018,000	$ 2,528,000

Summarized Balance Sheet
Adjusted for Changing Prices
At December 31, 1983

		Adjusted for	
	As reported	General Inflation (constant 1983 $)	Specific (current) Costs
Assets			
Inventories	$ 5,600,000	$ 6,175,000	$ 5,670,000
Property, plant and equipment	12,110,000	13,354,000	16,327,000
All other assets	8,290,000	9,141,000	7,506,000
Total assets	$26,000,000	$28,670,000	$29,503,000
Total liabilities	8,000,000	7,600,000	7,600,000
Shareholders' equity	$18,000,000	$21,070,000	$21,903,000

EXHIBIT 5 *(concluded)*

Supplementary financial data
Five-Year Comparison of Selected Data
Adjusted for Changing Prices

	Years Ended December 31				
	1979	1980	1981	1982	1983
Sales					
As reported	$14,020,000	$15,610,000	$17,240,000	$19,810,000	$23,850,000
1983 constant dollars	19,543,000	20,211,000	20,063,000	20,970,000	23,850,000
Net income					
As reported					$ 3,820,000
1983 constant dollars					3,017,000
Current costs					3,404,000
Earnings per share					
As reported					$4.92
1983 constant dollars					3.86
Current costs					4.37
Common stock dividends					
declared per share					
As reported	$1.40	$1.43	$1.55	$1.75	$2.00
1983 constant dollars	1.95	1.85	1.80	1.85	2.00
Net assets at year-end					
As reported					$18,000,000
1983 constant dollars					21,070,000
Current costs					21,903,000
Purchasing power gain on					
net monetary liabilities					1,000
Market price per common share					
at year-end					
Actual	$69.25	$68.13	$55.50	$67.63	$72.25
1983 constant dollars	90.50	84.95	64.80	72.45	68.50
Average consumer price index*	181.5	195.4	217.4	239.0	253.0

* Hypothetical, for illustrative purposes only.

NOTES TO FINANCIAL STATEMENTS

Notes disclose additional information regarding entries in all four primary statements, and usually are considered an integral part of the statements, included in and covered by the auditor's certification. Some corporations include the next three items to be discussed, segment information, effects of inflation, and long-term comparative summary of operations, in the notes. If included in some place other than the notes, then look for whether the statement was excluded from the auditor's audit.

SEGMENT INFORMATION

Notes disclosing geographic area and industry segment information usually summarize selected items such as net sales, operating income, total assets, depreciation and amortization, and capital expenditures for industry segments (business segments or product groups) and foreign operations.

Exhibit 4 shows the segment information for UMC's two segments.

As you can see from Exhibit 4, industry segment number one, Human and Animal Health Products, accounts for 84 percent ($20,044,000 divided by $23,850,000) of total sales, and 92 percent ($5,435,000 divided by $5,878,000) of UMC's operating income; all supported by 83.46 percent ($21,700,000 divided by

$26,000,000) of total assets. Eleven percent ($234,100 divided by $2,118,400) of total capital expenditures were made in industry segment number two, Environmental Health Products and Services for the treatment of water and air pollution.

Exhibit 4 also shows, based on the following ratios, that UMC's business is roughly 60 percent domestic United States; 40 percent nondomestic:

Net Sales:

$$\frac{\text{United States}}{\text{Total company}} = \frac{\$14,818,000}{\$23,850,000} = 62.13\%$$

Operating income:

$$\frac{\text{United States}}{\text{Total company}} = \frac{\$3,690,000}{\$5,037,000} = 62.78\%$$

Total assets:

$$\frac{\text{United States}}{\text{Total company}} = \frac{\$16,549,000}{\$26,000,000} = 63.65\%$$

SUPPLEMENTAL INFORMATION ON INFLATION ACCOUNTING

Pursuant to Financial Accounting Standards Board (FASB) *Statement of Financial Accounting Standards No. 33*, public enterprises that have either (1) inventories and property, plant, and equipment (before deducting accumulated

EXHIBIT 6

TEN-YEAR FINANCIAL SUMMARY
UNIVERSAL MANUFACTURING CORPORATION

	1983	1982	1981	1980	1979	1978	1977	1976	1975	1974
Net sales	$23,850,000	$19,810,000	$17,240,000	$15,610,000	$14,020,000	$12,604,000	$11,040,000	$9,426,000	$8,324,000	$7,611,000
Total income before tax	6,060,000	5,060,000	4,535,000	4,164,000	3,783,000	3,619,000	3,195,000	2,747,000	2,521,000	2,286,000
Net profit for the year	3,820,000	3,080,000	2,775,000	2,555,000	2,288,000	2,105,000	1,827,000	1,512,000	1,314,000	1,179,000
Earnings per share	4.92	3.95	3.56	3.28	2.94	2.71	2.36	1.95	1.70	1.53
Dividends per share	2.00	1.75	1.55	1.43	1.40	1.40	1.24	1.12	1.10	1.03
Net working capital	7,600,000	6,700,000	6,300,000	5,500,000	5,023,000	3,596,000	3,424,000	2,964,000	2,604,000	2,261,000
Total assets	26,000,000	22,481,600	19,934,000	17,594,000	15,390,000	12,433,000	9,890,000	8,348,000	7,365,000	6,643,000
Net plant and equipment	12,110,000	10,820,000	9,918,000	8,747,000	6,743,000	4,740,000	3,635,000	3,150,000	2,830,000	2,479,000
Long term debt	2,000,000	2,000,000	2,000,000	2,000,000	2,000,000	2,000,000	2,000,000	1,000,000	1,000,000	1,000,000
Preferred stock	1,360,000	1,360,000	1,360,000	1,360,000	1,360,000	1,360,000	1,360,000	1,360,000	1,360,000	1,360,000
Common stock and surplus	1,340,000	1,340,000	1,340,000	1,340,000	1,340,000	1,340,000	1,340,000	1,340,000	1,340,000	1,340,000
Book value per share	21.63									

depreciation) amounting to more than $125 million or (2) total assets amounting to more than $1 billion (after deducting accumulated depreciation) are required to report supplementary information in addition to the primary financial statements. FASB *Standards No. 33* are:

For fiscal years ended on or after December 25, 1979, enterprises are required to report:

a. Income from continuing operations adjusted for the effects of general inflation.
b. The purchasing power gain or loss on net monetary items.

For fiscal years ended on or after December 25, 1979, enterprises are also required to report:

a. Income from continuing operations on a current cost basis.
b. The current cost amounts of inventory and property, plant, and equipment at the end of the fiscal year.
c. Increases or decreases in current cost amounts of inventory and property, plant, and equipment, net of inflation.

Enterprises are required to present a five-year summary of selected financial data, including information on income, sales and other operating revenues, net assets, dividends per common share, and market price per share. In the computation of net assets, only inventory and property, plant, and equipment need be adjusted for the effects of changing prices.

UMC, because of its "small company" asset size, would be exempt from FASB *No. 33*'s reporting requirement. However, Exhibit 5 restates UMC's statement of income from continuing operations, restated for changing prices, for the year ending December 31, 1983; and UMC's five-year comparison of selected data adjusted for changing prices.

A final note on Notes: Feel free to speak with your friendly auditor, or sleuth on your own, regarding additional information which might remain undisclosed and could pertain to:

a. Liabilities arising out of company pension plans (e.g., ERISA).
b. Contractual obligations (e.g., the capitalized value of lease payments).
c. Legal judgments currently enforceable.
d. Contingent liabilities (e.g., pending lawsuits or possible income tax assessment).

TEN-YEAR FINANCIAL SUMMARY

Long-term performance of UMC is summarized and reported on the ten-year financial summary statement, Exhibit 6.

The long-term view is used for detecting trends and changes in trends in important factors such as net sales, total assets, net operating income, earnings per share, and dividends per share. On balance, the trends for UMC look pretty good: upward.

A Guide to SEC Corporate Filings

A basic purpose of the Federal securities laws is to provide disclosure of material financial and other information on companies seeking to raise capital through the public offering of their securities, as well as companies whose securities are already publicly held. This aims at enabling investors to evaluate the securities of these companies on an informed and realistic basis.

The Securities Act of 1933 is a *disclosure* statute. It generally requires that, before securities may be offered to the public, a registration statement must be filed with the Commission disclosing prescribed categories of information. Before the sale of securities can begin, the registration statement must become "effective," and investors must be furnished a prospectus containing the most significant information in the registration statement.

The Securities Exchange Act of 1934 deals in large part with securities already outstanding and requires the registration of securities listed on a national securities exchange, as well as "Over-the-Counter" securities in which there is a substantial public interest. Issuers of registered securities must file annual and other periodic reports designed to provide a public file of current material information. The Exchange Act also requires disclosure of material information to holders of registered securities in solicitations of proxies for the election of directors or approval of corporate action at a stockholder's meeting, or in attempts to acquire control of a company through a tender offer or other planned stock acquisition. It provides that insiders of companies whose equity securities are registered must report their holdings and transactions in all equity securities of their companies.

Effective December 15, 1980, the Securities and Exchange Commission adopted and proposed major changes in its disclosure systems under the Securities Act of 1933 and the Securities Exchange Act of 1934. These changes were intended to reinforce the concept of an integrated disclosure system.

The changes that were adopted include amendments to Form 10-K, amendments to the Proxy rules, expansion of amendments to Regulation S-K (which governs non-financial statement disclosure rules), uniform financial statement instructions, a general revision of Regulation S-X (which governs the form, content and requirements of financial statements), as well as a new simplified optional form for the registration of securities issued in certain business combinations.

The integrated disclosure system is based on the belief that investors expect to be furnished the same basic information package, both to support current information requirements of an active trading market and to provide information in connection with the sale of newly issued securities under the Securities Act.

The program is intended to:

Improve disclosure to investors and other users of financial information

Achieve a single disclosure system at reduced cost

Reduce current impediments to combining shareholder communications with official SEC filings

Form 10-K
Items Reported
Part I

1. **Business.** Identifies principal products and services of the company, principal markets and methods of distribution and, if "material," competitive factors, backlog and expectation of fulfillment, availability of raw materials, importance of patents, licenses, and franchises, estimated cost of research, number of employees, and effects of compliance with ecological laws.

   If there is more than one line of business, for each of the last three fiscal years a statement of total sales and net income for each line which, during either of the last two fiscal years, accounted for 10 percent or more of total sales or pretax income.

2. **Properties.** Location and character of principal plants, mines, and other important properties and if held in fee or leased.

3. **Legal Proceedings.** Brief description of material legal proceedings pending; when civil rights or ecological statutes are involved, proceedings must be disclosed.

4. **Principal Security Holders and Security Holdings of Management.** Identification of owners of 10 percent or more of any class of securities and of securities held by directors and officers according to amount and percent of each class.

Source: A *Guide to SEC Corporate Filings*, Disclosure, Inc., 5161 River Road, Bethesda, MD 20816.

Form 10-K
Part II

5. **Market for the Registrants' Common Stock and Related Security Holder Matters.** Includes principal market in which voting securities are traded with high and low sales prices (in the absence thereof, the range of bid and asked quotations for each quarterly period during the past two years) and the dividends paid during the past two years. In addition to the frequency and amount of dividends paid, this item contains a discussion concerning future dividends.
6. **Selected Financial Data.** These are five-year selected data including net sales and operating revenue; income or loss from continuing operations, both total and per common share; total assets; long-term obligations including redeemable preferred stock; cash dividends declared per common share. Also, additional items that could enhance understanding and trends in financial condition and results of operations. Further, the effects of inflation and changing prices should be reflected in the five-year summary.
7. **Management's Discussion and Analysis of Financial Condition and Results of Operations.** Under broad guidelines, this includes: liquidity, capital resources and results of operations; trends that are favorable or unfavorable as well as significant events or uncertainties; causes of any material changes in the financial statements as a whole; limited data concerning subsidiaries; discussion of effects of inflation and changing prices. Projections or other forward-looking information may or may not be included.
8. **Financial Statements and Supplementary Data.** Two-year audited balance sheets as well as three-year audited statements of income and changes in financial condition.

Form 10-K
Part III

9. **Directors and Executive Officers of the Registrant.** Name, office, term of office and specific background data on each.
10. **Remuneration of Directors and Officers.** List of each director and 3 highest paid officers with aggregate annual remuneration exceeding $40,000 and total paid all officers and directors.

Form 10-K
Part IV

11. **Exhibits, Financial Statement Schedules and Reports on Form 8-K.** Complete, audited annual financial information and a list of exhibits filed. Also, any unscheduled material events or corporate changes filed in an 8-K during the year.

Form 10-K
Schedules

I. Marketable securities. Other security investments
II. Amounts due from directors, officers, and principal holders of equity securities other than affiliates
III. Investments in securities of affiliates
IV. Indebtedness of affiliates (not current)
V. Property, plant and equipment
VI. Reserves for depreciation, depletion, and amortization of property, plant and equipment
VII. Intangible assets
VIII. Reserves for depreciation and amortization of intangible assets
IX. Bonds, mortgages, and similar debt
X. Indebtedness to affiliates (not current)
XI. Guarantees of securities of other issuers
XII. Reserves
XIII. Capital shares
XIV. Warrants or rights
XV. Other securities
XVI. Supplementary profit and loss information
XVII. Income from dividends (equity in net profit and loss of affiliates)

18-K

Annual report for foreign governments and political subdivisions thereof.

19-K

For American certificates against foreign issues for the underlying securities of a foreign issuer.
1. Changes in ownership and control
2. Changes in character of the business
3. Changes in property
4. Modification of securities of the registrant
5. Limitations effecting security holders
6. Securities of other issuers guaranteed by the registrant

7. Increases and decreases in outstanding equity's securities
8. Exchange control
9. Directors and officers of the registrant
10. Remuneration of officers and directors
11. Amount set aside for pensions and similar benefits
12. Options to purchase securities from registrant or subsidiaries
13. Financial statements and exhibits

20-F

Annual report filed by certain foreign issuers of securities trading in the United States.

Item 1 Business
Item 2 Management Discussion & Analysis of the Statements of Income
Item 3 Property
Item 4 Control of Registrant
Item 5 Directors and Officers of Registrant
Item 6 Remuneration of Directors and Officers
Item 7 Options to Purchase Securities from Registrant or Subsidiaries
Item 8 Pending Legal Proceedings
Item 9 Nature of Trading Market
Item 10 Capital Stock to be Registered
Item 11 Debt Securities to be Registered
Item 12 Other Securities to be Registered
Item 13 Exchange Controls and other Limitations Affecting Security Holders
Item 14 Taxation
Item 15 Changes in Securities and Changes in Security for Registered Securities
Item 16 Defaults upon Senior Securities
Item 17 Interest of Management in Certain Transactions
Item 18 Financial Statements and Exhibits

10-Q

This is the quarterly financial report filed by most companies, which, although unaudited, provides a continuing view of a company's financial position during the year. It must be filed within 45 days of the close of a fiscal quarter.

Form 10-Q
Items Reported
Part I

FINANCIAL STATEMENTS

1. Income Statement
2. Balance Sheet

3. Statement of source and application of funds
4. A narrative analysis of material changes in the amount of revenue and expense items in relation to previous quarters, including the effect of any changes in accounting principals.

Form 10-Q
Part II

1. **Legal Proceedings.** Brief description of material legal proceedings pending; when civil rights or ecological statutes are involved, proceedings must be disclosed.
2. **Changes in Securities.** Material changes in the rights of holders of any class of registered security.
3. **Changes in Security for Registered Securities.** Material withdrawal or substitution of assets securing any class of registered securities of the registrant.
4. **Defaults upon Senior Securities.** Material defaults in the payment if principal, interest, sinking fund or purchase fund installment, dividend, or other material default not cured within 30 days.
5. **Increase in Amount Outstanding of Securities or Indebtedness.** Amounts of new issues, continuing issues or reissues of any class of security or indebtedness with a reasonable statement of the purposes for which the proceeds will be used.
6. **Decreases in amount Outstanding of Securities or Indebtedness.** Amounts of decreases, through one or more transactions, in any class of outstanding securities or indebtedness.
7. **Submission of Matters to a Vote of Security Holders.** Information relating to the convening of a meeting of shareholders, whether annual or special, and the matters voted upon, with particular emphasis on the election of directors.
8. **Other Materially Important Events.** Information on any other item of interest to shareholders not already provided for in this form.

8-K

This is a report of unscheduled material events or corporate changes deemed of importance to the shareholders or to the SEC.
1. Changes in Control of Registrant.
2. Acquisition or Disposition of Assets.
3. Bankruptcy or Receivership.
4. Changes in Registrant's Certifying Accountant.

5. Other Materially Important Events.
6. Resignations of Registrant's Directors.
7. Financial Statements and Exhibits.

10-C

"Over-the-counter" companies use this form to report changes in name and amount of NASDAQ-listed securities. It is similar in purpose to the 8-K.

13-F

A quarterly report of equity holdings required of all institutions with equity assets of $100 million or more. This includes banks, insurance companies, investment companies, investment advisors and large internally managed endowments, foundations and pension funds.

Proxy Statement

A proxy statement provides official notification to designated classes of stockholders of matters to be brought to a vote at a shareholders' meeting. Proxy votes may be solicited for changing the company name, transferring large blocks of stock, electing new officers, or many other matters. Disclosures normally made via a proxy statement may in some cases be made using Form 10-K (Part III).

Registration Statements

Registration statements are of two principal types: (1) "offering" registrations filed under the 1933 Securities Act, and (2) "trading" registrations filed under the 1934 Securities Exchange Act.

"Offering" registrations are used to register securities before they may be offered to investors. Part I of the registration, a preliminary prospectus or "red herring," is promotional in tone; it carries all the sales features that will be contained in the final prospectus. Part II of the registration contains detailed information about marketing agreements, expenses of issuance and distribution, relationship of the company with experts named in the registration, sales to special parties, recent sales of unregistered securities, subsidiaries of registrant, franchises and concessions, indemnification of directors and officers, treatment of proceeds from stock being registered, and financial statements and exhibits.

"Offering" registration statements vary in purpose and content according to the type of organization issuing stock:

S-1 A generalized form which may be used for registration by an issuer when no other form is authorized or prescribed.

S-2 Used by "development stage" companies other than insurance, investment or mining companies.

S-3 Used by operating or development stage companies which mine for minerals other than oil and natural gas.

N-1 (Formerly S-5) Used by open-end investment companies.

N-2 (Formerly S-4) Used by closed-end investment companies.

S-6 Used by unit investment trusts registered under the Investment Act of 1940 on Form N-8B-2.

S-7 A short form which may be used by companies which have a relatively healthy operating history and have filed under both the Securities Act of 1933 and 1934 in a timely manner.

S-8 Used to register securities to be offered to employees under stock option and various other benefit plans.

S-9 Rescinded in SEC Release No. 33–5791, December 20, 1976. Previously used as a short form similar to the S-7 for the registration of debt securities. The requirements are now incorporated in form S-7.

S-10 Used for the registration of landowners' royalty interests, overriding royalty interests, participating interests, working interests, oil or gas payments, oil or gas fee interests, oil or gas leasehold interests and other producing and nonproducing oil or gas interests or rights.

S-11 Used by real estate companies, primarily limited partnerships and investment trusts.

S-12 Used to register American Depository Receipts issued against securities of foreign issuers deposited with an American depository.

S-13 Used for the registration of certificates, agreements, etc. relating to voting and voting-trust agreements.

S-14 Used to register securities for the reorganization, merger, consolidation, transfer of assets or similar plan of acquisition.

S-15 This new, experimental, optional, short registration form provides an abbreviated Prospectus to be sent to securities holders with the latest Annual Report in certain business combinations. It is anticipated that S-15 will be used primarily to register offerings made to small numbers of offerees so that inclusion of the Annual Report would not involve significant costs.

QUICK REFERENCE CHART TO CONTENTS OF SEC FILINGS

REPORT CONTENTS	10-K	19-K/20-F	10-Q	8-K	10-C	6-K	Proxy Statement	Prospectus	'34 Act F-10 8-A 8-B	'33 Act "S" Type	ARS	Listing Application	N-1R	N-1Q
Auditor														
□ Name	A	A	■					A	A		A	■	A	
□ Opinion	A	A	■						A		A		A	
□ Changes				A				■						
Compensation Plans														
□ Equity	■		■				F	F	A	F		■		
□ Monetary							F	A	F		■			
Company Information														
□ Nature of Business	A	A					F	A	A		A	■		
□ History	F	A							A		A			
□ Organization and Change	F	F		A	■	F		■	A	F	A			
Debt Structure	A							F	A	A	A	A	A	
Depreciation & Other Schedules	A	A						F	A	A	A			
Dilution Factors	A	A		F		F			A	A	A			
Directors, Officers, Insiders														
□ Identification	F	A				F	A	A	A		A	F		
□ Background	■	A				F	F	A	■		A			
□ Holdings		A		■			A	A	A		A			
□ Compensation		A					A	A	A		A			
Earnings Per Share	A	A	A			F			A		A		A	
Financial Information														
□ Annual Audited	A	A							A		A		A	
□ Interim Audited		A						■	■		■			
□ Interim Unaudited	■		A	■		F		F		F				
Foreign Operations	A							■	A	A	A	F		
Labor Contracts		■		■					F		F			
Legal Agreements	F								F		F			
Legal Counsel								A			A	■	■	
Loan Agreements	F		F					■	F		F		■	
Plants and Properties	A	F						F		F	F	■		
Portfolio Operations														
□ Content (Listing of Securities)														A
□ Management														A
Product-Line Breakout	A							A			A			
Securities Structure	A	A			■			A	A		A			
Subsidiaries	A	A				■		A	A		A	■		
Underwriting				■				A	A		A			
Unregistered Securities	■			■				F			F			
Block Movements				F				■			A			

Legend　**A** – *always included* – *included* - *if occured or significant*　**F** – *frequently included*　■ *special circumstances only*

TENDER OFFER/ACQUISITION REPORTS	13D	13 G	14D-1	14D-9	13E-3	13E-4
Name of Issuer (Subject Company)	A	A	A	A	A	A
Filing Person (or Company)	A	A	A	A	A	A
Amount of Shares Owned	A	A				
Percent of Class Outstanding	A	A				
Financial Statements of Bidders			F		F	F
Purpose of Tender Offer			A	A	A	A
Source and Amount of Funds	A		A		A	
Identity and Background Information			A	A	A	
Persons Retained Employed or to be Compensated			A	A	A	A
Exhibits	F		F	F	F	F

S-16 A short form which may be used for the registration of securities to be offered for sale by current or future security holders.

S-18 Short form registration up to $5 million.

"Trading" registrations are filed to permit trading among investors on a securities exchange or in the over-the-counter market. Registration statements which serve to register securities for trading fall into three categories:

(1) Form 10 is used by companies during the first two years they are subject to the 1934 Act filing requirements. It is a combination registration statement and annual report with information content similar to that of SEC-required annual reports.

(2) Form 8-A is used by 1934 Act registrants wishing to register *additional* securities for trading.

(3) Form 8-B is used by "successor issuers" (usually companies which have changed their name or state of incorporation) as notification that previously registered securities are to be traded under a new corporate identification.

Prospectus

When the sale of securities as proposed in an "offering" registration statement is approved by the SEC, any changes required by the SEC are incorporated into the prospectus. This document must be made available to investors before the sale of the security is initiated. It also contains the actual offering price, which may have been changed after the registration statement was approved.

Annual Report to Shareholders

The Annual Report is the principal document used by most major companies to communicate directly with shareholders. Since it is not a required, official SEC filing, companies have considerable discretion in determining what types of information this report will contain and how it is to be presented.

Recent changes (effective December 15, 1980) required by the SEC were made to standardize the presentation of disclosure items in annual reports to make them consistent with similar requirements in SEC filings. For example, selected financial data relating to a registrant's financial condition and results of continuing operations will be presented in the Annual Report in the same manner as in the 10-K.

In addition to financial information, the Annual Report to Shareholders often provides nonfinancial details of the business which are not reported elsewhere. These may include marketing plans and forecasts of future programs and plans.

Form 8 (Amendment)

Form 8 is used to amend or supplement filings previously submitted. 1933 Act registration statements are amended by filing an amended registration statement (pre-effective amendment) or by the prospectus itself, as previously noted.

Listing Application

Like the ARS, a listing application is not an official SEC filing. It is filed by the company with the NYSE, AMEX or other stock exchange to document proposed new listings. Usually a Form 8-A registration is filed with the SEC at about the same time.

N-1R

This report is the equivalent of the 10-K for registered management-investment firms. In addition to annual financial statements, this report shows diversification of assets, portfolio turnover activity, and capital gains experience.

N-1Q

This is the quarterly report of registered management-investment firms, which must be filed within one month after the quarter has ended. The N-1Q shows changes in portfolio securities, including the number of shares bought, sold and owned at the end of the quarter for each stock in the company's portfolio.

TENDER OFFERS/ ACQUISITION REPORTS

13G

An annual report (short form of 13D) which must be filed by all reporting persons (primarily institutions) meeting the 5% equity ownership rule within 45 days after the end of each calendar year.

1. Name of issuer

2. Name of person filing
3. 13D-1 or 13D-2 applicability
4. Amount of shares beneficially owned:
   Percent of class outstanding
   Sole or shared power to vote
   Sole or shared power to dispose
5. Ownership of 5% or less of a class of stock
6. Ownership of more than 5% on behalf of another person
7. Identification of subsidiary which acquired the security being reported on by the parent holding company (if applicable)
8. Identification and classification of members of the group (if applicable)
9. Notice of dissolution of the group (if applicable)

8. Persons retained, employed or to be compensated
9. Financial statements of certain bidders
10. Additional information
11. Material to be filed as exhibits which may include but are not limited to:
    a. The actual offer to purchase
    b. The letter to shareholders
    c. The letter of transmittal with notice of guaranteed delivery
    d. The press release
    e. The summary publication in business newspapers or magazines
    f. The summary advertisement to appear in business newspapers or magazines

13D

Similar information of 5% equity ownership in connection with a tender offer filed within ten days of the acquisition date:
1. Security and issuer
2. Identity and background of person filing the statement
3. Source and amount of funds or other consideration
4. Purpose of the transaction
5. Interest in securities of the issuer
6. Contracts, arrangements or relationships with respect to securities of the issuer
7. Material to be filed as exhibits which may include but are not limited to:
   a. Letter agreements between the parties
   b. Formal offer to purchase

14D-9

A solicitation/recommendation statement that must be submitted to equity holders and filed at the SEC by the management of a firm subject to a tender offer within ten days of the making of the tender offer:
1. Security and subject company
2. Tender offer of the bidder
3. Identity and background
4. The solicitation or recommendation
5. Persons retained, employed or to be compensated
6. Recent transactions and intent with respect to securities
7. Certain negotiations and transactions by the subject company
8. Additional information
9. Material to be filed as exhibits

14D-1

Tender offer filing made with the SEC at time offer is made to holders of equity securities of target company, if acceptance of offer would give the offerer over 5% ownership of the subject securities:
1. Security and subject company
2. Identity and background information
3. Past contacts, transactions or negotiations with subject company
4. Source and amount of funds or other consideration
5. Purpose of the tender offer and plans or proposals of the bidder
6. Interest in securities of the subject company
7. Contracts, arrangements or relationships with respect to the subject company's securities

13E-4

Issuer tender offer statement pursuant to the Securities Exchange Act of 1934:
1. Security and issuer
2. Source and amount of funds
3. Purpose of the tender offer and plans or proposals of the issuer or affiliates
4. Interest in securities of the issuer
5. Contracts, arrangements or relationships with respect to the issuer's securities
6. Person retained, employed or to be compensated
7. Financial information
8. Additional information
9. Material to be filed as exhibits which may include but are not limited to:
   The offer to purchase which is being sent to the shareholders to whom the tender offer is being made

13E-3

Transaction statement pursuant to the Securities Exchange Act of 1934 with respect to a public company or affiliate going private-
1. Issuer and class of security subject to the transaction
2. Identity and background of the individuals
3. Past contacts, transactions or negotiations
4. Terms of the transaction
5. Plans or proposals of the issuer or affiliate
6. Source and amount of funds or other considerations
7. Purpose, alternatives, reasons and effects
8. Fairness of the transaction
9. Reports, opinions, appraisals and certain negotiations
10. Interest in securities of the issuer
11. Contracts, arrangements or relationships with respect to the issuer's securities
12. Present intention and recommendation of certain persons with regard to the transaction
13. Other provisions of the transaction
14. Financial information
15. Persons and assets employed, retained or utilized
16. Additional information
17. Material to be filed as exhibits

HOW TO READ THE NEW YORK STOCK EXCHANGE AND AMERICAN STOCK EXCHANGE QUOTATIONS

(1)	(2)	(3)	(4)	(5)	(6)	(7)	(8)	(9)	(10)	(11)
52 Weeks				Yld	P-E	Sales				Net
High	Low	Stock	Div.	%	Ratio	100s	High	low	Close	Chg.
					A A	A				
14¾	9⅛	AAR	.44	4.3	7	26	10½	10¼	10¼	¼
52¼	32¼	ACF	2.76	6.0	10	51	46	45½	46	
27	12⅞	AMF	1.24	5.1	12	1543	24¼	23¾	24⅛ +	¼
24¾	10⅞	AM Intl				51	13⅞	13¾	13¾	
11⅜	6⅜	APL				51	6⅜ d	6¼	6¼	⅛

Source: Reprinted by permission of *The Wall Street Journal*, Dow Jones & Co., Inc., 1981. All rights reserved.

The composite quotations take into account prices paid for a stock on the New York or American Exchanges, plus those prices paid on regional exchanges, Over-the-Counter (OTC) and elsewhere, as shown in the example from the Wall Street Journal.
The stock market quotations are explained below:

(1) The highest price per share paid in the past 52 weeks in terms of ⅛ of a dollar, i.e., 10⅛ means $10.125.
(2) The lowest price paid per share in the last 52 weeks.
(3) The name of the company in abbreviated form.
(4) The regular annual dividend paid. Special or extra dividends are specified by letters given in the footnotes in the Explanatory Notes shown below.
(5) The yield, that is, the annual dividend divided by the current price of the stock expressed in percent. For example, a stock that sells for $20.00 per share and pays a dividend of $2.00 per share has a yield of 10 percent (2/20).
(6) The P/E ratio is the current price of the stock divided by the company's last reported annual earnings per share. The P/E ratio is generally high for companies which are thought to have a relatively large and persistent earning's growth rate. The average P/E ratio for the Dow Jones stocks varied from 7.7 to 10.2 during the last five years.
(7) The number of shares sold on the day reported in 100s of shares.
(8) The highest price paid per share on the day reported.
(9) The lowest price paid per share on the day reported.
(10) The last price paid per share on the day reported.
(11) The change in the closing price from the previous day's closing price.

EXPLANATORY NOTES
(For New York and American Exchange listed issues)

Sales figures are unofficial.

The 52-Week High and Low columns show the highest and the lowest price of the stock in consolidated trading during the preceding 52 weeks plus the current week, but not the current trading day.

u—Indicates a new 52-week high. d—Indicates a new 52-week low.

s—Split or stock dividend of 25 percent or more in the past 52 weeks. The high-low range is adjusted from the old stock. Dividend begins with the date of split or stock dividend.

n—New issue in the past 52 weeks. The high-low range begins with the start of trading in the new issue and does not cover the entire 52-week period.

g—Dividend or earnings in Canadian money. Stock trades in U.S. dollars. No yield or PE shown unless stated in U.S. money.

Unless otherwise noted, rates of dividends in the foregoing table are annual disbursements based on the last quarterly or semi-annual declaration. Special or extra dividends or payments not designated as regular are identified in the following footnotes.

a—Also extra or extras. b—Annual rate plus stock dividend. c—Liquidating dividend. e—Declared or paid in preceding 12 months. i—Declared or paid after stock dividend or split up. j—Paid this year, dividend omitted, deferred or no action taken at last dividend meeting. k—Declared or paid this year, an accumulative issue with dividends in arrears. r—Declared or paid in preceding 12 months plus stock dividend. t—Paid in stock in preceding 12 months, estimated cash value on ex-dividend or ex-distribution date.

x—Ex-dividend or ex-rights. v—Ex-dividend and sales in full. z—Sales in full.

wd—When distributed. wi—When issued. ww—With warrants. xw—Without warrants.

vi—In bankruptcy or receivership or being reorganized under the Bankruptcy Act, or securities assumed by such companies.

Source: Reprinted by permission of *The Wall Street Journal*, Dow Jones & Co., Inc., 1981. All rights reserved.

HOW TO READ OVER-THE-COUNTER NASDAQ LISTINGS

The over-the-counter quotations are explained below.

(1) The company's name, usually abbreviated.

(2) Annual regular dividend per share, unless accompanied by a notation which is explained in the OTC Explanatory Notes (below).

(3) Number of shares sold that day in hundreds, i.e., 2 means 200 shares.

(4) Bid price per share at closing time, i.e., the price at which broker-dealer will buy the stock from the investor. Prices do not include mark-up or commission.

(5) Ask price per share at closing time, i.e., the price at which the broker-dealer will sell the stock.*

(6) The change in the closing bid price from the previous day.

(1) (2)	(3)	(4)	(5)	(6)
	Sales			Net
Stock & Div.	100s	Bid	Asked	Chg.
CentVtPS 1.92	8	13⅝	13¾ +	⅛
Centrn Cp 2.56	4	23¼	23½	...
Centura Enrg	135	10½	10¾ −	½
CenturyBK .48	573	13	13⅛ −	⅛
CenturyOil Gs	49	7⅜	7⅝	...
Cetus Corptn	231	17⅛	17⅜ +	⅛
CFS Cont .40	18	13⅝	13⅞ +	⅛
CGA Assc Inc	155	10½	11 −	¼
Chalco Ind Inc	2	6	6½ −	¼

Source: Reprinted by permission of *The Wall Street Journal*, Dow Jones & Co., Inc., 1981. All rights reserved.

* Bid and ask prices are usually quoted in ⅛ (12.5 cents) of a dollar, i.e., 12⅛ means $12.125, 12½ means $12.50, etc. Very inexpensive stocks are quoted at ¹⁄₁₆ (6.25 cents) and ¹⁄₃₂ (3.125 cents) of a dollar.

OTC EXPLANATORY NOTES

z—Sales in full.

a—Annual rate plus cash extra. b—Paid so far in 1981, no regular rate. c—Payment of accumulated dividends. d—Paid in 1980. e—Cash plus stock paid in 1980. f—Cash plus stock paid in 1981. g—Annual rate plus stock dividend. h—Paid in 1981, latest dividend omitted. i—Percent paid in stock in 1980. j—Percent in stock paid in 1981, latest dividend omitted. k—Percent in stock paid in 1981. n—Asked price not applicable. p—Granted temporary exception from Nasdaq qualifications. q—In bankruptcy proceedings. ut—Units. wt—Warrants. x—Ex-dividend, ex-rights or ex-distribution. (z) No representative quote.

Source: Reprinted by permission of *The Wall Street Journal*, Dow Jones Co., Inc., 1981. All rights reserved.

THE EX-DIVIDEND EXPLAINED

The ex-dividend status of a stock is indicated by an *x* in the newspaper quotation or *xd* on the ticker tape. This is an abbreviation for *without dividend.*

A stock that is purchased during the ex-dividend period will not pay a previously declared dividend to its new owner. The ex-dividend period spans four business days before the so-called record date—the date a dividend issuing corporation uses to tally its shareowners. An ex-dividend stock buyer is not entitled to a dividend because his name is not recorded with the dividend issuing corporation until after the record date.

The New York Stock Exchange requires that the buyer in every transaction be recorded with the issuing corporation on the fifth business day following a trade. A stock buyer, therefore, must purchase his shares at least five business days

before the record date in order for the corporation to record his name in time for him to receive his dividend. A purchase one day later disqualifies a buyer from a dividend because the transfer of ownership cannot be completed by the record date. Therefore, on the fourth business day prior to the record date, a stock is sold ex-dividend.

In our example below, the corporation's Board has decided to pay a 50¢ dividend to shareholders of record on Monday, the 10th. A person buying shares up to the close of business on Monday, the 3rd, would be eligible for the dividend because normal settlement (5 business days) will be made on Monday the 10th. On Tuesday, the 4th, however, the stock would begin selling ex-dividend because a stock purchaser as of that date could not settle till after the record date.

On the ex-dividend date, the Exchange specialist will reduce all open buy orders and open sell stop orders by the amount of the dividend. This is done to more equitably reflect the stock's value since purchasers of stock on or after the ex-dividend date are ineligible for a dividend.

EX-DIVIDEND EXPLANATION

Any Month	Date	Calendar Day	Status
	3	Monday	With/Dividend
	4	Tuesday	Ex-Dividend (Without Dividend)
	5	Wednesday	" "
	6	Thursday	" "
	7	Friday	" "
	8	Saturday	Not a trading day
	9	Sunday	Not a trading day
	10	Monday	Record Date/Business Day
	11	Tuesday	Business Day

Source: *Taking The Mystery Out of Ex-Dividend,* The New York Stock Exchange, Inc.

MARGIN ACCOUNTS EXPLAINED

Stocks may be purchased by paying the purchase price in full (plus commissions and taxes) or on a margin account. With the margin account, the investors put up part of the purchase price in cash or securities, and the broker lends the remainder. The margin investor must pay the usual commissions as well as interest on the broker's loan. The stocks purchased on margin are held by the broker as collateral on the loan. Dividends are applied to the margin account and help offset the interest payments.

Margin (M) is defined as the market value (V) of the securities less the broker's loan (L), divided by the market value of the securities. The ratio is expressed as a percentage:

$$M = \frac{V - L}{V} \times 100$$

Example: You buy 100 shares of a stock at $20 per share at a total cost (V) of $2,000. You put up $1,200 in cash and borrow (L) $800 from the broker. The margin at the time of purchase is

$$M = \frac{\$2,000 - \$800}{\$2,000} \times 100 = 60\%$$

The margin at the time of purchase is called *initial margin.* The smallest allowed value of initial margin (set by the Federal Reserve) is currently 50%. Thus, with the above stock, if you buy 100 shares at $20 per share on 50% initial margin, you put up $1,000 (.5 × $2,000), and the broker's loan is $1,000.

After the purchase there is a *maintenance margin* (set by the Exchange) below which the margin is not permitted to decrease. The maintenance margin on the New York Stock Exchange is 25%. Some brokers, however, require a higher maintenance margin of about 30%. Thus, if the 100 shares of stocks discussed above decrease in price from $20 to $13 per share, then the margin is

$$M = \left(\frac{\$1,300 - \$1,000}{\$1,300}\right) \times 100 = 23\%$$

The margin of 23% is now below the maintenance margin of 25% set by the Exchange. The securities are said to be *under margined*, and a call for additional cash (or securities) is issued by the broker in order to bring up the margin to 25%. If the investor does not meet the call for additional cash (margin call) within a specified time, the stocks in the margin account are immediately sold.

MARGIN REQUIREMENTS (percent of market value and effective date)

	Mar. 11, 1968	June 8, 1968	May 6, 1970	Dec. 6, 1971	Nov. 24, 1972	Jan. 3, 1974
Margin stocks	70	80	65	55	65	50
Convertible bonds	50	60	50	50	50	50
Short sales	70	80	65	55	65	50

Note: Regulations G, T, and U of the Federal Reserve Board of Governors, prescribed in accordance with the Securities Exchange Act of 1934, limit the amount of credit to purchase and carry margin stocks that may be extended on securities as collateral by prescribing a maximum loan value, which is a specified percentage of the market value of the collateral at the time the credit is extended. Margin requirements are the difference between the market value (100 percent) and the maximum loan value. The term "margin stocks" is defined in the corresponding regulation.

Source: *Federal Reserve Bulletin.*

SHORT SELLING EXPLAINED

Short selling provides an opportunity to profit from a decline in the price of a stock. If you believe that a stock is due for a substantial decline, you arrange to have your broker borrow the stock from another investor who owns the shares. The borrowed stock is then sold. This cash is held as collateral against the borrowed shares. When (and if) the stock price declines, you purchase the stock at the market price and use it to replace the borrowed shares. The broker arranges the return of your cash collateral less the cost of the repurchased stock. Your profit per share is the price received on the sale of the stock less the purchase price.

There are certain cash outlays and costs associated with the short sale. Generally there is no charge for borrowing the stock, although occasionally stock lenders may charge a premium over the market price. You must deposit $2,000 or the required initial margin, whichever is the greater, at the time the stock is borrowed. Thus, if you borrow 100 shares of a stock priced at $50 per share and the margin required is 50%,

you must put up $2,500 (.5 × $50 × 100) in cash or securities. The margin deposit is returned when you close out the short sale. You pay commission when the stock is sold and when it is repurchased. In addition, you must pay the stock lender any dividends which are declared during the period you are short the stock. It is well to remember that if cash is used for the deposit, there is a loss of the interest which you would have obtained if the cash had been invested.

The dividend payments and interest loss can be reduced or eliminated if you short stocks which pay little or no dividends and use interest-bearing securities (such as T-bills or negotiable certificates of deposit) as the margin deposit.

An increase in the price of the stock can result in substantial losses since you may be forced to repurchase at a higher price than you sold. If there are many short sellers seeking to purchase the stock in order to close out their position, prices may be driven to very high levels.

The short sale cannot be executed while the stock price is declining on the exchange. According to the rules of the SEC, the stock must undergo an increase in price prior to the execution of a short sale.

HOW TO READ MUTUAL FUND QUOTATIONS

The following is an example of typical fund quotations as reported in the Wall Street Journal. The mutual fund quotations are explained in the adjacent column.

(1)	(2) NAV	(3) Offer Price	(4) NAV Chg.
Able Assoc	24.33	N.L. +	.80
Acorn Fnd	28.28	N.L. +	.03
ADV Fund	15.38	N.L. +	.02
Afuture Fd	15.59	N.L. +	.10
AIM Funds			
Conv Yld	15.42	16.49 +	.09
Edsn Gld	14.59	15.60 +	.09
HiYld Sc	8.98	9.60 +	.02
Alpha Fnd	17.82	N.L. +	.01
Am Birthrt	12.29	13.43 −	.03
American Funds Group			
Am Bal	8.73	9.54	...
Amcap F	6.21	6.79 +	.01
Am Mutl	12.46	13.62 −	.01

Source: Reprinted by permission of *The Wall Street Journal*, Dow Jones & Co., Inc. All rights reserved.

(1) Name of fund in abbreviated form.

(2) NAV means "net asset value" per share of the stock. It is the price at which the fund will buy shares from investors. The NAV is obtained from

$$NAV = \frac{M + C - L}{N}$$

M = market value of all stock in the fund's portfolio at the end of the trading day

C = fund's cash or cash equivalent position

L = fund's liabilities

N = number of shares issued by fund

(3) Offer price is the price per share at which the fund will sell shares to investors. With no load (NL, no sale's charge) funds, the offer price and the NAV are the same. With load funds, a sale's charge (load) is added to the NAV to arrive at the sale's price.

(4) The NAV change is the change in net asset value (at the close of the stock market) from that of the previous day.

Top 50 Performing Mutual Funds for 5 Years

Top 50 Funds, 1979-1983 Based on What $10,000 Grew To In 5-Year Period[1]

1	US Gold Fund*	$ 63,985
2	Magellan Fund†	61,823
3	International Investors	60,331
4	Strategic Investments	60,017
5	Franklin Gold	55,917
6	A-C Pace	43,956
7	Phoenix Stock Fund Series	40,894
8	Twentieth Century Select*	40,847
9	United Vanguard	39,834
10	Mass Capital Development	39,556
11	Loomis-Sayles Capital Dev.*	39,281
12	NEL Growth	38,835
13	Twentieth Century Growth*	38,730
14	St. Paul Growth	38,662
15	IDS Growth	38,302
16	Tudor Fund*	37,051
17	Hartwell Leverage*	36,966
18	A-C Venture	36,774
19	Weingarten Equity*	36,674
20	Lindner Fund*	36,444
21	Constellation Growth*	36,405
22	Stein Roe Special*	36,355
23	Delta Trend	36,299
24	A-C Comstock	36,273
25	(Vanguard) Explorer*	36,071
26	Janus*	36,041
27	Seligman Capital Fund	35,408
28	Fund of America	35,131
29	St. Paul Capital	34,902
30	St. Paul Special*	34,147
31	Columbia Growth*	33,846
32	Kemper Summit	33,774
33	Growth Fund of America	33,431
34	IDS New Dimensions	33,406
35	Evergreen Fund*	32,822
36	First Investors Discovery	32,805
37	Founders Special*	32,707
38	Putnam Vista	32,507
39	Nicholas*	32,455
40	A-C Enterprise	32,379
41	Ivy*	32,366
42	Hartwell Growth*	32,331
43	Fidelity Equity Income	32,121
44	Pennsylvania Mutual*	32,106
45	Investors Research	31,911
46	AMCAP	31,842
47	Value Line Special Situations*	31,811
48	Fund of the Southwest	31,759
49	Lord Abbett Developing Gr.	31,242
50	New York Venture	31,203

*—No-Load Fund
†—Low-Load Fund

Top 50 Performing Mutual Funds for 10 Years

Top 50 Funds, 1974-1983 Based on What $10,000 Grew To In 10-Year Period[1]

1	Magellan Fund†	$132,960
2	Lindner Fund*	113,704
3	Oppenheimer Special	111,570
4	Evergreen Fund*	106,405
5	Twentieth Century Growth*	103,002
6	A-C Pace	101,344
7	Twentieth Century Select*	98,337
8	Sequoia*	88,895
9	A-C Comstock	85,870
10	Mutual Shares Corp.*	82,546
11	Value Line Leveraged Growth*	82,384
12	Pennsylvania Mutual*	81,920
13	A-C Venture	80,314
14	Leverage Fund of Boston*	79,795
15	Pioneer II	77,267
16	Fidelity Destiny	75,070
17	Sigma Venture Shares	74,653
18	O-T-C Securities	74,207
19	Value Line Special Situations*	68,779
20	Valley Forge Fund*	66,822
21	Seligman Capital Fund	66,397
22	Hartwell Leverage*	66,282
23	Security Ultra	65,545
24	Forty Four Wall Street*	65,211
25	AMCAP	64,358
26	SAFECO Growth*	63,727
27	Fidelity Equity Income	63,550
28	Tudor Fund*	63,247
29	St. Paul Growth	63,107
30	Kemper Summit	62,130
31	Growth Fund of America	61,147
32	Partners Fund*	61,098
33	American National Growth	60,042
34	Nicholas*	59,294
35	Templeton Growth	59,178
36	Guardian Park Avenue	58,205
37	Acorn*	57,813
38	Mass Capital Development	57,575
39	Weingarten Equity*	57,191
40	(Vanguard) Windsor*	56,630
41	Hartwell Growth*	55,489
42	American National Income	55,077
43	Janus*	54,872
44	Vance Sanders Special	54,659
45	Value Line Fund*	54,327
46	Constellation Growth*	53,867
47	Dreyfus Growth Opportunity*	53,734
48	Stein Roe Special*	53,677
49	Scudder Development*	52,898
50	Sigma Capital Shares	52,700

[1] Does not take into account sales commission on initial investment or any capital gains or income taxes that would have to be paid.

Source: Donoghue's *Mutual Funds Almanac* © 1984. The Donoghue Organization, Inc., Box 540 Holliston, MA 01746. Telephone: 1–800–543–3413.

PERFORMANCE OF MUTUAL FUNDS

BARRON'S / LIPPER GAUGE

FUND NAME	OBJ.	TOTAL NET ASTS (MIL) 6/30/84	NAV 6/30/84	PERFORMANCE (RETURN ON INITIAL $10,000 INVESTMENT) 12/31/83–6/30/84	6/30/83–6/30/84	6/30/79–6/30/84	YIELD % 6/30/84	PER SHARE LATEST 12 MONTHS CAP GAINS	INC DIVS	LATEST AVAILABLE PRICE/EARNINGS	ANNUAL % TURNOVER
ABT EMERGING GROWTH	CA	$5.7	$10.32	$9,398.90	$7,938.50	☆	0.0	$0.00	$0.00	N/A	67
ABT SECURITY INCOME	OI	21.5	10.32	9,559.60	9,782.00	☆	7.5	0.75	0.80	N/A	90
ACORN FUND	SG	172.0	27.55	9,300.60	9,047.50	19,789.10	1.9	1.63	0.55	17.4	22
ADV FUND	CA	31.5	17.87	8,935.00	8,409.10	☆	1.9	0.54	0.34	16.9	63
AETNA INCOME SHARES	FI	108.3	10.45	9,710.60	10,052.80	14,738.60	9.4	0.00	0.98	8.7	117
AFFILIATED FUND	GI	1,878.3	8.43	9,225.20	9,874.20	20,230.30	5.9	0.82	0.52	14.5	41
AFUTURE FUND	G	26.2	11.09	8,000.10	6,816.20	18,547.40	0.7	2.01	0.08	17.4	152
AGE HIGH INCOME	I	71.4	3.40	9,687.80	10,129.40	15,275.60	14.7	0.00	0.50	N/A	20
AGGRESSIVE GROWTH SHARES	G	7.2	8.06	7,727.70	6,248.10	☆	0.0	0.00	0.00	N/A	289
ALLIANCE MORTGAGE INC	FI	216.3	8.99	#9,941.50	☆	☆	0.0	0.00	0.31	N/A	N/A
ALLIANCE TECHNOLOGY	G	142.4	16.14	8,131.00	6,868.70	☆	0.1	1.38	0.01	N/A	220
ALPHA FUND	G	20.5	19.30	9,226.00	8,726.20	☆	2.0	4.00	0.42	N/A	40
AMCAP FUND	G	924.1	7.63	9,143.90	9,112.70	23,578.80	3.3	0.11	0.25	16.9	15
AMERICAN BALANCED FUND	B	111.1	9.10	9,573.90	9,698.20	24,582.60	7.4	0.98	0.71	11.0	51
AMERICAN BIRTHRIGHT TR	GI	134.5	11.42	9,158.00	8,145.90	17,315.30	1.4	3.02	0.17	14.7	129
AMER CAPITAL COMSTOCK	CA	538.9	12.48	9,371.00	9,763.40	18,479.20	3.4	0.87	0.46	12.4	40
AMER CAPITAL CORP BOND	FI	79.5	6.20	9,691.40	9,934.00	27,953.00	12.4	0.00	0.77	N/A	33
AMER CAPITAL ENTERPRISE	G	492.3	10.55	8,952.90	8,329.90	13,345.00	2.6	3.06	0.35	18.9	73
AMER CAPITAL GROWTH	G	24.1	22.53	8,289.40	7,131.60	25,113.50	1.4	1.58	0.33	21.1	46
AMER CAPITAL HARBOR	GI	163.3	11.76	8,964.40	9,416.80	24,036.80	6.5	2.86	0.86	25.9	56
AMER CAPITAL HIGH YIELD	FI	372.1	9.02	9,649.80	10,053.80	22,762.80	14.0	0.00	1.26	43.9	60
AMER CAPITAL OTC	G	65.1	9.12	9,056.60	☆	14,977.50	0.0	0.00	0.00	22.7	N/A
AMER CAPITAL PACE	CA	1,125.1	18.80	9,188.70	9,537.30	☆	2.2	0.48	0.41	16.5	20
AMER CAPITAL VENTURE	CA	371.2	13.67	9,047.00	8,329.60	34,043.20	1.8	0.23	0.25	18.9	15
AMERICAN GROWTH	G	58.5	8.18	9,446.00	9,482.20	26,814.10	4.6	0.81	0.38	10.0	69
AMERICAN HERITAGE	CA	0.6	3.07	8,434.10	7,156.20	22,464.90	0.0	0.00	0.00	N/A	N/A
AMERICAN INDUSTRY SHARES	G	0.5	11.31	9,135.30	9,552.70	15,427.10	3.4	0.00	0.38	N/A	N/A
AMERICAN INVESTORS	G	93.4	7.26	8,250.00	6,635.00	11,561.10	13.6	0.00	0.99	24.5	59
AMERICAN INV INCOME	FI	16.4	8.81	8,835.00	8,840.10	☆	14.2	0.00	1.25	N/A	132
AMERICAN LEADERS	GI	41.6	9.65	9,977.90	10,574.50	14,483.20	5.2	1.36	0.57	10.9	42
AMERICAN MUTUAL	GI	873.9	13.55	9,397.40	9,773.40	20,905.60	4.8	0.64	0.66	12.5	20
AMERICAN NATIONAL BOND	FI	4.3	13.31	10,108.60	10,493.60	22,663.60	11.1	0.00	1.48	N/A	7
AMERICAN NATIONAL GROWTH	G	85.3	3.79	8,146.30	7,318.10	15,592.20	1.8	1.02	0.07	14.8	44
AMERICAN NATIONAL INCOME	EI	42.0	17.68	9,497.90	9,845.40	18,887.10	6.3	2.16	1.11	16.1	30
ANALYTIC OPTIONED EQU	OI	69.6	133.36	9,794.20	10,288.70	22,583.20	3.7	2.35	4.92	N/A	49
ARMSTRONG ASSOCIATES	G	9.7	7.29	8,596.70	7,599.40	17,395.50	4.0	0.28	0.30	N/A	59
AXE-HOUGHTON FUND B	B	128.6	8.72	9,194.80	8,881.30	18,891.70	6.7	0.13	0.59	15.9	64
AXE-HOUGHTON INCOME	FI	30.2	4.01	9,436.40	9,571.90	15,617.50	12.5	0.00	0.50	N/A	30
AXE-HOUGHTON STOCK	G	96.9	6.42	7,937.20	6,860.60	14,687.90	3.0	5.01	0.27	21.0	119
BABSON BOND TRUST	FI	36.8	1.40	9,921.50	10,260.10	18,674.40	12.1	0.00	0.17	N/A	49
BABSON ENTERPRISE	SG	5.5	8.75	8,820.60	☆	14,626.30	0.0	0.00	0.00	N/A	N/A
DAVID L BABSON GROWTH	G	208.3	10.85	9,151.60	8,905.80	15,791.50	3.1	1.61	0.38	15.8	26
BANK STOCK FUND	S	0.3	4.15	10,122.00	10,026.70	16,966.60	6.1	0.24	0.26	N/A	N/A
BASCOM HILL INVESTORS	GI	3.6	14.69	9,342.20	9,130.50	22,913.60	5.0	0.80	0.76	N/A	37

Copyright© Lipper Analytical Services, Inc.

PERFORMANCE OF MUTUAL FUNDS (continued)

FUND NAME	OBJ.	TOTAL NET ASTS (MIL) 6/30/84	NAV 6/30/84	PERFORMANCE (RETURN ON INITIAL $10,000 INVESTMENT) 12/31/83-6/30/84	6/30/83-6/30/84	6/30/79-6/30/84	YIELD % 6/30/84	PER SHARE LATEST 12 MONTHS CAP GAINS	INC DIVS	LATEST AVAILABLE PRICE/EARNINGS	ANNUAL % TURNOVER
BEACON GROWTH	G	5.6	13.21	9,297.80	8,898.10	15,967.80	1.9	0.00	0.25	N/A	8
BEACON HILL MUTUAL	G	2.3	15.74	9,380.20	9,391.40	16,637.80	0.0	0.00	0.00	N/A	N/A
BEACON INCOME	I	0.1	2.26	8,828.10	8,100.40	7,997.90	0.0	0.00	0.00	N/A	N/A
BERWYN FUND	GI	0.7	8.83	#9,001.00	☆	☆	0.0	0.00	0.00	N/A	N/A
BLC GROWTH FUND	G	16.4	15.94	8,693.90	8,768.90	18,570.00	2.2	0.97	0.35	N/A	30
BLC INCOME FUND	EI	22.2	14.68	9,394.40	10,167.30	20,758.80	5.8	1.35	0.85	N/A	24
BMI EQUITY FUND	CA	2.4	26.22	8,879.10	7,815.00	☆	0.5	0.00	0.12	N/A	38
BOND FUND OF AMERICA	FI	318.9	11.54	9,874.30	10,070.10	15,472.10	12.5	0.00	1.44	N/A	104
BOND PORT FOR ENDOWMENTS	FI	20.0	745.67	9,957.10	10,131.30	15,225.20	11.8	0.00	88.00	N/A	190
BOSTON CO CAPITAL APPREC	G	213.5	23.02	9,324.60	9,438.40	17,685.20	2.5	2.91	0.61	12.6	47
BOSTON CO GOVT INCOME	FI	5.5	10.08	10,032.30	10,352.80	☆	10.3	0.00	1.04	N/A	N/A
BOSTON CO SPECIAL GROWTH	G	28.8	15.84	8,871.90	8,022.90	☆	0.6	0.11	0.09	N/A	247
BOSTON FOUNDATION	B	26.5	12.21	9,866.60	10,375.80	18,793.60	7.2	0.00	0.88	11.3	33
BOSTON MUTUAL FUND	G	4.7	9.11	9,196.40	9,154.20	17,147.50	2.4	1.38	0.24	N/A	N/A
BRUCE FUND	G	1.2	185.98	8,866.30	8,645.00	19,068.20	2.1	30.25	3.83	13.0	34
BULL&BEAR CAPITAL GROWTH	G	50.2	12.26	8,925.10	8,140.30	19,310.50	0.8	1.93	0.10	13.0	36
BULL&BEAR EQUITY INCOME	EI	4.3	10.14	9,588.00	9,676.00	16,528.70	6.3	0.24	0.65	N/A	N/A
BULL&BEAR HIGH YIELD	FI	8.6	13.25	9,674.20	☆	☆	3.9	0.00	1.61	N/A	N/A
BULLOCK FUND	GI	125.2	15.78	9,123.10	8,874.10	17,679.70	3.9	1.00	0.64	13.8	29
CALVERT EQUITY	G	5.8	15.79	8,806.50	8,317.90	☆	2.6	0.00	0.41	N/A	12
CALVERT INCOME	FI	7.3	13.29	9,624.40	9,772.10	☆	12.6	0.03	1.67	N/A	49
CALVERT SOCIAL INV GRO	GI	9.0	16.03	9,646.20	9,087.20	☆	4.3	0.00	0.69	N/A	179
CANADIAN FUND	IF	21.4	7.64	8,753.00	9,040.30	15,097.40	3.7	0.37	0.29	13.0	7
CAPITAL PRES T NOTE TR	FI	9.6	9.76	10,273.60	10,710.20	☆	9.7	0.00	0.95	N/A	N/A
CARDINAL FUND	GI	19.0	11.10	9,628.80	9,822.80	20,734.00	3.2	0.60	0.36	N/A	5
CARNEGIE CAPPIELLO GROW	FI	16.4	10.30	‡10,228.40	☆	☆	0.0	0.00	0.00	N/A	N/A
CARNEGIE GOVT ITS	GI	12.7	8.95	10,013.40	10,306.90	☆	11.8	0.00	1.05	N/A	108
CENTENNIAL GROWTH	FI	17.2	8.96	8,405.30	6,433.80	15,768.00	0.1	1.04	0.63	N/A	4
CENTURY SHARES TRUST	S	65.5	11.62	9,343.20	9,815.20	16,499.00	5.2	0.91	0.17	9.3	68
CHARTER FUND	CA	70.9	5.77	8,799.80	8,322.40	21,041.80	2.8	0.65	0.29	N/A	82
CHEAPSIDE DOLLAR	G	53.6	9.45	8,880.20	7,943.60	15,072.10	2.5	4.74	0.24	14.8	34
CHEMICAL FUND	CA	914.0	8.91	9,005.70	8,272.10	17,272.70	2.5	1.46	0.00	13.9	N/A
CIGNA AGGRESSIVE GROW	CA	0.1	9.94	‡9,940.00	☆	☆	0.0	0.00	0.00	15.3	45
CIGNA GROWTH	G	174.3	12.17	9,166.40	8,870.30	18,837.60	3.4	1.69	0.44	15.4	40
CIGNA INCOME	FI	190.5	6.37	9,971.40	9,974.90	14,577.20	12.1	0.00	0.77	N/A	65
CIGNA HIGH YIELD	FI	76.1	9.08	9,863.20	10,251.40	15,579.60	14.1	0.00	1.27	N/A	N/A
CIGNA VALUE	GI	1.8	10.17	‡10,170.00	☆	☆	0.0	0.00	0.00	12.2	N/A
COLONIAL CORP CASH	EI	324.9	44.80	10,136.80	10,579.20	☆	9.3	0.00	4.22	N/A	318
COLONIAL CORP CASH II	EI	12.6	45.63	‡9,693.40	☆	☆	0.0	0.00	1.66	N/A	N/A
COLONIAL FUND	GI	83.2	13.02	9,608.40	10,110.70	18,471.90	6.5	1.20	0.85	18.7	12
COLONIAL GOVT SEC PLUS	FI	399.4	10.87	‡10,132.50	☆	☆	0.0	0.00	0.21	N/A	N/A
COLONIAL GROWTH SHARES	G	61.2	9.02	9,246.00	8,844.30	20,617.20	3.6	0.09	0.33	20.9	73
COLONIAL HIGH YIELD	FI	81.1	6.74	9,833.30	10,282.20	15,221.60	14.2	0.45	0.96	N/A	107
COLONIAL INCOME FUND	FI	139.3	6.16	9,648.90	9,895.20	14,065.70	13.5	0.00	0.83	N/A	30
COLONIAL OPTION GRO	OG	6.2	12.53	9,286.00	8,963.50	☆	2.5	2.12	0.36	N/A	152
COLONIAL OPTION INC	OI	1,417.0	7.97	9,558.90	9,952.40	16,751.70	3.1	1.29	0.27	14.4	171
COLONIAL TAX-MGD TRUST	EI	451.7	12.31	9,983.80	10,445.50	17,423.90	0.0	0.79	0.00	7.9	74
COLUMBIA FIXED INCOME	FI	32.5	11.33	9,853.90	10,351.40	☆	12.4	0.00	1.39	N/A	47
COLUMBIA GROWTH	G	128.0	19.55	8,577.50	8,166.60	24,925.90	0.9	2.41	0.19	15.8	95
COMMERCE INCOME SHARES	I	46.4	8.38	9,286.40	8,889.90	18,316.40	7.0	0.00	0.59	14.2	145
COMMONWEALTH A&B	GI	8.9	1.27	9,477.50	9,525.40	19,474.00	6.7	0.00	0.08	N/A	122
COMMONWEALTH C	GI	33.1	1.75	9,406.30	9,380.10	18,089.30	6.1	0.03	0.10	N/A	119
COMPANION FUND	**G**	**68.1**	**11.32**	**9,226.40**	**9,058.20**	**19,547.60**	**3.7**	**2.46**	**0.46**	**12.1**	**34**

Fund	Type	NAV	Assets ($Mil)	Value A	Value B	Value C	%	Col 1	Col 2	Col 3	Rank
COMPANION INCOME FUND	FI	7.53	10.7	9,979.10	10,123.50	14,471.50	13.1	0.00	0.98	N/A	21
COMPOSITE BOND & STOCK	B	8.92	23.6	9,083.30	9,459.10	17,465.60	8.2	0.64	0.76	14.5	10
COMPOSITE FUND	GI	9.74	36.5	9,117.00	9,835.30	20,302.80	4.5	0.99	0.46	16.9	31
COMPOSITE INCOME FUND	FI	8.52	3.4	9,702.90	10,036.90	13,238.90	11.7	0.00	1.00	N/A	13
CONCORD FUND	G	25.54	1.7	10,294.20	6,508.00	23,991.60	3.1	1.25	0.78	20.8	N/A
CONSTELLATION GROWTH	CA	16.27	90.0	8,136.60	8,920.60	14,466.40	0.0	0.73	0.00	N/A	90
CONTINENTAL MUTUAL INV	GI	5.79	1.2	9,298.00	8,860.20	18,024.50	2.4	0.90	0.15	N/A	N/A
CONVERTIBLE YIELD SEC	FI	11.48	20.4	9,328.80	10,370.40	17,111.10	6.4	0.00	0.76	N/A	173
COPLEY TAX-MANAGED	GI	6.16	5.6	10,165.00	☆	☆	0.0	0.74	0.00	N/A	N/A
CORPORATE CASH MGT	FI	45.65	194.5	9,919.10	10,252.70	19,770.00	15.2	1.04	4.58	N/A	29
CORPORATE LEADERS TR-B	GI	10.72	49.5	9,734.00	8,516.90	18,885.90	6.2	0.00	1.68	18.7	N/A
COUNTRY CAPITAL GROWTH	G	15.01	52.0	9,031.30	10,080.30	13,980.00	9.9	0.99	0.93	N/A	53
COUNTRY CAPITAL INCOME	FI	8.67	3.5	9,699.60	8,602.70	☆	3.0	0.00	0.85	N/A	N/A
CUMBERLAND GROWTH	CA	24.43	0.8	8,885.40	7,639.60	☆	2.0	0.04	0.74	N/A	N/A
DEAN WITTER DEV GRO (R)	SG	7.71	179.4	8,435.40	9,946.20	☆	4.4	0.06	0.15	N/A	N/A
DEAN WITTER DIVIDEND GRO	GI	11.76	50.4	9,647.50	9,811.90	☆	16.0	1.32	0.52	20.9	3
DEAN WITTER HIGH YIELD	FI	12.61	417.9	9,749.30	7,706.40	☆	2.0	0.09	2.02	N/A	115
DEAN WITTER IND VALUE	G	9.29	36.6	8,343.20	8,466.30	☆	2.4	0.16	0.20	N/A	100
DEAN WITTER NTRL RES DEV	NR	6.92	28.5	9,091.10	☆	☆	0.0	0.00	0.16	N/A	83
DEAN WITTER WORLD WIDE (R)	GL	9.52	101.6	9,357.60	10,251.40	21,632.40	5.3	1.54	0.12	12.5	5
DECATUR INCOME	EI	14.43	573.2	9,709.00	8,181.00	22,250.90	4.9	2.83	0.80	13.3	73
DELAWARE FUND	GI	17.00	262.1	8,861.60	9,730.20	14,668.70	12.8	0.00	0.91	N/A	78
DELCHESTER BOND FUND	FI	6.97	40.9	9,575.50	6,348.90	25,100.10	0.0	0.00	0.89	11.8	131
DELTA TREND FUND	CA	10.99	71.6	7,986.90	7,994.10	16,189.30	1.6	2.32	0.00	15.6	280
DE VEGH MUTUAL	FI	35.06	51.4	10,440.30	☆	☆	0.0	0.00	0.60	N/A	77
DFA-INFLATION HEDGE A	FI	100.28	148.6	9,205.90	8,856.90	☆	1.1	6.36	8.29	18.2	N/A
DFA-SMALL COMPANY	SG	153.95	444.7	7,476.60	7,142.90	2,666.70	0.0	0.00	1.68	N/A	N/A
DIRECTORS CAPITAL	OG	0.80	0.4	9,577.90	9,817.30	15,924.70	4.0	0.00	0.00	N/A	N/A
DIV/GROWTH DIVIDEND SR	EI	21.52	3.4	8,584.50	☆	☆	0.0	0.00	0.87	N/A	N/A
DIV/GROWTH LASER SR	S	11.28	0.2	8,524.10	9,667.30	18,375.50	3.9	0.23	0.00	N/A	8
DIVIDEND SHARES	GI	2.99	252.5	9,430.30	9,633.60	17,009.20	7.2	0.83	0.12	11.7	10
DODGE & COX BALANCED	B	24.14	17.8	9,530.70	9,802.30	20,726.70	4.3	1.88	1.77	12.7	17
DODGE & COX STOCK	GI	22.59	25.8	9,713.30	9,534.60	19,525.90	5.2	0.15	1.02	11.9	80
DREXEL BURNHAM FUND	FI	16.33	69.9	9,621.30	9,808.60	15,221.40	12.6	0.00	0.86	N/A	5
DREYFUS A BONDS PLUS	GI	11.94	94.4	9,232.30	9,657.70	19,402.40	5.9	2.66	1.50	12.4	80
DREYFUS FUND	GI	11.28	1,678.1	8,944.30	8,898.80	19,242.40	1.8	0.88	0.74	18.9	60
DREYFUS GRO OPPORTUNITY	CA	9.55	372.9	9,458.50	9,963.00	19,609.20	6.4	3.23	0.17	10.6	92
DREYFUS LEVERAGE FUND	I	15.37	334.4	9,785.10	10,175.70	17,098.10	8.7	0.28	1.08	19.5	27
DREYFUS SPECIAL INCOME	G	7.04	86.3	9,112.70	8,845.30	18,074.60	3.9	0.55	0.63	20.4	63
DREYFUS THIRD CENTURY	G	6.47	116.8	8,597.40	8,200.10	18,149.80	3.3	2.68	0.25	N/A	254
EAGLE GROWTH SHARES	B	6.62	5.0	9,440.40	9,624.50	16,493.90	7.0	0.95	0.26	12.4	30
EATON & HOWARD BALANCED	GI	7.07	53.3	9,699.10	9,901.00	17,701.80	5.0	2.00	0.53	11.8	69
EATON & HOWARD STOCK	I	10.85	61.9	9,222.00	9,087.20	19,652.50	2.2	1.51	0.59	15.5	73
EATON VANCE GROWTH	B	4.37	57.5	9,753.80	10,001.60	14,159.70	12.6	0.00	0.14	N/A	41
EATON VANCE HIGH YIELD	OG	7.90	20.9	9,770.00	9,904.10	15,446.60	12.2	0.00	0.55	8.7	68
EATON VANCE INC OF BOSTN	EI	7.22	33.4	9,525.30	9,780.40	18,426.30	7.0	0.52	0.96	12.5	28
EATON VANCE INVESTORS	NR	17.68	135.8	9,135.50	8,560.00	24,365.30	0.3	4.05	0.52	16.4	65
EATON VANCE SPL EQUITIES	G	12.84	41.8	9,727.30	10,338.20	☆	0.0	0.00	0.06	8.2	N/A
EATON VANCE TX-MGD TRUST	GI	11.41	553.2	10,041.20	9,841.80	20,648.80	2.1	0.24	0.00	N/A	95
EBRSTDT ENERGY-RESOURCE	NR	20.81	42.2	9,462.20	9,137.40	20,587.70	4.5	0.96	0.24	18.1	N/A
ELFUN TRUSTS	G	1,585.34	311.6	9,549.60	9,709.30	19,028.00	4.7	163.00	0.95	13.7	37
ENDOWMENTS INC	GI	17.68	24.9	9,871.60	9,948.50	14,871.60	5.7	0.79	74.00	12.4	32
ENERGY FUND	NR	18.98	347.8	9,758.10	9,981.10	☆	10.4	0.00	1.01	14.2	30
ENERGY & UTILITY SHARES	S	13.39	8.6	#9,752.40	☆	25,101.20	0.0	1.98	1.98	N/A	N/A
EUROPACIFIC GROWTH	IF	36.45	12.7	9,167.30	25,101.20	23,922.30	1.8	0.00	0.00	13.9	78
EVERGREEN FUND (R)	EI	13.80	215.6	8,774.50	23,922.30	26,337.30	5.9	4.79	0.68	10.2	113
EVERGREEN TOTAL RETURN	SG		49.5	9,798.60	26,337.30	20,109.30		1.32	0.88		N/A
EXPLORER FUND	SG	31.06	237.3	8,460.90	20,109.30		2.0	1.66	0.64	24.3	N/A
FAIRFIELD FUND	SG	7.42	45.1	8,162.80			0.5	1.06	0.04	26.0	127

Copyright® Lipper Analytical Services, Inc.

FUND NAME	OBJ.	TOTAL NET ASTS (MIL) 6/30/84	NAV 6/30/84	PERFORMANCE (RETURN ON INITIAL $10,000 INVESTMENT) 12/31/83-6/30/84	6/30/83-6/30/84	6/30/79-6/30/84	YIELD % 6/30/84	PER SHARE LATEST 12 MONTHS CAP GAINS	INC DIVS	LATEST AVAILABLE PRICE/EARNINGS	ANNUAL % TURNOVER
FAIRMONT FUND	CA	16.9	156.29	9,772.60	9,840.20	☆	2.0	5.72	3.13	N/A	N/A
FARM BUREAU GROWTH FUND	GI	42.1	12.74	9,022.70	8,878.30	16,391.70	9.0	0.73	1.24	16.1	29
FEDERATED GNMA TRUST	FI	180.1	9.59	9,720.10	10,153.10	☆	13.0	0.00	1.24	N/A	N/A
FEDERATED HIGH INCOME	FI	149.3	10.98	9,835.10	10,198.50	15,539.80	13.9	0.00	1.53	N/A	19
FEDERATED INCOME TRUST	I	141.3	9.45	9,801.60	10,303.60	☆	12.9	0.00	1.21	N/A	N/A
FEDERATED INTMDT GOVT	FI	149.5	9.06	10,117.70	10,451.80	☆	11.7	0.18	1.06	N/A	N/A
FEDERATED STOCK TRUST	GI	33.2	14.10	9,989.70	10,681.10	☆	4.5	0.00	0.63	28	N/A
FEDERATED SH-INTMDT GOVT	FI	17.7	9.84	‡10,169.50	☆		0.0	0.00	0.32	N/A	28
FIDELITY CONTRAFUND	G	73.4	9.19	8,373.40	8,273.30	17,707.10	4.5	1.69	0.45	22.8	452
FIDELITY CORPORATE BOND	FI	133.7	6.08	9,711.10	9,900.30	13,680.40	12.5	0.00	0.76	N/A	164
FIDELITY DESTINY	G	532.5	12.12	9,195.80	9,109.80	25,024.90	2.9	2.25	0.35	12.2	105
FIDELITY DISCOVERER	CA	92.5	17.11	8,374.90	8,100.70	21,615.10	1.4	3.63	0.27	17.2	353
FIDELITY EQUITY-INCOME	EI	837.2	21.32	9,455.20	9,711.10	25,601.30	7.4	3.12	1.70	11.1	118
FIDELITY FUND	GI	557.8	13.58	9,027.10	8,960.00	20,955.10	4.9	4.40	0.77	10.8	210
FIDELITY FREEDOM FUND	CA	285.3	11.16	9,204.90	8,948.60	☆	0.4	0.42	0.04	14.0	116
FIDELITY GOVT SECURITIES	FI	72.9	8.61	9,784.40	10,047.40	15,829.10	10.9	0.00	0.94	N/A	N/A
FIDELITY HIGH INCOME	FI	261.9	8.10	9,734.40	10,326.40	16,753.70	14.0	0.00	1.13	17.1	129
FIDELITY MAGELLAN FUND	G	1,617.6	29.72	9,000.40	8,637.10	43,684.00	1.1	3.69	0.37	14.3	85
FIDELITY MERCURY	EI	110.4	11.21	8,728.50	8,069.90	☆	0.3	0.24	0.03	17.9	136
FIDELITY PURITAN	EI	783.4	11.30	9,547.80	10,233.40	21,380.20	8.8	1.37	1.00	9.2	90
FIDELITY QUALIFIED DVD	NR	173.7	11.54	10,060.50	10,829.00	☆	11.1	0.01	1.27	7.3	28
FIDELITY SEL ENERGY (R)	S	65.5	9.70	10,102.10	9,790.10	☆	1.3	0.00	0.13	14.8	87
FIDELITY SEL FINANCIAL (R)	S	111.8	15.93	9,416.70	9,959.90	☆	0.6	0.04	0.09	N/A	105
FIDELITY SEL HEALTH (R)	S	66.9	16.05	9,307.60	7,435.90	☆	0.4	0.09	0.06	17.5	32
FIDELITY SEL PREC-MTLS (R)	AU	178.2	13.45	10,058.60	9,010.90	☆	1.4	0.02	0.19	20.6	37
FIDELITY SEL TECH (R)	S	426.6	20.17	8,032.60	7,527.70	☆	0.0	0.08	0.00	25.6	128
FIDELITY SEL UTILITIES (R)	S	16.2	14.17	9,882.90	10,983.50	☆	1.6	0.00	0.23	N/A	24
FIDELITY SPL SITUATIONS	CA	7.2	9.98	9,970.00	☆	☆	0.0	0.00	0.00	14.8	N/A
FIDELITY THRIFT TRUST	FI	111.3	8.97	9,767.20	10,087.10	16,740.50	11.7	0.00	1.04	N/A	238
FIDELITY TREND	G	549.4	34.42	8,928.70	8,992.10	17,223.50	2.3	0.00	0.78	N/A	71
FIDUCIARY CAPITAL GROWTH	G	26.0	16.53	9,224.30	8,635.60	☆	2.3	0.07	0.37	N/A	30
FINANCIAL BOND SHARES	FI	7.2	5.84	9,339.40	9,441.70	14,286.10	13.1	0.04	0.77	N/A	33
FINANCIAL DYNAMICS	CA	66.2	6.66	8,554.90	7,590.20	18,775.40	1.9	1.38	0.15	19.4	56
FINANCIAL HIGH YIELD BND	FI	1.7	6.96	‡9,737.90	☆	☆	0.0	0.00	0.34	N/A	N/A
FINANCIAL INDUST FUND	GI	303.1	3.83	8,822.60	8,285.50	17,505.80	3.7	0.88	0.14	12.8	88
FINANCIAL INDUST INCOME	EI	182.6	7.30	9,532.80	9,801.00	20,242.40	6.5	0.96	0.54	N/A	57
FINANCIAL PORT-ENERGY	NR	0.3	6.82	‡9,362.50	☆	☆	0.0	0.00	0.00	N/A	N/A
FINANCIAL PORT-GOLD	AU	1.6	7.49	8,525.00	☆	☆	0.0	0.00	0.00	N/A	N/A
FINANCIAL PORT-HEALTH	S	0.3	8.10	☆	☆	☆	0.0	0.00	0.00	N/A	N/A
FINANCIAL PORT-LEISURE	S	0.2	6.76	‡10,125.00	☆	☆	0.0	0.00	0.00	N/A	N/A
FINANCIAL PORT-PACIFIC	IF	0.6	7.59	☆	☆	☆	0.0	0.00	0.00	N/A	N/A
FINANCIAL PORT-TECH	S	0.4	6.34	‡9,487.50	☆	☆	0.0	0.00	0.00	N/A	N/A
FINOMIC INVESTMENT FUND	CA	4.1	12.01	8,320.20	6,143.40	18,672.10	11.5	0.75	1.43	13.8	N/A
FIRST INV BOND APPREC	FI	85.2	12.57	9,550.80	9,517.30	16,414.60	0.6	1.93	0.08	N/A	186
FIRST INV DISCOVERY	SG	40.5	7.18	8,126.50	6,905.60	20,383.40	1.8	1.59	0.14	14.4	58
FIRST INV FD FOR GROWTH	G	75.9		8,184.70	7,381.50	19,901.90	0.0	0.00	0.00	24.9	82
FIRST INV FD FOR INCOME	FI	856.0	5.74	9,547.90	9,692.80	13,900.10	15.3	0.48	0.88	N/A	123
FIRST INV INTERNATIONAL	GL	35.8	14.05	9,706.70	9,572.30	☆	0.3	0.39	0.05	N/A	57
FIRST INV NTRL RESOURCES	NR	12.6	6.31	9,541.80	8,114.20	☆	0.6	0.00	0.04	21.0	74
FIRST INV 90/10	OG	50.6	12.98	10,013.30	10,422.00	10,258.50	7.3	0.78	0.95	N/A	159
FIRST INV OPTION FD	OI	128.0	5.36	9,864.40	9,927.40	☆	2.1	1.25	0.12	N/A	267
FPA CAPITAL	G	35.5	8.57	8,609.20	8,668.30	17,343.10	3.6	0.00	0.35	13.8	130
FPA NEW INCOME	FI	4.4	7.49	9,718.60	9,714.20	16,366.30	12.1	1.36	0.91	N/A	30
FPA PARAMOUNT	GI	108.2	12.26	9,706.10	10,234.70	13,875.10	4.0	0.00	0.52	N/A	130
FPA PERENNIAL FUND	CA	5.7	14.18	‡10,201.40	☆	23,172.60	0.0	1.06	0.00	N/A	N/A
FLEX FUND	CA	44.5	10.51	9,915.80	9,694.10	☆	4.2	0.00	0.46	N/A	N/A
FLORIDA MUT US GOVT 2	FI	0.1	0.98	10,303.00	10,768.70	☆	8.5	0.00	0.08	N/A	N/A

Fund	Type	Net Assets	NAV	Value	Value	Value	%	%	%	%	Rank
44 WALL STREET	CA	82.0	7.56	5,990.50	4,416.00	9,274.80	0.0	4.02	0.00	27.2	113
44 WALL STREET EQUITY	CA	12.4	4.93	7,549.80	5,524.80		0.0	3.57	0.00	N/A	101
FOUNDATION GROWTH STOCK	G	1.3	4.43	9,548.90	9,297.20	14,130.20	3.2	0.39	0.15	N/A	N/A
FOUNDERS GROWTH	G	37.6	6.29	10,040.90	7,948.10	22,938.50	23.8	1.04	1.62	13.9	150
FOUNDERS INCOME	EI	6.9	13.86	9,072.90	10,385.40	19,853.30	5.9	0.49	0.82	13.4	159
FOUNDERS MUTUAL	GI	127.7	9.61	8,435.30	9,391.20	17,600.00	3.4	0.70	0.32	N/A	N/A
FOUNDERS SPECIAL	CA	13.4	23.02	#9,735.20	7,159.60	22,427.60 ☆	8.0	1.39	1.89	14.4	141
FRANKLIN CORP CASH	EI	39.4	9.12	9,057.80	8,192.90	24,552.40	0.0	0.00	0.33	N/A	88
FRANKLIN DYNATECH	CA	139.4	9.67	10,146.90	9,488.80	38,472.80	1.2	0.71	0.12	16.6	3
FRANKLIN GOLD FUND	AU	18.1	11.52	9,124.10	8,763.00	18,132.40	4.6	0.12	0.53	23.8	10
FRANKLIN GROWTH	G	65.5	10.55	9,522.10	9,819.60	19,887.60	1.9	0.53	0.23	N/A	8
FRANKLIN INCOME		6.4	1.79	9,699.90	9,991.70		12.8	0.23	0.23	6.2	50
FRANKLIN OPTION	OI	1,686.7	6.14	9,643.50	9,630.90	12,660.10	0.2	0.04	0.01	N/A	60
FRANKLIN US GOVERNMENT	FI	26.4	6.48	9,676.90	10,420.70	17,857.30	13.9	0.61	0.90	N/A	N/A
FRANKLIN UTILITIES	S	47.8	7.74	9,733.20	10,226.90	13,937.00	9.8	0.00	0.51	N/A	N/A
FUND FOR US GOVT SEC	FI	137.3	10.93	9,813.60	10,110.70		11.8	0.00	0.91	15.7	58
FUND OF AMERICA	GI	7.2	10.48	8,193.90	7,583.20	28,236.90	3.8	3.47	0.48	12.9	96
FUND OF THE SOUTHWEST	CA	349.5	10.43	9,081.50	9,416.20	23,529.00	0.5	2.60	0.06	13.4	21
FUNDAMENTAL INVESTORS	GI	23.3	13.48	9,588.50	9,829.80	19,677.70	3.8	0.43	0.40	N/A	170
GATEWAY OPTION INCOME	OI	0.6	12.36	#10,957.40	☆	15,470.40	3.0	1.70	0.43	N/A	N/A
GENERAL AGGRESSIVE GRO	G	173.3	9.67	9,864.50	9,323.10		12.1	0.00	0.00	N/A	N/A
GENL ELEC LT INTEREST	FI	583.4	30.36	9,268.30	8,976.60	16,833.40	5.1	1.40	1.17	11.4	N/A
GENL ELEC S&S PROGRAM	G	11.5	10.56	9,073.80		16,938.40	5.1	1.50	1.57	N/A	13
GENERAL SECURITIES	CA	0.2	10.10	10,049.80	10,364.90		0.0	0.00	0.58	N/A	N/A
GIBRALTAR FUND	GI	61.3	33.26	9,796.50	8,666.20		2.5	2.75	0.00	20.6	59
GINTEL ERISA	GI	106.1	71.59	9,308.30	9,299.60		1.9	8.24	0.85	19.3	43
GINTEL FUND	G	23.0	12.04	9,526.10	☆	20,246.30	1.7	0.00	1.51	22.7	12
GOLCONDA INVESTORS LTD	AU	12.7	11.91	9,407.60	☆		0.9	0.00	0.20	N/A	2
GOOD & BAD TIMES FUND	GI	3.1	9.19	9,676.20	☆		0.0	0.39	0.39	N/A	N/A
GT EQUITY INCOME	EI	3.6	8.73	9,873.90	☆		0.0	1.12	1.12	N/A	N/A
GT INCOME A RATED	FI	0.4	8.59	9,694.30	☆		0.0	1.22	1.22	N/A	N/A
GT INCOME MAX INC	FI	0.7	9.10	9,688.10	☆		0.0	0.24	0.24	N/A	N/A
GT PACIFIC FUND	G	3.8	9.55	8,987.60	☆		0.0	0.19	0.19	N/A	N/A
GT SELECT GROWTH	SG	6.9	7.99	9,178.40	8,103.30	18,496.00	0.3	0.00	0.00	N/A	82
GT SPECIAL GROWTH	SG	4.9	9.71	10,176.70	8,897.20	24,745.60	0.1	0.15	0.15	27.3	125
GRADISON EMERGING GROWTH	G	3.6	11.39	9,680.60	8,232.20	22,612.70	3.3	0.02	0.02	20.2	26
GRADISON ESTABLISHED GRO	G	434.6	8.13	8,954.30	6,232.90		1.9	3.52	0.01	N/A	10
GREENSPRING FUND	CA	59.4	12.16	9,282.10	10,719.80	15,136.30	0.4	0.27	0.40	N/A	757
GREENWAY FUND	G	7.2	10.12	8,631.40	9,127.80		4.6	0.66	0.20	13.7	130
GROWTH FUND OF AMERICA	G	39.2	6.37	8,952.20	9,424.70		0.0	0.36	0.06	N/A	34
GROWTH INDUSTRY SHARES	CA	0.5	15.67	9,921.80	9,127.80	22,001.00	4.3	0.03	0.05	16.4	4
GSC PERFORMANCE FUND	IF	3.2	1.28	9,388.40	9,640.90	23,370.70	2.8	0.00	0.00	N/A	50
GT PACIFIC FUND		300.7	9.21	9,294.20	9,622.30		4.2	2.38	1.55	10.6	66
GUIDANCE INVESTMENTS	I	51.4	35.10	9,820.10	7,838.80		12.7	2.36	0.48	10.7	23
GUARDIAN BOND FUND	FI	5.9	16.24	9,596.40	9,975.40	14,683.80	1.6	0.00	0.00	N/A	241
GUARDIAN MUTUAL	GI	190.5	10.70	8,736.50	8,773.70	13,116.40	11.0	0.21	0.21	13.7	23
GUARDIAN PARK AVENUE	G	687.7	5.06	9,719.30	10,282.00	20,909.90	4.2	1.62	1.62	N/A	45
GUARDIAN STOCK FUND	GI	52.2	12.82	9,932.70	7,581.00	14,425.90	0.0	0.93	0.19	16.4	N/A
HAMILTON FUNDS	FI	101.8	11.52	9,290.80	5,513.50	25,004.70	14.7	0.00	0.87	N/A	70
J HANCOCK BOND	FI	11.0	7.93	10,282.00	25,004.70	23,137.00	13.0	1.65	0.47	27.5	80
J HANCOCK GROWTH	G	38.6	10.47	8,694.00	23,137.00		0.0	1.39	0.00	N/A	33
J HANCOCK US GOVT SEC	FI	76.4	11.17	7,164.80		16,154.70	0.0	0.03	1.53	N/A	52
HARTWELL GROWTH FUND	CA	88.0	10.37	9,509.40			10.1	0.00	1.24	N/A	10
HARTWELL LEVERAGE FUND	CA	18.3	9.53	9,813.80			9.0	0.01	0.93	N/A	346
HIGH INCOME SHARES	FI	152.4	9.23	9,689.80			0.5	1.24	0.87	N/A	185
HIGH YIELD SECURITIES	FI	138.5	9.61	10,169.20			0.0	0.93	0.18	N/A	N/A
HOME INVESTORS FUND	SG	20.7	9.76	9,645.70				0.87	0.70		
HUTTON INV SR-BOND (R)	FI		9.58	7,527.80 ☆	7,527.80 ☆			0.18	0.05		
HUTTON INV SR-EMER GRO (R)	SG			#9,580.00 ☆				0.70	0.00		
HUTTON INV SR-GOVT	FI			☆				0.00	0.00		

Copyright® Lipper Analytical Services, Inc.

PERFORMANCE OF MUTUAL FUNDS *(continued)*

FUND NAME	OBJ.	TOTAL NET ASTS (MIL) 6/30/84	NAV 6/30/84	PERFORMANCE (RETURN ON INITIAL $10,000 INVESTMENT) 12/31/83–6/30/84	6/30/83–6/30/84	6/30/79–6/30/84	YIELD % 6/30/84	PER SHARE LATEST 12 MONTHS — CAP GAINS	INC DIVS	LATEST AVAILABLE PRICE/EARNINGS	ANNUAL % TURNOVER
HUTTON INV SR-GROWTH (R)	G	637.5	12.07	9,164.60	8,814.50	☆	2.1	1.67	0.27	N/A	437
HUTTON INV SR-OPTION	OI	90.3	9.34	9,668.00	☆	15,503.70	0.0	0.00	0.42	N/A	4
IDS BOND FUND	FI	1,061.3	4.39	9,832.40	10,065.60	☆	13.4	0.00	0.58	N/A	59
IDS DISCOVERY FUND	SG	290.1	6.67	8,475.20	7,114.60	31,388.20	1.4	0.35	0.09	21.9	36
IDS EXTRA INCOME	I	109.9	4.64	9,934.20	☆	☆	0.0	0.00	0.35	N/A	N/A
IDS GROWTH FUND	G	608.8	15.05	8,546.30	6,990.70	☆	0.1	0.94	0.01	26.8	38
IDS LIFE CAPITAL RES I	G	20.8	12.91	9,051.10	8,354.00	☆	2.6	0.65	0.33	N/A	60
IDS LIFE CAPITAL RES II	G	94.6	13.38	9,059.40	8,367.70	☆	2.6	0.20	0.34	N/A	33
IDS LIFE SPEC INC I	FI	22.3	10.09	9,911.60	10,052.60	☆	12.6	0.42	1.27	N/A	67
IDS LIFE SPEC INC II	FI	63.4	10.18	9,918.20	10,071.60	☆	12.6	0.35	1.28	N/A	52
IDS NEW DIMENSIONS	G	337.0	8.25	9,197.30	8,197.00	27,648.50	1.4	1.25	0.11	22.0	88
IDS PROGRESSIVE	CA	155.5	6.50	9,434.00	9,606.00	24,339.80	3.5	0.97	0.22	17.2	218
IDS SELECTIVE	FI	713.0	7.29	9,810.40	10,154.40	15,545.00	14.8	0.00	1.08	N/A	80
IDS STOCK	GI	1,291.1	14.86	9,287.10	9,182.50	17,550.20	3.4	5.78	0.60	15.5	152
IDS STRATEGY AGGR EQ (R)	CA	1.5	5.34	‡10,680.00	☆	☆	0.0	0.00	0.00	N/A	N/A
IDS STRATEGY EQUITY (R)	GI	1.1	5.12	‡10,274.80	☆	☆	0.0	0.00	0.01	N/A	N/A
IDS STRATEGY INCOME (R)	FI	1.0	4.97	‡10,055.20	☆	☆	0.0	0.00	0.05	N/A	N/A
IDS VARIABLE	GI	322.3	7.27	8,931.20	8,182.40	17,923.80	3.0	2.60	0.25	17.1	137
INCOME FUND OF AMERICA	EI	267.9	9.85	9,744.60	10,209.90	18,819.80	8.4	0.33	0.84	12.0	52
INDUSTRY FUND OF AMERICA	CA	0.5	6.70	8,567.80	7,827.10	14,316.20	0.0	0.00	0.00	N/A	N/A
INTERNATIONAL INVESTORS	AU	927.4	13.88	10,182.00	9,686.90	40,080.30	4.6	0.64	0.64	28.4	N/A
INVESTMENT CO OF AMERICA	GI	2,189.4	9.93	9,432.90	9,552.50	20,372.90	4.1	0.51	0.42	12.6	20
INVEST PORT-EQUITY (R)	CA	8.2	8.57	‡10,140.10	☆	☆	0.0	0.00	0.05	N/A	N/A
INVEST PORT-HIGH YLD (R)	FI	4.8	8.32	9,882.60	☆	☆	0.0	0.00	0.08	N/A	N/A
INVESTMENT QUAL INTEREST	FI	68.2	8.47	9,459.90	9,675.40	☆	13.3	0.09	1.14	N/A	59
INVESTMENT TRUST BOSTON	GI	51.8	8.84	9,018.00	8,268.50	16,580.10	2.5	1.13	0.25	13.6	42
ITB HIGH INCOME	FI	8.2	13.14	‡9,663.00	☆	☆	8.3	0.30	0.83	N/A	81
INVESTORS MUTUAL	B	1,000.8	10.09	9,578.60	9,995.00	17,478.00	0.0	0.53	0.00	14.5	56
INVESTORS RESEARCH	CA	36.3	4.87	9,293.90	7,732.20	26,251.00	0.0	0.91	0.00	21.6	59
IRI STOCK FUND	G	9.2	13.01	8,878.10	8,617.70	☆	1.1	0.70	0.15	N/A	612
ISI GROWTH FUND	I	13.3	6.09	9,841.50	9,911.80	15,208.50	7.4	0.00	0.45	N/A	N/A
ISI INCOME FUND	I	6.9	3.38	9,876.50	10,095.70	15,110.30	10.1	0.00	0.34	N/A	670
ISI TRUST FUND	GI	103.0	10.22	10,400.90	10,756.60	15,088.20	8.8	0.00	0.90	16.1	27
ISTEL FUND	GI	92.8	13.37	9,161.80	9,017.00	15,534.60	4.7	0.73	0.65	13.0	95
IVEST FUND	GL	168.9	15.47	9,567.10	9,506.60	20,615.40	2.2	2.08	0.34	12.1	59
IVY GROWTH	G	58.0	12.17	9,466.10	10,111.90	25,958.40	6.0	1.78	0.78	N/A	N/A
IVY INSTITUTIONAL	CA	53.4	95.10	‡9,536.70	☆	☆	0.0	0.00	0.00	18.0	94
JANUS FUND	G	282.0	11.38	9,399.30	8,924.30	31,222.40	7.1	0.35	0.82	N/A	77
JP GROWTH FUND	FI	17.3	12.68	9,645.00	9,273.20	20,225.60	4.5	1.50	0.60	16.7	11
JP INCOME FUND	G	18.7	7.16	9,409.00	9,452.40	12,772.70	12.6	0.00	0.90	N/A	73
KEMPER GROWTH FUND	G	215.1	12.21	9,044.20	8,700.70	23,213.10	2.1	1.74	0.27	N/A	108
KEMPER HIGH YIELD	FI	180.4	9.61	9,942.80	10,417.60	16,704.30	13.5	0.00	1.30	15.1	68
KEMPER INCOME & CAP PRES	IF	95.6	7.75	9,996.50	10,380.90	14,504.80	13.2	0.00	1.02	19.9	137
KEMPER INTERNATIONAL FUND	OI	44.5	13.90	9,302.20	10,047.60	☆	1.0	0.20	0.14	18.0	204
KEMPER OPTION INCOME	G	192.6	11.31	9,913.60	10,135.60	18,589.20	3.7	1.50	0.45	N/A	45
KEMPER SUMMIT FUND	B	150.0	22.01	8,961.70	8,246.50	24,893.20	1.5	2.02	0.35	N/A	98
KEMPER TOTAL RETURN	FI	246.5	12.21	9,097.90	8,632.70	22,229.70	4.6	1.60	0.60	N/A	N/A
KEMPER US GOVT SEC	FI	227.2	8.28	9,995.30	10,443.90	13,335.00	12.7	0.00	1.05	N/A	79
KEYSTONE B-1 (R)	FI	57.5	13.84	9,392.60	9,475.20	14,665.60	12.1	0.00	1.68	N/A	158
KEYSTONE B-2 (R)	FI	94.4	16.38	9,502.50	9,333.60	15,990.60	13.2	0.00	2.16	N/A	61
KEYSTONE B-4 (R)	FI	392.6	7.47	9,687.50	9,737.60	16,817.60	13.1	0.00	0.98	17.4	40
KEYSTONE INTERNATIONAL (R)	GL	26.9	4.67	8,895.20	8,700.90	15,101.90	1.1	0.00	0.05	13.1	N/A
KEYSTONE K-1 (R)	I	63.5	8.17	9,467.70	9,517.60	17,354.50	8.8	0.00	0.72	10.3	51
KEYSTONE K-2 (R)	G	163.2	5.86	8,854.30	8,478.00	17,902.20	2.7	2.19	0.20	14.9	63

Fund	Type	(1)	(2)	(3)	(4)	(5)	(6)	(7)	(8)	(9)	Rank
KEYSTONE S-1 (R)	GI	18.04	67.3	8,926.00	8,954.70	15,454.60	3.5	1.08	0.64	12.2	50
KEYSTONE S-3 (R)	G	8.16	141.3	8,644.10	8,418.10	19,637.80	2.5	1.02	0.20	21.9	66
KEYSTONE S-4 (R)	G	5.04	477.4	7,963.30	6,608.30	23,987.80	0.4	0.61	0.02	22.6	93
LBKL CAPITAL OPP	CA	18.69	44.0	9,609.70	9,609.30		2.2	1.38	0.42	12.7	46
LEGG MASON VALUE TRUST	G	18.35	70.4	9,613.70	10,454.90		1.6	0.34	0.30	N/A	18
LEHMAN CAPITAL FUND	CA	19.22	105.3	9,244.80	9,190.80	31,743.80	2.0	4.17	0.39	20.9	114
LEHMAN INVESTORS	GI	16.51	335.0	9,145.30	9,145.30	21,193.00	3.4	3.18	0.61	13.5	42
LEVERAGE FUND OF BOSTON	CA	6.65	29.5	8,021.70	7,656.80	15,990.50	11.4	3.04	0.00	22.1	75
LEXINGTON GNMA INCOME	FI	6.99	23.0	9,551.00	9,984.10	12,557.90	0.4	0.00	0.80	N/A	207
LEXINGTON GOLDFUND	AU	4.07	8.9	10,141.50	9,369.30	20,953.60	2.2	0.10	0.09	N/A	16
LEXINGTON GROWTH	G	7.29	18.8	8,054.40	6,907.60	13,019.50	2.3	0.73	0.30	15.5	57
LEXINGTON RESEARCH	G	14.22	92.7	8,698.10	8,643.90	19,701.40	5.1	2.73	0.80	11.9	64
LG FUND FOR GROWTH	G	8.90	2.5	9,609.40	9,133.90	☆	1.6	0.00	0.14	N/A	23
LG FUND FOR INCOME	EI	8.67	0.8	9,950.50	9,852.70	☆	6.0	0.00	0.52	N/A	10
LIBERTY FUND	FI	3.74	7.6	9,664.60	10,102.50	13,910.60	9.4	0.00	0.35	N/A	225
LIBRA FUND	G	5.15	0.3	#10,300.00	☆	☆	0.0	0.00	0.00	N/A	N/A
LINDNER FUND	G	18.30	339.8	10,300.10	10,539.80	30,709.50	4.7	0.45	0.86	11.0	15
LINDNER DIVIDEND	EI	20.45	1.2	10,287.00	11,219.10	31,897.10	5.5	6.10	1.32	N/A	30
LMH FUND	GI	20.55	30.5	10,009.70	☆	☆	0.0	0.00	0.00	N/A	N/A
LOOMIS-SAYLES CAPITAL	G	16.19	120.7	8,598.70	7,695.10	31,408.30	0.6	6.15	0.11	18.9	174
LOOMIS-SAYLES MUTUAL	B	15.06	81.7	9,173.50	9,182.00	17,256.20	5.9	1.86	0.95	10.9	194
LORD ABBETT BOND-DEB	FI	9.57	190.4	9,618.30	9,613.50	15,967.60	11.8	0.15	1.14	7.0	89
LORD ABBETT DEVEL GROWTH	SG	7.37	300.4	7,998.80	7,159.60	21,068.20	0.7	0.17	0.05	23.2	6
LORD ABBETT INCOME	I	2.77	47.9	9,862.80	10,002.90	15,930.00	12.5	0.00	0.34	7.1	52
LORD ABBETT VALUE APPREC	G	7.79	309.2	8,526.00	☆	☆	0.0	0.00	0.22	15.9	6
LOWRY MARKET TIMING	CA	8.90	56.6	9,684.00	☆	☆	0.0	0.00	0.00	N/A	N/A
LUTHERAN BRO FUND	GI	13.20	50.6	9,969.40	10,521.90	21,244.30	5.9	0.73	0.80	11.6	39
LUTHERAN BRO INCOME	I	7.84	122.0	9,752.90	10,133.70	15,605.70	13.3	0.00	1.04	5.7	78
MAGNA INCOME TRUST	FI	7.24	7.3	9,571.90	9,704.40	14,809.40	12.6	0.00	0.92	N/A	20
MAGNACAP FUND	G	6.17	9.8	10,028.30	10,440.10	20,336.30	5.3	0.00	0.33	N/A	70
MANHATTAN FUND	CA	5.82	69.1	9,485.40	9,515.60	24,206.70	3.1	0.00	0.18	11.9	173
HORACE MANN GROWTH	G	21.29	63.3	9,390.30	8,652.50	20,108.60	1.3	7.25	0.29	17.6	26
MASS CAPITAL DEVELOPMENT	G	9.90	577.8	8,529.90	8,151.40	29,836.20	2.1	0.62	0.21	16.4	67
MASS FINL BOND	FI	11.76	224.7	9,817.70	10,069.10	14,558.50	11.9	2.00	1.40	N/A	238
MASS FINL DEVELOPMENT	G	10.50	181.9	8,676.30	7,996.80	21,197.50	2.9	2.40	0.30	14.6	66
MASS FINL EMERGING GRO	SG	12.62	156.6	8,965.40	7,837.30	☆	1.6	0.00	0.20	21.8	41
MASS FINL HIGH INCOME	FI	6.59	344.8	9,752.90	9,773.20	18,749.90	13.3	0.48	0.91	N/A	101
MASS FINL INTL TR-BOND	GL	9.23	35.5	9,688.00	10,001.00	☆	8.7	0.00	0.80	17.3	192
MASS FINL SPECIAL	CA	6.59	79.4	8,402.80	8,256.30	☆	1.7	0.00	0.11	N/A	N/A
MASSACHUSETTS FUND	B	11.39	185.8	9,230.40	9,146.80	18,002.30	6.6	0.86	0.78	13.1	53
MASS INCOME DEVELOPMENT	I	7.96	186.7	9,370.00	9,699.20	18,058.80	7.8	0.64	0.62	11.1	121
MASS INVESTORS GROWTH	G	10.69	796.4	9,019.00	8,419.90	20,544.70	2.6	1.94	0.30	15.2	34
MASS INVESTORS TRUST	GI	10.40	985.3	9,147.10	9,229.60	17,983.80	4.2	1.25	0.46	13.2	25
MATHERS FUND	G	18.29	179.3	8,922.40	8,652.80	18,219.40	5.6	2.45	1.09	12.5	85
MAXIM BOND	FI	0.96	0.9	9,669.50	10,007.50	☆	11.7	0.00	0.11	N/A	N/A
MAXIM INCOME EQUITY	EI	0.91	1.3	9,291.70	9,427.70	☆	16.9	0.00	0.15	N/A	N/A
MBL GROWTH FUND	G	10.51	21.0	9,342.20	9,326.70	☆	4.2	1.11	0.47	N/A	35
MEDICAL TECHNOLOGY FUND	S	8.46	49.8	8,615.10	6,555.40	☆	0.7	0.00	0.05	29.7	8
MEESCHAERT CAPITAL	GI	21.16	13.1	10,061.80	10,081.00	☆	0.0	0.00	0.00	N/A	49
MERRILL LYN BASIC VALUE	GI	13.23	269.3	9,473.80	9,981.80	15,885.90	4.7	0.92	0.62	14.1	34
MERRILL LYN CAPITAL	GI	16.99	260.8	9,306.50	9,684.90	22,056.80	3.4	1.99	0.65	13.1	101
MERRILL LYN EQUI-BOND	FI	9.97	13.4	9,476.80	9,452.00	21,193.90	6.6	0.00	0.66	N/A	69
MERRILL LYN HIGH INCOME	FI	7.45	229.0	9,814.80	10,170.60	14,311.00	13.6	0.00	1.01	13.6	136
MERRILL LYN HIGH QUALITY	FI	9.37	113.1	9,730.70	9,948.30	15,073.00	12.9	0.00	1.21	12.9	145
MERRILL LYN INTERMEDIATE	FI	9.59	27.0	9,802.40	10,125.70		12.3	0.00	1.18	12.3	100
MERRILL LYN PACIFIC	IF	13.83	92.7	9,224.40	11,294.60		0.6	0.95	0.09	N/A	82
MERRILL LYN PHOENIX	GI	11.45	104.8	10,007.40	10,532.30	21,799.10	3.4	0.47	0.40	12.8	37
MERRILL LYN SPEC VALUE	G	11.07	84.4	9,171.90	8,104.80	17,197.20	0.7	0.29	0.08	17.8	46

Copyright© Lipper Analytical Services, Inc.

PERFORMANCE OF MUTUAL FUNDS (continued)

FUND NAME	OBJ.	TOTAL NET ASTS (MIL) 6/30/84	NAV 6/30/84	PERFORMANCE (RETURN ON INITIAL $10,000 INVESTMENT) 12/31/83-6/30/84	6/30/83-6/30/84	6/30/79-6/30/84	YIELD % 6/30/84	PER SHARE LATEST 12 MONTHS CAP GAINS	INC DIVS	LATEST AVAILABLE PRICE/EARNINGS	ANNUAL % TURNOVER
MIDAMERICA HIGH GROWTH	CA	12.2	4.42	8,822.40	8,634.60	17,381.70	2.2	1.02	0.10	N/A	96
MIDAMERICA MUTUAL	G	27.6	5.90	9,106.80	9,107.10	17,873.30	4.4	0.97	0.27	15.7	69
MIDWEST/BARLETT VALUE	GI	15.0	10.11	10,099.00	10,565.30	☆	5.2	0.00	0.53	N/A	8
MIDWEST INCOME TR/INTMDT	FI	24.5	9.60	10,057.80	10,285.80	☆	9.4	0.00	0.90	N/A	N/A
MONEY MARKET/OPTIONS	OG	13.4	16.72	9,405.70	9,324.10	17,356.10	8.3	0.00	1.38	N/A	N/A
MONTHLY INCOME SHARES	FI	34.2	9.82	9,594.10	9,704.70	13,228.60	12.7	0.00	1.25	6.2	27
WL MORGAN GROWTH	G	370.7	10.76	8,827.70	8,567.70	20,722.40	2.7	1.39	0.31	15.4	31
MUTUAL BENEFIT FUND	G	9.3	10.31	9,230.10	9,233.90	19,995.90	4.4	2.51	0.51	N/A	N/A
MUTUAL OMAHA AMERICA	FI	17.9	9.01	9,767.80	10,177.10	14,202.30	11.0	0.00	0.99	N/A	222
MUTUAL OMAHA GROWTH	G	18.7	5.27	9,197.20	8,405.90	17,047.00	5.3	0.00	0.28	18.5	164
MUTUAL OMAHA INCOME	I	44.6	7.62	9,785.30	9,986.80	14,534.50	11.7	0.00	0.89	24.7	79
MUTUAL QUALIFIED INCOME	CA	109.8	16.65	10,578.80	11,690.10	24,890.10	2.3	1.40	0.40	23.4	70
MUTUAL SHARES CORP	GI	370.3	51.29	10,566.80	11,502.70	23,116.80	4.9	3.40	2.60	27.5	70
NAESS & THOMAS SPECIAL	SG	36.0	39.04	8,146.90	6,680.80	16,532.00	4.8	5.52	2.01	16.6	83
NATL AVIATION & TECH	SG	75.4	8.40	8,652.40	7,711.50	17,944.60	2.9	0.34	0.25	N/A	10
NATL BALANCED	B	1.7	12.49	9,786.80	10,052.60	13,760.00	6.7	0.00	0.84	N/A	61
NATL BOND	FI	214.4	3.01	9,656.00	9,689.90	15,284.90	15.4	0.00	0.46	N/A	102
NATL GROWTH	G	68.8	7.86	8,444.20	6,996.20	19,495.50	1.5	0.38	0.12	18.4	51
NATL INCOME	EI	52.8	6.37	9,959.60	10,268.80	14,765.00	8.4	1.17	0.57	11.6	18
NATL INDUSTRIES (R)	GI	27.7	11.24	9,163.90	9,026.90	16,056.60	3.3	0.00	0.39	15.0	50
NATL PREFERRED	FI	3.5	6.78	10,024.00	10,257.00	17,600.80	10.6	0.64	0.72	10.3	41
NATL STOCK	FI	230.3	7.99	9,520.40	9,385.70	21,302.10	6.0	0.45	0.52	N/A	53
NATL TELECOM & TECH	GI	96.2	11.82	8,686.40	7,984.20	☆	4.1	0.01	0.48	18.8	6
NATL TOTAL RETURN	EI	128.6	5.45	9,680.60	9,824.80	16,690.30	6.5	0.13	0.38	13.7	29
NATIONWIDE BOND	FI	5.2	8.46	9,816.10	10,055.70	21,696.50	12.0	0.79	1.02	N/A	4
NATIONWIDE FUND	GI	218.6	9.27	9,585.40	9,720.90	16,621.80	5.7	0.21	0.53	13.3	10
NATIONWIDE GROWTH	G	56.7	7.72	9,772.20	9,916.20	19,382.80	1.5	3.38	0.12	13.3	36
NATION-WIDE SECURITIES	B	33.6	10.03	9,865.30	10,149.30	31,468.50	7.5	2.47	0.75	8.6	59
NEL EQUITY FUND	G	15.9	16.86	9,012.80	9,430.40	13,323.90	4.1	3.72	0.76	15.9	136
NEL GROWTH FUND	G	164.6	18.43	8,739.10	7,717.30	21,297.50	0.6	0.11	0.11	17.6	171
NEL INCOME FUND	FI	33.7	9.78	8,924.20	9,924.20	☆	10.7	0.49	1.05	N/A	289
NEL RETIREMENT EQUITY	GI	61.8	16.80	9,066.70	9,054.70	☆	2.6	0.55	0.48	N/A	180
NEL SERIES BOND INCOME	FI	10.3	99.31	9,990.20	☆	☆	0.0	1.16	3.76	N/A	N/A
NEL SERIES CAPITAL GRO	CA	1.1	96.62	8,911.50	☆	☆	0.0	0.39	0.21	N/A	N/A
NEUWIRTH FUND	G	18.0	15.17	8,314.30	6,825.40	17,654.20	0.0	0.45	0.54	N/A	81
NEW ALTERNATIVES FUND	NR	0.2	52.33	8,826.00	8,413.30	☆	1.0	1.16	1.26	N/A	1
"NEW BEGINNING" GROWTH	SG	13.3	18.88	9,538.70	8,447.60	☆	6.5	0.39	1.12	N/A	67
"NEW BEGINNING" INC & GR	GI	1.1	12.23	9,230.30	8,544.60	☆	8.9	0.45	0.00	N/A	139
NEW ECONOMY FUND	GL	348.0	12.93	9,410.50	☆	☆	3.3	0.60	0.27	16.9	N/A
NEW PERSPECTIVE FUND	GL	578.9	7.77	9,271.40	9,723.20	20,902.50	2.5	1.64	0.18	16.9	50
NEW YORK VENTURE	G	85.3	7.25	9,337.40	9,343.20	25,254.00	0.7	1.88	0.19	12.0	97
NEWTON GROWTH FUND	G	29.0	24.39	9,013.30	7,726.40	24,438.00	11.0	0.00	0.86	21.6	55
NEWTON INCOME FUND	FI	7.1	7.90	10,225.40	10,503.10	14,565.80	2.6	1.57	0.64	N/A	41
NICHOLAS FUND	G	157.1	22.73	9,673.70	9,313.30	27,330.10	13.0	0.00	0.44	12.2	22
NICHOLAS II	G	15.1	3.41	9,879.60	10,221.20	13,858.70	0.0	0.00	0.00	N/A	19
NICHOLAS INCOME	I	6.4	10.51	10,174.20	☆	☆	0.0	0.14	0.08	N/A	N/A
NORTH STAR APOLLO	CA	14.8	9.21	8,889.10	9,832.40	☆	0.0	0.00	0.90	N/A	20
NORTH STAR BOND FUND	FI	17.8	8.43	9,630.40	8,727.10	14,685.80	10.8	0.00	0.43	N/A	27
NORTH STAR REGIONAL FUND	GI	44.2	14.61	9,045.90	9,209.90	☆	2.7	1.11	0.36	18.5	77
NORTH STAR STOCK FUND	CA	45.9	11.41	9,132.20	8,811.90	20,169.50	2.9	1.39	0.11	12.1	69
NORTHEAST INV GROWTH	G	3.6	10.13	9,207.00	9,701.10	☆	1.1	0.30	1.46	N/A	63
NORTHEAST INV TRUST	FI	153.7	10.36	9,627.80	8,341.10	14,532.60	14.1	0.00	0.19	4.7	30
NOVA FUND	G	28.1	11.90	8,941.50	☆	☆	1.4	3.22	1.04	28.2	158
OHIO NATIONAL-BOND	FI	1.8	8.46	9,619.90	9,666.90	☆	12.4	0.00	—	N/A	N/A

Fund	Obj.	Net Assets	NAV							%	Rank
OHIO NATIONAL-EQUITY	CA	17.5	12.18	9,034.10	9,132.80	☆	4.7	0.64	0.58	N/A	N/A
OMEGA FUND	CA	23.1	9.50	8,765.60	7,934.00	13,627.90	0.9	1.65	0.09	N/A	242
ONE HUNDRED FUND	G	10.0	14.83	8,378.50	6,585.30	18,085.90	0.0	1.00	0.00	N/A	155
ONE HUNDRED & ONE FUND	GI	13	12.96	9,648.20	8,607.00	18,607.00	2.5	2.50	0.33	22.4	168
OPPENHEIMER A I M	GL	227.2	16.69	8,574.30	7,844.30	22,264.70	0.6	2.50	0.11	22.4	91
OPPENHEIMER CHALLENGER	CA	20.2	9.34	9,340.00	6,607.50	☆	0.0	3.16	0.00	N/A	N/A
OPPENHEIMER DIRECTORS	CA	244.3	17.33	7,913.20	8,937.50	20,805.30	6.6	1.99	0.45	14.6	280
OPPENHEIMER EQUITY	EI	66.3	6.83	9,117.20	7,493.50	22,364.10	2.0	0.27	0.16	11.0	287
OPPENHEIMER FUND		234.9	7.89	8,144.00	☆	16,110.80	14.6	0.24	0.00	12.8	241
OPPENHEIMER GLD & SP MIN	AU	29.4	8.21	8,837.50	9,843.30	☆	1.4	2.44	2.44	N/A	N/A
OPPENHEIMER HIGH YIELD	FI	388.8	16.70	9,582.30	10,213.90	14,543.20	0.0	3.11	0.34	14.0	201
OPPENHEIMER PREMIUM INC	OI	98.2	22.23	9,973.90	7,676.30	18,185.10	2.7	1.63	0.52	19.2	238
OPPENHEIMER REGENCY	CA	97.7	12.95	8,191.00	8,910.40	20,753.00	0.7	0.60	0.11	18.4	187
OPPENHEIMER SPECIAL	G	644.1	19.45	8,449.20	7,387.20	22,841.40	1.1	0.39	0.13	16.4	193
OPPENHEIMER TARGET (OT)	CA	150.3	15.57	8,476.30	7,657.40	23,980.20	1.1	1.38	0.17	15.7	49
OPPENHEIMER TIME	CA	159.9	12.00	8,614.50	9,026.50	18,114.50	6.0	0.00	0.71	27	173
OVER-THE-COUNTER SEC	SG	77.8	14.30	9,276.50	☆	☆	0.0	0.71	0.71	N/A	27
P-C CAPITAL FUND	CA	0.7	11.79	8,979.40	☆	☆	0.0	0.00	0.00	N/A	N/A
PACIFIC HORIZON AGG GRO	CA	0.6	14.24	#12,382.60	☆	☆	0.0	0.00	0.34	N/A	N/A
PACIFIC HORIZON HI YLD	FI	19.8	13.89	#10,608.00	☆	☆	0.0	0.00	0.54	N/A	N/A
PAINE WEBBER AMERICA	GI	78.4	12.05	#9,618.00	☆	☆	0.0	0.00	0.00	N/A	N/A
PAINE WEBBER ATLAS	GL	1.0	8.34	#9,114.80	☆	☆	0.0	0.12	0.12	N/A	N/A
PDC&J PERFORMANCE	CA	146.3	10.17	#10,167.00	9,800.10	24,581.70	5.9	1.96	0.84	10.3	232
PARTNERS FUND	G	13.7	14.13	9,573.20	9,885.50	17,431.50	4.5	0.77	0.49	15.0	29
PAX WORLD FUND	B	161.5	10.43	9,522.10	9,636.70	19,654.80	5.0	0.70	0.42	15.3	34
PENN SQUARE MUTUAL	GI	148.0	8.05	9,238.30	9,717.50	25,152.80	1.2	0.55	0.07	N/A	35
PENNSYLVANIA MUTUAL	SG	75.0	5.65	9,569.20	8,793.20	☆	3.9	0.00	0.00	14.7	2
PERMANENT PORTFOLIO	S	101.3	10.93	9,200.30	8,983.90	18,335.40	8.1	0.83	0.34	10.7	28
PHILADELPHIA FUND	GI	61.9	8.20	9,173.30	10,052.80	20,836.30	7.5	1.69	0.86	14.1	178
PHOENIX BALANCED	B	58.6	9.73	9,737.40	10,059.10	23,744.90	3.6	3.76	1.30	13.2	171
PHOENIX CONVERTIBLE	I	68.7	15.46	9,606.60	9,534.30	31,122.20	10.9	2.86	0.49	N/A	208
PHOENIX GROWTH	G	4.1	12.11	9,742.60	10,201.20	☆	14.0	0.39	0.87	14.3	54
PHOENIX HIGH QUAL BOND	FI	45.2	8.06	9,534.30	9,582.60	☆	3.1	3.92	1.22	11.2	104
PHOENIX HIGH YIELD	FI	46.4	8.55	9,635.80	10,406.50	32,638.50	10.7	0.00	0.38	21.5	227
PHOENIX STOCK	CA	486.9	10.34	9,832.10	9,794.50	☆	4.9	2.29	2.29	11.6	30
PILGRIM ADJUSTABLE RATE	FI	35.7	21.50	9,408.60	9,585.70	14,933.70	0.9	0.59	0.59	N/A	54
PILGRIM FUND	G	62.4	12.10	9,794.50	8,916.90	21,172.10	3.8	3.91	0.09	14.3	161
PILOT FUND	CA	39.4	7.77	9,585.70	9,272.30	17,578.50	11.9	1.44	0.47	15.6	103
PINE STREET FUND	GI	14.7	8.37	8,916.90	9,984.70	14,594.20	4.2	0.00	1.00	15.2	50
PIONEER BOND FUND	FI	1,195.1	18.59	9,272.30	8,985.50	17,810.60	1.8	0.99	0.80	17.0	12
PIONEER FUND	GI	202.3	12.37	9,984.70	9,873.20	☆	3.8	0.16	0.23	26.5	12
PIONEER THREE	GI	1,231.4	14.19	8,985.50	8,884.80	22,035.40	1.8	0.88	0.56	22.4	16
PIONEER II	GI	61.5	11.67	9,873.20	8,646.10	18,093.60	4.1	2.10	0.23	15.1	68
PLITREND FUND	AU	59.8	18.01	8,884.80	9,995.50	29,022.90	6.6	0.67	0.76	15.9	32
PRECIOUS METALS HOLDINGS	GI	277.3	11.72	8,646.10	9,292.60	☆	2.8	0.06	0.78	N/A	48
T ROWE PRICE GRO & INC	GI	868.9	12.80	9,995.50	8,883.30	13,996.90	1.1	0.45	0.36	N/A	63
T ROWE PRICE GROWTH STK	IF	178.5	12.99	9,292.60	8,471.20	☆	3.7	0.16	0.15	N/A	69
T ROWE PRICE INTL FUND	NR	452.6	15.85	8,883.30	9,276.50	20,141.00	1.1	1.29	0.61	12.8	37
T ROWE PRICE NEW ERA	SG	1,187.1	12.70	9,276.50	9,693.80	23,457.50	11.3	3.72	0.16	14.5	45
T ROWE PRICE NEW HORIZON	FI	615.6	8.05	8,980.40	10,613.60	15,773.50	0.0	0.00	0.91	N/A	84
T ROWE PRICE NEW INCOME	FI	18.4	4.89	10,279.40	☆	☆	5.4	0.00	0.17	N/A	N/A
T ROWE PRICE SH-TERM BD	G	0.9	5.28	#10,129.20	9,113.60	☆	4.9	0.00	0.28	N/A	N/A
PRINCIPAL EQUITY	GL	1.4	5.73	9,113.20	9,683.80	13,956.80	2.5	0.00	0.27	12.8	114
PRINCIPAL WORLD	G	28.9	8.92	9,683.80	8,462.20	13,687.00	10.3	0.00	0.22	14.5	105
PRO FUND	FI	21.2	8.00	9,423.20	9,717.50	21,393.40	6.8	0.82	0.82	N/A	42
PRO INCOME FUND	I	100.7	4.45	9,803.80	9,749.60	☆	0.0	0.34	0.34	N/A	N/A
PROVIDENT FD FOR INCOME	FI	221.3	23.10	9,749.60	9,783.40	☆	0.0	1.09	1.43	N/A	N/A
PRUDENTIAL-BACHE ARP	G	42.4	13.05	9,513.40	9,689.20	☆	1.1	0.57	0.15	N/A	133

PERFORMANCE OF MUTUAL FUNDS (continued)

FUND NAME	OBJ.	TOTAL NET ASTS (MIL) 6/30/84	NAV 6/30/84	PERFORMANCE (RETURN ON INITIAL $10,000 INVESTMENT) 12/31/83-6/30/84	PERFORMANCE 6/30/83-6/30/84	$10,000 INVESTMENT 6/30/79-6/30/84	YIELD % 6/30/84	PER SHARE LATEST 12 MONTHS CAP GAINS	INC DIVS	LATEST AVAILABLE PRICE/ EARNINGS	ANNUAL % TURNOVER
PRUDENTIAL-BACHE GOV INT	FI	41.4	9.38	10,122.60	10,378.00	☆	10.8	0.00	1.01	N/A	209
PRUDENTIAL-BACHE HIGH YD	FI	224.7	9.36	9,870.60	10,358.50	15,537.20	13.5	0.00	1.26	N/A	57
PRUDENTIAL-BACHE NEW DEC	G	59.8	11.57	8,778.50	7,547.30	☆	2.6	0.16	0.30	20.4	71
PRUDENTIAL-BACHE OPN GRO	OG	59.5	13.30	8,942.50	8,644.70	☆	1.2	0.00	0.16	N/A	N/A
PRUDENTIAL-BACHE QU INC	FI	23.4	13.92	9,961.50	10,267.00	☆	11.2	0.00	1.56	N/A	56
PRUDENTIAL-BACHE TX-MGD	G	156.8	8.20	9,184.50	8,451.60	☆	2.3	0.00	0.19	N/A	N/A
PRUDENTIAL-BACHE RESCH (R)	EI	122.2	20.36	10,094.20	10,698.90	23,146.50	0.0	1.60	0.00	21.6	69
PUTNAM CONVERTIBLE FUND	FI	45.1	12.12	9,495.40	9,228.30	☆	7.7	0.00	1.00	N/A	N/A
PUTNAM CORP CASH ARP	EI	275.5	45.84	☆	#9,896.40	☆	0.0	0.00	2.47	N/A	N/A
PUTNAM CORP CASH DSP	EI	67.0	46.24	#10,013.20	☆	☆	8.9	2.24	2.59	N/A	162
GEORGE PUTNAM FD BOSTON	B	257.3	10.11	8,648.90	8,651.50	17,718.60	4.3	2.17	1.00	15.5	197
PUTNAM GROWTH	G	722.5	10.02	9,442.70	9,580.70	20,872.70	2.2	0.57	0.48	15.1	31
PUTNAM HEALTH SCIENCE	S	245.4	14.53	9,019.20	7,171.80	☆		0.73	0.32	18.4	325
PUTNAM HIGH YIELD TRUST	FI	589.3	14.52	9,580.60	10,033.30	16,576.00	14.9	0.00	2.22	N/A	207
PUTNAM INCOME	FI	135.7	6.14	9,724.70	10,198.70	14,799.60	12.9	0.00	0.79	N/A	N/A
PUTNAM INFO SCIENCE	CA	198.0	10.96	8,636.70	8,370.80	☆	0.5	3.97	0.16	22.1	132
PUTNAM INTL EQUITIES	GL	44.5	14.86	9,500.20	9,445.70	18,652.80	2.1	1.24	0.09	14.1	50
PUTNAM INVESTORS	G	926.9	9.05	9,126.90	7,849.40	19,748.60	4.0	1.76	0.20	15.1	111
PUTNAM OPTION INCOME	OI	476.3	10.72	9,545.70	7,633.90	17,171.30	4.3	3.13	0.46	12.7	312
PUTNAM VISTA	CA	137.9	13.26	8,050.00	9,917.00	23,338.00	0.6	1.07	0.63	14.6	65
PUTNAM VOYAGER	CA	196.9	14.69	8,712.90	9,136.70	21,237.80	0.3	11.67	0.09	17.4	106
QUASAR ASSOCIATES	G	42.9	41.17	8,595.00	9,372.00	27,942.80	1.5	3.82	0.15	16.9	N/A
QUEST FOR VALUE FUND	CA	14.1	18.76	9,691.20	☆	☆	1.5	0.00	0.34	N/A	N/A
RAINBOW FUND	CA	1.6	3.81	9,361.20	9,500.90	14,431.80	0.0	0.28	0.00	N/A	417
REA-GRAHAM FUND	GI	9.2	11.17	9,125.20	10,181.40	19,232.50	6.5	0.63	0.74	N/A	31
RESEARCH EQUITY FUND	FI	55.5	5.86	9,704.60	8,392.90	12,667.60	2.1	0.00	0.12	16.1	64
RETIREMENT PLAN AM-BOND	FI	2.8	7.29	9,991.80	☆	☆	11.5	0.00	0.92	N/A	4
RETIREMENT PLAN AM-EQU	EI	2.8	14.30	9,667.80	☆	☆	2.8	0.00	0.40	N/A	31
ROCHESTER GROWTH FUND	G	2.0	8.25	9,972.90	☆	☆	0.8	0.00	0.06	N/A	N/A
ROCHESTER TAX-MGD	G	17.6	14.15	9,957.80	9,893.50	16,009.40	0.0	0.17	0.00	N/A	26
ROYCE VALUE FUND	SG	22.5	6.54	9,367.70	9,271.90	22,615.80	0.0	0.57	0.44	15.4	16
SAFECO EQUITY FUND	GI	30.1	9.19	9,263.70	8,861.70	16,762.50	4.7	1.19	0.45	16.3	19
SAFECO GROWTH FUND	G	58.0	16.32	8,633.90	10,276.10	21,474.80	2.7	0.86	0.82	N/A	32
SAFECO INCOME FUND	EI	19.5	11.77	9,621.80	10,226.50	21,123.10	6.8	0.00	0.72	N/A	N/A
SAFECO SPECIAL BOND	FI	1.9	7.17	10,048.30	8,339.80	15,077.60	10.1	3.04	0.34	16.1	126
ST PAUL CAPITAL	GI	61.6	9.03	8,965.70	8,485.80	28,808.40	3.3	2.30	0.27	N/A	116
ST PAUL FIDUCIARY	CA	6.9	11.96	9,018.50	☆	☆	2.1	2.87	0.21	20.4	131
ST PAUL GROWTH	CA	75.6	10.47	8,939.90	7,848.30	29,528.40	1.8	0.00	1.08	N/A	269
ST PAUL INCOME	FI	12.7	8.74	9,618.40	9,431.50	14,786.70	12.4	5.18	0.26	N/A	137
ST PAUL SPECIAL	CA	16.0	15.31	8,823.80	7,683.60	26,533.60	1.5	0.00	0.14	25.2	N/A
SCI/TECH HOLDINGS	GL	472.3	9.03	9,505.20	☆	☆	1.5	0.72	0.26	19.2	48
SCUDDER CAPITAL GROWTH	G	223.0	13.08	9,416.80	9,233.30	21,251.20	2.0	1.78	0.42	13.5	84
SCUDDER COMMON STOCK	G	223.7	10.99	8,677.10	9,157.90	17,474.50	3.5	1.30	1.02	20.9	22
SCUDDER DEVELOPMENT	SG	206.6	55.80	8,958.10	8,292.40	22,470.40	1.8	1.25	1.25	15.2	40
SCUDDER INCOME	FI	105.6	10.68	9,675.30	9,934.70	14,086.10	11.7	0.57	0.41	N/A	17
SCUDDER INTERNATIONAL	IF	173.4	20.94	9,731.30	10,527.40	17,794.30	1.9	0.41	0.61	N/A	27
SCUDDER TARGET GENL 1984	FI	1.0	10.11	10,369.90	10,818.90	☆	6.0	0.00	0.72	N/A	N/A
SCUDDER TARGET GENL 1985	FI	3.2	9.85	10,311.70	10,711.90	☆	7.3	0.00	0.71	N/A	N/A
SCUDDER TARGET GENL 1986	FI	2.3	9.54	10,191.60	10,455.90	☆	7.5	0.00	0.73	N/A	N/A
SCUDDER TARGET GENL 1987	FI	3.2	9.44	10,089.40	10,319.70	☆	7.8	0.00	0.80	N/A	4
SCUDDER TARGET GENL 1990	FI	7.7	8.74	9,936.80	9,897.70	☆	9.3	0.00	0.56	N/A	N/A
SCUDDER TARGET USGT 1984	FI	0.4	10.09	10,400.20	10,797.20	☆	5.6	0.00	0.78	N/A	N/A
SCUDDER TARGET USGT 1985	FI	1.7	9.70	10,312.70	10,655.70	☆	8.1	0.00	0.73	N/A	N/A
SCUDDER TARGET USGT 1986	FI	1.0	9.49	10,127.10	10,401.50	☆	7.8	0.00	0.75	N/A	N/A
SCUDDER TARGET USGT 1987	FI	1.9	9.08	9,906.80	10,155.20	☆	8.3	0.00	0.82	N/A	N/A
SCUDDER TARGET USGT 1990	FI	2.4	8.69	9,780.30	10,045.80	☆	9.5	0.00		N/A	N/A
SECURITY ACTION FUND	G	10.8	6.89	9,339.50	8,210.80	☆	0.6	0.00	0.04	N/A	51

Fund	Type										
SECURITY BOND FUND	FI	29.8	7.24	9,856.60	9,999.00	14,288.50	13.1	0.00	0.95	N/A	45
SECURITY EQUITY FUND	G	217.5	6.09	9,020.80	7,753.50	19,991.70	3.7	0.72	0.24	14.5	56
SECURITY INVESTMENT FUND	GI	103.0	8.43	9,474.20	8,325.30	17,883.20	6.5	0.40	0.56	11.4	41
SECURITY ULTRA FUND	CA	73.4	7.24	9,476.40	8,101.10	23,643.70	10.8	1.38	0.86	23.0	133
SELECTED AMERICAN SHARES	B	76.0	9.44	10,167.80	11,038.60	18,746.90	5.6	0.00	0.53	10.8	66
SELECTED SPECIAL SHARES	G	31.4	16.74	9,018.50	8,903.90	17,274.80	3.0	4.28	0.56	19.6	101
SELIGMAN CAPITAL	CA	125.2	9.33	8,062.40	6,975.20	26,324.80	0.0	1.42	0.00	16.8	68
SELIGMAN COMM & INFORMTN	G	45.5	7.11	8,393.40	☆	☆	0.0	1.86	0.07	21.1	N/A
SELIGMAN COMMON STOCK	GI	358.1	10.68	8,779.60	9,055.50	20,159.10	5.1	1.26	0.59	11.9	44
SELIGMAN GROWTH	GI	560.5	5.31	8,509.90	7,794.20	16,867.50	2.2	0.27	0.13	13.8	48
SELIGMAN INCOME	I	71.9	10.38	9,562.30	9,842.00	16,678.60	10.8	1.14	0.69	18.6	25
SENTINEL BALANCED FUND	B	12.4	8.61	9,758.10	10,191.00	18,248.10	7.9	0.30	0.69	N/A	39
SENTINEL BOND FUND	FI	12.3	5.74	9,874.20	10,110.50	14,334.00	12.1	0.00	0.86	9.7	24
SENTINEL COMMON STOCK	GI	311.6	16.10	9,759.70	10,257.60	21,505.00	5.2	0.78	0.25	19.4	40
SENTINEL GROWTH FUND	G	36.2	11.94	8,566.90	7,833.80	23,604.40	1.9	3.07	0.22	11.8	127
SENTRY FUND	G	27.6	9.30	9,111.70	7,896.50	18,038.90	2.2	1.43	1.58	10.4	45
SEQUOIA FUND	G	384.4	35.53	10,526.20	11,674.60	25,604.90	4.3	2.58	0.00	26.3	17
SHEARSON AGGRESSIVE GRO	CA	121.1	9.90	8,653.80	☆	☆	1.5	0.33	0.25	13.7	74
SHEARSON APPRECIATION	G	112.0	16.23	9,220.60	9,337.70	23,515.80	1.8	0.53	0.11	11.7	67
SHEARSON FUNDAMENTAL VAL	GI	36.8	6.05	9,680.00	10,116.90	☆	14.0	0.00	2.40	N/A	45
SHEARSON HIGH YIELD	FI	145.7	17.10	9,983.80	9,983.80	13,532.30	0.5	2.40	0.00	N/A	N/A
SHERMAN, DEAN FUND	CA	4.1	6.59	9,165.50	7,155.40	14,074.20	1.3	0.03	0.03	N/A	10
SIERRA GROWTH FUND	G	6.0	11.10	8,949.60	7,857.70	24,534.90	1.6	1.67	0.15	15.4	16
SIGMA CAPITAL SHARES	CA	36.0	11.93	9,205.20	9,226.60	13,259.80	11.8	0.00	0.19	11.4	12
SIGMA INCOME SHARES	FI	16.6	6.76	9,506.50	9,684.20	19,431.90	4.4	0.79	0.00	N/A	33
SIGMA INVESTMENT SHARES	GI	51.8	6.97	9,608.20	8,894.20	18,266.00	2.1	0.31	0.31	N/A	10
SIGMA SPECIAL FUND	G	14.8	6.35	9,166.90	8,774.20	16,370.80	7.1	0.20	0.13	N/A	13
SIGMA TRUST SHARES	B	23.8	10.07	9,655.60	9,971.70	22,221.00	1.0	0.07	0.72	20.2	10
SIGMA VENTURE SHARES	SG	46.9	8.78	8,591.00	7,641.60	20,484.00	2.7	0.12	0.09	14.0	46
SMITH, BARNEY EQUITY	G	54.9	12.35	9,188.70	8,812.80	23,091.20	7.4	2.40	0.37	N/A	44
SMITH, BARNEY INC & GR	GI	8.5	8.00	9,697.00	9,776.10	25,824.60	13.8	1.35	0.64	15.5	64
SOGEN INTERNATIONAL	G	40.6	13.32	9,751.60	10,012.90	13,143.40	11.0	0.84	1.95	N/A	147
SOUTHWESTERN INV INCOME	FI	9.4	4.31	9,595.00	9,926.30	19,333.90	4.3	0.00	0.47	N/A	17
SOVEREIGN INVESTORS	GI	13.3	17.35	9,683.60	9,938.50	☆	0.0	0.00	0.75	N/A	N/A
SBSF FUND	CA	17.6	9.93	9,841.40	☆	14,794.60	0.0	0.00	0.00	13.2	61
STATE BOND COMMON STOCK	G	27.4	4.73	8,636.60	8,027.10	17,897.10	2.5	0.29	0.12	N/A	39
STATE BOND DIVERSIFIED	GI	9.7	5.64	9,525.00	9,769.30	18,764.30	5.5	0.26	0.32	N/A	63
STATE BOND PROGRESS	G	6.8	7.56	8,298.30	7,202.40	16,299.50	1.6	0.51	0.12	18.6	N/A
STATE FARM BALANCED	B	21.4	11.77	9,129.60	8,868.60	17,925.80	6.4	0.66	0.78	15.9	24
STATE FARM GROWTH	G	152.0	8.76	9,040.80	8,475.70	14,902.80	4.0	0.85	0.37	N/A	N/A
STATE FARM INTERIM	FI	4.4	8.96	10,086.80	10,405.70	17,224.70	10.1	0.00	0.90	15.3	9
STATE STREET INVESTMENT (R)	GI	434.9	65.12	9,451.10	8,870.30	12,559.90	3.4	3.20	2.30	N/A	78
STEADMAN AMER INDUSTRY	CA	9.7	2.96	8,481.40	7,237.20	13,253.00	0.0	0.00	0.05	12.0	78
STEADMAN ASSOCIATED FUND	EI	25.0	0.84	9,162.80	8,540.40	13,070.50	6.2	0.05	0.00	N/A	186
STEADMAN INVESTMENT	G	10.2	1.36	8,636.70	7,753.40	13,279.80	0.4	0.00	0.00	N/A	225
STEADMAN OCEANOGRAPHIC	G	6.9	6.04	9,137.70	7,540.60	14,114.60	11.9	0.00	0.93	N/A	185
STEINROE BOND FUND	FI	86.5	7.75	9,703.90	9,866.00	22,496.80	0.6	0.21	0.00	22.8	72
STEIN R&F CAPITAL OPP	G	206.0	20.23	8,635.80	☆	☆	0.0	2.55	0.12	27.3	N/A
STEINROE DISCOVERY	SG	33.2	7.49	8,453.70	6,744.80	24,987.30	1.6	0.00	0.00	17.6	81
STEINROE SPECIAL FUND	CA	109.4	13.43	8,934.30	8,969.70	19,370.30	1.7	2.29	0.23	21.3	173
STEIN R&F STOCK	B	214.1	13.39	8,367.60	7,066.90	15,338.90	6.6	4.69	0.00	11.8	79
STEINROE TOTAL RETURN	G	86.9	19.66	9,317.00	9,037.20	☆	1.1	1.55	1.35	18.1	75
STEINROE UNIVERSE FUND	B	182.5	14.98	8,123.60	6,923.00	☆	0.0	0.65	0.17	N/A	42
STRATEGIC CAPITAL GAINS	CA	10.2	7.10	9,293.20	8,472.60	☆	6.4	0.00	0.00	N/A	12
STRATEGIC INVESTMENTS	EI	174.0	9.25	8,981.10	8,981.10	38,605.00	0.8	0.38	0.59	N/A	70
STRATTON GROWTH FUND	AU	11.8	16.21	8,901.70	8,682.70	18,977.10	1.8	0.00	0.13	N/A	587
STRONG INVESTMENT	B	91.2	16.45	10,247.90	10,555.90	☆	2.3	1.10	0.31	N/A	581
STRONG TOTAL RETURN	G	59.8	15.10	10,205.10	10,362.30	☆	0.4	1.29	0.37	15.5	117
SUMMIT FUND	CA	6.7	4.77	8,852.80	7,726.60	☆	0.6	0.00	0.02	26.8	39
SUNBELT GROWTH FUND	G	155.7	13.50	9,316.80	7,911.10	☆	0.7	0.00	0.08		37
SURVEYOR FUND	G	85.8	13.02	8,773.60	7,620.10	18,584.90		2.39	0.10		

Copyright© Lipper Analytical Services, Inc.

PERFORMANCE OF MUTUAL FUNDS (concluded)

FUND NAME	OBJ.	TOTAL NET ASTS (MIL) 6/30/84	NAV 6/30/84	PERFORMANCE 12/31/83–6/30/84	PERFORMANCE 6/30/83–6/30/84	$10,000 INVESTMENT 6/30/79–6/30/84	YIELD % 6/30/84	PER SHARE CAP GAINS	PER SHARE INC DIVS	PRICE/EARNINGS	ANNUAL % TURNOVER
TAX-MGD FUND UTILITY SHS	EI	107.8	12.91	9,584.30	8,836.40	11,084.00	0.0	0.00	0.00	8.0	141
TECHNOLOGY FUND	G	558.8	11.21	9,004.60	8,570.30	20,543.60	2.1	2.13	0.26	15.0	43
TEMPLETON FOREIGN	IF	61.8	10.39	9,293.40	10,372.70	☆	1.5	0.16	0.16	N/A	4
TEMPLETON GLOBAL I	GL	221.1	31.25	9,150.80	9,624.80	☆	2.6	3.72	0.87	14.7	21
TEMPLETON GLOBAL II	GL	144.4	9.36	9,140.60	☆	☆	2.1	0.00	0.19	15.8	N/A
TEMPLETON GROWTH	GL	842.9	8.78	9,412.70	9,937.90	19,047.20	3.0	0.29	0.36	16.3	10
TEMPLETON WORLD	GL	1,485.0	11.69	9,488.60	10,133.00	21,732.80	0.0	0.55	0.08	15.3	13
THOMSON MCKINNON GRO (R)	G	29.5	10.10	#10,179.40	☆	☆	0.0	0.00	0.27	N/A	N/A
THOMSON MCKINNON INC (R)	I	39.2	9.23	#9,496.80	☆	☆	0.0	0.00	0.04	N/A	N/A
THOMSON MCKINNON OPPTY (R)	CA	11.5	10.24	#10,279.80	☆	☆	0.0	0.00	0.70	N/A	N/A
TRANSATLANTIC FUND	IF	29.5	48.39	8,631.20	9,330.50	14,001.90	1.4	3.37	1.20	N/A	96
TRUSTEES COMMINGLED BOND	FI	47.5	22.50	9,449.60	9,177.60	☆	4.7	0.00	1.52	N/A	N/A
TRUSTEES COMMINGLED EQU	GI	237.2	31.11	8,885.10	10,341.80	☆	2.7	2.15	0.68	15.7	30
TRUSTEES COMMINGLED INTL	IF	196.5	24.87	9,682.60	7,610.70	☆	0.4	0.02	0.07	N/A	N/A
TUDOR FUND	CA	85.1	16.56	8,198.80	7,634.80	29,729.80	0.4	1.56	0.00	25.0	99
TWENTIETH CENTURY GIFT	G	1.5	3.96	8,371.40	☆	☆	0.4	0.00	0.05	N/A	N/A
TWENTIETH CENTURY GROWTH	CA	616.4	11.55	8,478.70	7,885.80	26,577.00	0.7	1.82	0.13	16.0	98
TWENTIETH CENTURY SELECT	G	745.9	20.73	8,030.10	6,546.90	31,044.30	0.0	0.68	0.00	16.5	57
TWENTIETH CENTURY ULTRA (R)	CA	435.9	6.39	10,047.10	10,427.40	☆	0.0	0.25	0.00	24.9	58
TWENTIETH CENTURY US GOV	FI	60.4	92.66	8,294.10	☆	☆	11.0	0.00	10.16	N/A	N/A
TWENTIETH CENTURY VISTA	CA	9.2	4.23	9,498.80	10,051.70	☆	0.0	0.00	0.00	23.4	75
UNIFIED ACCUMULATION	CA	90.7	7.77	9,610.40	8,897.50	18,544.20	0.0	0.00	0.55	N/A	16
UNIFIED GROWTH FUND	G	10.4	15.40	9,354.30	9,404.30	19,688.70	3.6	0.00	1.25	N/A	51
UNIFIED INCOME FUND	I	6.9	11.14	9,449.80	9,539.00	17,649.50	11.1	0.25	0.54	N/A	149
UNIFIED MUTUAL SHARES	GI	9.0	11.42	9,458.90	9,326.80	16,420.20	4.7	1.25	0.36	10.5	40
UNITED ACCUMULATIVE	G	456.9	6.94	9,577.40	9,759.00	22,581.30	4.4	0.54	0.66	N/A	111
UNITED BOND FUND	B	272.4	4.93	9,605.20	9,702.40	13,642.70	13.4	0.00	0.87	N/A	53
UNITED CONTL INCOME	FI	46.2	12.62	9,717.60	10,006.40	19,568.20	6.9	0.66	1.70	8.0	30
UNITED HIGH INCOME	FI	481.5	12.12	9,189.10	9,641.20	☆	13.7	0.00	0.33	16.7	135
UNITED INCOME	EI	480.5	11.62	9,253.10	9,863.40	19,214.40	5.4	0.33	0.48	13.1	N/A
UNITED INTL GROWTH	GL	96.3	5.92	9,937.90	10,167.80	23,738.10	3.5	0.48	0.00	15.7	76
UNITED MISSOURI BK BOND	FI	6.0	9.08	9,540.70	9,725.70	☆	11.7	0.00	0.20	N/A	108
UNITED MISSOURI BK STOCK	GI	10.9	10.09	9,489.00	9,288.30	☆	8.8	0.11	1.06	21.5	N/A
UNITED NEW CONCEPTS	SG	29.1	4.68	8,850.60	☆	☆	3.2	0.00	0.90	35.7	43
UNITED PROSPECTOR (R)	AU	48.0	0.77	9,639.60	9,232.50	20,408.20	3.4	0.00	0.15	17.8	4
UNITED RETIREMENT SHARES	GI	61.3	5.56	9,560.50	9,178.00	20,222.90	3.5	0.41	0.18	14.3	N/A
UNITED SCIENCE & ENERGY	GI	162.0	9.19	10,350.40	9,298.90	42,564.50	5.2	1.40	0.35	22.1	N/A
UNITED SERVICES GOLD SHS	AU	442.8	7.92	8,392.50	☆	☆	0.0	0.00	0.41	N/A	163
UNITED SERVICES GROWTH	CA	5.6	7.57	9,196.70	☆	☆	0.0	0.00	0.00	N/A	94
UNITED SERVICES INCOME	G	1.2	9.12	9,220.00	8,418.80	32,783.90	0.0	0.00	0.11	15.5	166
UNITED VANGUARD FUND	G	325.5	5.22	8,464.80	7,491.00	17,184.90	3.7	0.61	0.20	18.0	49
USAA GROWTH FUND	G	112.4	12.13	9,755.40	10,214.50	15,506.60	1.2	0.47	0.14	19.8	39
USAA INCOME FUND	I	83.5	10.07	10,214.50	☆	24,585.30	10.2	0.12	1.03	N/A	97
USAA SUNBELT ERA	CA	86.1	13.67	8,205.30	☆	☆	1.1	0.15	0.15	19.8	7
VALLEY FORGE FUND	G	5.4	10.23	10,198.20	10,777.80	19,117.40	5.5	0.91	0.59	11.0	72
VALUE LINE	GI	162.1	10.44	8,186.00	7,063.60	20,357.20	2.4	0.00	0.25	11.0	105
VALUE LINE BOND	FI	48.4	10.73	9,571.00	9,851.40	19,833.50	12.0	0.28	1.30	N/A	63
VALUE LINE INCOME	EI	107.8	5.62	8,995.90	8,450.90	20,777.10	9.0	0.26	0.52	5.1	90
VALUE LINE LVGE GROWTH	CA	173.8	15.17	8,347.40	7,483.40	20,603.20	2.0	0.99	0.31	11.2	21
VALUE LINE SPECIAL SIT	G	239.7	12.58	7,864.80	6,871.00	☆	0.2	0.08	0.02	15.5	82
VANCE, SANDERS SPECIAL	G	109.9	11.21	8,623.40	8,687.50	15,603.60	1.0	1.54	0.13	19.9	N/A
VANGUARD FI GNMA PORT	FI	200.2	8.31	9,697.80	10,201.10	☆	12.9	0.00	1.07	N/A	62
VANGUARD FI HIGH YIELD	FI	132.3	7.92	9,572.30	10,028.30	14,402.50	15.2	0.00	1.20	N/A	35
VANGUARD FI INC SHT TERM	FI	118.3	9.50	10,142.40	10,557.80	18,781.90	10.7	0.00	1.01	N/A	56
VANGUARD FI INV GRADE	FI	71.4	7.08	9,728.00	9,841.30	24,627.40	13.8	0.00	0.97	N/A	27
VANGUARD QUAL DVD I	GI	230.5	18.40	9,520.20	9,513.70	☆	4.6	0.97	0.71	12.7	N/A
VANGUARD QUAL DVD II	EI	57.6	14.24	9,680.20	10,522.70	☆	8.6	0.71	1.30	7.6	N/A
VANGUARD QUAL DVD III	FI	142.1	22.35	9,609.30	☆	☆	0.0	1.81	2.26	N/A	N/A

FUND NAME	OBJ	NAV	TOTAL NET ASSETS	FIVE YEARS	ONE YEAR	SIX MONTHS	YIELD	CAP GAINS	INC DIVS	P/E	TURNOVER
(VANGUARD ... — top row cut off)				☆	N/A					N/A	N/A
VANGUARD SPECIAL-ENERGY	NR	8.92	0.2	☆	$8,920.00	☆	0.0	0.00	0.00	N/A	N/A
VANGUARD SPECIAL-GOLD	AU	9.32	1.1	☆	#9,320.00	☆	0.0	0.00	0.00	N/A	N/A
VANGUARD SPECIAL-HEALTH	S	9.68	0.4	☆	#9,680.00	☆	0.0	0.00	0.00	N/A	N/A
VANGUARD SPECIAL-SERVICE	S	10.31	0.5	☆	#10,310.00	☆	0.0	0.00	0.00	N/A	N/A
VANGUARD SPECIAL-TECH	S	10.16	0.4	☆	#10,160.00	☆	0.0	0.00	0.00	N/A	N/A
VAN KAMPEN MERRITT-GOVT	FI	0.00	56.0	☆	N/A	9,275.00	0.0	0.00	0.00	N/A	N/A
VARIABLE STOCK FUND	G	8.87	6.2	17,865.90	9,370.80	10,434.00	3.1	0.88	0.29	N/A	N/A
VENTURE INCOME (+) PLUS	FI	10.04	28.7	☆	9,832.70	9,792.10	14.1	0.15	1.43	N/A	120
WADE FUND	G	40.70	0.5	☆	9,660.60		0.7	1.29	0.28	N/A	15
WALL STREET FUND	G	7.61	5.7	17,036.50	9,057.40		0.7	0.46	0.05	N/A	27
WASHINGTON MUTUAL INV	GI	8.38	526.2	14,516.40	9,428.70		5.0	0.89	0.46	12.1	118
WEINGARTEN EQUITY	CA	12.60	93.3	22,315.50	8,800.00		0.3	4.26	0.04	15.2	38
WELLESLEY INCOME	I	11.84	98.1	28,344.80	9,787.40		11.1	0.00	1.31	8.9	19
WELLINGTON FUND	B	11.63	563.4	17,031.50	9,572.70		7.7	0.44	0.91	10.1	N/A
WESTERGAARD FUND	CA	10.08	26.1	19,128.10	8,803.50		0.0	0.00	0.00	N/A	37
WINDSOR FUND	GI	11.14	1,887.3	23,165.20	9,773.40		6.2	1.03	0.72	8.8	56
WORLD OF TECHNOLOGY	GL	7.19	11.6	☆	8,327.10		0.1	0.00	0.00	N/A	

How to read the Barron's/Lipper gauge. These tables show the return on a $10,000 investment over three periods: five years, one year, and six months.

FUND NAME–Mutual fund name, occasionally shortened, appearing in alphabetical order. The majority of open-end funds registered with the Securities and Exchange Commission are included with the exception of the money market and municipal bond funds.

OBJ.–Investment objective of the fund as determined by both the language in the prospectus and a review of the funds' investment characteristics, such as yield, turnover, etc.

INVESTMENT OBJECTIVE DEFINITIONS:

AU–GOLD ORIENTED FUND-A fund which has at least 50% of its assets in shares of gold mines, gold-oriented mining finance houses, gold coins or bullion.

B–BALANCED FUND-A fund whose primary objective is stability of net asset value, achieved by maintaining a balanced portfolio of both stocks and bonds. Typically, the stock/bond ratio ranges around 60%/40%.

CA–CAPITAL APPRECIATION FUND-Any fund which meets at least two of the following criteria: (1) The investment objective shown in the prospectus is capital appreciation or similar wording. (2) A turnover rate of 100% or more is either expected or realized. (3) The fund is permitted to borrow more than 10% of the value of its portfolio. (4) The prospectus permits short selling, the purchase of options, or investing in common stocks or unregistered securities.

EI–EQUITY INCOME FUND-A fund which normally has 60% or more of its assets in equities and has an above average yield.

FI–FIXED INCOME FUND-A fund which typically has more than 75% of its assets in fixed income issues, such as money market instruments, bonds and preferred stocks.

G–GROWTH FUND-A fund which normally invests in companies whose long-term earnings are expected to grow significantly faster than the earnings of the stocks represented in the major unmanaged stock averages.

GI–GROWTH & INCOME FUND-A fund which combines a growth of earnings objective and an income requirement for level and/or rising dividends.

GL–GLOBAL FUND-A fund which invests at least 25% of its portfolio in securities traded outside of the United States and may own U.S. securities as well.

FUND-I–INCOME FUND-A fund which normally invests less than 75% in fixed income issues and less than 50% in equities, and whose principal aim is the generation of income.

IF–INTERNATIONAL FUND-A fund which invests more than 50% of its assets in securities whose primary trading markets are outside of the United States.

OG–OPTION GROWTH FUND-A fund which attempts to increase its net asset value by investing at least 5% of its portfolio in options.

OI–OPTION INCOME FUND-A fund which writes covered options on at least 50% of its portfolio.

NR–NATURAL RESOURCE FUND-A fund which typically invests more than 50% of its equity commitment in natural resource stocks.

S–SPECIALTY FUND-A fund which, by prospectus, limits its investments to a well-defined specialty, such as banks and utilities.

SG–SMALL COMPANY GROWTH FUND-A fund whose prospectus language and portfolio practice limits its investment to companies on the basis of the size of the company. (Those funds that use smaller companies some of the time or in conjunction with larger companies will not be considered a Small Company Growth Fund.)

TOTAL NET ASSETS–Fund assets minus liabilities, fund expenses, advisory fees and commissions.

NAV (Net Asset Value)–Total net assets divided by the number of shares outstanding.

PERFORMANCE–The theoretical ending value of an initial investment of $10,000 for the period analyzed. The amount shown excludes sales and redemptions charges, if any. All income dividends and capital gains distributions are assumed to be reinvested at net asset value on the ex-dividend date.

YIELD–The latest 12 months' worth of income dividends divided by the adjusted ending net asset value. The ending net asset value is adjusted periodically for the impact of capital gains paid during the previous 12 months.

PER SHARE–LATEST 12 MONTHS CAP GAINS–Total amount of capital gains per share paid during the last 12 months.

PER SHARE–LATEST 12 MONTHS INC DIVS–Total amount of income dividends per share paid during the last 12 months.

LATEST AVAILABLE–PRICE/EARNINGS–The weighted, average reported price/earnings per share ratio of the underlying equities in the portfolio, based on latest 12 months earnings reported in the latest issue of the "Lipper-Equity Analysis Report on the Weighted Average Holdings of Large Investment Companies."

LATEST AVAILABLE–ANNUAL TURNOVER–The ratio of the smaller of purchases and sales divided by average total net assets expressed as a percentage. The turnover shown is for the latest reported fiscal year.

☆–Fund not in existence for full time period covered.

#–Fund's first public offering occurred during the present calendar year.

N/A–Not available due either to size or availability of data.

(W)–Fund writes options; (PW)–Purchase/Write options; and (P)–Purchases options; (R)–Fund charges ½ of 1% each on sales and redemption. Fees going to the fund.

Copyright© Lipper Analytical Services, Inc.

Source: Publisher; Lipper Analytical Services, Inc. Reprinted by courtesy of *Barron's National Business and Financial Weekly*, August 13, 1984.

Largest Money Market Funds Invested in Government Securities

	Telephone	
	In State	Out-of-State
AARP US Government Money Market Trust	(412) 392–6300	(800) 245–4770
Capital Preservation	(800) 982–6150	(800) 227–8380
Merrill Lynch Government	(617) 357–1460	(800) 225–1576
Merrill Lynch CMA Government Securities	(617) 357–1460	(800) 225–1576
Fund for Government Investors	(202) 861–1800	—
Dreyfus Money Market Instruments Government	(212) 895–1206	(800) 645–6561
Hutton Government Fund	(212) 742–3992	(212) 742–6003 —
First Variable Rate Fund	(202) 951–4830	(800) 368–2748
Capital Preservation Fund II	(800) 982–6150	(800) 227–8380
Cash Equivalent Fund	(312) 781–1121	(800) 621–0322

Mutual Funds Which Invest Abroad

	Telephone	
	In State	Out-of-State
Alliance International Fund	(800) 522–2323	(800) 221–5672
Canadian Fund	(212) 269–8800	(800) 221–5757
G. T. Pacific Fund	(415) 392–6181	(800) 824–1580
First Investors International Securities Fund	(212) 825–7900	(800) 221–3846
International Investors Inc.	(212) 687–5200	(800) 547–3428
Japan Fund (Closed-End, New York Stock Exchange)	(212) 319–7813	—
Kemper International	(312) 781–1121	(800) 621–1048
Keystone International Fund	(617) 338–3200	(800) 225–1587
Mass Financial International Trust	(617) 423–3500	(800) 343–2829
Merrill Lynch Pacific Fund	(212) 692–2940	—
Putnam International Equities Fund	(617) 292–1000	(800) 225–1581
Scudder International Fund	(617) 426–8300	(800) 225–2470
Templeton Foreign Fund	(813) 823–8712	(800) 237–0738
Transatlantic Fund	(212) 747–0440	—
T. Rowe Price International Fund	(301) 547–2308	(800) 638–5660
Trustees' Commingled Equity International Portfolio	(800) 362–0530	(800) 523–7025
United International Growth Fund	(816) 283–4000	(800) 821–5664

Closed-end Equity Funds: 10 Largest in Market Value

Closed-end investment companies are traded on the New York Stock Exchange. Unlike the open-end companies (mutual funds), the closed-end investment companies do not redeem their shares and only issue new shares.

Adams Express
American Capital Bond Fund
ASA Ltd.
General American Investors
Japan Fund
Lehman Corp.
Mass Mutual Corp.
Petroleum & Resources
Source Cap Inc.
Tri-Continental Corp.

Mutual Funds Investing in Gold and Precious Metals

Fidelity Select Portfolio-Precious Metals
82 Devonshire Street
Boston, MA 02109
Telephone: (800) 225–6198
               (617) 523–1919

Golconda Investors
11 Hanover Square
New York, NY 10005
Telephone: (800) 431–6060
               (212) 785–0900

International Investors
122 E. 42 Street
New York, NY 10168
Telephone: (800) 221–2220
               (212) 687–5200

Research Capital
155 Bovet Road
San Mateo, CA 94402
Telephone: (800) 632–2180
               (415) 570–3000

Strategic Investments
P.O. Box 20066
Dallas, TX 752220
Telephone: (800) 527–5027
               (214) 484–1326

United Services Gold Shares
P.O. Box 29467
San Antonio, TX 78229
Telephone: (800) 531–5777
               (512) 696–1234

Selected No Load/Low Load Mutual Fund Families with Switching Privileges

No load funds do not charge an initial sales fee while low load funds apply an initial sales fee of 1% to 3%. In comparison load funds charge a sales fee of about 8½%. With no load funds all of your investment is put to work immediately. The performance of no load funds is comparable to that of load funds.

The funds listed below permit switching (exchanges) between other members of the fund family (including money market funds) unless otherwise indicated. Thus, investors who expect a marked decline have the option of switching into a money market fund while investors who expect a bull market may choose to switch into a growth oriented fund. Switching may be done by mail or by phone. Unless otherwise indicated, the fund families listed below permit telephone switching.

Since the performance of funds is quite variable, it is probably best for investors to diversify among three or four fund families.

Investors should study the fund prospectus carefully prior to investing, paying particular attention to average rates of return over the last five and ten year periods, and to risk level (fluctuations in the net asset value). Investors should also familiarize themselves with the switching procedures and restrictions, if any. The information can be obtained by phoning the fund.

Fund objectives vary and it is important to select the fund with objectives similar to yours. A detailed listing of funds by objective, perfor-

mance record, and much more is given in Donoghues's *Mutual Fund Almanac* (Box 540, Holliston, MA 01746).

We employ the following classifications:

M = Money market fund
B = Bond funds with income as the primary objective
I = Income funds provide income through investments in a mixture of high dividend stocks and bonds with limited capital gains opportunity
GI = Growth income funds invest in common stock and attempt to achieve both capital gains and income through dividend payments and interest. Similar to so called balanced funds. Suited for many conservative investors seeking capital gains.
G = These funds primarily seek capital gains though equity investment in companies with high growth potential. For the more aggressive investor willing to assume greater risks to obtain greater gains.

Babson Group of Funds
3 Crown Center
2440 Pershing Road
Kansas City, MO 64108
(800) 821-5591
(816) 471-5200

Babson Growth Fund (G)
Babson Income (B)
Babson MMF Federal Portfolio (M)
Babson MMF Prime Portfolio (M)
Babson Tax-Free Income Fund MMP (M)
Babson Tax Free Inc P Long Term (I)
Babson Tax Free Inc P Short Term (I)
UMB M.M.F. Federal Portfolio (M)
UMB M.M.F. Prime Portfolio (M)

Bull & Bear Management Corporation
    11 Hanover Square
    New York, NY 10005
    (800) 847-4200
    (212) 785-0900
Bull & Bear Capital Growth (G)
Bull & Bear Dollar Reserves (M)
Bull & Bear Equity Income (I)
Golconda Investors (Goldfund) (GI)

Columbia Management Company
    P.O. Box 1350
    Portland, OR 97205
    (800) 547-1037
    (503) 222-3600
Columbia Daily Income(I)
Columbia Fixed Income Securities (I)
Columbia Growth (G)

Dreyfus Corporation
    767 Fifth Avenue
    New York, NY 10022
    (212) 895-1206 (within NY)
    (516) 794-5200 (Long Island)
    (800) 645-6561 (out of state)
Dreyfus A Bonds Plus (I)
[2] Dreyfus Fund (G)
Dreyfus Growth Opportunity (G)
Dreyfus Inst. MMF Gov't Sec. Series (M)
Dreyfus Inst. MMF Money Market Series (M)
[2] Dreyful Leverage (G)
Dreyfus Liquid Assets (M)
Dreyfus Money Market Instruments Government Series (M)
Dreyfus Money Market Instruments MM Series (M)
Dreyfus Tax-Exempt MMF, Inc. (M)
Dreyfus Special Income (I)
Dreyfus Tax-Exempt Bond (B)
Dreyfus Third Century (G)
General Money Market Fund (M)

Fidelity Investments Corporation
    82 Devonshire Street
    Boston, MA 02109
    (800) 225-6190
    (617) 726-0200
Fidelity Cash Reserves (M)
Contrafund (G)
Financial Reserves Fund (M)
Fidelity Corp. Bond (B)
Fidelity Daily Income (M)
[2] Fidelity Destiny (G)

Fidelity Discoverer (G)
Fidelity Equity Income (I)
Fidelity Freedom Fund (GI)
Fidelity Fund (GI)
Fidelity Gov't Securities (I)
Fidelity High Income (B)
Fidelity High Yield Muni (I)
Fidelity Limited Term (B)
[3] Fidelity Mercury (G)
Fidelity MMT/Domestic (M)
Fidelity MMT/Government (M)
Fidelity MMT/U.S. Treasury (M)
Fidelity Muni Bond (B)
Fidelity Thrift Trust (B)
Fidelity Trend (G)
[3] Fidelity Select-Energy (G)
[3] Fidelity Select-Financial Services (G)
[3] Fidelity Select-Health CR (G)
[3] Fidelity Select-Precious Metals (G)
[3] Fidelity Select-Technology (G)
[3] Fidelity Select-Utilities (G)
Fidelity Tax-Exempt MM Trust (M)
Fidelity U.S. Gov't Reserves (M)
Freedom Fund (GI)
[3] Magellan Fund (G)
Puritan (I)
Ready Cash Fund Money Market (M)
Ready Cash Fund U.S. Treasury (M)
Rodney Square Fund Money Market (M)
Rodney Square Fund U.S. Government (M)

Financial Programs Inc.
    P.O. Box 2040
    Denver, CO 80201
    (800) 525-9831
    (303) 779-1233 (Denver)
    (800) 332-9145 (Colorado)
Financial Daily Income Shares (M)
Financial Tax-Free Income (I)
Financial Tax-Free Money Fund (M)
Financial Bond Shares (I)
Financial Dynamics (G)
Financial Industrial Fund (GI)
Financial Industrial Inc. (I)

[1] Investors Research Corp.
    605 W. 47 Street
    Kansas City, MO 64112
    (816) 531-5575
[2] American Growth (G)
Twentieth Century Growth (G)
Twentieth Century US Government (I)
[3] Twentieth Century UI (G)
Twentieth Century Select (GI)

[1] Lehman Management Co.
    55 Water Street
    New York, NY 10041

---

[1] Telephone Exchange not permitted.
[2] Load fund (8.5% sales charge).
[3] Low load fund (2%–3% sales charge); 20th Century Utra (1% sales charge).

(800) 221-5350
(212) 558-3288 (within NY)
Lehman Cash Management (M)
Lehman Government Fund (M)
Lehman Tax-Free MMF, Inc. (M)
Mariner Cash Management Fund (M)
Mariner Government Fund (M)
Mariner Tax-Free MMF (M)
Mariner U.S. Treasury (M)
One William Street (GI)

Lexington Management Corp.
    580 Sylvan Avenue
    P.O. Box 1515
    Englewood Cliffs, NJ 07632
    (800) 526-4791
    (201) 567-2375
Lexington GNMA Income (I)
Lexington Goldfund Inc. (G)
Lexington Growth (G)
Lexington Government Secs. MMF (M)
Lexington Money Market Trust (M)
Lexington Tax Free Money Fund (M)
Lexington Research (G)

Neuberger & Berman Management Inc.
    342 Madison Avenue
    New York, NY 10036
    (800) 367-0770
    (212) 850-8300
Energy (G)
Guardian Mutual (GI)
Liberty (I)
Manhattan (G)
Neuberger & Berman Government MF (M)
Partners Fund (G)

Scudder Stevens & Clark
    175 Federal Street
    Boston, MA 02110
    (800) 225-2470
    (617) 482-3990
Scudder Capital Growth (G)
Scudder Cash Investment Trust (M)
Scudder Common Stock (GI)
Scudder Development (G)
Scudder Gov't Money Fund (M)
Scudder Income (GI)
Scudder International (G)
Scudder Managed Muni Bond (B)
Scudder Tax-Free Money Fund (M)

Stein Roe & Farnham
    150 South Wacker Drive
    Chicago, IL 60606
    (800) 621-0320
    (312) 368-7700
Stein Roe Tax Exempt Bond Fund (B)
Stein Roe Universe (G)
SteinRoe Cash Reserves (M)
SteinRoe Gov't Reserves (M)
SteinRoe Tax-Exempt MF (M)
SteinRoe Total Return (G)
Stein Roe & Farnham Capital Opportunity (G)

Stein Roe & Farnham Stock (G)
Stein Roe Bond (I)
Stein Roe Special Fund (G)

T. Rowe Price Associates
    100 E. Pratt Street
    Baltimore, MD 21202
    (800) 638-5660
    (301) 547-2000
Price Growth Income Fund (GI)
Price Growth Stock (G)
Price International Fund (G)
Price New Era (G)
Price New Horizons (G)
Price New Income (I)
Price Tax Free Income (I)
T. Rowe Price Prime Reserve (B)
T. Rowe Price Tax-Exempt MF (M)
T. Rowe Price U.S. Treasury MF (M)

Value Line
    711 Third Avenue
    New York, NY 10017
    (800) 223-0818
    (212) 687-3965
The Value Line Cash Fund, Inc (M)
Value Line Bond (I)
Value Line Fund (G)
Value Line Income (I)
Value Line Leveraged Growth (G)
Value Line Special Situations (G)

Vanguard Group
    Drummers Lane
    Valley Forge, PA 19482
    (800) 523-7025
    (800) 362-0530 (Pennsylvania)
Energy (G)
Explorer (G)
Gold & Precious Metals (G)
Health Care (G)
Ivest (G)
Morgan Growth (G)
Qualified Dividend Port II (I)
Qualified Dividend Port I (GI)
Service Economy (G)
Technology (G)
Trustees' Commingled Equities (GI)
Vanguard Fixed Income GNMA (B)
Vanguard MMT Federal Fund (M)
Vanguard MMT Insured Portfolio (M)
Vanguard MMT Prime (M)
Vanguard Muni. Bond Fund M.M. (M)
Vanguard Fixed Income High Yield (B)
Vanguard Fixed Income Investment Grade (B)
Vanguard Index Trust (G)
Vanguard Muni High Yield (B)
Vanguard Muni Intermediate Term (B)
Vanguard Muni Long Term (B)
Vanguard Muni Short Term (B)
Wellesley Income (I)
Wellington (GI)
Windsor (G)

PERFORMANCES OF FOREIGN SECURITIES MARKETS

STOCK MARKET INDEXES
EUROPE

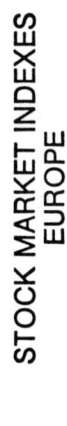

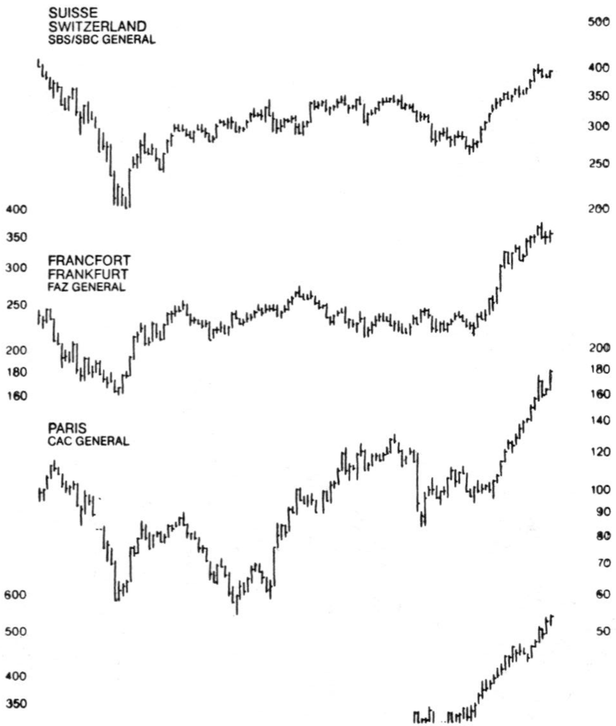
SUISSE
SWITZERLAND
SBS/SBC GENERAL
FRANCFORT
FRANKFURT
FAZ GENERAL
PARIS
CAC GENERAL
400
350
300
250
200
180
160
600
500
400
350
500
400
350
300
250
200
200
180
160
140
120
100
90
80
70
60
50

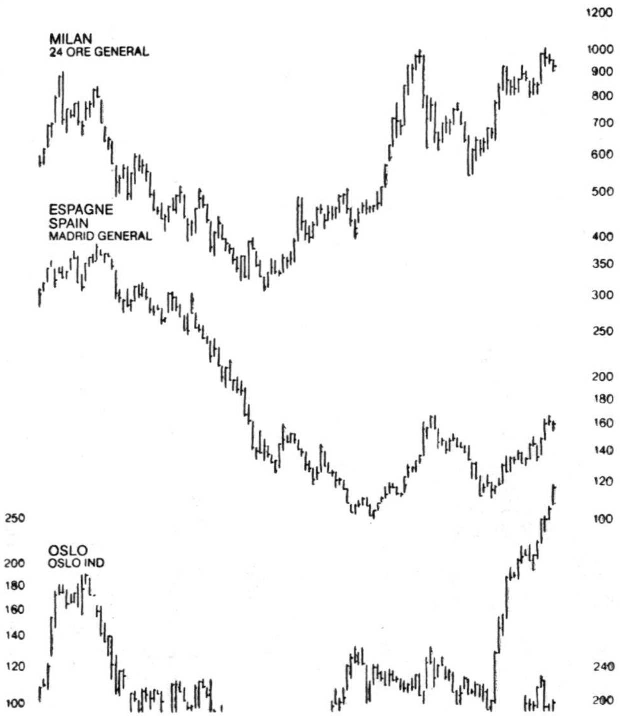
MILAN
24 ORE GENERAL
ESPAGNE
SPAIN
MADRID GENERAL
OSLO
OSLO IND
250
200
180
160
140
120
100
1200
1000
900
800
700
600
500
400
350
300
250
200
180
160
140
120
100
240
200

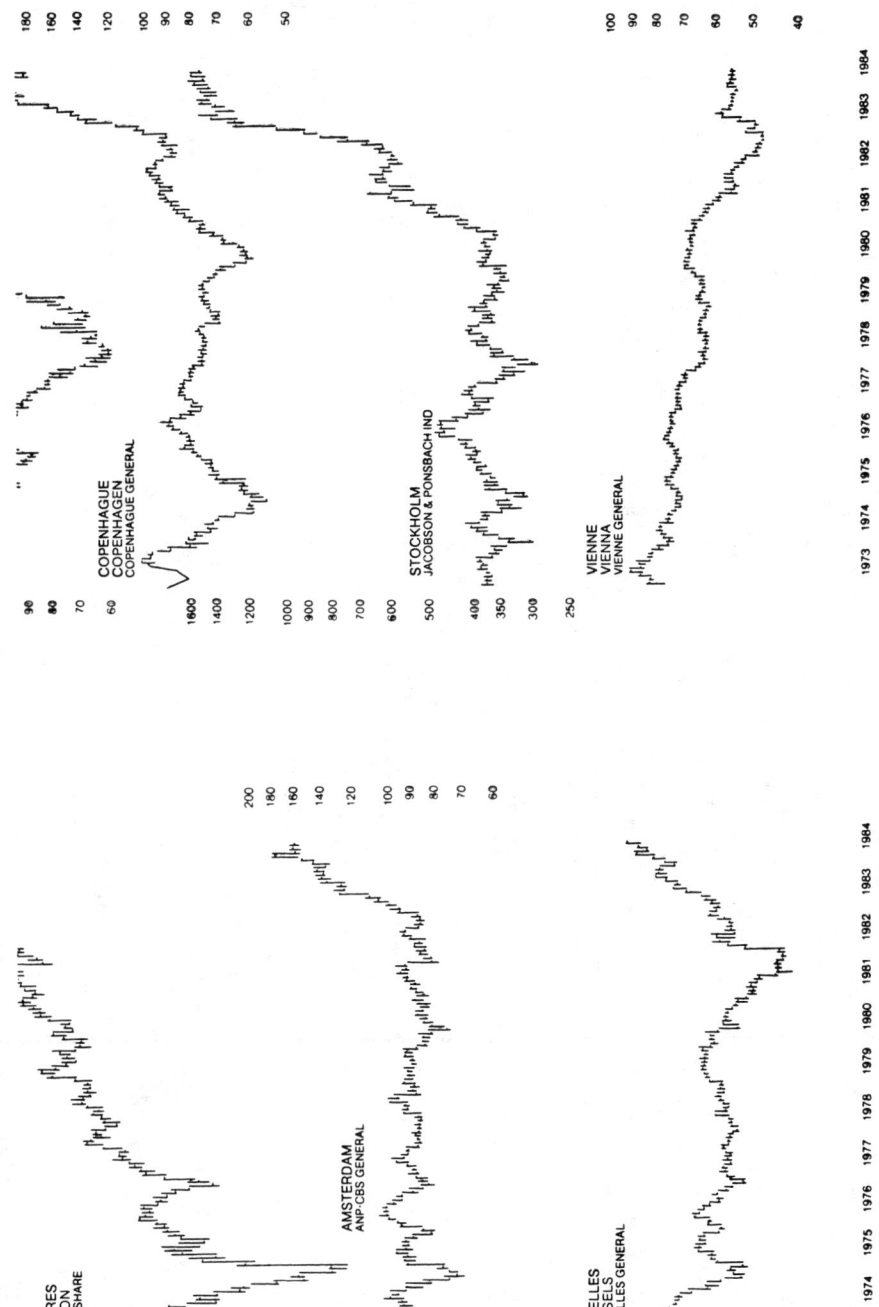

PERFORMANCES OF FOREIGN SECURITIES MARKETS *(continued)*

PACIFIC

NORTH AMERICA

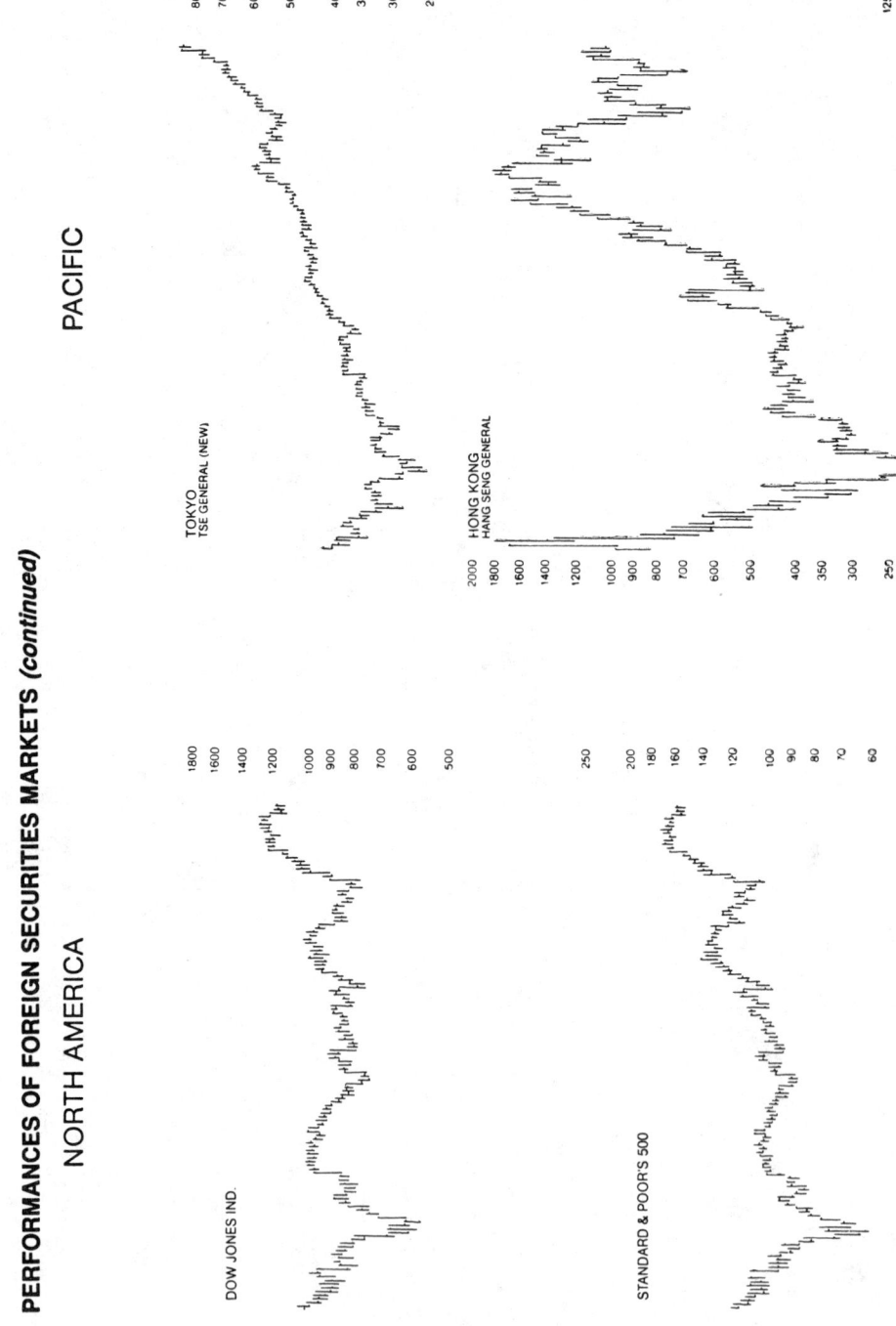

TOKYO
TSE GENERAL (NEW)

HONG KONG
HANG SENG GENERAL

DOW JONES IND.

STANDARD & POOR'S 500

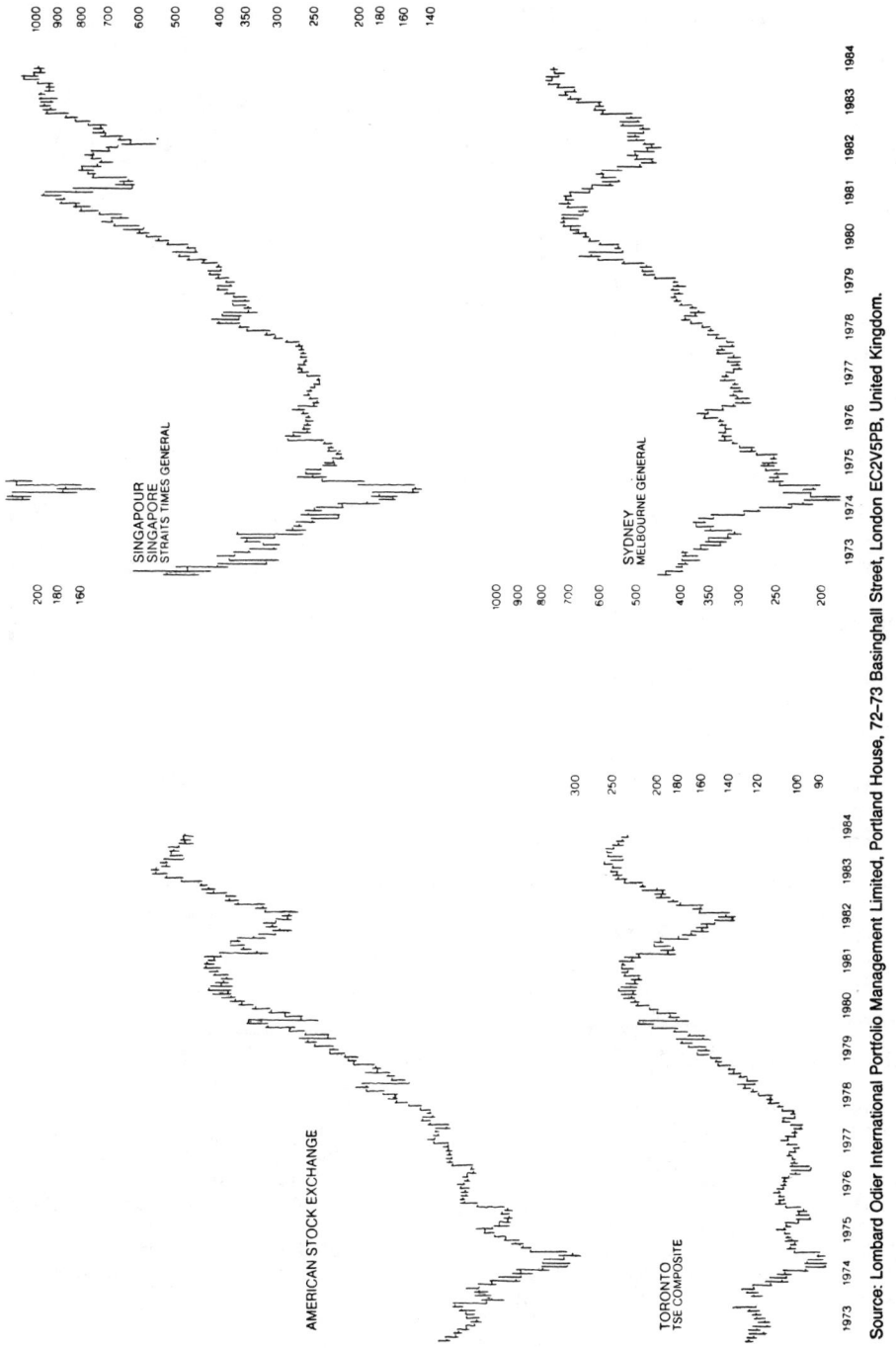

Source: Lombard Odier International Portfolio Management Limited, Portland House, 72–73 Basinghall Street, London EC2V5PB, United Kingdom.

RETURN ON WORLD STOCK MARKETS

	Market Value	Return in each Currency %			Currency Valuation %			Return in U.S. Dollar %		
	Billion Dollar	3 m	1 y	5 y Ⓐ	3 m	1 y	5 y Ⓑ	3 m	1 y	5 y Ⓒ
New York	1528.9	-3.5	4.1	9.4	0.0	0.0	0.0	-3.5	4.1	9.4
Tokyo	635.3	13.6	34.6	13.1	3.1	6.5	-1.4	17.1	43.3	11.5
London	242.8	13.1	33.9	10.6	-0.9	-2.8	-7.0	12.1	30.2	2.8
Toronto	123.1	-6.7	10.5	10.2	-2.5	-3.1	-1.9	-9.0	7.1	8.1
Frankfurt	86.1	-1.9	12.5	5.4	5.5	-6.0	-6.3	3.5	5.7	-1.3
Sydney	60.0	-2.5	46.4	13.5	4.1	8.4	-3.5	1.5	58.7	9.6
Paris	41.4	2.0	42.5	13.1	4.7	-8.6	-11.6	6.8	30.3	0.0
Zurich	45.3	-4.0	17.2	3.0	1.6	-2.9	-4.6	-2.5	13.8	-1.7
Hong Kong	22.0	15.9	1.8	13.5	-0.4	-13.9	-8.7	15.5	-12.3	3.6
Milano	24.9	14.3	2.7	23.0	2.8	-10.3	-12.2	17.5	-7.9	8.0
Amsterdam	32.6	0.6	20.0	10.8	5.0	-6.2	-7.1	5.6	12.5	2.9
Singapore	35.2	-0.8	14.6	21.7	1.6	0.0	0.9	0.8	14.6	22.9
Total	**2877.7**							**2.8**	**15.6**	**10.0**

Source: *Tokyo Stock Market Quarterly Review,* 1984 Vol. 2. A publication of Daiwa Securities Co. Ltd. Available through Daiwa Securities America, Inc. One Liberty Plaza, New York, NY 10038.

NOTES

Market Value Estimate for the end of March, 1984.

Return in each currency Return derived solely based upon each market's Stock Price Index (dividends are not included) for the periods ending on the last trading date of the latest quarter. Five-years data are shown in the annual compound rate. Stock price indices referred to are; S & P500, Tokyo Stock Price Index, FT industrial, Toronto composite, Commerzbank general index, Sydney Stock Exchange all ordinaries, CAC industrial, Swiss Bank Corporation general, index, Hang Seng Bank index, Banca Commerciale Italiana index, ANP-CBS industrial, and Straits Times industrial.

Currency valuation Rate of change of each currency's value in U.S. dollar terms (NY market) for the corresponding periods. Five-years data are shown in the annual compound rate.

Return in U.S. Dollar Return of each market in U.S. $ terms. Five-years data are shown in the annual compound rate.

FOREIGN STOCKS LISTED ON THE NEW YORK STOCK EXCHANGE

Foreign security listings by geographic region, end of 1983

Region	Number of listings	Stocks	Corporate bonds	Government bonds	Total
Africa	1	$ 532.800	–	–	$ 532,800
Asia	12	2,007,501	$ 54,898	$ 193,255	2,255,654
Australia	15	–	–	1,412,273	1,412,273
Europe	93	23,116,719	429,933	4,652,516	28,199,167
Centr. & So. America	11	2,263,833	2,917	278,057	2,544,806
North America	43	34,074,011	1,105,883	268,755	35,448,649
Total	**175**	**$61,994,864**	**$1,593,630**	**$6,804,856**	**$70,393,350**

Listed foreign stocks

Country	Company	Industry
Bahamas	Commodore International Ltd.	Integrated microcomputer systems
Bermuda	Sea Containers Ltd. (3 Pfd. issues)	Cargo container leasing
Canada	Alcan Aluminium Ltd.	Aluminum
	AMCA International Limited	Industrial prods.;construct.;engineer.
	Bell Canada Enterprises Inc.	Telecommunication services & equip.
	Campbell Red Lake Mines Ltd.	Gold mining
	Campbell Resources Inc. (2 issues)	Holding co.-coal; oil & gas interests
	Canadian Pacific Enterprises Ltd.	Iron & steel production; mining
	Canadian Pacific Limited	Integrated transportation system
	Carling O'Keefe Limited	Breweries
	Dome Mines Limited	Gold mining
	Genstar Limited (2 issues)	Land, building development
	Hiram Walker Resources Ltd.	Distilleries; gas utility
	Inco Ltd.	Nickel & copper production
	Inspiration Resources Corporation	Metals mining; petroleum
	MacMillan Bloedel Ltd.	Forest products, pulp & paper
	Massey-Ferguson Ltd.	Farm equipment
	McIntyre Mines Ltd.	Coal mining
	Mitel Corporation	Electronic telecomm. equip.
	Moore Corporation Ltd.	Business forms
	Northern Telecom Ltd.	Telecommunications equip.
	Northgate Exploration Limited	Holding co. - explor.; mining; invest.
	Ranger Oil Limited	Oil & gas exploration, production
	Seagram Co. Ltd.	Distilleries
	Westcoast Transmission Co., Ltd.	Natural gas transmission
Denmark	Novo Industri A/S	Industrial enzymes; drugs
Great Britain	British Petroleum Company Ltd.	Holding co.–integrated oil company
	Imperial Chemical Industries PLC	Diversified chemicals
	Plessey Company Ltd.	Telecommun. and electronic equip.
	"Shell" Transport and Trading Public Ltd. Co.	Holding co., - integrated oil company
	Tricentrol PLC	Oil & gas prod., oil trading
	Unilever PLC	Foods; consumer goods
Japan	Hitachi, Ltd.	Indust. equip., consumer products
	Honda Motor Co., Ltd.	Motor vehicles and parts
	Kubota, Ltd.	Agricultural equipment; piping
	Kyocera Corp.	Ceramic electronic products
	Matsushita Electric Industrial Co., Ltd.	Consumer electronic products
	Pioneer Electronic Corporation	Consumer electronic products
	Sony Corporation	Consumer electronic products
	TDK Corporation	Electronic components; magnetic tapes
Netherlands	KLM Royal Dutch Airlines	Air transportation
	Royal Dutch Petroleum Co.	Holding company-integrated oil co.
Netherlands Antilles	Erbamont N.V.	Pharmaceuticals
	Schlumberger, Ltd.	Oilfield serv.; electronics
	Unilever, N.V.	Foods; consumer goods
Panama	Norlin Corporation	Organs, pianos, guitars
	Syntex Corporation	Pharmaceuticals
Philippines	Benguet Corporation	Mining; construction
South Africa	ASA Limited	Closed-end investment company
Spain	Banco Central, S.A.	Holding company–bank

Source: New York Stock Exchange *1984 Fact Book.*

Securities Markets: Notable Dates

1792 Original brokers' agreement subscribed to by 24 brokers (May 17).

1817 Constitution and the name "New York Stock Exchange Board" adopted (March 8).

1830 Dullest day in history of exchange—31 shares traded (March 16).

1840s Outdoor trading in unlisted securities begins at Wall and Hanover Streets, moves to Wall and Broad, then shifts south along Broad Street.*

1863 Name changed to "New York Stock Exchange" (NYSE) (January 29).

1867 Stock tickers first introduced (November 15).

1868 Membership made salable (October 23).

1869 Gold speculation resulted in "Black Friday" (September 24).

1871 Continuous markets in stocks established.

1873 NYSE closed September 18–29.
Failure of Jay Cooke & Co. and others (September 18).
Trading hours set at 10 A.M. to 3 P.M.; Saturdays, 10 A.M. to noon (December 1).

1878 First telephones introduced in the exchange (November 13).

1881 Annunciator board installed for paging members (January 29).

1885 Unlisted Securities Department established (March 25).

1886 First million-share day—1,200,000 shares traded (December 15).

1908 E. S. Mendels forms New York Curb Agency in first departure from informal trading.*

1910 Unlisted Securities Department abolished (March 31).

1911 Trading rules established with formation of New York Curb Market Association.*

1914 Exchange closed from July 31 through December 11—World War I.

1915 Stock prices quoted in dollars as against percent of par value (October 13).

1919 Separate ticker system installed for bonds (January 2).

1920 Stock Clearing Corporation established (April 26).

1921 New York Curb Market association

moves indoors at 86 Trinity Place; name shortened to New York Curb Market and ticker service initiated (June 21).*

1927 Start of ten-share unit of trading for inactive stocks (January 3).

1929 Stock market crash; 16,410,000 shares traded (October 29).
New York Curb Market modifies its name to New York Curb Exchange.*

1930 Faster ticker—500 characters per minute—installed (September 2).

1931 Exchange building expanded; Telephone Quotation Department formed to send stock quotes to member firm offices.*

1933 New York Stock Exchange closed for bank holiday, March 4–14.

1934 Enactment of Securities Exchange Act of 1934 (June 6).

1938 First salaried president elected—Wm. McC. Martin, Jr. (June 30).

1946 Listed stocks outnumber unlisted stocks for first time since the 1934 act imposed restrictions on unlisted trading.*

1952 Trading hours changed: weekdays, 10 A.M. to 3:30 P.M. Closed Saturdays (September 29).*

1953 Name of New York Curb Exchange changed to American Stock Exchange.*

1958 First member corporation—Woodcock, Hess & Co. (June 4).
Mary C. Roebling becomes first woman governor.*

1962 Committee system of administration replaced by expanded paid staff reporting to president. Specialist system strengthened, surveillance of trading increased, listing and delisting standards introduced, and board restructured to give greater representation to commission and out-of-town brokers.*

1964 New member classification—Registered Trader (August 3).
New ticker—900 characters per minute—put into service (December 1).†
Am-Quote computerized telephone-quotation service was completed as first step in major automation program.*

1965 Fully automated quotation service introduced (March 8).
Electronic Systems Center created (October 15).
First women, Phyllis S. Peterson and Julia Montgomery Walsh, elected to regular membership.*

1966 New NYSE Stock Price Index inaugurated (July 14).
AMEX Price Change Index System introduced; computer complex installed

---

* Refers to American Exchange (AMEX) (formerly Curb Exchange).

† Applies to both the New York Stock Exchange and the American Exchange. Other entries refer to the New York Stock Exchange.

Sources: New York Stock Exchange *1984 Fact Book* and American Stock Exchange *Data Book* and *The Wall Street Journal.*

for ticker, surveillance, and compared-clearance operations.*

1967   First woman member admitted—Muriel F. Siebert (December 28).

1968   Ticker speed increased to maximum 900 characters per minute; transmission begun to six European countries. Trading floor modernized; line capacity for communications doubled. Visitors gallery expanded.*

1969   Central Certificate Service fully activated (February 26).

1970   Public ownership of member firms approved (March 26).
       Securities Investor Protection Corporation Act signed (December 30).

1971   First negotiated commission rates effective (April 5).
       First member organization listed—Merrill Lynch (July 27).
       AMEX incorporates and marks 50th anniversary of move indoors; Listed Company Advisory Committee formed, composed of nine chief executives of AMEX-listed companies.*

1972   NYSE reorganization, based on Martin Report, approved (January 20).
       Board of Directors, with ten public members, replaced Board of Governors (July 13).
       Securities Industry Automation Corporation established with AMEX to consolidate facilities of both exchanges (July 17).*
       First salaried chairman took office—James J. Needham (August 28).
       Board of Governors reorganized to include ten public and ten industry representatives plus full-time salaried chairman as chief executive officer.*

1973   Depository Trust Company succeeded Central Certificate Service (May 11).
       Chicago Board of Options Exchange opened with trading in 16 classes of call options (April 26).
       AMEX formally adopts affirmative action employment plan; Market Value Index System introduced to replace Price Change Index.*

1974   Trading hours extended to 4 P.M. (October 1).
       Consolidated tape begun; 15 stocks reported (October 18).

1975   Fixed commission system abolished (April 30).
       Full consolidated tape begun (June 16).
       AMEX trades call options.*
       Trading begins in call options and odd lots of U.S. government instruments.*

1976   New data line installed, handling 36,000 characters per minute (January 19).
       Specialists began handling odd lots in their stocks (May 24).

Varo, Inc.—first stock traded on both NYSE and AMEX (August 23).
Competition between specialists begun (October 11).

1977   Independent audit committee on listed companies' boards required (January 6).
       Competitive Trader category for members approved (January 19).
       National Securities Clearing Corporation (NSCC) began merging the clearing operations of the Stock Clearing Corporation of NYSE with American Stock Exchange Clearing Corporation and National Clearing Corporation of the NASD (January 20).
       Foreign broker/dealers permitted to obtain membership (February 3).
       Full Automated Bond System in effect (July 27).

1978   First 60 million share day in history (63,493,000 shares) (April 17).
       Intermarket Trading System (ITS) began.
       Registered Competitive Market-Maker category for members approved (May 2).
       First 65 million share day in history (66,370,000 shares) (August 3).
       Trading in Ginnie Maes inaugurated on the AMEX Commodities Exchange (ACE)* (September 12).
       AMEX reached an index high of 176.87 (September 13).

1979   Trading began at pilot post on the exchange floor. First stage in a $12-million upgrading of exchange facilities (January 29).
       Board of Directors of NYSE approved plan for the creation of the New York Futures Exchange, a wholly owned subsidiary of NYSE. Futures contracts in seven financial instruments will be traded on the NYSE (March 1).
       New York Commodities Exchange and NYSE terminated merger talks (March 15).
       81,619,000 shares were traded on the NYSE, making it the heaviest trade day in exchange history (October 10).

1980   American Stock Exchange reached an all-time daily stock volume record of 14,980,680 shares sold (January 15).*
       NYSE volume of 67,752,000 shares traded was second largest volume on record to date (January 16).
       NYSE Futures Exchange opened (August 7).
       Option seat on the American Stock Exchange sold at an all-time high of $160,000 (December 24).*
       NYSE index reached an all time high of 81.02 (November 28).

1981 First 90 million share day in the history of the Exchange, 92,881,000 (January 7).

The New York Stock Exchange subsidiary, the New York Futures Exchange, started trading futures in Domestic Bank Certificates of Deposit.

1982 A new AMEX subsidiary The American Gold Coin Exchange (AGCE) began trading in the Canadian Maple Leaf (January 21).*

Trading in NYSE Common Stock Index Futures began on the New York Futures Exchange (May 6).*

Trading started through experimental linkage between ITS operated by NYSE and six other exchanges and Computer Assisted Execution Service (CAES) operated by NASD, in 30 stocks exempted from exchange off-board trading rules under SEC Rule 19c-3. (May 17)

Record advance of 38.81 points reached in NYSE trading as measured by Dow Jones Industrial Average (August 17).

First 100 million share day (132,681,120 shares. (August 18).

Trading in Interest Rate Options on U.S. Treasury Bills & Notes started in May on the AMEX.*

Trading soared to an all time high of 147,081,070 shares on the NYSE (October 7).

All time options high of 340,550 contracts were traded on the AMEX (October 7).*

Dow Jones Industrial Average plunged 36.33 points, the largest one-day loss since the record plunge of 38.33 points on October 28, 1929 (October 25).

1983 Trading in options on NYSE Common Stock Index Futures started on New York Futures Exchange (January 28).

NYSE started trading options on the NYSE Common Stock Index (September 23).

Dow Jones Industrial Average reached an all time high of 1260.77 (September 26).

New shares of common stocks of seven regional telephone companies and shares of the "new" AT&T began trading on a "when issued" basis. Divestiture of AT&T effective January 1, 1984 (November 21).

AMEX stock trading went over the two billion share mark for the first time.

The AMEX list of stock options increased by four index options, two on specific industry groups, one on the AMEX Market Value Index.*

1984 Largest NYSE trading day of 159,999,031 shares traded (January 5).

NYSE volume soared to a record 236,565,110 shares traded (August 3).

INVESTMENT AND FINANCIAL TERMS*†**

Abandonment value The amount that can be realized by liquidating a project before its economic life has ended.*

Accelerated depreciation Depreciation methods that write off the cost of an asset at a faster rate than the write-off under the straight-line method. The three principal methods of accelerated depreciation are: (1) sum-of-the-years'-digits, (2) double-declining balance, and (3) units-of-production.*

Accruals Continuing recurring short-term liabilities. Examples are accrued wages, accrued taxes, and accrued interest.*

Accrued interest Interest accrued on a bond since the last interest payment was made. The buyer of the bond pays the market price plus accrued interest. Exceptions include bonds that are in default and income bonds. (See: *Flat income bond.*)†

Ad valorem tax A tax based on the value (or assessed value) of property.**

Aging schedule A report showing how long accounts receivable have been outstanding. It gives the percent of receivables not past due and the percent past due by, for example, one month, two months, or other periods.*

Amortization Accounting for expenses or charges as applicable rather than as paid. Includes such practices as depreciation, depletion, write-off of intangibles, prepaid expenses, and deferred charges.†

Amortize To liquidate on an installment basis; an amortized loan is one in which the principal amount of the loan is repaid in installments during the life of the loan.*

Annual report The formal financial statement issued yearly by a corporation. The annual report shows assets, liabilities, earnings—how the company stood at the close of the business year, how it fared profit-wise during the year and other information of interest to shareowners.†

Sources: From *Managerial Finance*, 6th ed., by J. Fred Weston and Eugene F. Brigham. Copyright © 1978 by The Dryden Press. Copyright © 1962, 1966, 1969, 1972, 1975 by Holt, Rinehart and Winston. Reprinted by permission of Holt, Rinehart and Winston, CBS College Publishing.

The *Language of Investing Glossary* published by the New York Stock Exchange, Inc.

Tax-Exempt Securities & the Investor published by the Securities Industry Association.

* Entries from *Managerial Finance*, 6th edition, by J. Fred Weston and Eugene F. Brigham.

† Entries from *The Language of Investing Glossary*.

** Entries from *Tax-Exempt Securities & the Investor*.

Annuity A series of payments of a fixed amount for a specified number of years.*

Arbitrage The process of selling overvalued and buying undervalued assets so as to bring about an equilibrium where all assets are properly valued. One who engages in arbitrage is called an arbitrager.*

Arrearage Overdue payment; frequently omitted dividend on preferred stock.

Assessed valuation The valuation placed on property for purposes of taxation.**

Assets Everything a corporation owns or due to it: Cash, investments, money due it, materials and inventories, which are called current assets; buildings and machinery, which are known as fixed assets; and patents and good will, called intangible assets. (See: *Liabilities.*)†

Assignment A relatively inexpensive way of liquidating a failing firm that does not involve going through the courts.*

Ask (See: *Bid and asked.*)†

Auction market The system of trading securities through brokers or agents on an exchange such as the New York Stock Exchange. Buyers compete with other buyers while sellers compete with other sellers for the most advantageous price. Most transactions are executed with public customers on both sides since the specialist buys or sells for his own account primarily to offset imbalances in public supply and demand. (See: *Dealers, Quotation, Specialist.*)†

Averages Various ways of measuring the trend of securities prices, one of the most popular of which is the Dow-Jones average of 30 industrial stocks listed on the New York Stock Exchange.

Formulas—some very elaborate—have been devised to compensate for stock splits and stock dividends and thus give continuity to the average.

In the case of the Dow-Jones industrial average, the prices of the 30 stocks are totaled and then divided by a divisor which is intended to compensate for past stock splits and stock dividends and which is changed from time to time. As a result point changes in the average have only the vaguest relationship to dollar price changes in stocks included in the average. Currently, the divisor is 1.465. (See: *NYSE common stock index, Point, Split.*)†

Balance sheet A condensed financial statement showing the nature and amount of a company's assets, liabilities and capital on a given date. In dollar amounts the balance sheet shows what the company owned, what it owed, and the ownership interest in the company of its stockholders. (See: *Assets, Earnings report.*)†

Balloon payment When a debt is not fully amortized, the final payment is larger than the preceding payments and is called a *balloon* payment.*

Bankruptcy A legal procedure for formally liquidating a business, carried out under the jurisdiction of courts of law.*

Basis book A book of mathematical tables used to convert yields to equivalent dollar prices.**

Basis price The price expressed in yield or percentage of return on the investment.**

Bear market A declining market. (See: *Bull market*.)†

Bearer bond A bond which does not have the owner's name registered on the books of the issuer and which is payable to the holder. (See: *Coupon bond, Registered bond*.)†

Bearer security A security that has no identification as to owner. It is presumed to be owned, therefore, by the bearer or the person who holds it. Bearer securities are freely and easily negotiable since ownership can be quickly transferred from seller to buyer.**

Beta coefficient Measures the extent to which the returns on a given stock move with "the stock market."*

Bid and asked Often referred to as a quotation or quote. The bid is the highest price anyone has declared that he wants to pay for a security at a given time, the asked is the lowest price anyone will take at the same time. (See *Quotation*.)†

Block A large holding or transaction of stock—popularly considered to be 10,000 shares or more.†

Blue chip A company known nationally for the quality and wide acceptance of its products or services, and for its ability to make money and pay dividends.†

Blue-sky laws A popular name for laws various states have enacted to protect the public against securities frauds. The term is believed to have originated when a judge ruled that a particular stock had about the same value as a patch of blue sky.†

Board room A room for registered representatives and customers in a broker's office where opening, high, low, and last prices of leading stocks used to be posted on a board throughout the market day. Today such price displays are normally electronically controlled although most board rooms have replaced the board with the ticker and/or individual quotation machines.†

Bond A long-term debt instrument.*

Bond funds Registered investment companies whose assets are invested in diversified portfolios of bonds.**

Book A notebook the specialist in a stock uses to keep a record of the buy and sell orders at specified prices, in sequence of receipt, which are left with him by other brokers. (See *Specialist*.)†

Book value the accounting value of an asset. The book value of a share of common stock is equal to the net worth (common stock plus retained earnings) of the corporation divided by the number of shares of stock outstanding.*

Break-even analysis An analytical technique for studying the relation between fixed cost, variable cost, and profits. A break-even *chart* graphically depicts the nature of break-even analysis. The break-even *point* represents the volume of sales at which total costs equal total revenues (that is, profits equal zero).*

Broker An agent, who handles the public's orders to buy and sell securities, commodities, or other property. For this service a commission is charged. (See: *Commission broker, dealer*.)†

Brokers' loans Money borrowed by brokers from banks or other brokers for a variety of uses. It may be used by specialists and to help finance inventories of stock they deal in; by brokerage firms to finance the underwriting of new issues of corporate and municipal securities; to help finance a firm's own investments; and to help finance the purchase of securities for customers who prefer to use the broker's credit when they buy securities. (See: *Margin*.)†

Bull market An advancing market. (See: *Bear market*.)†

Business risk The basic risk inherent in a firm's operations. Business risk plus financial risk resulting from the use of debt equals total corporate risk.*

Call (1) An option to buy (or "call") a share of stock at a specified price within a specified period. (2) The process of redeeming a bond or preferred stock issue before its normal maturity.*

Call premium The amount in excess of par value that a company must pay when it calls a security.*

Call price The price that must be paid when a security is called. The call price is equal to the par value plus the call premium.*

Call privilege A provision incorporated into a bond or a share of preferred stock that gives the issuer the right to redeem (call) the security at a specified price.*

Callable A bond issue, all or part of which may be redeemed by the issuing corporation under definite conditions before maturity. The term also applies to preferred shares which may be redeemed by the issuing corporation.†

Capital asset An asset with a life of more than one year that is not bought and sold in the ordinary course of business.*

Capital budgeting The process of planning expenditures on assets whose returns are expected to extend beyond one year.*

Capital gain or capital loss Profit or loss from the sale of a capital asset. A capital gain, under current federal income tax laws, may be either short-term (12 months or less) or long-term (more than 12 months). A short-term capital gain is taxed at the reporting individual's full income tax rate. A long-term capital gain is subject to a lower tax. The capital gains provisions of the tax law are complicated. You should consult your tax advisor for specific information.†

Capital market line A graphical representation of the relationship between risk and the required rate of return on an efficient portfolio.*

Capital markets Financial transactions involving instruments with maturities greater than one year.*

Capital rationing A situation where a constraint is placed on the total size of the capital investment during a particular period.*

Capital stock All shares representing ownership of a business, including preferred and common. (See: *Common stock, Preferred stock*.)†

Capital structure The permanent long-term financing of the firm represented by long-term debt, preferred stock, and net worth (net worth consists of capital, capital surplus, and retained earnings). Capital structure is distinguished from *financial structure*, which includes short-term debt plus all reserve accounts.*

Capitalization Total amount of the various securities issued by a corporation. Capitalization may include bonds, debentures, preferred and common stock, and surplus. Bonds and debentures are usually carried on the books of the issuing company in terms of their par or face value. Preferred and common shares may be carried in terms of par or stated value. Stated value may be an arbitrary figure decided upon by the directors or may represent the amount received by the company from the sale of the securities at the time of issuance. (See: *Par*.)†

Capitalization rate A discount rate used to find the present value of a series of future cash receipts; sometimes called *discount rate*.*

Carry-back; carry forward For income tax purposes, losses than can be carried backward or forward to reduce federal income taxes.*

Cash budget A schedule showing cash flows (receipts, disbursements, and net cash) for a firm over a specified period.*

Cash cycle The length of time between the purchase of raw materials and the collection of accounts receivable generated in the sale of the final product.*

Cash flow Reported net income of a corporation *plus* amounts charged off for depreciation, depletion, amortization, extraordinary charges to reserves, which are bookkeeping deductions and not paid out in actual dollars and cents. (See: *Amortization, Depletion, Depreciation*.)†

Cash sale A transaction on the floor of the Stock Exchange which calls for delivery of the securities the same day. In "regular way" trades, the seller is to deliver on the fifth business day except for bonds, which is the next day. (See: *Regular way delivery*.)†

Certainty equivalents The amount of cash (or rate of return) that someone would require *with certainty* to make him indifferent between this certain sum (or *rate of return*) and a particular uncertain, risky sum (or rate of return).*

Certificate The actual piece of paper which is evidence of ownership of stock in a corporation. Watermarked paper is finely engraved with delicate etchings to discourage forgery. Loss of a certificate may at the least cause a great deal of inconvenience—at the worst, financial loss.†

Characteristic line A linear least-squares regression line that shows the relationship between an individual security's return and returns on "the market." The slope of the characteristic line is the beta coefficient.*

Chattel mortgage A mortgage on personal property (not real estate). A mortgage on equipment would be a chattel mortgage.*

Closed-end investment company (See: *Investment company*.)

Coefficient of variation Standard deviation divided by the mean: CV.*

Collateral Assets that are used to secure a loan.*

Collateral trust bond A bond secured by collateral deposited with a trustee. The collateral is often the stocks or bonds of companies controlled by the issuing company but may be other securities.†

Commercial paper Unsecured, short-term promissory notes of large firms, usually issued in denominations of $1 million or more. The rate of interest on commercial paper is typically somewhat below the prime rate of interest.*

Commission The broker's basic fee for purchasing or selling securities or property as an agent.†

Commission broker An agent who executes the public's orders for the purchase or sale of securities or commodities.†

Commitment fee The fee paid to a lender for a formal line of credit.*

Common stock Securities which represent an ownership interest in a corporation. If the company has also issued preferred stock, both common and preferred have ownership rights. The preferred normally is limited to a fixed dividend but has prior claim on dividends and, in the event of liquidation, assets. Claims of both common and preferred stockholders are junior to claims of bondholders or other creditors of the company. Common stockholders assume the greater risk, but generally exercise the greater control and may gain the greater reward in the form of dividends and capital appreciation. The terms common stock and capital stock are often used interchangeably when the company has no preferred stock.†

Compensating balance A required minimum checking account balance that a firm must maintain with a commercial bank. The required balance is generally equal to 15 to 20 percent of the amount of loans outstanding. Compensating balances can raise the effective rate of interest on bank loans.*

Competitive trader A member of the Exchange who trades in stocks on the Floor for an account in which he has an interest. Also known as a Registered Trader.†

Composite cost of capital A weighted average of the component costs of debt, preferred stock, and common equity. Also called the *weighted-average cost of capital*, but it reflects the cost of each additional dollar raised, not the average cost of all capital the firm has raised throughout its history.*

Composition An informal method of reorganization that voluntarily reduces creditors' claims on the debtor firm.*

Compound interest An interest rate that is applicable when interest in succeeding periods is earned not only on the initial principal but also on the accumulated interest of prior periods. Compound interest is contrasted to *simple interest*, in which returns are not earned on interest received.*

Compounding The arithmetic process of determining the final value of a payment or series of payments when compound interest is applied.*

Conditional sales contract A method of financing new equipment by paying it off in installments over a one-to-five-year period. The seller retains title to the equipment until payment has been completed.*

Conglomerate A corporation that has diversified its operations, usually by acquiring enterprises in widely varied industries.†

Consolidated balance sheet A balance sheet showing the financial condition of a corporation and its subsidiaries. (See: *Balance sheet*.)†

Consolidated tape Under the Consolidated Tape Plan, the NYSE and AMEX ticker systems became the "Consolidated Tape," Network A and Network B respectively, on June 16, 1975. Network A reports transactions in NYSE listed securities that take place on the NYSE or any of the participating regional stock exchanges and other markets. Each transaction is identified according to its originating market. Similarly, transactions in AMEX-listed securities, and certain other securities listed on regional stock exchanges, are reported and identified on Network B.†

Consolidated tax return An income tax return that combines the income statement of several affiliated firms.*

Continuous compounding (discounting) As opposed to discrete compounding, interest is added continuously rather than at discrete points in time.*

Conversion price The effective price paid for common stock when the stock is obtained by converting either convertible preferred stocks or convertible bonds. For example, if a $1,000 bond is convertible into 20 shares of stock, the conversion price is $50 ($1,000/20).*

Conversion ratio or conversion rate The number of shares of common stock that may be obtained by converting a convertible bond or share of convertible preferred stock.*

Convertibles Securities (generally bonds or preferred stocks) that are exchangeable at the option of the holder for common stock of the issuing firm.*

Correlation coefficient Measures the degree of relationship between two variables.*

Correspondent A securities firm, bank, or other financial organization which regularly performs services for another in a place or market to which the other does not have direct access. Securities firms may have correspondents in foreign countries or on exchanges of which they are not members. Correspondents are frequently linked by private wires. Member organizations of the N.Y.S.E. with offices in New York City may also act as correspondents for out-of-town member organizations which do not maintain New York City offices.†

Cost of capital The discount rate that should be used in the capital budgeting process.*

Coupon bond Bond with interest coupons attached. The coupons are clipped as they come due and are presented by the holder for payment of interest. (See: *Bearer bond, Registered bond*.)†

Coupon rate The stated rate of interest on a bond.*

Covariance The correlation between two variables multiplied by the standard deviation of each variable:

$$\text{Cov} = r_{xy}\sigma_x\sigma_y.*$$

Covenant Detailed clauses contained in loan agreements. Covenants are designed to protect the lender and include such items as limits on total indebtedness, restrictions on dividends, minimum current ratio, and similar provisions.*

Coverage A term usually connected with revenue bonds. It is a ratio of net revenues pledged to principal and interest payments to debt service requirements. It is one of the factors used in evaluating the quality of an issue.**

Covering Buying a security previously sold short. (See: *Short sale, Short covering.*)†

Cumulative dividends A protective feature on preferred stock that requires all past preferred dividends to be paid before any common dividends are paid.*

Cumulative preferred A stock having a provision that if one or more dividends are omitted, the omitted dividends must be paid before dividends may be paid on the company's common stock.†

Cumulative voting A method of voting for corporate directors which enables the shareholder to multiply the number of his shares by the number of directorships being voted on and cast the total for one director or a selected group of directors. A 10-share holder normally casts 10 votes for each of, say 12 nominees to the board of directors. He thus has 120 votes. Under the cumulative voting principle he may do that or he may cast 120 (10 × 12) votes for only one nominee, 60 for two, 40 for three, or any other distribution he chooses. Cumulative voting is required under the corporate laws of some states, is permitted in most others.†

Curb exchange Former name of the American Stock Exchange, second largest exchange in the country. The term comes from the market's origin on a street in downtown New York.†

Current assets Those assets of a company which are reasonably expected to be realized in cash, or sold, or consumed during the normal operating cycle of the business. These include cash, U.S. government bonds, receivables and money due usually within one year, and inventories.†

Current liabilities Money owed and payable by a company, usually within one year.†

Current return (See: *Yield.*)

Current yield A relation stated as a percent of the annual interest to the actual market price of the bond.**

Cut-off point In the capital budgeting process, the minimum rate of return on acceptable investment opportunities.*

Day order An order to buy or sell which, if not executed expires at the end of the trading day on which it was entered.†

Dealer An individual or firm in the securities business acting as a principal rather than as an agent. Typically, a dealer buys for his own account and sells to a customer from his own inventory. The dealer's profit or loss is the difference between the price he pays and the price he receives for the same security. The dealer's confirmation must disclose to his customer that he has acted as principal. The same individual or firm may function, at different times, either as broker or dealer. (See: *NASD, Specialist.*)†

Debenture A long-term debt instrument that is not secured by a mortgage on specific property.*

Debit balance In a customer's margin account that portion of purchase price of stock, bonds, or commodities covered by credit extended by the broker to the margin customer.†

Debt limit The statutory or constitutional maximum debt that a municipality can legally incur.**

Debt ratio Total debt divided by total assets.*

Debt service Refers to the payments required for interest and retirement of the principal amount of a debt.**

Decision tree A device for setting forth graphically the pattern of relationship between decisions and chance events.*

Default The failure to fulfill a contract. Generally, default refers to the failure to pay interest or principal on debt obligations.*

Degree of leverage The percentage increase in profits resulting from a given percentage increase in sales. The degree of leverage may be calculated for financial leverage, operating leverage, or both combined.*

Denomination The face amount or par value of a security which the issuer promises to pay on the maturity date. Most municipal bonds are issued with a minimum denomination of $5,000, although a few older issues are available in $1,000 denominations.**

Depletion accounting Natural resources, such as metals, oil and gas, and timber, which conceivably can be reduced to zero over the years, present a special problem in capital management. Depletion is an accounting practice consisting of charges against earnings based upon the amount of the asset taken out of the total reserves in the period for which accounting is made. A bookkeeping entry, it does not represent any cash outlay nor are any funds earmarked for the purpose.†

Depository trust company (DTC) A central securities certificate depository through which members effect security deliveries between each other via computerized bookkeeping entries thereby reducing the physical movement of stock certificates.†

Depreciation Normally, charges against earnings to write off the cost, less salvage value, of an asset over its estimated useful life. It is a bookkeeping entry and does not represent any cash outlay nor are any funds earmarked for the purpose.†

Devaluation The process of reducing the value of a country's currency stated in terms of other currencies; for example, the British pound might be devalued from $2.30 for one pound to $2.00 for one pound.*

Director Person elected by shareholders to establish company policies. The directors appoint the president, vice presidents, and all other operating officers. Directors decide, among other matters, if and when dividends shall be paid. (See: *Management, Proxy.*)†

Discount The amount by which a preferred stock or bond may sell below its par value. Also used as a verb to mean "takes into account" as the price of the stock has discounted the expected dividend cut. (See: *Premium.*)†

Discount rate The interest rate used in the discounting process; sometimes called *capitalization rate.**

Discounted cash flow techniques Methods of ranking investment proposals. Included are (1) internal rate of return method, (2) net present value method, and (3) profitability index or benefit/cost ratio.*

Discounting The process of finding the present value of a series of future cash flows. Discounting is the reverse of compounding.*

Discounting of accounts receivable Short-term financing where accounts receivable are used to secure the loan. The lender does not *buy* the accounts receivable but simply uses them as collateral for the loan. Also called *assigning accounts receivable.**

Discretionary account An account in which the customer gives the broker or someone else discretion, which may be complete or within specific limits, either to the purchases, or sale of securities or commodities including selection, timing, amount, and price to be paid or received.†

Diversification Spreading investments among different companies in different fields. Another type of diversification is also offered by the securities of many individual companies because of the wide range of their activities. (See: *Investment trust.*)†

Dividend The payment designed by the board of directors to be distributed pro rata among the shares outstanding. On preferred shares, it is generally a fixed amount. On common shares, the dividend varies with the fortunes of the company and the amount of cash on hand, and may be omitted if business is poor or the directors determine to withhold earnings to invest in plant and equipment. Sometimes a company will pay a dividend out of past earnings even if it is not currently operating at a profit.†

Dividend yield The ratio of the current dividend to the current price of a share of stock.*

Dollar bond A bond that is quoted and traded in dollars rather than in terms of yield.**

Dollar cost averaging A system of buying securities at regular intervals with a fixed dollar amount. Under this system the investor buys by the dollars' worth rather than by the number of shares. If each investment is of the same number of dollars, payments buy more when the

price is low and fewer when it rises. Thus temporary downswings in price benefit the investor if he continues periodic purchases in both good times and bad and the price at which the shares are sold is more than their average cost. (See: *Formula investing.*)†

Double-barrelled bond A bond secured by the pledge of two or more sources of repayment, e.g., secured by taxes as well as revenues.**

Double exemption Refers to securities that are exempt from state as well as Federal income taxes.**

Double taxation Short for *double taxation of dividends.* The federal government taxes corporate profits once as corporate income; any part of the remaining profits distributed as dividends to stockholders may be taxed again as income to the recipient stockholder.†

Dow theory A theory of market analysis based upon the performance of the Dow-Jones industrial and transportation stock price averages. The theory says that the market is in a basic upward trend if one of these averages advances above a previous important high, accompanied or followed by a similar advance in the other. When the averages both dip below previous important lows, this is regarded as confirmation of a basic downward trend. The theory does not attempt to predict how long either trend will continue, although it is widely misinterpreted as a method of forecasting future action.†

Down tick (See: *Up tick.*)

Du Pont system A system of analysis designed to show the relationship between return on investment, asset turnover, and the profit margin.*

Earnings report A statement—also called an *income statement*—issued by a company showing its earnings or losses over a given period. The earnings report lists the income earned, expenses, and the net result. (See: *Balance sheet.*)†

EBIT Acronym for *earnings before interest and taxes.**

Economical ordering quantity (EOQ) The optimum (least cost) quantity of merchandise which should be ordered.*

EPS Acronym for *earnings per share.**

Equipment trust certificate A type of security, generally issued by a railroad, to pay for new equipment. Title to the equipment, such as a locomotive, is held by a trustee until the notes are paid off. An equipment trust certificate is usually secured by a first claim on the equipment.†

Equity The net worth of a business, consisting of capital stock, capital (or paid-in) surplus, earned surplus (or retained earnings), and occasionally, certain net worth reserves. *Common* *equity* is that part of the total net worth belonging to the common stockholders. *Total equity* would include preferred stockholders. The terms *common stock, net worth,* and *common equity* are frequently used interchangeably.†

Exchange acquisition A method of filling an order to buy a large block of stock on the floor of the exchange. Under certain circumstances, a member-broker can facilitate the purchase of a block by soliciting orders to sell. All orders to sell the security are lumped together and crossed with the buy order in the regular action market. The price to the buyer may be on a net basis or on a commission basis.†

Exchange distribution A method of selling large blocks of stock on the floor of the exchange. Under certain circumstances, a member-broker can facilitate the sale of a block of stock by soliciting and getting other member-brokers to solicit orders to buy. Individual buy orders are lumped together and crossed with the sell order in the regular auction market. A special commission is usually paid by the seller; ordinarily the buyer pays no commission.†

Exchange rate The rate at which one currency can be exchanged for another; for example, $2.30 can be exchanged for one British pound.*

Excise tax A tax on the manufacture, sale, or consumption of specified commodities.*

Exdividend A synonym for "without dividend." The buyer of a stock selling exdividend does not receive the recently declared dividend. Every dividend is payable on a fixed date to all shareholders recorded on the books of the company as of a previous date of record. For example, a dividend may be declared as payable to holders of record on the books of the company on a given Friday. Since five business days are allowed for delivery of stock in a "regular way" transaction on the New York Stock Exchange, the exchange would declare the stock "exdividend" as of the opening of the market on the preceding Monday. That means anyone who bought it on and after Monday would not be entitled to that dividend. When stocks go exdividend, the stock tables include the symbol "x" following the name. (See: *Cash sale, Net change, Transfer.*)†

Ex-dividend date The date on which the right to the current dividend no longer accompanies a stock. (For listed stock, the ex-dividend date is four working days prior to the date of record.).*

Exercise price The price that must be paid for a share of common stock when it is bought by exercising a warrant.*

Expected return The rate of return a firm expects to realize from an investment. The expected return is the mean value of the probability distribution of possible returns.*

Ex-rights The date on which stock purchase rights are no longer transferred to the purchaser of the stock.*

Extension An informal method of reorganization in which the creditors voluntarily postpone the date of required payment on past-due obligations.*

External funds Funds acquired through borrowing or by selling new common or preferred stock.

Extra The short form of *extra dividend.* A dividend in the form of stock or cash in addition to the regular or usual dividend the company has been paying.†

Face value The value of a bond that appears on the face of the bond, unless the value is otherwise specified by the issuing company. Face value is ordinarily the amount the issuing company promises to pay at maturity. Face value is not an indication of market value. Sometimes referred to as par value. (See: *Par.*)†

Factoring A method of financing accounts receivable under which a firm sells its accounts receivable (generally without recourse) to a financial institution (the *factor*).*

Field warehousing A method of financing inventories in which a "warehouse" is established at the place of business of the borrowing firm.*

Financial accounting standards board (FASB) A private (nongovernment) agency which functions as an accounting standards-setting body.*

Financial intermediation Financial transactions which bring savings surplus units together with savings deficit units so that savings can be redistributed into their most productive uses.*

Financial lease A lease that does not provide for maintenance services, is not cancellable, and is fully amortized over the life of the lease.*

Financial leverage The ratio of total debt to total assets. There are other measures of financial leverage, especially ones that relate cash inflows to required cash outflows.*

Financial markets Transactions in which the creation and transfer of financial assets and financial liabilities take place.*

Financial risk That portion of total corporate risk, over and above basic business risk, that results from using debt.*

Financial structure The entire right side of the balance sheet—the way in which a firm is financed.*

Fiscal year A corporation's accounting year. Due to the nature of their particular business, some companies do not use the calendar year for their bookkeeping. A typical example is the department store which finds December 31 too early a date to close its books after the Christmas rush. For that reason many stores wind up their accounting year January 31. Their fiscal year, therefore, runs from February 1 of one year through January 31 of the next. The fiscal year of other companies may run from July 1 through the following June 30. Most companies, though, operate on a calendar year basis.†

Fisher effect The increase in the nominal interest rates over real (purchasing power adjusted) interest rates reflecting anticipated inflation.*

Fixed charges Costs that do not vary with the level of output, especially fixed financial costs such as interest, lease payments, and sinking fund payments.*

Flat income bond This term means that the price at which a bond is traded includes consideration for all unpaid accruals of interest. Bonds which are in default of interest or principal are traded flat. Income bonds, which pay interest only to the extent earned are usually traded flat. All other bonds are usually dealt in "and interest," which means that the buyer pays to the seller the market price plus interest accrued since the last payment date.†

Float The amount of funds tied up in checks that have been written but are still in process and have not yet been collected.*

Floating exchange rates Exchange rates may be fixed by government policy *(pegged)* or allowed to *float* up or down in accordance with supply and demand. When market forces are allowed to function, exchange rates are said to be floating.*

Floor The huge trading area—about two-thirds the size of a football field—where stocks and bonds are bought and sold on the New York Stock Exchange.†

Floor broker A member of the Stock Exchange who executes orders on the floor of the exchange to buy or sell any listed securities. (See: *Commission broker, Two-dollar broker.*)†

Flotation cost The cost of issuing new stocks or bonds.*

Formula investing An investment technique. One formula calls for the shifting of funds from common shares to preferred shares or bonds as the market, on average, rises above a certain predetermined point—and the return of funds to common share investments as the market average declines. (See: *Dollar cost averaging.*)†

Free and open market A market in which supply and demand are freely expressed in terms of price. Contrasts with a controlled market in which supply, demand, and price may all be regulated.†

Fundamental research Analysis of industries and companies based on factors such as sales, assets, earnings, products or services, markets, and management. As applied to the economy, fundamental research includes consideration of gross national product, interest rates, unemployment, inventories, savings, and so on. (See: *Technical research.*)†

Funded debt Usually long-term, interest-bearing bonds or debentures of a company. Could include long-term bank loans. Does *not* include short-term loans, preferred, or common stock.†

Funding The process of replacing short-term debt with long-term securities (stocks or bonds).*

General mortgage bond A bond which is secured by a blanket mortgage on the company's property, but which may be outranked by one or more other mortgages.†

General obligation bond A bond secured by the pledge of the issuer's full faith, credit and taxing power.**

General purchasing power reporting A proposal by the FASB that the current values of nonmonetary items in financial statements be adjusted by a general price index.*

Gilt-edged High-grade bond issued by a company which has demonstrated its ability to earn a comfortable profit over a period of years and pay its bondholders their interest without interruption.†

Give up A term with many different meanings. For one, a member of the exchange on the floor may act for a second member by executing an order for him with a third member. The first member tells the third member that he is acting on behalf of the second member and "gives up" the second member's name rather than his own. For another, if you have an account with Doe & Company but you're in a town where Doe has no office, you go to another member firm, tell them you have an account with Doe & Company and would like to buy some stock. After verifying your account with Doe & Company, the firm may execute your order and tell the broker who sells the stock that the firm is acting on behalf of Doe & Company. They give up the name of Doe & Company to the selling broker. Or the firm may simply wire your order to Doe & Company who will execute it for you.†

Good delivery Certain basic qualifications must be met before a security sold on the exchange may be delivered. The security must be in proper form to comply with the contract of sale and to transfer title to the purchaser.†

Good 'til cancelled order (GTC) or open order An order to buy or sell which remains in effect until it is either executed or cancelled.†

Goodwill Intangible assets of a firm established by the excess of the price paid for the going concern over its book value.*

Government bonds Obligations of the U.S. government, regarded as the highest grade issues in existence.†

Growth stock Stock of a company with a record of growth in earnings at a relatively rapid rate.†

Guaranteed bond A bond which has interest or principal, or both, guaranteed by a company other than the issuer. Usually found in the railroad industry when large roads, leasing sections of trackage owned by small railroads, may guarantee the bonds of the smaller road.†

Guaranteed stock Usually preferred stock on which dividends are guaranteed by another company; under much the same circumstances as a bond is guaranteed.†

Hedge (See: *Arbitrage, Puts & Calls, Short sale.*)†

Holding company A corporation which owns the securities of another, in most cases with voting control.†

Hurdle rate In capital budgeting, the minimum acceptable rate of return on a project. If the expected rate of return is below the hurdle rate, the project is not accepted. The hurdle rate should be the marginal cost of capital.*

Hypothecation The pledging of securities as collateral—for example, to secure the debit balance in a margin account.†

Improper accumulation Earnings retained by a business for the purpose of enabling stockholders to avoid personal income taxes.*

Inactive stock An issue traded on an exchange or in the over-the-counter market in which there is a relatively low volume of transactions. Volume may be no more than a few hundred shares a week or even less. On the New York Stock Exchange many inactive stocks are traded in 10-share units rather than the customary 100. (See: *Round lot.*)†

In-and-out Purchase and sale of the same security within a short period—a day, a week, even a month. An in-and-out trader is generally more interested in day-to-day price fluctuations than dividends or long-term growth.†

Income bond Generally income bonds promise to repay principal but to pay interest only when earned. In some cases unpaid interest on an income bond may accumulate as a claim against the corporation when the bond becomes due. An income bond may also be issued in lieu of preferred stock.†

Incremental cash flow Net cash flow attributable to an investment project.*

Incremental cost of capital The average cost of the increment of capital raised during a given year.*

Indenture A written agreement under which bonds and debentures are issued, setting forth maturity date, interest rate, and other terms.†

Independent broker Members on the floor of the NYSE who execute orders for other brokers having more business at that time than they can handle themselves, or for firms who do not have their exchange member on the floor. Formerly known as *two-dollar brokers* from the time when these independent brokers received $2 per hundred shares for executing such orders. Their fees are paid by the commission brokers. (See: *Commission broker.*)†

Index A statistical yardstick expressed in terms of percentages of a base year or years. For instance, the Federal Reserve Board's index of industrial production is based on 1967 as 100. An index is not an average. (See: *Averages, NYSE common stock index.*)†

Industrial revenue bond A security backed by private enterprises that have been financed by a municipal issue.**

Insolvency The inability to meet maturing debt obligations.*

Institutional Investor An organization whose primary purpose is to invest its own assets or those held in trust by it for others. Includes pension funds, investment companies, insurance companies, universities, and banks.†

Interest Payments a borrower pays a lender for the use of his money. A corporation pays interest on its bonds to its bondholders. (See: *Bond, dividend.*)†

Interest factor (IF) Numbers found in compound interest and annuity tables.*

Internal financing Funds made available for capital budgeting and working-capital expansion through the normal operations of the firm; internal financing is approximately equal to retained earnings plus depreciation.*

Internal rate of return (IRR) The rate of return on an asset investment. The internal rate of return is calculated by finding the discount rate that equates the present value of future cash flows to the cost of the investment.*

Intrinsic value That value which, in the mind of the analyst, is justified by the facts. It is often used to distinguish between the *true value* of an asset (the intrinsic value) and the asset's current market price.*

Investment The use of money for the purpose of making more money, to gain income or increase capital, or both. Safety of principal is an important consideration. (See: *Speculation.*)†

Investment banker Also known as an *underwriter.* He is the middleman between the corporation issuing new securities and the public. The usual practice is for one or more investment bankers to buy outright from a corporation a new issue of stocks or bonds. The group forms a syndicate to sell the securities to individuals and institutions. Investment bankers also distribute very large blocks of stocks or bonds—perhaps held by an estate. Thereafter the market in the security may be over-the-counter, on a regional stock exchange, the American Exchange, or the New York Stock Exchange. (See: *Over-the-counter, primary distribution, syndicate.*)†

Investment company A company or trust which uses its capital to invest in other companies. There are two principal types: the closed-end and the open-end, or mutual fund. Shares in closed-end investment companies, some of which are listed on the New York Stock Exchange, are readily transferable in the open market and are bought and sold like other shares. Capitalization of these companies remains the same unless action is taken to change, which is seldom. Open-end funds sell their own new shares to investors, stand ready to buy back their old shares, and are not listed. Open-end funds are so called because their capitalization is not fixed; they issue more shares as people want them.†

Investment counsel One whose principal business consists of acting as investment adviser and a substantial part of his business consists of rendering investment supervisory services.†

Investment tax credit Business firms can deduct as a credit against their income taxes a specified percentage of the dollar amount of new investments in each of certain categories of assets.*

Investors service bureau A facility of the New York Stock Exchange which answers written inquiries from individual investors on all aspects of securities investing. Major areas of inquiries involve: finding local brokerage firms which take small orders or accounts, explaining investing methods and listed securities, clarifying exchange operations, providing instructions for tracing dubious securities.†

Issue Any of a company's securities, or the act of distributing such securities.†

Issuer A municipal unit that borrows money through the sale of bonds or notes.**

Legal list A list of securities in which mutual savings banks, pensions funds, insurance companies, and other fiduciary institutions are permitted to invest.*

Legal opinion An opinion concerning the legality of a bond issue usually written by a recognized law firm specializing in public borrowings.**

Leverage The effect on the per-share earnings of the common stock of a company when large sums must be paid for bond interest or preferred stock dividends, or both, before the common stock is entitled to share in earnings. Leverage may be advantageous for the common stock when earnings are good but may work against the common when earnings decline. Example: Company A has 1,000,000 shares of common stock outstanding, no other securities. Earnings drop from $1,000,000 to $800,000 or from $1 to 80 cents a share, a decline of 20 percent. Company B also has 1,000,000 shares of common but must pay $500,000 annually in bond interest. If earnings amount to $1,000,000, there is $500,000 available for the common or 50 cents a share. But earnings drop to $800,000

so there is only $300,000 available for the common, or 30 cents a share—a drop of 40 percent. Or suppose earnings of the company with only common stock increased from $1,000,000 to $1,500,000—earnings per share would go from $1 to $1.50, or an increase of 50 percent. But if earnings of the company which had to pay $500,000 in bond interest increased that much—earnings per common share would jump from 50 cents to $1 a share, or 100 percent. When a company has common stock only, no leverage exists because all earnings are available for the common, although relatively large fixed charges payable for lease of substantial plant assets may have an effect similar to that of a bond issue.†

Leverage factor The ratio of debt to total assets.*

Liabilities All the claims against a corporation. Liabilities include accounts and wages and salaries payable, dividends declared payable, accrued taxes payable, fixed or long-term liabilities such as mortgage bonds, debentures, and bank loans. (See: *Assets, balance sheet.*)†

Lien A lender's claim on assets that are pledged for a loan.*

Limit, limited order, or limited price order An order to buy or sell a stated amount of a security at a specified price, or at a better price, if obtainable after the order is represented in the Trading Crowd.†

Limited tax bond A bond secured by a pledge of a tax or group of taxes limited as to rate or amount.**

Line of credit An arrangement whereby a financial institution (bank or insurance company) commits itself to lend up to a specified maximum amount of funds during a specified period. Sometimes the interest rate on the loan is specified, at other times, it is not. Sometimes a commitment fee is imposed for obtaining the line of credit.*

Liquidation The process of converting securities or other property into cash. The dissolution of a company, with cash remaining after sale of its assets and payment of all indebtedness being distributed to the shareholders.†

Liquidity Refers to a firm's cash position and its ability to meet maturing obligations.*

Listed stock The stock of a company which is traded on a securities exchange, and for which a listing application and a registration statement, giving detailed information about the company and its operations, have been filed with the Securities and Exchange Commission, unless otherwise exempted, and the exchange itself. The various stock exchanges have different standards for listing. Some of the guides used by the New York Stock Exchange for an original listing are national interest in the company, a minimum of 1-million shares publicly held among not less than 2,000 round-lot stockholders. The publicly held common shares should have a minimum aggregate market value of $16 million. The company should have net income in the latest year of over $2.5-million before federal income tax and $2-million in each of the preceding two years.†

Load The portion of the offering price of shares of open-end investment companies in excess of the value of the underlying assets which cover sales commissions and all other costs of distribution. The load is usually incurred only on purchase, there being, in most cases, no charge when the shares are sold (redeemed).†

Lock-box plan A procedure used to speed up collections and to reduce float.*

Locked in An investor is said to be locked in when he has a profit on a security he owns but does not sell because his profit would immediately become subject to the capital gains tax. (See: *Capital gain.*)†

Long Signifies ownership of securities: "I am long 100 U.S. Steel" means the speaker owns 100 shares. (See: *Short position, short sale.*)†

Management The board of directors, elected by the stockholders, and the officers of the corporation, appointed by the board of directors.†

Manipulation An illegal operation. Buying or selling a security for the purpose of creating a false or misleading appearance of active trading or for the purpose of raising or depressing the price to induce purchase or sale by others.†

Margin The amount paid by the customer when he uses his broker's credit to buy a security. Under Federal Reserve regulations, the initial margin required in past years has ranged from 50 percent of the purchase price all the way to 100 percent. (See: *Brokers' loans, Equity, Margin call.*)†

Margin call A demand upon a customer to put up money or securities with the broker. The call is made when a purchase is made; also if a customer's equity in a margin account declines below a minimum standard set by the exchange or by the firm. (See: *Margin.*)†

Margin—profit on sales The *profit margin* is the percentage of profit after tax to sales.*

Marginal cost The cost of an additional unit. The marginal cost of capital is the cost of an additional dollar of new funds.*

Marginal efficiency of capital A schedule showing the internal rate of return on investment opportunities.*

Marginal revenue The additional gross revenue produced by selling one additional unit of output.*

Marketability The measure of the ease with which a security can be sold in the secondary market.**

Market order An order to buy or sell a stated amount of a security at the most advantageous price obtainable. (See: *Good 'til cancelled order, Limit order, Stop order.*)†

Market price In the case of a security, market price is usually considered the last reported price at which the stock or bond sold.†

Matched and lost When two bids to buy the same stock are made on the trading floor simultaneously, and each bid is equal to or larger than the amount of stock offered, both bids are considered to be on an equal basis. So the two bidders flip a coin to decide who buys the stock. Also applies to offers to sell.†

Maturity The date on which a loan or a bond or debenture comes due and is to be paid off.†

Member corporation A securities brokerage firm, organized as a corporation, with at least one member of the New York Stock Exchange, Inc., who is an officer and a holder of voting stock in the corporation. (See: *Member firm.*)†

Member firm A securities brokerage firm organized as a partnership and having at least one general partner who is a member of the New York Stock Exchange, Inc. (See: *Member corporation.*)†

Member organization This term includes New York Stock Exchange Member Firm *and* Member Corporation. (See: *Member corporation, Member firm.*)†

Merger Any combination that forms one company from two or more previously existing companies.*

Money market Financial markets in which funds are borrowed or lent for short periods (i.e., less than one year). (The money market is distinguished from the capital market, which is the market for long-term funds.)*

Mortgage A pledge of designated property as security for a loan.*

Mortgage bond A bond secured by a mortgage on a property. The value of the property may or may not equal the value of the so-called mortgage bonds issued against it. (See: *Bond, Debenture.*)†

Municipal bond A bond issued by a state or a political subdivision, such as county, city, town, or village. The term also designates bonds issued by state agencies and authorities. In general, interest paid on municipal bonds is exempt from federal income taxes and state and local income taxes within the state of issue.†

Mutual fund (See: *Investment company.*)

NASD The National Association of Securities Dealers, Inc. An association of brokers and dealers in the over-the-counter securities business. The association has the power to expel members who have been declared guilty of unethical practices. NASD is dedicated to—among other objectives—"adopt, administer and enforce rules of fair practice and rules to prevent fraudulent and manipulative acts and practices, and in general to promote just and equitable principles of trade for the protection of investors."†

NASDAQ An automated information network which provides brokers and dealers with price quotations on securities traded over-the-counter. NASDAQ is an acronym for National Association of Securities Dealers Automated Quotations.†

Negotiable Refers to a security, title to which is transferable by delivery. (See: *Good delivery.*)†

Net asset value A term usually used in connection with investment companies, meaning net asset value per share. It is common practice for an investment company to compute its assets daily, or even twice daily, by totaling the market value of all securities owned. All liabilities are deducted, and the balance divided by the number of shares outstanding. The resulting figure is the net asset value per share. (See: *Assets, Investment company.*)†

Net change The change in the price of a security from the closing price on one day and the closing price on the following day on which the stock is traded. The net change is ordinarily the last figure on the stock price list. The mark + 1⅛ means up $1.125 a share from the last sale on the previous day the stock traded.†

Net debt Gross debt less sinking fund accumulations and all self-supporting debt.**

Net present value (NPV) method A method of ranking investment proposals. The NPV is equal to the present value of future returns, discounted at the marginal cost of capital, minus the present value of the cost of the investment.*

Net worth The capital and surplus of a firm— capital stock, capital surplus (paid-in capital), earned surplus (retained earnings), and, occasionally, certain reserves. For some purposes, preferred stock is included; generally, net worth refers only to the common stockholders' position.*

New housing authority bonds A bond issued by a local public housing authority to finance public housing. It is backed by Federal funds and the solemn pledge of the U.S. Government that payment will be made in full.**

New issue A stock or bond sold by a corporation for the first time. Proceeds may be issued to retire outstanding securities of the company, for new plant or equipment, or for additional working capital.†

New issue market Market for new issues of municipal bonds and notes.**

Nominal interest rate The contracted or stated interest rate, undeflated for price-level changes.*

Noncumulative A preferred stock on which unpaid dividends do not accrue. Omitted dividends are, as a rule, gone forever. (See: *Cumulative preferred.*)†

Normal probability distribution A symmetrical, bell-shaped probability function.*

Notes Short-term unsecured promises to pay specified amounts of money. For municipal notes maturities generally range from six to twelve months.**

NYSE common stock index A composite index covering price movements of all common stocks listed on the "Big Board." It is based on the close of the market December 31, 1965 as 50.00 and is weighted according to the number of shares listed for each issue. The index is computed continuously and printed on the ticker tape each half hour. Point changes in the index are converted to dollars and cents so as to provide a meaningful measure of changes in the average price of listed stocks. The composite index is supplemented by separate indexes for four industry groups: industrials, transportation, utilities, and finances, (See: *Averages.*)†

Objective probability distributions Probability distributions determined by statistical procedures.*

Odd lot An amount of stock less than the established 100-share unit or 10-share unit of trading: from 1 to 99 shares for the great majority of issues, 1 to 9 for so-called inactive stocks. (See: *Round lot, Inactive stock.*)†

Off-board This term may refer to transactions over-the-counter in unlisted securities, or to a transaction involving listed shares which was not executed on a national securities exchange. (See: *Over-the-counter, Secondary distribution.*)†

Offer The price at which a person is ready to sell. Opposed to bid, the price at which one is ready to buy. (See: *Bid and asked.*)†

Official statement Document prepared by or for the issuer that gives in detail the security and financial information about the issue.**

Open order (See: *Good 'til cancelled order.*)

Open-end investment company (See: *Investment company.*)

Operating leverage The extent to which fixed costs are used in a firm's operation. Break-even analysis is used to measure the extent to which operating leverage is employed.*

Opportunity cost The rate of return on the best *alternative* investment that is available. It is the highest return that will *not* be earned if the funds are invested in a particular project. For example, the opportunity cost of *not* investing in bond A yielding 8 percent might be 7.99 percent, which could be earned on bond B.*

Option A right to buy (call) or sell (put) a fixed amount of a given stock at a specified price within a limited period of time. The purchaser hopes that the stock's price will go up (if he bought a call) or down (if he bought a put) by an amount sufficient to provide a profit greater than the cost of the contract and the commission and other fees required to exercise the contract. If the stock price holds steady or moves in the opposite direction, the price paid for the option is lost entirely. There are several other types of options available to the public but these are basically combinations of puts and calls. Individuals may write (sell) as well as purchase options and are thereby obliged to deliver or buy the stock at the specified price.

There are also listed call option markets on the Chicago Board Options Exchange, the American, Midwest, Pacific, and PBW Stock Exchanges. These differ from the over-the-counter market in that trading is limited to selected issues, expiration of contracts is standardized at four dates during the year, exercise prices are set at multiples of 5 below 50 and multiples of 10 above 50, and option prices are determined through a continuous competitive-auction market system.†

Orders good until a specified time A market or limited price order which is to be represented in the Trading Crowd until a specified time, after which such order or the portion thereof not executed is to be treated as cancelled.†

Ordinary income Income from the normal operations of a firm. Operating income specifically excludes income from the sale of capital assets.*

Organized security exchanges Formal organizations having tangible, physical locations. Organized exchanges conduct an auction market in designated ("listed") investment securities. For example, the New York Stock Exchange is an organized exchange.*

Overbought An opinion as to price levels. May refer to a security which has had a sharp rise or to the market as a whole after a period of vigorous buying, which it may be argued, has left prices "too high."†

Overdraft system A system where a depositor may write checks in excess of his balance, with his bank automatically extending a loan to cover the shortage.*

Overlapping debt That portion of the debt of other governmental units for which residents of a particular muncipality are responsible.**

Oversold An opinion—the reverse of overbought. A single security or a market which, it is believed, has declined to an unreasonable level.†

Over-the-counter A market for securities made up of securities dealers who may or may not be members of a securities exchange. Over-the-counter is mainly a market made over the telephone. Thousands of companies have insufficient shares outstanding, stockholders, or earnings to warrant application for listing on the New York Stock Exchange, Inc. Securities of these companies are traded in the over-the-counter market between dealers who act either as principals or as brokers for customers. The over-the-counter market is the principal market for U.S. government and municipal bonds. (See: *NASD, NASDAQ, Off-board.*)†

Paper profit An unrealized profit on a security still held. Paper profits become realized profits only when the security is sold. (See: *Profit taking.*)†

Par In the case of a common share, par means a dollar amount assigned to the share by the company's charter. Par value may also be used to compute the dollar amount of the common shares on the balance sheet. Par value has little significance so far as market value of common stock is concerned. Many companies today issue no-par stock but give a stated per share value on the balance sheet. In the case of preferred shares and bonds, however, par is important. It often signifies the dollar value upon which dividends on preferred stocks, and interest on bonds, are figured. The issuer of a 6 percent bond promises to pay that percentage of the bond's par value annually. (See: *Capitalization, Transfer tax.*)†

Par value The nominal or face value of stock or bond.*

Participating preferred A preferred stock which is entitled to its stated dividend and, also, to additional dividends on a specified basis upon payment of dividends on the common stock.†

Passed dividend Omission of a regular or scheduled dividend.†

Payback period The length of time required for the net revenues of an investment to return the cost of the investment.*

Paying agent Place where principal and interest is payable. Usually a designated bank or the treasurer's office of the issuer.**

Payout ratio The percentage of earnings paid out in the form of dividends.*

Pegging A market stabilization action taken by the manager of an underwriting group during the offering of new securities. He does this by continually placing orders to buy at a specified price in the market.*

Penny stocks Low-priced issues often highly speculative, selling at less than $1 a share. Frequently used as a term of disparagement, although a few penny stocks have developed into investment-caliber issues.†

Percentage order A limited price order to buy (or sell) a stated amount of a specified stock after a fixed number of shares of such stock have traded.†

Perpetuity A stream of equal future payments expected to continue forever.*

Pledging of accounts receivable Short-term

borrowing from financial institutions where the loan is secured by accounts receivable. The lender may physically take the accounts receivable but typically has recourse to the borrower; also called *discounting of accounts receivable.**

Point In the case of shares of stock, a point means $1. If ABC shares rises 3 points, each share has risen $3. In the case of bonds a point means $10, since a bond is quoted as a percentage of $1,000. A bond which rises 3 points gains 3 percent of $1,000, or $30 in value. An advance from 87 to 90 would mean an advance in dollar value from $870 to $900 for each $1,000 bond. In the case of market averages, the word point means merely that and no more. If, for example, the Dow-Jones Industrial averages rises from 870.25 to 871.25, it has risen a point. A point in this average, however, is not equivalent to $1. (See: *Averages.*)†

Pooling of interest An accounting method for combining the financial statements of firms that merge. Under the pooling-of-interest procedure, the assets of the merged firms are simply added to form the balance sheet of the surviving corporation. This method is different from the "purchase" method, where goodwill is put on the balance sheet to reflect a premium (or discount) paid in excess of book value.*

Portfolio Holdings of securities by an individual or institution. A portfolio may contain bonds, preferred stocks, and common stocks of various types of enterprises.†

Portfolio effect The extent to which the variation in returns on a combination of assets (a "portfolio") is less than the sum of the variations of the individual assets.*

Portfolio theory Deals with the selection of optimal portfolios; that is, portfolios that provide the highest possible return for any specified degree of risk.*

Preemptive right A provision contained in the corporate charter and by laws that gives holders of common stock the right to purchase on a pro rata basis new issues of common stock (or securities convertible into common stock.)*

Preferred stock A class of stock with a claim on the company's earnings before payment may be made on the common stock and usually entitled to priority over common stock if the company liquidates. Usually entitled to dividends at a specified rate—when declared by the board of directors and before payment of a dividend on the common stock—depending upon the terms of the issue. (See: *Cumulative preferred, Participating preferred.*)†

Premium The amount by which a preferred stock, bond, or option may sell above its par value. In the case of a new issue of bonds or stocks, premium is the amount the market price rises over the original selling price. Also refers to a charge sometimes made when a stock is borrowed to make delivery on a short sale. May refer, also, to redemption price of a bond or preferred stock if it is higher than face value. (See: *Discount, Short sale.*)†

Present value (PV) The value today of a future payment, or stream of payments, discounted at the appropriate discount rate.*

Price-earnings ratio The price of a share of stock divided by earnings per share for a twelve-month period. For example, a stock selling for $50 a share and earning $5 a share is said to be selling at a price-earnings ratio of 10 to 1.†

Primary distribution Also called primary offering. The original sale of a company's securities. (See: *Investment banker, Secondary distribution.*)†

Primary market Market for new issues of securities.

Prime rate The lowest rate of interest commercial banks charge very large, strong corporations.*

Principal The person for whom a broker executes an order, or a dealer buying or selling for his own account. The term *principal* may also refer to a person's capital or to the face amount of a bond.†

Pro forma A projection. A *pro forma* financial statement is one that shows how the actual statement will look if certain specified assumptions are realized. *Pro forma* statements may be either furture or past projections. An example of a backward *pro forma* statement occurs when two firms are planning to merge and shows what their consolidated financial statements would have looked like if they had been merged in preceding years.*

Profit center A unit of a large, decentralized firm that has its own investments and for which a rate of return on investment can be calculated.*

Profit margin The ratio of profits after taxes to sales.*

Profitability index (PI) The present value of future returns divided by the present value of the investment outlay.*

Profit-taking Selling stock which has appreciated in value since purchase, in order to realize the profit which has been made possible. The term is often used to explain a downturn in the market following a period of rising prices. (See: *Paper profit.*)†

Progressive tax A tax that requires a higher percentage payment on higher incomes. The personal income tax in the United States, which is at a rate of 14 percent on the lowest increments of income to 70 percent on the highest increments, is progressive.*

Prospectus The official selling circular that must be given to purchasers of new securities registered with the Securities and Exchange

Commission so investors can evaluate those securities before or at the time of purchase. It highlights the much longer Registration Statement filed with the commission. It warns the issue has not been approved (or disapproved) by the commission and discloses such material information as the issuer's property and business, the nature of the security offered, use of proceeds, issuer's competition and prospects, management's experience, history, and remuneration, and certified financial statements. A preliminary version of the prospectus, used by brokers to obtain buying indications from investors, is called a *red herring*. This is because of a front-page notice (printed in red ink) that the preliminary prospectus is "subject to completion or amendment" and "shall not constitute an offer to sell . . ."†

Proxy A document giving one person the authority or power to act for another. Typically, the authority in question is the power to vote shares of common stock.*

Proxy statement Information required by SEC to be given stockholders as a prerequisite to solicitation of proxies for a security subject to the requirements of Securities Exchange Act.†

Prudent man rule An investment standard. In some states, the law requires that a fiduciary, such as a trustee, may invest the fund's money only in a list of securities designated by the state—the so-called legal list. In other states, the trustee may invest in a security if it is one which a prudent man of discretion and intelligence, who is seeking a reasonable income and preservation of capital, would buy.†

Pure (or primitive) security A security that pays off $1 if one particular state of the world occurs and pays off nothing if any other state of the world occurs.*

Put An option to sell a specific security at a specified price within a designated period.*

Puts and calls (See: *Option*.)

Quotation Often shortened to *quote*. The highest bid to buy and the lowest offer to sell a security in a given market at a given time. If you ask your broker for a "quote" on a stock, he may come back with something like "45¼ to 45½." This means that $45.25 is the highest price any buyer wanted to pay at the time the quote was given on the floor of the exchange and that $45.50 was the lowest price which any seller would take at the same time. (See: *Bid and asked*.)†

Rally A brisk rise following a decline in the general price level of the market, or in an individual stock.†

Rate of return The internal rate of return on an investment.*

Ratings Designations used by investors' services to give relative indications of quality.**

Record date The date on which you must be registered as a shareholder on the stock book of a company in order to receive a declared dividend or, among other things, to vote on company affairs. (See: *Ex dividend, Transfer*.)†

Recourse arrangement A term used in connection with accounts-receivable financing. If a firm sells its accounts receivable to a financial institution under a recourse agreement, then, if the accounts receivable cannot be collected, the selling firm must repurchase the account from the financial institution.*

Redemption price The price at which a bond may be redeemed before maturity, at the option of the issuing company. Redemption value also applies to the price the company must pay to call in certain types of preferred stock. (See: *Callable*.)†

Rediscount rate The rate of interest at which a bank may borrow from a Federal Reserve Bank.*

Refinancing Same as refunding. New securities are sold by a company and the money is used to retire existing securities. Object may be to save interest costs, extend the maturity of the loan, or both.*

Refunding Sale of new debt securities to replace an old debt issue.*

Registered bond A bond which is registered on the books of the issuing company in the name of the owner. It can be transferred only when endorsed by the registered owner. (See: *Bearer bond, Coupon bond*.)†

Registered representative Present name for the older term *customer's man*. In a New York Stock Exchange Member Organizations, a *registered representative* is an employee who has met the requirements of the exchange as to background and knowledge of the securities business. Also known as an *account executive* or *customer's broker*.†

Registrar Usually a trust company or bank charged with the responsibility of preventing the issuance of more stock than authorized by a company. (See: *Transfer*.)†

Registration Before a public offering may be made of new securities by a company, or of outstanding securities by controlling stockholders—through the mails or in interstate commerce—the securities must be registered under the Securities Act of 1933. The registration statement is filed with the SEC by the issuer. It must disclose pertinent information relating to the company's operations, securities, management, and purpose of the public offering. Securities of railroads under jurisdiction of the Interstate Commerce Commission, and certain other types of securities, are exempted. On security offerings involving less than $300,000, less information is required.

Before a security may be admitted to dealings on a national securities exchange, it must be registered under the Securities Exchange Act of 1934. The application for registration must be filed with the exchange and the SEC by the company issuing the securities. It must disclose pertinent information relating to the company's operations, securities, and management.†

Regression analysis A statistical procedure for predicting the value of one variable (dependent variable) on the basis of knowledge about one or more other variables (independent variables).*

Regular way delivery Unless otherwise specified, securities sold on the N.Y. Stock Exchange are to be delivered to the buying broker by the selling broker and payment made to the selling broker by the buying broker on the fifth business day after the transaction. Regular way delivery for bonds is the following business day. (See: *Transfer.*)†

Regulation T The federal regulation governing the amount of credit which may be advanced by brokers and dealers to customers for the purchase of securities. (See: *Margin.*)†

Regulation U The federal regulation governing the amount of credit which may be advanced by a bank to its customers for the purchase of listed stocks. (See: *Margin.*)†

Reinvestment rate The rate of return at which cash flows from an investment are reinvested. The reinvestment rate may or may not be constant from year to year.*

REIT Real Estate Investment Trust, an organization similar to an investment company in some respects but concentrating its holdings in real estate investments. The yield is generally liberal since REIT's are required to distribute as much as 90 percent of their income. (See: *Investment company.*)†

Reorganization When a financially troubled firm goes through reorganization, its assets are restated to reflect their current market value, and its financial structure is restated to reflect any changes on the asset side of the statement. Under a reorganizations the firm continues in existence; this is contrasted to bankruptcy, where the firm is liquidated and ceases to exist.*

Replacement-cost accounting A requirement under SEC release no. 190 (1976) that large companies disclose the replacement costs of inventory items and depreciable plant.*

Required rate of return The rate of return that stockholders expect to receive on common stock investments.*

Residual value The value of leased property at the end of the lease term.*

Retained earnings That portion of earnings not paid out in dividends. The figure that appears on the balance sheet is the sum of the retained earnings for each year throughout the company's history.*

Return (See: *Yield.*)

Revenue bond A bond payable from revenues derived from tolls, charges, or rents paid by users of the facility constructed from the proceeds of the bond issue.**

Rights When a company wants to raise more funds by issuing additional securities, it may give its stockholders the opportunity, ahead of others, to buy the new securities in proportion to the number of shares each owns. The piece of paper evidencing this privilege is called a right. Because the additional stock is usually offered to stockholders below the current market price, rights ordinarily have a market value of their own and are actively traded. In most cases they must be exercised within a relatively short period. Failure to exercise or sell rights may result in actual loss to the holder. (See: *Warrant.*)†

Rights offering A securities flotation offered to existing stockholders.*

Risk The probability that actual future returns will be below expected returns. It is measured by standard deviation or coefficient of variation of expected returns.*

Risk-adjusted discount rates The discount rate applicable for a particular risky (uncertain) stream of income: the riskless rate of interest plus a risk premium appropriate to the level of risk attached to the particular income stream.*

Risk premium The difference between the required rate of return on a particular risky asset and the rate of return on a riskless asset with the the the same expected life.*

Risk-return trade-off function (See *Security market line.*)

Round lot A unit of trading or a multiple thereof. On the NYSE the unit of trading is generally 100 shares in stocks and $1,000 par value in the case of bonds. In some inactive stocks, the unit of trading is ten shares.†

Sale and leaseback An operation whereby a firm sells land, buildings, or equipment to a financial institution and simultaneously executes an agreement to lease the property back for a specified period under specific terms.*

Salvage value The value of a capital asset at the end of a specified period. It is the current market price of an asset being considered for replacement in a capital budgeting problem.*

Scale order An order to buy (or sell) a security which specifies the total amount to be bought (or sold) and the amount to be bought (or sold) at specified price variations.†

Seat A traditional figure-of-speech for a membership on an exchange. Price and admission requirements vary.†

SEC The Securities and Exchange Commission, established by Congress to help protect investors. The SEC administers the Securities Act of 1933, the Securities Exchange Act of 1934, the Securities Act Amendments of 1975, the Trust Indenture Act, the Investment Company Act, the Investment Advisers Act, and the Public Utility Holding Company Act.†

Secondary distribution Also known as a secondary offering. The redistribution of a block of stock, sometimes after it has been sold by the issuing company. The sale is handled off the NYSE by a securities firm or group of firms and the shares are usually offered at a fixed price which is related to the current market price of the stock. Usually the block is a large one, such as might be involved in the settlement of an estate. The security may be listed or unlisted. (See: *Exchange distribution, Investment banker, Primary distribution, Special offering, Syndicate.*)†

Secondary market Market for issues previously offered or sold.**

Securities and exchange commission (See *SEC.*)

Securities, junior Securities that have lower priority in claims on assets and income than other securities *(senior securities)*. For example, preferred stock is junior to debentures, but debentures are junior to mortgage bonds. Common stock is the most junior of all corporate securities.*

Securities, senior Securities having claims on income and assets that rank higher than certain other securities *(junior securities)*. For example, mortgage bonds are senior to debentures, but debentures are senior to common stock.*

Security market line A graphic representation of the relation between the required return on a security and the product of its risk times a normalized market measure of risk. Risk-return relationships for individual securities or investments.*

Self-supporting debt Debt incurred for a project or enterprise requiring no tax support other than the specific tax or revenue earmarked for that purpose.**

Seller's option A special transaction on the NYSE which gives the seller the right to deliver the stock or bond at any time within a specified period, ranging from not less than 6 business days to not more than 60 days. (See: *Delivery.*)†

Selling group A group of stock brokerage firms formed for the purpose of distributing a new issue of securities; part of the investment banking process.*

Sensitivity analysis Simulation analysis in which key variables are changed and the resulting change in the rate of return is observed. Typically, the rate of return will be more sensitive to changes in some variables than it will in others.*

Serial bond An issue which matures in part at periodic stated intervals.†

Service lease A lease under which the lessor maintains and services the asset.*

Settlement Conclusion of a securities transactions in which a customer pays a debit balance he owes a broker or receives from the broker the proceeds from a sale. The term also applies to continuous daily netting out of transactions among brokerage houses, usually through centralized securities clearing corporations. (See: *Regular delivery, Cash sale, Depository trust company.*)†

Short covering Buying stock to return stock previously borrowed to make delivery on a short sale.†

Short position Stocks sold short and not covered as of a particular date. On the NYSE, a tabulation is issued once a month listing all issues on the exchange in which there was a short position of 5,000 or more shares and issues in which the short position had changed by 2,000 or more shares in the preceding month. *Short position* also means the total amount of stock an individual has sold short and has not covered, as of a particular date.†

Short sale A person who believes a stock will decline and sells it though he does not own any has made a short sale. For instance: You instruct your broker to sell short 100 shares of ABC. Your broker borrows the stock so he can deliver the 100 shares to the buyer. The money value of the shares borrowed is deposited by your broker with the lender. Sooner or later you must cover your short sale by buying the same amount of stock you borrowed for return to the lender. If you are able to buy ABC at a lower price than you sold it for, your profit is the difference between the two prices—not counting commissions and taxes. But if you have to pay more for the stock than the price you received, that is the amount of your loss. Stock exchange and federal regulations govern and limit the conditions under which a short sale may be made on a national securities exchange. Sometimes a person will sell short a stock he already owns in order to protect a paper profit. This is known as selling short against the box. (See: *Up tick.*)†

SIAC Securities Industry Automation Corporation, an independent organization established by the New York and American Stock Exchanges as a jointly owned subsidiary to provide automation, data processing, clearing, and communications services.†

Simulation A technique whereby probable future events are simulated on a computer. Estimated rates of return and risk indexes can be generated.*

Sinking fund A required annual payment designed to amortize a bond or a preferred stock issue. The sinking fund may be held in the form of cash or marketable securities, but more generally the money put into the sinking fund is used to retire each year some of the securities in question.*

SIPC Securities Investor Protection Corporation, which provides funds for use, if necessary, to protect customers' cash and securities which may be on deposit with a SIPC member firm in the event the firm fails and is liquidated under the provisions of the SIPC Act. SIPC is not a government agency. It is a nonprofit membership corporation created, however, by an act of Congress.†

Small business administration (SBA) A government agency organized to aid small firms with their financing and other problems.*

Special bid A method of filling an order to buy a large block of stock on the floor of the New York Stock Exchange. In a special bid, the bidder for the block of stock—a pension fund, for instance, will pay a special commission to the broker who represents him in making the purchase. The seller does not pay a commission. The special bid is made on the floor of the exchange at a fixed price which may not be below the last sale of the security or the current bid in the regular market, whichever is higher. Member firms may sell this stock for customers directly to the buyer's broker during trading hours.†

Special offering Opposite of special bid. A notice is printed on the ticker tape announcing the stock sale at a fixed price usually based on the last transaction in the regular auction market. If there are more buyers than stock, allotments are made. Only the seller pays the commission. (See: *Secondary distribution*.)†

Special tax bond A bond secured by a special tax, such as a gasoline tax.**

Specialist A member of the New York Stock Exchange, Inc., who has two functions: First, to maintain an orderly market, insofar as reasonably practicable, in the stocks in which he is registered as a specialist. In order to maintain an orderly market, the exchange expects the specialist to buy or sell for his own account, to a reasonable degree, when there is a temporary disparity between supply and demand. Second, the specialist acts as a broker's broker. When a commission broker on the exchange floor receives a limit order, say, to buy at $50 a stock then selling at $60—and he cannot wait at the post where the stock is traded to see if the price reaches the specified level. So he leaves the order with the specialist, who will try to execute it in the market if and when the stock declines to the specified price. At all times the specialist must put his customers' interests above his own. There are about 400 specialists on the NYSE. (See: *Book, Limited order*.)†

Speculation The employment of funds by a speculator. Safety of principal is a secondary factor. (See: *Investment*.)†

Speculator One who is willing to assume a relatively large risk in the hope of gain. The speculator may buy and sell the same day or speculate in an enterprise which he does not expect to be profitable for years.†

Split The division of the outstanding shares of a corporation into a larger number of shares. A 3-for-1 split by a company with 1 million shares outstanding results in 3 million shares outstanding. Each holder of 100 shares before the 3-for-1 split would have 300 shares, although his proportionate equity in the company would remain the same; 100 parts of 1 million are the equivalent of 300 parts of 3 million. Ordinarily splits must be voted by directors and approved by shareholders. (See: *Stock dividends*.)†

Standard deviation A statistical term that measures the variability of a set of observations from the mean of the distribution (σ.)*

State-preference model A framework in which decisions are based on probabilities of payoffs under alternative states of the world.*

Stock ahead Sometimes an investor who has entered an order to buy or sell a stock at a certain price will see transactions at that price reported on the ticker tape while his own order has not been executed. The reason is that other buy and sell orders at the same price came in to the specialist ahead of his and had priority. (See: *Book, Specialist*.)†

Stock dividend A dividend paid in securities rather than cash. The dividend may be additional shares of the issuing company, or shares of another company (usually a subsidiary) held by the company. (See: *Ex-dividend, Split*.)†

Stock split An accounting action to increase the number of shares outstanding; for example, in a 3-for-1 split, shares outstanding would be tripled and each stockholder would be tripled and each stockholder would receive three new shares for each one formerly held. Stock splits involve no transfer from surplus to the capital account.*

Stockholder of record A stockholder whose name is registered on the books of the issuing corporation.†

Stop limit order A stop order which becomes a limit order after the specified stop price has been reached. (See: *Limit order, Stop order*.)†

Stop order An order to buy at a price above or sell at a price below the current market. Stop buy orders are generally used to limit loss or protect unrealized profits on a short sale. Stop sell orders are generally used to protect unrealized profits or limit loss on a holding. A stop order becomes a market order when the stock sells at or beyond the specified price and, thus, may not necessarily be executed at that price.†

Stopped stock A service performed—in most cases by the specialist—for an order given him by a commission broker. Let's say XYZ just sold at $50 a share. Broker A comes along with an order to buy 100 shares at the market. The lowest offer is $50.50. Broker A believes he can do better for his client than $50.50, perhaps might get the stock at $50.25. But he doesn't want to take a chance that he'll miss the market—that is, the next sale might be $50.50 and the following one even higher. So he asks the specialist if he will stop 100 at ½ ($50.50). The specialist agrees. The specialist guarantees Broker A he will get 100 shares at 50½ if the stock sells at that price. In the meantime, if the specialist or broker A succeeds in executing the order at $50.25, the stop is called off. (See: *Specialist*.)†

Street The New York financial community in the Wall Street area.†

Street name Securities held in the name of a broker instead of his customer's name are said to be carried in a *street name*. This occurs when the securities have been bought on margin or when the customer wishes the security to be held by the broker.†

Subdivision Any legal and authorized political entity under a state's jurisdiction (county, city, water district, school district, etc.).**

Subjective probability distributions Probability distributions determined through subjective procedures without the use of statistics.*

Subordinated debenture A bond having a claim on assets only after the senior debt has been paid off in the event of liquidation.*

Subscription price The price at which a security may be purchased in a rights offering.*

Switch order or contingent order An order for the purchase (sale) of one stock and the sale (purchase) of another stock at a stipulated price difference.†

Switching Selling one security and buying another.†

Syndicate A group of investment bankers who together underwrite and distribute a new issue of securities or a large block of an outstanding issue.†

Synergy A situation where "the whole is greater than the sum of its parts"; in a synergistic merger, the postmerger earnings exceed the sum of the separate companies' premerger earnings.*

Systematic risk That part of a security's risk that cannot be eliminated by diversification.*

Take-over The acquiring of one corporation by another—usually in a friendly merger but sometimes marked by a "proxy fight." In "unfriendly" take-over attempts, the potential buying company may offer a price well above current market values, new securities, and other inducements to stockholders. The management of the subject company might ask for a better price or fight the take-over or merger with another company. (See: *Proxy*.)†

Tangible assets Physical assets as opposed to intangible assets such as goodwill and the stated value of patents.*

Tax base The total resources available for taxation.**

Tax-exempt bond Another name for a municipal bond. The interest on a municipal bond is presently exempt from Federal income tax.**

Technical research Analysis of the market and stocks based on supply and demand. The technician studies price movements, volume, and trends and patterns which are revealed by charting these factors, and attempts to assess the possible effect of current market action on future supply and demand for securities and individual issues. (See: *Fundamental research*.)†

Tender offers A situation wherein one firm offers to buy the stock of another, going directly to the stockholders, frequently over the opposition of the management of the firm whose stock is being sought.*

Term issue An issue that has a single maturity.**

Term loan A loan generally obtained from a bank or an insurance company with a maturity greater than one year. Term loans are generally amortized.*

Thin market A market in which there are comparatively few bids to buy or offers to sell, or both. The phrase may apply to a single security or to the entire stock market. In a thin market, price fluctuations between transactions are usually larger than when the market is liquid. A thin market in a particular stock may reflect lack of interest in that issue or a limited supply of or demand for stock in the market. (See: *Bid and asked, Liquidity, Offer*.)†

Third market Trading of stock exchange listed securities in the over-the-counter market by non-exchange-member brokers and all types of investors.†

Ticker The instruments which display prices and volume of securities transactions worldwide within minutes after each trade.†

Time order An order which becomes a market or limited price order at a specified time.†

Tips Supposedly "inside" information on corporation affairs.†

Trade credit Interfirm debt arising through credit sales and recorded as an account receivable by the seller and as an account payable by the buyer.*

Trader One who buys and sells for his own account for short-term profit. (See *Investor, Speculator*.)†

Trading floor (See: *Floor*.)

Trading market The secondary market for outstanding securities.**

Trading post One of 23 trading locations on the floor of the New York Stock Exchange at which stocks assigned to that location are bought and sold. About 75 stocks are traded at each post.†

Transfer This term may refer to two different operations. One is the delivery of a stock certificate from the seller's broker to the buyer's broker and legal change of ownership, normally accomplished within a few days. The other is to record the change of ownership on the books of the corporation by the transfer agent. When the purchaser's name is recorded on the books of the company, dividends, notices of meetings, proxies, financial reports, and all pertinent literature sent by the issuer to its securities holders are mailed direct to the new owner. (See: *Registrar, Street name.*)†

Transfer agent A transfer agent keeps a record of the name of each registered shareowner, his or her address, the number of shares owned, and sees that certificates presented to his office for transfer are properly cancelled and new certificates issued in the name of the transferee. (See: *Registrar, Transfer.*)†

Treasury stock Common stock that has been repurchased by the issuing firm.* It may be held in the company's treasury indefinitely, reissued to the public, or retired. Treasury stock receives no dividends and has no vote while held by the company.†

Trust receipt An instrument acknowledging that the borrower holds certain goods in trust for the lender. Trust receipt financing is used in connection with the financing of inventories for automobile dealers, construction equipment dealers, appliance dealers, and other dealers in expensive durable goods.*

Trustee The representative of bondholders who acts in their interest and facilitates communication between them and the issuer. Typically these duties are handled by a department of a commercial bank.*

Turnover rate The volume of shares traded in a year as a percentage of total shares listed on an exchange, outstanding for an individual issue, or held in an institutional portfolio.

Underwriter (See: *Investment banker.*)

Underwriting (1) The entire process of issuing new corporate securities. (2) The insurance function of bearing the risk of adverse price fluctuations during the period in which a new issue of stock or bonds is being distributed.*

Underwriting syndicate A syndicate of investment firms formed to spread the risk associated with the purchase and distribution of a new issue of securities. The larger the issue, the more firms typically are involved in the syndicate.*

Unlimited tax bond A bond secured by pledge of taxes that are not limited by rate or amount.**

Unlisted A security not listed on a stock exchange. (See: *Over-the-counter.*)†

Unlisted Securities Securities that are traded in the over-the-counter market period.*

Unlisted trading privileges On some exchanges a stock may be traded at the request of a member without any prior application by the company itself. The company has no agreement to conform with standards of the exchange. Today admission of a stock to unlisted trading privileges requires SEC approval of an application filed by the exchange. The information in the application must be made available by the exchange to the public. No unlisted stocks are traded on the New York Stock Exchange. (See: *Listed stock.*)†

Unsystematic risk That part of a security's risk associated with random events; unsystematic risk can be eliminated by proper diversification.*

Up tick A term used to designate a transaction made at a price higher than the preceding transaction. Also called a *plus-tick*. A stock may be sold short only on an up tick, or on a "zero-plus" tick. A *zero-plus* tick is a term used for a transaction at the same price as the preceding trade but higher than the preceding different price.

Conversely, a *down tick*, or *minus* tick, is a term used to designate a transaction made at a price lower than the preceding trade. A *zero minus* tick is a transaction made at the same price as the preceding sale but lower than the preceding different price.

A plus sign, or a minus sign, is displayed throughout the day next to the last price of each company's stock traded at each trading post on the floor of the New York Stock Exchange. (See: *Short sale.*)†

Utility theory A body of theory dealing with the relationships among money income, utility (or "happiness"), and the willingness to accept risk.*

Value additivity principle Neither fragmenting cash flows or recombining them will affect the resulting values of the cash flows.*

Volume The number of shares traded in a security or an entire market during a given period. Volume is usually considered on a daily basis and a daily average is computed for longer periods.†

Voting right The stockholder's right to vote his stock in the affairs of his company. Most common shares have one vote each. Preferred stock usually has the right to vote when preferred dividends are in default for a specified period. The right to vote may be delegated by the stockholder to another person. (See: *Cumulative voting, Proxy.*)†

Warrant A long-term option to buy a stated number of shares of common stock at a specified price. The specified price is generally called the *exercise price.**

Weighted cost of capital A weighted average of the component costs of debt, preferred stock, and common equity. Also called the *composite cost of capital.**

When issued A short form of "when, as, and if issued." The term indicates a conditional transaction in a security authorized for issuance but not as yet actually issued. All "when issued" transactions are on an "if" basis, to be settled if and when the actual security is issued and the exchange or National Association of Securities Dealers rules the transactions are to be settled.†

Wire house A member firm of an exchange maintaining a communications network linking either its own branch offices, offices of correspondent firms, or a combination of such offices.†

Working capital Refers to a firm's investment in short-term assets—cash, short-term securities, accounts receivable, and inventories. *Gross working capital* is defined as a firm's total current assets. *Net working capital* is defined as current assets minus current liabilities. If the term *working capital* is used without further qualification, it generally refers to gross working capital.**

Working control Theoretically, ownership of 51 percent of a company's voting stock is necessary to exercise control. In practice—and this is particularly true in the case of a large corporation—effective control sometimes can be exerted through ownership, individually or by a group acting in concert, of less than 50 percent.†

Yield Also known as return. The dividends or interest paid by a company expressed as a percentage of the current price. A stock with a current market value of $40 a share paying dividends at the rate of $2.00 is said to return 5 percent ($2 ÷ $40). The current return on a bond is figured the same way. A 3 percent $1,000 bond selling at $600 offers a current yield return of 5 percent ($30 ÷ $600). (See: *Dividend, Interest*.)†

Yield to maturity The yield of a bond to maturity takes into account the price discount from or premium over the face amount. It is greater than the current yield when the bond is selling at a discount and less than the current yield when the bond is selling at a premium.†

Zero coupon bonds Bonds which do not convey a coupon (i.e., do not pay interest) but which are offered at a substantial discount from par value and appreciate to their full value (usually $1,000) at maturity. However, under U.S. tax law, the imputed interest is taxed as it accrues.

The appeal of Zero coupon bonds is primarily for IRA and other tax sheltered retirement accounts.

Securities and Exchange Commission

JUDICIARY PLAZA
450 FIFTH STREET, NW
WASHINGTON, DC 20549
INFORMATION: 202-272-2650
FREEDOM OF INFORMATION ACT:
202-272-7420
FILINGS BY REGISTERED COMPANIES:
202-272-2624

FULL AND FAIR DISCLOSURE

The Securities Act of 1933 requires issuers of securities making public offerings of securities in interstate commerce or through the mails, directly or by others on their behalf, to file registration statements containing financial and other pertinent data about the issuer and the securities being offered. A similar requirement applies to such offerings on behalf of a controlling person of the issuer. Unless a registration statement is in effect with respect to such securities, it is unlawful to sell the securities in interstate commerce or through the mails. (There are certain limited exemptions, such as government securities, nonpublic offerings, and intrastate offerings, as well as offerings not exceeding $1,500,000 in amount, which comply with the commission's Regulation A.) The effectiveness of a registration statement may be refused or suspended after a public hearing, if the statement contains material misstatements or omissions, thus barring sale of the securities until it is appropriately amended. Registration of securities does not imply approval of the issue by the commission or that the commission has found the registration disclosures to be accurate. It does not insure investors against loss in their purchase but serves rather to provide information upon which investors may make an informed and realistic evaluation of the worth of the securities.

Persons responsible for filing false information with the commission subject themselves to the risk of fine or imprisonment or both; and persons connected with the public offering may be liable in damages to purchasers of the securities if the disclosures in the registration statement and prospectus are materially defective. Also, the above act contains antifraud provisions

---

Source: This material was abstracted from the United States Government Manual.

which apply generally to the sale of securities, whether or not registered (48 Stat. 74; 15 U.S.C. 77a et seq.).

REGULATION OF SECURITIES MARKETS AND PERSONS CONDUCTING A SECURITIES BUSINESS

The Securities Exchange Act of 1934 assigns to the commission broad regulatory responsibilities over the securities markets, the self-regulatory organizations within the securities industry, and persons conducting a business in securities. The commission is directed to facilitate the establishment of a national market system for securities and a national system for the clearance and settlement of securities transactions. Securities exchanges and certain clearing agencies are required to register with the commission, and associations of brokers or dealers are permitted to register with the commission. The Securities Exchange Act also provides for the establishment of the Municipal Securities Rulemaking Board to formulate rules for the municipal securities industry. The commission oversees the self-regulatory activities of the national securities exchanges and associations, registered clearing agencies, and the Municipal Securities Rulemaking Board. In addition, the commission regulates industry professionals, such as securities brokers and dealers, certain municipal securities professionals, and transfer agents.

The Securities Exchange Act authorizes national securities exchanges, national securities associations, clearing agencies, and the Municipal Securities Rulemaking Board to adopt rules that are designed, among other things to promote just and equitable principles of trade and to protect investors. The commission is required to approve or disapprove most proposed rules of these self-regulatory organizations and has the power to abrogate or amend existing rules of the national securities exchanges, national securities associations, and the Municipal Securities Rulemaking Board.

In addition, the commission has broad rulemaking authority over the activities of brokers, dealers, municipal securities dealers, securities information processors, and transfer agents. The commission may regulate such securities trading practices as short sales and stabilizing transactions. It may regulate the trading of options on national securities exchanges and the activities of members of exchanges who trade on the trading floors and may adopt rules governing broker-dealer sales practices in dealing with investors. The commission also is authorized to adopt rules concerning the financial responsibility of brokers and dealers and reports to be made by brokers and dealers. The Securities Exchange Act also empowers the Board of Governors of the Federal Reserve System to prescribe rules relating to the extension of credit by brokers and dealers for securities transactions. Such rules include the establishment of minimum margin requirements with respect to securities registered on national securities exchanges and certain securities traded over-the-counter (48 Stat. 881; U.S.C. 78a et seq.).

The Securities Exchange Act also requires the filing of registration applications and annual and other reports with national securities exchanges and the commission by companies whose securities are listed upon the exchanges, by companies that have assets of $3 million or more and 500 or more shareholders of record, and by companies that distributed securities pursuant to a registration statement declared effective by the commission under the Securities Act of 1933. Such applications and reports must contain financial and other data prescribed by the commission as necessary or appropriate for the protection of investors and to insure fair dealing. In addition, the solicitation of proxies, authorizations, or consents from holders of such registered securities must be made in accordance with rules and regulations prescribed by the commission. These rules provide for disclosures to securities holders of information relevant to the subject matter of the solicitation.

Disclosure of the holdings and transactions by officers, directors, and large (10 percent) holders of equity securities of companies is also required, and any and all persons who acquire more than 5 percent of certain equity securities are required to file detailed information with the commission and any exchange upon which such securities may be traded. Moreover, any person making a tender offer for certain classes of equity securities is required to file reports with the commission, if as a result of the tender offer such person would own more than 5 percent of the outstanding shares of the particular class of equity involved. The commission also is authorized to promulgate rules governing the repurchase by a corporate issuer of its own securities.

REGULATION OF MUTUAL FUNDS AND OTHER INVESTMENT COMPANIES

The Investment Company Act of 1940 provides for the registration with the commission of investment companies and subjects their activities to regulation to protect investors. The regulation covers sales and management fees, composition of boards of directors, and capital structure. Also, various transactions of investment companies, including transactions with affiliated interests, are prohibited unless the commission first determines that such transactions are fair. Under the act, the commission may institute court action to enjoin the consummation of mergers and other plans of reorganization of investment companies if such plans are unfair to security holders. It also may impose sanctions by administrative proceedings against investment company managements for violations of the act and other federal securities laws, and file court actions to enjoin acts and practices of management officials involving breaches of fiduciary duty involving personal misconduct and to disqualify such officials from office (54 Stat. 789; 15 U.S.C. 80a–1—80a–52).

REGULATION OF COMPANIES CONTROLLING ELECTRIC OR GAS UTILITIES

The Public Utility Holding Company Act of 1935 provides for regulation by the commission of the purchase and sale of securities and assets by companies in electric and gas utility holding company systems, their intra-system transactions and service and management arrangements. It limits holding companies to a single coordinated utility system and requires simplification of complex corporate and capital structures and elimination of unfair distribution of voting power among holders of system securities.

The issuance and sale of securities by holding companies and their subsidiaries, unless exempt (subject to conditions and terms which the commission is empowered to impose) as an issue expressly authorized by the state commission in the state in which the issuer is incorporated, must be found by the commission to meet statutory standards, namely: that the new security is reasonably adapted to the security structure and earning power of the issuer; that the proposed financing is necessary and appropriate to the economical and efficient operation of the company's business; that the consideration received, and fees, commissions, and other remuneration paid, are fair; and that the terms and conditions of the sale are not detrimental to investors, consumers, or the public.

The purchase and sale of utility properties and other assets may not be made in contravention of rules, regulations, or orders of the commission regarding the consideration to be received, maintenance of competitive conditions, fees and commissions, accounts, disclosure of interest, and similar matters. In passing upon proposals for reorganization, merger, or consolidation, the commission must be satisfied that the objectives of the act generally are complied with and that the terms of the proposal are fair and equitable to all classes of security holders affected (49 Stat. 803; 15 U.S.C. 79–92z–6).

REGULATION OF INVESTMENT COUNSELORS AND ADVISERS

The Investment Advisers Act of 1940 provides that persons who, for compensation, engage in the business of advising others with respect to their security transactions must register with the commission. The act prohibits certain

REGIONAL OFFICES (Securities and Exchange Commission)

Region	Address
1. New York, New Jersey	26 Federal Plaza, New York, NY 10078
2. Maine, Vermont, New Hampshire, Massachusetts, Connecticut, Rhode Island	150 Causeway Street, Boston, MA 02114
3. Tennessee, North Carolina, South Carolina, Mississippi, Alabama, Georgia, Florida, Louisiana (southeastern portion only)	1375 Peachtree Street NE, Atlanta GA 30367
4. Minnesota, Wisconsin, Michigan, Iowa, Missouri, Illinois, Indiana, Ohio, Kentucky	219 S. Dearborn Street, Chicago, IL 60604
5. Kansas, Oklahoma, Texas, Arkansas, Louisiana (except southeastern portion)	411 W. 7th Street, Fort Worth, TX 76102
6. North Dakota, South Dakota, Colorado, Kansas, Utah, Wyoming, New Mexico	410 17th Street, Denver, CO 80202
7. California, Nevada, Arizona, Hawaii	5757 Wilshire Boulevard, Los Angeles, CA 90036
8. Washington, Oregon	915 Second Avenue, Seattle, WA 98174
9. Pennsylvania, West Virginia, Virginia, Maryland, Delaware	4015 Wilson Boulevard, Arlington, VA 22203

types of fee arrangements, makes unlawful practices of investment advisers involving fraud or deceit, and requires, among other things, disclosure of any adverse interests the advisers may have in transactions executed for clients. The act authorizes the commission to issue rules proscribing acts and practices that may operate as a fraud or deceit upon investors (54 Stat. 847; 15 U.S.C. 80b–1—80b–21).

REHABILITATION OF FAILING CORPORATIONS

Chapter X of the Bankruptcy Act provides for commission participation as adviser to federal courts in proceedings for the reorganization of insolvent corporations. An important aspect of this activity is the advice rendered to the parties and the court with respect to the fairness and feasibility of proposed plans of reorganization (52 Stat. 883; 11 U.S.C. 501–676).

INDEPENDENT REPRESENTATION OF THE INTERESTS OF HOLDERS OF DEBT SECURITIES

The interests of purchasers of publicly offered debt securities issued pursuant to trust indentures are safeguarded under the provisions of the Trust Indenture Act of 1939. This act, among other things, requires the exclusion from such indentures of certain types of exculpatory clauses and the inclusion of certain protective provisions. The independence of the indenture trustee, who is a representative of the debt holder, is assured by proscribing certain relationships that might conflict with the proper exercise of his duties (53 Stat. 1149; 15 U.S.C. 77aaa–77bbbb).

ENFORCEMENT ACTIVITIES

The commission's enforcement activities are designed to secure compliance with the federal securities laws administered by the commission and the rules and regulations adopted thereunder. These activities include measures to compel obedience to the disclosure requirements of the registration and other provisions of the acts; to prevent fraud and deception in the purchase and sale of securities; to obtain court orders enjoining acts and practices that operate as a fraud upon investors or otherwise violate the laws; to revoke the registrations of brokers, dealers, and investment advisers who willfully engage in such acts and practices; to suspend or expel from national securities exchanges or the National Association of Securities Dealers, Inc., any member or officer who has violated any provision of the federal securities laws; and to prosecute persons who have engaged in fraudulent activities or other willful violations of those laws. In addition, attorneys or accountants who violate the securities laws face possible loss of their privilege to practice before the commission. To this end, private investigations are conducted into complaints or other evidences of securities violations. Evidence thus established of law violations in the purchase and sale of securities is used in appropriate administrative proceedings to revoke registration or in actions instituted in federal courts to restrain or enjoin such activities. Where the evidence tends to establish fraud or other willful violation of the securities laws, the facts are referred to the Attorney General for criminal prosecution of the offenders. The commission may assist in such prosecutions.

INVESTOR INFORMATION AND PROTECTION

Complaints and inquiries may be directed to the home office or to any regional office. Registration statements and other public documents filed with the commission are available for public inspection in the public reference room at the home office. Much of the information also is available in its New York, Chicago, and Los Angeles regional offices, and to a lesser extent in the other regional offices of the commission. Reproduction of the public material may be purchased from the commission at prescribed rates.

Fidelity/Source

STOCKS—LEVEL 1

Dollar Amount of Transaction	Commission Rate
Under $5,000	$28 + .008 of dollar amount
$ 5,001–15,000	$28 + .006 of dollar amount
$15,001–25,000	$28 + .005 of dollar amount
$25,001–50,000	$28 + .004 of dollar amount
$50,001 and over	$28 + .0033 of dollar amount

Maximum charge—40¢ per share on the first 100 shares, 30¢ per share from 101–500 shares, and 20¢ per share thereafter.

Minimum charge—2¢ per share.

OPTIONS—LEVEL 1

Dollar Amount of Transaction	Commission Rate
Under $3,000	$28 + .013 of dollar amount
$3,000–9,999.99	$28 + .010 of dollar amount
$10,000 and over	$28 + .007 of dollar amount

Minimum Options Commissions: 1–10 contracts, $3.00 per contract; 11 and over, $2.50.

Maximum Options Commission: $20 per contract.

BONDS—LEVEL 1

1st through 25th bonds	$28 + $4.00 per bond
26 or more bonds	additional $3.00 per bond

Source: Fidelity/Source, (Fidelity Brokerage Service, Inc.) 161 Devonshire Street, Boston, MA 02110.

ADDITIONAL DISCOUNTS FOR LARGE ORDERS

On Commissions of	This Additional Discount Will Apply
$ 80–100	4%
$101–150	5%
$151–200	6%
$201 and over	7%

Commission Schedule—Level 2

Accounts generating more than $2,500 in commissions in a 12-month period will automatically receive an extra 10% discount from the rates in Level 1.

Commission Schedule—Level 3

Accounts generating more than $5,000 in commissions in a 12-month period will automatically receive an extra 15% discount from the rates in Level 1.

Margin Rates

Debit Balance	Interest Will Be Charged at Brokers' Call Rate, Plus
$ 0– 9,999	2%
$10,000–24,999	1½%
$25,000–49,999	1%
$50,000–99,999	½%
$100,000 and over	¼%

NOTE: In calculating a commission, apply the discount for large orders before any Level 2 or Level 3 discount. Discounts do not reduce commissions below stated minimums. All transactions are subject to a $30.00 minimum commission, regardless of any other applicable discount.

REPRESENTATIVE DISCOUNT COMMISSION RATES

Number of shares bought or sold at a given price	Charles Schwab & Co., Inc.	Fidelity/Source	Quick & Reilly
100 shares @ $15	$ 36.00	$ 40.00	$ 35.00
@ 20	42.00	40.00	35.00
@ 30	45.00	40.00	35.00
@ 40	45.00	40.00	41.34
@ 50	45.00	40.00	43.33
200 shares @ $15	54.00	52.00	43.38
@ 20	60.00	60.00	49.90
@ 30	72.00	64.00	65.58
@ 40	81.00	70.00	78.99
@ 50	87.00	70.00	92.41
300 shares @ $15	63.00	64.00	38.25
@ 20	72.00	64.00	58.38
@ 30	84.00	78.72	75.14
@ 40	93.00	96.00	91.91
@ 50	102.00	100.00	108.68
400 shares @ $15	72.00	64.00	50.00
@ 20	81.00	76.00	73.28
@ 30	93.00	96.00	95.63
@ 40	105.00	102.60	117.99
@ 50	117.00	121.60	140.34

The above discount commissions are those of the larger national firms. Frequently even lower commissions are available from smaller discount brokerage firms, as for example the rates offered by Discount Brokerage Corporation of America (67 Wall Street, New York, NY 10005), as illustrated below.

Number of shares bought or sold at a given price	Discount Brokerage Corporation
100 shares @ $15	$ 35.00
@ 20	35.00
@ 30	35.00
@ 40	35.00
@ 50	35.00
200 shares @ $15	35.00
@ 20	35.00
@ 30	38.26
@ 40	46.08
@ 50	53.90
300 shares @ $15	35.00
@ 20	40.86
@ 30	52.60
@ 40	64.34
@ 50	76.07
400 shares @ $15	43.47
@ 20	51.30
@ 30	66.95
@ 40	82.59
@ 50	98.24

Dow Jones Industrial Average Price, Earnings, Dividends

The table below lists the earnings (losses) of the Dow Jones Industrial Average based upon generally accepted accounting principles. The latest P/E ratio for the DJI correctly reflects deficit/negative earnings for the 1982 September and December quarters.

Quarter Ended	Clos. Avg.	Qtrly Earns	12-Mth. Earns	P/E Ratio	Qtrly Divs
1984 June 29	1132.40	35.02	102.07	11.1	14.98
Mar. 30	1164.89	30.12	87.38	13.3	13.94
1983 Dec. 30	1258.94	13.89	72.45	17.4	14.77
Sept. 30	1233.13	23.04	56.12	30.0	13.98
June 30	1221.96	20.33	11.59	105.4	13.70
Mar. 31	1130.03	15.19	9.52	118.7	13.88
Yr. End		72.45			56.33
1982 Dec. 31	1046.54	d2.44	9.15		13.03
Sept. 30	896.25	d21.49	35.15	25.5	13.44
June 30	811.93	18.26	79.90	10.2	13.75
Mar. 31	822.77	14.82	97.13	8.5	13.92
Yr. End		9.15			54.14
1981 Dec. 31	875.00	23.56	113.71	7.7	14.44
Sept. 30	849.98	23.26	123.32	6.9	13.73
June 30	976.88	35.49	128.91	7.6	14.19
Mar. 31	1003.87	31.40	123.60	8.1	13.86
Yr. End		113.71			56.22
1980 Dec. 31	963.99	33.17	121.86	7.9	14.40
Sept. 30	932.42	28.85	111.58	8.4	13.53
June 30	867.92	30.18	116.40	7.5	13.20
Mar. 31	785.75	29.66	120.77	6.5	13.23
Yr. End		121.86			54.36
1979 Dec. 31	838.74	22.89	124.46	6.7	13.87
Sept. 28	878.67	33.67	136.26	6.4	12.51
June 29	841.98	34.55	128.99	6.5	12.49
Mar. 30	862.18	33.35	124.10	6.9	12.11
Yr. End		124.46			50.98
1978 Dec. 29	805.01	34.69	112.79	7.1	14.34
Sept. 29	865.82	26.40	101.59	8.5	11.41
June 30	818.95	29.66	91.37	9.0	11.62
Mar. 31	757.36	22.04	89.23	8.5	11.15
Yr. End		112.79			48.52
1977 Dec. 30	831.17	23.49	89.10	9.3	13.24
Sept. 30	847.11	16.18	89.86	9.4	10.73
June 30	916.30	27.52	97.18	9.4	11.41
Mar. 31	919.13	21.91	95.51	9.6	10.46
Yr. End		89.10			45.84
1976 Dec. 31	1004.65	24.25	96.72	10.4	12.13
Sept. 30	990.19	23.50	95.81	10.3	9.85
June 30	1002.78	25.85	90.68	11.1	10.19
Mar. 31	999.45	23.12	81.87	12.2	9.23
Yr. End		96.72			41.40
1975 Dec. 31	852.41	23.34	75.66	11.3	9.63
Sept. 30	793.88	18.37	75.47	10.5	9.05
June 30	878.99	17.04	83.83	10.5	8.97
Mar. 31	768.15	16.91	93.47	8.2	9.81
Yr. End		75.66			37.46
1974 Dec. 31	616.24	23.15	99.04	6.2	10.45
Sept. 30	607.87	26.73	99.73	6.1	9.43
June 28	802.41	26.68	93.26	8.6	8.87
Mar. 29	846.68	22.48	89.46	9.5	8.97
Yr. End		99.04			37.72
1973 Dec. 31	850.86	23.84	86.17	9.9	10.62
Sept. 28	947.10	20.26	82.09	11.5	8.36
June 29	891.71	22.88	77.56	11.5	8.27
Mar. 30	951.01	19.19	71.98	13.2	8.08
Yr. End		86.17			35.33
1972 Dec. 29	1020.02	19.76	67.11	15.2	8.99
Sept. 29	953.27	15.73	62.15	15.3	7.76
June 30	929.03	17.30	58.87	15.8	7.87
Mar. 30	940.70	14.32	56.76	16.6	7.65
Yr. End		67.11			32.27
1971 Dec. 31	890.20	14.80	55.09	16.2	7.85
Sept. 30	887.19	12.45	53.43	16.6	7.51
June 30	891.14	15.19	53.45	16.7	7.80
Mar. 31	904.37	12.65	52.36	17.3	7.70
Yr. End		55.09			30.86

Quarter Ended	Clos. Avg.	Qtrly Earns	12-Mth. Earns	P/E Ratio	Qtrly Divs
1970 Dec. 31	838.92	13.14	51.02	16.4	8.25
Sept. 30	760.68	12.47	51.83	14.7	7.80
June 30	683.53	14.10	53.18	12.8	7.80
Mar. 31	785.57	11.31	54.07	14.5	7.68
Yr. End		51.02			31.53
1969 Dec. 31	800.36	13.95	57.02	14.0	8.63
Sept. 30	813.09	13.82	59.60	13.6	7.82
June 30	873.19	14.99	59.47	14.7	8.08
Mar 28	935.48	14.26	59.34	15.8	9.37
Yr. End		57.02			33.90
1968 Dec. 31	943.75	16.53	57.89	16.3	8.59
Sept. 30	935.79	13.69	57.05	16.4	7.73
June 28	897.80	14.86	55.71	16.1	7.73
Mar. 29	840.67	12.81	53.98	15.6	7.29
Yr. End		57.89			31.34
1967 Dec. 29	905.11	15.69	53.87	16.8	8.03
Sept. 29	926.66	12.35	52.73	17.6	7.25
June 30	860.26	13.13	54.27	15.8	7.36
Mar. 31	865.98	12.70	56.67	15.3	7.55
Yr. End		53.87			30.19
1966 Dec. 30	785.69	14.55	57.68	13.6	10.01
Sept. 30	774.22	13.89	57.36	13.5	7.18
June 30	870.10	15.53	56.23	15.5	7.26
Mar. 31	924.77	13.71	55.05	16.8	7.44
Yr. End		57.68			31.89
1965 Dec. 31	969.26	14.23	53.67	18.1	8.54
Sept. 30	930.58	12.76	52.74	17.6	6.58
June 30	868.03	14.35	50.84	17.1	6.79
Mar. 31	889.05	12.33	48.55	18.3	6.70
Yr. End		53.67			28.61
1964 Dec. 31	874.13	13.30	46.43	18.8	10.46
Sept. 30	875.37	10.86	45.88	19.1	5.79
June 30	831.50	12.06	44.46	18.7	7.16
Mar 31	813.29	10.21	42.60	19.1	7.83
Yr. End		46.43			31.24
1963 Dec. 31	762.95	12.75	41.21	18.5	7.39
Sept. 30	732.79	9.44	40.18	18.2	5.35
June 28	706.68	10.20	38.71	18.3	5.52
Mar. 29	682.52	8.82	37.35	18.3	5.15
Yr. End		41.21			23.41
1962 Dec. 31	652.10	11.72	36.43	17.9	7.66
Sept. 28	578.98	7.97	35.52	16.3	5.26
June 29	561.28	8.84	34.74	16.2	5.23
Mar. 30	706.95	7.90	34.11	20.7	5.15
Yr. End		36.43			23.30
1961 Dec. 29	731.13	10.81	31.91	22.9	7.57
Sept. 29	701.21	7.19	29.03	24.2	5.09
June 30	683.96	8.21	29.29	23.4	5.05
Mar. 30	676.63	5.70	29.53	22.9	5.00
Yr. End		31.91			22.71
1960 Dec. 31	615.89	7.93	32.21	19.1	6.55
Sept. 30	580.14	7.45	31.64	18.3	4.86
June 30	640.62	8.45	31.26	20.5	4.83
Mar. 31	610.59	8.38	33.82	18.2	5.12
Yr. End		32.21			21.36
1959 Dec. 31	679.36	7.36	34.31	19.8	6.73
Sept. 30	631.68	7.07	35.70	17.7	4.53
June 30	643.60	11.01	35.71	18.0	4.59
Mar. 31	601.71	8.87	31.04	19.4	4.89
Yr. End		34.31			20.74
1958 Dec. 31	583.65	8.75	27.94	20.9	5.83
Sept. 30	532.09	7.08	27.97	19.0	4.59
June 30	478.18	6.34	29.41	16.3	4.62
Mar. 31	446.76	5.78	32.56	13.7	4.96
Yr. End		27.95			20.00
1957 Dec. 31	435.69	8.78	36.08	12.1	6.91
Sept. 30	456.30	8.51	36.70	12.4	4.91
June 28	503.29	9.49	34.82	14.4	4.79
Mar. 29	474.81	9.30	34.30	13.8	5.00
Yr. End		36.08			21.61

Source: Reprinted by courtesy of *Barron's National Business and Financial Weekly*, August 20, 1984.

Bonds and Money Market Investments

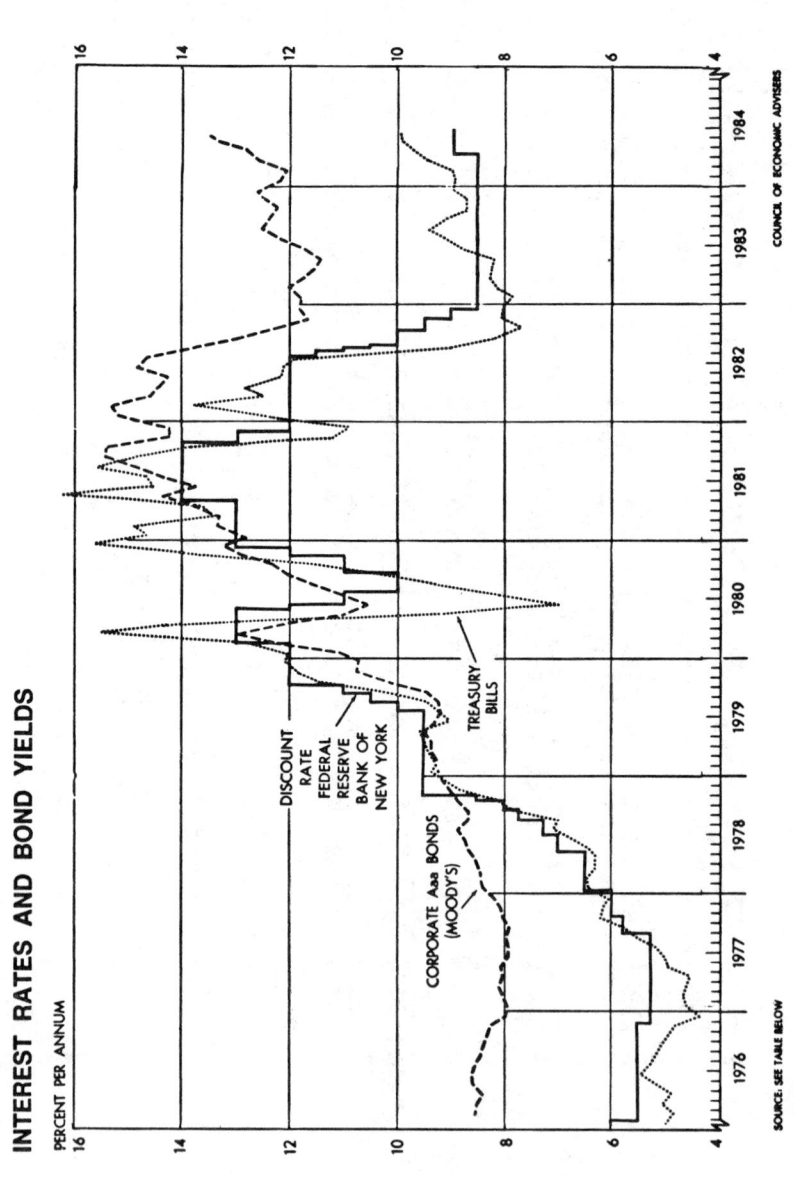

INTEREST RATES AND BOND YIELDS

PERCENT PER ANNUM

COUNCIL OF ECONOMIC ADVISERS

SOURCE: SEE TABLE BELOW

[Percent per annum]

Period	U.S. Treasury security yields			High-grade municipal bonds (Standard & Poor's) [3]	Corporate Aaa bonds (Moody's)	Prime commercial paper, 6 months [4]	Discount rate (N.Y. F.R. Bank) [5]	Prime rate charged by banks [5]	New-home mortgage yields (FHLBB) [6]
	3-month bills [1]	Constant maturities [2]							
		3-year	10-year						
1978	7.221	8.29	8.41	5.90	8.73	4 7.99	7.46	9.06	9.56
1979	10.041	9.72	9.44	6.39	9.63	10.91	10.28	12.67	10.78
1980	11.506	11.55	11.46	8.51	11.94	12.29	11.77	15.27	12.66
1981	14.029	14.44	13.91	11.23	14.17	14.76	13.41	18.87	14.70
1982	10.686	12.92	13.00	11.57	13.79	11.89	11.02	14.86	15.14
1983	8.63	10.45	11.10	9.47	12.04	8.89	8.50	10.79	12.57
							High-low	High-low	
1983: June	8.82	10.32	10.85	9.51	11.74	9.03	8.50–8.50	10.50–10.50	12.36
July	9.12	10.90	11.38	9.46	12.15	9.36	8.50–8.50	10.50–10.50	12.50
Aug	9.39	11.30	11.85	9.72	12.51	9.68	8.50–8.50	11.00–10.50	12.38
Sept	9.05	11.07	11.65	9.57	12.37	9.28	8.50–8.50	11.00–11.00	12.54
Oct	8.71	10.87	11.54	9.64	12.25	8.98	8.50–8.50	11.00–11.00	12.25
Nov	8.71	10.96	11.69	9.79	12.41	9.09	8.50–8.50	11.00–11.00	12.34
Dec	8.96	11.13	11.83	9.90	12.57	9.50	8.50–8.50	11.00–11.00	12.42
1984: Jan	8.93	10.93	11.67	9.61	12.20	9.18	8.50–8.50	11.00–11.00	12.29
Feb	9.03	11.05	11.84	9.63	12.08	9.31	8.50–8.50	11.00–11.00	12.23
Mar	9.44	11.59	12.32	9.92	12.57	9.86	8.50–8.50	11.50–11.00	12.02
Apr	9.69	11.98	12.63	9.98	12.81	10.22	9.00–8.50	12.00–11.50	r 12.04
May P	9.90	12.75	13.41	10.55	13.28	10.87	9.00–9.00	12.00–11.00	12.17
June P	9.94	13.16	13.55	10.71	13.53	11.22			
Week ended:									
1984: May 19	10.07	12.78	13.49	10.45	13.33	11.05	9.00–9.00	12.50–12.50	
26	9.95	12.93	13.59	10.80	13.42	10.96	9.00–9.00	12.50–12.50	
June 2	9.83	13.25	13.86	11.14	13.56	11.08	9.00–9.00	12.50–12.50	
9	9.90	12.99	13.47	10.78	13.46	11.13	9.00–9.00	12.50–12.50	
16	10.07	13.08	13.43	10.68	13.48	11.19	9.00–9.00	12.50–12.50	
23	10.01	13.24	13.55	10.63	13.55	11.24	9.00–9.00	12.50–12.50	
30	9.77			10.73			9.00–9.00	12.50–12.50	

1 Rate on new issues within period; bank-discount basis.
2 Yields on the more actively traded issues adjusted to constant maturities by the Treasury Department.
3 Weekly data are Wednesday figures.
4 Bank-discount basis. Prior to November 1, 1979, data are for 4-6 months paper.
5 Average effective rate for year; high and low rate for month and week.
6 Effective rate (in the primary market) on conventional mortgages, reflecting fees and charges as well as contract rate and assumed, on the average, repayment at end of 10 years. Rates beginning January 1973 not strictly comparable with prior rates.

Sources: Department of the Treasury, Board of Governors of the Federal Reserve System, Federal Home Loan Bank Board, Moody's Investors Service, and Standard & Poor's Corporation.

Source: *Economic Indicators,* Council of Economic Advisers.

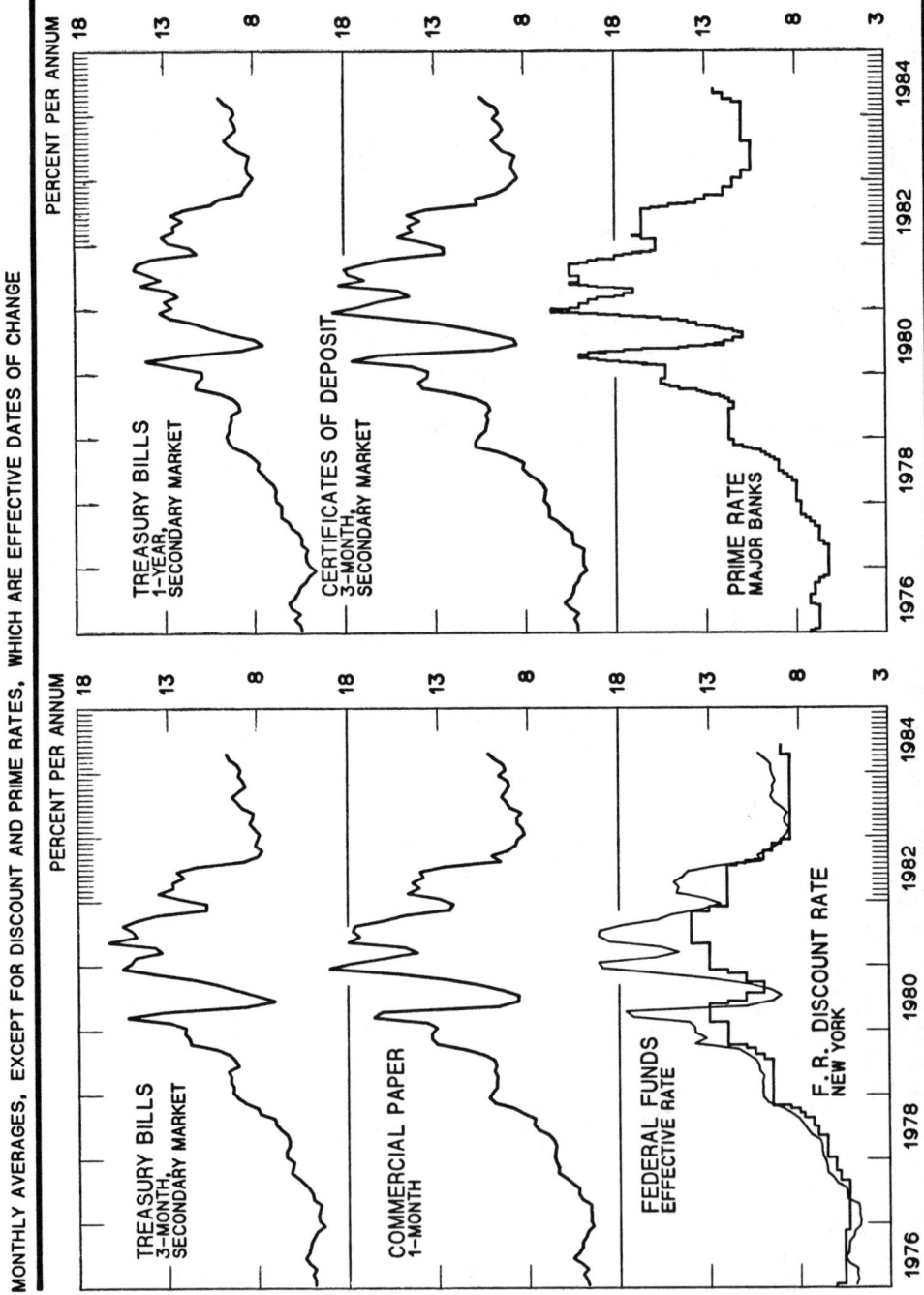

SHORT-TERM INTEREST RATES

MONTHLY AVERAGES, EXCEPT FOR DISCOUNT AND PRIME RATES, WHICH ARE EFFECTIVE DATES OF CHANGE

Source: Federal Reserve Chart Book, Board of Governors of the Federal Reserve System.

LONG-TERM INTEREST RATES

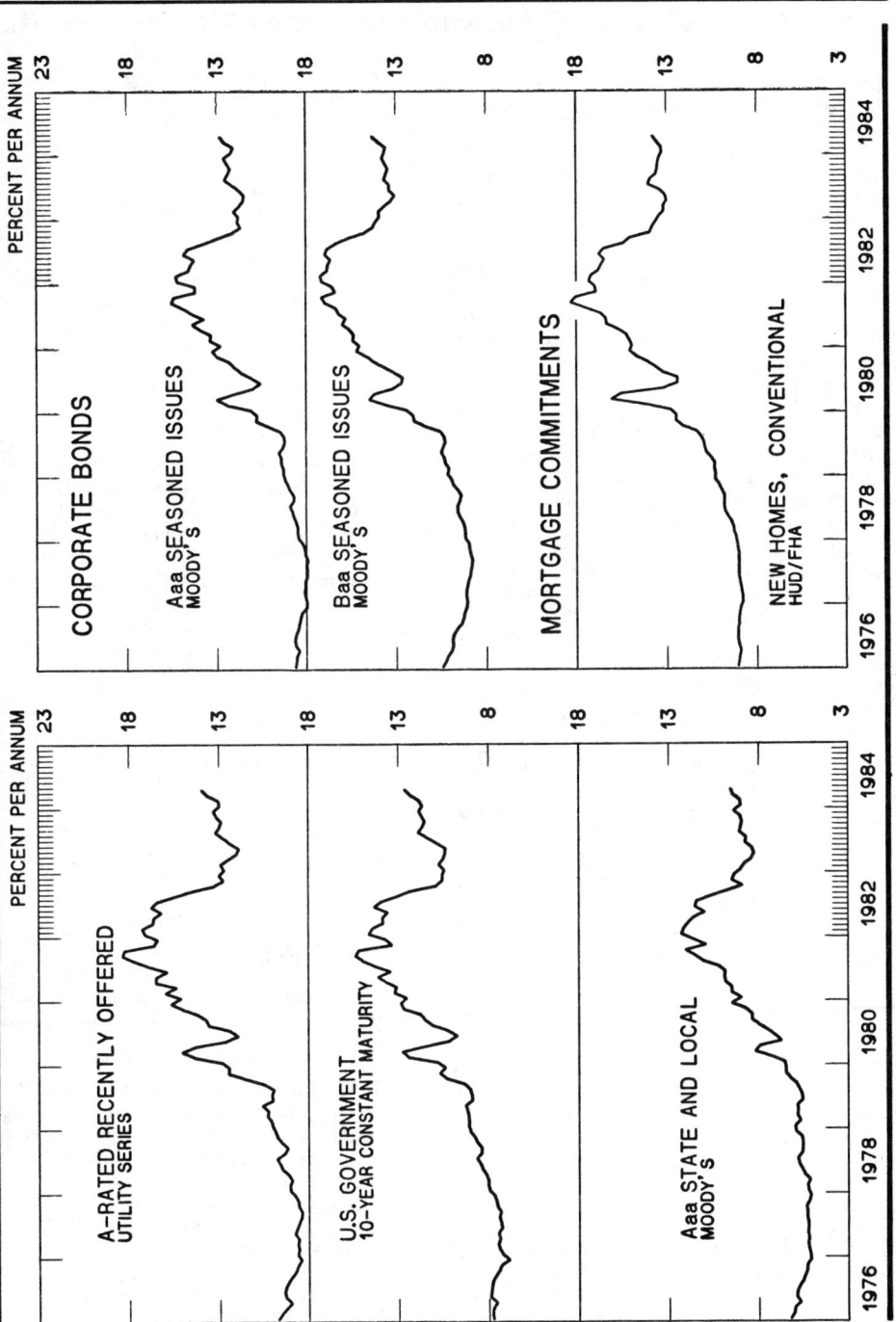

MONTHLY AVERAGES

PERCENT PER ANNUM

CORPORATE BONDS

Aaa SEASONED ISSUES
MOODY'S

Baa SEASONED ISSUES
MOODY'S

MORTGAGE COMMITMENTS

NEW HOMES, CONVENTIONAL
HUD/FHA

PERCENT PER ANNUM

A–RATED RECENTLY OFFERED
UTILITY SERIES

U.S. GOVERNMENT
10-YEAR CONSTANT MATURITY

Aaa STATE AND LOCAL
MOODY'S

Source: *Federal Reserve Chart Book,* Board of Governors of the Federal Reserve System.

Credit Ratings of Fixed Income and Money Market Securities

KEY TO STANDARD & POOR'S CORPORATE AND MUNICIPAL BOND RATING DEFINITIONS

A Standard & Poor's corporate or municipal debt rating is a current assessment of the creditworthiness of an obligor with respect to a specific debt obligation. This assessment may take into consideration obligors such as guarantors, insurers, or lessees.

The debt rating is not a recommendation to purchase, sell or hold a security, inasmuch as it does not comment as to market price or suitability for a particular investor.

The ratings are based on current information furnished by the issuer or obtained by Standard & Poor's from other sources it considers reliable. Standard & Poor's does not perform an audit in connection with any rating and may, on occasion, rely on unaudited financial information. The ratings may be changed, suspended or withdrawn as a result of changes in, or unavailability of, such information, or for other circumstances.

The ratings are based, in varying degrees, on the following considerations:

    I. Likelihood of default—capacity and willingness of the obligor as to the timely payment of interest and repayment of principal in accordance with the terms of the obligation;

    II. Nature of and provisions of the obligation;

    III. Protection afforded by, and relative position of, the obligation in the event of bankruptcy, reorganization or other arrangement under the laws of bankruptcy and other laws affecting creditors' rights.

AAA

Debt rated **AAA** have the highest rating assigned by Standard & Poor's to a debt obligation. Capacity to pay interest and repay principal is extremely strong.

AA

Debt rated **AA** have a very strong capacity to pay interest and repay principal and differ from the highest rated issues only in small degree.

A

Debt rated **A** have a strong capacity to pay interest and repay principal although they are somewhat more susceptible to the adverse effects of changes in circumstances and economic conditions than debts in higher rated categories.

BBB

Debt rated **BBB** are regarded as having an adequate capacity to pay interest and repay principal. Whereas they normally exhibit adequate protection parameters, adverse economic conditions or changing circumstances are more likely to lead to a weakened capacity to pay interest and repay principal for debts in this category than for debts in higher rated categories.

BB, B, CCC, CC

Debt rated **BB, B, CCC,** and **CC** are regarded, on balance, as predominantly speculative with respect to capacity to pay interest and repay principal in accordance with the terms of the obligation. **BB** indicates the lowest degree of speculation and **CC** the highest degree of speculation. While such debts will likely have some quality and protective characteristics, these are outweighed by large uncertainties or major risk exposures to adverse conditions.

C

The rating **C** is reserved for income bonds on which no interest is being paid.

D

Debt rated **D** are in default, and payment of interest and/or repayment of principal is in arrears.

Plus (+) or minus (−)

The ratings from **AA** to **BB** may be modified by the addition of a plus or minus sign to show relative standing within the major rating categories.

Provisional ratings

The letter *p* indicates that the rating is provisional. A provisional rating assumes the successful completion of the project being financed by the debts being rated and indicates that payment of debt service requirements is largely or entirely dependent upon the successful and timely completion of the project. This rating, however, while addressing credit quality subsequent to completion of the project, makes no comment on the likelihood of, or the risk of default upon failure of, such completion. The investor should exercise his own judgment with respect to such likelihood and risk.

NR

Indicates that no rating has been requested, that there is insufficient information on which

Source: From Standard & Poor's Debt Rating Division.

to base a rating or that S&P does not rate a particular type of obligation as a matter of policy.

DEBT OBLIGATIONS

Debt Obligations of issuers outside the United States and its territories are rated on the same basis as domestic corporate and municipal issues. The ratings measure the creditworthiness of the obligor but do not take into account currency exchange and other uncertainties.

BOND INVESTMENT QUALITY STANDARDS

Under present commerical bank regulations issued by the Comptroller of the Currency, bonds rated in the top four categories (AAA, AA, A, BBB, commonly known as "Investment Grade" ratings) are generally regarded as eligible for bank investment. In addition, the Legal Investment Laws of various states impose certain rating or other standards for obligations eligible for investment by savings banks, trust companies, insurance companies and fiduciaries generally.

KEY TO STANDARD & POOR'S PREFERRED STOCK RATING DEFINITIONS

A Standard & Poor's preferred stock rating is an assessment of the capacity and willingness of an issuer to pay preferred stock dividends and any applicable sinking fund obligations. A preferred stock rating differs from a bond rating inasmuch as it is assigned to an equity issue, which issue is intrinsically different from, and subordinated to, a debt issue. Therefore, to reflect this difference, the preferred stock rating symbol will normally not be higher than the bond rating symbol assigned to, or that would be assigned to, the senior debt of the same issuer.

The preferred stock ratings are based on the following considerations:

I. Likelihood of payment—capacity and willingness of the issuer to meet the timely payment of preferred stock dividends and any applicable sinking fund requirements in accordance with the terms of the obligation.
II. Nature of, and provisions of, the issue.
III. Relative position of the issue in the event of bankruptcy, reorganization, or other arrangements affecting creditors' rights.

AAA

This is the highest rating that may be assigned by Standard & Poor's to a preferred stock issue and indicates in extremely strong capacity to pay the preferred stock obligations.

AA

A preferred stock issue rated AA also qualifies as a high-quality fixed income security. The capacity to pay preferred stock obligations is very strong, although not as overwhelming as for issues rated AAA.

A

An issue rated A is backed by a sound capacity to pay the preferred stock obligations, although it is somewhat more susceptible to the adverse effects of changes in circumstances and economic conditions.

BBB

An issue rated BBB is regarded as backed by an adequate capacity to pay the preferred stock obligations. Whereas it normally exhibits adequate protection parameters, adverse economic conditions or changing circumstances are more likely to lead to a weakened capacity to make payments for a preferred stock in this category than for issues in the A category.

BB, B, CCC

Preferred stock rated BB, B, and CCC are regarded, on balance, as predominately speculative with respect to the issuer's capacity to pay preferred stock obligations. BB indicates the lowest degree of speculation and CCC the highest degree of speculation. While such issues will likely have some quality and protective characteristics, these are outweighed by large uncertainties or major risk exposures to adverse conditions.

CC

The rating CC is reserved for a preferred stock issue in arrears on dividends or sinking fund payments but that is currently paying.

C

A preferred stock rated C is a non-paying issue.

D

A preferred stock rated D is a non-paying issue with the issuer in default on debt instruments.

NR indicates that no rating has been requested, that there is insufficient information on which to base a rating, or that S&P does not rate a particular type of obligation as a matter of policy.

Plus (+) or Minus (−) To provide more detailed indications of preferred stock quality, the ratings from AA to B may be modified by the addition of a plus or minus sign to show relative standing within the major rating categories.

The preferred stock rating is not a recommendation to purchase or sell a security, inasmuch as market price is not considered in arriving at the rating. Preferred stock *ratings* are wholly unrelated to Standard & Poor's earnings and dividend *rankings* for common stocks.

The ratings are based on current information furnished to Standard & Poor's by the issuer, and obtained by Standard & Poor's from other sources it considers reliable. The ratings may be changed, suspended, or withdrawn as a result of changes in, or unavailability of, such information.

Standard & Poor's Corporation receives compensation for rating securities. Such compensation is based on the work done and is paid either by issuers of such securities or by the underwriters participating in the distribution thereof. The fees generally vary from $1,500 to $20,000 for corporate securities.

KEY TO STANDARD & POOR'S COMMERCIAL PAPER RATING DEFINITIONS

A Standard & Poor's Commercial Paper Rating is a current assessment of the likelihood of timely payment of debt having an original maturity of no more than 365 days.

Ratings are graded into four categories, ranging from **A** for the highest quality obligations to **D** for the lowest. The four categories are as follows:

A

Issues assigned this highest rating are regarded as having the greatest capacity for timely payment. Issues in this category are further refined with the designations 1, 2, and 3 to indicate the relative degree of safety.

A-1 This designation indicates that the degree of safety regarding timely payment is very strong.

A-2 Capacity for timely payment on issues with this designation is strong. However, the relative degree of safety is not as overwhelming as for issues designated **A-1**.

A-3 Issues carrying this designation have a satisfactory capacity for timely payment. They are, however, somewhat more vulnerable to the adverse effects of changes in circumstances than obligations carrying the higher designations.

B

Issues rated **B** are regarded as having only an adequate capacity for timely payment. However, such capacity may be damaged by changing conditions for short-term adversities.

C

This rating is assigned to short-term obligations with a doubtful capacity for payment.

D

This rating indicates that the issue is either a default or is expected to be in default upon maturity.

The Commercial Paper Rating is not a recommendation to purchase or sell a security. The rating applies only to the actual debt securities being rated and not to any other debt obligations of the same issuer. The ratings are based on current information furnished to Standard & Poor's by the issuer and obtained by Standard & Poor's from other sources it considers reliable. The ratings may be changed, suspended, or withdrawn as a result of changes in, or unavailability of, such information.

KEY TO MOODY'S MUNICIPAL RATINGS

Aaa

Bonds which are rated **Aaa** are judged to be of the best quality. They carry the smallest degree of investment risk and are generally referred to as "gilt edge." Interest payments are protected by a large or by an exceptionally stable margin and principal is secure. While the various protective elements are likely to change, such changes as can be visualized are

---

General Note: Those bonds in the A and Baa groups which Moody's believes possess the strongest investment attributes are designated by the symbols **A 1** and **Baa 1**. Other A and Baa bonds comprise the balance of their respective groups. These rankings (1) designate the bonds which offer the maximum in security within their quality group, (2) designate bonds which can be bought for possible upgrading in quality and (3) additionally afford the investor an opportunity to gauge more precisely the relative attractiveness of offerings in the market place.

Generally speaking, bonds in Moody's highest rating categories can be characterized as follows: Aaa obligations, their safety is so absolute that with the occasional exception of oversupply in a few specific instances, characteristically, their market value is affected solely by money market fluctuations; Aa bonds, their market value is virtually immune to all but money market influences, with the occasional exception of oversupply in a few specific instances; A-rated bonds may be influenced to some degree by economic performance during a sustained period of depressed business conditions but during periods of normalcy A-rated bonds frequently move in parallel with Aaa and Aa obligations, with the occasional exception of oversupply in a few specific instances: Baa-rated are more sensitive to changes in economic circumstances, and aside from occasional speculative factors applying to some bonds of this class, Baa issues will move in parallel with Aaa, Aa, and A obligations during periods of economic normalcy, except in instances of oversupply; Ba bonds are speculative, their market value may be affected by varying economic circumstances not necessarily geared to the business cycle; B-rated bonds are usually quite sensitive to day-to-day circumstances affecting the borrower's ability to service debt on schedule, especially during down trending economic cycle; Caa bonds reflect the market's concept of the probability and imminence of a workout; Ca bonds are speculative in high degree and usually indicate nominal workout value; and C-rated bonds appear to be hopelessly in default and usually have only a nominal speculative market value.

Unless otherwise noted, municipal ratings are for "general obligations" which are defined as validly issued and legally binding evidences of indebtedness secured by the full faith, credit and taxing powers of the issuer.

Source: Moody's Investors Service, Inc.

most unlikely to impair the fundamentally strong position of such issues.

Aa

Bonds which are rated **Aa** are judged to be of high quality by all standards. Together with the **Aaa** group they comprise what are generally known as high grade bonds. They are rated lower than the best bonds because margins of protection may not be as large as in **Aaa** securities or fluctuation of protective elements may be of greater amplitude or there may be other elements present which make the long term risks appear somewhat larger than in **Aaa** securities.

A

Bonds which are rated **A** possess many favorable investment attributes and are to be considered as upper medium grade obligations. Factors giving security to principal and interest are considered adequate, but elements may be present which suggest a susceptibility to impairment sometime in the future. See general note on preceding page.

Baa

Bonds which are rated **Baa** are considered as medium grade obligations; i.e., they are neither highly protected nor poorly secured. Interest payments and principal security appear adequate for the present but certain protective elements may be lacking or may be characteristically unreliable over any great length of time. Such bonds lack outstanding investment characteristics and in fact have speculative characteristics as well. See general note on preceding page.

Ba

Bonds which are rated **Ba** are judged to have speculative elements; their future cannot be considered as well assured. Often the protection of interest and principal payments may be very moderate, and thereby not well safeguarded during both good and bad times over the future. Uncertainty of position characterizes bonds in this class.

B

Bonds which are rated **B** generally lack characteristics of the desirable investment. Assurance of interest and principal payments or of maintenance of other terms of the contract over any long period of time may be small.

Caa

Bonds which are rated **Caa** are of poor standing. Such issues may be in default or there may

be present elements of danger with respect to principal or interest.

Ca

Bonds which are rated **Ca** represent obligations which are speculative in a high degree. Such issues are often in default or have other marked shortcomings.

C

Bonds which are rated **C** are the lowest rated class of bonds, and issues so rated can be regarded as having extremely poor prospects of ever attaining any real investment standing.

Con.(—)

Bonds for which the security depends upon the completion of some act or the fulfillment of some condition are rated conditionally. These are bonds secured by (a) earnings of projects under construction, (b) earnings of projects unseasoned in operation experience, (c) rentals which begin when facilities are completed, or (d) payments to which some other limiting condition attaches. Parenthetical rating denotes probable credit stature upon completion of construction or elimination of basis of condition.

KEY TO MOODY'S CORPORATE RATINGS*

Aaa

Bonds which are rated **Aaa** are judged to be of the best quality. They carry the smallest degree of investment risk and are generally referred to as "gilt edge." Interest payments are protected by a large or by an exceptionally stable margin and principal is secure. While the various protective elements are likely to change, such changes as can be visualized are most unlikely to impair the fundamentally strong position of such issues.

---

* Since April 26, 1982 Moody's applies numerical modifiers, **1, 2,** and **3** in each generic rating classification from **Aa** through **B** in its corporate bond rating system. The modifier **1** indicates that the security ranks in the higher end of its generic rating category; the modifier **2** indicates a mid-range ranking; and the modifier **3** indicates that the issue ranks in the lower end of its generic rating category.

A triple-A rating will have no numerical modifier; it remains Moody's highest corporate bond rating. Also, generic ratings **Caa, Ca,** and **C** will not have numerical modifiers. The new system comprises the following symbols:

Aaa	Baa1, Baa2, Baa3	Caa
Aa1, Aa2, Aa3	Ba1, Ba2, Ba3	Ca
A1, A2, A3	B1, B2, B3	C

Aa

Bonds which are rated **Aa** are judged to be of high quality by all standards. Together with the Aaa group they comprise what are generally known as high grade bonds. They are rated lower than the best bonds because margins of protection may not be as large as in Aaa securities or fluctuation of protective elements may be of greater amplitude or there may be other elements present which make the long term risks appear somewhat larger than in Aaa securities.

A

Bonds which are rated **A** possess many favorable investment attributes and are to be considered as upper medium grade obligations. Factors giving security to principal and interest are considered adequate but elements may be present which suggest a susceptibility to impairment sometime in the future.

Baa

Bonds which are rated **Baa** are considered as medium grade obligations, i.e., they are neither highly protected nor poorly secured. Interest payments and principal security appear adequate for the present but certain protective elements may be lacking or may be characteristically unreliable over any great length of time. Such bonds lack outstanding investment characteristics and in fact have speculative characteristics as well.

Ba

Bonds which are rated **Ba** are judged to have speculative elements; their future cannot be considered as well assured. Often the protection of interest and principal payments may be very moderate and thereby not well safeguarded during both good and bad times over the future. Uncertainty of position characterizes bonds in this class.

B

Bonds which are rated **B** generally lack characteristics of the desirable investment. Assurance of interest and principal payments or of maintenance of other terms of the contract over any long period of time may be small.

Caa

Bonds which are rated **Caa** are of poor standing. Such issues may be in default or there may be present elements of danger with respect to principal or interest.

Ca

Bonds which are rated **Ca** represent obligations which are speculative in a high degree.

Such issues are often in default or have other marked shortcomings.

C

Bonds which are rated **C** are the lowest rated class of bonds and issues so rated can be regarded as having extremely poor prospects of ever attaining any real investment standing.

KEY TO MOODY'S COMMERCIAL PAPER RATINGS*

Moody's Commercial Paper ratings are opinions of the ability of issuers to repay punctually promissory obligations not having an original maturity in excess of nine months. Moody's makes no representation that such obligations are exempt from registration under the Securities Act of 1933, nor does it represent that any specific note is a valid obligation of a rated issuer or issued in conformity with any applicable law. Moody's employs the following three designations, all judged to be investment grade, to indicate the relative repayment capacity of rated issuers:

Prime-1	Highest Quality
Prime-2	Higher Quality
Prime-3	High Quality

If an issuer represents to Moody's that its Commercial Paper obligations are supported by the credit of another entity or entities, the name or names of such supporting entity or entities are listed within parenthesis beneath the name of the issuer. In assigning ratings to such issuers, Moody's evaluates the financial strength of the indicated affiliated corporations, commercial banks, insurance companies, foreign governments or other entities, but only as one factor in the total rating assessment. Moody's makes no representation and gives no opinion on the legal validity or enforceability of any support arrangement. You are cautioned to review with your counsel any questions regarding particular support arrangements.

KEY TO MOODY'S PREFERRED STOCK RATINGS

Moody's Rating Policy Review Board Extended its rating services to include quality designations on preferred stocks on October 1, 1973. The decision to rate preferred stocks, which Moody's had done prior to 1935, was prompted by evidence of investor interest. Moody's believes that its rating of preferred

---

* The term "Commercial Paper" as used by Moody's means promissory obligations not having an original maturity in excess of nine months. Moody's makes no representation as to whether such Commercial Paper is by any other definition "Commercial Paper" or is exempt from registration under the Securities Act of 1933, as amended.

Source: Moody's Investors Service, Inc.

stocks is especially appropriate in view of the ever-increasing amount of these securities outstanding, and the fact that continuing inflation and its ramifications have resulted generally in the dilution of some of the protection afforded them as well as other fixed-income securities.

Because of the fundamental differences between preferred stocks and bonds, a variation of our familiar bond rating symbols is being used in the quality ranking of preferred stocks. The symbols, presented below, are designed to avoid comparison with bond quality in absolute terms. It should always be borne in mind that preferred stocks occupy a junior position to bonds within a particular capital structure.

Preferred stock rating symbols and their definitions are as follows:

aaa

An issue which is rated **aaa** is considered to be a top-quality preferred stock. This rating indicates good asset protection and the least risk of dividend impairment within the universe of preferred stocks.

aa

An issue which is rated **aa** is considered a high-grade preferred stock. This rating indicates that there is reasonable assurance that earnings and asset protection will remain relatively well maintained in the foreseeable future.

a

An issue which is rated **a** is considered to be an upper-medium grade preferred stock. While risks are judged to be somewhat greater than in the "aaa" and "aa" classifications, earnings and asset protection are, nevertheless, expected to be maintained at adequate levels.

baa

An issue which is rated **baa** is considered to be medium grade, neither highly protected nor poorly secured. Earnings and asset protection appear adequate at present but may be questionable over any great length of time.

ba

An issue which is rated **ba** is considered to have speculative elements and its future cannot be considered well assured. Earnings and asset protection may be very moderate and not well safeguarded during adverse periods. Uncertainty of position characterizes preferred stocks in this class.

b

An issue which is rated **b** generally lacks the characteristics of a desirable investment. Assur-

ance of dividend payments and maintenance of other terms of the issue over any long period of time may be small.

caa

An issue which is rated **caa** is likely to be in arrears on dividend payments. This rating designation does not purport to indicate the future status of payments.

KEY TO CUMULATIVE INDEX OF SHORT-TERM LOAN RATINGS

Moody's ratings for state and municipal notes and other short-term loans are designated **Moody's Investment Grade (MIG)**. This distinction is in recognition of the differences between short-term credit risk and long-term risk. Factors affecting the liquidity of the borrower are uppermost in importance in short-term borrowing, while various factors of the first importance in bond risk are of lesser importance in the short run. Symbols used are as follows:

MIG 1

Loans bearing this designation are of the best quality, enjoying strong protection from established cash flows of funds of their servicing or from established and broad-based access to the market for refinancing, or both.

MIG 2

Loans bearing this designation are of high quality, with margins of protection ample although not so large as in the preceding group.

MIG 3

Loans bearing this designation are of favorable quality, with all security elements accounted for but lacking the undeniable strength of the preceding grades. Market access for refinancing, in particular, is likely to be less well established.

MIG 4

Loans bearing this designation are of adequate quality, carrying specific risk but having protection commonly regarded as required of an investment security and not distinctly or predominantly speculative.

All state and municipal short-term loan or note ratings in effect are listed below. Issues are identified by date of issue, date of maturity or maturities, and description to distinguish each issue from other issues. The rating of any given issue carries no implications as to any other similar issue of the same obligor. Only issues listed below are rated. Ratings terminate at retirement of the note and may be withdrawn for failure to provide current information or for other reasons.

MAJOR MONEY MARKET AND FIXED INCOME SECURITIES

Type	Interest: When Paid	Marketability	Minimum Amount of Issue	Maturity
A. Interest Fully Taxable				
Corporate Bonds and Notes	S[1]	Very good to poor depending on quality	$1,000	1 to 50 years
Corporate Preferred Stock (Pays dividends as a fixed percentage of face value. Dividends not obligatory, but if declared must be paid before that of the common stock. Dividends fully taxable for individuals, but 85% exempt from federal tax for corporations)	Generally quarterly	Good to poor depending on quality	$100 or less	No maturity
Federal Home Loan Mortgage Corporate Bonds	S	Fair	$25,000	Up to 25 years
Federal Home Loan Mortgage Certificates	S	Fair	$100,000	Up to 3 years
Farmers' Home Administration Notes and Certificates	Annual	Fair	$25,000	1 to 25 years
Federal Housing Administration Debentures (Guaranteed by the U.S. Government)	S	Very good	$50	1 to 40 years
Federal National Mortgage Association Bonds	S	Fair	$25,000	2 to 25 years
Government National Mortgage Modified Pass through Certificates (interest plus some repayment of principal, guaranteed by U.S. Government)	Monthly	Good	$25,000	30 years; average life 12 years
Federal Home Loan Bank Bonds and Notes	S	Good	$10,000	1 to 20 years
Export-Import Bank Debentures and Certificates	S	Good	$5,000	3 to 7 years
International Bank for Reconstruction Development (World Bank), Inter-American Development Bank, Asia Development Bank	S	Fair to poor	$1,000	3 to 25 years
Foreign and Eurodollar Bonds and Notes	May be Annual or S	Poor	$1,000 (amounts vary in foreign currencies)	1 to 30 years
Bankers Acceptances (short-term debt obligations (resulting from international trade and guaranteed by a major bank)	Discounted[2] on a 360-day year basis	Fair	$5,000	1 to 270 days
Commercial Paper (short-term debt issued by a major corporation)	Discounted on a 360-day year basis	No secondary market	$100,000 (occasionally smaller)	1 to 270 days
Negotiable Certificates of Deposit (short-term debt issued by banks and which can be sold on the open market)	Interest paid on maturity; 360-day year basis	Fair	$100,000 (occasionally smaller)	30 days to 1 year
Non-negotiable Certificate of Deposit (savings certificates)	Interest paid on maturity; 360-day year basis	Non-negotiable	$500 $10,000	30 months 6 months
Collateralized Mortgage Obligations (CMO)	S or monthly	Good	$1,000	typically 2 to 20 years

MAJOR MONEY MARKET AND FIXED INCOME SECURITIES *(concluded)*

Type	Interest: When Paid	Marketability	Minimum Amount of Issue	Maturity
Repurchase Agreements (generally short term loans by large investors, secured by U.S. Government or other high quality issues)[3]	Interest paid on maturity; 360-day year basis	No secondary market	$100,000	1 to 30 days (sometimes more)
Zero Coupon Bonds (Bonds stripped of coupons)	Bonds issued at deep discount. Full yield realized at maturity	Good	$1,000 on maturity	1 to 30 years
B. *Interest Exempt from State and Local Income Taxes*				
U.S. Treasury Bonds and Notes	S	Very good	$1,000	1 to 20 years
U.S. Treasury Bills	Discounted on a 360-day basis	Very good	$10,000	90 days to 1 year
U.S. Series EE Savings Bonds[4]	Issued at discount, full interest, paid on maturity	No secondary market: available for resale	$50 minimum $15,000 maximum	11 years (can be redeemed before maturity at reduced yields
U.S. Series HH Savings Bonds	S	No secondary market	$500 $15,000 maximum	10 years
Federal Land Bank Bonds	S	Good	$1,000	1 to 10 years
Federal Financing Bank Notes and Bonds	S	Good	$1,000	1 to 20 years
Tennessee Valley Authority Notes and Bonds	S	Fair	$1,000	5 to 25 years
Banks for Cooperatives Bonds	Interest: 360-day year basis	Good	$5,000	180 days
Federal Intermediate Credit Bank Bonds	Interest: 360-day year basis	Good	$5,000.	270 days
Federal Home Loan Bank Notes and Bonds	Discounted: 360-day year basis	Good	$10,000.	30 to 360-day year basis (some more)
Farm Credit Bank Notes and Bonds	Interest: 360-day year basis	Good	$50,000.	270 days (some more)
C. *Interest Exempt from Federal Income Tax*				
State and Local Notes and Bonds (in-State issues, usually exempt from State and local income taxes)	S	Good to fair depending on rating	$5,000.	1 to 50 years
Housing Authority Bonds (in-State issues usually exempt from State and local income taxes)	S	Good to fair	$5,000.	1 to 40 years

[1] S means semiannually.

[2] A discount means interest paid in advance, thus a 10% discounted security maturing at $10,000 would cost $9,000 to purchase.

[3] Recently some banks have issued repurchase agreements for smaller amounts of money, i.e., several thousands of dollars.

[4] Since November 1982, U.S. Savings Bonds pay variable interest equal to 85% of the 5 year Treasury securities' rate adjusted semi-annually and have a minimum guaranteed rate of 7.5%.

U.S. Treasury Bonds, Notes, and Bills: Terms Defined*

U.S. Treasury bonds, notes and bills are interest paying securities representing a debt on the part of the U.S. Government. Treasury bonds have a maturity of over 5 years, while notes mature within 5 to 7 years. Bills are discussed below. Both Treasury bonds and notes are generally issued in minimum denominations of $1,000 and pay interest semiannually. The amount of semiannual interest paid is determined by the coupon rate specified on the bond and is calculated on a 365-day year basis. For a $1,000 face value† bond the interest is given by:

$$\text{semiannual interest} = 1/2\ (\$1,000 \times \text{coupon rate})$$

Bonds may be priced higher (at a premium) or lower (at a discount) than the face value (par) depending on current interest rates. The *current yield* is the rate the investor receives based on the prices actually paid for a bond. The price is given by:

$$\text{current yield} = \frac{\$1,000 \times \text{coupon rate}}{\text{purchase price}}$$

Thus, a $1,000 face value bond with an 8% coupon rate purchased at $850 has a current yield by:

$$\text{current yield} = \frac{\$1,000 \times 8\%}{\$850} = 9.41\%$$

The *yield to maturity* (YTM) is the yield obtained on taking into account the years remaining to maturity, annual interest payments, and the capital gain (or loss) realized at maturity. It is obtained from special tables.

However, the yield to maturity (YTM) may be found approximately from the formula

$$\text{YTM} = \frac{I + A}{B}$$

$I = $ annual interest rate

$$A = \frac{\$1,000 - M}{N}$$

$$B = \frac{\$1,000 + M}{2}$$

where M = current market price of the bond
N = years remaining to maturity

---

* The terms *current yield, yield to maturity*, etc. defined in this section are generally applicable to all fixed incomes.

† Face value is the amount of the bond or note payable upon maturity.

As an example, a bond ($1,000 face value) has a 10% coupon and is currently priced at $1,100 with 10 years remaining to maturity. What is the approximate YTM?

$$I = \$1,000 \times .1 = \$100 \text{ interest per year}$$

$$A = \frac{\$1,000 - \$1,100}{10} = \$-10$$

$$B = \frac{\$1,000 + \$1,100}{2} = \$1,050$$

$$\text{YTM} = \frac{\$100 - \$10}{\$1,050} = .0857 = 8.57\%$$

U.S. Treasury bills (T-bills) are U.S. Government debt obligations which mature within one year. They are offered by the Federal Reserve Bank with maturities of 90 days (3 month bills) and 182 days (six month bills). Nine-month bills and one-year bills are also available. Treasury bills are sold in a minimum denomination of $10,000. Interest is paid by the discount method based on a 360-day year. With the discount method, interest is, in effect, paid at the time the bill is purchased. Thus a 91-day $10,000 bill (face value) with an 8% discount interest rate would provide the buyer with $202.22 ($10,000 × .08 × $^{91}/_{360}$) interest at the time of purchase. This amount is deducted from the face value of the bill at the time of purchase so the buyer actually pays a net amount of $9,797.78 ($10,000 − $202.22). When the bill matures, the buyer receives $10,000 on redemption.

Since T-bills pay interest at the time of purchase (discount basis) on a 360-day year basis, while bonds (and notes) pay interest semiannually on a 365-day year basis, the two rates cannot be compared directly. To compare the two rates, the discount rate must be converted to the so-called *bond equivalent yield*, given by

$$\text{bond equivalent yield} = \frac{365 \times \text{discount rate}}{360 - (\text{discount rate} \times \text{days to maturity})}$$

As an example, a newly issued 91-day note with a discount rate of 12% has a

$$\text{bond equivalent yield} = \frac{365 \times (.12)}{360 - (.12 \times 91)}$$
$$= 12.55\%$$

Interest from U.S. Treasury bonds, notes, and bills are subject to federal income tax, but are exempt from state and local income taxes.

How to Read U.S. Government Bond and Note Quotations

TREASURY BONDS AND NOTES

(1) Rate	(2) Mat.	(3) Date	(4) Bid	(5) Asked	(6) Bid Chg.	(7) Yld.
6¾s,	1981	Jun n ...	99.3	99.7	+ .1	16.51
9⅛s,	1981	Jun n ...	99.12	99.16	+ .2	15.10
9⅜s,	1981	Jul n	98.21	98.25	+ .3	16.54
7s,	1981	Aug.....	97.26	98.10	+ .2	15.19
7⅝s,	1981	Aug n ...	97.30	98.2	+ .6	17.66
8⅜s,	1981	Aug n ...	98.2	98.6	+ .2	17.15
9⅝s,	1981	Aug n ...	98.5	98.9	+ .4	16.53
6¾s,	1981	Sep n ...	96.29	97.1	+ .5	16.10
10⅛s,	1981	Sep n ...	97.28	98	+ .4	16.28
12⅝s,	1981	Oct n ...	98.14	98.18	+ .4	16.18
7s,	1981	Nov n ...	96.4	96.8	+ .10	15.86
7¾s,	1981	Nov n ...	96.18	96.22	+ .13	15.55
12⅛s,	1981	Nov n ...	98.1	98.5	+ .3	16.14
7¼s,	1981	Dec n ...	95.12	95.16	+ .10	15.14

Source: Reprinted by permission of *The Wall Street Journal*, Dow Jones & Co., Inc., 1981. All rights reserved.

The above exhibit is an example of U.S. Government bond and note quotations as it appears in *The Wall Street Journal.*

(1) Indicates the coupon rate of interest which is designated by *s*. Rates are quoted to ⅛ of a percent. Thus 8⅜ means 8.375%. The semiannual interest payments are calculated, as described elsewhere, using this rate.

(2) Indicates the year of maturity.

(3) Indicates the month (of the above year) in which the bond or note matures. The letter *n* means the security is a note. Otherwise a bond is implied.

(4) The *bid price* per bond or note (the price at which the bond can be sold to the dealer), expressed as a percentage of the face value ($1,000) of the bond. Prices are quoted in terms of 1/32 of a percent. Thus 98.5 means 98 5/32. To find the dollar value of the price, convert 98 5/32 to a decimal (98 5/32 = .98156) and multiply by the face value of the bond to give $981.56 (.98156 × $1,000).

(5) The *ask price* per bond or note (the price at which the dealer will sell the bond). The dollar value is found as indicated above.

(6) The change in the bid price from the closing price of the previous day.

(7) The yield if the bond is held to maturity, based on the ask price.

Some U.S. Treasury bonds can be called back for redemption prior to maturity. These are shown with two dates (under item 2 for example)—*1993–98* indicating that the bonds mature in 1998, but may be called back and redeemed any time after 1993.

Some newspapers (such as *The New York Times*) use a slight modification of the above arrangement, though the various terms have the same meaning as defined above. Thus, a bond maturing in June of 1985 and bearing a 10⅜% coupon is indicated by *May '85 10⅜.*

How to Read U.S. Treasury Bill Quotations

(1) U.S. Treas. Mat. date	(2) Bills Bid	(3) Asked Discount	(4) Yield
-1981-			
6–18	17.62	17.44	17.69
6–25	17.15	17.03	17.33
7– 2	15.39	15.01	15.31
7– 9	15.18	15.04	15.39
7–16	15.02	14.78	15.17
7–23	14.83	14.67	15.10
7–30	14.72	14.42	14.88
8– 6	14.11	13.89	14.36
8–13	13.94	13.72	14.22
8–20	13.94	13.72	14.26
8–27	13.92	13.70	14.28
9– 3	13.97	13.63	14.24
9–10	13.72	13.64	14.29
9–17	13.52	13.34	14.00
9–24	13.63	13.43	14.14
10– 1	13.74	13.54	14.30

Source: Reprinted by permission of *The Wall Street Journal*, Dow Jones & Co., Inc. 1981. All rights reserved.

The above exhibit is an example of Treasury bill quotations as it appears in *The Wall Street Journal.*

(1) The date of maturity, i.e., 6–18 means June 18, 1981.

(2) The bid price at market close quoted as a *discount* rate in percent. This bid price is the price at which the dealer will buy the bill. To convert the discount rate to a dollar price use the formula

$$\text{dollar price} = \$10{,}000 - (\text{discount rate} \times \text{days to maturity} \times .2778)$$

In the above, the discount must be expressed in percent. For example, if the dealer bids 16.18% discount for a bill which will mature in 110 days, the dollar price is given by

$$\text{dollar price} = \$10{,}000 - (16.18 \times 110 \times .2778) = \$9{,}505.57 \text{ per bill}$$

(3) The asked price at market close expressed as a discount rate in percent. The asked price is the price at which the dealer will sell a bill to a buyer. To convert to a dollar price use the above formula.

(4) The bond equivalent yield expressed in percent. This is calculated (as explained elsewhere) from the asked price expressed as a dis-

count rate. This rate is used to compare T-bill yields to that of bonds, notes and certificates of deposit.

Some newspapers (e.g., *The New York Times*) use a somewhat different arrangement, though the meaning of the terms is the same as defined above. Thus, a bill maturing on June 4, 1981, is indicated as such. Also included in some newspapers is the change in bid price expressed as a discount rate.

How to Read Corporate Bond Quotations*

Corporate bonds are debt securities issued by private corporations. They generally have a face value (the amount due on maturity) of $1,000 and a specified interest rate (coupon rate) paid semiannually. Many corporate bonds have a *call* provision which permits the company to recall and redeem the bond after a specified date. Call privileges are usually exercised when interest rates fall sufficiently. Investors, therefore, cannot count on *locking in* high interest rates with corporate bonds. Bond quality designations used by Moody's and Standard & Poor's are given elsewhere in the Almanac (pp. 372–377).

The following is an example of price quotations for bonds traded on The New York Stock Exchange as they appear in *The Wall Street Journal.*

CORPORATION BONDS

VOLUME, $18,990,000

(1) Bonds		(2) Cur YlD	(3) Vol	(4) High	(5) Low	(6) Close	(7) Net Chg.
AlaP	9s2000	14.	6	63	62	63	2
AlaP	8½s01	15.	10	57½	57½	57½	...
AlaP	8⅞s03	15.	25	60	59½	60	+ ½
AlaP	10⅞05	15.	3	72	72	72	− 2¼
AlaP	10½05	15.	12	70½	70½	70½	− 1
AlaP	12⅝10	16.	7	81¼	81⅛	81⅛	− 1⅝
AlaP	15¼10	16.	111	94⅝	93⅝	94	...
AlaP	14¾91	15.	31	97	96½	96½	...
AlaP	17⅜11	17.	99	104	103½	103¾	− ¼
Alexn	5½96	cv	34	61¾	61⅝	61¾	+ ¾
Allgl	10¾99	15.	2	70½	70½	70½	...
AllstF	8⅛87	11.	2	76⅜	76⅜	76⅜	+ 1⅞
AllstF	9⅝86	12.	10	83⅛	83	83	+ 1⅞

Source: Reprinted by permission of *The Wall Street Journal,* Dow Jones and Company, Inc. 1981. All rights reserved.

(1) The name of the issue in abbreviated form, followed by the coupon rate of interest in percent (designated by the letter *s*), and the year in which the bond matures. The coupon rate is stated in terms of ⅛ of a percent; 9⅜ means 9.375%.

(2) This is the current yield which is calculated as stated elsewhere. (See U.S. Treasury Bonds, Notes, and Bills, p. 380.)

(3) This item is the number of bonds sold that day.

(4) This is the highest price quoted for the bond sold on that day, expressed as a percentage of face value ($1,000). To convert to dollars, express the price as a decimal and multiply by the face value of the bond. As an example:

$$58\tfrac{1}{2} = (.5850 \times \$1{,}000.) = \$585$$

(5) This is the lowest price quoted that day. It is converted into dollars as described above.

(6) This is the price at the close of the market that day.

(7) This is the change in the closing price from that of the previous day. To convert to dollars, express as a decimal and multiply by $1,000. Thus, −1⅞ means a decrease per bond of $18.75 (.01875 × $1,000) from that of the previous day.

* Yield terms are the same as those defined in the section on U.S. Treasury Bonds, Notes and Bills, p. 404.

Tax-Exempt Bonds

Tax exempt (municipal) bonds are issued by state and local governments and are free from federal income tax on interest payments. The bonds are often issued in $5,000 denominations and pay interest semiannually. Capital gains are taxable. In addition, holders of out-of-state bonds may be subject to state and local income taxes of the state in which they reside. For example, a New York City resident holding Los Angeles municipal bonds would be subject to New York State and City income taxes on the interest.

The taxable equivalent yield of a tax exempt bond is obtained by means of the expression

$$\text{taxable equivalent yield} = \frac{\text{tax exempt yield}}{1 - (F + S + L)}$$

where

F is the federal tax bracket of the investor
S is the state tax bracket of the investor
L is the local tax bracket of the investor

Thus, an investor in the 50% federal bracket, 10% state bracket and 3% local bracket who holds a bond with a current yield of 6% which is exempt from all income taxes would enjoy a taxable equivalent yield (TEY) given by

$$\text{TEY} = \frac{6\%}{1 - (.5 + .1 + .03)} = 16.21\%$$

Section continues on p. 408.

TAX EXEMPT VERSUS TAXABLE YIELDS

tax bracket	To equal a tax-free yield of:											
	5½%	6%	6½%	7%	7½%	8%	8½%	9%	9½%	10%	10½%	11%
	a taxable investment has to earn:											
28%	7.64%	8.33%	9.03%	9.72%	10.42%	11.11%	11.81%	12.50%	13.19%	13.89%	14.58%	15.28%
30	7.86	8.57	9.29	10.00	10.71	11.43	12.14	12.86	13.57	14.29	15.00	15.71
31	7.97	8.70	9.42	10.14	10.87	11.59	12.32	13.04	13.77	14.49	15.22	15.94
32	8.09	8.82	9.56	10.29	11.03	11.76	12.50	13.24	13.97	14.71	15.44	16.18
34	8.33	9.09	9.85	10.61	11.36	12.12	12.88	13.64	14.39	15.15	15.91	16.67
36	8.59	9.38	10.16	10.94	11.72	12.50	13.28	14.06	14.84	15.63	16.41	17.19
37	8.73	9.52	10.32	11.11	11.90	12.70	13.49	14.29	15.08	15.87	16.67	17.47
39	9.02	9.84	10.66	11.48	12.30	13.11	13.93	14.75	15.57	16.39	17.21	18.03
42	9.48	10.34	11.21	12.07	12.93	13.79	14.66	15.52	16.38	17.24	18.10	18.97
43	9.65	10.53	11.40	12.28	13.16	14.04	14.91	15.79	16.67	17.54	18.42	19.30
44	9.82	10.71	11.61	12.50	13.39	14.29	15.18	16.07	16.96	17.86	18.75	19.64
46	10.19	11.11	12.03	12.96	13.89	14.81	15.74	16.67	17.59	18.52	19.44	20.37
49	10.78	11.76	12.75	13.73	14.71	15.69	16.67	17.65	18.63	19.61	20.59	21.57
54	11.96	13.04	14.13	15.22	16.30	17.39	18.48	19.57	20.65	21.74	22.83	23.91
55	12.22	13.33	14.44	15.56	16.67	17.78	18.89	20.00	21.11	22.22	23.33	24.44
59	13.41	14.63	15.85	17.07	18.29	19.51	20.73	21.95	23.17	24.39	25.61	26.83
63	14.86	16.22	17.57	18.92	20.27	21.62	22.97	24.32	25.68	27.03	28.38	29.73
64	15.28	16.67	18.06	19.44	20.83	22.22	23.61	25.00	26.39	27.78	29.17	30.56
68	17.19	18.75	20.31	21.88	23.44	25.00	26.56	28.13	29.69	31.25	32.81	34.38
70	18.33	20.00	21.67	23.33	25.00	26.67	28.33	30.00	31.67	33.33	35.00	36.67

A taxable yield of 16.21% would be necessary to provide the same yield as the 6% current yield on the tax exempt security.

TYPES OF TAX EXEMPT BONDS AND NOTES

General Obligation bonds, also known as GO's, are backed by a pledge of a city's or state's full faith and credit for the prompt repayment of both principal and interest. Most city, county and school district bonds are secured by a pledge of unlimited property taxes. Since general obligation bonds depend on tax resources, they are normally analyzed in terms of the size of the resources being taxed.

Revenue bonds are payable from the earnings of a revenue-producing enterprise such as a sewer, water, gas or electric system, airport, toll bridge, college dormitory, lease payments from property rented to industrial companies, and other income-producing facilities. Revenue bonds are analyzed in terms of their earnings.

Limited and Special Tax bonds are payable from the pledge of the proceeds derived by the issuer from a specific tax such as a property tax levied at a fixed rate, a special assessment, or a tax on gasoline.

Municipal notes are short term obligations maturing from 30 days to a year and are issued in anticipation of revenues coming from the sales of bonds (BANS), taxes (TANS), or other revenues (RANS).

Project notes, issued by local housing and urban renewal agencies, are backed by a U.S. Government guarantee and are also tax exempt.

How to Understand Tax-Exempt Bond Quotations

Generally the prices of municipal bonds are quoted in terms of the yield to maturity (defined elsewhere) rather than in percentage of face value, as with other bonds. The yield to maturity can be converted to a dollar price if the years remaining to maturity and the rate of interest due are known. Certain tables used for this purpose are given in the *Basis Book* (published by the Financial Publishing Company, 82 Brookline Avenue, Boston, Massachusetts). The books list the dollar price (per $1,000 face value of the bond) corresponding to a given coupon rate, yield, and years to maturity.

Some municipal bonds, however, are quoted directly in terms of percentage of face value. Thus, a bid price (the price at which the dealer will buy the bonds from the investor) of 98⅝ for a $5,000 face value bond can be converted to a dollar price by first converting the bid to a decimal expression (.98625) and then multiplying by the face value of the bond. The result

in this case is $4,931.25 (.98625 × $5,000). The same calculation applies to the ask price (the price at which the dealer will sell the bond to the investor).

Prices of tax exempt bonds are not quoted in the daily press. They can be obtained by calling municipal bond dealers. Extensive quotations are given in some relatively expensive publications:

The Blue List
Standard & Poor's
25 Broadway
New York, New York 10004
(212–248–3463)

The Daily Bond Buyer
and
The Weekly Bond Buyer
The Bond Buyer
1 State Street Plaza
New York, New York 10004
(212–964–8270)

Bond Week (Formerly Money Manager)
Institutional Investor
488 Madison Avenue
New York, New York 10022
(212–832–8888)

Government National Mortgage Association (GNMA) Modified Pass Through Certificates

A GNMA Mortgage-Backed Security is a government-guaranteed security which is collateralized by a pool of federally-underwritten residential mortgages. The investor receives a monthly check for a proportionate share of the principal and interest on a pool of mortgages whether or not the payments have actually been collected from the borrowers.

The GNMA Mortgage-Backed Security offers the highest yield of any federally-guaranteed security. In addition, the GNMA security offers a very competitive return in comparison to private corporation debt issues. Moreover, the investor receives a monthly return on the GNMA guaranteed investment, rather than semi-annual payments as on most bonds. This monthly payment represents a cash flow available for reinvestment and has the effect of increasing the yield on GNMAs by 10 to 18 basis points (a basis point is 0.1%) when compared to the yield equivalent received on a bond investment with the same "coupon" rate but paying interest semi-annually.

On single-family securities (the most popular form) the maturity is typically 30 years. However, statistical studies have determined that the average life of a single-family security is approximately 12 years, due to prepayments of principal. Nevertheless, some of the mortgages in any pool are likely to remain outstanding for the full 30-year period.

The minimum size of original individual certificates is $25,000 with increments of $5,000 above that amount.

Due to the uncertainties in the maturity of the above mentioned pass-through certificates, collateralized mortgage obligations (CMOs)

have been introduced. CMOs are bonds backed by Ginnie Maes, Freddie Macs, and other mortgage instruments providing investors with a wide choice of maturities ranging from 2 to 20 years. Essentially, the monthly payments from the underlying mortgage instruments are initially allocated to the nearest maturity CMO and subsequently to CMO maturities of successively longer duration. CMO interest payments are made semiannually or monthly.

Top Ten General Purpose Money Funds Ranked by 12-Month Performance*

Fund	1983 Yield (%)	Assets ($ Millions) Dec. 31, 1983
Calvert Social Invest./M.M. Port (k)	9.31	15.6
Kemper Money Market Fund	9.21	3,611.1
Guardian Cash Management Trust (k)	9.10	12.2
Calvert Cash Reserves/Prime Port. (k)	9.09	9.9
Financial Daily Income Shares, Inc.	9.09	213.8
Transamerica Cash Reserves, Inc.	9.07	299.2
SAFECO Money Market Mutual Fund	9.05	23.2
Cash Equivalent Fund/Money Market Port.	9.04	3,818.4
First American Money Fund	9.02	48.3
MoneyMart Assets	9.00	2,597.4

* (k) Manager absorbing a portion of fund expenses.
Source: *Donoghue's Mutual Funds Almanac* © 1984. The Donoghue Organization, Inc., Box 540, Holliston, MA. 01746. Telephone: 1-800-543-3413.

Tax-Exempt Mutual Funds: Selected No Loads

Funds listed below invest in municipal bonds. Interest is free of federal income tax. However, capital gains are subject to federal income tax and state income taxes generally apply.

	Telephone
Dreyfus Tax-Exempt Bond Fund	800-645-6561
Fidelity:	
High Yield Municipals	800-225-6190
Limited Term Municipals	800-225-6190
Municipal Bond Fund	800-225-6190
Keystone Tax-Free Fund	800-225-1587
Nuveen Municipal Bond Fund	800-621-1227
Scudder Managed Municipal Bond Fund	800-225-2471
Stein Roe Tax-Exempt Bond Fund	800-621-0321
Vanguard:	
Municipal Bond-High Yield	800-523-7025
Municipal Bond-Intermediate	800-523-7025
Municipal Bond-Long Term	800-523-7025

10 Largest Tax-Exempt Money Market Funds by Assets[1,2]

	Assets (millions)
Dreyfus Tax-Exempt Money Market Fund	1,764
Daily Tax Free	402
Federated Tax Free Instruments	564
Federated Tax-Free Trust	3,214
Fidelity Tax-Exempt Money Market	2,370
Merrill Lynch CMA Tax-Exempt Fund	3,169
Municipal Cash Reserve Management	891
Nuveen Tax-Exempt Money Market Trust	1,372
Provident Municipal Temp. Investments	1,029
T. Rowe Price Tax-Exempt Money Fund	785

[1] As of June 6, 1984.
[2] Interest exempt from Federal Income Tax.

How to Understand Convertible Securities

The term "Convertible Securities" refers to securities that can be exchanged for another type of security, usually the common stock of the company issuing the convertible.

The two basic types of convertible securities are debentures (commonly known as bonds) and preferred stock. These securities have intrinsic value. Bonds represent a debt of the issuing company. Preferred stock represents an ownership interest. Intrinsic value may be enhanced by the convertible feature.

There are other certificates or contracts which are sometimes considered to be convertible securities but which have no intrinsic value based on ownership interest or debt. Their value is derived solely from their ability to be converted into another type of security. To do so requires a payment in addition to the surrender of the security. These are rights, warrants and options. To many investors these securities may offer certain advantages. However, our emphasis here will be on convertible securities—bonds and preferred stock—which have broader application as investment vehicles.

CONVERTIBLE BONDS

Convertible debt securities are almost always issued in the form of debentures. That is, there is no specific collateral pledged by the issuing corporation in the indenture which states the terms under which the security is issued. Rather, the promise to pay interest on stated dates and the principal amount at maturity is backed by the full faith and credit of the corporation. However, even the most sophisticated investors and those in the securities industry commonly refer to this type of security as a convertible bond.

Convertible bonds have been extolled as the ultimate investment medium offering the desirable features of other securities without the normal risks. If this were so, it would not be for long. Demand for such a security would be so great that the price would be driven up to the point where the element of risk would be very evident. Convertible bonds like all other securities have both advantages and disadvantages and the informed investor can measure these against his own objectives.

Here are the three most important characteristics:

Source: Reprinted, with permission, from *Understanding Convertible Securities*, © New York Stock Exchange, Inc., 1982. Further reprinting is prohibited without express written approval of New York Stock Exchange, Inc.

1. Convertible bonds pay interest—which, as a general rule yields more than the dividends on common stock of comparable quality and less than the interest on straight (non-convertible) bonds of equivalent quality and maturity.

   The issuing company's obligation to pay this interest comes before dividends on preferred and common stock.

2. Convertible bonds offer appreciable possibilities linked to the earnings and growth of the company. As the common stock rises in value to reflect this growth, the price of the convertible bond should also increase. Conversely, as the common stock declines in value, so should the convertible bond decline.

3. Convertible bonds enjoy some of the stability and relative safety associated with straight bonds and preferred stock. For each outstanding convertible bond, it is possible to estimate an investment value. This is the price below which the convertible bond is not expected to fall, if interest rates remain constant, even if the common stock price falls to such an extent as to render the convertible feature virtually valueless. Investment value is arrived at by estimating a price that would produce a yield comparable to straight bonds of equivalent quality. Investment value, it should be stressed, is only an estimate and subject to change from many influences such as fluctuating interest rates, economic and business conditions, ratings given by investment advisory services and the general well-being of the issuing company.

These characteristics can perhaps best be understood by examining how convertible bonds come into existence and how they behave in various circumstances.

XYZ COMPANY ISSUES CONVERTIBLE BONDS

Let's assume that the XYZ Company wants to raise more capital to expand its business. Interest rates are high and XYZ does not want to pay 12% or more to borrow money in the conventional bond market. XYZ is also reluctant at this time to issue additional common stock as a means of raising additional capital. This could be due to a number of reasons, one of which might be unwillingness to dilute the equity interest of its present stockholders. For example, if there are presently ten million shares outstanding and an additional million are issued, earnings per share will normally be reduced by ten percent at the moment of issue, and the market price of the common stock probably would fall proportionately unless it could support the higher price earnings ratio. (The dilution problem is not quite the same when additional stock is issued to acquire an interest in or control of another company. The acquired company will presumably have its own earnings to contribute to earnings per share.) The XYZ Company is also mindful of the fact that dividends on stock are paid after federal income taxes, whereas interest on debt securities, like bonds, is a deduction before taxes.

Accordingly, the management of the XYZ Company decides to issue convertible bonds. In conjunction with the underwriting firm, the interest is set at 10% and the bonds are priced at par—an even $1,000 per $1,000 face amount bond. Bond prices are commonly stated as a percentage of par which, in this case, would be 100. It is further stipulated that each $1,000 bond can be converted into 25 shares of XYZ common stock. At the time that the bonds are marketed, the common stocks is trading at $32 per share.

DEFINITION OF TERMS

In any discussion of convertible bonds, various terms, related to the above figures, are widely used. Before proceeding, these should be defined.

Market Price Price at which a convertible bond can be bought or sold at a given point in time. Market price is stated as a percentage of par, usually $1,000. 100 means $1,000, 90 means $900, 110 means $1,100, etc.

Conversion Ratio Number of shares of common stock obtainable through conversion of one bond. In the case of XYZ, conversion ratio is 25.

Conversion Price The reciprocal of conversion ratio or the price of the stock when the number of shares obtainable through conversion of one $1,000 bond equals exactly $1,000. Conversion price is $40 when conversion ratio is 25.

Conversion Value Current value of total shares into which a bond can be converted. Conversion value of XYZ $1,000 bond with conversion ratio of 25 shares is $800 when XYZ common stock is trading at $32 per share.

Conversion Premium Percentage difference between conversion value and market value of bond. When conversion value is $800 and market value is $1,000, conversion premium is 25% since difference between conversion and market values ($1,000 − $800 = $200) is 25% of conversion value ($800). This figure represents the judgment of investors, as expressed in the marketplace, with respect to the worth of the three characteristics of convertible securities discussed above. These were yield, appreciation

potential and relative safety. With some issues, supply and demand is also a factor in the premium.

Investment Value Estimated price, usually set by investment advisory services, at which bond would be selling if it had no convertible feature. Investment value is arrived at by estimating the price at which the convertible bond would have to sell to provide a percentage yield comparable to percentage yield on a non-convertible bond of equivalent quality and maturity. Investment value, like market price, is normally stated as a percentage of $1,000. For the XYZ Bonds, investment value will be assumed to be 75 providing a current yield of 13.33%.

Premium Over Investment Value Percentage difference between estimated investment value and market price of bond. When market price is 100 and investment value is estimated at 75, the difference is 25 which is 33% of 75. Thus, the premium over investment value is 33%. This figure can be considered a measurement of the worth of the conversion privilege as well as an indication of the proportion of the price that is subject to the risks associated with common stock.

To summarize, the position of XYZ Convertible Bonds, and the related stock at the time the bonds are marketed, is as follows:

Market Price of Bond.............100		($1,000)
Yield 10%		
Conversion Ratio.............................25		
Conversion Price $40	$\left(\dfrac{\$1,000}{25}\right)$	
Market Price of Stock...................$32		
Conversion Value............$800	(25 × $32)	
Conversion Premium ...25%	$\left(\dfrac{\$1,000 - \$800}{\$800}\right)$	
Investment Value.........75	($750)	
Premium Over Investment Value 33%	$\left(\dfrac{\$1,000 - \$750}{\$750}\right)$	

Obviously, no owners of the bonds would convert them into the common stock at this time, since they would be exchanging $1,000 for $800. However, it is not necessary to convert a convertible bond into stock in order to enjoy its advantages. Bonds are frequently sold many times before they are finally converted into stock and many investors have actively participated in the convertible bond market without ever exercising the conversion privilege. Let's now explore what could happen to the XYZ Convertible Bonds under various circumstances.

IF THE STOCK GOES UP

If the XYZ Company prospers and is considered to have appreciation potential, the price of the common stock should go up. By the same token, the price of the XYZ Convertible Bond should also rise. Let's assume the stock goes up by 25% to $40 per share. Normally, the bond will also go up but not necessarily at the same rate as the stock. There is a good reason for this. As the bond price increases, it acts more like a stock and less like a bond. Investment value is left further behind. The risk increases. Yield diminishes too. Accordingly, even though the appreciation potential of the stock may not have changed, the other factors (greater risk and lower yield) will tend to hold back the price of the bond. Therefore, a rise in the XYZ stock of 25% from $32 to $40 might be reflected in a rise in the bond of 20% from 100 to 120. The most significant figures are now as follows:

Market Price of Bond.............120	($1,200)	
Current Yield 8.33%	$\left(\dfrac{\$100}{\$1,200}\right)$	
Market Price of Stock....................$40		
Conversion Value $1,000	(25 × $40)	
Conversion Premium..20%	$\left(\dfrac{\$1,200 - \$1,000}{\$1,000}\right)$	
Premium Over Investment Value 60%	$\left(\dfrac{\$1,200 - \$750}{\$750}\right)$	

Conversion is still unrealistic. But bondholders who bought at the offering may want to take profits by selling their bonds to other investors who believe the stock will continue to go up but are not quite certain enough in their belief to buy the stock itself. Let's assume now that XYZ common stock goes up to $60 per share, an increase of 87½% since the bonds were issued. What is likely to happen to the XYZ bonds? The bond price may now rise to the level where virtually all of the bond-like characteristics are lost and, from the standpoint of risk, the bond is interchangeable with the stock. If we assume this is so, the bond's conversion value should be approximately the same as its market value and conversion premium will disappear. The picture would now look like this:

Market Price of Bond.............150	($1,500)	
Current Yield..........6.67%	$\left(\dfrac{\$100}{\$1,500}\right)$	
Market Price of Stock....................$60		
Conversion Value $1,500	(25 × $60)	
Conversion Premium 0	$\left(\dfrac{\$1,500 - \$1,500}{\$1,500}\right)$	
Premium Over Investment Value 100%		

Now the owner of the bond will think very seriously about converting. His decision may depend to some extent on the comparative yields of the bond and the stock. Interest on the bond is $100 per year. If the dividend on the stock is less than $4.00 per share, conversion would result in less income. If, on the other hand, the dividend is $4.20 (a yield of 7%) conversion would result in more current income.

In the meantime, while the stock has been rising from $32 to $60 per share, the company has presumably been using the money received from the sale of the convertible bonds to expand its business and improve its earnings. This should have put it in a better position to absorb the dilution that conversion into common stock entails.

When a convertible bond's conversion value and market price become the same, the stock and the bond should move up and down together within a limited range to maintain this relationship. It is virtually impossible for a convertible bond to sell with a negative conversion premium (below its conversion value) for any length of time. If this should happen, professional traders will quickly move in and employ a device known as arbitrage to make a small but rapid profit. They will buy the bonds and simultaneously sell the stock short. Converting the bonds enables them to replace the stock borrowed for the short sale. If, for example, XYZ convertibles are selling at $1,450 while the conversion value is $1,500, the trader can buy ten bonds for $14,500. By selling short 250 shares, he receives $15,000 for an immediate gross profit of $500. This activity will tend to drive the price of the bond back up to or above conversion value.

IF THE STOCK GOES DOWN

Let us now consider what might happen to the XYZ convertible bonds if the common stock took an opposite course and declined from the price of $32 per share which it was enjoying at the time that the convertible bonds were issued. As the price falls the convertible bond's price will also fall. However, the bond's downside potential is less than that of the stock, since the bond should not decline below its investment value which is the estimated value of the bond when we disregard the conversion feature. We have assumed this to be a price of 75 which is 25% below par. Therefore, while the stock is falling from $32 to an unknown level, the bond should only travel from 100 to 75. This factor serves as a brake on the bond and is the reason why convertible bonds are generally considered to be a more conservative investment than the stock of the same issuing company. In reality, conditions which would cause a stock to decline drastically would probably produce a re-adjustment in the investment value of the convertible bond. Investment value is also subject to adjustment when money rates change.

To see how the convertible bond might be affected by a decline in the common stock of the XYZ Company, let's assume that the market price of the stock sags from its original price of $32 all the way down to $16 per share. It has lost half its value. If we estimated correctly the investment value of the convertible bond, and if other factors are the same, it will be selling in the area of $750. Thus, a drop of 50% in the price of the stock produces a drop of 25% in the price of the bond. The table of values will now be as follows:

Market Price of Bond 75	($750)
Current Yield...........13.33%	$\left(\dfrac{\$100}{\$750}\right)$
Market Price of Stock....................$16	
Conversion Value............$400	(25 × $16)
Conversion Premium ...87½%	$\left(\dfrac{\$750 - \$400}{\$400}\right)$
Premium Over Investment Value 0	

Thus, we have seen in this example that the price of a convertible bond is controlled primarily by the price of the stock into which it is convertible. However, when the stock goes up, the bond's rise should be held back somewhat as risk increases and yield decreases. Conversely, when the stock goes down, the bond's decline is cushioned as yield increases and investment value is approached. This is an oversimplification which disregards other influences but, hopefully, it provides a basic understanding of how convertible bonds behave. Prices, yields

and ratios were chosen in order to illustrate the example and simplify the arithmetic. They are not intended to reflect actual market conditions at any time.

HEDGING

We have seen that convertible bonds offer an investor opportunities to participate in the stock market with somewhat less risk (and less profit potential) than is normally encountered with direct investment in common stocks. This opportunity can be pursued even further by employing hedges. Although extremely complex in practice, the basic principles of hedging are actually quite simple.

Typically, a hedge is established when an investor buys convertible bonds and, at the same time, sells short the stock into which the bond is convertible. If the stock goes up, there should be a profit in the bonds and a loss in the stock. If the stock goes down, there should be a profit in the stock and a loss in the bonds. Obviously, there is no advantage in a hedge unless the profit exceeds the loss and expenses. There is no way to assure a profit but the skillful and judicious use of hedges can greatly reduce the risk of loss and enhance the possibility of profit. An essential feature is the ability to sell stock short without margin when the corresponding convertible security is held.

Convertible hedges are a highly sophisticated investment technique and should not be attempted without a complete understanding of all of their ramifications.

CALLABILITY AND OTHER LIMITATIONS

An important factor to consider with convertible bonds is the call feature. This is the right of the issuing company to redeem the bonds before maturity at a stated price slightly above par. Usually the original purchasers of a bond are given some protection against this privilege of the company through an initial period during which the bond is non-callable. If a bond has been on the market for four years and commands a price of 130, this price may be short lived if the bond can be called at 105 after five years. When a convertible bond issue listed on the New York Stock Exchange is called for redemption some notice is always given in a newspaper of general circulation to permit the holders to exercise their conversion privilege or sell the bond to someone else who may convert it. Holders of record of registered bonds are notified directly. If, for some reason, the bond is not converted before expiration date for conversion, which may be the same or a few days before the redemption date, it is then worth no more nor less than the call price. It is, therefore, most important for holders of convertible bonds to know what the call features are and to be sure that they will receive information about calls when and if they occur. Obviously, the best way to do this is to hold registered bonds.

Most convertible bonds are convertible into stock at a fixed rate during the entire life of the bond. However, this rate may change because of a stock split, stock dividend, merger or other circumstances. The conversion privilege may expire before the bond matures or it may not be effective until some time after the bond is issued. Sometimes the conversion rate declines at regular intervals. A bond that is convertible into 25 shares of common stock when first issued may become convertible into only 20 shares after five years, 15 shares after ten years, etc. Although the typical convertible bond is exchangeable for the common stock of the issuing company, this is also subject to variation. Conversion may be made into a combination of common and preferred stock. Or a bond of one company may be convertible into the stock of a parent company.

All of these possible limitations should be checked by investors when investigating convertible securities. A member firm of the New York Stock Exchange, Inc. can usually supply the essential information.

MARGIN AND COMMISSION

Two other features of convertible bonds have traditionally appealed to investors—margin requirements and commission rates. Although the current margin requirement for the purchase of common stock or convertible bonds is the same—50%, the convertible bond rate has usually been significantly less. In 1973, for instance, an investor with $6,500 available in cash could have bought $10,000 worth of common stock or $13,000 of convertible bonds. (Margin requirements are subject to change by the Federal Reserve Board).

The commission paid to a member firm broker for the purchase or sale of listed stocks is one of the lowest fees paid for the transfer of property of any kind. However, in most cases, the commission paid for the purchase or sale of bonds is even lower on a given dollar investment.

CONVERTIBLE PREFERRED STOCK

Convertible preferred stock possesses many of the basic characteristics of convertible bonds and will normally perform in approximately the same manner when subject to the same conditions and influences. However, there are also basic differences which should be pointed out.

Convertible preferred stock represents an equity interest and is, therefore, junior to all debt securities including convertible bonds and would not—all else being equal—have as high a degree of relative safety as convertible bonds. However, all else is rarely equal and the convertible preferred stock of Company A could have more relative safety than the convertible bonds of Company B. Convertible preferred stocks do not have maturity dates as do bonds but are usually subject to redemption.

Convertible preferreds, like common stock, require 50% margin currently, and are subject to the same commission structure.

FOREIGN SHORT-TERM AND LONG-TERM INTEREST RATES: SELECTED COUNTRIES

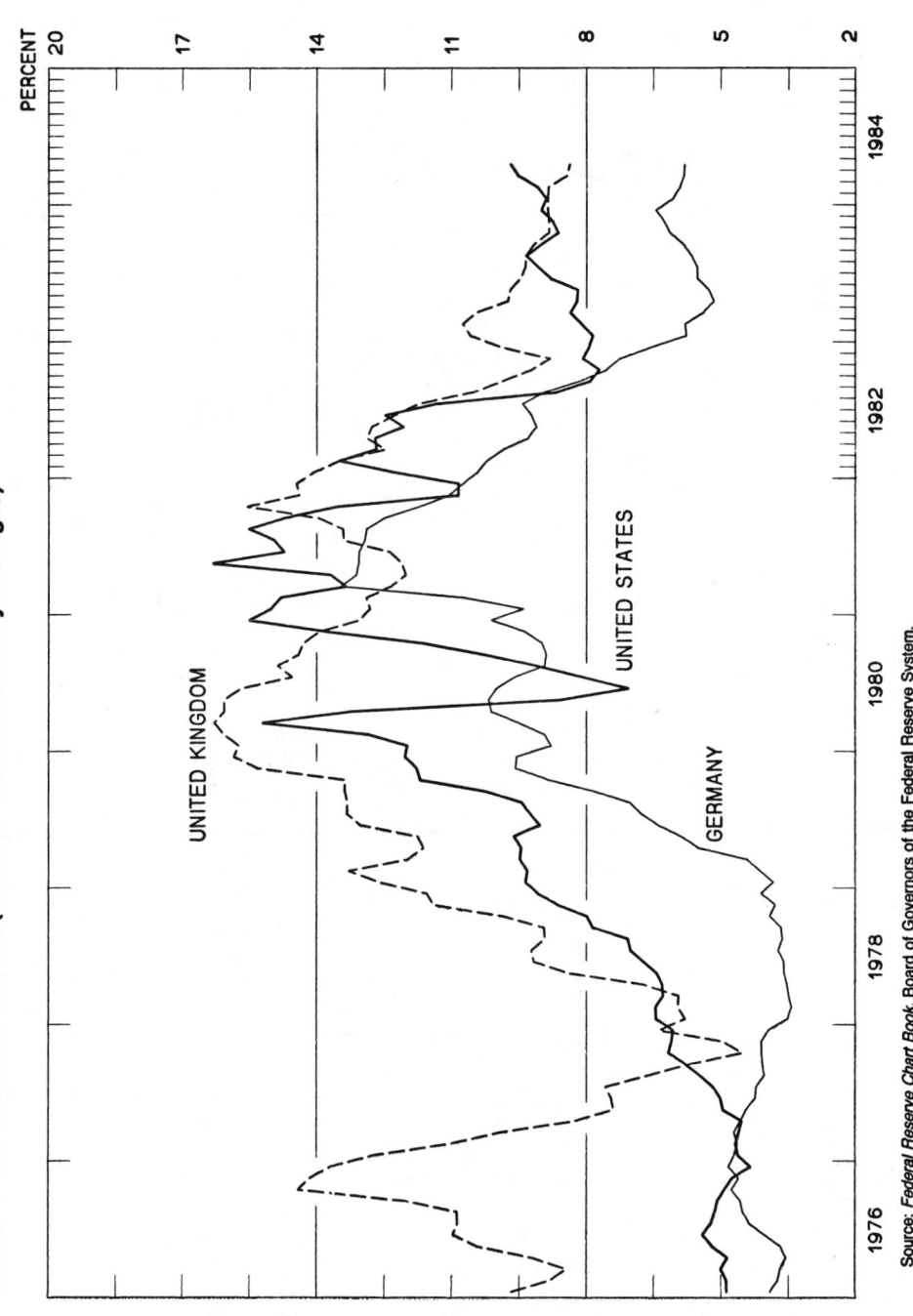

SHORT-TERM INTEREST RATES (selected countries monthly averages)

Source: *Federal Reserve Chart Book*, Board of Governors of the Federal Reserve System.

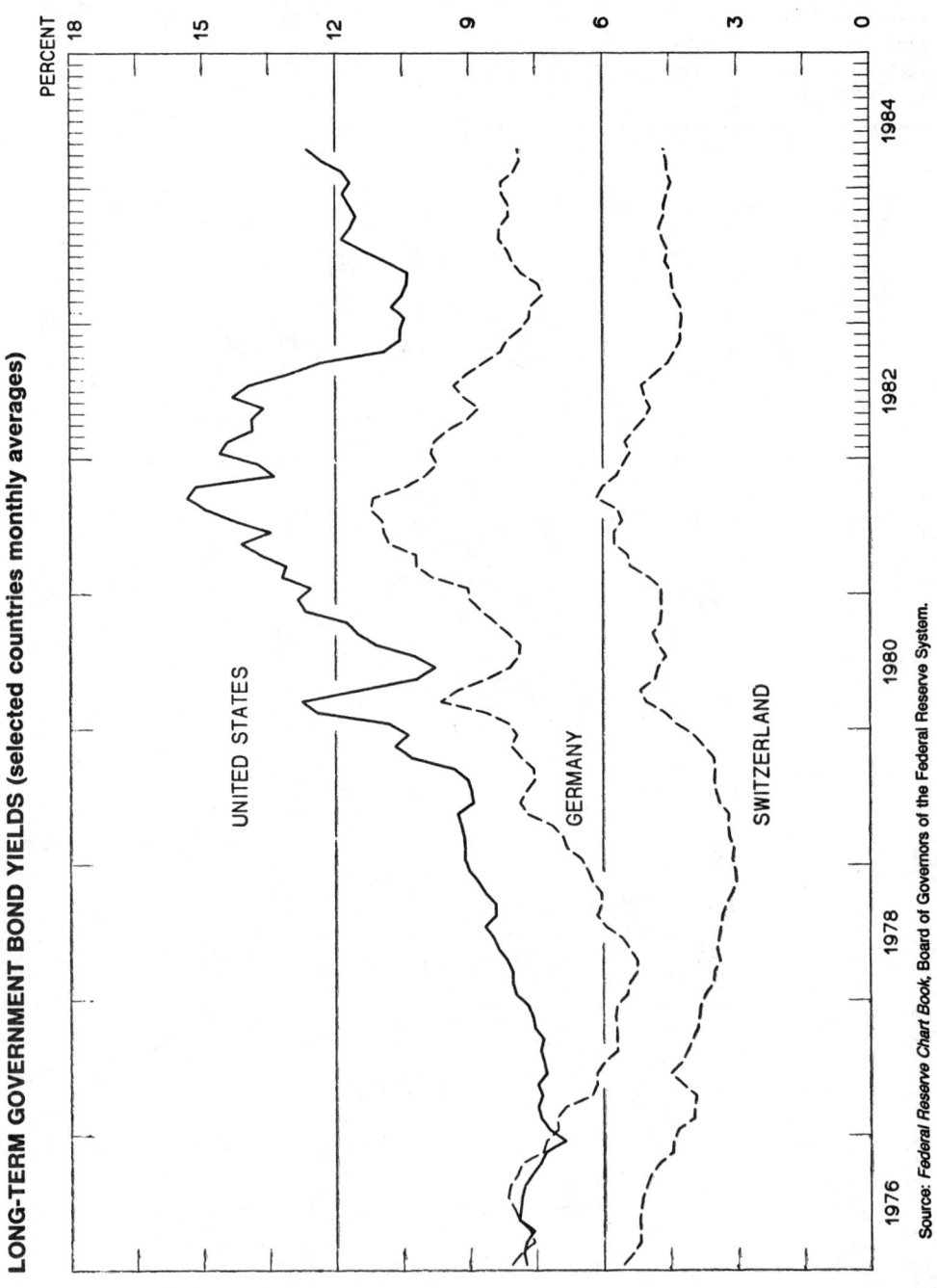

LONG-TERM GOVERNMENT BOND YIELDS (selected countries monthly averages)

PERCENT

UNITED STATES

GERMANY

SWITZERLAND

Source: *Federal Reserve Chart Book*, Board of Governors of the Federal Reserve System.

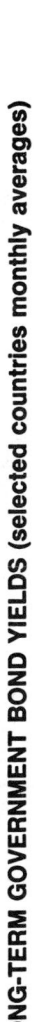

LONG-TERM GOVERNMENT BOND YIELDS (selected countries monthly averages)

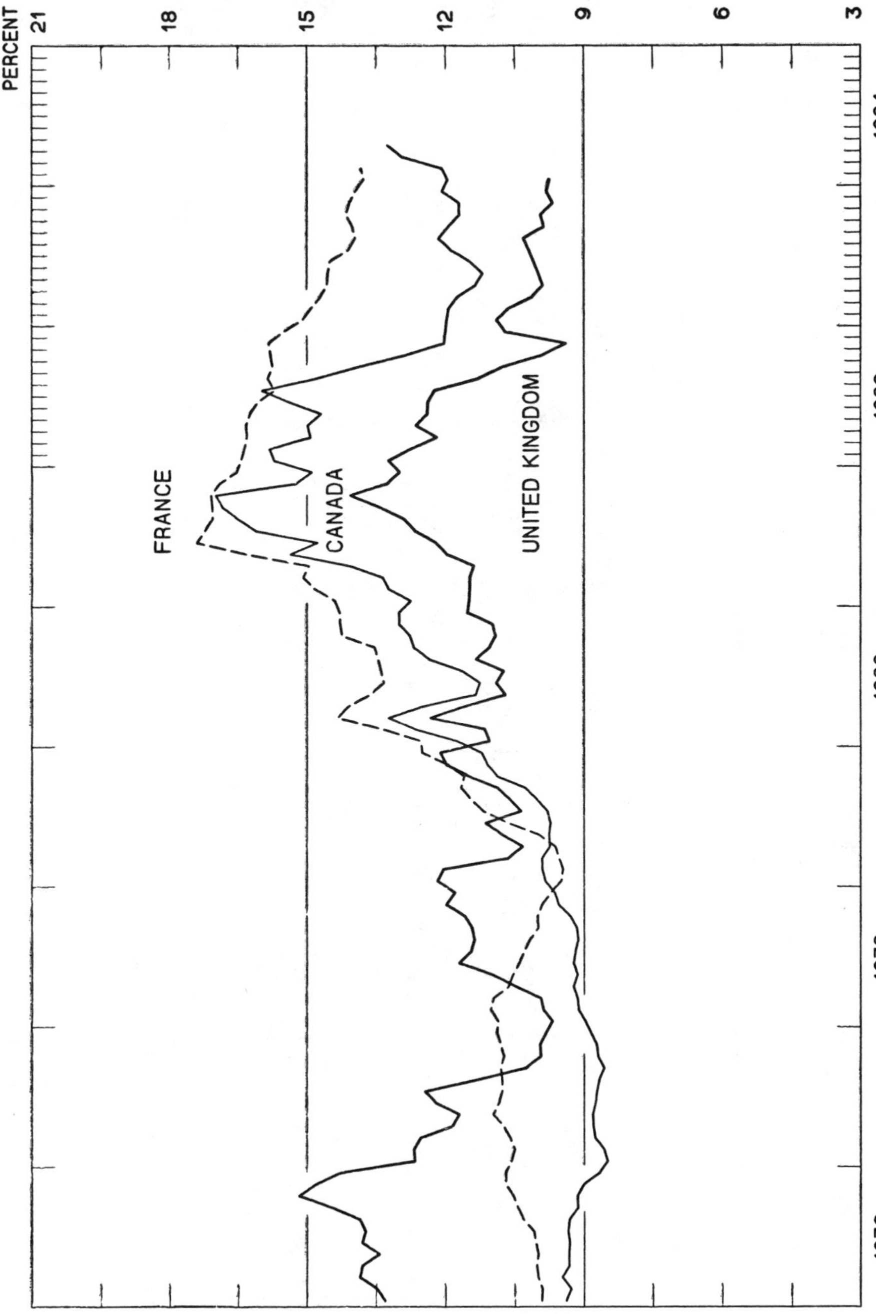
PERCENT
21
18
15
12
9
6
3
FRANCE
CANADA
UNITED KINGDOM
1976
1978
1980
1982
1984

Source: *Federal Reserve Chart Book*, Board of Governors of the Federal Reserve System.

FOREIGN TREASURY BILL RATES (bond-equivalent yields, at or near end of month)

	1980 Dec	1981 Dec	1982 Dec	1983 Nov	1983 Dec	1984 Jan	Feb	Mar	Apr	May	Jun
United States	14.87	11.90	8.15	9.05	9.28	9.20	9.48	10.09	10.02	10.13	10.29
Canada	17.01	14.41	9.80	9.38	9.71	9.73	9.79	10.53	10.59	11.29	12.11
Belgium	12.75	16.00	12.25	10.85	10.85	10.85	12.25	12.25	11.75	11.75	11.75
Ireland	12.84	17.35	14.70	11.66	11.63	11.80	12.16	12.59	12.35	12.10	12.08
Italy	16.87	21.36	19.11	17.05	16.95	15.74	15.81	15.61	15.45	14.99	n.a.
Netherlands	8.00	9.75	5.62	5.63	5.63	5.75	6.12	5.88	5.38	5.63	5.88
Spain	n.a.	n.a.	15.28	14.53	14.46	13.61	13.66	13.20	12.64	12.04	11.17
Sweden	n.a.	n.a.	12.90	12.10	11.75	11.10	11.15	10.80	10.99	11.83	14.20
United Kingdom	13.45	15.31	9.90	9.08	9.08	9.08	9.08	8.59	8.59	9.99	9.08
Australia	12.17	13.27	9.39	9.32	8.54	9.43	10.35	13.11	11.89	11.81	11.24
Japan	5.93	5.42	5.42	4.91	4.91	4.91	4.91	4.91	4.91	4.91	4.91
New Zealand	11.25	11.25	11.25	7.80	7.80	7.80	7.80	7.80	7.80	7.80	7.80
South Africa	6.31	14.55	14.62	17.47	18.43	18.55	18.57	18.57	18.64	18.64	18.44
Brazil	65.87	92.62	115.40	179.15	179.15	179.15	179.15	179.15	179.15	179.15	179.15
Mexico	27.73	33.33	57.44	53.85	53.78	53.02	50.32	46.16	46.63	n.a.	n.a.
Philippines	12.70	13.22	14.54	15.63	15.99	16.27	17.01	17.25	17.61	20.81	n.a.
Singapore	6.77	3.03	2.74	2.62	2.59	2.67	2.65	2.66	2.87	3.00	3.01

Source: *World Financial Markets*, a publication of Morgan Guaranty Trust Company of New York.

FOREIGN MONEY-MARKET RATES (bond-equivalent yields on major short-term (mostly 3–4-month) money-market instruments, other than Treasury bills, at or near end of month)

	1980	1981	1982	1983		1984					
	Dec	Dec	Dec	Nov	Dec	Jan	Feb	Mar	Apr	May	Jun
United States	17.62	12.78	8.81	9.31	9.75	9.36	9.68	10.30	10.50	10.94	11.63
Canada	17.50	15.25	9.95	9.60	9.87	9.85	9.95	10.70	10.75	11.55	12.50
Belgium	13.10	16.00	12.35	10.75	11.00	11.00	12.50	12.35	11.90	11.90	11.90
France	11.56	15.25	12.75	12.31	12.19	12.25	12.54	12.56	12.31	12.25	12.06
Germany	10.20	10.50	6.20	6.25	6.30	6.10	5.85	5.80	5.70	6.25	6.10
Ireland	13.62	18.50	15.75	12.37	12.19	12.25	12.56	13.00	12.88	12.75	12.50
Italy	17.37	21.00	19.00	17.88	17.88	17.88	17.00	17.25	17.25	16.75	16.63
Netherlands	9.37	11.00	5.25	6.31	6.00	5.94	6.00	6.06	5.88	6.13	6.19
Portugal	11.00	13.80	15.04	24.17	24.11	24.06	23.79	23.99	24.04	24.00	25.25
Spain	17.40	15.52	16.55	20.29	18.48	17.30	18.30	16.42	15.07	14.66	13.45
Switzerland	7.50	10.12	3.87	4.25	3.87	3.62	3.75	3.94	3.88	4.25	4.50
United Kingdom	14.75	15.69	10.50	9.25	9.31	9.37	9.21	8.88	8.81	9.75	9.44
Australia	13.00	16.00	10.65	10.60	9.50	11.00	13.00	13.55	14.20	13.55	12.70
Japan	9.80	6.30	6.80	6.42	6.42	6.30	6.40	6.40	6.20	8.35	8.40
New Zealand	14.25	16.05	16.75	12.00	12.10	13.85	15.00	14.75	15.00	17.00	17.00
South Africa	7.12	15.47	15.26	18.19	19.12	19.07	19.01	18.30	19.07	18.00	17.90
Chile	26.79	34.54	71.44	25.34	22.42	19.56	14.03	11.35	18.16	18.16	18.16
Hong Kong	17.69	14.18	10.13	11.50	12.84	11.37	7.87	7.90	9.93	12.38	13.13
Indonesia	12.54	14.48	18.50	15.00	19.50	19.00	20.50	19.50	18.50	19.00	20.00
Korea	16.35	15.69	8.00	8.00	8.00	8.00	8.00	8.00	8.00	8.00	8.00
Malaysia	9.41	9.50	8.50	8.65	9.80	9.47	8.51	8.95	9.10	9.20	9.70
Philippines	14.99	17.70	15.96	17.34	15.61	16.08	17.41	17.14	15.83	26.51	n.a.
Singapore	14.12	7.81	8.69	7.62	8.44	7.75	7.75	8.50	8.63	9.13	9.00
Taiwan	14.49	10.94	9.94	7.26	7.65	9.22	9.42	7.81	7.31	6.15	7.77
Thailand	16.55	14.29	12.25	14.50	16.00	16.50	17.00	15.50	13.50	14.00	13.50

Source: *World Financial Markets*, a publication of Morgan Guaranty Trust Company of New York.

FOREIGN GOVERNMENT BOND YIELDS (long-term issues, at or near end of month)

	1980 Dec	1981 Dec	1982 Dec	1983 Nov	1983 Dec	1984 Jan	Feb	Mar	Apr	May	Jun
United States	11.46	14.33	10.61	11.89	12.00	11.72	12.13	12.49	12.79	13.58	13.75
Canada	12.69	15.27	11.69	11.80	12.02	11.92	12.40	13.06	13.31	13.93	13.81
Austria	9.62	10.37	8.81	8.06	8.02	7.96	7.88	7.88	7.94	7.99	8.06
Belgium	13.04	13.99	12.66	11.75	11.89	11.97	12.35	12.20	12.08	12.19	12.13
Denmark	19.98	20.91	20.14	14.22	12.96	13.39	14.02	14.78	14.27	15.20	15.54
Finland	10.42	10.98	10.64	11.16	11.16	11.17	10.62	11.19	10.80	11.20	11.29
France	14.31	16.44	15.40	14.12	13.96	13.76	13.78	14.05	13.81	13.82	13.99
Germany	9.19	9.71	7.90	8.34	8.38	8.33	8.13	8.18	8.18	8.29	8.25
Ireland	15.63	18.28	14.54	13.72	14.25	13.94	14.16	14.08	14.14	14.49	14.58
Italy	16.23	21.39	19.70	17.78	17.69	16.91	16.34	15.69	15.75	15.75	n.a.
Netherlands	10.48	11.28	8.16	8.57	8.58	8.57	8.56	8.40	8.45	8.52	8.68
Norway	10.44	12.37	13.32	12.50	12.50	12.50	12.25	12.25	12.25	12.00	12.00
Portugal	17.19	17.39	16.63	22.80	22.11	21.19	21.57	21.97	22.37	n.a.	n.a.
Spain	16.15	16.20	15.92	19.50	18.71	18.33	18.68	18.74	18.64	n.a.	n.a.
Sweden	12.61	12.80	13.01	13.05	12.30	11.70	11.50	11.50	11.65	12.60	14.01
Switzerland	4.63	5.40	4.22	4.63	4.54	4.50	4.56	4.37	4.47	4.61	4.69
United Kingdom	13.05	15.02	10.62	9.93	9.94	9.97	10.04	9.89	10.16	10.73	10.81
Australia	13.00	15.00	13.00	13.40	13.65	13.70	14.05	14.00	14.00	14.10	14.00
Japan	9.04	8.32	7.76	7.39	7.19	7.20	7.06	6.74	6.68	7.45	7.46
New Zealand	12.99	12.55	12.84	10.61	10.50	10.84	11.33	10.42	n.a.	n.a.	n.a.
South Africa	11.81	13.33	11.31	13.63	13.64	14.13	13.80	13.78	14.46	14.68	14.72
Philippines	13.20	13.01	13.64	13.76	14.47	14.42	14.61	13.67	18.47	18.45	n.a.
Venezuela	7.39	12.50	15.00	14.00	13.50	13.00	13.00	13.00	13.50	14.00	14.00

Source: *World Financial Markets*, a publication of Morgan Guaranty Trust Company of New York.

FOREIGN CORPORATE BOND YIELDS (long-term issues, at or near end of month)

	1980 Dec	1981 Dec	1982 Dec	1983 Nov	1983 Dec	1984 Jan	Feb	Mar	Apr	May	Jun
United States	13.00	15.50	11.75	12.38	12.63	12.38	12.88	13.25	13.88	13.58	14.50
Canada	13.53	16.18	12.74	12.58	12.89	12.78	13.27	13.84	14.13	14.59	14.69
France	15.23	17.33	15.91	14.30	14.06	13.96	14.28	14.37	14.23	13.88	13.77
Germany	9.50	10.50	8.20	8.30	8.30	8.30	8.00	8.00	8.00	8.00	8.00
Netherlands	10.71	11.03	7.80	8.53	8.51	8.44	8.39	8.26	8.28	8.35	8.43
Norway	11.24	13.36	14.13	13.25	13.25	13.25	13.00	13.00	13.00	12.75	12.75
Spain	14.82	14.76	17.10	20.03	19.84	20.19	20.69	21.90	22.54	22.06	21.63
Sweden	11.95	12.94	13.37	12.51	12.21	12.15	11.96	11.84	12.04	12.23	14.03
Switzerland	n.a.	n.a.	4.87	4.94	4.94	4.93	4.91	4.85	4.91	5.10	5.07
United Kingdom	14.21	16.65	12.34	11.51	11.57	11.52	11.61	11.29	11.48	12.11	12.69
Australia	14.25	16.50	15.00	15.00	13.50	14.00	14.50	14.50	n.a.	n.a.	n.a.
Japan	8.60	7.70	7.55	7.27	7.09	7.05	7.04	6.92	6.89	7.16	7.13
Korea	28.20	26.90	15.90	14.20	14.20	14.30	14.00	13.60	13.00	13.20	n.a.
Venezuela	16.15	17.00	18.00	18.00	18.00	18.00	17.50	17.50	17.50	18.00	18.00

Source: *World Financial Markets*, a publication of Morgan Guaranty Trust Company of New York.

Composition of Dow Jones Bond Averages

10 PUBLIC UTILITIES

Alabama Pwr 9¾s,2004
Amer T&T 8.8s,2005
Comwlth Edis 8¾s, 2005
Cons Ed 7.9s, 2001
Cons Pwr 9¾s, 2006

Detroit Edison 9s, '99
New York Tel 4½s, '91
Pac G&E 7¾s, 2005
Phil Elec 7⅜s, 2001
Pub Svc Ind 9.6s, 2005

10 INDUSTRIALS

BankAm 7⅞s, 2003
Beth Steel 6⅞s, '99
Dow Chem 4.35s, '88
Exxon 6s, '97
Ford Mtr 8⅛s, '90

Gen Mtrs Accept 4½s, '85
NCR 4⅜s, '87
Pfizer 9⅛s, 2000
Socony 4⅛s, '93
Weyerhaeuser 5.20s, '91

Components of U.S. Government Bond Avg.

13⅛'s, 1984 July
4¼'s, 1975-85 May
6⅛'s, 1986 Nov.
14½'s, 1989 July
3½'s, 1990 Feb.

4¼'s, 1987-92 Aug.
6¾'s, 1993 Feb.
4⅛'s, 1989-94 May
7's, 1993-98 May
7⅞'s, 1995-00 Feb.

Source: Reprinted by courtesy of *Barron's National Business and Financial Weekly.*

Components Confidence Index

BEST GRADE BONDS

Amer Tel & Tel 3⅞s, '90
Atchison Topeka & Santa Fe, 4s '95
Chesapeake & Ohio, 4½s, '92
Consumers Pwr 1st 5⅞s, '96
Exxon 6s, '97
Gen El 8½s, 2004
Illinois Bell Telephone, 8s, '04
Norfolk & Western, 4s, '96
Union Pacific, 2½s, '91
US Steel, 4½s, '86

INTERMEDIATE GRADE BONDS

Alabama Power 9¾s, 2004
Bethlehem Steel 6⅞s, '99
Detroit Edison 9s, '99
Ford Motor 8⅛s, '90
Louisville Nash 7⅜s, '93
Missouri Pac 4¼s, 2005
Pacific G&E 7¾s, 2005
Pfizer 9¼s, 2000
Philadelphia El 7⅜s, 2001
St. Louis San Fr 4s, '97

Federal Reserve Banks

Federal Reserve Bank of

BOSTON — 600 Atlantic Avenue, Boston, Massachusetts 02106—(617) 973-3462

NEW YORK — 33 Liberty Street (Federal Reserve P.O. Station). New York, New York 10045—(212) 791-5823 (Telephone 24 hours a day, including Saturday & Sunday)

Buffalo Branch — 160 Delaware Avenue (P.O. Box 961), Buffalo, New York 14240—(716) 849-5046

PHILADELPHIA — 100 North Sixth Street (P.O. Box 90), Philadelphia, Pennsylvania 19105—(215) 574-6580

CLEVELAND — 1455 East Sixth Street (P.O. Box 6387), Cleveland, Ohio 44101—(216) 241-2800

Cincinnati Branch — 150 East Fourth Street (P.O. Box 999), Cincinnati, Ohio 45201—(513) 721-4787 ext 333

Pittsburgh Branch — 717 Grant Street (P.O. Box 867), Pittsburgh, Pennsylvania 15230—(412) 261-7864

RICHMOND — 701 East Byrd Street (P.O. Box 27622), Richmond, Virginia 23261—(804) 643-1250

Baltimore Branch — 114-120 East Lexington Street (P.O. Box 1378), Baltimore, Maryland 21203—(301) 539-6552

Charlotte Branch — 401 South Tryon Street (P.O. Box 300), Charlotte, North Carolina 28230—(704) 373-0200

ATLANTA — 104 Marietta Street, N.W., (P.O. Box 1731) Atlanta, Georgia 30301—(404) 586-8657

Birmingham Branch — 1801 Fifth Avenue, North (P.O. Box 10447), Birmingham, Alabama 35202—(205) 252-3141 ext. 215

Jacksonville Branch — 515 Julia Street, Jacksonville, Florida 32231—(904) 632-4245

Miami Branch — 9100 N.W. Thirty-sixth Street Extension, Miami, Florida 33178 (P.O. Box 520847, Miami, Florida 33152)—(305) 591-2065

Nashville Branch — 301 Eighth Avenue, North, Nashville, Tennessee 37203—(615) 259-4006

New Orleans Branch — 525 St. Charles Avenue (P.O. Box 61630), New Orleans, Louisiana 70161 (504) 586-1505 ext. 230, 240, 242

CHICAGO	230 South LaSalle Street (P.O. Box 834), Chicago, Illinois 60690—(312) 786–1110 (Telephone 24 hours a day, including Saturday & Sunday)
Detroit Branch	160 Fort Street, West (P.O. Box 1059), Detroit, Michigan 48231—(313) 961–6880 ext. 372, 373
ST. LOUIS	411 Locust Street (P.O. Box 442), St. Louis, Missouri 63166—(314) 444–8444
Little Rock Branch	325 West Capitol Avenue (P.O. Box 1261), Little Rock, Arkansas 72203—(501) 372–5451 ext. 270
Louisville Branch	410 South Fifth Street (P.O. Box 32710), Louisville, Kentucky 40232 (502) 587–7351 ext. 237, 301
Memphis Branch	200 North Main Street (P.O. Box 407), Memphis, Tennessee 38101—(800) 238–5293 ext. 225
MINNEAPOLIS	250 Marquette Avenue, Minneapolis, Minnesota 55480—(612) 340–2051
Helena Branch	400 North Park Avenue, Helena, Montana 59601—(406) 442–3860
KANSAS CITY	925 Grand Avenue (Federal Reserve Station), Kansas City, Missouri 64198—(816) 881–2783
Denver Branch	1020 16th Street (P.O. Box 5228, Terminal Annex), Denver, Colorado 80217 (303) 292–4020
Oklahoma City Branch	226 Northwest Third Street (P.O. Box 25129), Oklahoma City, Oklahoma 73125 (405) 235–1721 ext. 182
Omaha Branch	102 South Seventeenth Street, Omaha, Nebraska 68102—(402) 341–3610 ext. 242
DALLAS	400 South Akard Street (Station K), Dallas, Texas 75222—(214) 651–6177
El Paso Branch	301 East Main Street (P.O. Box 100), El Paso, Texas 79999—(915) 544–4730 ext. 57
Houston Branch	1701 San Jacinto Street (P.O. Box 2578), Houston, Texas 77001—(713) 659–4433 ext 19, 74, 75, 76
San Antonio Branch	126 East Nueva Street (P.O. Box 1471), San Antonio, Texas 78295—(512) 224–2141 ext 61, 66
SAN FRANCISCO	400 Sansome Street (P.O. Box 7702), San Francisco, California 94120—(415) 392–6639
Los Angeles Branch	409 West Olympic Boulevard (P.O. Box 2077, Terminal Annex), Los Angeles, California 90051 (213) 683–8563
Portland Branch	915 S.W. Stark Street (P.O. Box 3436), Portland, Oregon 97208—(503) 228–7584
Salt Lake City Branch	120 South State Street (P.O. Box 30780), Salt Lake City, Utah 84130—(801) 355–3131
Seattle Branch	1015 Second Avenue (P.O. Box 3567), Seattle, Washington 98124—(206) 442–1650
TREASURY	**General information concerning Treasury Securities and requests for forms:**

TREASURY

General information concerning Treasury Securities and requests for forms:
Bureau of the Public Debt, Dept. F
Washington, D.C. 20226
Telephone: (202) 287-4113

Specific questions concerning Bills:
Bureau of the Public Debt, Dept. X
Washington, D.C. 20226
Telephone: (202) 287-4113

Specific questions concerning registered Notes or Bonds:
Bureau of the Public Debt, Dept A
Washington, D.C. 20226
Telephone: (202) 287-4113

BANK FAILURES (1983)

Name and location	Date of deposit payout or assumption
1. The Madison County Bank, Fredericktown, Missouri	January 21, 1983
2. State Bank of Barnum, Barnum, Minnesota	February 9, 1983
3. Dry Dock Savings Bank, New York, New York	February 9, 1983
4. American State Bank, Bradley, Illinois	February 12, 1983
5. United American Bank in Knoxville, Knoxville, Tennessee	February 14, 1983
6. Merchants and Farmers State Bank, Blythe, California	February 18, 1983
7. American City Bank, Los Angeles, California	February 25, 1983
8. Newport Harbour National Bank, Newport Beach, California	March 11, 1983
9. Columbia Pacific Bank and Trust Company, Portland, Oregon	March 18, 1983
10. Pan American National Bank, Union City, New Jersey	March 18, 1983
11. Prairie County Bank, Hazen, Arkansas	March 24, 1983
12. Bear Creek Valley Bank, Phoenix, Oregon	March 25, 1983
13. The Ina State Bank, Ina, Illinois	April 8, 1983
14. Bank of San Marino, San Marino, California	April 8, 1983
15. Sparta-Sanders State Bank, Sparta, Kentucky	April 15, 1983
16. Heritage Bank, Ashland, Oregon	April 29, 1983
17. First National Bank of Oak Lawn, Oak Lawn, Illinois	April 29, 1983
18. Smith County Bank, Carthage, Tennessee	May 6, 1983
19. City and County Bank of Knox County, Knoxville, Tennessee	May 27, 1983
20. United Southern Bank of Nashville, Nashville, Tennessee	May 27, 1983
21. United American Bank in Hamilton County, Chattanooga, Tennessee	May 27, 1983
22. City and County Bank of Roane County, Kingston, Tennessee	May 27, 1983
23. City and County Bank of Anderson County, Lake City, Tennessee	May 27, 1983
24. The Commercial Bank of California, Los Angeles, California	May 27, 1983
25. Community Bank, Hartford, South Dakota	June 17, 1983
26. Western National Bank of Lovell, Lovell, Wyoming	June 24, 1983
27. Mineral Bank of Nevada, Las Vegas, Nevada	June 30, 1983
28. Union National Bank of Chicago, Chicago, Illinois	July 8, 1983
29. The First Central Bank, Smithville, Tennessee	July 8, 1983
30. Bank of Niobrara, Niobrara, Nebraska	July 8, 1983
31. First Peoples Bank of Washington County, Johnson City, Tennessee	July 29, 1983
32. Metro Bank, Midland, Texas	July 29, 1983
33. Oregon Mutual Savings Bank, Portland, Oregon	August 5, 1983
34. The First National Bank of Danvers, Danvers, Illinois	August 5, 1983
35. First Commerce Bank of Hawkins County, Rogersville, Tennessee	August 12, 1983
36. United Southern Bank of Clarksville, Clarksville, Tennessee	August 26, 1983
37. The Douglass State Bank, Kansas City, Kansas	September 2, 1983
38. Warren County Bank, McMinnville, Tennessee	September 16, 1983
39. Dominion Bank of Denver, Denver, Colorado	September 30, 1983
40. National Bank of Odessa, Odessa, Texas	September 30, 1983
41. Auburn Savings Bank, Auburn, New York	October 1, 1983
42. The Deschutes Bank, Redmond, Oregon	October 7, 1983
43. The First National Bank of Midland, Midland, Texas	October 14, 1983
44. First National Bank of Browning, Browning, Montana	November 10, 1983
45. Atkinson Trust and Savings Bank, Atkinson, Illinois	November 25, 1983
46. Union Trust Company, San Juan, Puerto Rico	December 9, 1983
47. Bank of Hackleburg, Hackleburg, Alabama	December 13, 1983
48. The Bank of Red Oak, Red Oak, Oklahoma	December 16, 1983

Source: *1983 Annual Report*, Federal Deposit Insurance Corporation.

Options and Futures

What Are Stock Options?

There are two types of stock options—call and put. A call option is the right to buy a specified number of shares of a stock at a given price before a specific date. A put option is the right to sell a specific number of shares of a stock at a given price before a specific date. Options, unlike a futures contract, are a right *not an obligation* to buy or sell stock. The price at which the stock may be bought or sold is referred to as the exercise (or striking) price. The date at which the option expires is the *expiration* date. The term "in-the-money" option refers to either a call option with an exercise price less than that of the market price of the stock, or a put option with an exercise price above the market price of the stock.

Expiration months are set at intervals of three months for the cycles: the January–April–July–October cycle, February–May–August–November cycle, and the March–June–September–December cycle. Options expire at 11:59 P.M. Eastern Standard Time on the Saturday immediately following the third Friday of the expiration month.

The exercise prices are set at 5 point (dollar) intervals for stocks trading below $50, 10 point intervals for stocks trading between $50 to $200, and 20 point intervals for securities trading above $200. Initial exercise prices are set above and below the price of the security. Thus, if a security is priced at 32½ on the New York Stock Exchange at the time new options are opened, the opening exercise prices would be set at 30 and 40. If the price of the security is close to a standard exercise price, three prices are set: at the standard price, as well as above and below the latter.

Standard option contracts are written for 100 shares of stock of the underlying security. The price at which the seller (writer) agrees to sell an option to the buyer is called the *premium*. The premium is quoted *per share* of the underlying stock so that the price per contract is 100 times the quote.

After the option is issued, the premium will fluctuate with the price of the stocks. With call options the premium will increase with an increase in the price of stock. With put options the premium will increase when the stock price declines. The reason should be clear from the following examples. Assume that in January a

July call option is written at the exercise price of 50 ($50 per share) on the XYZ Corporation stock. We assume that the stock is selling at $51. The call option writer (seller) asks and receives a premium of $2 ($200 per option contract). After brokerage commission on the sale (say $25 per contract) the option writer nets a profit of $175 per contract. The call option buyer pays $200 for the contract plus the commission or $225. Assume that the stock increases to 60 per share. The option holder (buyer) can, in principle, purchase the stock at 50 (the Exercise price) and sell it at 60 netting a profit on transaction of $10 per share (neglecting commissions). Clearly the call option has acquired increased value which will be reflected in the premium (option price). Let us assume that the premium increases from 2 to 10 ($200 to $1,000 per contract). If the option holder now sells the option, he will make a profit (after commissions) of $750 on a $250 investment ($200 premium and $50 commission).

Alternatively, the option holder may elect to exercise the option and acquire the shares at 50 (the exercise price). The option writer must then deliver 100 shares of XYZ Corporation at $50 per share.

If the stock price drops below the exercise price and remains so until expiration of the option, the call option buyer can lose his entire investment. Sometimes the loss may be reduced if the option is sold before it matures. The holder then is said to have *closed out* his position.

Similar arguments apply to put options. In this case the option holder benefits if the price of the stock decreases below the exercise price. Assume that the above stock drops to 40. The put holder could, in principle, buy the stock at 40 and sell it at 50 (the exercise price) to the put writer. The put holder would make a profit of $10 per share (neglecting commissions). The put premium would reflect this situation and, as a result, increase.

Instead of selling the option and taking a profit, the put holder may elect to exercise the option and sell 100 shares to the put writer who must purchase these shares at the 50 exercise price.

If the market price of the stock is greater than the exercise price when the put option expires, the holder will lose his investment.

Options are traded on the Chicago Board of Options Exchange, the American Stock Exchange, the Pacific Stock Exchange and the Philadelphia Stock Exchange.

How to Read Option Quotations

(1) Option & NY Close	(2) Strike Price	(3) Calls—Last			(4) Puts—Last		
		Aug	Nov	Feb	Aug	Nov	Feb
Slb							
94¾	100	2½	7	9½	5⅞	7¾	a
94¾	110	⅝	3⅜	5½	a	16	a
94¾	120	⅛	1⅛	b	a	a	b
94¾	130	¹⁄₁₆	b	b	a	b	b
Skylin	15	3⅜	4	a	a	⅝	a
17⅝	20	⅝	1¹¹⁄₁₆	2¼	a	a	a
Southn	10	a	2⅜	2⁷⁄₁₆	b	b	b

Source: Reprinted by permission of *The Wall Street Journal* © Dow Jones and Company, Inc., 1981. All rights reserved.

(1) The name of the company in abbreviated form. Below the company name is the New York or American Exchange closing price of the stock in terms of ⅛ of a dollar.

(2) The striking (exercise) price of the option.

(3) The expiration month of the call option, beneath which is the option's premium (price) per share of stock. Contracts are for 100 shares of stock so that, for example, the price of a contract quoted as 2⅛ ($2.125 per share) is $212.50. Options expire on the Saturday following the third Friday of the expiration month. The premium does not include commissions.

(4) The same as item 3, but for a put option. The letter *a* means the option was not traded that day, and *b* means the option is not offered.

Stock Market Futures*

Standard & Poor's 500 Stock Index futures† combine the unique aspects of the futures market with the opportunities of stock ownership and stock options by helping many investors manage their inherent stock market risks, and at the same time allowing others to participate in broad market moves. S&P 500 Index futures can play an important role in an individual's or institution's overall market strategy.

Stock ownership is subject to several risks. Lower earnings reports or changes in industry fundamentals can cause severe declines in individual issues. Or, a promising industry or company might drop because the entire market is heading down. A myriad of decisions go into individual stock selection—but the first question is usually what is the state and direction of the entire market.

The introduction of the Standard & Poor's 500 Stock Index contract allows investors to hedge, and therefore, virtually eliminate their portfolio exposure in a declining market without disturbing their holdings. At the same time, others can purchase or sell the contract according to their expectations of future market activity. This simultaneous ability to hedge the risks of stock ownership and to take advantage of broad market moves creates opportunities for everyone with positions in or opinions about the stock market.

A NEW MARKET FOR TODAY'S INVESTOR

S&P 500 Index futures are traded on the Index and Option Market division of the Chicago Mercantile Exchange. One of the largest commodity exchanges in the world, the CME introduced financial futures trading in 1972 when it formed the International Monetary Market to trade contracts in foreign currencies. Later, the IMM added futures contracts in Gold, 90-Day Treasury Bills, Three-Month Domestic Certificates of Deposit, and Three-Month Eurodollar Time Deposits.

THE S&P 500 INDEX

The Standard & Poor's Stock Price Index has been the standard by which professional portfolio managers and individuals have measured their performance for 65 years. Begun in 1917 as an index based on 200 stocks, the list was expanded to 500 issues in 1957.

Currently, the Index is one of the U.S. Commerce Department's 12 leading economic indicators.

The S&P 500 Index is made up of 400 industrial, 40 public utilities, 20 transportation, and 40 financial companies and represents approximately 80% of the value of all issues traded on the New York Stock Exchange.

The S&P 500 Index is calculated by giving more "weight" to companies with more stock issued and outstanding in the market. Basically, each stock's price is multiplied by its number of shares outstanding. This assures that each

---

* Although every attempt has been made to ensure the accuracy of the information in this section, the Chicago Mercantile Exchange assumes no responsibility for any errors or omissions. All matters pertaining to rules and specifications herein are made subject to and are superseded by official Exchange rules.

† Editor's Note: Futures based on the Value Line (Kansas City Exchange) and the New York Stock Exchange (New York Futures Exchange) indices are also traded. The principles are the same as with the S&P 500 futures.

Source: *Opportunities in Stock Futures*, Index and Option Market, Chicago Mercantile Exchange, 444 West Jackson Street, Chicago, IL 60606.

stock influences the Index with the same importance that it carries in the actual stock market.

The Index is calculated by multiplying the shares outstanding of each of the 500 stocks by its market price. These amounts are then totaled and compared to a 1941–43 base period.

Calculations are performed continually while the market is open for each of the 500 stocks in the Index. The resulting Index is available minute-by-minute via quote machines throughout the world.

WHAT IS FUTURES TRADING?

The practice of buying or selling goods at prices agreed upon today, but with actual delivery made in the future, dates back to the 12th century. In the United States, organized futures exchanges were active as early as the 1840s. Today, the markets offer futures in grains, meats, lumber, metals, poultry products, currencies and interest-bearing securities.

The ability to contract today at a fixed price for future delivery performs two vital economic functions: risk transfer and price discovery.

For example, suppose a producer of cattle sees that someone is willing to buy his animals for delivery six months hence at a price that insures him an adequate profit. He decides to sell his production, with delivery after the animal matures, at the contracted price. In the process, he has locked in a price that is satisfactory to him and has insulated himself against the risk that the price may fall. In other words, he has transferred the risk of lower prices to someone else. Conversely, the purchaser of his animals has locked in his price and is assured that he will not have to pay a higher price in the future. This transaction could take place directly between the two men, or could be accomplished through futures trading at the CME—without the need for buyer and seller to actually meet. The open public trading system at the CME makes it easy to discover what the market currently considers to be a fair price for future delivery.

If the sale takes place on the Chicago Mercantile Exchange, the Exchange guarantees that both parties adhere to their agreement by placing itself and its resources between them. The Exchange thus becomes the buyer and the seller of the contract. This assures both parties that the contract will be carried out because the Exchange stands behind both parts of the agreement.

When delivery day arrives, the product is delivered to designated delivery points and inspected to make sure it is of the quality stipulated by the contract. The seller receives payment at the agreed price and buyer receives the produce.

Since full payment does not occur until the delivery day, the performance of both parties to the contract requires a good faith deposit or performance bond—known as the margin—when the contract is entered. Margins usually amount to a small percentage of the contract's total face value.

This payment differs from margin for stock purchases in that it is not a partial payment. It serves as a guarantee for both buyer and seller that there are sufficient funds on either side to cover adverse price movements that might otherwise bring the ability to meet contract terms into question.

At the close of business each day, each futures position is revalued at the contract's current closing price. This price is compared to the previous day's close (or if an initial position, the purchase or sale price) and the net gain or loss is calculated. Gains and losses are taken or made from the margin account each day in cash. There are no paper gains or losses in futures trading. If a margin account falls below a specified level, futures traders are required to deposit more money to maintain their positions.

All futures market participants should understand the operation of futures markets and consult with a Registered Commodity Representative before opening a futures trading account.

The S&P 500 Index futures contract is quoted in terms of the actual Index, but carries a face value of 500 times the Index. The contract does not move point-for-point with the actual Index, but it says close enough to act as an effective proxy for the Index, and by extension, for the stock market as a whole.

If, for example, the futures price is quoted at 108.75, then the face value of the contract would be $54,375 (500 × 108.75). Minimum futures price increments, or movements, are .05 of the Index or $25. So if the futures quote is at 108.75, trades can continue to take place at that level, or move to 108.80 or to 108.70, with each .05 move equal to $25.

Trading opens at 9:00 A.M. and closes at 3:15 P.M. (Chicago time) with contracts trading for settlement in March, June, September and December. The final settlement day is the third Thursday of the contract month. At the close of business on that day all open positions have one final mark-to-market calculation—only on this day the expiration of the contract is marked to the actual closing level of the S&P 500 Index itself. Unlike traditional commodities, there is no physical delivery of the underlying commodity or resulting payment for the commodity in S&P 500 futures.

It is this unique cash settlement feature of the S&P 500 futures contract that eliminates the prohibitively expensive costs of delivering 500 individual issues in varying amounts. Since there are little or no delivery costs, investors are assured that there will be no institutional factors to influence the futures contract's price. Thus, the price of the futures contract will reflect the current expectations about the direction of future stock prices. The International Monetary Market division of the CME pioneered this innovative concept in 1981, when its Eurodollar Time Deposit contract became the first cash settlement futures contract ever traded.

The S&P 500 futures contract should be viewed as a complement to equity ownership, not a substitute for it. Among the many benefits of S&P futures is the hedging ability that holders of stock can employ to provide an effective, cost efficient means of protecting security holdings against temporary market declines rather than selling and disturbing stock holdings. In addition, investors find the futures market equally as liquid for both buyers and sellers. Unlike the stock exchanges, short sellers do not require an up-tic before a trade can take place and there are no additional margin requirements.

SITUATIONS & STRATEGIES

Outright positions, either long or short, spreading and hedging are all uses for S&P futures. The contract also offers an unusually large number of hedging strategies when combined with equity portfolios and options. The following examples will show some of these uses in more detail.

LONG POSITION

Situation: An individual sees that interest rates are declining, the economy is firming and believes the entire market is undervalued. He notes that the S&P 500 futures contract for September delivery is at 108.85 and the actual S&P 500 Index is at 108.70.

It is apparent that most futures market participants also believe a move up is imminent. As supply and demand factors are balanced in an open marketplace, the intrinsic value of the September contract is established. The market is willing to pay a slight premium (.15) for the futures contract over the actual Index.

He calls his Registered Commodity Representative, enters an order to buy one September S&P 500 futures contract at the market and makes a good faith deposit to his account to guarantee his ability to meet his contractual commitment. For purposes of the following example, a margin account balance of $5,000 will be used. Margin requirements for actual positions vary. Individuals should contact their Registered Commodity Representatives for current information.

Day	Position	Cost	S&P Future Closing Price	Gain or (Loss) Points X $5 (.01 equals 1 point)		Account Balance	Cumulative Gain or (Loss)
1	Long one contract	108.85	108.90	.05	$ 25	$5.025	$ 25
2	same	108.85	108.60	(.30)	(150)	4.875	(125)
3	same	108.85	108.40	(.20)	(100)	4.775	(225)
4	same	108.85	107.00	(1.40)	(700)	4.075	(925)
5	same	108.85	108.00	1.00	500	4.575	(425)
6	same	108.85	108.70	.70	350	4.925	(75)
7	same	108.85	109.50	.80	400	5.325	325
Sub Total Period one		108.85	109.50	.65	$325	$5.325	$325

Period one: Our investor was a little off on his timing and his margin account was debited each day that losses occurred. If his margin balance had fallen to the maintenance minimum ($2.000 per contract) in this example he would have been required to make an additional payment to bring his balance back to the initial margin level ($5.000). As it is, he ended the period with a credit of $325 in cash.

Period two: With minor backing and filling, the trend is up and the S&P futures price closes period two at a level of 115.65.

	Position	Cost	S&P Future Closing Price	Gain or (Loss) Points X $5 (.01 equals 1 point)		Account Balance	Cumulative Gain or (Loss)
Sub Total Period Two:	Long one contract	108.85	115.65	6.80	$3.400	$8.400	$3.400

Observations: During the first two weeks our investor's judgment of the market was correct and the S&P futures price advanced 680 index points or 6.25%. This translated into a gain of $3.400 on his initial investment of $5.000, or a gain of 68%.

At this point our investor believes that the market is due for a correction and decides to lock in his profit. He calls his RCR and instructs him to "cover" his September long position. His broker will then enter a sell order. After the close of business, the Exchange Clearing House will match the investor's previous long position and his new short position for a net zero position. All margins will be returned with cash credited to the investor's account with his broker the next day. Brokerage commissions have not been included in this example, but they are usually extremely reasonable and generally are quoted to include *both* the purchase and sale of the contract.

SHORT POSITION

If, instead of a rising market our investor believed that tight money would increase interest rates and the economy was weakening, he might have concluded that the S&P 500 Index

pany's own growth, the expectation is that the growth will be reflected in higher share prices. However carefully constructed and diversified a portfolio may be, it is still subject in varying degrees to the risk that the market will decline. In order to protect principal values in a declin-

Day	Position	Cost	S&P Future Closing Price	Gain or (Loss) Points X $5 (.01 equals 1 point)		Account Balance	Cumulative Gain or (Loss)
1	Short one contract	108.85	110.05	(1.20)	$ 600	$4,400	($ 600)
2	same	108.85	112.50	(2.45)	(1,225)	3,175	(1,825)
3	same	108.85	112.00	(.50)	(250)	3,425	(1,575)
4	same	108.85	109.50	(2.50)	(1,250)	4,675	(325)
5	same	108.85	108.75	.75	375	5,050	50
6	same	108.85	107.40	1.35	675	5,725	725
7	same	108.85	107.05	.35	175	5,900	900
Sub Total		108.85	107.05	1.80	$ 900	$5,900	$ 900

In our hypothetical example, the short position eventually worked. If the price had gone to a closing level of 114.85, the investor's account balance would have dropped to the maintenance margin level of $2,000 and he would have been required to add additional funds to bring his balance back to $5,000.

futures price of 108.85 was an overvaluation and that the price was vulnerable to a decline.

He decides to call his Registered Commodity Representative and enter a sell order for one September S&P 500 Stock Index future. Selling is just as easy as buying in an open outcry market. All bids to buy and offers to sell must be made publicly in the trading arena and are subject to immediate acceptance by any member. This differs greatly from stock exchanges where specialists or market makers require an up-tic from the previous sale to transact a short sale.

Let's again assume the initial margin required is $5,000. The above table shows the status of the short position over the course of seven trading days.

Our investor decides at this point that he wants to cover his short position and lock in his profit. The next morning before the opening of trading, he enters an order to buy one September S&P Index contract to cover his short at the opening.

The opening is down on news that industrial production was weak and his position is covered at 106.55. His gain on his short then amounts to 2.30 at $25 per .05 or $1,150. The money is credited to his account the following day.

REDUCING THE VOLATILITY OF A STOCK PORTFOLIO

One reason for equity ownership is to take advantage of the long-term growth prospects of the company in which stock is purchased. Over time, higher earnings per share might be translated into a higher dividend payout. In the case of a company with a high return on investment and profits that are reinvested in the com-

ing market, investors have traditionally sold stock to raise cash or shifted to more defensive issues with less volatility. These tactics very often are short-run solutions that disturb carefully tailored long-run objectives. S&P 500 Index futures can be used to add protection against a market downturn and allow an investor to maintain his equity holdings based on the prospects of the companies rather than the direction of the market.

SHORT HEDGE AGAINST A DIVERSIFIED PORTFOLIO

Situation: An investor owns a well-diversified portfolio with a current market value of $110,000. The S&P 500 futures contract is at 108.85. The market appears weak and the investor believes that there is substantial downside risk during the next three months. He decides to short S&P 500 futures to protect his portfolio.

Action: The S&P 500 futures contract at 108.85 represents a contract value of $54,425 (500 × 108.85). In order to protect his portfolio, he sells two contracts ($110,000 divided by $54,425 equals 2.02).

This hypothetical example assumed that the volatility of the portfolio very closely matched that of the market as measured by the S&P 500 futures contract prices. In reality, portfolios may be more or less sensitive to market moves. Statistical regression analysis for individual issues and entire portfolios can be calculated to measure past price volatility relative to the market. Expressed as "beta," it is a statistical measure of past movements which may change in the future. However, it is useful when hedging market risk in portfolios that are more volatile than the market.

Day	Position Short 2 Contracts	Closing Price S&P Contract	Gain or (Loss) Contract Points X $5 X 2 Contracts (.01 equals 1 point)		Value of Stock Portfolio	Portfolio Gain or (Loss)
1	108.85	110.05	(1.20)	($1,200)	$111,213	$1,213
18	108.85	109.50	(.65)	(650)	110,657	657
36	108.85	107.40	1.45	1,450	108,535	(1,465)
54	108.85	106.05	2.80	2,800	107,171	(2,829)
72	108.85	103.10	5.75	5,750	104,190	(5,810)
90	108.85	100.65	8.20	8,200	101,714	(8,286)
Position Closed	108.85	100.65	8.20	$8,200	$101,714	($8,286)

Observations: The market dropped and our investor hedged the cash decline in his portfolio with an offsetting gain in his futures position. Of course, if he were wrong about the direction of the market and it went up, he would have had losses in his futures positions but his stocks may have participated in the advance. The investor, throughout this period, did not have to disturb his holdings and continued to receive his dividend payments.

Let us assume that the S&P 500 has a beta of 1.00, (that is, a given percentage move in the market gives rise to the same percentage move in the S&P 500) and our hypothetical portfolio has a beta of 1.50. Our portfolio's past market action relative to moves in the market was 50% greater than a given move in the general market. To compensate for this greater volatility, our hedger would require more S&P contracts to offset a greater decline in the value of his portfolio. Known as a hedge ratio, the dollar value of the portfolio is divided by the dollar value of the S&P 500 futures contract, the resulting figure is multiplied by the beta of the portfolio. Using our investor's portfolio and having calculated a beta of 1.5, we arrive at three contracts instead of two when the beta was 1.00:

$$\frac{\$110,000}{54,425} \times 1.5 = 3.03 \text{ contracts}$$

Thus, our investor would have sold three contracts to offset the portfolio's greater volatility to the market.

The concept of volatility and hedge ratios also may be applied to industry groupings and individual stocks. However, as the number of individual stock holdings that are being hedged decreases, then the greater is the chance that factors affecting that smaller group will make their prices react differently relative to the market than they have in the past.

ADDITIONAL USES OF THE S&P 500 FUTURES CONTRACT

Spreads: The simultaneous purchase and sale of different contract months to take advantage of perceived price discrepancies is called "spreading." The technique is considered by many to be less volatile than an outright long or short position, and as such, spreads generally carry lower margin requirements.

A characteristic of the futures market is that the closest contract date behaves more like the cash market. (In the S&P 500 futures contract, the cash market is the actual S&P 500 Index.) More distant months or back months have a greater component of their price determined by the expectations of what the price will be in the future.

These changing expectations of price levels of the S&P 500 contract into the future creates spreading opportunities. Options strategists will use the S&P 500 futures contract to reduce market risk when writing uncovered puts and calls. Block traders, investment bankers, stock specialists, options principals and anyone with the risk of stock market volatility, now have a vehicle and a well-capitalized liquid market to buy and sell market risk—the Standard & Poor's 500 Stock Index futures contract.

CONTRACT TERMS SUMMARY

Size	500 times the value of the S&P 500 Index
Delivery	Mark-to-market at closing value of the actual S&P 500 Index on Settlement Date
Hours	9:00 am to 3:15 pm Central Time
Months Traded	March, June, September, December
Clearing House Symbol	SP
Ticker Symbol	SP
Prices	Contract quoted in terms of S&P 500 Index
Minimum Fluctuation in Price	.05 ($25)
Limit Move	3.00 ($1,500)
Last Day of Trading	3rd Thursday of Contract Month
Settlement Date	Last Day of Trading

Understanding the Commodities Market

COMMODITY EXCHANGES

A Commodity Exchange is an organized market of buyers and sellers of various types of commodities. It is public to the extent that anyone can trade through member firms. It provides a trading place for commodities, regulates the trading practices of the members, gathers and transmits price information, inspects and governs commodities traded on the Exchange, supervises warehouses that store the commodity, and provides means for settling disputes between members. All transactions must be conducted in a pit on the Exchange floor within certain hours.

FUTURES CONTRACT

A futures contract is a contract between two parties where the buyer agrees to accept delivery at a specified price from the seller of a particular commodity, in a designated month in the future, if it is not liquidated before the contract reaches maturity. A futures contract is not an option; nothing in it is conditional. Each contract calls for a specified amount, and grade of product. For example: *A person buying a February Pork Belly contract at 52.40 in effect is making a legal obligation, now, to accept delivery of 38,000 pounds of frozen Pork Bellies, to be delivered during the month of February, for which the buyer will pay 52.40 per pound.*

The average trader does not take delivery of a futures contract, since he normally will close out his position before the futures contract matures. As a matter of fact, a survey conducted by a leading exchange has estimated that less than 3% of the contracts traded are settled by actual delivery.

Editor's Note: The scope of the commodities market has been broadened in recent years to include contracts on financial (debt) instruments (T-bills, bonds, etc.) and composite stock market indices such as Value Line, S&P 500, and the New York Stock Exchange. With the stock market index futures, settlement is made in cash in amount based on the underlying index. Cash, not the securities, is used to offset the long and short positions. The cash value of the contract is defined as the index quotation × 500.

THE HEDGER AND SPECULATOR

A hedger buys or sells a futures contract in order to reduce the risk of loss through price

Source: Commodity Educational Services, Division of Commodity Cassettes, Inc., 778 Frontage Road, Northfield, IL 60093.

variation. A short hedger sells a futures contract to protect the possible decline in the actual commodity owned by him. A long hedger purchases a futures contract to protect the possible advance in the value of an actual commodity needed to be purchased in the future.

The speculator is an important factor in the volume of future trading today. He, in effect, voluntarily assumes the risk, which the hedger tries to avoid, with the expectations of making a profit. He is somewhat of an insurance underwriter. The largest number of traders on any commodity exchange is the speculator. In order for the hedger to participate, he must have continuous trading interests and activity in the market. This trading activity stems from the role of the speculator, because he involves himself in buying or selling of futures contracts with the idea of making a profit on the advance or decline of prices. The speculator tries to forecast prices in advance of delivery and is willing to buy or sell on this basis. A speculator involves himself in an inescapable risk.

CAN YOU BE A SPECULATOR?

Now, can you be a speculator? Before considering entering into the futures market as a speculator, there are several facts which you should understand about the market and also about yourself. In order to enter into the futures market, you must understand that you are dealing with a margin account. Margins are as low as 5 to 10% of the total value of the futures contract, so you are obtaining a greater leverage on your capital.

Fluctuations in price are rapid, volatile, and wide. It is possible to make a very large profit in a short period of time, but also, it is possible to take a substantial loss. In fact, surveys taken by the Agricultural Department have shown that up to 75% of the individuals speculating in commodity markets have lost money. This does not mean that some of their trades were not profitable, but after a period of time with a given sum of money they ended up being a loser.

Now taking you as an individual, let us see whether you have the characteristics to become a commodity trader. Number one and the most important is that you do not take money that you have set aside for your future, or money you need daily to support your family or yourself. Number two, and almost equally important, is that you must be willing to assume losses and be willing to assume these losses with such a temperament that it is not going to affect your everyday life. Money used in the futures market should be money that has been set aside for strictly risk purposes, and if this money is not risk capital, your methods of trading could be seriously affected, because you cannot afford to be a loser.

Another very important factor is that you must not feel that you are going to take a thousand, two thousand, five or ten thousand dollars and place this with a brokerage firm and not follow the daily happenings of the market. Price fluctuations are fast, and as stated before, wide, so you must not only be in contact with your Account Executive daily, but know and study the technical facts that may be affecting the particular market in which you are speculating.

The individual who makes his first trade by buying a contract on Monday and selling this contract on the following Wednesday, making six hundred dollars on a $1,000 investment, in a period of two days, suddenly says to himself, *"Where has this market been all my life? Why am I working? Why not just concentrate on this market, if every two days or so I can make six hundred dollars?"* This is a fallacy, since this is an individual that is going to destroy himself and most likely his family. The next trade he will feel confident that because of his first profitable trade the market will always go his way even though he is now showing a loss in his position. He still feels that the market will turn around in his direction. If you become married to a particular commodity futures contract and constantly feel that the losses you are taking at the present time will reverse into profits, you are really fighting the market and in most cases fighting a losing battle. This could lead to disaster. There is a saying that you let your profits ride, but liquidate your losses fast.

In any way that you are uneasy with a position that you are holding, it is better to liquidate it. If, prior to the time of buying or selling a contract, you are not sure that this is the right step to take, do not take it. To protect yourself against this hazard you should pre-decide on every trade and exactly how much you intend to lose.

Another important point is not to involve yourself in too many markets. It is difficult to know all the technical facts and be able to follow numerous markets. In addition, if you are in a winning position, be conservative as to how you add additional contracts or pyramid your position. Being conservative will sometimes cause you to miss certain moves in certain markets and you may feel this to be wrong, but over a long period of time, this conservatism will be profitable to you.

If at this point you feel that you are ready, both financially and mentally to trade commodities, the next step is to begin the actual mechanics of trading a futures contract.

OPENING AN ACCOUNT

The first important factor is to decide which brokerage firm will afford you the best service. To accomplish this, you should do a little research by checking with the various exchanges about different brokerage firms. You should study their advertising, market letters, and other information. These should all be presented in a business-like manner and have no unwarranted claims, such as a guarantee of profit without indicating the possibility of loss.

The brokerage firm must be able to handle orders on all commodity exchanges. Do not pick just any Account Executive in a firm, but one you feel confident to help you make market decisions. Become acquainted with the Account Executive through phone or personal conversations. His knowledge of the factors entering into the market and the understanding of current market trends are important in your final choice.

After making a decision on the brokerage firm and the Account Executive that would be best for you, contact him and have him send you the literature concerning different contracts, and also, any additional information as to his organization. He will then send you the necessary signature cards required by the firm to open an account, and ask you for a deposit of margin money.

You will be trading in regulated commodities, and margin money will be deposited in a segregated fund at the brokerage firm's bank. A segregated account means that the money will only be used for margin and not for expenses of the brokerage firm.

Now you decide to enter into your first trade. Your Account Executive and you decide to enter into a December Live Cattle contract on the Chicago Mercantile Exchange. Your order will be executed as follows: Your Account Executive will place this order with his order desk who will then transmit the order to the floor of the Chicago Mercantile Exchange. There your order will be executed on the trading floor, in the pit. All technical details connected with the transaction will be handled by the brokerage firm.

Upon filling of your order, the filled order will be transmitted back to your Account Executive, who will then contact you, advising you that you have purchased one December Live Cattle contract at a given price. You will also receive a written confirmation on this transaction. You will now show an open position in December Live Cattle on the books of the brokerage firm.

MECHANICS OF A TRADE

Let us go back one step to explain in detail just how your order to buy one December Cattle was handled on the floor of the exchange. All buying and selling in the pit is done by open out-cry, and every price change is reported on the exchange ticker system. Each firm has brokers in the different pits, a pit meaning a trading area for the purpose of buying and selling contracts.

When your order was received on the exchange floor, it was time stamped and then given to a runner. This is a person who takes the order from the desk on the exchange floor and gives it to one of the brokers in the December Cattle trading pit. He is then responsible to the brokerage firm to fill that order, if possible, at the stated price. After filling the order, he then has the runner return it to the desk where it is time stamped and transmitted back to the order desk at the brokerage house, and the filled order is reported to you.

MARGIN

Futures trading requires the trader to place margin with his brokerage firm. Initial margin is required and this amount varies with each commodity. The minimum margin is established by each commodity exchange. Additional funds are needed when the equity of your account falls below this level. This is known as a maintenance margin call.

All margin calls must be met immediately. Normally you will be given a reasonable amount of time to comply with this request. If you do not comply, the firm has the right to liquidate your trades or a sufficient number of trades to restore your account to margin requirements.

The brokerage firm has the right to raise margin requirements to the customer at any time. This is normally done if the price of the commodity is changing sharply or if it is the brokerage firm's opinion that due to the volatility of the market the margin requirement is not sufficient at that particular time.

Most commodity contracts have a minimum fluctuation and also a maximum fluctuation for any one particular day. For example, if you are trading frozen Pork Bellies on the Chicago Mercantile Exchange the fluctuation is considered in points. A point equals three dollars and eighty cents. This means that if you buy a contract at 52.40 and the next price tick is 52.45, you have made a paper profit of five points or nineteen dollars. The maximum fluctuation on a belly contract is 200 points, so your profit or loss cannot exceed in one day more than 200 points from the previous day's settlement. There are exceptions in some commodity contracts, where the spot month has no limit.

Let us assume that you had originally placed in the hands of your brokerage firm two thousand dollars margin money, and that you and your Account Executive decide to purchase a December Live Cattle contract whose initial margin is $1200 with maintenance of $900.00. After the purchase of the contract your account would show initial margin required $1200 dollars with excess funds of eight hundred dollars. At the end of each day the settlement price of December Cattle would be applied to your purchase price and your account would be adjusted to either an increase due to profit or decrease due to loss in your contract.

Further, assume that in a period of two or three days there is a decline in the price of the December Cattle contract and your account now shows a loss of three hundred dollars. Since maintenance margin is only nine hundred dollars on this contract, you will still show an excess of eight hundred dollars over and above maintenance margin. But, in the next four days suppose there is an additional loss of nine hundred dollars. Your account will now need one hundred dollars to maintain the maintenance margin and four hundred dollars additional in order to bring your account up to initial margin. Your Account Executive, or a man from the margin department of the brokerage firm will then contact you, stating that you must place additional money with the firm in order to maintain the December Cattle contract.

At this point, you must decide whether you should continue with the contract, feeling that it may be profitable in the next few days, and thus sending the brokerage firm the required four hundred dollars to maintain your position, or whether to assume your loss and sell the contract.

Let us assume that you decide to sell your December contract at this point and that the selling price causes a loss of four hundred dollars. Added to this loss would be the commission of forty dollars, so your total loss on the transaction would be four hundred forty dollars. A confirmation and purchase and sales statement will be sent to you, showing the original price paid for the contract, the price for which it was sold, the gross loss of four hundred dollars plus the commission of forty dollars making the total loss four hundred forty dollars, and your new ledger balance on deposit with the firm as fifteen hundred sixty dollars.

As shown in our example, commission was charged only when the contract was closed out. A single commission is charged for each round-turn transaction consisting of the creation and liquidation of a single contract.

CONTROLLED, DISCRETIONARY, AND MANAGED ACCOUNTS

There are two methods of trading your account. The first is the professional approach where you and your Account Executive decide on each trade with no discretion being given directly to your Account Executive. This method was illustrated in the discussion about margins. The second method is called a controlled discretionary or managed account. Under this method, you are giving your Account Executive authorization to trade your account at his discretion at any time and as many times that he considers that a trade should be made. The Chicago Mercantile Exchange, and the Board of Trade have rules governing this type of relationship. The following is an excerpt from the C.M.E. rule regarding controlled, discretionary and managed accounts.

REQUIREMENTS

No clearing member shall accept or carry an account over which any individual or organization, other than the person in whose name the account is carried, exercises trading authority or control, hereinafter referred to as controlled accounts, unless:

The account is initiated with a minimum of $5000*, and maintained at a minimum equity of $3,750*, regardless of lesser applicable margin requirements. In determining equity the accounts or ledger balances and positions in all commodities traded at the clearing member shall be included. Whenever at the close of any business day the equity, calculated with all open positions figured to the settling price, in any such account is below the required minimum, the clearing member shall immediately notify the customer in person, by telephone or telegraph and by written confirmation of such notice mailed directly to the customer, not later than the close of the following business day. Such notice shall advise the customer that unless additional funds are promptly received to restore the customer's controlled account to no less than $5,000*, the clearing member shall liquidate all of the customer's open futures positions at the Exchange.

In the event the call for additional equity is not met within a reasonable time, the customer's entire open position shall be liquidated. No period of time in excess of five business days shall be considered reasonable unless such longer period is approved in writing by an officer or partner of the clearing member upon good cause shown.

REVIEWING YOUR CONFIRMATIONS AND STATEMENTS

An important factor in trading is that you must be sure that no errors occur in your account. For every trade made you should receive a confirmation, and for every close-out a profit and loss statement known as a Purchase-and-Sale, showing the financial results of each transaction closed out in your account. In addition, a monthly statement showing your ledger balance, your open position, the net profit or loss in all contracts liquidated since the date of your

last previous statement, and the net unrealized profit and loss on all open contracts figured to the market should be sent to you.

You should carefully review these statements. Upon receiving a confirmation of a trade you should immediately check its accuracy as far as type of commodity, month, trading price and quantity of contracts. If this does not agree with your original order, it should be immediately reported to the main office of your brokerage firm, and any differences should be explained and adjustments should be made.

If you do not receive a confirmation on a trade after it was orally reported to you by your Account Executive, be sure to contact him and the main office so that if an error was made it can be corrected immediately. You should receive written confirmation when you deposit money with your brokerage firm. If within a few days, you have not received this confirmation, report it immediately to the main office of your brokerage firm.

Never assume that an order has been filled until you receive an oral confirmation from your broker. A ticker or a board that you may be observing can be running several minutes behind and is not the determining factor as to whether your trade was executed or not. Until you receive this oral confirmation, never re-enter an order to buy or sell, against that position.

If you receive a confirmation in the mail showing a trade not belonging to you, immediately notify the main office of your brokerage firm and have them explain why this is on a confirmation with your account number. If it is an error, be sure that it is adjusted immediately and a written confirmation sent to you showing the adjustment of the error. If an error is made and it is profitable to you do not consider this any differently than if it was not profitable. Regardless of whether there is a profit or loss, all errors should be immediately reported to the brokerage firm.

Be sure that when you request funds to be mailed from your account that they are received within a few days from the time of your request. If not, contact the accounting department of the brokerage firm to see what is the cause of the delay.

Never make a check out to an individual. Always make your check out to the brokerage firm.

DAY TRADING

Day trading is where there is a buy and sell made during the trading hours on one particular day. Day trading is not considered to be a sound practice for the new speculator and inexperienced trader. Day trading is something that should be executed only by a sophisticated trader who is in frequent communication with the floor, and even then, on a limited basis.

---

* Minimums can be changed by each exchange, so consult your Account Executive for current regulations.

ORDERS

In order to trade effectively in the commodity market there are several basic types of orders. The most common order is a market order. A market order is one which you authorize your Account Executive to buy or sell at the existing price. This is definitely not a predetermined price, but is executed at a bid or offer at that particular moment.

Example: Buy 5 Feb Pork Bellies at the market.

LIMITED OR PRICE ORDERS AND "OB" DESIGNATION

This type of order to buy or sell commodities at a fixed or "limited" price and the ordinary "market" order are the most common types of orders.

Example: Buy Three Jan Silver 463.10. This limit order instructs the floor broker to buy three contracts of January Silver futures at 463.10. Even with this simple order, however, one presumption is necessary—that the market price prevailing when the order enters the pit is 463.10 or higher. If the price is below 463.10, the broker could challenge on the basis that the client may have meant *"Buy Three Jan Silver 463.10 stop."* Therefore, while it is always assumed that a "limit: order means 'or better,' " if possible, it saves confusion and challenges if the "OB" designation is added to the limit price. This is particularly true on orders near the market, or on pre-opening orders with the limit price based on the previous close, because no one knows whether the opening will be higher or lower than the close, *i.e., Buy Three Jan Silver 463.10 OB.*

STOP ORDERS *(Orders having the effect of market orders)*

Buy Stop Buy stop orders must be written at a price higher than the price prevailing at the time of entry. If the prevailing price for December Wheat is 456 per bushel, a buy stop order must designate a price above 456.

Example: "Buy 20 Dec Wht 456½ Day Stop." The effect of this order is that if December Wheat touches 456½ the order to buy 20 December Wheat becomes a market order. From that point, 456½ on, all the above discussion regarding market orders applies.

Sell Stop Sell stop orders must be written at a price lower than the price prevailing at the time of entry in the trading pit. If the prevailing price of December Wheat is 456 per bushel, a sell stop order must designate a price below 456.

Example: "Sell 20 Dec Wht 455 Day Stop." If this order enters the trading pit with the above price of 456 prevailing, the order to sell 20 December Wheat becomes a market order. From that point 455 on, all the above discussion regarding market orders applies.

Buy stop orders have several specific uses. If you are short a December Wheat at 456, and wish to limit your loss to ½ cent per bushel, the above buy stop order at 456½ would serve this purpose. However, it is important to realize that such *"stop loss"* orders do not actually limit the loss to exactly ½ cent when *"elected"* or *"touched off"* because they become market orders and must be executed at whatever price the market conditions dictate.

Another use is when you are without a position and believe that, because of chart analysis or for other reasons, a buy of December Wheat at 456½ would signal the beginning of an important uptrend in Wheat prices. Thus, the same order to *"Buy 20 Dec Wheat 456½ Day Stop"* would serve this purpose.

Sell stop orders have the same uses in reverse. That is, if you are long 20 December Wheat at 456 and wish to limit this loss to 1 cent per bushel, the above sell stop order at 455 would serve this purpose, within the limitations of the market order possibilities. Similarly, if you are without a position and believe that a sale of December Wheat at 455 would signal a downtrend in wheat prices, and you wish to be short the market, you could use the order to *"Sell 20 December Wheat 455 Day Stop"* for this purpose.

STOP LIMIT ORDERS *(Variations of stop orders)*

Stop limit orders should be used by you when you wish to give the floor broker a limit beyond which he cannot go in executing the order which results when a stop price is *"elected."*

Example: "Buy 20 Dec Wheat 456½ Day Stop Limit." This instructs the broker that when the price of 456½ is reached and *"elects"* this stop order, instead of making it a market order, it becomes a limited order to be executed at 456½ *(or lower),* but no higher than 456½. Another possibility:

Example: "Buy One February Pork Belly 58.10 Day Stop Limit 58.25 (or any other price above 58.10)." This instructs the broker that when the price of 58.10 *"elects"* the stop order instead of making it a market order, it becomes a limited order to buy at 58.25 *(or lower),* but no higher as with any limit order.

Stop limit orders are particularly useful to you when you have no position and wish to enter a market via the stop order, but want to put some reasonable limit as to what you will pay. On the other hand, stop limit orders are not useful to you when you have an open position and wish to prevent a loss beyond a certain point. The reason is that by limiting the broker to a certain price after a *"stop loss"* order is elected, **you also run the risk that the market may exceed the limit too fast for the broker to execute.** This would leave you with your original position because the broker would have to wait for the return to the limit before executing. With a straight stop *(no limit)* order, the broker must execute *"at the market."*

Example: "Buy One February Pork Belly 58.10 Day Stop Limit 58.25." Suppose the market moves to 58.10 but then only 20 February Pork Bellies are offered at that price. Your broker bids for one at 58.10 but another broker in the pit catches the seller's eye first and buys 20 and your broker misses the sale. Your broker then bids 58.20 but the best offer is 58.30. He bids 58.25, but the offer at 58.30 remains unchanged. Then another broker bids for and buys February Pork Bellies at 58.30 and the market moves on up. Your broker is left with no execution to your order unless the market later declines to your limit making a fill possible.

If you did not have a position you might be disappointed, but you would be unhurt financially. However, if you had a position and were trying to limit your loss you would have defeated your purpose with the stop limit order, if you truly wanted *"out"* after the stop was elected.

Stop limit orders on the sell side have exactly the same uses, advantages and disadvantages as discussed above, but in reverse:

Example: "Sell 20 December Wheat 455 Day Stop Limit." This means that when the market declines to 455 per bushel, the broker may sell at 455 *(or higher)*, but no lower.

Another Example: "Sell One February Pork Belly 58.25 Stop Limit 58.10." This instructs the broker to sell a belly after the stop price of 58.25 is reached and *"elects"* the stop order, but no lower than 58.10.

M.I.T. ORDERS *(Market-if-touched)*

By adding MIT *(Market-If-Touched)* to a limit order, the limit order will have the effect of a market order when the limit price is reached or touched. This type of order is useful to you, when you have an open position and if a certain limit price is reached.

Example: "Sell One September Sugar 950 MIT." The floor broker is told that if and when the price of September Sugar rises to 9½¢ per pound, he is to sell one contract

at the market. At this price of 9½¢ all prior discussion on market orders applies.

Under certain market conditions, not enough contracts are bid at 9½ cents to fill all offers to sell. Thus, you may see your straight limit price appear on the ticker, but your broker fails to make the sale.

But by adding MIT to the limit price, you will receive an execution, because the order becomes a market order, if the price is touched. However, the price will not necessarily be a good one in your eyes, since it became a market order when touched.

The same reasoning is true on the buy side of MIT orders but in reverse. Assume you are short one contract of September Sugar, with the prevailing price at 9½¢ per pound and you want to cover or liquidate your short at 9¢.

Example: "Buy One September Sugar 9¢ MIT." If and when the price of September sugar declines to 9¢ per pound, the floor broker must buy one contract at the market. Aside from the disadvantages of any market order, the MIT designation on the buy order prevents the disappointment which might arise if a straight limit buy at 9¢ were entered without the MIT added.

SPREAD ORDERS

As explained in the Glossary, a spread is a simultaneous long or short position in the same or related commodity. Thus a spread order would be to buy one month of a certain commodity and sell another month of the same commodity, or buy one month of one commodity and sell the same or another month of a related commodity.

Example: "Buy 5 July Beans Market and Sell 5 May Beans Market" or *"Buy 10 Kansas City Dec Wheat Market and Sell 10 Chicago May Wheat Market."*

Another Example: "Buy 5 May Corn Market and Sell 5 May Wheat Market."

In the example of the related commodity spread, normally the reason you would use such a spread, is that you expect to make a profit out of an expected tightness in the Corn Market, in the hope the corn contract will gain in value faster than wheat.

There may be a situation where you have a position either long or short in a commodity and want to change to a nearer or more distant option of the same commodity. For example you are long 5,000 bushels of May Soybeans on May 20 and want to avoid a delivery notice by moving your position forward into the July option. The basic spread order would be:

"Buy 5 July Beans Market and Sell 5 May Beans Market."

Sometimes you may prefer not to use market orders, in which case you use the difference spread.

Example: "Buy 5 July Beans and Sell 5 May Beans July 2¢ Over." Even though the prices of the two options are not specified, the broker is allowed to execute at any time he can do so with July selling at 2¢ or less above May. Over or under designations are a necessity for clarity to the floor broker. Omitting either is like omitting the price.

All orders, except market orders, can be cancelled, prior to execution. Naturally, a market order is executed immediately upon reaching the pit, so its cancellation is almost impossible.

There are other variations of orders, but for you the new speculator, the types mentioned are sufficient for your trading.

Options on Stock Market Indices, Bond Futures, and Gold Futures

STOCK MARKET INDEX OPTIONS

Stock market index related options are options whose prices are determined by the value of a stock market average such as the Standard and Poor (S&P) 500 Index or the New York Stock Exchange Composite Index, among others. Two types of such options are currently traded; index options and index futures options. The former are settled in cash while the latter are settled by delivery of the appropriate index futures contract.

Both types of options move in the same way in response to the underlying market index, therby providing investors the opportunity to speculate on the market averages. The buyer of a call index option is betting that the underlying market index value will increase significantly above the strike price (before the option expires) so as to provide a profit when the option is sold. On the other hand, the buyer of a put option is speculating that the market index value will fall sufficiently below the strike price before the option expires so as to provide a profit when the put option is sold. Options writers (sellers), on the other hand, assume an opposite position.

While index futures (page 426) also permit speculation on the market averages, index option tend to be less risky since option *buyers* are not subject to margin calls and losses are limited to the price (premium) paid for the option. However, index option writers (sellers), in return for the premium received, are subject to margin calls and are exposed to losses of indeterminate magnitude. However, writers of

call options on index *futures* can protect themselves by holding the underlying futures contract.

Index Options

Currently five index options on the broad market averages are traded; options on the S&P 100 and S&P 500 Indices (on the Chicago Board of Options Exchange), the New York Stock Exchange Composite Index (on the New York Stock Exchange), the Major Market Index (MMI) and the AMEX Market Indexes (on the American Stock Exchange).

The S&P 100 Index is a so-called weighted index obtained by multiplying the current price of each of the 100 stocks by the number of shares outstanding and then adding all of the products to obtain the weighted sum. The weighted sum is then multiplied by a scaling factor to provide an index of a convenient magnitude. The S&P 500 Index is calculated simularly except that all of the S&P 500 stocks are included.

The NYSE Index is based on the weighted sum of all of the stocks traded on the New York Exchange while the AMEX Index is based on the weighted sum of all of the issues traded on the American Exchange.

The Major Market Index differs from the above in that it is just the simple (unweighted) sum of 20 blue chip stocks multiplied by a factor of one tenth. This index behaves very similarly to the Dow Jones Index.

Generally index options expire on the Saturday following the third Friday of the expiration month. Hence the last trading day is on the third Friday of the expiration month. The price of an index option contract is $100 times the premium as quoted in the financial press.

Example: The July 120 (an option with a strike price of 120 expiring in July) Major Market Index call option is quoted (Exhibit 1, see page 438) at 3.00. The cost of an option contract is $300 ($100 × 3).

Option premiums consist of the sum of two components; the intrinsic value and the time value. The intrinsic value of a *call* option is $100 times the difference obtained by subtracting the strike price from the current value of the index. The instrinsic value of a *put* option is $100 times the difference obtained by subtracting the current value of the index from the strike price. The time value is the money which an option buyer is willing to pay in the expectation that the option will become more valuable (*increase its intrinsic value*) before it expires. Obviously the time value decreases as the time to expiration decreases.

It should be noted that there is a distinction between exercising an index option and selling an index option to close out a position. Exercising an option gives the holder the right to a cash amount equal to the *intrinsic* value of the

EXHIBIT 1   INDEX OPTIONS QUOTATIONS

CHICAGO BOARD

CBOE 100 INDEX

Strike Price	Calls—Last			Puts—Last		
	June	Sept	Dec	June	Sept	Dec
145	15¼	....	....	1/16	1	....
150	13¾	....	....	⅛	1¾	....
155	9⅛	10	....	7/16	3⅛	....
160	5⅛	9¼	....	17/16	4⅝	8¼
165	2⅛	6½	8⅝	3⅞	7¼	10½
170	11/16	3¾	6	7⅝	12	13½

Total call volume 20846.   Total call open int. 62006.
Total put volume 25167.   Total put open int. 103733.
The index closed at 163.55, +1.91.

AMERICAN EXCHANGE

MAJOR MARKET INDEX

Strike Price	Calls—Last			Puts—Last		
	Jul	Oct	Jan	Jul	Oct	Jan
115	5¾	8⅝	10	1⅞	3¾	5½
120	3	5¾	7	4	5⅞	7½
125	1⅛	3¼	....	7⅜	....	....
130	7/16	2¼	3⅝	....	....	....

Total call volume 2351.   Total call open int. 14572.
Total put volume 5276.   Total put open int. 9593.
The index closed at 118.69, +1.00.

Source: Reprinted by permission of *The Wall Street Journal,* Dow Jones & Co., Inc. All rights reserved.

option. Hence, the time value of the option is lost. When an option is sold to close out a position, the option holder receives a cash amount equal to the *premium* which contains both the intrinsic value and the time value of the option. Thus, in most cases it is more profitable to sell the option. The profit realized (before commissions and taxes) on the *sale* of an option contract is equal to $100 times the difference obtained by subtracting the premium paid when the option was purchased from the premium received when the option was sold.

Example: On May 24 the CBOE 100 Index was 163.55. In anticipation of a market decline, an investor buys a September 165-put option quoted at 7¼ for a total premium of $725 (7.25 × 100) per option. Assume that on August 10 the puts were selling at a total premium of $850 due to a decline in the CBOE 100 Index to 160.10. If the investor sells the put option he will realize a profit, before commissions and taxes, of $125 (850 − 725). If the market moves in a contrary direction he could lose his entire investment.

Index Futures Options

Index futures options (also called futures options) are the right to buy (call) or sell (put) the underlying index futures contracts (see page 426). Futures options are currently traded on the New York Futures Exchange and the Chi-

cago Mercantile Exchange. The dollar value of the underlying contract for the New York Futures Exchange option is equal to the New York Stock Exchange Composite Index multiplied by 500 while that for the Chicago Mercantile Exchange option is equal to the S&P 500 Index multiplied by 500. Quotations for futures options as they appear in *The Wall Street Journal* are shown in Exhibit 2. The total futures option premium per option is equal to the quoted value multiplied by 500. Gains and losses are calculated in the same way as index options.

The expiration day of the S&P 500 futures option is on the third Thursday of the expiration month while that for the NYSE futures option is the business day prior to the last business day of the expiration month.

Example: On May 24, 1983, the New York Composite Index is 94.39. An investor expects the Index to increase during the next six months and buys a September 96 futures call option at a total premium of $1750 (3.50 × 500), as indicated in Exhibit 2. Assume that by August

EXHIBIT 2   FUTURES OPTIONS

CHICAGO MERCANTILE EXCHANGE

S&P 500 STOCK INDEX — Price = $500 times premium.

Strike Price	Calls—Settle			Puts—Settle		
	Jun	Sep	Dec	Jun	Sep	Dec
135	....	....	....	.05	....	....
140	23.90	24.25	....	.05	.45	....
145	18.90	20.20	....	.05	.90	....
150	13.95	15.25	....	.10	1.25	....
155	9.20	11.50	....	.30	2.30	4.50
160	4.95	8.60	....	1.05	3.60	....
165	1.90	5.50	8.75	3.00	5.75	7.80
170	.45	3.50	....	6.50	9.50	....
175	.10	1.80	....	11.15	14.00	....

Estimated total vol. 1,440
Calls: Fri. vol. 766; open int. 6,216
Puts: Fri. vol 532; open int. 6,552

N.Y. FUTURES EXCHANGE

NYSE COMPOSITE INDEX — Price = $500 times premium.

Strike Price	Calls—Settle			Puts—Settle		
	Jun	Sep	Dec	Jun	Sep	Dec
84	10.90	11.70	....	.05	.40	.75
86	8.90	10.00	11.00	.05	.70	1.50
88	5.95	8.50	9.70	.05	1.00	1.75
90	5.15	7.00	8.30	.25	1.50	2.30
92	3.35	5.50	7.00	.50	2.00	2.95
94	1.95	4.50	6.00	1.15	3.00	3.75
96	.95	3.50	5.00	2.10	3.90	4.95
98	.40	2.75	3.95	3.50	5.25	6.05
100	.15	1.75	3.25	....	6.25	7.00

Estimated total vol. 1,405
Calls: Fri. vol. 844; open int. 4,836
Puts: Fri. vol. 549; open int. 4,801
S&P 500 Index 163.43
New York Composite Index = 94.39

Source: Reprinted by permission of *The Wall Street Journal,* Dow Jones & Co., Inc. All rights reserved.

10 the Index is at 100 and that the September call premium is quoted at 8.00 corresponding to a total premium per option of $4000 (8.00 × 500). By selling the option at the current value the investor can realize a profit of $2250 (4000 − 1750) before commissions and taxes.

Example: Assume that on May 24, 1983 when the S&P 500 Index is at 163.43, an investor expects a market decline within six months. He purchases a September 155 S&P put option at a total premium per option of $1150 (2.30 × 500), as indicated in the quotations shown in Exhibit 2. Assume that the Index declines to 150 on August 10 and that the quoted put premium is 6.50 corresponding to a total premium per option of $3250 (6.50 × 500). By selling the option at the current value the investor can realize a profit of $2100 (3250 − 1150), before commissions and taxes.

While a number of the same basic concepts apply to both index options and future options, there are differences between the two because the futures options have underlying index futures contracts which are traded on the open market. This makes possible a number of trading strategies with futures options which are not available with index options; for example, simultaneously buying an index futures contract and writing a corresponding call option. Also, for the reason given above, there is a distinction between selling a futures option, the usual procedure, and exercising the option. When a futures option is exercised, the option is exchanged for a position in the index futures market which may result in a loss in the time value of the option.

Investors planning to trade options should read two free booklets available from any of the options exchanges:

Understanding the Risks and Uses of Options

Listed Options On Stock Indices

Subindex Options

Subindex options are based on an index made up of leading publicly traded companies within a specific industry. These options permit speculation on an industry without the necessity of selecting specific stocks within the industry. As with all stock index options they are settled in cash.

Subindex options currently traded are indicated below:

American Stock Exchange (AMEX)
  Computer Technology Index Option
  Oil and Gas Index Option
  Transportation Index Option

Chicago Board of Options Exchange (CBOE)
  S&P Computer/Business Index Option
  S&P Integrated International Oil
    Index Option
  S&P Telephone Index Option
  S&P Transportation Index Option

New York Stock Exchange
  Telephone Index Option

Pacific Stock Exchange
  Technology Index Option

Philadelphia Stock Exchange
  Gambling/Hotel Index Option
  Gold/Silver Index Option

U.S. TREASURY BOND FUTURES OPTIONS

Options on U.S. Treasury Bonds (T-Bonds), traded on the Chicago Board of Trade, are the right to buy (call) or sell (put) a T-Bond futures contract. The T-Bond futures contract underlying the option is for $100,000 of Treasury Bonds, bearing an 8% or equivalent coupon, which do not mature (and are non-callable) for at least 15 years. When long term interest rates decline, the value of the futures contract and the call option increases while the value of a put option decreases. The reverse is true when long terms rates increase.

Premiums for T-bond futures *options* are quoted in $1/64$ of 1% (point): Hence each $1/64$ of a point is equal to $15.63 ($100,000 × .01 × $1/64$) per option. Thus a premium quote of 2–16 means 2 $16/64$ or (2 × 64 + 16) × $15.63 or $2250.72 per option. It should be noted that prices of T-bond *futures* are quoted in $1/32$ (of a point) worth $31.25 per futures contract.

As with options trades in general, the profit (before taxes and commissions) is the premium received (per option) when the option is sold minus the premium paid when the option was purchased.

The last trading day for the options is the first Friday, preceded by at least five business days, in the month *prior* to the month in which the underlying futures contract expires. For example, in 1983 a December option stops trading on November 18, 1983.

GOLD FUTURES OPTIONS

The most widely traded gold futures option is on the New York Comex Exchange. The option is the right to buy (call) or sell (put) a gold futures contract for 100 Troy ounces of pure gold. Both the futures contract and the corresponding call option increase or decrease with the price of gold. Put option premiums move in the opposite direction to the price of gold.

Option premiums are in dollars per ounce of gold. Thus a quoted premium of 2.50 corresponds to total premium of $2500 (2.50 × 100) per option.

The profit (before commissions and taxes) to an option buyer is simply the premium received when the option is sold less the premium paid when the option was purchased.

The last trading day for gold futures options

is the second Friday in the month *prior* to the expiration date of the underlying gold futures contract. Thus in 1983 a December option expires on Friday November 11, 1983. Example: In August an investor buys a December 400 (an option with a strike price of 400 on a December gold futures contract) Comex call option quoted at 25.00. The total price per option is $2500 (25.00 × 100).

On November 5, the price of gold has increased and the investor sells the option at a quoted premium of 50.00 or $5000.00 (50 × 100) per option. His profit is $2500 (5000 − 2500).

The Commodities Glossary

Acreage allotment The portion of a farmer's total acreage that he can harvest and still qualify for government price supports, low interest crop loans and other programs. It currently applies to specialty crops—tobacco, peanuts and extra long staple cotton—for which complex federal marketing orders have been written to control production closely. Before the 1977 farm bill was passed, the same term also applied more loosely to the portion of a farmer's wheat or feed grain acreage for which government payments would be made. A farmer could harvest 100 acres of wheat, for instance, but he'd receive price support payments only for 70 acres if that was his allotment. The allotment in this sense is called "program acreage" in the new farm bill.

Arbitrage The simultaneous buying and selling of futures contracts to profit from what the trader perceives as a discrepancy in prices. Usually this is done in futures in the same commodity traded on different exchanges, such as cocoa in New York and cocoa in London or silver in New York and silver in Chicago. Some arbitrage occurs between cash markets and futures markets.

Asking price The price offered by one wishing to sell a physical commodity or a futures contract. Sometimes a futures market will close with an asking price when no buyers are around.

Backwardation An expression peculiar to New York markets. It means "nearby" contracts are trading at a higher price, or "premium," to the deferreds. See also *Inverted market*.

Basis A couple of meanings: (1) The difference between the price of the physical commodity (the cash price) and the futures price of that commodity. (2) A geographic reference point for a cash price; for example, the price of a beef carcass is quoted "basis Midwest packing plants."

Bear A trader who thinks prices will decline. "Bearish" is often used to describe news or developments that have, or are expected to have,

a downward influence on prices. A bear market is one in which the predominant price trend is down. Some think this term originated with an old axiom about "selling the skin before you've caught the bear."

Bid The price offered by one who wishes to purchase a physical commodity or a futures contract. Sometimes a futures market will close with a bid price when no sellers are around.

Broker An agent who buys and sells futures on behalf of a client for a fee. They work for brokerage firms, some of which have extensive research and analysis departments that occasionally issue trading advice. A few firms have so many customers who follow such advisories that recommendations to buy or sell can influence market prices materially.

Bull A trader who thinks prices will go up. "Bullish" describes developments that have, or are expected to have, an upward influence on prices. A bull market is one in which the predominant price trend is up. Some theorize this term originally related to a bull's habit of tossing its head upward.

Butterfly An unusual sort of spread involving three contract months rather than two. Often used to move profits or losses from one year to the next for tax purposes.

Cash The price at which dealings in the physical commodity take place. Used more sweepingly, it can mean simply the physical commodity itself (as in "cash corn" or "cash lumber"), or refer to a market. For example, the cash hog market is a terminal (or, collectively, all terminals) where live hogs are sold by farmers and bought by meat packers.

Chart A graph of futures prices (and sometimes other statistical trading information) plotted in such a way that the charter believes gives insight into future price movements. Several futures markets regularly are influenced by buying or selling based on traders' price-chart indications.

Clearing house The part of all futures exchanges (usually a separate corporation with its own members, fees, etc.) which clears all trades made on the exchange during the day. It

Source: The *Dow Jones Commodities Handbook*, edited by Dan Ruck, Dow Jones Books, Dow Jones Company, Inc. 1979.

matches the buy transactions with the equal number of sell transactions to provide orderly control over who owns what and who owes what to whom. Although futures traders theoretically trade contracts among themselves, the clearing house technically is in the middle of each transaction—being the buyer to every seller and the seller to every buyer. That's how it keeps track of what is going on.

Close The end of the trading session. On some exchanges, the "close" lasts for several minutes to accommodate customers who have entered buy or sell orders to be consummated "at the close." On those exchanges, the closing price may be a range encompassing the highest and lowest prices of trades consummated at the close. Other exchanges officially use settlement prices as the closing prices.

Cold storage Refrigerated warehouses where perishable commodities are stored. In effect, the warehouses are secondary sources of commodities that aren't immediately available from the producers. The Agriculture Department periodically reports the quantities of various commodities stored in warehouses. Futures traders watch these reports to see if the supplies are building or dwindling abnormally fast, which indicates how closely supply and demand are balanced.

Commission The fee charged by a broker for making a trade on behalf of customers.

Contract In the case of futures, an agreement between two parties to make and in turn accept delivery of a specified quantity and quality of a commodity (or whatever is being traded) at a certain place (the delivery point) by a specified time (indicated by the month and year of the contract).

Country Refers to a place relatively close to a farmer where he can sell or deliver his crop or animals. For instance, a country elevator typically is located in a small town and accepts grain from farmers in the immediate vicinity. A country shipping point is a place where farmers in an area combine their marketings for shipment. A country price is the one these elevators, shipping points or whatever pay for the farmers' goods; it's based on the terminal-market prices, less transportation and handling costs.

Covering Buying futures contracts to offset those previously sold. "Short covering" often causes prices to rise even though the overall market trend may be down.

Crop report Estimates issued periodically by the Department of Agriculture on estimated size and condition of major U.S. crops. Similar reports are made on livestock.

Crush The process of reducing the raw, unusable soybean into its two major components, oil and meal. A "crush spread" is a futures spreading position in which a trader attempts to profit from what he believes to be discrepancies in the price relationships between soybeans and the two products. The "crush margin" is the gross profit that a processor makes from selling oil and meal minus the cost of buying the soybeans.

Deferred contracts In futures, those delivery months that are due to expire sometime beyond the next two or three months.

Delivery The tendering of the physical commodity to fulfill a short position in futures. This takes place only during the delivery month and normally takes the form of a warehouse receipt (from an exchange-accredited warehouse, elevator or whatever) that shows where the cash commodity is.

Delivery point The place(s) at which the cash commodity may be delivered to fulfill an expiring futures contract.

Discretionary accounts A futures trading account in which the customer puts up the money but the trading decisions are made at the discretion of the broker or some other person, or maybe a computer. Also known as "managed accounts."

Evening up Liquidating a futures position in advance of a significant crop report or some other scheduled development so as not to be caught on the wrong side of a surprise. In concentrated doses, evening up can cause a bull market to retreat somewhat and a bear market to rebound somewhat.

First notice day The first day of a delivery period when holders of short futures positions can give notice of their intention to deliver the cash commodity to holders of long positions. The number of contracts circulated on first notice day and how they are accepted or not accepted by the longs is often interpreted as an indication of future supply-demand expectations and thus often influence prices of all futures being traded, not just the delivery-month price. This effect also sometimes occurs on subsequent notice days. Rules concerning notices to deliver vary from contract to contract.

F.O.B. Free on Board, meaning that the commodity will be placed aboard the shipping vehicle at no cost to the purchaser, but thereafter the purchaser must bear all shipping costs.

Forward Contract A commercial agreement for the merchandising of commodities in which actual delivery is contemplated but is deferred for purposes of commercial convenience or necessity. Such agreements normally specify the quality and quantity of goods to be delivered at the particular future date. The forward contract may specify the price at which the commodity will be exchanged, or the agreement may stipulate that the price will be determined at some time prior to delivery.

Fundamentalist A trader who bases his buy-sell decisions on supply and demand trends or developments rather than on technical or chart considerations.

Futures Contracts traded on an exchange that call for a cash commodity to be delivered and received at a specified future time, at a specified place and at a specified price. Similar arrangements made directly between buyer and seller are called "forward contracts." They aren't traded on an exchange.

Hedge Using the futures market to reduce the risks of unforeseen price changes that are inherent in buying and selling cash commodities. For example, as an elevator operator buys cash grain from farmer, he can "hedge" his purchases by selling futures contracts; when he sells the cash commodity, he purchases an offsetting number of futures contracts to liquidate his position. If prices rise while he owns the cash grain, he sells the cash grain at a profit and closes out his futures at a loss, which almost always is no greater than his profit in the cash transaction. If prices fall while he owns the cash grain, he sells the cash grain at a loss but recoups all or almost all of the loss by buying back futures contracts at a price correspondingly lower than at which he first sold them. Some users of commodities assure themselves of supplies of their raw materials at a set price by buying futures, which is another form of hedging. When the time comes to acquire inventories, they can either take delivery on their futures contracts or, more likely, simply buy their supplies in the cash market. Futures-contract prices tend to match cash prices at the time the futures expire, so if cash prices have risen the users' higher costs are offset by profits on their futures contracts.

Hedger The Commodity Futures Trading Commission says a hedger in a general sense is someone who uses futures trading as a temporary, risk-reducing substitute for a cash transaction planned later in his main line of business. All other futures traders are classified as speculators. There are more legally specific definitions of hedging and hedgers in such markets as grains, soybeans, potatoes and cotton, where limits are placed on the number of contracts speculators may trade or own. The Commission has broadened these limits to allow hedging in closely related, rather than exactly matching, commodities. A sorghum producer, for instance, can use corn futures as a hedging tool where he couldn't before this rule-broadening. The more general distinction between hedgers and speculators may be important to potential traders. Some may want to use a market like interest rate futures to offset some expected heavy borrowing. The government hasn't set any speculative trading limits in those markets, but lenders or company directors are more apt to back a plan to trade futures for hedging purposes rather than speculation.

Inverted market A futures market where prices for deferred contracts are lower than those for nearby-delivery contracts because of great near-term demand for the cash commodity. Normally, prices of deferred contracts are higher, in part reflecting storage costs.

Last trading day The day when trading in an expiring contract ceases, and traders must either liquidate their positions or prepare to make or accept delivery of the cash commodity. After that, there is no more futures trading for that particular contract month and year.

Life of contract The period of time during which futures trading in a particular contract month and year may take place. This is usually less than a year, but sometimes up to 18 months.

Limit move The maximum that a futures price can rise or fall from the previous session's settlement price. This limit, set by each exchange, varies from commodity to commodity. Some exchanges have variable limits, whereby the limit is expanded automatically if the market moves by the limit for a certain number of consecutive trading sessions. When prices fail to move the expanded limit, or after a specified period of time, the limits revert to normal.

Liquidation Closing out a previous position by taking an opposite position in the same contract. Thus, a previous buyer liquidates by selling, and a previous seller liquidates by buying.

Long A trader who has bought futures, speculating the prices will rise. He is "long" until he liquidates by selling or fulfills his contracts by making delivery.

Margin The amount of "good faith" money that commodity traders must put in order to trade futures. The margins, set by each exchange, usually amount to 5% to 10% of the total value of the commodity contract. The "initial margin" is the amount of money that must be put up to establish a position in a futures market. Exchanges establish this margin, too, but brokerage firms often require even larger amounts to protect their own financial interests. "Maintenance margin" is the money that traders must put up to retain their position in the futures markets.

Margin call A request by a brokerage firm that a customer put up more money. That means the market price has gone against the customer's position and the brokerage firm wants the customer to cover his paper loss, which would become a real loss if the position were liquidated.

Nearby contracts The futures that expire the soonest. Those that expire later are called deferred contracts.

New crop The supply of a commodity that will be available after harvest. The term also is sometimes used in connection with pigs and hogs because the major farrowing periods in the spring and fall are referred to as "crops." There sometimes are substantial price differences between futures contracts related to new-crop supplies and those related to old-crop supplies.

Nominal price An artificial price—usually the midpoint between a bid and an asked price—that gives an indication of the market price level even though no actual transactions may have taken place at that price.

Old crop The supply from previous harvests.

Open The period each session when futures trading commences. Sometimes the open lasts several minutes to accommodate customers who have placed orders to buy or sell contracts "on the open." On these exchanges, opening prices often are reported by the exchange as a range, although these seldom are widely disseminated because of space restrictions in newspapers and periodicals; they are carried on tickers and display panels during that trading day, however.

Open interest Outstanding futures contracts that haven't been liquidated by purchase or sale of offsetting contracts, or by delivery or acceptance of the physical commodity.

Option The right to buy or sell a futures contract over a specified period of time at a set price.

Overbought A term used to express the opinion that prices have risen too high too fast and so will decline as traders liquidate their positions.

Oversold Like "overbought," except the opinion is that prices have fallen too far too fast and so probably will rebound.

Pit The areas on exchange floors where futures trading takes place. Pits usually have three or more levels and can accommodate a large number of traders. On several New York exchanges the trading areas are called rings and consist of open-center, circular tables around which traders sit or stand.

Position A trader's holdings, either long or short. A position limit is the maximum number of contracts a speculator can hold under law; it doesn't apply to bona-fide hedgers, although there really isn't any objective way of telling whether a person in position to hedge actually is hedging or is speculating instead.

Profit taking A trader holding a long position turns paper profits into real ones by selling his contracts. A trader holding a short position takes profits by buying back contracts.

Reaction A decline in prices following a substantial advance.

Recovery An increase in prices following a substantial decline.

Settlement price The single closing price, determined by each exchange's price committee of directors. It is used primarily by the exchange clearing house to determine the need for margin capital to be put up by brokerage-firm members to protect the net position of that firm's total accounts. It's also issued by some exchanges as the official closing price, and it is used to determine the price limits and net price changes on the following trading day. (See also: *Close.*)

Set-aside Acreage withdrawn from crop production for a season and used for soil conservation under a production-control program. Wheat farmers this year must set aside two acres of land for each 10 acres they plant to wheat in order to get any federal price support or disaster aid. The Agriculture Department has also said corn, sorghum and barley producers similarly may be required to set aside some of their acreage if it appears that surpluses will grow too much otherwise.

Short A trader who has sold futures, speculating that prices will decline. He is "short" until he liquidates by buying back contracts or fulfills his contracts by taking delivery.

Short squeeze A situation in which "short" futures traders are unable to buy the cash commodity to deliver against their positions and so are forced to buy offsetting futures at prices much higher than they'd ordinarily be willing to pay.

Speculation Buying or selling in hopes of making a profit. The word connotes a high degree of risk.

Spot The same as cash commodities. Literally, delivery "on the spot" rather than in the future.

Spreads and straddles Terms for the simultaneous buying of futures in one delivery month and selling of futures in another delivery month (or even the simultaneous buying of futures in one commodity and selling of futures in a different but related commodity). One purpose is to profit from perceived discrepancies in price relationships. Another purpose is to transfer current trading profits to some future time to avoid immediate tax liability.

Stop-loss order An open order given to a brokerage firm to liquidate a position when the market reaches a certain price so as to prevent losses from mounting or profits from eroding. Sometimes market price trends are accelerated when concentrations of stop-loss orders are touched off.

Support price A level below which the government tries to keep the agricultural-commodity prices that farmers receive from falling. They're set basically by Congress when farm legislation is passed and adjusted from time to time by the President or Agriculture Secretary. Subsidy payments, commodity purchases, production controls or commodity-secured loans are among the devices used to make up the difference when market prices dip below the support level. Futures and cash prices often tend to remain near the support level when there are large crop surpluses because lower prices keep commodities off the market and higher ones quickly draw willing sellers.

Switch A trading maneuver in which a trader liquidates his position in one futures delivery and takes the position in another delivery month in expectation that prices will change more rapidly in the second contract than in the first. Thus, a trader might switch out of a position in an October silver futures contract into a position in a December silver futures contract. Warning: Some people use the word "switch" when they mean "spread" or "straddle." Feel free to correct them.

Technical factors Futures prices often are affected by influences related to the market itself, rather than to supply-demand fundamentals of the commodity with which the market is concerned. For example, if a market moves up or down the limit several days in succession there frequently is a subsequent "technical reaction" caused in part by the liquidation of contracts held by traders on the wrong side of the price move.

Terminal Refers to an elevator or livestock market at key distribution points to which commodities are sent from a wide area.

Trading range The amount that futures prices can fluctuate during one trading session—essentially, the price "distance" between limit up and limit down. If, for instance, the soybean futures price can advance or fall by a maximum of 20 cents per bushel in one day, the trading range is double that, or 40 cents per bushel. In one market, cocoa, price movements are restricted to a daily range of six cents a pound.

Visible supply The amount of a commodity that can be accounted for and computed accurately, usually because it is being kept in major known storage places.

Warehouse or elevator receipt The negotiable slip of paper that a short can hand over to fulfill an expiring futures contract's delivery requirement. The receipt shows how much of the commodity is in storage.

Dow Jones Futures and Spot Commodity Indexes

The method for arriving at the Dow Jones Futures and Spot Commodity Indexes differs from some others in the order in which the computations are made. Instead of first weighting each price, then adding them up and finally calculating the percentage or index, this method first turns each price into an index or percentage of its base-year price, then weights each individual index, and finally adds them up. Stated mathematically, the more usual method calculates the percentage relation of one average to another, while the Dow Jones Commodity Index method calculates the average of a set of percentage changes. These two methods do not result in exactly the same figures. However, they are equally valid when used consistently, and the indexes they produce are of the same general magnitude.

The Dow Jones Commodity Index method has two advantages. One is that it saves computation, because the factors or multipliers perform two computations at once. They calculate the individual percentages and weight them at one stroke. The other advantage is that if you have yesterday's index, you can apply the multipliers to today's individual price changes. Then all you do is add the resulting figures to yesterday's index, or subtract them from it, depending on whether they're up or down. That gives today's index. No need to recalculate the whole thing each day.

As for the weights, they were obtained by the usual mathematical methods. Basically, the weight of each commodity is the percentage of its commercial production value to the total commercial production value of all commodities in the index, in this case for the years 1927–31. In calculating the weights, consideration also was given to the relation between volume of trading in each commodity and its commercial production.

A further refinement was necessary because price changes of the various commodities are quoted in different units. Grain prices change in eighths of a cent, wool prices change in tenths of a cent, and all the other staples in the Dow Jones index move in hundredths of a cent. This adjustment merely required appropriate treatment in each case of the multiplier, so that it would give the right figure for any price change. In the case of grains it meant an adjustment of 20%, since one-tenth is that much smaller than one-eighth. In other cases a mere adjustment of decimal points was sufficient.

The twelve commodities, with the weight of each and the multiplier applied to the price changes of each, are:

Source: The *Dow Jones Commodities Handbook*, edited by Dan Ruck, Dow Jones Books, Dow Jones & Company, Inc.

	Weight	Multiplier
Wheat	19.5	16
Corn	8	11
Oats	5	13
Rye	4	5
Wool Tops	5.5	4
Cotton	23	10
Cottonseed Oil	4.5	4
Coffee	7	3
Sugar	8.5	27
Cocoa	5	5
Rubber	6	3
Hides	4	3

These are the essentials for calculating the spot index. However, the futures index requires one more set of unusual steps. That's because several times a year an actual quoted "future" disappears. For instance, while early in the year it is possible to buy wheat to be delivered in December, when the month of December actually arrives that "delivery" expires and is no longer quoted.

The result is that futures prices are affected not only by market conditions but also by how close the delivery date looms. Interest charges and other such factors influence them. On July 1, the December delivery is just five months off, but a month later it is only four months away, and a five-month delivery should not, in a precise index, be compared with a four-month delivery.

This problem is overcome by the use of two futures quotations for each commodity. They are combined to produce on each market day the calculated price that would apply to a delivery exactly five months off.

On the first day of July, only the December delivery is used, since it is just five months away and thus no adjustment need be made. On the second day, the two quotations used are those for the same December delivery and the one for May of the following year. The quoted price for December is adjusted by one day's proportion of the difference between it and May's quoted price. Since there are 151 days between December and May (except in leap years) the figure for one day's proportion is 1/151 of the price difference between the two. The resulting fraction is added to December's price, or subtracted from it, depending on whether May is quoted above or below December.

The following day 2/151 of the difference are added or subtracted, the third day 3/151 and so on until December 1, on which day only the May contract's price is used. On December 2, the combination used is May and July, and so on around the year.

To facilitate the work of calculating the futures index every hour of each business day and the spot index once a day, tables have been prepared—resembling somewhat tables of logarithms or bond yields—which give the figures arrived at by multiplying the various quotational units of each commodity by its factor or multiplier. For instance, the tables show the proper multiples for one-eighth, one-quarter, three-eighths, etc., when each is multiplied by each grain's factor or multiplier.

The commodity futures index is published once an hour and as of the close of commodity markets each day on the Dow Jones News Service, where also the spot index is published once daily. Both are published likewise in *The Wall Street Journal.*

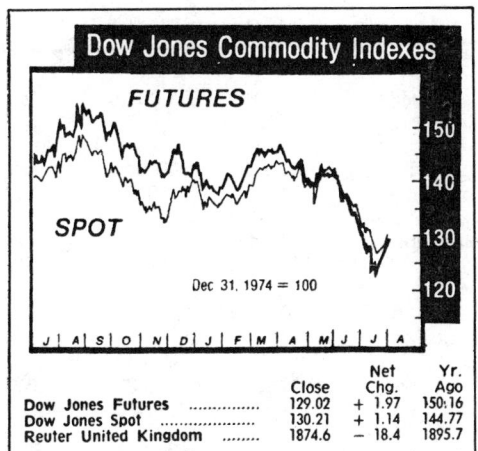

	Close	Net Chg.	Yr. Ago
Dow Jones Futures	129.02	+ 1.97	150.16
Dow Jones Spot	130.21	+ 1.14	144.77
Reuter United Kingdom	1874.6	– 18.4	1895.7

Source: Reprinted by permission of *The Wall Street Journal* © Dow Jones & Company, Inc., August 6, 1984. All rights reserved.

Commodity Trading Facts and Figures

The following provides as complete a list of futures, options on futures and options on actuals contracts as we could put together. It is possible we may have overlooked some contract because of the number of new contracts that have been introduced in the last year, or we may have listed a contract that has quietly become inactive. The list includes some contracts that are awaiting approval by the CFTC or SEC and are not trading yet, but it does not include all contracts awaiting such government action.

Details of all contracts are current, to the best of our knowledge, but any one of the areas listed is subject to change. The daily limit figure given is the normal limit that prices can move up or down from the previous day's close. A number of exchanges have variable limit policies which can alter these limits in a volatile market. For more information on limit changes, current minimum margin requirements or other contract details, you should check with your broker.

Futures Contracts

Commodity	Trading months	Trading hours (local time)	Contract size	Minimum price fluctuation	Daily limit
Chicago Board of Trade					
Corn	Mar/May/July Sept/Dec	9:30-1:15	5,000 bu.	1/4¢/bu. = $12.50	10¢/bu. = $500
Oats	Mar/May/July Sept/Dec	9:30-1:15	5,000 bu.	1/4¢/bu. = $12.50	6¢/bu. = $300
Soybeans	Jan/Mar/May/July Aug/Sept/Nov	9:30-1:15	5,000 bu.	1/4¢/bu. = $12.50	30¢/bu. = $1,500
Soybean Meal	Jan/Mar/May/July Aug/Sept/Oct/Dec	9:30-1:15	100 tons	10¢/ton = $10	$10/ton = $1,000
Soybean Oil	Jan/Mar/May/July Aug/Sept/Oct/Dec	9:30-1:15	60,000 lb.	1/100¢/lb. = $6	1¢/lb. = $600
Wheat	Mar/May/July Sept/Dec	9:30-1:15	5,000 bu.	1/4¢/bu. = $12.50	20¢/bu. = $1,000
Crude Oil	Feb/June/July/Aug Sept/Oct/Dec	8:30-2:10	1,000 barrels (42,000 gal.)	1¢/barrel = $10	$1/barrel = $1,000
GNMA CDR	Mar/June Sept/Dec	8:00-2:00	$100,000 principal	1/32 pt. = $31.25	64/32 pt. = $2,000
U.S. Treasury Bonds	Mar/June Sept/Dec	8:00-2:00	$100,000 8% coupon	1/32 pt. = $31.25	64/32 pt. = $2,000
U.S. Treasury Notes (6½-10 yr.)	Mar/June Sept/Dec	8:00-2:00	$100,000 8% coupon	1/32 pt. = $31.25	64/32 pt. = $2,000

Source: Reproduced with permission of *Futures Magazine*, 219 Parkade, Cedar Falls, Iowa 50613.

Commodity	Trading months	Trading hours (local time)	Contract size	Minimum price fluctuation	Daily limit
GNMA II	Mar/June Sept/Dec	8:00-2:00	$100.000 principal	1/32 pt. = $31.25	64/32 pt. = $2,000
Long-term Municipal Bond Index	Mar/June Sept/Dec	8:00-2:00	$1,000 × Bond Buyer Municipal Bond Index	1/32 pt. = $31.25	64/32 pt. = $2,000
30-Day Repurchase Agreements	Mar/June Sept/Dec	8:00-2:00	$2,500,000	1/100 pt. = $20.83	1 pt. = $2,083
90-Day Repurchase Agreements	Mar/June Sept/Dec	8:00-2:00	$1,000,000	1/100 pt. = $25	1 pt. = $2,500
Commodity Index	Mar/June Sept/Dec	Not determined	$500 × Commodity Index	1/40 = $12.50	None
Major Market Index	March cycle and consecutive months	8:45-3:15	$100 × Major Market Index*	1/8 = $12.50	None
AMEX Market Value Index	March cycle and consecutive months	8:45-3:15	$100 × Market Value Index*	1/8 = $12.50	None
Gold	Feb/Apr/June Aug/Oct/Dec	8:00-1:30	1 kilogram = 32.15 oz.	10¢/oz. = $3.22	$50/oz. = $1,607.50
Silver	Feb/Mar/Apr June/Aug/Oct/Dec	8:05-1:25	1,000 troy oz.	1/10¢/oz. = $5	50¢/oz. = $500
Western Plywood	Jan/Mar/May July/Sept/Nov	9:00-1:05	76,032 sq. ft.	10¢/1,000 sq. ft. = $7.60	$7/1,000 sq. ft. = $532

*Under review.

Chicago Mercantile Exchange

Commodity	Trading months	Trading hours (local time)	Contract size	Minimum price fluctuation	Daily limit
Broilers, Fresh	Feb/Apr/June/July Aug/Oct/Dec	9:10-1:00	30,000 lb.	2.5/100¢/lb. = $7.50	2¢/lb. = $600
Cattle, Feeder	Jan/Mar/Apr/May Aug/Sept/Oct/Nov	9:05-12:45	44,000 lb.	2.5/100¢/lb. = $11	1.5¢/lb. = $660
Cattle, Live	Feb/Apr/June Aug/Oct/Dec	9:05-12:45	40,000 lb.	2.5/100¢/lb. = $10	1.5¢/lb. = $600
Eggs, Fresh White	All months except August	9:20-1:00	22,500 doz.	5/100¢/doz. = $11.25	2¢/doz. = $450
Hogs, Live	Feb/Apr/June/July Aug/Oct/Dec	9:10-1:00	30,000 lb.	2.5/100¢/lb. = $7.50	1.5¢/lb. = $450
Pork Bellies	Feb/Mar/May July/Aug	9:10-1:00	38,000 lb.	2.5/100¢/lb. = $9.50	2¢/lb. = $760

Commodity	Trading Months	Trading Hours (Local Time)	Contract Size	Minimum Price Fluctuation	Daily Limit

International Monetary Market of the Chicago Mercantile Exchange

Commodity	Trading Months	Trading Hours (Local Time)	Contract Size	Minimum Price Fluctuation	Daily Limit
Deutsche Mark	Jan/Mar/Apr/June July/Sept/Oct/Dec and spot month	7:30-1:20	125,000 DM	$0.0001/DM = $12.50	$0.01 = $1,250
Canadian Dollar	Jan/Mar/Apr/June July/Sept/Oct/Dec and spot month	7:30-1:26	100,000 CD	$0.0001/CD = $10	$0.0075 = $750
French Franc	Jan/Mar/Apr/June July/Sept/Oct/Dec and spot month	7:30-1:28	250,000 FF	$0.00005/FF = $12.50	$0.005 = $1,250
Swiss Franc	Jan/Mar/Apr/June July/Sept/Oct/Dec and spot month	7:30-1:16	125,000 SF	$0.0001/SF = $12.50	$0.0150 = $1,875
British Pound	Jan/Mar/Apr/June July/Sept/Oct/Dec and spot month	7:30-1:24	25,000 BP	$0.0005/BP = $12.50	$0.05 = $1,250
Mexican Peso	Jan/Mar/Apr/June July/Sept/Oct/Dec and spot month	7:30-1:18	1,000,000 MP	$0.00001/MP = $10	$0.00150 = $1,500
Japanese Yen	Jan/Mar/Apr/June July/Sept/Oct/Dec and spot month	7:30-1:22	12,500,000 JY	$0.000001/JY = $12.50	$0.0001 = $1,250
Gold	Jan/Mar/Apr/June July/Sept/Oct/Dec and spot month	8:00-1:30	100 troy oz.	10¢/oz. = $10	$50/oz. = $5,000
Treasury Bills (90-day)	Mar/June Sept/Dec	8:00-2:00	$1,000,000	1 pt. = $25	60 pt. = $1,500
Domestic Certificates of Deposit (3-month)	Mar/June Sept/Dec	7:30-2:00	$1,000,000	1 pt. = $25	80 pt. = $2,000
Eurodollar Time Deposit (3-month)	Mar/June/Sept/Dec and spot month	7:30-2:00	$1,000,000	1 pt. = $25	100 pt. = $2,500

Index and Option Market of the Chicago Mercantile Exchange

Commodity	Trading Months	Trading Hours (Local Time)	Contract Size	Minimum Price Fluctuation	Daily Limit
Standard & Poor's 500 Stock Index	Mar/June Sept/Dec	9:00-3:15	500 × S&P Stock Index	5 pt. = $25	None
Standard & Poor's 100 Stock Index	Next four months and Mar/June Sept/Dec	9:00-3:15	200 × S&P 100 Stock Index	5 pt. = $10	None

Commodity	Trading Months	Trading Hours (Local Time)	Contract Size	Minimum Price Fluctuation	Daily Limit
No. 2 Fuel Oil	Every calendar month	8:30-2:30	1,000 barrels (42,000 gal.)	0.025¢ = $10.50	3¢/gal. = $1,260
Leaded Regular Gasoline	Every calendar month	8:30-2:30	1,000 barrels (42,000 gal.)	0.025¢ = $10.50	3¢/gal. = $1,260
Lumber (random-length)	Jan/Mar/May July/Sept/Nov	9:00-1:05	130,000 bd. ft.	10¢/1,000 bd. ft. = $13	$5/1,000 bd. ft. = $650

Chicago Rice and Cotton Exchange (Formerly New Orleans Commodity Exchange; now trades on floor of MidAmerica Commodity Exchange)

Commodity	Trading Months	Trading Hours	Contract Size	Minimum Price Fluctuation	Daily Limit
Rough Rice	Jan/Mar/May July/Sept/Nov	8:45-1:45	2,000 cwt. (200,000 lb.)	1¢/cwt. = $20	30¢/cwt. = $600

Coffee, Sugar & Cocoa Exchange, Inc.

Commodity	Trading Months	Trading Hours	Contract Size	Minimum Price Fluctuation	Daily Limit
Cocoa	Mar/May/July Sept/Dec	9:30-3:00	10 metric tons	$1/metric ton = $10	$88/metric ton = $880
Coffee "C"	Mar/May/July Sept/Dec	9:45-2:30	37,500 lb.	1/100¢/lb. = $3.75	4¢/lb. = $1,500
Sugar No. 11 (world)	Jan/Mar/May July/Sept/Oct	10:00-1:45	112,000 lb.	1/100¢/lb. = $11.20	1/2¢/lb. = $560
Sugar No. 12 (domestic)	Jan/Mar/May July/Sept/Nov	10:00-1:45	112,000 lb.	1/100¢/lb. = $11.20	1/2¢/lb. = $560

Commodity Exchange (Comex)

Commodity	Trading Months	Trading Hours	Contract Size	Minimum Price Fluctuation	Daily Limit
Aluminum	Current calendar month, next two months and Jan/Mar/May July/Sept/Dec	9:30-2:15	40,000 lb.	0.05¢/lb. = $20	5¢/lb. = $2,000
Copper	"	9:50-2:00	25,000 lb.	5/100¢/lb. = $12.50	5¢/lb. = $1,250
Silver	"	9:05-2:25	5,000 troy oz.	10/100¢/oz. = $5	50¢/oz. = $2,500
Gold	Current calendar month, next two months and Feb/Apr/June Aug/Oct/Dec	9:00-2:30	100 troy oz.	10¢/oz. = $10	$25/oz. = $2,500

Commodity	Trading months	Trading hours (local time)	Contract size	Minimum price fluctuation	Daily limit
Kansas City Board of Trade					
Wheat (hard red winter)	Mar/May/July Sept/Dec	9:30-1:15	5,000 bu.	1/4¢/bu. = $12.50	25¢/bu. = $1,250
Value Line Stock Index	Mar/June Sept/Dec	9:00-3:15	500 times the futures price	0.05 = $25	None
Mini Value Line Stock Index	Mar/June Sept/Dec	9:00-3:15	100 times the futures price	0.05 = $5	None
MidAmerica Commodity Exchange					
Cattle, Live	Feb/Apr/June Aug/Oct/Dec	9:05-1:00	20,000 lb.	2.5/100¢/lb. = $5	1.5¢/lb. = $300
Hogs, Live	Feb/Apr/June July/Aug/Oct/Dec	9:10-1:15	15,000 lb.	2.5/100¢/lb. = $3.75	1.5¢/lb. = $225
Corn	Mar/May/July Sept/Dec	9:30-1:30	1,000 bu.	1/8¢/bu. = $1.25	10¢/bu. = $100
Oats	Mar/May/July Sept/Dec	9:30-1:30	1,000 bu.	1/8¢/bu. = $10	6¢/bu. = $60
Soybeans	Jan/Mar/May July/Aug/Sept/Nov	9:30-1:30	1,000 bu.	1/8¢/bu. = $1.25	30¢/bu. = $300
Wheat	Mar/May/July Sept/Dec	9:30-1:30	1,000 bu.	1/8¢/bu. = $1.25	20¢/bu. = $200
Gold	Mar/June/Sept Dec	8:00-1:40	33.2 fine troy oz.	10¢/oz. = $3.32	$50/oz. = $1,660
Silver (Chicago contract)	Current month and any subsequent months, up to 12-15 months ahead	8:05-1:40	1,000 troy oz.	10/100¢/oz. = $1	50¢/oz. = $500
Silver (New York contract)	Same as above for Chicago contract				
U.S. Treasury Bonds	Mar/June Sept/Dec	8:00-2:15	$50,000 face value	1/32 pt. = $15.62	64/32 pt. = $1,000
U.S. Treasury Bills (90-day)	Mar/June Sept/Dec	8:00-2:15	$500,000 face value	1/10 pt. = $12.50	60 pt. = $750
Sugar (domestic refined)	Jan/Mar/May July/Sept/Nov	9:00-1:00	40,000 lb.	1/100¢/lb. = $4	1/2¢/lb. = $200
British Pound	Mar/June Sept/Dec	7:30-1:34	12,500 BP	$0.0005/BP = $6.25	$0.05/BP = $625

Commodity	Trading months	Trading hours (local time)	Contract size	Minimum price fluctuation	Daily limit
Canadian Dollar	Mar/June Sept/Dec	7:30-1:36	50,000 CD	$0.0001/ CD = $5	$0.0075/ CD = $375
Deutsche Mark	Mar/June Sept/Dec	7:30-1:30	62,500 DM	$0.0001/DM = $6.25	$0.01/DM = $625
Japanese Yen	Mar/June Sept/Dec	7:30-1:32	6,250,000 JY	$0.000001/ JY = $6.25	$0.0001/JY = $625
Swiss Franc	Mar/June Sept/Dec	7:30-1:26	62,000 SF	$0.0001/SF = $6.25	$0.015/SF = $937

Minneapolis Grain Exchange

Commodity	Trading months	Trading hours (local time)	Contract size	Minimum price fluctuation	Daily limit
Spring Wheat	Mar/May/July Sept/Dec	9:30-1:15	5,000 bu.	1/8¢/bu. = $6.25	20¢/bu. = $1,000
Sunflower Seeds	Jan/Mar/May July/Nov	9:25-1:20	100,000 lb.	1/100¢/lb. = $10	1/2¢/lb. = $500

New York Cotton Exchange

Commodity	Trading months	Trading hours (local time)	Contract size	Minimum price fluctuation	Daily limit
Cotton No. 2	Mar/May/July Oct/Dec	10:30-3:00	50,000 lb. (approx. 100 bales)	1/100¢/lb. = $5	2¢/lb. = $1,000
Orange Juice	Jan/Mar/May July/Sept/Nov	10:15-2:45	15,000 lb.	5/100¢/lb. = $7.50	5¢/lb. = $750
Propane Gas (liquified)	All months	10:45-3:15	1,000 barrels (42,000 gal.)	1/100¢/gal. = $4.20	2¢/gal. = $840

New York Futures Exchange

Commodity	Trading months	Trading hours (local time)	Contract size	Minimum price fluctuation	Daily limit
NYSE Composite Stock Index	Mar/June Sept/Dec	10:00-4:15	500 × index	5 pt. = $25	None

New York Mercantile Exchange

Commodity	Trading months	Trading hours (local time)	Contract size	Minimum price fluctuation	Daily limit
Palladium	All months	9:00-2:20	100 troy oz.	5¢/oz. = $5	$6/oz. = $600
Platinum	All months	9:10-2:30	50 troy oz.	10¢/oz. = $5	$20/oz. = $1,000
Potatoes	Mar/Apr May/Nov	9:45-2:00	100,000 lb.	1¢/50 lb. = $20	40¢/50 lb. = $800

Commodity	Trading months	Trading hours (local time)	Contract size	Minimum price fluctuation	Daily limit
No. 2 Heating Oil (New York)	All months	10:00-3:05	42,000 gal.	1/100¢/gal. = $4.20	2¢/gal. = $840
Leaded Gasoline	All months	9:45-3:00	42,000 gal.	1/100¢/gal. = $4.20	2¢/gal. = $840
Crude Oil (light sweet)	All months	9:30-3:10	1,000 barrels (42,000 gal.)	1¢/barrel = $10	$1/barrel = $1,000

The Montreal Exchange Mercantile Division

Commodity	Trading months	Trading hours (local time)	Contract size	Minimum price fluctuation	Daily limit
Eastern Lumber	Jan/Mar/May July/Sept/Nov	9:00-3:00	130,000 bd. ft.	U.S. 10¢/ 1,000 bd. ft. = $13	U.S. $5/ 1,000 bd. ft. = $650

Toronto Futures Exchange

Commodity	Trading months	Trading hours (local time)	Contract size	Minimum price fluctuation	Daily limit
Canadian Bonds (18-year)	Mar/June Sept/Dec	9:00-3:15	CD $100,000	1/32 pt. = $31.25	2 pt. = $2,000
Canadian T-Bills (13-week)	Mar/June Sept/Dec	9:00-3:15	CD $1,000,000	0.005 pt. = $50	0.150 pt. = $1,500
Toronto Stock Exchange (TSE) 300 Index	Mar/June Sept/Dec	10:00-4:15	10 × index	1 pt. = $10	150 pt. = $1,500
U.S. Dollar	Mar/June Sept/Dec	8:30-3:30	U.S. $100,000	0.01¢ = $10	1¢ = $1,000

The Winnipeg Commodity Exchange

Commodity	Trading months	Trading hours (local time)	Contract size	Minimum price fluctuation	Daily limit
Domestic Feed Barley	Mar/May/July Oct/Dec	9:30-1:15	100 metric tons	10¢/ton = $10	$5/ton = $500
Alberta Domestic Feed Barley	Feb/Apr/June Sept/Nov	9:30-1:15	20 metric tons	10¢/ton = $2	$5/ton = $100
Flaxseed	Mar/May/July Oct/Dec	9:30-1:15	100 metric tons	10¢/ton = $10	$10/ton = $1,000
Domestic Feed Oats	Mar/May/July Oct/Dec	9:30-1:15	100 metric tons	10¢/ton = $10	$5/ton = $500
Rapeseed	Jan/Mar/June Sept/Nov	9:30-1:15	100 metric tons	10¢/ton = $10	$10/ton = $1,000
Rye	Mar/May/July Oct/Dec	9:30-1:15	100 metric tons	10¢/ton = $10	$5/ton = $500

Commodity	Trading months	Trading hours (local time)	Contract size	Minimum price fluctuation	Daily limit
Domestic Feed Wheat	Mar/May/July Oct/Dec	9:30-1:15	100 metric tons	10¢/ton = $10	$5/ton = $500
Gold	Mar/June/Sept Dec	8:25-1:30	20 oz.	10¢/oz.	$25/oz.
Silver	Jan/Apr/July Oct	8:30-1:35	200 oz.	1¢/oz. = $2	50¢/oz. = $100
Treasury Bills (13-week)	Mar/June/Sept Dec	8:20-1:25	$200,000	One index point	Sixty index points
Long-Term Bonds	Mar/June/Sept Dec	8:20-1:25	$20,000	1/32 of $1 per $100 face value	64/32 of $1 per $100 face value

Options on Futures

Options on futures have the same contract months, trading hours, limits, etc., as their underlying futures contracts. This list does not include all those options that may be included in the agricultural options program scheduled to begin in the fall of 1984. Some exchanges had not made a final determination on contracts by our deadline date.

Underlying futures contract	Contract size	Strike price increments	Minimum fluctuation	Expiration date

Chicago Board of Trade

U.S. Treasury Bonds	$100,000	2 pt.	1/64 pt. = $15.62 (1.0 = $1,000)	Noon on Friday at least five business days before first notice day
GNMA II	$100,000 principal	2 pt.	1/64 pt. = $15.625 (1.0 = $1,000)	Second Friday preceding last day of trading in underlying futures
Soybeans	5,000 bu.	25¢ under $8; 50¢ above $8	1/8¢/bu. = $6.25 (1.0 = $50)	Saturday following last trading day

Index and Option Market of the Chicago Mercantile Exchange

S&P 500 Stock Index	500 × S&P Index	5 pt.	0.05 pt. = $25 (1.0 = $500)	Third Thursday of contract month
Deutsche Mark	125,000 DM	1¢	0.01¢/DM = $12.50 (1.0 = $1,250)	

Source: Reproduced with permission of *Futures Magazine*, 219 Parkade, Cedar Falls, Iowa 50613.

Underlying futures contract	Contract size	Strike price increments	Minimum fluctuation	Expiration date

Coffee, Sugar and Cocoa Exchange

Sugar No. 11 — 112,000 lb. (50 long tons) — Varies* — 1/100¢/lb. = $11.20 (1.0 = $1,120) — Second Friday of month before futures expire

*1/2¢/lb. for two nearby options and 1¢/lb. for deferreds when futures price is below 15¢/lb. (will be 1¢ for all contracts beginning with October 1984). When the futures contract price is 15¢-40¢ per lb., the increment will be 1¢ for two nearby months and 2¢ for deferred months. When the futures contract price is above 40¢, the increment will be 2¢ for two nearby months and 4¢ for deferred months.

Commodity Exchange Inc. (Comex)

Gold — 100 troy oz. — Varies* — 10¢/oz. = $10 (1.0 = $100) — Second Friday of month before futures expire

*$10/oz. below $300; $20/oz. $300-$500; $30/oz. $500-$800; $40/oz. above $800

Silver — 5,000 troy oz. — 50¢ between $5-$14.99/oz,; $1 above $15/oz. — 1/10¢/oz. = $5 (1.0 = $100) — Second Friday of month prior to futures month

MidAmerica Commodity Exchange

Gold — 33.2 troy oz. — $10/oz. — 10¢/oz. = $3.32 (1 = $33.20) — Second Friday of month prior to futures delivery

New York Cotton Exchange

Cotton — 50,000 lb. — Nearest two delivery months: 1¢ up to 74¢/lb., 2¢ at 75¢/lb. and above. — 1/100¢/lb. = $5 (1.0 = $500) — First Friday preceding delivery month

New York Futures Exchange

NYSE Composite Stock Index — 500 × NYSE Composite Index — 2 pt. — 0.05 pt = $25 (1.0 = $500) — Last trading day of underlying futures contract

Winnipeg Commodity Exchange

Gold (Calls only) — 20 oz. — $20/oz. — 10¢/oz. = $2 (1.0 = $20) — Six business days before delivery month

Options on Actuals

New options were being introduced as this issue was being put together so the following list may not be complete. Options on futures (see page 453) required Commodity Futures Trading Commission approval. U.S. options in the list below have gone through the Securities and Exchange Commission.

Underlying instrument	Contract months	Local trading hours	Contract size	Strike price increments	Minimum fluctuation
American Stock Exchange (Amex)					
Major Market Index (20 stocks)	Four sequential expiration months	10:00-4:10	100 × index value	5 pt.	Premium less than $3: 1/16; above $3: 1/8 (1.0 = $100)
(Same details apply to **AMEX Market Value Index, Computer Technology Index, Oil and Gas Index and Transportation Index**)					
U.S. Treasury Bills (90-day)	Mar/June Sept/Dec	9:00-3:00	$1 million principal	1 pt.	0.01 pt. = $25 (1.0 = $2,500)
U.S. Treasury Notes (10-year)	Feb/May Aug/Nov	9:00-3:00	$100,000	2 pt.	1/32 pt. = $31.25 (1.0 = $1,000)
Chicago Board Options Exchange (CBOE)					
S&P 100 Stock Index	Four sequential months	9:00-3:10	100 × index	5 pt.	Premium less than $3: 1/16; above $3: 1/8. (1.0 = $100)
(Same details apply to **S&P Telephone Index and S&P Transportation Index**)					
S&P 500 Stock Index	Mar/June Sept/Dec	"	"	"	"
U.S. Treasury Bonds (12% and 10⅜%)	Mar/June Sept/Dec	8:00-2:00	$100,000	2 pt.	1/32 pt. = $31.25 (1.0 = $1,000)
New York Stock Exchange					
NYSE Index	Next three months and then December cycle	10:00-4:10	100 × index	5 pt.	1/16 up to $3; 1/8 above $3 (1.0 = $100)
NYSE Telephone Index	Next three months and then January cycle	"	"	"	"

Source: Reproduced with permission of *Futures Magazine,* 219 Parkade, Cedar Falls, Iowa 50613.

Underlying instrument	Contract months	Local trading hours	Contract size	Strike price increments	Minimum fluctuation

Pacific Stock Exchange

PSE Technology Index	Four sequential months	7:00-1:10	100 × index	5 pt.	1/16 (1.0 = $100)

Philadelphia Stock Exchange (PHLX)

Deutsche Mark	Mar/June Sept/Dec	8:30-2:30	DM 62,500	$0.01	$0.0001/DM = $6.25 (1.0 = $625)
Swiss Franc	Mar/June Sept/Dec	8:30-2:30	SF 62,500	$0.01	$0.0001/SF = $6.25 (1.0 = $625)
Canadian Dollar	Mar/June Sept/Dec	8:30-2:30	CD $50,000	$0.01	$0.0001/CD = $5 (1.0 = $500)
British Pound	Mar/June Sept/Dec	8:30-2:30	£12,500	$0.05	$0.0005/£ = $6.25 (1.0 = $125)
Japanese Yen	Mar/June Sept/Dec	8:30-2:30	JY 6,250,000	$0.01	$0.000001/ JY = $6.25 (1.0 = $625)
French Franc	Mar/June Sept/Dec	8:30-2:30	FF 125,000	$0.005	$0.00005/FF = $6.25 (1.0 = $1,250)
Gaming/Hotel Stock Index	Next three months and two deferred months	10:00-4:10	100 × index	5 pt.	1/16 (1.0 = $100)
Gold/Silver Stock Index	"	"	"	"	"

International Options Market (IOM) Division of the Montreal Stock Exchange*

(All times EST/EDT)

Gold	Feb/May Aug/Nov	Amsterdam: 4:30-10:30 Montreal: 9:00-2:30 Vancouver: 2:30-7:00	10 oz.	U.S. $25 under $500; $50 above $500	10¢/oz. = $1
Canadian Dollar	Mar/June Sept/Dec	Montreal: 9:00-2:30 Vancouver: 2:30-7:00	CD $50,000	U.S. $0.01	$0.0001/CD = $5

*Some options also traded on the European Options Exchange at the Amsterdam Stock Exchange and at the Vancouver Stock Exchange.

Underlying instrument	Contract months	Local trading hours	Contract size	Strike price increments	Minimum fluctuation
Deutsche Mark	Mar/June Sept/Dec	Montreal: 9:00-4:00	DM 25,000	U.S. $0.01	$0.0001/DM = $2.50
Swiss Franc	Mar/June Sept/Dec	Montreal: 9:00-4:00	SF 25,000	U.S. $0.01	$0.0001/SF = $2.50
British Pound	Mar/June Sept/Dec	Montreal: 9:00-4:00	£5,000	U.S. $0.05	$0.0005/£ = $2.50
Japanese Yen	Mar/June Sept/Dec	Montreal: 9:00-4:00	JY 2,500,000	U.S. $0.01	$0.000001/ JY = $2.50
Canadian Bonds	Mar/June Sept/Dec	Montreal: 9:00-4:00	CD $25,000	CD $2.50	Premium under $2: 5¢; above $2: 1/8

Toronto Futures Exchange

Silver	Mar/June Sept/Dec	9:30-2:30	100 oz.	$1 below $15/oz.; $2.50 from $15-$35/oz.	5¢ below $2; 12½¢ above $2

Toronto Stock Exchange

TSE 300 Index	Next three months	10:00-4:10	100 × index	$1	5¢ under $2; 1/8 above $2

Commodity Futures Trading Commission

Federal laws regulating commodity futures trading are enforced by the Commodity Futures Trading Commission. For information on commodity brokers call (202) 254-8630.

National Office

Commodity Futures Trading Commission
2033 K Street, NW
Washington, DC 20581
  Telephone: (202) 254-6387

Regional Offices

Eastern Region
1 World Trade Center, Suite 4747
New York, NY 10048
  Telephone: (212) 466-2071

Central Region
233 S. Wacker Drive, Suite 4600
Chicago, IL 60606
  Telephone: (312) 353-9031

Source: U.S. Government Manual.

Southwestern Region
4901 Main Street, Room 400
Kansas City, MO 64112
  Telephone: (816) 374-2994

510 Grain Exchange Building
Minneapolis, MN 55415
  Telephone: (612) 349-3255

Western Region
10850 Wilshire Boulevard, Suite 510
Los Angeles, CA 90024
  Telephone: (213) 6783

The Commodity Futures Trading Commission (CFTC), the Federal regulatory agency for futures trading, was established by the Commodity Futures Trading Commission Act of 1974 (88 Stat. 1389; 7 U.S.C. 4a), approved October 23, 1974. The Commission began operation in April 1975, and its authority to regulate futures trading was renewed by Congress in 1978 and in 1982.

The CFTC consists of five Commissioners who are appointed by the President with the advice and consent of the Senate. One Commissioner is designated by the President to serve as Chairman. The Commissioners serve staggered 5-year terms, and by law no more than three Commissioners can belong to the same political party.

FUNCTIONS AND ACTIVITIES

The Commission consists of five major operating components: the divisions of enforcement, economics and education, trading and markets, and the offices of the executive director and the general counsel.

The Commission regulates trading on the 11 U.S. futures exchanges, which at the end of fiscal 1982 were offering 80 active futures contracts. It also regulates the activities of some 5,025 commodity exchange members, 420 public brokerage houses (futures Commission merchants), about 49,000 Commission-registered futures industry salespeople and associated persons, and 3,600 commodity trading advisers and commodity pool operators. Some off-exchange transactions involving instruments similar in nature to futures contracts also fall under CFTC jurisdiction.

The Commission's regulatory and enforcement efforts are designed to ensure that the futures trading process is fair and that it protects both the rights of customers and the financial integrity of the marketplace. The CFTC approves the rules under which an exchange proposes to operate and monitors exchange enforcement of those rules. It reviews the terms of proposed futures contracts, and registers companies and individuals who handle customer funds or give trading advice. The Commission also protects the public by enforcing rules that require that customer funds be kept in bank accounts separate from accounts maintained by firms for their own use, and that such customer accounts be marked to present market value at the close of trading each day.

Futures contracts for agricultural commodities were traded in the United States for more than 100 years before futures trading was diversified to include trading in contracts for precious metals, raw materials, foreign currencies, commercial interest rates, and U.S. Government and mortgage securities. Contract diversification has grown in exchange trading volume, a growth not limited to the newer commodities.

Futures and Options Exchanges: Addresses

UNITED STATES
American Stock Exchange
86 Trinity Place
New York, NY 10006
   (212) 306-1000

Chicago Board of Trade (CBT)
141 West Jackson Boulevard
Chicago, IL 60604
   (312) 435-3500

Chicago Board Options Exchange
LaSalle at Van Buren
Chicago, IL 60605
   (312) 786-5600

Chicago Mercantile Exchange (CME) and International Monetary Market (IMM)
444 West Jackson Boulevard
Chicago, IL 60606
   (312) 930-1000

Chicago Rice & Cotton Exchange
444 W. Jackson Boulevard
Chicago, IL 60606
   (312) 341-3078

Coffee, Sugar & Cocoa Exchange (CSCE)
4 World Trade Center
New York, NY 10048
   (212) 938-2800

Commodity Exchange, Inc. (COMEX)
4 World Trade Center
New York, NY 10048
   (212) 938-2900

International Monetary Market [IMM] (see Chicago Merchantile Exchange [CME]

Kansas City Board of Trade (KCBT)
4800 Main Street
Kansas City, MO 64112
   (816) 753-7500

Midamerica Commodity Exchange (MACE)
444 West Jackson Boulevard
Chicago, IL 60604
   (312) 341-3000 & (800) 572-3276

Minneapolis Grain Exchange (MGE)
150 Grain Exchange Building
Minneapolis, MN 55415
   (612) 338-6212

New York Cotton Exchange
4 World Trade Center
New York, NY 10048
   (212) 938-2702

New York Futures Exchange (NYFE)
20 Broad Street
New York, NY 10005
   (212) 623-4949 & (800) 221-7722

New York Mercantile Exchange (NYME)
4 World Trade Center
New York, NY 10048
   (212) 938-2222

New York Stock Exchange
11 Wall St.
New York, NY 10005
    (800) 692-6973

Pacific Stock Exchange
301 Pine St.
San Francisco, CA 94104
    (415) 393-4000

Philadelphia Stock Exchange
1900 Market St.
Philadelphia, PA 19103
    (215) 496-5000

CANADIAN
Montreal Stock Exchange
800 Victoria Square
Montreal, Quebec, Canada H4Z 1A9
    (514) 871-2424

Toronto Futures Exchange
2 First Canadian Place
Exchange Tower
Toronto, Ontario, Canada M5X 1J2
    (416) 947-4485

Toronto Stock Exchange
2 First Canadian Place
Exchange Tower
Toronto, Ontario, Canada M5X 1J2
    (416) 947-4700

Vancouver Stock Exchange
609 Granville
Vancouver, British Columbia
Canada V7Y 1H1
    (604) 689-3334

The Winnipeg Commodity Exchange
500 Commodity Exchange Tower
360 Main Street
Winnipeg, Manitoba
Canada R3C 3Z4
    (204) 949-0495

SELECTED FOREIGN EXCHANGES
London Commodity Exchange Co. Ltd.
Cereal House, 58 Mark Lane
London, England EC3R 7NE
    01-481-2080

The London International Financial Futures Exchange Ltd. (LIFFE)
Royal Exchange
London, England EC3
    01-623-0444

The Hong Kong Futures Exchange Ltd.
Hutchison House, Second Floor
Harcourt Road
Hong Kong
    5-251005

European Options Exchange (EOE)
DAM 21
1012 JS Amsterdam
The Netherlands
    20-26 27 21

Paris Commodity Exchange
Bourse de Commerce
2, rue de Viarmes B.P. 53/01
75040 Paris, Cedex 01 France
1-508-82-50
    (212) 751-9050-New York

The Singapore International Monetary Exchange Ltd.
24 Raffles Place
29-04 Clifford Centre
Singapore 0104

Sydney Futures Exchange Ltd.
13-15 O'Connell St.
Sydney, NSW, Australia 2000
    02-233-7633

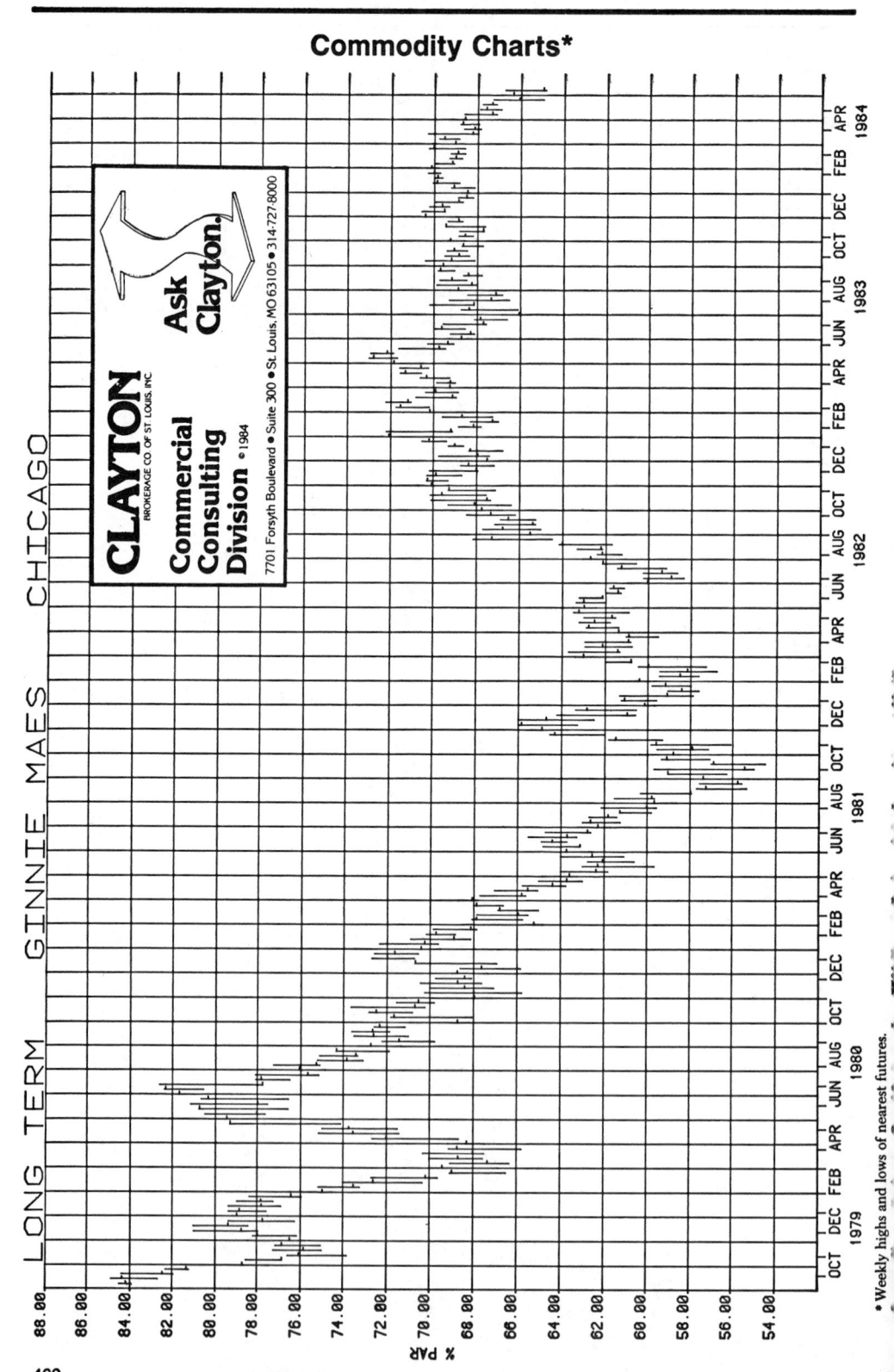

Commodity Charts*

LONG TERM GINNIE MAES CHICAGO

CLAYTON
BROKERAGE CO OF ST LOUIS, INC

Commercial
Consulting
Division. © 1984

7701 Forsyth Boulevard • Suite 300 • St. Louis, MO 63105 • 314-727-8000

Ask
Clayton.

* Weekly highs and lows of nearest futures.

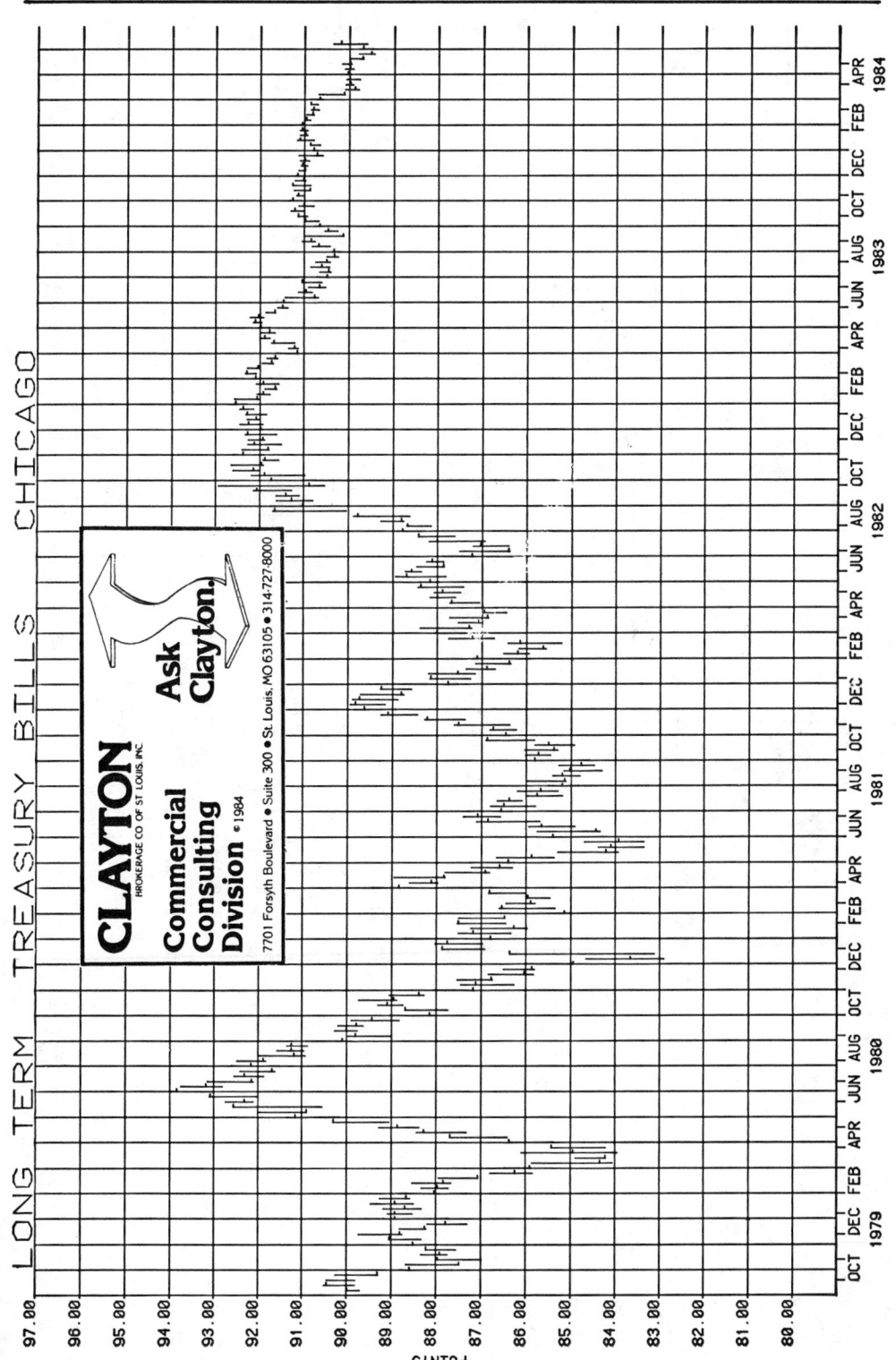

LONG TERM TREASURY BILLS CHICAGO

POINTS

CLAYTON
BROKERAGE CO OF ST LOUIS, INC.

Ask Clayton.

Commercial
Consulting
Division ®1984

7701 Forsyth Boulevard ● Suite 300 ● St. Louis, MO 63105 ● 314-727-8000

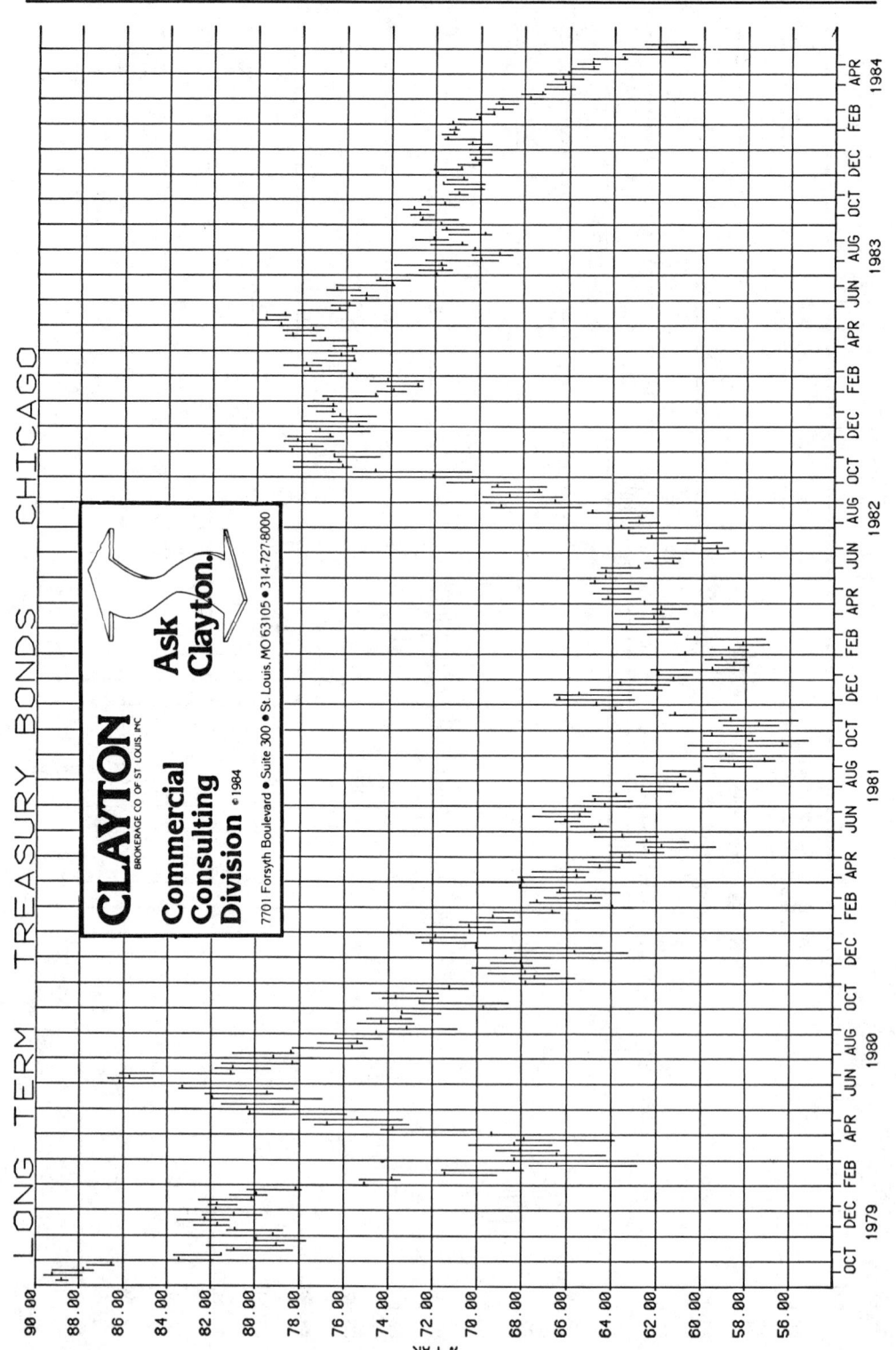

CLAYTON
BROKERAGE CO OF ST. LOUIS, INC

Commercial
Consulting
Division ©1984

7701 Forsyth Boulevard • Suite 300 • St. Louis, MO 63105 • 314-727-8000

Ask
Clayton.

LONG TERM TREASURY BONDS CHICAGO

% PAR

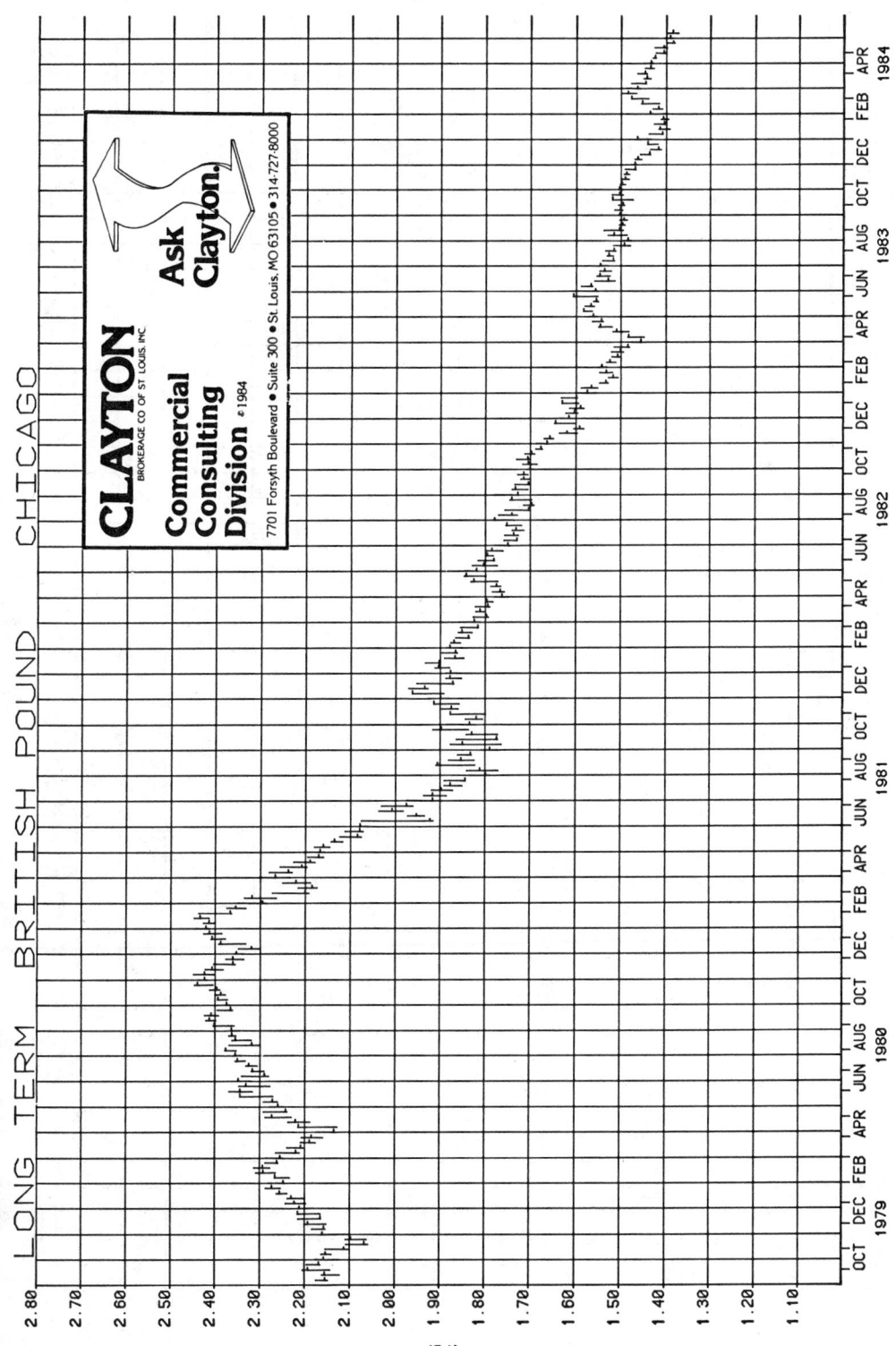

CLAYTON
BROKERAGE CO OF ST LOUIS, INC.

Commercial
Consulting
Division ©1984

Ask
Clayton.

7701 Forsyth Boulevard ● Suite 300 ● St. Louis, MO 63105 ● 314-727-8000

LONG TERM BRITISH POUND CHICAGO

dB/$

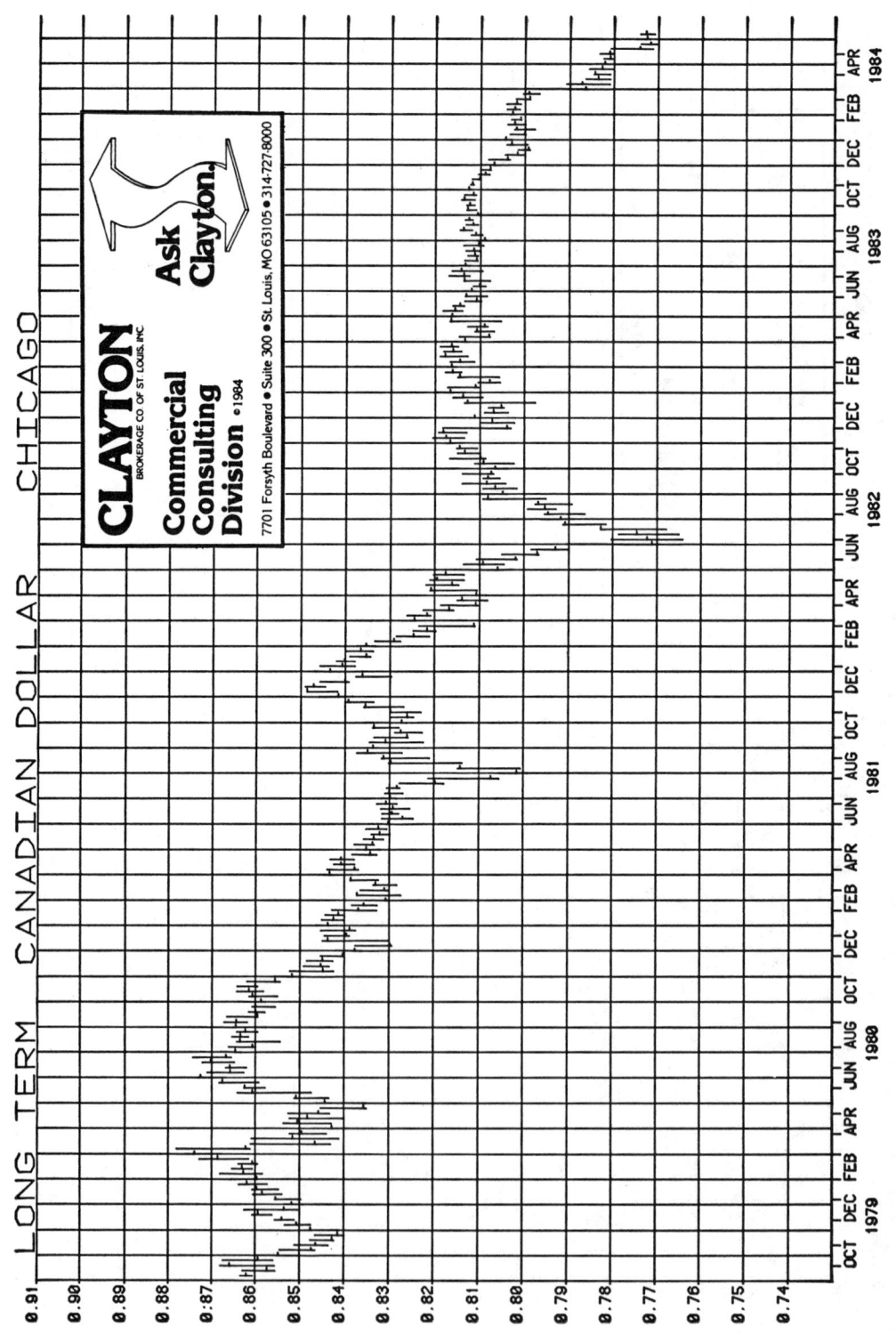

CLAYTON
BROKERAGE CO OF ST. LOUIS INC

Commercial
Consulting
Division ©1984

Ask
Clayton.

7701 Forsyth Boulevard ● Suite 300 ● St. Louis, MO 63105 ● 314-727-8000

LONG TERM CANADIAN DOLLAR CHICAGO

CD/$

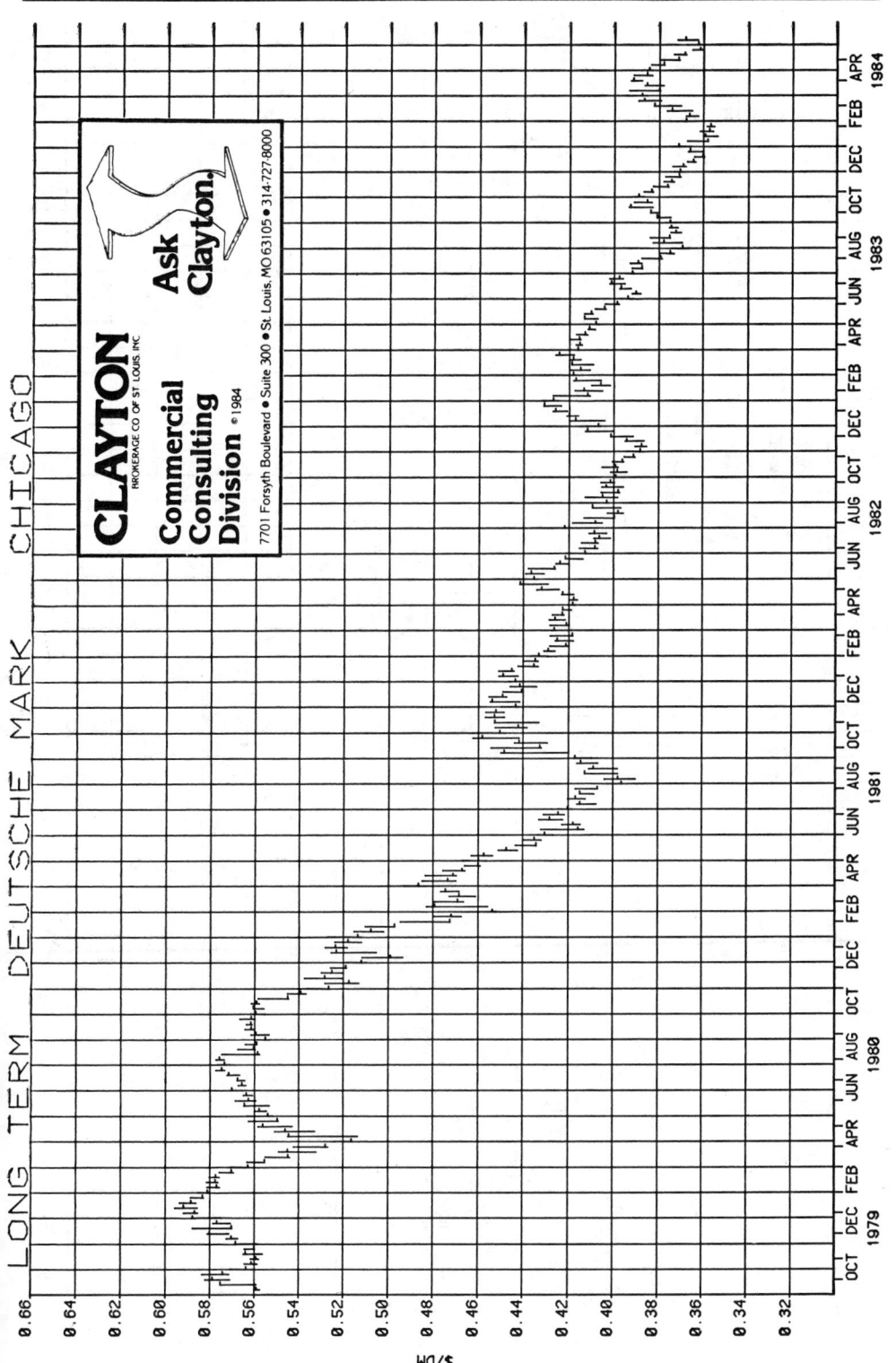

LONG TERM DEUTSCHE MARK CHICAGO

CLAYTON
BROKERAGE CO OF ST LOUIS INC

Commercial
Consulting
Division ©1984

Ask
Clayton.

7701 Forsyth Boulevard • Suite 300 • St. Louis, MO 63105 • 314-727-8000

$/DM

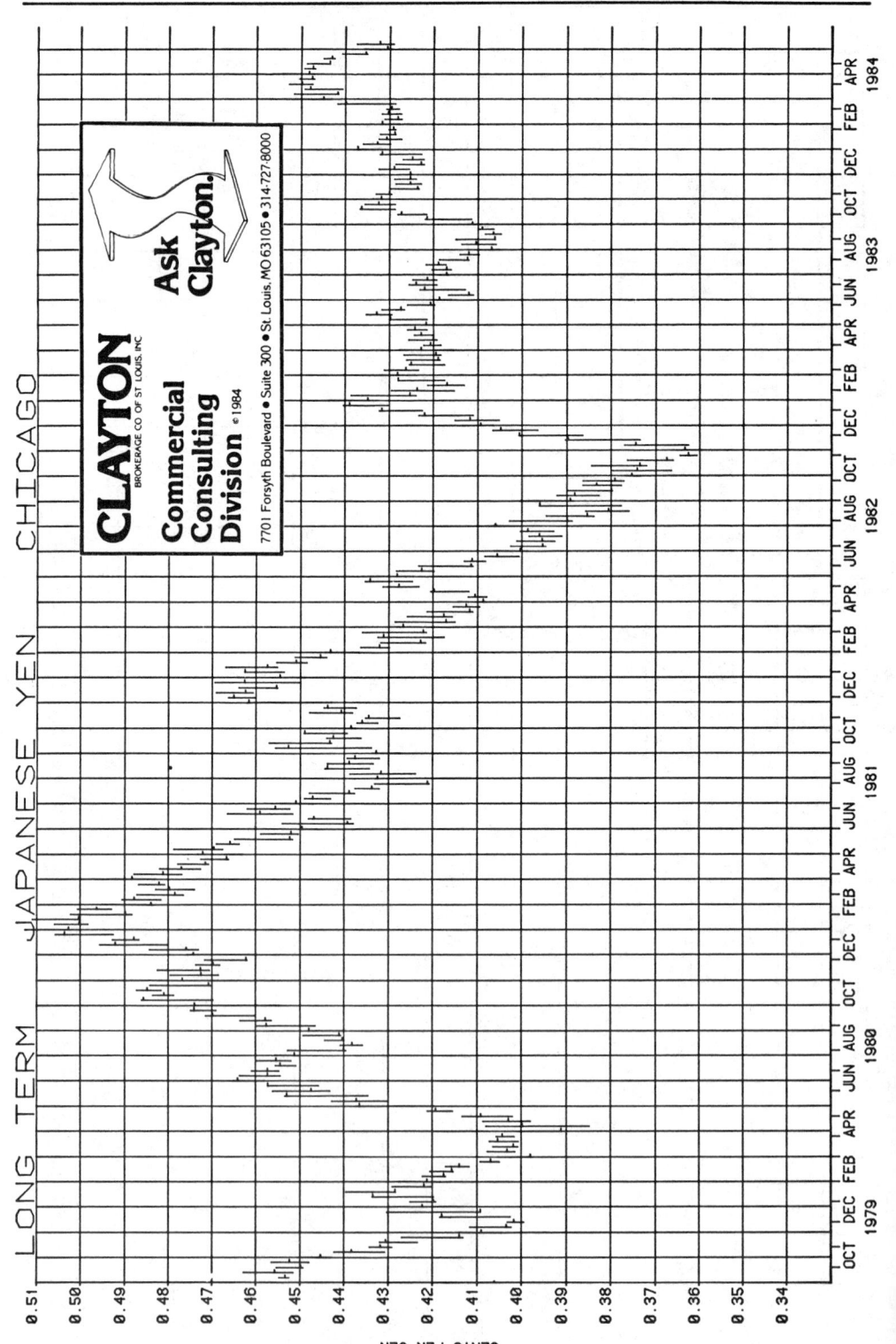

CLAYTON
BROKERAGE CO OF ST LOUIS, INC

Ask Clayton.

Commercial
Consulting
Division ©1984

7701 Forsyth Boulevard • Suite 300 • St. Louis, MO 63105 • 314-727-8000

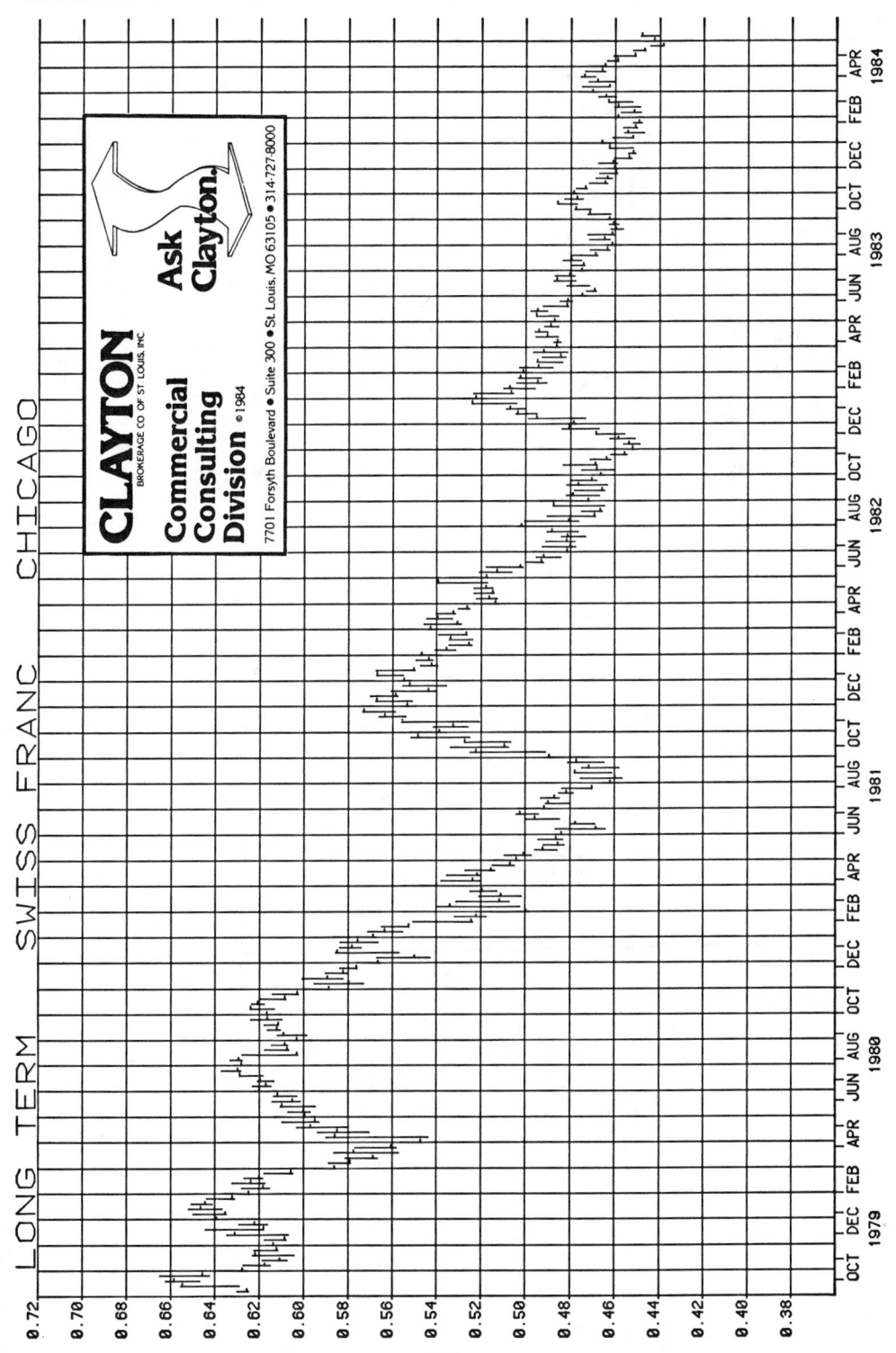

LONG TERM   SWISS FRANC   CHICAGO

CLAYTON
BROKERAGE CO OF ST LOUIS, INC

Commercial
Consulting
Division © 1984

Ask
Clayton.

7701 Forsyth Boulevard ● Suite 300 ● St. Louis, MO 63105 ● 314-727-8000

$/SF

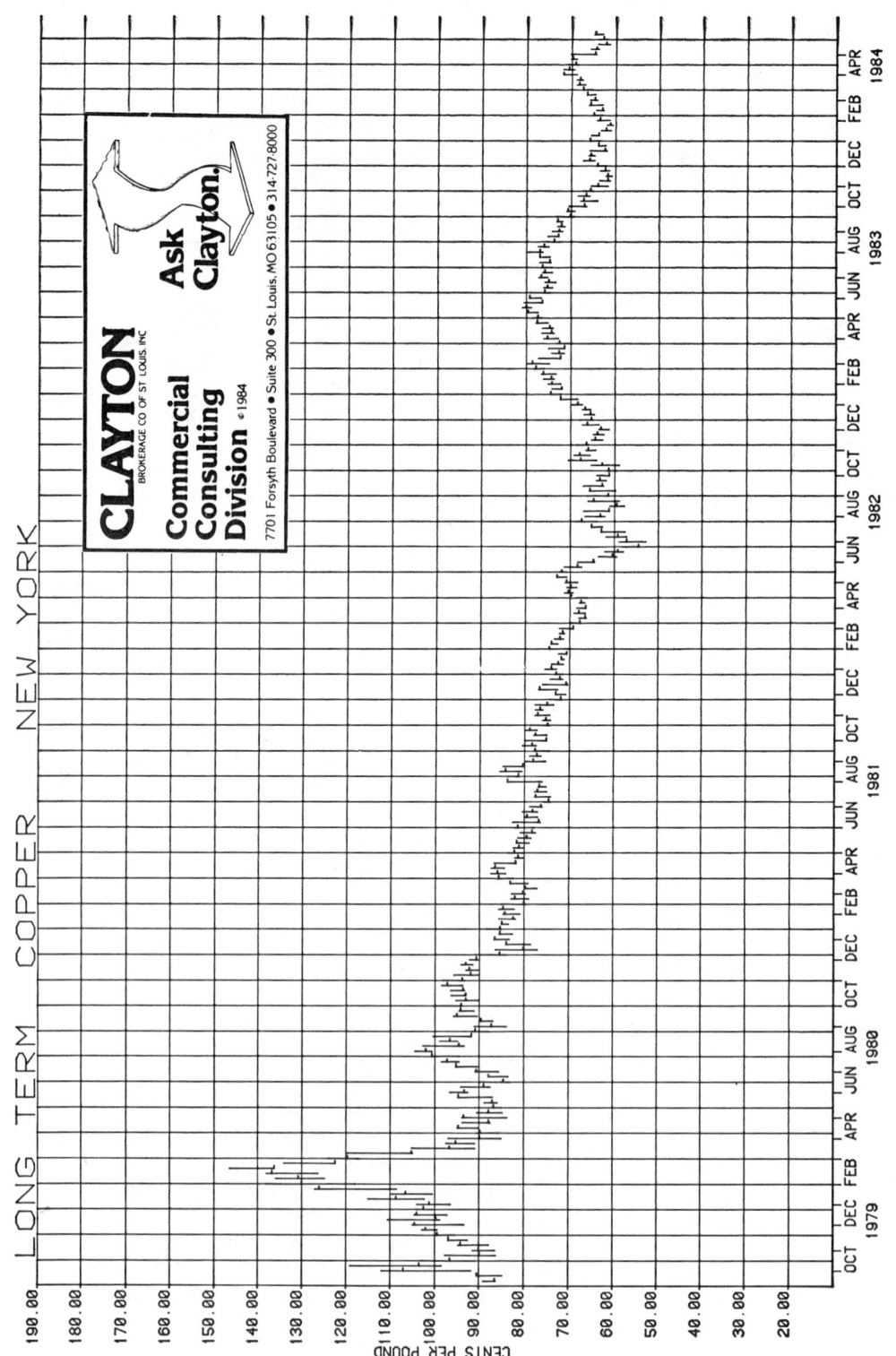

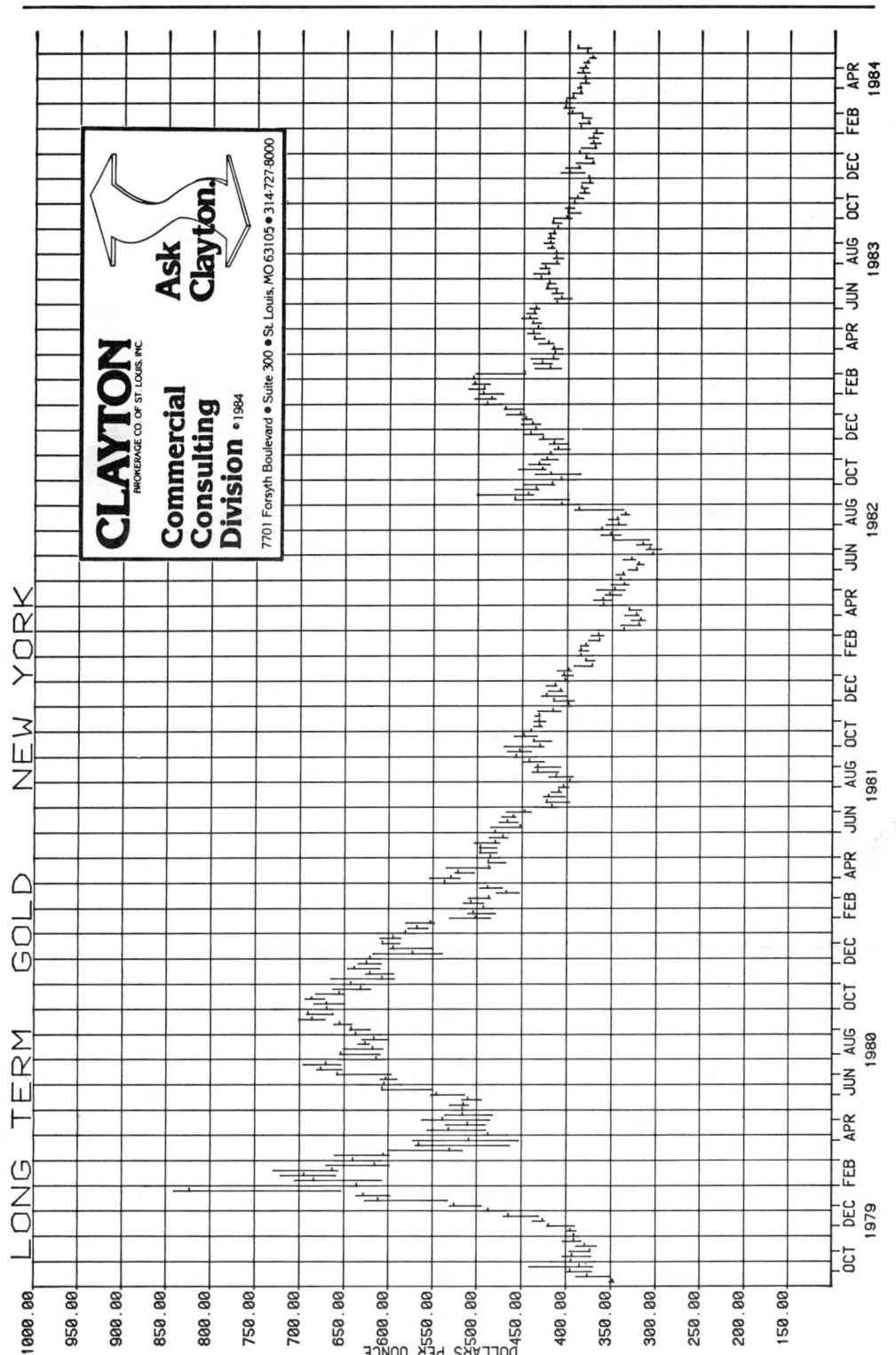

LONG TERM GOLD NEW YORK

DOLLARS PER OUNCE

CLAYTON
BROKERAGE CO. OF ST. LOUIS, INC.

Commercial
Consulting
Division ●1984

Ask
Clayton.

7701 Forsyth Boulevard ● Suite 300 ● St. Louis, MO 63105 ● 314-727-8000

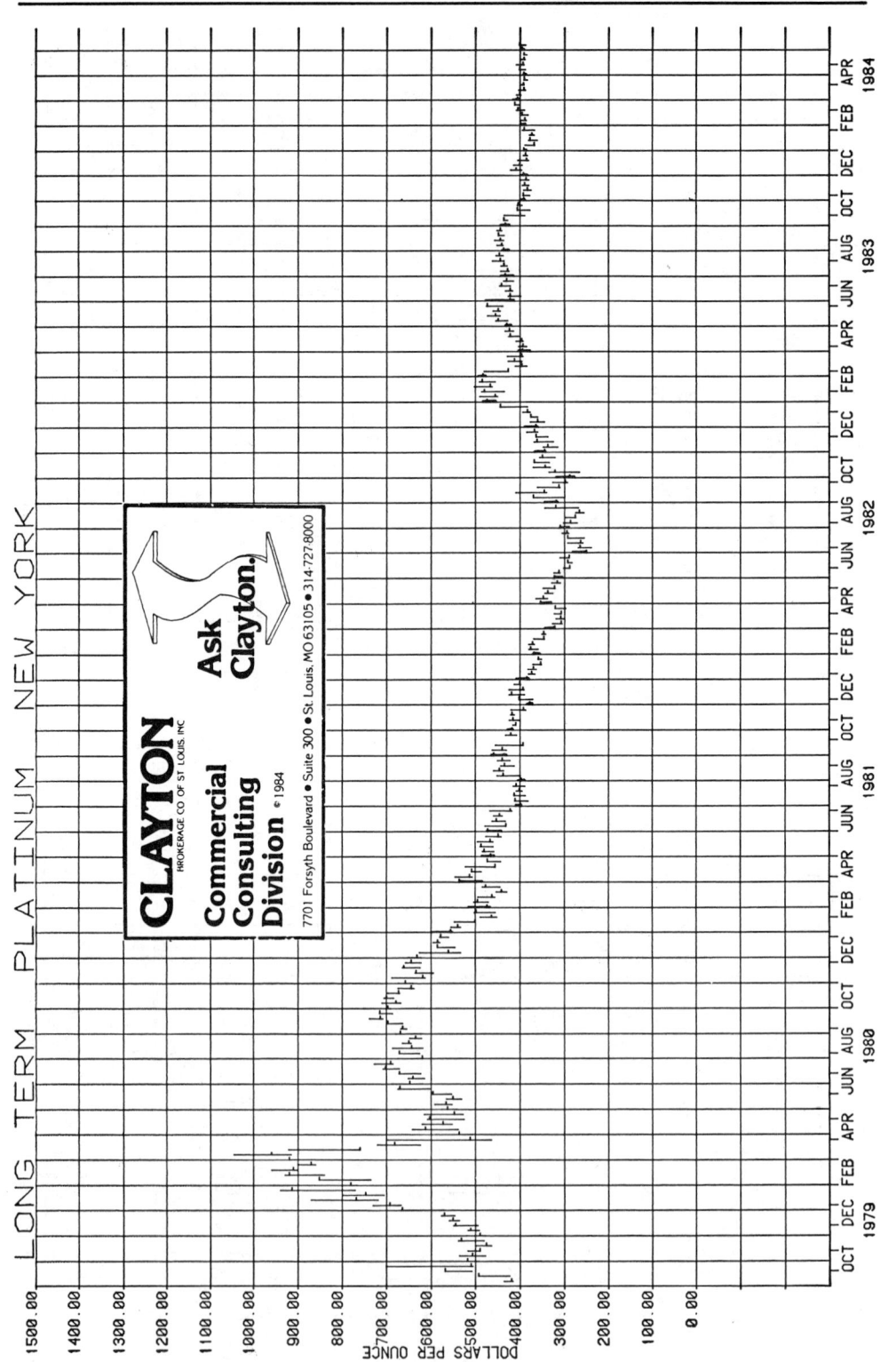

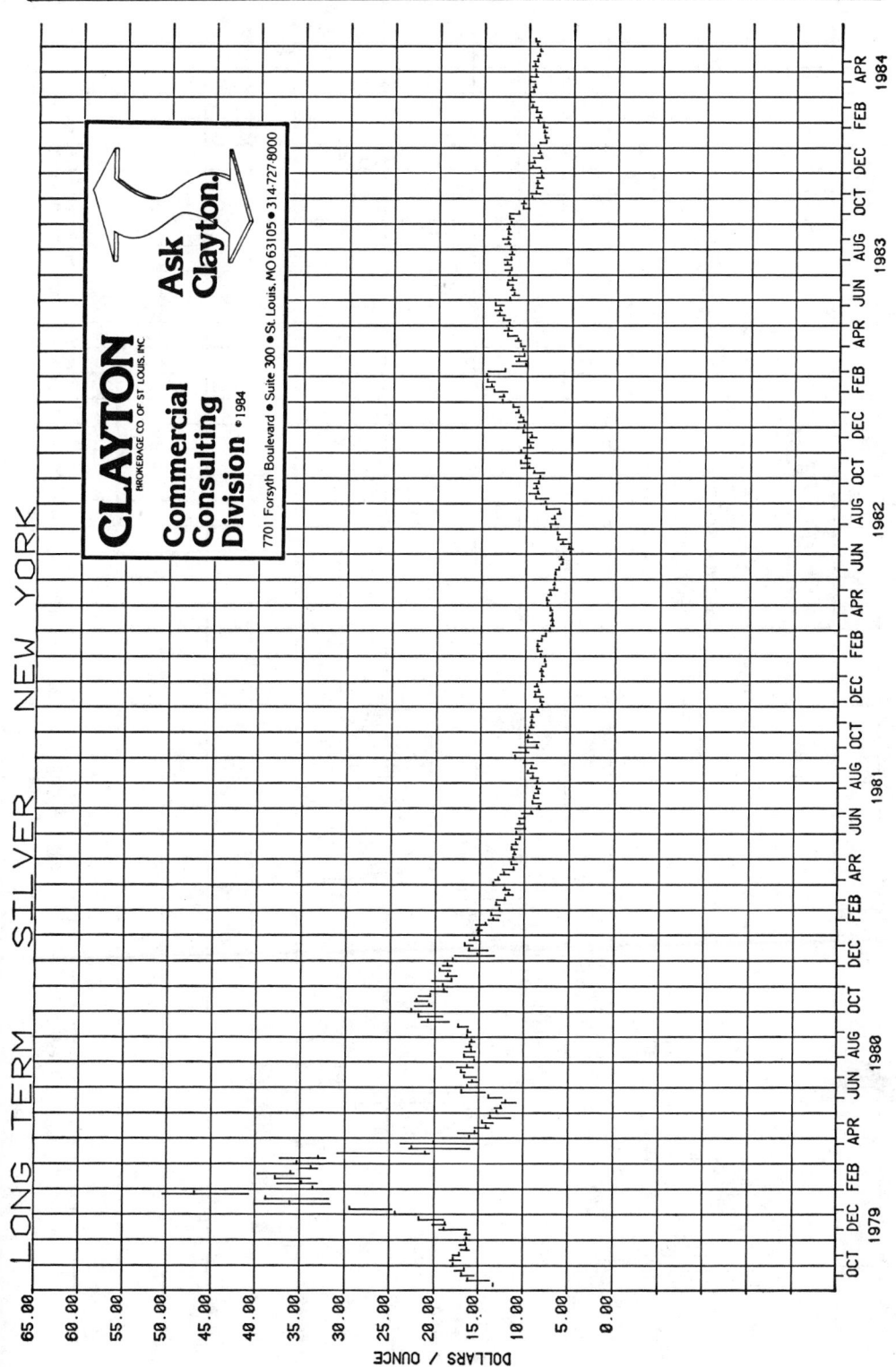

LONG TERM SILVER NEW YORK

DOLLARS / OUNCE

CLAYTON
BROKERAGE CO OF ST LOUIS INC

Commercial
Consulting
Division © 1984

Ask
Clayton.

7701 Forsyth Boulevard • Suite 300 • St. Louis, MO 63105 • 314 727 8000

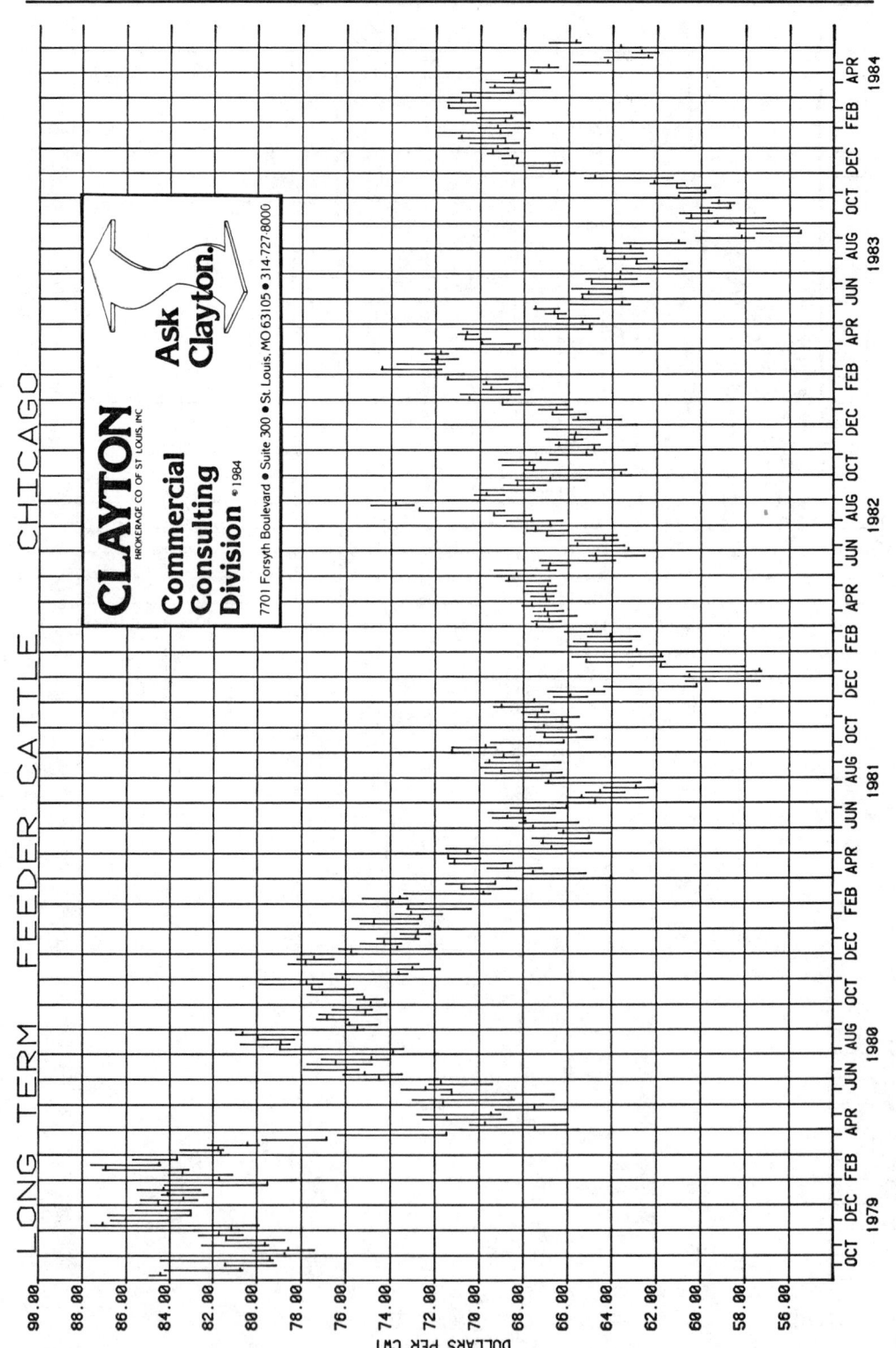

LONG TERM FEEDER CATTLE CHICAGO

DOLLARS PER CWT

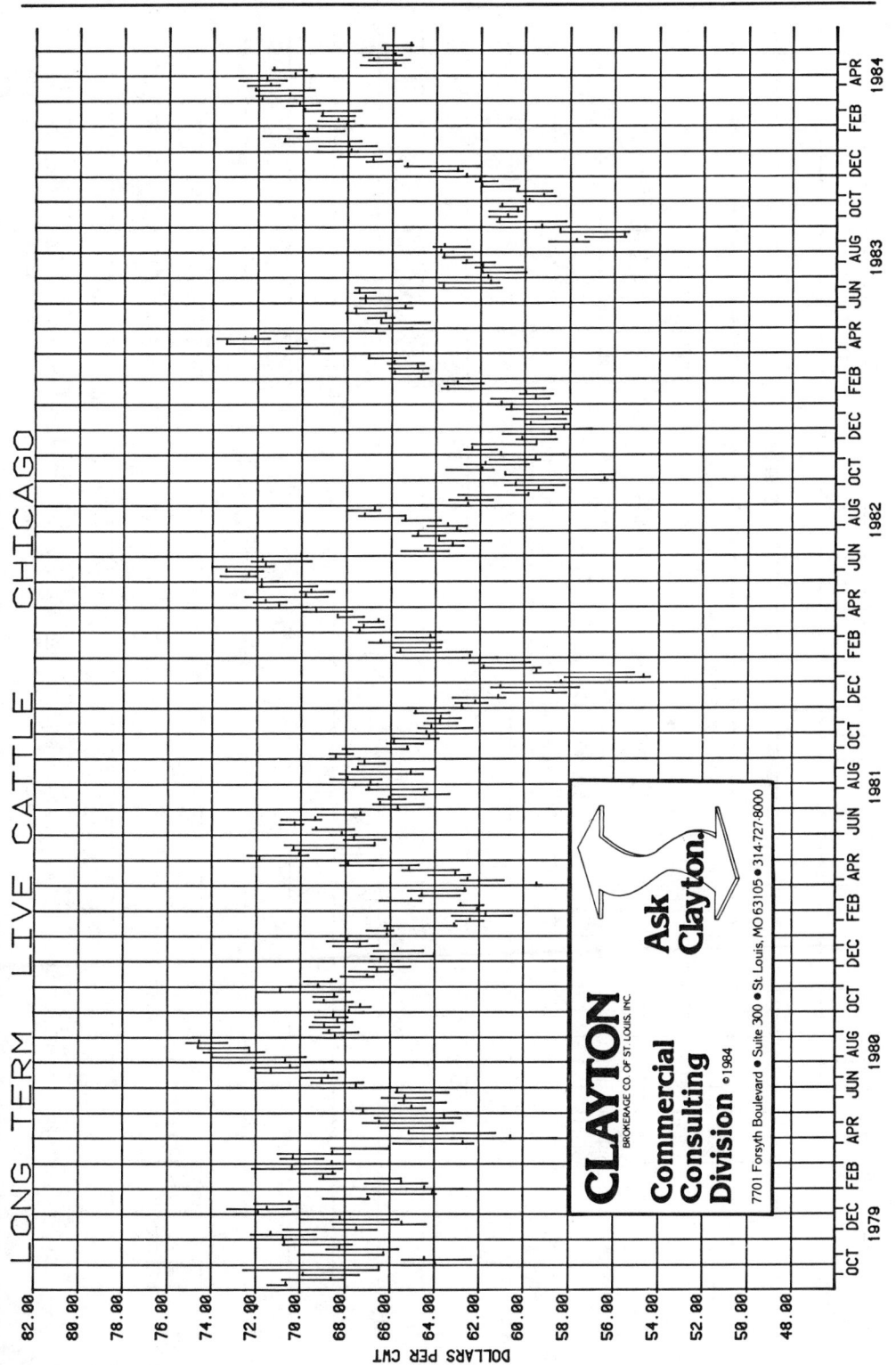

LONG TERM LIVE CATTLE CHICAGO

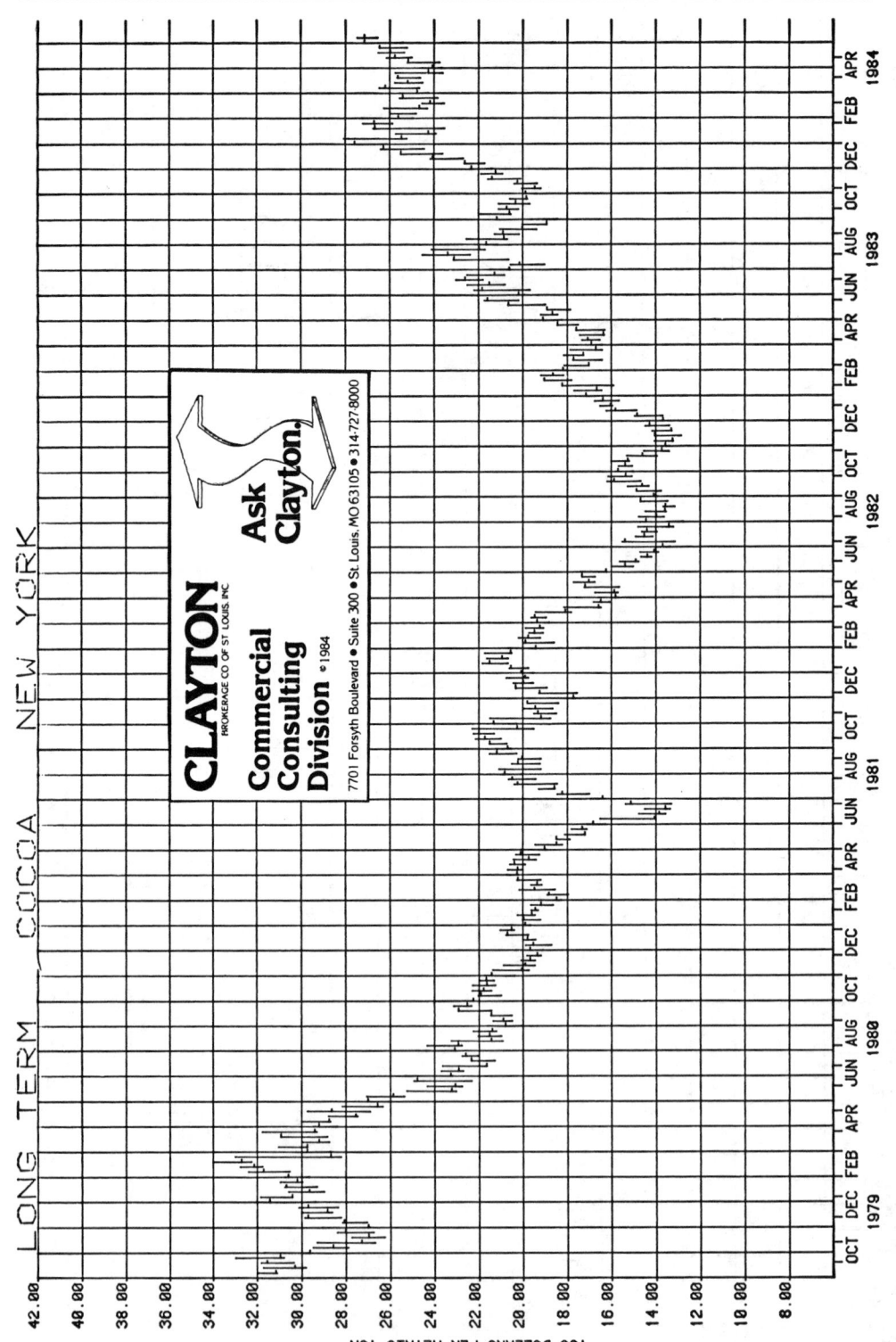

LONG TERM COCOA NEW YORK

CLAYTON
BROKERAGE CO OF ST LOUIS, INC

Commercial
Consulting
Division ©1984

Ask
Clayton.

7701 Forsyth Boulevard • Suite 300 • St. Louis, MO 63105 • 314·727·8000

100 DOLLARS PER METRIC TON

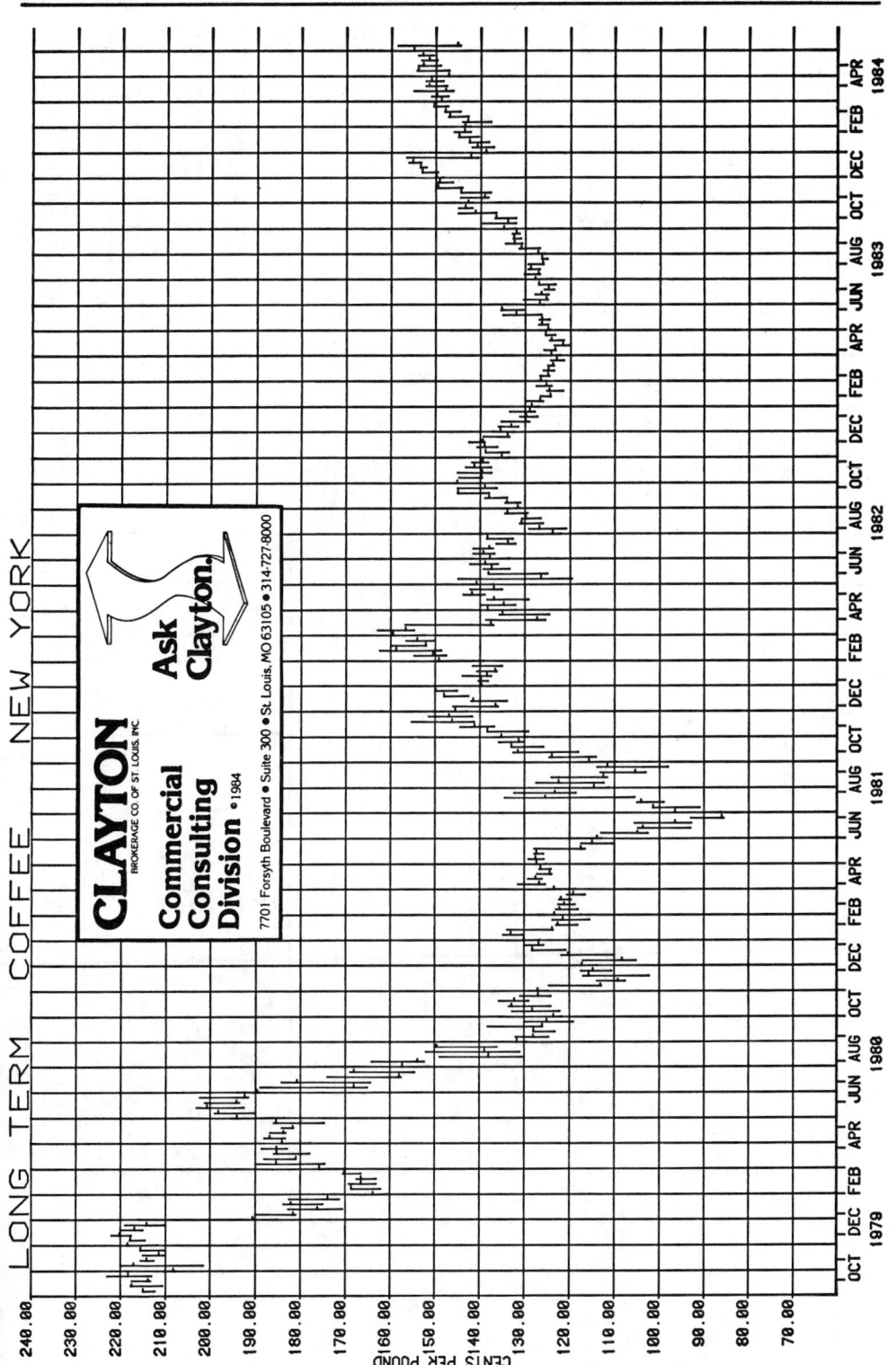

LONG TERM COFFEE NEW YORK

CENTS PER POUND

CLAYTON
BROKERAGE CO. OF ST. LOUIS, INC.

Commercial
Consulting
Division ©1984

Ask
Clayton.

7701 Forsyth Boulevard ● Suite 300 ● St. Louis, MO 63105 ● 314-727-8000

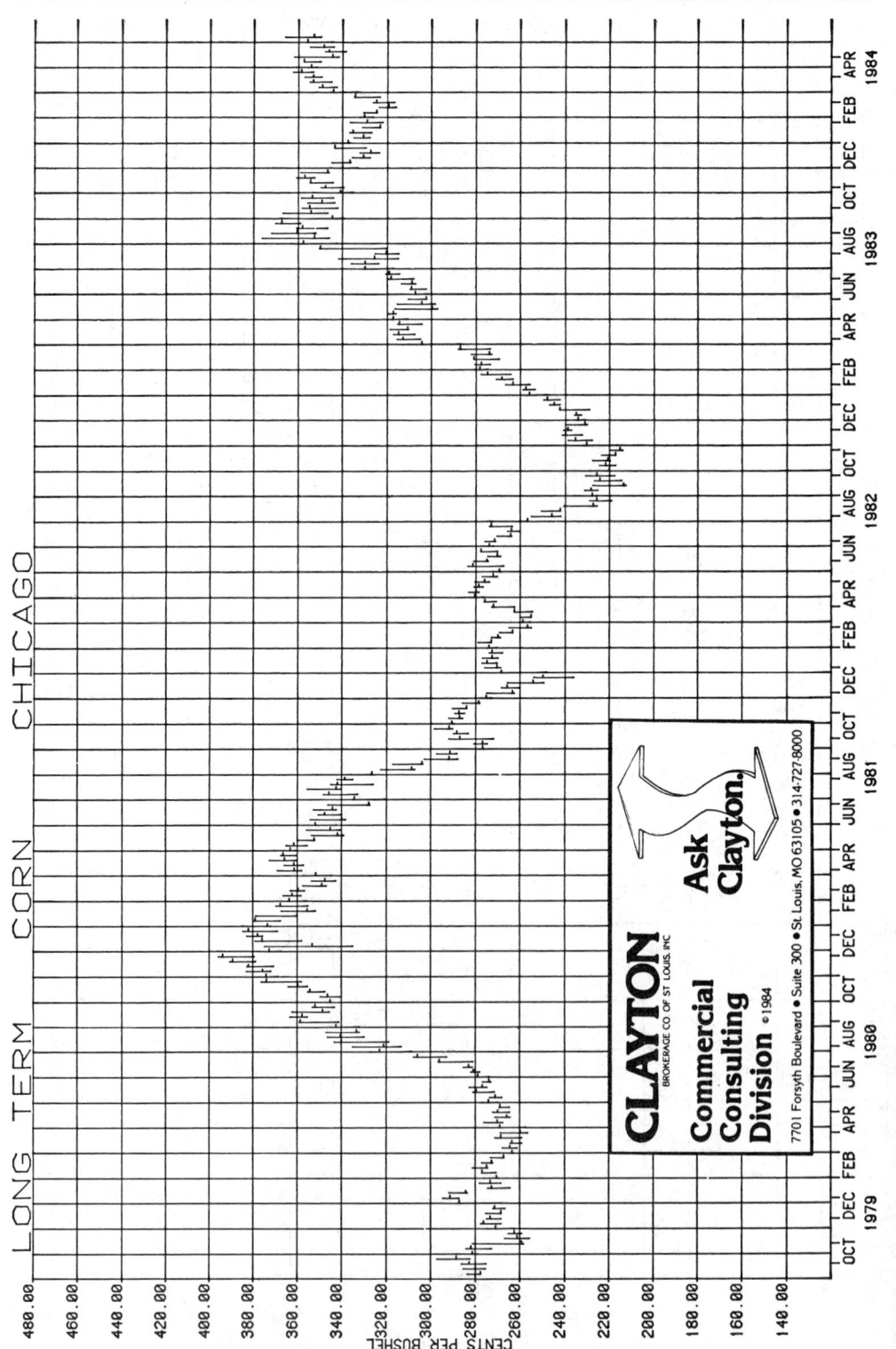

LONG TERM CORN CHICAGO

CENTS PER BUSHEL

480.00 460.00 440.00 420.00 400.00 380.00 360.00 340.00 320.00 300.00 280.00 260.00 240.00 220.00 200.00 180.00 160.00 140.00

OCT DEC 1979 FEB APR JUN AUG OCT 1980 DEC FEB APR JUN AUG 1981 OCT DEC FEB APR JUN AUG 1982 OCT DEC FEB APR JUN AUG 1983 OCT DEC FEB APR 1984

CLAYTON
BROKERAGE CO OF ST LOUIS, INC

Commercial
Consulting
Division ©1984

Ask
Clayton.

7701 Forsyth Boulevard • Suite 300 • St. Louis, MO 63105 • 314-727-8000

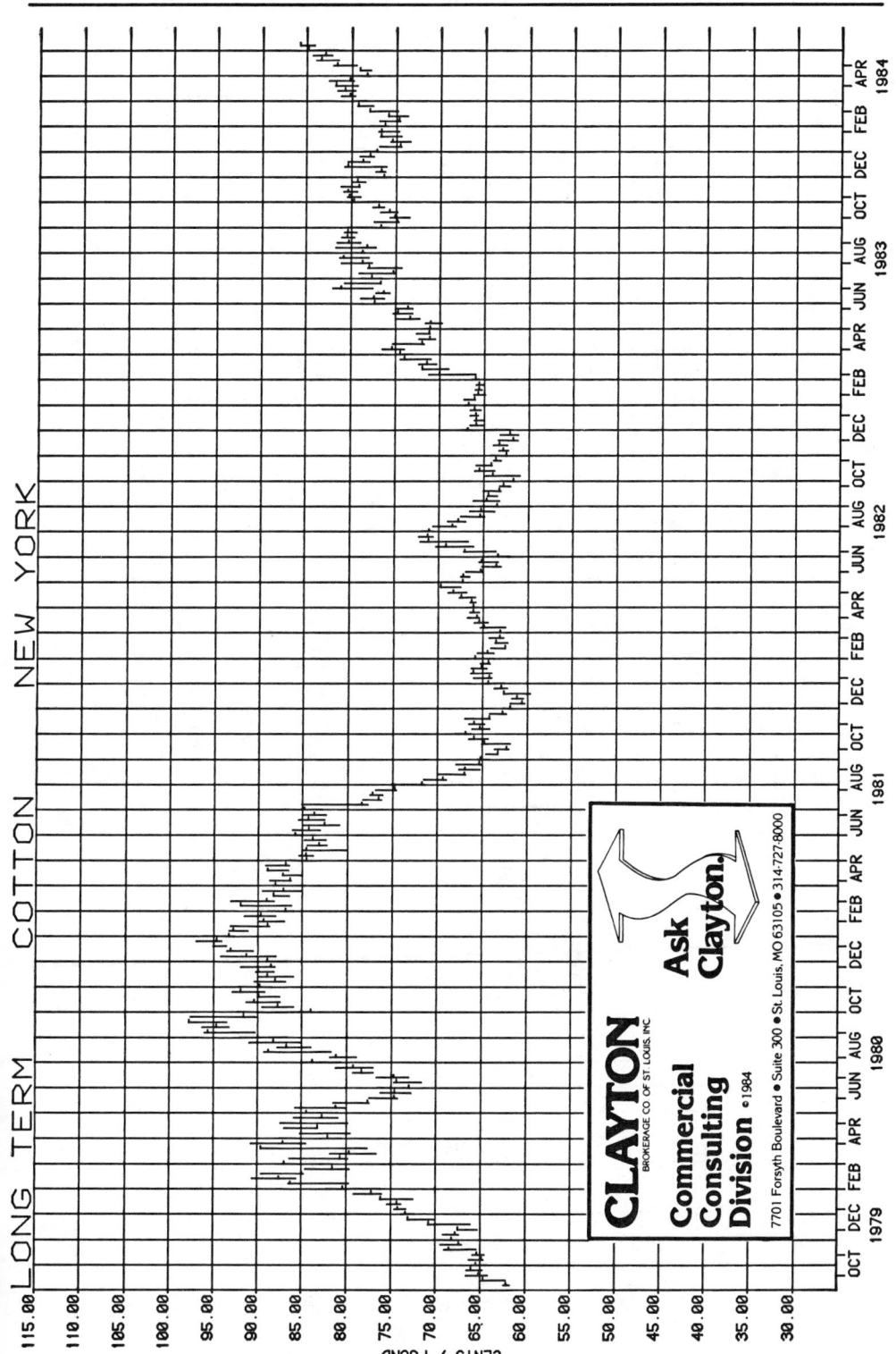

LONG TERM   COTTON   NEW YORK

CENTS / POUND

115.00
110.00
105.00
100.00
95.00
90.00
85.00
80.00
75.00
70.00
65.00
60.00
55.00
50.00
45.00
40.00
35.00
30.00

OCT DEC FEB APR JUN AUG OCT DEC FEB APR JUN AUG OCT DEC FEB APR JUN AUG OCT DEC FEB APR JUN AUG OCT DEC FEB APR
1979   1980   1981   1982   1983   1984

CLAYTON
BROKERAGE CO OF ST LOUIS, INC

Commercial
Consulting
Division ©1984

7701 Forsyth Boulevard ● Suite 300 ● St. Louis, MO 63105 ● 314-727-8000

Ask
Clayton.

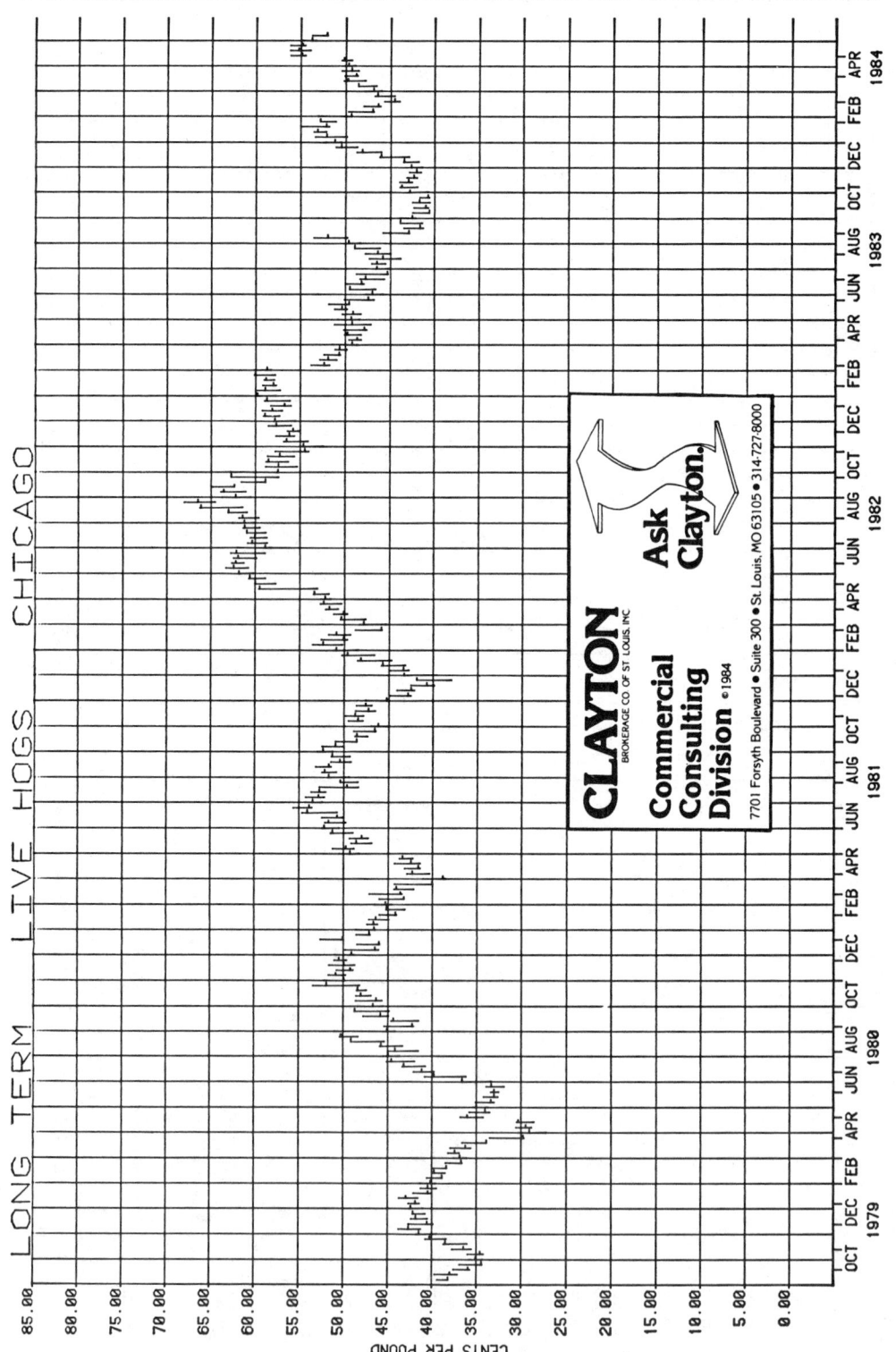

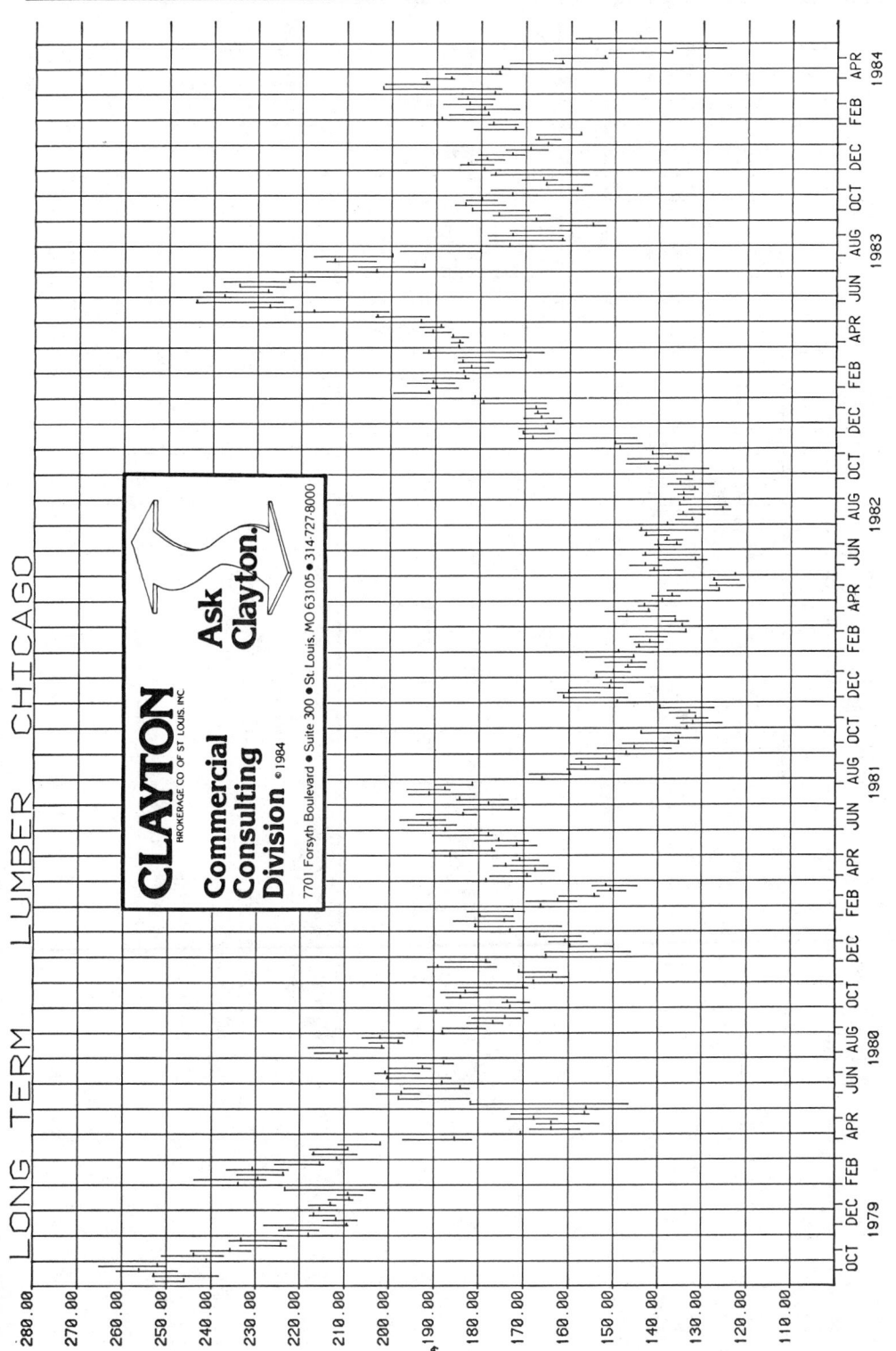

LONG TERM   LUMBER   CHICAGO

CLAYTON
BROKERAGE CO OF ST LOUIS, INC

Commercial
Consulting
Division ®1984

Ask
Clayton.

7701 Forsyth Boulevard ● Suite 300 ● St. Louis, MO 63105 ● 314·727·8000

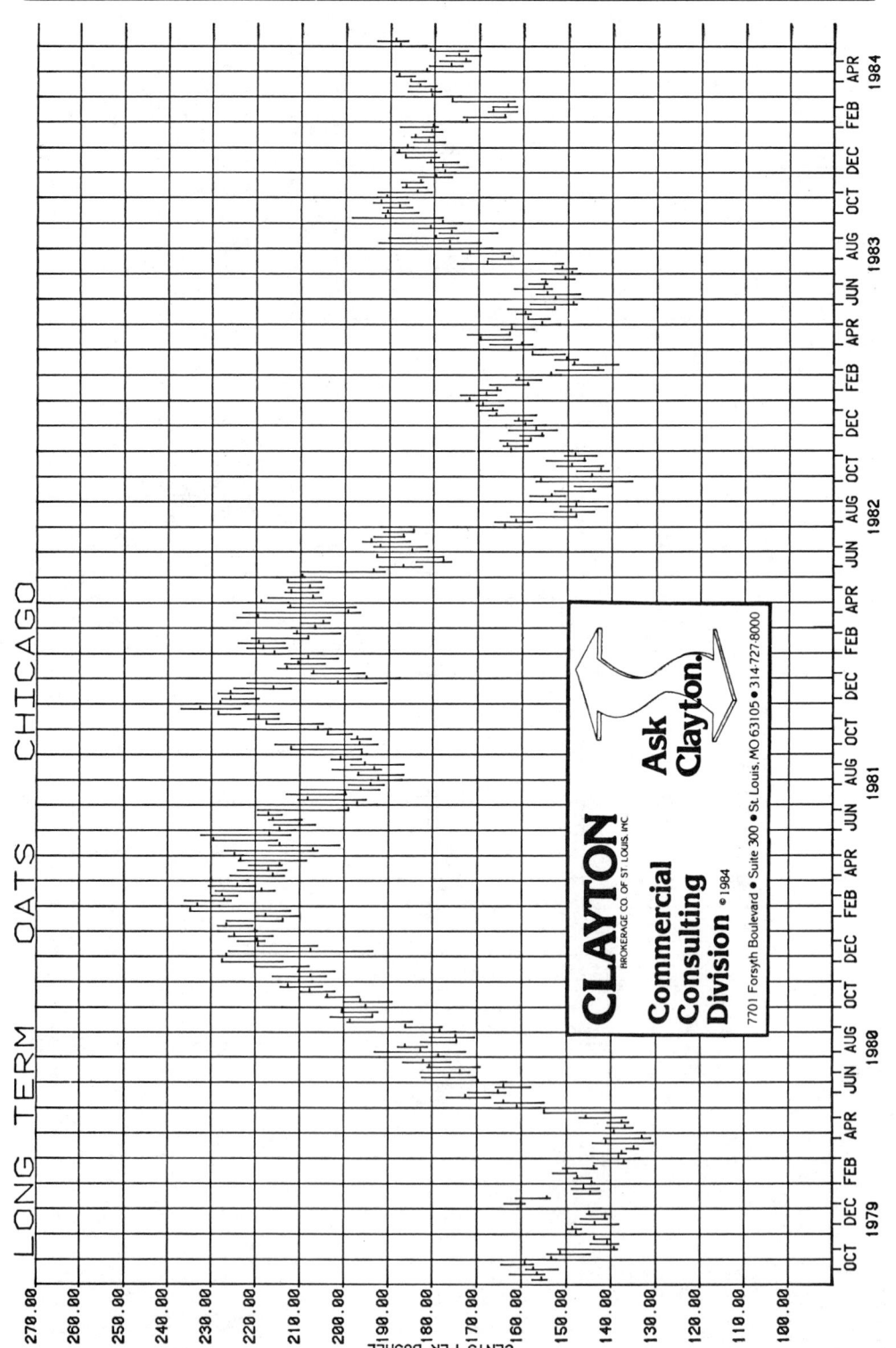

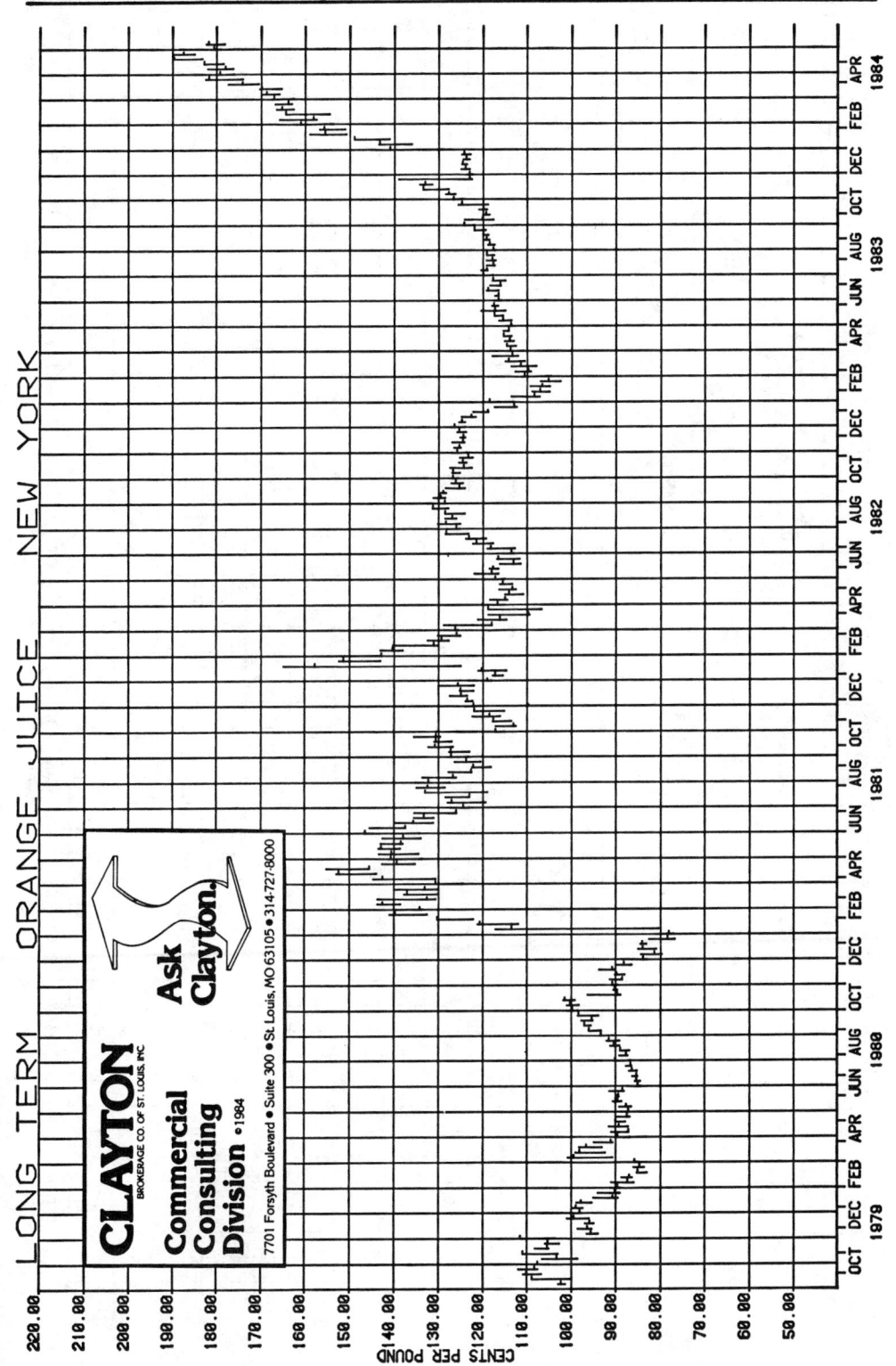

LONG TERM ORANGE JUICE NEW YORK

CENTS PER POUND

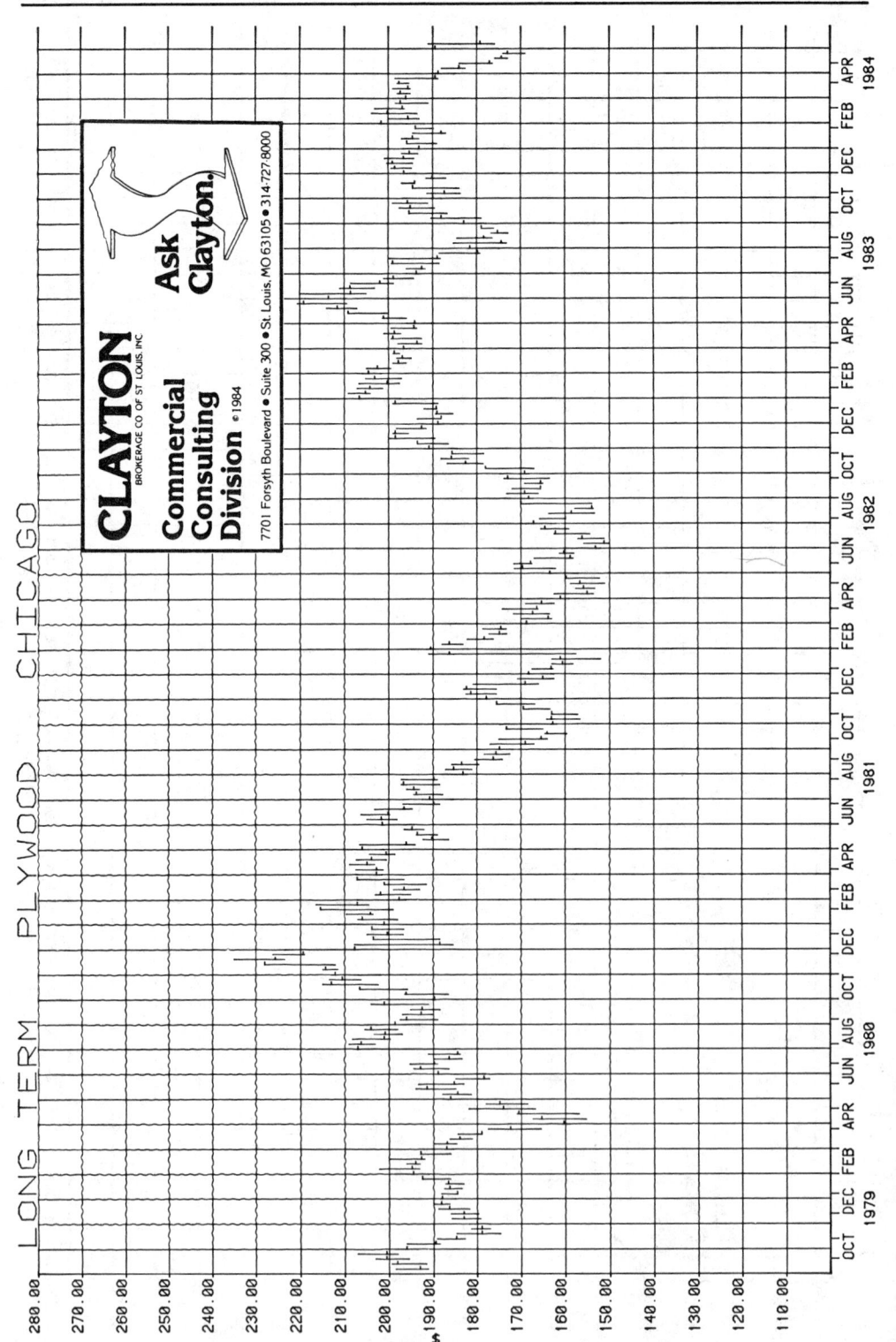

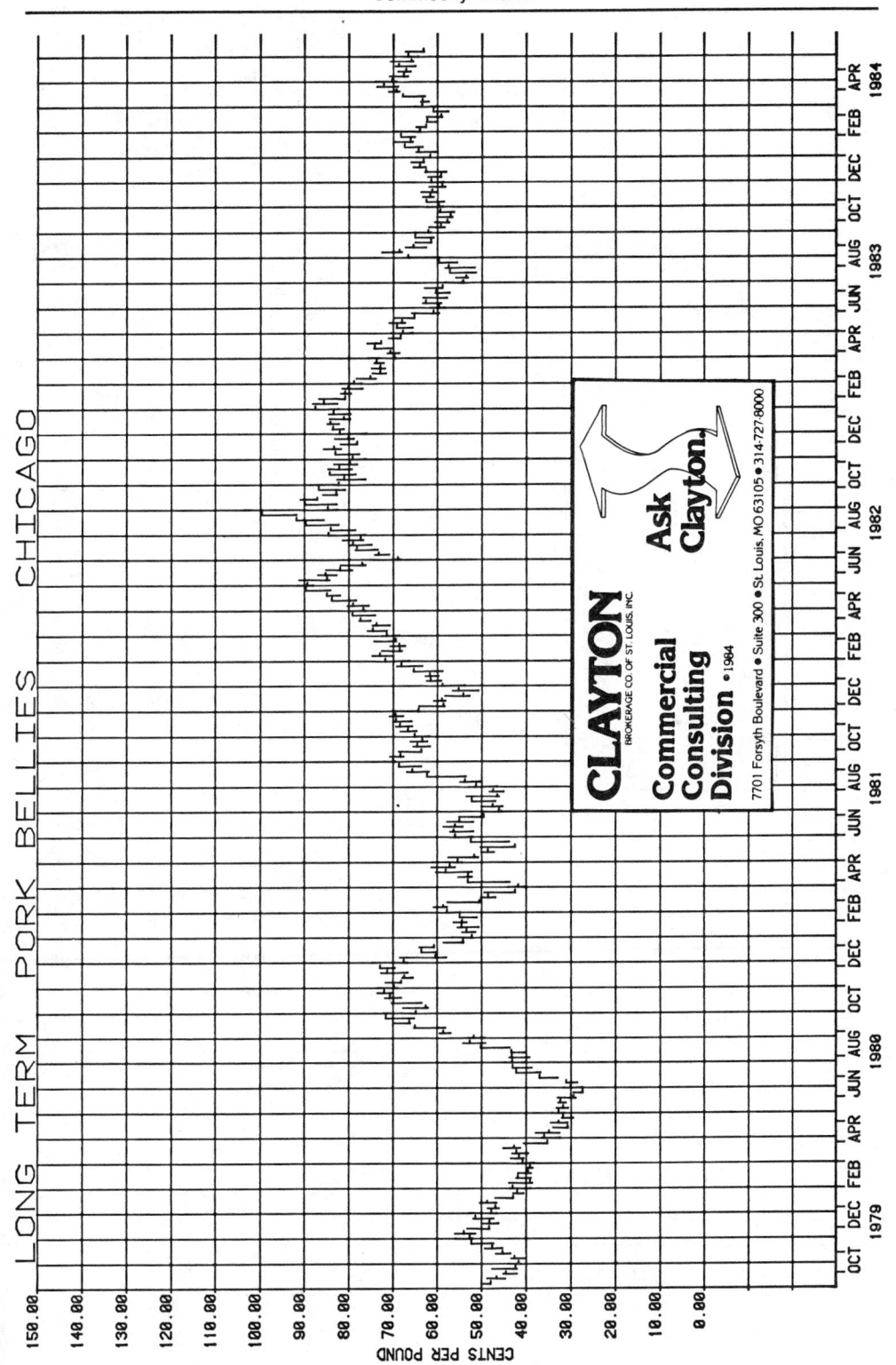

LONG TERM PORK BELLIES CHICAGO

CENTS PER POUND

150.00 140.00 130.00 120.00 110.00 100.00 90.00 80.00 70.00 60.00 50.00 40.00 30.00 20.00 10.00 0.00

OCT 1979 DEC FEB APR JUN AUG 1980 OCT DEC FEB APR JUN 1981 AUG OCT DEC FEB APR 1982 JUN AUG OCT DEC FEB APR 1983 JUN AUG OCT DEC FEB 1984 APR

CLAYTON
BROKERAGE CO. OF ST. LOUIS, INC.

Commercial
Consulting
Division • 1984

Ask
Clayton.

7701 Forsyth Boulevard • Suite 300 • St. Louis, MO 63105 • 314-727-8000

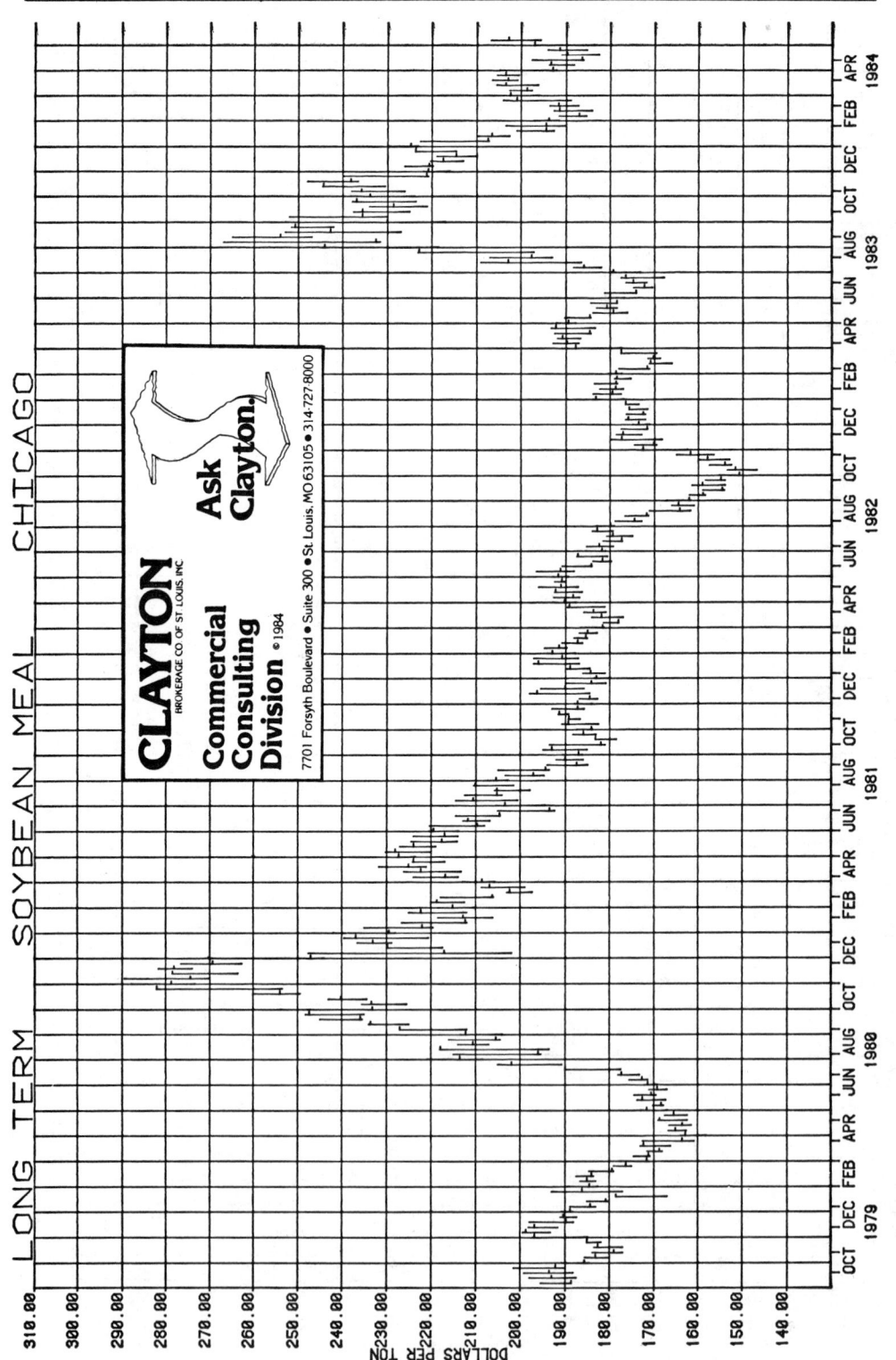

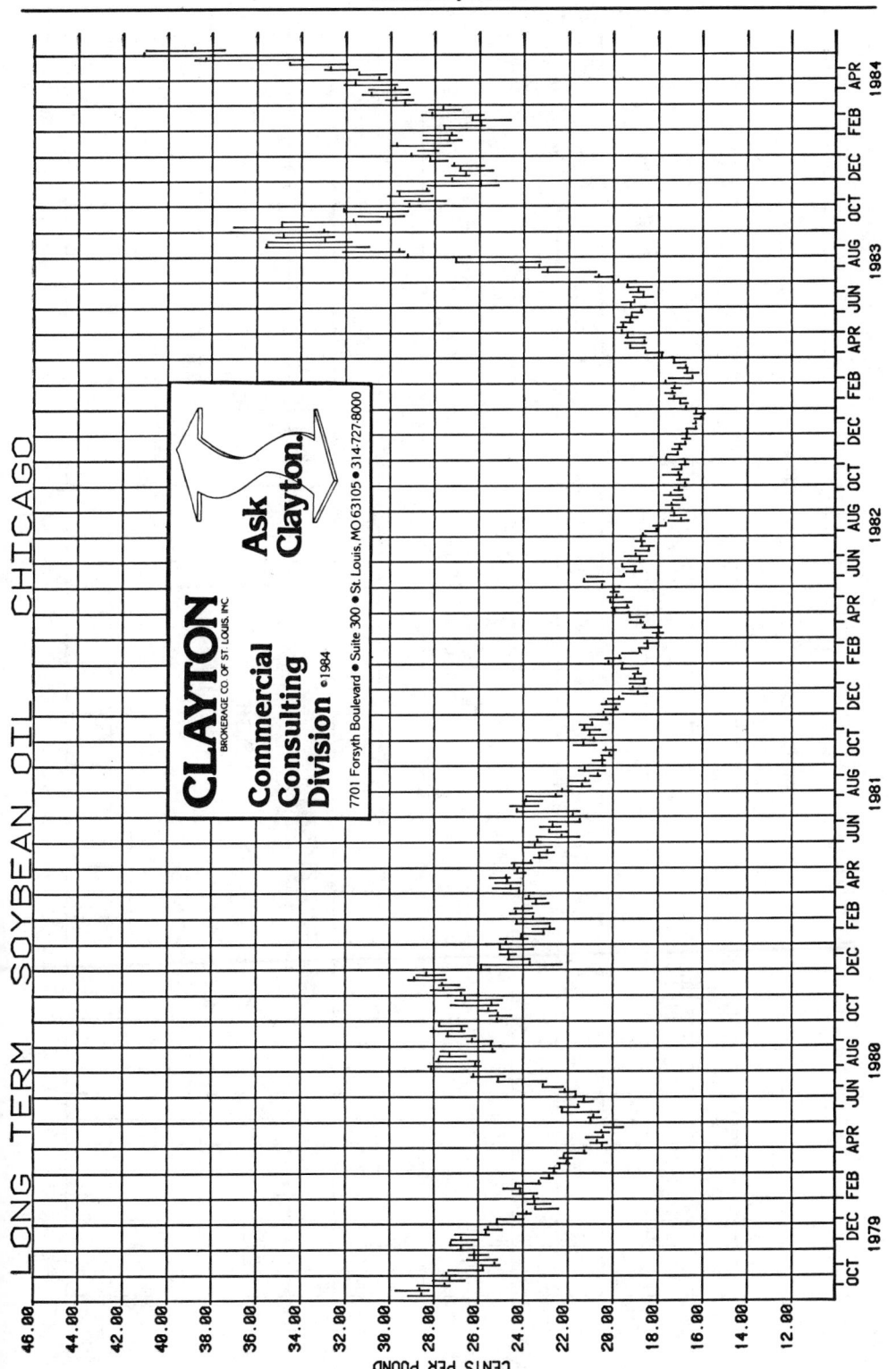

LONG TERM SOYBEAN OIL CHICAGO

CENTS PER POUND

CLAYTON
BROKERAGE CO OF ST. LOUIS, INC

Commercial
Consulting
Division ©1984

7701 Forsyth Boulevard ● Suite 300 ● St. Louis, MO 63105 ● 314-727-8000

Ask
Clayton.

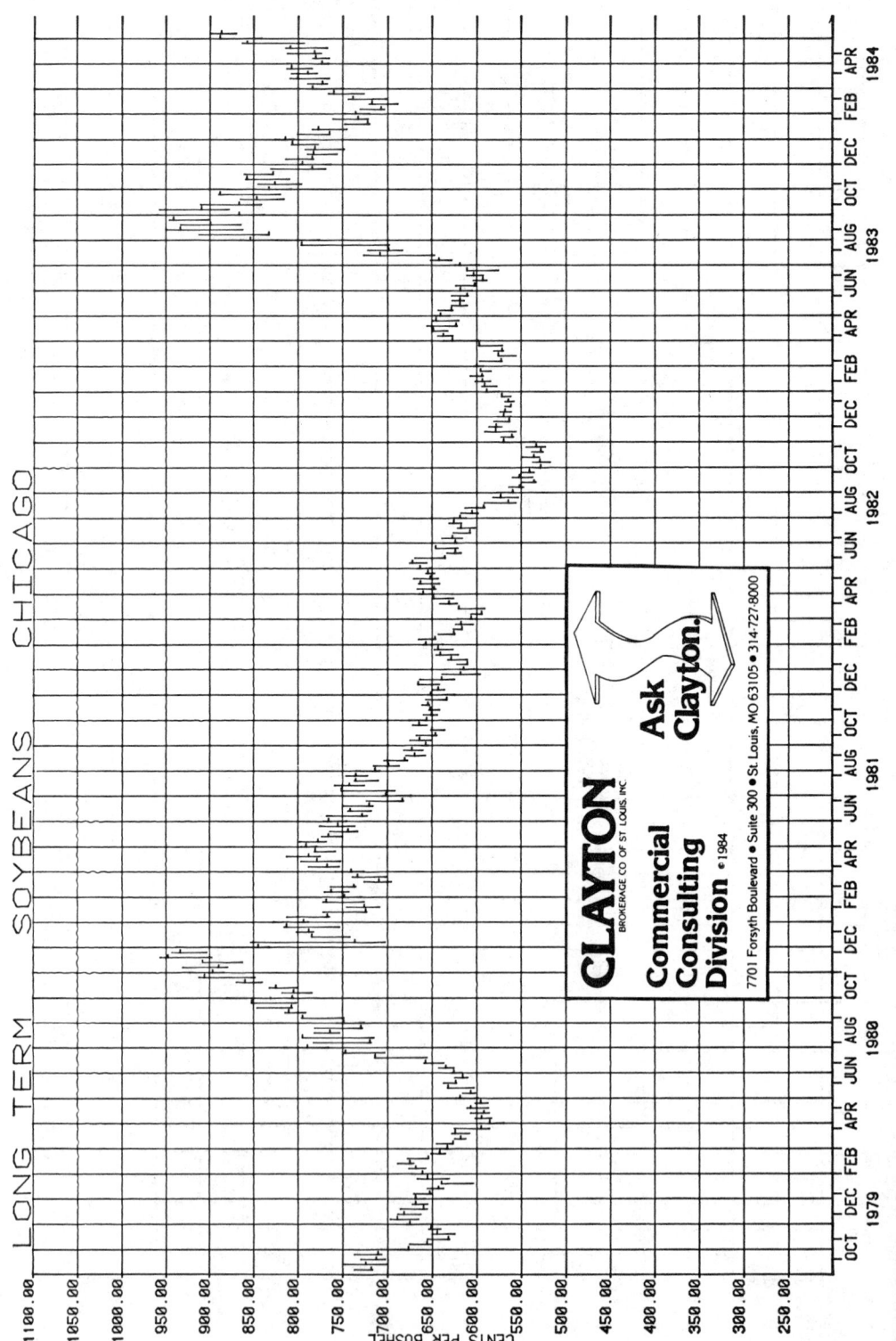

CLAYTON
BROKERAGE CO OF ST LOUIS, INC.

Commercial
Consulting
Division ©1984

Ask
Clayton.

7701 Forsyth Boulevard ● Suite 300 ● St. Louis, MO 63105 ● 314-727-8000

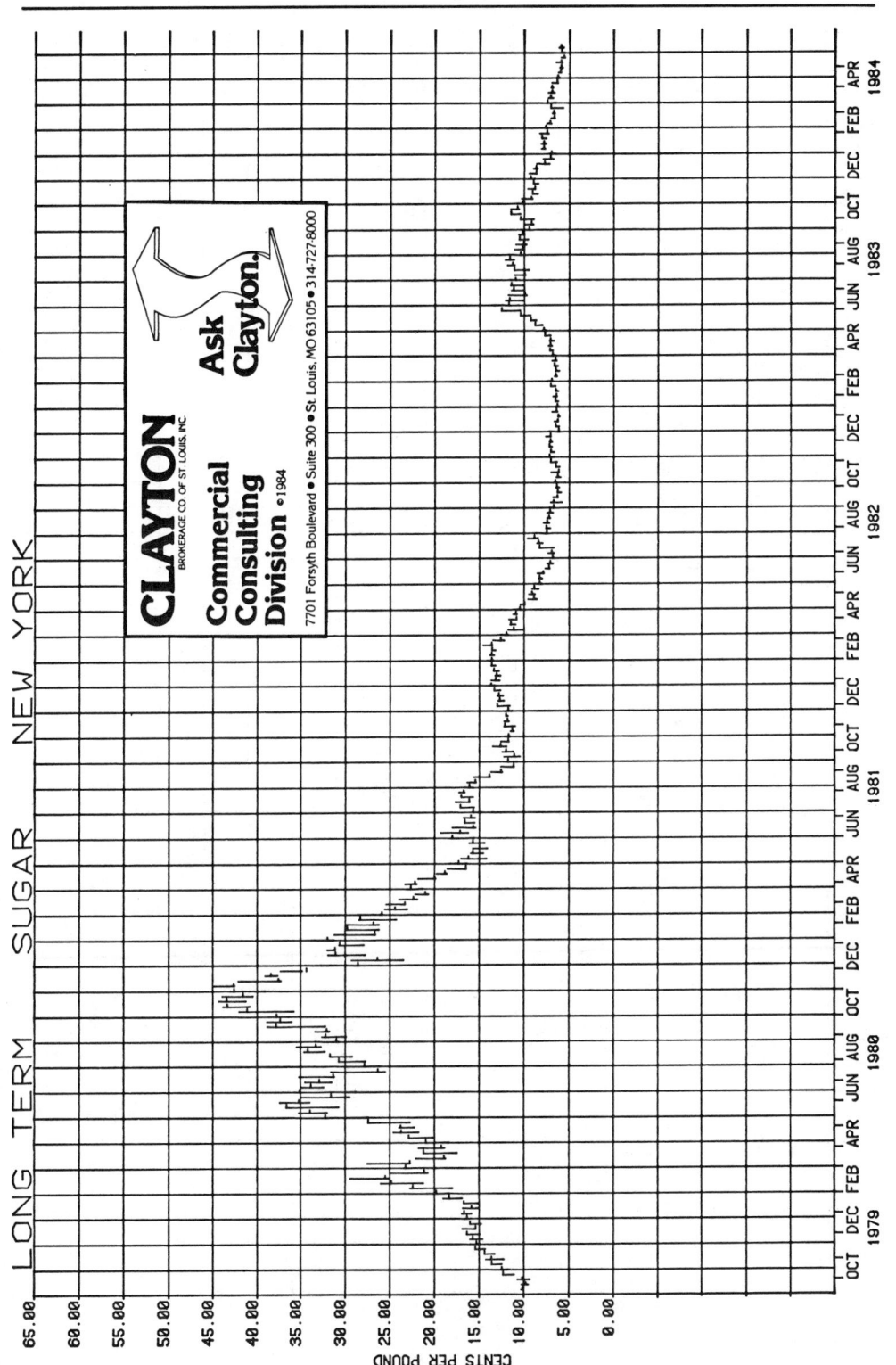

LONG TERM SUGAR NEW YORK

CENTS PER POUND

CLAYTON
BROKERAGE CO OF ST LOUIS, INC

Commercial
Consulting
Division ©1984

Ask
Clayton.

7701 Forsyth Boulevard • Suite 300 • St. Louis, MO 63105 • 314-727-8000

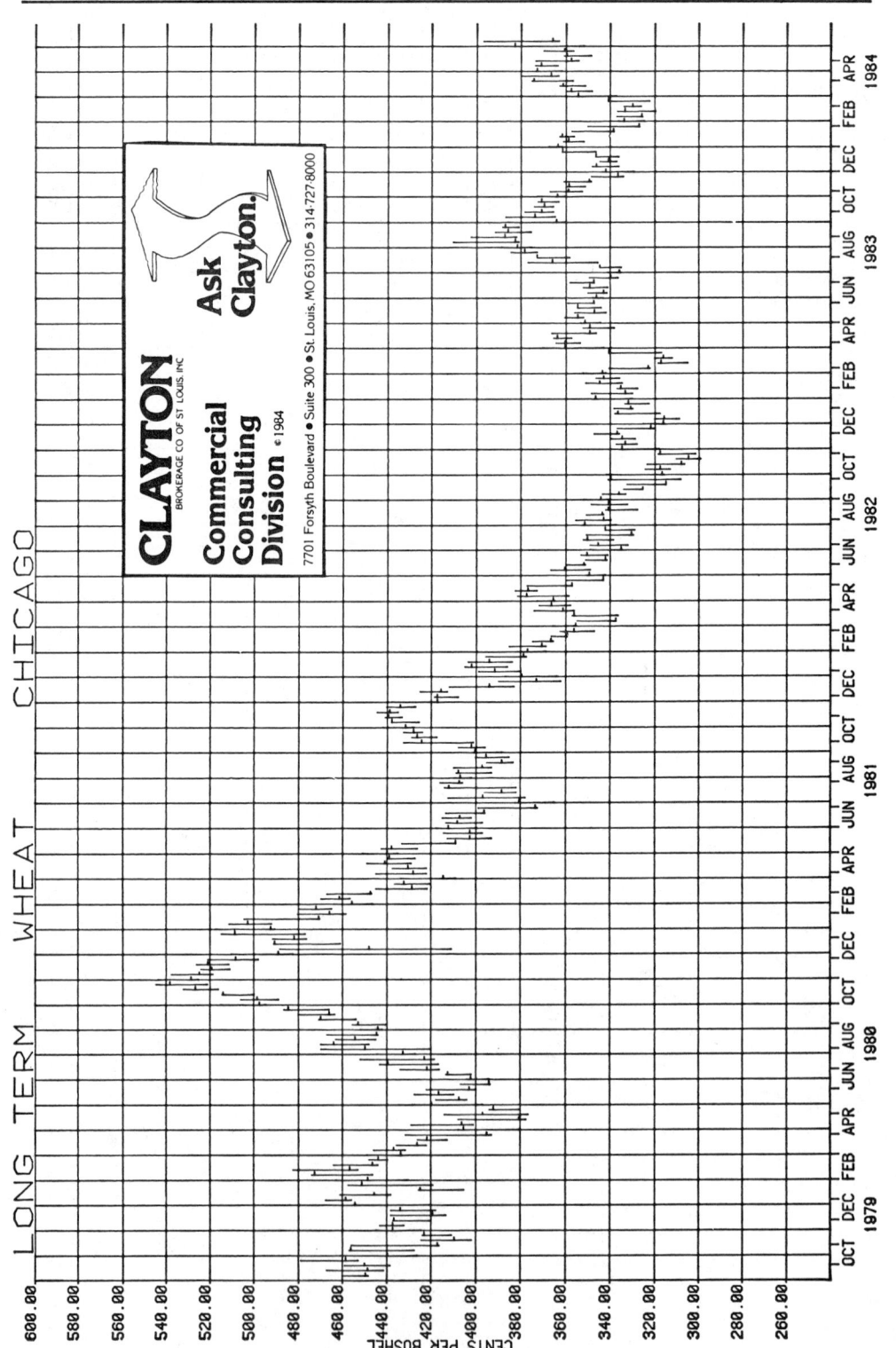

LONG TERM WHEAT CHICAGO

CENTS PER BUSHEL

Taxes

Tax Sheltered Investments*

Highlights

- Worthwhile tax investments offer both investment merit and tax benefits.

- A tax investment is a form of investment in which tax benefits play a significant role in the realization of economic return. The concept includes deferral, conversion, and leverage.

- As an investor, you should have:
  (1) substantial net worth and assets;
  (2) sufficient current assets and liquidity; and
  (3) an understanding of tax investment risk.

- The three major investment goals of a tax investment offering—tax savings, tax-sheltered cash flow and capital gains—in some cases can't all be realized simultaneously.

- Most tax investments involve public and private programs organized as limited partnerships in existing income producing real estate; newly constructed real estate; energy programs, such as oil and gas drilling, income/royalty funds, equipment leasing, agriculture and research and development.

- Certain investors find specialized tax advantaged investments well suited to their needs.

- Selecting a tax investment offering requires analysis of your own qualifications and characteristics, your investment goals and desired results.

- Always consult your tax advisor before finalizing any tax investment decisions.

Introduction

Tax investment offerings are based on specific provisions of the tax laws enacted by Con-

gress to encourage investment capital to flow directly into the basic areas of our economy such as housing, petroleum and manufacturing. In one sense, a tax investment means investing in vital industries in a way that permits you—rather than the companies you invest with—to keep the tax benefits, while retaining your opportunities for significant profits.

Because of the Economic Recovery Tax Act of 1981, and the Tax Equity and Fiscal Responsibility Act of 1982 offerings have become more attractive.

The Acts provide the lowering of the maximum tax rate on unearned or investment income from 70% to 50%. Previously, the 70% tax bite discouraged income-oriented tax investments, while encouraging risk-oriented tax investments. The 50% maximum will now provide investors with the incentive to consider the economic aspects of tax investment programs. Therefore, it is anticipated that borderline or the more exotic tax investment schemes will fall by the wayside.

Also, tax investments look much more appealing under the Acts when they begin to generate income. The reason: any ordinary income returns will be taxed at the maximum rate of 50% and not 70%; and long-term capital gains will be taxable at the maximum tax rate of 20% versus 28%.

In the following pages, we will help you evaluate tax investment offerings in the context of the Acts, as well as your financial and tax situation. The initial section introduces tax investment concepts and objectives. The next section deals with the *Major Tax Investments* available in today's marketplace. There is also a section on the mechanics of *Investing in Tax Investment Offerings*.

Finally, we have prepared a glossary covering tax investment terms. It is widely held that tax investments are very complicated; actually, they are relatively simple, it is the *language* of tax investments that cause the problems. Some things needing explanation are taxation principles; others are part of the specialized vocabulary of tax investments. To simplify the explanation process, we have put the key terms in *italics* in the text and defined them in the glossary. The glossary begins on page 502.

---

* For changes under the 1984 Tax Act see pages 509, 518.

Source: *A Tax Investment Guide for the '80s,* Prudential-Bache Securities Inc., 1984. With permission.

Tax Investment Concepts and Objectives

TAX INVESTMENT INDUSTRIES

The majority of quality tax investment offerings are found in five areas:

Real Estate
Energy
Equipment Leasing
Agriculture
Research and Development

TAX INVESTMENTS—THE CONCEPTS

In order to understand the basics of tax advantaged investing, it is important to define the concepts.

A tax investment is a form of investment in which tax benefits play a significant role in the realization of economic return. The concepts include:

(1) **Deferral:** Postponing the payments of tax liability. These dollars can then be used for further investment, allowing additional growth of assets.

(2) **Conversion:** Obtaining current tax deductions against ordinary income, while turning future revenues into income taxable at more favorable *capital gains* rates or lower rates derived from favorable tax features such as *depletion* or *depreciation*.

(3) **Leverage:** Obtaining current deductions in excess of your cash investment through the use of loans: either *non-recourse loans* which increases *deductions* without increasing your investment or personal liability, or through *recourse loans* for which you are personally liable. Non-recourse loans apply to all investments although are used most often in real estate transactions. Since the enactment of the Tax Reform Act of 1976 and the Revenue Act of 1978, recourse loans must be used for all tax investments other than real estate, if you are to have deductions in excess of 100% of your investment.

If you have unusually high income for one year, but do not expect to be at the same level in subsequent years, you may select a tax investment offering emphasizing *deferral*. On the other hand, if your income continually puts you in a high tax bracket you may want a tax investment which will generate deductions for several years. In both cases the use of *leverage* may help you increase your tax benefits.

TAX INVESTMENTS—DIVERSIFIED FORMS

Probably the most frequent question asked by clients about tax investments is: "Just what is a tax investment?"

The answer is: A tax investment is a form of investment. What you receive when you invest in a tax investment is an interest in a *limited partnership, joint venture* or, in rare instances, a *Reit, grantor trust,* or *S Corporation.*

TAX INVESTMENTS—LIMITED PARTNERSHIPS

To fully understand a limited partnership, you need to study its five basic features: the limited partnership concept, the general partner, the limited partner, limited liability and flow-through of tax benefits. In addition, you should understand the difference between a "public" program and a "private" program.

THE LIMITED PARTNERSHIP CONCEPT

The most common organizational structure for a tax investment offering is the limited partnership. The fundamental reason for selecting this structure for tax investment offerings is that it is usually not a taxable entity for Federal income tax purposes. Instead, the tax benefits generated by the investment flow through directly to the investor. A second reason for using the limited partnership is that it permits the investor to limit his liability to his investment in the project. A limited partnership is an undertaking between an individual and/or company that has expertise in the particular venture and a group of investors seeking specific benefits. The person or company with the expertise is called the general partner and the investors are called limited partners.

THE GENERAL PARTNER'S ROLE

The general partner's role is to collect the investors' money, make the investments, keep the partnership books, report the results and make distributions to the investors if there are profits. Essentially the general partner is responsible for the overall management of the partnership.

THE LIMITED PARTNER'S ROLE

The limited partner provides the money to fund the partnership. To preserve the tax status of the partnership, the limited partner must not take any active role in the management of the partnership. In other words, he is a passive investor. Tax benefits normally accrue to the limited partners. Profits from the operation are shared according to a stated formula designed to compensate the general partner and the limited partners for their respective contributions.

LIMITED LIABILITY

Your personal liability as a limited partner is legally limited to what you have actually invested or committed to invest, plus your share of any undistributed profits. If something goes wrong (a major fire or an earthquake for example), the partnership's creditors cannot attach your personal assets except to the extent of any *recourse loans* for which you have agreed to become personally liable. Limited liability is the principal reason why tax investment recommendations are concentrated on limited partnerships.

FLOW-THROUGH OF TAX BENEFITS

The partnership itself pays no taxes; benefits pass directly to the partners. You include your share of partnership profits and losses (usually losses in the early years) on your own tax return. Later, if your partnership begins generating taxable profits, those profits are added to your other income.

PUBLIC OR PRIVATE

Tax investment programs are offered to investors as either public or private offerings. Essentially the difference between the two offering formats has to do with investment size and investor suitability.

Public programs are registered with the SEC and are offered in unit sizes as small as $1,000, although the usual offering amount is $5,000. Public programs can be offered as "blind pools" which simply means that the partnership does not specify the properties it intends to invest in prior to purchase by the investor. This is a common offering technique, which gives the sponsor flexibility in selecting a diversified group of projects designed to meet partnership goals.

Private programs are not registered with the SEC due to an exemption which allows such offerings. These offerings have stricter investor suitability standards and a larger minimum investment size. Private offerings generally require an investment of at least $50,000 which may be paid-in over a number of years. Private programs usually specify the projects to be invested in and may be more suitable for wealthier investors.

Investment Goals

Before considering a tax investment limited partnership you should determine whether your own financial and tax position justifies such an investment.

PREREQUISITES

Before getting into tax investments, you should conduct a "personal audit" to determine whether you have the prerequisites to become

an investor in tax investment offerings, and more important, whether you can really benefit.

As an investor in tax investments, it is required that you have: (1) substantial net worth and income; (2) sufficient current assets to avoid impairing other investment goals; and (3) an understanding of the risks and lack of liquidity.

NET WORTH AND INCOME

The definition of "substantial" net worth and income varies from person to person and from tax investment to tax investment; however, there are some guidelines. Many states require that prospective investors in tax investment programs meet "suitability requirements." For example, state regulators usually require that oil and gas investors have a minimum net worth of $225,000; or a net worth of $60,000 and a taxable income of $60,000 exclusive of illiquid assets. (When we talk about net worth, we mean assets excluding the value of your home, cars and personal possessions).

Tax investments with lesser risk, i.e., income oriented real estate and income producing energy programs, as well as equipment leasing have correspondingly lower suitability requirements.

CURRENT ASSETS

Another way to analyze whether you are "suitable" is to evaluate your assets and other possible sources for investment capital. Your investment should not come out of funds earmarked for college education or retirement. Tax investment funds should be derived from current income. Remember, your objective is sheltering current taxable income.

UNDERSTANDING RISK AND LIQUIDITY

The reason for concern about current assets, income and net worth relate to two characteristics of all tax investment offerings: investment risk and lack of liquidity.

It's difficult to quantify investment risk, but in every type of investment there's underlying danger of the possibility of a disappointing performance. Even if you have sufficient income, net worth and available cash, you should understand that you may be faced with this factor. "Investment risk" implies a range of returns—some great years, and some less than great. With some tax investments, you must be prepared to continue reinvesting for enough years to average your investment performance.

An understanding of *liquidity* is also required. Whatever tax investment you choose, it may be some time before you begin receiving any cash distributions and before you can sell out and receive the *cash liquidating value* of your chosen partnership. Don't count on being able to sell a partnership interest like a stock or a bond on a moment's notice, even in an emergency.

If you meet the suitability requirements . . . if you're prepared to invest in your chosen tax investment industry long enough to smooth out the effect of investment risk . . . if you realize that it may be a number of years before you get your money out . . . then you can probably benefit from a long-term investment program.

POSSIBLE BENEFITS

Once you have determined that tax investments are suitable for your portfolio, you will have to decide what combinations of benefits offered by tax investments fits your own investment goals: (1) tax savings, (2) tax-sheltered cash flow, or (3) capital gains.

TAX SAVINGS

Reducing current taxes is the principal goal of most tax investment investors. Limited partnerships are usually structured to maximize tax *deductions* in the first year. The objective is to have *tax losses*, i.e., a tax investment that generates more deductions than income the first year or first few years. When combined with other income on your tax return, your share of partnership deductions offsets an equal amount of your taxable income from other sources on April 15th. For example, if you are in a 50% Federal tax bracket, each dollar of your share of net partnership deductions generates *tax savings* of up to 50¢.

Let us illustrate the effect of various degrees of deductibility in a tax investment offering. Assume you are in a 50% Federal tax bracket, file a joint return, have $162,400 of taxable income and invest $10,000.

Using the 50% Federal Tax bracket, the deduction on a $10,000 investment, for example, saves $2,500 in taxes, so the net cost is only $7,500 even though you have $10,000 invested. The 100% and 150% deductible tax investments produce tax savings of $5,000 and $7,500 respectively.

Try to resist the urge to conclude that the 150% deductible tax investment is "best" because it saves the most taxes. It may be the best if reducing current taxes is your only goal. But remember, deductions in excess of your investment are achieved only through borrowing which utilizes either *non-recourse* loans or *recourse* loans.

You cannot deduct more than your share of partnership expenses; without borrowing, your partnership cannot expend more than you invest. Also remember, borrowing has to be repaid; this will involve additional risk especially if recourse loans are used. The funds used to make those repayments may increase your tax bill in later years and reduce your potential economic benefits.

TAX-SHELTERED CASH FLOW

Any income received from a tax investment offering may be partially or wholly offset by ongoing deductions for *depreciation, depletion,* in-

TAX DEDUCTION FROM A $10,000 TAX INVESTMENT IN FIRST YEAR AS A PERCENTAGE OF THE INVESTMENT

Joint Return — 50% Tax Bracket

	Nothing Deductible	50% Deductible	100% Deductible	150% Deductible
Taxable Income*	$162,400	$162,400	$162,400	$162,400
Deductions from Tax Investment	—	($ 5,000)	($ 10,000)	($ 15,000)
Revised Taxable Income	$162,400	$157,400	$152,400	$147,400
Tax Due	$ 62,600	$ 60,150	$ 57,700	$ 55,250
Tax Savings	—	$ 2,500	$ 5,000	$ 7,500
Net Investment Cost ($10,000 minus Tax Savings)	—	$ 7,500	$ 5,000	$ 2,500

*Income after exemptions and itemized deductions.

terest and operating costs. Depreciation and depletion are particularly important because they are *non-cash charges;* your taxable income is reduced by the deductions, but no cash is actually paid to anyone—it is only a bookkeeping transaction. Let's look at how $100 of tax sheltered income from a hypothetical tax investment might yield *tax sheltered cash flow:*

maximum tax rate for other types of income—capital gains treatment should provide a significant degree of tax shelter and increase your net worth.

Any investment plan seeking maximum tax savings in the first few years, or maximum tax-sheltered cash flow in later years, may limit capital gains possibilities. Here is why: In certain

Joint Return 50% Tax Bracket

	Cash Flow	Tax Statement
Tax Investment Gross Income	$100	$100
Operating Expenses	(46)	(46)
Operating Income	$ 54	$ 54
Deductions:		
Depreciation (Non-Cash)	—	(34)
Interest Payments	(30)	(30)
Principal Payments	(6)	(—)
Cash Flow Received	$ 18	
Taxable Income (Loss)		$(10)

In this example, you receive $18 in cash out of each $100 of gross income received by the partnership. In addition, deductions reduce your taxable income from the same $100 to minus $10, which offsets $10 in taxable income from other sources and reduces your tax bill by $5. Because deductions offset the tax liability, you receive $18 of tax-sheltered cash flow. The *non-cash deduction* is creating the tax benefits.

Some tax investments yield fully tax-sheltered cash flow plus additional tax losses, as in the example above. Other tax investments produce some deductions but not enough to absorb all the tax liability, thus partially sheltering your cash flow received. Still other tax investments generate: (1) fully taxable cash flow; (2) tax losses but no cash flow; or (3) taxable income but no cash flow received, as in some high *leverage* situations requiring large loan repayments.

Because of the necessity to repay borrowed funds, leverage will reduce the possibility of receiving cash flow. Thus, a tax investment offering maximum first year deductions through leverage will not generally satisfy a need for tax-sheltered cash flow in later years.

CAPITAL GAINS

If your partnership sells any assets, or you sell your interest in a partnership, you have to pay a tax on your share of any profits.

If the assets sold are *capital assets,* the sale may qualify for taxation at long-term capital gains rates rather than ordinary income tax rates. Since long-term capital gains are taxed at a maximum tax rate of 20% against a 50%

instances when *accelerated depreciation* or *intangible drilling costs* have been claimed as *deductions,* a portion of those deductions are subject to *recapture* as ordinary income in the year of the sale. This feature may limit capital gains, particularly if leverage has been employed.

In summary, you will not find a tax investment that offers maximum tax savings, maximum tax-sheltered cash flow and maximum capital gains opportunities. You will have to decide which investment goals are best for your situation. For example, if you have a very high annual income continuing for several years, some combination of tax savings and capital gains may be your goal. On the other hand, if you are nearing retirement, you may want to forego maximum tax savings in favor of tax-sheltered cash flow to augment your retirement fund; alternatively, you may decide to seek ways to defer your current taxes and pay them at your lower, post-retirement tax rate.

SPECIAL TAX CONSIDERATIONS

To insure that substantial investors did not utilize tax investments to avoid all taxes, Congress enacted the *alternative mimum tax* on *tax preference items.*

Under the minimum tax provisions, the 15% add-on tax is repealed after 1982. In its place, the alternative minimum tax has been expanded. The new alternative minimum tax will be payable to the extent that it exceeds the taxpayer's regular tax.

Minimum taxable income is computed by adding preference amounts to adjusted gross income. Special minimum tax deductions are subtracted. The exemption for filers has been increased to $20,000 for single individuals, and $30,000 for married and individuals filing separately $30,000 for estates and trusts and $40,000 for joint filers. The resulting sum is subject to a flat 20% tax rate.

Tax preference items include:

1. Excess of mining exploration and development costs (other than oil and gas), research and experimental costs and magazine and prepublication expenses (over the amount of deduction allowed had such expenses been capitalized and amortized over 10 years).
2. Excess of accelerated depreciation on real property over deduction allowable using the straight-line method.
3. Excess of accelerated depreciation on leased personal property over deduction allowable using the straight-line method.
4. Percentage depletion in excess of the adjusted basis of the property.
5. Intangible drilling cost deductions on successful wells that have not reached total depth by April 1 of the year following the tax year.
6. The bargain element of incentive stock options.
7. All-Savers interest exclusion.
8. The 15% net interest exclusion taking effect after 1984.
9. The dividend income exclusion.
10. Net capital gain (deduction (usually 60% of long-term capital gains).

These concepts are complex, but in general, the larger your taxable income and the more you invest in tax investments, the more likely you are to be affected. All factors should be evaluated in light of your asset base, cash position, risk tolerance and income level.

The Major Tax Investment Industries

The majority of tax investment recommendations are concentrated in the areas of real estate, energy, equipment leasing, agriculture and research and development. This group offers: (1) a wide range of benefits satisfying virtually any tax investment goal; (2) a broad spectrum of risk/reward relationships; (3) well established principles of taxation; and (4) a variety of offerings from which to select.

REAL ESTATE

Real estate is undoubtedly the most popular tax investment. Because of its similarity to home ownership, it is more easily understood. The obvious distinction between a home and investment real estate is that tenants occupy investment buildings and make periodic lease or rental payments to cover costs of operations, maintenance and debt retirement as well as profit. The not-so-obvious difference relates to taxation. Owners of investment real estate are allowed deductions for taxes, operating and maintenance expenses, interest on mortgage money and depreciation on buildings (but not land). Homeowners are allowed *deductions* for taxes and interest paid on mortgages, thus making home ownership probably the most widely used tax investment. However, homeowners are denied the primary tax advantage of the *depreciation* deduction. Depreciation is a *non-cash deduction* in which taxable income is reduced, but no cash is paid to anyone.

Real estate, a collective term, describes a variety of investments. Real estate limited partnerships involve commercial properties, conventionally financed apartment complexes or government subsidized housing programs. These can be further categorized into existing and newly constructed real estate.

Some real estate partnerships are *specified property programs*, others are *blind pool programs* involving properties selected after partnership operations begin.

EXISTING PROPERTIES COMMERCIAL/INDUSTRIAL PROPERTIES

If a partnership plans to invest in commercial/industrial properties, these properties will usually include office buildings, hotels, shopping centers, warehouses or mini-warehouses.

Existing commercial/industrial properties are rented with long-term leases which can provide investors with a predictable income stream. Also, escalation clauses protect investors against rising operating costs because property management can pass on increases in these costs to the tenant. This arrangement is commonly referred to as a net lease, whereby the tenant is responsible for lease payments, plus all taxes, insurance and other operating expenses. The most common net lease partnership is where a major corporation sells its property to the partnership and, in turn, becomes the tenant and makes lease payments to the partnership. The partnership benefits as it has a credit-worthy tenant, and is secured by a long-term lease.

In many cases, net lease transactions are highly leveraged with a minimum of a 2 to 1 write-off over pay-in. Typically, these are tax-oriented investments with very little cash flow to the investor.

The economic-oriented net lease transaction employs lower leverage. Most of these limited partnerships offer investors minimal first year write-offs (remember, the tenants pay operating costs; the partnership's only deductions are interest and *depreciation*) and significant opportunities for *tax-sheltered cash flow*, as well as the potential for a long-term *capital gain* when the property is sold.

RESIDENTIAL PROPERTIES

Limited partnerships concentrating on residential properties generally purchase garden apartments. The potential for increased value of such properties is affected by the following important facts:

- Increased housing demand—the trend of high interest rates and unaffordable mortgages forces investors to rent and not buy; and

- Insufficient housing supply—because there is little new construction activity at the present time, existing rental properties tend to become more valuable.

Limited partners can enjoy:

- Cash flow—lease periods are usually no more than a year which permits increased rental income by re-leasing at market rates.

- Equity build-up—through the reduction of mortgage loans by payment of principal; and

- Appreciation—provided by the supply/demand factor previously mentioned, as well as inflationary pressures in the economy.

NEWLY CONSTRUCTED COMMERCIAL/ INDUSTRIAL/RESIDENTIAL PROPERTIES

These programs construct new buildings. Typically, this type of real estate involves *leverage*. High leverage from *non-recourse loans* and *depreciation* can mean tax losses for the partnership for at least 5 years.

New buildings financed with high leverage imply higher risk. However, through a combination of high tax write-off, tax-sheltered cash flow and property appreciation, newly constructed properties are attractive for those investors willing to bear the risk associated with these types of properties.

GOVERNMENT SUBSIDIZED HOUSING

Primarily there are two types of housing investments which are made possible through federal, state and city programs.

The first, known as Section 8, receives subsidies from the Department of Housing and Ur-

ban Development (HUD). HUD makes up the difference between the "fair market rent" and the portion of rent paid by the tenant on a newly constructed or rehabilitated property. The rent subsidies are usually combined with state financing or federal mortgage insurance programs. These programs provide loans at favorable interest rates and have long-repayment periods.

Limited partnerships formed to develop and/or operate Section 8 housing can now deduct interest and taxes during construction, therefore, providing limited partners with additional tax shelter. The second type of program is a Section 221 (d)(4) which receives the benefit of a mortgage subsidy. That is, the developer can get a larger loan than from a commercial bank; below-the-market interest rates; and long-term financing, usually 10 to 15 years longer than most other conventional mortgages. Unlike Section 8 programs there are no rent subsidies or income limitations governing tenant admission to the apartment building.

REAL ESTATE PARTNERSHIP OPERATIONS

All real estate limited partnerships function similarly—only the properties purchased and the tax treatment vary. Typically, the *general partner* manages the partnership. He subtracts a *management fee*, and organization and offering expenses. Then he applies partnership proceeds to a group of properties which meet stated partnership objectives. Tax losses are derived from partnership and property operating expenses, depreciation, and interest deductions, etc.

After partnership properties are in operation, rental income is designated for property management, maintenance and repayment of loans. Any excess is divided among the general and limited partners according to an established formula.

HISTORIC REHABILITATIONS

The historic rehabilitation transaction offers investors significant tax benefits and the potential for future economic return, while enriching the American heritage.

Essentially, any building which individually or is situated within an area that has significant impact on American history (i.e., it may be associated with historical events or figures or embody distinctive architectural characteristics or aesthetic qualities) is an historic structure. Any structure displaying such features can be nominated for certification as a historic landmark.

Currently, there are between 700,000 and 1 million certified historic structures ("landmarks"). These represent only a small percentage of all potentially certifiable structures. By

1985, the U.S. Treasury Department expects $2 billion of historic structures to be certified landmarks.

The approved rehabilitation of all historic structures qualifies for the investment tax credit (ITC). The ITC is utilized the year rehabilitation is completed. The renovation of commercial buildings more than 30-years-old qualify for a 15% ITC and those over 40-years-old for a 20% ITC. The rehabilitation of an historic landmark, however, results in a 25% ITC, the highest credit available for any investment.

In addition, other benefits result. The basis of historic rehab property is reduced by only one half of the tax credit when depreciation is determined (in any other form of real estate investment, the basis of the property is reduced by the amount of the entire credit). Restored property may provide substantial capital appreciation.

Energy

OIL & GAS

Since 1970, oil and natural gas prices have risen dramatically. As witnessed, oil prices have risen 1100% from 1970 to 1981, while natural gas prices rose 1500% for the same period. The costs to develop wells have increased only 400%. An atmosphere which is favorable to oil and gas investments, resulted due to the profit margins existing between the cost of drilling and the price of oil and gas.

However, not only profit margins make oil and gas a viable investment, consider these factors:

- There is not enough oil being discovered to satisfy even reduced consumption levels in the long-term.
- It is anticipated that OPEC production potential will decline materially in this decade.
- A rebound in the Western economies will increase demand.
- Oil and gas will remain the paramount commercial fuels for the remainder of this century.
- A disruption of Middle-Eastern supplies would create an immediate world oil crisis.
- Little attention is paid to the excellent investment opportunities associated with natural gas.
- Natural gas is still underpriced with price deregulation scheduled to occur in 1985.

One way for investors to participate in this industry is through oil and gas limited partnerships.

TYPES OF PROGRAMS

A key decision for investors is whether to participate in a program which is primarily exploratory, developmental, balanced or income producing in nature.

- Exploratory programs drill prospects in an area where no oil or gas has ever been found.
- Developmental well sites result from someone's wildcat discovery, that is drilling takes place in areas where oil and gas have previously been found.
- Balanced drilling programs combine exploratory with developmental drilling. Investors have the opportunity for potentially higher returns while the developmental drilling reduces risk.
- Income/royalty funds primarily acquire and own interests in oil and gas producing properties. However, the partnership may acquire non-producing royalty interests which can add significantly to the cash flow, if substantial reserves are found.

No matter what type program the investor chooses, an oil and gas limited partnership provides a number of benefits.

- The investor reduces his risk and increases his profit potential by participating in the drilling of a number of oil and gas wells;
- The investor receives professional management and is aware of his monetary commitment from the outset of the program;
- General and administrative expenses, offering expenses and *intangible drilling costs* combine to offer first year tax losses of 70% to 90% of the amount invested. Once successful wells are producing, *depletion* partially shelters oil and gas gross income. An investor can deduct up to 15% of his share of the gross oil and gas production revenue from the property.
- *Capital gains* opportunities can arise from the sale of productive oil and gas properties by the partnership. Capital gains will now be taxed at the maximum tax rate of 20%, however, they may be reduced when previously claimed deductions for *intangible drilling costs* are taken back as ordinary income or *recaptured.*

RECAP

In an effort to encourage domestic oil and gas exploration and development, Congress has given investors the following tax incentives:

- Immediate tax deductions;
- Tax-sheltered income; and
- *Conversion* of income to long-term capital gains.

Summary

	Balanced
Exploratory	Development Income/Royalty Funds
High Risk	Low Risk

Equipment Leasing

Equipment of all types plays an important part in our daily lives. In the past, companies often acquired equipment by purchasing it outright or financing it at a bank. Recently, however, the advantages of equipment leasing—the rental by owners (lessors) of an endless variety of goods, have made it a popular alternative to buying.

The minimal cash outlay required and flexibility of terms may influence a company's decision to lease. Probably the most significant factor is the better overall cost of financing that leasing provides. Usually, lease costs are lower than the overall costs of a loan taken out to purchase equipment.

In addition to the business that uses leased equipment (lessee), two other parties benefit from a leasing transaction:

- The equipment manufacturer or seller of the equipment; and
- The leasing company (lessor).

By selling to a leasing company, the manufacturer is able to book a cash sale and use the proceeds to continue to produce equipment. The leasing company leases equipment to the users and benefits from monthly payments, gains from residual value,* as well as certain tax considerations. An investor assumes the role

---

* It is important to keep in mind that new technology can eliminate or reduce the residual value of some types of equipment.

of a lessor in an equipment leasing limited partnership.

Investing in equipment leasing transactions is not new. The idea has been used for some time by institutions and by individuals with considerable wealth. Now, through equipment leasing partnerships, the concept is available to a wider segment of the investing public.

LEASE TERMS

There are, from a generic point of view, two types of leases—full payout and an operating lease.

Full Payout Lease—is a financing device whereby a lessee can acquire the use of an asset for most of its useful life. Rental payments to the lessors over the life of the lease are sufficient to enable them to recover the cost of the equipment plus the interest on their investments. The rental payments to the lessors are net of all costs associated with the operation of the equipment. The lessee pays taxes, insurance and maintenance. At the end of the lease, there is a possibility of selling the equipment at a profit.

Operating Lease—is a short-term lease whereby the lessee can acquire the use of an asset for part of its useful life. In an operating lease, rental payments to the lessors are not sufficient to enable them to fully recover the cost of the equipment. The lessor is responsible for maintenance, insurance and taxes. However, the short lease term enables the lessor to re-lease the equipment or possibly sell it at a profit after the initial lease term.

BENEFITS TO THE LIMITED PARTNERS (LESSORS):

Tax Savings Via:

- Depreciation of the equipment.
- Interest deductions from any loans used to buy the equipment. In an equipment leasing transaction, a significant portion of the equipment is financed through borrowings from an institutional lender. Interest expense incurred from the use of

borrowed funds is deductible for tax purposes.

- Investment tax credit is now 6% for 3-year assets and 10% for all other equipment. *Individual* taxpayers are subject to operating lease and expense guidelines for *investment tax credits*. Equipment must be leased for less than half the useful life of the asset. If the initial lease is longer, no ITC can be taken. The ITC is applied directly against the investor's Federal income tax liability. In a full payout lease, the ITC is not available to an individual investor.

Cash Flow Via:

- Rent on lease payments made to the lease company by the user, plus some return of capital. Assuming a financially stable lessee, there is usually predictable cash flow.
- Residual or end value from the sale of the asset after expiration of the lease.

Agriculture

BREEDING

Investments in livestock breeding ventures have become increasingly popular due to the tax attractions offered (significant tax-sheltered cash flow, asset appreciation and tax benefits) and the market demand for a tangible asset. Breeding programs may include horses, cattle or other animals. Although the "livestock" varies, program operations are similar.

A herd is acquired, offspring produced and the female animals are reimpregnated. Tax losses arise from depreciation of the herd as well as expenses incurred (i.e., feed costs). In cattle breeding programs, the investment tax credit is available on the initial herd, but not on the offspring. The ITC does not apply to horse breeding transactions.

Sale of the herd generates income. Offspring are sold annually. Superior males and females may be retained to increase herd size and/or quality. Adult animals may be sold as they age. Capital gains are realized on the sale of horses or cattle held for more than 24 months.

RESEARCH AND DEVELOPMENT

In the past few years, the world economy has begun a shift from manufacturing to higher valued, more technologically sophisticated businesses. Major American corporations are approaching product development from innovations in technology.

Research and Development (R & D) part-nership financing is offered by hundreds of technology- and research-oriented firms and has become a sought after tax investment throughout the financial community. Funds raised aid a vital industry while providing the potential for high returns.

Through the limited partnership structure, individuals can participate in the research and development of new technologies having commercial applications. The partnership contracts with a company or companies to fund the research and/or development of a product(s). The partnership structure generally takes the form of a joint venture or royalty transaction.

The economic aspects of R & D partnership funding are significant. Tax losses resulting from funding the research are currently deductible. If the technology is successfully developed, the partners share in the income generated from product sales. (Rights to developed products accrue to the partnership. Warrants or an immediate equity position may be negotiated in order to participate in future growth.)

Upon completion of research, the developed product is marketed. The partnership receives either a share of the profits (joint venture transaction) or royalty payments during a specified period of review (royalty transaction).

The company may opt to purchase the partnership's interest in the technology. Purchase takes the form of royalties representing a return between three to five times the amount of the partnership's original investment over a 3–10 year period. Early prepayment is usually arranged for.

BENEFITS TO THE LIMITED PARTNERS
TAX SAVINGS VIA:

- Immediate deductions (up to 100%) for R & D expenditures.

CAPITAL RETURN VIA:

- An equity position in the R & D entity. Shares of stock are authorized but unissued.
- Cash flow is provided by marketing rights and/or royalty payments based on the sales of the developed product(s). Royalty payments take the form of licensing fees (a percentage of the sales price of the product(s) over several years) usually ranging between 6–7% of sales and beginning in 1–3 years.
- Repurchase of rights. The R & D entity usually retains the option to repurchase the rights after a specified period for a specified amount.
- Purchase of the patent.
- Long-term capital gains treatment of gains on the sale or licensing of a patent.

The investor is entitled to capital gains treatment even if an outright sale of the product for a fixed price has not been made.

TAX TREATMENT OF INCOME

Income to the partnership may take several forms. Joint venture income or royalties paid to the partnership during the specified period of review (approximately a year) result in ordinary income. If the patentable technology is sold during this time, the partnership realizes short-term capital gains. Assuming the company exercises its option to purchase the partnership's interest in the joint venture or technology after this time, long-term capital gains result.

Investing in Tax Investment Offerings

SELECTING THE INDUSTRY

Unfortunately, there are no hard and fast industry-selection rules. Your situation, which is different from the next person's, changes each year. This year's tax-investment need—maximum tax losses, maximum tax-sheltered cash flow or maximum capital gains—will depend on your individual package of assets, liabilities and lifestyle, plus your present and anticipated future income.

SELECTING THE PROGRAM

Analyzing any program requires in-depth knowledge of partnership law, taxation, the industry and the General Partner's management and operations.

The following are some tenets of a tax investment philosophy to guide your decision making:

Diversification Pooling capital of several investors and spreading risk among several projects is a key benefit of *limited partnerships.*

Program size Too small a program may offer only limited diversification, or it may be excessively burdened by *front-end load.* Too large a program may force the sponsor into unwise decisions if he is under pressure to complete partnership projects before year-end.

Management Decisions are based on integrity, past performance, experience in the operating area, financial stability, limited partnership experience, experience with comparable-size programs and quality of investor communications.

Sharing arrangement The General Partner's compensation should encourage superior performance. Compensation should be derived from operation profits and appreciation, not front-end fees.

Tax features Well accepted taxation principles avoid unnecessary "tax-risk." Programs promising excessive deductions or unreasonable expectation of investment returns are avoided.

Liquidity Any liquidity is better than none; however, all tax investment offerings are, at best, illiquid. Emphasis is placed on the General Partner's financial ability to provide liquidity at the appropriate time.

INVESTMENT APPLICATIONS

An integral part of selecting the "right" industry and "right" program is what you hope to accomplish by making the investment. Applications of tax investments invlude: (1) saving taxes by sheltering high-level recurring income; (2) reducing tax effects of major capital gains; (3) building retirement income; (4) increasing charitable contributions; (5) employing sophisticated estate planning tactics; and (6) enhancing corporate tax planning.

RECURRING INCOME

The most familiar use of tax investments is related to softening the burden of taxes on high-level, recurring income. If you are a high-salaried corporate executive, doctor or lawyer, for example, you know that, short of some unpredictable economic or personal calamity, you will earn at least X dollars each year for the next Y years. You can use this knowledge and apply tax investments to help reduce your annual tax liability.

Let's assume that each year for the next 10 years, you will file a joint return with $200,000* taxable income (after exemptions and itemized deductions). Also, assume you will purchase a 100% deductible, $10,000 annual tax investment offering and you are in the 50% Federal tax bracket.

Over a 10-year period, you will invest $100,000, and because of the tax savings the out-of-pocket cost is only $50,000. You will have accomplished four things: (1) reduced your annual tax bill by $5,000; (2) invested $100,000 at an out-of-pocket cost of only $50,000; (3) purchased assets which can yield an investment return with dollars that normally go to pay taxes; and (4) diluted your risk.

CAPITAL GAINS

Let's suppose that in 1 year you have, in addition to your $200,000 recurring taxable in-

---

* No adjustments made for tax bracket on a yearly basis.

Joint Return—50% Tax Bracket	Without Tax Investment	With Tax Investment
Taxable Income* 1984	$400,000	$400,000
60% Capital Gains Deduction	(120,000)	(120,000)
Net Taxable Income	$280,000	$280,000
100% Deductible Tax Investment**	—	(80,000)
Revised Taxable Income	$280,000	$200,000
Tax Due (Including Tax Preference)	$121,400	$ 81,400
Tax Savings	—	$ 40,000
Net Investment Cost	—	$ 40,000

*Net income $200,000; capital gains $200,000
**Assumes $40,000 of tax preference items from the tax investment.

come, a $200,000 capital gain. A good rule of thumb is to consider investing 40% of a large capital gain in a tax investment offering, in this case $80,000.

This technique: (1) puts $80,000 to work for a net cost of 50¢ on the dollar, (2) reduces your tax bill 33%, and (3) still leaves you at least $120,000 cash remaining from your capital gain . . . a very powerful tax and investment planning tool.

RETIREMENT PLANNING

If you are a few years from retirement, tax investments—particularly those with a *deferral* feature—can help you take advantage of needed tax savings up to your retirement date. After retirement your tax investment offering may yield ordinary income which will be taxed at your lower post-retirement tax rate.

CHARITY CONTRIBUTIONS

You can invest in a tax investment limited partnership and hold it until the *cash liquidating value* or other fair market value is determined. Tax laws permit a deduction up to the fair market value of an asset contributed to a qualified charitable organization. Using this technique, you have the opportunity—assuming a successful tax investment—to take two deductions on the same dollars: first when you invest, and then when you contribute. Your charity receives an income producing asset free of any administrative responsibilities. Note, however, that charity giving is a very sensitive tax area requiring advance consultation with both your tax advisor and charity.

ESTATE PLANNING

The same invest-hold-contribute technique used for charity giving can be used to transfer tax investment assets out of your estate to your children. This technique: (1) decreases your taxable estate and, ultimately, reduces inheritance taxes; also, (2) reduces overall family tax liability by shifting your high-bracket taxable income into your children's lower tax bracket. Like charity contributions, estate planning requires careful study by your tax advisor.

CORPORATE TAX PLANNING

Corporations—particularly closely-held entities—can employ tax investments in a number of creative ways, including: (1) sheltering recurring income; (2) utilizing tax benefits, then contributing the investment to employee pension and profit sharing plans; (3) avoiding the penalty tax on accumulated earnings; and (4) providing executive compensation through tax investment loan plans.

INVESTMENT RETURNS

Because of risk, it is impossible to say what rate of return you may receive from a given tax shelter program; losses or less-than-anticipated returns are always possible. However, with tax savings (which reduce your initial out-of-pocket investment costs), proper diversification, a proven management term and, when feasible, a 3- to 5-year program of recurring investments, risks are significantly reduced.

As soon as possible, your General Partner will begin distributing your share of any partnership profits. After distributions begin, you'll probably continue receiving them on a fairly regular basis; quarterly is the most common distribution pattern.

SUMMARY

This section is intended only to acquaint you with some of the various facets of tax investment offerings. Therefore, it is suggested that you consult your own tax advisor before considering a tax investment offering.

Investment Objectives

Type	Investor Suitability*	Minimum Investment[1]	Economic Benefits	Tax Benefits
REAL ESTATE				
Existing	Net worth of $30.000 & $30.000 taxable income. or net worth of $75.000.	$5.000	Appreciation potential: Cash flow: Equity build-up. Leverage	Tax-sheltered cash flow; Minimal write-off: Capital gains.
Newly Constructed	Net worth of $50.000 & $50.000 taxable income: or net worth of $200.000.	$5.000	Appreciation potential: Low cash flow: Leverage	Tax-sheltered cash flow Write-off; Capital gains
Government Assisted Housing	Net worth of $75.000 & $75.000 taxable income: or net worth of $200.000.	$5.000	Mortgage guarantee: Rental assistance — (Section 8) Highly leveraged: Inexpensive financing.	Multiple write-offs.
ENERGY				
Oil and Gas Income Producing	Net worth of $25.000 & $25.000 taxable income. or net worth of $90.000.	$5.000	Lower risk: Early cash flow	Partially tax-sheltered cash flow: No write-off.
Development	Net worth of $60.000 & $60.000 taxable income: or net worth of $225.000.	$5.000	Lower risk: Potential for early cash flow	Partially tax-sheltered cash flow. Write off.
Balanced	Net worth of $60.000 & $60.000 taxable income: or net worth of $225.000.	$5.000	Exploratory-upside potential. Development-low risk.	Partially tax-sheltered cash flow: Moderate write-off.
Exploratory	Net worth of $60.000 & $60.000 taxable income: or net worth of $225.000.	$5.000	Higher risk. Cash flow to begin in later years.	Partially tax-sheltered cash flow: Higher write-off.
Coal	Net worth of $25.000 & $25.000 taxable income: or net worth of $90.000.	$5.000	Cash flow.	Write-off. Partially tax-sheltered cash flow
EQUIPMENT LEASING				
	Net worth of $30.000 & $30.000 taxable income: or net worth of $75.000.	$5.000	Cash flow from rental of equipment. Residual value (possible appreciation). Leverage.	Write-off. Investment tax credit: Partially tax-sheltered cash flow
RESEARCH & DEVELOPMENT				
	Net worth exceeding the greater of $100,000 or 4 times the purchase price of units subscribed for AND anticipated income during the current and the next year of at least $75,000 (if married) or $60,000 (if single), OR net worth of at least $200,000 or 10 times his proposed investment. Certain states may differ.	$5,000	Early cash flow and possible participation in future growth of companies contracted with.	Write-off, Capital gains.

Excluding value of home, cars and personal possessions.

[1] Editor's note: Minimum investments are for the Prudential Bache partnerships and are given for illustrative purposes only.

Glossary

Note: Terms in *italics* are defined elsewhere in the glossary.

Accelerated Depreciation Any method of *depreciation* which permits a *deduction* of a greater percentage of the cost of an asset in the early years of the asset's useful life with smaller deductions in later years. Note that the accelerated portion of the depreciation deduction is a *tax preference item.*

Alternative Minimum Tax The alternative minimum tax will be payable to the extent that it exceeds the taxpayer's regular tax. Minimum taxable income is computed by adding preference amounts to adjusted gross income. Special minimum tax deductions are subtracted. The exemption for filers has been increased to $20,000 for single individuals, $30,000 for married individuals filing separately, $30,000 for estates and trusts and $40,000 for joint filers. The resulting sum is subject to a flat 20% tax rate.

Assessment Additional amounts of money which a *limited partner* in a *tax investment partnership* may be required to furnish beyond his original *subscription*. A given program, depending on the terms, may be either "assessable" or "non-assessable." An assessable program may have limited or unlimited assessments. Assessments may be optional or mandatory.

"At Risk" Limitations This limitation is designed to prevent non-corporate taxpayers from deducting losses in excess of their economic investment in the activity involved. These rules now apply to all activities except real estate. In addition, where your amount of investment deemed to be "at risk" is reduced below zero (by distributions or change of status of liabilities from *recourse* to *non-recourse*), income recognition may be required of *deductions* previously taken.

Blind Pool Program A *tax investment limited partnership* which, at the time that the sale of *subscriptions* begins, does not have the *proceeds* of the offering allocated to specific projects or properties. (Contrast with *specified property program.*)

Capital Asset Any asset (property, equipment, livestock, etc.) which is (1) used in a trade or business (except inventories or items held for sale to customers); (2) held for production of income; or (3) given the effect of a capital asset by a tax law provision. With certain exceptions, capital assets—including interests in *tax invest-*ment limited partnerships—are subject to *capital gains* treatment on any profit (or loss) arising from sale or exchange.

Capital Gains Usually gain (or loss) from sale or exchange of any property is included in income and taxed at ordinary income tax rates. However, if the gain is from the sale or exchange of a *capital asset* owned for more than 12 months, the tax is calculated at the lower long-term capital gains rate, generally no more than 20%. Almost all types of *tax investment offerings* except cattle feeding and equipment leasing offer some capital gains opportunities. Certain types of real estate, and oil and gas offer the most potential. It has been said that capital gains offer the major source of tax relief. Note however, that capital gains benefits may be reduced by *recapture*. Note also that 60% of long-term capital gains may be taxed under the alternative minimum tax.

Cash Liquidating Value The amount, generally based on an evaluation of a qualified independent appraiser, which will be paid by the *general partner* for an interest in a *tax investment partnership* upon exercise by a *limited partner* of his right to receive such value.

Conversion Obtaining current tax *deductions* against ordinary income, while turning future revenues into income taxable at more favorable *capital gains* rates or lower rates derived from favorable tax features such as *depletion* or *depreciation.*

Deductions In this context, the interest, taxes, *depreciation, depletion* and other expenses incurred in the trade or business of a *tax investment limited partnership* which are passed on to the *limited partners* thereby reducing their taxable income and, ultimately, their tax liability. The "ordinary and necessary" expenses of any business are allowable as deductions; for example (1) certain forms of *tax investment intangible drilling costs* associated with oil and gas; (2) depreciation and interest costs associated with real estate and equipment leasing tax investments, particularly when *leverage* is employed. Ideally, a *tax investment limited partnership* will generate deductions in excess of income for the first year or first few years thereby permitting the program's *limited partners* to recover part or all of their investments through *tax losses.*

Deferral Resulting from a tax investment timed so that *deductions* take place during the investor's high income years and taxable income is realized at a later time. Equipment leasing and certain types of real estate offer the best deferral opportunities.

Depletion A form of *deduction* that applies to a "wasting asset" interest. The purpose is to encourage exploration for new deposits by permitting recovery of exploration and development costs out of tax savings. The annual depletion deduction for any mineral property is the greater of "cost depletion" (based on the ratio of annual percent). The major advantage of percentage depletion is that benefits are available each year that a property produces income and does not cease even when the cost of the property has been recovered. Oil and gas, timber and minerals all offer some depletion. Percentage depletion on oil and gas is 15% of gross income from each property limited to the lesser of 65% of the individual's taxable income or 50% of the taxable income from the property. Note that percentage depletion is a tax preference item.

Depreciation A form of *deduction* to permit recovery of the cost of an asset in the form of tax savings. This cost recovery is spread over a specified cost recovery period established by ERTA as an annual deduction from taxable income. Depreciation is most attractive in real estate and equipment leasing especially if *leverage* is employed.

Front-End Load A slang term for the total of *organizational* and *offering expenses* plus *management fees:* i.e., the total deductions from the *offering amount* to arrive at the *proceeds* of a *tax investment limited partnership*. (See also: *management fees*.)

General Partner In this context, the manager or sponsor of a *tax investment offering* which has been organized as a *limited partnership*. (See *limited partnership* for details.)

Grantor Trust An entity that's sole purpose is to protect and conserve property for its beneficiaries. A grantor trust cannot operate with the aim of conducting business for profit. This arrangement consists of the trustee (who gains legal title to the trust property) and the beneficiaries (the "grantors" of the trust or investors). The grantor trust is an attractive format in a leasing transaction because it allows for a full year's depreciation under circumstances in which limited partners would receive a pro-rated amount.

Intangible Drilling Costs A tax *deduction* for certain expenditures incurred in drilling and completing oil and gas wells. "Intangibles" are the items which have no salvage value (commonly non-material costs such as labor, chemicals, drill-site preparation, etc.) Intangibles frequently account for 50% to 80% of the cost of drilling and completing a given well. Note

that intangible drilling costs on producing wells in excess of oil and gas net income is a *tax preference item*.

Investment Tax Credit It reduces dollar for dollar the amount of tax owed, up to statutory limitations. A tax credit is subtracted directly from the amount of tax due. (Contrast with *tax deductions*.)

Joint Venture A form of business organization. In this context, a *tax investment offering* in which the manager and the investors share jointly in the ownership, management authority and liability. (Contrast with *limited partnership*.)

Leverage In this context, a method of increasing tax benefits through borrowing (see *non-recourse loans* and *recourse loans*) as a part of a *tax investment offering*. The investor (in a real estate limited partnership) is permitted *deductions* for interest, *management fees, depreciation*, etc., on the amount he invests plus his pro-rata share of the amount the partnership borrows on a *non-recourse* basis, or any amounts for which he is personally liable on a *recourse* basis in other types of tax investments. Any properly-structured loan, therefore, serves to increase total deductions from income for tax purposes. Real estate offers excellent leverage possibilities, because of non-recourse debt.

Limited Partner In this context, the purchaser of a subscription in a *tax investment offering* which has been organized as a *limited partnership* i.e., an investor.

Limited Partnership A form of business organization in which some partners exchange their right to participate in management for a limitation of their liability. Commonly, *limited partners* have liability only to the extent of their investment in the business plus their share of any undistributed profits. To establish limited liability, there must be at least one *general partner* who is fully liable for all claims against the business. Limited partnerships are a popular organizational form for *tax investment offerings* because of the ease with which tax benefits flow through the partnership to the individual partners. (Contrast with *joint venture*.)

Liquidity The ability of an asset to be readily converted into cash. (Most tax investments are considered illiquid.)

Liquidating Value See: *cash liquidating value*.

Management Fee *An amount paid to the general partner of a tax investment limited part-*

nership to cover *organization* and *offering expenses* and/or to repay costs of operating and administrating the partnership, commonly expressed as a percentage of the total *offering amount*. Under present law, the management fee is claimed as a *deduction* by many limited partnerships. However, only the general partner's reimbursements to cover costs of operating and administrating the partnership are considered fully deductible.

Minimum Subscription The smallest dollar amount which an investor must initially commit in order to become a *limited partner* in a *tax investment limited partnership*. It is usually one or more *units*. In a *public program* the minimum subscription is generally $5,000 (See also: *subscription*.)

Non-Cash Charges *Deductions* for *depreciation* and *depletion* which are not actually paid to anyone, yet are subtracted from taxable income before calculating tax due. *Tax investment limited partnerships* such as real estate and equipment leasing which employ *leverage* may be able to pyramid non-cash charges to the point that limited partners receive *tax sheltered cash flow* in the early years against which there is limited or no tax liability.

Non-Recourse Loan In this context, any borrowing by a *tax investment limited partnership*, structured in such a way that lenders can look only to specific assets pledged for repayment and not to the individual assets of the various partners. However, in the event of a foreclosure, if partnership cash and assets are not sufficient to repay the loan balance, the *limited partners* may be left with a substantial tax bill because of "forgiveness of debt." Real estate is the only tax investment area where non-recourse financing is permitted. (Contrast with *recourse loan*; see also: *leverage*.)

Offering Amount The total dollar which will fund a program. This funding is provided by the sale of subscriptions to potential *limited partners*.

Organization and Offering Expenses Those expenses incurred in connection with preparing a *tax investment limited partnership* for registration with Federal and/or state securities agencies, and subsequently selling subscriptions to *limited partners*. Organizational and offering expenses typically include legal fees, printing costs, registration fees, sales commissions and selling costs. (See also: *management fee; front-end load*.)

Private Program A *tax investment limited partnership* which is offered and sold pursuant to the private offering exemption available under the Securities Act of 1933 and/or some registration exemption allowed under the securities laws of one or more states; i.e., a program which is not registered with the Securities and Exchange Commission. (Contrast with *public program*.)

Proceeds The dollar amount remaining for the general partner to conduct partnership operations after the deduction of *organization* and *operating expenses* or other items of *front-end load* from the total amount committed.

Program Manager An outside company in a grantor trust transaction that provides the same type of asset management and industry expertise as would the general partner of a limited partnership.

Public Program A *tax investment limited partnership* which is registered with the Securities and Exchange Commission (SEC) and distributed in a public offering by broker/dealers and/or employees of the *general partner*. The principal differences between a *public program* and a *private program* relate to: (1) the number of *investors*, which may be several thousand in a public program, but limited, in a private program; (2) *minimum subscription: $5,000 in a public program, $50,000 or more in a private program (payable at times in stages);* and (3) *the fact that "private" investors are subject to stricter suitability standards.*

Real Estate Investment Trust (REIT) A corporation, trust or association which fulfills requirements under federal tax laws. A REIT usually invests in real estate mortgages or equities and does not pay taxes on distributed income as long as 95% of its taxable income is distributed as dividends.

Recapture Upon profitable sale of certain assets, *capital gains* may be severely restricted when previously claimed *deductions* for *depreciation, intangible drilling costs* or *investment credit* are taken back into ordinary income (i.e., "recaptured"). Since ordinary income tax rates can run as high as 50% versus 20% for capital gains—recapture can severely reduce capital gains benefits. The amount of recapture depends on the type of asset, holding period, type of depreciation (straight-line or accelerated) as well as dollar amount of gain versus the amount of "recaptured" deductions.

Recourse Loans In this context, any borrowing by a *tax investment* investor for which he is personally liable. (Contrast with *non-recourse loan*.)

S Corporation A form of corporation with a limited number of qualified stockholders who elect to utilize a specific tax law provision which permits them to be taxed so the corporation pays no taxes and each stockholder reports his share of the corporate income (or loss) on his own tax return.

Specified Property Program A *tax investment limited partnership* which, at the time sale of *subscription* begins, has the proceeds of the offering allocated to definite projects or properties which are described in detail in the prospectus or offering circular. (Contrast with *blind pool program*.)

Straight Line Depreciation See: *depreciation*.

Subscription The total dollar amount for which a *limited partner* in a *tax investment limited partnership* commits. Legally it represents the amount he is obligated to pay, exclusive of any *assessment* amount which he normally has the option to reject. (See also: unit.)

Tax Investment Offering An investment that has the expectation of economic profit, made even more attractive because of the timing of the profit, or the way it is taxed, generally having some or all of the following characteristics:

(a) Tax write-off;
(b) Tax deferral; and
(c) Tax reduction.

The flow-through of tax benefits is a material factor whether the entity is organized as a *limited partnership, joint venture, grantor trust* or *S Corporation* and whether it is offered to investors as a *private program* or a *public program*. Common forms of tax investment offerings include: real estate, energy, equipment leasing and research and development.

Tax Investment Limited Partnership A *tax investment offering* organized as a *limited partnership*. Commonly, a tax investment program is created to mutually benefit a group of *limited partners* and a *general partner*. It may be organized as a *public program* or a *private program*.

Tax Loss A situation that occurs when the *deductions* generated by a *tax investment limited*

partnership exceed program revenues. These deductions are usually caused by non-cash expenditures such as *depreciation*. Thus, the *limited partner's* taxable income is lower, resulting in a tax saving.

Tax Preference Items Items of tax preference subject to the alternative *minimum tax* include:

Excess of mining exploration and development costs (other than oil and gas), research and experimental costs and magazine and prepublication expenses (over the amount of deduction allowed had such expenses been capitalized and amortized over 10 years); excess of accelerated depreciation on real property over deduction allowable using the straight-line method; excess of accelerated depreciation on leased personal property over deduction allowable using the straight-line method; percentage depletion in excess of the adjusted basis of the property; intangible drilling cost deductions on successful wells that have not reached total depth by April 1 of the year following the tax year; the bargain element of incentive stock options; All-Savers interest exclusion; the 15% net interest exclusion taking effect after 1984; the dividend income exclusion and the net capital gain deduction.

Tax Sheltered Cash Flow The situation that arises when *non-cash charges* and other *deductions* exceed gross income from a *tax investment limited partnership*. Therefore, the program has cash to distribute to *limited partners* even though the cash they may receive involves no current tax liability or is taxed at a lower rate. Real estate and equipment leasing programs employing *accelerated depreciation* and *leverage* are the best sources of tax sheltered cash flow.

Unit The smallest dollar amount into which *subscriptions* in a *tax investment limited partnership* may be divided. For example, a $10 million *public program* might consist of 2,000 units of $5,000 each. Alternately, it might consist of 10,000 units of $1,000 each. Each type would normally have a *minimum subscription* of $5,000.

Tax Rate Schedule for Heads of Household—1984

To find the tax, locate your taxable income and read off to the right. Your tax for a particular year is the sum of (1) the dollar amount shown, plus (2) the indicated percentage of taxable income in excess of the amount in Column (A). *Example:* Taxable income is $50,000. For tax year 1984, the tax is as follows:

Dollar amount shown	$10,696
$50,000 minus $44,700 (Amount in Column A) equals $5,300, times 42% equals.....................	2,226
Regular tax before credits	$12,922

Taxable Income Between (A) and (B)	Tax Year 1984
Up to $2,300	—0—
$ 2,300 - $ 4,400	11% over $2,300
$ 4,400 - $ 6,500	$ 231 + 12%
$ 6,500 - $ 8,700	$ 483 + 14%
$ 8,700 - $11,800	$ 791 + 17%
$11,800 - $15,000	$ 1,318 + 18%
$15,000 - $18,200	$ 1,894 + 20%
$18,200 - $23,500	$ 2,534 + 24%
$23,500 - $28,800	$ 3,806 + 28%
$28,800 - $34,100	$ 5,290 + 32%
$34,100 - $44,700	$ 6,986 + 35%
$44,700 - $60,600	$ 10,696 + 42%
$60,600 - $81,800	$ 17,374 + 45%
$81,800 - $108,300	$ 26,914 + 48%
Over $108,300	$ 39,634 + 50%

Tax Rate Schedule for Single Taxpayers—1984

To find the tax, locate your taxable income and read off to the right. Your tax for a particular year is the sum of (1) the dollar amount shown, plus (2) the indicated percentage of taxable income in excess of the amount in Column (A). *Example:* Taxable income is $50,000. For tax year 1984, the tax is as follows:

Dollar amount shown	$10,319
$50,000 minus $41,500 (Amount in Column A) equals $8,500, times 42% equals.....................	3,570
Regular tax before credits	$13,889

Taxable Income Between (A) and (B)	Tax Year 1984
Up to $2,300	—0—
$ 2,300 - $ 3,400	11% over $2,300
$ 3,400 - $ 4,400	$ 121 + 12%
$ 4,400 - $ 6,500	$ 241 + 14%
$ 6,500 - $ 8,500	$ 535 + 15%
$ 8,500 - $10,800	$ 835 + 16%
$10,800 - $12,900	$ 1,203 + 18%
$12,900 - $15,000	$ 1,581 + 20%
$15,000 - $18,200	$ 2,001 + 23%
$18,200 - $23,500	$ 2,737 + 26%
$23,500 - $28,800	$ 4,115 + 30%
$28,800 - $34,100	$ 5,705 + 34%
$34,100 - $41,500	$ 7,507 + 38%
$41,500 - $55,300	$ 10,319 + 42%
$55,300 - $81,800	$ 16,115 + 48%
Over $81,800	$ 28,835 + 50%

Tax Rate Schedule for Marrieds Filing Jointly and Surviving Spouses—1984

To find the tax, locate your taxable income on the chart, and read off to the right. Your tax for a particular year is the sum of (1) the dollar amount shown, plus (2) the indicated percentage of taxable income in excess of the amount in Column (A). *Example:* Taxable income is $50,000. For tax year 1984, the tax is as follows:

Dollar amount shown	$ 9,772
$50,000 minus $45,800 (Amount in Column A) equals $4,200, times 38% equals.....................	1,596
Regular tax before credits	$11,368

Taxable Income Between (A) and (B)	Tax Year 1984
Up to $3,400	—0—
$ 3,400–$ 5,500	11% over $3,400
$ 5,500–$ 7,600	$ 231 + 12%
$ 7,600–$ 11,900	$ 483 + 14%
$11,900–$ 16,000	$ 1,085 + 16%
$16,000–$ 20,200	$ 1,741 + 18%
$20,200–$ 24,600	$ 2,497 + 22%
$24,600–$ 29,900	$ 3,465 + 25%
$29,900–$ 35,200	$ 4,790 + 28%
$35,200–$ 45,800	$ 6,274 + 33%
$45,800–$ 60,000	$ 9,772 + 38%
$60,000–$ 85,600	$ 15,168 + 42%
$85,600–$109,400	$ 25,920 + 45%
$109,400–$162,400	$ 36,630 + 49%
Over $162,400	$ 62,600 + 50%

Tax Rate Schedule for Marrieds Filing Separate Returns—1984

To find the tax, locate your taxable income and read off to the right. Your tax for a particular year is the sum of (1) the dollar amount shown, plus (2) the indicated percentage of taxable income in excess of the amount in Column (A). *Example:* Taxable income is $50,000. For tax year 1984, the tax is as follows:

Dollar amount shown	$12,960
$50,000 minus $42,800 (Amount in Column A) equals $7,200, times 45% equals.....................	3,240
Regular tax before credits	$16,200

Taxable Income Between (A) and (B)	Tax Year 1984
Up to $1,700	—0—
$ 1,700–$ 2,750	11% over $1,700
$ 2,750–$ 3,800	$ 115.50 + 12%
$ 3,800–$ 5,950	$ 241.50 + 14%
$ 5,950–$ 8,000	$ 542.50 + 16%
$ 8,000–$10,100	$ 870.50 + 18%
$10,100–$12,300	$ 1,248.50 + 22%
$12,300–$14,950	$ 1,732.50 + 25%
$14,950–$17,600	$ 2,395 + 28%
$17,600–$22,900	$ 3,137 + 33%
$22,900–$30,000	$ 4,886 + 38%
$30,000–$42,800	$ 7,584 + 42%
$42,800–$54,700	$ 12,960 + 45%
$54,700–$81,200	$ 18,315 + 49%
Over $81,200	$ 31,300 + 50%

Tax Rate Schedule for Estates and Trusts—1984

For your convenience, the chart below shows the tax rate schedules for tax year 1984. To find the tax, locate your taxable income and read off to the right. Tax for a particular year is the sum of (1) the dollar amount shown, plus (2) the indicated percentage of taxable income in excess of the amount in Column (A).

Example: Taxable income is $40,000. For tax year 1984, the tax is as follows:

Dollar amount shown .... $ 7,584
$40,000 minus $28,300 (Amount in Column A) equals $11,700, times 42% equals...................... 4,914
Regular tax before credits $12,498

Taxable Income Between (A) and (B)	Tax Year 1984
Up to $1,050	11% of income
$ 1,050–$ 2,100	$ 115.50 + 12%
$ 2,100–$ 4,250	$ 241.50 + 14%
$ 4,250–$ 6,300	$ 542.50 + 16%
$ 6,300–$ 8,400	$ 870.50 + 18%
$ 8,400–$10,600	$ 1,248.50 + 22%
$10,600–$13,250	$ 1,732.50 + 25%
$13,250–$15,900	$ 2,395 + 28%
$15,900–$21,200	$ 3,137 + 33%
$21,200–$28,300	$ 4,886 + 38%
$28,300–$41,100	$ 7,584 + 42%
$41,100–$53,000	$ 12,960 + 45%
$53,000–$79,500	$ 18,315 + 49%
Over $79,500	$ 31,300 + 50%

This account has been prepared for informational purposes only and is not an offer to sell or the solicitation of an offer to buy any tax investment offering or any other security.

The material contained in this description of a tax investment offering is based upon the provisions of the Internal Revenue Code of 1954, as presently amended, the existing applicable regulations and current administrative rulings and practice. However, it is emphasized that no assurance can be given that legislative or administrative changes will not be forthcoming which would modify this description. Any such changes may or may not be retroactive with respect to transactions entered into prior to the effective date of such changes.

Participation in tax investment offerings may give rise to liability for state income, property or inheritance taxes which are not discussed herein and may create the necessity for ancillary probate proceedings. Due to the complex tax and other legal considerations surrounding an investment in a tax investment offering, each prospective investor is urged to consult with his own counsel before obligating himself to purchase an interest in a tax investment offering.

Highlights: 1984 Tax Act

Postponements, Freezes and Repeals of Tax Reductions

Recent tax legislation included a number of tax cuts scheduled to take effect in 1984 or later. These cuts were designed to encourage capital investment and to reduce tax burdens on individuals and corporations. This year, however, Congress decided to eliminate, postpone or freeze many of these scheduled tax reductions. You may refer to the chart at page 510 for a topical summary of these changes.

- The maximum amount of investment in used property eligible for the investment tax credit is limited to $125,000 through 1987 and $150,000 thereafter. This amount was scheduled to increase to $150,000 in 1985.

- The maximum amount of qualifying business property that may be expensed in the year placed in service is currently $5,000. This limitation was to have increased to $7,500 in 1984 and 1985 and to $10,000 for taxable years beginning after 1985. Under the Act, the limits are $5,000 for taxable years beginning before 1988, $7,500 for taxable years beginning in 1988 or 1989, and $10,000 for taxable years beginning after 1989.

- The tax credit for employer contributions to an Employee Stock Ownership Plan (ESOP) is limited to 0.5 percent of the aggregate compensation of all employees covered under the plan. This limitation will prevail through 1987 and no credit is provided after that year.

- Under the Act, the cost-of-living increases to the dollar limits on contributions and benefits under qualified pension plans, tax-sheltered annuity programs, and simplified employee pensions (SEPs) are postponed until 1988.

- ERTA permitted taxpayers, after 1984, to exclude up to 15 percent of $3,000 ($6,000 on a joint return) of net interest. The Act repeals this exclusion.

- The exclusion of foreign earned income for U.S. citizens living abroad is limited to $80,000 through 1987, $85,000 in 1988, $90,000 in 1989 and $95,000 thereafter.

- The maximum estate and gift tax rate had been scheduled to drop to 50 percent by 1985. The Act delays this reduction three years, keeping the top rate at 55 percent through 1987, and reducing it to 50 percent in 1988 and thereafter.

- The windfall profit tax rate applicable to newly discovered oil remains at 22.5 percent through 1987 and then drops to 20 percent for 1988 and to 15 percent for 1989 and subsequent years.

- Liberal leasing rules for limited-use property (property that can be used only by the lessee) and fixed price purchase options became effective January 1, 1984. The Act postpones until 1988 the liberal leasing rules for leases after March 6, 1984.

- The telephone excise tax will be continued at the rate of 3 percent through 1987.

Two tax reductions scheduled to take place after 1983 that escaped Congressional action are the increase in the unified gift and estate tax credit and in the royalty exemption under the windfall profit tax.

Taxation of Individuals

The Act contains a wide variety of provisions affecting individuals that are intended to eliminate perceived abuses, generate additional revenue, or clarify existing law.

BELOW-MARKET-RATE LOANS

For many years, individuals were able to make low interest or interest free loans to family members without income tax consequences. Such loans were used for specific purposes such as to provide education expenses, or, more generally, to reduce the tax impact on income by shifting it to family members in lower tax rate brackets. Below market loans were also used in other contexts, e.g., compensation arrangements to avoid taxation.

In general, the Act treats interest-free and low-interest loans as arms-length transactions. The new rules apply to gift or family loans, compensation-related loans, corporation-shareholder loans, tax avoidance loans, and other below-market loans designated by regulations.

Among family members, foregone interest on a loan is treated as a gift from the lender to the borrower and is subject to the gift tax.

For loans from a corporation to a shareholder, the interest element is treated as if a dividend includible in income was paid by the

Source: Excerpts reprinted by permission of Deloitte Haskins & Sells from its booklet *The Tax Provisions of the Deficit Reduction Act of 1984.*

Tax Freezes

	Present Law	Scheduled Change	Freeze Provision
Used Property Eligible for Investment Tax Credit	$125,000	1985 – $150,000	1988 – $150,000
Trade or Business Property Which May Be Expensed	$5,000	1984 & 1985 – $7,500 1986 & after – $10,000	1988 & 1989 – $7,500 1990 & after – $10,000
Credit for Contributions Of Stock or Cash to ESOP	.5%	1985-1987 – .75%	Remains at .5%
Cost-of-Living Increases on Contribution Limitations for Pension Plans	—	To become effective 1986	Postponed to 1988
Net Interest Exclusion	None	15% of interest up to $3,000	Repealed
Foreign Earned Income Exclusion	$80,000	1984 – $85,000 1985 – $90,000 1986 & After – $95,000	1988 – $85,000 1989 – $90,000 1990 – $95,000
Maximum Gift and Estate Tax Rates	1983 – 60%	1984 – 55% 1985 – 50%	1984-1987 – 55% 1988 & after – 50%
Windfall Profit Tax on Newly Discovered Oil	25%	1984 – 22.5% 1985 – 20% 1986 & after – 15%	1984-1987 – 22.5% 1988 – 20% 1989 & after – 15%
Finance Leasing Rules Available for Limited Use Property and Fixed Price Purchase Options	—	Became effective 1/1/84	To become effective 1/1/88
Telephone Excise	3%	To expire after 1985	Extended to 1987

corporation to the shareholder. A loan to a person providing services results in the foregone interest being treated as compensation.

The borrower is then deemed to retransfer the amount of gift, dividend, or compensation to the lender as interest.

The Act does provide exceptions to these rules for loans of less than $10,000. However, in the case of loans between individuals, the exception only applies if the loan proceeds are not used for business or investment purposes and the foregone interest charges are in the nature of gifts. The exceptions will not exclude a loan transaction if a principal purpose of the transaction is tax avoidance.

Comment: This change effectively eliminates demand loans between family members as a device to shift substantial amounts of income to a lower tax bracket. As an alternative to demand loans, individuals may want to use 10-year Clifford trusts or to make outright gifts to children.

Effective Dates: Term loans made after June 6, 1984 and demand loans outstanding after June 6, 1984. There is an exception for demand loans outstanding on June 6, 1984 and repaid within 60 days after July 18, 1984.

BUSINESS USE OF AUTOMOBILES, INCLUDING LUXURY AUTOMOBILES

Under prior law, a self-employed individual or an employee who owned a car used partly for business was required to allocate the cost of the car between business and personal use. A company was not denied tax benefits from supplying a car to an employee who used it partly for business and partly for personal use. Instead, the company was required to include the value of the personal use on the employee's W-2 form as other compensation, or the employee was required to reimburse the company for the value of the personal use. The Act, however, restricts the tax benefits of luxury automobiles, imposes a 50 percent business use test, and tightens compliance rules.

Under the new rules, the maximum amount of available investment tax credit is limited to $1,000 per car and the maximum amount of depreciation is limited to $4,000 in the first year of use and to $6,000 in all following years. The maximum amount of depreciation can be taken each year until the cost of the car is fully recovered. Thus, it will take 5 years fully to recover the cost of a $25,000 car compared to 3 years under prior law. The $1,000 and the $4,000/$6,000 limits will be reduced proportionally for any personal use and will be increased each year for inflation in automobile prices.

Comment: Personal use by an employee will be treated as business use if the employee pays a personal use charge or income is attributed to the employee.

The Act also requires that at least 50 percent of the use be for business purposes. If this requirement is not met, the investment tax credit is disallowed and 5-year straight line depreciation is mandatory. A car provided as compensation to a 5 percent owner of a business or to a related taxpayer will not be treated as a trade or business use. However, cars provided to other employees as compensation would be treated as trade or business use, as under prior law.

Comment: The 50 percent test primarily affects the self-employed and employees who own their own cars. These taxpayers previously had to allocate car expenses between personal and business use. Employees will be elgible for the investment tax credit and depreciation only if the use of the car is required for the convenience of the employer and as a condition of employment.

In the case of leased cars, the 50 percent test will be applied at the lessee level rather than the lessor level. If the lessee fails the 50 percent test, a deduction will be denied for a percentage of the lease payments.

A drop in the business-use percentage in a later taxable year will be treated as a partial sale for purposes of investment tax credit recapture and depreciation.

Comment: This treatment should eliminate the practice of purchasing a car in late December, using it 100 percent for business purposes for a few days, and claiming a 25 percent first-year depreciation deduction.

Finally, the Act establishes new compliance rules for business use of automobiles and other property. *Taxpayers must keep contemporaneous records (recording the date of the trip and the mileage driven for business purposes) and certify in writing their existence to a tax return preparer. Preparers must also advise taxpayers of the recordkeeping rules.*

Comment: Except for auto sales people, the personal use by an employee of a car owned or leased by an employer does not fall under any of the new statutory exclusions for fringe benefits. Thus, wage withholding will be imposed on the fair market value of the personal use of a company car in excess of any amount paid by the employee for such use. Many companies, in order to avoid withholding on employees, may want to raise reimbursement rates for use of company cars to the fair market value of the personal use.

Effective Date: For the 50 percent business use test and the ITC and depreciation limits, cars placed in service after June 18, 1984, with a binding contract exception. Compliance rules effective for taxable years beginning after 1984. Fringe benefit rules effective January 1, 1985.

PROPERTY OTHER THAN AUTOMOBILES

The 50 percent business use test also applies to other personal property, including property used for transportation (other than automobiles), entertainment and recreation property, computers, and other property listed by regulations. The rules for the use of such property are generally the same as for automobiles, with some exceptions.

In the case of a 5-percent owner or related taxpayer, an aircraft provided as compensation will constitute business use provided that the business use—without consideration of such compensation—is at least 25 percent of total use. Depreciation on property that fails the 50 percent business use test is straight-line over earnings and profits lives. The 50 percent test does not apply to a computer owned by the employer or proprietor and exclusively located at a regular business establishment of the employer or proprietor. Like the rule for automobiles, employees will be eligible for the investment tax credit and depreciation only when the use of the property is required for the convenience of the employer and as a condition of employment.

Comment: This requirement will severely restrict the tax benefits previously derived from the use of home computers.

Effective Date: Property placed in service after June 18, 1984, with a binding contract exception.

INCOME AVERAGING

The income averaging provisions of the tax Code effectively treat any increase in current year's income above a certain percentage of "averageable income" as if the increased income were earned in the prior lower income years. Because of the extensive loss of tax revenue due to income averaging, the Act makes three significant changes to these rules:

- the averaging period for determining the base income is decreased from the most recent *four* years to the most recent *three* years

- the specified percentage of base income above which current year actual earnings become averageable is increased from 120 percent to 140 percent

- tax is computed on averageable income as if spread over a *four year* period (the past three years plus the current year), instead of over 5 years as under old law.

Effective Date: Taxable years beginning after December 31, 1983.

The following example, for a single taxpayer, demonstrates the new provisions.

Taxable Income

1980	$30,000	1983	$37,700
1981	$32,000	1984	$46,000
1982	$34,500		

Old Law

4-Year average (1980–1983)	$33,550
120%	$40,260
Averageable Income, 1984	$ 5,740
Tax Liability, 1984 (income averaging)	$12,028
Tax Liability, Regular Method	$12,209

New Law

3-Year average (1981–1983)	$34,733
140%	$48,627
Averageable Income, 1984	$ -0-
Tax Liability 1984 (Regular Method —Income averaging is not available)	$12,209

DOMESTIC RELATIONS

Transfers of Property. In an attempt to simplify the tax laws relating to transfers of property between spouses or former spouses, the Act changes the rules dealing with divorce, alimony and related provisions.

Under prior law, gain was generally recognized on the transfer of property for the release of marital claims. The Act, however, provides that a transfer related to a divorce does not trigger recognition of gain or loss and that the transferee will take the transferor's basis in the property. This nonrecognition rule also applies in the case of transfers of property between married spouses.

Effective Date: Transfers after July 18, 1984 or after December 31, 1983 if both parties elect. There is an exception for transfers pursuant to instruments in effect on July 18, 1984 if both parties do not elect to have the provisions apply.

Alimony. The Act changes the definition of alimony for federal income tax purposes. Under prior law, payments were required to be periodic, in discharge of a legal obligation, and imposed under a decree of divorce or separate maintenance. The Act provides that for a payment to qualify as alimony, the payor must have no liability to make payments for any period following the death of the payee spouse, the spouses or former spouses must not reside in the same household, and the payment must be made under a decree of divorce or separate maintenance. The payments (in excess of $10,000) must continue for at least 6 years, assuming neither spouse dies during the period and that the payee does not remarry, and may not vary by more than $10,000 during any of those years, except for fluctuating payments due to a continuing liability to pay a fixed portion of the earnings of a business or property.

If the amount of alimony specified in the instrument of divorce or separation will be reduced to reflect a contingency relating to a child, an equal amount will be treated as child support instead of alimony. Child support is neither deductible nor includible in income. To provide added flexibility, the Act permits divorcing parties to agree that payments that would otherwise be treated as alimony will not be so treated and thus will not be deductible or includible in income.

Effective Date: Generally, agreements executed after December 31, 1984.

Dependency Exemption. In general, the $1,000 dependency exemption available to divorced or separated parents is allocated to the parent who has custody of the. child unless that parent agrees in writing to allow the noncustodial parent to take the deduction, or there is a multiple support agreement, or there is a pre-1985 agreement providing the dependency exemption to the noncustodial parent. Medical expense deductions, however, will be allowed to either parent who pays the expenses, regardless of which parent claims the dependency exemption.

Effective Date: Taxable years beginning after December 31, 1984.

Filing Status. Parents living apart for the last six months of the year, compared to the whole year under prior law, may be treated as single or as head of household if the other eligibility tests are met.

Effective Date: Taxable years beginning after December 31, 1984.

ESTIMATED TAXES

Under prior law, taxpayers who paid tax through estimated tax payments were subject to mandatory penalties for late payments. No penalties were applied if total tax payments for the year equalled or exceeded certain levels. Also, taxpayers did not have to pay estimated tax on the alternative minimum tax.

The Act requires estimated tax payments for the alternative minimum tax and changes the method for computing the underpayment penalty. Now, the penalty is based on the lesser of 80 percent of the tax shown on the return, 100 percent of the tax shown on the preceding year's return, or 80 percent of the current year's tax computed on income to date placed on an annualized basis.

The Act repeals two exceptions to the estimated tax penalty; specifically, that no penalty is imposed if payment equals 90 percent of tax

on income to date or if payment equals the tax based on prior year's facts and current year's rates and exemptions.

The Act also reverses an IRS ruling that had required that an income tax overpayment could not be credited against an estimated tax liability prior to the taxpayer's filing a return and making the proper election. Now, the taxpayer may elect to credit an overpayment to an estimated tax payment that arises after the overpayment but before the election is made.

The Act permits the IRS to waive the estimated tax penalty in the event of a casualty, disaster, or other unusual circumstance. Also, the IRS could waive the penalty if failure to make payment is due to reasonable cause during the first two years after the individual retires upon reaching age 62 or becoming disabled. Under prior law, the IRS could not waive the penalty.

Comment: Taxpayers may want to verify that amounts paid in 1985 are at least equal to the 1984 tax liability in order to avoid underpayment penalties.

Effective Date: Taxable years beginning after December 31, 1984; provision relating to crediting of overpayments effective January 1, 1984; provision relating to waiver of penalty effective for taxable years beginning after December 31, 1983.

TAX STRADDLES

The Act contains specific rules to prevent the use of straddles to defer income or to convert ordinary income and short-term capital gain to long-term capital gain.

Prior law provides a loss deferral rule, not applicable to equities, that limits the deduction of losses to the amount by which losses exceed gains on offsetting positions. This loss-deferral rule, in the past, applied to straddle positions involving actively traded personal property other than stock or domestic exchange-traded stock options with holding periods of less than one year.

A mark-to-market system also applies to regulated futures contracts under which taxes were paid on unrecognized gains and losses at the end of each year. Gains and losses are treated as 60 percent long-term and 40 percent short-term resulting in a maximum tax rate of 32 percent. The tax treatment of options on futures contracts and cash settlement options was unclear.

The Act changes the law applicable to straddles.

- The blanket exception from the loss deferral rule for stock options and stock offset by an option or by substantially similar or related property is repealed.

Effective Date: For positions established after December 31, 1983 in taxable years ending after such date.

- Loss on a covered call is considered long-term if the offsetting position has been held for the long-term holding period.

Effective Date: For positions established after June 30, 1984.

- A corporation formed to hold positions offsetting those held by the taxpayer, other than offsetting positions held by different members of an affiliated group, is subject to the straddle rules.

Effective Date: For positions taken on or after May 23, 1983.

- The mark-to-market system is extended to options on futures contracts (other than stock index futures contracts), to broad based equity index options, to options which are not equity based and to options held by options market makers.

Effective Date: For positions established after July 18, 1984, except in the case of options on regulated futures contracts for which the Act applies to positions established after October 31, 1983.

- Capitalized carrying costs of carrying a straddle position are reduced by dividends received, after allowance for the dividends received deduction, on stock included in a straddle.

Effective Date: For positions established after July 18, 1984.

- Hedging losses to the extent they do not exceed unrecognized hedging gains in the trade or business in which hedging transactions were entered into are allowed only against income from such trade or business.

Effective Date: For taxable years beginning after December 31, 1984.

- Treasury regulations are to be issued providing a taxpayer an election to adopt a separate netting rule for identified mixed straddles. If the election is not made, short term losses will be treated as 60 percent long-term and 40 percent short-term to the extent of offsetting 60/40 gains.

Effective Date: The regulations will apply only to mixed straddles for which all positions are not established by January 1, 1984.

- The wash sale rule is extended to apply to short sales, including short sales "against the box." However, the only exception to the general wash sale rules now available is to losses incurred by a dealer in stock or securities in the course of his trade or business.

Effective Date: Short sales of stock or securities made after July 18, 1984. Dealer exception—sales after December 31, 1984.

- The exercise of an option on a regulated futures contract is a recognition event and is treated as a general option to buy or sell property.

Effective Date: For options purchased or granted after October 31, 1983.

TAXATION OF LIFE INSURANCE

Life Insurance Annuities. The major goal of the life insurance policy holder provisions of the Act is to discourage the use of life insurance as a short-term tax-favored investment tool. Thus, the Act imposes more stringent rules with respect to premature annuity distributions.

Under prior law, a 5 percent penalty was applied to the ordinary income from distributions attributable to contract contributions from the previous 10 years. The Act eliminates the 10 year provision and taxes *any* premature distribution unless the taxpayer has attained age 59½.

New rules are provided in regard to the timing of distributions on an annuity contract upon the death of the contract holder. In order to be treated as an annuity contract:

- If the contract holder dies on or after the annuity starting date, any remaining distributions must be made at least as rapidly as the current distribution method;
- If the contract holder dies before the annuity starting date, a distribution of the proceeds must be made within 5 years of death or an annuity may be provided over the life of a designated beneficiary if payment begins within 1 year of the date of death;
- A spousal beneficiary may be treated as the original holder of the contract.

Effective Date: Contracts issued 6 months after July 18, 1984 with transitional rules.

Group Term Life Insurance. The cost (as determined under IRS tables) of providing group term life insurance in excess of $50,000 to employees is included in employees' gross income. Under prior law, retired and disabled employees were exempt, but the Act brings such employees within this provision. The cost is included in income for the year in which the coverage is received whether or not the benefit of retirement coverage vests upon retirement.

Discrimination rules are also extended to apply to retired employees. If a plan is found to be discriminatory, the cost of the coverage to be included in the employee's gross income is the actual cost of the coverage and not the amount determined under the IRS provided tables (as was the case under prior law).

Effective Date: Taxable years beginning after December 31, 1983 with exceptions for plans in existence on January 1, 1984.

Exchanges of Life Insurance Policies. Life insurance contracts and endowment contracts issued by life insurance companies were allowed to be exchanged tax-free under prior law. The new law allows this tax-free exchange for contracts issued by any insurance company taxable under the insurance company provisions of the Internal Revenue Code.

Effective Date: All exchanges before, on, or after July 18, 1984.

CHARITABLE EXPENSES AND DEDUCTIONS

Taxpayers who contribute their services to charitable organizations may either deduct the actual expenses of operating their vehicles for that purpose or use a new standard rate of $ .12 per mile.

Effective Date: Taxable years beginning after December 31, 1984.

TRANSFERS OF RESTRICTED STOCK

A 1982 Tax Court decision, *Alves v. Commissioner,* recently affirmed by the Ninth Circuit Court of Appeals, could prove troublesome to founders of new companies. The taxpayer in that case had paid fair market value for the stock but had not made an election under section 83 of the Code to include in income the difference between the fair market value of the stock and the amount he paid for the stock— or zero. This decision required the recognition of income at the time the restrictions lapsed even though the employee had paid fair market value for the stock.

The Act provides relief from this decision by enabling a taxpayer to make a one-time retroactive election to include zero in income on the transfer of property to the taxpayer in connection with the performance of services if not less than fair market value was paid for the property at the time of transfer and the employer consents to the election.

Comment: This provision does not eliminate the Alves "trap for the unwary" but only provides relief to taxpayers penalized by the original decision.

Effective Date: The election applies to a transfer of property between June 30, 1976 and November 19, 1982 and must be made with the income tax return for the first tax year ending after July 18, 1984.

PARTIAL ROLLOVERS

Whereas prior law allowed rollovers only of total distributions, the Act allows a partial tax-free rollover of distributions from qualified pension or annuity plans or tax sheltered annuities to an IRA. The rollover is allowed if at least 50 percent of the balance credited to the employee is distributed, the distribution is not one of a series of distributions, and the employee elects such treatment under applicable Treasury regulations. The rollover must be made within 60 days of the distribution. Subsequent distributions from the same plan do not qualify for special 10 year averaging and capital gain treatment.

Effective Date: Distributions made after July 18, 1984.

CASUALTY LOSSES

Under prior law personal casualty and theft losses were deductible only to the extent that the loss from each casualty exceeded $100 and the aggregate of these excess losses exceeded 10 percent of the adjusted gross income of the individual.

If there are net personal casualty gains for a year under the Act, all gains and losses are treated as capital and are not subject to the 10 percent floor. If the personal casualties result in a net loss for the year, the gains and losses are ordinary and only the net losses are subject to the 10 percent floor. Losses to the extent of the gains are deducted "above the line."

Effective Date: For taxable years beginning after December 31, 1983.

TAX BENEFIT RULE

In general, the tax benefit rule requires that a taxpayer who recovers an item that was deducted in an earlier taxable year must recognize income to the extent the deduction yielded a tax reduction in the earlier year. The Act provides that when an amount attributable to a prior year's deduction is received in a later year such amount may be excluded from gross income only to the extent it did not reduce income subject to tax.

Effective Date: Amounts recovered after December 31, 1983.

EARNED INCOME CREDIT

The refundable earned income credit is increased from 10 percent to 11 percent of the first $5,000 of earned income, providing a maximum allowable credit of $550. The credit is phased out as income increases from $6,500 to $11,000. The credit is reduced by the amount of a taxpayer's minimum tax liability.

Effective Date: Taxable years beginning after December 31, 1984.

ESTATE AND GIFT TAXES

In addition to the delay in the reduction of the top estate and gift tax rate described under the freezes, several minor provisions are contained in the Act that relate to the taxation of trusts and estates.

Trusts. Under the Act, as in prior law, a trust or estate does not recognize any gain or loss on the distribution of appreciated property. However, unlike prior law, the basis of the trust or estate in the appreciated property would carry over to the beneficiary who, on a later disposition, would pay tax on the appreciation. Alternatively, the trust or estate could elect to recognize gain or loss on the distribution and, if so, the beneficiaries would, in effect, receive a step-up in basis in the property equal to its fair market value at the time of distribution.

Multiple trusts established by substantially the same grantor for substantially the same beneficiary with a principal purpose of tax avoidance are now treated as one trust for tax purposes. This provision codifies Treasury regulations.

Effective Date: Taxable years beginning after March 1, 1984, for multiple trusts. Distributions after June 1, 1984 for appreciated property.

Alternate Valuation Date Election. The value of a decedent's gross estate is determined either at date of death, or, if elected, on an alternate valuation date six months after the date of death. The alternate valuation date was initially made available to provide relief in the case in which the value of the estate decreased after the date of death.

However, with the recent increases in the unified credit and the decrease in the number of estates subject to the estate tax, many estates have elected the alternate valuation date in situations in which the value of the estate increased and the estate was not subject to an estate tax. Therefore, the Act provides that no election to use the alternate valuation date can be made unless the total value of all property in the gross estate and the federal estate tax liability imposed thereon are reduced as a result of the election.

Effective Date: Applies to estates of decedents dying after July 18, 1984.

Business Taxation

DEPRECIATION

Prior law allowed the depreciation of certain real property (including low-income housing) under ACRS over 15 years. The taxpayer could use the 175 percent declining balance method (200 percent for low-income housing), switching to the straight line method or could elect straight line over 15, 35 or 45 years.

Year	15-Year Recovery Period	Present Value @ 12%	18-Year Recovery Period	Present Value @ 12%
1	36.000	34.017	24.000	22.678
2	66.000	55.682	54.000	45.558
3	60.000	45.197	48.000	36.157
4	54.000	36.319	48.000	32.283
5	48.000	28.824	42.000	25.221
6	42.000	22.519	36.000	19.302
7	36.000	17.233	36.000	17.234
8	30.000	12.823	30.000	12.823
9	30.000	11.449	30.000	11.449
10	30.000	10.222	24.000	8.178

Note: Depreciation amounts under the 15-year recovery period are based on tables prepared by the Treasury Department. Amounts under the 18-year recovery period are computed by DH&S based on the same method incorporated in the Treasury tables, using a mid-month convention as required by the Act.

Because of the rapid depreciation write offs, favorable recapture rules and installment sale relief, tax-oriented real estate partnerships have grown rapidly. Sale-leaseback transactions have also increased, especially by corporations whose taxable income is insufficient to absorb the accelerated depreciation deductions.

Congress believed that this generous depreciation may be diverting investment away from the more productive investment projects. Therefore, Congress changed the 15-year depreciation period to 18 years for real property (other than low-income housing property). In addition a mid-month convention is adopted, which treats all property regardless of the actual date placed in service during a month as though it were placed in service in the middle of the month. This convention will be incorporated in tables to be prescribed by Treasury. Taxpayers can continue to depreciate low-income housing property over 15 years.

If a $600,000 building is purchased in July of Year 1 the depreciation schedules (page 516) show the recovery amounts under both 15 and 18 years and the present value of those amounts using a 12 percent discount rate.

If the asset were sold at the end of Year 5, the sum of the present value of the deductions allowed under a 15-year recovery period is $200,039 as opposed to $161,897 over an 18-year period. If the aset is held until the end of Year 10, the amounts are $274,285 for 15-year and $230,883 for 18-year recovery.

Effective Date: For property placed in service after March 15, 1984. The 15-year recovery rules continue to apply to property placed in service before January 1, 1987 if a binding contract existed, or construction was commenced on or before March 15, 1984.

Compliance Measures

The Act continues the emphasis on tightening taxpayer compliance measures that has been so evident in recent tax legislation. Examples follow:

TAX SHELTER REGISTRATION

- Any organizer of a tax shelter must register it with the Treasury no later than the day on which the first offering is made. This registration must describe the shelter and its tax benefits to investors. A pur-

chaser of an interest in a shelter must receive the shelter's I.D. number and place it on his or her tax return. A shelter is defined as any investment in which it can reasonably be inferred from the representations made that the ratio of the deductions and 200 percent of the credits from the shelter to the cash and other property contributed to the shelter exceeds 2 to 1 as of the close of any of the first 5 years.

Effective Date: Tax shelter interests sold after August 31, 1984.

- Any person who organizes or sells an interest in a potentially abusive tax shelter must maintain a list that identifies each person purchasing an interest in the shelter and must make these lists available to the IRS upon request. A potentially abusive tax shelter is defined as any shelter requiring registration and any entity, investment plan or arrangement, or any other plan or arrangement which the Secretary, by regulation, has determined has a potential for tax avoidance or evasion.

Effective Date: Any interest first sold to an investor after August 31, 1984.

TAX SHELTER PROMOTER PENALTIES

The penalty imposed on persons who organize, assist or participate in the organization or sale of an abusive tax shelter is increased to the greater of $2,000 or 20 percent of the gross income derived from the activity.

Effective Date: Activity occurring after July 18, 1984.

INTEREST RATE FOR TAX SHELTER CASES

The interest rate to be applied to certain underpayments is 120 percent of the statutory rate. Such rate applies if the underpayment exceeds $1,000 and results from 1) a valuation overstatement of 150 percent or more, 2) disallowance of a loss or investment tax credit under the at-risk rules, 3) any tax shelter, 4) use of an accounting method potentially resulting in a substantial distortion of income, or 5) any other tax motivated transaction as prescribed by regulations.

Effective Date: Interest accruing after December 31, 1984.

Investment Overview of the 1984 Tax Act*

It's the Law!

On July 18, President Reagan signed the Deficit Reduction Act of 1984 into law. While the primary purpose of the new legislation is to raise tax dollars and reduce the budget deficit, the law does not necessarily mean bad news for investors. In fact, it may even provide opportunities for those who carefully review their portfolios and position their assets to take advantage of the law. The Act is not a simplification of tax rules; thus, many investors are confused by provisions of the law—and don't even know where to begin analyzing their portfolios. This issue of *Action Alert* gives you a head start on careful tax planning for 1984 and beyond. It seeks to summarize the provisions of the tax law that are pertinent to investors, and, where applicable, provide investment strategies to maximize opportunities.

Capital Gains Holding Period Now Six Months and One Day

The most widely publicized investment ramification of the new law is the reduction of the capital gains holding period from over one year to six months and one day. Now, a security need only be held for more than six months to qualify for the more favorable long-term capital gains tax treatment. This change applies to assets acquired after June 22, 1984

---

* Prudential-Bache Securities Inc. is not a tax advisor. Investors should consult their tax advisor(s) before taking action on any investment strategies or ideas suggested herein, and carefully determine their suitability requirements.

This publication was prepared with the assistance of Arthur Andersen & Co.; Harold I. Staub, Prudential-Bache Tax Department; and the Prudential-Bache Corporate Bond, Direct Investment, and Options Departments.

Any statements non-factual in nature constitute only current opinions, which are subject to change. Prudential-Bache Securities Inc. (or one of its affiliates) or their officers and directors may have positions in securities or commodities referred to herein, and may, as principal or agent, buy and sell such securities or commodities. Neither the information, nor any opinion expressed, shall be construed to be, or constitute an offer to sell or a solicitation of an offer to buy any securities or commodities mentioned herein. Opinions based on technical factors are suited primarily for the trader. Our fundamental opinions, however, are geared for the longer term investor. Therefore, there may be instances when these opinions may not be in concert. This firm (or one of its affiliates) may from time to time perform investment banking or other services for, or solicit investment banking or other business from, any company mentioned in this report.

Source: *Action Alert, 1984 Tax Act: Overview and Opportunities,* July 26, 1984. Prudential-Bache Securities with permission.

and before January 1, 1988, when a reversion to the one-year holding period is scheduled. Assets that were acquired before June 23 will still have to be held for over one year to qualify for long-term benefits. The amount of capital loss that a noncorporate taxpayer may offset against ordinary income in any taxable year has *not* changed; it remains at $3,000.

New Holding Period: Capitalize!

The shortened holding period under the new law mandates that you keep accurate records of when securities were purchased and the period they were held. For investors considering new securities purchases, the benefit is obvious. Position in stocks and bonds . . . mutual funds . . . unit trusts . . . options . . . there are many vehicles available to capitalize. What can you do if you already hold short-term positions? *Strategy: Swap to realize short-term losses whenever possible, with an eye to upgrading portfolio quality as well as healing the tax bite.*

If the short-term position was put on two or three months ago and is now breakeven or shows a small profit, you can *dramatically shorten the holding period.* Simply sell the security and repurchase it, thereby subjecting the new position to a shorter holding period requirement. It is recommended that you wait at least one day before repurchase. If you hold stocks with losses short-term, there are several appropriate strategies:

- *Swap.* Switch to another stock of a company in the same industry with similar or superior growth characteristics to realize losses now, and continue tax planning for the balance of this year.

- *Double Up.* If you wish to maintain a position, you should double up on your position, wait 31 days and then sell your original position. This will give you a short-term loss on the original holding and make the new position eligible for a long-term gain after six months and one day *if this stock rallies.*

- *Sell Put Options.* As an alternative to doubling up, you can avoid wash sale problems, take short-term losses and institute a reduced holding period through the use of options. If you sell the stock and simultaneously sell an *in-the-money put* expiring after thirty-one days, you can position advantageously. If the stock does not trade listed options, over-the-counter puts can be created. This creates a short-term loss, a six month holding period after the stock is put, and a hedge during the 31-day wash sale period.

NEW HOLDING PERIOD—OPTING FOR OPTIONS

The new six month capital gain holding period *means that outright long puts or calls acquired after June 22 and held for over six months will receive favorable long-term capital gains treatment.* This is especially significant for longer term bearish investors, since a long put position held for over six months will receive long-term treatment—as opposed to short sales, which can never receive long-term capital gains treatment. Uncovered short positions in puts or calls will continue to be taxed as short-term capital items. For more, see below.

Market Discount Securities Changes

Significant new provisions concern the character and timing of income from certain publicly traded debt obligations (i.e., corporate bonds, government securities with maturities of over one year, and other taxable fixed income vehicles).

With respect to bonds issued after July 18, 1984 (enactment date), any market discount (the difference between the acquisition price and the face amount, which is not original issue discount) must be accrued ratably to maturity. Such accrual will be ordinary income (to the extent of gain) on disposition of the security. For example, an investor buys a bond with four years to maturity and a market discount of eight points, the discount will accrue at two points per year. If he sells the bond after two years, he will have to accrue four points of the discount. If his profit is four points or less, the entire profit is considered to be interest income, but if the profit is more than four points, four points is considered interest income and the excess is capital gain.

With respect to bonds outstanding on July 18, realization of the market discount will continue to be capital gain, limited in certain instances by borrowings.

Under the new law, if an investor purchases post-enactment bonds, or purchases pre-enactment bonds after July 18 and *finances these bonds,* the interest cost will not be currently deductible to the extent that market discount accrues. This deduction will be available in the year bonds are sold or redeemed. Investors may elect to accrue the market discount each year and report such accrual as taxable income. In this case, interest cost is deductible in the year incurred.

WARNING

With respect to old bonds acquired after July 18, 1984, any discount will be ordinary income for the period the bonds were financed. Where market discount bonds were purchased before July 19, 1984, investors will realize capital gain on a subsequent disposition at a profit, even if the acquisition was financed. In cases where it is required to accrue discount, investors may elect to accrue on a yield to maturity basis.

This law does not affect the treatment of market discount municipals.

DISCOUNT ON SHORT-TERM OBLIGATIONS

For many investors, interest income on certain short-term obligations (term not exceeding one year), such as Treasury Bills, will no longer be deferred until redemption. Instead, a portion of the interest income will have to be accrued ratably over the remaining term of the obligation. Any interest expense incurred to purchase a short-term obligation is deductible only to the extent that interest income has been accrued for that year. Investors may elect, however, to accrue income currently, thereby avoiding the interest deduction limitation. Discount on tax-exempt obligations is not covered by these provisions.

Two-Tiered Bond Market: Ideas

As a result of this provision of the law, a two-tiered market in corporates and governments is expected to emerge. Market discount bonds issued pre-law are expected to assume a scarcity value, since these issues still enjoy capital gain treatment upon sale at a profit or redemption at par at maturity. Consider positioning these bonds now, as they may very well rise in price—and implement swap strategies early! Also consider swapping into municipals.

For investors seeking income, bonds issued after July 18 may offer potentially lower prices, while, of course, offering quality, attractive yield, and potential for high total return. Where tax consequences are not a consideration (i.e., retirement plan accounts), the new market discount securities could also provide an attractive alternative.

Your Account Executive can help you determine the suitability of various bonds for your portfolio. He or she can also recommend corporate income funds (professionally managed and diversified portfolios of corporate bonds) issued prelaw. These can provide investors with both capital gains and high monthly income. Also consider MITFs (municipal investment trust funds) and bond mutual funds for additional flexibility.

Exercising Your Options

A number of important provisions to rules affecting equity and non-equity options transactions have been added to the law.

1. "Anti-straddle" rules have been established for offsetting stock and option positions established after December 31, 1983.

Here, a straddle is meant to be a position consisting of two or more components where protection is provided irrespective of market movement, such as a *spread* or *long stock and short call positions*. The anti-straddle rules provide for:

- The disallowance of recognized loss to the extent of unrecognized gain in other legs of the straddle ("loss deferral").
- The elimination of holding period and conversion of short-term loss to long-term loss under the "short sale" rules of Section 1233.
- The disallowance of "carrying charges" (interest, in-lieu-of dividends).

DEFINITION

An *"offsetting"* position is one which "substantially diminishes the risk of loss" in other positions. This vague definition would include most option spreads, back spreads, conversions, and reversals involving the same underlying stock. It should not include long stock option "straddles" (the purchase of a put and call on the same underlying stock), but could include short option "straddles" (writing puts and calls on the same stock) which are deep-in-the-money.

BOTTOM LINE FOR INVESTORS

Investors are no longer able to use tax spreads to defer gains to future years, although it does appear that they can do the reverse and establish gains this year and losses next year. This latter strategy may be attractive to: 1) investors seeking to convert long-term losses into short-term losses; 2) corporate investors seeking to establish new holding periods for expiring capital loss carryforwards; and 3) investors requiring short-term gains because of excessive deductions under alternative minimum tax regulations.

2. "Qualified" covered calls will be generally exempt from the anti-straddle rules.

However, the loss deferral rule would apply to a loss realized on the option if the stock is sold in a subsequent tax year within 30 days after the option is closed out. Also, qualified covered calls which were in-the-money when written would be subject to modified short sale rules (effective for positions established after June 30, 1984) which would: 1) suspend, but

---

Options Opportunities

Regarding options, the new law provides some significant opportunities:

1. *Index option trading offers increased appeal,* since index option transactions will now be taxed at a maximum 32% rate versus the pre-law 50% rate. As one example, if investors are seeking to speculate on a declining overall market. OEX and XMI puts can be purchased with tax advantage. *There is no holding period requirement!*

2. *Capitalize on the new six months and one day holding period. Stock puts always were treated as short-term. Under the new law, if they are held for six months and one day, they qualify for long-term treatment. Buying long-term puts is the only way to obtain a long-term gain from a bearish equity position.* Ask your Account Executive to supply you with information on suitable shorts, and instead of

selling short, consider purchasing puts out 7–9 months.

3. *"Buy Stock, Buy Put" is a strategy that is especially effective now.* If you buy a stock and *simultaneously* purchase a seven month put, the married position can qualify for long-term treatment if held over six months. Many favorite stocks have inexpensive puts which can be married to the stock position to provide downside protection in uncertain markets.

4. *With the new anti-straddle rules, investors are no longer able to use tax spreads to defer gains to future years. However, it appears that they can do the reverse and establish gains this year and losses next year.*

5. *For investors with a loss position that is not yet long-term, the sale of a non-qualified in-the-money call will eliminate the holding period!* The holding period will begin anew when the call expires, or is repurchased.

not eliminate, the holding period in the underlying stock; and 2) treat any loss on the option as a long-term loss if the underlying stock had a long-term holding period at the time the loss on the call is realized.

DEFINITION

A *"qualified" covered call* is a covered call stock option which, when written:

- Has more than 30 days to expiration.
- Has a strike price no lower than *first* available strike price below the closing price of the stock on the previous day. For options written with more than 90 days to expiration and strike prices of more than $50, a strike price no lower than the *second* available strike price below the closing stock price on the previous day (but for stock prices of $150 or less, the option cannot be more than $10 in-the-money).
- If the stock price on the *previous day* is $25 or less, the strike price must be at least 85% of the stock price.

SUMMARY

Qualified in-the-money calls suspend the holding period, while non-qualified in-the-money calls nullify the holding period of short-term equity positions. Note that the writing of out-of-the-money calls does not affect the holding period of *short-term* equity positions. No option transaction affects the holding period of stocks that are already long-term.

3. Non-equity options will receive 60/40 mark-to-market treatment.

Non-equity options are options on currencies, debt securities and *broad based* stock index options such as the Standard & Poor's 100 Index and the Major Market Index. Gain or loss on property subject to 60/40 treatment is marked to market at year-end (if not disposed of during the year) and taxed as 60% long-term and 40% short-term gain or loss. Year-end mark-to-market means the transaction for tax purposes is treated as if it had been liquidated at the close of trading on the last business day of the year. *This results in a maximum tax rate of 32% for investors in the top 50% tax bracket. There is no holding period requirement and the 60/40 treatment applies to both long and short positions!*

RESULT

Index option trading will obviously be more appealing, since index option transactions will now be taxed at a maximum rate of 32% versus the current 50% rate. This new regulation is effective July 18, 1984, although investors may elect to make it effective retroactive to January 1, 1984.

Options: Other Changes

- Pre-law, taxpayers were required to capitalize otherwise deductible interest expense and carrying charges incurred on property held as part of an offsetting straddle position, although the amount could be reproduced by interest income from the property. *Under the new law, dividends on stock, if it is property held as part of an offsetting straddle position, may also offset amount required to be capitalized.*
- *The IRS is directed to issue regulations within six months clarifying the taxation of mixed straddles.* A straddle is mixed when one of the positions is subject to the mark-to-market rules and the other position is not. These regulations will allow mixed straddle gains and losses to be netted but limit the ability to derive more than 50% long-term capital gain or 40% short-term capital loss from such netted transactions.
- *New provisions are added to apply the wash sale rule to short sales.* Thus, any loss realized on closing a short sale will be deferred if within a period of 30 days before or after the short sale closing, substantially identical stock or securities were sold or sold short. *This should not preclude use of the traditional "short against the box" strategy.* This change is effective for short sales entered into after July 18, 1984.

Commodities: Tax Law Impact

Effective with all options acquired, purchased or granted after October 31, 1983, commodity futures options are treated exactly the same as regulated commodity futures contracts. The profit or loss will be 60% long-term, 40% short-term, irrespective of the holding period.

Corporate Revisions

DIVIDENDS RECEIVED DEDUCTION

Formerly, the 85% dividends received deduction was available to corporate shareholders who held the underlying stock for 16 days (91 days in the case of certain preferred stock distributions). Now the holding period necessary to secure the 85% deduction will increase from 16 to 46 days. This holding period does not include any period during which the corporate stockholder has "diminished his risk of loss" from holding the stock by holding other positions in "substantially similar or related property," such as a short sale, put or covered call (other than a qualified covered call) in that same stock. The amount of the deduction will be limited if all or a portion of the stock is debt financed. However, the debt must be directly traceable to the purchase of the stock. Moreover, the deduction will not be limited if the dividend is received from a subsidiary (eligible for a special 100% deduction), or a small business investment company.

EXTRAORDINARY DIVIDENDS

If an unusually large or "extraordinary dividend" is paid on stock that has been held one year or less, the dividends-received deduction will reduce the tax basis (adjusted cost) in the underlying stock. In the case of a corporate shareholder, the dividends received deduction will reduce the stock basis of a shareholder who held the stock for less than one year even though the stock was held for 91 days. Thus, the opportunity to generate short-term capital losses through purchasing stock before the ex-dividend date for a large distribution and then selling it when the price drops will be greatly reduced.

SHORT SALE EXPENSE DEDUCTION LIMITED

Under a new rule, investors who have used the short sale technique to generate profits may have to pay more tax. To receive an ordinary deduction for payments made in lieu of dividends to the owner of shares borrowed to make the short sale, the investor must now hold the short sale open for *at least 46 days* (more than one year for extraordinary dividends). Otherwise, the amount paid will be added to the short seller's basis in the stock acquired to close the short sale, and consequently, will reduce short-term capital gain or increase capital loss realized.

DISTRIBUTIONS FROM REGULATED INVESTMENT COMPANIES (RICs)

A regulated investment company (RIC) is not subject to taxation if it distributes a sufficient portion of its income to its shareholders. The income will retain the character it had in the RIC's hands even after distribution to shareholders. The new law increases the required holding period to 46 days for a RIC to be able to distribute dividends eligible for the dividends received deduction. In addition, if less than 100% of the ordinary income of a RIC is from qualifying dividends, a pro-rata portion of such distribution will be classified as a qualifying distribution. Investors receiving a long-term capital gain distribution from a RIC or a real estate investment trust (REIT), who subsequently incur a loss on the sale of the RIC or REIT stock, will have long-term capital losses if the stock has been held six months or less. This loss will be recharacterized only to the extent that the investor received distributions receiving long-term capital gain treatment. For example, if a $1,050 loss is recognized and a $1,000 long-term capital gain was previously recognized, $1,000 of the loss will be recharacterized as long-term capital loss.

Tax Shelters: Still Alive and Well!

A primary focus of the new legislation has been the curtailment of certain tax shelters which are perceived as "abusive"; i.e., not offering sound economics. In summary, the new legislation will affect certain tax shelters as follows:

PREPAID EXPENSES

The new bill significantly reduces the benefits from tax shelters, such as cattle feeding and oil and gas operations, that are based on prepaying expenses before the tax year in which they are actually incurred. These deductions will now be delayed until the tax year to which the expenses are properly allocable, i.e., the year when property or services are actually provided or when property is actually used. A deduction in the year of prepayment will be allowed if the property or service is provided or used within 90 days after the close of the taxable year and the deduction does not exceed the cash investment in the shelter. These restrictions will apply to deductions taken after March 31, 1984.

ACCRUED EXPENSES

Presently, investors use the accrual method of accounting to deduct the full amount of a liability, even though actual payment does not occur until several years later. The new bill effectively reduces the time period between accrual and payment. However, an exception is made for certain recurring business expenses, when the liability is discharged within eight and a half months after the end of the year in which the deduction is taken.

RETROACTIVE ALLOCATIONS AMONG PARTNERS

To prevent the retroactive allocation of losses to a partner when a cash basis partner's interest in the partnership changes, the new law provides that certain partnership items must be allocated on an accrual basis—by first allocating a portion of the item to each day in the tax year, and then allocating the daily portions to each partner in proportion to his interest in the partnership on that day. The items which must be allocated include: interest, taxes, payments for services or for the use of property, and additional items to be specified by regulation.

PARTNER'S BASIS

A general partner who guarantees an otherwise non-recourse debt of the partnership will now include the entire liability in the computation of his basis. Formerly, a portion of the debt would also be included in each limited partner's basis.

REAL ESTATE DEPRECIATION

The period for real estate depreciation, other than low income housing, has been extended from 15 to 18 years.

ITC AT-RISK RULES

Under the new law, the investment tax credit at-risk rules have been amended to provide that to the extent that property is financed with non-recourse borrowing, it will not qualify for the investment tax credit. These rules will generally not apply, however, to property used in an active trade or business of an S corporation, and where debt is obtained from a commercial lender, and is at risk for at least 20%.

In the case of pass-through leases, the law states that the lessor's at-risk position will determine the availability of the credit unless the lessor has manufactured or produced the property, the property has readily ascertainable fair market value, or the lessor is not normally subject to the at-risk rules.

Taxation of Certain Annuity Contracts: Act Now to Benefit!

Under present law, premature distributions (cash withdrawals prior to the starting date of the annuity) are includable in gross income to the extent that the annuity contract cash value exceeded the annuity investment. In addition, if the investment is made within ten years of the distribution, a penalty tax of 5% is imposed on the amount includable in gross income. This is true unless, at the time of distribution, the contractholder reached age 59½, became disabled, died, or received the distribution as a payment under an annuity for life or at least five years.

The new law generally retains the present-law provisions for annuity contracts. However, the 5% penalty for premature distributions will apply to amounts distributed, whether or not the investment was made within ten years of the distribution. In addition, to be treated as an annuity contract, the contract must provide that:

1. If the contractholder dies on or after the annuity starting date and before all interest in the contract has been distributed, the remaining portion of interest will be distributed at least as rapidly as under the distribution method in effect at the holder's death.
2. If the contractholder dies before the annuity starting date, the entire interest must be distributed within five years of the date of death.

This provision is effective for contracts issued more than six months after July 18, 1984.

Limitations on Deductions to Private Foundations

Under prior law, all contributions by individuals to private non-operating foundations (i.e., grant making foundations) and certain other organizations (i.e., veterans and fraternal organizations) were deductible up to 20% of the donor's adjusted gross income (or the excess of 50% of the donor's adjusted gross income over contributions to public charities and operating foundations, if less) with no carryover of excess contributions allowed. In addition, the amount deductible for contributions of appreciated capital-gain property was limited to the donor's basis in the property, increased by 60% of the excess of fair market value of the property over the donor's basis. The new law increases the amount deductible for contributions of cash or ordinary income property to 30% of the donor's taxable income, unless limited as discussed above. The 20% limitation remains in effect for all gifts of capital-gain property by individuals except as discussed below.

Finally, the new law generally allows individuals to deduct the full fair market value of "qualified appreciated stock" donated to private non-operating foundations. Qualified appreciated stock is defined as any stock of a corporation for which market quotations are readily available on an established securities market and long-term capital gain would result if sold. The new law is effective for contributions made in taxable years ending after enactment date. The deduction for qualified appreciated stock is limited to approximately ten years and will not apply to contributions made after 1994.

Employee Benefit Provisions

Major changes will affect the tax treatment of employee benefits. These changes include reducing the amount deductible for contributions to funded employee welfare benefit plans and applying new nondiscrimination standards to these plans. Additional miscellaneous provisions apply to fringe benefits, qualified pension and profit-sharing plans, employee stock ownership plans, and cafeteria plans. Highlights of some of these provisions follow.

FRINGE BENEFITS

Generally, specified benefits will be tax-free to employees if they are provided on a nondiscriminatory basis. If qualified benefits are provided in a manner that discriminates in favor of employees who are owners, shareholders, or highly compensated, these employees will not qualify for the income tax exclusion.

If non-statutory fringe benefits fall within one of five categories (no additional cost service, qualified employee discount, working condition fringe, *de minimis* fringe, and qualified tuition reduction), they are excluded from the employee's gross income for purposes of federal income tax and related payroll taxes.

VOLUNTARY EMPLOYEE BENEFIT ASSOCIATIONS (VEBAs)

The new provisions will affect all employers that contribute to and maintain funded welfare benefit plans, including VEBAs. A contribution that is otherwise deductible under the Code generally will be deductible only if it does not exceed what a cash basis employer could deduct if the benefits were paid directly to employees. In addition to these limitations, new anti-discrimination rules may lead to disqualification of the plan. These measures may reduce tax benefits of VEBAs to employers.

CAFETERIA PLANS

Cafeteria plans may now offer as benefits only cash, and group term life insurance, group legal services, accident and health benefits, and dependent care assistance programs. Also, "use it or lose it" rule will apply to salary reduction arrangements.

The legislation establishes a new nondiscrimination test, in addition to the test that currently exists for highly compensated employees. A plan will now be considered discriminatory if the amount of tax-free benefits provided for key employees exceeds 25% of total cafeteria plan benefits. If benefits for key employees exceed the 25% limit, key employees will be taxed on all benefits they receive under the plan.

EMPLOYEE STOCK OWNERSHIP PLANS (ESOP)

With the exception of the freeze on the tax credit increase, changes are generally favorable, and include:

- Tax credit for employer contributions to ESOPs is frozen at the current rate of ½% through 1987 and *eliminated* thereafter.
- Tax-free rollover of proceeds from sale of a business to an ESOP under certain conditions.
- A corporate deduction for dividends paid on ESOP stock.
- A 50% exclusion for interest income of banks and insurance companies making loans to ESOPs.
- Assumption of liability for estate taxes of a stockholder by the ESOP in exchange for stock of equal value, provided the company maintaining the ESOP guarantees payment of taxes.

FREEZE ON PLAN BENEFIT AND CONTRIBUTION INCREASES

The cost-of-living benefit freeze affecting maximum contribution and benefit levels is extended from 1986 to 1988. Accordingly, employer contributions to a defined contribution plan cannot exceed $30,000 and maximum benefits from a defined benefit plan cannot exceed $90,000.

GOLDEN PARACHUTES

Congress has enacted new rules that eliminate the deduction for any amount paid or incurred pursuant to a "golden parachute" contract. Golden parachutes are contractual arrangements entered into or renewed after June 14, 1984, that provide for payments in excess of 300% of a base amount and that are contingent upon change in corporate control or ownership. In addition to a loss of the corporate deduction for excess amount of payment, a nondeductible excise tax of 20% of the excess parachute payment will be imposed on the recipient.

Personal Finance

INTEREST-FREE LOANS

Specific rules dealing with interest-free loans will cause the value of the interest on the loan to be treated as either a taxable gift, a dividend, or compensation, depending on the relationship between the borrower and lender. The borrower will also be treated as having paid a market rate of interest to the lender. Thus, the lender will have to recognize income while the borrower will incur interest expense. Exceptions to these rules are provided for certain loans of minimal amount and where tax avoidance is not a principal purpose for the loan. For the most part, these rules apply to loans made after June 6, 1984. As an alternative to interest free loans, consider *Clifford Trusts.* Clifford Trusts allow individuals to transfer income to family members in lower tax brackets, provided that the property placed in trust does not revert to the grantor within ten years.

ESTIMATED TAXES

The exceptions that apply for avoiding a penalty for underpayment of estimated tax have been simplified and liberalized. The IRS has also been given the authority to waive the penalty in extraordinary circumstances. The Act provides that the Alternative Minimum Tax (AMT), where applicable, must be estimated and paid in installments.

ESTATE TAX EXCLUSION

The $100,000 exclusion of certain retirement plan distributions from the estate tax has been repealed. Starting with estates of decedents dying in 1985, such distributions will be included in the decedent's taxable estate. The 55% maximum estate tax rate will gradually drop to 50% in 1988, instead of 1985 as formerly scheduled.

Investing in Gold, Diamonds and Collectibles

Investing in Gold

Gold has been one of the more widely promoted investment vehicles over the last several years. Prices have moved from about $140 per ounce in early 1977 to over $800 in early 1980. However, by mid-1981 prices declined to $460 an ounce. Because of such large fluctuations, the metal has stimulated a great deal of speculative interest among many investors.

Investment in gold can be made in a variety of ways:

Gold bullion (bars and wafers) This can be purchased through many stock brokers, bullion currency dealers, and some investment (mutual fund) companies. The purity of gold is indicated by the fineness. Pure gold has a fineness of 1.000 and corresponds to 24 karats.* Each bar is stamped with the fineness as determined by an assay, the refiner's number, a bar identification number and the weight. A bar fineness of .995 or better is acceptable.

Individuals who accept delivery of gold bars and who subsequently wish to resell must have the bar reassayed prior to sale because of the possibility of adulteration with cheaper metals. Because of the latter possibility, individuals should always buy from reputable dealers, and the bar should bear the stamp of well recognized refiners or assayers. Individuals taking physical possession of the metal also have sales taxes, storage, and insurance costs.

The purchaser may arrange to have the dealer (or agent) retain physical possession of the bullion. In this case, evidence of ownership is provided by a *gold deposit certificate* (receipt) issued by the dealer. Since gold certificates are generally nonnegotiable or assignable, there is no loss if it is stolen. The gold deposit certificate method of buying bullion eliminates sales taxes, storage risks (though the dealer will charge a modest storage fee) and the need for assay on resale. It is probably the most convenient way of purchasing gold.

Gold bullion coins Bullion coins are issued in large number by several governments which guarantee their gold content. They have no numismatic value. The best known gold bullion coins are the South African Krugerand, Canadian Maple Leaf, Austrian 100 Corona and the Gold Mexican 50 peso. The first two coins have a pure gold content of one ounce. The Austrian Corona has a gold content of .9802 ounce and the Mexican peso 1.2057 ounces. The premium (cost above the gold value) varies from dealer to dealer. For those who do not want to take physical possession, deposit certificates are available for the coins.

Gold stocks The stocks of a number of Canadian and U.S. gold mining companies are traded on the New York (N), American (A) and Over-The-Counter (O) exchanges. Of course, with stocks, the investor is not just buying into gold, but also into the many special problems associated with running a company—production costs, quality of the ore, lifetime of the deposit, etc. However, many gold stocks pay dividends, whereas other gold investments do not pay any return during the holding period.

Some listed stocks are given below:
Agnico-Eagle Mines (O)
Campbell Red Lake Mines (N)
Dome Mines (N)
Sunshine Mining (N)
Homestake Mining Company (N)

A publicly-held New York Stock Exchange closed-end gold fund is ASA Limited. Several mutual funds which invest in gold are given in the mutual fund section of the Almanac (page 351).

To locate reputable gem dealers check with:

American Gem Society
3460 Wilshire Boulevard
Los Angeles, CA 90010
(213) 387–7375

Accredited Gemologists Association
36 NE 1st Street
Miami, FL 33132
(305) 372–0872

South African gold mines are traded on the Over-The-Counter Market by means of ADR (American Depository Receipt). ADR is a claim on foreign stocks (South African gold shares, in this case) held by the foreign branches of large U.S. banks. Holders of ADRs are entitled to dividends which, in the case of South African gold shares, may be substantial. The ADRs of these companies

---

* This "karats" is not to be confused with the "carats" that apply to diamonds.

are listed in *The Wall Street Journal* under the Foreign Securities section, which follows the OTC quotations.

Some major South African gold mining companies are:

Blyvooruitzicht
Buffelsfontein
East Driefontein
Kloof
President Brand
President Steyn
Randfontein
West Dreifontein
Western Deep Levels
Western Holdings

Mutual funds specializing in gold and precious metals A number of mutual funds (see page 351) specialize in gold and precious metals stocks. These funds provide diversification among a number of issues thereby reducing risk associated with any particular stock.

Options on gold stocks Put and call options are available on Homestake Mining (Chicago Options Exchange) and on ASA Limited (American Options Exchange). These options may be used for leveraged speculation or for hedging existing gold holdings. Holders of call options gain if the gold shares increase, while holders of put options benefit if prices decline.

The Philadelphia Stock Exchange trades a gold/silver option based on an index of seven different stocks in the industry.

Options on gold bullion Put and call options on gold bullion are traded on the International Options Market (IOM) of the Montreal Stock Exchange. IOM options are on 10 ounces of gold. Contract months are Feb/May/Aug/Nov.

Monex (Newport Beach, CA) provides put and call options on 32.15 ounces of gold. The Monex options are not tradeable but can be exercized during the option period. Expiration periods are 30, 60, 90, and 180 days. Mocatta Metals (New York) offers a somewhat similar contract.

Since options are paid in full, they are not subject to margin calls or forced liquidation as is the case with futures contracts. At this time, quotations on bullion options are not available in the daily press.

Gold futures contract Gold futures contracts are obligations to buy or sell 100 ounces of gold on or before a specified date at a specified price. Futures contracts must be exercised if held to maturity, while options contracts need not be exercised if held to maturity. Futures contracts are purchased on margin, and hence, are subject to margin call and possible forced liquidation. They are widely quoted in the financial press, and the market is highly organized.

As with options, futures contracts may be used for leveraged speculation or for hedging. Speculators will buy contracts if they anticipate a price increase or sell contracts in anticipation of a price decrease.

Gold futures are traded on the N.Y. Commodity Exchange, the International Monetary Market of the Chicago Mercantile Exchange, and other markets.

Options on Gold Futures Contracts Options on Gold Futures contracts (the right to buy and sell a gold futures contract rather than the metal) are actively traded on the New York Comex. The futures contract underlying the options is for 100 ounces of gold. Contract months are April/Aug/Dec. Gold futures options premiums are reported daily in the *Wall Street Journal.*

Investing in Diamonds

Diamonds have appreciated on the average of about 12.6% over the ten-year period 1969–1979 (compared to a consumer price index of 6.1% during the same period of time). There have been periods (the recession of 1973—1974 and in 1981) when the price of investment quality diamonds slipped as much as 40%. A major factor stabilizing the market is DeBeers, a South African diamond company which handles as much as 80% of the world's diamonds. While the appreciation of diamonds has been impressive, potential buyers should be aware that prices are not quoted in the daily newspapers; therefore, selling the stones at a profit may be difficult. *The PreciouStones Newsletter,* 7315 Wisconsin Avenue, Bethesda, MD 20814, Telephone (301) 986–0666 is one of the few reliable sources of prices. Buyers should only deal with reputable firms, and the stones should be certified by an independent laboratory such as the Gemological Institute of America, International Gemological Institute and the European Gemological Laboratories. They maintain offices in New York and Los Angeles.

Diamonds are ranked in terms of the 4 C's—carat (one carat equals 1/142 ounces weight), color, clarity, and cut.

Carat For investment purposes the diamond should be more than .5 carat. However, diamonds of more than 2 carats may be difficult to sell.

Color There are six main categories, each with subdivisions:

D,E,F—Colorless
G,H,I,J—Near colorless
K,L,M—Faint yellow
N,O,P,Q,R—Very light yellow
S,T,U,V,W,X,Y,Z—Light yellow
Fancy yellow stone

Color should be in the range from to D to H. However, Fancy Yellow Stones often command very high prices because of their scarcity.

Clarity Although bubbles, lines, and specks (inclusions) are natural to diamonds, they may interfere with the passage of light through the diamond. With a 10X magnification, a professional appraiser can grade the diamond according to the ten clarity grades:

FL—Flawless
IF—Internally flawless
VVS-1, VVS-2—Very, very slight inclusions
VS-1, VS-2—Very slight inclusions
SI-1, SI-2—Slight inclusions
I-1, I-2, I-3—Imperfect

Investment grade stones should be in the range FL to VS-2.

Cut There are several types of cuts—oval, marquise, pear shaped, round brilliant and emerald. Round brilliant stones are preferred for investment purposes. Proportions are important, and the preferred values are:

Depth % (total depth divided by girdle diameter): 57% to 63%.
Table (table diameter divided by girdle diameter): 57% to 66%.
Girdle thickness should be neither very thick nor very thin.

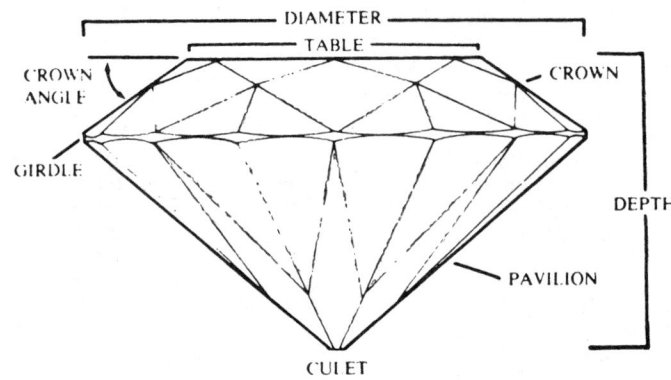

THE ROUND BRILLIANT DIAMOND

Investing in Collectibles

THE SOTHEBY INDEX®

Category	Wgt	June 19	June 12	Sept. 1983	Sept. 1982
Old Master Paintings	17	245	245	217	199
19th Century European Paintings	12	245	209	197	183
Impressionist & Post-Impressionist Paintings	18	317	317	298	255
Modern Paintings (1900–1950)	10	301	301	275	245
American Paintings (1800-pre-WW II)	3	589	589	501	459
Continental Ceramics	3	284	284	272	266
Chinese Ceramics	10	459	459	445	460
English Silver	5	237	237	219	183
Continental Silver	5	161	161	156	134
American Furniture	3	241	241	239	213
French & Continental Furniture	7	270	270	254	234
English Furniture	7	360	342	309	263
Weighted Aggregate	...	**297**	**296**	**275**	**251**

Sept. 1975 = 100.
© 1984 Sotheby Parke Bernet Inc.
    The data reflected in the Sotheby Index are based on results of auction sales by affiliated companies of the Sotheby Parke Bernet Group and other information deemed relevant by Sotheby's. Sotheby's does not warrant the accuracy of the data reflected therein. Nothing in any commentary furnished by Sotheby's nor any of the Sotheby's Indices is intended or should be relied upon as investment advice or as a prediction, warranty or guaranty as to future performance or otherwise. All individual prices quoted in the review are aggregate prices, inclusive of the buyer's premium.

Source: Reprinted by courtesy of *Barron's National Business and Financial Weekly*, June 25, 1984.

Investing in Real Estate

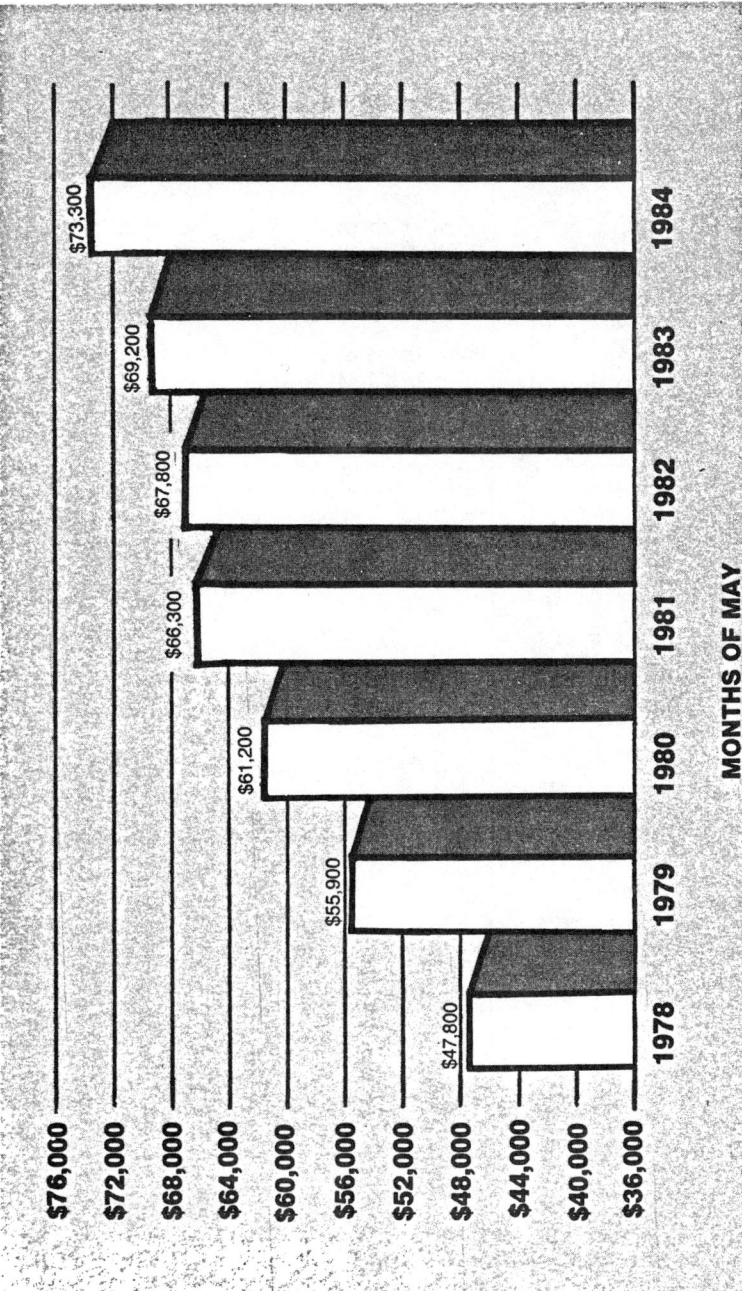

MEDIAN SALES PRICE OF EXISTING SINGLE-FAMILY HOMES IN THE UNITED STATES FOR THE MONTH OF MAY 1978–1984

Months of May	Median Sales Price
1978	$47,800
1979	$55,900
1980	$61,200
1981	$66,300
1982	$67,800
1983	$69,200
1984	$73,300

MONTHS OF MAY

Source: National Association of Realtors, Economics and Research Division, 777 14th Street, N.W., Washington, D.C. 20005.

MEDIAN SALES PRICE OF EXISTING SINGLE-FAMILY HOMES FOR METROPOLITAN AREAS (not seasonally adjusted in thousands of dollars)

| | Years | | | Quarters | | | | |
	1981	1982	1983	1983 I	II	III	IV	1984 I^r
Albany	$46.1	$47.1	$49.4	$46.5	$49.0	$50.6	$51.0	$52.0
Anaheim/Santa Ana*	131.4	133.0	134.9	131.5	134.9	139.1	133.7	133.5
Atlanta	n/a	55.3	63.0	57.5	58.4	67.1	65.8	67.9
Baltimore	57.7	62.0	n/a	62.9	64.8	65.5	n/a	64.2
Birmingham	59.2	60.6	62.8	59.8	62.9	65.4	61.4	65.0
Boston	n/a	80.2	82.6	78.6	80.1	85.4	84.9	89.4
Chicago	70.3	73.0	76.4	76.0	78.8	78.7	75.9	77.8
Cincinnati	n/a	n/a	57.2	56.8	58.5	57.6	56.0	58.7
Cleveland	n/a	n/a	n/a	n/a	n/a	64.9	61.7	59.8
Columbus	55.0	57.8	59.4	57.9	60.4	59.6	58.8	60.2
Dallas/Ft. Worth	67.3	74.0	76.0	73.2	75.9	78.8	77.1	81.0
Denver	n/a	76.2	78.3	76.2	78.2	79.6	78.2	79.6
Detroit	48.5	47.5	47.5	46.8	48.3	47.1	47.8	48.1
Ft. Lauderdale	72.8	74.2	73.9	72.9	74.5	75.5	72.3	69.9
Houston	72.7	77.2	79.9	76.8	80.3	83.0	80.0	78.4
Indianapolis	49.7	50.6	52.8	52.0	54.2	53.7	49.8	50.6
Kansas City	46.1	58.1	58.8	59.0	59.9	59.2	56.4	60.8
Los Angeles*	111.4	113.4	112.7	111.9	112.7	114.3	111.5	114.2
Louisville	47.6	46.0	47.4	52.1	46.3	49.3	46.5	47.9

Memphis	55.9	59.3	61.6	59.6	60.0	64.1	61.8	62.0
Miami	n/a	n/a	n/a	n/a	76.7	78.0	75.9	79.8
Milwaukee	64.5	65.8	68.0	66.1	68.0	70.5	66.7	69.8
Minneapolis/St. Paul	69.7	72.4	73.6	72.5	74.3	73.7	73.7	73.4
Nashville	n/a	n/a	61.0	61.5	60.8	60.8	61.0	60.0
New York Met Area**	73.8	70.5	88.9	83.1	87.1	93.0	94.4	100.6
Oklahoma City	54.1	58.4	61.6	60.4	60.8	62.4	62.5	62.1
Philadelphia	59.2	58.1	59.6	59.1	59.8	60.7	58.6	59.8
Providence	50.0	49.7	54.7	50.4	53.7	57.8	56.2	56.5
Rochester	45.9	49.5	54.8	55.2	55.7	55.4	54.9	55.4
St. Louis	n/a	57.0	58.9	57.2	59.2	59.6	58.7	57.5
Salt Lake City	62.9	64.6	64.3	63.7	64.1	65.7	63.1	64.0
San Antonio	53.6	58.3	62.6	58.1	61.9	67.6	62.3	64.5
San Diego*	97.4	98.6	98.9	97.0	99.6	100.2	98.6	96.3
San Francisco*	121.6	124.9	129.5	122.0	128.6	136.5	129.4	126.6
San Jose	109.0	122.6	127.6	122.8	126.8	130.6	128.6	125.0
Tampa	51.9	53.9	55.5	52.0	55.2	58.2	55.4	55.6
Washington, D.C.	88.3	87.2	89.4	87.9	89.7	90.8	89.0	91.3

n/a Not Available
*   Provided by the California Association of REALTORS®
**   Including Long Island and Newark
r Revised

Source: National Association of Realtors, Economics and Research Division, 777 14th Street, N.W., Washington, D.C. 20005.

HOUSING AFFORDABILITY

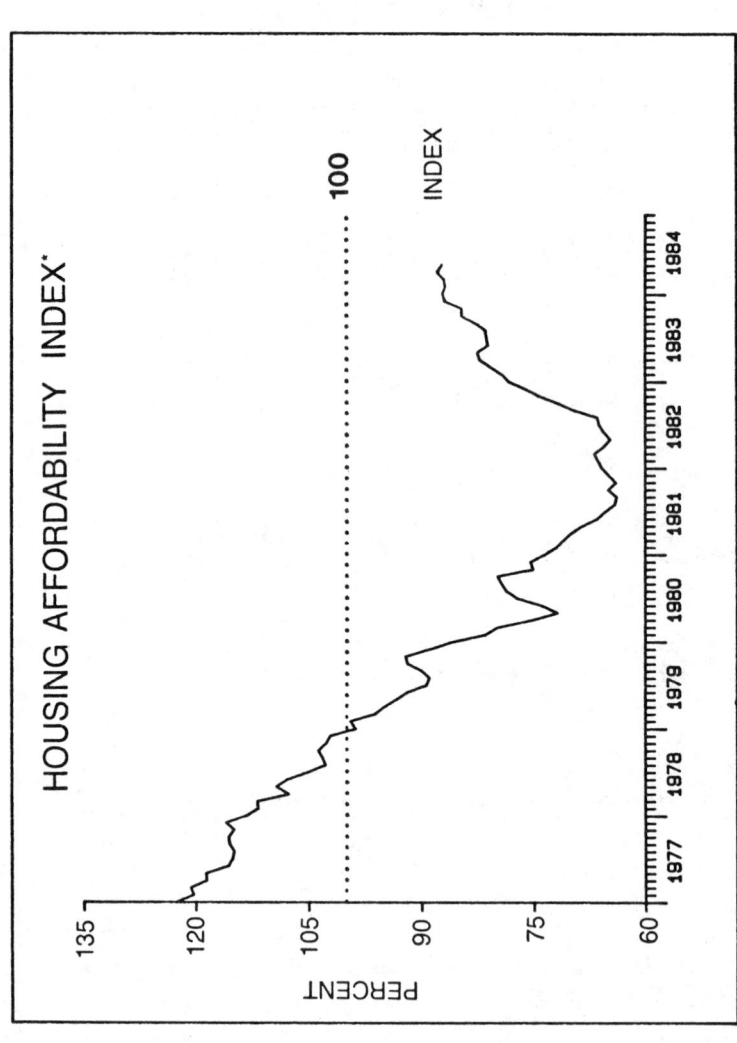

Year	Median-Priced Existing Single-Family Home	Mortgage Rate**	Monthly P & I Payment	Payment as % Income	Median Family Income	Qualifying Income***	Affordability Index
1977	$42,900	9.02%	$277	20.7%	$16,010	$13,279	120.6
1978	48,700	9.58	330	22.4	17,640	15,834	111.4
1979	55,700	10.92	422	25.7	19,680	20,240	97.2
1980	62,200	12.95	549	31.3	21,023	26,328	79.9
1981	66,400	15.12	677	36.3	22,388	32,485	68.9
1982	67,800	15.38	702	35.9	23,433	33,713	69.5
1983	70,300	12.85	616	29.9	24,700	29,546	83.6
1983							
May	$69,200	12.82%	$605	30.3%	$23,961	$29,021	82.6
Jun	71,400	12.67	617	30.8	24,066	29,624	81.2
Jul	71,800	12.63	619	30.7	24,172	29,704	81.4
Aug	71,500	12.72	620	30.6	24,278	29,772	81.5
Sep	69,900	12.85	612	30.1	24,383	29,378	83.0
Oct	69,800	12.65	602	29.5	24,489	28,918	84.7
Nov	70,400	12.58	605	29.5	24,594	29,020	84.8
Dec	69,900	12.39	592	28.8	24,700	28,418	86.9
1984							
Jan	$71,300	12.16%	$594	28.7%	$24,844	$28,500	87.2
Feb	71,800	12.19	599	28.8	24,988	28,764	86.9
Mar	72,200	12.17	602	28.7	25,132	28,881	87.0
Apr^r	72,500	12.07	600	28.5	25,276	28,787	87.8
May^p	73,300	12.09	607	28.7	25,420	29,148	87.2

r   Revised   p   Preliminary

* Index equals 100 when median family income equals qualifying income.

** Effective rate on loans closed on existing homes—Federal Home Loan Bank Board.

*** Based on current lending requirements of the Federal National Mortgage Association using a 20 percent downpayment.

Source: National Association of Realtors, Economics and Research Division, 777 14th Street, N.W., Washington, D.C. 20005.

FARM REAL ESTATE VALUES: AVERAGE VALUE PER ACRE OF LAND AND BUILDINGS, BY STATE, GROUPED BY FARM PRODUCTION REGION, FEB. 1, 1976–81; AND APRIL 1, 1982–84[1]

State	1976	1977	1978	1979	1980	1981	1982	1983	1984
					Dollars				
Northeast									
Maine	375	414	464	538	579	612	636	649	691
New Hampshire	625	696	787	919	988	1,045	1,087	1,109	1,181
Vermont	496	533	584	660	710	751	781	797	849
Massachusetts	1,044	1,138	1,261	1,443	1,552	1,641	1,707	1,741	1,854
Rhode Island	1,650	1,821	2,045	2,370	2,548	2,696	2,804	2,860	3,046
Connecticut	1,645	1,780	1,960	2,227	2,395	2,533	2,634	2,687	2,862
New York	553	587	600	670	708	749	786	770	793
New Jersey	2,106	2,211	2,386	2,701	2,926	2,998	3,118	3,056	3,148
Pennsylvania	820	994	1,115	1,273	1,404	1,447	1,332	1,279	1,381
Delaware	1,114	1,250	1,350	1,500	1,755	1,843	1,659	1,659	1,692
Maryland	1,280	1,353	1,579	1,800	2,251	2,556	2,416	2,174	2,239
Lake States									
Michigan	609	778	877	975	1,082	1,232	1,192	1,109	1,109
Wisconsin	496	598	718	856	980	1,105	1,073	1,019	958
Minnesota	529	672	761	901	1,061	1,231	1,197	1,065	990
Corn Belt									
Ohio	846	1,099	1,224	1,483	1,678	1,727	1,474	1,297	1,245
Indiana	888	1,188	1,357	1,589	1,833	1,972	1,715	1,492	1,477
Illinois	1,062	1,458	1,625	1,858	2,013	2,133	1,940	1,727	1,692
Iowa	920	1,259	1,331	1,550	1,811	1,941	1,802	1,568	1,396
Missouri	456	548	641	726	878	941	872	759	759
Northern Plains									
North Dakota	236	274	300	347	399	423	436	414	414
South Dakota	163	194	227	256	273	290	291	271	263
Nebraska	363	420	412	525	600	660	626	563	495
Kansas	342	398	418	501	573	590	585	544	528

Appalachian									
Virginia	633	701	774	930	1,009	1,080	1,040	1,050	1,040
West Virginia	393	430	459	592	704	751	829	829	804
North Carolina	676	759	830	1,051	1,215	1,331	1,284	1,297	1,362
Kentucky	514	619	715	861	955	991	996	966	927
Tennessee	528	618	736	860	953	1,024	972	923	951
Southeast									
South Carolina	515	600	653	773	879	930	918	863	846
Georgia	507	581	685	777	868	915	842	817	801
Florida	763	861	981	1,149	1,352	1,507	1,432	1,461	1,490
Alabama	425	477	527	639	792	935	922	876	858
Delta States									
Mississippi	408	461	567	681	825	1,047	1,000	920	966
Arkansas	475	542	606	770	921	1,061	1,104	983	944
Louisiana	575	665	818	1,001	1,288	1,519	1,511	1,481	1,481
Southern Plains									
Oklahoma	345	394	450	512	604	662	696	661	661
Texas	274	299	337	386	448	492	576	593	646
Mountain States									
Montana	134	157	176	196	229	239	254	236	241
Idaho	386	454	515	585	669	717	753	700	700
Wyoming	98	110	121	144	153	164	170	162	165
Colorado	219	256	273	322	376	412	419	411	423
New Mexico	86	101	112	143	190	203	211	200	204
Arizona	122	138	154	199	264	282	294	279	285
Utah	227	271	308	400	530	567	590	561	572
Nevada	98	112	140	191	253	271	282	268	273
Pacific States									
Washington	438	535	602	692	725	854	888	888	915
Oregon	294	342	414	504	556	605	611	580	574
California	711	759	914	1,186	1,426	1,735	1,905	1,925	1,925
48 States	397	474	531	628	725	795	789	743	739

[1]These values are based on land-value benchmarks obtained from the Census of Agriculture.

Source: *Farm Real Estate Development,* Economics and Statistics Service, U.S. Department of Agriculture.

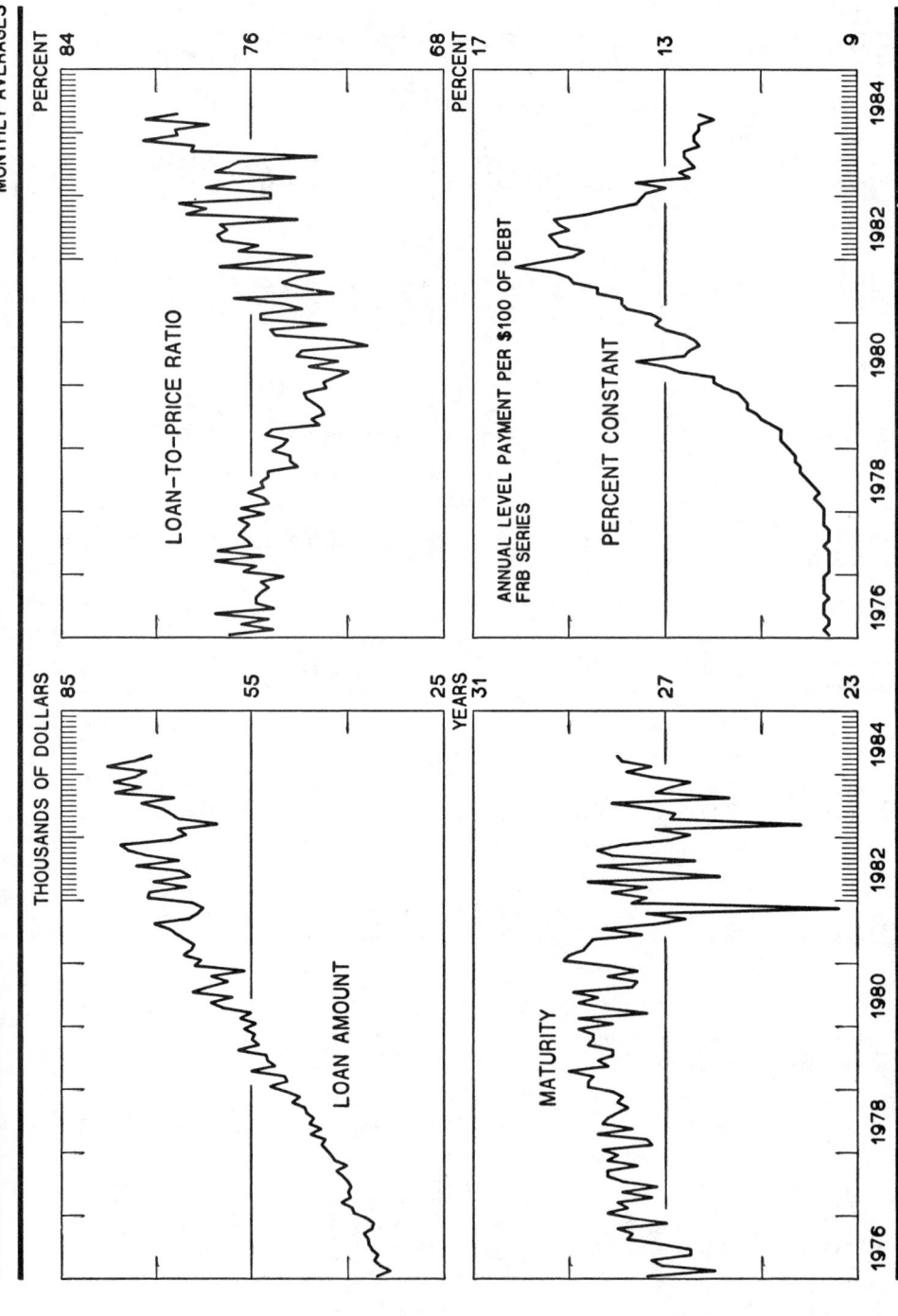

CONVENTIONAL LOANS ON NEW HOMES

MONTHLY AVERAGES

PERCENT

LOAN-TO-PRICE RATIO

ANNUAL LEVEL PAYMENT PER $100 OF DEBT
FRB SERIES

PERCENT CONSTANT

PERCENT

THOUSANDS OF DOLLARS

LOAN AMOUNT

YEARS

MATURITY

Source: *Federal Reserve Chart Book*, Board of Governors of the Federal Reserve System.

Glossary of Real Estate and REIT Terms

This glossary of terminology used in conjunction with discussions of real estate investment trusts has been prepared by the Research Department of the National Association of Real Estate Investment Trusts. Credit should be given to Realty Income Trust, a NAREIT member, which produced a glossary of terms upon which NAREIT drew heavily.

Acceleration clause A condition in a loan contract or mortgage note which permits the lender to demand immediate repayment of the entire balance if the contract is breached or conditions for repayment occur, such as sale or demolition.

Accrued interest or rent An amount of interest or rent which has been earned but which may not have been received in the same period as earned. On many short-term first mortgages, accrued interest is not received in cash until permanent financing is obtained.

Acquisition loan See C&D loan.

Advisor A REIT's investment advisor (usually pursuant to a renewable one-year contract) provides analysis of proposed investments, servicing of the portfolio, and other advisory services. Fee limits for advisory services are prescribed by many state securities regulators. Also spelled "adviser."

Amortization The process of retiring debt or recovering a capital investment through scheduled, systematic repayments of principal; that portion of fixed mortgage payment applied to reduction of the principal amount owed.

Anchor Tenant An important tenant, usually with an excellent credit rating (also known as a triple-A tenant), which takes a large amount of space in a shopping center or office building and is usually one of the first tenants to commit to lease. The anchor tenant usually is given lower rent because of the desirability of having that tenant at the property, both because of its credit rating and its ability to generate traffic.

Appraisal An opinion by an expert of the value of a property as of a specified date, supported by the presentation and analysis of relevant data. The appraisal may be arrived at by any or all of three methods: the cost approach (cost to reproduce), the market approach (comparison with other similar properties), or the income approach (capitalization of actual or projected income figures).

Assessed value The value of a property which is assigned to it by a taxing authority for purposes of assessing property taxes; often assessed value bears a fixed relationship by local statute to market value.

Asset swaps See swap program.

Assets Anything of value owned by the company. Assets are either financial, as cash or bonds; or physical, as real or personal property. For REIT tax purposes, more than 75% of the trust's assets must be property owned or securities backed by real estate.

Assumption of mortgage When the responsibility for repaying existing indebtedness secured by property is "assumed" by the second purchaser. In most jurisdictions, this relieves the first owner of the original obligations, at least to the extent that can be satisfied by sale of this asset after foreclosure.

Attribution More than 50% of a REIT's shares cannot be held by fewer than six people (otherwise it becomes a personal holding company for tax purposes). When someone has indirect control over someone else's shares (such as a trustee over shares held for the benefit of another) then "control" for personal holding company purposes may be "attributed." This complicated legal topic of "attribution" arises, however, only when the REIT's shares are held by a few.

Audit An examination of the financial status and operations of an enterprise, based mostly on the books of account, and undertaken to assure conformity to generally accepted accounting principles and to secure information for, or to check the accuracy of, the enterprise's balance sheet, income statement, and/or cash flow statement.

Balloon mortgage A mortgage loan which provides for periodic payments, which may include both interest and principal, but which leaves the loan less than fully ammortized at maturity, requiring a final large payment which is the "balloon." Usually the term does not apply to an "interest only" loan whose full principal is due upon maturity or upon call during its life.

Bankrupt When liabilities exceed assets, Federal laws enable the entity to dissolve in an orderly fashion (Chapter VII), or permit a court officer to restructure the company into a survivor "going business" (Chapter X), or permit existing management to do the same under court supervision (Chapter XI), or to do so despite the preferred position of secured creditors if real property is the only asset of the business (Chapter XII).

Beneficial owner The person who ultimately benefits from ownership of shares or other securities—in contrast to "nominees" (often pseudonyms for control of investment professionals so as to facilitate security transactions without having to track down beneficial owners to participate in each step of the procedures).

Source: National Association of Real Estate Trusts, 1101 Seventeenth Street, N.W., Washington, D.C. 20036.

Blue sky laws State laws regulating conditions of sale of securities of companies, (particularly those just starting out of the "clear blue sky") for the protection of the investing public. National stock exchange rules usually supercede state laws pursuant to a "blue chip" exemption contained in such state laws. The federal securities laws dovetail with state laws and pertain to publicly held companies, primarily as to accounting and disclosure practices.

Bond A debt certificate which (a) represents a loan to a trust, (b) bears interest, and (c) matures on a stated future date. Short term bonds (generally with a maturity of five years or less from the date of issuance) are often called notes. See debentures.

Book value per share Shareholder equity as adjusted to tangible net worth (assets minus liabilities plus paid-in capital) per share outstanding.

Borrower A person or entity who received something of value, ordinarily money, and is obligated to pay it back, as the debtor to the creditor, usually pursuant to a note or "IOU" containing terms and conditions.

Broker A person who is paid to act as an intermediary in connection with a transaction, in contrast to a dealer or principal who buys or sells for his own account. In the REIT world, the term "broker" usually refers to a real estate salesman, although the term is also used for "stockbrokers" too.

Building lien An encumbrance upon the property by the contractor or subcontractors. Also known as a "mechanic's" or "materialman's" lien.

Building permit Written permission by the local municipality (usually through the building inspector or other agent) allowing construction work on a piece of property in accordance with plans which were submitted and conforming to local building codes and regulations.

Business trust An unincorporated business in which assets are given to trustees for management to hold or to sell, as investments. The business trust form was first fully developed in Massachusetts, under common law, and the term "Massachusetts business trust" is sometimes used to describe entities formed in other states. It is a form of business through a trustee or trustees who hold legal title to the property of the business. Capital contributions are made to the trustees by the beneficaries whose equitable title and interest in the property of the trust are evidenced by trust certificates, usually called shares of beneficial interest. The earnings of the trust are paid to them, as dividends are paid to stockholders. The beneficiaries generally enjoy limited liability, as the control and management of the trust rests solely with the trustees, but the trust form or organization can

be distinguished from a corporation. Early REIT tax laws relied on this distinction to define eligible real estate operations.

Capital gain The amount by which the net proceeds from resale of a capital item exceed the adjusted cost (or "book value") of the asset. If a capital asset is held for more than twelve months before disposition it is taxed on a more favorable basis than a gain after a shorter period of time.

Capitalization rate The rate of return utilized to value a given cash flow, the sum of a Discount Rate and a Capital Recapture Rate. It is applied to any income stream with a finite term over which the invested principal is to be returned to the investor or lender.

Cash flow The revenue remaining after all cash expenses are paid, i.e., non-cash charges such as depreciation are not included in the calculation.

Cash flow per share. Cash flow divided by the common shares outstanding. Shareholders must make this computation themselves since the SEC has prohibited companies from stating this calculation.

Net cash flow. Generally determined by net income plus depreciation less principal payments on long-term mortgages.

Cash on cash return The "cash flow" from a property expressed as a percentage of the cash "equity" invested in a property.

Chapter X See bankrupt.

Collateral An item of value, such as real estate or securities, which a borrower pledges as security. A mortgage gives the creditor the right to seize the real estate collateral after non-performance of the debtor.

Commitment A promise to make an investment at some time in the future if certain specified conditions are met. A REIT may charge a fee to the borrower at the time of making the commitment. A REIT's level of commitments minus expected repayments can be regarded as an indication of future funding requirements.

"Take-out" commitment is one provided by the anticipated long-term lender, usually with complicated terms and conditions that must be met before the "take out" becomes effective.

"Gap" commitment is an anticipated short-term loan to cover part of the final "take-out" that the long-term lender refuses to advance until certain conditions are met (like 90% rent-up of an apartment after construction is completed). The amount above the "floor" or basic part of the loan is the "gap," and the gap commitment is issued to enable the construction lender to make a construction loan commitment for the full amount of the takeout loan instead of only for the "floor" amount.

"Standby" commitment is one that the lender and borrower doubt will be used. It exists as reassurance to a short-term construction lender that if, after completion of a building, the borrower cannot find adequate long-term "take-out" financing, the construction lender will be repaid.

Compensating balances Money which is sometimes required by banks to be held in checking accounts by borrowers, as part of their loan agreement.

Condominium A form of fee ownership of whole units or separate portions of multi-unit buildings which facilitates the formal filing, recording and financing of a divided interest in real property. The condominium concept may be used for apartments, offices and other professional uses. See cooperatives.

Conduit tax treatment So long as most (if not all) earnings are passed along by an entity, then federal taxation is avoided at the entity's level. REITs, mutual funds, and certain kinds of holding companies are elibible for "conduit tax treatment" under certain conditions.

Constant The agreed-upon periodic (usually monthly) payment to pay the face interest rate, with any residual amount going to amortize the loan.

Construction and development loan (C&D) A short-term loan for the purpose of constructing a building, shopping center, or other improvement upon real estate, or developing a site in preparation for construction. A C&D loan is normally disbursed in increments (called *draws* or *draw-downs*) as building proceeds, rather than in a single disbursement, and is conditioned upon compliance with a variety of factors. It is usually repaid with the proceeds of the permanent loan. A land loan or purchase and development loan is sometimes made for the purpose of acquiring unimproved vacant land, usually as a future building site and for financing improvements to such land (street, sewers, etc.) as a prerequisite to construction of a building upon the site.

Contingent Interest Interest on a loan that is payable only if certain conditions occur, in contrast to interest that becomes an accrued liability (whether or not paid) at a specific time.

Cooperative A form of ownership whereby a structure is owned by a corporation or trust with each individual owner holding stock in the corporation representative of the value of his apartment. Title to the apartment is evidenced by a proprietary lease which often does not qualify as adequate collateral for some lenders.

Cost-to-carry The concept specified by the accounting profession to be used by REITs in computing anticipated interest cost on debt needed to "carry" non-earning or partially-earning assets until they're restored to earning status or sold.

Current Liabilities Money owed and due to be paid within one year.

Dealer Someone who buys property with the purpose of selling it at a profit rather than holding it as an investment. A dealer's profits are taxed at the ordinary income rate rather than the capital gains rate regardless of how long the property is held for resale (in contrast to the investor who sells a property after a year and pays at the capital gains rate). A REIT is not permitted to be a dealer unless it is willing to pay a 100% tax on gains from such sales in the year in which it is deemed to be a dealer; sales of foreclosed property do not fall within this definition. See principal.

Debenture An obligation which is secured only by the general credit of the issuing trust, as opposed to being secured by a direct lien on its assets, real estate or otherwise. A debenture is a form of a bond.

Declaration of Trust Similar to articles of incorporation for a corporation, this document contains rules for operation of the trust, selection of its governing trustees, etc., and is the keystone of a REIT.

Deed A legal instrument which conveys title from one to another. It must be (a) made between competent parties (b) have legally sound subject matter (c) correctly state what is being conveyed (d) contain good and valuable consideration (e) be properly executed by the parties involved and (f) be delivered to be valid.

Deed in lieu of foreclosure The device by which title to property is conveyed from the mortgagor (borrower) to the mortgagee (lender) as an alternative to foreclosure. While this procedure can transfer effective control more quickly, many lenders eschew it because undiscovered prior liens (from a workman who was never paid but hadn't gotten around to filing his valid, but late, claim for example) remain enforceable in contrast to the more formal foreclosure procedures which wipe out prior claims after due notice.

Deferred maintenance the amount of repairs that should have been made to keep a property in good running condition, but which have been put off. The term contemplates the desirability of immediate expenditures, although it does not necessarily denote inadequate maintenance in the past.

Deficiency dividend The process of paying an "extra" dividend after the close of the fiscal year so as to comply with REIT tax requirements to pay out more than 90% of income. See dividend.

Depreciation The loss in value of a capital asset, due to wear and tear which cannot be compensated for by ordinary repairs, or an allowance made to allow for the fact that the asset may become obsolete before it wears out. The purpose of a depreciation charge is to write off the original cost of an asset by equitably distributing charges against its operation over its useful life, matching "cost" to the period in which it was used to generate earnings. Depreciation is an optional noncash expense recognizable for tax purposes. If the REIT pays out more than its taxable earnings, then it is distributing a "return of capital" or—as is commonly stated in the industry—"paying out depreciation."

Development loans See Construction and development loan.

Dilution The situation which results when an increase occurs in a company's outstanding securities without a corresponding increase in the company's assets and/or income.

Discount rate An interest rate used to convert a future stream of payments into a single present value. See capitalization rate.

Dividend or distribution The distribution of cash or stock to shareholders of a company which is made periodically as a means of distributing all or a portion of net income or cash flow. Technically, a dividend can be paid only from net taxable income, so many REITs distribute cash and later characterize their distributions as capital gains or a tax-free return of capital if net taxable income is less than the cash paid out.

Dividend or distribution yield The annual dividend or distribution rate for a security expressed as a percent of its market price. For most REITs, the "annualized" rate is the previous quarter's distribution times four, regardless of how the distribution is characterized.

Draw A request from a borrower to obtain partial payment from the lender pursuant to a loan commitment. The lender reassures himself that the borrower has completed the required steps (such as putting in the concrete properly) before advancing money. Often, the borrower submits bills from subcontractors, which are then "paid" by the lender after inspecting the subcontractor's work. In such cases, the check is usually made out to the subcontractor but must be signed by the borrower, too, so that the lender ends up only with one borrower. See construction and development loan.

Effective Borrowing Costs The cost of borrowing after adjustment for compensating balances or fees in lieu of compensating balances, and selling expenses in the case of publicly sold debt.

Encumbrance A legal right or interest in real estate which diminishes its value. Encumbrances can take a number of forms, such as easements, zoning restrictions, mortgages, etc.

Entrepreneur An individual who is responsible for a commercial or real estate activity who takes a certain risk of loss in a transaction for the right to enjoy any profit which may result.

Equity The interest of the shareholders in a company as measured by their paid-in capital and undistributed income. The term is also used to describe (i) the difference between the current market value of a property and the liens or mortgages which encumber it or (ii) the cash which makes up the difference between the mortgage(s) and the construction or sale price.

Equity leveraging The process by which shares are sold at a premium above book value (in anticipation of greater earnings).

Equity participation Usually, the right of an investor to participate to some extent in the increased value of a project by receiving a percentage of the increased income from the project. If a REIT were to participate in a percentage of the net income of a venture (such as the shopping center's owner/lessor), then it could be deemed to be a partner in an active business. Thus, most REIT leases spell out the "equity participation" as a percentage of gross receipts or sales (which is a more stable measure of sales activity, anyway, and one readily identifiable from the lessor's federal income tax statement).

Escrow A deposit of "good faith" money which is entrusted to a third party (often a bank) until fulfillment of certain conditions and agreements, when the escrow may be released or applied as payment for the purchase of property or for services rendered.

Estoppel certificate An instrument used when a mortgage or lease is assigned to another. The certificate sets forth the exact remaining balance of the lease or mortgage as of a certain date and verifies any promises to tenants that may have been made by the first owner for which the second owner may be held accountable.

Exculpatory clause A clause which relieves one of liability for injuries or damages to another. Exculpatory clauses are placed in REIT documents with the intention of eliminating personal liability of its trustees, shareholders and officers.

Expenses The costs which are charges against current operations or earnings of a building, company or other reporting entity. They may have been "paid out" in cash, or accrued to be paid later, or charged as a bookkeeping procedure to reflect the "using up" of assets (as in depreciation) utilized in the production of income during the period of current operations.

Face value The value which is shown on the face of an instrument such as a bond, debenture or stock certificate. The "face rate" of a debt instrument is often known as its "coupon rate."

Fair market value See Market value.

Fee or fee simple Title to a property which is absolute, good and marketable; ownership without condition.

Fiduciary A relationship of trust and confidence between a person charged with the duty of acting for the benefit of another and the person to whom such duty is owed, as in the case of guardian and ward, trustee and beneficiary, executor and heir.

First mortgage That mortgage which has a prior claim over all other liens against real estate. In some jurisdictions, real estate taxes, mechanics liens, court costs, and other involuntary liens may take priority over such a contractual lien: title companies "clear" properties so as to reassure first mortgage lenders (and owners) of their uncontested position and to guarantee them of that position under certain conditions.

Fiscal year The 12-month period selected as a basis for computing and accounting for a business. A fiscal year need not coincide with the calendar year, except for all REITs initially qualifying for special tax treatment after 1976.

Fixed assets Assets, such as land, buildings and machinery, which cannot be quickly converted into cash. For REITs, most "fixed assets" are real property although some (like furniture in an apartment lobby) may be personal property.

Fixed charges Those interest charges, insurance costs, taxes and other expenses which remain relatively constant regardless of revenue. See net lease.

Floating rate A variable interest rate charged for the use of borrowed money. It is determined by charging a specific percentage above a fluctuating base rate, usually the prime rate as announced by a major commercial bank.

Floor loan A portion or portions of a mortgage loan commitment which is less than the full amount of the commitment and which may be funded upon conditions less stringent than those required for funding the full amount, or the "ceiling" of the loan. For example, the floor loan, equal to perhaps 80% of the full amount of the loan, may be funded upon completion of construction without any occupancy requirements, but substantial occupancy of the building may be required for funding the full amount of the loan, which is referred to as the "ceiling." See commitment, gap.

Foreclosure The legal process of enforcing payment of a debt by taking the properties which secure the debt, once the terms of the obligation are not followed. Upon foreclosure, the entire debt might not be fully discharged by transfer and disposition of the property (as determined by the courts). If so, a "deficiency judgment" may be obtained, at which point the lender is like any other creditor in attempting to get the debtor to pay the deficiency. Collection of the deficiency judgment in major real estate transactions is rare, but it becomes a major factor in negotiations if the borrower decides to return to the real estate business in the future.

Fully diluted earnings The hypothetical earnings per share of a company, computed after giving effect to the number of shares which would be outstanding if all convertible debt and warrants were exercised, and also to any reduction in interest payments resulting from such exercise.

Gap commitment See commitment, gap. Also see floor loan.

General lien A lien against the property of an individual or other entity generally, rather than against specific items of realty or personal property.

Ground lease See sale-leaseback.

Holding company A corporation that owns or controls the operations of various other companies. Many REITs were sponsored by bank or insurance holding companies whose subsidiary companies advise and manage REITs, pursuant to contracts with the REIT's trustees.

Independent contractor A firm hired to actively manage property investments. A tax-qualified REIT must hire an independent contractor to manage and operate its property, so as to distinguish itself as an investor rather than an active manager.

Income property Developed real estate, such as office buildings, shopping centers, apartments, hotels and motels, warehouses and some kinds of agricultural or industrial property, which produce a flow of income—in contrast to non-income generating real estate like raw land which would be bought and held for a speculative profit upon resale or development.

Indenture The legal document prepared in connection with, for example, a bond issue, setting forth the terms of the issue, its specific security, remedies in case of default, etc. It may also be called the "deed of trust."

Indentured trustee A trustee, generally the trust department of a major bank, which represents the interest of bondholders under a publicly offered issue.

Insider A person close to a trust who has intimate knowledge of financial developments before they become public knowledge.

Interest rate The percentage rate which an individual pays for the use of borrowed money for a given period of time.

Intermediate-term loan A loan for a term of three to ten years which is usually not fully amortized at maturity. Often, developers will seek interim loans by which to pay off construction financing, in anticipation of obtaining long-term financing at a later date on more favorable terms, either because long-term rates decline generally or because the project can show an established, stable earnings history.

Interim loan A type of loan which is to be repaid out of the proceeds of another loan. Ordinarily, not self-liquidating (amortized), the lender evaluates the risk of obtaining refinancing as much as the period risk. See C&D loans.

Investment advisor See advisor.

Joint venture The entity which is created when two or more persons or corporate entities join together to carry out a specific business transaction of real estate development. A joint venture is usually of limited duration and usually for a specific property; it can be treated as a partnership for tax purposes. The parties have reciprocal and paralleling rights and obligations.

Junior mortgage loan Any mortgage loan in which the lien and the right of repayment is subordinate to that of another mortgage loan or loans. A "second mortgage" is a junior mortgage. "Third, fourth," etc. mortgages are always deemed to be secondary.

Land loan See Construction and development loan.

Land-purchase leaseback See sale-leaseback.

Late charge The charge which is levied against a borrower for a payment which was not made in a timely manner.

Lease A contract between the owner of property (lessor) and a tenant (lessee) setting forth the terms, conditions and consideration for the use of the property for a specified period of time at a specified rental. See sale-leaseback and net lease.

Leasehold improvements The cost of improvements or betterments to property leased for a period of years, often paid for by the tenant. Such improvements ordinarily become the property of the lessor (owner) on expiration of the lease; consequently their cost is normally amortized over the life of the lease if the lessor pays for them.

Leverage The process of borrowing upon one's capital base with the expectation of generating a profit above the cost of borrowing.

Liability management The aspect of the management of a company concerned with the planning and procurement of funds for investment through the sale of equity, public debt and bank borrowings. In the REIT industry, the phrase contrasts to "asset management" or the real estate side of the business.

Line of credit Usually, an agreement between a commercial bank and a borrower under which the bank agrees to provide unsecured credit to the borrower upon certain terms and conditions. Normally, the borrower may draw on all or any part of the credit from time to time.

Limited partnership A partnership which limits certain of the partners' (the limited partners) liability to the amount of their investment. At least one partner (the "general partner") is fully liable for the obligations of the partnership and

its operations, usually with the limited partners participating as investors only.

Loan loss reserve A reserve set up to offset asset values in anticipation of losses that are reasonably expected. Initially, REITs had insufficient operating experience to anticipate losses in any one class of investments or for a portfolio as a whole, so tax authorities would not permit substantial contributions toward a reserve as an allowable period expense. When difficulties arose, the conversion of short-term loans to longer-term property holdings required some form of recognition of likely losses in the financial statements. A novel procedure for REITs was devised by requiring, for book purposes, computation of additions to the reserve based in part on the probable cost of sustaining the troubled assets over the longer period of time necessary to "cure" the problem. Also known as "allowance for losses."

Loan run-off The rate at which an existing mortgage portfolio will reduce (or "run-off") to zero if no new loans are added to the portfolio.

Loan swaps See asset swaps.

Long-term mortgage Any financing, whether in the form of a first or junior mortgage, the term of which is ten years or more. It is generally fully amortized.

Loss carry forwards The net operating loss (NOL) incurred in prior years, which may be applied for tax purposes against future earnings, thereby reducing taxable income. For REITs (which must pay out most of their taxable income), NOLs can be carried forward eight years; for non-REIT-taxed companies, NOL can be carried forward for only seven years.

Market value The highest price in terms of money which a property will bring in a competitive and open market under all conditions requisite to a fair sale—the buyer and the seller each acting prudently, knowledgeably, and at arm's length. See appraisal.

Moratorium A period in which payments of debts or other performance of a legal obligation is suspended temporarily, usually because of unforeseen circumstances which make timely payment or performance difficult or impossible. This forebearance can be whole or partial.

Mortgage A publicly recorded lien by which the property is pledged as security for the payment of a debt valid even beyond death ("mort" is death in French). In some states a mortgage is an actual conveyance of the property to the creditor until the terms of the mortgage are satisfied. While there is always a "note" secured by a mortgage document, both the note and mortgage instrument are commonly called "the mortgage." For types, see: first, junior, short-term, long-term, wrap-around and construction and development mortgage definitions.

Mortgage banker A non-depository lender who makes loans secured by real estate and then usually packages and sells those loans in large groups to institutional investors, pursuant to a "long-term commitment" he has negotiated with the life insurance company or other institutional investor. Mortgage bankers frequently arrange to service these mortgages for the out-of-town institutions, collecting regular payments, keeping the lender up to date on the progress of the loan, escrowing payments for taxes and insurance premiums, and, if necessary, administering foreclosure proceedings. Many REITs were sponsored by mortgage bankers.

Mortgage constant The total annual payments of principal and interest (annual debt service) on a mortgage with level-payment amortization schedule, expressed as a percentage of the initial principal amount of the loan.

Mortgagee in possession A lender or one who holds a mortgage who has taken possession of a property in order to protect an interest in the property. Usually, this is done with commercial properties as to which rents, management fees and other disbursements continue even if the mortgage is in default. The possession must be taken with the consent of the mortgagor (or a court, in cases of foreclosure) and the mortgagee must be careful to do only those things to the property that the mortgagor (or court) will agree to accept, should it resume its role as a credit-worthy owner.

Net Income The dollar amount that remains after all expenses, including taxes, are deducted from gross income. For regular companies, it is also called after-tax profit, the "bottom line" figure of how a company has performed with its investors' money. For REITs, it is net taxable income which, if fully distributed, is not taxed.

Net lease A lease, sometimes called a net-net (insurance and taxes) or even a net-net-net lease (insurance, taxes, and maintenance) in which the tenant pays all costs, including insurance, taxes, repairs, upkeep and other expenses, and the rental payments are "net" of all these expenses. See lease and fixed charges.

Net worth The remaining asset value of a property company or other entity after deduction of all liabilities against it.

Non-accrual loans See non-earning investments.

Non-earning investments The category of loans or investments which are not earning the originally anticipated rate of return. Some may be characterized as "partially earning." When interest is recorded as earned rather than as received (accrued interest), "non-accrual investments" are those which management expects not to receive interest as originally contemplated. In the vernacular, nonearning investments are "problem loans" or "troubled properties."

Non-qualified REIT A REIT that was formerly qualified, or conducts its affairs as if it is qualified, but that has elected for the tax year in question to be treated like a normal business corporation for tax purposes. Thus, some restraints (primarily against active management and holding property for sale) are lifted, while REIT conduit tax treatment is lost.

Occupancy rate The amount of space or number of apartments or offices or hotel rooms which are rented as compared with the total amount or number available. The rate is usually expressed as a percentage.

Operating expenses Expenses arising out of or relating to business activity such as interest expense, professional fees, salaries, etc.

Operating income Income received directly from business activity in the normal course, as contrasted with capital gains income, or other extraordinary income.

Option A right to buy or lease property at a certain specified price for specified terms. Consideration is typically given for the option, which is exercisable over a limited time span. If the option is not exercised, the consideration is forfeited. A loan to a developer secured by his option to obtain real estate is considered a "qualified" REIT asset.

Origination The process by which a loan is created, including the search for (or receipt of) the initial plans, the analysis and structuring of the proposed financing, and the review and acceptance procedures by which the commitment to make the investment is finally issued.

Overage income Rental income above a guaranteed minimum depending on a particular level of profit or retail sales volume by the tenant, payable under the terms of a lease.

Participations A lender often "participates out" or sells a portion of his loan to another lender while retaining a portion and managing the investment. REITs buy real estate secured participations as well as originating them.

Par Value The face value assigned to a security when it is issued. The stated par value of a security generally has nothing to do with its market or book value.

Passivity The state of owning investments but not actively managing them (as a property management firm does for the investor) or engaging in trading the securities (like a broker or dealer). This "passivity" test is implicit behind several of the REIT tax requirements.

Pension funds Money which is accumulated in trust to fund pensions for companies or unions and which is frequently invested in part in real estate. A co-mingled real estate pension fund account is managed, usually under contract to a financial institution, much like a REIT except that its shares are not publicly traded but instead sold to other pension funds.

Permanent financing See long-term loan.

Point An amount which represents 1% of the maximum principal amount of an investment. Used in connection with a discount from, or a share of, a principal amount deducted at the time funds are advanced, it represents additional compensation to the lender.

Portfolio The investments of a company, including investments in mortgages and/or ownership of real property. REIT portfolios usually consist of equity in property, short-term mortgages, long-term mortgages and/or subordinated land sale-lease-backs.

Portfolio turnover The average length of time from the funding of investments until they are paid off or sold.

Preferred shares Stocks which have prior claim on distributions (and/or assets in the event of dissolution) up to a certain definite amount before the shares of beneficial interest are entitled to anything. As a form of ownership, preferred shares stand behind senior subordinated and secured debtholders in dissolution, as well as other creditors.

Prepayment penalty The penalty which is imposed on the borrower for payment of the mortgage before it is due. Often a mortgage contains a clause specifying that there is to be no prepayment penalty, or limits the prepayment penalty to only the first few years of the mortgage term.

Price earning ratio A ratio which consists of the market price divided by current annualized earnings per share. Such a computation is now found in most daily stock listings. For REITs, annualization of quarterly earnings is computed by multiplying the most recent distribution by four, regardless of the distribution's later characterization as a dividend, return-of-capital, or capital gains.

Prime lending rate The rate at which commercial banks will lend money from time to time to their most credit-worthy customers, used as a base for most loans to financial intermediaries such as REITs.

Principal The buyer or seller in a real estate transaction as distinguished from an agent.

Principal The sum of money loaned. The amount of money to be repaid on a loan excluding interest charges.

Prior lien A lien or mortgage ranking ahead of some other lien. A prior lien need not itself be a first mortgage.

Pro forma Projected or hypothetical as opposed to actual as related, for example, to a balance sheet or income statement.

Problem investments See nonearning investments.

Prospectus A document describing an investment opportunity; the detailed description of new securities which must be supplied to prospective interstate purchasers under the Securities Act of 1933.

Provision for loan losses Periodic allocation of funds to loan loss reserves in recognition of a decline in the value of a loan or loans in a trust's portfolio due to a default on the part of the borrowers.

Proxy An authorization given by a registered security holder to vote stock at the annual meeting or at a special meeting of security holders.

Purchase and leaseback See sale-leaseback.

Pyramiding In stock market transactions, this term refers to the practice of borrowing against unrealized "paper" profits in securities to make additional purchases. In corporate finance, it refers to the practice of creating a speculative capital structure by a series of holding companies, whereby a relatively small amount of voting stock in the parent company controls a large corporate system. In real estate, it refers to the practice of financing 100% or more of the value of the property.

Qualified assets Assets which meet tax requirements for special REIT tax treatment, i.e. real property. In any tax year, 75% of a REIT's assets must be invested in real property, either through ownership or by securities secured by real estate. A "partially qualified" asset is one that qualifies under the 90% test of being a passive investment in a security, but not under the 75% real estate test.

Qualified income That portion of income which is classified as interest, rents, or other gain from real property, as spelled out in the REIT tax laws.

Raw land Land which has not been developed or improved.

RCA See revolving credit agreement.

Real estate investment trust (REIT, pronounced "reet") A trust established for the benefit of a group of investors which is managed by one or more trustees who hold title to the assets for the trust and control its acquisitions and investments, at least 75% of which are real estate related. A major advantage of a REIT is that no federal income tax need be paid by the trust if certain qualifications are met. Congress enacted these special tax provisions to encourage an assembly method, which is essentially designed to provide for investment in real estate what the mutual provided for investment in securities. The REIT provides the small investor with a means of combining his funds with those of others, and protects him from the double taxation that would be levied against an ordinary corporation or trust.

Revolving credit agreement (or "revolver") A formal credit agreement between a group of banks and a REIT, the terms of which are reviewed periodically when it is "rolled over" or "revolved" or refinanced by a similar agreement. For many trusts, "revolvers" have replaced informal lines of credit extended by individual banks to REITs, thereby providing a uniform (and usually restrictive) approach by all creditors, reassuring each bank that others in the RCA would not be paid off preferentially.

Registration statement The forms filed by a company with the Securities and Exchange Commission in connection with an offering of new securities or the listing of outstanding securities on a national exchange.

Reserves for loss See loan loss reserve.

Return of capital A distribution to shareholders in excess of the trust's earnings and profits, usually consisting of either depreciation or repayment of principal from properties or mortgages held by the trust. Each shareholder receiving such a distribution is required to reduce the tax basis of his shares by the amount of such distribution. For financial accounting purposes, what constitutes a return of capital may differ from that determined under Federal income tax requirements.

Return on equity A figure which consists of net income for the period divided by equity and which is normally expressed as a percentage.

Right of first refusal The right or option granted by a seller to a buyer, to have the first opportunity of acquiring a property.

Rights offering The privilege extended to a shareholder of subscribing to additional stock of the same or another class or to bonds, usually at a price below the market and in an amount proportional to the number of shares already held. Rights must be exercised within a time limit and often may be sold if the holder does not wish to purchase additional shares.

Sale-leaseback A common real estate transaction whereby the investor buys property from and simultaneously leases it back to, the seller. This enables the previous owner (often a developer) to "cash out" on an older property while retaining control.

Land sale-leaseback—this procedure, made common by several REITs that specialize in the transaction, affects only the land under income—producing improvements (such as shopping centers, etc.)—leaving the depreciable improvements in the hands of those who might benefit from the tax consequences. Since the improvements were probably financed with the proceeds of a first mortgage which remains in effect, the rights of the new investor are made second, or junior, to those of the first mortgage holder. Hence the common phrase "subordinated land sale-leaseback." In return for accepting a less secure position, the new investor usu-

ally obtains an "overage" clause whereby additional rent is paid anytime gross income of the shopping center (or whatever) exceeds a pre-determined floor.

Seasoned issues Securities of large, established companies which have been known to the investment public for a period of years, covering good times and bad.

Second mortgages See junior mortgage loan.

Secured debt For REITs, senior mortgage debt secured by specific properties. In case of default on "nonrecourse" debt, the lender may assume property ownership but may not pursue other assets of the lender.

Senior mortgage A mortgage which has first priority.

Senior unsecured debt Funds borrowed under open lines without security. Most bank lines to REITs were unsecured.

Shares of beneficial interest Tradable shares in a REIT. Analogous to common stock in a corporation.

Shareholders' equity Primarily money invested by shareholders through purchase of shares, plus the accumulation of that portion of net income that has been reinvested in the business since the commencement of operations.

Short-term mortgage A loan upon real estate for a term of three years or less, bearing interest payable periodically, with principal usually payable in full at maturity.

Sinking fund An arrangement under which a portion of a bond or preferred stock issue is retired periodically, in advance of its fixed maturity. The company may either purchase a stipulated quantity of the issue itself, or supply funds to a trustee or agent for that purpose. Retirement may be made by call at a fixed price, or by inviting tenders, or by purchase in the open market.

Sponsor The entity which initiated the formation of a REIT and usually acts (often via a subsidiary) as investment advisor to the trust thereafter. The sponsor puts the reputation of its institution on the line for the REIT and usually arranges lines of credit, provides support services and, occasionally, compensating balances.

Spread Difference between percentage return on an investment and cost of funds to support the investment.

Standby commitment See commitment, standby.

Standing loan Usually not amortized, the loan is secured by completed property that has not yet been refinanced with a "permanent" long-term mortgage.

Subordinated debt Debt which is junior to secured and unsecured senior debt, it may be convertible into shares of beneficial interest for

REITs. Senior subordinated debt is senior to other subordinated debt.

Subordinated ground lease See sale-leaseback.

Swap Program A procedure for reducing debt (by a troubled REIT) by trading an asset to the creditor in return for cancellation of part of a loan to the REIT. Often a cash premium payment is made in addition to reduction of the debt. The premium may then be distributed to the other creditors pro rata. The amount of the cash premium, or the ratio of cash-to-debt reduction to be applied against the value of the asset, is sometimes determined by a sealed-bid "auction" process as set forth in the "revolving credit agreement" between the creditors and the REIT. See RCA.

Syndicate A group of investors who transact business for a limited period of time and sometimes with a single purpose. It is a short-term partnership.

Take-out commitment See commitment.

Tax shelter The various aspects of an investment which offer relief from income taxes or opportunities to claim deductions from taxable income. Although tax shelters are an important facet of real estate investment, they do not have a direct influence on REIT investment choices because qualified trusts are exempt from income taxes.

Usury The charging of interest rates for the use of money higher than what's allowed by local law.

Warrants Stock purchase warrants or options give the holder rights to purchase shares of stock, generally running for a longer period of time than ordinary subscription rights given shareholders. Warrants are often attached to other securities, but they may be issued separately or detached after issuance.

Working capital Determined by subtracting current liabilities from current assets. It represents the amount available to carry on the day-to-day operation of the business.

Work-out When a borrower has problems, the process undertaken by the lender to help the borrower "work out" of the problems becomes known itself as a "work out." The presumption during a "work out" is that the borrower will eventually resume a more normal debtor's position once problems are solved within (presumably) a reasonably short time.

Wrap-around mortgage A type of junior mortgage used to refinance properties on which there is an existing first mortgage loan. The face amount of the wrap-around loan is equivalent to the unpaid balance on the existing mortgage plus cash advanced to the property owner upon funding. Such loans carry a higher interest rate than the existing mortgage. The wrap-around lender assumes the obligation to maintain payments of principal and interest on the existing mortgage so as to enhance his right to make claim from his secondary position.

Yield In the stock market, the rate of annual distribution or dividend expressed as a percentage of price. Current yield is found by dividing the market price into the distribution rate in dollars. In real estate, the term refers to the effective annual amount of income which is being accrued on an investment expressed as a percentage of its value.

Employee Benefits in Medium and Large Firms*

More employees in medium and large firms helped to pay the premiums on their group health insurance in 1983 than in 1982. According to surveys of employee benefits conducted by the Bureau of Labor Statistics, U.S. Department of Labor, 31 percent of the workers shared these costs for single person coverage in 1983, compared with 26 percent one year earlier. A greater proportion—up from 47 percent to 50 percent—paid part of the premiums for family coverage. At the same time, the average share for those employees paying part of the premiums rose 13 and 19 percent, respectively, to $10.13 per month for single coverage and $32.51 for families.

The fifth annual survey of employee benefits conducted by the Bureau of Labor Statistics of the U.S. Department of Labor provides representative data for 20 million full-time employees in a cross section of the Nation's private industries in 1983. The survey's scope generally was limited to establishments employing at least 100 or 250 workers, depending upon the industry.

The study provides information on paid leave, insurance, and private pension plans, as well as many other benefits that are paid, at least in part, by the employer. It covers both the extent of these benefits and the detailed characteristics of the benefit plans. Data are provided for all employees and for three employee groups—professional-administrative, technical-clerical, and production workers.

Paid Time Off

Time off with pay is available to employees in several different forms and amounts—from daily rest breaks of a few minutes to annual vacations of several weeks. Findings on paid leave provisions in 1983 are summarized below.

Paid holidays and vacations were provided to virtually all of the employees covered by the survey. The average number of holidays granted was 9.8 in 1983, down 0.2 of a day for

the second consecutive year following negotiated reductions, primarily in the auto industry. The amount of vacation, which generally varied by length of service, averaged 8.7 days after 1 year of service, 15.7 days after 10 years, and 20.5 days after 20 years of service—virtually unchanged from the previous survey.

Personal leave allows employees to be absent from work with pay for a variety of reasons not covered by other specific leave plans. Where such plans were in effect, employees typically were eligible for 2 to 5 days a year; the average number of days available was 3.7.

Paid lunch periods and formal provisions for *paid rest time* (for example, coffee breaks and cleanup time) were more common among production employees than among the other two groups. Paid lunch breaks typically were 20 to 30 minutes a day, while paid rest was most commonly provided as two daily breaks of 10 to 15 minutes each. Paid lunch and paid rest periods each averaged 2.1 hours per week.

Paid sick leave plans vary greatly depending on whether the number of days granted are available per year or per disability. Plan provisions that allow employees to carry over unused sick leave from one year to the next and coordinate sick leave with sickness and accident insurance also affect the amount of sick leave protection. For example, after 1 year of service, cumulative sick leave plans that were coordinated with sickness and accident insurance in 1983 allowed an average of 7.4 days off per year with full pay; coordinated plans that did not allow year-to-year carry-over of unused sick leave averaged 14.1 days. When days off were specified per disability, the average was 46.2 days after 1 year of service; these plans usually are not coordinated with sickness and accident insurance. In many plans, the number of days of sick leave increased with years of service.

Insurance

Sickness and accident insurance, paying a portion of an employee's usual wages, is often provided either in combination with sick leave or in place of it. As a result, ninety-four percent of the workers covered by the survey had income protection against short-term disabilities. Sickness and accident benefits are usually paid for a maximum of 26 weeks. Production workers, who have sick leave plans less frequently

* Detailed information of the benefit provisions studied are available in a bulletin "Employee Benefits in Medium and Large Firms, 1983 published by the Bureau of Labor Statistics.

Source: "Employee Benefits in Medium and Large Firms, 1983: More Employees Helped Pay Health Insurance Premiums in 1983," in *News*, May 1984, U.S. Department of Labor, Bureau of Labor Statistics, Washington, DC 20212. For further historical and technical data call 202-523-9444.

PERCENT OF FULL-TIME EMPLOYEES PARTICIPATING IN SELECTED EMPLOYEE BENEFIT PROGRAMS, MEDIUM AND LARGE ESTABLISHMENTS, UNITED STATES, 1983[1]

Employee Benefit Program	All Employees	Professional and Administrative Employees	Technical and Clerical Employees	Production Employees
Paid:				
Holidays	99	99	100	98
Vacations	100	100	100	99
Personal leave	25	31	35	17
Lunch period	11	4	5	17
Rest time	74	58	76	80
Sick leave	67	92	91	42
Sickness and accident insurance	49	29	34	67
Noncontributory[2]	41	22	26	57
Long-term disability insurance	45	66	58	28
Noncontributory[2]	34	47	42	23
Health insurance for employee.............	96	98	95	96
Noncontributory[2]	65	62	54	71
Health insurance for dependents	93	95	91	92
Noncontributory[2]	43	42	35	47
Life insurance	96	97	95	95
Noncontributory[2]	80	79	78	81
Private pension plan	82	86	84	79
Noncontributory[2]	75	79	79	72

[1] The survey excludes data for executives and employees in constant travel status, such as airline pilots, as well as for Alaska and Hawaii.
[2] Provided at no cost to employee.

than the other two groups, are the main participants in sickness and accident insurance. (See Exhibit.)

Long-term disability insurance (LTD) typically pays 50 to 60 percent of a worker's usual earnings when the employee is disabled for a prolonged period. Long-term disability payments generally begin after sick leave and sickness and accident insurance are exhausted, and they usually continue as long as the person is disabled or until retirement age. (LTD insurance is not the only source of private long-term disability benefits. Half of the survey's workers were covered under pension plans that provided immediate disability retirement benefits.)

Health insurance has experienced many changes in recent years, including dramatic growth in coverage for dental and vision care. During the 5-year history of the survey, participation in dental insurance, covering routine examinations and procedures, increased from 48 percent to 71 percent of the employees; participation in vision care, usually including payment for eyeglasses grew from 17 to 27 percent.

Also, there has been a shifting away from full payment of initial medical expenses, although first-dollar coverage for many expenses remained the typical practice in 1983. Another noticeable change since the surveys began has been in the method of determining payments. Few plans remain that specify a daily dollar amount of coverage for hospital room and board, while protection up to the "semi-private room rate" applied to 94 percent of plan participants with basic coverage. Similarly, payment schedules for surgical expenses have increasingly given way to the "usual and customary charge" limitation.

Ninety-two percent of health insurance participants were covered for specified expenses either wholly or partly through major medical insurance. As in earlier surveys, employees most often paid the first $100 of covered expenses (the deductible) and 20 percent of the balance incurred each year, but some increases in deductible amounts were recorded. On the other hand, stop-loss provisions under major medical plans have spread from 46 percent of the participants in 1979 to 71 percent in 1983. (These provisions limit the annual out-of-pocket costs employees would be required to pay for covered expenses.)

Life insurance for 65 percent of the insured was based on the employee's earnings, while 33 percent were provided flat dollar amounts. Flat amounts were most common among production workers, where they applied to just over half of the plan participants. The amounts were usually less than $15,000, but the proportion receiving $15,000 or more has climbed from 7 to 18 percent since the information was first recorded in 1981. Earnings-based formulas, typically paying one or two times earnings, applied to about four-fifths of the professional-administrative and technical-clerical workers participating in life insurance programs. The amount of insurance for 2 percent of the workers varied by length of service.

Retirement Pension Plans

Eighty-two percent of the workers were covered by retirement pension plans, down slightly from 84 percent in 1982. Over seven-tenths of the participants had plans with payment formulas based on earnings; most used a 5-year average during a worker's final years of employment. Formulas in most of the remaining plans used specified dollar amounts for each year of service.

Age requirements for retiring with full benefits became more liberal in 1983. Sixty-four percent of the plan participants could retire before age 65 with unreduced pensions; this compared with 58 percent in 1982. The greatest change in this percentage occurred among professional-administrative workers—nearly seven-tenths could retire before age 65 with unreduced pensions in 1983. For production worker participants, nearly one-fourth could retire at any age with 30 years of service; in 1982, the proportion had been about one-fifth.

The opportunity for increasing pension benefits for working beyond age 65 also improved. Fifty-five percent of participants in 1983, compared with 48 percent in 1982, were covered by plans that either credited the additional service or adjusted pensions upwards for the shorter retirement period.

Other Benefits

In addition to the major benefits described above, BLS collected information on the incidence of 18 other benefit plans including funeral and military leave; bonuses; employee discounts; recreation facilities; educational assistance; and parking. Data are available on the percent of full-time employees eligible for these benefits, although they do not indicate the proportion of employees actually using or receiving the benefit. Also included in this group of other benefits are several capital accumulation plans, such as profit sharing, saving and thrift, and stock ownership. The availability of each of these plans has risen over the past 3 years; most replace or supplement the conventional pension plan.

Computer Data Bases and Software

Selected On-Line Business/Financial Data Bases

On-line data bases are collections of computer stored data which are retrievable by remote terminals. The data bases are collected and organized by a so-called *producer*. The latter provides the data base to a *vendor* who distributes the data by means of a telecommunication network to the user. Often a vendor will offer a large number of different data bases. In some instances the producer and vendor are the same.

Using an on-line data base requires: (1) a *terminal* (a typewriter-like device usually equipped with a video display) to receive data and send commands to the vendor's computers, and (2) a *modem* for coupling the terminal to a telephone line. Printouts (hard copy) of the desired information can be obtained with the aid of electronic printers located at the user's terminal or, alternatively, ordered from the vendor.

The user accesses the data base by dialing a telephone number and then typing (on the terminal keyboard) a password provided by the vendor. Searching the data base is done with special commands and procedures peculiar to each base.

The contents of data bases vary. Some provide statistical data only—usually in the form of time series. Other bases provide bibliographic references and, in some instances, abstracts or the full text of articles.

Specifics concerning data base contents, instructions, and prices are available from vendors. Listed below are some major business data bases and vendors. More complete information concerning data bases is available from the sources given below.

ABI Inform
Provides references on all areas of business management with emphasis on "how-to" information.
Producer: Data Courier Inc. (Louisville, KY)
Vendors: BRS, DIALOG, SDC

Accountants Index
Contains reference information on accounting, auditing taxation, management and securities.
Producer: American Institute of Certified Public Accountants (New York, NY)
Vendors: SDC

Advertising and Marketing Intelligence
Covers consumer trends, new products, media planning, sale promotion.
Producer: New York Times Information Service and J. Walter Thompson Co. (Parsippany, NJ)
Vendors: N.Y. Times Information Service

American Profile
Provides statistical information on U.S. households including population, income, dependents, and also data on types of businesses in an area.
Producer: Donnelley Marketing (Stamford, CT)
Vendors: Business Information Service

BI Data
Maintains international statistical data including national accounts, labor, foreign trade, consumption, prices, production.
Producer: Business International Corp. (New York, NY)
Vendors: General Electric Information Service, I. P. Sharpe, DIALOG

Business Credit Service
Provides business credit and financial information.
Producer: TRW, Inc. (Orange, CA)
Vendors: TRW

Canadian Business Periodicals Index
Provides references to a wide variety of topics from Canadian business publications.
Producer: Micromedia Limited (Toronto, Canada)
Vendor: SDC

CIS Index
Contains references and abstracts from nearly every publication resulting from Senate and House Committee meetings since 1970.
Producer: Congressional Information Services, Inc. (Washington, DC)
Vendors: Dialog, SDC

Commodities Market Data Bank
Provides statistical data on all traded commodities.

Producer: Data Resources Inc. (Lexington, MA)
Vendors: Data Resources, Inc.

CompuServe, Inc.
Provides reference, statistical and full text retrieval of information of personal interest including health, recipes, gardening, financial and investment data including the Compustat and Value Line data bases.

Producer: CompuServe, Inc. (Columbus, OH)
Vendor: CompuServe

Compustat
Provides very extensive financial data on companies.

Producer: Standard And Poor's Compustat Service, Inc. (Englewood, CO)
Vendors: ADP, Business Information Services, CompuServe, Data Resources, Chase Econometrics/Interactive Data Corp.

Computerized Engineering Index
Provides a broad coverage of the international literature on engineering and technology.

Producer: Engineering Index (New York, NY)
Vendors: BRS, DIALOG, SDC

Disclosure II
Provides extracts of 10K and other reports filed with the Securities and Exchange Commission.

Producer: Disclosure Inc. (Bethesda, Maryland)
Vendors: Business Information Services (Control Data). Dialog, Dow Jones, New York Times Information Services, Mead Data Central.

Dow Jones News/Retrieval Service and Stock Quote Reporters
Contains text of articles appearing in major financial publications including the *Wall Street Journal* and *Barrons*. Quote Service provides quotes on stocks, bonds, mutual funds.

Producer: Dow Jones & Company (New York, NY)
Vendors: BRS, Dow Jones & Company

DRI Capsule/EEI Capsule
Provides over 3700 U.S. social and economic statistical time series such as population, income, money supply data, etc.

Producers: Data Resources, Inc. (Lexington, MA) and Evans Economics Inc. (Washington, DC)

Vendors: Business Information Services, United Telecom Group, I. P. Sharp

EIS Industrial Plants
Offers statistical data pertaining to industrial establishments with annual sales of more than $500,000 and with more than 20 employees. Data includes location of each plant, shipment values, market share.

Producer: Economic Information Systems (New York, NY)
Vendors: Business Information Services (Control Data), DIALOG

Federal Register Abstracts
Provides coverage of federal regulatory agencies as published in the Federal Register.

Producer: Capitol Services (Washington, DC)
Vendors: DIALOG, SDC

GTE Financial System One Quotation Service
Provides current U.S. and Canadian quotations and statistical data on stocks, bonds, options, commodities and other market data.

Producer: GTE Information Systems (Mount Laurel, NJ)
Vendor: GTE Information Systems, Inc.

The Information Bank
Provides an extensive current affairs data source consisting of abstracts from numerous English language publications.

Producer: The New York Times Information Service
Vendor: The New York Times Information Service

LEXIS
Contains full text references to a wide range of legal information including court decisions, regulations, government statutes.

Producer: Mead Data Central (New York, NY)
Vendor: Mead Data Central

NEXIS
Provides full text business and general news including management, technology, finance, science, politics, religion.

Producer: Mead Data Central (New York, NY)
Vendor: Mead Data Central

Quick Quote
Provides current quotations, volume, high-low data for securities of U.S. public corporations.

Producer: CompuServe Inc.
Vendor: CompuServe

Quotron 800

Provides up to the minute quotation and statistics on a broad range of securities such as stocks, bonds, options, commodities.

Producer: Quotron Systems Inc. (Los Angeles, CA)

Vendor: Quotron Systems Inc.

The Source

Covers a broad variety of consumer services business and financial information including travel information, reservations, restaurant reviews etc.

Producer: Source Telecomputing (McLean, VA)

Vendor: Source Telecomputing Corp.

Value Line II

Provides extensive financial data from the Value Line Investment Survey covering over 1600 major companies.

Producer: Arnold Bernhard & Co. (New York, NY)

Vendors: ADP Service, Chase Econometrics/Interactive Data Corp., CompuServe Data Resources, Inc.

For further information:

A. T. Kruzas and J. Schmittroth, *Encyclopedia of Information Systems,* Gale Research (Book Tower, Detroit, MI 48226) revised periodically.

Information Industry Market Place, R. R. Bowker (New York, NY) annual.

On Line Data Base Services Directory; Gale Research (address above) revised periodically.

The Federal Data Base Finder. A guide to more than 3,000 free and fee based data bases provided by the US Government. Available from Information USA, 1200 Beall Mt. Road, Potomac, MD 20854.

Guidance on Software Maintenance. Superintendent of Documents, Government Printing Office, Washington, DC 20402. Offers advice on maintaining software and suggestions on how to streamline your system.

Introduction to Software Packages. Superintendent of Documents (address given above). Sources of information on available software packages.

Data Base Vendors

ADP Network Services, Inc.
175 Jackson Plaza
Ann Arbor, MI 48106
313-769-6800

BRS, Inc.
1200 Route 7
Latham, NY 12110
518-783-1161
800-833-4707

Business Information Services

Control Data Corporation
500 West Putnam Avenue
Greenwich, CT 06830
203-622-2000

Chaes Econometrics/Interactive Data Corporation
486 Totten Pond Road
Waltham, MA 02154
617-890-1234

CompuServe, Inc.
5000 Arlington Centre Boulevard
Columbus, OH 43220
614-457-8600

Data Resources, Inc. (DRI)
29 Hartwell Avenue
Lexington, MA 02173
617-861-0165

DIALOG Information Services, Inc.
3460 Hillview Avenue
Palo Alto, CA 94304
415-858-3810
800-227-1960

Dow Jones & Company, Inc.
P.O. Box 300
Princeton, NJ 08540
609-452-2000
800-257-5114

General Electric Information Services Company
401 North Washington Street
Rockville, MD 20850
301-340-4000

GTE Information Systems, Inc.
East Park Drive
Mount Laurel, NJ 08054
609-235-7300

Mead Data Central
200 Park Avenue
New York, NY 10017
212-883-8560

The New York Times Information Services, Inc.
1719-A Route 10
Parsippany, NJ 07054
201-539-5850

Quotron Systems, Inc.
5454 Beethoven Street
Los Angeles, CA 90066
213-398-2761

SDC Search Service
2500 Colorado Avenue
Santa Monica, CA 90406
203-820-4111
800-421-7229

I. P. Sharp Associates
145 King Street West
Toronto, Ontario, Canada M5H IJ8
416-364-5361

Source Telecomputing Corporation
1515 Anderson Road
McLean, VA 22102
703-734-7500X546
800-336-3366

TRW Information Services Division
1 City Boulevard
Orange, CA 92668
714-937-2700

United Telecom Computer Group
5454 West 110 Street
Overland Park, KA 66211
913-341-9161

How to Find Software Packages

The task of learning about software packages can seem staggering at first. The following section is a guide to reference material which will make this task much simpler. It describes sources of information which are available; which sources are the most useful; and how to make the best of them.

OVERCOMING THE TERMINOLOGY HURDLE

No matter which sources of information about software packages are used, understanding computer terminology is one of the first problems that those who are unfamiliar with computers will encounter. The evolution of computer science and its related fields has led to the proliferation of a special language with technical meanings that are often unfamiliar to the lay person. Some of these terms are heard quite often—for instance, almost everyone has been told at some time that he/she can't do something because "the computer is DOWN." Fortunately, many of these terms are becoming so common they are listed in recent dictionaries (for instance, the term "down time" is listed in *Webster's New Collegiate Dictionary*). In addition, there are a number of sources dealing specifically with the technical language of computing which may be useful. Three of those sources are:

Computer Dictionary and Handbook, Charles J. Sippl, ed. [Howard W. Sams and Company, Inc.: 4300 West 62nd Street, Indianapolis, IN 46268].

Encyclopedia of Computer Science, Anthony Ralston, ed. [Van Nostrand Reinhold Company, Inc.: 135 West 50th Street, New York, NY 10020].

Dictionary for Information Processing [FIPS PUB 11–1, National Bureau of Standards].

The most important thing to remember when attempting to overcome the terminology hurdle is that the software to be purchased is intended to provide a service to its users. It should make life easier, not more complicated. The special terminology associated with computer technology need not have much impact upon the users of that technology. It is only in making sense of the available information on software packages and in dealing with vendors that understanding the special terminology is necessary.

INFORMATION SOURCES

A major problem encountered when attempting to select a software package is finding the information upon which to base a decision. At first, information is difficult to find, and then, when it is found, it may seem staggeringly complex—especially for a computer novice or a nontechnical computer user.

There are numerous sources of information on applications software packages. The following sections discuss several of these sources and describe how to best use them. Many of the sources which are discussed here may be found in local public and university libraries or Federal agency libraries and reference rooms.

PERIODICALS

Periodicals are one of the most widely available sources of information on software pack-

Source: Excerpted from *Introduction to Software Packages,* Sheila Frankel, editor. [NBS Special Publication 500–114], Systems and Software Technology Division, National Bureau of Standards, U.S. Department of Commerce, April 1984.

ages; the problems which confront those who are attempting to computerize specific functions; and techniques to follow when computerizing. Computer journals are not the only periodicals which print useful articles. While computer trade magazines typically have more in-depth analyses of the technical aspects of software packages (e.g., process requirements and storage requirements), application area trade magazines typically are more oriented toward the procedures a package supports. Both sources are valuable in early evaluation of various packages. When evaluating software for a specific business application area, an evaluation team that is not particularly conversant with computers might find trade journals which concentrate on the specific application area useful. For instance, to automate an accounting system, accounting magazines are probably, initially at least, the best source of information.

Valuable information, such as how current users rate packages, is often available in computer periodicals. A good example of this is the magazine *Datamation*, which provides a yearly users' survey of software packages. In addition, some periodicals publish articles which give tips on where to buy software. Some of them also reference additional sources of software package information.

While trade journals are good sources of information on computerizing specific functions, they are unlikely to have articles on computing in each edition. Therefore, it is best to make use of periodical indexes. Two indexes which are especially useful are:

Business Index [Information Access Corporation: 404 6th Avenue, Menlo Park, CA 94025].

Business Index is provided on microfilm. Listings are filed alphabetically by subject headings and by magazine titles. *Business Index* includes listings from 640 periodicals (approximately 90,000 articles per year).

Business Periodicals Index [H. W. Wilson Company: 950 University Avenue, Bronx, NY 10452].

Business Periodicals Index is in book form. It lists magazines by subject headings followed by subheadings. In this index, which is less extensive than *Business Index*, but more readily available, articles on automation are usually under the heading Data Processing.

DIRECTORIES

There are several directories available which catalog software, often according to the hardware on which it is available. Because of the explosion in sales of personal computers, most such directories are for microcomputer applications. Examples of these directories follow:

The Apple Software Directory [WIDL Video: 5245 W. Diversey Ave., Chicago, IL 60639] Software for Apple Computers.

Commodore Software Encyclopedia [Commodore Business Machines, Computer Systems Division: 300 Valley Forge Sp., 681 Moore Rd., King of Prussia, PA 19046] Software for Commodore Computers.

Dataguide [Sentry Database Publishing: 5 Kane Industrial Dr., Hudson, MA 01749] Hardware, software and accessories.

Directory of Microcomputer Software [DATAPRO: 1805 Underwood Blvd., Delran, NJ 08075] Software, updated monthly, comes with telephone inquiry service.

International Microcomputer Software Directory [Imprint: 420 South Howes, Fort Collins, CO 80521] Software, vendor lists.

Software Directory [Digital Research: P.O. Box 579, Pacific Grove, CA 93950] Applications and system software.

Software Vendor Directory [Micro-Serve: P.O. Box 482, Nyack, NY 10960] Applications and system software, vendors. Also available on computer diskette.

TRS-80 Applications Software Sourcebook [Available at Radio Shack stores] Applications software for TRS-80 computers.

REFERENCE SERVICES

Services have been developed which aid in the process of sorting through the vast quantity of computer information which is available. Some of these services are computerized, while others are not. In general, they can be very useful.

Datapro is one such reference service that is well established and maintains a good reputation in the data processing community. *Datapro Reports* [Datapro Research Corporation: 1805 Underwood Blvd., Delran, NJ 08075] is published in a three-ring binder format and is updated monthly. The Datapro subscription fee not only includes the basic volumes of the service, but also includes updates and an inquiry service. Datapro covers a variety of subject areas related to computing. Two volumes of particular interest to software package research are the following:

Datapro Applications Software (part of the solutions series)—especially designed for those "with line or staff responsibilities in planning, designing, programming or maintaining applications software solutions to business problems." Includes "Software Development Concepts," "How to Buy Software Packages," "Make or Buy Tradeoffs," "Selection and Acquisition," "Reliability and Vendor Support" and "User Ratings." Software packages are identified by applications area and detailed descriptions of each package are provided. Vendor lists are also provided.

Datapro Reports on Minicomputers—provides "detailed coverage of all types of minicomputers." Includes "Software" (user's ratings) and "Computers" ("individual, detailed analyses of minicomputer and small business computer systems from all important suppliers"). These analyses include users' reactions and software information.

Another well established reference service similar to Datapro is Auerbach. *Auerbach Technology Reports* [Auerbach Publishers, Inc.: 6560 North Park Drive, Pennsauken, NJ 08109]. The Auerbach volume on applications software includes discussions of special problems involved in computerizing specific applications areas and lists available packages in each application area. Listings include the package price, hardware requirements, capabilities, the number of installations, date of first installation, and the address of the package developer. Some of the many application areas which are covered include:

Human resource management
Accounts receivable
Accounts payable
General ledger
Inventory control
Integrated accounting
General business management
Manufacturing
Banking
Transportation
Medical
Insurance
Utilities
Scientific/engineering

A third reference service is Data Sources. *Data Sources* [Ziff-Davis Publishing Co.: P.O. Box 5845, Cherry Hill, NJ 08034] is published quarterly. As with Auerbach, software packages are identified by application area and hardware compatibility. Application areas include those mentioned above and others, such as those listed below:

Project management
Legal
Bill of materials
Civil engineering
Health
Economic modeling
Financial analysis
Government (Federal)
Government (local and state)
Library services
Office automation
Professional time accounting
Research and survey analysis

One company which provides a customized search utilizing a computerized listing of software packages is SofSearch. SofSearch's data base includes some 30,000 software packages offered by 8,500 vendors. Provided with a description of the application, the target computer and operating system and the industry, SofSearch will perform a search and provide one page reports on each package which meets these briefly described requirements.

To help you locate the software you want, P.C. Telemart offers a free service in about 100 retail stores. To find the location of the nearest store, call 703-352-0721 or write: P.C. Telemart, 11787 Lee Jackson Highway Fairfax, VA 22033.

Other sources of reference material are:

Directory of Systems Houses and Computer Distributors [Sentry Database Publishing: 5 Kane Industrial Drive, Hudson, MA 01749]

Computer Software Industry: A Financial and Strategic Analysis [Dun & Bradstreet Credit Services: New York, NY]

Software News [Sentry Database Publishing: 5 Kane Industrial Drive, Hudson, MA 01749]

Computerworld Software Buyer's Guide [C. W. Communications, Inc.: Box 880, 375 Cochituate Road, Framingham, MA 01701]

Microcomputer Software Letter [610 Fifth Avenue, Suite 706, New York, NY 10020]

PERIODICAL DESCRIPTIONS

The following section provides detailed descriptions of the periodicals.

Accountancy [The Institute of Chartered Accountants in England and Wales: 56/66 Goswell Road, London, England EL1B 7LD—American distributors: Expediters of the Printed Word LTD.: 527 Madison Avenue, Suite 1217, New York, NY 10022]. A British publication which often includes articles on the computerization of accounting practices. Articles are of high depth. One to two articles per issue are related to computerization. Published monthly.

Administrative Management [Geyer-McAllister Publications, Inc.: 51 Madison Avenue, New York, NY 10010]. This periodical contains an average of two computer articles and one article on new technologies per issue. Sample titles include: "A Buyer's Guide to Word Processing Software," by Alan Hoffberg, Contributing Editor; "What You Get With a '90-Day Trial,'" by Patrick Flanagan; "Superminis: In the Mainstream of Business DP," by Randi T. Sachs, Associate Editor; "Software for Sorts, Retrieval and Other Filing Tasks," by Bonnie Canning and Karen Michaels. Published monthly.

Byte [Byte Publications, Inc.: 70 Main St., Peterborough, NH 03458]. This monthly magazine is subtitled "The Small Systems Journal." Most articles are on computers (approximately 98%) with about half of the articles on hardware and half on software. About 60% of the advertisements are for hardware, 40% for software. Example articles are on how to select a text editor, and "Adapting Microcomputers to Wall Street." Issues are very long, averaging about 550 pages. Published monthly.

Chilton's Iron Age [Chilton Company: Wayne, PA 19089]. *Chilton's Iron Age* is subtitled "The Magazine for Metalworking Management." It contains some articles on computing and a few advertisements for computers. Articles are of low to medium depth. *Chilton's Iron Age* includes an advertisers' index. Free to qualified managers in US metal-working companies. Published every 10 days.

Computer Business News [C. W. Communications, Inc.: P.O. Box 880, 375 Cochituate Rd., Framingham, MA 01701]. This newspaper-format magazine is subtitled "The Newsweekly for the OEM Community." All articles are in some way related to computers. The focus is on marketing computers and computer industry investment information. A majority of articles and advertisements relate to hardware. Articles are of medium to low depth. A software applications directory is included annually. Published bi-monthly.

Computer Decisions [Hayden Publishing Co.: 50 Essex St., Rochelle Park, NJ 07662]. This magazine is subtitled "The Management Magazine of Computing." The magazine includes departments which appear in each issue such as "Snyder on Software" (including pros and cons of reviewed software), "Software" (write-ups by vendors) and an "Advertisers' Index." Example articles include: "Choosing the Right Turnkey Mini Supplier," by David Whieldon; "Office Automation Rolls Along," interview of Professor Howard Morgan; "How to Pick 'Friendly' Terminals," by David Whieldon; and "Don't Make—Buy! Support From Timesharing Services," by David Whieldon. There are many advertisements, both for hardware and business-applications software. Free subscriptions for executives of companies that deal with or use computers. Published monthly.

Computer Design [Computer Design Publishing Co.: 119 Russell St., Littleton, MA 01460]. Though a few useful articles are presented in this magazine on recent software developments, the orientation is toward hardware architecture issues and not business applications. Free subscriptions for engineers and those who manage engineers. Published monthly.

Computerworld [C. W. Communications, Inc.: P.O. Box 880, 375 Cochitaute Rd., Framingham, MA 01701]. This periodical, organized in a large newspaper format, is usually about 100 pages long. Many articles provide discussions of financial trends in the computer industry, while some discuss business applications. *Computerworld* includes many advertisements, including coupons for requesting specific information from vendors. It typically contains a software advertising section, often features special sections on software, and usually lists new product announcements. Published weekly.

Data Management [Data Processing Management Association: 505 Busse Highway, Park Ridge, IL 60068]. This magazine is business- and computer-oriented with a concentration on data management and processing. Most computer articles and advertisements are on software. Published monthly.

Datamation [Technical Publishing Company: 875 Third Avenue, New York, NY 10022].

This magazine has a business orientation and provides extensive information on all aspects of computing. User surveys of software are often included—for instance, the May 1982 issue included the "Applications Software Survey." Each edition includes an Advertisers' Index, which is an easy way to get a quick overview of what is available. Free subscriptions for qualified personnel. Published monthly.

Decision Sciences [American Institute for Decision Sciences: University Plaza, Atlanta, GA 30303]. *Decision Sciences* is designed for managers. On the average, one article per issue is concerned with computers. Articles contain in-depth analysis. Very few advertisements are included. Articles stress the use of behavioral, economic and quantitative methods of analysis for decision-making in public and private organizations. Published monthly.

Electronic Business [Cahners Publishing Co., Inc.: 270 Saint Paul Street, Denver, CO 80206]. *Electronic Business* has an electronic equipment orientation with an emphasis on text equipment. It occasionally provides application area articles.

Harvard Business Review [Subscription Service Department: P.O. Box 3010, Woburn, MA 01888]. This journal is published by Harvard Graduate School of Business Administration as part of a program in executive education. It is designed for a management audience. Approximately one article in each issue relates to computers. The depth of articles is medium to high, and the number of advertisements of any sort is low. Published bi-monthly.

IEEE Micro [IEEE, Inc., Computer Society: 445 Hoes Lane, Piscataway, NJ 08854]. All articles in this magazine are on computers. Few, however, address business applications. The technical level is high, as is the depth of articles. Published quarterly.

Infosystems [Hitchcock Publishing Companies, Inc.: Hitchcock Building, P.O. Box 3007, Wheaton, IL 60187]. This periodical is subtitled "The Magazine for Information Systems Managers." It includes many advertisements, both for software and hardware, and some comparison articles. Example articles include: "Programming Tools: Impacting DP Productivity," by Carol Tomme Thiel; "Keys to Successful Office Automation: Company Strategies and User Needs," by Alan G. Rockhold, Senior Editor; "Bottom Line Report: Remote Computing Services: You've Got to Watch the Meter," by Wayne L. Rhodes, Jr., Senior Editor; and "Summer Bonanza: What's New in Software Packages," by Carol Tomme Thiel, Software Editor. Published monthly.

Interface: Data Processing Management [International Computer Programs, Inc.: 9000 Keystone Crossing, P.O. Box 40946, Indianapolis, IN 46240]. All articles are on computers and many are business related. Approximately 70%

of the advertisements are for software, while the other 30% are for hardware and business services. A sample article is "In House Timesharing," by Ken Ross. Free subscription for qualified USA residents employed by one of the industries addressed by the publication. Published quarterly.

Interface Age [McPheters, Wolfe and Jones: 16704 Marquardt Ave., Cerritos, CA 90701]. This periodical is subtitled "Computing for Business." There are numerous advertisements, though more of them are for hardware than for software. All articles have something to do with computers, with about 40% pertaining to business applications. Many reviews of new hardware systems and software packages are provided. Some package comparisons, and useful articles on where to purchase software and how to negotiate for software packages are also provided. Published monthly.

Interfaces [The Institute of Management Sciences: 345 Whitney Avenue, New Haven, CT 06511]. This magazine is designed for managers and ADP specialists. Articles are of medium to high depth. Software advertisements and product comparisons are few. Published bi-monthly.

Journal of Accountancy [American Institute of Certified Public Accountants, Inc.: 1211 Avenue of the Americas, New York, NY 10036]. This magazine does not include articles on computing. However, it does include many advertisements for packages related to accounting. Published monthly.

Journal of Small Business Management [International Council for Small Business: West Virginia University, Bureau of Business Research, Morgantown, WV 26506]. This publication has an academic orientation and each edition has a particular theme. Only about one in five issues includes an article on computerization, although one entire issue was devoted to computerization with at least 60% of that issue's articles being on computers. No advertisements for either hardware or software are included. Articles are of medium depth. Published quarterly.

Journal of Systems Management [Association for Systems Management: 24587 Bagley Road, Cleveland, OH 44138]. This journal is designed for managers. All articles are on computers. Articles are of medium depth and include such titles as "The V-Curve: A Road Map For Avoiding People Problems in Systems Changes" and "The Main-Frame Computer: A Glimpse Into the Future." Published monthly.

Management Accounting [National Association of Accountants: 919 Third Ave., New York, NY 10022]. Computer advertisements are mostly for software (primarily accounting and financial packages). Only about one in five issues contains articles on computers, but one edition was a computer special and approximately 50% of its articles were on computing. The depth of these articles is from medium to high. Published monthly.

Management Review [American Management Associations: ARACOM Division, P.O. Box 319, Saranac Lake, NY 12983]. One in twelve issues includes an article on computing, and these articles are not directed toward the issues or audience addressed in this document. Articles are often very general. Published monthly.

Management Science [Institute of Management Sciences: 146 Westminister St., Providence, RI 02903]. This periodical is highly quantitative and academic. There are few advertisements. It is not recommended as a source for software package information. Published monthly.

Management Today [Management Publishing LTD.: 76 Dean Street, London, W1A 1BU]. *Management Today* is a British magazine. One in five issues includes an article on computers. Articles are of medium to high depth. Published monthly.

Merchandising [Gralla Publications: 1515 Broadway, New York, NY 10036]. This magazine has a large, glossy-newspaper format. While every issue has at least one article on computers, the orientation is not toward software packages, but on computer industry marketing information. Advertisements are also marketing-oriented. Published monthly.

Microcomputing [P.O. Box 997, Farmingdale, NY 11737]. All the articles in this magazine relate to microcomputers. Some articles address business concerns. An example article is "Meet the Monthly Billing Deadline," by Sam Davis. Monthly sections include descriptions of new products and software ratings. Most advertisements focus on hardware; however, some relate to software. Published monthly.

Mini-Micro Systems [Cahners Publishing Company, Inc.: 270 Saint Paul Street, Denver, CO 80206]. All articles in this magazine deal with computers. Articles are technically detailed and are rarely geared to business concerns. Articles do include comparisons, but the major emphasis is on hardware rather than software. This magazine provides articles directly related to a Government audience. Free subscriptions for qualified individuals. Published monthly.

Modern Office Procedures [Penton-IPC: Penton Plaza, 111 Chester Ave., Cleveland, OH 44114]. Approximately three articles per issue are on word processing. Occasionally, there are other articles on some type of computing. The articles concentrate on procedures rather than on types of software. The advertisements in this magazine are more often for hardware than for software. Published monthly.

The Office [Office Publications, Inc.: 1200 Summer St., Stamford, CT 06904]. This periodical is subtitled "Magazine of Management, Equipment, Automation." It contains many articles on office automation, word processing, etc. Articles are of medium depth. More articles are on procedures than on software, but some articles do include comparisons. Advertisements for software products are included. *The Office* has a business orientation. Published monthly.

Output [Technical Publishing: 1301 S. Grove Ave., Barrington, IL 60010]. This magazine is subtitled "The Information Systems Magazine for the General Management User." All of its articles are related in some way to computers and to business. Advertisements are for both software and hardware; however, the overall number of advertisements in these areas is low. Articles do include comparisons, such as in the article "Choosing a Vendor For the Automated Office," by Margaret Coffey. Published monthly.

Personal Computing [Hayden Publishing Company, Inc.: 50 Essex St., Rochelle Park, NJ 07662]. *Personal Computing* describes the uses of personal computers. Most articles are on how to use computers more effectively in the home. Some articles address the use of personal computers for business concerns as "When the Boss Got Into Computing," by Marvin Grosswirth. Articles are of medium depth. Approximately 20% of the advertisements are for software products. Published monthly.

Personnel Journal [A. C. Croft, Inc.: P.O. Box 2440, Costa Mesa, CA 92626]. One in three issues has an article on computerization. One such article is "A Guide For Building a Human Resource Data System," by Vincent R. Ceriello. Published monthly.

Personnel Management [Business Publications LTD.: Audit House, Field End Road, Ruislip, Middlesex HA4 9LT]. This magazine is a British publication. It includes advertisements for Personnel System Software packages. Most advertisements represent British products. Articles are of medium depth. Published monthly.

Purchasing [Cahners Publishing Company, Inc.: 270 Saint Paul Street, Denver CO 80206]. This periodical is business oriented. It does not include computer advertisements. Every issue has something on computers, but often the depth is low. An example article is "Computers in Purchasing: Part 30," by Robert Porter and Gilbert Trill. Published bi-monthly.

Software News [Sentry Database Publishing: 5 Kane Industrial Drive, Hudson, MA 01749]. All the articles in this periodical are concerned with computers; some also discuss business concerns. This periodical is designed like a newspaper. Articles are datelined, and are of medium depth. Sample articles include "Software and the Automated Office," by John A. Murphy and "Productivity Tools Mean Better Code," by Dave Ferris. Published monthly.

Today's Office [United Technical Publications, Inc.: 645 Stewart Ave., Garden City, NY 11530]. Most articles are on computers in business applications and comparisons are often included in these articles. Advertisements generally relate to office products while some (about 40%) are for computer software. Free to administrative executives and qualified Government offices. Published monthly.

Business Information Directory

General Information Sources

GENERAL SOURCES

The *United States Government Manual* is an annual publication. It describes the organization, purposes, and programs of most government agencies and lists top personnel. Available from the Superintendent of Documents, Government Printing Office, Washington, DC 20402.

Washington Information Directory is an annual publication listing, by topic, organizations and publications which provide information on a wide range of subjects. It also lists congressional committee assignments, regional federal offices, embassies, and state and local officials. Published by the Congressional Quarterly, Inc., 1414 22nd Street NW, Washington, DC 20037.

Statistical Abstracts of the United States, published annually, is the standard summary on the social, political, and economic statistics of the United States. It includes data from both government and private sources. Appendix II gives a comprehensive list of sources. (Available from the Superintendent of Documents, Government Printing Office, Washington, DC 20402)

Professional and trade organizations and publications are a major source of contacts and information. Key directories to these sources are listed below:

Encyclopedia of Associations, published by Gale Research Co., Book Tower, Detroit, MI 48226.

The World Guide to Trade Associations gives a comprehensive national and international listing of associations. Published by R. R. Bowker Co., 1180 Avenue of the Americas, New York, NY 10036.

Ulrich's International Periodical Directory covers both domestic and foreign periodicals. Published by R. R. Bowker Co., 1180 Avenue of the Americas, New York, NY 10036.

Standard Periodical Directory covers U.S. and Canadian periodicals. Published by Oxbridge Communications, Inc., 150 Fifth Avenue, New York, NY 10011.

The IMS 83 Ayer's Directory of Publications provides titles of trade newspapers and periodicals. Published by IMS Press, 426 Pennsylvania Avenue, Fort Washington, PA 19034.

Standard Rate and Data Service provides information on periodical circulation and advertising rates. Published by Standard Rates and Data Service, Inc., 3004 Glen View Road, Wilmette, IL 60091.

Encyclopedia of Information Systems and Services. Descriptions of U.S. organizations (and some foreign) that produce, process, store, and use bibliographic and non-bibliographic information. About 1500 data bases covered. Published by Gale Research Co., Book Tower, Detroit, MI 48226.

National Directory of Addresses and Telephone Numbers. A national business directory that lists all SEC registered companies, major accounting and law firms, banks, and financial institutions, associations, unions, etc. Available from Concord Reference Books, 135 W. 50th Street, New York, NY 10020.

Encyclopedia of Business Information, a comprehensive single-volume source, is updated periodically. Available from Gale Research Co., Book Tower, Detroit, MI 48226.

Researcher's Guide to Washington Experts, Washington Researchers, 2612 P Street NW, Washington, D.C. 20007.

Information USA is a reference book with leads about how to tap the information mine of the federal government. Published by Penguin Books, 624 Madison Avenue, New York, NY 10022.

FEDfind explains how to get services and publications from the U.S. Government. Published by ICUC Press, P.O. Box 1447-NR, Springfield, VA 22151.

Library of Congress National Referral Center, 110 2nd S.E. Street, Washington, DC 20540 (202–287–5670) provides referrals to a wide range of services.

Encyclopedia of Banking and Finance, a comprehensive source on subjects indicated in title. Bankers Publishing Co., Boston, MA.

Listings of trade directories are given in the following:

Guide to American Directories, published by B. Klein Publications, Inc., P.O. Box 8503, Coral Springs, FL 33065.

Directory of Directories, distributed by Gale Research Co., Book Tower, Detroit, MI 48226.

BUSINESS AND ECONOMICS INFORMATION

Government publications referred to below may be obtained from the Government Printing Office (GPO), Washington, DC, 20402, unless other indicated.

Business and economic information is provided by the following key references.

Survey of Current Business is a major publication which is supplemented on a weekly basis with *Current Statistics.* The publication contains articles as well as comprehensive statistics on all aspects of the economy, including data on the GNP, employment, wages, prices, finance, foreign trade, and production by industrial sector. (GPO)

Business Conditions Digest is a monthly with an extensive collection of charts and tables on the national income and products, leading coincident and lagging cyclical indicators, foreign trade, prices, wages, analytical ratios, and international production and stock prices. (GPO)

Economic Indicators is a monthly summary-type publication prepared by the Council of Economic Advisers. It contains charts and tables on natural output, income, spending, employment, unemployment, wages, industrial production, construction, prices, money, credit, federal finance, and international statistics. (GPO)

Federal Reserve Bulletin is a monthly issued by the Federal Reserve System, containing articles and very extensive tabulated data on all aspects of the monetary situation, credit, mortgage markets, interest rates, and stock and bond yields. A monthly *Chart Book* is available which contains charts of financial and monetary data. Both are available from the Board of Governors, Federal Reserve System, Washington, DC 20551.

Monthly Labor Review. This monthly publication provides articles and statistics on employment, productivity, wages, earnings, prices, wage settlements, and work stoppages. (GPO)

U.S. Industrial Outlook is an annual providing evaluations and projections of all major industrial and commercial segments of the domestic economy. (GPO)

Quarterly Financial Report for Manufacturing, Mining, and Trade Corporations is issued by the Bureau of the Census of the U.S. Department of Commerce. It covers corporate financial statistics including sales, profits, assets, and financial ratios, classified by industry group and size. (GPO)

Current Industrial Reports are a series of over 100 monthly, quarterly, semiannual, and annual reports on major products manufactured in the United States. For subscription, contact the Bureau of the Census, U.S. Department of Commerce, Washington, DC 20233. (GPO)

Annual Survey of Manufacturers. General statistics of manufacturing activity for industry groups, individual industries, states, and geographical regions are provided. (GPO)

County Business Patterns is an annual publication on employment and payrolls, which include a separate paperbound report for each state. (GPO)

Foreign Trade is a Bureau of the Census publication giving monthly reports on U.S. foreign trade. (GPO)

Population: Current Report is a series of monthly and annual reports covering population changes and socioeconomic characteristics of the population. (GPO)

Retail Sales: Current Business Report is a weekly report which provides retail statistics. (GPO)

Wholesale Trade, Sales and Inventories: Current Business Report provides a monthly report on wholesale trade. (GPO)

Directory of Marketing Research Houses and Services is an annual available from the American Marketing Association, 420 Lexington Avenue, New York, NY 10022.

CORPORATE INFORMATION

The major sources of information on publicly held corporations (as well as government and municipal issues) are: *Moody's Investor Services, Inc.,* owned by Dun & Bradstreet, 99 Church Street, New York, NY 10007, and *Standard & Poor's Corp.,* owned by McGraw-Hill, 345 Hudson Street, New York, NY 10014.

Standard & Poor's *Corporate Records* and Moody's *Manuals* are large multivolume works published annually and kept up to date with daily (for Standard & Poor's) or semiweekly (for Moody's) reports. The services provide extensive coverage of industrials, public utilities, transportation, banks, and financial companies. Also included are municipal and government issues.

In addition, the above corporations provide computerized data services and magnetic tapes. Compustat tapes, containing major corporate financial data, are available from Investor's Management Services, Inc., Denver, CO, a subsidiary of Standard & Poor's. Time-sharing access to Compustat and other financial data bases is available through Interactive Data Corporation, Waltham, MA (617) 890–1234.

DISCLOSURE II, available from Disclosure, Inc., 5161 River Road, Bethesda, MD 20816) provides an on line data base of corporate information for more than 8,000 companies. Disclosure II can be used via the Dow Jones Retrieval Service, New York Times Information Service, Lockheed's DIALOG Information Services, Inc. NEXIS and the Service Bureau Company.

The 10-K and other corporate reports are filed with the Securities and Exchange Commission and are available at local SEC offices, investor relations departments of publicly traded companies, as well as various private services, such as Disclosure Inc. which provides a complete microfiche service. *The SEC News Digest,* formerly published by the government, is now available from Disclosure, Inc. (address above). Included in the *Digest* is a daily listing of 8K reports, a daily Acquisitions of Securities Report, as well as information about what's happening inside the SEC.

How to Find Information About Companies, Washington Researchers, 2612 P Street NW, Washington, DC 20007.

Major trade directories include the *Thomas Register of American Manufacturers* (published by Thomas Publishing Company, 1 Pennsylvania Plaza, New York, NY) and Dun & Bradstreet's *Reference Book of Manufacturers.*

Thomas Register includes in one volume an alphabetical listing of manufacturers, giving address, phone number, product, subsidiaries, plant location, and an indication of assets. Dun & Bradstreet's *Reference Book* covers similar information, including sales and credit. Dun & Bradstreet's *Million Dollar Directory* series provides data on more than 120,000 U.S. companies whose net worth is $500,000 and up, including information on privately held corporations; also published is a companion volume the *Billion Dollar Directory* which tracks America's corporate families.

Register of Corporations is published by Standard and Poor's Corp., 345 Hudson Street, New York, NY 10014.

Directory of Corporate Affiliations and International Directory of Corporate Affiliations are references to the structure of major domestic and international corporations. Published by NRPC, 3004 Glen View Road, Wilmette, IL 60091.

Sources of State Information on Corporations, provides information filed by companies with the state governments and also business related data collected by the states. Washington Researchers, 2612 P Street NW, Washington, DC 20007.

Future earnings projections of listed companies based on surveys by securities analysts is provided by Lynch, Jones, and Ryan, 325 Hudson Street, New York, NY (212-243-3132).

TRACKING FEDERAL GOVERNMENT DEVELOPMENTS

Commerce Business Daily. This daily provides information on contract awards and subcontract opportunities, Defense Department awards, and surplus sales. (GPO)

Federal Register. This daily provides information on federal agency regulations and other legal documents (GPO).

CQ Weekly Report. This major service follows every important piece of legislation through both houses of Congress and reports on the political and lobbying pressures being applied. Available from the Congressional Quarterly Service, 1414 22nd Street, Washington, DC 20037.

Daily Report for Executives. A daily series of reports giving Washington developments that affect all aspects of business operations. Available from the Bureau of National Affairs, Inc., 1231 25th Street NW, Washington, DC 20037. Call: 301-258-1033.

Two major services, the *Bureau of National Affairs, Inc.* (address above) and the *Commerce Clearing House, Inc.* (4025 West Peterson Avenue, Chicago, IL 60646), publish a large number of valuable weekly loose-leaf reports covering developments in all aspects of law, government regulations, and taxation.

INDEX PUBLICATIONS

Indexes of a wide variety of articles appearing in periodicals, trade presses, and financial services dealing with corporations, industry, and finance are given in the following:

Business Periodicals Index published by H. W. Wilson Co., 950 University Avenue, Bronx, NY.

Funk and Scott Index of Corporations and Industries, published by Predicast, Inc., 11001 Cedar Street, Cleveland, OH 44141.

Major newspaper indexes are:

Wall Street Journal Index published by Dow Jones & Co. Inc., 22 Cortland Street, New York, NY 10007 (monthly).

New York Times Index published by the New York Times Company, 229 W. 43rd Street, New York, NY 10036 (semimonthly, cumulates annually).

TRACKING ECONOMIC INDICATORS

Composite Index of Leading Ecnomic Indicators: Each month the Bureau of Economic Analysis compiles this data from the 12 leading economic indicators. This material appears each month in the *Bureau's Business Conditions Digest* (BCD) available by subscription from:

Superintendent of Documents
Government Printing Office
Washington, DC 20402

For current index values call: 202-523-0589.

Consumer Price Index (changes in cost of goods to customers): For these monthly reports prepared by the Bureau of Labor Statistics write:

Bureau of Labor Statistics
Department of Labor
441 G Street NW
Washington, DC 20212

Data from these reports is available within 24 hours of their release by subscription to the Consumer Price Index Mailgram Service. Contact:

National Technical Information Service
5285 Port Royal Road
Springfield, VA 22161
703-487-4630

Producer Price Index (measures changes in prices received in primary markets by producers). For monthly reports write:

Bureau of Labor Statistics
Department of Labor
441 G Street NW
Washington, DC 20212

Available from the Bureau of Labor Statistics are press releases on *State and Metropolitan Area Unemployment* (issued monthly), the *Employment Cost Index* (issued quarterly, and the *Employment Situation Study* (released monthly). For a sample copy call 202-523-1221. To subscribe write:

Bureau of Labor Statistics
Department of Labor
Washington, DC 20230

Unemployment Insurance Claims Weekly may be obtained by calling 202-376-6908 or by writing:

Employment and Training Administration
Department of Labor
601 D Street, NW
Washington, DC 20213

Releases on the *Money Supply* (Report H-6, issued weekly) and on *Consumer Credit* (Report G-19, issued monthly) may be obtained from the

Publications Services
Federal Reserve Board
Washington, DC 20551
202-452-3244

Personal Consumption Expenditure Deflator is prepared monthly by the Bureau of Economic Analysis of the Department of Commerce. This information appears in a press release *Personal Income and Outlays* and can be obtained in writing from the

Current Business Analysis
Bureau of Economic Analysis
Department of Commerce
Washington, DC 20230

For information on the above call 202-523-0777.
Monthly Trade Report (index of retail sales and accounts receivable) is compiled by the Bureau of the Census and published in *Current Business Reports* as part of what is known as the BR series. To subscribe contact the Superintendent of Documents (Address given above). For a sample copy call: 301-763-4040
Survey of US Export and Import Merchandise (value of imports and exports) is available by subscription from:

Subscriber Services Section
Bureau of the Census
Washington, DC 20233

For a sample copy call: 301-763-5140
Value of New Construction Put in Place is a Census Bureau monthly report (part of the C-30 Series) which charts the dollar amount of new construction. It is available on an annual subscription basis from the Superintendent of Documents, Government Printing Office, Washington, DC 20402. For a sample copy call: 301-763-4040.

JOINT ECONOMIC COMMITTEE OF CONGRESS REPORTS

Reports on the economic issues studied by the Joint Economic committee are available free of charge from:

Joint Economic Committee of Congress
Dirksen Senate Office Building
Washington, DC 20510
202–224–5321

FEDERAL INFORMATION CENTERS (FICs)

FICS located in key cities throughout the country are a joint venture of the U.S. General Services Administration and the U.S. Civil Services. Each center is a focal point for obtaining information about the federal government and often about state and local governments. A member of the center's staff can either provide information or direct inquiries to an expert who can. Some centers have specialists who speak foreign languages. The coordinator of the FICS is located at 18th and F Streets, NW, Washington, DC 20405; call 202–566–1937. The Federal Information Centers and their telephone numbers are listed below.

Alabama
Birmingham: (205) 322–8591
Mobile: (205) 438–1421

Alaska
Anchorage: (907) 271–3650

Arizona
Phoenix: (602) 261–3313

Arkansas
Little Rock: (501) 378–6177

California
Los Angeles: (213) 688–3800
Sacramento: (916) 440–3344
San Diego: (619) 293–6030
San Francisco: (415) 556–6600
Santa Ana: (714) 836–2386

Colorado
Colorado Springs: (303) 471–9491
Denver: (303) 236–7181
Pueblo: (303) 544–9523

Connecticut
Hartford: (203) 527–2617
New Haven: (203) 624–4720

Florida
Ft. Lauderdale: (305) 522–8531
Jacksonville: (904) 354–4756
Miami: (305) 350–4155
Orlando: (305) 442–1800
St. Petersburg: (813) 893–3495
Tampa: (813) 229–7911
West Palm Beach: (305) 833–7566

Georgia
Atlanta: (404) 221–6891

Hawaii
Honolulu: (808) 546–8620

Illinois
Chicago: (312) 353–4242

Indiana
Gary: (219) 883–4110.
Indianapolis: (317) 269–7373

Iowa
From all points in Iowa (800) 532–1556

Kansas
From all points in Kansas: (800) 432–2934

Kentucky
Louisville: (502) 582–6261

Louisiana
New Orleans: (504) 589–6696

Maryland
Baltimore: (301) 962–4980

Massachusetts
Boston: (617) 223–7121

Michigan
Detroit: (313) 226–7016
Grand Rapids: (616) 451–2628

Minnesota
Minneapolis: (612) 349–5333

Missouri
St. Louis: (314) 425–4106
From elsewhere in Missouri: (800) 392–7711

Nebraska
Omaha: (402) 221–3353
From elsewhere in Nebraska: (800) 642–8383

New Jersey
Newark: (201) 645–3600
Trenton: (609) 396–4400

New Mexico
Albuquerque: (505) 766–3091

New York
Albany: (518) 463–4421
Buffalo: (716) 846–4010
New York: (212) 264–4464
Rochester: (716) 546–5075
Syracuse: (315) 476–8545

North Carolina
Charlotte: (704) 376–3600

Ohio
Akron: (216) 375–5638
Cincinnati: (513) 684–2801
Cleveland: (216) 522–4040
Columbus: (614) 221–1014
Dayton: (513) 223–7377
Toledo: (419) 241–3223

Oklahoma
Oklahoma City: (405) 231–4868
Tulsa: (918) 584–4193

Oregon
Portland: (503) 221–2222

Pennsylvania
Philadelphia: (215) 597–7042
Pittsburgh: (412) 644–3456

Rhode Island
Providence: (401) 331–5565

Tennessee
Chattanooga: (615) 265–8231
Memphis: (901) 521–3285
Nashville: (615) 242–5056

Texas
Austin: (512) 472–5494
Dallas: (214) 767–8585
Fort Worth: (817) 334–3624
Houston: (713) 229–2552
San Antonio: (512) 224–4471

Utah
Salt Lake City: (801) 524–5353

Virginia
Norfolk: (804) 441–3101
Richmond: (804) 643–4928.
Roanoke: (703) 982–8591

Washington
Seattle: (206) 442–0570
Tacoma: (206) 383–5230

Wisconsin
Milwaukee: (414) 271–2273

Useful Contacts for Business Information

Association addresses of any organization may be obtained by writing the Director of Information Central, American Society of Association Executives, 1575 "Eye" Street NW, Washington, DC 20005, or calling 202–626–2723.

Congressional action information can be obtained from several sources. The Legis Office will provide information on whether legislation has been introduced, who sponsored it, and its current status. For House or Senate action, call 202–225–1772.

Cloakrooms of both houses will provide details on what is happening on the floor of the chamber. House cloakrooms: Democrat 202–225–7330; Republican 202–225–7350. Senate cloakrooms: Democrat 202–224–4691; Republican 202–224–6396.

Corporate reports filed with the SEC can be ordered from Discosure, Inc., 5161 River Road, Bethesda, MD 20816; or call 301–951–1300, 212–732–5955.

The Commerce Department's ombudsman operates throughout the entire government complex to assist both business and consumers. Services include dissemination of information and reports such as *Outlook*. Write Office of Business Liaison, U.S. Department of Commerce, Washington, DC 20230, or call 202–377–3176. This office is also a focal point for handling inquiries for domestic business information.

European Community country information is available free from the European Community

Information Service, 2100 M Street NW, Washington, DC 20037; or call 202–862–9500.

Industry experts in the International Trade Administration can provide specifics about an industry. To locate the proper authority contact the appropriate office:

Office of Basic Industries	202–377–0614
Office of Consumer Goods and Services	202–377–0823
Office of Business Analysis	202–377–1985
Office of Producer Goods	202–377–5023
Office of Research Analysis and Statistics	202–377–1316

Economic data and indicators provided by the Bureau of Census on a weekly, monthly, or quarterly basis may be obtained as released. Telephone numbers of the offices publishing and producing the information are given in the table below.

DEMOGRAPHIC FIELDS

Center for Demographic Studies	(301)763-7720
Center for International Research	763-2870
Decennial Operations Division	763-5613
Decennial Planning Division	763-7670
Demographic Surveys Division	763-2776
Housing Division	763-2863
International Statistical Programs Center	763-2832
Population Division	763-7646
Statistical Methods Division	763-2672

Population and Housing Subjects

Age and Sex:	
States (age only)	763-5072
United States	763-5072
Aging Population	763-7553
Aliens	763-7571
Annexation Population Counts	763-7955
Apportionment	763-7955
Births and Birth Expectations; Fertility Statistics	763-5303
Census Tracts:	
Boundary Information	763-2364
Census Data	763-5002
Citizenship:	
Foreign Born Persons, Country of Birth; Foreign Stock Persons	763-7571
Commuting:	
Means of Transportation; Place of Work	763-3850
Congressional Districts:	
Census Data	763-5002
Address Locations	763-5692
Population Estimates	763-5072
Consumer Expenditure Survey	763-2764
Crime Surveys:	
Data Analysis and Publication	763-7984
Victimization, General Information	763-1735
Current Population Survey	763-2773
Decennial Census:	
Content and Tabulations	763-1840
Count Complaints	763-1146
General	763-2748
Minority Statistics Program	763-5987

Special Tabulations:
  Population Data .... (301)763–7962
  Housing Data 763–2873
Disability 763–7946
Education; School Enrollment and Social Stratification 763–1154
Employment; Unemployment; Labor Force 763–2825
Farm Population:
  Census 763–7955
  Current Surveys 763–7955
Health Surveys 763–5508
Households and Families:
  Marriage and Divorce... 763–7950
  Projections 763–7950
  Size; Number; Social Characteristics 763–7950
Housing:
  Annual Housing Survey 763–2881
  Components of Inventory Change Survey 763–5840
  Contract Block Program 763–2873
  Housing Information, Decennial Census................................. 763–2873
  Housing Vacancy Data 763–2880
  Market Absorption 763–2866
  Residential Finance 763–2866
    (See also Economic Subjects—Construction Statistics)
Income Statistics:
  After Tax Income... 763–5060
  Child Support and Alimony 763–5060
  Current Surveys 763–5060
  Decennial Statistics 763–5060
  Discretionary Income 763–5060
  Household 763–5060
  Lifetime Earnings 763–5060
  Noncash Benefits 763–5060
  Revenue Sharing 763–5060
Income Surveys 763–2063
Incorporated/Unincorporated Places 763–7955
Industry and Occupation Statistics
  (See also Economic Fields) 763–5144
Institutional Population... 763–7950
International Statistics:
  Africa.. 763–4086
  Asia and Oceania 763-2834
  China, People's Republic of 763–4012
  Europe 763–4221
  International Data Base 763–4286
  Latin America and Caribbean 763–4086
  USSR-Population/Manpower 763–4020
  USSR-Economics 763-4022
  Women in Development 763–4232
Journey to Work 763–3850
Language, Current; Mother Tongue 763–1154
Longitudinal Surveys 763–2380
Marital Status; Living Arrangements 763–7950
Metropolitan Statistical Areas (MSA's)
  Census and Estimates Data; Current Definitions 763–5002
  New Criteria 763–5184/5368
Migration.. 763–3850
Neighborhood Statistics... 763–5024
Outlying Areas (Puerto Rico, etc.)
  Decennial Census 763–5002
  Population Estimates 763–5072
  Place of Birth 763–3850
Population:
  General Information; Published Data from Censuses,
    Surveys, Estimates, and Projections .... , ... 763–5020(TTY)/763–5002
Population Estimates Methodology:
  Congressional Districts; SMSA's 763–5072
  Counties; Federal-State Cooperative
    Program for Local Population Estimates 763–7722
  Estimates Research; Age Estimates 763–7883
  Local Areas; Revenue Sharing....................................... 763–7722
  Race Estimates 763–7883

ECONOMIC FIELDS

Economic Subjects

Enterprise Statistics	(301)763–5470
Foreign Owned US Firms	763–5182
Foreign Trade Information..	763–5140
Governments:	
Criminal Justice Statistics	763–7789
Eastern States Government Sector	763–7783
Employment	763–5086
Federal Expenditure Data	763–5276
Finance	763–7664
Governmental Organization and Special Projects......................	763–7789
Revenue Sharing (See also Demographic Fields)	763–5120
Taxation	763–5308
Western States Government Sector	763–5344
Industry and Commodities Classification	763–1935
Manufactures:	
Census/Annual Survey of Manufactures	763–7666
Durables	763–7304
Nondurables..	763–2510
Subject Reports (Concentration, Production	
Index, Water, etc.)	763–1503
Current Programs	763–7800
Durables	763–2518
Environmental Surveys	763–5616
Fuels/Electric Energy Consumed by Manufactures	763–5938
Nondurables..	763–5911
Origin of Exports...	763–5566
Shipments, Inventories, and Orders	763–2502
Mineral Industries	763–5938
Fuels/Electric Energy Consumed	
by Manufacturers..	763-7067
Water Used in Mineral	
and Manufacturing Industries	763-7066
Minority and Women Owned Businesses................................	763–5470
Puerto Rico:	
Censuses of Retail Trade, Wholesale Trade, and	
Selected Service Industries.......................................	763–7778
Quarterly Financial Report	763–4270
Retail Trade:	
Advance Monthly Sales; Annual Sales; Monthly Inventories	763–7561
Census	763–7038
Monthly Retail Trade Report	763–7128
Service Industries:	
Census	763–7039
Current Selected Services Reports	763–3916
Transportation:	
Commodity Transportation Survey; Truck Inventory and	
Use; Domestic Movement of Foreign Trade Data	763–1744
Wholesale Trade:	
Census	763–5281
Current Wholesale Sales and Inventories	763–3916

Source: User Training Branch, Data User Services Division, Bureau of the Census, Washington DC 20233.

Economic news and highlights of the day are provided by phone from the Department of Commerce. For economic news call 202–393–4100. For news highlights call 202–393–1847.

The Energy Information Center will provide free information on energy and related matters. Write National Energy Information Center, Forrestal Building, 1000 Independence Avenue SW, Washington, DC 20585. Call 202–252–8800.

Industry information statistics and details on specific industries can be obtained from the Bureau of Industrial Economics Department of Commerce, Washington, DC 20230; or call 202–377–4356.

Technical and scientific information is provided by the National Technical Information Service of the Department of Commerce, 5285 Port Royal, Springfield, VA 22161, which handles requests about government-sponsored research of all kinds. The basic charge to research a subject is $125. For information call 703–487–4600. For orders call 703–487–4650. For rush orders within the local calling area call 703–487–4700. For rush order outside the local calling area call 800–336–4700.

The reference section of the Library of Congress, Science and Technology Division, 10 First Street SE, Washington, DC 20540, provides answers to specific questions; call 202–287–5580. The National Referral Center provides names, addresses, and descriptions of information resources; call 202–287–5670.

Population information on all aspects of national and world population is provided by the Population Reference Bureau, Inc., 2213 M Street NW, Washington, DC 20037, or call 202–785–4664.

The Washington Information Research Service provides reports and guidance to information on a fee basis. Write Washington Researchers, 2612 P Street NW, Washington, DC 20007, or call 202–333–3499.

Foreign trade information as well as general business data are provided by the World Trade Information Center, One World Trade Center, New York, NY 10048, which maintains extensive data banks. The charge for a preliminary search is $30 an hour. Call 212–466–3063.

Information Sources in the U.S. Department of Commerce (by subject)

Abbreviations

USEA	Under Secretary for Economic Affairs	NOAA	National Oceanic & Atmospheric Administration
BEA	Bureau of Economic Analysis	NTIA	National Telecommunications & Information Administration
CEN	Bureau of the Census	NTIS	National Technical Information Service
EDA	Economic Development Administration	PTO	Patent and Trademark Office
ITA	International Trade Administration	SEC	Office of the Secretary
MBDA	Minority Business Development Agency	USTTA	United States Travel & Tourism Administration
NBS	National Bureau of Standards		

Subject	Source	Telephone Number
Aeronautical Charting	NOAA	(202) 377-8090
Agriculture Census	CEN	(301) 763-4040
Air-Quality Research	NOAA	(202) 377-8090
Arab Boycott	ITA	(202) 377-2253
Atmospheric Remote Sensing	NOAA	(303) 497-6286
Atmospheric Research	NOAA	(303) 497-6286
Atomic, Nuclear, Isotopic Research	NBS	(301) 921-3181
Auto Imports	ITA	(202) 377-3259
Automation Technology	NBS	(301) 921-3181
Broadcast News	SEC	(202) 377-5610
Building Technology	NBS	(301) 921-3181
Business Censuses	CEN	(301) 763-4040
Business Conditions Digest	BEA	(202) 523-0777
Business Conditions Report	ITA	(202) 377-4356
Business Liaison	SEC	(202) 377-3942
Capacity Utilization, Manufacturing	BEA	(202) 523-0874
Capital Equipment	ITA	(202) 377-5087
Censuses	CEN	(301) 763-4040
Chemical Analysis	NBS	(301) 921-3181
Chemical Engineering	NBS	(301) 921-3181
Climate Monitoring	NOAA	(202) 377-8090
Coastal Zone Management	NOAA	(202) 377-8090
Commerce Business Daily	ITA	(202) 377-4853
Commerce Publications Update	SEC	(202) 377-4233

Subject	Source	Telephone Number
Computer Science & Technology	NBS	(301) 921-3181
Construction & Forest Products	ITA	(202) 377-5087
Construction Review	ITA	(202) 377-5087
Consumer Affairs	SEC	(202) 377-5001
Consumer Goods	ITA	(202) 377-5087
Corporate Profits	BEA	(202) 523-0888
Decennial 1980 Census	CEN	(301) 763-4040
District Offices	ITA	(202) 377-3259
East-West Trade	ITA	(202) 377-3259
Economic Affairs	USEA	(202) 377-2235
Economic Development	EDA	(202) 377-5113
Economic Censuses	CEN	(301) 763-4040
Education Statistics	CEN	(301) 763-4040
Electromagnetic Radiation	NBS	(303) 497-3246
Electronics	NBS	(301) 921-3181
Employment & Unemployment Surveys	CEN	(301) 763-4040
Energy (Conservation)	NBS	(301) 921-3181
Energy (Inventions)	NBS	(301) 921-3181
Environment (Pollution)	NBS	(301) 921-3181
Environment Data Services	NOAA	(301) 763-7820
Environmental Research	NOAA	(303) 497-6286
Environmental Satellites	NOAA	(202) 377-3263
Export Development	ITA	(202) 377-3253
Export Information	ITA	(202) 377-3253
Export licenses	ITA	(202) 377-2253
Exports Awards	ITA	(202) 377-5205
Export Trading Companies	ITA	(202) 377-2253
Expositions (International)	SEC	(202) 377-4987
Failure Analysis (Buildings)	NBS	(301) 921-3181
Federal Economic Indicators	USEA	(202) 377-2235
Federal Receipts Expenditures	BEA	(202) 523-0744
Fire Protection	NBS	(301) 921-3181
Fisheries	NOAA	(202) 634-7281
Flash Floods	NOAA	(301) 427-7622
Foreign Commercial Service	ITA	(202) 377-3259
Foreign Investment Statistics	BEA	(202) 523-0645
Foreign Trade Opportunities	ITA	(202) 377-3253
Foreign Trade Analysis	ITA	(202) 377-2253
Foreign Trade Statistics	CEN	(301) 763-4040
Foreign Trade Zones	ITA	(202) 377-2253
Franchising	ITA	(202) 377-5087
Freedom Of Information	SEC	(202) 377-3271
Frequency Allocations (Federal Use)	NTIA	(202) 377-1551
Geodetic Surveys	NOAA	(202) 377-8090
Government Finances (State & Local)	CEN	(301) 763-4040
Great Lakes Research	NOAA	(303) 497-6286
Gross National Product	BEA	(202) 523-0777
Housing & Construction Statistics	CEN	(301) 763-4040
Hurricane Research	NOAA	(303) 497-6286
Hurricane Warning	NOAA	(301) 427-7622

Subject	Source	Telephone Number
Hydrology, Office Of	NOAA	(301) 427-7622
Import Programs	ITA	(202) 377-2253
Income, Family	CEN	(301) 763-4040
Industrial Outlook	ITA	(202) 377-4356
Industry Surveys	CEN	(301) 763-4040
Information Policy	NTIA	(202) 377-1551
Input-Output Analysis	BEA	(202) 523-0683
Interdepartment Radio Advisory Committee (IRAC)	NTIA	(202) 377-1551
International Finance, Investment & Marketing	ITA	(202) 377-3259
International Investment Statistics	BEA	(202) 523-0645
International Transactions	BEA	(202) 523-0620
Investment Services	ITA	(202) 377-3259
Law Enforcement Standards	NBS	(301) 921-3181
Leading Economic Indicators	BEA	(202) 523-0777
Manufacturing Engineering	NBS	(301) 921-3131
Manufacturing Industries (By Product)	ITA	(202) 377-5087
Marine Ecosystem Studies	NOAA	(303) 497-6286
Marine Mammals	NOAA	(202) 634-7281
Marine Technology	NOAA	(202) 377-8090
Materials Research	NBS	(301) 921-3181
Merchandise Trade	BEA	(202) 523-0668
Meteorological Center	NOAA	(301) 427-7622
Metric	OMP	(202) 377-0944
Minority Business Development Programs	MBDA	(202) 377-1936
Multinational Corporations	ITA	(202) 377-3259
National Marine Fisheries	NOAA	(202) 634-7281
Nautical Charts (Also Aviation Charts)	NOAA	(202) 377-8090
News Releases & Speeches (See Also PIO's)	SEC	(202) 377-4901
Non-ferrous Metals	ITA	(202) 377-5087
Occupation And Industry Statistics	CEN	(301) 763-4040
Overseas Business Opportunities	ITA	(202) 377-3253
Patent & Trademarks	PTO	(703) 557-3428
Patents, Government-owned, Foreign Filing	NTIS	(703) 487-4738
Personal Income & Outlays	BEA	(202) 523-0777
Plant & Equipment Expenditures	BEA	(202) 523-0874
Pollution Abatement And Control Expenditures	BEA	(202) 523-0687
Population Information	CEN	(301) 763-4040
Product Statistics	ITA	(202) 377-5087
Productivity	USEA	(202) 377-2235
Publications, Requests	SEC	(202) 377-4233
Publications, Sales & Distribution	SEC	(202) 377-5494
Radiation Measurements	NBS	(301) 921-3181
Regional Economic Statistics	BEA	(202) 523-0966
Research (Economic)	USEA	(202) 377-3685
Retail, Wholesale, & Service Trade Statistics	CEN	(301) 763-4040
Satellites	NOAA	(202) 377-3263
Sea Grants	NOAA	(202) 377-8090
Secretarial Statements	SEC	(202) 377-4901
Service Industries (Statistics)	ITA	(202) 377-5087
Solar Forecasts	NOAA	(303) 497-6286

Subject	Source	Telephone Number
Space Environment Research	NOAA	(303) 497-6286
Spectrum Management	NTIA	(202) 377-1551
Standard Reference Materials And Data	NBS	(301) 921-3181
Standards Information	NBS	(301) 921-3181
Stratospheric Research	NOAA	(303) 497-6286
Survey Of Current Business	BEA	(202) 523-0777
Technical Document Sales (All Govt. Agencies)	NTIS	(703) 487-4600
Technical Help To Exporters	NTIS	(703) 487-4733
Technology Transfer To Developing Countries	NTIS	(703) 487-4820
Telecommunications Applications	NTIA	(202) 377-1551
Telecommunications Policy (Int'l & Domestic)	NTIA	(202) 377-1551
Telecommunications Research	NTIA	(202) 377-1551
Telecommunications Technology	NTIA	(202) 377-1551
Textiles	ITA	(202) 377-3259
Time And Frequency (Standards)	NBS	(303) 323-3198
Tornado & Severe Storms Research	NOAA	(303) 497-6286
Tornado Warning	NOAA	(301) 427-7622
Tourism, International, To USA	USTTA	(202) 377-0137
Trade Fairs, Trade Centers And Missions	ITA	(202) 377-3253
Trademarks	PAT	(703) 557-3428
Trade Negotiations	ITA	(202) 377-3259
Trade Opportunities	ITA	(202) 377-3253
Trade Zone Board	ITA	(202) 377-2253
Transportation Equipment	ITA	(202) 377-5087
Travel To USA	USTTA	(202) 377-0137
Trigger Price Mechanism	ITA	(202) 377-2253
Weather Modification (Cloud Seeding)	NOAA	(303) 497-6286
Weather Service	NOAA	(301) 427-7622
Weights And Measures	NBS	(301) 921-3181

ADDRESSES OF U.S. DEPARTMENT OF COMMERCE INFORMATION SOURCES

Office of the Under Secretary for Economic Affairs
Rm. 4857, Main Commerce
14th and Constitution Ave., N.W.
Washington, D.C. 20230
Telephone: (202) 377–2235

Bureau of the Census
Rm. 2705, Fed. Office Bldg. No. 3
Suitland, MD 20023
Telephone: (301) 763–4051

Bureau of Economic Analysis
Rm. 713, Tower Bldg.
1401 K Street, N.W.
Mailing Address:
U.S. Department of Commerce
14th & Constitution Ave., N.W.
Washington, D.C. 20230
Telephone: (202) 523–0777

Economic Development Administration
Rm. 7800B, Main Commerce
14th & Constitution Ave., N.W.
Washington, D.C. 20230
Telephone: (202) 377–5113

International Trade Administration
Rm. 4805, Main Commerce
14th & Constitution Ave., N.W.
Washington, D.C. 20230
Telephone: (202) 377–3808

Minority Business Development Agency
Rm. 5063, Main Commerce
14th & Constitution Ave., N.W.
Washington, D.C. 20230
Telephone: (202) 377–1936

National Bureau of Standards
Rm. A903 Admin. Bldg.
Gaithersburg, Maryland
Mailing address:
National Bureau of Standards
Washington, D.C. 20234
Telephone: (301) 921–3112

National Oceanic and Atmospheric Admin.
Rm. 5806, Main Commerce

14th & Constitution Ave., N.W.
Washington, D.C. 20230
Telephone: (202) 377–4190
**National Technical Information
Service**
Room 1067, Main Commerce
14th & Constitution Ave., N.W.
Washington, D.C. 20230
Telephone: (202) 377–0365
**National Telecommunications
and Information Administration**
Room 4889, Main Commerce
14th & Constitution Ave., N.W.
Washington, D.C. 20230
Telephone: (202) 377–1551
Patent and Trademark Office
Rm. 1D01, Crystal Plaza Building 3
2021 Jefferson Davis Highway
Arlington, VA 20231
Telephone: (703) 557–3428
**United States Travel and
Tourism Administration**
Rm. 5410, Main Commerce Building
14th & Constitution Ave., N.W.
Washington, D.C. 20230
Telephone: (202) 377–0137

Commerce Department Data Base Research Services*

Fourteen field offices of the U.S. Department of Commerce offer computerized literature searches on most any business topic. The field

----

* Source: *The Information Report,* Washington Researchers, 2612 P Street, NW, Washington, DC 20007.

offices have access to Lockheed's DIALOG system as well as data generated by the Commerce Department. The offices charge out-of-pocket expenses plus an overhead fee. The offices that provide this service are located in Alabama, Arizona, California, Georgia, Illinois, Massachusetts, Michigan, Minnesota, Missouri, New York, North Carolina, Ohio, Texas and Washington.

Commerce Department Roadmap Program for Business Information

Designed to shorten the time it takes a businessperson to track down information within the labyrinth of government bureaus and agencies. Roadmap staffers can provide information or direct inquiries to the proper authority on such subjects as regulatory changes, government programs, services, policies, and even relevant government publications for the business community. For information call 202–377–3176 or write: Roadmap Program, Business Liason Office, Rm 5898-C, Department of Commerce, Washington, DC 20230.

U.S. General Services Administration: Business Service Centers

Business representatives interested in selling products and services to the Government should contact the nearest Business Service Center given below.

Mailing Address and Telephone	Area of Service
Business Service Center General Services Administration John W. McCormack Post Office and Courthouse Boston, MA 02109 (617) 223–2868	Connecticut, Maine, Massachusetts, New Hampshire, Rhode Island, and Vermont
Business Service Center General Services Administration 26 Federal Plaza New York, NY 10007 (212) 264–1234	New Jersey, New York, Puerto Rico, and Virgin Islands
Business Service Center General Services Administration 7th and D Streets, SW., Rm. 1050 Washington, DC 20407 (202) 472–1804	District of Columbia, nearby Maryland, Virginia
Business Service Center General Services Administration 9th and Market Streets Room 1300 Philadelphia, PA 19107 (215) 597–9613	Delaware, Pennsylvania, West Virginia, Maryland, Virginia

Mailing Address and Telephone	Area of Service
Business Service Center General Services Administration Richard B. Russell Federal Building and Court House 75 Spring Street Atlanta, GA 30303 (404) 221–5103/3032	Alabama, Florida, Georgia, Kentucky, Mississippi, North Carolina, South Carolina, and Tennessee
Business Service Center General Services Administration 230 South Dearborn Street Chicago, IL 60604 (312) 353–5383	Illinois, Indiana, Ohio, Michigan, Minnesota, and Wisconsin
Business Service Center General Services Administration 1500 East Bannister Road Kansas City, MO 64131 (816) 926–7203	Iowa, Kansas, Missouri, and Nebraska
Business Service Center General Services Administration 819 Taylor Street Fort Worth, TX 76102 (817) 334–3284	Arkansas, Louisiana, New Mexico, Oklahoma, and Texas
Business Service Center General Services Administration Building 41, Denver Federal Center Denver, CO 80225 (303) 234–2216	Colorado, Montana, North Dakota, South Dakota, Utah, and Wyoming
Business Service Center General Services Administration 525 Market Street San Francisco, CA 94105 (415) 454–9000	California (northern), Hawaii, and Nevada (except Clark County)
Business Service Center General Services Administration 525 Market Street San Francisco, CA 94105 (415) 556–2122	
Business Service Center General Services Administration 300 North Los Angeles Street Los Angeles, CA 90012 (213) 688–3210	Arizona, Los Angeles, California (southern), and Nevada (Clark County only)
Business Service Center General Services Administration 440 Federal Building 915 Second Avenue Seattle, WA 98174 (206) 442–5556	Alaska, Idaho, Oregon, and Washington

State Information Guide

Regional Directories

Central Atlantic States Manufacturing Directory, T. K. Sanderson Organization, 200 E. 25 Street, Baltimore, MD 21218

Daltons' Greater Philadelphia Industrial Directory, Dalton Corp., 2925 N. Broad Street, Philadelphia, PA 19132

Directory of Central Atlantic States Manufacturers, Manufacturers' News, Inc., 4 E. Huron Street, Chicago, IL 60611; George D. Hall Company, 20 Kilby Street, Boston, MA 02109

Directory of New England Manufacturers, The, George D. Hall Company, 20 Kilby Street, Boston, MA 02109

Eastern Manufacturers' and Industrial Directory, Bell Directory Publishers, Inc., 2112 Broadway, New York, NY 10023

MacRae's Blue Book, The National Industrial Directory, 87 Terminal Drive, Plainview, NY 11803

Midwest Manufacturers' and Industrial Directory, Industrial Directory Publishers, 1002 Park Avenue Building, Detroit, MI 48226

New England Apparel Directory, Register Publication, Inc., 99 Chauncey Street, Boston, MA 02111

New England Industrial Service Directory, George D. Hall Company, 20 Kilby Street, Boston, MA 02109

New England Manufacturers Directory, Manufacturers' News, Inc., 3 E. Huron Street, Chicago, IL 60611

State Executive Directory, Carroll Publishing Company, 1058 Thomas Jefferson NW, Washington, DC 20007

State Sales Guides, Dun & Bradstreet, Inc., 99 Church Street, New York, NY 10007

Survey of Industries in Texarkana (Arkansas-Texas), Texarkana Chamber of Commerce, Box 1468, Texarkana, AK 75501

State Business Assistance

Directory of Incentives for Business Investment and Development in the U.S., The Urban Institute Press, P.O. Box 19958 Hampden Station, Baltimore, MD 21211. State by state guide to economic business incentives. Included are descriptions of state assistance and financial assistance programs.

Alabama*

STATE CAPITOL, MONTGOMERY, AL 36130
(205) 862–6400 or 6980

INFORMATION OFFICES

Commerce/Economic Development
Office of State Planning and Federal Programs
State Capitol
Montgomery, AL 36130

Corporate
Secretary of State
State Office Building
Montgomery, AL 36130

Alabama Development Office
State Capitol
Montgomery, AL 36130

Office of Minority Business Enterprise
State Capitol
Montgomery, AL 36130

Taxation
Department of Revenue
Administrative Building
Montgomery, AL 36130

State Chamber of Commerce
Alabama Chamber of Commerce
468 S. Perry Street
P.O. Box 76
Montgomery, AL 36101

International Commerce
Governor's Office
State Capitol
Montgomery, AL 36130

Banking
State Banking Department
State Capitol
Montgomery, AL 36130

Securities
Alabama Securities Exchange Commission
State Capitol
Montgomery, AL 36130

Labor and Industrial Relations
Department of Industrial Relations
State Capitol
Montgomery, AL 36130

Alabama Department of Labor
State Capitol
Montgomery, AL 36130

---

* For Small Business Administration offices see page 258.

Insurance
Department of Insurance
State Capitol
Montgomery, AL 36130
Uniform Industrial Code
Alabama Development Office
State Capitol
Montgomery, AL 36130
Business Ombudsman
Business Ombudsman
State Capitol
Montgomery, AL 36130

INDUSTRIAL AND BUSINESS DIRECTORIES

Alabama Directory of Mining and Manufacturing, Alabama Development Office, State Capitol, Montgomery, AL 36130
Alabama Industrial Directory, Manufacturers' News, Inc., 3 E. Huron Street, Chicago, IL 60611; State Industrial Directories Corp., 2 Penn Plaza, New York, NY 10001
Alabama International Trade Directory, Office of State Planning and Federal Programs, State Capitol, Montgomery, AL 36130
Birmingham Industrial Directory, Birmingham Chamber of Commerce, 1914 6th Avenue, Birmingham, AL 35203
Alabama Metalworking Directory, Office of State Planning and Federal Programs, State Capitol, Montgomery, AL 36130

Alaska

STATE CAPITOL, JUNEAU, AK 99811
(907) 465–2111

INFORMATION OFFICES

Commerce/Economic Development
Department of Commerce & Economic Development
Pouch D
Juneau, AK 99811
Corporate
Department of Commerce & Economic Development
Corporation Section
Pouch D
Juneau, AK 99811
Taxation
Department of Revenue
Pouch S
Juneau, AK 99811
State Chamber of Commerce
Alaska State Chamber of Commerce
310 2nd Street
Juneau, AK 99801

International Commerce
Office of International Trade
Department of Commerce & Economic Development
Pouch D
Juneau, AK 99811
Banking
Division of Banking
Department of Commerce & Economic Development
Pouch D
Juneau, AK 99811
Securities
Division of Securities and Corporations
Department of Commerce and Economic Development
Pouch D
Juneau, AK 99811
Labor and Industrial Relations
Department of Labor
1111 W. 8th Street
Juneau, AK 99801
Insurance
Division of Insurance
Department of Commerce and Economic Development
Pouch D
Juneau, AK 99811
Uniform Industrial Code
Department of Natural Resources
Uniform Commercial Code
P.O. Box 103336
Anchorage, AK 99510

INDUSTRIAL AND BUSINESS DIRECTORIES

Alaska Directory of Commercial Establishments, Manufacturers' News, Inc., 4 E. Huron Street, Chicago, IL 60611; State Industrial Directories Corp., 2 Penn Plaza, New York, NY 10001
Alaska Petroleum and Industrial Directory, 409 W. Northern Lights Boulevard, Anchorage, AK 99603

Arizona

STATE CAPITOL, PHOENIX, AZ 85007
(602) 255–4900

INFORMATION OFFICES

Commerce/Economic Development
Office of Economic Planning and Development
1700 W. Washington Avenue
Phoenix, AZ 85007
Corporate
Arizona Corporation Commission

1210 W. Washington Avenue
P.O. Box 6019
Phoenix, AZ 85007
Taxation
Department of Revenue
State Capitol
Phoenix, AZ 85007
State Chamber of Commerce
Arizona State Chamber of Commerce
3216 N. Third Street
Phoenix, AZ 85012
Banking
Banking Department
1601 W. Jefferson
Phoenix, AZ 85007
Insurance
Insurance Department
1601 W. Jefferson
Phoenix, AZ 85007
Securities
Arizona Corporation Commission
1200 W. Washington
Phoenix, AZ 85007
International Commerce
Office of Economic Planning and Development
1700 W. Washington
Phoenix, AZ 85007
Labor and Industrial Relations
Industrial Commission
1601 W. Jefferson
Phoenix, AZ 85007

INDUSTRIAL AND BUSINESS DIRECTORIES

Arizona Directory of Industries, Manufacturers' News, 3 E. Huron Street, Chicago, IL 60611
Arizona Directory of Manufacturers, Manufacturers' News, Inc., 3 E. Huron Street, Chicago, IL 60611; State Industrial Directories Corp., 2 Penn Plaza, New York, NY 10001
Arizona USA International Trade Directory, Arizona State Department of Economic Planning and Development, 1700 W. Washington Avenue, Phoenix, AZ 85007
Directory of Arizona Manufacturers, Phoenix Chamber of Commerce, Phoenix, AZ 85001

Arkansas

STATE CAPITOL, LITTLE ROCK, AR 72201
(501) 371–1010

INFORMATION OFFICES

Commerce/Economic Development
Industrial Development Commission
One State Capitol Mall
Little Rock, AR 72201

Corporate
Secretary of State
Corporation Department
State Capitol
Little Rock, AR 72201
Taxation
Division of Revenue Services
Department of Finance and Administration
7th and Wolfe Streets
Little Rock, AR 72201
State Chamber of Commerce
Arkansas State Chamber of Commerce
911 Wallace Building
Little Rock, AR 72201
International Commerce
Industrial Development Commission
International Marketing Division
One State Capitol Mall
Little Rock, AR 72201
Banking
Banking Department
One State Capitol Mall
Little Rock, AR 72201
Securities
Securities Department
One State Capitol Mall
Little Rock, AR 72201
Labor and Industrial Relations
Arkansas Department of Labor
1022 High Street
Little Rock, AR 72201
Insurance
Insurance Division
University Towers Building
Little Rock, AR 72204

INDUSTRIAL AND BUSINESS DIRECTORIES

Arkansas Directory of Industries, Manufacturers' News, 3 E. Huron Street, Chicago, IL 60611
Directory of Arkansas Manufacturers, Arkansas Industrial Development Foundation, P.O. Box 1784, Little Rock, AR 72203; State Industrial Directories Corp., 2 Penn Plaza, New York, NY 10001
State and County Economic Data (annual), University of Arkansas Industrial Research Center, University of Arkansas, Little Rock College of Business Administration, 33rd and University Avenue, Little Rock, AR 72204

California

STATE CAPITOL, SACRAMENTO, CA 95814
(916) 332–9900

INFORMATION OFFICES

Commerce/Economic Development
Economic and Business Development
1030 13th Street
Sacramento, CA 95814
Corporate
Secretary of State
1230 "J" Street
Sacramento, CA 95814
Taxation
Franchise Tax Board
Aerojet Center
Sacramento, CA 95857
Board of Equalization
1020 N Street
Sacramento, CA 95814
State Chamber of Commerce
California Chamber of Commerce
1027 10th Street
P.O. Box 1736
Sacramento, CA 95808
International Commerce
California State World Trade Commission
1121 L Street
Sacramento, CA 95814
Banking
State Banking Department
235 Montgomery Street
San Francisco, CA 94104-2980
Securities
Department of Corporations
1025 P Street
Sacramento, CA 95814
Labor and Industrial Relations
Department of Industrial Relations
1121 L Street
Sacramento, CA 95814
Insurance
Department of Insurance
100 Van Ness Avenue
San Francisco, CA 94102

INDUSTRIAL AND BUSINESS DIRECTORIES

California Handbook, Center for California Public Affairs, 226 W. Foothill Boulevard, Claremont, CA 91711
California International Business Directory, Center for International Business, 333 S. Flower Street, Los Angeles, CA 90071
California Manufacturers Register, Time-Mirror Press, 1115 S. Boyle Avenue, Los Angeles, CA 90023; Manufacturers' News, Inc., 4 E. Huron Street, Chicago, IL 60611; State Industrial Directories Corp., 2 Penn Plaza, New York, NY 10001
Los Angeles Area Chamber of Commerce Southern California Business Directory and Buyers Guide, Los Angeles Chamber of Commerce, 404 S. Bixel Street, Los Angeles, CA 95113

San Francisco Manufacturers Directory, San Francisco Chamber of Commerce, 333 Pine Street, San Francisco, CA 94577

Colorado

STATE CAPITOL, DENVER, CO 80203
(303) 866–5000

INFORMATION OFFICES

Commerce/Economic Development
Division of Commerce and Development
Department of Local Affairs
Centennial Building
1313 Sherman Street
Denver, CO 80203
Corporate
Secretary of State
Corporation Division
1575 Sherman Street
Denver, CO 80203
Taxation
Administrative Division
Department of Revenue
1375 Sherman Street
Denver, CO 80203
State Chamber of Commerce
Colorado Association of Commerce and Industry
1390 Logan Street
Denver, CO 80203
International Commerce
Foreign Trade Office
Division of Commerce & Development
1313 Sherman Street
Denver, CO 80203
Banking
Division of Banking
303 W. Colfax Street
Denver, CO 80203
Securities
Division of Securities
1525 Sherman Street
Denver, CO 80203
Labor and Industrial Relations
Division of Labor
1313 Sherman Street
Denver, CO 80203
Insurance
Division of Insurance
303 W. Colfax Street
Denver, CO 80203
Uniform Industrial Code
Commercial Recordings Division
1575 Sherman Street
Denver, CO 80203
Business Ombudsman
Business Information Center
1525 Sherman Street
Denver, CO 80203

INDUSTRIAL AND BUSINESS DIRECTORIES

Directory of Colorado Manufacturers, Business Research Division, Graduate School of Business Administration, Campus Box 420, University of Colorado, Boulder, CO 80309

Connecticut

STATE CAPITOL, HARTFORD, CT 06106
(203) 566-4840

INFORMATION OFFICES

Commerce/Economic Development
Department of Economic Development
210 Washington Street
Hartford, CT 06106
Corporate
Secretary of State
Corporate Division
30 Trinity Street
Hartford, CT 06115
Taxation
Department of Revenue Services
92 Farmington Avenue
Hartford, CT 06115
State Chamber of Commerce
Connecticut Business and Industry Association
60 Washington Street
Hartford, CT 06106
International Commerce
Department of Economic Development
210 Washington Street
Hartford, CT 06106
Banking
Department of Banking
State Office Building
Hartford, CT 06106
Securities
State Treasurer
20 Trinity Street
Hartford, CT 06106
Labor and Industrial Relations
Department of Labor
200 Folly Brook Boulevard
Wethersfield, CT 06109
Insurance
Department of Insurance
State Office Building
Hartford, CT 06106
Uniform Industrial Code
Department of Economic Development
210 Washington Street
Hartford, CT 06106
Business Ombudsman
Department of Economic Development
210 Washington Street
Hartford, CT 06106

INDUSTRIAL AND BUSINESS DIRECTORIES

Classified Business Directory—State of Connecticut, Connecticut Directory Co., Inc., 322 Main Street, Stamford, CT 06901
Connecticut Classified Business Directory, Connecticut Directory Co., Inc., 322 Main Street, Stamford, CT 06901
Connecticut State Industrial Directory, Manufacturers' News, 3 E. Huron Street, Chicago, IL 60611; State Industrial Directories Corp., 2 Penn Plaza, New York, NY 10001
Directory of Connecticut Manufacturing Establishments, Connecticut Department of Labor, 200 Folly Brook Boulevard, Wethersfield, CT 06109

Delaware

LEGISLATIVE HALL, DOVER, DE 19901
(302) 736-4101

INFORMATION OFFICES

Commerce/Economic Development
Delaware Development Office
99 Kings Highway
P.O. Box 1401
Dover, DE 19903
Corporate
Secretary of State
Corporations Department
P.O. Box 898
Dover, DE 19903
Taxation
Department of Finance
Division of Revenue
Carvel State Office Building
820 N. French Street
Wilmington, DE 19801
State Chamber of Commerce
Delaware State Chamber of Commerce, Inc.
One Commerce Center
Wilmington, DE 19801
Banking
State Bank Commission
15 The Green
Dover, DE 19901
Labor and Industrial Relations
Division of Industrial Affairs
Department of Labor
Carvel State Office Building
820 N. French Street
Wilmington, DE 19801
Insurance
State Insurance Commission
21 The Green
Dover, DE 19901

INDUSTRIAL AND BUSINESS DIRECTORIES

Delaware Directory of Commerce and Industry, Delaware State Chamber of Commerce, One Commerce Center, Wilmington, DE 19801
Delaware State Industrial Directory, State Industrial Directories Corp., 2 Penn Plaza, New York, NY 10001

Florida

STATE CAPITOL, TALLAHASSEE, FL 32301
(904) 488-1234

INFORMATION OFFICES

Commerce/Economic Development
  Department of Commerce
  Collins Building
  Tallahassee, FL 32301
  Division of Economic Development
  Department of Commerce
  Collins Building
  Tallahassee, FL 32301
Corporate
  Secretary of State
  Division of Corporations
  Capitol Building
  Tallahassee, FL 32304
Taxation
  Department of Revenue
  Carlton Building
  Tallahassee, FL 32301
State Chamber of Commerce
  Florida State Chamber of Commerce
  P.O. Box 11309
  Tallahassee, FL 32302
International Commerce
  Florida Department of Commerce
  Bureau of International Trade
  Collins Building
  Tallahassee, FL 32301
Banking
  Florida Department of Banking & Finance
  The Capitol
  Tallahassee, FL 32301
Securities
  Florida Department of Banking & Finance
  Division of Securities
  1402 Capitol
  Tallahassee, FL 32301
Labor and Industrial Relations
  Florida Department of Labor and Employment Security
  Berkeley Building
  2590 Executive Center Circle, East
  Tallahassee, FL 32301
Insurance
  Florida Department of Insurance
  The Capitol

Tallahassee, FL 32301
Uniform Industrial Code
  Florida Department of State
  Bureau of Uniform Commercial Code
  P.O. Box 5588
  Tallahassee, FL 32314
Business Ombudsman
  Florida Department of Commerce
  Bureau of Business and Community Development
  Collins Building
  Tallahassee, FL 32301

INDUSTRIAL AND BUSINESS DIRECTORIES

Directory of Florida Industries, Manufacturers' News, Inc., 4 E. Huron Street, Chicago, IL 60611; Florida State Chamber of Commerce, P.O. Box 11309, Tallahassee, FL 32302; State Industrial Directories Corp., 2 Penn Plaza, New York, NY 10001
Florida Industries Guide, McHenry Publishing Co., Inc., Box 935, Orlando, FL 32802

Georgia

STATE CAPITOL, ATLANTA, GA 30334
(404) 656-2000

INFORMATION OFFICES

Commerce/Economic Development
  Department of Industry and Trade
  230 Peachtree Street NE
  Atlanta, GA 30303
Corporate
  Corporations Division
  Secretary of State
  2 Martin Luther King Jr. Drive, SE
  Atlanta, GA 30334
Taxation
  Department of Revenue
  270 Washington Street, SW
  Atlanta, GA 30334
State Chamber of Commerce
  Business Council of Georgia
  575 N. Omni Boulevard
  Atlanta, GA 30335
International Commerce
  Department of Industry and Trade
  230 Peachtree Street, NE
  Atlanta, GA 30303
Banking
  Department of Banking and Finance
  2990 Brandywine Road
  Atlanta, GA 30341
Securities
  Securities Division
  Secretary of State

2 Martin Luther King Jr. Drive, SE
Atlanta, GA 30334
Labor and Industrial Relations
Department of Labor
254 Washington Street, SW
Atlanta, GA 30334
Insurance
Comptroller General's Office
Floyd Building
Atlanta, GA 30334

INDUSTRIAL AND BUSINESS DIRECTORIES

Directory of Associations in Georgia, 1974–1975, Basic Data Research, Industrial Development Division, Engineering Experiment Station, Atlanta, GA 30332

Georgia Manufacturing Directory, Department of Industry and Trade, 230 Peachtree Street, NE, Atlanta, GA 30303

Georgia World Trade Directory, Business Council of Georgia, 575 N. Omni International, Atlanta, GA 30335

Industrial Sites in Georgia, Georgia Power Company, Box 4545DJ, Atlanta, GA 30302

Georgia Industrial Survey (in French, German and Japanese), Department of Industry and Trade, 575 N. Omni International, Atlanta, GA 30335

Georgia International Trade Directory, Department of Industry and Trade, 230 Peachtree Street NE, Atlanta, GA 30303

Georgia Directory of International Services, Department of Industry and Trade, 230 Peachtree Street NE, Atlanta, GA 30303

International Companies with Facilities in Georgia. Department of Industry and Trade, 230 Peachtree Street, NE, Atlanta, GA 30303

Industrial Survey of Georgia, Business Council of Georgia, 575 N. Omni International, Atlanta, GA 30335

Hawaii

STATE CAPITOL, HONOLULU, HI 96813
(808) 548–2211

INFORMATION OFFICES

Commerce/Economic Development
Department of Planning and Economic Development
250 S. King Street
Honolulu, HI 96813

Department of Commerce and Consumer Affairs
250 S. King Street
Honolulu, HI 96813

Corporate
Department of Commerce and Consumer Affairs
Business Registration
P.O. Box 40
Honolulu, HI 96810
Taxation
Department of Taxation
425 Queen Street
Honolulu, HI 96813
State Chamber of Commerce
Chamber of Commerce of Hawaii
735 Bishop Street
Dillingham Building
Honolulu, HI 96813
International Commerce
Hawaii International Services Agency, State Department of Planning and Economic Development
P.O. Box 2359
Honolulu, HI 96804

Hawaii Foreign-Trade Zone No. 9, Pier 2
Honolulu, HI 96813
Banking
Bank Examination Division
State Department of Commerce and Consumer Affairs
1010 Richards Street
Honolulu, HI 96813
Securities
Bank Examination Division
State Department of Commerce and Consumer Affairs
1010 Richards Street
Honolulu, HI 96813
Labor and Industrial Relations
State Department of Labor and Industrial Relations
P.O. Box 3680
Honolulu, HI 96811
Insurance
Insurance Division
State Department of Commerce and Consumer Affairs
1010 Richards Street
Honolulu, HI 96813
Business Ombudsman
Office of the Ombudsman
465 S. King Street
Honolulu, HI 96813

INDUSTRIAL AND BUSINESS DIRECTORIES

Directory of Manufacturers, State of Hawaii, Chamber of Commerce of Hawaii, Dillingham Building, 735 Bishop Street, Honolulu, HI 96813

Hawaii Business Directory, Hawaii Business Directory, Inc., 1164 Bishop Street, Honolulu, HI 96813

Hawaii Directory of Manufacturers, Manufacturers' News, Inc., 4 E. Huron Street, Chicago, IL 60611; State Industrial Directories Corp., 2 Penn Plaza, New York, NY 10001

Idaho

STATE CAPITOL, BOISE, ID 83720
(208) 334-2470

INFORMATION OFFICES

Commerce/Economic Development
Division of Economic and Community Affairs
Capitol Building
Boise, ID 83720
Corporate
Secretary of State
State Capitol
Boise, ID 83720
Taxation
Department of Revenue and Taxation
Capitol Building
Boise, ID 83720
State Chamber of Commerce
Idaho Association of Commerce and Industry
805 Idaho Street
Boise, ID 83720
International Commerce
U.S. and Foreign Commercial Service
International Trade Administration
Statehouse
Boise, ID 83720
Banking
Department of Finance
700 W. State Street
Boise, ID 83720
Securities
Department of Finance
700 W. State Street
Boise, ID 83720
Labor and Industrial Relations
Department of Labor and Industrial Services
317 Main Street
Boise, ID 83720
Insurance
Department of Insurance
700 W. State Street
Boise, ID 83720
Uniform Industrial Code
Department of Labor and Industrial Services
317 Main Street
Boise, ID 83720
Business Ombudsman
Division of Economic and Community Affairs
Statehouse
Boise, ID 83720

INDUSTRIAL AND BUSINESS DIRECTORIES

Manufacturing Directory of Idaho, Center for Business and Research, University of Idaho, Moscow, ID 83843

Idaho Opportunities, Division of Economic and Community Affairs, Capitol Building, Boise, ID 83720

Illinois

STATE HOUSE, SPRINGFIELD, IL 62706
(217) 782-2000

INFORMATION OFFICES

Commerce/Economic Development
Department of Commerce and Community Affairs
222 S. College Street
Springfield, IL 62706
Corporate
Corporate Division
Centennial Building
Springfield, IL 62756
Taxation
Department of Revenue
1515 S. 9th Street
Springfield, IL 62708
State Chamber of Commerce
Illinois State Chamber of Commerce
20 N. Wacker Drive
Chicago, IL 60606
International Commerce
Department of Commerce & Community Affairs
620 E. Adams Street
Springfield, IL 62701
Banking
Department of Financial Institutions
160 N. LaSalle Street
Chicago, IL 60601
Securities
Secretary of State
840 S. Spring Street
Springfield, IL 62704
Labor and Industrial Relations
Department of Labor
100 N. 1st, Alzina Building
Springfield, IL 62706
Department of Commerce & Community Affairs
620 E. Adams Street
Springfield, IL 62701
Insurance
Department of Insurance
320 W. Washington Street
Springfield, IL 62767
Uniform Industrial Code
Department of Commerce & Community Affairs
620 E. Adams Street
Springfield, IL 62701
Business Ombudsman
Department of Commerce & Community Affairs

620 E. Adams Street
Springfield, IL 62701

INDUSTRIAL AND BUSINESS DIRECTORIES

Chicago Buyers' Guide, Chicago Association of Commerce and Industry, 130 S. Michigan Avenue, Chicago, IL 60603

Chicago Cook County and Illinois Industrial Directory, National Publishing Corp., 3150 Des Plaines Avenue, Des Plaines, IL 60018

Chicago Geographic Edition, Manufacturers' News, Inc., 4 E. Huron Street, Chicago, IL 60611; State Industrial Directories Corp., 2 Penn Plaza, New York, NY 10001

Illinois Industrial Directory, Illinois Industrial Directories National Publishing Corp., 3150 Des Plaines Avenue, Des Plaines, IL 60018

Illinois Manufacturers Directory, Manufacturers' News, Inc., 3 E. Huron Street, Chicago, IL 60611; State Industrial Directories Corp., 2 Penn Plaza, New York, NY 10001

Illinois Services Directory, Manufacturers' News, Inc., 3 E. Huron Street, Chicago, IL 60611

International Buyers' Directory to Illinois Products, Department of Business and Economic Development, 222 S. College Street, Springfield, IL 62706

Illinois Financial Sources Directory, Department of Commerce and Community Affairs, 222 S. College Street, Springfield, IL 62706

Indiana

STATE HOUSE, INDIANAPOLIS, IN 46204
State Information Center
(317) 232-3140

INFORMATION OFFICES

Commerce/Economic Development
Department of Commerce
1 N. Capitol Avenue
Indianapolis, IN 46204
Corporate
Secretary of State
Corporation Division
State House
Indianapolis, IN 46204
Taxation
Department of Revenue
State Office Building
Indianapolis, IN 46204
State Board of Tax Commissioners
201 State Office Building
Indianapolis, IN 46204
State Chamber of Commerce
Indiana State Chamber of Commerce, Inc.

1 N. Capitol Avenue, Ste 200
Indianapolis, IN 46204
International Commerce
International Trade Division
Indiana Department of Commerce
1 N. Capitol Avenue
Indianapolis, IN 46204-2243
Banking
Indiana Bankers Association
1 N. Capitol Avenue
Indianapolis, IN 46204-2243
Securities
Secretary of State
Securities Commission
1 N. Capitol Avenue
Indianapolis, IN 46204-2243
Labor and Industrial Relations
Indiana Industrial Board
State Office Building
100 N. Senate Avenue
Indianapolis, IN 46204
Insurance
Indiana Department of Insurance
State Office Building
100 N. Senate Avenue
Indianapolis, IN 46204
Uniform Industrial Code
Uniform Commercial Code Division
Secretary of State Office
State House
Indianapolis, IN 46204
Business Ombudsman
Office of Regulatory Ombudsman
Indiana Department of Commerce
1 North Capitol Avenue
Indianapolis, IN 46204-2243

INDUSTRIAL AND BUSINESS DIRECTORIES

Indiana Industrial Directory, Harris Publishing Co., 2057-2 Aurora Rd., Twinsburg, OH 44087 Indiana State Chamber of Commerce, 1 N. Capitol Avenue, Ste 200, Indianapolis, IN 46204

Iowa

STATE CAPITOL, DES MOINES, IA 50319
(515) 281-5011

INFORMATION OFFICES

Commerce/Economic Development
Development Commission
Capitol Center Building
600 E. Court Avenue
Des Moines, IA 50309
Corporate
Secretary of State
Corporation Division

Hoover Building
Des Moines, IA 50319
Taxation
Department of Revenue
Hoover Building
Des Moines, IA 50319
International Commerce
Iowa Development Commission
600 E. Court Avenue
Des Moines, IA 50309
Banking
Iowa Banking Department
Liberty Building
Des Moines, IA 50309
Securities
Securities Division
Insurance Department of Iowa
Lucas Building
Des Moines, IA 50317
Insurance
Insurance Department
Lucas Building
Des Moines, IA 50317

INDUSTRIAL AND BUSINESS DIRECTORIES

Directory of Iowa Manufacturers, Iowa Development Commission, 600 E. Court Avenue, Des Moines, IA 50309

Kansas

STATE HOUSE, TOPEKA, KS 66612
(913) 296–0111

INFORMATION OFFICES

Commerce/Economic Development
Department of Economic Development
503 Kansas Avenue
Topeka, KS 66603
Corporate
Secretary of State
State House
Corporation Department
Topeka, KS 66612
Taxation
Department of Revenue
State Office Building
Topeka, KS 66612
State Chamber of Commerce
Kansas Chamber of Commerce and Industry
500 First National Tower
1 Townsite Plaza
Topeka, KS 66603
International Commerce
Department of Economic Development
503 Kansas Avenue
Topeka, KS 66603

Banking
Banking Department
700 Jackson Street
Topeka, KS 66603
Securities
Securities Commissioner of Kansas
109 W. 9th Street
Topeka, KS 66612
Labor and Industrial Relations
Department of Human Resources
401 Topeka Boulevard
Topeka, KS 66603
Insurance
Insurance Department
420 SW 9th Street
Topeka, KS 66612
Business Ombudsman
Department of Economic Development
503 Kansas Avenue
Topeka, KS 66603

INDUSTRIAL AND BUSINESS DIRECTORIES

Directory of Kansas Manufacturers and Products, Kansas Department of Economic Development, 503 Kansas Avenue, Topeda, KS 66603; State Industrial Directories Corp., 2 Penn Plaza, New York, NY 10001
Directory of Manufacturers, Wichita, Kansas, Wichita Area Chamber of Commerce, 350 West Douglas, Wichita, KS 67202

Kentucky

STATE CAPITOL, FRANKFORT, KY 40601
(502) 564–3130

INFORMATION OFFICES

Commerce/Economic Development
Department of Economic Development
Capitol Plaza Office Tower
Frankfort, KY 40601
Corporate
Office of Secretary of State
Corporation Division
Capitol Building
Frankfort, KY 40601
Taxation
Revenue Cabinet
Capitol Annex
Frankfort, KY 40601
State Chamber of Commerce
Kentucky Chamber of Commerce
Versailles Road
Frankfort, KY 40601
International Commerce
Kentucky Commerce Cabinet
Office of International Marketing

Capital Plaza Tower
Frankfort, KY 40601
Banking
Kentucky Department of Banking and Securities
911 Leawood Drive
Frankfort, KY 40601
Securities
Kentucky Department of Banking and Securities
911 Leawood Drive
Frankfort, KY 40601
Labor Industrial Relations
Kentucky Labor Cabinet
The 127 Building
Frankfort, KY 40601
Insurance
Kentucky Department of Insurance
229 West Main Street
Frankfort, KY 40601
Uniform Industrial Code
Kentucky Department of Housing, Buildings, and Construction
U.S. 127 South
Frankfort, KY 40601
Business Ombudsman
Kentucky Department of Economic Development
Capital Plaza Tower
Frankfort, KY 40601

INDUSTRIAL AND BUSINESS DIRECTORIES

Exporters Directory, Kentucky Commerce Cabinet, Capitol Plaza Tower, Frankfort, KY 40601

Kentucky Directory of Manufacturers, Department of Economic Development, Capitol Plaza Tower, Frankfort, KY 40601; and from Manufacturers' News, 4 E. Huron Street, Chicago, IL 60611; State Industrial Directories Corp., 2 Penn Plaza, New York, NY 10001; Harris Publishing Co., 20572 Aurora Road, Twinsburg, OH 44087

Louisiana

STATE CAPITOL, BATON ROUGE, LA 70804
(504) 342-6600

INFORMATION OFFICES

Commerce/Economic Development
Department of Commerce
P.O. Box 44185
Baton Rouge, LA 70804
Corporate
Secretary of State
Division of Corporation

P.O. Box 44125
Baton Rouge, LA 70804
Taxation
Department of Revenue
P.O. Box 201
Baton Rouge, LA 70821
State Chamber of Commerce
Louisiana Association of Business and Industry
P.O. Box 3988
Baton Rouge, LA 70821
International Commerce
International Division
Office of Commerce and Industry
324 International Trade Mart
#2 Canal Street
New Orleans, LA 70130
Securities
Louisiana Securities Commission
315 Louisiana State Office Building
New Orleans, LA 70112
Insurance
Office of Insurance Rating Commission
P.O. Box 44157
Baton Rouge, LA 70804
Business Ombudsman
Department of Commerce
P.O. Box 44185
Baton Rouge, LA 70804

INDUSTRIAL AND BUSINESS DIRECTORIES

Louisiana Directory of Manufacturers, Department of Commerce, State Land and Natural Resources Building, Baton Rouge, LA 70804; and from Manufacturers' News, Inc., 4 E. Huron Street, Chicago, IL 60611; State Industrial Directories Corp., 2 Penn Plaza, New York, NY 10001

Louisiana International Trade Directory, International House, New Orleans, LA 70150

Maine

STATE HOUSE, AUGUSTA, ME 04333
(207) 289-1110

INFORMATION OFFICES

Commerce/Economic Development
State Development Office
State House Station
Augusta, ME 04333
Corporate
Department of State
Division of Corporations
State House Station #101
Augusta, ME 04333
Private Development Associations
Maine Development Foundation

1 Memorial Circle
Augusta, ME 04330
Taxation
Bureau of Taxation
Department of Finance and Administration
State House Station #24
Augusta, ME 04333
State Chamber of Commerce
Maine State Chamber of Commerce and Industry
126 Sewall Street
Augusta, ME 04330
International Commerce
State Development Office
State House Station #59
Augusta, ME 04333
Banking
Bureau of Banking
State House Station #36
Augusta, ME 04333
Securities
Bureau of Banking
Securities Division
State House Station #36
Augusta, ME 04333
Labor and Industrial Relations
Department of Labor
Bureau of Labor Standards
State House Station #45
Augusta, ME 04333
Insurance
Bureau of Insurance
State House Station #34
Augusta, ME 04333
Business Ombudsman
State Development Office
State House Station #59
Augusta, ME 04333

INDUSTRIAL AND BUSINESS DIRECTORIES

Maine Marketing Directory, State Development Office, State House Station #59, Augusta, ME 04333
Maine Register, Tower Publishing Company, Portland, ME 04101

Maryland

STATE HOUSE, ANNAPOLIS, MD 21404
(301) 269–3901

INFORMATION OFFICES

Commerce/Economic Development
Department of Economic and Community Development
45 Calvert Street
Annapolis, MD 21401

Corporate
State Department of Assessments and Taxation
301 W. Preston Street
Baltimore, MD 21201
Taxation
Comptroller of the Treasury
Louis L. Goldstein Treasury Building
P.O. Box 466
Annapolis, MD 21404
State Chamber of Commerce
Maryland State Chamber of Commerce
60 West Street
Annapolis, MD 21401
International Commerce
Department of Economic and Community Development
45 Calvert Street
Annapolis, MD 21401

Maryland Port Administrator
Office of the Port Administrator
World Trade Center
Baltimore, MD 21202
Banking
State Banking Commission
1301 Baustein Building
1 N. Charles Street
Baltimore, MD 21201
Securities
Division of Securities
7 N. Calvert Street
Baltimore, MD 21201
Labor and Industrial Relations
Division of Labor and Industry
501 St. Paul Place
Baltimore, MD 21202
Insurance
State Insurance Division
501 St. Paul Place
Baltimore, MD 21202
Business Ombudsman
Department of Economic and Community Development
45 Calvert Street
Annapolis, MD 21401

INDUSTRIAL AND BUSINESS DIRECTORIES

Directory of Maryland Manufacturers, Maryland Department of Economic and Community Development, 45 Calvert Street, Annapolis, MD 21401
Maryland State Industrial Directory, State Industrial Directories Corp., 2 Penn Plaza, New York, NY 10001

Massachusetts

STATE HOUSE, BOSTON, MA 02133
(617) 727–2121

INFORMATION OFFICES

Commerce/Economic Development
Governor's Office of Economic Development
Room 109
State House
Boston, MA 02133
Executive Office of Economic Affairs
2101 McCormack Building
Boston, MA 02108
Department of Commerce and Development
Leverett Saltonstall Building
100 Cambridge Street
Boston, MA 02202

Corporate
Secretary of State
1 Ashburton Place
Boston, MA 02108

Taxation
Department of Revenue
Leverett Saltonstall Building
100 Cambridge Street
Boston, MA 02202

International Commerce
Office of International Trade and Investment
1 Ashburton Place
Boston, MA 02108

Banking
Division of Banks and Loan Agencies
100 Cambridge Street
Boston, MA 02202

Securities
Secretary of State, Securities
1 Ashburton Place
Boston, MA 02108

Labor and Industrial Relations
Executive Office of Labor
1 Ashburton Place
Boston, MA 02108

Insurance
Division of Insurance
100 Cambridge Street
Boston, MA 02202

INDUSTRIAL AND BUSINESS DIRECTORIES

Directory of Directors in the City of Boston and Vicinity, Bankers Service Co., 14 Beacon Street, Boston, MA 02108

Directory of Massachusetts Manufacturers, George D. Hall Company, 20 Kilby Street, Boston, MA 02109

Massachusetts Directory of Manufacturers, Manufacturers' News, Inc., 4 E. Huron Street, Chicago, IL 60611

Massachusetts State Industrial Directory, State Industrial Directories Corp., 2 Penn Plaza, New York, NY 10001

Michigan

STATE CAPITOL, LANSING, MI 48913
(517) 373-1837

INFORMATION OFFICES

Commerce/Economic Development
Department of Commerce
525 W. Ottawa Street
P.O. Box 30225
Lansing, MI 48909

Corporate
Corporation and Securities Bureau
6546 Mercantile Way
P.O. Box 30054
Lansing, MI 48909

Taxation
Bureau of Collection
Department of Treasury
Treasury Building
Lansing, MI 48922

State Chamber of Commerce
Michigan State Chamber of Commerce
200 N. Washington Square
Lansing, MI 48922

International Commerce
Office of International Development
Department of Commerce
P.O. Box 30105
Lansing, MI 48909

Banking
Financial Institutions Bureau
Department of Commerce
Law Building
P.O. Box 30224
Lansing, MI 48909

Securities
Corporation and Securities Bureau
Department of Commerce
6546 Mercantile Way
Lansing, MI 48909

Labor and Industrial Relations
Bureau of Labor Relations
Department of Labor
State of Michigan Plaza Building
1200 Sixth Street
Detroit, MI 48226

Department of Labor
Lansing Plaza
309 North Washington
P.O. Box 30015
Lansing, MI 48909

Insurance
Insurance Bureau
Department of Licensing and Regulation
611 West Ottawa
North Ottawa Tower
P.O. Box 30220
Lansing, MI 48909

INDUSTRIAL AND BUSINESS DIRECTORIES

Directory of Michigan Manufacturers, Manufacturers' News, Inc., 4 E. Huron Street, Chicago, IL 60611; Manufacturers Publishing Co., 8543 Puritan Avenue, Detroit, MI 48238

Harris Michigan Marketers Industrial Directory, Harris Publishing Company, 33140 Aurora Road, Cleveland, OH 44139

Michigan State Industrial Directory, State Industrial Directories Corp., 2 Penn Plaza, New York, NY 10001

MacRae's Michigan State Industrial Directory, MacRae Publishing, 817 Broadway, New York, NY 10003

Economic Development Corporations Directory for the State of Michigan, Department of Commerce, Office of Business and Community Development, Lansing, MI 48909

Minnesota

STATE CAPITOL, ST. PAUL, MN 55155
(612) 296–6013

INFORMATION OFFICES

Commerce/Economic Development
Department of Energy and Economic Development
900 American Center Building
St. Paul, MN 55101
Corporate
Corporation Division
180 State Office Building
St. Paul, MN 55155
Taxation
Department of Revenue
Centennial Office Building
St. Paul, MN 55145
State Chamber of Commerce
Minnesota Association of Commerce and Industry
Hanover Building
480 Cedar Street
St. Paul, MN 55101
International Commerce
Minnesota Trade Office
90 W. Plato Boulevard
St. Paul, MN 55107
Banking
Minnesota Department of Banking
Metro Square Building
7th & Robert Streets
St. Paul, MN 55101
Securities
Minnesota Department of Securities
Metro Square Building
7th & Robert Streets
St. Paul, MN 55101

Labor and Industrial Relations
Minnesota Department of Labor and Industry
444 Lafayette Road
St. Paul, MN 55101
Insurance
Minnesota Department of Insurance
Metro Square Building
7th & Robert Streets
St. Paul, MN 55101
Business Ombudsman
Department of Energy and Economic Development
900 American Center Building
St. Paul, MN 55101

INDUSTRIAL AND BUSINESS DIRECTORIES

Minnesota Directory of Manufacturers, Manufacturers' News, Inc., 4 E. Huron Street, Chicago, IL 60611; State Industrial Directories Corp., 2 Penn Plaza, New York, NY 10001

Mississippi

NEW CAPITOL, JACKSON, MS 39205
(601) 948–7321

INFORMATION OFFICES

Commerce/Economic Development
Mississippi Department of Economic Development
P.O. Box 849
Jackson, MS 39205
Department of Agriculture and Commerce
1604 Sillers Building
Jackson, MS 39205
Corporate
Secretary of State
Corporation Division
P.O. Box 136
Jackson, MS 39205
Taxation
Tax Commission
102 Woolfolk Building
Jackson, MS 39201
State Chamber of Commerce
P.O. Box 1849
Depositors Savings Building
Jackson, MS 39205
Banking
Department of Banking and Consumer Finance
Woolfolk State Office Building
Jackson, MS 39205
Securities
Department of State
Securities Division

P.O. Box 136
Jackson, MS 39205
Labor and Industrial Relations
1520 W. Capitol Street
Jackson, MS 39205
Insurance
Department of Insurance
Sillers Building
Jackson, MS 39205

INDUSTRIAL AND BUSINESS DIRECTORIES

Mississippi International Trade Directory, Mississippi Marketing Council, Box 849, Sillers State Office Building, Jackson, MS 39205

Mississippi Manufacturers' Directory, Manufacturers' News, Inc., 4 E. Huron Street, Chicago, IL 60611; Public Information Office, Mississippi Research and Development Center, Jackson, MS 39205; State Industrial Directories Corp., 2 Penn Plaza, New York, NY 10001

Missouri

STATE CAPITOL, JEFFERSON CITY, MO 65101
(314) 751-2151

INFORMATION OFFICES

Commerce/Economic Development
Department of Consumer Affairs, Regulation and Licensing
Truman State Office Building
P.O. Box 118
Jefferson City, MO 65102
Corporate
Secretary of State
Corporations Division
P.O. Box 778
Jefferson City, MO 65102
Taxation
Department of Revenue
Division of Taxation
Truman State Office Building
P.O. Box 629
Jefferson City, MO 65105
State Chamber of Commerce
Missouri Chamber of Commerce
428 East Capitol Avenue
P.O. Box 149
Jefferson City, MO 65102
International Commerce
International Business Development
Missouri Division of Community & Economic Development
Truman State Office Building
Jefferson City, MO 65102
Banking
Missouri Division of Finance

Truman State Office Building
Jefferson City, MO 65102
Securities
Office of the Secretary of State
Securities Division
Truman State Office Building
Jefferson City, MO 65102
Labor and Industrial Relations
Missouri Dept. of Labor & Industrial Relations
421 E. Dunklin
Jefferson City, MO 65102
Insurance
Missouri Division of Insurance
Truman State Office Building
Jefferson City, MO 65102
Uniform Industrial Code
Missouri Division of Labor Standards
P.O. Box 449
Jefferson City, MO 65102
Business Ombudsman
Office of the Lieutenant Governor
Missouri State Capitol
Jefferson City, MO 65102

INDUSTRIAL AND BUSINESS DIRECTORY

Contacts Influential: Commerce and Industrial Directory (for Kansas City Area), Contacts Influential, Inc., 6347 Brookside Boulevard, Suite 204, Kansas City, MO 64113

Missouri Directory of Manufacturing and Mining (annual), Informative Data Co., 3546 Watson Road, St. Louis, MO 63139

Montana

STATE CAPITOL, HELENA, MT 59620
(406) 449-3111

INFORMATION OFFICES

Commerce/Economic Development
Department of Commerce
Capitol Station
Helena, MT 59620
Economic Development and Research
Department of Commerce
1429 9th Avenue
Helena, MT 59620
Corporate
Secretary of State
Corporation Bureau
State Capitol Building
Helena, MT 59620
State Chamber of Commerce
Montana Chamber of Commerce
P.O. Box 1730
Helena, MT 59601

International Commerce
  International Export Officer
  Montana Department of Commerce
  1424 9th Avenue
  Helena, MT 59620
Banking
  Commissioner of Financial Institutions
  Montana Department of Commerce
  1424 9th Avenue
  Helena, MT 59620
Securities
  Securities Division
  State Auditor's Office
  Sam Mitchell Building
  Helena, MT 59620
Labor & Industrial Relations
  Commissioner's Office
  Montana Department of Labor & Industry
  Lockey and Roberts
  Helena, MT 59620
Insurance
  Insurance Division
  State Auditor's Office
  Sam Mitchell Building
  Helena, MT 59620
Uniform Commercial Code
  Secretary of State
  Uniform Commercial Code Bureau
  State Capitol Building
  Capitol Station
  Helena, MT 59620
Business Ombudsman
  Small Business Advocate
  Montana Department of Commerce
  1424 9th Avenue
  Helena, MT 59620

INDUSTRIAL AND BUSINESS DIRECTORIES

Montana Manufacturers and Products Directory, Department of Commerce, 1424 9th Avenue, Helena, MT 59620

Nebraska

STATE CAPITOL, LINCOLN, NE 68509
(402) 471–3111

INFORMATION OFFICES

Commerce/Economic Development
  Department of Economic Development
  301 Centennial Mall South
  P.O. Box 94666
  Lincoln, NE 68509
Corporate
  Secretary of State
  Corporation Division
  State Capitol
  Lincoln, NE 68509

Taxation
  Department of Revenue
  P.O. Box 94818
  Lincoln, NE 68509
State Chamber of Commerce
  Nebraska Association of Commerce and Industry
  P.O. Box 81556
  Lincoln, NE 68501
International Commerce
  Nebraska Department of Economic Development
  International Division
  Nebraska State Office Building
  Lincoln, NE 68509
Banking
  Department of Banking and Finance
  Nebraska State Office Building
  Lincoln, NE 68509
Securities
  Department of Banking and Finance
  Bureau of Securities
  Nebraska State Office Building
  Lincoln, NE 68509
Labor and Industrial Relations
  Nebraska Department of Labor
  550 South 16th Street
  Lincoln, NE 68509
Insurance
  Department of Insurance
  Nebraska State Office Building
  Lincoln, NE 68509
Uniform Industrial Code
  Uniform Commercial Code Division
  Nebraska State Office Building
  Lincoln, NE 68509
Business Ombudsman
  State Claims Board
  Office of Risk Management
  Nebraska State Office Building
  Lincoln, NE 68509

INDUSTRIAL AND BUSINESS DIRECTORIES

Directory of Nebraska Manufacturers and Their Products, Manufacturers' News, Inc., 4 E. Huron Street, Chicago, IL 60611
Directory of Nebraska Manufacturers and Their Products, Nebraska State Department of Economic Development, Lincoln, NE 68509
Manufacturers and Wholesalers Directory, Lincoln Chamber of Commerce, 200 Lincoln Building, Lincoln, NE 68508
Directory of Manufacturers for the Omaha Metropolitan Area, Omaha Economic Development Council, 1606 Douglas, Omaha, NE 68102.
Directory of Major Employers for the Omaha Area, Omaha Economic Development Council, 1606 Douglas, Omaha, NE 68102.

Nevada

LEGISLATIVE BUILDING, CARSON CITY, NV 89710
(702) 885–5627

INFORMATION OFFICES

Commerce/Economic Development
Department of Commerce
321 Nye Building
Carson City, NV 89710

Department of Economic Development
Capitol Complex
Carson City, NV 89710

Corporate
Secretary of State
Capitol Complex
Carson City, NV 89710

Taxation
Tax Commission
1340 S. Curry Street
Carson City, NV 89710

State Chamber of Commerce
Nevada Chamber of Commerce Association
P.O. Box 2806
Reno, NV 89505

International Commerce
Department of Commerce
Nye Building
Carson City, NV 89710

Banking
Banking Division
Department of Commerce
406 E. Second Street
Carson City, NV 89710

Securities
Office of Secretary of State
State Capitol Building
Carson City, NV 89710

Labor and Industrial Relations
Office of Labor Commissioner
Kinkead Building
505 E. King Street
Carson City, NV 89710

Department of Industrial Relations
1390 S. Curry Street
Carson City, NV 89710

Insurance
Insurance Division
201 S. Fall Street
Carson City, NV 89710

INDUSTRIAL AND BUSINESS DIRECTORIES

Nevada Industrial Directory, Department of Economic Development, Capitol Complex, Carson City, NV 89710
Nevada Directory of Business, Manufacturers'

News, Inc., 4 E. Huron Street, Chicago, IL 60611

New Hampshire

STATE HOUSE, CONCORD, NH 03301
(603) 271–1110

INFORMATION OFFICES

Commerce/Economic Development
Department of Resources and Economic Development
Division of Economic Development
105 Loudon Road, Building #2
Prescott Park
Concord, NH 03301

Corporate
Secretary of State
Corporations Division
State House Annex
Concord, NH 03301

Taxation
Board of Taxation
61 S. Spring Street
Concord, NH 03301

Department of Revenue Administration
61 S. Spring Street
Concord, NH 03301

State Chamber of Commerce
Business and Industry Association of New Hampshire
23 School Street
Concord, NH 03301

International Commerce
Department of Resources & Economic Development
Division of Economic Development
105 Loudon Road, Building #2
Prescott Park—Concord, NH 03301

Banking
Banking Department
State of New Hampshire
97 N. Main Street
Concord, NH 03301

New Hampshire Banking Association
125 N. Main Street
Concord, NH 03301

Securities
Insurance Department, Securities Division
State of New Hampshire
169 Manchester Street
Concord, NH 03301

Labor and Industrial Relations
Department of Employment Security
State of New Hampshire
32 S. Main Street
Concord, NH 03301

Department of Labor
State of New Hampshire

32 S. Main Street
Concord, NH 03301
Insurance
Insurance Department
State of New Hampshire
169 Manchester Street
Concord, NH 03301
Standard Industrial Code
Department of Employment Security
State of New Hampshire
32 S. Main Street
Concord, NH 03301

INDUSTRIAL AND BUSINESS DIRECTORIES

Made in New Hampshire, New Hampshire Office of Industrial Development, Department of Resources, Concord, NH 03301
New Hampshire Register, Tower Publishing Company, 163 Middle Street, Portland, ME 04111

New Jersey

STATE HOUSE, TRENTON, NJ 08625
(609) 292–2121

INFORMATION OFFICES

Commerce/Economic Development
Department of Commerce and Economic Development
1 W. State Street CN 820
Trenton, NJ 08625
Division of Travel and Tourism
CN 826
Trenton, NJ 08625
Economic Development Authority
Capitol Place
Trenton, NJ 08625
Corporate
Secretary of State
State House
CN 300
Trenton, NJ 08625
Taxation
Division of Taxation
West State and Willow Streets, CN 240
Trenton, NJ 08625
State Chamber of Commerce
New Jersey State Chamber of Commerce
240 W. State Street
Trenton, NJ 07102
International Commerce
Division of International Trade
744 Broad Street
Newark, NJ 07102
Banking
Department of Banking

36 W. State Street CN 040
Trenton, NJ 08625
Securities
Bureau of Securities
36 W. State Street
Trenton, NJ 08625
Labor and Labor Relations
Department of Labor and Industry
John Fitch Plaza
Trenton, NJ 08625
Insurance
Department of Insurance
201 E. State Street CN 325
Trenton, NJ 08625
Business Ombudsman
Office of Business Advocacy
1 W. State Street CN 823
Trenton, NJ 08625

INDUSTRIAL AND BUSINESS DIRECTORIES

New Jersey State Industrial Directory, Manufacturers' News, Inc., 4 E. Huron Street, Chicago, IL 60611; State Industrial Directories Corp., 2 Penn Plaza, New York, NY 10001

New Mexico

STATE CAPITOL, SANTE FE, NM 87503
(505) 827–4011

INFORMATION OFFICES

Commerce/Economic Development
Economic Development and Tourism
Bataan Memorial Building
Sante Fe, NM 87503
Corporate
State Corporation Commission
P.O. Drawer 1269
Sante Fe, NM 87501
Taxation
Bureau of Revenue
Manuel Lujan Sr. Building
Santa Fe, NM 87501
State Chamber of Commerce
Association of Commerce and Industry of New Mexico
117 Quincy NE
Albuquerque, NM 87108
International Commerce
Department of International Trade
Bataan Memorial Building
Sante Fe, NM 87503
Banking
Lew Wallace Building
Sante Fe, NM 87503
Securities
Lew Wallace Building
Sante Fe, NM 87503

Labor and Industrial Commission
509 Camino de Los Marques
Sante Fe, NM 87501
Insurance
State Corporation Commission
P.O. Box 1269
Sante Fe, NM 87501

INDUSTRIAL AND BUSINESS DIRECTORIES

New Mexico Directory of Manufacturing, Manufacturers' News, Inc., 4 E. Huron Street, Chicago, IL 60611; New Mexico Commerce and Industry Department, Bataan Memorial Building, Santa Fe, NM 87503; State Industrial Directories Corp., 2 Penn Plaza, New York, NY 10001

New York

STATE CAPITOL, ALBANY, NY 12224
(518) 474-8390

INFORMATION OFFICES

Commerce/Economic Development
Department of Commerce
One Commerce Plaza
Albany, NY 12245

Division of Industrial and Corporate Development
One Commerce Plaza
Albany, NY 12245

Office of Development Planning
Executive Chamber
Albany, NY 12224
Corporate
Secretary of State
162 Washington Avenue
Albany, NY 12231
Taxation
State Tax Commission
Department of Taxation and Finance
State Campus Building #9
Albany, NY 12227
State Chamber of Commerce
New York State Business Council
152 Washington Avenue
Albany, NY 12210
Small Business Advisory Board
Division of Small Business Services
230 Park Avenue
New York, NY 10169
International Commerce
Department of Commerce
230 Park Avenue
New York, NY 10169
Banking
Department of Banking

194 Washington Avenue
New York, NY 12210
Labor and Industrial Relations
Department of Labor
State Campus
Albany, NY 12240
Insurance
Department of Insurance
Empire State Plaza
Agency Building #1
Albany, NY 12257
Business Ombudsman
Department of Commerce
Small Business Services Division
230 Park Avenue
New York, NY 10169

INDUSTRIAL AND BUSINESS DIRECTORIES

New York and Surrounding Territory Classified Business Directory, New York Directory Co., Inc., 1440 Broadway, New York, NY 10018
New York Classified Business Directory, New York Directory Co., Inc., 1440 Broadway, New York, NY 10018
New York State Industrial Directory, State Industrial Directories Corp., 2 Penn Plaza, New York, NY 10001; Manufacturers' News, Inc., 4 E. Huron Street, Chicago, IL 60611
Directory of Minority and Woman's Business, Minority and Woman's Business Division, New York State Department of Commerce, 230 Park Avenue, New York, NY 10169

North Carolina

STATE LEGISLATIVE BUILDING, RALEIGH, NC 27602
(919) 733-1110

INFORMATION OFFICES

Commerce/Economic Development
Department of Commerce
430 N. Salisbury Street
Raleigh, NC 27611
Corporate
Secretary of State
Corporation Division
300 N. Salisbury Street
Raleigh, NC 27611
Taxation
Department of Revenue
2 S. Salisbury Street
Raleigh, NC 22760
State Chamber of Commerce
North Carolina Citizens for Business and Industry

P.O. Box 2508
Raleigh, NC 27602
International Commerce
International Development
Department of Commerce
430 N. Salisbury Street
Raleigh, NC 27611
Banking and Securities
Banking Commission
Department of Commerce
430 N. Salisbury Street
Raleigh, NC 27611
Labor and Industrial Relations
Department of Labor
4 W. Edenton Street
Raleigh, NC 27611
Insurance
Department of Insurance
430 N. Salisbury Street
Raleigh, NC 27611
Uniform Industrial Code
Business Ombudsman
Business Assistance
Department of Commerce
430 N. Salisbury Street
Raleigh, NC 27611

INDUSTRIAL AND BUSINESS DIRECTORIES

Directory of North Carolina Manufacturing Firms, North Carolina Department of Commerce, Raleigh, NC 27611; State Industrial Directories Corp., 2 Penn Plaza, New York, NY 10001; Manufacturers' News, Inc., 4 E. Huron Street, Chicago, IL 60611

North Dakota

STATE CAPITOL, BISMARCK, ND 58505
(701) 224–2000

INFORMATION OFFICES

Commerce/Economic Development
Economic Development Commission
Liberty Memorial Building
Bismarck, ND 58505
Corporate
Corporation Department
Office of the Secretary of State
Bismarck, ND 58505
Taxation
Tax Department
State Capitol
Bismarck, ND 58505
State Chamber of Commerce
Greater North Dakota Association—State Chamber of Commerce
P.O. Box 2467
Fargo, ND 58102

International Commerce
International Trade Department
Economic Development Commission
Liberty Memorial Building
Bismarck, ND 58505
Banking
State Banking Commission
State Capitol
Bismarck, ND 58505
Securities
Securities Commissioner
State Capitol
Bismarck, ND 58505
Labor and Industrial Relations
State Commissioner of Labor
State Capitol
Bismarck, ND 58505
Insurance
Insurance Commissioner
State Capitol
Bismarck, ND 58505
Uniform Industrial Code
Secretary of State
State Capitol
Bismarck, ND 58505
Business Ombudsman
Economic Development Commission
Liberty Memorial Building
Bismarck, ND 58505

INDUSTRIAL AND BUSINESS DIRECTORIES

North Dakota Manufacturers Directory, Economic Development Commission, Liberty Memorial Building, Bismarck, ND 58505; Manufacturers' News, Inc., 4 E. Huron Street, Chicago, IL 60611; State Industrial Directories Corp., 2 Penn Plaza, New York, NY 10001
Strictly Business, Frontier Directory Co., Inc., 222 W. Bowen Avenue, Bismarck, ND 58501

Ohio

STATE HOUSE, COLUMBUS, OH 43215
(614) 466–2000

INFORMATION OFFICES

Commerce/Economic Development
Ohio Department of Development
30 E. Broad Street
Columbus, OH 43215
Corporate
Secretary of State
Corporation Section
30 East Broad Street
Columbus, OH 43216
Taxation
Department of Taxation

30 E. Broad Street
Columbus, OH 43215
State Chamber of Commerce
Ohio Chamber of Commerce
Huntington Bank Building
17 South High Street
Columbus, OH 43215
International Commerce
Ohio Department of Development
International Trade Division
P.O. Box 1001
Columbus, OH 43216
Banking
Ohio Department of Commerce
Division of Banks
Two Nationwide Plaza
Columbus, OH 43215
Securities
Ohio Department of Commerce
Division of Securities
Two Nationwide Plaza
Columbus, OH 43215
Labor and Industrial Relations
Ohio Department of Industrial Relations
2323 W. Fifth Avenue
P.O. Box 825
Columbus, OH 43216
Insurance
Ohio Department of Insurance
2100 Stella Court
Columbus, OH 43215
Uniform Industrial Code
Industrial Commission of Ohio
Division of Safety and Hygiene
246 N. High Street
Columbus, OH 43215
Business Ombudsman
Ohio Department of Development
Small and Developing Business Division
Minority Business Development Division
P.O. Box 1001
Columbus, OH 43216

INDUSTRIAL AND BUSINESS DIRECTORIES

Akron, Ohio Membership Directory and Buyers Guide, Akron Area Chamber of Commerce, P.O. Box 436, Crystal Lake, IL 60014

Directory of Manufacturers in the Toledo Area, Toledo Area Chamber of Commerce, 218 Huron Street, Toledo, OH 43604

Directory of Ohio Manufacturers, Harris Publishing Co., 2057-2 Aurora Road, Twinsburg, OH 44087; Manufacturers' News, Inc., 4 E. Huron Street, Chicago, IL 60611

Manufacturers Directory, Columbus Area Chamber of Commerce, 50 W. Broad Street, Columbus, OH 43215

Ohio and International Trade, Division of International Trade, Department of Development, P.O. Box 1001, Columbus, OH 43216

Oklahoma

STATE CAPITOL, OKLAHOMA CITY, OK 73105
(405) 521-2011

INFORMATION OFFICES

Commerce/Economic Development
Department of Economic Development
4024 N. Lincoln
Oklahoma City, OK 73105
Department of Economic and Community Affairs
4545 Lincoln Boulevard
Oklahoma City, OK 73105
Corporate
Secretary of State
State Capitol
Oklahoma City, OK 73105
Taxation
Tax Commission
M. C. Connors Building
Oklahoma City, OK 73105
State Chamber of Commerce
Oklahoma State Chamber of Commerce
4020 North Lincoln
Oklahoma City, OK 73105
International Commerce
International Export Services
P.O. Box 53424
Oklahoma City, OK 73152
Banking
Oklahoma Banking Services
4100 Lincoln Boulevard
Oklahoma City, OK 73105
Securities
Oklahoma Securities Commission
2915 Lincoln Boulevard
Oklahoma City, OK 73152
Labor and Industrial Relations
Oklahoma Labor Department
State Capitol
Oklahoma City, OK 73105
Insurance
Insurance Commission
408 Will Rogers Memorial Office Building
Oklahoma City, OK 73105
Uniform Industrial Code
Universal Commercial Code Division
County Clerk's Office
County Court House
Oklahoma City, OK 73102

INDUSTRIAL AND BUSINESS DIRECTORIES

Oklahoma Directory of Manufacturers and Products, Industrial Development Department, P.O. Box 53424, Oklahoma City, OK 73152

Oregon

STATE CAPITOL, SALEM, OR 97310
(503) 378–3131

INFORMATION OFFICES

Commerce/Economic Development
Department of Economic Development
595 Cottage Street, N.E.
Salem, OR 97310
Corporate
Corporation Commission
Commerce Building
158 12th Street N.E.
Salem, OR 97310
Taxation
Department of Revenue
Revenue Building
955 Center Street
Salem, OR 97310
International Commerce
Economic Development Department
International Trade Division
921 S.W. Washington
Portland, OR 97205
Banking
Department of Commerce
Banking Division
280 Court Street N.E.
Salem, OR 97310
Securities
Department of Commerce
Corporation Division—Securities Section
Commerce Building
158 12th Street N.E.
Salem, OR 97310
Labor and Industrial Relations
Bureau of Labor and Industries
1400 S.W. 5th Avenue
Portland, OR 97201
Insurance
Department of Commerce
Insurance Division
Commerce Building
158 12th Street N.E.
Salem, OR 97310
Uniform Industrial Code
Department of Commerce
Building Codes Division
401 Labor and Industries Building
Salem, OR 97310

INDUSTRIAL AND BUSINESS DIRECTORIES

Oregon Manufacturers Directory, Department of Economic Development, 595 Cottage Street, N.E., Salem, OR 97310; State Industrial Directories Corp., 2 Penn Plaza, New York, NY 10001; Manufacturers' News, Inc., 4 E. Huron Street, Chicago, IL 60611

Pennsylvania

MAIN CAPITOL BUILDING, HARRISBURG, PA 17120
(717) 787–2121

INFORMATION OFFICES

Department of Commerce
Department of Commerce
433 Forum Building
Harrisburg, PA 17120
Bureau of Domestic and International Commerce
Department of Commerce
454 Forum Building
Harrisburg, PA 17120
Bureau of Economic Assistance
Department of Commerce
405 Forum Building
Harrisburg, PA 17120
Small Business Action Center
Department of Commerce
400 S. Office Building
Harrisburg, PA 17120
Corporate
Department of State
Bureau of Corporations
North Office Building
Harrisburg, PA 17120
Taxation
Department of Revenue
Information Service
P.O. Box 8056
Harrisburg, PA 17120
State Chamber of Commerce
Pennsylvania Chamber of Commerce
222 N. Third Street
Harrisburg, PA 17101
International Commerce
Department of Commerce
Bureau of Domestic & International Commerce
453 Forum Building
Harrisburg, PA 17120
Banking
Banking
333 Market Street
Harristown II
Harrisburg, PA 17101-2290
Securities
Securities Commission
471 Forum Building
Harrisburg, PA 17120
Labor and Industrial Relations
Department of Labor & Industry

Labor & Industry Building
Harrisburg, PA 17120
Insurance
Insurance
Strawberry Square
Harrisburg, PA 17120
Business Ombudsman
Small Business Action Center
Department of Commerce
South Office Building
Harrisburg, PA 17120

INDUSTRIAL AND BUSINESS DIRECTORIES

Industrial Directory of the Commonwealth of Pennsylvania, Department of General Services, Harris Publishing Company, 2057-2 Aurora Road, Twinsburg, OH 44087

Rhode Island

STATE HOUSE, PROVIDENCE, RI 02903
(401) 277–2000

INFORMATION OFFICES

Commerce/Economic Development
Department of Economic Development
7 Jackson Walkway
Providence, RI 02903
Taxation
Division of Taxation
Department of Administration
289 Promenade Street
CIC Complex
Providence, RI 02908
Corporate
Secretary of State
Corporation Department
State House
Providence, RI 02903
State Chamber of Commerce
Rhode Island Chamber of Commerce
206 Smith Street
Providence, RI 02908
International Commerce
Rhode Island Department of Economic Development
European Office
Meir 24
2000 Antwerp
Belgium
Banking
Department of Business Regulation
Banking Division
100 N. Main Street
Providence, RI 02903
Securities
Department of Business Regulation
Banking Division

100 N. Main Street
Providence, RI 02903
Labor and Industrial Relations
Department of Labor
200 Elmwood Avenue
Providence, RI 02907
Insurance
Department of Business Regulation
Insurance Division
100 N. Main Street
Providence, RI 02903
Uniform Industrial Code
Department of Labor
200 Elmwood Avenue
Providence, RI 02907

INDUSTRIAL AND BUSINESS DIRECTORIES

Rhode Island Directory of Manufacturers, Department of Economic Development, 7 Jackson Walkway, Providence, RI 02903
Rhode Island State Industrial Directory, State Industrial Directories Corp., 2 Penn Plaza, New York, NY 10001

South Carolina

STATE HOUSE, COLUMBIA, SC 29211
(803) 758–0221

INFORMATION OFFICES

Commerce/Economic Development
South Carolina State Development Board
P.O. Box 927
1301 Gervais Street
Columbia, SC 29202
Taxation
Tax Commission
P.O. Box 125
John C. Calhoun Office Building
Columbia, SC 29214
Corporate
Secretary of State
P.O. Box 11350
Columbia, SC 29211
State Chamber of Commerce
South Carolina Chamber of Commerce
1301 Gervais Street
Columbia, SC 29202
International Commerce
South Carolina State Development Board
1301 Gervais Street
P.O. Box 927
Columbia, SC 29202
Labor and Industrial Relations
South Carolina Labor Department
Landmark Center, 3600 Forest Drive
P.O. Box 11329
Columbia, SC 29211

Insurance
South Carolina Department of Insurance
2711 Middleburg Drive
P.O. Box 4067
Columbia, SC 29240
Business Ombudsman
South Carolina State Development Board
1301 Gervais Street
P.O. Box 927
Columbia, SC 29202

INDUSTRIAL AND BUSINESS DIRECTORIES

Industrial Directory of South Carolina, South Carolina State Development Board, P.O. Box 927, 1301 Gervais Street, Columbia, SC 29202
South Carolina International Trade Directory, South Carolina State Development Board, P.O. Box 927, 1301 Gervais Street, Columbia, SC 29202

South Dakota

STATE CAPITOL, PIERRE, SD 57501
(605) 773–3011

INFORMATION OFFICES

Commerce/Economic Development
Department of State Development
P.O. Box 6000
Pierre, SD 57501
Department of Commerce and Regulation
State Capitol
Pierre, SD 57501
Corporate
Secretary of State
Corporation Division
Capitol Building
Pierre, SD 57501
Taxation
Department of Revenue
Knelp Building
Pierre, SD 57501
State Chamber of Commerce
South Dakota State Chamber of Commerce
P.O. Box 190
Pierre, SD 57501
International Commerce
Department of State Development
P.O. Box 6000
Pierre, SD 57501
Banking
Department of Commerce and Regulation
Division of Banking
116 North Euclid
Pierre, SD 57501
Securities
Department of Commerce and Regulation

Division of Securities
State Capitol
Pierre, SD 57501
Labor and Industrial Relations
Department of Labor
Division of Labor and Management
Kneip Building
Pierre, SD 57501
Insurance
Department of Commerce and Regulation
Division of Insurance
Insurance Building
Pierre, SD 57501

INDUSTRIAL AND BUSINESS DIRECTORIES

Directory of South Dakota Industries, Manufacturers' News, Inc., 4 E. Huron Street, Chicago, IL 60611
South Dakota Manufacturers and Processors Directory, South Dakota Department of State Development, P.O. Box 6000, Pierre, SD 57501; State Industrial Directories Corp., 2 Penn Plaza, New York, NY 10001
South Dakota Export Directory, South Dakota Department of State Development, 221 S. Central, Pierre, SD 57501

Tennessee

STATE CAPITOL, NASHVILLE, TN 37219
(615) 741–3011

INFORMATION OFFICES

Commerce/Economic Development
Department of Economic and Community Development
1007 Andrew Jackson Building
Nashville, TN 37219
Corporate
Secretary of State
Records Division
James K. Polk Building
Nashville, TN 37219
Taxation
Department of Revenue
927 Andrew Jackson Building
Nashville, TN 37219
State Chamber of Commerce
State Chamber Division of the Tennessee Taxpayers Association
242 Doctors Building
Nashville, TN 37203
International Commerce
Department of Economic & Community Development
International Sales & Marketing
Andrew Jackson Building
Nashville, TN 37219

Banking
Department of Financial Institutions
James K. Polk State Office Building
505 Deaderick Street
Nashville, TN 37219
Securities
Department of Commerce & Insurance
Securities Division
State Office Building
Nashville, TN 37219
Labor and Industrial Relations
Department of Labor
501 Union Building
Nashville, TN 37219
Insurance
Department of Commerce & Insurance
Insurance Division
State Office Building
Nashville, TN 37219
Business Ombudsman
Department of Economic & Community Development Business & Industry Services Division
Andrew Jackson Division
Nashville, TN 37219

INDUSTRIAL AND BUSINESS DIRECTORIES

Directory of Tennessee Industries, Manufacturers' News, Inc., 4 E. Huron Street, Chicago, IL 60611; State Industrial Directories Corp., 2 Penn Plaza, New York, NY 10001
Tennessee Directory of Manufacturers, Industrial Development Division, Andrew Jackson Building, Nashville, TN 37219

Texas

STATE CAPITOL, AUSTIN, TX 78701
State Information: (512) 475–2323

INFORMATION OFFICES

Commerce/Economic Development
Texas Economic Development Commission
410 East 5th Street
Austin, TX 78711
Corporate
Secretary of State
P.O. Box 13701
Sam Houston Building
Austin, TX 78711
Taxation
Comptroller of Public Accounts
104 LBJ State Office Building
Austin, TX 78711
State Chamber of Commerce
Texas State Chamber of Commerce
77001 N. Lamar
Suite 302

Austin, TX 78752
Tourism Department
P.O. Box 12008
Austin, TX 78711
Lower Rio Grand Valley Chamber of Commerce
P.O. Box 975
Weslaco, TX 75896
South Texas Chamber of Commerce
6222 NW IH 19
San Antonio, TX 78201
East Texas Chamber of Commerce
P.O. Box 1592
Longview, TX 75601
West Texas Chamber of Commerce
P.O. Box 1516
Abilene, TX 79604
International Commerce
International Division
Texas Economic Development Commission
P.O. Box 12728, Capitol Station
Austin, TX 78711
Banking
Texas Department of Banking
2601 North Lamar
Austin, TX 78705
Securities
Securities Board
1800 San Jacinto St.
Austin, TX 78701
Labor and Industrial Relations
Texas Department of Labor and Standards
P.O. Box 12157, Capitol Station
Austin, TX 78711
Insurance
Texas State Board of Insurance
State Insurance Building
1110 San Jacinto
Austin, TX 78786
Uniform Industrial Code
Uniform Commercial Code Section
Secretary of State's Office
P.O. Box 13193, Capitol Station
Austin, TX 78711
Business Ombudsman
Governor's Office of Economic Development
P.O. Box 13561
Austin, TX 78711

INDUSTRIAL AND BUSINESS DIRECTORIES

Dallas Business Guide, Dallas Chamber of Commerce, Fidelity Tower, Dallas, TX 75201
Directory of Texas Manufacturers, Bureau of Business Research, University of Texas, Austin, TX 78712; State Industrial Directories Corp., 2 Penn Plaza, New York, NY 10001
Fort Worth Directory of Manufacturers, Fort Worth Area Chamber of Commerce, 700 Throckmorton Street, Fort Worth, TX 76102
Texas Exporter-Importer Directory, Gulf Inter-

national Trades, Box 52717, Houston, TX 77052

Texas Manufacturers Directory, Manufacturers' News, Inc., 4 E. Huron Street, Chicago, IL 60611

Utah

STATE CAPITOL, SALT LAKE CITY, UT 84114
(801) 533-4000

INFORMATION OFFICES

Commerce/Economic Development
Department of Business Regulation
160 East 300 South Street
Salt Lake City, UT 84111
Department of Community and Economic Development
Division of Economic and Industrial Development
6150 State Office Building
Salt Lake City, UT 84114
Office of Planning & Budget
Data Resources Section
116 Capitol Building
Salt Lake City, UT 84114
Corporate
Secretary of State
State Capitol
Salt Lake City, UT 84114
Taxation
Tax Commission
160 East 300 South Street Building
Salt Lake City, UT 84111
International Commerce
International Business Development
Division of Economic & Industrial Development
6150 State Office Building
Salt Lake City, UT 84114
Banking
Department of Financial Institutions
160 E. 300 South
P.O. Box 89
Salt Lake City, UT 84110
Securities
Department of Financial Institutions
160 E. 300 South
P.O. Box 89
Salt Lake City, UT 84110
Labor and Industrial Relations
Industrial Commission of Utah
160 E. 300 South
Salt Lake City, UT 84110-5800
Insurance
Department of Insurance
160 E. 300 South
Salt Lake City, UT 84110-5803
Uniform Industrial Code
Employment Security/Job Service

174 Social Hall Avenue
Salt Lake City, UT 84147
Business Ombudsman
Division of Economic & Industrial Development
Department of Community & Economic Development
6150 State Office Building
Salt Lake City, UT 84114

INDUSTRIAL AND BUSINESS DIRECTORIES

Directory of Utah Manufacturers, Manufacturers' News, Inc., 4 E. Huron Street, Chicago, IL 60611; Department of Employment Security, 1234 S. Main Street, Salt Lake City, UT 84147

Vermont

STATE HOUSE, MONTPELIER, VT 05602
(802) 828-2228

INFORMATION OFFICES

Commerce/Economic Development
Agency of Development and Community Affairs
Department of Economic Development
109 State Street
Montpelier, VT 05602
Corporate
Secretary of State
Corporation Department
26 Terrace Street
Montpelier, VT 05602
Taxation
Department of Texas
Agency of Administration
109 State Street
Montpelier, VT 05602
State Chamber of Commerce
Vermont State Chamber of Commerce
P.O. Box 37
Montpelier, VT 05602
Insurance
Department of Banking and Insurance
120 State Street
Montpelier, VT 05602
Banking
Department of Banking and Insurance
120 State Street
Montpelier, VT 05602

INDUSTRIAL AND BUSINESS DIRECTORIES

Vermont Directory of Manufacturers, Vermont Agency of Development and Community Affairs, Montpelier, VT 05602

Vermont State Industrial Directory, Manufacturers' News, Inc., 4 E. Huron Street, Chicago, IL 60611; State Industrial Directories Corp., 2 Penn Plaza, New York, NY 10001
Vermont Yearbook, The National Survey, Chester, VT 05143

Virginia

STATE CAPITOL, RICHMOND, VA 23219
(804) 786-0000

INFORMATION OFFICES

Commerce/Economic Development
Division of Industrial Development
1000 Washington Building
Richmond, VA 23219

Department of Conservation and Economic
Development
1100 Washington Building
Richmond, VA 23219
Corporate
State Corporation Commission
1220 Bank Street
Richmond, VA 23209
Taxation
Department of Taxation
2200 W. Broad Street
Richmond, VA 23219
State Chamber of Commerce
Virginia State Chamber of Commerce
611 E. Franklin Street
Richmond, VA 23219
International Commerce
Department of Economic Development
1000 Washington Building
Richmond, VA 23219
Banking
State Corporation Commission
Bureau of Financial Institutions
701 E. Byrd Street
Richmond, VA 23205
Securities
State Corporation Commission
Division of Securities and Retail Franchising
11 S. 12th Street
Richmond, VA 23219
Labor and Industrial Relations
Department of Labor and Industry
205 N. 4th Street
Richmond, VA 23241
Insurance
State Corporation Commission
Bureau of Insurance
1220 Bank Street
Richmond, VA 23209
Uniform Industrial Code
Virginia Employment Commission
Research and Analysis Division

703 E. Main Street
Richmond, VA 23211
Business Ombudsman
Department of Agricultural and Consumer
Services
Office of Consumer Affairs
1100 Bank Street
Richmond, VA 23219

INDUSTRIAL AND BUSINESS DIRECTORIES

Industrial Directory of Virginia, Chamber of Commerce, 611 E. Franklin Street, Richmond, VA 23219
Virginia Industrial Directory, Manufacturers' News, Inc., 4 E. Huron Street, Chicago, IL 60611; State Industrial Directories Corp., 2 Penn Plaza, New York, NY 10001

Washington

10 GENERAL ADMINISTRATION BUILDING, OLYMPIA, WA 98504
(206) 753-5630

INFORMATION OFFICES

Commerce/Economic Development
Department of Commerce and Economic
Development
101 General Administration Building
Olympia, WA 98504
Corporate
Secretary of State
Corporate Division
Legislative Building
Olympia, WA 98504
Taxation
Department of Revenue
412 General Administration Building
Olympia, WA 98504
State Chamber of Commerce
Association of Washington Business
1414 S. Cherry Street
Olympia, WA 98501
Small Business Development Centers
441 Todd Hall
Washington State University
Pullman, WA 99164

180 Nickerson
Suite 310
Seattle, WA 98109

101 General Administration Building
Olympia, WA 98504

303 E. D Street
Suite 2
Yakima, WA 98901

7th Floor Bon Building
Spokane, WA 99201

Western Washington University
Bellingham, WA 98225
International Commerce
Department of Commerce & Economic Development
International Business Development Division
312 First Avenue North
Seattle, WA 98109
Banking
General Administration Building
Banking & Small Loans
218 General Administration Building
Olympia, WA 98504
Securities
Department of Licensing Building
Att: Securities Division
12th & Franklin
Olympia, WA 98504
Labor and Industrial Relations
Department of Labor & Industries
Employment Standards Division
General Administration Building
Olympia, WA 98504
Insurance
Insurance Commissioner's Office
Insurance Building
Olympia, WA 98504
Uniform Commercial Code
Department of Licensing
Business License Centre
1300 Quint Street
East Side Plaza
Olympia, WA 98504
Business Ombudsman
Department of Commerce & Economic Development
Office of Small Business
101 General Administration Building
Olympia, WA 98506

INDUSTRIAL AND BUSINESS DIRECTORIES

1984 Directory of Advanced Technology Industries in Washington State, Economic Development Council of Puget Sound, 1900 Seattle Tower, 1218 Third Avenue, Seattle, WA 98101

Business Associations in Washington State, Washington State International Trade Directory, Department of Commerce and Economic Development, 101 General Administration Building, Olympia, WA 98504

Minority Women Business Enterprises, Office of Minority Women Business Enterprise, 406 S. Water Street, Olympia, WA 98504

Washington Manufacturers Register, Times Mirror Press, 1115 S. Boyle, Los Angeles, CA 90023

MacRae's Washington State Industrial Directory, 87 Terminal Drive, Plainview, NY 11803

West Virginia

STATE CAPITOL, CHARLESTON, WV 25305
(304) 348-3456

INFORMATION OFFICES

Commerce/Economic Development
Governor's Office of Economic and Community Development
State Office Building R-150
Charleston, WV 25305
Corporate
Secretary of State
Corporate Division
State Capitol
Charleston, WV 25305
Taxation
Tax Department
West Wing
State Capitol
Charleston, WV 25305
State Chamber of Commerce
P.O. Box 2789
1101 Kanawha Valley Building
Charleston, WV 25301
International Commerce
Governor's Office of Economic Development
Industrial Development Division
1900 Washington Street, East
Building 6
Charleston, WV 25305
Banking
Department of Banking
1900 Washington Street, East
Building 5
Charleston, WV 25305
Securities
Auditor's Office
1900 Washington Street, East
Building 1, WW-100
Charleston, WV 25305
Labor & Industrial Relations
Governor's Office of Economic Development
Industrial Development Division
1900 Washington Street, East
Building 6
Charleston, WV 25305
Insurance
Insurance Department
2100 Washington Street, East
Charleston, WV 25305
Uniform Industrial Code
Governor's Office of Economic Development
Industrial Development Division
1900 Washington Street, East
Building 6
Charleston, WV 25305
Business Ombudsman
Governor's Office of Economic Development

Industrial Development Division
Building 6
Charleston, WV 25305

INDUSTRIAL AND BUSINESS DIRECTORIES

West Virginia Manufacturing Directory, Governor's Office of Economic and Community Development, State Office Building #6, Charleston, WV 25305; State Industrial Directories Corp., 2 Penn Plaza, New York, NY 10001

Wisconsin

STATE CAPITOL, MADISON, WI 53702
(608) 266-2211

INFORMATION OFFICES

Commerce/Economic Development
Department of Development
123 W. Washington Avenue
Madison, WI 53702
Corporate
Secretary of State
Corporate Division
201 E. Washington Avenue
Madison, WI 53702
Taxation
Department of Revenue
125 S. Webster Avenue
Madison, WI 53702
State Chamber of Commerce
Wisconsin Association of Manufacturers and
Commerce
111 E. Wisconsin Avenue
Milwaukee, WI 53202
International Commerce
International Business Services
Department of Development
123 W. Washington Avenue
Madison, WI 53702
Banking
Banking, Office of the Commissioner
123 West Washington Avenue
Madison, WI 53702
Securities
Securities—Office of the Commissioner
111 West Wilson Avenue
Madison, WI 53703
Labor and Industrial Relations
Department of Industry, Labor, and Human
Relations
201 E. Washington Avenue
Madison, WI 53702
Insurance
Office of the Commissioner—Insurance
123 West Washington Avenue
Madison, WI 53702

Uniform Industrial Code
Department of Industry, Labor and Human
Relations
201 E. Washington Avenue
Madison, WI 53702
Business Ombudsman
Small Business Ombudsman
Department of Development
123 W. Washington Avenue
Madison, WI 53702

INDUSTRIAL AND BUSINESS DIRECTORIES

Classified Directory of Wisconsin Manufacturers, Wisconsin Association of Manufacturers and Commerce, 111 E. Wisconsin Avenue, Milwaukee, WI 53202; State Industrial Directories Corp., 2 Penn Plaza, New York, NY 10001
Wisconsin Manufacturers Directory, Manufacturers' News, Inc., 4 E. Huron Street, Chicago, IL 60611
Wisconsin Local Development Organizations (annual), Wisconsin Department of Development, 123 W. Washington Avenue, Madison, WI 53702

Wyoming

STATE CAPITOL, CHEYENNE, WY 82002
(307) 777-7011

INFORMATION OFFICES

Commerce/Economic Development
Department of Economic Planning and Development
Herschler Building
Cheyenne, WY 82002
Corporate
Secretary of State
Corporate Division
State Capitol
Cheyenne, WY 82002
Taxation
Department of Revenue and Taxation
Herschler Building
Cheyenne, WY 82002
International Commerce
International Trade Office
Industrial Development Division
Department of Economic Planning and Development
Herschler Building
Cheyenne, WY 82002
Banking
State Examiner
Herschler Building
Cheyenne, WY 82002

Securities
Secretary of State
Securities Division
State Capitol
Cheyenne, WY 82002
Labor and Industrial Relations
Department of Labor and Statistics
Herschler Building
Cheyenne, WY 82002
Insurance
Insurance Commission
Herschler Building
Cheyenne, WY 82002
Uniform Industrial Code
Industrial Siting Commission
Boyd Building
1720 Carey Avenue
Cheyenne, WY 82002

Industrial Development Division
Department of Economic Planning and Development
Herschler Building
Cheyenne, WY 82002

INDUSTRIAL AND BUSINESS DIRECTORIES

Wyoming Directory of Manufacturing and Mining, Manufacturers' News, Inc., 4 E. Huron Street, Chicago, IL 60611; Department of Economic Planning and Development, Herschler Building, Cheyenne, WY 82002; State Industrial Directories Corp. 2 Penn Plaza, New York, NY 10001

Puerto Rico

CAPITOL, SAN JUAN, PR 00901
(809) 724–6040 (House of Representatives)
(809) 724-2030 (Senate)

INFORMATION OFFICES

Commerce/Economic Development
Puerto Rico Department of Commerce
P.O. Box S 4275
San Juan, PR 00905

Puerto Rico Economic Development Administration
P.O. Box 2350
San Juan, PR 00936

Puerto Rico Planning Board
P.O. Box 41119
San Juan, PR 00940

Government Development Bank
P.O. Box 42001
Minillas Station
Santurce, PR 00940

Taxation
Income Tax Bureau
Puerto Rico Department of Treasury
P.O. Box S-4515
San Juan, PR 00905

Office of Industrial Tax Exemption
Fomento Building
Hato Rey, PR 00918
Chamber of Commerce
Camara De Comercio de Puerto Rico
P.O. Box 3789
San Juan, PR 00904
Securities
Puerto Rico Treasury Department
Securities, Banks and Financial Institutions
Administration
P.O. Box 4515
San Juan, PR 00905
Labor and Industrial Relations
Labor Affairs Office
GPO Box 3088
San Juan, PR 00936

Puerto Rico Labor Relations Board
P.O. Box 4048
San Juan, PR 00905

National Labor Relations Board
Federal Building
Hato Rey, PR 00918-2272
Insurance
Office of the Insurance Commissioner
P.O. Box 8330
Santurce, PR

Puerto Rico Insurance Companies Association, Inc.
Housing Investment Building
San Juan, PR
Uniform Industrial Code
Labor and Human Resources Department
Labor Statistics Bureau
505 Muñoz Rivera Avenue
Prudencio Rivera Martínez Building
Hato Rey, PR 00918
Business Ombudsman
Ombudsman Office
1205 Ponce de León Avenue
Banco de San Juan
Santurce, PR 00908
International Commerce
Puerto Rico Department of Commerce
External Trade Promotion Program
P.O. Box S 4275
San Juan, PR 00905

US Department of Commerce
International Trade Administration
San Juan Field Office
Federal Building
Hato Rey, PR 00918

Puerto Rico Chamber of Commerce
International Trade Division
P.O. Box 3789
San Juan, PR 00930

Banking

Puerto Rico Treasury Department
Bureau of Banks and Financial Institutions
P.O. Box S 4515
San Juan, PR

Puerto Rico Bankers Association
Banco Popular Center
Hato Rey, PR 00918

INDUSTRIAL AND BUSINESS DIRECTORIES

Puerto Rico Official Industrial and Trade Directory, Witcom Group, Inc., P.O. Box 2310, San Juan, PR 00902

The Businessman's Guide to Puerto Rico, Puerto Rico Almanacs, Inc., P.O. Box 9582, Santurce, Puerto Rico 00908

International Information Sources

Foreign Trade Information

Business people seeking information about foreign commercial opportunities or sources of business contacts have available a number of government and private services that are described in this and subsequent sections. The extensive nature of these services is not always fully appreciated by members of the business community. Some of the most helpful services are provided by the International Trade Administration (ITA) 202–377–3808 of the Department of Commerce, described below. This agency is particularly helpful in establishing initial contacts and in evaluating foreign markets.

Business people traveling abroad will find the following services of help in initiating contacts:

1. Office of Business Counselling, U.S. Department of Commerce. Telephone: 202-377-3181
2. Commercial offices at U.S. embassies or consulates.

Foreign credit information sources are provided at the end of this section.

DEPARTMENT OF COMMERCE

Address: Constitution and 14th Street NW, Washington, DC 20230. Information phone: 202–377–3181.

The central export information source within the Department of Commerce is the **International Trade Administration** (ITA), which promotes the growth of U.S. industry and commerce, both foreign and domestic. Several units including the U.S. and Foreign Commercial Service, International Economic Policy, Trade Development, and Trade Administration have functions relevant to exporters.

International Economic Policy (IEP)*

Organized geographically to deal with all issues which are country-specific or region-specific; multilateral issues are handled by an office reporting to the principal Deputy Assistant Secretary for IEP.

Four regional units, each under a Deputy Assistant Secretary, are established:

Europe
The Western Hemisphere
East Asia, and the Pacific
Africa, the Near East and South Asia

Single-country offices (example: Japan) or multi-country offices (example: USSR and Eastern Europe) are under each Deputy Assistant Secretary.

The IEP regional Deputy Assistant Secretaries provide geographic program supervision of Foreign Commercial Service (FCS) country senior officers overseas, and (jointly with the Director-General) appraise their performance.

The IEP country offices are the day-to-day contact point in ITA for the FCS overseas post activities and communications.

Trade Development (TD)

Organized to develop and manage export trade issues bearing on specific industries, and to manage ITA's data collection and analysis.

A key feature of the organization is its focus on seven major industry sectors: Aerospace; Automotive Affairs and Consumer Goods; Basic Industries; Capital Goods and International Construction; Science and Electronics; Services and Textiles and Apparel. Rounding out TD are two units that cover issues cutting across industry sectors: Trade Information and Analysis gathers, analyzes and disseminates trade and investment data for use in trade promotion and policy for-

---

* Excerpted from *Business America*, U.S. Department of Commerce and other Department of Commerce sources.

mulation; and Trade Adjustment assistance helps firms to adjust to international competition.

The U.S. and Foreign Commercial Service (USFCS)

The only government organization involved in international trade with a worldwide field presence and delivery system, the USFCS is designed to help the U.S. business community enter export trade.

Through USFCS, a U.S. firm has access to more than 95 percent of the global marketplace for U.S. exports. It has 68 U.S. offices linked to 124 overseas posts in 68 countries. The Office of Export Promotion in Washington, D.C. designs and tests products for the business community, thereby ensuring responsiveness to market demand and a better quality product.

The USFCS also coordinates the administration's Carribbean Basin Initiative.

ITA Publications and Services

Many of the ITA publications listed below are provided by USFCS. Except as otherwise noted they may be ordered from:

Office of Trade Information Services
Room 1324
U.S. Department of Commerce
P.O. Box 1427
Washington, D.C. 20044

A Basic Guide to Exporting contains information on selling goods and services abroad and covers such topics as export techniques, government regulations, and export programs. The guide is aimed, among other things, at helping small businesses benefit from the export market. Available from the Superintendent of Documents, General Printing Office, Washington, DC 20402.

World Traders Data Reports (WTDRs) are background reports on individual foreign firms, containing information about each firm's business activities, its standing in the local business community, its credit-worthiness, and its overall reliability and suitability as a trade contact for U.S. exporters. WTDRs are designed to help U.S. firms locate and evaluate potential foreign customers before making a business commitment.

Foreign Traders Index: Information on more than 140,000 foreign importing organizations in 130 countries is stored in ITA's *Foreign Traders Index* (FTI), a computerized file. New information on listed firms and information on newly identified firms are constantly added to the index. The information in the file is collected and supplied to Commerce by the U.S. Foreign Service—Department of State.

Most of the lists or services described here are products of the *Foreign Traders Index*.

Some, however, are prepared from special source material.

Export Mailing List Service: U.S. firms wishing to make export contacts may obtain lists of foreign organizations selected by electronic data processing techniques from the *Foreign Traders Index*. Selection of firms in one or more countries or geographic areas may be made according to the products or product groups handled by the foreign organizations.

The information is available either on pressure-sensitive mailing labels or in standard printout format.

Data Tape Service: U.S. firms with computer facilities may purchase magnetic tapes containing information on all firms in selected countries or in all countries covered in the *Foreign Traders Index*. This service makes it possible for users to retrieve various segments of data from the *Foreign Traders Index* through their own computer facilities.

The Agent/Distributor Service: ITA's *Agent/Distributor Service* (A/DS) helps U.S. firms find agents or distributors for their products in almost every country of the world. U.S. commercial officers overseas will identify up to six foreign firms that have expressed interest in a specific U.S. proposal.

Application forms (ITA-424P) may be obtained from any Commerce Department district office. Trade specialists at district offices will help a U.S. firm prepare an application. They will offer guidance and determine whether there are factors to discourage a business relationship.

Trade List Service: The names and addresses of foreign distributors, agents, purchasers, and other firms, classified by products they handle and services they offer, are made available to U.S. firms through printed *Trade Lists* (TL). Some of the lists are produced from information in the *Foreign Traders Index*. Others are prepared from data compiled in connection with ITA's export promotion programs and from other sources.

Trade Opportunities Program: Up-to-the-minute direct sales leads and representation opportunities from overseas are now available to interested U.S. companies through a computerized mail service, the *Trade Opportunities Program* (TOP). A U.S. businessman, as a subscriber to TOP, specifies the products and the countries for which he wants trade opportunities, and that information is fed into the TOP computer.

The *Annual Worldwide Industry Review (AWIR)* is a multi-country "view for the year" which focuses on a particular U.S. industry's export prospects in a number of selected countries. Each report includes three parts: (1) A worldwide profile of U.S. export trends for the industry, (2) Country-by-country market assessments for the industry as reported annually by U.S. Foreign Commercial Service Officers, and

(3) Statistical tables showing U.S. exports of the industry's products to each country over the latest 5 years.

Foreign Economic Trends (FET) present current business and economic developments and the latest economic indicators in more than 100 countries. They are prepared on an annual or semiannual basis by the U.S. Foreign Service and U.S. Foreign Commercial Service. Available from the Superintendent of Documents, U.S. Government Printing Office, Washington, D.C. 20402.

Overseas Business Reports (OBR) include current and detailed marketing information, trade outlooks, statistics, regulations, and market profiles. They are available from the Superintendent of Documents, U.S. Government Printing Office, Washington, DC 20402.

Global and Country Market Surveys (GMS) provide detailed information on 15 to 30 of the best foreign markets for the products of a single U.S. industry or a group of related industries.

International Marketing Information are reports prepared by U.S. Embassies describing market opportunities or conditions within a country, but not in accordance with IMR specifications.

Custom Service Statistics—the new "custom" service complements the standard *Export Statistics Profiles (ESP)*. It includes data on products not covered in the standard ESP industries. It also provides data on specific countries which may not appear in the standard ESP country rankings for a particular industry.

Country Market Sectoral Surveys pinpoint the best U.S. export opportunities in a single foreign country. They provide detailed reports on 13 to 15 leading industrial sectors. Copies may be purchased from the Superintendent of Documents, U.S. Government Printing Office, Washington, DC 20402.

International Economic Indicators presents a wide variety of comparative economic statistics for the United States and seven major competitor nations for recent periods. This quarterly publication is available from the Superintendent of Documents, U.S. Government Printing Office, Washington, DC 20402.

Two publications designed to assist U.S. exporters identify and evaluate export markets are the *Export Statistical Profiles* and the *International Market Research Reports*.

Export Statistical Profiles includes tables which help identify whether a product or industry has export potential and information on how much of what products in an industry have been exported to specific countries and regions of the world over the past five years. Also given are the industry's leading and fastest growing export products and markets, and the best prospect countries for the next two years. *International Market Research Reports* cover single industries in selected countries or markets and are chosen according to their potential for U.S. export sales. These reports are produced abroad under contract with experienced local research analysts according to detailed specifications prepared in Washington.

The following are some additional publications on international commerce available from the Government Printing Office, Washington, DC 20402 unless otherwise indicated.

Foreign Trade Report FT 410: U.S. Exports Commodity by Country is one of the best sources for locating export markets. These monthly publications provide a statistical record of the shipments of all merchandise from the United States to foreign countries.

Market Share Reports. These annual reports provide a five-year record of U.S. participation in foreign markets for manufactured products. Both country and product series are available. For a free catalogue write:

National Technical Information Service
5285 Port Royal Road
Springfield, VA 22161

Business America published by International Trade Administration is Commerce Department's principal periodical for domestic and international business news and covers a wide range of topics. Available from Publications Sales Branch, U.S. Department of Commerce, Washington, DC 20230.

Commerce Business Daily is a daily record containing synopses of U.S. government procurement limitations, subcontracting leads, contract awards, sales of surplus property, and foreign business opportunities.

The Overseas Export Promotion Calendar lists U.S. trade-promotion events held abroad. These include exhibitions, missions, and seminars featuring U.S. products and services. The calendar is indexed by product, gives the location and date of each event, and also identifies U.S. Export Development Offices (i.e., International Marketing Centers) promoting sales of U.S. goods and services. Subscription information may be obtained by calling ITA's Export Awareness Division of Event Management and Support Services at 202–377–5367.

Country Trade Lists and *Industry/Product Trade Lists* are published by the Office of Trade Information Services (OTIS) to provide U.S. exporters with the names and addresses of potential overseas buyers in selected industries and countries. Contact and other basic information (size, number of employees, year established, business activities/interests, etc.) on overseas distributors, agents, manufacturers, retailers and other potential importing firms are given. For publications or updated Index write to: U.S. Department of Commerce, International Trade

Administration/OTIS, Trade Lists, Room 1324, P.O. Box 1427, Washington, DC 20230 or nearest Commerce District Office.

Current International Trade Position of the United States is a free reference guide from the Department of Commerce on U.S. imports of petroleum, U.S. trading by type and area, balance of payments and U.S. share of world exports. Order from the U.S. Department of Commerce, Publications Sales Branch, Washington, DC 20230.

Growth Markets of the 1980's: Western Europe describes the market conditions in some 21 countries and examines their market potentials. Also included is a product category index. Order from the U.S. Department of Commerce, Publications Sales Branch, Washington, D.C. 20230.

Export Counseling Unit: Counseling services are provided by the U.S. Departments of Commerce and State in Washington, DC, and by the Commerce district offices located in major commercial and industrial centers throughout the United States and Puerto Rico.

The Export Counseling Unit (202–377–3181) offers guidance, in-depth counseling, and scheduling of appointments with appropriate Commerce officials as well as with officials in other agencies. This service is designed to give the businessperson a maximum amount of information in a minimum of time.

An important part of this program is an Export Information Reference Room where businesspeople can review a wide range of major foreign projects under consideration by international financial institutions—World Bank Group, Inter-American Development Bank, Asian Development Bank, and the United Nations Development Programme.

For further information on all of the above publications and services, contact the nearest Department of Commerce District Office.

Trade Administration of ITA administers controls on exports that may be limited for national security, foreign policy, or short-supply reasons. This office also administers the antiforeign boycott program, U.S. foreign-trade zones program, and duty-free importation for scientific or educational reasons. The bureau indicates quotas for duty-free import of watches and watch parts from the Virgin Islands, Guam, and American Samoa.

International Trade Administration Desk Officers

Information on a specific country as well as assistance or information about marketing there may be obtained from an International Economic Policy desk officer assigned to cover that particular country. To locate the proper desk officer, call 202-377-5087.

DISTRICT OFFICES OF THE U.S. DEPARTMENT OF COMMERCE

NORTHEASTERN REGION I
Connecticut
Hartford
Federal Office Bldg.
450 Main Street 06103
203–244–3530

Maine
• **Augusta (Boston, Massachusetts District)**
1 Memorial Circle
Casco Bank Bldg. 04330
207–622–8249

Massachusetts
Boston
441 Stuart Street 02116
617–223–2312

New Hampshire
Serviced by Boston District Office
New York
Buffalo
1312 Federal Bldg.
111 West Huron Street 14202
716–846–4191

• **Rochester**
183 E. Main Street 16404
716–263–6480

New York
Federal Office Bldg.
26 Federal Plaza 10278
212–264–0634

Rhode Island
• **Providence (Boston, Massachusetts District)**
7 Jackson Walkway 02903
401–277–2605, Ext. 22

Vermont
Serviced by Boston District Office

MID-ATLANTIC REGION II
Delaware
Serviced by Philadelphia District Office
District of Columbia
Serviced by Baltimore District Office
Maryland
Baltimore
415 U.S. Customhouse
Gay and Lombard Streets 21202
301–962–3560

• **Rockville**
101 Monroe Street 20850
301–251–2345

New Jersey
∗ **Trenton**
Capitol Plaza

• Trade Specialist at Post of Duty Station
  ∗ Regional Office with Supervisory Regional Responsibilities

240 West State Street 08608
609-989-2100

Pennsylvania

Philadelphia
9448 Federal Bldg.
600 Arch Street 19106
215-597-2866

Pittsburgh
2002 Federal Bldg.
1000 Liberty Ave. 15222
412-644-2850

APPALACHIAN REGION III

Kentucky

Louisville
U.S. Post Office and
    Courthouse Bldg. 40202
502-582-5066

North Carolina

* **Greensboro**
203 Federal Bldg.
West Market Street
P.O. Box 1950 27402
919-378-5345

• **Raleigh**
Dobbs Bldg.
430 N. Salisbury Street 27611
919-755-4687

South Carolina

Columbia
Strom Thurmond Federal Bldg.
1835 Assembly Street 29201
803-765-5345

• **Charleston**
505 Federal Bldg.
334 Meeting Street 29403
803-677-4361

• **Greenville**
P.O. Box 5823
Station B, 29606
803-235-5919

Tennessee

Nashville
One Commerce Place 37239
615-251-5161

* **Memphis**
3693 Central Ave. 38111
901-521-4826

Virginia

Richmond
8010 Federal Bldg.
400 North 8th Street 23240
804-771-2246

• **(Fairfax County)**
Dumn Loring
8100 Oak Street 22027
703-573-9460

West Virginia

Charleston
3000 New Federal Bldg.

500 Quarrier Street 25301
304-343-6181, Ext. 375

SOUTHEASTERN REGION IV

ALABAMA

* **Birmingham**
908 South 20th Street 35205
205-254-1331

Florida

Miami
Federal Bldg.
51 S.W. First Ave. 33130
305-350-5267

• **Clearwater**
128 North Osceola Ave. 33515
813-461-0011

• **Jacksonville**
3 Independent Drive 32202
904-791-2796

• **Orlando**
75 East Ivanhoe Blvd. 32802
305-425-1247

• **Tallahassee**
Collins Bldg. 32304
904-488-6469

Georgia

Atlanta
1365 Peachtree Street, N.E. 30309
404-881-7000.

Savannah
27 E Bay Street
P.O. Box 9746 31401
912-944-4204

Mississippi

Jackson
Jackson Mall Office Center
220 Woodrow Wilson Blvd. 39213
601-960-4388

Puerto Rico

San Juan (Hato Rey)
Federal Bldg. 00918
809-753-4555 Ext. 555

GREAT LAKES REGION V

Illinois

Chicago
1406 Mid Continental Plaza Bldg.
55 East Monroe Street 60603
312-353-4450

• **Palatine**
W.R. Harper College
Algonquin & Roselle Road 60067
312-397-3000, Ext. 532

Indiana

Indianapolis
357 U.S. Courthouse & Federal Office
    Bldg.
46 East Ohio Street 46204
317-269-6214

Michigan
Detroit
445 Federal Bldg.
231 West Layfayette 48226
313-226-3650

• **Grand Rapids**
300 Monroe N.W.
Room 409 49503
616-456-2411

Minnesota
Minneapolis
108 Federal Bldg.
110 S. 4th Street 55401
612-349-3338

Ohio
* **Cincinnati**
9504 Federal Office Bldg.
550 Main Street 45202
513-684-2944

Cleveland
666 Euclid Ave. 44114
216-522-4750

Wisconsin
Milwaukee
U.S. Courthouse
517 E. Wisconsin Ave. 53202
414-291-3473

PLAINS REGION VI
Iowa
Des Moines
817 Federal Bldg.
210 Walnut Street 50309
515-284-4222

Kansas
• **Wichita (Kansas City, Missouri District)**
P.O. Box 48
Wichita State University 67208
316-269-6160

Missouri
* **St. Louis**
120 South Central Ave. 63105
314-425-3302-4

Kansas City
601 East 12th Street 64106
816-374-3142

Nebraska
Omaha
Empire State Bldg.
300 South 19th Street 68102
402-221-3664

North Dakota
Serviced by Omaha District Office
South Dakota
Serviced by Omaha District Office

CENTRAL REGION VII
Arkansas
Little Rock
Savers Federal Bldg.

320 W. Capitol Ave. 72201
501-378-5794

Louisiana
New Orleans
432 International Trade Mart
No. 2 Canal Street 70130
504-589-6546

New Mexico
Albuquerque
505 Marquette Ave., NW
Suite 1015
505-766-2386

Oklahoma
Oklahoma City
4024 Lincoln Blvd. 73105
405-231-5302

• **Tulsa**
440 S. Houston Street 74127
918-581-7650

Texas
* **Dallas**
1100 Commerce Street 75242
214-767-0542

Houston
2625 Federal Courthouse Bldg.
515 Rusk Street 77002
713-229-2578

ROCKY-MOUNTAIN REGION VIII
Arizona
Phoenix
Valley Bank Center
201 North Central Ave. 85073
602-261-3285

Colorado
* **Denver**
U.S. Customhouse
721-19th Street 80202
303-837-3240

Idaho
• **Boise**
Statehouse 83720
208-334-2470

Montana
Serviced by Denver District Office

Nevada
Reno
1755 E. Plumb Lane, #152 89502
702-784-5203

Utah
Salt Lake City
U.S. Courthouse
350 S. Main Street 84101
801-524-5116

Wyoming
Serviced by Denver District Office

PACIFIC REGION IX

Alaska

Anchorage
701 C Street
P.O. Box 32 99513
907–271–5041

California

Los Angeles
Room 800
11777 San Vicente Blvd. 90049
213–209–6707

• **San Diego**
Port Administration Bldg.
3165 Pacific Hwy. 92101
619–293–5395

* **San Francisco**
Federal Bldg.
Box 36013
450 Golden Gate Ave. 94102
415–556–5860

• **San Jose**
111 West Saint John Street 95113
408–275–7648

Hawaii

Honolulu
4106 Federal Bldg.
P.O. Box 50026
300 Ala Moana Blvd. 96850
808–546–8694

Oregon

Portland
1220 S.W. 3rd Ave. 97204
503–221–3001

Washington

Seattle
Room 706
Lake Union Bldg.
1700 Westlake Ave. North 98109
206–442–5616

• **Spokane**
P.O. Box 2170 99210
509–838–8202

U.S. EXPORT DEVELOPMENT OFFICES (EDO'S)

The Department of Commerce provides worldwide opportunities for both new and established exporters to enter export markets through its trade promotion activities. These activities are coordinated by the Department's Export Development Offices (EDO's). Regional Export Development Offices (REDO's) provide overall event coordination among the EDO's within specific geographic regions of responsibility.

Source: *Overseas Export Promotion Calendar*, U.S. Department of Commerce, International Trade Administration.

EDO's with On-Site Exhibition Facilities

MEXICO CITY
(Mexico and Central America
U.S. Export Development Office
31 Liverpool
Mexico 6, D.F.; or
c/o American Embassy
P.O. Box 3087
Laredo, Texas 78041
Phone: 591–0155.
Telex: 01773471 USTC ME

MILAN
(Southern Europe)
U.S. Export Development Office
Via Gattamelata 5
20149 Milan Italy; or
c/o American Embassy
Box M, APO New York 09794
Phone: 011–392–469–6451
Telex: 330208 USIMC I

SAO PAULO
(Brazil and River Plate)
U.S. Export Development Office
Edificio Eloy Chaves
Avenida Paulista
2439
Sao Paulo, Brazil; or
c/o American Consulate General
APO Miami 34030
Phone: (011) 55–11–853–2011
Telex: (391) 1125274

SYDNEY
(Australia and New Zealand)
U.S. Export Development Office
4 Cliff Street
Milsons Point, Sydney N.S.W. 2061
Australia; or
c/o American Embassy
APO San Francisco 96209
Phone: (02) 929–0977
Telex: 27619

TOKYO
(Japan, Hong Kong and
the People's Republic of China)
U.S. Export Development Center
7th Floor, World Import Mart
1–3 Higashi Ikebukuro 3-chome
Toshima-ku, Tokyo 170
Japan; or
c/o American Embassy
APO San Francisco 96503
Phone: (03) 987–2441
Telex: 2722446 USTC J
Cable: USTRACEN TOKYO

EDO's and U.S. Commercial Offices without On-Site Exhibition Facilities

REGIONAL EXPORT DEVELOPMENT
OFFICE—EUROPE (R/EDO-E)

All U.S. Department of Commerce trade promotion events in Europe are coordinated by the Regional Export Development Office-Europe, located in Bonn, West Germany. Inquiries regarding the Department's schedule of promotion activities should be directed to:

U.S. Regional Export Development Office-
   Europe
U.S. Embassy
Delchmannsaue
5300 Bonn 2
Germany; or
c/o American Embassy
APO New York 09080
Phone: (0228) 339-2081/2
Telex: 08-85-624

EXPORT DEVELOPMENT OFFICES (EDO's)

The following EDO's do not have on-site exhibit facilities but coordinate trade events for the U.S. Foreign Commercial posts within their jurisdiction.

U.S. Export Development Office
Suite 100
Springfield Bldg.
8125 NW. 53rd Street
Miami, Florida 33166 U.S.A.
Phone: 305-350-4913
TWX: 810-848-4187 (ITC DOC MIA)
Cable: RUEVH DG
Jurisdiction: Andean/Caribbean

U.S. Export Development Office
Vienna 1
Friedrich Schmidtplatz 2
Vienna, Austria 1060
Phone: 011-43-222-31-55-11
Telex: 76103
Jurisdiction: Eastern Europe

U.S. Export Development Office
Middle East/North Africa/Sub-Saharan
   Africa
Room 2204
Office of Event Management and
   Support Services
U.S. Department of Commerce
Washington, D.C. 20230
Phone: 202-377-1209
Jurisdiction: Middle East/North Africa/
   Sub-Saharan Africa

U.S. Export Development Office
Singapore
Unit 1501 Peninsula Plaza
111 N. Bridge Road
Singapore 0617; or
c/o American Embassy
FPO San Francisco 96699
Telex: RS25079 (SINGTC)
Jurisdiction: East and South Asia

U.S. COMMERCIAL OFFICES

U.S. Commercial Office
15 U. Chaikovskogo
Moscow, U.S.S.R.
Phone: 001-7-95-255-46-60
Telex: 413-205 USCO SU

U.S. Trade Development Center
Wiejska Street 20
Warsaw, Poland
Phone: 21-45-15
Telex: 813934 USTDOPL

NON-EDO FACILITIES AT
FOREIGN COMMERCIAL SERVICE POSTS
LONDON
(Ireland and United Kingdom)
U.S. Embassy
Grosvenor Square
London W1A 1AE
England; or
c/o American Embassy
Box 40, FPO New York 09510
Phone: 01-629-4304
Telex: 24196 USIMC G
OSAKA/KOBE
American Merchandise Display
American Consulate General in Osaka
Sankei Kaikan Bldg., 9th Floor
27 Umeda-Cho, Kita-ku, Osaka 530
Japan; or
c/o American Consulate General
APO San Francisco 96503
Phone: (06) 341-2755 c/o American
Consulate General Osaka
Telex: 5623023 AMCON J
FUKUOKA
Foreign Commercial Office—ACE
American Consulate in Fukuoka
5-26 Ohori 2-chome
Chuo-ku, Fukuoka 810
Japan; or
c/o American Consulate
Box 10, FPO Seattle 98766
Phone: (029) 751-9331 c/o American
Consulate Fukuoka
Telex: 725679

SAPPORO
American Products Display Area
American Consulate in Sapporo
North 1, West 28
Chuo-Ku, Sapporo 064
Japan; or
c/o American Consulate
APO San Francisco 96503
Telephone: (011) 641-1115 c/o American
   Consulate Sapporo
SEOUL
(Korea)
U.S. Embassy
82 Sejong-Ro

Chongro-ku
Seoul, Korea; or
c/o American Embassy
APO San Francisco 96301
Phone: 722–2601 through 19
Telex: AMEMB 23108

U.S. Foreign-Trade Zones (FTZs)*

Firms involved in certain operations subject to significant customs duties should consider using Foreign Trade Zones (FTZs), which are now available in nearly 100 port of entry communities throughout the United States. The advantages of using an FTZ include the following:

1. Foreign and domestic merchandise may be moved into an FTZ for storage, exhibition, assembly, manufacture, or other processing free of duties and quotas;
2. Duties are payable and quotas are applied if and when the merchandise enters the U.S. market;
3. Domestic goods entering the FTZ for export are considered exported when they enter the zone.

Information on FTZs is available from the International Trade Administration at 202–377–2862.

Financing Exports*

Many sources of financial assistance are available to exporters. In addition to your own working capital or bank line of credit, the following are brief descriptions of some important sources of export financing assistance.

COMMERCIAL BANKS

A wide choice of financial institutions that provide marketing assistance, as well as international financing is available to exporters. More than 250 U.S. banks have qualified international banking departments with specialists familiar with specific foreign countries and/or various types of commodities and transactions. These banks, located in all major U.S. cities, maintain correspondent relationships with smaller banks throughout the country. This banking network enables exporters to find export financing assistance for themselves or their foreign customers. Larger banks also maintain correspondent rela-

tionships with banks in most foreign countries or operate their own overseas branches, providing a direct channel to foreign customers.

Firms that are seriously interested in developing an export trade will probably wish to work directly with a bank that offers at least one full-time international banker. These specialists are generally well-informed about export matters, even in areas that fall outside the usual limits of international banking. If they are unable to provide direct guidance or assistance, they may be able to refer you to other specialists who can. In short, the international banker is a valuable source of expertise which beginning exporters should not overlook. Best of all, since they primarily derive income from loans to the exporter and from fees for special services, banks are able to provide consultation and guidance free of charge to their clients.

The variety of services and resources available from many commercial banks throughout the United States include: advice on export regulations, exchange of currencies, collection of foreign invoices, drafts, letters of credit, and other foreign receivables, transfer of funds to other countries, letters of introduction and credit, credit information on potential buyers overseas, and credit assistance to the exporter's foreign buyers.

FACTORING HOUSES

Certain companies, known as "factoring houses" or simply "factors" will purchase your export receivables (i.e., your invoices to foreign buyers) for a somewhat discounted price, perhaps 2 to 4 percent less than their face value. The actual amount of the discount will depend on the factoring house, the kind of product(s) involved, the customer, and the country. Factors offer two important advantages: (1) They enable you to receive immediate payment for your goods, freeing cash that could otherwise be tied up for months. (2) They relieve you of the burden of collection.

Arrangements with factoring houses are made either with or without "recourse." Arrangements "with recourse" leave you, the exporter, ultimately liable for repaying the factor if the foreign buyer defaults or other problems prevent payment within a reasonable period. Arrangements "without recourse" free you from this responsibility. Naturally, factors that accept export receivables "without recourse" generally require a large discount.

EXPORT MANAGEMENT COMPANIES (EMCs)

Export management companies (EMCs) will not only act as your export representative but, in some cases, will carry the financing for your export sale, assuring you of immediate payment

---

* Source: Excerpted from *A Basic Guide to Exporting*, U.S. Department of Commerce.

and removing from your firm any foreign credit risk. EMCs solicit and transact business in the name of the manufacturers they represent for a commission, salary, or retainer plus commission. Many EMCs will also carry the financing for export sales, ensuring immediate payment for the manufacturer's products.

An agreement with an EMC can be an especially advantageous arrangement for smaller firms that do not have the time, personnel, or money to develop foreign markets, but wish nonetheless to establish a corporate and product identity overseas. For a description of services rendered to exporters by EMCs (and suggestions for choosing an appropriate firm) request Commerce's pamphlet, *"The EMC—Your Export Department."* Commerce also publishes a *"U.S. Export Management Companies Directory"* listing the names, addresses, and industry specialties of more than 1,100 EMCs in the United States. A copy of the first publication may be requested from the Publications Sales Branch, International Trade Administration, U.S. Department of Commerce, Washington, D.C. 20230. The "EMC Directory" can be purchased from: Superintendent of Documents, U.S. Government Printing Office, Washington, D.C. 20402.

CONFORMING

Designed to help exporters and importers expand their markets, improve cash flow, and create greater profit leverage, "confirming" is a financial service in which an independent company confirms an export order in the vendor's own country and makes payment for the goods in the currency of that country. This service can pay for and finance on terms the following items: The goods themselves, transportation (ocean or air), inland transportation at both ends, forwarding fees, customs brokerage fees, duties, etc. For the U.S. exporter, this means that the entire export transaction, from factory to end-user, can be fully coordinated and paid for with terms. Though common in Europe, confirming is still in its infancy in the United States. There are, however, U.S. firms that will provide such assistance. For further information, contact: Director, Office of Export Marketing Assistance, International Trade Administration, U.S. Department of Commerce, Washington, D.C. 20230.

EXPORT-IMPORT BANK

Address: 811 Vermont Avenue NW, Washington, DC 20471. Phone: 202–566–8990.

Small Business Advisory Hotline Service
800–424–5201
202–566–8860 [within Washington, DC]

In addition to its other export-related assistance, the U.S. Government participates in the financing of America's exports. The Export-Import Bank of the United States (Eximbank) offers direct loans for large projects and equipment sales that usually require longer-term financing. It cooperates with commercial banks in the United States and abroad in providing a number of financial arrangements to help U.S. exporters offer credit guarantees to commercial banks that finance export sales. Through the Foreign Credit Insurance Association it also provides insurance to U.S. exporters, enabling them to extend credit terms to their overseas buyers. In all cases, the Bank must find a "reasonable assurance of repayment" as a precondition of participating in the transaction.

Eximbank's support for short-term (up to 180 days) export sales rests exclusively with the export credit insurance program that it jointly operates with the Foreign Credit Insurance Association. The advantages of export credit insurance are significant. Most importantly, it offers protection in what is usually the riskiest part of an exporter's business—foreign sales receivables. In addition, prudent use of export credit insurance can:

- Protect exporters against political and commercial risks over which they have no control.
- Encourage exporters to make competitive offers by extending terms of payments.
- Broaden potential markets by minimizing exporter risks.
- Give leveraging possibility on exporter accounts receivable.

Three Eximbank programs are specifically designed to support medium-term (181 days–5 years) export sales:

- FCIA's medium-term export credit insurance.
- Discount Loan Program.
- U.S. Commercial Bank Guarantee Program.

For complete information on the above programs contact the Export-Import Bank at the phone numbers given above.

FOREIGN CREDIT INSURANCE ASSOCIATION (FCIA)

Address: 40 Rector Street, New York, NY 10006. Phone: 212–306–5000.

The export credit insurance offered by FCIA provides three basic incentives for American exporters when they do offer competitive terms to buyers. It enables them to (1) protect corporate assets as credit is extended; (2) maximize the rate of plant utilization as overseas competition is matched and orders won; and (3) improve corporate liquidity when insured foreign receivables are financed.

FCIA administers the U.S. export credit insurance program on behalf of its member insurance companies and the Export-Import Bank, an agency of the U.S. Government. The private insurers cover the normal commercial credit risks, primarily the insolvency of or protracted payment default by overseas buyers.

U.S. SMALL BUSINESS ADMINISTRATION [SBA]

Through financial assistance programs, the SBA can promote small business participation in international trade by making funds available for export-oriented activities.

Funds may be used to purchase machinery, equipment, facilities, supplies, or materials needed to manufacture or sell products overseas, as well as for working capital. Working capital loans may be used to defray the costs of developing or penetrating foreign markets. Specifically, this can include costs for professional foreign marketing advice and services, foreign business travel, shipping sample merchandise abroad, shopping foreign markets, participating in overseas trade center shows and international fairs, foreign advertising and preparation of promotional materials, and other related purposes.

For information on the SBA financial assistance programs, policies and requirements, contact the nearest SBA field office (see page 258).

PRIVATE EXPORT FUNDING CORPORATION (PEFCO)

Address: 280 Park Avenue, New York, NY 10017. Telephone: 212–557–3100.

PEFCO, owned by 62 investors (mostly commercial banks), lends only to finance export of goods and services of U.S. manufacture and origin. PEFCO's loans generally have maturities in the medium-term area and all are unconditionally guaranteed by Eximbank as to payment of interest and repayment of principal. PEFCO's funds supplement the financing of U.S. exports available through commercial banks and Eximbank.

OVERSEAS PRIVATE INVESTMENT CORPORATION (OPIC)

Address: 1129 20th Street NW, Washington, DC. 20527. Information phone: 202–653–2920.

OPIC, established in 1971, is an independent agency of the U.S. government with the mission of reducing or eliminating private investment risks in the developing countries. OPIC insures U.S. investors against political risks of expropriation, inconvertibility of local currency holdings, and damage from war, revolution, or insurrection. The agency offers lenders protection by guaranteeing payment of principal, interest, and loans.

The corporation offers investment information and counseling to business and participates in the cost of locating and developing projects.

Domestic International Sales Corporation

A DISC—Domestic International Sales Corporation—is a category of corporation added to the Tax Code by the Revenue Act of 1971. A DISC is entitled to defer Federal income taxes on 50 percent of its export income. The deferral is limited to 25 percent of export income for sales of military property.

Deferral continues as long as the DISC remains qualified or until the DISC makes a distribution to shareholders. Once a distribution to shareholders is made (and the law requires 50 percent or more of export income be deemed distributed during each tax year), it is taxed to the shareholders at their normal rates.

Any company exporting or interested in exporting can form a DISC to handle its export sales. Basically, a DISC is a domestic corporation that meets the following requirements:

- Has at least $2,500 paid-in capital.
- Has only one class of stock.
- Files a statement of election to be treated as a DISC with the Internal Revenue Service.
- Demonstrates shareholder consent to such election.
- Maintains its own-bank account and accounting records.

A DISC also must meet certain tests to qualify for the deferral benefit:

- At least 95 percent of its income must be from qualified export receipts.
- At least 95 percent of its assets must be export related.

A corporation wishing to be treated as a DISC must file a statement of election (IRS Form 4876) with the Internal Revenue Service within 90 days preceding the beginning of the

Source: International Trade Administration, U.S. Department of Commerce.

year for which it seeks DISC status, or if newly formed within 90 days after the date of incorporations.

Under the 1984 Tax Act the status of the DISC has undergone revision. For details contact the Department of Commerce.

Foreign Sales Corporation (FSC)

A Foreign Sales Corporation (FSC) is a foreign chartered corporation through which exports can be made. A portion of the foreign income thus generated will be exempt from Federal taxation as of 1985.

In order to qualify as a FSC certain criteria must be met with respect to the management of the FSC and the exports made through it. Among the requirements are:

- The FSC must not have more than 25 shareholders.
- A statement of election to be treated as a FSC must be filed with the Internal Revenue Service.
- A bank account must be maintained in a foreign bank and accounting records kept in a foreign office.

There are two exceptions for small exporters. (1) Small exporters may use the FSC without meeting some of the export activities test or (2) small exporters may maintain their DISC (Domestic International Sales Corporation) by paying an annual interest charge on the DISC deferred tax liability.

Further information can be obtained by calling 202–566–5485.

Export Assistance from State Governments

State development agencies, departments of commerce, and other departments within State governments often provide valuable assistance to exporters within the State. These groups may provide assistance in marketing, market development, and in arranging for trade shows and trade missions. The agencies in each state responsible for international trade and export assistance to local firms are given under each state in the State Information Guide section of the *Almanac,* page 574. Information is also obtainable from the National Association of State Development Agencies, (NASDA) 444 N. Capitol Street, Washington, DC 20001. Telephone: 202–624–5411.

Source: International Trade Administration, U.S. Department of Commerce.

Private and Government Sources of Interest to U.S. Exporters

Advisory Council on Japan-U.S. Economic Relations (U.S. Section)[1]
Phone: (202) 659–3054

African Development Bank and Fund
B.P. No. 1387
Abijan, Ivory Coast

Asean-U.S. Business Council (U.S. Section)[1]
Phone: (202) 659–6117

Asian Development Bank
Roxas Blvd.
P.O. Box 789
Manila, Philippines

Association of American Chambers of Commerce in Latin America
1615 H Street, NW.
Washington, D.C. 20062
Phone: (202) 659–3055

Brazil-U.S. Business Council (U.S. Section)[1]
Phone: (202) 659–3055

Bulgarian-U.S. Economic Council (U.S. Section)[1]
Phone: (202) 659–2024

The Business Roundtable
200 Park Ave.
New York, N.Y. 10017
Phone: (212) 682–6370

Caribbean Development Bank
P.O. Box 408 Wildey
St. Michael, Barbados
West Indies

Chamber of Commerce of the United States
1615 H Street, NW.
Washington, D.C. 20062
Phone: (202) 659–6000

Committee for the Caribbean
1333 New Hampshire Ave., NW.
Washington, D.C. 20036
Phone: (202) 466–7464

Committee on Canada-United States Relations (U.S. Section)[1]
Phone: (202) 659–3054

[1] Address: Chamber of Commerce of the United States, International Division, 1615 H Street NW, Washington, DC 20062.
Source: *Basic Guide to Exporting,* International Trade Administration, U.S. Department of Commerce.

Czechoslovak-U.S. Economic Council (U.S. Section)[1]
Phone: (202) 659-2024

Department of Commerce International Trade Administration
14th Street and Constitution Ave., NW.
Washington, D.C. 20230
Phone: (202) 377-3808

Department of State Bureau of Economic and Business Affairs
2201 C Street, NW.
Washington, D.C. 20520
Phone: (202) 632-0354

East-West Trade Council
1700 Pennsylvania Ave., NW.
Suite 670
Washington, D.C. 20006
Phone: (202) 393-6240

Egypt-U.S. Business Council (U.S. Section)[1]
Phone: (202) 659-3058

Export-Import Bank of the United States
811 Vermont Ave., NW.
Washington, D.C. 20571
Phone: (202) 566-2117

FCIB (Foreign Credit Interchange Bureau/National Association of Credit Management Corporation)
475 Park Ave. South
New York, N.Y. 10016
Phone: (212) 725-1700

Federal Trade Commission
Pennsylvania Ave. at Sixth Street, NW.
Washington, D.C. 20580
Phone: (202) 523-3625

Foreign Credit Insurance Association
One World Trade Center
New York, N.Y. 10048
Phone: (212) 432-6200

Hungarian-U.S. Economic Council (U.S. Section)[1]
Phone: (202) 659-2024

India-U.S. Business Council (U.S. Section)[1]
Phone: (202) 659-3058

Inter-American Development Bank
308 17th Street, NW.
Washington, D.C. 20557
Phone: (202) 634-8152

International Advertising Association, Inc.
475 Fifth Ave.
New York, N.Y. 10017
Phone: (212) 684-1583

International Centre for Settlement of Investment Disputes
1818 H Street, NW.
Washington, D.C. 20433
Phone: (202) 676-1438

International Monetary Fund
700 19th Street, NW.
Washington, D.C. 20431
Phone: (202) 477-7000

International Trade Centre (UNCTAD/GATT)
4, Route des Morillons
CH-1211, Geneva 22
Switzerland

Israel-U.S. Business Council (U.S. Section)[1]
Phone: (202) 659-6116

National Association of Export Management Companies, Inc.
65 Liberty Street
New York, N.Y. 10005
Phone: (212) 766-1343

National Association of Manufacturers
1776 F Street, NW.
Washington, D.C. 20006
Phone: (202) 331-3700

The National Council for U.S.-China Trade
1050 17th Street, NW.
Washington, D.C. 20036
Phone: (202) 828-8300

National Foreign Trade Council, Inc.
10 Rockefeller Plaza, Room 530
New York, N.Y. 10020
Phone: (212) 581-6420

Office of the United States Trade Representative
1800 G Street, NW.
Washington, D.C. 20506
Phone: (202) 395-4647

Organization for Economic Cooperation and Development
1750 Pennsylvania Ave., NW.
Washington, D.C. 20006
Phone: (202) 724-1857

Overseas Private Investment Corporation
1129 20th Street, NW.
Washington, D.C. 20527
Phone: (202) 653-2920

Polish-U.S. Economic Council (U.S. Section)[1]
Phone: (202) 659-2024

President's Export Council
Washington, D.C. 20230
Phone: (202) 377-5719

Romanian-U.S. Economic Council (U.S. Section)[1]
Phone: (202) 659–2026

Small Business Administration Office of International Trade
1441 L Street, NW.
Washington, D.C. 20416
Phone: (202) 653–6600

Sudan-U.S. Business Council (U.S. Section)[1]
Phone: (202) 659–3057

U.S. Council of the International Chamber of Commerce
1212 Avenue of the Americas
New York, N.Y. 10036
Phone: (212) 354–4480

U.S.-European Community Conference on Agriculture[1]
Phone: (202) 659–2022

U.S.-German Democratic Republic Trade and Economic Council
40 Westminister Street
Providence, Rhode Island 02903
Phone: (401) 331–2400

U.S. International Trade Commission
701 E Street, NW.
Washington, D.C. 20004
Phone: (202) 523–0161

U.S.-Korea Economic Council
88 Morningside Drive
New York, N.Y. 10027
Phone: (212) 749–4200

U.S.-Republic of China Economic Council
200 Main Street
Crystal Lake, IL 60014
Phone: (815) 459–5875

U.S.-U.S.S.R. Trade and Economic Council
1211 Avenue of the Americas
New York, N.Y. 10036
Phone: (212) 840–5500

U.S.-Yugoslav Economic Council, Inc.
51 East 42nd Street
New York, N.Y. 10017
Phone: (212) 687–7797

DUN & BRADSTREET

Address: 99 Church Street, New York, NY. 10007 Phone: 212–285–7000.

Dun & Bradstreet provides a number of valuable services and publications in the area of international business, i.e., international credit reports on companies, international marketing guides and services, and directories of foreign firms. Dun & Bradstreet publishes the comprehensive annual, *Exporters Encyclopedia*, with monthly supplements. It details the rules and regulations in over 220 world markets and is arranged alphabetically by country and market area. *Principal International Businesses* is a useful marketing publication providing addresses, lines of business, sales figures, and other information on nearly 50,000 foreign firms.

INTERNATIONAL REPORTS

Address: 200 Park Avenue South, New York, NY 10003.

International Reports publishes reports on sources of worldwide export credit insurance, foreign investment guarantees, and export financing under the title of *Insurance in International Finance*.

It also publishes the monthly *International Commercial Finance Service*, containing extensive information and data on financing and interest rates, surveys of credit ratings, and foreign payment records of individual countries.

BUSINESS INTERNATIONAL

Address: One Dag Hammarskjold Plaza, New York, NY 10017. Phone: 212–750–6300.

Business International publishes a series of weekly reports: *Business International* (a global view of business); *Business Europe; Business Latin America; Business Asia; Eastern Europe Report; Business China* (People's Republic); *Business International Money Report; Investing, Licensing, Trading Report;* and *Financing Foreign Operations*. It publishes a multivolume series, *Doing Business with Eastern Europe*.

COMMERCE CLEARING HOUSE

Address: 4025 West Peterson Avenue, Chicago, IL 60646. Phone 312–583–8500.

Commerce Clearing House publishes a number of widely used looseleaf series updated on a weekly or monthly basis. In the international field these include: *Euromarket News; Doing Business in Europe; Balance of Payment Reports; Common Market Reports;* and *Income Taxes World Wide*. It also publishes a number of detailed tax and legal guides for specific countries, i.e., Canada, Mexico, Australia, England, and Germany.

U.S. DEPARTMENT OF STATE

Address: New State Building, 2201 C Street, NW, Washington, DC 20520.
Information: 202–632–9884.

PUBLICATIONS

Background Notes of the Countries of the World gives profiles of foreign countries.

Key Officers of Foreign Service Posts lists the addresses and phone numbers of all American embassies and consulates and their key personnel.

Department of State Bulletin is a weekly publication devoted to the latest developments in international politics and trade agreements.

THE LIBRARY OF CONGRESS

The Library of Congress's international divisions provide overseas free research assistance on social, economic, and political topics. Call:

African and Middle East
  Division   202–287–7937
Asian Division   202–287–5420
European Division   202–287–5413
Hispanic Division   202–287–5400

Write: Library of Congress, 10 First Street SE, Washington, D.C. 20540.

UNITED STATES INTERNATIONAL TRADE COMMISSION*

Address: 701 E Street NW, Washington, DC 20436. Information phone: 202–523–0161.

Formerly the U.S. Tariff Commission, the name was changed to the U.S. International Trade Commission in 1974.

The commission is given broad powers of investigation relating to the customs laws of the United States and foreign countries, the volume of importation in comparison with domestic production and consumption, the conditions, causes, and effects relating to competition of foreign industries with those of the United States and all other factors affecting competition between articles of the United States and imported articles.

Businesspersons who believe they have been injured by unfair trade methods from abroad may file a complaint with this commission.

Summaries of trade and tariff information may be obtained directly from the commission.

OTHER PUBLICATIONS

Europa Year Book is an annual two-volume work covering a wide range of commercial, economic, and political statistics and information about every country in the world. Volume I deals with international organizations and the countries of Europe, while Volume II covers Africa, the Americas, Asia, and Australia. It is published by Europe Publications, Ltd., 18 Bedford Square, London, England.

Jane's Major Companies of Europe is an annual providing extensive information about all

major European companies. It is available from Jane's Yearbooks, 8 Shepherdess, London N1 7LW, England.

Foreign Commerce Handbook provides information on international trade and foreign markets. Included are addresses and phone numbers of organizations involved with foreign trade, a glossary of foreign commercial terms and a bibliography of indexes and periodicals. Available from the Chamber of Commerce of the United States, 1615 H Street NW, Washington, DC 20062.

International Marketing Handbook contains marketing profiles for 138 countries, near term trade outlooks for major countries, as well as business guides to the Near East, North Africa and Eastern bloc countries Available in the U.S. from Gale Research Company, Book Tower, Detroit, MI 48226.

Lambert's World Government Directory identifies government officials in 168 countries as well as officials in Inter-Governmental organizations. Published by International Executive Reports, 115 Massachusetts Avenue NW, Washington, DC 20005.

Country Experts in the Federal Government is a guide to U.S. government analysts for almost all countries. Published by Washington Researchers, 2612 P Street, NW, Washington, DC 20007.

International Research Center Directory edited by Anthony F. Kruzas and Kay Gill identifies 15,000 university-related, independent and government research organizations throughout the world. Available from Gale Research Company (address above).

Croner's Reference Book for World Traders is a three volume work covering basic data and hard-to-locate information for international traders and market researchers. Available from Croner Publications, 211–05 Jamaica Avenue, Queens Village, New York, 11428.

Incoterms is a booklet providing a set of international rules for interpreting the main terms used in foreign trade contracts. Available from the U.S. Council of the International Chamber of Commerce, Inc. 1212 Avenue of the Americas, New York, NY 10036. Also publishes other useful material.

Revised American Foreign Trade Definitions, is a compilation from the National Council of Importers, the Chamber of Commerce of the U.S., and the National Foreign Trade Council. Available from the National Foreign Trade Council at 100 E. 42nd Street, New York, NY 10017.

European Markets: A Guide to Company and Industry Information Sources is a three volume resource for accessing information on European companies and markets. Available from Washington Researchers, 2612 P Street NW, Washington, DC 20007.

---

* Source: *U.S. Government Organization Manual.*

Sources of International Credit Information

International Trade Administration, U.S. Department of Commerce, Washington, DC.

Dun & Bradstreet, 99 Church Street, New York, NY 10007.

FCIB-NACM Corp., 475 Park Avenue South, New York, NY 10015.

Major Commercial Banks

International Organizations

UNITED NATIONS (UN)

Address: New York, NY 10017. Information phone: 212–754–1234.

The UN and its affiliated organizations publish a large number of reports and statistical tables covering all member nations. Publications may be obtained by writing: Sales Section, United Nations Publications, New York, NY 10017. A periodic check list of UN publications is available on request.

PUBLICATIONS

Economic Survey of Europe.
Journal of Development Planning.
Guidelines for Contracting for Industrial Projects in Developing Countries.
World Economic Survey.
Annual Bulletin of Exports of Chemical Products.
Annual Bulletin of Coal Statistics for Europe.
Statistics of World Trade in Steel.
Annual Bulletin of Gas Statistics for Europe.
Annual Bulletin of Electric Energy Statistics for Europe.
Economic Bulletin for Europe.
Economic Bulletin for Asia and the Pacific.
Economic Bulletin for Africa.
Economic Bulletin for Latin America.
Quarterly Bulletin of Statistics for Asia and the Pacific.
Statistical Yearbook for Asia and the Pacific
Demographic Yearbook.
Yearbook of International Trade Statistics Vol. I: Trade by Country; Vol. II: Trade by Commodity.
Monthly Bulletin of Statistics provides monthly statistics on 70 subjects from more than 200 countries and territories together with special tables illustrating important economic developments. Quarterly data for significant world and regional aggregates are also prepared regularly for the bulletin.

Statistical Yearbook is a comprehensive compilation of international statistics relating to: population and manpower; agricultural, mineral, and manufacturing production; construction; energy; trade; transport; communications; consumption; balance of payments; wages and prices; national accounts; finance; development assistance; health; housing; education; science and technology; and culture.

Population and Vital Statistics Reports (quarterly).
Yearbook of National Accounts Statistics.
Yearbook of International Trade Statistics.
Yearbook of Construction Statistics.
Commodity Trade Statistics (quarterly).
World Trade Annual
The Growth of World Industry: Vol. I General Industrial Statistics; Vol. II Commodities Production Data.

INTERNATIONAL MONETARY FUND (IMF)

Address: 19th and H Streets NW, Washington, DC 20431. Phone: 202–477–7000.

The IMF was organized in 1945 with the purpose of promoting international monetary cooperation and consultation. The fund also seeks to facilitate the expansion of international trade and currency exchange stability. The fund issues Special Drawing Rights (SDR), a form of reserve currency used by central banks for settling balance of payment obligations.

PUBLICATIONS

The IMF issues a broad range of publications (some in conjunction with the World Bank Group) of interest to the business community.

Foreign Trade Statistics. Series A. This monthly bulletin provides a breakdown of overall trade by main commodity categories and available indices of foreign trade unit values and volumes. *Series B. Trade by Commodities. Analytical Abstracts* (quarterly). *Series C. Trade by Commodities. Market Summaries* (yearly).

Provisional Oil Statistics (quarterly).

The Annual Report of the Executive Directors reviews the funds' activities, policies, organization, and administration and surveys the world economy, with special emphasis on international liquidity, payments problems, exchange rates, and world trade.

Annual Report on Exchange Restrictions reviews developments in exchange controls and restrictions and other measures that may have direct implications for the balance of payments of member countries.

International Financial Statistics (monthly) reports for most countries of the world current data needed for analyzing problems of international payments and inflation and deflation, i.e., data on exchange rates, international liquidity, money and banking, international trade, prices, production, government finance, interest rates, and other items. Information is presented in country tables for each country and in tables with area and world aggregates. Charts on each country page show recent changes in important series.

Balance of Payments Yearbook presents statistics in a standard form, expressed in a common unit of account, for countries that report information to the fund on their balance of payments transactions. In the tables that are designated as "standard presentations," these transactions are classified in terms of objective criteria; in the tables designated as "analytic presentations," they are regrouped to facilitate further analysis and certain cumulative balances are drawn.

Direction of Trade is published jointly by the International Monetary Fund and the International Bank for Reconstruction and Development. The monthly issues provide the latest available information on each country's direction of trade, with comparative data for the corresponding period of the preceding year.

The *IMF Survey* is a topical report of the fund's activities (including all press releases, texts of communiques and major statements, SDR valuations, and exchange rates) presented in the broader context of developments in national economics and international finance.

ORGANIZATION FOR ECONOMIC COOPERATION AND DEVELOPMENT (OECD)

Address: Rue Andre Pascal, Paris, France. 1750 Pennsylvania Avenue NW, Washington, DC 20026. Phone: 202–724–1857.

The OECD, established in 1961, is an outgrowth of the Organization for European Economic Cooperation, set up under the Marshall Plan in 1948. It consists of 24 developed countries: Canada, United States, Japan, Australia, New Zealand, Austria, Belgium, Denmark, England, Finland, France, West Germany, Greece, Iceland, Italy, Luxembourg, Netherlands, Norway, Portugal, Spain, Sweden, Turkey, Switzerland, and Yugoslavia. Together, the OECD countries account for 20 percent of world population, 60 percent of world industrial production, and 73 percent of world trade.

PUBLICATIONS

OECD Observer is intended for people who are interested in and concerned with economic and social planning in the broadest sense and who want to have relevant information in the most succinct form possible. It presents in readable fashion the entire range of OECD's work— in economic affairs, trade, manpower, social affairs, science and education, the environment,

financial affairs, and development assistance. (Published bimonthly.)

The *OECD Economic Outlook* is a twice yearly, detailed survey of economic trends and prospects for the immediate future.

OECD Financial Statistics supplies complete, up-to-date, authoritative information on financial markets in 16 European countries, the United States, Canada, and Japan. (Published yearly with bimonthly supplements.)

OECD Economic Surveys is an annual analysis of the economic policy of each OECD country as seen by the others.

Main Economic Indicators, a monthly publication, is an essential source of statistics for the student of the international business cycle.

GENERAL AGREEMENT ON TRADE AND TARIFFS (GATT)

Address: Centre William Rappard, 154 Rue de Lausanne, Geneva, Switzerland.

GATT is a multilateral trade treaty (entered into force in 1948) among 83 countries providing for the reduction of tariffs and other trade barriers, standardization of trade procedures, and the resolution of trade disputes. GATT publishes *Compilations of Basic Information on Export Markets; Guide to Sources of Foreign Trade Information; Analytical Bibliography: A Compendium of Sources: International Trade Statistics;* and *World Directory of Industry and Trade Associations.*

International Information Available in the U.S. by Country

This section lists helpful addresses in the United States for those doing business with countries where business practices may present certain problems.

JAPAN

Exporters and importers generally find it essential to use the services of the Japanese trading companies, which offer a wide range of services including negotiation of overseas deals, transportation, storage, finance, and marketing. The largest trading companies are listed below. The small exporter will often do better using smaller trading companies that specialize in one or two types of products. Exporters seeking an appropriate trading company should contact the local office of the Japan Trade Center:

Bank of America Tower*
555 S. Flower Street
Los Angeles, CA 90071

1737 Post Street*
San Francisco, CA 94115

230 N. Michigan Avenue*
Chicago, IL 60601

1221 Avenue of the Americas*
New York, NY 10020

One World Trade Center
2100 Stemmons Freeway
Dallas, TX 75258

1221 McKinney*
One Houston Center
Houston, TX 77010

P.O. Box 3356
Marina Station
Mayaguez, PR 00708

* Problems and or inquiries concerning non-tariff barriers can be handled in the United States at the action desks at specific Japan Trade Centers indicated above by an asterisk. The inquiry will be directed to the proper authority in Japan at JETRO (Japan External Trade Organization). Inquiries can of course, be made directly to Japan at one of the following:

Ministry of Foreign Affairs
  First International Organizations Division
  Economic Affairs Bureau
  Tokyo, Japan

Ministry of International Trade and Industry
  Import Division, International
  Trade and Administration
  Bureau
  Tokyo, Japan

Economic Planning Agency
  First International Economic Affairs Division
  Coordination Bureau
  Tokyo, Japan

Ministry of Finance
  Import Division
  Customs and Tariffs Bureau
  Tokyo, Japan

MAJOR TRADING COMPANIES (U.S. OFFICES)

Mitsubishi
  520 Madison Avenue
  New York, NY 10022

  Bank of America Tower
  555 S. Flower Street
  Los Angeles, CA 90071

  601 California Street
  San Francisco, CA 94108

Mitsui & Co. (USA), Inc.
  200 Park Avenue
  New York, NY 10017

  611 W. Sixth Street
  Los Angeles, CA 90017

Marubeni Corporation
  200 Park Avenue
  New York, NY 10017

One Wilshire Building
624 S. Grand Avenue
Los Angeles, CA 90017

C. Itoh & Co. (America), Inc.
  270 Park Avenue
  New York, NY 10017

  555 S. Flower Street
  Los Angeles, CA 90017

Sumitomo Shoji America, Inc.
  345 Park Avenue
  New York, NY 10022

  606 S. Olive Street
  Los Angeles, CA 90014

Nissho-Iwai American Corp.
  1211 Avenue of the Americas
  New York, NY 10036

  One Wilshire Building
  624 S. Grand Avenue
  Los Angeles, CA 90017

Toyomenka (America), Inc.
  One World Trade Center
  New York, NY 10048

  445 South Figueroa Street
  Los Angeles, CA 90017

Kanematsu-Gosho (USA), Inc.
  One World Trade Center
  New York, NY 10048

  350 California Street
  San Francisco, CA 94104

Itoman USA Inc.
  1211 Avenue of the Americas
  New York, NY 10036

Nichimen Co., Inc.
  1185 Avenue of the Americas
  New York, NY 10036

Occidental Center
  1150 S. Olive Street
  Los Angeles, CA 90015

Chori New York, Inc.
  350 Fifth Avenue
  New York, NY 10001

HELP FOR TRADING PROBLEMS IN JAPAN

Help is available for firms, groups, and trade associations which have trouble gaining access to the Japanese market. The Joint U.S. Japan Trade Facilitation Committee staff will intervene with Japanese authorities on behalf of the U.S. companies or groups when Japanese regulations present trade problems.

For more information and aid, contact:

International Trade Administration
Department of Commerce

Source: *The Information Report*, Washington Researchers, 918 16th Street NW, Washington, DC 20006.

14th & Constitution Ave. NW, Room 3053
Washington, DC 20230
202–377–4527

THE PEOPLE'S REPUBLIC OF CHINA (PRC)

For information or advice on contacting the Chinese on commercial matters, call or write to:

U.S. Department of Commerce
International Trade Administration Office of
   PRC and Hong Kong
Washington, DC 20230
Telephone: 202–377–3583/4681

Commercial Office
Embassy of the People's Republic of China
2300 Connecticut Avenue, N.W.
Washington, DC 20008

THE NATIONAL COUNCIL FOR U.S.-CHINA TRADE

Address: 1050 17th Street NW, Suite 350, Washington, DC 20036. Phone: 202–429–0340.

The Council, a nonprofit, private organization maintaining close liaison with the U.S. government, serves as a forum for the discussion of trade policy and issues. It also serves as a focal point for business contact and the dissemination of information on marketing in the PRC. The council maintains a business counseling service; it also publishes the *China Business Review* bimonthly. The council facilitates the reciprocal arrangements of trade missions and trade exhibitions in the United States and China.

USSR AND EASTERN EUROPE*

USSR

USSR Affairs Division, International Economic Policy (202–377–4655). This division collects, analyzes, and disseminates current information on economic, commercial, and other developments in the USSR and estimates their impact on the U.S. business community. The division develops policy guidance in our commercial relationship with the Soviet Union and provides staff support to and representation on the Joint Commercial Commission. It also maintains close contact with the U.S. Commercial Office in Moscow and with USSR commercial officials in the United States in order to initiate and pursue official representations on behalf of the American business community.

The U.S. Commercial Office (USCO), Moscow. The USCO should be a firm's first stop when visiting the USSR.

It may also be to the company's advantage to touch base with the following USSR commercial organizations in the United States to try to obtain some indication of Soviet interest and to identify contacts in the Soviet Union:

The Trade Representation of the USSR in the U.S.A., 2001 Connecticut Avenue NW, Washington, DC 20008, telephone 202–234–7170.

The Amtorg Trading Corporation, 750 Third Avenue, New York, NY 10017, telephone 212–972–1220.

The staffs of both Amtorg and the Trade Representation include representatives of individual foreign trade organizations (FTOs).

The USSR Consulate General, 2790 Green Street, San Francisco, CA 94123, telephone 415–922–6642, may have information conveniently available for companies on the West Coast.

Insurance Coverage

Insurance coverage for U.S.-USSR. trade is available from a number of U.S. insurance companies on a case-by-case basis in the areas of export insurance, transportation insurance, and insurance on fixed locations. No political or commercial credit risk coverage is currently available for the USSR from the Foreign Credit Insurance Association (FCIA) or the Export-Import Bank because of the 1974 Trade Act provisions. Many of the private U.S. companies, however, have established working and contractual relationships with the USSR State Insurance Company (Ingosstrakh) and with the wholly owned Soviet insurance companies, Black Sea and Baltic Company, Ltd., in London, Schwarzmeer und Ostee A.G. in Hamburg, and Garant A.G. in Vienna.

Private American insurers which write policies on some or all of the areas of standard property, casualty transportation, marine and war risk insurance, and more specialized insurance for Soviet-American cooperative projects in the USSR or a third country are:*

AFIA Reinsurance Insurance
North American Control Office
110 William Street
New York, NY 10038
Telephone: 212–732–9070

Members of the American Institute of
   Marine Underwriters
14 Wall Street
New York, NY 10005
Telephone 212–233–0550

American International Underwriters Corporation

* Source: Excerpted from Department of Commerce Overseas Reports, "Trading with the USSR."

* This listing is not to be considered an endorsement by the Department of Commerce, the U.S. government or the *Business and Investment Almanac.*

70 Pine Street
New York, NY 10005
Telephone: 212–770–7000

Chubb and Son, Inc.
International Department
100 William Street
New York, NY 10038
Telephone: 212–285–2850

Insurance Company of North America
International Insurance Section
2 INA Plaza
1600 Arch Street
Philadelphia, PA 19101
Telephone: 215–241–4000

EASTERN EUROPE

Commercial transactions with Bulgaria, Czechoslovakia, East Germany, Hungary, Poland, and Romania are similar to those with the USSR. Contracts are negotiated with the appropriate Foreign Trade Organization. For detailed information about trade shows, missions, export licenses, and FTOs, contact the Office of East-West Trade, Department of Commerce in Washington, or the Commerce Department Offices at the district level. Another key source of information is the U.S. East-West Trade Development Office in Vienna.

BULGARIA

Bulgarian Embassy
2100 16th Street NW
Washington, DC 20009

Bulgarian Commercial Counselor
121 E. 62nd Street
New York, NY 10021

CZECHOSLOVAKIA

Czechoslovakian Embassy
3900 Linnean Avenue NW
Washington, DC 20008

Office of the Czechoslovakian Commercial
  Counselor
292 Madison Avenue
New York, NY 10016

EAST GERMANY
(German Democratic Republic)

Embassy of the German Democratic Republic
1717 Massachusetts Avenue NW
Washington, DC 20036

Permanent Mission of German Democratic
  Republic to the United Nations
58 Park Avenue
New York, NY 10016

U.S. banks with offices in Berlin
Citibank, New York NY

HUNGARY

Embassy of Hungary to the United States
2437 15th Street NW
Washington, DC 20009

Office of the Commercial Counselor of the Embassy of Hungary
2401 Calvert Street
Washington, DC 20008

Hungarian Consulate
8 E. 75th Street
New York, NY 10021

POLAND

Economic Counselor's Office
Embassy of the Polish People's Republic
2540 16th Street NW
Washington, DC 20008

Polish Consulate General
233 Madison Avenue
New York, NY 10016

Polish Commercial Counselor's Office
1 Daghammarskjold Plaza
New York, NY 10017

Office of Polish Commercial Consul
333 E. Ontario Street
Chicago, IL 60611

Polish Chamber of Foreign Trade
44 Montgomery Street
San Francisco, CA 94104

U.S. banks with offices in Warsaw
First National Bank, Chicago

ROMANIA

Romanian Embassy
1607 23rd Street NW
Washington, DC 20008

Romanian Office of the Economic Counselor
200 E. 38th Street
New York, NY 10016

Romanian Foreign Trade Promotion Office
100 W. Monroe Street
Chicago, IL 60603

Romanian Foreign Trade Promotion Office
22 Battery Street
San Francisco, CA 94111

U.S. banks with offices in Bucharest
Manufacturer's Hanover Trust, New York, NY

NEAR EAST AND NORTH AFRICA*

The Office of the Near East within the International Trade Administration serves as the focal point for the U.S. Department of Commerce response to the dramatically changed economic

* Source: *A Business Guide to the Near East & North Africa*, International Trade Administration, U.S. Department of Commerce.

situation and significant business opportunities in the Near East and North Africa. The group assembles, analyzes, and disseminates to the U.S. business community information on economic conditions and new opportunities in the area, provides counseling for and makes representations on behalf of U.S. exporters, and plans promotional programs to assist U.S. firms to take advantage of the market boom. The Office of The Near East also coordinates Department of Commerce participation in joint commission activities.

To take advantage of these programs call 202–377–5737 (Arab Near East); 202–377–5737 (North Africa); 202–377–4652 (Iran, Israel, Egypt). For information concerning major projects call 202–377–4441. The mailing address is The Office of the Near East, International Trade Administration, Washington, DC 20230.

ALGERIA

Embassy of Algeria
2118 Kalorama Road NW
Washington, DC 20008
Telephone: 202–328–5300

BAHRAIN

Embassy of Bahrain
3502 International Drive NW
Washington, DC 20008
Telephone: 202–342–0741

ARAB REPUBLIC OF EGYPT

Embassy of the Arab Republic of Egypt
2310 Decatur Place NW
Washington, DC 20008
Telephone: 202–232–5400

Commercial and Economic Office
2232 Connecticut Avenue NW
Washington, DC 20008
Telephone: 202–234–1414

Egyptian Commercial Office
20 E. 46th Street
New York, NY 10017
Telephone: 212–286–0060

Consulate of the Arab Republic of Egypt
1110 Second Avenue
2nd Floor
New York, NY 10022
Telephone: 212–759–7120

Consulate of the Arab Republic of Egypt
3001 Pacific Avenue
San Francisco, CA 94115
Telephone: 415–346–9700

IRAQ

Iraqi Interests Section
Indian Embassy

1801 P Street NW
Washington, DC 20008
Telephone: 202–483–7500

ISRAEL

Embassy of Israel
3514 International Drive NW
Washington, DC 20008
Telephone: 202–364–5500

Israel Supply Mission
Empire State Building
350 Fifth Avenue
New York, NY 10001
Telephone: (212) 560–0680

Israel Consulates General
    Atlanta, Boston, Chicago, Houston, Los Angeles, New York City, Philadelphia, and San Francisco

Investment Authority and Branches:
350 Fifth Avenue
New York, NY 10001
Telephone: 212–560–0610

174 N. Michigan Avenue
Chicago, IL 60601
Telephone: 312–332–2160

Israel Trade Center
350 Fifth Avenue
New York, NY 10001
Telephone: 212–560–0680

Israel Supply Mission
350 Fifth Avenue
New York, NY 10001
Telephone: 212–560–0680

6380 Wilshire Boulevard
Los Angeles, CA 90048
Telephone: 213–651–5700

805 Peachtree Street, NE
Atlanta, GA 30308
Telephone: 404–875–6947

JORDAN (HASHEMITE KINGDOM OF)

Embassy of Jordan
2319 Wyoming Avenue, NW
Washington, DC 20008
Telephone: 202–265–1606

Consulate General
866 U.N. Plaza
New York, NY 10017
Telephone: 212–752–0135

Consulates are also located in Houston, Texas; Chicago, Illinois; Scottsdale, Arizona; and Palm Beach, Florida.

STATE OF KUWAIT

Embassy of Kuwait
2940 Tilden Street NW
Washington, DC 20008
Telephone: 202–966–0702

LEBANON

Embassy of Lebanon
2560 28th Street NW
Washington, DC 20008
Telephone: 202–462–8600

Consulate General
9 E. 76th Street
New York, NY 10021
Telephone: 212–744–7905

Consulate General
1300 Lafayette East, Suite 407
Detroit, Michigan 48207
Telephone: 313–963–0233

MOROCCO

Embassy of Morocco
1601 21st Street NW
Washington, DC 20009
Telephone: 202–462–7979/82

Consulate General
437 Fifth Avenue
New York, NY 10016
Telephone: 212–683–3062

OMAN

Embassy of the Sultanate of Oman
2342 Massachusetts Avenue NW
Washington, DC 20008
Telephone: 202–387–1980

Combined Consulate and Permanent Mission
to the United Nations
605 Third Avenue
Room 3304
New York, NY 10016
Telephone: 202–682–0447

QATAR

Embassy of Qatar
600 New Hampshire Avenue NW
Washington, DC 20037
Telephone: 202–338–0111

SAUDI ARABIA

Saudi Arabian Embassy
1520 18th Street NW
Washington, DC 20036
Telephone: 202–483–2100

Consulate General
866 United Nations Plaza
New York, NY 10017
Telephone: 212–752–2740

Consulate
5433 West Heimer, Suite 825
Houston, Texas 77056
Telephone: (713) 961–3351

Commercial Attache
1155 15th Street NW
Washington, DC 20005
Telephone: 202–331–0422

SYRIAN ARAB REPUBLIC

Embassy of the Syrian Arab Republic
2215 Wyoming Avenue NW
Washington, DC 20008
Telephone: 202–232–6313

TUNISIA

Embassy of Tunisia
2408 Massachusetts Avenue NW
Washington, DC 20008
Telephone: 202–234–6644

Tunisian Investment Promotion Agency
Tunisian National Tourist Office
2408 Massachusetts Avenue NW
Washington, DC 20008
Telephone: 202–234–6650

UNITED ARAB EMIRATES

Embassy of the United Arab Emirates
Suite 740
600 New Hampshire Avenue, N.W.
Washington, DC 20037
Telephone: 202–338–6500

YEMEN ARAB REPUBLIC

Embassy of the Yemen Arab Republic
600 New Hampshire Avenue, NW
Suite 860
Washington, DC 20037
Telephone: 202–965–4760

Consulate of the Yemen Arab Republic
211 East 43rd Street
Room 2402
New York, NY 10017
Telephone: 212–986–0990

FAST—MATCH

A quick, easy way to match your
international business requirements
to the appropriate Government
programs or services designed to
satisfy those needs

**IF YOU ARE SEEKING
INFORMATION REGARDING** ➡

USE ⬇

	Potential Markets	Market Research *	Direct Sales Leads	Agents/Distributors	Licenses	Credit Analysis	Financial Assistance	Risk Insurance	Tax Incentives
Foreign Trade Statistics (FT-410)	•								
Global Market Surveys	•	•							
Foreign Market Reports	•	•							
Market Share Reports	•	•							
Foreign Economic Trends	•	•							
Business America	•	•	•	•	•				
Commercial Exhibitions	✿✿	✿✿	•	•	•				
Overseas Business Reports (OBR)		•							
Overseas Private Investment Corp.		•					•	•	
Commerce Business Daily			•						
New Product Information Service			•	•	•				
Trade Opportunity Program (TOP)			•	•	•				
Industry Trade Lists			•	•	•				
Special Trade Lists			•	•	•				
Export Mailing List Service (EMLS)			•	•	•				
Agent/Distributor Service (ADS)				•					
World Traders Data Reports (WTDR)						•			
Export—Import Bank							•	•	
Foreign Credit Insurance Assoc. (FCIA)								•	
Domestic Int'l. Sales Corp. (DISC)							•		•

* Foreign Trade Outlook Market Profiles; Industry Trends; Distribution and Sales
Channels; Transportation Facilities; Local Business Practices and Customs;
Investment Criteria; Import Procedures and Trade Regulations; and Industrial
Property Rights.
** Research material developed regarding a planned exhibition and released to
support promotional activities.
Cost of services may be obtained from Commerce District Offices.
Source: Industry and Trade Administration, U.S. Department of Commerce.

Index

DISCARD